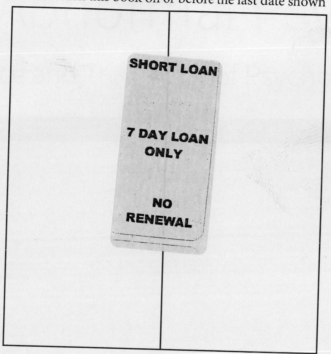
...nology

The Scie... ...cal Disorders

Fourteenth Edition

WileyPLUS

The next generation of WileyPLUS gives you the freedom and flexibility to tailor curated content and easily manage your course in order to keep students engaged and on track.

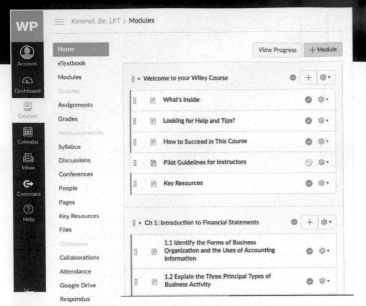

When course materials are presented in an organized way, students are more likely to stay focused, develop mastery, and participate in class. WileyPLUS Next Gen gives students a clear path through the course material.

Starting with Wiley's quality curated content, you can customize your course by hiding or rearranging learning objectives, setting the pacing of content, and even integrating videos, files, or links to relevant material. The easy-to-use, intuitive interface saves you time getting started, managing day-to-day class activities, and helping individual students stay on track.

Customized Content
Using the content editor, you can add videos, documents, pages, or relevant links to keep students motivated.

Interactive eTextbook
Students can easily search content, highlight and take notes, access instructor's notes and highlights, and read offline.

Drag-and-Drop Customization
Quick reordering of learning objectives and modules lets you match content to your needs.

Linear Design and Organization
Customizable modules organized by learning objective include eTextbook content, videos, animations, interactives, and practice questions.

Calendar
The drag-and-drop calendar syncs with other features in WileyPLUS—like assignments, syllabus, and grades—so that one change on the calendar shows up in all places.

Instructor App
You can modify due dates, monitor assignment submissions, change grades, and communicate with your students all from your phone.

Wileyplus.com/nextgen

Abnormal Psychology

The Science and Treatment of Psychological Disorders

Fourteenth Edition

ANN M. KRING
University of California, Berkeley

SHERI L. JOHNSON
University of California, Berkeley

WILEY

VICE PRESIDENT & EXECUTIVE DIRECTOR	George Hoffman
DIRECTOR EDITORIAL – PSYCHOLOGY	Veronica Visentin
SENIOR MARKETING MANAGER	Glenn Wilson
PRODUCT DESIGNER	Karen Staudinger
SENIOR CONTENT MANAGER	Dorothy Sinclair
SENIOR PRODUCTION EDITOR	Sandra Rigby
CREATIVE DIRECTOR	Jon Boylan
SENIOR DESIGNER	Thomas Nery
PHOTO DEPARTMENT MANAGER	Melinda Patelli
SENIOR PHOTO EDITOR	Mary Ann Price

Cover Photo: Shutterstock/© PinkCat

This book was typeset in 9.5/11.5 Source Sans Pro at Aptara.

Founded in 1807, John Wiley & Sons, Inc. has been a valued source of knowledge and understanding for more than 200 years, helping people around the world meet their needs and fulfill their aspirations. Our company is built on a foundation of principles that include responsibility to the communities we serve and where we live and work. In 2008, we launched a Corporate Citizenship Initiative, a global effort to address the environmental, social, economic, and ethical challenges we face in our business. Among the issues we are addressing are carbon impact, paper specifications and procurement, ethical conduct within our business and among our vendors, and community and charitable support. For more information, please visit our website: www.wiley.com/go/citizenship.

This book is printed on acid-free paper.

EPUB ISBN: 978-1-119-39523-2
ISBN: 978-1-119-58630-2

The inside back cover will contain printing identification and country of origin if omitted from this page. In addition, if the ISBN on the cover differs from the ISBN on this page, the one on the cover is correct.

To

Angela Hawk

Daniel Rose

About the Authors

Courtesy Angela Hawk

Courtesy Sheri Johnson

ANN M. KRING is Professor and Chair of Psychology at the University of California at Berkeley. She received her B.S. from Ball State University and her M.A. and Ph.D. from the State University of New York at Stony Brook. Her internship in clinical psychology was completed at Bellevue Hospital and Kirby Forensic Psychiatric Center, both in New York. From 1991 to 1998, she taught at Vanderbilt University. She joined the faculty at UC Berkeley in 1999 and served two terms as Director of the Clinical Science Program and Psychology Clinic. She received a Distinguished Teaching Award from UC Berkeley in 2008. She is on the editorial boards of *Schizophrenia Bulletin, Journal of Abnormal Psychology*, and *Psychological Science in the Public Interest*, and she is a former Associate Editor for *Journal of Abnormal Psychology, Cognition and Emotion,* and *Applied & Preventive Psychology*. She was elected President of the Society for Research in Psychopathology, and President of the Society for Affective Science.

She was awarded a Young Investigator Award from the National Alliance for Research on Schizophrenia and Depression (NARSAD) in 1997 and the Joseph Zubin Memorial Fund Award in 2006 in recognition of her research in schizophrenia. In 2005, she was named a fellow of the Association for Psychological Science. Her research has been supported by grants from the Scottish Rite Schizophrenia Research Program, NARSAD, and the National Institute of Mental Health. She is a co-editor (with Denise Sloan) of *Emotion Regulation and Psychopathology* (Guilford Press) and co-author (with Janelle Caponigro, Erica Lee, and Sheri Johnson) of *Bipolar Disorder for the Newly Diagnosed* (New Harbinger Press). She is also the author of more than 100 articles and book chapters. Her current research focus is on emotion and psychopathology, with a specific interest in the emotional features of schizophrenia, negative symptoms in schizophrenia, and the linkage between cognition and emotion in schizophrenia.

SHERI L. JOHNSON is Professor of Psychology at the University of California at Berkeley, where she directs the Cal Mania (CALM) Program. She received her B.A. from Salem College and her Ph.D. from the University of Pittsburgh. She completed an internship and postdoctoral fellowship at Brown University, and she was a clinical assistant professor at Brown from 1993 to 1995. From 1995 to 2008, she taught in the Department of Psychology at the University of Miami, where she was recognized three times with the Excellence in Graduate Teaching Award. In 1993, she received a Young Investigator Award from the National Alliance for Research in Schizophrenia and Depression. She is a consulting editor for *Clinical Psychological Science* and *Journal of Abnormal Psychology*, and she serves on editorial boards for six journals. She has served as the president for the Society for Research in Psychopathology and is a Fellow of the Academy of Behavioral Medicine Research, the Association for Behavioral and Cognitive Therapies, and the Association for Psychological Science.

For the past 25 years, her work has focused on understanding the factors that predict the course of mania and depression. She uses social, psychological, and neurobiological paradigms to understand these processes. Her work has been funded by the National Alliance for Research on Schizophrenia and Depression, the National Cancer Institute, the National Science Foundation, and the National Institute of Mental Health. She has published over 200 articles and book chapters, and her findings have been published in leading journals such as the *Journal of Abnormal Psychology, Psychological Bulletin*, and the *American Journal of Psychiatry*. She is co-editor or co-author of several books, including *Psychological Treatment of Bipolar Disorder* (Guilford Press), *Bipolar Disorder for the Newly Diagnosed* (New Harbinger Press), *Bipolar Disorder: Advances in Psychotherapy Evidence-Based Practice* (Hogrefe Publishing), and *Emotion and Psychopathology* (American Psychological Association).

A bit of history...

For the past 13 years, Ann Kring and Sheri Johnson have been the sole authors of this book, but its history dates back more than 40 years. The first edition was published in 1974, the result of conversations between Gerald Davison and John Neale about their experiences teaching the undergraduate abnormal psychology course at the State University of New York at Stony Brook that sparked their collaboration as textbook authors. Ann Kring joined the team in 2001, and she invited Sheri Johnson to join in 2004, when Kring and Johnson took over full authorship responsibilities. We are forever indebted to these two pioneering authors who developed and wrote many editions of this textbook. Near the end of our work on the twelfth edition, John Neale passed away after a long illness. He is greatly missed by many.

Courtesy of Christine McDowell

GERALD C. DAVISON is Professor of Psychology at the University of Southern California.

Courtesy of John M. Neale

JOHN M. NEALE was Professor of Psychology at the State University of New York at Stony Brook until his retirement in 2000.

Preface

From the beginning, the focus of this book has always been on the balance and blending of research and clinical application, on the use of paradigms as an organizing principle, and on the effort to involve the learner in the problem solving engaged in by clinicians and scientists. We continue to emphasize an integrated approach, showing how psychopathology is best understood by considering multiple perspectives and how these varying perspectives can provide us with the clearest accounting of the causes of these disorders as well as the best possible treatments.

With the fourteenth edition, we continue to emphasize the recent and comprehensive research coverage that has been the hallmark of the book. Of equal importance, however, we have worked to make the prose ever more accessible to a variety of students. Finally, Wiley has integrated this edition with the powerful capabilities of WileyPLUS for those who wish to have a resource-rich online learning environment to go along with the book.

WileyPLUS is an online teaching and learning platform that integrates text with interactive and multimedia content, online tools and resources to provide a contemporary and appealing learning experience. The complete program in WileyPLUS, along with a stand-alone eText and practical printed text options, offer the flexibility to suit any course format, whether it be face-to-face, a hybrid/blended learning environment, or an online class. Some of the resources and capabilities of WileyPLUS include:

- A **digital version** of the complete textbook with integrated media and quizzes.
- The **ORION** adaptive learning module, which maximizes study time.
- **Case Study Videos.** Available in WileyPLUS or for those who adopt the print version of the book, this collection of 7- to 10-minute videos presents an encompassing view of 16 psychological disorders. Produced by documentary filmmaker Nathan Friedkin in collaboration with Ann Kring and Sheri Johnson, each case study features people with psychological disorders and their families, describing symptoms from their own perspective. In addition, each video also provides concise information about the available treatment options and commentary from a mental health professional.
- **ScienCentral Videos.** This collection of clips applies the concepts of clinical psychology to current class material.
- **Review Questions.** These learning features give students a way to test themselves on course material before exams. Each review question contains fill-in-the-blank and multiple-choice questions that provide immediate feedback. Each question is also linked to a learning objective within the book to aid students in concept mastery.

- **Flashcards.** This interactive module gives students the opportunity to easily test their knowledge of vocabulary terms.
- **Web Resources.** Annotated web links put useful electronic resources for psychology into the context of your Abnormal Psychology course.

Goals of the Book

With each new edition, we update, make changes, and streamline features to enhance both the scholarly and pedagogical characteristics of the book. We also devote considerable effort to couching complex concepts in prose that is sharp, clear, and vivid. The domains of psychopathology and intervention continue to become increasingly multifaceted and technical. Therefore, good coverage of psychological disorders must engage students and foster the focused attention necessary to acquire a deep, critical understanding of the material. Some of the most exciting breakthroughs in psychopathology research and treatment that we present in the book have come in complex areas such as molecular genetics, neuroscience, and cognitive science. Rather than oversimplify these knotty issues, we have instead worked to make the explanations clear and accessible.

We strive to present up-to-date theories and research in psychopathology and intervention as well as to convey some of the intellectual excitement of the search for answers to some of the most puzzling questions facing us today. We encourage students to participate with us in a process of discovery as we sift through the evidence on the origins of psychopathology and the effectiveness of specific interventions.

As always, we continue to emphasize ways in which we can do away with the stigma that is unfortunately still associated with psychological disorders. Despite the ubiquity of psychopathology, such stigma can keep some individuals from seeking treatment, keep our legislatures from providing adequate funding for treatment and research, and keep myths about psychological disorders alive and well. A major goal for this book is to combat this stigma and present a positive and hopeful view on the causes and treatments of mental illness.

Another difference in our book is the broadening of our title. The term *abnormal psychology* is a vestige of the past in many ways, even though many courses covering the causes and treatment of psychological disorders retain this title. It is our hope that *abnormal psychology* will soon be replaced because it can perpetuate the stigma that people with psychological disorders are "abnormal" in many ways. Our contention is that people with psychological disorders are first and foremost people, and that the term *abnormal* can be overly broad and misconstrued to the detriment of people who have psychological disorders.

Organization of the Fourteenth Edition

In Chapters 1 through 4, we place the field in historical context, present the concept of paradigms in science, describe the major paradigms in psychopathology, describe the fifth edition of the *Diagnostic and Statistical Manual of Mental Disorders* (DSM-5), critically discuss its validity and reliability, provide an overview of major approaches and techniques in clinical assessment, and then describe the major research methods of the field. These chapters are the foundation on which the later chapters can be interpreted and understood. As in the thirteenth edition, specific psychological disorders and their treatment are discussed in Chapters 5 through 15.

Throughout the book, we discuss three major perspectives or paradigms: genetic, neuroscience, and cognitive behavioral. We also emphasize the importance of factors that are important to all paradigms: emotion, gender, culture, ethnicity, and socioeconomic status. A related issue is the use of more than one paradigm in studying psychological disorders. Rather than force an entire field into, for example, a cognitive behavioral paradigm, we argue from the available information that different problems in psychopathology are amenable to analyses within different frameworks. For instance, genetic factors are important in bipolar disorder and attention-deficit/hyperactivity disorder, but genes do their work via the environment. In disorders such as depression, cognitive behavioral factors are essential, but neurotransmitters also exert an influence. For still other disorders—for example, dissociative disorders—cognitive factors involving consciousness are important to consider. Furthermore, the importance of a diathesis–stress approach remains a cornerstone to the field. Emerging data indicate that nearly all psychological disorders arise from subtle interactions between genetic or psychological predispositions and stressful life events.

We continue to include considerable material on culture, race, and ethnicity in the study of causes and treatment of psychological disorders. In Chapter 2, we present a separate section that emphasizes the importance of culture, race, and ethnicity in all paradigms. We point to the important role of culture and ethnicity in the other chapters as well. For example, in Chapter 3, Diagnosis and Assessment, we discuss cultural bias in assessment and ways to guard against this selectivity in perception. We also add new information on the role of culture in anxiety and depression in Chapters 5, 6, and 7.

New to This Edition

The fourteenth edition has many new and exciting additions and changes. We no longer apologetically cover theories that don't work or don't have empirical support. As the research on each disorder has burgeoned, we've decided to highlight only the most exciting and accepted theories, research, and treatments. This edition, as always, contains hundreds (*n* = 831) of updated references. Throughout the book, we have streamlined the writing to increase the clarity of presentation and to highlight the key issues in the field. We have included new figures and tables to carefully illustrate various concepts. We have also included several new Clinical Cases to illustrate the ways in which psychological disorders are experienced by people.

We have continued to add additional pedagogy based on feedback from students and professors. For example, we have added new Focus on Discovery sections to showcase cutting-edge research on selected topics. In addition, we have modified and added new Check Your Knowledge questions in nearly all chapters so that students can do a quick check to see if they are learning and integrating the material. Drawing on evidence for the importance of generative thinking for learning, we also include open-ended questions. There are many new photos to provide students with additional real-world examples and applications of psychopathology, including examples of some of the highly successful and well-known people who have come forward in the past several years to discuss their own psychological disorders. The end-of-chapter summaries continue to be consistent across the chapters, using a bulleted format and summarizing the descriptions, causes, and treatments of the disorders covered.

New and Expanded Coverage

We are excited about the new features of this edition. Throughout the book, chapters have been restructured for smoother online presentation of material, which often involves more frequent Check Your Knowledge questions and section summaries. Material comparing DSM-IV to DSM-5 has been removed. The major new material in this edition is outlined by chapter here:

Chapter 1: Introduction and Historical Overview

- Chapter is refocused to concentrate on key moments in history that influence contemporary thinking
- Updated Focus on Discovery on stigma
- Added material on reducing stigma
- Streamlined the section defining abnormal/disorder
- Added two new Focus on Discovery sections covering Freud and neo-Freudians
- Streamlined the mental health professionals section

Chapter 2: Current Paradigms in Psychopathology

- Removed material from neuroscience sections not covered in later chapters
- Added new material on epigenetics, genome-wide association studies (GWAS), behavioral genetics, and cytokines
- Streamlined section on immune system to include material covered in later chapters
- Provided new information on cognitive science
- Included new information on culture

Chapter 3: Diagnosis and Assessment

- Entire chapter is streamlined to focus on diagnostic and assessment issues that are covered throughout the book
- Streamlined the discussion of validity
- Removed material on distinctions between DSM-IV-TR and DSM-5 (history of the DSM is still covered in a Focus on Discovery section)
- Updated and expanded discussion of internalizing versus externalizing disorders, and included very brief description of work on the p-factor
- New information on research domain criteria (RDoC)
- New information on culture
- Updated prevalence statistics from the World Mental Health Survey
- Removed neurotransmitter assessment, which is not covered in other chapters
- New information on connectivity analyses
- New information on single photon emission computed tomography (SPECT) as a neuroimaging technique
- Added new personality inventory: the Big Five Inventory-2 (BFI-2)
- New Focus on Discovery covering projective tests

Chapter 4: Research Methods in Psychopathology

- Removed Focus on Discovery on case studies
- Included evidence that lifetime prevalence estimates from epidemiological studies may be low due to failures of memory, as suggested by multiple large longitudinal studies
- Consolidated details on GWAS and association studies with the section on genetics in Chapter 2.
- Provided a more clinically relevant example of an experiment
- Simplified the discussion of treatment manuals

- Updated material on culture and ethnicity in psychological treatment
- Simplified the example of a single-case experiment
- Moved material on analogues, as not all are experiments
- Integrated and updated sections on efficacy and dissemination
- Added new section on reproducibility and replication

Chapter 5: Mood Disorders

- Removed specifiers section (except the Focus on Discovery coverage of seasonal affective disorder and anxious features)
- Provided more epidemiological data regarding income disparity, prevalence, treatment costs, medical and mortality outcomes of the mood disorders
- Updated research on creativity and bipolar disorder, including a study of over 1 million persons
- Updated and clarified findings on gender differences in depression
- Integrated literature on an internalizing factor to explain anxiety and depression overlap
- Expanded discussion of culture and somatic symptoms of depression
- Trimmed outdated case study on bipolar disorder; retained Kay Jamison Redfield autobiographical account of manic symptoms
- New data on gene-environment interactions in the prediction of major depressive disorder (MDD) onset.
- Reduced focus on interpersonal factors as an outcome of depression, given longitudinal predictive power of interpersonal effects
- Updated cortisol section focuses on cortisol awakening response rather than the Dex/CRH test
- New section on the mixed findings from imaging studies on neurotransmitters
- Removed tryptophan depletion studies
- New section on the lack of replicability of GWAS findings
- New material on connectivity in imaging studies
- Covered more longitudinal research on the hopelessness model of depression
- Simplified the discussion of rumination in depression
- Noted racial disparities in the treatment of bipolar disorder
- Updated findings on mindfulness treatment, Internet-based treatment, serotonin and norepinephrine reuptake inhibitors (SNRIs) for depression
- Removed deep brain stimulation after two major trials provided poor results
- Updated statistics and graph concerning the epidemiology of suicidality, including international as well as U.S. data

- New findings regarding the interpersonal predictors of non-suicidal self-injury (NSSI)
- Streamlined focus on major empirical research in suicidality, with reduced focus on myths of suicide and reasons to live
- Updated references on media and suicide, and on means-reduction approaches

Chapter 6: Anxiety Disorders

- Updated findings regarding prevalence and gender differences in anxiety disorders
- New evidence regarding culture and anxiety
- New material on heritability, neural circuity, SPECT and positron emission tomography (PET) findings regarding neurotransmitters, and behavioral indicators of responsivity to unpredictable threats
- NPSR1 gene findings removed due to inconsistent findings in relation to anxiety disorders
- Original Borkovec model replaced with newer contrast avoidance model of generalized anxiety disorder (GAD)
- Removed trauma exposure from the GAD section; appears to be a general risk factor
- New evidence that cognitive behavioral therapy (CBT) for anxiety disorders is helpful for Latino clients
- New evidence that mindfulness-based approaches are more helpful than placebo, but are best integrated with exposure-based treatment
- New mixed findings concerning psychodynamic therapy for panic disorder
- Removed d-cycloserine after failed trials

Chapter 7: Obsessive-Compulsive-Related and Trauma-Related Disorders

- Tables added to illustrate common obsessions and compulsions
- New material on culture shaping the prevalence and form of obsessive-compulsive disorder (OCD) symptoms
- New material on outcomes of OCD and hoarding
- Added new evidence from a large-scale twin study for shared genetic contributions to OCD, body-dysmorphic disorder (BDD), and hoarding.
- Removed yedasentience model
- Improved coverage of OCD-related treatments, including the addition of Internet-based treatment, recent trials, racial disparities, and effects on fronto-striatal abnormalities
- Updated information about the chronicity of posttraumatic stress disorder (PTSD) with evidence that some vets meet criteria in a 40-year follow-up

- New content about cross-national prevalence of PTSD and related risk factors
- Removed findings that have not been replicated, including smaller hippocampi among twins of those diagnosed with PTSD and specific forms of memory deficits in PTSD
- Updated treatment outcome research and dissemination for medications, exposure treatment, eye movement desensitization and reprocessing (EMDR), and Internet-based treatment of PTSD

Chapter 8: Dissociative Disorders and Somatic Symptom-Related Disorders

- New findings regarding sleep disturbance and dissociation
- New findings regarding false memories
- In the clinical description of dissociative identity disorder (DID), described relevant cultural experiences and symptom validity measures (moved from the etiology section)
- Moved material on epidemiology of the dissociative disorders integrated into one section.
- Removed information that is no longer supported, such as visual changes across alters or that very few clinicians diagnose DID
- Updated findings on the ability to role-play DID
- Removed the criticism that DSM-5 somatic symptom and related disorders would be overly diagnosed; research suggests that these conditions are more narrowly diagnosed than the DSM-IV-TR somatoform disorders.
- Noted that as many as two-thirds of medical complaints in primary care are not given a medical explanation
- Removed statement that all somatic symptom and related disorders are more common in women than men; this appears to be more specific to somatic symptom disorder in recent work
- Removed material on family illness and somatic symptoms; although effects are consistent, they appear quite small
- Described experimental evidence regarding the importance of beliefs and safety behaviors to the genesis of somatic symptoms
- Noted that findings on dissociation, stress, and trauma have been mixed for conversion disorder
- Updated information on the neuroscience of unconscious processing in conversion disorder
- Updated treatment findings to note that more than a dozen findings support CBT in the treatment of disorders involving health anxiety, and two randomized controlled trials (RCTs) support CBT for DID

Chapter 9: Schizophrenia

- New information on urbanicity and migration
- New and updated genetic information
- New and updated neurotransmitter information
- Streamlined section on symptom descriptions
- Streamlined section on medications
- New table on medication side effects

Chapter 10: Substance Use Disorders

- New organization for better comprehension
- New information on opioids
- Three new tables on prevalence rates of substance use and disorders
- New figure on drug use
- New Focus on Discovery on gambling disorder
- New Clinical Case on opioid use disorder
- Changed term *opiates* to *opioids* to be more consistent with reports about this category
- New table on prescription pain medicines
- New information on e-cigarettes
- New information on marijuana legalization
- New information on dopamine's role in substance use disorders

Chapter 11: Eating Disorders

- New information on obesity added to Focus on Discovery 11.1
- New information on medication and psychological treatments for eating disorders
- New information on stigma and eating disorders
- Removed older references to culture and eating disorder
- Updated information on prognosis for eating disorders
- New GWAS data on anorexia
- New information on the brain's reward system, dopamine, and eating disorders
- New information on perfectionism and negative emotions
- New information on prevention programs

Chapter 12: Sexual Disorders

- Updated information from newer community-based representative samples on sexual norms and gender differences in sexuality

- Updated information on outcomes of sexual reassignment surgery
- Updated research on the influence of sexual dysfunction on relationships, the effects of anxiety and depression on sexual dysfunction
- Reorganized and updated the material on treatment of sexual dysfunction
- Replaced two clinical cases illustrating sexual dysfunction
- Updated information from large-scale surveys on the prevalence of paraphilic interests
- Removed material on the prevalence, comorbidity, clinical characteristics, and outcomes of paraphilias drawn from biased samples
- Removed material on cognitive distortions in paraphilia
- Restructured the material on paraphilic disorder treatment outcome
- Shortened Focus on Discovery sections

Chapter 13: Disorders of Childhood

- New table on prevalence rate of mood and anxiety disorders
- New information on girls and attention-deficit/hyperactivity disorder (ADHD) and longitudinal outcomes
- New information on ADHD in adulthood
- New studies on ADHD treatment
- New information on genetics and conduct disorder
- New information on callous and unemotional traits in conduct disorder
- Updated information on treatments and prevention programs for conduct disorder
- Updated information on treating OCD in children and adolescents
- New information on separation anxiety disorder
- Updated information on disruptive mood dysregulation disorder
- New Quick Summary and Check Your Knowledge questions for dyslexia section
- New information on depression prevention
- Reorganized and streamlined section on specific learning disorders focusing on dyslexia
- Removed discussion of dyscalculia
- New information on autism spectrum disorder prognosis
- Updated information on autism spectrum disorder genetics
- Updated information on the brain and autism
- Updated information on medication treatment for autism

Chapter 14: Late Life and Neurocognitive Disorders

- New information about worldwide aging of populations
- More detailed information about the peak ages for different aspects of cognition
- New findings about the effects of negative stereotypes about aging
- Updated findings on polypharmacy and medications deemed dangerous in late life
- New section on adapting treatments of psychological conditions
- New section on neuropsychiatric syndromes in dementia
- Updated information on alternative diagnostic criteria for mild cognitive impairment
- New clinical case to illustrate mild cognitive impairment
- Updated information on the epidemiology of dementia
- Updated material on genetic risk and biomarkers, lifestyle variables, and depression related to Alzheimer's disease
- New material regarding treatment, including addressing cardiovascular disease, limited effects of antidepressants
- Basic research findings on electrical stimulation to improve memory
- Updated findings on behavioral interventions, exercise, and cognitive training

Chapter 15: Personality Disorders

- Added the DSM-5 general criteria for personality disorder
- Added a paragraph about culture and diagnosis
- New evidence for the clinical utility of the alternative DSM model of personality disorder
- Reduced emphasis on the personality disorders that were excluded from the DSM-5 alternative model of personality disorders, such as schizoid and dependent personality disorder. Case studies and etiological sections now focus on the six personality disorders that were retained in that system.
- Discussion of differential psychological correlates of antisocial personality disorder versus psychopathy
- Updated findings on neurobiology, parenting, and emotion vulnerability related to borderline personality disorder
- Reorganized material on narcissistic personality disorder to discuss social consequences of these symptoms as part of the clinical description
- Updated section on fragile self-esteem and narcissistic personality disorder
- Removed Focus on Discovery describing longitudinal changes in narcissistic personality disorder

- New data on the malleability of personality traits
- Removed discussion of cognitive therapy for borderline personality disorder because findings have been mixed.
- Noted that both dialectical behavior therapy (DBT) and psychodynamic therapy have received support for the treatment of borderline personality disorder.

Chapter 16: Legal and Ethical Issues

- Trimmed older material substantially
- New Focus on Discovery covers recent insanity verdicts
- New Focus on Discovery on the "Goldwater Rule"
- New information on violence and mental illness
- New information on ethics

Special Features for Students

Several features of this book are designed to make it easier for students to master and enjoy the material.

Clinical Cases We include Clinical Cases throughout the book to provide a clinical context for the theories and research that occupy most of our attention in the chapters and to help make vivid the real-life implications of the empirical work of psychopathologists and clinicians.

Focus on Discovery These in-depth discussions of selected topics appear as stand-alone features throughout the book, allowing us to involve readers in specialized topics without detracting from the flow of the main chapter text. Sometimes a Focus on Discovery expands on a point discussed in the chapter; sometimes it deals with an entirely separate but relevant issue—often a controversial one. We have added new Focus on Discovery elements and removed several older ones.

Quick Summaries We include short summaries of sections throughout the chapters to allow students to pause and assimilate the material. These should help students keep track of the multifaceted and complex issues that surround the study of psychopathology.

End-of-Chapter Summaries At the end of each chapter we review the material in bulleted summaries. In Chapters 5–15, we organize these by clinical descriptions, etiology, and treatment—the major sections of every chapter covering the disorders. We believe this format makes it easier for readers to review and remember the material. In fact, we even suggest that students read the summary before beginning the chapter itself to get a good sense of what lies ahead. Reading the summary again after completing the chapter will also enhance students' understanding and provide an immediate sense of the knowledge that can be acquired in just one reading of the chapter.

Check Your Knowledge Questions

Throughout each chapter, we provide three to seven sets of review questions covering the material discussed. These questions are intended to help students assess their understanding and retention of the material as well as to provide them with samples of the types of questions that often are found in course exams. We believe that these will be useful aids for students as they make their way through the chapters.

Glossary

When an important term is introduced, it is boldfaced and defined or discussed immediately. Most such terms appear again later in the book, in which case they will not be highlighted in this way. All these terms are listed again at the end of each chapter, and definitions appear at the end of the book in a glossary.

DSM-5 Diagnoses

We include a summary of the psychiatric nomenclature for the fifth edition of the *Diagnostic and Statistical Manual of Mental Disorders*, known as DSM-5. This provides a handy guide to where disorders appear in the "official" taxonomy or classification. We make considerable use of DSM-5, though in a selective and sometimes critical manner. Sometimes we find it more effective to discuss theory and research on a problem in a way that is different from DSM's conceptualization.

To Learn More

To review samples of the rich program of teaching and learning material that accompanies **Abnormal Psychology: The Science and Treatment of Psychological Disorders**, please visit www.wileyplus.com or contact your Wiley account manager to arrange a live demonstration of WileyPLUS.

Acknowledgments

We are grateful for the contributions of our colleagues and staff, for it was with their assistance that this edition was able to become the book that it is. Sheri is deeply thankful to Kiara Timpano for her thoughts about exciting new findings; to Jennifer Pearlstein, Ben Swerdlow, and Manon Ironside for their suggestions regarding writing; and to Katie Mohr for her assistance with library research. We have also benefited from the skills and dedication of the folks at Wiley. For this edition, we have many people to thank. Specifically, we thank Editorial Director, Veronica Visentin and Associate Development Editor Courtney Luzzi; working with the two of you on this edition has been a delight.

From time to time, students and faculty colleagues have written us their comments; these communications are always welcome. Readers can e-mail us at kring@berkeley.edu, sljohnson@berkeley.edu.

Finally, and most important, our heartfelt thanks go to the most important people in our lives for their continued support and encouragement along the way. A great big thanks to Angela Hawk (AMK) and Daniel Rose (SLJ), to whom this book is dedicated with love and gratitude.

September 2017

ANN M. KRING,
Berkeley, CA

SHERI L. JOHNSON,
Berkeley, CA

Brief Contents

Contents

16 Legal and Ethical Issues   485

CHAPTER 1

Introduction and Historical Overview

LEARNING GOALS

1. Explain the meaning of stigma as it applies to people with psychological disorders.

2. Compare different definitions of psychological disorder.

3. Explain how the causes and treatments of psychological disorders have changed over the course of history.

4. Describe the historical forces that have helped to shape our current view of psychological disorders, including biological, psychoanalytic, behavioral, and cognitive views.

5. Describe the different mental health professions, including the training involved and the expertise developed.

Clinical Case

Jack

Jack dreaded family gatherings. His parents' house would be filled with his brothers and their families, and all the little kids would run around making a lot of noise. His parents would urge him to "be social" and spend time with the family, even though Jack preferred to be alone. He knew that the kids called him "crazy Uncle Jack." In fact, he had even heard his younger brother Kevin call him "crazy Jack" when he'd stopped by to see their mother the other day. Jack's mother admonished Kevin, reminding him that Jack had been doing very well on his new medication. "Schizophrenia is an illness," his mother had said.

Jack had not been hospitalized with an acute episode of schizophrenia for over 2 years. Even though Jack still heard voices, he learned not to talk about them in front of his mother

because she would then start hassling him about taking his medication or ask him all sorts of questions about whether he needed to go back to the hospital. He hoped he would soon be able to move out of his parents' house and into his own apartment. The landlord at the last apartment he had tried to rent rejected his application once he learned that Jack had schizophrenia. His mother and father needed to cosign the lease, and they had inadvertently said that Jack was doing very well with his illness. The landlord asked about the illness, and once his parents mentioned schizophrenia, the landlord became visibly uncomfortable. The landlord called later that night and said the apartment had already been rented. When Jack's father pressed him, the landlord admitted he "didn't want any trouble" and that he was worried that people like Jack were violent.

Clinical Case

Felicia

Felicia didn't like to think back to her early school years. Elementary school was not a very fun time. She couldn't sit still or follow directions very well. She often blurted out answers when it wasn't her turn to talk, and she never seemed to be able to finish her class papers without many mistakes. As if that wasn't bad enough, the other girls often laughed at her and called her names. She still remembers the time she tried to join in with a group of girls during recess. They kept running away, whispering to each other, and giggling. When Felicia asked what was so funny, one of the girls laughed and said, "You are hyper, girl! You fidget so much in class, you must have ants in your pants!"

When Felicia started fourth grade, her parents took her to a psychologist. She took several tests and answered all sorts of questions. At the end of these testing sessions, the psychologist diagnosed Felicia with attention-deficit/hyperactivity disorder (ADHD). Felicia began seeing a different psychologist, and her pediatrician prescribed the medication Ritalin. She enjoyed seeing the psychologist because she helped her learn how to deal with the other kids' teasing and how to do a better job of paying attention. The medication helped, too—she could concentrate better and didn't seem to blurt out things as much anymore.

Now in high school, Felicia is much happier. She has a good group of close friends, and her grades are better than they have ever been. Though it is still hard to focus sometimes, she has learned several ways to deal with her distractibility. She is looking forward to college, hoping she can get into the top state school. Her guidance counselor has encouraged her, thinking her grades and extracurricular activities will make for a strong application.

We all try to understand other people. Determining why another person does or feels something is not easy to do. In fact, we do not always understand our own feelings and behavior. Figuring out why people behave in normal, expected ways is difficult enough; understanding seemingly abnormal behavior, such as the behavior of Jack and Felicia, can be even more difficult.

Psychological Disorders and Stigmas

In this book, we will consider the description, causes, and treatments of several different **psychological disorders**. We will also demonstrate the numerous challenges professionals in this field face. As you approach the study of **psychopathology**, the field concerned with the nature, development, and treatment of psychological disorders, keep in mind that the field is continually developing and adding new findings. As we proceed, you will see that the field's interest and importance are ever growing.

Our subject matter, human behavior, is personal and powerfully affecting. Who has not experienced irrational thoughts or feelings? Most of us have known someone, a friend or a relative, whose behavior was upsetting or difficult to understand, and we realize how frustrating it can be to try to understand and help a person with psychological difficulties.

Our closeness to the subject matter also adds to its intrinsic fascination; undergraduate courses in clinical or abnormal psychology are among the most popular in the entire college curriculum, not just in psychology departments. Our feeling of familiarity with the subject matter draws us to the study of psychopathology, but it also has a distinct disadvantage: We bring to the study our preconceived notions of what the subject matter is. Each of us has developed certain ways of thinking and talking about psychological disorders, certain words and concepts that somehow seem to fit. As you read this book and try to understand the psychological disorders it discusses, we may be asking you to adopt different ways of thinking about psychological disorders from those to which you are accustomed.

Perhaps most challenging of all, we must not only recognize our own preconceived notions of psychological disorders, but we must also confront and work to change the **stigma** we often associate with these conditions. Stigma refers to the destructive beliefs and attitudes held by a society that are ascribed to groups considered different in some manner, such as people with psychological disorders. More specifically, stigma has four characteristics (see **Figure 1.1**):

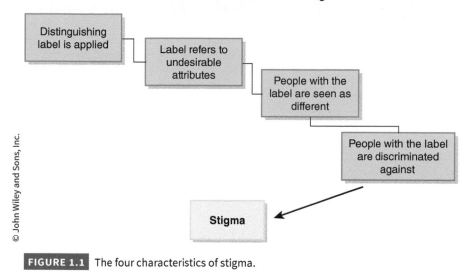

The Four Characteristics of Stigma

© John Wiley and Sons, Inc.

FIGURE 1.1   The four characteristics of stigma.

1. A label is applied to a group of people that distinguishes them from others (e.g., "crazy").

2. The label is linked to deviant or undesirable attributes by society (e.g., crazy people are dangerous).

3. People with the label are seen as essentially different from those without the label, contributing to an "us" versus "them" mentality (e.g., we are not like those crazy people).

4. People with the label are discriminated against unfairly (e.g., a clinic for crazy people can't be built in our neighborhood).

The case of Jack illustrates how stigma can lead to discrimination. Jack was denied an apartment because of his schizophrenia. The landlord believed Jack's schizophrenia meant he would be violent. This belief is based more in fiction than reality, however. A person with a psychological disorder is not necessarily any more likely to be violent than a person without such a disorder (Steadman, Mulvey, et al., 1998; Swanson, Holzer, et al. 1990), even though people with psychological disorders can be violent if they do not receive treatment (Torrey, 2014).

As we will see, the treatment of people with psychological disorders throughout recorded history has not generally been good, and this has contributed to their stigmatization, to the extent that they have often been brutalized and shunned by society. In the past, torturous treatments were held up to the public as miracle cures, and even today, terms such as *crazy, insane, retard*, and *schizo* are tossed about without thought of the people who have psychological disorders and for whom these insults and the intensely distressing feelings and behaviors they refer to are a reality of daily life. The cases of Jack and Felicia illustrate how hurtful using such careless and mean-spirited names can be.

Psychological disorders remain the most stigmatized of conditions in the twenty-first century, despite advances in the public's knowledge about the origins of psychological disorders (Hinshaw, 2007). In 1999, then Surgeon General of the United States David Satcher, in his groundbreaking report on mental illness, wrote that stigma is the "most formidable obstacle to future progress in the arena of mental illness and mental health" (U.S. Department of Health and Human Services, 1999). Sadly, this is still true today. In 2010, a staff person working with then Wisconsin gubernatorial candidate Scott Walker wrote dismissively about an election opponent's plan to make mental health care a focus of the campaign, "No one cares about crazy people." This awful phrase was turned into something hopeful when author Ron Powers opted to use it as the title of his book, an unflinchingly honest memoir about his two sons with schizophrenia and the current state of mental health care in the United States (Powers, 2017).

Throughout this book, we hope to fight this stigma by showing you the latest evidence about the nature and causes of these disorders, together with treatments, dispelling myths and other misconceptions as we proceed. As part of this effort, we will try to put a human face on psychological disorders by including descriptions of actual people with these disorders. Additional ways to fight stigma are presented in **Focus on Discovery 1.1**.

Focus on Discovery 1.1

Fighting Against Stigma: A Strategic Approach

In 2007, psychologist Stephen Hinshaw published a book entitled *The Mark of Shame: The Stigma of Mental Illness and an Agenda for Change*. In this important book, Hinshaw discusses several steps that can be taken to end stigma surrounding psychological disorders. Here we briefly discuss some of the key suggestions for fighting stigma in many arenas, including community, mental health professions, and individual/family behaviors and attitudes.

Community Strategies

Housing Options Rates of homelessness in people with psychological disorders are too high, and more programs to provide community residences and group homes are needed. However, many neighborhoods are reluctant to embrace the idea of people with a psychological disorder living among them. Lobbying legislatures and community leaders about the importance of adequate housing is a critically important step toward providing housing for people with psychological disorders and reducing stigma.

Education Educating people about psychological disorders (one of the goals of this book!) is an important step toward reducing stigma. Education alone won't completely eradicate stigma, however. By learning about psychological disorders, though, people may be less hesitant to interact with people who have different disorders. Many of you already know someone with a psychological disorder. Sadly, though, stigma often prevents people from disclosing their history with a psychological disorder. Education may help lessen people's hesitancy to talk about their illnesses.

Personal Contact Providing greater housing opportunities for people with psychological disorders will likely mean that people with these disorders will shop and eat in local establishments alongside people without these disorders. Research suggests that this type of contact—where status is relatively equal—can reduce stigma. In fact, personal contact is more effective than education in reducing stigma (Corrigan, Morris, et al., 2012). Informal settings, such as local parks and churches, can also help bridge the personal contact gap between people with and without psychological disorders.

Mental Health and Health Profession Strategies

Mental Health Evaluations Many children see their pediatricians for well-baby or well-child exams. The goal of these visits is to prevent illness before it occurs. Hinshaw (2007) makes a strong case for including similar preventive efforts for psychological disorders among children and adolescents by, for example, including rating scale assessments from parents and teachers to help identify problems before they become more serious.

Education and Training Mental health professionals should receive training in stigma issues. This type of training would undoubtedly help professionals recognize the pernicious signs of stigma, even within the very profession that is charged with helping people with psychological disorders. In addition, mental health professionals need to keep current on the descriptions, causes, and empirically supported treatments for psychological disorders. This would certainly lead to better interactions with people and might also help educate the public about the important work being done by mental health professionals.

Individual and Family Strategies

Education for Individuals and Families It can be frightening and disorienting for families to learn that a loved one has been diagnosed with an illness, and this may be particularly true for psychological disorders. Receiving current information about the causes and treatments of psychological disorders is crucial because it helps to alleviate blame and remove stereotypes families might hold about psychological disorders. Educating people with a psychological disorder is also extremely important. Sometimes termed *psychoeducation*, this type of information is built into many types of treatments, whether pharmacological or psychosocial. For people to understand why they should adhere to certain treatment regimens, it is important for them to know the nature of their illness and the treatment alternatives available.

Support and Advocacy Groups Participating in support or advocacy groups can be a helpful adjunct to treatment for people with psychological disorders and their families. Websites such as Mind Freedom International (http://www.mindfreedom.org) and the Icarus Project (http://www.theicarusproject.net) are designed to provide a forum for people with psychological disorders to find support. These sites, developed and run by people with psychological disorders, contain useful links, blogs, and other helpful resources. In-person support groups are also helpful, and many communities have groups supported by the National Alliance on Mental Illness (http://www.nami.org). Finding peers in the context of support groups can be beneficial, especially for emotional support and empowerment.

But you will have to help in this fight, for the mere acquisition of knowledge does not ensure the end of stigma (Corrigan, 2015). Many mental health practitioners and advocates have hoped that the more people learned about the neurobiological causes of psychological disorders, the less stigmatized these disorders would be. However, results from an important study show that this may not be true (Pescosolido, Martin, et al., 2010). People's knowledge has increased, but unfortunately stigma has not decreased. In the study, researchers surveyed people's attitudes and knowledge about psychological disorders at two points in time: 1996 and 2006. Compared with 1996, people in 2006 were more likely to believe that psychological disorders such as schizophrenia, depression, and alcohol addiction had a neurobiological cause, but stigma toward these disorders did not decrease. In fact, in some cases it increased.

For example, people in 2006 were less likely to want to have a person with schizophrenia as their neighbor compared with people in 1996. Clearly, there is work to be done to reduce stigma.

Recent efforts to reduce stigma have been quite creative in their use of social media and other means to get the message out that psychological disorders are common and affect us all in one way or another. Indeed, close to 44 million people in the United States (i.e., about 1 in 5 people) had some type of psychological disorder according to the Center for Behavioral Health Statistics and Quality (2015) report. For example, the site Bring Change to Mind (http://bringchange2mind.org) is a platform for personal stories that seeks to end stigma associated with psychological disorders, co-founded by the actress Glenn Close and her sister Jessie who has bipolar disorder (see Chapter 5) and her nephew Calen who has schizophrenia (see Chapter 9). Many blogs feature people talking poignantly about their lives with different psychological disorders, and these accounts help to demystify and therefore destigmatize it. For example, Allie Brosh wrote a blog called Hyperbole and a Half about her experiences with depression (http://hyperboleandahalf.blogspot.com) that culminated in a book (Brosh, 2013). The blog that is part of Strong365 (http://strong365.org) features stories of people living with different psychological disorders. The site Patients Like Me (http://www.patientslikeme.com) is a social networking site for people with all sorts of illnesses. Other creative efforts include the design of T-shirts by a graphic designer named Dani Balenson (http://danibalenson.com). In her work, she seeks to use color and graphics to depict the symptoms, behaviors, and struggles that characterize psychological disorders such as ADHD, obsessive-compulsive disorder, depression, and bipolar disorder (http://www.livingwith.co).

Celebrities or public figures with psychological disorders can also help reduce stigma. For example, the singer and songwriter Demi Lovato openly discusses her life with bipolar disorder and has joined the campaign BeVocal (http://www.bevocalspeakup.com/) to help reduce stigma.

In this chapter, we first discuss what we mean by the term *psychological disorder.* Then we look briefly at how our views of psychological disorders have evolved through history to the more scientific perspectives of today. We conclude with a discussion of the current mental health professions.

Tinseltown/Shutterstock

This book focuses on the description, causes, and treatments of several different psychological disorders. It is important to note at the outset that the personal impact of our subject matter requires us to make a conscious, determined effort to remain objective. Stigma remains a central problem in the field of psychopathology. Stigma has four components that involve the labels for psychological disorders and their uses. Even the use of everyday terms such as *crazy* or *schizo* can contribute to the stigmatization of people with psychological disorders.

Check Your Knowledge 1.1
(Answers are at the end of the chapter.)

1. Characteristics of stigma include all the following *except*:
    a. a label reflecting desirable characteristics
    b. discrimination against those with the label
    c. focus on differences between those with and without the label
    d. labeling a group of people who are different

2. True/False

Psychological disorders remain the most stigmatized of conditions in the twenty-first century.

3. True/False

Close to 20 million people in the United States had some type of psychological disorder according to the Center for Behavior Health Statistics and Quality (2015) report.

Defining Psychological Disorder

A difficult but fundamental task facing those in the field of psychopathology is to define psychological disorder. The best current definition of psychological disorder is one that contains several characteristics. The definition of *mental disorder* presented in the fifth edition of the American diagnostic manual, the *Diagnostic and Statistical Manual of Mental Disorders* (DSM-5), includes several characteristics essential to the concept of psychological disorder (Stein, Phillips, et al., 2010) as shown in **Table 1.1**.

In the following sections, we consider three key characteristics that should be part of any comprehensive psychological disorder definition: personal distress, disability/dysfunction, and violation of social norms (see **Figure 1.2**). We will see that no single characteristic can fully define the concept, although each has merit and each captures some part of what might be a full definition. Consequently, psychological disorder is usually determined based on the presence of several characteristics at one time.

FIGURE 1.2 Three characteristics of a comprehensive definition of psychological disorder.

Personal Distress

One characteristic used to define psychological disorder is personal distress—that is, a person's behavior may be classified as disordered if it causes him or her great distress. Felicia felt distress about her difficulty in paying attention and the social consequences of this difficulty—that is, being called names by other schoolgirls. Personal distress also characterizes many of the forms of psychological disorder considered in this book—people experiencing anxiety disorders and depression suffer greatly. But not all psychological disorders cause distress. For example, an individual with antisocial personality disorder may treat others coldheartedly and violate the law without experiencing any guilt, remorse, anxiety, or other type of distress. And not all behavior that causes distress is disordered—for example, the distress of hunger due to religious fasting or the pain of childbirth.

Personal distress can be part of the definition of psychological disorder.

Disability and Dysfunction

Disability—that is, impairment in some important area of life (e.g., work or personal relationships)—can also characterize psychological disorder. For example, substance use disorders are defined in part by the social or occupational disability (e.g., serious arguments with one's spouse or poor work performance) created by substance abuse. Being rejected by

TABLE 1.1 **The DSM-5 Definition of Mental Disorder**

The DSM-5 was released in 2013. The definition of mental disorder includes the following:

- The disorder occurs within the individual.
- It involves clinically significant difficulties in thinking, feeling, or behaving.
- It usually involves personal distress of some sort, such as in social relationships or occupational functioning.
- It involves dysfunction in psychological, developmental, and/or neurobiological processes that support mental functioning.
- It is not a culturally specific reaction to an event (e.g., death of a loved one).
- It is not primarily a result of social deviance or conflict with society.

Clinical Case

José

José didn't know what to think about his nightmares. Ever since he returned from the war, he couldn't get the bloody images out of his head. He woke up nearly every night with nightmares about the carnage he witnessed as a soldier stationed in Fallujah. Even during the day, he would have flashbacks to the moment his Humvee was nearly sliced in half by a rocket-propelled grenade. Watching his friend die sitting next to him was the worst part; even the occasional pain from shrapnel still embedded in his shoulder was not as bad as the recurring dreams and flashbacks. He seemed to be sweating all the time now, and whenever he heard a loud noise, he jumped out of his chair. Just the other day, his grandmother stepped on a balloon left over from his "welcome home" party. To José, it sounded like a gunshot, and he immediately dropped to the ground.

His grandmother was worried about him. She thought he must have *ataque de nervios*, just like her father had back home in Puerto Rico. She said her father had been afraid all the time and felt like he was going crazy. She kept going to Mass and praying for José, which he appreciated. The army doctor said he had posttraumatic stress disorder (PTSD). José was supposed to go to the Veterans Administration (VA) hospital for an evaluation, but he didn't really think there was anything wrong with him. Yet his buddy Jorge had been to a group session at the VA, and he said it made him feel better. Maybe he would check it out. He wanted these images to get out of his head.

peers, as Felicia was, is also an example of this characteristic. Phobias can produce both distress and disability—for example, if a severe fear of flying prevents someone living in California from taking a job in New York. Like distress, however, disability alone cannot be used to define psychological disorder because some, but not all, disorders involve disability. For example, the disorder bulimia nervosa involves binge eating and compensatory purging (e.g., vomiting) to control weight, but it does not necessarily involve disability. Many people with bulimia lead lives without impairment, while bingeing and purging in private. Other characteristics that might, in some circumstances, be considered disabilities—such as being blind and wanting to become a professional race car driver—do not fall within the domain of psychopathology. We do not have a rule that tells us which disabilities belong in our domain of study and which do not.

Dysfunction refers to something that has gone wrong and is not working as it should. The DSM-5 definition, shown in Table 1.1, provides a broad concept of dysfunction, which is supported by our current body of evidence. Specifically, the DSM definition of dysfunction refers to the fact that developmental, psychological, and biological dysfunctions are all interrelated. That is, the brain impacts behavior, and behavior impacts the brain; thus, dysfunction in these areas is interrelated.

Violation of Social Norms

In the realm of behavior, social norms are widely held standards (beliefs and attitudes) that people use consciously or intuitively to make judgments about where behaviors are situated on such scales as good–bad, right–wrong, justified–unjustified, and acceptable–unacceptable. Behavior that violates social norms might be classified as disordered. For example, the repetitive rituals performed by people with obsessive-compulsive disorder (see Chapter 7) and the conversations with imaginary voices that some people with schizophrenia engage in (see Chapter 9) are behaviors that violate social norms. José's dropping to the floor at the sound of a popping balloon does not fit within most social norms. Yet this way of defining psychological disorder is both too broad and too narrow. For example, it is too broad in that criminals violate social norms but are not usually studied within the domain of psychopathology; it is too narrow in that highly anxious people typically do not violate social norms.

Also, of course, social norms vary a great deal across cultures and ethnic groups, so behavior that clearly violates a social norm in one group may not do so at all in another. For example, in some cultures but not in others, it violates a social norm to directly disagree with someone. In Puerto Rico, José's behavior would not likely have been interpreted in the same way as it would be in the United States. Throughout this book, we will address this important issue of cultural and ethnic diversity as it applies to the descriptions, causes, and treatments of psychological disorders.

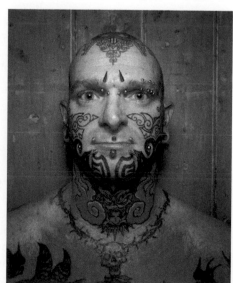

To some people, extreme tattoos are a violation of the social norm. However, social norm violations are not necessarily signs of a psychological disorder.

Quick Summary

Defining psychological disorder remains difficult. Several different definitions have been offered, but none can entirely account for the full range of disorders. Whether a behavior causes personal distress can be a characteristic of psychological disorder. But not all behaviors that we consider to be part of psychological disorders cause distress. Behaviors that cause a disability or are unexpected can be considered part of a psychological disorder. But again, some behaviors do not cause disability, nor are they unexpected. Behavior that violates social norms can also be considered part of a psychological disorder. However, not all such behavior is considered part of a psychological disorder, and some behaviors that are characteristic of psychological disorders do not necessarily violate social norms. Taken together, each definition of psychological disorder has something helpful to offer in the study of psychopathology.

Check Your Knowledge 1.2

1. True/False

Phobias can produce both distress and disability.

2. Which of the following definitions of psychological disorder is currently thought best?
    a. personal distress
    b. disability and dysfunction
    c. norm violation
    d. none of the above
3. What is an advantage of the DSM-5 definition of psychological disorder?
    a. It includes information about both violation of social norms and dysfunction.
    b. It includes many components, none of which alone can account for psychological disorder.
    c. It is part of the current diagnostic system.
    d. It recognizes the limits of our current understanding.

History of Psychopathology

Many textbooks begin with a chapter on the history of the field. Why? It is important to consider how concepts and approaches have changed (or not) over time, because we can learn from mistakes made in the past and because we can see that our current concepts and approaches are likely to change in the future. As we consider the history of psychopathology, we will see that many new approaches to the treatment of psychological disorders throughout time appear to go well at first and are heralded with much excitement and fanfare. But these treatments eventually fall into disrepute. These are lessons that should not be forgotten as we consider more contemporary approaches to treatment and their attendant excitement and fanfare.

Supernatural Explanations

Before the age of scientific inquiry, all good and bad manifestations of power beyond human control—eclipses, earthquakes, storms, fire, diseases, the changing seasons—were regarded as supernatural. Behavior seemingly out of individual control was also ascribed to supernatural causes. Many early philosophers, theologians, and physicians who studied the troubled mind believed that disturbed behavior reflected the displeasure of the gods or possession by demons.

Examples of supernatural explanations are found in the records of the early Chinese, Egyptians, Babylonians, and Greeks. Among the Hebrews, odd behavior was attributed to possession of the person by bad spirits, after God in his wrath had withdrawn protection. The New Testament includes the story of Christ curing a man with an unclean spirit by casting out the devils from within him and hurling them onto a herd of swine (Mark 5:8–13).

The belief that odd behavior was caused by possession led to treating it by **exorcism**, the ritualistic casting out of evil spirits. Exorcism typically took the form of elaborate rites of prayer, noisemaking, forcing the afflicted to drink terrible-tasting brews, and on occasion more extreme measures, such as flogging and starvation, to render the body uninhabitable to devils.

Early Biological Explanations

In the fifth century B.C., Hippocrates (460?–377? B.C.), often called the father of modern medicine, separated medicine from religion, magic, and superstition. He rejected the prevailing Greek belief that the gods sent mental disturbances as punishment and insisted instead that such illnesses had natural causes and hence should be treated like other, more common maladies, such as colds and constipation. Hippocrates regarded the brain as the organ of consciousness, intellectual life, and emotion; thus, he thought that disordered thinking and behavior were indications of some kind of brain pathology. Hippocrates is often considered one of the earliest proponents of the notion that something wrong with the brain contributes to psychological disorders.

Hippocrates (see photo) classified psychological disorders into three categories: mania, melancholia, and phrenitis, or brain fever. He believed that healthy brain functioning, and therefore mental health, depended on a delicate balance among four humors, or fluids of the body, namely, blood, black bile, yellow bile, and phlegm. An imbalance of these humors produced disorders. For example, if a person had a preponderance of black bile, the explanation was melancholia; too much yellow bile explained irritability and anxiousness; and too much blood, changeable temperament.

Through Hippocrates' teachings, the phenomena associated with psychological disorders became more clearly the province of physicians rather than religious figures. The treatments he suggested were quite different from exorcism. For melancholia, for example, he prescribed tranquility, sobriety, care in choosing food and drink, and abstinence from sexual activity. Because Hippocrates believed in natural rather than supernatural causes, he depended on his own keen observations and made valuable contributions as a clinician. He also left behind remarkably detailed records clearly describing many of the symptoms now recognized in seizure disorders, alcohol use disorder, stroke, and paranoia.

Hippocrates' ideas, of course, did not withstand later scientific scrutiny. However, his basic premise—that human behavior is markedly affected by bodily structures or substances and that odd behavior is produced by physical imbalance or even damage—did foreshadow aspects of contemporary thought. In the next seven centuries, Hippocrates' naturalistic approach to disease and disorder was generally accepted by other Greeks as well as by the Romans, who adopted the medicine of the Greeks after the Roman Empire became the major power in the ancient European world.

The Greek physician Hippocrates held a biological view of psychological disorders, considering psychological disorders to be diseases of the brain.

© Bruce Miller/Alamy

The Dark Ages: Back to the Supernatural

Historians have often pointed to the death of Galen (A.D. 130–200), the second-century Greek who is regarded as the last great physician of the classical era, as the beginning of the so-called Dark Ages in western European medicine and in the treatment and investigation of psychological disorders (see photo). Over several centuries of decay, Greek and Roman civilization ceased to be. The Church now gained in influence, and the papacy was declared independent of the state. Christian monasteries, through their missionary and educational work, replaced physicians as healers and as authorities on psychological disorder.[1]

The monks in the monasteries cared for and nursed the sick, and a few of the monasteries were repositories for the classic Greek medical manuscripts, even though the

Galen was a Greek physician who followed Hippocrates' ideas and is regarded as the last great physician of the classical era.

Corbis Historical/Getty Images

---

[1]The teachings of Galen continued to be influential in the Islamic world. For example, the Persian physician al-Razi (865–925) established a facility for the treatment of people with psychological disorders in Baghdad and was an early practitioner of psychotherapy.

monks may not have made use of the knowledge in these works. Monks cared for people with psychological disorders by praying over them and touching them with relics; they also concocted fantastic potions for them to drink in the waning phase of the moon. Many people with psychological disorders roamed the countryside, destitute and progressively becoming worse. During this period, there was a return to a belief in supernatural causes of psychological disorders.

Lunacy Trials From the thirteenth century on, as the cities of Europe grew larger, hospitals began to come under secular jurisdiction. Municipal authorities, gaining in power, tended to supplement or take over some of the activities of the Church, one of these being the care of people with psychological disorders. The foundation deed for the Holy Trinity Hospital in Salisbury, England, dating from the mid-fourteenth century, specified the purposes of the hospital, one of which was that the "mad are kept safe until they are restored of reason." English laws during this period allowed people with psychological disorders to be hospitalized. Notably, the people who were hospitalized were not described as being possessed (Alldderidge, 1979).

Beginning in the thirteenth century, lunacy trials to determine a person's mental health were held in England. As explained by Neugebauer (1979), the trials were conducted under the Crown's right to protect people with psychological disorders, and a judgment of insanity allowed the Crown to become guardian of the person's estate. The defendant's orientation, memory, intellect, daily life, and habits were at issue in the trial. Usually, strange behavior was attributed to physical illness or injury or to some emotional shock. In all the cases that Neugebauer examined, only one referred to demonic possession. Interestingly, the term *lunacy* comes from a theory espoused by the Swiss physician Paracelsus (1493–1541), who attributed odd behavior to a misalignment of the moon and stars (the Latin word for "moon" is *luna*). Even today, many people believe that a full moon is linked to odd behavior; however, there is no scientific evidence to support this belief.

Bettmann/Getty Images, Inc.

In the dunking test, if the woman did not drown, she was considered to be in league with the devil (and punished accordingly); this is the ultimate no-win situation.

Development of Asylums

Until the fifteenth century, there were very few hospitals for people with psychological disorders in Europe. However, there were many hospitals for people with leprosy. As leprosy gradually disappeared from Europe (probably because with the end of wars came a break with the sources of the infection), these buildings were now underused. Attention seems to have turned to people with psychological disorders, and the old leprosy hospitals were converted to **asylums**, refuges for the housing and care of people with psychological disorders.

Bethlehem and Other Early Asylums The Priory of St. Mary of Bethlehem was founded in 1243. Records indicate that in 1403 it housed six men with psychological disorders. In 1547, Henry VIII handed it over to the city of London, thereafter to be a hospital devoted solely to the housing of people with psychological disorders. The conditions in Bethlehem were deplorable. Over the years the word *bedlam*, the popular name for this hospital, came to mean a place or scene of wild uproar and confusion. Bethlehem eventually became one of London's great tourist attractions, by the eighteenth century rivaling both Westminster Abbey and the Tower of London. Even as late as the nineteenth century, viewing the people housed in Bethlehem was considered entertainment, and people bought tickets to see them. Similarly, in the Lunatics Tower, which was constructed in Vienna in 1784, people were confined in the spaces between inner square rooms and the outer walls, where they could be viewed by passersby.

Unfortunately, housing people with psychological disorders in hospitals and placing their care in the domain of medicine did not necessarily lead to more humane and effective treatment. In fact, the medical treatments were often crude and painful. Benjamin Rush (1745–1813), for example, began practicing medicine in Philadelphia in 1769 and is considered the father of American psychiatry. Yet he believed that psychological disorder was caused by an excess of blood in the brain, for which his favored treatment was to draw great quantities of blood from people with psychological disorders (Farina, 1976). Rush also believed that many people with psychological disorders could be cured by being frightened. Thus, one of his recommended procedures was for the physician to convince the patient that death was near!

In this eighteenth-century painting by Hogarth, two upper-class women find amusement in touring St. Mary's of Bethlehem (Bedlam).

Bettmann/Getty Images

Pinel's Reforms

Philippe Pinel (1745–1826) has often been considered a primary figure in the movement for more humane treatment of people with psychological disorders in asylums. In 1793, while the French Revolution raged, he was put in charge of a large asylum in Paris known as La Bicêtre. A historian described the conditions at this particular hospital:

> [The patients were] shackled to the walls of their cells, by iron collars which held them flat against the wall and permitted little movement. They could not lie down at night, as a rule. Oftentimes there was a hoop of iron around the waist of the patient and in addition chains on both the hands and the feet. These chains [were] sufficiently long so that the patient could feed himself out of a bowl, the food usually being a mushy gruel—bread soaked in a weak soup. Since little was known about dietetics, [no attention] was paid to the type of diet given the patients. They were presumed to be animals and not to care whether the food was good or bad. (Selling, 1940, p. 54)

Many texts assert that Pinel removed the chains of the people imprisoned in La Bicêtre. Historical research, however, indicates that it was not Pinel who released the people from their chains. Rather, it was a former patient, Jean-Baptiste Pussin, who had become an orderly at the hospital. In fact, Pinel was not even present when the people were released (Weiner, 1994). Several years later, though, Pinel praised Pussin's efforts and began to follow the same practices.

Pinel came to believe that people in his care were first and foremost human beings, and thus these people should be approached with compassion and understanding and treated with dignity. He surmised that if their reason had left them because of severe personal and social problems, it might be restored to them through comforting counsel and purposeful activity. Thus, light and airy rooms replaced dungeons. People formerly considered dangerous now strolled through the hospital and grounds without creating disturbances or harming anyone.

Although Pinel did much good for people with psychological disorders, he was no paragon of enlightenment and egalitarianism. He reserved the more humanitarian treatment for the upper classes; people of the lower classes were still subjected to terror and coercion as a means of control, with straitjackets replacing chains.

Moral Treatment

For a time, mental hospitals established in Europe and the United States were relatively small, privately supported, and operated along the lines of the humanitarian changes at La Bicêtre. In the United States, the Friends' Asylum, founded in 1817 in Pennsylvania, and the Hartford Retreat, established in 1824 in Connecticut, were established to provide humane treatment. In accordance with this approach, which became known as **moral treatment**, people had close contact with attendants, who talked and read to them and encouraged them to engage in purposeful activity; residents led lives as close to normal as possible and in general took responsibility for themselves within the constraints of their disorders. Further, there were to be no more than 250 people in any given hospital (Whitaker, 2002).

Moral treatment was largely abandoned in the latter part of the nineteenth century. Ironically, the efforts of Dorothea Dix (1802–1887), a crusader for improved conditions for people with psychological disorders who fought to have hospitals created for their care, helped effect this change (see photo). Dix, a Boston schoolteacher, taught a Sunday school class at the local prison and was shocked at the deplorable conditions in which the inmates lived. Her interest spread to the conditions at mental hospitals and to people with psychological disorders who had nowhere to go for treatment. She campaigned vigorously to improve the lives of people with psychological disorders and personally helped see that 32 hospitals were built. These large public hospitals took in many of the people whom the private hospitals could not accommodate. Unfortunately, the small staffs of these new hospitals were unable to provide the individual attention that was a hallmark of moral treatment (Bockhoven, 1963, Powers; 2017). (See **Focus on Discovery 1.2** for an examination of whether the conditions in today's mental hospitals have improved.)

Focus on Discovery 1.2

The Mental Hospital Today

frank60/Shutterstock

More people with psychological disorders are found in jails and prisons than in mental hospitals in the United States—a national disgrace.

In the late 1960s and early 1970s, concerns about the restrictive nature of confinement in a mental hospital along with unrealistic enthusiasm about community-based treatments (Torrey, 2014) led to the so-called deinstitutionalization (i.e., release from the hospital) of a large number of people with psychological disorders. Budget cuts beginning in 1980 and continuing today have caused this trend to continue. But sometimes people with a psychological disorder do need treatment in a hospital setting and, unfortunately, we still do not do a good job of this, even in the twenty-first century (as we will discuss in more detail in Chapter 16). Treatment in public mental hospitals today is often "just enough" to provide some protection, food, shelter, and in most cases medication. Indeed, people with psychological disorders in a public hospital may receive little treatment beyond medication; their existence is monotonous and sedentary for the most part.

Public mental hospitals in the United States are funded either by the federal government or, more likely, by the state in which they are located. Many Veterans Administration hospitals and general medical hospitals also contain units for people with psychological disorders. Since the mid-1950s, the number of public mental hospitals has decreased substantially. In 1955, there were 340 beds in public hospitals for people with psychological disorders for every 100,000 people; by 2010 there were just 14 beds for every 100,000 people (Torrey, 2014).

A somewhat specialized mental hospital, sometimes called a forensic hospital, is reserved for people who have been arrested and judged unable to stand trial and for those who have been acquitted of a crime by reason of insanity (see Chapter 16). Although these people have not been sent to prison, security staff and other tight security measures regiment their lives even as they receive treatment during their stay. There is some evidence to suggest that people who receive treatment at forensic hospitals are less likely to reoffend than people who are sent to regular prisons and do not receive treatment (Harris, 2000).

One of the many unfortunate consequences of fewer mental hospitals today is overcrowding in existing hospitals. One longitudinal study of 13 public mental hospitals in Finland showed that nearly half the hospitals were overcrowded (defined as having 10 percent more occupancy than the hospital was designed for). The researchers also found that overcrowding was associated with an increased risk of violence against hospital staff by patients (Virtanen, Vahtera, et al., 2011). Although we have developed more effective treatments for many psychological disorders, as we will see throughout this book, the mental hospital of today is still in need of improvement.

Another very unfortunate consequence of fewer mental hospitals is the fact that jails have become the *de facto* mental hospitals in many cities in the United States (Baillargeon, Binswanger, et al., 2009; Torrey, 2014). Sadly, jails in Los Angeles County and Cook County (in Chicago) are now the largest "mental hospitals" in the United States, housing 10 times more people with psychological disorders than any actual mental hospital (Steinberg, Mills, & Romano, 2015). Moreover, a report from the Treatment Advocacy Center and the National Sheriffs Association that drew from 2004–2005 data in the United States indicated that there are more people with psychological disorders in jails or prisons than in mental hospitals (Torrey, Kennard, et al., 2010). Furthermore, of the people currently in prison or jail, over half have a psychological disorder (James & Glaze, 2006).

© Amanda Brown/Star Ledger

Most rooms at state mental hospitals are bleak and unstimulating.

Quick Summary

Early concepts of psychological disorders included not only supernatural but also biological approaches, as evidenced by the ideas of Hippocrates. During the Dark Ages, some people with psychological disorders were cared for in monasteries, but many simply roamed the countryside. Treatments for people with psychological disorders have changed over time, though not always for the better. Exorcisms did not help. Treatments in asylums could also be cruel and unhelpful, but pioneering work by Dix and others made asylums more humane places for treatment. Unfortunately, their good ideas did not last, as the mental hospitals became overcrowded and understaffed.

Check Your Knowledge 1.3

True or false?

1. Benjamin Rush is credited with beginning moral treatment in the United States.

2. Exorcism was an early biological treatment.

3. Hippocrates was one of the first to propose that psychological disorders had a biological cause.

4. The term *lunatic* is derived from the ideas of Paracelsus.

In the nineteenth century, Dorothea Dix played a major role in establishing more mental hospitals in the United States.

The Evolution of Contemporary Thought

As horrific as the conditions in Bethlehem Hospital were (and in some ways, continue to be; see Focus on Discovery 1.2), the physicians at the time were nonetheless interested in what caused the maladies of their patients. **Table 1.2** lists the hypothesized causes of the illnesses exhibited

TABLE 1.2	Causes of Maladies Observed Among People in Bethlehem in 1810
Cause	**Number of People**
Childbed*	79
Contusions/fractures of skull	12
Drink/intoxication	58
Family/hereditary	115
Fevers	110
Fright	31
Grief	206
Jealousy	9
Love	90
Obstruction	10
Pride	8
Religion/Methodism	90
Smallpox	7
Study	15
Venereal	14
Ulcers/scabs dried up	5

Source: Adapted from Appignanesi (2008), Hunter & Macalpine (1963).

*Childbed refers to childbirth—perhaps akin to what we now call postpartum depression.

by people in 1810 that were recorded by William Black, a physician working at Bethlehem at the time (Appignanesi, 2008). It is interesting to observe that about half of the presumed causes were biological (e.g., fever, hereditary, venereal) and half were psychological (e.g., grief, love, jealousy). Only around 10 percent of the causes were supernatural.

Contemporary developments in biological and psychological approaches to the causes and treatments of psychological disorders were heavily influenced by theorists and scientists working in the late nineteenth and early twentieth centuries. We will discuss, compare, and evaluate these approaches more fully in Chapter 2. In this section, we review the historical antecedents of these more contemporary approaches.

Recall that in the West, the death of Galen and the decline of Greco-Roman civilization temporarily ended inquiries into the nature of both physical and mental illness. Not until much later did any new facts begin to come to light, thanks to an emerging empirical approach to medical science, which emphasized gathering knowledge by direct observation.

Biological Approaches

Discovering Biological Origins in General Paresis and Syphilis

The anatomy and workings of the nervous system were partially understood by the mid-1800s, but not enough was known to let investigators conclude whether or not the structural brain abnormalities presumed to cause various psychological disorders were present. One striking medical success was the elucidation of the nature and origin of syphilis, a sexually transmitted disease that had been recognized for several centuries.

The story of this discovery regarding syphilis provides a good illustration of how an empirical approach, the basis for contemporary science, works. Since the late 1700s, it had been known that a number of people with psychological disorders manifested a syndrome characterized by a steady deterioration of both mental and physical abilities, and progressive paralysis; the presumed disease associated with this syndrome was given the name general paresis. By the mid-1800s, it had been established that some people with general paresis also had syphilis, but a connection between the two conditions had not yet been made.

In the 1860s and 1870s, Louis Pasteur established the germ theory of disease, which posited that disease is caused by infection of the body by minute organisms. This theory laid the groundwork for demonstrating the relation between syphilis and general paresis. Finally, in 1905, the specific microorganism that causes syphilis was discovered. For the first time, a causal link had been established between infection, damage to certain areas of the brain, and a form of psychopathology (general paresis). If one type of psychopathology had a biological cause, so could others. Biological approaches gained credibility, and searches for more biological causes were off and running.

Genetics

Francis Galton (1822–1911), often considered the originator of genetic research with twins because of his study of twins in the late 1800s in England, attributed many behavioral characteristics to heredity (see photo). He is credited with coining the terms *nature* and *nurture* to talk about differences in genetics (nature) and environment (nurture). In the early twentieth century, investigators became intrigued by the idea that psychological disorders may run in families, and beginning at that time, many studies documented the heritability of psychological disorders such as schizophrenia, bipolar disorder, and depression. These studies would set the stage for later theories about the causes of psychological disorders.

Unfortunately, Galton is also credited with creating the eugenics movement in 1883 (Brooks, 2004). Advocates of this movement sought to eliminate undesirable characteristics from the population by restricting the ability of certain people to have children (e.g., by enforced sterilization). Many of the early efforts in the United States to determine whether psychological disorders could be inherited were associated with the eugenics movement, and this stalled research progress. Indeed, in a sad page from U.S. history, state laws in the late 1800s and early 1900s prohibited people with psychological disorders from marrying and forced them to be sterilized to prevent

Bettmann/Getty Images

Francis Galton is considered the originator of genetics research.

them from "passing on" their illness. Such laws were upheld by the U.S. Supreme Court in 1927 (Stern, 2015), and it wasn't until much later that these abhorrent practices were halted. For example, the eugenics law in California was not repealed until 1979. Still, investigative reporting uncovered 148 sterilizations of women in California prisons between 2006 and 2010, prompting a new law signed in 2014 that bans the practice in prisons. In the past 10 years, some states have provided compensation to survivors of this horrible practice (Stern, Novak, et al., 2017).

Biological Treatments The general warehousing of people in mental hospitals earlier in the twentieth century, coupled with the shortage of professional staff, created a climate that allowed, perhaps even subtly encouraged, experimentation with radical interventions. In the early 1930s, the practice of inducing a coma with large dosages of insulin was introduced by Sakel (1938), who claimed that up to three-quarters of the people with schizophrenia whom he treated showed significant improvement. Later findings by other researchers were less encouraging, and insulin-coma therapy—which presented serious risks to health, including irreversible coma and death—was gradually abandoned.

In the early twentieth century, **electroconvulsive therapy (ECT)** was originated by two Italian physicians, Ugo Cerletti and Lucino Bini. Cerletti was interested in epilepsy and was seeking a way to induce seizures experimentally. Shortly thereafter he found that by applying electric shocks to the sides of the human head, he could produce full epileptic seizures. Then, in Rome in 1938, he used the technique on a person with schizophrenia.

In the decades that followed, ECT was administered to people with schizophrenia and severe depression, usually in hospital settings. As we will discuss in Chapter 5, it is still used today for people with severe depression. Fortunately, important refinements in the ECT procedures have made it less problematic, and it can be an effective treatment.

In 1935, Egas Moniz, a Portuguese psychiatrist, introduced the *prefrontal lobotomy*, a surgical procedure that destroys the tracts connecting the frontal lobes to other areas of the brain. His initial reports claimed high rates of success (Moniz, 1936), and for 20 years thereafter thousands of people with psychological disorders underwent variations of this psychosurgery. The procedure was used especially for those whose behavior was violent. Many people did indeed quiet down and could even be discharged from hospitals, but largely because their brains were damaged. During the 1950s, this intervention fell into disrepute for several reasons. After surgery, many people became dull and listless and suffered serious losses in their emotional experience and cognitive capacities—for example, becoming unable to carry on a coherent conversation with another person—which is not surprising given the destruction of parts of their brains that support emotion, thought, and language.

Scene from *One Flew Over the Cuckoo's Nest.* The character portrayed by Jack Nicholson was lobotomized in the film.

Psychological Approaches

The search for biological causes dominated the field of psychopathology until well into the twentieth century, no doubt partly because of the discoveries made about the brain and genetics. But beginning in the late eighteenth century, various psychological points of view emerged that attributed psychological disorders to psychological malfunctions. These theories were fashionable first in France and Austria, and later in the United States, leading to the development of psychotherapeutic interventions based on the tenets of the individual theories.

Mesmer and Charcot During the eighteenth century in western Europe, many people were observed to be subject to *hysteria*, which referred to physical incapacities, such as blindness or paralysis, for which no physical cause could be found. Franz Anton Mesmer (1734–1815), an Austrian physician practicing in Vienna and Paris in the late eighteenth century, believed that hysteria was caused by a distribution of a universal magnetic fluid in the body. Moreover, he felt that one person could influence the fluid of another to bring about a change in the other's behavior.

Mesmer conducted meetings cloaked in mystery and mysticism, and he originally developed a technique using rods to influence a person's alleged magnetic fields. Later, Mesmer perfected his routines by simply looking at people rather than using rods.

Although Mesmer regarded hysteria as having strictly biological causes, we discuss his work here because he is generally considered one of the earlier practitioners of modern-day hypnosis. (The word *mesmerism* is a synonym for *hypnotism*; the phenomenon itself was known to the ancients of many cultures, where it was part of the sorcery and magic of conjurers and faith healers.)

Mesmer came to be regarded as a quack by his contemporaries, which is ironic, since he had earlier helped discredit an exorcist, Father Johann Joseph Gassner, who was performing similar rituals (Harrington, 2008). Nevertheless, hypnosis gradually became respectable. The great Parisian neurologist Jean-Martin Charcot (1825–1893) also studied hysterical states. Although Charcot believed that hysteria was a problem with the nervous system and had a biological cause, he was also persuaded by psychological explanations. One day, some of his enterprising students hypnotized a healthy woman and, by suggestion, induced her to display certain hysterical symptoms. Charcot was deceived into believing that she was an actual patient with hysteria. When the students showed him how readily they could remove the symptoms by waking the woman, Charcot became interested in psychological interpretations of these very puzzling phenomena. Given Charcot's prominence in Parisian society, his support of hypnosis as a worthy treatment for hysteria helped to legitimize this form of treatment among medical professionals of the time (Harrington, 2008; Hustvedt, 2011).

Mesmer's procedure for manipulating magnetism was generally considered a form of hypnosis.

Breuer and the Cathartic Method

In the nineteenth century, a Viennese physician, Josef Breuer (1842–1925) (see photo), treated a young woman, whose identity was disguised under the pseudonym Anna O., with a number of hysterical symptoms, including partial paralysis, impairment of sight and hearing, and often difficulty speaking. She also sometimes went into a dreamlike state, or "absence," during which she mumbled to herself, seemingly preoccupied with troubling thoughts. Breuer hypnotized her, and while hypnotized, she began talking more freely and, ultimately, with considerable emotion about upsetting events from her past. Frequently, on awakening from a hypnotic session she felt much better. Breuer found that the relief of a particular symptom seemed to last longer if, under hypnosis, she was able to recall the event associated with the first appearance of that symptom and if she was able to express the emotion she had felt at the time. Reliving an earlier emotional trauma and releasing emotional tension by expressing previously forgotten thoughts about the event was called catharsis, and Breuer's method became known as the **cathartic method**. In 1895, Breuer and a younger colleague, Sigmund Freud (1856–1939), jointly published *Studies in Hysteria*, partly based on the case of Anna O.

Josef Breuer, an Austrian physician and physiologist, collaborated with Freud in the early development of psychoanalysis.

The case of Anna O. became one of the best-known clinical cases in the psychoanalytic literature. Ironically, later investigation revealed that Breuer and Freud reported the case incorrectly. Historical study by Ellenberger (1972) indicates that Breuer's talking cure helped the young woman only temporarily. This claim is supported by Carl Jung, a renowned colleague of Freud's, who is quoted as saying that during a conference in 1925, Freud told him that Anna O. had never been cured. Hospital records discovered by Ellenberger confirmed that Anna O. continued to rely on morphine to ease the "hysterical" problems that Breuer is reputed to have cured by catharsis.

Freud and Psychoanalysis

The apparently powerful role played by factors of which people seemed unaware led Freud to postulate that much of human behavior is determined by forces that are inaccessible to awareness. The central assumption of Freud's theorizing, often referred to as **psychoanalytic theory**, is that psychopathology results from **unconscious** conflicts in the individual. In the next sections, we take a look at Freud's theory.

Structure of the Mind

Freud divided the mind into three principal parts: id, ego, and superego. According to Freud, the id is present at birth and is the repository of all the energy needed to run the mind, including the basic urges for food, water, elimination, warmth, affection, and sex. Trained as a neurologist, Freud saw the source of the id's energy as biological and unconscious. That is, a person cannot consciously perceive this energy—it is below the level of awareness.

The **id** seeks immediate gratification of its urges. When the id is not satisfied, tension is produced, and the id drives a person to get rid of this tension as quickly as possible. For example, a baby feels hunger and is impelled to move about, sucking, in an attempt to reduce the tension arising from the hunger urge.

According to Freud, the **ego** begins to develop from the id during the second 6 months of life. Unlike the contents of the id, those of the ego are primarily conscious. The task of the ego is to deal with reality, and it mediates between the demands of reality and the id's demands for immediate gratification.

The **superego**—the third part of the mind in Freud's theory—can be roughly conceived of as a person's conscience. Freud believed that the superego develops throughout childhood, arising from the ego much as the ego arises from the id. As children discover that many of their impulses—for example, biting—are not acceptable to their parents, they begin to incorporate parental values as their own to receive the pleasure of parental approval and avoid the pain of disapproval.

Sigmund Freud developed psychoanalytic theory, a theory of the structure and functions of the mind (including explanations of the causes of psychological disorders), and psychoanalysis, a method of therapy based on it.

Defense Mechanisms

According to Freud, and as elaborated by his daughter Anna (A. A. Freud, 1946/1966), herself an influential psychoanalyst, discomforts experienced by the ego as it attempts to resolve conflicts and satisfy the demands of the id and superego can be reduced in several ways. A **defense mechanism** is a strategy used by the ego to protect itself from anxiety. Examples of defense mechanisms are presented in **Table 1.3**.

TABLE 1.3   Selected Defense Mechanisms

Defense Mechanism	Definition	Example
Repression	Keeping unacceptable impulses or wishes from conscious awareness	A professor starting a lecture she dreaded giving says, "In conclusion."
Denial	Not accepting a painful reality into conscious awareness	A victim of childhood abuse does not acknowledge it as an adult.
Projection	Attributing to someone else one's own unacceptable thoughts or feelings	A man who hates members of a racial group believes that it is they who dislike him.
Displacement	Redirecting emotional responses from their real target to someone else	A child gets mad at her brother but instead acts angrily toward her friend.
Reaction formation	Converting an unacceptable feeling into its opposite	A person with sexual feelings toward children leads a campaign against child sexual abuse.
Regression	Retreating to the behavioral patterns of an earlier stage of development	An adolescent dealing with unacceptable feelings of social inadequacy attempts to mask those feelings by seeking oral gratification.
Rationalization	Offering acceptable reasons for an unacceptable action or attitude	A parent berates a child out of impatience, then indicates that she did so to "build character."
Sublimation	Converting unacceptable aggressive or sexual impulses into socially valued behaviors	Someone who has aggressive feelings toward his father becomes a surgeon.

Corbis Historical/Getty Images

TABLE 1.4	Major Techniques of Psychoanalysis
Technique	**Description**
Free association	A person tries to say whatever comes to mind without censoring anything.
Interpretation	The analyst points out the meaning of certain of a person's behaviors.
Analysis of transference	The person responds to the analyst in ways that the person has previously responded to other important figures in his or her life, and the analyst helps the person understand and interpret these responses.

Psychoanalytic Therapy **Psychotherapy** based on Freud's theory is called **psychoanalysis** or psychoanalytic therapy. It is still practiced today, although not as commonly as it once was. In psychoanalytic and newer psychodynamic treatments, the goal of the therapist is to understand the person's early-childhood experiences, the nature of key relationships, and the patterns in current relationships. The therapist is listening for core emotional and relationship themes that surface again and again (see **Table 1.4** for a summary of psychoanalysis techniques).

Freud developed several techniques in his efforts to help people resolve repressed conflicts. With *free association*, a person reclines on a couch, facing away from the analyst, and is encouraged to give free rein to his or her thoughts, verbalizing whatever comes to mind, without censoring anything.

Another key component of psychoanalytic therapy is the analysis of **transference**. Transference refers to the person's responses to his or her analyst that seem to reflect attitudes and ways of behaving toward important people in the person's past. For example, a person might feel that the analyst is generally bored by what he or she is saying and as a result might struggle to be entertaining; this pattern of response might reflect the person's childhood relationship with a parent rather than what's going on between the person and the analyst. Through careful observation and analysis of these transferred attitudes, Freud believed the analyst could gain insight into the childhood origins of a person's repressed conflicts. In the example above, the analyst might suggest that the person was made to feel boring and unimportant as a child and could only gain parental attention through humor.

In the technique of *interpretation*, the analyst points out the meanings of a person's behavior. Defense mechanisms (see Table 1.3) are a principal focus of interpretation. For instance, a man who appears to have trouble with intimacy may look out the window and change the subject whenever the conversation touches on closeness during the course of a session.

The analyst will attempt at some point to interpret the person's behavior, pointing out its defensive nature in the hope of helping the person acknowledge that he is in fact avoiding the topic.

Continuing Influences of Freud and His Followers Freud's original ideas and methods have been heavily criticized over the years. For example, Freud conducted no formal research on the causes and treatments of psychological disorders. This remains one of the main criticisms today: because they are based on anecdotal evidence gathered during therapy sessions, some psychodynamic theories are not grounded in objectivity and therefore are not scientific. However, other contemporary psychodynamic theories, such as object relations theory (discussed in Chapter 2), have built a limited base of supportive research. Offshoots of object relations theory, such as attachment theory and the idea of the relational self (discussed in Chapter 2), have accumulated research support, both in children and adults. In **Focus on Discovery 1.3**, we discuss two influential theorists who began with Freud but then developed their own theories.

Focus on Discovery 1.3

Extensions and Variations on Freud's Theories

Several of Freud's contemporaries met with him periodically to discuss psychoanalytic theory and therapy. As often happens when a brilliant leader attracts brilliant followers and colleagues, disagreements arose about many general issues, such as the relative importance of id versus ego, of biological versus sociocultural forces on psychological development, of unconscious versus conscious processes, and of childhood versus adult experiences. We discuss two influential historical figures here: Carl Jung and Alfred Adler.

Carl Jung was the founder of analytical psychology.

Jung and Analytical Psychology

Carl Gustav Jung (1875–1961) (see photo) originally considered Freud's heir apparent, broke with Freud in 1914 over many issues. After a 7-year period of intense correspondence about their disagreements. Jung proposed ideas radically different from Freud's, ultimately establishing *analytical psychology.*

Jung hypothesized that in addition to the personal unconscious postulated by Freud, there is a *collective unconscious*, the part of the unconscious that is common to all human beings and that consists primarily of what Jung called *archetypes*, or basic categories that all human beings use in conceptualizing about the world.

Adler and Individual Psychology

Alfred Adler (1870–1937) (see photo), also an early adherent of Freud's theories, came to be even less dependent on Freud's views than was Jung, and Freud remained quite bitter toward Adler after their relationship ended. Adler's theory, which came to be known as *individual psychology*, regarded people as inextricably tied to their society because he believed that fulfillment was found in doing things for the social good. Like Jung, he stressed the importance of working toward goals (Adler, 1930).

A central element in Adler's work was his focus on helping people change their illogical and mistaken ideas and expectations. He believed that feeling and behaving better depend on thinking more rationally, an approach that anticipated contemporary developments in cognitive behavior therapy (discussed in Chapter 2).

Alfred Adler was the founder of individual psychology.

Though perhaps not as influential as it once was, the work of Freud and his followers continues to have an impact on the field of psychopathology (Westen, 1998). This influence is most evident in the following three commonly held assumptions:

1. *Childhood experiences help shape adult personality.* Contemporary clinicians and researchers still view childhood experiences and other environmental events as crucial. They seldom focus on the psychosexual stages about which Freud wrote, but some emphasize problematic parent–child relationships in general and how they can influence later adult relationships in negative ways.

2. *There are unconscious influences on behavior.* As we will discuss in Chapter 2, the unconscious is a focus of contemporary research in cognitive neuroscience and psychopathology. This research shows that people can be unaware of the causes of their behavior. However, most current researchers and clinicians do not think of the unconscious as a repository of id instincts.

3. *The causes and purposes of human behavior are not always obvious.* Freud and his followers sensitized generations of clinicians and researchers to the nonobviousness of the causes and purposes of human behavior. Contemporary psychodynamic theorists continue to caution us against taking everything at face value. A person expressing disdain for another, for example, may actually like the other person very much, yet be fearful of admitting positive feelings. This tendency to look under the surface, to find hidden meanings in behavior, is perhaps Freud's best-known legacy.

The Rise of Behaviorism After some years, many in the field began to lose faith in Freud's approach. Instead, the experimental procedures of the psychologists who were investigating learning in animals became a more dominant focus of psychology. **Behaviorism** focuses on observable behavior rather than on consciousness or mental functioning. We will look at three types of learning that influenced the behaviorist approach in the early and middle parts of the twentieth century and that continue to be influential today: **classical conditioning**, **operant conditioning**, and **modeling**.

Ivan Pavlov, a Russian physiologist and Nobel laureate, made important contributions to the research and theory of classical conditioning.

Classical Conditioning Around the turn of the twentieth century, the Russian physiologist and Nobel laureate Ivan Pavlov (1849–1936) (see photo) discovered classical conditioning, quite by accident. As part of his study of the digestive system, Pavlov gave a dog meat powder to make it salivate. Before long, Pavlov's laboratory assistants became aware that the dog began salivating when it saw the person who fed it. As the experiment continued, the dog began to salivate even earlier, when it heard the footsteps of its feeder. Pavlov was intrigued by these findings and decided to study the dog's reactions systematically. In the first of many experiments, a bell was rung behind the dog and then the meat powder was placed in its mouth. After this procedure had been repeated several times, the dog began salivating as soon as it heard the bell and before it received the meat powder.

In this experiment, because the meat powder automatically elicits salivation with no prior learning, the powder is termed an **unconditioned stimulus (UCS)** and the response of salivation an **unconditioned response (UCR)**. When the offering of meat powder is preceded several times by a neutral stimulus, the ringing of a bell, the sound of the bell alone (the **conditioned stimulus**, or **CS**) can elicit the salivary response (the **conditioned response**, or **CR**) (see **Figure 1.3**). As the number of paired presentations of the bell and the meat powder increases, the number of salivations elicited by the bell alone increases. What happens to an established CR if the CS is no longer followed by the UCS—for example, if repeated soundings of the bell are not followed by meat powder? The answer is that fewer and fewer CRs (salivations) are elicited, and the CR gradually disappears. This is termed **extinction**.

Classical conditioning can even instill fear. A famous but ethically questionable experiment conducted by John Watson (see photo) and Rosalie Rayner (Watson & Rayner, 1920) involved introducing a white rat to an 11-month-old boy, Little Albert. The boy showed no fear of the animal and appeared to want to play with it. But whenever

John B. Watson, an American psychologist, was a major figure in establishing behaviorism.

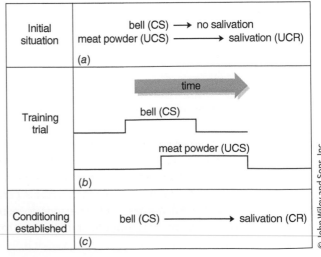

FIGURE 1.3 The process of classical conditioning. (**a**) Before learning, the meat powder (UCS) elicits salivation (UCR), but the bell (CS) does not. (**b**) A training or learning trial consists of presentations of the CS, followed closely by the UCS. (**c**) Classical conditioning has been accomplished when the previously neutral bell elicits salivation (CR).

the boy reached for the rat, the experimenter made a loud noise (the UCS) by striking a steel bar behind Albert's head. This caused Little Albert great fright (the UCR). After five such experiences, Albert became very frightened (the CR) by the sight of the white rat, even when the steel bar was not struck. The fear initially associated with the loud noise had come to be elicited by the previously neutral stimulus, the white rat (now the CS). This study suggests a possible relationship between classical conditioning and the development of certain disorders, in this instance a phobia. It is important to note that this type of study could never be done today because it breaches ethical standards. However, the work of John Watson (1878–1958) helped to establish the promise of behavioral approaches.

Operant Conditioning In the 1890s, Edward Thorndike (1874–1949) began work that led to the discovery of another type of learning. Rather than investigate the association between stimuli, as Pavlov did, Thorndike studied the effects of consequences on behavior. Thorndike formulated what was to become an extremely important principle, the **law of effect**: Behavior that is followed by consequences satisfying to the organism will be repeated, and behavior that is followed by unpleasant consequences will be discouraged.

B. F. Skinner (1904–1990) (see photo) introduced the concept of operant conditioning, so called because it applies to behavior that operates on the environment. Renaming Thorndike's "law of effect" the "principle of reinforcement," Skinner distinguished two types of reinforcement. **Positive reinforcement** refers to the strengthening of a tendency to respond by virtue of the presentation of a pleasant event, called a positive reinforcer. For example, a puppy will be more likely to sit if it is given a treat after doing so. **Negative reinforcement** also strengthens a response, but it does so via the removal of an aversive event, such as when the beeping noise in your car stops once you fasten your seatbelt.

B. F. Skinner originated the study of operant conditioning and the extension of this approach to education, psychotherapy, and society as a whole.

Operant conditioning principles may contribute to the persistence of aggressive behavior, a key feature of conduct disorder (see Chapter 13). Aggression is often rewarded, as when one child hits another to secure the possession of a toy (getting the toy is the reinforcer). Parents may also unwittingly reinforce aggression by giving in when their child becomes angry or threatens violence to achieve some goal, such as staying up late to watch Netflix or play video games.

Modeling Learning often goes on even in the absence of reinforcers. We all learn by watching and imitating others, a process called modeling. In the 1960s, experimental work demonstrated that witnessing someone perform certain activities can increase or decrease diverse kinds of behavior, such as sharing, aggression, and fear. For example, Bandura and Menlove (1968) used a modeling treatment to reduce fear of dogs in children. After witnessing a fearless model engage in various activities with a dog, initially fearful children showed an increased willingness to approach and touch a dog. Children of parents with phobias or substance use problems may acquire similar behavior patterns in part by observing their parents' behavior.

Behavior Therapy Behavior therapy emerged in the 1950s. In its initial form, this therapy applied procedures based on classical and operant conditioning to alter clinical problems.

One important behavior therapy technique that is still used to treat phobias and anxiety today is called **systematic desensitization**. Developed by Joseph Wolpe in 1958, it includes two components: (1) deep muscle relaxation and (2) gradual exposure to a list of feared situations, starting with those that arouse minimal anxiety and progressing to those that are the most frightening. Wolpe hypothesized that a state or response opposite to anxiety is substituted for anxiety as the person is exposed gradually to stronger and stronger doses of what he or she fears.

Ken Cavanagh/Science Source

Aggressive responses in children are often rewarded, which makes them more likely to occur in the future. In this photo, the more aggressive child gets to keep the toy.

Operant techniques such as systematically rewarding desirable behavior and extinguishing undesirable behavior have been particularly successful in the treatment of many childhood problems (Kazdin & Weisz, 1998). One challenge with these approaches is maintaining the effects of treatment. After all, a therapist or teacher cannot keep providing reinforcement forever! This issue has been addressed in several ways. Because laboratory findings indicate that intermittent reinforcement—rewarding a response only a portion of the times it appears—makes new behavior more enduring, many behavior therapies move away from reinforcing a desired behavior every time it occurs. For example, if a teacher has succeeded in helping a child spend more time sitting by praising the child generously for each math problem finished while seated, the teacher will gradually reward the child for every other success, and ultimately only infrequently.

The Importance of Cognition Although behaviorism remains influential in many ways today, clinicians and researchers have recognized the limitations of focusing only on behavior. Human beings don't just behave; they think and feel, too! Early behavior theories did not leave much room for cognition and emotion. Beginning in the 1960s, the study of cognition began to become very prominent. Researchers and clinicians realized that the ways in which people think about, or *appraise*, situations can influence behavior in dramatic ways. For example, walking into a room of strangers can elicit thoughts such as "Great! I am so excited to meet all sorts of new and interesting people" or "I do not know any of these people and I am going to look and sound like a complete moron!" A person who has the first thought is likely to join a group of people enthusiastically and join in the conversation. The person who has the second thought, however, is likely to turn right around and leave the room.

© 2000 Bil Keane, Inc. King Features Syndicate

Appraisals are an important part of cognitive therapy. As illustrated, appraisals can change the meaning of a situation.

Cognitive Therapy Cognitive therapy, as mentioned earlier, is based on the idea that people not only behave, but also think and feel. All cognitive approaches have one thing in common. They emphasize that how people construe themselves and the world is a major determinant of psychological disorders. In cognitive therapy, the therapist typically begins by helping clients become more aware of their maladaptive thoughts. By changing cognition, therapists hope that people can change their feelings, behaviors, and symptoms.

The roots of cognitive therapy included Aaron Beck's cognitive therapy (discussed in Chapter 2) and Albert Ellis's *rational-emotive behavior therapy (REBT)*. Ellis's (1913–2007) principal thesis was that sustained emotional reactions are caused by internal sentences that people repeat to themselves; these self-statements reflect sometimes unspoken assumptions—irrational beliefs—about what is necessary to lead a meaningful life. In Ellis's REBT (Ellis, 1993, 1995), the aim is to eliminate these ultimately self-defeating beliefs. A person with depression, for example, may say several times a day, "What a worthless jerk I am." Ellis proposed that people interpret what is happening around them, that sometimes these interpretations can cause emotional turmoil, and that a therapist's attention should be focused on these beliefs rather than on historical causes or, indeed, on overt behavior.

Have We Learned From History?

Many students of psychopathology grumble about having to read about the history of our field; they are excited to get right into learning about the clinical descriptions, causes, and treatments for psychological disorders. After all, many students of psychopathology aspire to a career as a mental health professional, not a historian. As we began our tour of history, however, we noted that it was important for us to consider the history of our field so that we could see how things have and have not changed over time. Ideally, we will learn from our historical mistakes.

Certainly, we have made many advancements over the centuries. We've learned that many people will experience a psychological disorder in their lifetime, and major models are available that integrate biology, psychology, and social influences for almost every psychological disorder we will cover in this book. Many psychological treatments have been developed, and thousands of publications each year focus on the genetic, neurobiological, and psychosocial causes of psychological disorders.

Despite these advances, we still have much to learn from history when it comes to reducing stigma and treating people with psychological disorders with respect, compassion, and dignity. Consider, for example, recent popular "reality" television shows of today such as *Hoarders*, *Beyond Scared Straight*, *Obsessed*, or *Intervention* that, respectively, showcase the lives of people with hoarding disorder (see Chapter 7), conduct disorder (see Chapter 13), obsessive compulsive disorder (see Chapter 7), or substance use disorder (see Chapter 10). Perhaps these shows help to educate people about psychological disorders, but perhaps also they perpetuate stigma by serving as the twenty-first-century version of viewing people in asylums for entertainment, as was done in the eighteenth century. On the other hand, other television shows present realistic and compassionate portrayals of psychological disorders, such as *Homeland* (bipolar disorder; see Chapter 5) or *The United States of Tara* (dissociative identity disorder; see Chapter 8). Yet even these shows can simplify or magnify some of the rarer aspects of psychological disorders, perhaps to amplify their entertainment value.

Are contemporary television shows such as *Hoarders* a modern equivalent of aristocrats viewing people in St. Mary's of Bethlehem (aka Bedlam) for entertainment?

What about the living conditions for people with psychological disorders? People with serious disorders, such as schizophrenia, bipolar disorder, or severe depression, are often in need of short stays in hospitals. Unfortunately, many hospitals have closed since the 1950s, making it extremely difficult to be able to stay in a hospital when needed. As we will discuss in more detail in Chapter 16, many of the conditions inside the hospitals were deplorable. Yet, instead of improving these conditions, many hospitals simply closed, leaving a large gap in treatment services for people with particularly severe disorders. In 2014, the new "hospital" for psychological disorders is jail. That is, people with severe psychological disorders are more likely to be housed in jails than in a hospital (Torrey, 2014). Many people with psychological disorders are not able to work and thus have very little income. These economic realities increase the likelihood of living in low-income housing, such as a single-room occupancy hotel, or SRO, to avoid homelessness. A recent study of such living accommodations found that nearly 75 percent of the residents of an SRO in Vancouver, Canada, had some type of psychological disorder and that 95 percent of the residents had a substance use disorder (Vila-Rodriguez, Panenka, et al., 2013).

As we will see in the following chapters, we still have some way to go when it comes to finding effective treatments with a tolerable set of side effects. Many people take medications to help with the symptoms of psychological disorders: In 2013, nearly 17 percent of adults in the United States had at least one prescription for such a medication (Moore & Mattison, 2017). However, these medications can have some very unpleasant side effects. For example, medications commonly used to treat schizophrenia can cause weight gain, dry mouth, blurred vision, and extreme fatigue. Imagine your life as a student if you had blurred vision nearly all the time! Some of these side effects contribute to the development of other health problems (e.g., weight gain increases the risk of developing type 2 diabetes). It is perhaps not surprising then, that some people with schizophrenia opt not to take these medications to avoid the side effects. Of course, current medications may not be as horrid as treatments of old like bleeding or prefrontal lobotomy. In addition, there are effective psychotherapy treatments that do not involve medication at all for some psychological disorders. However, even though we will see in the coming chapters that cognitive behavior therapy is an effective treatment for several psychological disorders, it does not help all people.

Have we learned from history? It seems that the answer is both yes and no. These lessons of history are therefore important for those who are headed toward careers as clinical scientists and mental health professionals. And we hope that readers of this book, regardless of their current or future careers, will recognize that we can all do something to reduce stigma, first and foremost by understanding that our current approaches to psychological disorders can and must continue to improve.

Quick Summary

The nineteenth and twentieth centuries saw a return to biological explanations for psychological disorders. Developments outside the field of psychopathology, such as the germ theory of disease and the discovery of the cause of syphilis, illustrated how the brain and behavior are linked. Early investigations into the genetics of psychological disorders led to a tragic emphasis on eugenics and the enforced sterilization of many thousands of people with psychological disorders. Biological approaches to treatment such as induced insulin coma and lobotomy eventually gave way to drug treatments. Psychological approaches to psychopathology began with Mesmer's manipulation of "magnetism" to treat hysteria (late eighteenth century), proceeded through Breuer's conceptualization of the cathartic method in his treatment of Anna O. (late nineteenth century), and culminated in Freud's psychoanalytic theories and treatment techniques (early twentieth century). The theories of Freud and other psychodynamic theorists do not lend themselves to systematic study, which has limited their acceptance by some in the field. Although Freud's early work is often criticized, his theorizing has been influential in the study of psychopathology in that it has made clear the importance of early experiences, the notion that we can do things without conscious awareness, and the insight that the causes of behavior are not always obvious.

Behaviorism began its ascendancy in the 1920s and continues to be an important part of various psychotherapies. John Watson built on the work of Ivan Pavlov in showing how some behaviors can be conditioned. B. F. Skinner, building on the work of Edward Thorndike, emphasized the contingencies associated with behavior, showing how positive and negative reinforcement could shape behavior. Research on modeling helped to explain how people can learn even when no obvious reinforcers are present. Early behavior therapy techniques that are still used today include systematic desensitization, intermittent reinforcement, and modeling. The study of cognition became popular beginning in the 1960s. Cognitive therapy was developed, and one of its pioneers, Albert Ellis, developed a cognitive treatment that focuses on beliefs. Rational-emotive behavior therapy emphasizes that the thoughts and "demands" that people impose on themselves (I should do this; I must do that) are counterproductive and lead to different types of emotional distress.

Check Your Knowledge 1.4

Fill in the blanks.

1. _____ was a French neurologist who was influenced by the work of _____.

2. _____ developed the cathartic method, which _____ later built on in the development of psychoanalysis.

3. The _____ is driven by the pleasure principle, but the _____ is driven by the reality principle.

4. In psychoanalysis, _____ refers to interpreting the relationship between therapist and client as indicative of the client's relationship to others.

True or false?

1. Positive reinforcement refers to increasing a desired behavior, while negative reinforcement refers to eliminating an undesirable behavior.

2. Systematic desensitization involves meditation and relaxation.

3. A cat comes running at the sound of a treat jar rattling, and his human friend then gives him a treat. The conditioned stimulus in this example is the sound of the jar rattling.

4. REBT focuses on changing emotions first so that thoughts can then change.

The Mental Health Professions

As views of psychological disorders have evolved, so, too, have the professions associated with the field. Professionals authorized to provide psychological services include clinical psychologists, psychiatrists, psychiatric nurses, and social workers. The need for such professions has never been greater. For example, the cost of psychological disorders in the United States is nearly $200 billion a year in lost earnings (Kessler, Heeringa, et al., 2008). People with serious psychological disorders are often not able to work due to their illness, and as a result their yearly earnings are substantially less than those of people without psychological disorders (by as much as $16,000 a year!). In addition, people with psychological disorders used to be much more likely to be without health insurance than people without psychological disorders (Garfield, Zuvekas, et al., 2011), a situation that changed in the United States with the Affordable Care Act passed in 2010 that mandated mental health treatment be covered as an "essential health benefit." In this section, we discuss the different types of mental health professionals who treat people with psychological disorders and the different types of training they receive.

Clinical psychologists (such as the authors of this textbook) must have a Ph.D. (or Psy.D.) degree, which entails 4 to 8 years of graduate study. Training for the Ph.D. in clinical psychology is similar to the training in other psychological specialties, such as developmental or cognitive neuroscience. It requires a heavy emphasis on research, statistics, and the empirically based study of human behavior. As in other fields of psychology, the Ph.D. is basically a research degree, and candidates are required to produce independent research. But candidates in clinical psychology learn skills in two additional areas, which distinguish them from other Ph.D. candidates in psychology. First, they learn techniques of assessment and diagnosis of psychopathology; that is, they learn the skills necessary to determine whether a person's symptoms or problems indicate a particular disorder. Second, they learn how to practice psychotherapy, a primarily verbal means of helping people change their thoughts, feelings, and behavior to reduce distress and to achieve greater life satisfaction. Students take courses in which they master specific techniques and treat people under close professional supervision; then, during an intensive internship, they assume increasing responsibility for the care of people. As we shall see throughout the book, many psychotherapies have research support showing that they are effective for many psychological disorders. According to a recent meta-analysis (see Chapter 4 for more on this method) of 34 studies, people with depression or anxiety were three times more likely to prefer psychotherapeutic treatment over medication (McHugh, Whitton, et al., 2013).

Clinical psychologists are trained to deliver psychotherapy.

© PhotoStock-Israel/Alamy

Another degree option for clinical psychologists is the Psy.D. (doctor of psychology), for which the curriculum is similar to that required of Ph.D. students, but with less emphasis on research and more on clinical training. The thinking behind this approach is that clinical psychology has advanced to a level of knowledge and certainty that justifies intensive training in specific techniques of assessment and therapeutic intervention rather than combining practice with research. On the other hand, conducting assessment or therapy without a sufficient research basis is professionally dubious.

Psychiatrists hold an M.D. degree and have had postgraduate training, called a residency, in which they have received supervision in the practice of diagnosis and pharmacotherapy (administering medications). By virtue of the medical degree, and in contrast to psychologists, psychiatrists can function as physicians—giving physical examinations, diagnosing medical problems, and the like. Most often, however, the only aspect of medical practice in which psychiatrists engage is prescribing medications, chemical compounds that can influence how people feel and think. Psychiatrists may receive some training in psychotherapy as well, though this is not a strong focus of their training.

A **psychiatric nurse** typically receives training at the bachelor's or master's level. Nurses can also receive more specialized training as a nurse practitioner that will allow them to prescribe psychoactive medications. There are currently over 18,000 psychiatric nurses in the United States, but the trend appears to be more toward emphasizing training as a nurse practitioner in order to secure prescription privileges (Robiner, 2006).

Social workers have an M.S.W. (master of social work) degree. Training programs are shorter than Ph.D. programs, typically requiring 2 years of graduate study. The focus of training is on psychotherapy. Those in social work graduate programs do not receive training in psychological assessment. Some M.S.W. programs offer specialized training and certification in marriage and family therapy.

Summary

- The study of psychopathology is a search to explain why people behave, think, and feel in unexpected, sometimes odd, and possibly self-defeating ways. Unfortunately, people who have a psychological disorder are often stigmatized. Reducing the stigma associated with psychological disorders remains a great challenge for the field.

- In evaluating whether a behavior is part of a psychological disorder, psychologists consider several different characteristics, notably, personal distress, disability/dysfunction, and violation of social norms. Each characteristic tells us something about what can be considered psychological disorder, but no one by itself provides a fully satisfactory definition.

- Since the beginning of scientific inquiry into psychological disorders, supernatural, biological, and psychological points of view have vied for attention. More supernatural viewpoints posited that people with psychological disorders are possessed by demons or evil spirits, leading to treatments such as exorcism. Early biological viewpoints originated in the writings of Hippocrates. After the fall of Greco-Roman civilization, the biological perspective became less prominent in western Europe, and supernatural thinking regained ascendancy. Beginning in the fifteenth century, people with psychological disorders were often confined in asylums, such as London's Bethlehem; treatment in asylums was generally poor or nonexistent until various humanitarian reforms were instituted in the eighteenth century. In the twentieth century, genetics and psychological disorders became an important area of inquiry, though the findings from genetic studies were used to the detriment of people with psychological disorders during the eugenics movement.

- Psychological viewpoints emerged in the nineteenth century from the work of Charcot and the writings of Breuer and Freud. Freud's theory emphasized the importance of unconscious processes and defense mechanisms. Therapeutic interventions based on psychoanalytic theory make use of techniques such as free association and the analysis of transference in attempting to overcome repression so that people can confront and understand their conflicts and find healthier ways of dealing with them.

- Behaviorism suggested that behavior develops through classical conditioning, operant conditioning, or modeling. B. F. Skinner introduced the ideas of positive and negative reinforcement and showed that operant conditioning can influence behavior. Behavior therapists try to apply these ideas to change undesired behavior, thoughts, and feelings.

- The study of cognition became widespread in the 1960s. Appraisals and thinking are part of cognitive therapy. Ellis was an influential theorist in cognitive therapy.

- There are several different mental health professions, including clinical psychologist, psychiatrist, psychiatric nurse, social worker, and marriage and family therapist. Each involves different training programs of different lengths and with different emphases on research, psychological assessment, psychotherapy, and psychopharmacology.

Answers to Check Your Knowledge Questions

1.1 1. a; 2. T; 3. F

1.2 1. T; 2. d; 3. b

1.3 1. F; 2. F; 3. T; 4. T

1.4 1. Charcot, Mesmer; 2. Breuer, Freud; 3. id, ego; 4. transference; 5. F; 6. F; 7. T; 4 F

Key Terms

asylums
behaviorism
cathartic method
classical conditioning
clinical psychologist
conditioned response (CR)
conditioned stimulus (CS)
defense mechanism
ego
electroconvulsive therapy (ECT)
exorcism
extinction

id
law of effect
modeling
moral treatment
negative reinforcement
operant conditioning
positive reinforcement
psychiatric nurse
psychiatrist
psychoanalysis
psychoanalytic theory
psychological disorder

psychopathology
psychotherapy
social worker
stigma
superego
systematic desensitization
transference
unconditioned response (UCR)
unconditioned stimulus (UCS)
unconscious

Current Paradigms in Psychopathology

1. Describe the essentials of the genetic, neuroscience, and cognitive behavioral paradigms.

2. Describe the concept of emotion and how it may be relevant to psychopathology.

3. Explain how culture, ethnicity, and interpersonal factors figure into the study and treatment of psychopathology.

4. Recognize the limits of adopting any one paradigm and the importance of integration across multiple levels of analysis, as in the diathesis–stress integrative paradigm.

Science is a human enterprise that is bound by scientists' human limitations; it is also bound by the current state of scientific knowledge. Our view is that every effort should be made to study psychopathology according to scientific principles.

In this chapter, we present three paradigms that guide the study and treatment of psychopathology: genetic, neuroscience, and cognitive behavioral. We also consider the important role of emotion and sociocultural factors in psychopathology. These factors cut across all the paradigms and are significant in terms of the description, causes, and treatments of all the disorders we will discuss in this book.

Current thinking about psychopathology is multifaceted. The work of clinicians and researchers is informed by an awareness of the strengths and limitations of all the paradigms. For this reason, current views of psychopathology and its treatment typically integrate several paradigms. That is, no one paradigm offers the "best" conceptualization of psychopathology. Rather, for most disorders, each paradigm offers some important information about causes and treatment, but only part of the picture. At the end of this chapter we describe an integrative paradigm—diathesis–stress—that provides the basis for a multifaceted approach.

The Genetic Paradigm

Genes do not, on their own, make us smart, dumb, sassy, polite, depressed, joyful, musical, tone-deaf, athletic, clumsy, literary or incurious. Those characteristics come from a complex interplay within a dynamic system. Every day in every way you are helping to shape which genes become active. Your life is interacting with your genes. (Shenk, 2010, p. 27)

Central to scientific activity, suggested by philosopher of science Thomas Kuhn (1962/1970), is the notion of a **paradigm**, a conceptual framework or approach within which a scientist works—that is, a set of basic assumptions, a general perspective, that defines how to conceptualize and study a subject, how to gather and interpret relevant data, even how to think about a particular subject.[1] A paradigm has important implications for how scientists operate at any given time. Paradigms specify what problems scientists will investigate and how they will go about the investigation.

It has been over 15 years since researchers decoded the human genome. That exciting milestone has been augmented with the virtual explosion of information regarding human genetics. The changes that have occurred in the **genetic paradigm** have transformed the way we think about genes and behavior. We no longer must wonder, "Is nature or nurture responsible for human behavior?" We now know that (1) almost all behavior is heritable to some degree (i.e., it involves genes) and (2) despite this, genes do not operate in isolation from the environment. Instead, throughout the life span, the environment shapes how our genes are expressed, and our genes also shape our environments (Plomin, DeFries, et al., 2003; Rutter & Silberg, 2002; Turkheimer, 2000).

The current way to think about genes and the environment is cast as "nature via nurture" (Ridley, 2003). In other words, researchers are learning how environmental influences, such as stress, relationships, and culture (the nurture part), shape which of our genes are turned on or off and how our genes (the nature part) influence our bodies and brain. We know that without genes, a behavior might not be possible. But without the environment, genes could not express themselves and thus contribute to the behavior.

People have 23 pairs of chromosomes; 46 total. Each chromosome is made up of many **genes**, the carriers of the genetic information (DNA) passed from parents to child. People have between 20,000 and 25,000 genes; the absolute number is hard to fully estimate (Human Genome Project, 2008).

Surprisingly, people don't have many more genes than insects; the mere fruit fly has around 14,000 genes! How can this be? Surely human beings are several times more complex than a fly! As it turns out, however, one of the exciting discoveries about genes was the revelation from dozens of genetic labs that the number of genes was not all that important. Instead, it is the sequencing, or ordering, of these genes as well as what the genes actually *do* that make us unique. What genes do is make proteins that in turn make the body and brain work. Some of these proteins switch other genes on and off, a process called **gene expression**. Learning about the flexibility of genes and how they turn on or off has closed the door on beliefs about the inevitability of the effects of genes, good or bad. And with respect to most psychological disorders, there is not one gene that contributes vulnerability. Instead, psychopathology is **polygenic**, meaning several genes, perhaps operating at different times during development, turning themselves on and off as they interact with a person's environment, is the essence of genetic vulnerability.

We now know that we do not inherit psychological disorders from our genes alone; we develop them through the interaction of our genes with our environments (Mukherjee, 2016; Shenk, 2010). This is a subtle but very important point. It is easy to fall into the trap of thinking a person inherits a disorder like schizophrenia from his or her genes. What genetics research today is telling us, however, is that a person *develops* schizophrenia from the interaction between genes and the environment [as well as the body (e.g., hormones) and brain].

An important term that will be used throughout the book is **heritability**. Unfortunately, it is a term that is easily misunderstood and often misused. Heritability refers to the extent to which variability in a particular behavior (or disorder) in a population can be accounted for by genetic factors. There are two important points about heritability to keep in mind.

1. Heritability estimates range from 0.0 to 1.0: the higher the number, the greater the heritability.
2. Heritability is relevant *only* for a large population of people, not a particular individual. Thus, it is incorrect to talk about any one person's heritability for a particular behavior or disorder. Knowing that the heritability of attention-deficit/hyperactivity disorder (ADHD) is around

[1]O'Donohue (1993) has criticized Kuhn's use of the concept of paradigm, noting that he was inconsistent in its definition. The complexities of this argument are beyond the scope of this book. Suffice to say that we find it useful to organize our thinking about psychological disorders around the paradigm concept. We use the term to refer to the general perspectives that constrain the way scientists collect and interpret information in their efforts to understand the world.

Blend Images/SuperStock, Inc.

Shared environment refers to things families have in common, like marital quality.

0.70 does not mean that 70 percent of Jane's ADHD is the product of her genes and 30 percent, other factors. Rather, it means that in a population (e.g., a large sample in a study), the variation in ADHD is understood as being attributed to 70 percent genetic factors and 30 percent environmental factors. There is no heritability in ADHD (or any disorder) for a particular individual.

Other factors that are just as important as genes in genetic research are environmental factors. **Shared environment** factors include those things that members of a family have in common, such as family income level, child-rearing practices, and parents' marital status and quality. **Nonshared environment** (sometimes referred to as *unique environment*) factors are those things believed to be distinct among members of a family, such as relationships with friends or specific events unique to a person (e.g., being in a car accident or on the swim team), and these are believed to be important in understanding why two siblings from the same family can be so different. Consider an example. Jason is a 34-year-old man who is dependent on alcohol and struggling to keep his job. His sister Joan is a 32-year-old executive in a computer company in San Jose and has no alcohol or drug problems. Jason did not have many friends as a child; Joan was one of the most popular girls in high school. Jason and Joan shared several influences, including their family atmosphere growing up. They also had unique, nonshared experiences, such as differences in peer relationships. Behavior genetics research suggests that shared environmental factors are important for the development of child psychopathology (Burt, 2009, 2014). The nonshared, or unique, environmental experiences can also play a role, although these can be difficult to measure and change a great deal, at least during childhood and adolescence (Burt, Klahr, & Klump, 2015).

We now turn to review two broad approaches in the genetic paradigm, including behavior genetics and molecular genetics. We then discuss the exciting evidence on the ways in which genes and environments interact. This sets the stage for our discussion of an integrative paradigm later in the chapter.

Behavior Genetics

Behavior genetics is the study of the degree to which genes and environmental factors influence behavior. To be clear, behavior genetics is not the study of *how* genes or the environment determine behavior. Many behavior genetics studies estimate the heritability of a psychological disorder without providing any information about how the genes might work. The total genetic makeup of an individual, consisting of inherited genes, is referred to as the **genotype** (physical sequence of DNA); the genotype cannot be observed outwardly. In contrast, the totality of observable behavioral characteristics, such as level of anxiety, is referred to as the **phenotype**.

We defined gene expression earlier and learned that the genotype should not be viewed as a static entity. Instead it is dynamic: Genes switch off and on at specific times, for example, to control various aspects of development. Indeed, genetic programs are quite flexible—they respond in remarkable ways to things that happen to us throughout our lives.

The phenotype also changes over time and is the product of an interaction between the genotype and the environment. For example, a person may be born with the capacity for high intellectual achievement, but whether he or she develops this

Pixland/SuperStock, Inc.

Nonshared environment refers to factors that are distinct among family members, such as having different groups of friends.

genetically given potential depends on environmental factors such as upbringing and education. Hence, intelligence is an index of the phenotype.

A study by Turkheimer and colleagues (2003) shows how genes and environment may interact to influence IQ. Research has demonstrated high heritability for IQ (e.g., Plomin, 1999), and has even identified a constellation of over 50 genes that may be involved (Sniekers, Stringer, et al., 2017). What Turkheimer and colleagues found, though, was that heritability depends on environment. The study included 319 twin pairs of 7-year-olds (114 identical, 205 fraternal). Many of the children were living in families either below the poverty line or with a low family income. Among the families of lower socioeconomic status (SES), 60 percent of the variability in children's IQ was attributable to the environment. Among the higher SES families, the opposite was found. That is, variability in IQ was more attributable to genes than to environment. Thus, being in an impoverished environment may have deleterious effects on IQ, whereas being in a more affluent environment may not help out all that much. It is important to point out that these interesting findings deal with IQ scores, a measure of what psychologists consider to be intelligence, not achievement (we discuss this issue in more detail in Chapter 3). In Chapter 4, we will discuss the major research designs used in behavior genetics research—including family, twin, and adoption studies—to estimate the heritability of different disorders.

Behavior genetics studies the degree to which characteristics, such as physical resemblance or psychopathology, are shared by family members with shared genes.

Molecular Genetics

Molecular genetics studies seek to identify **genes** and their functions. Recall that a human being has 46 chromosomes (23 chromosome pairs) and that each chromosome is made up of hundreds or thousands of genes that contain DNA (see **Figure 2.1**). Different forms of the same gene are called **alleles**. The alleles of a gene are found at the same location, or locus, of a chromosome pair. A genetic **polymorphism** refers to a difference in DNA sequence on a gene that has occurred in a population.

The DNA in genes is transcribed to RNA. In some cases, the RNA is then translated into amino acids, which then form proteins, and proteins make cells (see **Figure 2.2**). All of this is a remarkably complex system, and variations along the way, such as different combinations or sequences of events, lead to different outcomes.

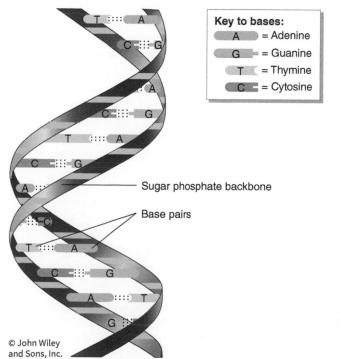

Key to bases:
A = Adenine
G = Guanine
T = Thymine
C = Cytosine

Sugar phosphate backbone

Base pairs

© John Wiley and Sons, Inc.

FIGURE 2.1 This figure shows a strand of DNA with four chemical bases: A (adenine), T (thymine), G (guanine), and C (cytosine).

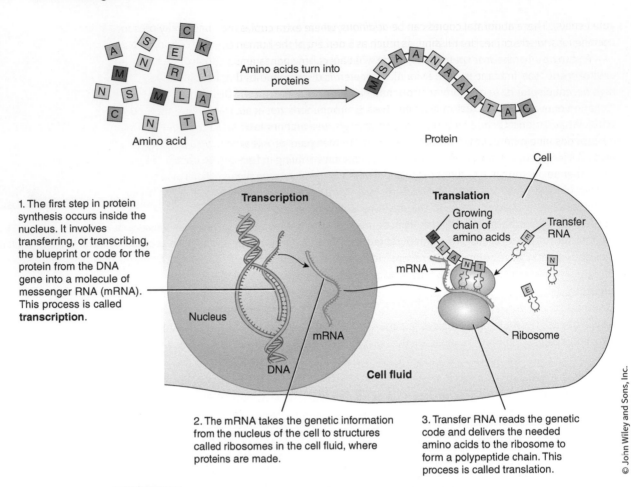

1. The first step in protein synthesis occurs inside the nucleus. It involves transferring, or transcribing, the blueprint or code for the protein from the DNA gene into a molecule of messenger RNA (mRNA). This process is called **transcription**.

2. The mRNA takes the genetic information from the nucleus of the cell to structures called ribosomes in the cell fluid, where proteins are made.

3. Transfer RNA reads the genetic code and delivers the needed amino acids to the ribosome to form a polypeptide chain. This process is called translation.

FIGURE 2.2 This figure shows gene transcription, the process by which DNA is transcribed to RNA. In some cases, the RNA is then translated into amino acids, which then form proteins, and proteins make cells.

Current molecular genetics research has focused on identifying differences between people in the *sequence* of their genes and in the *structure* of their genes. One area of interest in the study of gene sequence involves identifying what are called **single nucleotide polymorphisms** or **SNPs** (pronounced *snips*). A SNP refers to differences between people in a single nucleotide (A, T, G, or C; see **Figure 2.3**) in the DNA sequence of a particular gene. Figure 2.1 illustrates what a SNP looks like in a strand of DNA. The SNP is circled, pointing to the single nucleotide difference between the two strands. These are the most common types of polymorphisms in the human genome, with nearly 10 million different SNPs identified thus far. SNPs have been studied in schizophrenia, autism, and mood disorders, to name but a few disorders.

Another area of interest is the study of differences between people in gene structure, including the identification of so-called **copy number variations (CNVs)**. A CNV can be present in a single gene or multiple genes. The name refers to an abnormal copy of one or more sections of DNA within

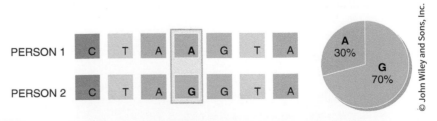

FIGURE 2.3 Illustration of what a single nucleotide polymorphism, or SNP, looks like in a comparison of two people. The two strands are the same except for a single nucleotide. To the right, an illustration showing that the position of G in the sequence is far more common in a large population of people than the position of A in the sequence.

the gene(s). These abnormal copies can be *additions*, where extra copies are abnormally present, or *deletions*, where copies are missing. As much as 5 percent of the human genome contains CNVs, which can be inherited from parents or can be what are called spontaneous (*de novo*) mutations—appearing for the first time in an individual. Later we will discuss studies that have identified CNVs in different disorders, particularly schizophrenia (Chapter 9), autism, and ADHD (Chapter 13).

Genome-wide association studies (**GWAS**, pronounced *gee-waas*) are a key method to examine SNPs and CNVs. Using powerful computers, researchers look at all the nearly 21,000 genes to isolate differences in the sequence of genes between people who have a psychological disorder and people who do not. Remarkably, a person's entire genome can be obtained from a simple swab on the inside of the cheek! The saliva is then analyzed to reveal millions of sequences across the thousands of genes for each person. Because millions of sequences are analyzed, GWAS require very large samples. To date, GWAS with thousands of participants are available for schizophrenia, bipolar disorder, autism, depression, and Alzheimer's disease (Sullivan, Daly, & O'Donovan, 2012). If certain SNPs are found more often in the group of people with certain diagnoses, such as schizophrenia, they are said to be associated with schizophrenia.

Gene–Environment Interactions

As we noted earlier, we know now that genes and environments work together. Life experience shapes how our genes are expressed, and our genes guide us in behaviors that lead to the selection of different experiences. A **gene–environment interaction** means that a given person's sensitivity to an environmental event is influenced by genes.

Take a simple (and made-up) example. If a person has gene XYZ, he or she might respond to a snakebite by developing a fear of snakes. A person without the XYZ gene would not develop a fear of snakes after being bitten. This simple relationship involves both genes (the XYZ gene) and an environmental event (snakebite). We will discuss a real example of this in Chapter 5 where we present a **gene-environment interaction** study in major depressive disorder.

The study of how the environment can alter gene expression or function is called **epigenetics**. The term *epigenetic* means "above or outside the gene" and refers to the chemical "marks," such as DNA methyl tags or histones, that are attached to and protect the DNA in each gene. These epigenetic marks are what control gene expression, and the environment can directly influence the work of these marks, as shown in **Figure 2.4** (Champagne, 2016; Zhang & Meaney, 2010). In studies with animals, research has shown that epigenetic effects can be passed down across multiple generations from parents (mothers *and* fathers; Braun & Champagne, 2014) to children, and even from grandparents to grandchildren (Champagne, 2016).

Evaluating the Genetic Paradigm

Our discussion of each paradigm will conclude with an evaluation section. Genetics is an important part of the study of psychopathology, and there are many ways in which genes might be involved in psychopathology. The models that will help us understand how genes are implicated in psychopathology are the ones that take the contemporary view that genes do their work through the environment.

There are two huge challenges facing scientists working within the genetic paradigm. The first is to specify exactly how genes and environments reciprocally influence one another. Making

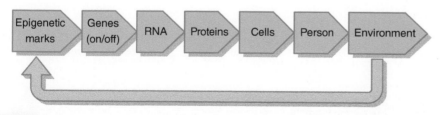

FIGURE 2.4   The dynamic process by which epigenetics influences whether genes are switched on or off. Importantly, the environment influences epigenetics.

the leap to understanding how genes interact with complex human environments throughout the course of development is a great challenge. The second is to recognize the complexity of the task, knowing that several genes (not just one) will contribute to a specific disorder and that currently there is a long pathway between the genes and the complex behaviors that make up psychological disorders, with several biological processes unfolding along the way. For example, the pathway between genes and eye color is short: genes give instructions for production of the chemicals that produce pigment. Indeed, just one SNP accounts for blue eye color (Sturm, Duffy, et al., 2008). By contrast, the pathway between genes and the behavioral phenotypes of psychological disorders is a long and winding road, filled with many biological and psychosocial processes, each of which is influenced by multiple genes. Thus, each individual gene or genetic mutation may reveal a very small effect. Putting all the small genetic pieces together to tell the gene-via-environment story for psychological disorders remains a very big challenge (Chabris, Lee, et al., 2013).

This is an exciting time for genetics research, and important discoveries about genes, environments, and psychopathology are being made at a rapid rate. In addition, some of the most exciting breakthroughs in genetics have involved a combination of methods from genetics and neuroscience. Although we present the genetic and neuroscience paradigms separately, they go hand in hand when it comes to understanding the possible causes of psychopathology.

Quick Summary

The genetic paradigm focuses on questions such as whether certain disorders are heritable and, if so, what is actually inherited. Heritability is a population statistic, not a metric of the likelihood a person will inherit a disorder. Environmental effects can be classified as shared and not shared (sometimes called unique). Molecular genetics studies seek to identify differences in the sequence and structure of genes as well as gene polymorphisms, such as SNPs, that may be involved in psychopathology. Research has emphasized the importance of gene–environment interactions. In most cases genes do their work via the environment. Recent examples of genetic influence being manifested only under certain environmental conditions (e.g., poverty and IQ) make clear that we must look not just for the genes associated with psychological disorders but also for the conditions under which these genes may be expressed.

Check Your Knowledge 2.1
(Answers are at the end of the chapter.)

1. The process by which genes are turned on or off is referred to as:
   a. heritability
   b. gene expression
   c. polygenic
   d. gene switching

2. Sam and Sally are twins raised by their biological parents. Sam excelled in music and was in the high school band; Sally was the star basketball player on the team. They both received top-notch grades, and they both had part-time jobs at the bagel store. An example of a shared environment variable would be _____; an example of a nonshared environment variable would be _____.
   a. school activities; their parents' relationship
   b. band for Sam; basketball for Sally
   c. their parents' relationship; work
   d. their parents' relationship; school activities

3. _____ refers to different forms of the same gene; _____ refers to different genes contributing to a disorder.
   a. Allele; polygenic
   b. Polygenic; allele
   c. Allele; polymorphism
   d. Polymorphism; allele

4. SNPs tell us about the _____ of genes, and CNVs tell us about the _____ of genes.

    a. DNA; RNA

    b. sequence; structure

    c. structure; sequence

    d. DNA; polymorphism

5. GWAS involve:

    a. examining the entire genomes of people.

    b. large samples of participants.

    c. analysis of millions of gene sequences to look for SNPs.

    d. All of the above.

The Neuroscience Paradigm

The **neuroscience paradigm** holds that psychological disorders are linked to aberrant processes in the brain. For example, aspects of schizophrenia are associated with neurotransmitter problems; anxiety disorders may be related to a problem within the autonomic nervous system; dementia can be traced to impairments in structures of the brain. In this section, we look at three components of this paradigm in which the data are particularly interesting: neurons and neurotransmitters, brain structure and function, and the neuroendocrine system. We then consider some of the key treatments that follow from the paradigm.

Neurons and Neurotransmitters

The cells in the nervous system are called neurons, and the nervous system is comprised of billions of neurons. Although neurons differ in some respects, each **neuron** has four major parts: (1) the cell body; (2) several dendrites, the short and thick extensions; (3) one or more axons of varying lengths, but usually only one long and thin axon that extends a considerable distance from the cell body; and (4) terminal buttons on the many end branches of the axon (**Figure 2.5**). When a neuron is appropriately stimulated at its cell body or through its dendrites, a nerve impulse travels down the axon to the terminal endings. Between the terminal endings of the sending axon and the cell membrane of the receiving neuron there is a small gap, called the **synapse** (**Figure 2.6**).

For neurons to send a signal to the next neuron so that communication can occur, the nerve impulse must have a way of bridging the synaptic space. The terminal buttons of each axon contain synaptic vesicles, small structures that are filled with **neurotransmitters**. Neurotransmitters are chemicals that allow neurons to send a signal across the synapse to another neuron. As the neurotransmitter flows into the synapse, some of the molecules reach the receiving, or postsynaptic, neuron. The cell membrane of the postsynaptic neuron contains receptors. Receptors are configured so that only specific neurotransmitters can fit into them. When a neurotransmitter fits into a receptor site, a message can be sent to the postsynaptic cell. What actually happens to the postsynaptic neuron depends on integrating thousands of similar messages. Sometimes these messages are excitatory, leading to the creation

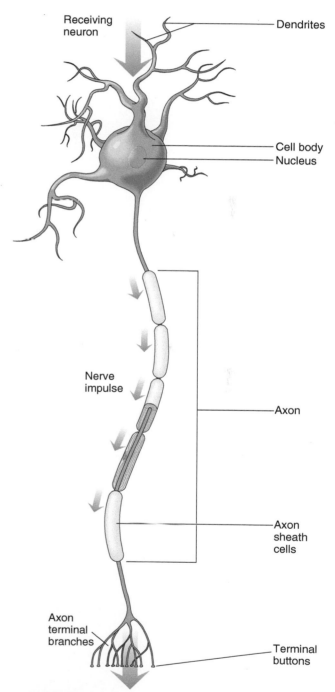

© John Wiley and Sons, Inc.

FIGURE 2.5 The neuron, the basic unit of the nervous system.

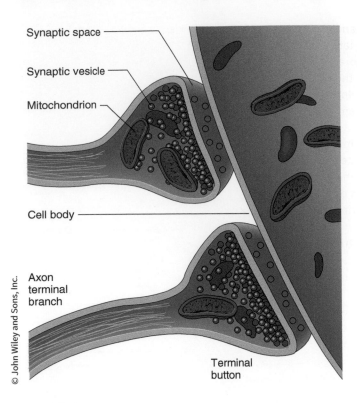

Synaptic space

Synaptic vesicle

Mitochondrion

Cell body

Axon terminal branch

Terminal button

© John Wiley and Sons, Inc.

FIGURE 2.6 A synapse, showing the terminal buttons of two axon branches in close contact with a very small portion of the cell body of another neuron.

of a nerve impulse in the postsynaptic cell; at other times the messages are inhibitory, making the postsynaptic cell less likely to create a nerve impulse.

Once a presynaptic neuron (the sending neuron) has released its neurotransmitter, the last step is for the synapse to return to its normal state. Not all of the released neurotransmitter has found its way to postsynaptic receptors. Some of what remains in the synapse is broken down by enzymes, and some is taken back into the presynaptic cell through a process called **reuptake**.

Several key neurotransmitters have been implicated in psychopathology, including **dopamine**, **serotonin**, **norepinephrine**, and **gamma-aminobutyric acid (GABA)**. Serotonin and dopamine may be involved in depression, mania, and schizophrenia. Norepinephrine is a neurotransmitter that communicates with the sympathetic nervous system, where it is involved in producing states of high arousal and may be involved in the anxiety disorders and other stress-related conditions (see **Focus on Discovery 2.1** for more on the sympathetic nervous system). GABA inhibits nerve impulses throughout most areas of the brain and may be involved in the anxiety disorders.

There are several ways in which neurotransmitters may contribute to psychopathology, though the mechanisms by which this happens are not currently well understood. Early theories linking neurotransmitters to psychopathology proposed that a given disorder was caused by either too much or too little of a neurotransmitter (e.g., mania is associated with too much norepinephrine, anxiety disorders with too little GABA). Later research has found, however, that these ideas were too simple. Neurotransmitters are synthesized in the neuron through a series of metabolic steps, beginning with an amino acid. Each reaction along the way to producing an actual neurotransmitter is catalyzed by an enzyme. Neurotransmitter activity can be influenced by errors in these metabolic steps. Other problems with neurotransmitters might result from alterations in the usual processes by which transmitters are deactivated after being released into the synapse. For example, a failure to pump leftover neurotransmitter back into the presynaptic cell (reuptake) would leave excess neurotransmitter in the synapse. Other research has focused on the possibility that the neurotransmitter receptors are at fault in some disorders. This reasoning comes largely from our understanding of how medications used to treat psychological disorders have an impact on receptors.

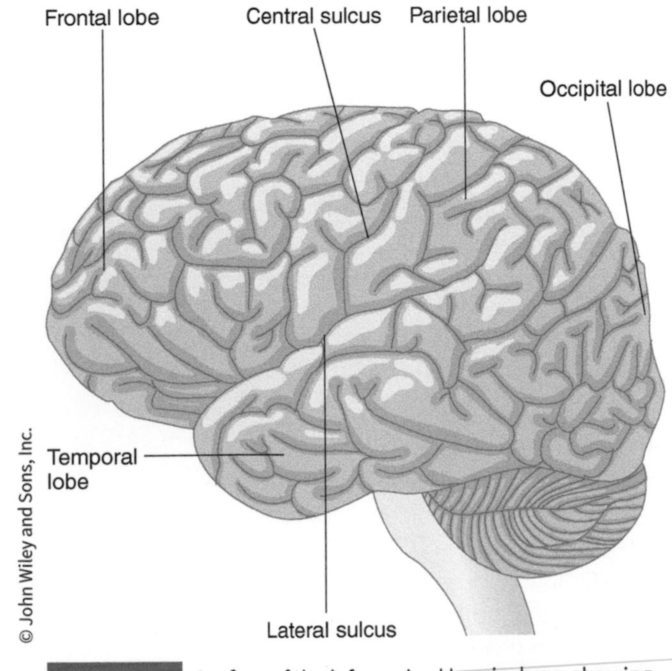

Structure and Function of the Human Brain

The cortex of the human brain is comprised of the neurons that form the thin outer covering of the brain, the so-called **gray matter** of the brain. **Figure 2.7** shows the surface of the cortex on one side of the brain. The cortex consists of six layers of tightly packed neurons, estimated to number close to 16 billion. The cortex is vastly convoluted; the ridges are called gyri, and the depressions between them sulci. The sulci are used to define different regions of the brain, much like guide points on a map. The frontal

Frontal lobe

Central sulcus

Parietal lobe

Occipital lobe

Temporal lobe

Lateral sulcus

© John Wiley and Sons, Inc.

FIGURE 2.7 Surface of the left cerebral hemisphere, showing the four lobes and the central and lateral sulci.

lobe lies in front of the central sulcus, the parietal lobe is behind it and above the lateral sulcus, the temporal lobe is located below the lateral sulcus, and the occipital lobe lies behind the parietal and temporal lobes (see Figure 2.7). One important area of the cortex is called the **prefrontal cortex**. This region, in the very front of the cortex, helps to regulate the amygdala (discussed below) and is important in many different disorders.

If the brain is sliced in half, separating the two cerebral hemispheres, additional important structures can be seen. The gray matter of the cerebral cortex does not extend throughout the interior of the brain. Much of the interior is **white matter**, made up of large tracts of myelinated (sheathed) fibers that connect cell bodies in the cortex with those in the spinal cord and in other areas of the brain.

Deep within the brain are cavities called **ventricles**. These ventricles are filled with cerebrospinal fluid. Cerebrospinal fluid circulates through the brain through these ventricles, which are connected with the spinal cord.

A set of deeper, mostly subcortical, structures are often implicated in different forms of psychopathology. Some of these structures are shown in **Figure 2.8**. Important structures are the **anterior cingulate**; the **hippocampus**, which is associated with memory; the **hypothalamus**, which regulates metabolism, temperature, perspiration, blood pressure, sleeping, and appetite; and the **amygdala**, which is an important area for attention to emotionally salient stimuli. This is one of the key brain structures for psychopathology researchers, given the ubiquity of emotional problems in the psychological disorders.

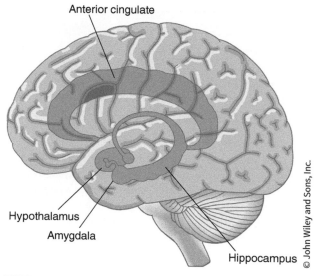

FIGURE 2.8 Subcortical structures of the brain.

© John Wiley and Sons, Inc.

The development of the human brain is a complex process that begins early in the first trimester of pregnancy and continues into early adulthood. It has been estimated that about a third of our genes are expressed in the brain, and many of these genes are responsible for laying out the structure of the brain. The development of the cells and the migration of these cells to the appropriate layers of cortex comprise an intricate dance. Unfortunately, missteps can happen, and current thinking about several disorders, such as schizophrenia, places the beginnings of the problem in these early developmental stages. Brain development continues throughout childhood, adolescence, and even into adulthood. What is happening during this time is cell development and a honing of the connections between cells and brain areas. The gray matter of the brain continues to develop, filling with cells, until early adolescence. Then, somewhat surprisingly, a number of synaptic connections begin to be eliminated—a process called **pruning**. Throughout early adulthood, the connections in the brain may become fewer, but they also become faster. The areas that develop the quickest are areas linked to sensory processes, like the cerebellum and occipital lobe. The area that develops last is the frontal lobe.

Most current research on the brain and psychopathology examines not just areas or regions of the brain, but rather the connectivity between different areas of the brain. In Chapter 9, we discuss brain connectivity methods. These connectivity methods have revealed several **brain networks**. Networks are clusters of brain regions that are connected to one another in that activation in these regions is reliably correlated when people perform certain types of tasks or are at rest. For example, the frontoparietal network involves activation of the frontal and parietal cortices, and this network is activated when people are doing cognitive tasks. The default-mode network involves areas of the prefrontal cortex and temporal cortex and is activated when people are daydreaming or thinking about the future and recalling memories.

We will discuss several of these brain areas and networks throughout the book. For example, people with schizophrenia have been found to have enlarged ventricles (Chapter 9); the size of the hippocampus is reduced among some people with posttraumatic stress disorder, depression, and schizophrenia, perhaps due to overactivity of their stress response systems (Chapters 5, 7, and 9); brain size among some children with autism expands at a much greater rate than it should in typical development (Chapter 13).

Focus on Discovery 2.1

The Autonomic Nervous System

The **autonomic nervous system (ANS)** innervates the endocrine glands, the heart, and the smooth muscles that are found in the walls of the blood vessels, stomach, intestines, kidneys, and other organs. Much of our behavior is dependent on a nervous system that operates very quickly, generally without our awareness, and that has traditionally been viewed as beyond voluntary control; hence, the term *autonomic.* This nervous system is itself divided into two parts, the **sympathetic nervous system** and the **parasympathetic nervous system** (**Figure 2.9**). A simple way to think about these two components of the ANS is that the sympathetic nervous system prepares the body for "fight or flight" and the parasympathetic nervous system helps "calm down" the body. Things are not actually that simple, though. The sympathetic portion of the ANS, when energized, accelerates the heartbeat, dilates the pupils, inhibits intestinal activity, increases electrodermal activity (i.e., sweat on the skin), and initiates other smooth muscle and glandular responses that prepare the organism for sudden activity and stress. Division of activities is not quite so clear-cut, however, for it is the parasympathetic system that increases blood flow to the genitals during sexual excitement.

The autonomic nervous system figures prominently in many anxiety disorders, such as panic disorder and posttraumatic stress disorder. For example, people with panic disorder tend to misinterpret normal changes in their nervous system, such as shortness of breath after running up a flight of stairs. Instead of attributing this to being out of shape, people with panic disorder may think they are about to have another panic attack. In essence, they come to fear the sensations of their own autonomic nervous system.

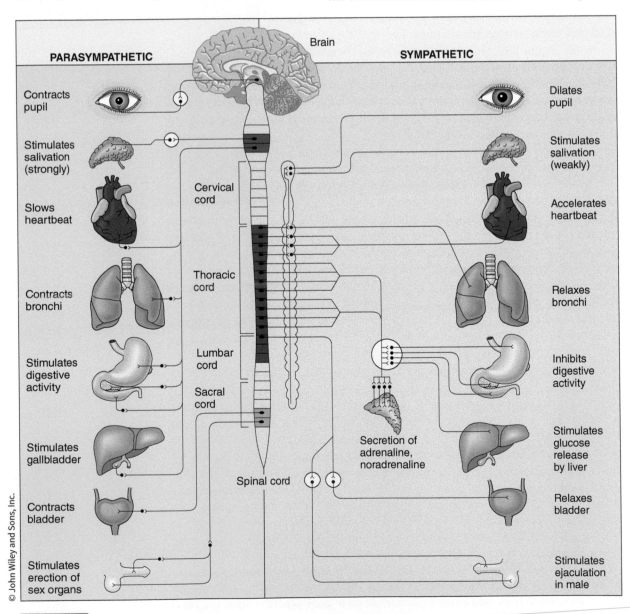

FIGURE 2.9 The autonomic nervous system.

The Neuroendocrine System

The neuroendocrine system has been implicated in psychopathology as well, and we will consider this evidence throughout this book. One of the systems we will return to again and again is the hypothalamic-pituitary-adrenal (HPA) axis (shown in **Figure 2.10**). The **HPA axis** is central to the body's response to stress, and stress figures prominently in many of the disorders we discuss in this book.

When people are faced with threat, the hypothalamus releases corticotropin-releasing factor (CRF), which then communicates with the *pituitary gland*. The pituitary then releases adrenocorticotropic hormone, which travels via the blood to the adrenal glands. The outer layers of the adrenal glands are referred to as the *adrenal cortex*; this area promotes the release of the hormone cortisol. **Cortisol** is often referred to as the stress hormone. This is not a fast-moving system, like the autonomic nervous system, reviewed in Focus on Discovery 2.1. Rather, it takes about 20 to 40 minutes for cortisol release to peak. After the stress or threat has remitted, it can take up to an hour for cortisol to return to baseline (i.e., prior to stress) levels (Dickerson & Kemeny, 2004).

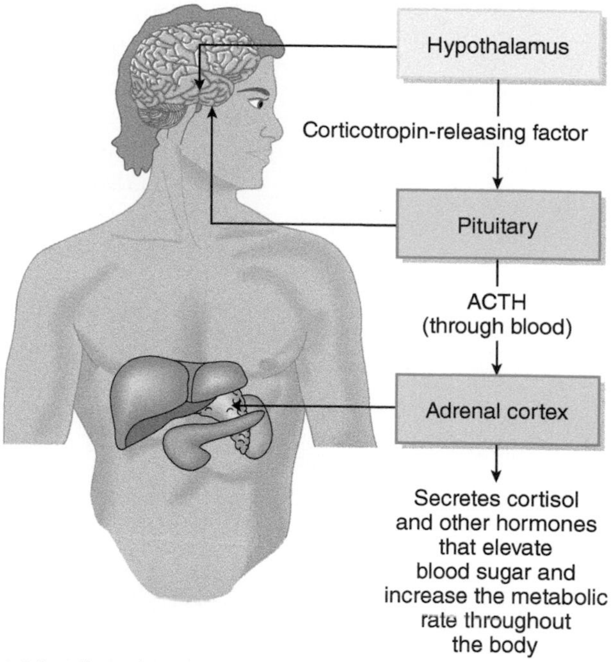

Studies of stress and the HPA axis are uniquely integrative. That is, they begin with a psychological concept (stress) and examine how stress is manifested in the body (the HPA axis). As in our discussion of the genetic paradigm earlier, it is hard to consider biology and environment separately—biology may create increased reactivity to the environment, and early experiences may influence biology. As we will see, chronic stress and its effects on the HPA axis are linked to disorders as diverse as schizophrenia, depression, and posttraumatic stress disorder.

© John Wiley and Sons, Inc.

FIGURE 2.10   The HPA axis.

The Immune System

Stress also has effects on the immune system. Reviews of nearly 300 studies confirmed that a wide range of stressors produce problematic changes in the immune system, including medical school examinations, depression and bereavement, marital discord and divorce, job loss, and caring for a relative with Alzheimer's disease, among others (Kiecolt-Glaser & Glaser, 2002; Segerstrom & Miller, 2004). Given that stress is important in psychological disorders, it is perhaps not surprising that the immune system is involved as well.

The immune system involves a broad array of cells and proteins that respond when the body is infected or invaded. The body's first and quickest line of defense against infectious microorganisms is to unleash cells, such as macrophages and natural killer cells, and T-cells to destroy these invaders. Inflammation or swelling is a sign of these immunity cells at work. Activation of macrophages in turn stimulates the release of proteins called **cytokines**, which help initiate such bodily responses to infection as fatigue, inflammation, and activation of the HPA axis. Cytokines that produce helpful inflammation are called pro-inflammatory cytokines. Pro-inflammatory cytokines such as interleukin-1 (IL-1) and tumor necrosis factor alpha (TNF-alpha) have been implicated in depression (see Chapter 5). Other cytokines such as IL-6 and IL-8 have been implicated in schizophrenia (Fineberg & Ellman, 2013).

Neuroscience Approaches to Treatment

The use of psychiatric drugs continues to increase. For example, between 2005 and 2010, just over 6 percent of adolescents in the United States ages 12–19 took some type of psychiatric medication (Jonas, Gu, & Albertorio-Diaz, 2013), and nearly 17 percent of adults between the ages of 18 and 85 had at least one prescription for a psychiatric medication in 2013 (Moore & Mattison, 2017). Antidepressants were the third most commonly prescribed medication for any type of health issue in 2013, behind only blood pressure and cholesterol medications (IMS Health, 2014). Spending on antipsychotic drugs increased from $1.3 billion in 1997 to $5.6 billion in 2006 (Barber, 2008).

Antidepressants, such as Prozac, increase neural transmission in neurons that use serotonin as a neurotransmitter by inhibiting the reuptake of serotonin. Benzodiazepines, such as Xanax, can be effective in reducing the tension associated with some anxiety disorders, perhaps by stimulating GABA neurons to inhibit other neural systems that create the physical symptoms of anxiety. Antipsychotic drugs, such as Olanzapine, used in the treatment of schizophrenia, work on dopamine and serotonin. Stimulants, such as Adderall, are often used to treat children with attention-deficit/hyperactivity disorder; they operate on several neurotransmitters that help children focus.

It should be noted that a person could hold a neuroscience view about the nature of a disorder and yet recommend psychological intervention. Contemporary scientists and clinicians also appreciate that nonbiological interventions can influence brain functioning. For example, psychotherapy that teaches a person how to stop performing compulsive rituals, which is an effective and widely used behavioral treatment for obsessive-compulsive disorder, has measurable effects on brain activity (Baxter, Ackerman, et al., 2000).

Evaluating the Neuroscience Paradigm

Over the past several decades, neuroscientists have made great progress in elucidating brain–behavior relationships. Neuroscience research on both the causes and treatment of psychopathology is proceeding at a rapid rate, as we will see when we discuss specific disorders in later chapters. Although we view these developments in a positive light, we also want to caution against reductionism.

Reductionism refers to the view that whatever is being studied can and should be reduced to its most basic elements or constituents. In the case of psychological disorders, reductionism happens when scientists try to reduce complex mental and emotional responses to biology. In its extreme form, reductionism asserts that psychology and psychopathology are ultimately nothing more than biology.

Basic elements, such as individual nerve cells, are organized into more complex brain networks. The properties of these networks cannot be deduced from the properties of the individual nerve cells. The whole is greater than the sum of its parts. A good example is provided by computers. Students writing papers for their courses use programs like Google Docs. These programs consist of many levels of code that communicate with the computer. The program necessarily involves low-level communication with the computer, involving a series of 0's and 1's and even electronics. Yet we don't conceptualize the program in terms of binary digits or electrical impulses. If the spell-checker stopped working, our first place to begin repairs would not be with the computer chips. Instead, we would want the programmer to fix the bug in the code. To be sure, the program could not run without the computer, but the program is more than just the impulses sent by the chips. In the same way, although a complex behavior like a hallucination necessarily involves the brain and nerve impulses, it is not likely that we can fully capture this by knowing about specific nerve impulses.

Although you might assume that we have learned which neurotransmitters are involved in a disorder and then used that to determine pharmacological treatments, this is often not the case. Rather, the reverse has often happened: A drug is found that influences symptoms, and then researchers are inspired to study the neurotransmitters influenced by that drug. But as we will see, the evidence linking neurotransmitters as causal factors in psychopathology is not very strong.

Quick Summary

The neuroscience paradigm is concerned with the ways in which the brain contributes to psychopathology. Neurotransmitters such as serotonin, norepinephrine, dopamine, and GABA have been implicated in many disorders. Several different brain areas are also a focus of research. The autonomic nervous system, which includes the sympathetic and parasympathetic nervous systems, is also implicated in the manifestations of some disorders. The HPA axis is responsible for the body's response to stress and thus is relevant for several stress-related disorders. Stress can also produce problematic changes in the immune system, and this can have an impact on psychological disorders, such as major depressive disorder. Cytokines help initiate such bodily responses to infection as fatigue, inflammation, and activation of the HPA axis. Pro-inflammatory cytokines have been linked to different psychological disorders. Treatments derived from neuroscience, primarily medications, are effective for different disorders, but they are not necessarily treating the cause of the disorders. Although the brain plays an important role in our understanding of the causes of psychopathology, we must be careful to avoid reductionism.

Check Your Knowledge 2.2

Fill in the blanks.

1. Important subcortical areas of the brain include: _____, _____, _____, and _____.
2. The _____ matter of the brain consists of the tracts of myelinated fibers that connect cells; the _____ matter of the brain refers to the brain's cells or neurons.
3. Neurotransmitters that are studied in psychopathology include _____, which can produce states of high arousal, and _____, which inhibits nerve impulses.
4. The HPA axis consists of the _____, _____, and _____.
5. _____are part of the immune system and are associated with disorders such as _____ and _____.

The Cognitive Behavioral Paradigm

The **cognitive behavioral paradigm** traces its roots to learning principles and to cognitive science. As we will see, the basic principles from classical and operant conditioning (see Chapter 1) as well as cognitive science have shaped the development of many cognitive behavioral therapies.

Influences from Behavior Therapy

As discussed in Chapter 1, a key influence from behaviorism is the notion that problem behavior is likely to continue if it is reinforced. Once the source of reinforcement has been identified, treatment is then tailored to alter the consequences of the problem behavior. For example, if it was established that getting attention reinforced the problem behavior, the treatment might be to ignore the behavior. Alternatively, the problem behavior could be followed by **time-out**— the person is sent for a period of time to a location where positive reinforcers are not available. Today, time-out is a commonly used parenting technique for children who exhibit a problematic behavior of some sort (see photo).

Another successful example of operant conditioning is **behavioral activation (BA) therapy** of depression (Dimidjian, Barrera, et al., 2011), which involves helping a person engage in tasks that provide an opportunity for positive reinforcement.

We introduced the technique called systematic desensitization in Chapter 1. Recall that this involves two components: (1) deep muscle relaxation and (2) gradual exposure to a list of feared situations, starting with those that arouse minimal anxiety and progressing to those that are the most frightening. The still-influential contribution from this behavioral approach is the **exposure** component of this treatment. The basic idea is that the anxiety will extinguish if the person can face the object or situation long enough with no actual harm occurring. Sometimes this exposure can be conducted in real-life situations (see photo). For example, if someone has a fear of flying, you might have him or her take an actual flight. At times, exposure cannot be conducted in real life, so *imaginal exposure* will be used to address fears, such as rape, trauma, or contamination. In other situations, both types of exposure are used.

Exposure continues to be a centrally important component of many forms of cognitive behavior therapy today, as we discuss in more detail in Chapters 6 and 7. In the years since exposure treatments were first developed, much has been learned about them.

Jeff Greenberg/PhotoEdit

Time-out is a behavioral therapy technique based on operant conditioning; the consequence for misbehavior is removal to an environment with no positive reinforcers.

Exposure treatment is one of the most well-supported approaches for anxiety disorders.

For instance, exposure to the real thing, when practical, is more effective than imagining situations. Also, even though relaxation training helps people experience less arousal when they first face the feared stimulus, there is limited evidence that such training is required for good outcomes. As a result, it has been possible to develop briefer psychological treatments that do not include relaxation training.

As influential as these behavior therapy techniques were (and still are), behaviorism and behavior therapy were often criticized for minimizing the importance of two important factors: thinking and feeling. In other words, the way we think and feel about things undoubtedly influences our behavior. These limitations of behavioral points of view led some behavioral researchers and clinicians to include cognitive and emotion variables in their conceptualizations of psychopathology and therapy.

Cognitive Science

Cognition is a term that groups together the mental processes of perceiving, recognizing, conceiving, judging, and reasoning. Cognitive science focuses on how people structure their experiences, how they make sense of them, and how they relate their current experiences to past ones that have been stored in memory.

At any given moment, we are bombarded by far more stimuli than we can possibly respond to. How do we filter this overwhelming input, put it into words or images, form hypotheses, and arrive at a perception of what is out there?

Cognitive scientists regard people as active interpreters of a situation, with people's past knowledge imposing a perceptual funnel on the experience. A person fits new information into an organized network of already accumulated knowledge, often referred to as a **schema**, or cognitive set (Neisser, 1976). New information may fit the schema; if not, the person reorganizes the schema to fit the information or construes the information in such a way as to fit the schema. The following scenario, inspired by the pioneering work of Bransford and Johnson (1973), illustrates how a schema may alter the way in which information is processed and remembered.

> *The woman worked all night finalizing the code for the new dating app. She rushed home to take a quick shower and grab some breakfast before the presentation to the VC firm. She picked out an outfit that was professional yet casual. While eating breakfast, she quickly scanned several apps on her phone and sent a few text messages. As she was leaving, she ran into the landlord who asked about the rent again. She rushed past, realizing she had left her car keys in the apartment. Not wanting to return for her keys and pass the landlord, she requested Uber even though she was going to be charged premium pricing given the time of day, which soured her mood. And having to wait might make her late.*

Now read the excerpt again, but add the word *unemployed* before the word *woman*. Now read it a third time, substituting *Google employee* for *woman*. Notice how differently you understand the passage. Ask yourself what apps these women might have checked. If you were asked on a questionnaire to recall this information and you no longer had access to the excerpt, you might answer "Craigslist jobs" for the unemployed woman and "a technology site like ReCode" for the Google employee. Since the passage does not specify what was read, these answers are wrong, but in each instance the error would have been a meaningful, predictable one.

Other important contributions from cognitive science include the study of attention. As we will see, people with disorders as diverse as anxiety disorders, mood disorders, and schizophrenia have problems with attention. For example, individuals with anxiety disorders tend to focus their attention on threatening or anxiety-producing events or situations in the environment, as we discuss in more detail in Chapter 6. People with schizophrenia have a hard time concentrating their attention.

Of course, the concepts of schema and attention are related to each other. If a person has a particular set or schema about the world (e.g., the world is dangerous), that person may be more likely to pay attention to threatening or dangerous things in the environment. Furthermore, this person may be more likely to interpret ambiguous things in the environment as threatening. For example, seeing a stranger standing on a front porch may be interpreted as a sign of danger to someone with such a "danger" schema. For someone without such a schema, this person may be viewed simply as the person who lives in that house.

One of the exciting advances in cognitive science in the past 10 years is the access to and analysis of "big data." Traditional cognitive science experiments involve bringing a sample (say, of 50 to 100 people) into a laboratory to do a set of tasks. Big data approaches, by contrast, can include thousands of participants completing experiments online. Griffiths (2015) describes several exciting new ways in which cognitive scientists are testing theories and hypotheses about cognitive and behavioral processes like decision making, memory, preference learning, or categorization using many participants or huge online databases. Understanding why people make such choices can be enormously useful for psychopathology research to understand, for example, why certain people may be more prone to gambling problems than others (Chapter 10) or which people might benefit more from online interventions for various problems.

Indeed, cognitive explanations are central in the search for the causes of psychopathology and for new methods of intervention. Cognitive theorizing will be included in discussions of most of the disorders presented in subsequent chapters.

The Role of the Unconscious

As far back as Freud (see Chapter 1), much of human behavior was presumed to be unconscious, or outside the awareness of the individual. The unconscious has been a hot topic of study among cognitive psychologists for over 30 years. For example, in one study, participants were presented with different shapes for 1 millisecond (one-thousandth of a second) (Kunst-Wilson & Zajonc, 1980). Later they showed virtually no ability to recognize the shapes they had seen, but when they rated how much they liked the shapes, they preferred the ones they had been shown to other ones. We know that familiarity affects judgments of stimuli; people tend to like familiar stimuli more than unfamiliar ones. This study indicates that some aspects of the stimuli must have been absorbed, even though participants said that they did not recognize the shapes.

Cognitive neuroscientists have more recently explored how the brain supports behavior that is outside conscious awareness. For example, the concept of *implicit memory* refers to the idea that a person can, without being aware of it, be influenced by prior learning. A person may be shown a list of words so quickly that he or she cannot identify the words. Later, the person will be able to recall those words even though the words were not consciously perceived during the rapid initial presentation. Thus, a memory is formed implicitly (i.e., without conscious awareness). Implicit memory paradigms have been adopted by psychopathology researchers, who have found, for example, that people with social anxiety and depression have trouble with these tasks (Amir, Foa, & Coles, 1998; Watkins, 2002).

Contemporary studies of the unconscious, such as studies of implicit memory, are a long way from Freud's original theorizing about the unconscious. For cognitive neuroscientists, the unconscious reflects the incredible efficiency and automaticity of the brain. That is, there are simply too many things going on around us all the time for us to be aware of everything. Thus, our brains have developed the capacity to register information for later use even if we are not aware of it.

Cognitive Behavior Therapy

Cognitive behavior therapy (CBT) incorporates theory and research on cognitive processes. Cognitive behavior therapists pay attention to private events—thoughts, perceptions, judgments, self-statements, and even tacit (unconscious) assumptions—and have studied and manipulated these processes in their attempts to understand and modify overt and covert disturbed behavior. **Cognitive restructuring** is a general term for changing a pattern of thought. People with depression may not realize how often they think self-critically, and those with anxiety disorders may not realize that they tend to be overly sensitive to possible threats in the world. Therapists hope that people can change their feelings, behaviors, and symptoms by changing their cognition. The therapist begins by tracking the daily thoughts a person experiences but then moves to understanding more about core cognitive biases and schemata that might shape those daily negative thoughts.

Dr. Aaron T. Beck, University Professor of Psychiatry, University of Pennsylvania

Aaron Beck developed a cognitive theory of depression and a cognitive behavioral therapy for people with depression.

Beck's Cognitive Therapy Psychiatrist Aaron Beck (see photo), one of the leading cognitive behavior therapists, developed a cognitive therapy for depression based on the idea that depressed mood is caused by distortions in the way people perceive life experiences (Beck, 1976; Salkovskis, 1996). For example, a person with depression may focus exclusively on negative happenings and ignore positive ones. Imagine that a woman's romantic partner both praises and criticizes her. If the woman attends to the praise and remembers it the next day, she is likely to feel happy. But if she focuses on the criticism and continues to dwell on it the next day, she is likely to feel unhappy. Beck's therapy, which has now been adapted for many other disorders in addition to depression, is a collaborative treatment between a therapist and the person seeking treatment. When a person with depression expresses feelings that nothing ever goes right, for example, the therapist offers counterexamples, pointing out how the person has overlooked favorable happenings. The general goal of Beck's therapy is to provide people with experiences, both inside and outside the therapy room, that will alter their negative schemas, enabling them to have hope rather than despair.

Clinical Case

An Example of Beck's Cognitive Therapy

The following examples illustrate ways of beginning to help a person change negative cognitions.

Therapist: You said that you feel like a failure since Bill left you. How would you define "failure"?

Patient: *Well, the marriage didn't work out.*

Therapist: So, you believe that the marriage didn't work out because you, as a person, are a failure?

Patient: *If I had been successful, then he would still be with me.*

Therapist: So, would we conclude that we can say, "People whose marriages don't work out are failures"?

Patient: *No, I guess I wouldn't go that far.*

Therapist: Why not? Should we have one definition of failure for you and another for everyone else?

People who define *failure* as less than "extraordinarily successful" can see that their definitions are polarized in all-or-nothing terms—that is, "complete success" versus "complete failure." A variation on this technique is to ask the patient how others would define "success" or "failure."

Therapist: You can see that your definition of failure is quite different from the way other people might see it. Few people would say that a person who is divorced is a failure. Let's focus on the positive end right now. How would most people define "success" in a person?

Patient: *Well, they might say that someone has success when they accomplish some of their goals.*

Therapist: OK. So, would we say that if someone accomplishes some goals they have success?

Patient: *Right.*

Therapist: Would we also say that people can have different degrees of success? Some people accomplish more goals than others?

Patient: *That sounds right.*

Therapist: So, if we applied this to you, would we say that you have accomplished some of your goals in life?

Patient: *Yes, I did graduate from college and I have been working for the past six years. I've been busy raising Ted—he had some medical problems a couple of years ago, but I got the right doctors for him.*

Therapist: So, would we call these some successful behaviors on your part?

Patient: *Right, I've had some successes.*

Therapist: Is there a contradiction, then, in your thinking—calling yourself a "failure" but saying that you have had several successes?

Patient: *Yes, that doesn't make sense, does it? Source: Leahy, R. L., (2017) Cognitive Therapy Techniques: A Practitioner's Guide, pp. 52–53, Published by Guilford Press.*

There have also been many extensions of behavior therapy and CBT. The so-called "third wave" behavioral treatments include dialectical behavior therapy (see Chapter 15), mindfulness-based cognitive therapy (see Chapter 5), and acceptance and commitment therapy. The newer treatments differ from traditional CBT by incorporating a focus on spirituality, values, emotion, and acceptance. Another theme involves strategies to minimize emotional avoidance. For example, in acceptance and commitment therapy (Hayes, 2005), a person might be taught that much of the destructive power of emotions lies in the way we respond to them cognitively and behaviorally. An overarching goal of these therapies is to help a person learn to be more aware of emotions but to avoid immediate, impulsive reactions to that emotion. In the case of mindfulness-based cognitive therapy, this is facilitated through the use of meditation (Segal, Williams, & Teasdale, 2003). Overall, a rich array of cognitive behavioral approaches has been developed.

Evaluating the Cognitive Behavioral Paradigm

Cognitive behavioral explanations of psychopathology have generated a great deal of research over the past several decades. Yet some cognitive explanations do not appear to explain much. That a person with depression has a negative schema tells us that the person thinks gloomy thoughts. But such a pattern of thinking is actually part of the diagnosis of depression. What is distinctive in the cognitive behavioral paradigm is that the thoughts are given causal status; that is, the thoughts are regarded as causing the other features of the disorder, such as sadness. Left unanswered is the question of where the negative schema came from in the first place. Much of the current research is focused on understanding what types of mechanisms sustain the negative thoughts typical of many different psychopathologies.

Quick Summary

The cognitive behavioral paradigm reflects influences from behavior therapy and cognitive science. Treatment techniques designed to alter the consequences or reinforcers of a behavior, such as time-out and exposure, are still used today. Cognitive science focuses on concepts such as schemas (a network of accumulated knowledge or set), attention, memory, and the unconscious, and these concepts are part of cognitive behavioral theories and treatments of psychopathology. For example, research on implicit memory promoted acceptance of the ideas of unconscious influences on behavior. Cognitive behavior therapy uses behavior therapy techniques and cognitive restructuring. Aaron Beck is an influential cognitive behavior therapist.

Check Your Knowledge 2.3

True or false?

1. A schema refers to an organized network of cognitive knowledge.
2. Beck's theory suggests that people have distortions in the way they perceive life's experiences.
3. Current research on the unconscious is conducted in much the same way as it was when Freud talked about the unconscious.

Factors That Cut Across Paradigms

Three important sets of factors that we will consider throughout this book are emotional, sociocultural, and interpersonal factors. Some type of disturbance in emotion can be found in nearly all psychological disorders. In addition, we will see that gender, culture, ethnicity, and social relationships bear importantly on the descriptions, causes, and treatments of different disorders. In the next sections, we introduce these concepts and give some examples of why they are so important in psychopathology, regardless of what paradigm has been adopted.

Emotion and Psychopathology

Emotions influence how we respond to problems and challenges in our environment. They help us organize our thoughts and actions, both explicitly and implicitly, and they guide our behavior. Perhaps because our emotions exert such widespread influence, we spend a good deal of time trying to regulate how we feel and how we present our emotions to others. Given their centrality, it is not surprising that disturbances in emotion figure prominently in many different forms of psychopathology. By one analysis, as many as 85 percent of psychological disorders include disturbances in emotional processing of some kind (Thoits, 1985).

What is emotion? The answer to that question could fill an entire textbook on its own. Emotions are believed to be fairly short-lived states, lasting for a few seconds, minutes, or at most hours. Sometimes the word *affect* is used to describe short-lasting emotional feelings. Moods, on the other hand, are emotional experiences that endure for a longer period of time.

An emotional response has different components, including (but not limited to) expressive, experiential, and physiological components. The *expressive*, or *behavioral*, *component* of emotion typically refers to facial expressions of emotion. The *experience*, or *subjective feeling*, component of emotion refers to how someone reports he or she feels at any given moment or in response to some event. For example, learning that you received an A on your midterm might elicit feelings of happiness, pride, and relief. Learning you received a C might elicit feelings of anger, anxiety, or embarrassment. The *physiological component* of emotion involves changes in the body, such as those due to the autonomic nervous system activity that accompanies emotion. For example, if a car almost runs you down as you are crossing the street, you may show a frightened look on your face, feel fear, and experience an increase in your heart rate and breathing rate.

When we consider emotional disturbances in psychological disorders, it is important to consider which of the emotion components are affected. In some disorders, all emotion components may be disrupted, whereas in others, just one might be problematic. For example, people with schizophrenia do not readily express their emotions outwardly, but they report feeling emotions very strongly. People with panic disorder experience excessive fear when no actual danger is present. People with depression may experience prolonged sadness and other negative feelings. A person with antisocial personality disorder may not feel empathy. We will try to be clear in this book as to what component of emotion is being considered.

Another important consideration in the study of emotion and psychopathology is the concept of *ideal affect*, which simply refers to the kinds of emotional states that a person ideally wants to feel. At first glance, you might presume that happiness is the ideal affect for everyone. After all, who doesn't want to feel happy? However, research shows that ideal affects vary depending on cultural factors (Tsai, 2007). Thus, people from Western cultures, such as the United States, do indeed value happiness as their ideal state. However, people from East Asian cultures, like China, value less arousing positive emotions, such as calmness, more than happiness (Tsai, Knutson, & Fung, 2006). Tsai and colleagues have also shown a linkage between people's ideal affect and drug usage; if the ideal affect is a state of low arousal, like calmness, a person is less likely, for example, to use cocaine (Tsai, Knutson, & Rothman, 2007). Cross-nationally, more people in the United States seek treatment for cocaine and amphetamines, drugs that are stimulating and associated with feelings of excitement and happiness; more people in China seek

Emotion consists of many components, including expression (shown here), experience, and physiology.

treatment for heroin, a drug that has calming effects (Tsai, 2007; for more on the effects of these drugs, see Chapter 10).

The study of emotion figures prominently in the work of neuroscientists who are examining the ways in which the brain contributes to the different emotion components. Geneticists have also begun to examine how tendencies to experience a lot of positive or negative emotion may run in families. Cognitive behavioral therapies also consider how emotion influences thinking and behavior. Emotion thus cuts across the paradigms and can be studied from multiple perspectives, depending on the paradigm that is adopted.

Sociocultural Factors and Psychopathology

A good deal of research has focused on the ways in which sociocultural factors, such as gender, race, culture, ethnicity, and socioeconomic status, can contribute to different psychological disorders. Researchers who study such sociocultural factors and psychopathology all share the premise that environmental factors can trigger, exacerbate, or maintain the symptoms that make up the different disorders. But the range of variables considered and the ways of studying those variables cover a lot of ground.

Several studies consider the role of gender in different disorders. These studies have shown that some disorders affect men and women differently. For example, depression is nearly twice as common among women as among men. On the other hand, antisocial personality disorder and alcohol use disorder are more common among men than women. Childhood disorders, such as attention-deficit/hyperactivity disorder, affect boys more than girls, but some researchers question whether this reflects a true difference between boys and girls or a bias in the diagnostic criteria. Current research is looking beyond whether men and women differ in the prevalence rates of certain disorders to asking questions about risk factors that may differently impact men and women in the development of certain disorders. For example, father-to-son genetic transmission appears to be an important risk factor in the development of alcohol use disorder for men, whereas sociocultural standards of thinness may be a risk factor in the development of eating disorders for women.

Other studies show that poverty is a major influence on psychological disorders. For example, poverty is related to antisocial personality disorder, anxiety disorders, and depression.

Cultural and ethnic factors in psychopathology have also been examined. Some questions, such as whether the disorders we diagnose and treat in the United States are observed in other parts of the world, have been fairly well studied. This research has demonstrated that several disorders are observed in diverse parts of the world. Indeed, no country or culture is without psychopathology of some sort. For example, schizophrenia is observed in diverse cultures, but the conceptualization and meaning of the symptoms may vary. For example, *nuthkavihak* in the Eskimo culture and *were* in the Yoruba culture includes talking to oneself, refusing to talk, delusional beliefs, and bizarre behavior (Murphy, 1976). People with schizophrenia in the United States consider their auditory hallucinations (hearing voices) to be part of their illness, but people with schizophrenia in India and Ghana are less likely to consider these hallucinations as part of their illness (Luhrmann, Padmavati, et al., 2015). In Chapter 6, we discuss a few anxiety conditions around the world that look very similar to the symptoms of panic disorder.

Although some disorders appear to occur in different cultures, other disorders are apparently specific to particular cultures. In Chapter 11, we consider the evidence that eating disorders are specific to Western culture. The Japanese term *hikikomori* refers to a condition in which a person completely withdraws from his social world (although women are affected, it is observed predominantly among men). People with hikikomori may completely shut themselves into their room or house—in some cases, for many years—refusing to interact with other people and leaving only occasionally to buy food. As we discuss in Chapter 3, the current diagnostic system includes cultural factors in the discussion

Betsie Van der Meer/Stone/Getty Images

Culture and ethnicity play an important role in the descriptions, causes, and treatments of psychological disorders.

of every category of disorder, and this may be an important step toward increasing research in this area.

Even though there are some cross-cultural similarities in psychological disorders across cultures, there are also many profound cultural influences on the symptoms expressed in different disorders, the availability of treatment, and the willingness to seek treatment. We consider these issues throughout this book.

We must also consider the role of race and ethnicity in psychopathology. Some disorders, such as schizophrenia, are diagnosed more often among blacks than whites. Does this mean schizophrenia occurs more often in this group, or does it mean that some type of ethnic bias might be operating in diagnostic assessments? The use of drugs and their effects vary by ethnicity. Whites are more likely to use or abuse many drugs, such as nicotine; hallucinogens; methamphetamine; prescription painkillers; and, depending on the age group, alcohol. Yet African American smokers are more likely to die from lung cancer. Eating disturbances and body dissatisfaction are greater among white women than black women, particularly in college, but differences in actual eating disorders, particularly bulimia, do not appear to be as great. The reasons for these differences are not yet well understood and are the focus of current research. **Table 2.1** shows data on ethnic and racial differences in the lifetime prevalence of different disorders.

The study of sociocultural factors has become more prominent in genetics and neuroscience. For example, *social neuroscience* seeks to understand what happens in the brain during complex social situations. Culture, too, has figured into neuroscience research (Kitayama & Uskul, 2011). Gene–environment interaction studies are uncovering the ways in which the social environment in combination with certain genes can increase the risk for disorders. A multinational project called the 1000 Genomes Project (http://www.1000genomes.org) seeks to sequence the genomes of a representative sample of people around the world. In one study from this project, researchers found that people from each country had about the same number of rare variants in the genomes (Gravel, Henn, et al., 2011). However, the rare variants were not the same in the different countries, suggesting that culture may also be influencing gene expression. Cognitive behavioral traditions have tended to focus more on the individual rather than on how the individual interacts with the social world. However, this, too, is changing. Efforts are under way,

TABLE 2.1	Lifetime Prevalence Rates of DSM Disorders Among Different Ethnic Groups		
Disorder	**White**	**Hispanic**	**Black**
ADHD	4.6	4.6	3.4
Alcohol abuse or dependence	13.4	15.0*	9.5
Bipolar disorder	3.2	4.3	4.9*
Depression	17.9*	13.5	10.8
Drug abuse or dependence	7.9	9.1	6.3
Generalized anxiety disorder	8.6*	4.8	5.1
Panic disorder	4.9	5.4	3.1
PTSD	6.8	5.9	7.1

Table values are percentages. *indicates group with significantly highest prevalence rate.

Source: Adapted from Breslau, Lucia, & Alvarado (2006). Sample came from the National Comorbidity Survey Replication study, which included a representative sample of people age 18 or older in the United States. Diagnoses made based on DSM-IV-TR criteria.

for example, to develop cognitive behavior therapy for people from different cultures and ethnicities.

Interpersonal Factors and Psychopathology

Beyond the role of culture, ethnicity, and poverty, thousands of articles have been published on how the quality of relationships influences different disorders. Family and marital relationships, social support, and even the amount of casual social contact all play a role in influencing the course of disorders. In **Focus on Discovery 2.2**, we discuss couples and family approaches to psychotherapy. Within relationships, researchers have looked for ways to measure not only the relative closeness and support offered but also the degree of hostility displayed.

Other researchers are interested in understanding the role of trauma, serious life events, and stress in psychopathology. We will describe some of the ways people measure life events in the next chapter. But the influence of stress within the context of social relationships plays a role in just about all the disorders we will consider.

Focus on Discovery 2.2

Couples and Family Therapies

Given that interpersonal factors are important in nearly all disorders we discuss in this book, it is not surprising that therapies have been developed to focus on these relationships. In addition to interpersonal therapy, discussed in the text, we consider here two other types of therapies: couples therapy and family therapy.

Couples Therapy

Conflict is inevitable in any long-term partner relationship. About 50 percent of marriages in the United States end in divorce, and most of these divorces happen within the first seven years of marriage (Snyder, Castellani, & Whisman, 2006). People in a distressed marriage are two to three times as likely to experience a psychological disorder (Whisman & Uebelacker, 2006). In some couples, distress may be a consequence of the psychological disorder, but it is also clear that distress can contribute to psychological disorders. Couples therapy is often used in the treatment of

psychological disorders, particularly when they occur in the context of major relationship distress.

In couples therapy, the therapist works with both partners together to reduce relationship distress. Treatments for most couples focus on improving communication, problem solving, satisfaction, trust, and positive feelings.

Family Therapy

Family therapy is based on the idea that the problems of the family influence each member and that the problems of each member influence the family. As such, family therapy is used to address specific symptoms of a given family member, particularly for the treatment of childhood problems.

Some family therapists focus on roles within the family, asking questions about whether parents assume an appropriate level of responsibility. Sometimes family therapists attend to whether a given person in the family has been "scapegoated," or unfairly blamed for a broader issue in the family. Many family therapists teach strategies to help families communicate and solve problems more effectively.

Family therapy is often tailored to the specific disorder. In family approaches for conduct disorder, the therapist may focus on improving parental monitoring and discipline. For adolescents with other externalizing problems, the goal of family therapy may be to improve communication, to change roles, or to address a range of family problems. With disorders like schizophrenia and bipolar disorder, family therapy often includes psychoeducation as a supplement for the medication treatment provided to the individual. Psychoeducation focuses on improving understanding of the disorder, reducing expressed family criticism and hostility, and helping families learn skills for managing symptoms, as in the Clinical Case of Clare (Miklowitz, George, et al., 2003). In anorexia nervosa, family members are used strategically to help the adolescent gain weight. In sum, the goals and strategies of family therapy will be adjusted to meet the needs of different clients.

Gary Conner/Alamy

When a problem involves a couple, treatment is most effective if the couple is seen together.

Clinical Case

Clare

Clare, a 17-year-old girl who lived with her parents and her 15-year-old brother, was referred for family-focused treatment (FFT) of bipolar disorder as an adjunct to medication treatment. She had received a diagnosis of bipolar I disorder in early adolescence and was treated with lithium carbonate and quetiapine but had never fully responded to medications.

During an individual assessment session, Clare explained that she thought about suicide almost daily and had made two prior attempts, both by overdosing on her parents' medications. Clare had kept both attempts secret from her parents. Ethically, clinicians need to take steps to keep a client safe, and in this case, one measure would be to let Clare's parents know about her suicidality. The clinician explained this to Clare.

The first goal in FFT is to provide psychoeducation about bipolar disorder. As the symptoms of bipolar disorder were being reviewed, the clinician asked Clare to discuss her suicide attempts with her parents. When Clare did so, her parents were surprised. Her father, who had experienced his own father's suicide, was particularly concerned.

After psychoeducation, a goal in FFT is to choose one problem for the family to address and to help them learn new problem-solving skills in the process. In this family, the focus of problem solving was how to keep Clare safe from her suicidal impulses. To begin problem solving, the therapist worked with the family to define the problem and its context. The therapist asked the family to discuss situations that seemed to place Clare at most risk for suicide. The family was able to pinpoint that both previous attempts had followed interpersonal losses.

The next phase of problem solving is to generate potential solutions. To help with this process, the clinician framed questions in the problem-solving process for the family, including whether Clare could share her suicidal thoughts with her parents, how to establish whether she was safe, what responses would be helpful from them, and what other protective actions should be taken. Using this structure, the family was able to agree on the plan that Clare would phone or page her parents when she was feeling self-destructive. Clare and her parents generated a plan in which her parents would help Clare engage in positive and calming activities until her suicidal thoughts were less intrusive. Clare and her parents reported feeling closer and more optimistic.

The therapist then began to conduct the next phase of therapy, which focused directly on symptom management. This phase consisted of training Clare to monitor her moods, to identify triggers for mood changes, and to help her cope with those triggers.

As is typical in FFT, the clinician introduced the communication enhancement module during her eighth session. A goal of this module is to role-play new communication skills. Family members practice skills such as "active listening" by paraphrasing and labeling the others' statements and by asking clarifying questions. At first, Clare and her brother protested against the role-play exercises.

Clare experienced another loss during this period when her one and only close, long-term friend announced that she was going to be moving out of state. Clare took an overdose of Tylenol in a suicide attempt. Soon after overdosing, she became afraid, induced vomiting, and later told her parents about the attempt.

The next session focused on the suicide attempt. Her parents, particularly her father, were hurt and angry. Clare in turn reacted angrily and defensively. The therapist asked the family to practice active listening skills regarding Clare's suicidality. Clare explained that she had acted without even thinking about the family agreement because she had been so distressed about the idea of losing her friend. Clare's parents were able to validate her feelings using active listening skills. The therapist reminded the parents that suicidal actions are common in bipolar disorder and noted that Clare's ability to be honest about her suicide attempt was an indicator of better family connectedness. The therapist also recommended that Clare see her psychiatrist, who increased her dosage of lithium.

By the end of treatment after 9 months, Clare had not made any more suicide attempts, had become more willing to take her medications, and felt closer to her parents. Like many people with bipolar disorder, though, she remained mildly depressed. Clare and her family continued to see the therapist once every 3 months for ongoing support. [Adapted from Miklowitz and Taylor (2005) with permission of the authors.]

Recall from Chapter 1 that one of the central features of psychoanalysis is transference, which refers to a person's responses to the analyst that seem to reflect attitudes and ways of behaving toward important people in the patient's past rather than reflecting actual aspects of the relationship between the person and the analyst. Contemporary psychodynamic theorists have built on the concept of transference to emphasize the importance of a person's interpersonal relationships for psychological well-being. One example is **object relations theory**, which stresses the importance of long-standing patterns in close relationships, particularly within the family, that are shaped by the ways in which people think and feel. The "object" refers to another person in most versions of this theory. This theory goes beyond transference to emphasize the way in which a person comes to understand, whether consciously or not, how the self is situated in relation to other people. For example, a woman may come to understand herself as a worthless person based on her cold and critical relationship with her mother.

Another influential theory, **attachment theory**, grew out of object relations theory. John Bowlby (1907–1990) first proposed this theory in 1969, and Mary Ainsworth (1913–1999) and colleagues (1978) developed a method to measure attachment styles in infants. The essence of the theory is that the type or style of an infant's attachment to his or her caregivers can set the stage for psychological health or problems later in life. For example, infants who are securely attached to their caregivers are more likely to grow up to be psychologically healthy adults, whereas infants who are anxiously attached to their caregivers are more likely to experience psychological difficulties. Attachment theory has been extended to adults (Main, Kaplan, & Cassidy, 1985; Pietromonaco & Barrett, 1997), and couples (e.g., Fraley & Shaver, 2000); and therapies based on attachment theory have been developed for children and adults, though these treatments have not yet been empirically scrutinized.

Children who are securely attached to parents are more likely to be psychologically healthy adults.

Blend Images/SuperStock, Inc.

Social psychologists have integrated both of these theories into the concept of the *relational self*, which refers to the self in relation to others (Chen, Boucher, et al., 2013; Chen, Boucher, & Parker Tapias, 2006). The concept of the relational self has garnered a tremendous amount of empirical support. For example, people will describe themselves differently depending on what other close relationships they have been asked to think about (Chen et al., 2006). Other studies show that describing a stranger in terms that are similar to a description of a close significant other will trigger positive feelings and facial expressions, presumably linked to the view of the self in relation to the close other person (Andersen, Reznik, & Manzella, 1996). Thus, if you are given a description of a stranger you must interact with that resembles a description of a close friend from high school, you will be more likely to smile, perhaps as a result of thinking about yourself and your interactions with your high school friend. The idea of the relational self has not yet been fully extended to the study of psychopathology, but given its theoretical basis and empirical support, it is ripe for translation to the study of interpersonal difficulties across many different psychological disorders.

Interpersonal Therapy

Interpersonal therapy (IPT) emphasizes the importance of current relationships in a person's life and how problems in these relationships can contribute to psychological symptoms. The therapist first encourages the patient to identify feelings about his or her relationships and to express these feelings, and then helps the patient generate solutions to interpersonal problems. IPT has been shown to be an effective treatment for depression (a topic we turn to in more detail in Chapter 5). IPT has also been used to treat eating disorders, anxiety disorders, and personality disorders.

In IPT, four interpersonal issues are assessed to examine whether one or more of them might be having an impact on symptoms:

- *Unresolved grief*—for example, experiencing delayed or incomplete grieving following a loss
- *Role transitions*—for example, transitioning from child to parent or from worker to retired person
- *Role disputes*—for example, resolving different relationship expectations between romantic partners
- *Interpersonal or social deficits*—for example, not being able to begin a conversation with an unfamiliar person or finding it difficult to negotiate with a boss at work

In sum, the therapist helps the patient understand that psychopathology occurs in a social or relationship context and that getting a better handle on relationship patterns is necessary to reduce symptoms of psychopathology.

Unresolved grief is one of the issues discussed in interpersonal therapy.

PhotoDisc/SuperStock, Inc.

Stressors that may activate a diathesis range from minor, such as having car trouble, to major, such as the aftermath of a tornado.

Diathesis–Stress: An Integrative Paradigm

Psychopathology is much too diverse to be fully explained or treated adequately by any one of the current paradigms. Most of the disorders we will discuss in this book likely develop through an interaction of neurobiological and environmental factors, a view that we turn to next.

The **diathesis–stress** paradigm is an integrative paradigm that links genetic, neurobiological, psychological, and environmental factors. It is not limited to one particular school of thought, such as cognitive behavioral, genetic, or neurobiological. The diathesis–stress concept was introduced in the 1970s as a way to account for the multiple causes of schizophrenia (Zubin & Spring, 1977). Its appeal continues today for many disorders, however, because, like the gene–environment interaction model reviewed earlier, it is a model that focuses on the interaction between a predisposition toward disease—the **diathesis**—and environmental, or life, disturbances—the stress. Diathesis refers most precisely to a constitutional predisposition toward illness, but the term may be extended to any characteristic or set of characteristics of a person that increases his or her chance of developing a disorder.

In the realm of neurobiology, for example, several disorders considered in later chapters appear to have a genetically influenced diathesis. Other neurobiological diatheses include oxygen deprivation at birth, poor nutrition, and a maternal viral infection or smoking during pregnancy. Each of these conditions may lead to changes in the brain that predispose a person toward psychopathology.

In the psychological realm, a diathesis for depression may be a cognitive schema or the chronic feeling of hopelessness sometimes found in people with depression. Other psychological diatheses include the ability to be easily hypnotized, which may be a diathesis for dissociative identity disorder (formerly called multiple personality disorder), and an intense fear of becoming fat, which is a vulnerability factor for some eating disorders.

Possessing the diathesis for a disorder increases a person's risk of developing it but does not by any means guarantee that a disorder will develop. The stress part of diathesis–stress is meant to account for how a diathesis may be translated into an actual disorder. Psychological stressors include major traumatic events (e.g., becoming unemployed, divorce, death of a spouse, serving in combat) as well as more chronic stressors (e.g., living in poverty throughout childhood).

The key point of the diathesis–stress model is that both diathesis and stress are necessary in the development of disorders. Some people, for example, have inherited a predisposition that places them at high risk for mania (see Chapter 5): a certain amount of stress increases the possibility of developing mania. Other people, those at low genetic risk, are not likely to develop mania regardless of how difficult their lives are.

Another major feature of the diathesis–stress paradigm is that psychopathology is unlikely to result from the impact of any single factor. A genetic diathesis may be necessary for some disorders, but it is embedded in a network of other factors that also contribute to the disorder. These factors could include genetic diatheses for other personality characteristics; childhood experiences that shape personality; the development of behavioral competencies, and coping strategies; stressors encountered in adulthood; cultural influences; and numerous other factors.

Finally, we should note that within this framework, the data gathered by researchers holding different paradigms are not incompatible with one another. For example, stress may be needed to activate a predisposition toward a problem in neurotransmitter systems. Some of the differences between the paradigms also appear to be more semantic than substantive. A cognitive behavioral theorist may propose that maladaptive cognitions cause depression, whereas a neurobiological theorist may speak of the activity of a certain neural pathway. The two positions are not contradictory but merely reflect different levels of description, just as we could describe a table as pieces of wood in a particular configuration or as a collection of atoms.

In **Focus on Discovery 2.3** we illustrate how adopting one paradigm to the exclusion of others can bias your view of the critical targets for treatment.

Focus on Discovery 2.3

Multiple Perspectives on a Clinical Problem

To provide a concrete example of how it is possible to conceptualize a clinical case using multiple paradigms, we present a case and discuss how the information provided is open to several interpretations, depending on the paradigm adopted.

Clinical Case

Arthur

Arthur's childhood had not been a particularly happy one. His mother died suddenly when he was 6, and for the next 10 years he lived either with his father or with a maternal aunt. His father drank heavily, seldom managing to get through a day without some alcohol. His father's income was so irregular that he could seldom pay bills on time or afford to live in any but the most run-down neighborhoods. At times Arthur's father was totally incapable of caring for himself, let alone his son. Arthur would then spend weeks, sometimes months, with his aunt in a nearby suburb.

Despite these early life circumstances, Arthur completed high school and entered college. He qualified for student loans and other financial aid, but he also needed to wait tables and tend bar to make ends meet. During these college years, he felt an acute self-consciousness with people he felt had authority over him—his boss, his professors, and even some of his classmates, with whom he compared himself unfavorably.

Like many people in college, Arthur attended his fair share of parties. He pledged a fraternity at the end of his freshman year, and this was the source of most of his socializing. It was also the source of a lot of alcohol. He drank heavily at the weekend parties. By his senior year, however, he was drinking daily, often to deal with the stress of being in school and working at the same time.

Two years after college, Arthur married his college girlfriend. He could never quite believe that his wife, as intelligent as she was beautiful, really cared for him. As the years wore on, his doubts about himself and about her feelings toward him would continue to grow.

After college, Arthur began a job at a publishing company, serving as an assistant editor. This job proved to be even more stressful than college. The deadlines and demands of the senior editors were difficult. He constantly questioned whether he had what it took to be an editor. Like his father, he often drank to deal with this stress.

Several years later, when it seemed that life should be getting easier, he found himself in even greater turmoil. Now 35 years old, with a fairly secure job that paid reasonably well, he was arguing more often with his wife. She continually complained about his drinking; he denied that there was a problem. After all, he was only drinking four beers a night. His wife wanted to start a family, but he was not sure if he wanted to have this additional stress in his life. His brooding over his marriage led him to drink even more heavily until finally, one day, he realized he was drinking too much and needed to seek help.

Depending on the paradigm you adopt, your conceptualization of this case may differ. If you hold a genetic point of view, you are attentive to the family history, noting that Arthur's father had similar difficulties with alcohol. You are probably aware of the research (to be reviewed in Chapter 10) that suggests a genetic contribution to alcohol use disorder. You understand, though, that genes do their work via the environment, and you hypothesize about the ways in which genetic factors interact with different environmental factors (e.g., stress at work and in his relationships), which may in turn increase the likelihood that he will turn to alcohol to cope.

Now suppose that you are committed to a cognitive behavioral perspective, which encourages you to approach psychological disorders in terms of reinforcement patterns as well as cognitive variables. You may focus on Arthur's self-consciousness at college, which seems related to the fact that, compared with his fellow students, he grew up with few advantages. Economic insecurity and hardship may have made him unduly sensitive to criticism and rejection. Alcohol has been his escape from such tensions. But heavy drinking, coupled with persistent doubt about his own worth as a human being, has worsened an already deteriorating marital relationship, further undermining his confidence. As a cognitive behavior therapist, you may decide on cognitive behavior therapy to convince Arthur that he need not obtain universal approval for every undertaking.

If you adopt an integrative perspective, you might follow more than one of these strategies. You would acknowledge the likely genetic contribution to Arthur's alcohol use disorder, but you would also identify key triggers (e.g., job stress) that might lead to greater bouts of drinking. You would likely employ many of the therapeutic techniques noted in this chapter.

Quick Summary

Disturbances in emotion figure prominently in psychopathology, but the ways in which emotions can be disrupted vary quite a bit. It is important to distinguish between components of emotion, including expression, experience, and physiology. In addition, mood can be distinguished from emotion. The concept of ideal affect points to important cultural differences in emotion that may be important in psychopathology. Psychological disorders have different types of emotion disturbances, and thus it is important to consider which of the emotion components are affected. In some disorders, all emotion components may be disrupted, whereas in others just one might be problematic. Emotion is an important focus in the paradigms.

Sociocultural factors, such as culture, ethnicity, gender, and socioeconomic status, are important factors in the study of psychopathology. Some disorders, like schizophrenia or anxiety, appear to be universal across cultures, yet their manifestations may differ somewhat and the ways in which society regards them may also differ. Other disorders, like eating disorders or hikikomori, may be specific to particular cultures. Some disorders are more frequently diagnosed in some ethnic groups than in others. It is not clear whether this reflects a true difference in the presence of disorder or perhaps a bias on the part of diagnosticians.

Current research is also examining whether risk factors associated with various disorders differ for men and women. Sociocultural factors have recently become the focus of people working in the other paradigms, and this trend will continue. Interpersonal relationships can be important buffers against stress and have benefits for physical and mental health. Object relations theory, which stresses the importance of relationships, and its offshoot, attachment theory, which emphasizes the role of attachment styles in infancy through adulthood, are also important in psychopathology research.

Check Your Knowledge 2.4

True or false?

1. Emotion consists of at least three components: expression, experience, and physiology.

2. Sociocultural factors such as gender, culture, ethnicity, and social relationships are less important to consider in the neuroscience paradigm.

3. Examining the problem-solving interactions of family members is useful for understanding key dimensions in relationships.

4. The relational self is a concept from social psychology that incorporates ideas from object relations and attachment theories.

5. Interpersonal therapy may focus on four types of interpersonal problems: unresolved grief, role transitions, role disputes, and social deficits.

Summary

- A paradigm is a conceptual framework or general perspective. Paradigms specify what problems scientists will investigate and how they will go about the investigation and inform the way we approach psychopathology.

- The genetic paradigm holds that psychopathology is influenced by heritable factors. Research shows how genes and the environment interact, and it is this type of interaction that will figure prominently in psychopathology. Molecular genetics research is identifying differences in gene sequence and structure that may be associated with vulnerability to psychopathology. Epigenetics refers to the ways in which environments influence the expression of genes.

- The neuroscience paradigm emphasizes the role of the brain, neurotransmitters, and other systems, such as the HPA axis. Biological treatments, including medications, are widely used.

- The cognitive behavioral paradigm emphasizes schemas, attention, and cognitive distortions about life experiences and their influence on behavior as major factors in psychopathology. Cognitive neuroscience research follows from the early work of Freud, highlighting the importance of childhood experiences, the unconscious, and the fact that the causes of behavior are not always obvious. Cognitive behavior therapy focuses on cognitive restructuring.

- Emotion plays a prominent role in many disorders. It is important to distinguish among components of emotion that may be disrupted, including expression, experience, and physiology.

- Sociocultural factors, including culture, ethnicity, gender, and poverty, are also important in conceptions of psychopathology. The prevalence and meaning of disorders may vary by culture and ethnicity, men and women may have different risk factors for different disorders, and social relationships can be an important buffer against stress.

- Interpersonal factors, including social support and relationships, are also factors that cut across paradigms. Social relationships

can be an important buffer against stress, and relationships, including current conceptualizations of attachment and the relational self, are important. Sociocultural and interpersonal factors are included in the work of geneticists, neuroscientists, and cognitive behaviorists.

- Because each paradigm seems to have something to offer in enhancing our understanding of psychological disorders, an integrative paradigm such as the diathesis-stress paradigm is perhaps the most comprehensive. The diathesis may be genetic, neurobiological, or psychological and may be caused by early-childhood experiences, genetically influenced personality traits, or sociocultural influences, among other things.

Answers to Check Your Knowledge Questions

2.1 1. b; 2. d; 3. a; 4. b; 5.d

2.2 1. hypothalamus, anterior cingulate, hippocampus, amygdala; 2. white, gray; 3. norepinephrine, GABA; 4. hypothalamus, pituitary gland, adrenal cortex; 5. pro-inflammatory cytokines; depression; schizophrenia

2.3 1. T; 2. T; 3. F

2.4 1. T; 2. F; 3. T; 4. T; 5. T

Key Terms

allele
amygdala
anterior cingulate
attachment theory
autonomic nervous system (ANS)
behavioral activation (BA) therapy
behavior genetics
brain networks
cognition
cognitive behavioral paradigm
cognitive behavior therapy (CBT)
cognitive restructuring
copy number variation (CNV)
cortisol
diathesis
diathesis–stress
dopamine
emotion
epigenetics

exposure
gamma-aminobutyric acid (GABA)
gene
gene–environment interaction
gene expression
genetic paradigm
genome-wide association studies (GWAS)
genotype
gray matter
heritability
hippocampus
HPA axis
hypothalamus
interpersonal therapy (IPT)
molecular genetics
neuron
neuroscience paradigm
neurotransmitters
nonshared environment

norepinephrine
object relations theory
paradigm
parasympathetic nervous system
phenotype
polygenic
polymorphism
prefrontal cortex
pruning
reuptake
schema
serotonin
shared environment
single nucleotide polymorphism (SNP)
sympathetic nervous system
synapse
time-out
ventricles
white matter

CHAPTER 3

Diagnosis and Assessment

LEARNING GOALS

1. Describe the purposes of diagnosis and assessment, and distinguish the different types of reliability and validity.

2. Identify the basic features, strengths, and weaknesses of the DSM, and concerns about diagnosis more broadly.

3. Describe the goals, strengths, and weaknesses of psychological approaches to assessment.

4. Understand key approaches to neurobiological assessment.

5. Understand the ways in which culture and ethnicity impact diagnosis and assessment.

Clinical Case

Aaron

Hearing the sirens in the distance, Aaron realized that someone must have called the police. He didn't mean to get upset with the people sitting next to him at the bar, but he just knew that they were talking about him and plotting to have his special status with the CIA revoked. He could not let this happen again. The last time people conspired against him, he wound up in the hospital. He did not want to go to the hospital again and endure all the evaluations. Different doctors would ask him all sorts of questions about his work with the CIA, which he simply was not at liberty to discuss. They asked other odd questions, such as whether he heard voices or believed others were putting thoughts into his head. He was never sure how they knew that he had those experiences, but he suspected that there were electronic bugging devices in his room at his parents' house, perhaps in the electrical outlets.

Just yesterday, Aaron began to suspect that someone was watching and listening to him through the electrical outlets. He decided that the safest thing to do was to stop speaking to his parents. Besides, they were constantly hounding him to take his medication. But when he took this medication, his vision got blurry and he had trouble sitting still. He reasoned that his parents must somehow be part of the group of people trying to remove him from the CIA. If he took this medication, he would lose his special powers that allowed him to spot terrorists in any setting, and the CIA would stop leaving messages for him in phone booths or in the commercials on Channel 2. Just the other day, he found a tattered paperback book in a phone booth, which he interpreted to mean that a new assignment was imminent. The voices in his head were giving him new clues about terrorist activity. They were currently telling him that he should be wary of people wearing the color purple, as this was a sign of a terrorist. If his parents were trying to sabotage his career with the CIA, he needed to keep out of the house at all costs. That was what had led him to the bar in the first place. If only the people next to him hadn't laughed and looked toward the door. He knew this meant that they were about to expose him as a CIA operative. If he hadn't yelled at them to stop, his cover would have been blown.

In this chapter, we will describe the official diagnostic system used by many mental health professionals, as well as the strengths and weaknesses of this system. We will then turn to a discussion of the most widely used assessment techniques, including interviews, psychological assessment, and neurobiological assessment. We then conclude the chapter with an examination of a sometimes neglected aspect of assessment, the role of cultural bias. Before considering diagnosis and assessment in detail, however, we begin with a discussion of two concepts that play a key role in diagnosis and assessment: reliability and validity.

Cornerstones of Diagnosis and Assessment: Reliability and Validity

Diagnosis and assessment are the critically important first steps in the study and treatment of psychopathology. In the case of Aaron, a clinician may begin treatment by determining whether he meets the diagnostic criteria for a mood disorder, schizophrenia, or perhaps a substance use disorder. Diagnosis can be the first major step in good clinical care. Having a correct **diagnosis** will allow the clinician to describe base rates, causes, and treatment for Aaron and his family, all of which are important aspects of good clinical care. More broadly, imagine that your doctor told you, "There is no diagnosis for what you have." Rather than this alarming scenario, hearing a diagnosis can provide relief in several different ways. Many disorders, such as depression and anxiety, are extremely common; knowing that his or her diagnosis is common can also help a person feel less unusual. A diagnosis also can help a person begin to understand why certain symptoms are occurring, which can be a huge relief.

Diagnosis enables clinicians and scientists to communicate accurately with one another about cases or research. Indeed, establishing a new diagnosis often fosters research on the topic. For example, autism spectrum disorder (ASD) was only recognized in the *Diagnostic and Statistical Manual* in 1980. Since that time, research on the causes and treatments of ASD has grown exponentially.

To help make the correct diagnosis, clinicians and researchers use a variety of assessment procedures, beginning with a clinical interview. Broadly speaking, all clinical assessment procedures are more or less formal ways of finding out what is wrong with a person, what may have caused problems, and what can be done to improve the person's condition. Assessment procedures can help in making a diagnosis, and they can also provide information beyond a diagnosis. Indeed, a diagnosis is only a starting point. In the case of Aaron, for example, many other questions remain unanswered. Why does Aaron behave as he does? Why does he believe he is working for the CIA? What can be done to resolve his conflicts with his parents? Has he performed up to his intellectual potential in school and in his career? What obstacles might interfere with treatment? These are the types of questions that mental health professionals address in their assessments.

The concepts of reliability and validity are the cornerstones of any diagnostic or assessment procedure. Without them, the usefulness of our methods is seriously limited. That said, these two concepts are quite complex. Here, we provide a general overview.

Reliability

Reliability refers to consistency of measurement. An example of a reliable measure would be a wooden ruler, which produces the same value every time it is used to measure an object. In contrast, an unreliable measure would be a flexible, elastic-like ruler whose length changes every time it is used. Several types of reliability exist, and here we will discuss the types that are most central to assessment and diagnosis.

Inter-rater reliability refers to the degree to which two independent observers agree on what they have observed. To take an example from baseball, two umpires may or may not agree as to whether the ball is fair or foul.

NewMedia Inc./Reuters

Reliability is an essential property of all assessment procedures. One means of establishing reliability is to determine whether different judges agree, as happens when two umpires witness the same event in a baseball game.

Test—retest reliability measures the extent to which people being observed twice or taking the same test twice, perhaps several weeks or months apart, receive similar scores. This kind of reliability makes sense only when we can assume that the people will not change appreciably between test sessions on the underlying variable being measured; a prime example of a situation in which this type of reliability is typically high is in evaluating intelligence tests. On the other hand, we cannot expect people to be in the same mood at a baseline and a follow-up assessment 4 weeks later, and thus the test—retest reliability of a mood measure would likely be low.

Sometimes psychologists use two forms of a test rather than giving the same test twice, perhaps when there is concern that test takers will remember their answers from the first round of taking the test and aim merely to be consistent. This approach enables the tester to determine **alternate-form reliability**, the extent to which scores on the two forms of the test are consistent.

Finally, **internal consistency reliability** assesses whether the items on a test are related to one another. For example, one would expect the items on an anxiety questionnaire to correlate with one another, if they truly tap anxiety. A person who reports a dry mouth in a threatening situation would be expected to report increases in muscle tension as well, since both are common characteristics of anxiety.

Reliability is typically measured on a scale from 0 to 1.0. For all types of reliability, the closer the number is to 1.0, the better the reliability. For example, a test with an internal consistency reliability of .65 is only moderately reliable; a different test with an internal consistency reliability of .91 is very reliable.

Validity

Validity is a complex concept, generally related to whether a measure measures what it is supposed to measure. For example, if a questionnaire is supposed to measure a person's hostility, does it do so? Before we describe types of validity, it is important to note that validity is related to reliability—unreliable measures will not have good validity. Because an unreliable measure does not yield consistent results (recall our example of a ruler whose length is constantly changing), it will not relate very strongly to other measures. For example, an unreliable measure of coping is not likely to show how a person adjusts to stressful life experiences. Reliability, however, does not guarantee validity. Height can be measured very reliably, but height would not be a valid measure of anxiety. Perhaps the most common form of validity in developing tests is criterion validity, which assesses whether a test predicts related measures. Here we focus on two types of validity that are often used in considering diagnosis and symptoms.

Content validity refers to whether a measure adequately samples the domain of interest. For example, a test to assess social anxiety ought to include items that cover feelings of anxiety in different social situations. It would have excellent content validity if it contained questions about all the symptoms associated with social anxiety (see Chapter 6). For certain uses, though, the same test might have poor content validity. The test doesn't cover questions about anxiety in nonsocial situations, and if one were trying to assess specific phobias about heights or snakes, this test would have poor content validity.

Construct validity is a more complex concept. It is relevant when we want to interpret a test as a measure of some characteristic or construct that is not observed directly or overtly (Cronbach & Meehl, 1955). A construct is an inferred attribute, such as anxiousness or distorted cognition. Consider an anxiety-proneness questionnaire as an example. If the questionnaire has construct validity, people who obtain different scores on our test really will differ in anxiety proneness. Content validity does not ensure high construct validity.

As shown in **Figure 3.1**, construct validity is evaluated by looking at a wide variety of data. For example, people diagnosed as having an anxiety disorder and people without such a diagnosis could be compared using their scores on our self-report measure of anxiety proneness. The self-report measure would achieve some construct validity if the people with anxiety disorders scored higher than the people without anxiety disorders. Greater construct validity would be achieved by showing that the self-report measure was related to other measures thought to reflect anxiety, such as observations of fidgeting and trembling, and physiological indicators, such as increased heart rate and rapid breathing. When the self-report measure is associated with these multiple measures (diagnosis, observational indicators, physiological measures), its construct validity is increased.

More broadly, construct validity is related to theory. For example, we might hypothesize that being prone to anxiety is in part caused by a family history of anxiety. We could then obtain further evidence for the construct validity of our questionnaire by showing that it relates to a family history of anxiety. At the same time, we would also have gathered support for our theory of anxiety proneness. Thus, construct validation is an important part of the process of theory testing.

Quick Summary

With all assessments, the reliability (the consistency of measurement) and validity (whether an assessment measures what it is designed to measure) should be evaluated. Reliability can be estimated by examining how well raters agree, how consistent test scores are over time, how scores from alternate forms of a test compare, or how well items correlate with each other.

Although criterion validity is commonly considered in developing a test, content and construct validity are critically important in the assessment of psychopathology.

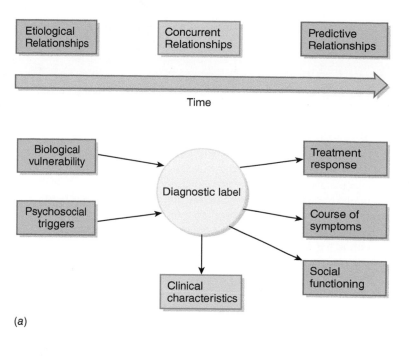

(a)

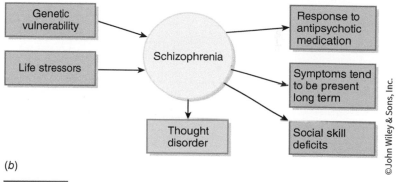

(b)

FIGURE 3.1 Construct validity. An example of the types of information a diagnosis might help predict.

Check Your Knowledge 3.1
(Answers are at the end of the chapter.)

Answer the questions.

1. Which type of reliability or validity is tested with the following procedures?

_____ A group of high school students is given the same IQ test 2 years in a row.

_____ A measure of the tendency to blame oneself is developed, and researchers then test whether it predicts depression, whether it is related to childhood abuse, and whether it is related to less assertiveness in the workplace.

_____ People are interviewed by two different doctors. Researchers examine whether the doctors agree about the diagnosis.

   a. inter-rater reliability

   b. test–retest reliability

   c. construct validity

Diagnosis

Roxanne

Roxanne is a middle-aged woman who was brought to the local psychiatric emergency room by the police. They had found her running through a crowded street, laughing loudly and running into people. Her clothes were dirty and torn. When they questioned her, she was speaking rapidly, and her thoughts were hard to follow. At the ER, she wrestled free of the police and began running down the hallway. She knocked over two staff members during her flight, while bellowing at the top of her lungs, "I am the resurrection! Come follow me!" Police brought her back to the exam room, and the staff began to form hypotheses. Clearly, she was full of energy. Had she been through some trauma? She believed she had special religious powers—could this be a delusion? Unfortunately, the staff was unable to gain much information from an interview due to her rapid and incoherent speech.

Roxanne sat restlessly, occasionally laughing and shouting; treatment could not proceed without understanding the reason for her unusual behavior. When efforts to calm Roxanne failed, police helped the staff to contact family members, who were relieved to hear that Roxanne was safe. She had disappeared from home the day before. Family members described a long history of bipolar disorder, and they reported having been concerned for the past couple weeks because Roxanne had stopped taking medications for both her bipolar disorder and her high blood pressure. Treatment was able to proceed based on the idea that Roxanne was experiencing a new manic episode of her long-standing bipolar disorder.

The DSM-5 diagnosis for Roxanne might look as follows.

Diagnoses: Bipolar I disorder, current or most recent episode manic; high blood pressure

The Diagnostic System of the American Psychiatric Association: DSM-5

In this section, we focus on the diagnostic system used by many mental health professionals, the **DSM-5** or the ***Diagnostic and Statistical Manual of Mental Disorder*, Fifth Edition**. In 1952, the American Psychiatric Association published its first *Diagnostic and Statistical Manual* (DSM). The DSM has been revised many times since 1952 (see **Focus on Discovery 3.1** for more on the history of the DSM). The fifth edition of the DSM, referred to as DSM-5, was released in 2013 (www.dsm5.org). We will review the major features of DSM-5, and then we will outline some strengths and criticisms of the DSM as well as of diagnosis in general.

The DSM-5 provides information about each disorder. To begin, the DSM-5 provides specific diagnostic criteria—symptoms for a given diagnosis. These criteria have become more detailed over time. **Table 3.1** compares the descriptions of a manic episode given in DSM-II

TABLE 3.1   **Mania in DSM-II Versus DSM-5**

DSM-II (1968)

Mania was described in DSM-II in just a short paragraph. The paragraph described mania with five symptoms (elevated mood, irritable mood, racing thoughts, rapid talking, and rapid movement). There was no mention of how many symptoms were needed to meet the criteria for a manic episode.

DSM-5 (2013)

DSM-5 provides a list of symptoms with descriptive detail for each symptom. The symptom description is divided into four parts, which we briefly summarize here. The actual DSM-5 offers more detail for all four parts.

1. The first part describes the mood and energy symptoms for mania. A person must show an elevated or irritable mood as well as a great deal of goal-directed behavior and energy. These mood and energy symptoms must last for at least 1 week or be severe enough to require hospitalization.

2. In addition to the mood and energy symptoms, a person must also have three or more symptoms, including racing thoughts, rapid talking, very little need for sleep, very high self-esteem or grandiose ideas about the self, difficulty maintaining focused attention, participation in behaviors that cause trouble (e.g., excessive spending or sexual encounters), and excessive activity.

3. These symptoms interfere with work or social interactions.

4. The last part of the diagnosis is a "rule out" section to clarify whether the symptoms cannot be better accounted for by something else, such as another disorder or the effects of a drug (legal or not).

Focus on Discovery 3.1

A History of Classification and Diagnosis

By the end of the nineteenth century, medical diagnostic procedures were improving as physicians began to understand the advantages of tailoring treatments to different illnesses. During the same period, other sciences, such as botany and chemistry, advanced after classification systems were developed. Impressed by these successes, investigators of psychological disorders also sought to develop classification schemes. Unfortunately, progress in classifying psychological disorders did not come easily.

Early Efforts at Classification of Psychological Disorders

Emil Kraepelin (1856–1926) authored an influential early classification system in his textbook of psychiatry first published in 1883. Kraepelin noted that certain symptoms clustered together as a *syndrome*. He labeled a set of syndromes and hypothesized that each had its own biological cause, course, and outcome. Even though effective treatments had not been identified, at least the course of the disease could be predicted.

Kraepelin proposed two major groups of severe psychological disorders: dementia praecox (an early term for schizophrenia) and manic-depressive psychosis (an early term for bipolar disorder). He postulated a chemical imbalance as the cause of dementia praecox and an irregularity in metabolism as the explanation of manic-depressive psychosis. Though his theories about causes were not quite correct, Kraepelin's classification scheme nonetheless influenced the current diagnostic categories.

Development of the WHO and DSM Systems

In 1939 the World Health Organization (WHO) added psychological disorders to the *International List of Causes of Death*. In 1948 the list was expanded to become *the International Statistical Classification of Diseases, Injuries, and Causes of Death*. Unfortunately, the psychological disorders section was not widely accepted. Even though American psychiatrists had played a prominent role in the WHO effort, the American Psychiatric Association published its own *Diagnostic and Statistical Manual* (DSM) in 1952.

In 1969 the WHO published a new version, now referred to as the *International Classification of Disease* (ICD), which was more widely accepted. In the United Kingdom, a glossary of definitions was produced to accompany the WHO system. A second version of the American Psychiatric Association's DSM, DSM-II, also published in 1968, was similar to the WHO system. But true consensus still eluded the field. Even though DSM-II and the British *Glossary of Mental Disorders* specified some symptoms of diagnoses, the two systems defined different symptoms for a given disorder! Thus diagnostic practices still varied widely. With each revision of the DSM and ICD, authors have tried to achieve greater consensus between the two systems. The ICD is currently in its 10th edition (the 11th edition is expected in 2018).

In 1980 the American Psychiatric Association published an extensively revised diagnostic manual, DSM-III, and a somewhat revised version, DSM-III-R, followed in 1987. One of the big changes in DSM-III that remained in place for 33 years was the introduction of the multiaxial system. Diagnoses were listed on separate dimensions, or axes, as shown in **Figure 3.2**. This multiaxial classification system, by requiring judgments on each of the five axes, forced the diagnostician to consider a broad range of information. DSM-5 no longer uses these distinct axes.

In 1988 the American Psychiatric Association began work on DSM-IV, which was published in 1994. For the first time, the committees shaping the new DSM were tasked with explicitly reviewing research data and describing the data guiding any changes in diagnoses. A revision to the supporting text of the DSM-IV, not the actual diagnostic criteria, was published in 2000 and named DSM-IV-TR, with the "TR" standing for "text revision".

The development of DSM-5 began in 1999. As with the process for DSM-IV, work groups reviewed each set of diagnoses. Study groups were also formed to consider issues that cut across diagnostic categories, such as life-span developmental approaches, gender and cross-cultural issues, general medical issues, impairment and disability, and diagnostic assessment instruments. To protect the process from commercial interests, all work group members signed conflict-of-interest agreements stating that they would limit their

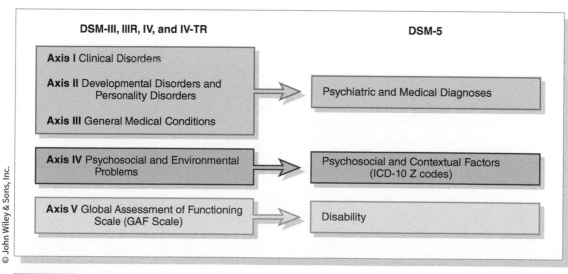

© John Wiley & Sons, Inc.

FIGURE 3.2 DSM-5 does not use the five axes of DSM-IV-TR.

income to $10,000 or less per year from pharmaceutical and industry groups. As was done with DSM-IV, field trials were conducted to assess how the new DSM-5 criteria performed in mental health settings. Additional revisions were made based on these data. In the final stages of DSM-5 development, the leaders made changes that were not always consistent with the data and recommendations of the work groups (see Chapter 15 on Personality Disorders for a stark example of this problem).

The DSM-5 includes many changes from the DSM-IV-TR. Indeed, even conventions for labeling the edition have shifted—the Roman numerals used to denote the edition (e.g., DSM-IV) are replaced with Arabic numbers (i.e., DSM-5) to facilitate electronic printing.

As has happened with each new edition of the DSM, several new diagnoses were added to DSM-5. For example, disruptive

mood dysregulation disorder, hoarding disorder, binge-eating disorder, premenstrual dysphoric disorder, and gambling disorder were added.

Some of the DSM-IV-TR diagnoses were combined in the DSM-5 because there was not enough evidence for differential etiology, course, or treatment response to justify separate diagnostic categories. For example, the DSM-IV-TR diagnoses of substance abuse and dependence were replaced with the DSM-5 diagnosis of substance use disorder. The DSM-IV-TR diagnoses of autism and Asperger's disorder were replaced with the DSM-5 diagnosis of autism spectrum disorder.

The crafters of the DSM-5 aimed to create a living document that will change as new research evidence emerges. New editions, then, are already on the horizon.

---

to those given in DSM-5. Notice how DSM-5 is much more detailed and concrete. For each disorder, the DSM-5 also describes diagnostic features as well as associated features, such as laboratory findings (e.g., enlarged ventricles in schizophrenia) and results from physical exams (e.g., electrolyte imbalances in people who have eating disorders). Next, the DSM-5 provides information about age of onset, course, prevalence, risk, prognosis, cultural factors, gender ratios, and differential diagnosis (i.e., how to distinguish similar diagnoses from each other).

Organizing Diagnoses by Symptoms Versus Causes DSM-5 defines diagnoses on the basis of symptoms. Some have argued that advances in our understanding of etiology (causes) could help us rethink this approach. For example, should symptoms that emerge in the context of serious life adversity be treated in the same way as symptoms that emerge out of the blue? Perhaps the social context could be weighted more heavily in considering whether to diagnose a set of symptoms (Lewis-Fernandez & Aggarwal, 2013; Wakefield, 2013). Others argue that biology should be weighted more heavily in the diagnostic system. For example, schizophrenia and schizotypal personality disorder share a great deal of genetic overlap. Could these ties be reflected in the diagnostic system? Others have proposed organizing diagnoses based on parallels in neurotransmitter activity, temperament, or emotion dysregulation. After considerable review during the development of DSM-5, it became clear that our knowledge base is not yet strong enough to organize diagnoses around etiology (Hyman, 2010). With the exception of IQ tests to help with the diagnosis of intellectual disability or polysomnography for sleep disorders, we have no laboratory tests, neurobiological markers, or genetic indicators to use in making diagnoses. The DSM-5 uses symptoms as the basis for diagnosis.

DSM-5 is the current diagnostic system of the American Psychiatric Association. It was published in 2013.

Although the DSM-5 relies on symptoms as the criteria for diagnoses, overlap in the causes of disorders is considered in a different way—the DSM-5 chapters are organized to reflect patterns of comorbidity and shared causes (see **Figure 3.3**). For example, the DSM-5 includes a chapter for obsessive-compulsive and other related disorders. This chapter includes disorders that often co-occur and share some risk factors, including obsessive-compulsive disorder, hoarding disorder, and body dysmorphic disorder.

Ethnic and Cultural Considerations in Diagnosis

Psychological disorders are universal. There is not a single culture in which people are free of psychological disorders. But culture influences the risk factors for psychological disorders (e.g., social cohesion, income inequality, access to drugs of abuse, and stress), the types of symptoms experienced, stigma, the willingness to seek help, and the treatments available. Sometimes the differences across cultures are profound. For example, although mental health care is widely available in the United States, it is estimated that there is less than one psychiatrist for every million people living in sub-Saharan Africa (WHO, 2015).

Cultural differences do not always play out in the way one might expect. For example, even though they are only half as likely to receive mental health treatment as those in the United States, people with serious mental health concerns in Nigeria remain much more engaged in key roles than do those in other countries (Demyttenaere, Bruffaerts, et al., 2004). This fits with previous findings that outcomes for schizophrenia were more favorable in Nigeria, India, and Colombia than in more industrialized countries, including the United States (Sartorius, Jablensky, et al. 1986). As shown in **Table 3.2**, rates of psychological disorders tend to be higher in the United States than in many other countries. People who immigrate from Mexico to the United States are initially about half as likely to meet the criteria for a psychological disorder as native-born citizens in the United States, but over time, they and their children begin to show an increase in certain disorders, such as substance abuse, such that their risk for disorder begins to approximate that of people born in the United States (Alegria, Canino, et al., 2008). A similar profile has been shown among Asian-Americans; those who immigrate to the United States have a markedly lower prevalence of mental health diagnoses than Asian Americans who are born in the United States (Hong, Walton, et al., 2014). If we hope to understand how culture influences risk, symptom expression, and outcomes, we need a diagnostic system that can be applied reliably and validly in different countries and cultures.

Previous editions of the DSM were criticized for their lack of attention to cultural and ethnic variations in psychopathology. DSM-5 added several features to enhance cultural sensitivity:

- Culture-related issues are discussed in the text for almost all of the disorders.

- A cultural formulation interview provides 16 questions clinicians can use to help understand how culture may be shaping the clinical presentation.

- An appendix describes syndromes that appear in particular cultures, culturally specific ways of expressing distress, and cultural explanations about the causes of symptoms, illness, and distress.

The DSM-5 cautions clinicians not to diagnose symptoms unless they are atypical and problematic within a person's culture. Extremely quiet behavior and reticence to speak may

DSM-5 Chapters

- Neurodevelopmental Disorders
- Elimination Disorders
- Neurocognitive Disorders
- Substance-Related and Other Addictive Disorders
- Schizophrenia Spectrum and Psychotic Disorders
- Bipolar and Related Disorders
- Depressive Disorders
- Anxiety Disorders
- Obsessive-Compulsive and Related Disorders
- Trauma- and Stressor-Related Disorders
- Somatic Symptom and Related Disorders
- Dissociative Disorders
- Sexual Dysfunctions
- Gender Dysphoria
- Paraphilic Disorders
- Feeding and Eating Disorders
- Sleep–Wake Disorders
- Disruptive, Impulse Control, and Conduct Disorders
- Personality Disorders
- Other Disorders
- Medication-Movement Disorders and Other Adverse Effects of Medication
- Other Conditions That May Be a Focus of Clinical Attention

FIGURE 3.3 Chapters in DSM-5.

© John Wiley & Sons, Inc.

TABLE 3.2	Twelve-Month Prevalence Rates of the Most Common DSM-IV-TR Diagnoses by Country			
Country	Anxiety Disorders	Mood Disorders	Substance Disorders	Any Psychological Disorder
Americas				
Colombia	14.4	7.0	2.8	21.0
Mexico	8.4	4.7	2.3	13.4
United States	19.0	9.7	3.8	27.0
Europe				
Belgium	8.4	5.4	1.8	13.2
France	13.7	6.5	1.3	18.9
Germany	.8.3	3.3	1.2	11.0
Italy	6.5	3.4	0.2	8.8
Netherlands	8.9	5.1	1.9	13.6
Spain	6.6	4.4	0.7	9.7
Middle East and Africa				
Lebanon	12.2	6.8	1.3	17.9
Nigeria	4.2	1.1	0.9	6.0
Asia				
Japan	4.2	2.5	1.2	7.4
China	3.0	1.9	1.6	7.1

Source: (Kessler, Aguilar-Gaxiola, et al., 2009).

Diagnoses were assessed with the Composite International Diagnostic Interview. Values are percentages.

Note: In the European countries, bipolar disorder (a form of mood disorder) and non–alcohol-related substance use disorders were not assessed. Obsessive-compulsive disorder (which was considered an anxiety disorder in this survey) was not assessed in Asian countries.

seem like social anxiety in one culture, but could be a sign of respect in another culture (Lewis-Fernandez & Aggarwal, 2013).

The DSM-5 provides information about ways in which culture can shape the symptoms and expression of a given disorder. For example, it is more likely in Japan than in the United States for anxiety to be focused around fears of offending others (Kirmayer, 2001). In evaluating symptoms, clinicians also need to be aware that cultures may shape the language used to describe distress. In many cultures, for example, it is common to describe grief or anxiety in physical terms—"I am sick in my heart" or "My heart is heavy"—rather than in psychological terms. In general, clinicians are advised to be constantly mindful of how culture and ethnicity influence diagnosis and treatment.

The DSM-5 appendix includes nine **cultural concepts of distress** to describe syndromes that are observed within specific regions of the world or cultural groups. The following are some examples of these cultural concepts of distress:

- *Dhat Syndrome.* A term used in India to refer to severe anxiety about the discharge of semen.
- ***Shenjing shuairuo***. A syndrome commonly diagnosed in China, characterized by weakness, mental fatigue, negative emotions, and sleep problems. People describing these symptoms often report concerns about work or family stressors, loss of face, or failure. Although people with this disorder often will meet diagnostic criteria for DSM diagnoses of anxiety, depression, and somatoform conditions, about half will not meet diagnostic criteria for any DSM diagnosis (Lim, 2015).
- ***Taijin kyofusho*** (interpersonal fear disorder). The fear that one could offend others through inappropriate eye contact, blushing, a perceived body deformation, or body odor. This disorder is most common in Japan, but similar syndromes are observed in cultures that place a strong emphasis on social appropriateness and hierarchy (Lim, 2015).

- *Khyâl cap* (wind attacks). A syndrome observed in Cambodian, Thai, and Vietnamese cultural groups. Symptoms share overlap with panic attacks, including dizziness, rapid heart rate, shortness of breath, and other indicators of intense anxiety and autonomic arousal. These attacks are accompanied by the belief that *khyâl* (a windlike substance) is rising in the body and may cause serious physical harm (Hinton, Pich, et al., 2010).

- *Ataque de nervios.* Intense anxiety, anger, fear, or grief; screaming and shouting uncontrollably; crying; trembling; sensations of heat rising from the chest into the head; and verbal or physical aggression. The symptoms are most commonly observed among people from Latino cultures and are usually preceded by an acute life stressor (Lim, 2015).

- *Ghost sickness.* An extreme preoccupation with death and those who have died, found among certain Native American tribes.

- *Hikikomori* (withdrawal). A syndrome observed in Japan, Taiwan, and South Korea in which an individual, most often an adolescent boy or young adult man, shuts himself into a room (e.g., bedroom) for a period of 6 months or more and does not socialize with anyone outside the room.

The core symptoms of depression appear to be similar cross-culturally.

Richard Nowitz/Science Source

Cultural influences on well-being change over time. Between 2000 and 2005, more than 400 children were brought to Swedish doctors with coma-like symptoms that had no medical explanation—they did not move, were mute, did not consume food or drink independently, and showed no response to conversation, or even to physically painful stimuli. Almost all were the children of refugees, and almost all were from families who had heard that asylum might be denied. The Swedish government published guidance on the syndrome, which they labeled as resignation syndrome (*uppgivenhetssyndrome*). Symptoms for the children would last for months and were found to remit only after the families were granted asylum. After the Swedish government changed their guidelines concerning asylum in 2006, the number of cases dwindled to dozens per year (Aviv, 2017).

Clinical Case

Lola

An Example of Diagnosis

Lola is a 17-year-old high school junior. She moved to the United States from Mexico with her parents and brother when she was 14 years old. A few months after they arrived, Lola's father returned to Mexico to attend the funeral of his brother. He was denied reentry to the United States due to a problem with his visa, and he has been unable to reunite with the family for nearly 3 years. Lola's mother found it difficult to make ends meet on her salary as a bookkeeper, and the family was forced to move to a rougher neighborhood a year ago. Lola's English was fairly good when she came to the United States, and she picked up many of the nuances of the language since arriving in the country. For the past 2 years, she has been dating a boy in her school. They have been fairly constant companions, and she describes him as the one person she would turn to if she was feeling upset.

If her mother had any previous concern about Lola, it was that she relied too much on her boyfriend—she asked for his advice on both small and large decisions, and she seemed wary of social interactions when he wasn't present. Lola's mother stated, "It is as though she is afraid to think for herself." Lola's mother noted that Lola had always been shy and had tended to count on

her brother a lot for decisions and social support when she was younger.

With little warning, her boyfriend announced that he wanted to break up with her. Lola was extremely distressed by this change and reported that almost immediately she was unable to sleep or eat well. She lost weight rapidly and found herself unable to concentrate on her schoolwork. Friends complained that she no longer wanted to talk during lunch or by phone. After 2 weeks of steadily feeling worse, Lola left a suicide note and disappeared. Police found her the next day in an abandoned home, holding a bottle of medicines. She reported that she had been sitting there all night, considering ending her life. Lola's mother reported that she had never seen her so distressed but noted that a few other family members had struggled with periods of sadness. Still, these family members in Mexico had neither attempted suicide nor received any formal treatment. Instead, the family learned to give these family members support and time to heal on their own. After the police found Lola, she was hospitalized for intensive treatment.

DSM-5 Diagnosis

Diagnoses: Major depressive disorder, dependent personality disorder

Important Psychosocial/Contextual Factors: Low income (ICD-10 Z59.6)

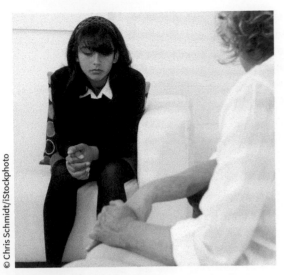

A therapist must be mindful of the role of culture in shaping how people describe their problems.

Some have argued that we should try to identify broad syndromes that can be identified across cultures and, in this light, have argued against differentiating cultural concepts of distress from other diagnostic syndromes (Lopez-Ibor, 2003). In support of this position, they point toward several cultural concepts of distress that are not so different from the main DSM diagnoses. For example, many Chinese people who have been diagnosed with shenjing shuairuo meet criteria for major depressive disorder and will respond to antidepressant medication (Kleinman, 1986). The symptoms of taijin kyofusho overlap with those of social anxiety disorder (excessive fear of social interaction and evaluation) and body dysmorphic disorder (the mistaken belief that one is deformed or ugly), which are more commonly diagnosed in the United States. In one study, 100% of the attacks of khyâl cap met diagnostic criteria for panic disorder (Hinton et al., 2010). Hence, some researchers believe it is important to look for commonalities across cultures.

In contrast, others believe that cultural concepts of distress are central. Surveys that estimate prevalence of anxiety disorders may vastly underestimate prevalence if cultural concepts of distress are not assessed (Steel, Silove, et al., 2009). Moreover, the local beliefs that shape cultural concepts of distress are a key issue in understanding and treating psychological disorders (Hinton et al., 2010). Whether one advocates for a cross-cultural or culture-specific approach to diagnosis, all mental health professionals ought to, at the very least, be aware of the cultural influences that can and do influence the expression of symptoms as well as attitudes toward treatment (Sue, Yan Cheng, et al., 2012).

Specific Criticisms of the DSM

Some specific questions and concerns have been raised about the DSM. We review some of these concerns in the following sections.

Too Many Diagnoses? In the past, up to half of the people seeking treatment described mild symptoms that fell just below the threshold for a diagnosis (Helmuth, 2003). The DSM-5 made it "easier" for these more minor symptoms to receive a diagnosis, by increasing the number of diagnoses, decreasing the number of months that symptoms must persist for some diagnoses, and decreasing the number of symptoms required for other diagnoses. The DSM-5 contains 347 different diagnoses. Even if a person does not meet one of the 347 DSM-5 diagnoses, the DSM-5 includes the category "unspecified," which is to be used when a person meets many but not all of the criteria for a diagnosis.

Some have criticized the burgeoning number and scope of diagnostic categories (see **Table 3.3**). As one example, the DSM-5 includes a diagnosis for caffeine intoxication—should the person who drinks too much caffeine in one day be considered to have a mental disorder? The DSM-5 also continues to include a category for acute stress disorder in order to capture symptoms in the first month after a severe trauma. Should these relatively common reactions to trauma be pathologized by diagnosing them as a psychological disorder (Harvey & Bryant, 2002)? By expanding its coverage, the authors of the DSM seem to have made too many problems into psychological disorders without good justification for doing so (Wakefield, 2015).

Others argue that the DSM system includes too many minute distinctions based on small differences in symptoms. One side effect of the huge number of diagnostic categories is a phenomenon called **comorbidity**, which refers to the presence of a second diagnosis. Comorbidity is the norm rather than the exception. Among people who met criteria for at least one DSM-IV psychological diagnosis, 45 percent meet criteria for at least one more psychological diagnosis (Kessler, Berglund, et al., 2005). Some argue that this overlap is a sign that we are dividing syndromes too finely (Hyman, 2010).

TABLE 3.3	Number of Diagnostic Categories per Edition of DSM	
Edition of DSM	**Number of Categories**
DSM I	106
DSM-II	182
DSM-III	265
DSM-III-R	292
DSM-IV-TR	297
DSM-5	347

Does this mean that we should lump some of the disorders into one category? Beliefs about lumping versus splitting differ. Some think we should keep the finer distinctions, whereas others believe we should lump (Caspi, Houts, et al., 2014). Among people who think there are too many diagnostic categories, several researchers have considered ways to collapse disorders into broader categories. To begin, some disorders co-occur more frequently than do others. For example, a person with antisocial personality disorder is highly likely to meet the diagnostic criteria for a substance use disorder. In the DSM, these are diagnosed as separate disorders. Some have argued that childhood conduct disorder, adult antisocial personality disorder, alcohol use disorder, and substance use disorder co-occur so often that they should be considered different manifestations of one underlying disease process or vulnerability and jointly labeled as "externalizing disorders" (Krueger, Markon, et al., 2005). Similarly, anxiety disorders, posttraumatic stress disorder, and depressive disorders, which often co-occur, could be considered "internalizing disorders." Symptoms of different psychotic disorders often co-occur and could be considered indicators of a broader category of thought disorders (Kotov, Krueger, et al., 2017).

A subtler issue about the large number of diagnoses is that many risk factors relate to more than one disorder. As one example, in one study of more than 600 adolescents, neuroticism was highly correlated with tendencies toward internalizing disorders. The association with internalizing disorders (as a group) was much stronger than the association of neuroticism with any one of the internalizing disorders (Griffith, Zinbarg, et al., 2009). This study suggests that risk factors may set the stage for internalizing disorders as a whole.

Like neuroticism, many risk variables predict the onset of multiple disorders. For example, some genes are associated with an increase in the risk of externalizing disorders as a whole (Kendler, Prescott, et al., 2003). Anxiety and mood disorders also share overlap in genetic risk (Kendler, Jacobson, et al., 2003). Tendencies to attend to and remember negative information about the self both increase risk for many different internalizing disorders (Harvey, Watkins, et al., 2004). Similarly, as we will see throughout this book, selective serotonin reuptake inhibitors (SSRIs), such as Prozac, often relieve symptoms of depression, anxiety, and many other diagnoses. Different diagnoses do not seem to be distinct in their etiology or treatment.

To take the idea of lumping a step further, people who have an internalizing disorder are at higher risk for an externalizing disorder, and vice versa. Some researchers have suggested that we consider a general "psychopathology" factor or "p" factor (Caspi et al., 2014). According to this view, some risk factors are probably related to all of the psychopathologies and work in concert with risk factors that predict more specific syndromes. In this book, we will focus on some risk factors that help explain a specific disorder, but you will see that some of the same risk factors—such as early adversity, serotonin dysfunction, poor function of the prefrontal cortex, and the personality trait neuroticism, will appear in multiple chapters because they are important to many different disorders.

The National Institute of Mental Health is tackling this problem of overlap in risk factors with the **Research Domain Criteria**, or **RDoC** (https://www.nimh.nih.gov/research-priorities/rdoc/index.shtml). The RDoC domains refer to psychological variables that are relevant for many different conditions, such as problems in responses to negative stimuli or contexts, problems in responses to positive stimuli or contexts, cognitive problems, social problems, or lack of ability to regulate emotion or behavior. Funding is being invested in identifying the genetic and neuroscience mechanisms that drive these dimensions. The hope is that basic science advances will allow the field to develop a new classification system that is based on neuroscience and genetic data rather than just clinical symptoms (Insel, 2014).

Categorical Classification Versus Dimensional Classification In the DSM-5, clinical diagnoses are based on **categorical classification**. Does the person have schizophrenia or not? Do the symptoms fit the category of mania or not? For example, in Table 3.1 we see that the diagnosis of mania requires the presence of three symptoms plus high mood and excessive energy. But why require three symptoms rather than two or five? A categorical system forces clinicians to define one threshold as "diagnosable." There is often little research support for the DSM diagnostic threshold, and indeed, there is a good deal of evidence that many individuals with subthreshold symptoms are experiencing considerable distress and difficulty with

Categorical Classification

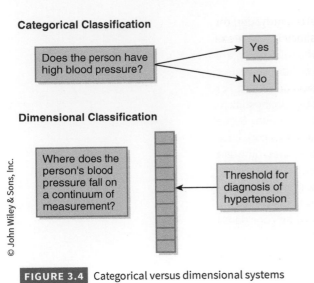

Dimensional Classification

© John Wiley & Sons, Inc.

FIGURE 3.4 Categorical versus dimensional systems of diagnosis.

functioning (Rodriguez-Seijas, Eaton, & Krueger, 2015). Categorical diagnoses foster a false impression that psychological disorders have actual, hard boundaries.

It may be more helpful to know the severity of symptoms as well as whether they are present. In contrast to a categorical system, a **dimensional diagnostic system** describes the *degree* of an entity that is present (e.g., a 1-to-10 scale of anxiety, where 1 represents minimal and 10, extremely severe). See **Figure 3.4** for an illustration of the difference between dimensional and categorical approaches. Dimensional systems provide a way to describe subthreshold symptoms, as well as symptoms that are particularly severe.

One reason categorical systems are popular is that they define a threshold for treatment. Consider high blood pressure (hypertension). Blood pressure measurements form a continuum, which clearly fits a dimensional approach; yet by defining a threshold for high blood pressure, doctors can feel more certain about when to offer treatment. Similarly, a threshold for clinical depression may help demarcate a point where treatment is recommended. Although the cutoffs are likely to be somewhat arbitrary, they can provide helpful guidance.

DSM-5 preserved a categorical approach to diagnosis. The DSM-5 work group for personality disorders recommended a shift to a dimensional approach to diagnosing personality concerns, but this recommended system is included only in a section on emerging models and measures that is placed after the main section on diagnostic classification. The diagnoses in the main body of the DSM are based on categorical classification. DSM-5 did add severity ratings for nearly all disorders, however. Thus, DSM-5 is taking a first step toward including dimensions alongside the current categories.

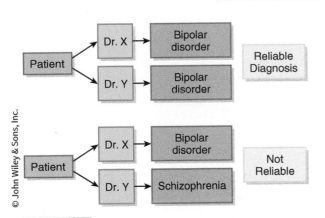

© John Wiley & Sons, Inc.

FIGURE 3.5 Inter-rater reliability. In this example, the diagnosis of the first person is reliable—both clinicians diagnose bipolar disorder—whereas the diagnosis of the second is not reliable.

Reliability of the DSM in Everyday Practice
Suppose you were concerned about your mental health, and you went to see two psychologists. Consider the distress you would feel if the two psychologists disagreed—one told you that you had schizophrenia, and the other told you that you had bipolar disorder. Diagnostic systems must have high inter-rater reliability to be useful. Before DSM-III, reliability for DSM diagnoses was poor, mainly because the criteria for making a diagnosis were not clear (see **Figure 3.5** for an illustration of inter-rater reliability).

The increased explicitness of the DSM criteria has improved reliability for many diagnoses (see Table 3.1). Nonetheless, because clinicians might not rely on the criteria precisely, the reliability of the DSM in everyday usage may be lower than that seen in research studies. Even when following criteria, there is some room for disagreement in DSM-5. For example, in the criteria for mania, mood is supposed to be "abnormally" elevated. What is abnormal? When criteria are vague, diagnosticians are more likely to insert their personal biases, or those based on their cultural background, into deciding what the average person should be doing. Because different clinicians may adopt different definitions for symptoms such as "abnormally elevated mood," achieving high reliability can be a challenge.

Evidence from the DSM-5 field trials where the diagnostic criteria were tested at several different mental health treatment facilities across the country suggests that the DSM still has work to do when it comes to reliability (see **Table 3.4**). Some have argued that expecting high reliability is unrealistic, particularly since the reliability of

TABLE 3.4 **Reliability Data from the DSM-5 Field Trials**

Diagnosis	Pooled Reliability Estimate
Schizophrenia	.46
Bipolar I disorder	.56
Posttraumatic stress disorder	.67
Borderline personality disorder	.54
ADHD	.61
Autism Spectrum Disorder	.69

Source: Adapted from Narrow, Clarke, et al. (2013). Numbers are kappa statistics—the closer to 1.0, the better the reliability. Kappa scores between .40 and .60 are generally considered moderate (Altman, 1991).

these diagnoses was comparable to most medical diagnoses (Kraemer, 2014). Although this may be true, it is disconcerting to think that mental health professionals may not agree on a particular person's diagnosis.

How Valid Are Diagnostic Categories? The DSM diagnoses are based on a pattern of symptoms. A diagnosis of schizophrenia, then, does not have the same status as a diagnosis of, say, diabetes, for which we have laboratory tests.

One way of thinking about diagnosis is to ask whether the system helps organize different observations (see Figure 3.1). Diagnoses have construct validity if they help make accurate predictions. What types of predictions should a good diagnostic category facilitate? One would hope that a diagnosis would inform us about related clinical characteristics and about functional impairments. The DSM specifies that impairment or distress must be present to meet criteria for a diagnosis, so perhaps it is not surprising that diagnoses are related to functional impairments such as marital distress and missed days at work (see **Table 3.5**). Beyond capturing the most common difficulties for a person with a diagnosis, one would hope that a diagnosis would inform us about what to expect next—the likely course of the disorder and response to different treatments. Perhaps most importantly, one would hope that the diagnosis relates to possible causes of the disorder, for example, a genetic predisposition or a biochemical imbalance. A diagnosis with strong construct validity should help predict a broad range of characteristics.

We have organized this book around the major DSM diagnostic categories because we believe that they do indeed possess some construct validity. Certain categories have less validity than others, however, and we will discuss these gaps in the validity of specific diagnostic categories in later chapters.

General Criticisms of Diagnosing Psychological Disorders

Although we described some advantages of diagnosis in the beginning of this chapter, it is also clear that diagnoses can have negative effects. Consider how your life might be changed by receiving the diagnosis of schizophrenia. You might become worried that someone will recognize your disorder. Or you might fear the onset of another episode. You might worry about your ability to deal with new challenges. The fact that you have a diagnosis of a psychological disorder could have a stigmatizing effect. Friends and loved ones might treat you differently, and employment might be hard to find.

TABLE 3.5	**Rates of Marital Distress and Missed Work Days Among People with Psychological Disorders in the Past Year**	
Disorder	**Odds of Marital Distress for a Given Diagnosis Compared to No Psychological Disorder**	**Odds of Missed Work Days for a Given Diagnosis Compared to No Psychological Disorder**
Panic disorder	1.28	3.32
Specific phobia	1.34	2.82
Social phobia	1.93	2.74
Generalized anxiety disorder	2.54	1.15
Posttraumatic stress disorder	2.30	2.05
Major depressive disorder	1.68	2.14
Bipolar I or II disorder	3.60	Not assessed
Alcohol use disorder	2.78	2.54

Note: Age, gender, education, and race/ethnicity are controlled for in marital distress analyses, and age and gender are controlled for in work-loss analyses. Diagnoses were based on the Composite International Diagnostic Interview. Marital distress was measured using a 14-item version of the Dyadic Adjustment Scale. Missed work days were measured during the month before the interview.

Source: Information on marital distress drawn from Whisman (2007). Information on work-loss days drawn from Alonso, Angermeyer, et al. (2004).

Without doubt, hearing a diagnosis can be difficult. Research shows that psychological disorders are widely viewed negatively (Evans-Lacko, Brohan, et al., 2011), and people with psychological disorders and their families often encounter stigma as a result (Wahl, 1999), which remains a huge problem. Many have raised concerns that a diagnosis might contribute to stigma. To study this problem, researchers have given people brief written descriptions of a person. Beyond including a bit of information about the person's life and personality, the descriptions include either a psychological disorder diagnosis (such as schizophrenia or bipolar disorder), a description of their symptoms (such as periods of high moods, decreased sleep, and restlessness), both (a diagnosis and symptoms), or neither. In this way, researchers can examine whether people tend to be more negative about diagnostic category labels or symptomatic behavior. Research suggests that people tend to view the behaviors negatively more than the category labels. Sometimes labels may actually relieve stigma by providing an explanation for the symptomatic behavior (Lilienfeld, Lynn, et al., 2010). Of course, making a diagnosis is still a serious process that warrants sensitivity and privacy. But it may not be fair to presume that diagnostic labels are the major source of stigma.

Another concern is that when a diagnostic category is applied, we may lose sight of the uniqueness of that person. Because of this concern, the American Psychological Association recommends that people avoid using words like *schizophrenic* or *depressive* to describe people. After all, we do not call people with medical illnesses by their disease (e.g., you aren't likely to hear someone with cancer described as the *canceric*). Rather, psychologists are encouraged to use phrases such as *a person with schizophrenia*.

Quick Summary

Diagnostic systems for psychological disorders have changed a great deal in the past 100 years.

The DSM provides specific criteria for each disorder, as well as a summary of research on prevalence, comorbidity, and other features. The DSM also provides guidance to enhance sensitivity to culturally specific expressions of symptoms, and to help clinicians consider the cultural influences on diagnoses.

There are several concerns about the DSM-5. Some argue that there are too many diagnoses. Others challenge the use of a categorical rather than a dimensional approach. Reliability is higher than it was in earlier editions of the DSM, but clinicians still disagree regarding some diagnoses, and the reliability achieved in practice may not be as high as the reliability achieved in research studies. Finally, the field as a whole faces a huge challenge. Researchers are focused on validating this diagnostic system by identifying the course of symptoms over time, causal factors, and treatment outcomes predicted by a given diagnosis, but it is clear that there is considerable overlap in the causes and treatments for the different DSM diagnoses.

Regardless of which diagnostic system is used, certain problems are inherent in diagnosing people with psychological disorders. The American Psychological Association recommends using phrases such as *person with schizophrenia* rather than *schizophrenic* as one way to acknowledge that a person is much more than his or her diagnosis. Although many worry that applying labels may increase stigma, diagnoses can sometimes relieve stigma by providing a way of understanding symptoms.

Check Your Knowledge 3.2

Answer the questions.

1. Describe three ways in which the DSM-5 considers the role of culture in mental health.
2. List three reasons why some think DSM should lump diagnoses.
3. What are three broad types of characteristics that a valid diagnosis should help predict?

Psychological Assessment

To make a diagnosis, mental health professionals can use a variety of assessment measures and tools. Beyond helping to make a diagnosis, psychological assessment techniques are used in other important ways. For example, assessment methods are often used to identify appropriate therapeutic interventions. And repeated assessments are very useful in monitoring the effects of treatment over time. In addition, assessments are fundamental to conducting research on the causes of disorder.

We will see that many of the assessment techniques stem from the paradigms presented in Chapter 2. Here we discuss clinical interviews; measures for assessing stress; personality tests; intelligence tests; and behavioral and cognitive assessment techniques. Although we present these methods individually, a complete psychological assessment of a person will often entail combining several assessment techniques. The data from the various techniques complement each other and provide a more complete picture of the person. In short, there is no one best assessment measure. Rather, using multiple techniques and multiple sources of information will provide the best assessment.

Clinical Interviews

Mental health professionals use both formal and structured as well as informal and less structured clinical interviews in psychopathological assessment.

Although it is illegal to discriminate against those with psychological disorders, many employers do so. Stigma must be considered when giving a person a diagnosis of a psychological disorder.

Ryan McVay/Getty Images

Characteristics of Clinical Interviews
Carrying out a good **clinical interview** requires great skill. Clinicians, regardless of the paradigm adopted, recognize the importance of establishing rapport with a person who seeks their professional help. The interviewer must obtain the trust of the person; it is naive to assume that a person will easily reveal information to another, even to someone with the title "Doctor." Even a person who sincerely, perhaps desperately, wants to recount intensely personal problems to a professional may not be able to do so without help.

Most clinicians empathize with their clients to draw them out and to encourage them to elaborate on their concerns. An accurate summary statement, or reflection, of what a person has been saying can help sustain the momentum of talk about painful and possibly embarrassing events and feelings, and an accepting attitude toward personal disclosures.

Interviews vary in the degree to which they are structured. In practice, most clinicians probably operate from only the vaguest outlines. Exactly how information is collected is left largely up to the particular interviewer and depends, too, on the responsiveness and responses of the interviewee. Through years of training and clinical experience, each clinician develops ways of asking questions that he or she is comfortable with and that seem to draw out the information that will be of maximum benefit to the person. Thus, to the extent that an interview is unstructured, the interviewer must rely on intuition and general experience. As a consequence, unstructured clinical interviews are less reliable than structured interviews; that is, two interviewers may reach different conclusions about the same person.

Structured interviews are widely used to make reliable diagnoses.

© BSIP/Medical Images

Structured Interviews
At times, mental health professionals need to collect standardized information, particularly for making diagnostic judgments based on the DSM. To meet that need, investigators use a **structured interview**, in which the questions are set out in a prescribed fashion for the interviewer. One example of a commonly used structured interview is the Structured Clinical Interview (SCID) (First, Williams, et al. 2015). The general format of this interview is shown in **Figure 3.6**.

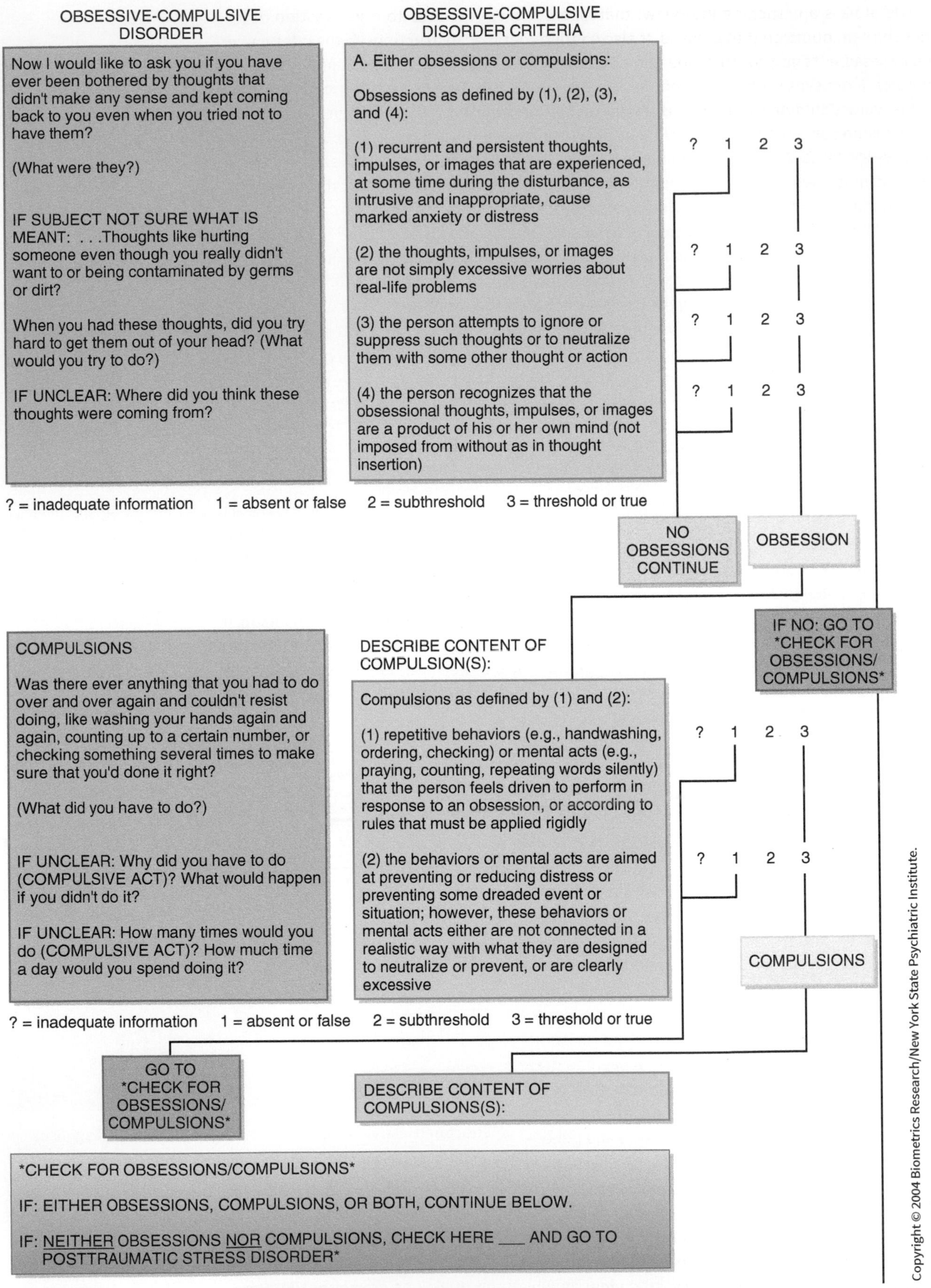

OBSESSIVE-COMPULSIVE DISORDER

Now I would like to ask you if you have ever been bothered by thoughts that didn't make any sense and kept coming back to you even when you tried not to have them?

(What were they?)

IF SUBJECT NOT SURE WHAT IS MEANT: . . .Thoughts like hurting someone even though you really didn't want to or being contaminated by germs or dirt?

When you had these thoughts, did you try hard to get them out of your head? (What would you try to do?)

IF UNCLEAR: Where did you think these thoughts were coming from?

OBSESSIVE-COMPULSIVE DISORDER CRITERIA

A. Either obsessions or compulsions:

Obsessions as defined by (1), (2), (3), and (4):

(1) recurrent and persistent thoughts, impulses, or images that are experienced, at some time during the disturbance, as intrusive and inappropriate, cause marked anxiety or distress   ? 1 2 3

(2) the thoughts, impulses, or images are not simply excessive worries about real-life problems   ? 1 2 3

(3) the person attempts to ignore or suppress such thoughts or to neutralize them with some other thought or action   ? 1 2 3

(4) the person recognizes that the obsessional thoughts, impulses, or images are a product of his or her own mind (not imposed from without as in thought insertion)   ? 1 2 3

? = inadequate information   1 = absent or false   2 = subthreshold   3 = threshold or true

NO OBSESSIONS CONTINUE   OBSESSION

IF NO: GO TO *CHECK FOR OBSESSIONS/ COMPULSIONS*

COMPULSIONS

Was there ever anything that you had to do over and over again and couldn't resist doing, like washing your hands again and again, counting up to a certain number, or checking something several times to make sure that you'd done it right?

(What did you have to do?)

IF UNCLEAR: Why did you have to do (COMPULSIVE ACT)? What would happen if you didn't do it?

IF UNCLEAR: How many times would you do (COMPULSIVE ACT)? How much time a day would you spend doing it?

DESCRIBE CONTENT OF COMPULSION(S):

Compulsions as defined by (1) and (2):

(1) repetitive behaviors (e.g., handwashing, ordering, checking) or mental acts (e.g., praying, counting, repeating words silently) that the person feels driven to perform in response to an obsession, or according to rules that must be applied rigidly   ? 1 2 3

(2) the behaviors or mental acts are aimed at preventing or reducing distress or preventing some dreaded event or situation; however, these behaviors or mental acts either are not connected in a realistic way with what they are designed to neutralize or prevent, or are clearly excessive   ? 1 2 3

? = inadequate information   1 = absent or false   2 = subthreshold   3 = threshold or true

COMPULSIONS

GO TO *CHECK FOR OBSESSIONS/ COMPULSIONS*

DESCRIBE CONTENT OF COMPULSIONS(S):

CHECK FOR OBSESSIONS/COMPULSIONS

IF: EITHER OBSESSIONS, COMPULSIONS, OR BOTH, CONTINUE BELOW.

IF: NEITHER OBSESSIONS NOR COMPULSIONS, CHECK HERE ___ AND GO TO POSTTRAUMATIC STRESS DISORDER*

FIGURE 3.6 Sample item from the SCID. Reprinted by permission of New York State Psychiatric Institute Biometrics Research Division.

The SCID is a branching interview; that is, a person's response to one question determines the next question that is asked. It also contains detailed instructions to the interviewer concerning when and how to probe in detail and when to go on to questions about another diagnosis. Most symptoms are rated on a three-point scale of severity, with instructions in the interview schedule for directly translating the symptom ratings into diagnoses. The initial questions pertaining to obsessive-compulsive disorder (discussed in Chapter 7) are presented in Figure 3.6. The interviewer begins by asking about obsessions. If the responses elicit a rating of 1 (absent), the interviewer turns to questions about compulsions. If the person's responses again elicit a rating of 1, the interviewer is instructed to go to the questions for the next disorder. On the other hand, if positive responses (rating of 2 or 3) are elicited about obsessive-compulsive disorder, the interviewer continues with further questions about that problem.

In practice, most clinicians review the DSM symptoms in an informal manner without using a structured interview. Note, however, that clinicians using unstructured diagnostic interviews tend to miss comorbid diagnoses that often accompany a primary diagnosis (Zimmerman & Mattia, 1999). When clinicians use an informal interview rather than a structured interview, the reliability of diagnoses also tends to be much lower (Garb, 2005). With adequate training, inter-rater reliability for structured interviews is generally quite good (Blanchard & Brown, 1998).

Assessment of Stress

Given its centrality to nearly all the disorders we consider in this book, measuring stress is clearly important in the total assessment picture. To understand the role of stress, we must first be able to define and measure it. Neither task is simple, as stress has been defined in many ways. See **Focus on Discovery 3.2** for influential antecedents to our current conceptualizations of stress. Broadly, **stress** can be conceptualized as the subjective experience of distress in response to perceived environmental problems. Life stressors can be defined as the environmental problems that trigger the subjective sense of stress. Various self-report scales and interviews have been developed to measure life stress. Many self-report scales, though quick and easy to administer, are limited in coverage, based on different definitions of stress, and have limited validity (Harkness & Monroe, 2016). Here we examine the most comprehensive interview measure of life stress: the Bedford College Life Events and Difficulties Schedule.

The Life Events and Difficulties Schedule (LEDS) is widely used to study life stressors (Brown & Harris, 1978). The LEDS includes an interview that covers over 200 different kinds of stressors. Because the interview is only semistructured, the interviewer can tailor questions to cover stressors that might only occur to a small number of people. The interviewer and the interviewee work collaboratively to produce a calendar of each of the major events within a given time period (see **Figure 3.8** for an example). After the interview, raters evaluate the severity and several other dimensions of each stressor. The LEDS was designed to address several problems in life stress assessment, including the need to evaluate the importance of any given life event in the context of a person's life circumstances. For example, pregnancy might have quite a different meaning for an unmarried 14-year-old girl compared to a 38-year-old woman who has been trying to conceive for a long time. A second goal of the LEDS is to exclude life events that might just be consequences of symptoms. For example, if a person

Stress can include major life events or daily hassles.

The LEDS focuses on major stressors, such as deaths, job losses, and romantic breakups.

Focus on Discovery 3.2

A Brief History of Stress

The pioneering work by the physician Hans Selye set the stage for our current conceptualizations of stress. He introduced the term *general adaptation syndrome* (GAS) to describe the biological response to sustained and high levels of stress (see **Figure 3.7**). In Selye's model there are three phases of the response:

1. During the first phase, the alarm reaction, the autonomic nervous system is activated by the stress.

2. During the second phase, resistance, the organism tries to adapt to the stress through available coping mechanisms.

3. If the stressor persists or the organism is unable to adapt effectively, the third phase, exhaustion, follows, and the organism dies or suffers irreversible damage (Selye, 1950).

Phase 1 The Alarm Reaction	Phase 2 Resistance	Phase 3 Exhaustion
ANS activated by stress	Damage occurs or organism adapts to stress	Organism dies or suffers irreversible damage

© John Wiley & Sons, Inc.

FIGURE 3.7 Selye's general adaptation syndrome.

In Selye's syndrome, the emphasis was on the body's response, not the environmental events that trigger that response. Psychological researchers later broadened Selye's concept to account for the diverse stress responses that people exhibited, including emotional upset, deterioration of performance, or physiological changes such as increases in the levels of certain hormones. The problem with these response-focused definitions of stress is that the criteria are not clear-cut. Physiological changes in the body can occur in response to many things that we would not consider stressful (e.g., anticipating a pleasurable event).

Other researchers defined stress as exposure to a difficult life event, often referred to as a stressor. Events that are considered stressors can be major (the death of a loved one), minor (daily hassles, such as being stuck in traffic), acute (failing an exam), or chronic (a persistently unpleasant work environment). For the most part, they are experiences that people regard as unpleasant, but they can also be pleasant events (a wedding).

It is important to acknowledge that people vary widely in how they respond to life's challenges. A given event does not elicit the same amount of stress in everyone. For example, one person may be devastated by a failing grade, and another may shrug off the disappointment. Current conceptualizations of stress often emphasize that how we perceive the environment shapes our response to a stressor. This raises the very important point that the life stressors and the response to life stressors are two different variables (Harkness & Monroe, 2016). Both of these variables appear important to psychopathology.

---

misses work because he or she is too depressed to get out of bed, any consequent job problems should really be seen as symptoms of the disorder rather than a triggering life event. Finally, the LEDS includes a set of strategies to carefully date when a life stressor occurred. Using this more careful assessment method, researchers have found that life stressors are robust predictors of episodes of anxiety, depression, schizophrenia, and even the common cold (Brown & Harris, 1989; Cohen, Frank, et al., 1998).

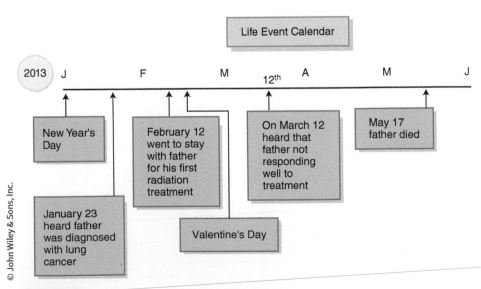

FIGURE 3.8 Example of a life events timeline. The LEDS interview is designed to capture the major stressors a person has encountered in the past year.

Personality Tests

Psychological tests further structure the process of assessment. The two most common types of psychological tests are personality tests and intelligence tests. In **Focus on Discovery 3.3**, we discuss older personality measures called projective tests.

Focus on Discovery 3.3

Projective Tests: Another Type of Personality Test

A **projective test** is an older psychological assessment tool in which a set of standard stimuli—inkblots or drawings—ambiguous enough to allow variation in responses is presented to the person. The assumption is that because the stimulus materials are unstructured and ambiguous, the person's responses will be determined primarily by unconscious processes and will reveal his or her true attitudes, motivations, and modes of behavior.

The use of projective tests assumes that the respondent would be either unable or unwilling to express his or her true feelings if asked directly. As you might have guessed, projective techniques are derived from the work of Freud and his followers (see Chapter 1).

In the Thematic Apperception Test (TAT) a person is shown a series of black-and-white pictures one-by-one and asked to tell a story related to each. For example, a person seeing a picture of a boy observing a youth baseball game from behind a fence may tell a story that contains angry references to the boy's parents. The clinician may infer that the person harbors resentment toward his or her parents. There are few reliable scoring methods for this test, and the norms are based on a small and limited sample (i.e., few

norms for people of different ethnic or cultural backgrounds). The construct validity of the TAT is also limited (Lilienfeld, Wood, & Garb, 2000).

The Rorschach Inkblot Test is perhaps the best-known projective technique. In the Rorschach test, a person is shown 10 inkblots (for similar inkblots, see **Figure 3.9**), one at a time, and asked to tell what the blots look like.

Exner (1978) designed the most commonly used system for scoring the Rorschach test. The Exner scoring system concentrates on the perceptual and cognitive patterns in a person's responses. The person's responses are viewed as a sample of how he or she perceptually and cognitively organizes real-life situations (Exner, 1986).

The Exner scoring system has norms, although the sample on which they are based was rather small and did not represent different ethnicities and cultures well. Regarding its reliability and validity, this work has enthusiastic supporters as well as equally harsh critics (Hunsley & Bailey, 1999; Lilienfeld et al., 2000; Meyer & Archer, 2001).

Projective tests, like the Rorschach or TAT, are not as widely used today, likely due to their poor validity. Reliability can be achieved using scoring systems such as Exner's.

© John Wiley & Sons, Inc.

FIGURE 3.9 In the Rorschach test, the person is shown a series of inkblots and is asked what the blots look like.

In a **personality inventory**, the person is asked to complete a self-report questionnaire indicating whether statements assessing habitual tendencies apply to him or her. When these tests are developed, they are typically administered to many people to analyze how certain kinds of people tend to respond. Statistical norms for the test can thereby be established. This process is called **standardization**. The responses of a particular person can then be compared with the statistical norms.

One well known test is the **Minnesota Multiphasic Personality Inventory-2 (MMPI-2;** Butcher, Dahlstrom, et al., 1989). The MMPI-2 is called multiphasic because it was designed to detect several psychological problems. Hundreds of items were tested in very large samples of people with and without a diagnosis. Sets of these items were established as scales. If a person answered many of the items in a scale in the same way as had people from a certain diagnostic group, his or her behavior was expected to resemble that of the particular diagnostic group. These 10 scales are described in **Table 3.6**.

The MMPI-2 (Butcher, Dahlstrom, et al., 1989) has been revised several times, most recently in 2009. An extensive research literature shows that the MMPI-2 is reliable and has adequate validity, in that it is related to diagnoses made by clinicians and to ratings made by spouses (Graham, 2011).

TABLE 3.6 **Typical Clinical Interpretations of Items Similar to Those on the MMPI-2**

	Scale	Sample Item	Interpretation
	(Cannot say)	This is merely the number of items left unanswered or marked both true and false.	A high score indicates evasiveness, reading difficulties, or other problems that could invalidate results of the test. A very high score could also suggest severe depression or obsessional tendencies.
L	(Lie)	I approve of every person I meet. (True)	Person is trying to look good, to present self as someone with an ideal personality.
F	(Infrequency)	Everything tastes sweet. (True)	Person is trying to look abnormal, perhaps to ensure getting special attention from the clinician.
K	(Correction)	Things couldn't be going any better for me. (True)	Person is guarded, defensive in taking the test, wishes to avoid appearing incompetent or poorly adjusted.
1.	Hs (Hypochondriasis)	I am seldom aware of tingling feelings in my body. (False)	Person is overly sensitive to and concerned about bodily sensations as signs of possible physical illness.
2.	D (Depression)	Life usually feels worthwhile to me. (False)	Person is discouraged, pessimistic, sad, self-deprecating, feeling inadequate.
3.	Hy (Hysteria)	My muscles often twitch for no apparent reason. (True)	Person has somatic complaints unlikely to be due to physical problems; also tends to be demanding and histrionic.
4.	Pd (Psychopathy)	I don't care about what people think of me. (True)	Person expresses little concern for social mores, is irresponsible, has only superficial relationships.
5.	Mf (Masculinity–Femininity)	I like taking care of plants and flowers. (True, female)	Person shows nontraditional gender characteristics (e.g., men with high scores tend to be artistic and sensitive).
6.	Pa (Paranoia)	If they were not afraid of being caught, most people would lie and cheat. (True)	Person tends to misinterpret the motives of others, is suspicious and jealous, vengeful and brooding.
7.	Pt (Psychasthenia)	I am not as competent as most other people I know. (True)	Person is overanxious, full of self-doubts, moralistic, and generally obsessive-compulsive.
8.	Sc (Schizophrenia)	I sometimes smell things others don't sense. (True)	Person has bizarre sensory experiences and beliefs, is socially reclusive.
9.	Ma (Hypomania)	Sometimes I have a strong impulse to do something that others will find appalling. (True)	Person has overly ambitious aspirations and can be hyperactive, impatient, and irritable.
10.	Si (Social Introversion)	Rather than spend time alone, I prefer to be around other people. (False)	Person is very modest and shy, preferring solitary activities.

Note: The first four scales assess the validity of the test; there are seven other scales and methods for assessing validity not shown here. The numbered scales are the clinical or content scales. The Restructured Clinical (RC) Scales are not shown here.

Sources: Hathaway & McKinley (1943); revised by Butcher et al. (1989).

Figure 3.10 shows a hypothetical MMPI-2 profile.

You may wonder whether it would be easy to fake answers that suggest no psychopathology. For example, a superficial knowledge of contemporary psychopathology research could alert someone that to be regarded as psychologically healthy, he or she must not admit to worrying a great deal about receiving messages from television.

As shown in Table 3.6, the MMPI-2 includes several "validity scales" designed to detect deliberately faked responses. For example, an item on the lie scale might be, "I read the newspaper editorials every day." The assumption is that few people would be able to endorse such a statement honestly. Persons who endorse many of the statements in the lie scale might be attempting to present themselves in a good light. High scores on the infrequency (F) scale also discriminate between people trying to fake psychopathology and people who actually have a psychological disorder (Bagby, Nicholson, et al., 2002). If a person obtains high scores on the lie or infrequency (F) scale, his or her profile might be viewed with skepticism. People who are aware of these validity scales, however, can still effectively fake their profile (Baer & Sekirnjak, 1997; Walters & Clopton, 2000). In most testing circumstances, however, people do not want to falsify their responses because they want to be helped.

Another well-known personality test is the **Big Five Inventory-2** (BFI-2; Soto & John, 2016; John, Naumann, & Soto, 2008). This measure assesses the broad five domains of personality: openness to experience, conscientiousness, extraversion, agreeableness, and neuroticism (often recalled by the acronym *ocean,* with each letter representing one of the personality domains). The BFI-2 expands the original BFI to include more specific aspects of each of the big five domains. Like the MMPI-2, the BFI-2 has measurement properties that allow clinicians and researchers to make sure respondents are responding the same way to all items. These

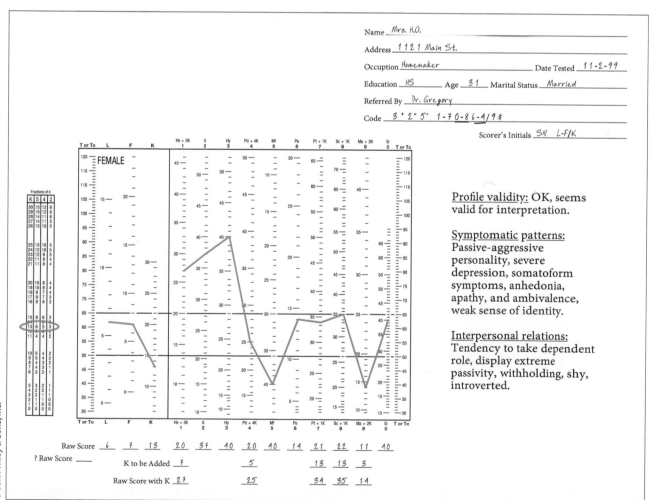

FIGURE 3.10 Hypothetical MMPI-2 profile.

dimensions are central to dimensional approaches to personality disorders (Chapter 14) but are also important in mood and anxiety disorders (Chapters 5 and 6).

Intelligence Tests

An **intelligence test**, often referred to as an IQ test, is a way of assessing a person's current cognitive ability. IQ tests are based on the assumption that a detailed sample of a person's current intellectual functioning can predict how well he or she will perform in school, and most such tests are individually administered. The most commonly administered tests include the Wechsler Adult Intelligence Scale, 4th edition (WAIS-IV, 2008); the Wechsler Intelligence Scale for Children, 5th edition (WISC-V, 2014); the Wechsler Preschool and Primary Scale of Intelligence, 4th edition (WPPSI-IV, 2012); and the Stanford–Binet, 5th edition (SB5, 2003); IQ tests are regularly updated, and, like personality inventories, they are standardized.

IQ tests tap several functions believed to constitute intelligence, including language skills, abstract thinking, nonverbal reasoning, visual-spatial skills, attention and concentration, and speed of processing. Beyond predicting school performance, intelligence tests are also used to diagnose learning disorders or intellectual ability (discussed in Chapter 13) and as part of neuropsychological evaluations (discussed in Neurobiological Assessment). IQ tests can also identify intellectually gifted children so that appropriate instruction can be provided them in school.

IQ tests are highly reliable (Canivez & Watkins, 1998) and have good validity. For example, they distinguish between people who are intellectually gifted and those with intellectual disability and between people with different occupations or educational attainment (Reynolds, Chastain, et al., 1997). They also predict educational attainment and occupational success (Hanson, Hunsley, & Parker, 1988), at least among Caucasians (we discuss cultural bias in assessment later). Although IQ and educational attainment are positively correlated (see Chapter 4 for a discussion of correlational methods), what remains less clear is whether more education causes an increase in IQ or whether IQ causes one to attain more education (Deary & Johnson, 2010). Furthermore, although correlations between IQ scores and school performance are statistically significant, IQ tests explain only a small part of school performance; much more is unexplained by IQ test scores than is explained.

Regarding construct validity, it is important to keep in mind that IQ tests measure only what psychologists consider intelligence. Factors other than what we think of as intelligence, however, also play an important role in how people will do in school, such as family and circumstances, motivation to do well, expectations, performance anxiety, and difficulty of the curriculum. Another factor relevant to IQ test performance is called stereotype threat. This concept refers to the notion that calling attention to stereotypes (e.g., African Americans do poorly on IQ tests; women perform more poorly than men on mathematics tests) actually interferes with their performance on these tests. In one study demonstrating this phenomenon, groups of men and women were given a difficult mathematics test. In one condition, the participants were told that men scored higher than women on the test they were going to take (stereotype threat condition), while in the other condition they were told there were no gender differences in performance on the test. Only when the test was described as yielding gender differences did the women perform more poorly than the men (Spencer, Steele, & Quinn, 1999).

Unfortunately, awareness of these stereotypes develops early. For example, a study revealed that children develop awareness of stereotypes regarding ethnicity and ability between the ages of 6 and 10, with 93 percent of children being aware of such stereotypes by age 10 (McKown & Weinstein, 2003). This awareness seems to influence stereotype threat (and performance). In the McKown and Weinstein (2003) study, children

Richard T. Nowitz/Corbis/Getty Images

IQ tests have many subtests, including this test to assess spatial ability.

were asked to complete a puzzle task. Half of the children received instructions that the task reflected their ability (stereotype threat condition), and half the children received instructions that the test did not reflect their ability. African American children who were aware of the stereotype about ethnicity and ability showed evidence of stereotype threat. Specifically, among African American children, those who received the ability instructions performed more poorly on the puzzle task than the children who did not, suggesting that the instructions activated the stereotype and thus influenced their performance.

Behavioral and Cognitive Assessment

Thus far, we have discussed assessment methods that measure personality traits and intellectual ability. Other types of assessment focus on behavioral and cognitive characteristics, including the following:

- Aspects of the environment that might contribute to symptoms (e.g., an office location next to a noisy hallway might contribute to concentration problems)
- Characteristics of the person (e.g., a person's fatigue may be caused in part by a cognitive tendency toward self-deprecation manifested in such statements as "I never do anything right, so what's the point in trying?")
- The frequency and form of problematic behaviors (e.g., procrastination taking the form of missing important deadlines)
- Consequences of problem behaviors (e.g., when a person avoids a feared situation, his or her partner offers sympathy and excuses, thereby unwittingly keeping the person from facing up to his or her fears)

The information necessary for a behavioral or cognitive assessment is gathered by several methods, including direct observation of behavior in real life as well as in laboratory or office settings, interviews and self-report measures, and various other methods of cognitive assessment.

Direct Observation of Behavior

In formal behavioral observation, the observer divides the sequence of behavior into various parts that make sense within a learning framework, including such things as the antecedents and consequences of particular behaviors. Behavioral observation is also often linked to intervention (O'Brien & Haynes, 1995).

It is difficult to observe most behavior as it actually takes place, and little control can be exercised over where and when it may occur. For this reason, many therapists contrive somewhat artificial situations in their consulting rooms or in a laboratory so that they can observe how a person or a family acts under certain conditions. For example, Barkley (1981) had a mother and her child spend time together in a laboratory living room, complete with sofas and a television. The mother was given a list of tasks for the child to complete, such as picking up toys or doing math problems. Observers behind a one-way mirror watched the proceedings and reliably coded the child's reactions to the mother's efforts to control as well as the mother's reactions to the child's compliant or noncompliant responses.

Behavioral assessment often involves direct observation of behavior, as in this case, where the observer is behind a one-way mirror.

© Marmaduke St. John/Alamy

These behavioral assessment procedures yielded data that could be used to measure the effects of treatment.

Self-monitoring can be done via apps on phones or text messages.

Cognitive assessment focuses on the person's perception of a situation, realizing that the same event can be perceived differently. For example, moving could be regarded as a very negative event or a very positive one, resulting in very different levels of stress.

Self-Monitoring

Cognitive behavior therapists and researchers often ask people to monitor and track their own behavior and responses. Self-monitoring is used to collect a wide variety of data, including moods, stressful experiences, coping behaviors, and thoughts (Stone, Schwartz, et al., 1998)

One version of self-monitoring is called **ecological momentary assessment**, or **EMA**. EMA involves the collection of data in real time as opposed to the more usual methods of having people reflect back over some time period and report on recently experienced thoughts, moods, or stressors. With EMA, a person is signaled (via text message or smartphone alert most typically) several times a day and asked to enter responses directly into the device (Stone & Shiffman, 1994). Self-monitoring with portable electronic devices like smartphones has also been included effectively in cognitive behavior therapy for different anxiety disorders (Przeworski & Newman, 2006).

Cognitive-Style Questionnaires

Cognitive questionnaires tend to be used to help plan targets for treatment as well as to determine whether clinical interventions are helping to change overly negative thought patterns as well as negative and positive emotions. In format, some of these questionnaires are similar to the personality tests we have already described.

One self-report questionnaire that was developed based on Beck's theory (see Chapters 2 and 5) is the Dysfunctional Attitude Scale (DAS). The DAS contains items such as "People will probably think less of me if I make a mistake" (Weissman & Beck, 1978). Supporting construct validity, researchers have shown that they can differentiate between people with and without depression on the basis of their scores on this scale and that scores decrease (i.e., improve) after interventions that relieve depression. Furthermore, the DAS relates to other aspects of cognition in ways consistent with Beck's theory (Glass & Arnkoff, 1997).

Quick Summary

The psychological assessments we have described are summarized in **Table 3.7**. A comprehensive psychological assessment draws on many different methods and tests. Interviews can be structured, with the questions predetermined and followed in a certain order, or unstructured, to follow more closely what the person tells the interviewer. Structured interviews are more reliable. Rapport is important to establish regardless of the type of interview.

Stress is best assessed via a semistructured interview that captures the importance of any given life event in the context of a person's life circumstances, as in the LEDS.

The MMPI-2 and BFI-2 are standardized personality tests. They have good reliability and validity and are widely used. Intelligence tests have been used for many years and are quite reliable. Like any test, there are limits to what an IQ test can tell a clinician or researcher.

Direct observation of behavior can be very useful in assessment, though it can take more time than a self-report inventory. Other behavioral and cognitive assessment methods include ecological momentary assessment (EMA) and questionnaires.

TABLE 3.7	**Psychological Assessment Methods**	
Interviews	Clinical interviews	The clinician learns about the person's problems through conversation.
	Structured interviews	Questions to be asked are spelled out in detail in a booklet. The Structured Clinical Interview is a structured interview that is commonly used to help make a diagnosis.
Stress measures		Self-report scales or interviews that assess stressful events and responses to these events.
Psychological tests	Personality tests	Self-report questionnaires, used to assess either a broad range of characteristics, as in the BFI-2, or a single characteristic, such as dysfunctional attitudes.
	Intelligence tests	Assessments of current cognitive functioning. Used to predict school performance and identify cognitive strengths and weaknesses.
Direct observation		Used by clinicians to identify problem behaviors as well as antecedents and consequences.
Self-monitoring		People monitor and keep records of their own behavior, as in ecological momentary assessment.

Check Your Knowledge 3.3

True or false?

1. If conducted properly, a psychological assessment typically includes just one measure most appropriate to the person.

2. Unstructured interviews may have poor reliability, but they can still be quite valuable in a psychological assessment.

3. The MMPI-2 contains scales to detect whether someone is faking answers.

4. The BFI-2 assesses five broad domains of personality.

5. Intelligence tests are highly reliable.

6. EMA is a method to assess unwanted impulses.

Neurobiological Assessment

Recall from Chapters 1 and 2 that throughout history people interested in psychopathology have assumed, quite reasonably, that some symptoms are likely to be due to or at least reflected in malfunctions of the brain. We turn now to contemporary work in neurobiological assessment. We'll look at three areas in particular: brain imaging, neuropsychological assessment, and psychophysiological assessment (see **Table 3.8** for a summary of these methods).

Brain Imaging: "Seeing" the Brain

There are several different types of brain imaging techniques that allow clinicians and researchers a direct look at both the structure and functioning of the brain.

Computerized axial tomography, the **CT** or **CAT scan**, helps to assess structural brain abnormalities (and is able to image other parts of the body for medical purposes). A moving beam of X-rays passes into a horizontal cross section of the person's brain, scanning it through 360 degrees; the moving X-ray detector on the other side measures the amount of radioactivity that penetrates, thus detecting subtle differences in tissue density. A computer uses the information to construct

TABLE 3.8   **Neurobiological Assessment Methods**

Brain imaging	CT and MRI scans reveal the structure of the brain. PET reveals brain function and, to a lesser extent, brain structure. fMRI is used to assess both brain structure and brain function.
Neuropsychological assessment	Behavioral tests such as the Halstead–Reitan and Luria–Nebraska assess abilities such as motor speed, memory, and spatial ability. Deficits on particular tests help point to an area of possible brain dysfunction.
Psychophysiological assessment	Includes measures of electrical activity in the autonomic nervous system, such as skin conductance, or in the central nervous system, such as EEG (electroencephalogram).

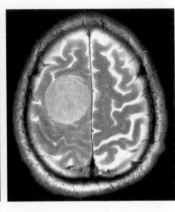

These two CT scans show a horizontal "slice" through the brain. The one on the left is normal; the one on the right has a tumor on the left side.

a two-dimensional, detailed image of the cross section, giving it optimal contrasts. Then the machine scans another cross section of the brain. The resulting images can show the enlargement of ventricles (which can be a sign of brain tissue degeneration) and the locations of tumors and blood clots (see photo).

Another method for seeing brain structure is **magnetic resonance imaging**, also known as **MRI**, which is superior to the CT scan because it produces pictures of higher quality and does not rely on even the small amount of radiation required by a CT scan. In MRI, the person is placed inside a large, circular magnet, which causes the hydrogen atoms in the body to move. When the magnetic force is turned off, the atoms return to their original positions and thereby produce an electromagnetic signal. These signals are then read by the computer and translated into pictures of brain tissue.

An even greater advance has been a technique called **functional MRI (fMRI),** which allows researchers to measure both brain structure and brain function. This technique takes MRI pictures so quickly that metabolic changes can be measured, providing a picture of the brain at work rather than of its structure alone. fMRI measures blood flow in the brain, and this is called the **BOLD** signal, which stands for **blood oxygenation level dependent**. As neurons fire, presumably blood flow increases to that area. Therefore, blood flow in a particular region of the brain is a reasonable proxy for neural activity in that brain region.

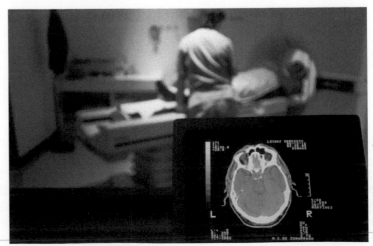

A person entering an fMRI scanner.

Positron emission tomography, the **PET scan**, a more expensive and invasive procedure, also allows measurement of both brain structure and brain function, although the measurement of brain structure is not as precise as with MRI or fMRI. A substance used by the brain is labeled with a short-lived radioactive isotope and injected into the bloodstream. The radioactive molecules of the substance emit a particle called a positron, which quickly collides with an electron. A pair of high-energy light particles shoot out from the skull in opposite directions and are detected by the scanner. The computer analyzes millions of such recordings and converts them into a picture of the functioning brain. The images are in color; fuzzy spots of lighter and warmer colors are areas in which metabolic rates for the substance are higher. Because this is more invasive than fMRI, it is used less often as a measure of brain function. Nevertheless, this method is useful for assessing neurotransmitter functioning in the brain.

A less expensive but still invasive way to measure neurotransmitter activity in the living brain is with single photon emission computed tomography or a **SPECT** scan. Like PET, this method involves injecting a radioisotope into the bloodstream. However, this method is less expensive because the isotopes are more readily available. SPECT directly measures gamma rays that are produced by injection of the radioisotope and generates images of activity in different regions of the brain.

Current neuroimaging studies in psychopathology are attempting to identify not only areas of the brain that may be dysfunctional (e.g., the prefrontal cortex) but also deficits in the ways in which different areas of the brain communicate and connect with one another. This type of inquiry is often referred to as **connectivity** since it aims to identify how different areas of the brain are connected with one another.

Broadly speaking, there are three types of connectivity. *Structural (or anatomical) connectivity* refers to how different structures of the brain are connected via white matter (see Chapter 2). *Functional connectivity* refers to the connectivity between brain regions based on correlations between their blood oxygen level dependent (BOLD) signal measured with fMRI (see Chapter 2). For example, several studies have found reduced functional connectivity in schizophrenia, particularly in the frontal cortex (Pettersson-Yeo, Allen, et al., 2011).

Effective connectivity combines both types of connectivity in that it not only reveals correlations between BOLD activations in different brain regions but also the direction and timing of those activations by showing, for example, that activation in the occipital cortex comes first, followed by activation on the frontal cortex when someone is viewing pictures of objects (Friston, 1994).

Clinicians and researchers in many disciplines are currently using brain-imaging assessment techniques both to discover previously undetectable brain problems and to conduct inquiries into the neurobiological contributions to thought, emotion, and behavior. It is a very lively and exciting area of research and application. Indeed, one might reasonably assume that researchers and clinicians could observe the brain and its functions and connectivity more or less directly and thus assess all brain abnormalities. Results

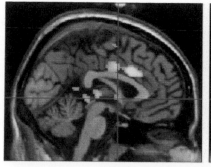
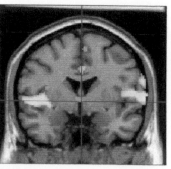

Functional magnetic resonance images (fMRI). With this method, researchers can measure how brain activity changes while a person is doing different tasks, such as viewing an emotional film, completing a memory test, looking at a visual puzzle, or hearing and learning a list of words.

Science Photo Library/Science Source

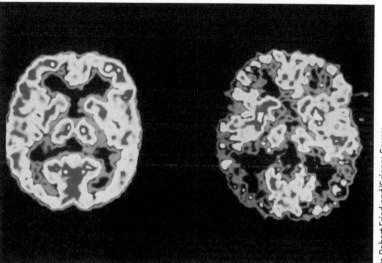

The PET scan on the left shows a normal brain; the one on the right shows the brain of a person with Alzheimer's disease.

Dr. Robert Fried and/Science Source

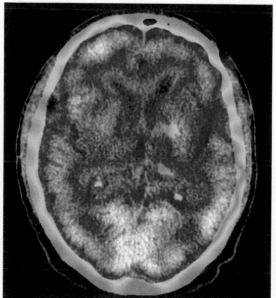

SPECT image. This type of imaging can show neurotransmitter activity.

Steven Needell/Science Source Images

to date, however, are not strong enough for these methods to be used in diagnosing psychopathology. Moreover, many brain abnormalities involve alterations in structure so subtle or slight in extent that they have thus far eluded direct examination. Furthermore, the problems in some disorders are so widespread that finding the contributing brain dysfunction is a daunting task. Take, for example, schizophrenia, which affects thinking, feeling, and behavior. Where in the brain might there be dysfunction? Looking for areas that influence thinking, feeling, and behavior requires looking at just about the entire brain.

Neuropsychological Assessment

Neuropsychological tests are often used in conjunction with the brain-imaging techniques just described, both to detect brain dysfunction and to help pinpoint specific areas of behavior that are impacted by problems in the brain. Neuropsychological tests are based on the idea that different psychological functions (e.g., motor speed, memory, language) rely on different areas of the brain. Thus, for example, neuropsychological testing might help identify the extent of brain damage suffered during a stroke, and it can provide clues about where in the brain the damage may exist that can then be confirmed with more expensive brain-imaging techniques. There are numerous neuropsychological tests used in psychopathology assessment. Here, we highlight two widely used batteries of tests.

One neuropsychological test is Reitan's modification of a battery, or group, of tests previously developed by Halstead, called the Halstead—Reitan neuropsychological test battery. The following are three of the Halstead—Reitan tests.

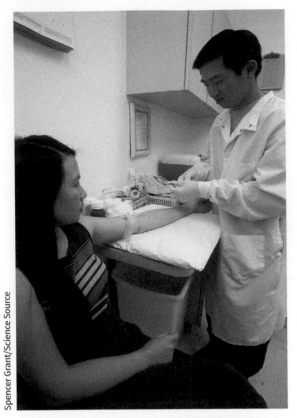

Spencer Grant/Science Source

Measures of neurotransmitter **metabolites** in blood or urine levels do not provide a very accurate index of neurotransmitter levels in the brain.

1. **Tactile Performance Test—Time.** While blindfolded, the person tries to fit variously shaped blocks into spaces of a form board, first using the preferred hand, then the other, and finally both.

2. **Tactile Performance Test—Memory.** After completing the timed test, the person is asked to draw the form board from memory, showing the blocks in their proper location. Both this and the timed test are sensitive to damage in the right parietal lobe.

3. **Speech Sounds Perception Test.** Participants listen to a series of nonsense words, each comprising two consonants with a long-*e* sound in the middle. They then select the "word" they heard from a set of alternatives. This test measures left-hemisphere function, especially temporal and parietal areas.

Extensive research has demonstrated that the battery is valid for detecting behavior changes linked to brain dysfunction resulting from a variety of conditions, such as tumors, stroke, and head injury (Horton, 2008).

The Luria–Nebraska battery (Golden, Hammeke, & Purisch, 1978) is also widely used. The battery includes 269 items divided into 11 sections designed to determine basic and complex motor skills, rhythm and pitch abilities, tactile and kinesthetic skills, verbal and spatial skills, receptive speech ability, expressive speech ability, writing, reading, arithmetic skills, memory, and intellectual processes.

Richard Nowitz/Science Source

Neuropsychological tests assess various performance deficits in the hope of detecting a specific area of brain malfunction. Shown here is the Tactile Performance Test.

The Luria–Nebraska is highly reliable (e.g., Kashden & Franzen, 1996). Validity has been established by findings that test scores can correctly distinguish 86 percent of people with and without neurological disease (Moses, Schefft, et al., 1992). A particular advantage of the Luria–Nebraska tests is that one can control for educational level so that a less educated person will not receive a lower score solely because of limited educational experience (Brickman, McManus, et al., 1984).

Psychophysiological Assessment

The discipline of **psychophysiology** is concerned with the bodily changes that are associated with psychological events. Experimenters have used measures such as heart rate, tension in the muscles, blood flow in various parts of the body, and electrical activity in the brain (so-called brain waves) to study physiological changes when people are afraid, depressed, asleep, imagining, solving problems, and so on. For example, in using exposure to treat a person with an anxiety disorder, it would be useful to know the extent to which the person shows physiological reactivity when exposed to the stimuli that create anxiety. People who show more physiological reactivity may be experiencing more fear, which predicts more benefit from the therapy (Foa, Riggs, et al., 1995).

The activities of the autonomic nervous system (also discussed in Chapter 2) are often assessed to understand aspects of emotion. One such measure is heart rate. Each heartbeat generates electrical changes, which can be recorded by electrodes placed on the chest that convey signals to an electrocardiograph or a polygraph. The signal is graphically depicted in an **electrocardiogram (EKG)**, which may be seen as waves on a computer screen.

Another measure of autonomic nervous system activity is **electrodermal responding**, or skin conductance. Anxiety, fear, anger, and other emotions increase activity in the sympathetic nervous system, which then boosts sweat-gland activity. Increased sweat-gland activity increases the electrical conductance of the skin. Conductance is typically measured by determining the current that flows through the skin as a small voltage is passed between two electrodes on the hand. When the sweat glands are activated, this current shows a pronounced increase. Since the sweat glands are activated by the sympathetic nervous system, increased sweat-gland activity indicates sympathetic autonomic excitation and is often taken as a measure of emotional arousal. These measures are widely used in research in psychopathology.

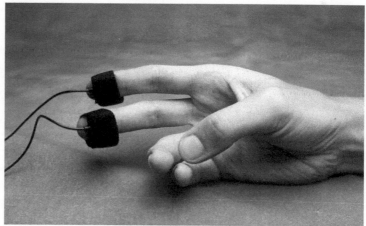

Courtesy of BIOPIC Systems, Inc. (biopic.com)

In psychophysiological assessment, physical changes in the body are measured. Skin conductance can be measured with sensors on two fingers.

A Cautionary Note About Neurobiological Assessment

A cautionary note regarding neurobiological assessment methods is in order here. Inasmuch as psychophysiology and brain imaging employ highly sophisticated electronic machinery, and many psychologists aspire to be as scientific as possible, researchers and clinicians sometimes believe uncritically in these apparently objective assessment devices without appreciating their real limitations and complications. Many of the measurements do not differentiate clearly among emotional states. Skin conductance, for example, increases not only with anxiety but also with other emotions—among them, happiness. In addition, being in a scanner is often a threatening experience. Thus, the investigator interested in measuring brain changes associated with emotion using fMRI must also take the scanning environment into account. It is also important to keep in mind that brain-imaging techniques do not allow us to manipulate brain activity and then measure a change in behavior (Barrett, 2003). In a typical study, we show people a list of emotionally evocative words and then measure blood flow in the brain. Does a person who fails to show the same level of activation in emotion regions during this task have a brain-based emotion deficit? Not necessarily. The person might not have paid attention, might not have understood the words, or might be focused on the loud clanging noises that the fMRI machine is making. It is important to be extremely careful in considering alternative explanations for the effects found in these studies.

Neither is there a one-to-one relationship between a score on a given neuropsychological test or a finding on an fMRI scan on the one hand and psychological dysfunction on the other. The reasons for these sometimes loose relationships have to do with such factors as how the person has, over time, developed different coping strategies. And the success of coping, in turn, has to do with the social environment in which the person has lived, for example, how understanding parents and friends have been or how well the school system has provided for the special educational needs of the person. Furthermore, the brain itself will change in response to these psychological and socioenvironmental factors over time. Therefore, in addition to the imperfect nature of the neurobiological assessment instruments themselves and our incomplete understanding of how the brain functions, clinicians and researchers must consider social and environmental factors that operate over time to contribute to the clinical picture. In other words, a complete assessment must include multiple methods (clinical interviews, psychological and neurobiological methods).

A final caution is reflected in the simple yet often unappreciated fact that in attempting to understand the consequences of any brain dysfunction, one must understand the preexisting abilities that the person had prior to diagnosis with a psychological disorder. This straightforward truth brings to mind the story of the man who, recovering from an accident that has broken all the fingers in both hands, earnestly asks the surgeon whether he will be able to play the piano when his wounds heal. "Yes, I'm sure you will," says the doctor reassuringly. "That's wonderful," exclaims the man, "I've always wanted to be able to play the piano."

Quick Summary

Advances in technology have allowed clinicians and researchers to "see" the living brain. Different imaging techniques, such as fMRI, PET, and SPECT, have the potential to show areas of the brain that might not be working optimally. Neuropsychological tests are designed to show how changes in behavior may reflect damage or disturbance in particular areas of the brain. Psychophysiological assessment methods can show how behaviors and cognitions are linked to changes in nervous system activity, such as heart rate or skin conductance. These methods have as many as or more limitations than other assessment measures, and the key concepts of reliability and validity are just as relevant with neurobiological assessment as with other forms of assessment.

Check Your Knowledge 3.4

True or false?

1. MRI is a technique that shows both the structure and function of the brain.

2. SPECT is invasive, but less expensive than PET and can be used to examine neurotransmitter function in the brain.

3. A neuropsychological battery assesses performance on tasks thought to rely on certain regions of the brain and can thus suggest possible brain dysfunction.

4. Electrodermal activity can be measured with the psychophysiological method called EKG.

Cultural and Ethnic Diversity and Assessment

Studies of the influences of culture and ethnicity on psychopathology and its assessment have proliferated in recent years. As you read about some of this research, it is critical to keep in mind that there are typically more differences within cultural, ethnic, and racial groups than there are between them. Remembering this important point can help you avoid the dangers of stereotyping members of a culture or ethnic group.

We should also note that the reliability and validity of various forms of psychological assessment have been questioned on the grounds that their content and scoring procedures reflect the culture of white European Americans and so may not accurately assess people from other cultures. In this section we discuss problems of cultural bias and what can be done about them.

Cultural Bias in Assessment

The issue of cultural bias in assessment refers to the notion that a measure developed for one culture or ethnic group may not be equally reliable and valid with a different cultural or ethnic group. Some tests that were developed in the United States have been translated into different languages and used in different cultures successfully. For example, Spanish-language versions of the WAIS and WISC have been available for nearly 50 years. The WISC-IV Spanish includes not just a translation from English to Spanish, but also includes norms for Spanish-speaking children and items designed explicitly to minimize cultural bias. Additionally, the MMPI-2 has been translated into more than two dozen languages (Tsai, Butcher, et al., 2001), and the BFI-2 has been translated into three other languages, with other translations underway.

Simply translating words into a different language, however, does not ensure that the meaning of those words will be the same across different cultures. Several steps in the translation process, including working with multiple translators, back-translating, and testing with multiple native speakers, can help to ensure that the test is similar in different languages. The International Test Commission released the revised *Guidelines for Translating and Adapting Tests* in 2010, updating the original guidelines published in 1996. These guidelines cover the context of a test, the development and adaption of a test to a different language, administration, and scoring interpretations (International Test Commission, 2010). This approach has been successful in achieving equivalence across different cultures and ethnic groups for some instruments, such as the MMPI-2 (Arbisi, Ben-Porath, & McNulty, 2002). Even with the MMPI-2, however, there are cultural differences that are not likely attributable to differences in psychopathology. For example, among Asian Americans who are not heavily assimilated into American culture, scores on most MMPI-2 scales are higher than those of Caucasians (Tsai & Pike, 2000). This is unlikely to reflect truly higher emotional disturbance among Asians.

Despite these efforts, the field has a way to go in reducing cultural and ethnic bias in clinical assessment. First, the guidelines are not always followed. A recent review of 61 articles of test translations found that the majority of the studies did not follow the guidelines (Rios & Sireci, 2014). Additionally, cultural assumptions or biases may cause clinicians to over- or underestimate psychological problems in members of other cultures (Lopez, 1989, 1996). At least since the 1970s, studies have found that African Americans are more likely to receive a diagnosis of schizophrenia than are Caucasian Americans; this does not likely reflect an actual difference but instead a form of ethnic bias on the part of clinicians (Arnold, Keck, et al., 2004; Trierweiler, Neighbors, et al., 2000). Yet take the example of an Asian American man who is very emotionally withdrawn. Should the clinician consider the notion that Asian cultures take a more positive view of lower emotional expressiveness in men than do European American cultures? A clinician who quickly attributes the

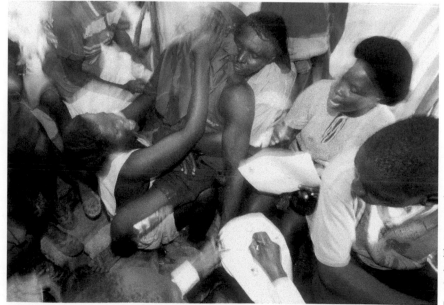

Assessment must take the person's cultural background into account. Belief in spirit possession in some cultures should not always be taken to mean that the believer is psychotic.

behavior to a cultural difference may overlook an emotional problem that he or she would be likely to diagnose if the person were a white male. Indeed, recent evidence shows that clinicians confuse the absence of excitement in the facial expressions of Asian people as a sign of depression. Even though Asians are less likely to show such expressions than European Americans, this has nothing to do with whether or not they have depression (Tsai, 2014).

How do such biases come about? Cultural factors may affect assessment in various ways. Language differences, differing religious and spiritual beliefs, the alienation or presumed timidity of members of ethnic groups when being assessed by clinicians of the European American culture— all these factors can play a role. For example, clinicians who encounter people claiming to be surrounded by spirits might view this belief as a sign of schizophrenia. Yet in Puerto Rican cultures, such a belief is common; therefore, believing that one is surrounded by spirits should probably not be taken as a sign of schizophrenia in a Puerto Rican person (Rogler & Hollingshead, 1985).

Cultural and ethnic differences in psychopathology must be examined more closely. Unfortunately, the cultural and ethnic biases that can creep into clinical assessment do not necessarily yield efforts to compensate for them. There is no simple answer. The DSM-5's emphasis on cultural factors in the discussion of every category of disorder, along with its new cultural formulation interview, may well sensitize clinicians and researchers to the issue. When practitioners were surveyed, they overwhelmingly reported taking culture into account in their clinical work (Lopez, 1994), so it appears that the problem, if not the solution, is clearly in focus.

Strategies for Avoiding Cultural Bias in Assessment

Clinicians can—and do—use various methods to minimize the negative effects of cultural biases when conducting assessments. Perhaps the place to begin is with graduate training programs. Lopez (2002) has noted three important issues that should be taught to graduate students in clinical psychology programs. First, students must learn about basic issues in assessment, such as reliability and validity. Second, students must become informed about the specific ways in which culture or ethnicity may impact assessment rather than relying on more global stereotypes about a particular cultural or ethnic group. Third, students must consider that culture or ethnicity may not impact assessment in every individual case.

Assessment procedures can also be modified to ensure that the person truly understands the requirements of the task. For example, suppose that a Native American child performed poorly on a test measuring psychomotor speed. The examiner's hunch is that the child did not understand the importance of working quickly and was overly concerned with accuracy instead. The test could be administered again after a more thorough explanation of the importance of working quickly without worrying about mistakes. If the child's performance improves, the examiner has gained an important understanding of the child's test-taking strategy and avoids diagnosing psychomotor speed deficits.

As Lopez (1994) points out, however, "the distance between cultural responsiveness and cultural stereotyping can be short" (p. 123). To minimize such problems, clinicians are encouraged to be particularly tentative about drawing conclusions regarding people from different cultural and ethnic backgrounds. Rather, they are advised to make hypotheses about the influence of culture on a person, entertain alternative hypotheses, and then test those hypotheses.

Training in cultural awareness is truly important, as a clinician's biases can influence diagnosis. As an example, because schizophrenia is often overdiagnosed among African Americans, this contributes to higher dosages of antipsychotic medications than may be necessary (Alarcon et al., 2009). One way to combat these biases is to use structured diagnostic interviews, like the SCID described

© Marmaduke St. John/Alamy

Cultural differences can lead to different results on an aptitude or IQ test. For example, Native American children may not recognize the need to perform quickly on some tests even if mistakes are made.

above. When clinicians use structured interviews, they are less likely to overdiagnose people from different ethnic groups (Garb, 2005).

Summary

Reliability and Validity

In gathering diagnostic and assessment information, clinicians and researchers must be concerned with both reliability and validity. Reliability refers to whether measurements are consistent and replicable, and validity refers to whether assessments are tapping into what they are meant to measure. Assessment procedures vary greatly in their reliability and validity.

Diagnosis

- Diagnosis is the process of assessing whether a person meets the criteria for a psychological disorder. Having an agreed-on diagnostic system allows clinicians to communicate effectively with each other and facilitates the search for causes and treatments. Clinically, diagnosis provides the foundation for treatment planning.

- *The Diagnostic and Statistical Manual of Mental Disorders* (DSM), published by the American Psychiatric Association, is an official diagnostic system widely used by mental health professionals. The latest edition of the manual, referred to as DSM-5, was published in 2013.

- Reliability of diagnosis has been improved dramatically by including specific criteria for each diagnosis. Criticisms of the DSM include the proliferation of diagnoses that are often related to the same risk factors and tend to co-occur; the reliance on a categorical rather than a dimensional approach to classification; the fact that reliability in practice may be lower than that achieved in research studies; and the ongoing need to validate diagnoses against etiology, course, and treatment. Most researchers and clinicians, though, recognize that the DSM is an enormous advance compared to previous systems.

- Some critics of the DSM argue against diagnosis in general. They point out that diagnostic classifications may ignore important information. Although many worry that diagnostic labels will increase stigma, there is some data that a diagnosis can reduce stigma by providing an explanation for worrisome behavior.

Assessment

- Clinicians rely on several types of assessment in trying to find out how best to describe an individual, search for the reasons the person is troubled, arrive at an accurate diagnosis, and implement effective treatments. The best assessment involves multiple types of methods.

- Psychological assessments include clinical interviews, assessments of stress, psychological tests, and behavioral and cognitive assessments.

- Clinical interviews are structured or relatively unstructured conversations in which the clinician probes the person for information about his or her problems. Assessing stress is key to the field of psychopathology. A very useful method for assessing stress is the LEDS.

- Psychological tests are standardized procedures designed to assess personality or measure performance. Personality assessments include empirically derived self-report questionnaires, such as the Minnesota Multiphasic Personality Inventory-2 or the Big Five Inventory-2. Intelligence tests, such as the Wechsler Adult Intelligence Scale, evaluate a person's intellectual ability and can predict how well he or she will perform academically.

- Behavioral and cognitive assessment is concerned with how people act, feel, and think in particular situations. Approaches include direct observation of behavior, self-monitoring, and self-report measures that are situational in their focus.

- Neurobiological assessments include brain-imaging techniques, such as fMRI, that enable clinicians and researchers to see various structures and access functions of the living brain; neuropsychological tests, such as the Luria-Nebraska battery, that seek to identify brain dysfunction based on variations in responses to psychological tests; and psychophysiological measurements, such as heart rate and electrodermal responding, that are associated with certain psychological events or characteristics.

- Cultural and ethnic factors play a role in clinical assessment. Assessment techniques developed on the basis of research with Caucasian populations may be inaccurate when used with people of differing ethnic or cultural backgrounds. Clinicians can have biases when evaluating people from different ethnic and cultural groups, which can lead to minimizing or exaggerating a person's psychopathology. Clinicians use various methods to guard against the negative effects of cultural biases in assessment.

Answers to Check Your Knowledge Questions

3.1 1. b, c, a

3.2 1. Culture-related issues are described for most of the specific disorders; a cultural formulation interview is provided; an appendix describes cultural concepts of distress, culturally specific ways of expressing distress, and cultural explanations of symptoms 2. high comorbidity, many different diagnoses are related to the same causes, symptoms of many different diagnoses respond to the same treatments; 3. any three of the following: etiology, course, social functioning, treatment

3.3 1. F; 2. T; 3. T; 4. T; 5. T; 6. F

3.4 1. F; 2. T; 3. T; 4. F

Key Terms

alternate-form reliability
Big Five Inventory-2 (BFI-2)
BOLD
categorical classification
clinical interview
comorbidity
connectivity
construct validity
content validity
CT or CAT scan
cultural concepts of distress
diagnosis
DSM-5; *Diagnostic and Statistical Manual of Mental Disorders*

dimensional diagnostic system
ecological momentary assessment (EMA)
electrocardiogram (EKG)
electrodermal responding
functional magnetic resonance imaging (fMRI)
intelligence test
internal consistency reliability
inter-rater reliability
magnetic resonance imaging (MRI)
Minnesota Multiphasic Personality Inventory (MMPI)
neuropsychological tests
personality inventory
PET scan

projective test
psychophysiology
reliability
Research Domain Criteria (RDoC)
shenjing shuairuo
SPECT
standardization
stress
structured interview
taijin kyofusho
test–retest reliability
validity

CHAPTER 4

Research Methods in Psychopathology

LEARNING GOALS

1. Describe issues in defining theory and hypotheses.

2. Discuss the advantages and disadvantages of case studies, correlational designs, and experimental designs, and identify common types of correlational and experimental designs.

3. Explain the standards and issues in conducting psychotherapy outcome research.

4. Describe the types of analogues that are most common in psychopathology research, and concerns about the use of analogues.

5. Discuss current debate concerning replicability in science, and the basic steps in conducting a meta-analysis.

The ability to conceptualize and treat psychological disorders has improved vastly over the past 50 years. Nonetheless, important questions remain unanswered about the causes and treatments of psychological disorders. Therefore, it is important to pursue new discoveries using scientific research methods.

In this chapter, we discuss key issues in designing and evaluating psychopathology research. We begin with defining theory and hypotheses. Then we discuss the pros and cons of common research designs, and we provide examples of how these different types of designs are used in psychopathology research. We discuss several types of analogue research that are used to overcome ethical and pragmatic barriers in the study of psychological disorders. We then consider another core facet of the scientific process—the need to replicate findings and to integrate findings from multiple studies. As we discuss these elements of the research process, bear in mind that researchers also must consider ethical issues in the conduct of research, as discussed in Chapter 16.

Even with carefully designed research on the causes of and treatments for psychological disorders, we will often encounter shortcomings in the predictive power of our research findings. Even if we knew all the variables controlling behavior—and no one would claim that we do—our ability to predict behavior would be limited by many unexpected and uncontrollable factors that are likely to affect a person over time. People do not behave in a social vacuum. Research participants and therapy clients live moment to moment in exquisitely complex interaction with others who themselves are affected on a moment-to-moment basis by hundreds of factors that are impossible to anticipate. We want to counsel humility, even awe, in an enterprise that tries to understand how things go awry with mental health.

Science, Theory, and Hypotheses

The term *science* comes from the Latin *scire*, meaning "to know." At its core, science is a way of knowing. More formally, it is the systematic pursuit of knowledge through observation. Science involves forming a theory and then systematically gathering data to test the theory.

A **theory** is a set of propositions meant to explain a class of observations. Usually, the goal of scientific theories is to understand cause–effect relationships. A theory permits the generation of more specific hypotheses—expectations about what should occur if a theory is true. For example, if the original classical conditioning theory of phobias is valid, people with dog phobias should be more likely than those without dog phobias to have had traumatic experiences with dogs. By collecting such data, you could test this **hypothesis**.

What makes a good theory? A scientific approach requires that the theory and hypotheses be stated clearly and precisely. This is needed for scientific claims to be exposed to systematic tests that could negate the scientist's expectations. That is, regardless of how plausible a theory seems, it must be subject to disproof. Science proceeds by disproving theories, never by "proving theories." Consequently, it is not enough to assert that traumatic experiences during childhood cause psychological maladjustment in adulthood. This is no more than a possibility. According to a scientific point of view, a hypothesis must be amenable to systematic testing that could show it to be false. That is, the focus of testing is on disproving rather than proving a theory.

Researchers must consider a set of principles in testing a theory. They must choose assessments with strong reliability and validity, as discussed in Chapter 3. Beyond choosing measures carefully, researchers in psychopathology choose among different types of research designs, a topic we turn to next.

Quick Summary

Science is the systematic pursuit of knowledge through observation. The first step of science is to define a theory and related hypotheses. A good theory is precise and could be disproven.

Check Your Knowledge 4.1
(Answers are at the end of the chapter.)

True or false?

1. A good theory can be proven.
2. Good research depends on validity, but not reliability, of measures.
3. Hypotheses are broader and more abstract than a theory is.

Research Designs in Psychopathology

In this section we describe the most common research methods in the study of psychopathology: the case study, correlational methods, and experimental methods. You will see these methods in the studies described throughout this book. In this chapter, we will describe some of the typical ways these different research methods are used in psychopathology research. **Table 4.1** provides a summary of the strengths and weaknesses of each.

The Case Study

The **case study**, perhaps the most familiar method of observing human behavior, involves recording detailed information about one person at a time. The clinical cases described in the last chapter are examples of case studies. A comprehensive case study covers developmental milestones, family history, medical history, educational background, employment history,

TABLE 4.1   **Research Methods in Psychopathology**

Method	Description	Evaluation
Case study	Collection of detailed biographical information	Excellent source of hypotheses Can provide information about novel cases or procedures Can disconfirm a relationship that was believed to be universal Cannot provide causal evidence because alternative hypotheses cannot be eliminated May be biased by observer's theoretical viewpoint
Correlation	Study of the relationship between two or more variables, measured as they exist in nature	Widely used because we cannot manipulate many risk variables (such as personality, trauma, or genes) or diagnoses in psychopathology research with humans Often used by epidemiologists to study the incidence, prevalence, and risk factors of disorders in a representative sample Often used in behavioral genetics research to study the heritability of different disorders Directionality and third-variable problems can interfere with determining causality
Experiment	Includes a manipulated independent variable, a dependent variable, preferably at least one control group, and random assignment	Most powerful method for determining causal relationships Often used in studies of treatment Single-case experimental designs also common but can have limited external validity Can also examine analogue versions of risk factors

marital history, social adjustment, personality, environment, and experiences in therapy over the life span.

Case studies lack the control and objectivity of other research methods. That is, the validity of the information gathered in a case study is sometimes questionable. The objectivity of case studies is limited because the author's paradigm will shape the kinds of information reported in a case study. As one example, case studies by psychodynamic clinicians typically contain more information about the client's early childhood and parental conflicts than do reports by behavioral clinicians.

Case studies do not provide good evidence in support of a particular theory because they do not provide a way to rule out alternative hypotheses. To illustrate this problem, consider a case study that describes a client who responds well to a novel therapy. Although it would be tempting to conclude that the therapy is effective, such a conclusion cannot be drawn legitimately because other factors could have produced the change. A stressful situation in the client's life may have resolved, or the client may have adopted better coping skills during the time period of the intervention. Thus, rival hypotheses could account for the clinical improvement. The data yielded by the case study do not allow us to determine the true cause of the change.

Despite their relative lack of control, case studies still play an important role in the study of psychological disorders. Specifically, the case study can be used:

1. to provide a rich description of a new or unusual clinical phenomenon or treatment,
2. to disprove an allegedly universal hypothesis, and
3. to generate hypotheses that can be tested through controlled research.

We discuss the latter two of these uses in more detail next.

The Case Study Can Disprove a Hypothesis Case histories can provide examples that contradict an assumed universal relationship. Consider, for example, the theory that all people with agoraphobia experience panic attacks. As researchers increasingly documented cases of agoraphobia in the absence of panic attacks, this negated the theory.

Using the Case Study to Generate Hypotheses Although the case study may not provide valid support for hypotheses, it does help generate hypotheses about causes and

Greg Smith/Corbis /Getty Images

Although the information yielded by a case study does not provide strong support for theory it is an important source of hypotheses.

treatments for disorders. As they hear the life histories of many different clients, clinicians may notice patterns and then formulate important hypotheses that they could not have formed otherwise. For example, in his clinical work, Kanner (1943) noticed that some disturbed children showed a similar constellation of symptoms, including failure to develop language and extreme isolation from other people. He therefore proposed a new diagnosis—infantile autism—that was subsequently confirmed by larger-scale research and adopted into the DSM (see Chapter 13).

The Correlational Method

A great deal of psychopathology research relies on the **correlational method**. Correlational studies address questions of the form "Do variable X and variable Y vary together (co-relate)?" In correlational research, variables are measured as they exist in nature. This is distinct from experimental research (discussed later in this chapter), in which the researcher manipulates variables.

To illustrate the difference, consider that the role of stress in hypertension (high blood pressure) can be assessed with either a correlational or an experimental design. In a correlational study, we might measure stress levels by interviewing people about their recent stressful experiences. Stress would then be correlated with blood pressure measurements collected from these same people. In an experimental study, in contrast, the experimenter might create stress in the laboratory; for example, half of the participants might be asked to give a speech to an audience about the aspect of their personal appearance that they find least appealing, and the other half might be assigned to a nonstressful condition (see **Figure 4.1**). The key difference between correlational and experimental designs is whether or not a variable is manipulated. Psychopathologists will rely on correlational methods when there are ethical reasons not to manipulate a variable; for example, no researcher would try to manipulate genes, trauma, severe stressors, or neurobiological deficits in humans.

Numerous examples of **correlation** can be drawn from mental health research. For example, depression tends to correlate with anxiety; people who feel depressed tend to report feeling anxious. Comparisons of people with and without a diagnosis can be correlational as well. See **Table 4.2** for a description of how such data might be coded. For example, two diagnostic groups may be compared to see how much stress was experienced before the onset of their disorders. In other words, questions are asked about relationships between a given diagnosis and some other variable; for example, "Is schizophrenia related to social class?" or "Are anxiety disorders related to neurotransmitter function?"

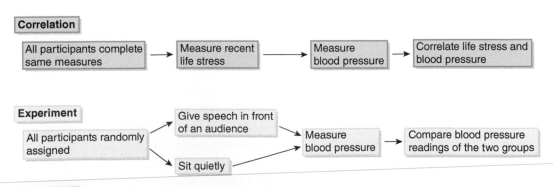

FIGURE 4.1 Correlational versus experimental studies.

TABLE 4.2   Data for a Correlational Study with Diagnosis

Participant	Diagnosis	Stress Score
1	1	65
2	1	72
3	0	40
4	1	86
5	0	72
6	0	21
7	1	65
8	0	40
9	1	37
10	0	28

Note: Diagnosis of an anxiety disorder is coded as 1 if present and 0 if not present. Recent life stress is assessed on a 0–100 scale. Higher scores indicate greater recent stress. This illustration includes a smaller sample of cases than would be used in an actual research study. Notice that diagnosis is correlated with recent life stress. Patients with an anxiety disorder tend to have higher stress scores than people without an anxiety disorder. In this example, the correlation between stress and anxiety scores is +.60.

In the next sections, we discuss how to measure the relationship (correlation) between two variables, how to test whether the relationship is statistically and clinically significant, and some issues involved in determining whether variables are causally related. Then we discuss two specific types of research that tend to use correlational designs: epidemiology and behavior genetics.

Measuring Correlation The first step in determining a correlation is to obtain pairs of observations of the two variables in question. One example would be the height and weight of each participant. Another example would be the intelligence of mothers and daughters. Once such pairs of measurements are obtained, the strength of the relationship between the paired observations can be computed to determine the **correlation coefficient**, denoted by the symbol r. This statistic may take any value between −1.00 and +1.00, and it measures both the magnitude and the direction of a relationship. The higher the absolute value of r, the stronger the relationship between the two variables. That is, an r of either +1.00 or −1.00 indicates the strongest possible, or perfect, relationship, whereas an r of .00 indicates that the variables are unrelated. If the sign of r is positive, the two variables are said to be positively related; in other words, as the values for variable X increase, those for variable Y also tend to increase. **Table 4.3** shows data for a correlation of +.88 between height and weight, indicating a very strong positive relationship; as height increases, so does weight. Conversely, when the sign of r is negative, variables are said to be negatively related; as scores on one variable increase, those for the other tend to decrease. For example, the number of hours spent watching television is negatively correlated with grade point average.

One way to think about the strength of a correlation is to plot the two variables. In **Figure 4.2**, each point represents the scores for a given person on variable X and variable Y. In a perfect correlation, all the points fall on a straight line; if we know the value of only one of the variables for a person, we can know the value of the other variable. Similarly, when the correlation is relatively large, there is only a small degree of scatter about the line of perfect correlation. The values tend to scatter increasingly far from the line as the correlations become lower. When the correlation reaches .00, knowledge of a person's score on one variable tells us nothing about his or her score on the other.

TABLE 4.3 **Data for Determining a Correlation**

	Height in Inches	Weight in Pounds
John	70	170
Asher	70	140
Eve	64	112
Gail	63	105
Jerry	70	177
Gayla	62	100
Steve	68	145
Margy	65	128
Gert	66	143
Sean	70	140
Kathleen	64	116

Note: For this data set, the *r* of height and weight = +.88.

Statistical and Clinical Significance Thus far we have established that the magnitude of a correlation coefficient tells us the strength of a relationship between two variables. But scientists use **statistical significance** for a more rigorous test of the importance of a relationship. (Although we focus on correlation coefficients here, significance is

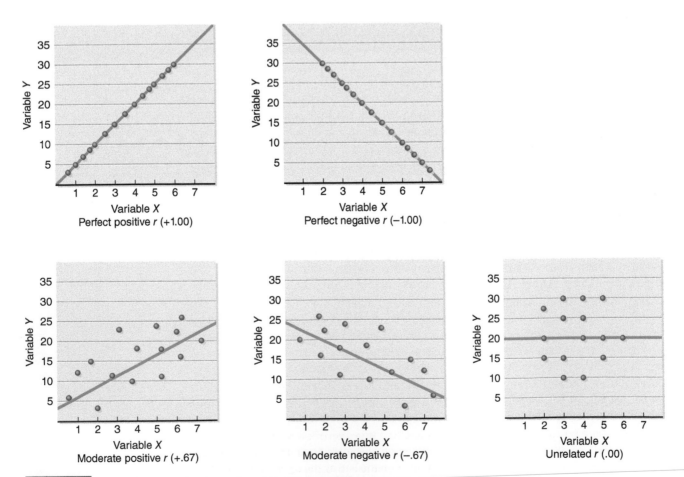

FIGURE 4.2 Scatter diagrams showing various degrees of correlation.

assessed with statistics other than correlation coefficients as well.) A statistically significant correlation (or other statistic) is large enough that it is unlikely to have occurred by chance. A nonsignificant correlation may have occurred by chance, so it does not provide evidence for an important relationship. What do scientists mean by chance? Imagine that a researcher conducted the same study again and again. You would not expect to see exactly the same results every time. For example, there might be differences in who signed up for the study that would influence the pattern of findings. This random variation, or chance, must be considered in evaluating the findings of any study. When a correlation is not statistically significant, it is highly likely that no significant relationship would be observed if the study is repeated.

A statistical finding is usually considered significant if the probability that it is a chance finding is 5 or less in 100. This level of significance is called the alpha level, commonly written as $p < .05$ (the p stands for probability). We will discuss the p value later in this chapter as we consider replicability of studies. In general, as the absolute size of the correlation coefficient increases, the result is more likely to be statistically significant. For example, a correlation of .80 (or −.80) is more likely to be significant than a correlation of .40.

Statistical significance is influenced not only by the size of the relationship between variables but also by the number of participants in a study. The fewer people studied, the larger the correlation must be to reach statistical significance. For example, a correlation of $r = .30$ is statistically significant when the number of observations is large—say, 300—but is not significant if only 20 observations were made. Thus, if the alcohol consumption of 20 men was studied and the correlation between depression and drinking was found to be .30, the correlation would not be statistically significant. The same correlation, however, would be significant if 300 men were studied.

Beyond statistical significance, it is important to consider **clinical significance**. Clinical significance is defined by whether a relationship between variables is large enough to matter. In a survey as large as the U.S. Census, almost every correlation you could conceive of would be statistically significant. Because of this issue, researchers also attend to whether a correlation is large enough to be clinically significant. For example, one might want to see that a risk factor has a moderately strong relationship with the severity of symptoms. Clinical significance is also considered with statistics other than correlations. For a treatment effect to be considered clinically significant, a researcher might want to see that at the end of active treatment, symptoms were decreased by 50 percent or that patients appeared comparable to those without disorder. In other words, researchers should evaluate not only whether an effect is statistically significant but also whether the effect is large enough to be meaningful in predicting or treating a psychological disorder (Jacobson, Roberts, et al., 1999).

Problems of Causality Even though correlational designs are commonly used, they have a critical drawback: they do not allow determination of cause–effect relationships. A large correlation between two variables tells us only that they are related to each other, but we do not know if either variable is the cause of the other. For example, there is a moderate correlation between the diagnosis of schizophrenia and social class; lower-class people are diagnosed with schizophrenia more often than middle- and upper-class people are. One possible explanation is that the stress of living in poverty could cause an increase in the prevalence of schizophrenia (Kwok, 2014). But a second hypothesis has been supported. It may be that the disorganized behavior patterns of persons with schizophrenia cause them to perform poorly in their occupational endeavors and thus to become impoverished (Dohrenwend & Dohrenwend, 1974).

The **directionality problem** is present in most correlational research designs—hence the often-cited dictum "correlation does not imply causation." One way of overcoming the directionality problem is based on the idea that causes must precede effects. In a **longitudinal design**, the researcher tests whether causes are present before a disorder has developed. This is in contrast to a **cross-sectional design**, in which the researcher measures the causes and effects at the same point in time. A longitudinal design to study the development of schizophrenia, for example, would involve selecting a large sample of babies, measuring risk variables repeatedly throughout development, and following the sample for 40 years to determine who develops schizophrenia. But such a method would be prohibitively expensive, for only about 1 person in 100 eventually develops schizophrenia. The yield of data from such a longitudinal study would be small indeed.

The **high-risk method** overcomes this problem; with this approach, researchers study only people with above-average risk of developing schizophrenia. For example, many research programs involve studying people who have a parent diagnosed with schizophrenia (having a parent with schizophrenia increases a person's risk for developing schizophrenia). The high-risk method is used to study several disorders, and we will examine these findings in subsequent chapters.

Even if a high-risk study identifies a variable that precedes schizophrenia, a researcher still faces the **third-variable problem:** a third factor may have produced the correlation. Such factors are labeled as *confounds*. Psychopathology research offers numerous examples of third variables. Researchers often report biochemical differences between people with and without schizophrenia. These differences could reflect the influence of medications used for schizophrenia or even dietary differences between groups; the differences might not reveal anything about the nature of schizophrenia. Are there ways to resolve the third-variable problem? Although some strategies can help address some of the confounds, the solutions are only partially satisfactory. Take the example of diet as a potential confound in biochemical differences in schizophrenia. Researchers can try to control for diet in statistical analyses, but they may not measure the most important aspects of diet. It is not feasible to measure every possible confound. Because of the third-variable problem, causal claims cannot be made from correlational data.

© sturti/iStockphoto

In some epidemiological research, interviewers go door to door to conduct interviews.

One Example of Correlational Research: Epidemiological Research

Epidemiology is the study of the distribution of disorders in a population. That is, data are gathered about the rates of disorder and the correlates of disorder in a large sample. Epidemiological research focuses on three features of a disorder:

1. **Prevalence.** The proportion of people with the disorder either currently or during their lifetime
2. **Incidence.** The proportion of people who develop *new* cases of the disorder in some period, usually a year
3. **Correlates.** Variables that are correlated with the presence of the disorder.

Epidemiological studies are usually correlational studies because they examine how variables relate to each other without manipulating any of the variables.

Epidemiological studies are designed to be *representative* of the population being studied—researchers test a group of people who match the population on key characteristics, like gender, economic status, and ethnicity. Unfortunately, much of mental health research does not follow these principles but rather draws on samples that are not representative. For example, many studies use undergraduate samples. Undergraduates, though, are likely to be wealthier and more educated than the general population. If we only studied undergraduates with anxiety disorders, we could end up concluding that people with anxiety disorders are above average in intelligence. Other studies use samples drawn from treatment centers, but people who seek treatment tend to be those with the more severe forms of disorders. For example, estimates of suicide rates for a given disorder are much higher when measured in hospitalized samples as compared with rates in representative community samples. These types of bias can skew our perceptions of factors related to psychological disorders. Epidemiological studies, then, are needed to carefully identify the correlates of and outcomes for disorders.

The National Comorbidity Survey–Replication (NCS-R) is an example of one large-scale national survey that used structured interviews to collect information on the prevalence of several diagnoses (Kessler, Berglund, et al., 2005). In the World Mental Health Survey, interviews that were parallel with those used in the NCS-R were conducted in dozens of countries to allow comparison of mental health prevalence cross-nationally (Kessler, Angermeyer, et al., 2007). **Table 4.4** shows some of the survey data that was gathered in the United States. The table presents lifetime prevalence rates—the proportion of people who experienced a disorder during their lifetime. From the table, we can see that major depression, alcoholism, and anxiety disorders are very common—so common, in fact, that about one out of every two people (46.4 percent) in the United States describe meeting criteria for a psychological disorder at some point during their lives.

Although the idea that almost half of people will meet diagnostic criteria may seem high, this number may even be an underestimate. In one study, researchers interviewed participants about psychological symptoms during their lifetime four different times—at ages 18, 21, 26, and 32. At any one of those four interviews, the rates of depressive and anxiety disorders appeared similar to the levels reported in the NCS-R study and observed in multiple other epidemiological studies. But about half of people who endorsed a given disorder in any one interview did not do so in other interviews (Moffitt, Caspi, et al., 2010). Because of this inaccuracy in any one interview, the researchers tallied how many people reported a psychological disorder in at least one interview. Using these tallies, the researchers estimated that 60 percent or more of people will meet criteria for a psychological disorder during their lifetime, findings that have been replicated in several longitudinal epidemiological studies (Schaefer, Caspi, et al., 2017).

Knowing that psychological disorders will strike so many people should help reduce stigma. People who experience the disorders may take comfort in knowing that so many other people struggle with similar issues.

Knowledge about the correlates of disorder may provide clues to the causes of disorders. For example, depression is about twice as common in women as in men. In Chapter 5, we will review theories about this gender difference. Trauma, poverty, and income inequality also are tied to many different psychological disorders. The results of epidemiological research may inform us about correlates of disorder (like gender, trauma, poverty, and income inequality) that can be more thoroughly investigated using other research methods.

Epidemiological research has shown that mood disorders, anxiety disorders, and substance abuse are extremely common.

Image Source/Getty Images, Inc.

TABLE 4.4   **Lifetime Prevalence Rates of Selected Diagnoses in the United States**

Disorder	Male	Female	Total
Major depressive disorder	13.2	20.2	16.6
Bipolar I or II disorder	na	na	3.9
Dysthymia	1.8	3.1	2.5
Panic disorder	3.1	6.2	4.7
Specific phobia	11.1	13.0	12.1
Social phobia	8.9	15.8	12.5
Generalized anxiety disorder	na	na	5.7
Alcohol abuse	19.6	7.5	13.2
Drug abuse	11.6	4.8	7.9

Source: From data collected in the National Comorbidity Survey–Replication Study (Kessler et al., 2005).

Another Example of Correlational Research: Behavior Genetics   Behavior genetics estimates genetic predisposition for disorder by considering whether relatives demonstrate similarity (correlations) in their patterns of disorder. This contrasts with the focus of molecular genetics (see Chapter 2) on identifying specific genes that contribute to the presence of a disorder. Both behavior genetics and molecular genetics rely on correlational techniques in the study of psychopathology in humans. Here we will focus on three common methods used in behavior genetics to examine the genetic contribution to psychopathology—comparison of members of a family, comparison of pairs of twins, and investigation of adoptees.

The **family method** can be used to study a genetic predisposition among members of a family because the average number of genes shared by two blood relatives is known. Children receive a random sample of half their genes from one parent and half from the other, so on average siblings as well as parents and their children share 50 percent of their genes. People who share 50 percent of their genes with a given person are called first-degree relatives of that person. Relatives who are not as closely related share fewer genes. For example, nephews and nieces share 25 percent of the genetic makeup of an uncle and are called second-degree relatives. If a predisposition for a psychological disorder can be inherited, a study of the family should reveal a relationship between the proportion of shared genes and the **concordance** of the disorder in relatives. When relatives are matched on presence or absence of a disorder, they are said to be concordant.

The starting point in such investigations is the collection of a sample of persons with the diagnosis in question. These people are referred to as **index cases** or **probands**. Then relatives are studied to determine the frequency with which the same diagnosis might be applied to them. If a genetic predisposition to the disorder being studied is present, first-degree relatives of the index cases should have the disorder at a rate higher than that found in the general population. This is the case with schizophrenia: about 10 percent of the first-degree relatives of index cases with schizophrenia can be diagnosed as having this disorder, compared with about 1 percent of the general population.

Although the methodology of family studies is clear, the data they yield are not always easy to interpret. For example, children of parents with agoraphobia—people suffering from a fear of being in places from which it would be hard to escape if they were to become highly anxious—are themselves more likely than average to have agoraphobia. Does this mean that a predisposition for this anxiety disorder is genetically transmitted? Not necessarily. The greater number of family members with agoraphobia could reflect the child-rearing practices and modeling of the agoraphobic parents. In other words, family studies show that agoraphobia runs in families but not necessarily that a genetic predisposition is involved.

In the **twin method**, both **monozygotic (MZ) twins** and **dizygotic (DZ) twins** are compared. MZ, or identical, twins develop from a single fertilized egg and are genetically the same. DZ, or fraternal, pairs develop from separate eggs and are on average 50 percent alike genetically, no more alike than are any two siblings. MZ twins are always of the same sex, but DZ twins can be either the same sex or opposite in sex. Twin studies begin with diagnosed cases and then assess the presence of the disorder in the other twin. To the extent that a predisposition for a psychological disorder can be inherited, concordance for the disorder should be greater in genetically identical MZ pairs than in DZ pairs. When the MZ concordance rate is higher than the DZ rate, the characteristic being studied is said to be heritable. As described in Chapter 2, heritability estimates range from 0 (no genetic contribution) to 1 (100 percent genetic contribution). We will see in later chapters that the concordance for most forms of psychopathology is higher in MZ twins than in DZ twins.

The **adoptees method** studies children who were adopted and reared completely apart from their biological parents. Though infrequent, findings from this method are more clear-cut because the child is not raised by the parent with a disorder. If a high frequency of agoraphobia was found in children reared apart from their parents who also had agoraphobia, we would have convincing support for the heritability of the disorder. In another adoptee method called **cross-fostering**, researchers assess children who are adopted and reared completely apart from their biological parents. In this case, however, the adoptive parent has a particular disorder, not the biological parent. The adoptee method is also used to examine gene–environment interactions. For example, one study found that adoptees who had a biological parent with antisocial personality disorder (APD) and were raised in an unhealthy adoptive family (e.g., parental conflict, abuse, alcohol/drugs in the adoptive family) were more likely to develop APD than two other groups of adoptees: (1) adoptees who had a biological parent with APD but were raised in a healthy family and (2) adoptees who had no biological parent with APD but were raised in an unhealthy adoptive family (Cadoret, Yates, et al., 1995). Thus, genes (APD in a biological parent) and environment (unhealthy adoptive family) worked together to increase the risk for developing antisocial personality disorder.

The Experiment

The **experiment** is the most powerful tool for determining causal relationships. It involves the **random assignment** of participants to conditions, the manipulation of an **independent variable**, and the measurement of a **dependent variable**. We will begin with a brief overview of the basic features of an experiment.

As an introduction to the basics of experimental research, let's consider a study designed to assess whether a specific form of cognitive behavioral therapy called dialectical behavior therapy has efficacy in reducing suicidal behavior (Linehan, Comtois, et al., 2006). In this study, researchers recruited women who had engaged in recent suicidal behavior and randomly assigned them to receive either one year of dialectical behavior therapy or treatment as usual by experts in the community. The researchers interviewed patients about their suicidal behavior at baseline before the treatment began, and then every 4 months for 2 years. At baseline, the patients in the two groups did not differ in the number or severity of their previous suicide attempts. During the two years of the study, patients assigned to receive DBT were less likely to make a suicide attempt (23.1 percent) than were those in the treatment as usual condition (46 percent).

Basic Features of Experimental Design   The treatment study just discussed illustrates many of the basic features of an experiment:

1. The investigator manipulates an independent variable. In this study, the independent variable was the treatment condition.

2. Participants are allocated to the two conditions (dialectical behavior therapy versus treatment as usual) by random assignment. To randomly assign participants in a two-group experiment, for example, the researchers could toss a coin for each participant. If the coin turned up heads, the participant would be assigned to one group; if tails, to the other group.

3. The researcher measures a dependent variable that is expected to vary with conditions of the independent variable. The dependent variable in this study was the presence or absence of a suicide attempt.

4. Differences between conditions on the dependent variable are called the **experimental effect**. In this example, the experimental effect is the difference in the probability of suicide attempts for those assigned to receive dialectical behavior therapy compared to those assigned to treatment as usual.

Internal Validity   **Internal validity** refers to the extent to which the experimental effect can be attributed to the independent variable. For a study to have internal validity, the researchers must include at least one **control group**. The control group does not receive the experimental treatment and is needed to claim that the effects of an experiment are due to the independent variable. The data from a control group provide a standard against which the effects of an independent variable can be assessed. In the study described, the control group—treatment as usual—allows for a test of whether dialectical behavior therapy was more efficacious than standard care in the community. We will describe control groups in more detail as we discuss treatment outcome studies.

The inclusion of a control group does not ensure internal validity, however. Random assignment is also important. **Random assignment** helps ensure that groups are similar on variables other than the independent variable. Consider a treatment study in which participants can enroll in their choice of two experimental conditions—psychotherapy or medication. In this study, the researcher cannot claim that group differences are the result of treatment because a competing hypothesis cannot be disproven: Patients in the two conditions might have differed in baseline characteristics such as their willingness to discuss difficult emotional issues or their beliefs about medications. This study design is poor because the researchers did not use random assignment. Without true random assignment, potential confounds make results hard to interpret so that internal validity can be limited.

External Validity

External validity is defined as the extent to which results can be generalized beyond the study. If investigators find that a particular treatment helps a particular group of patients, they will want to conclude that this treatment will be effective for other similar patients, at other times, and in other places. For example, Linehan and her colleagues would hope that their findings would generalize to men.

Determining the external validity of the results of an experiment is extremely difficult. For example, participants in studies often behave in certain ways because they are being observed, and thus results that are produced in the laboratory may not be reproduced in the natural environment. In psychological research today, perhaps the largest threat to external validity comes from the narrow range of participants in research—external validity may be threatened by including only a select group of persons in a study, such as college students or Caucasian middle-class Americans. Indeed, in a review of articles published in six journals of the American Psychological Association between 2003 and 2007, 68 percent of participants in studies were from the United States and 96 percent were from Western industrialized countries (Arnett, 2008). Findings from a specific group, such as college students in the United States, may not generalize to people from other contexts (Hanel & Vione, 2016). We will discuss these concerns further as we consider treatment outcome research below. Often researchers must perform similar studies in new settings or with a different sample to test whether findings generalize.

Single-Case Experiments

We have been discussing experimental research with groups of participants, but experiments are not always conducted on groups. In **single-case experimental design**, the experimenter studies how one person responds to manipulations of the independent variable (Kazdin, 2011). Unlike the traditional case studies described earlier, single-case experimental designs can have high internal validity. For an example of a single-case experiment with high internal validity, see **Focus on Discovery 4.1**.

Focus on Discovery 4.1

An Example of a Single-Case Experiment

Chorpita, Vitali, and Barlow (1997) provide an example of how single-case experimental studies can provide well-controlled data. They describe their treatment of a 13-year-old girl with a phobia (intense fear) of choking, such that she was no longer able to eat solid foods. At times, her fear was so intense that she would experience a fast heart rate, chest pain, and dizziness. She reported that the most frightening foods were hard foods, such as raw vegetables.

A behavioral treatment was designed based on exposure, a common strategy for treating anxiety. During the first 2 weeks, baseline assessments were taken of the amount of different foods eaten, along with her level of discomfort in eating those foods. Discomfort ratings were made on the Subjective Units of Distress Scale (SUDS), ranging from 0 to 9. **Figure 4.3** shows her SUDS ratings and

eating behavior over time for each food group. During week 3, she was asked to begin eating foods she described as mildly threatening—crackers and cookies—in three 4-minute blocks each day. The authors hoped that exposure to feared foods would reduce her anxiety. Despite this intervention, the patient's SUDS ratings and food consumption did not improve. When the therapist talked with the client and her parents, he discovered that the client was eating only the absolute minimum of foods, such that she was not getting enough exposure to the feared stimulus. To increase her exposure to foods, he added reinforcement to the program—he instructed her parents to give her ice cream at the end of any day in which the patient had consumed at least three servings of the target food. Within a week, she reported being able to consume crackers and cereals without distress. Gradually, she was asked to begin eating more frightening foods. One week she was asked to begin consuming soft vegetables, pasta, and cheese, followed the next week by meat, and the next week by raw vegetables, salad, and hard fruit. As shown by the graphs, as exposure to each new food group was introduced, the client experienced a reduction in SUDS ratings within the next week; these effects do not appear to have been due simply to time or maturation, as anxiety was reduced only after the client was first exposed to the new food group. The repeated decrements in anxiety are hard to explain using any variable other than treatment. Gains were maintained through a 19-month follow-up.

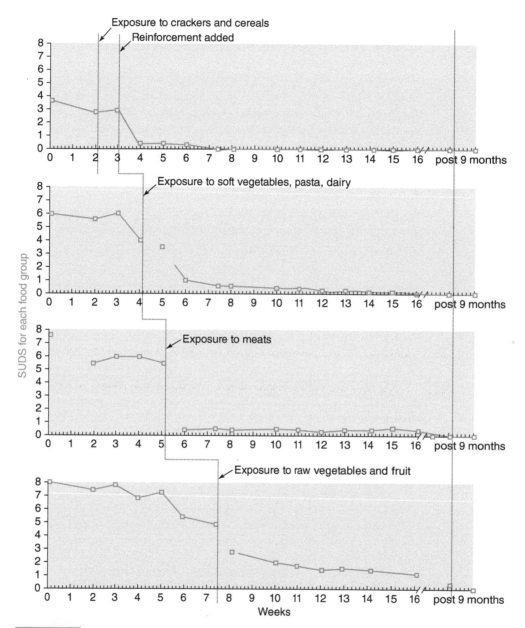

FIGURE 4.3 Effects of exposure treatment and reinforcement for food phobia in a single-case design. Note the rapid shifts in SUDS ratings as exposure for each new food group is introduced. Adapted from Chorpita et al., "Behavioral treatment of choking phobia in an adolescent: An experimental analysis," *Journal of Behavioral Therapy and Experimental Psychiatry, 38,* 307–315, copyright ©, 1997.

In one form of single-case design, referred to as a **reversal design** or **ABAB design**, the participant's behavior is carefully measured in a specific sequence:

1. An initial time period, the baseline (A)

2. A period when a treatment is introduced (B)

3. A reinstatement of the conditions of the baseline period (A)

4. A reintroduction of the treatment (B)

If behavior in the experimental period is different from that in the baseline period, reverses when the treatment is removed, and resumes when the treatment is again introduced, there is little doubt that the manipulation, rather than chance or uncontrolled factors, has produced the change. Hence, "A" time periods serve as control comparisons for the treatment.

The reversal technique cannot always be employed, however, because the initial state of a participant may not be recoverable. Remember that most treatments aim to produce enduring change, so just removing an intervention may not return a person to the pretreatment state. This reversal technique, then, is most applicable when researchers believe that the effects of their manipulation are temporary.

The biggest drawback of single-case designs is the potential lack of external validity. The fact that a treatment works for a single person does not necessarily imply that it will be effective for others. Findings may relate to a unique aspect of that one person. Some researchers use single-case experimental research to decide whether research with larger groups is warranted. Other researchers conduct a series of single-case experiments to see if findings generalize. In doing so, it is important to include participants who differ. With replication across diverse participants, single-case designs can provide a strong test of hypotheses. Indeed, single-case experimental research can be used as evidence that a treatment is efficacious. The APA (Task Force on Promotion and Dissemination of Psychological Procedures, 1995) considers a treatment to have gained empirical support if it has shown success compared to a well-designed control condition in at least nine single-case experiments.

Quick Summary

Case studies can provide detailed information about a novel phenomenon or treatment technique, and they can disprove a hypothesis. They do not provide good evidence for cause and effect, and they can be biased.

Correlational studies examine the strength of relation between variables, and they do not involve any variable being manipulated. Correlation does not imply causation. Longitudinal studies can help determine whether one variable precedes the other, but third variables (called confounds) could still explain any observed relationship.

Correlation coefficients provide an estimate of the strength and direction of the relationship. A correlation coefficient of –1 or +1 indicates a perfect relationship, and a correlation coefficient of 0 indicates that there is no systematic relationship between two variables.

A statistical finding is usually considered significant if the probability that it is a chance finding is 5 or less in 100. Statistical significance is influenced by the size of the sample.

A clinically significant finding is one in which the relationship is large enough to matter.

Epidemiology and behavior genetics are correlational approaches that are commonly used in psychopathology research.

Epidemiology is the science of obtaining and testing representative samples drawn from the community. Epidemiology is used to estimate the prevalence and incidence of disorders, and the correlates of those disorders.

Behavior genetics involves the study of concordance among first degree relatives, MZ versus DZ twins, and adoptees as a way to estimate the heritability of disorders, and interactions between genetic and environmental contributions to disorders.

The experimental method entails manipulating an independent variable and measuring the effect on a dependent variable. Generally, participants are randomly assigned to one of at least two groups: an experimental group, which experiences the active condition of the independent variable, and a control group, which does not. The researcher tests to see if the independent variable had an effect (the experimental effect) by looking for differences between the experimental and control groups on the dependent variable.

Internal validity refers to whether an effect can be confidently attributed to the independent variable. External validity refers to whether experimental effects can be generalized to situations and people outside this specific study. Experimental designs can provide internal validity, but external validity is sometimes of concern. Correlational studies can provide solid external validity but poorer internal validity.

In single-case experimental designs, the researcher examines the effects of manipulating an independent variable in a single person. These designs can have high internal validity, particularly if reversal designs are employed. External validity can be limited for single-case experimental designs.

Check Your Knowledge 4.2

Answer the questions.

1. Which of the following are good uses of case studies (circle all that apply)?
    a. to illustrate a rare disorder or treatment
    b. to show that a theory does not fit for everyone
    c. to prove a model
    d. to show cause and effect

2. Correlational studies involve:
    a. manipulating the independent variable
    b. manipulating the dependent variable
    c. manipulating the independent and dependent variables
    d. none of the above

3. What is the most central problem that is unique to correlational studies, regardless of how carefully a researcher designs a study?
    a. Findings are qualitative rather than statistical.
    b. It is impossible to know which variable changes first.
    c. Third variables may explain a relationship observed.
    d. Findings may not generalize.

4. Incidence refers to:
    a. the number of people who will develop a disorder during their lifetime
    b. the number of people who report a disorder at the time of an interview
    c. the number of people who develop a disorder during a given time period
    d. none of the above

5. In behavior genetics studies, researchers can rule out the influence of parenting variables most carefully if they conduct studies using the:
    a. correlational method
    b. family method
    c. twin method
    d. adoptees method

One Example of Experimental Research: Treatment Outcome Research

Treatment outcome research is designed to address a simple question: does treatment work? The clear answer is yes. Here we will focus on the issues in testing psychotherapy, but many of these same issues must be considered in evaluating medication treatments.

Treatment outcome studies are the most common form of experiment in the psychopathology field. Hundreds of studies have examined whether people who receive psychotherapy fare better than those who do not. In meta-analyses of more than 300 studies, researchers have found that there is a moderately positive effect of treatment. About 75 percent of people who enter treatment achieve at least some improvement (Lambert & Ogles, 2004). As shown in **Figure 4.4**, these effects appear to be more powerful than the passage of time or support from friends and family. On the other hand, it is also clear from this figure that therapy does not always work. That is, about 25 percent of people do not improve in therapy.

What standards must treatment outcome research meet to be seen as valid? Several different working groups have come up with slightly different answers to this question. At

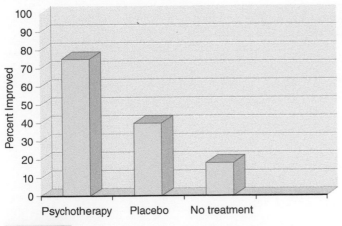

FIGURE 4.4 Summary of the percent of people who achieve improvement across outcome for psychotherapy, placebo, and no treatment across studies. Drawn from Lambert (2004).

a minimum, most researchers agree that a treatment study should include the following criteria:

- A clear definition of the sample being studied, such as a description of diagnoses or problem behavior to be addressed
- A clear description of the treatment being offered, as in a treatment manual (described below)
- Inclusion of a control or comparison treatment condition
- An experimental design that involves random assignment of clients to treatment or comparison conditions
- Reliable and valid outcome measures (see Chapter 3 for definitions of reliability and validity)
- A large enough sample size

Studies in which clients are randomly assigned to receive active treatment or a comparison (either no treatment, a placebo, or another treatment) are called **randomized controlled trials (RCTs)**. In this type of experiment, the independent variable is the treatment and the dependent variable is the clients' outcome.

The American Psychological Association (APA) publishes a report on the therapies that have received empirical support using standards like these. The APA standards also require that two independent research teams must find positive effects for a treatment before it is considered to be empirically supported (Task Force on Promotion and Dissemination of Psychological Procedures, 1995). The goal is to help clinicians, consumers, managed care agencies, and insurance companies draw more easily on the rapidly growing literature about **empirically supported treatments (ESTs)**. Some of the therapies the APA has found to have empirical support are shown in **Table 4.5**. We will describe empirically supported treatments throughout this book when we discuss specific psychological disorders.

Some have hotly debated aspects of the APA report on ESTs. For example, a treatment's failure to appear on the APA list of ESTs (Table 4.5) could simply reflect a lack of careful studies. As you can see, most of the treatments listed are cognitive behavioral. Research on other treatments had not met the APA's research standards at the time the report was published (a more recent list of ESTs is available at https://www.div12.org/psychological-treatments/disorders/). In 2015, the APA announced plans to update their reports on therapies, so as to provide guidelines for specific conditions. The new guidelines will consider not just the benefits of a given treatment, but also any evidence that treatments cause harm (see **Focus on Discovery 4.2**) (American Psychological Association, 2015).

We now turn to some of the major decisions researchers face as they design treatment outcome studies. These issues include defining the treatment procedures, choosing the best possible control group, and recruiting an appropriate sample of patients. Once a treatment has been shown to work well in a tightly controlled treatment outcome study, effectiveness research is designed to test how well treatments fare in the real world. As evidence accrues that a treatment works, dissemination encourages therapists in the community to adopt the treatment.

Defining the Treatment Condition

There are different ways to define the goals of psychological treatments. For several decades, most researchers have focused on designing treatments to address a given diagnosis, such as major depressive disorder. More recently, the National Institute of Mental Health (NIMH) has prioritized funding treatment studies designed to target a mechanism involved in psychopathology (e.g., lack of motivation) (Insel, 2015). This NIMH approach differs in that some mechanisms may be involved across a broad range of diagnoses.

A treatment manual provides specific procedures for a therapist to use in working with a client. They are standard in treatment outcome studies.

TABLE 4.5 **Examples of Empirically Supported Treatments for Adult Disorders**

Generalized anxiety disorder	*Depression*
Cognitive therapy	Cognitive therapy
Applied relaxation	Behavior therapy
Social phobia	Interpersonal psychotherapy
Exposure	Problem-solving therapy
Cognitive behavioral group therapy	Self-management/self-control therapy
Systematic desensitization	*Schizophrenia*
Simple phobia	Family psychoeducation
Exposure	Cognitive behavior therapy
Guided mastery	Social learning/token economy programs
Systematic desensitization	Cognitive remediation
Obsessive-compulsive disorder	Social skills training
Exposure and response prevention	Behavioral family therapy
Cognitive therapy	Supported employment programs
Agoraphobia	Assertive community treatment
Exposure	*Alcohol abuse and dependence*
Cognitive behavior therapy	Community reinforcement approach
Panic	*Relationship distress*
Cognitive behavior therapy	Behavioral couples therapy
Posttraumatic stress disorder	Emotion-focused therapy
Prolonged exposure	Insight-oriented couples therapy
Cognitive processing therapy	*Sexual dysfunctions*
Bulimia	Partner-assisted sexual skills training
Cognitive behavior therapy	*Borderline personality disorder*
Interpersonal psychotherapy	Dialectical behavior therapy
Anorexia nervosa	
Family-based treatment	

Drawn from Task Force on Promotion and Dissemination of Psychological Procedures (1995).

Regardless of whether a treatment aims to address a diagnostic condition or a mechanism, treatment manuals are widely recommended for psychotherapy research (e.g., Nathan & Gorman, 2015) and for training therapists (Crits-Christoph, Chambless, et al. 1995). Treatment manuals are books that provide details on how to conduct a particular psychological treatment, including specific procedures for the therapist to follow at each stage of treatment. With manuals, someone reading a psychotherapy study can have an idea of what happened in therapy sessions.

Focus on Discovery 4.2

Can Therapy Be Harmful?

Despite the substantial evidence that therapies, on average, tend to be helpful, this does not mean that they help everyone. Indeed, a small number of people may be in worse shape after therapy. Estimating how often therapy is harmful is not easy. Up to 10 percent of people are more symptomatic after therapy than they were before therapy began (Lilienfeld, 2007). Does this mean that therapy harmed them? Maybe not. Without a control group, it is hard to know whether symptoms would have worsened even without therapy. Unfortunately, few researchers report the percentage of people who worsened in the different branches of treatment trials.

Nonetheless, it is important to be aware that several treatments have been found to be harmful to some people. Table 4.6 lists treatments identified as resulting in worsened outcomes in randomized controlled trials or in multiple case reports (Lilienfeld, 2007). We should note that harmful effects are not exclusive to therapy; the U.S. Food and Drug Administration has issued warnings that antidepressants and antiseizure medications can increase the risk of suicidality and that antipsychotic medications can increase the risk of death among the elderly.

TABLE 4.6   Examples of Treatments Found to Be Harmful in Multiple Studies or Case Reports

Treatment	Negative Effects
Critical incident stress debriefing	Heightened risk for posttraumatic symptoms
Scared Straight	Exacerbation of conduct problems
Facilitated communication	False accusations of child abuse against family members
Attachment therapies (e.g., rebirthing)	Death and serious injury to children
Recovered-memory techniques	Production of false memories of trauma
Dissociative identity disorder-oriented therapy	Induction of "alter" personalities
Grief counseling for people with normal bereavement reactions	Increases in depressive symptoms
Expressive-experiential therapies	Exacerbation of painful emotions
Drug Abuse Resistance Education (DARE) programs	Increased intake of alcohol and cigarettes

Drawn from Lilienfeld (2007).

Some have expressed concern that manuals might constrain therapists to such an extent that they might not be sufficiently sensitive to a client's unique concerns (Haaga & Stiles, 2000). A good manual provides enough freedom so that therapists will not feel constrained—for example, describing ways to use exposure treatment to reduce conditioned fears in anxiety disorders but also giving a menu of options of how to conduct exposure (Kendall & Beidas, 2007).

Defining Control Groups

To illustrate the importance of a control group, consider a study of a particular therapy for anxiety. Let us assume that persons with anxiety disorders receive therapy and that, from the start to the end of a 16-week program, their anxiety symptoms diminish. With no control group against which to compare the improvement, we cannot argue that changes are due to the treatment. The improvement in anxiety could have been due to factors other than the treatment, such as the passage of time or support from friends. Without a control group, any changes during treatment are difficult to interpret.

Researchers use many different types of control groups in treatment outcome research. A no-treatment control group allows researchers to test whether the mere passage of time helps as much as treatment does. A treatment as usual control group allows for a comparison against standard treatment in the community. A stricter test compares the treatment group to a **placebo** control group. In psychotherapy research, the placebo might be a therapy that consists of support and encouragement (the "attention" component) but not the active ingredient of therapy under study (e.g., exposure to a feared stimulus in a behavioral treatment of a phobia). In medication studies, a placebo might be a sugar pill that is described to the patient as a proven treatment. A placebo condition allows researchers to control for expectations of symptom relief. The strictest type of design includes an active-treatment control group in which researchers compare the new treatment against a well-tested treatment. This type of design allows researchers to make comparative statements about two treatments.

Some have argued that placebos and no-treatment controls are unethical, in that active treatment is being

Troubled people may talk about their problems with friends or seek professional therapy. Treatment is typically sought by those for whom the advice and support of family or friends have not provided relief.

Esbin-Anderson/The Image Works

withheld from patients who might suffer as a consequence (Wolitzky, 1995). An active-treatment control group may not raise ethical concerns, but it can be hard to show a difference between different types of active treatments. Choosing the best control group, then, is a difficult decision!

When including a placebo condition in a medication trial, researchers use a **double-blind procedure**. That is, the psychiatrist and the patient are not told whether the patient receives active medication or a placebo, so as to reduce bias in evaluating outcomes. A double-blind procedure can be hard to implement. Treatment providers and patients may guess who is getting the active treatment because medications are much more likely to produce side effects than are placebos (Salamone, 2000). Researchers often measure whether participants guessed that they were in the placebo condition, as well as how much they expected their treatment to help them.

The **placebo effect** refers to a physical or psychological improvement that is due to a patient's expectations of help rather than to any active ingredient in a treatment. The placebo effect is often significant and even long-lasting. For example, a meta-analysis of 75 research studies revealed that 29.7 percent of patients with depression improved after they received a placebo (Walsh, Seidman, et al., 2002). Because the placebo effect can be so powerful, many researchers continue to believe this is an important type of control condition to use.

Defining a Sample

In selecting samples, it is important for researchers to recruit people who mirror the characteristics of the real-world people seeking help for psychological syndromes. Many studies exclude groups of potential participants, and this can limit the external validity of findings. For example, researchers might exclude people who have more than one disorder or who are acutely suicidal (for ethical reasons). In response to criticism that treatment studies exclude many potential participants (Westen, Novotny, & Thompson-Brenner, 2004), some researchers have included a broader range of individuals in studies, without seeing any decay in outcomes (Foa, Gillihan, & Bryant, 2013). Nonetheless, some participants might be unwilling to enroll in a study in which they might be assigned to an ineffective treatment (the control condition).

One major concern in treatment outcome studies has been whether findings are relevant to people from different cultural backgrounds. Members of minority groups and those from non-Western cultures are less likely to seek or to receive treatment than are white, non-Hispanic adults in the United States (U.S. Department of Health and Human Services, 2014; Snowden, 2012). As shown in **Table 4.7**, there are also dramatic differences between countries in rates of treatment seeking among people with psychological disorders (Wang, Aguilar-Gaxiola, et al., 2007). Cultural and ethnic differences in willingness to seek treatment, particularly treatment in a research study, can limit the relevance of findings to minority populations. In 2001, the National Institute of Mental Health mandated that researchers consider whether findings from projects they funded would be relevant to women and members of minority groups, and hundreds of RCTs of psychological interventions are now available with a minority focus. Those studies indicate that psychological therapies are helpful in addressing a broad range of concerns for minority populations (Huey, Tilley, et al., 2014). See **Focus on Discovery 4.3** for other ways to consider culture and ethnicity in treatment

Assessing and Implementing Treatments in the Real World

RCTs, typically conducted in academic research settings, are designed to determine the **efficacy** of a treatment, that is, whether a treatment works under the purest of conditions. Because of the kinds of concerns just raised, some RCTs might not inform us about how these treatments work with broader samples in the hands of nonacademic therapists. That is, the external validity of controlled RCTs is sometimes criticized. We need to determine not just the efficacy of a treatment but also its **effectiveness**—that is, how well the treatment works in the real world. Studies of effectiveness might include clients with a broader range of problems and provide less intensive supervision of therapists. Effectiveness studies often rely on briefer assessments as well. As you might expect, when clients have more serious diagnostic complications and

TABLE 4.7	Percentage of People Who Sought Treatment in the Past 12 Months for Emotions, Nerves, Mental Health, or Drug/Alcohol Concerns by Country (N=84,850)
Country	**Percentage of People Seeking Treatment**
Nigeria	1.6
China	3.4
Italy	4.3
Lebanon	4.4
Mexico	5.1
Colombia	5.5
Japan	5.6
Spain	6.8
Ukraine	7.2
Germany	8.1
Israel	8.8
Belgium	10.9
Netherlands	10.9
France	11.3
New Zealand	13.8
South Africa	15.4
United States	17.9

Drawn from a World Health Organization study reported by Wang et al. (2007).

Focus on Discovery 4.3

The Importance of Culture and Ethnicity in Psychological Treatment

We have already mentioned that racial and ethnic minorities are less likely to seek mental health care (Wang, Lane, et al., 2005). Even when they do seek care, they are more likely to stop treatment prematurely, and they are less likely to receive state-of-the-art effective treatments. A growing body of research is considering how to make treatments more accessible and effective for people from diverse backgrounds (Lopez, Barrio, et al., 2012; Snowden, 2012). As we consider this area, we do want to raise one caveat about the risks of stereotyping. People from minority groups can differ as much from each other as their racial or ethnic group differs from another racial or ethnic group.

Many minority clients report that they would prefer to see someone from a similar background (Lopez, Lopez, & Fong, 1991). Many clients believe that therapists of similar background, perhaps even of the same gender, will understand their life circumstances better and more quickly. Despite this assumption, it has *not* been demonstrated that better outcomes are achieved when client and therapist are similar in race or ethnicity (Griner & Smith, 2006) or that clients are more likely to continue treatment when there is such a match (Maramba & Nagayama-Hall, 2002).

Cultural competence matters more than ethnic matching. A therapist who is culturally competent has an appreciation for and understanding of cultural differences and similarities, appreciates

sociopolitical events that may have been salient for some cultural groups, and has an awareness of their own culturally based assumptions and biases. A large body of research indicates that therapists who are more culturally competent are more likely to have clients who feel satisfied and see the therapeutic relationship positively. Cultural competence also has small positive effects on the degree of symptom relief that clients achieve (Tao, Owen, et al., 2015).

In developing cultural competence, therapists need to consider that many members of minority groups have encountered prejudice and racism, and many have been subjected to hate crimes (Sue, Zane, et al., 2009). Many families immigrate to new countries to escape political turmoil and persecution, and these traumas may intensify the risks of posttraumatic stress disorder and emotional distress. Cultural background may shape values and beliefs about emotion (Boiger & Mesquita, 2012), as well as how to interact with authorities like treatment providers. These values and beliefs will influence the therapeutic interview. For example, Latino cultural values may inhibit men from expressing weakness and fear (USDHHS, 2002). Native American spiritual beliefs shape beliefs and rituals around healing that are not reflected in standard treatments developed for Western majority individuals (Walker & Bigelow, 2015). Hence cultural background may shape not only experiences relevant to the development of symptoms but also how people will communicate and set expectations in treatment.

Even though there is evidence that established treatments are helpful for minority populations, many theorists argue that treatments should be adapted to be more culturally sensitive. In one meta-analysis, 76 RCTs examining culturally competent psychotherapy were identified (Griner & Smith, 2006). The culturally adapted interventions were consistently beneficial compared to control conditions. Researchers have also considered a more difficult test—do these culturally sensitive interventions work better than empirically supported psychotherapies? Evidence on this front is more mixed. Cultural tailoring appears to be more helpful when clients are less acculturated into the majority culture (Huey et al., 2014).

There are several examples of researchers who have made culturally sensitive adaptations that do improve outcomes compared to empirically supported treatments. As an example of modifying the content of CBT for depression to be more specific to the concerns of African American women, one manual includes innovative suggestions, such as a focus on the social isolation, family concerns, and trauma that are common in this population, as well as strategies to challenge the myths of the superhuman African American woman. Among African American women, the tailored intervention was rated more positively and produced a larger reduction in depressive symptoms than a traditional CBT intervention (Kohn, Oden, et al., 2002).

Another approach to developing culturally sensitive interventions is to draw on the strengths of a given culture. For example, Latino culture emphasizes family values and spirituality. One team modified CBT for depression to incorporate more emphasis on family values. Puerto Rican adolescents who received culturally sensitive

Although many minority clients report that they would like to see a minority therapist, cultural sensitivity appears to be more important to outcome than a match of ethnicity between client and therapist.

Lew Merrim/Science Source

CBT demonstrated significantly more decrease in depressive symptoms than did those who received interpersonal psychotherapy or a control condition (Rossello, Bernal, & Rivera-Medina, 2008).

Despite the many positive examples of culturally sensitive interventions, there is some evidence that too much focus on how a given cultural group differs from others can backfire—perhaps because of the risk that individuals feel stereotyped (Huey et al., 2014). Researchers are continuing to consider the best ways to provide accessibility, support, and effective interventions for people from different backgrounds.

providers have less support, psychotherapies and even medications tend to look less powerful than they do in careful efficacy studies (Rush, Trivedi, et al., 2006).

Dissemination is the process of facilitating adoption of efficacious treatments in the community, most typically by developing guidelines about the best available treatments along with training for clinicians on how to conduct those treatments. Major policy efforts in England and in the U.S. Veterans Administration have focused on dissemination (McHugh & Barlow, 2010). For example, mental health outcomes were improved in the United States Veterans Health Care System by training thousands of mental health providers to provide ESTs for anxiety, depression, pain, and PTSD (Karlin & Cross, 2014). In Britain, a major dissemination initiative provides ESTs by phone, with over a million persons screened so far (Carey, 2017). Other dissemination research considers how to tailor empirically supported treatments to make their delivery feasible in countries with few mental health professionals—for example, by creating short versions of these treatments that can be offered online or by those without advanced degrees (Patel, Chisholm, et al., 2016). Dissemination is highly important because too few clients are offered ESTs.

Quick Summary

Treatment outcome studies are the most common form of experiment in the psychopathology field. These studies focus on whether a given treatment works well.

A number of groups have attempted to provide standards for psychotherapy research and to identify psychotherapies that have received empirical support. It is generally agreed that treatment outcome researchers should use treatment manuals, randomly assign participants to the active treatment or control comparison, clearly define the sample, and include reliable and valid measures of outcome.

Treatment manuals provide detailed guidance about how to conduct each phase of a psychotherapy.

There is some debate about the best type of control condition in that no-treatment and placebo-condition control groups involve withholding active treatments for those who may be suffering. Placebo conditions, however, are informative in that many people demonstrate symptom reduction after taking a placebo.

The external validity of randomized controlled trials (RCTs) has been criticized in the past because so many people are excluded or do not take part in studies. A growing body of research, though, shows that empirically supported treatments are helpful in addressing the concerns of people from different ethnic and cultural backgrounds. Effectiveness studies focus on whether treatment findings generalize to the real world.

Check Your Knowledge 4.3

Answer the questions.

1. What is an RCT?

2. Describe the major pro and con of placebo controlled designs.

3. Why are treatment manuals recommended in psychotherapy outcome research?

True or false?

4. Very little research is available on whether empirically supported treatments work well for minority individuals.

Match the word to the definition

5. Efficacy

6. Effectiveness

7. Dissemination

    a. The process of encouraging treatment providers in the community to adopt a treatment

    b. The degree to which a treatment appears to work well in a carefully controlled RCT

    c. The degree to which a treatment appears to work well when administered in a less carefully controlled study in the community

Analogues in Psychopathology Research

Researchers are often confronted with ethical and pragmatic barriers in conducting research on psychological disorders. Here we describe several types of analogue research that are commonly used to overcome those barriers.

The experimental method is the clearest way to determine cause–effect relationships. There are many situations in which the experimental method cannot be used to understand the causes of psychological disorders. Why? Suppose that a researcher has hypothesized that emotionally charged, overly dependent maternal relationships cause generalized anxiety disorder. An experimental test of this hypothesis would require randomly assigning infants to either of two groups of mothers. The mothers in one group would undergo an extensive training program to ensure that they would be able to create a highly emotional atmosphere and foster overdependence in children. The mothers in the second group would be trained not to create such a relationship with their children. The researcher would then wait until the participants in each group reached adulthood and determine how many of them had developed generalized anxiety disorder. Clearly, this is unethical.

In an effort to take advantage of the power of the experimental method, researchers sometimes use an **analogue experiment**. Investigators attempt to create or observe a related but less severe phenomenon—that is, an analogue of the risk variable—in the laboratory to allow more intensive study. Because a true experiment is conducted, results with good internal validity can be obtained. The problem of external validity arises, however, because the researchers are no longer studying the actual phenomenon of interest.

In one type of analogue experiment, temporary symptoms are produced through experimental manipulations. For example, lactate infusion can elicit a panic attack, and threats to self-esteem can produce anxiety or sadness. The success of experimental manipulations in producing mild symptoms provides clues into the causes of more severe symptoms.

In addition to analogue experiments, researchers sometimes use analogue samples in which participants are selected because they are considered similar to people with certain diagnoses. Thousands of studies, for example, have been conducted with college students who received high scores on questionnaire measures of anxiety or depression. These samples may be assessed in either experimental or correlational designs.

A third type of analogue study involves using animals as a way to understand human behavior. For example, researchers found that dogs that were exposed to electrical shocks that the dogs could not control developed many of the symptoms of depression, including seeming despair, passivity, and decreased appetite (Seligman, Maier, & Geer, 1968). Similarly, researchers often rely on animal models in the development of novel pharmacological treatments for psychopathologies (Micale, Kucerova, & Sulcova, 2013). Such animal models have helped us understand more about the neurobiology of depression, anxiety, and other disorders in humans. Sometimes, animal researchers use an experimental design, as when researchers manipulate stress; other times, animal researchers use correlational designs.

Studies of college students with mild symptoms may not provide a good analogue for major psychological disorders.

The key to interpreting such studies lies in the validity of the analogue. Is a stressor encountered in the laboratory fundamentally similar to the death of a parent or other serious stressors? Are distressed college students similar to people with clinically diagnosable depression? Are lethargy and decreased eating in dogs akin to depressive symptoms in humans? Some argue against analogue research, even when researchers are careful to discuss the limits of generalizability. For example, Coyne (1994) has argued that clinical depression is caused by different processes from those that cause common distress. He would argue that analogue studies of mild symptoms among undergraduates have poor external validity.

We believe that analogue studies can be very helpful but that findings from these types of studies must be considered conjointly with studies that do not rely on analogues. Science often depends on comparing the results of experimental analogue studies to those of longitudinal correlational studies. For example, analogue studies have shown that people with depression respond more negatively to laboratory stressors (an analogue of life stress) than do those without depression, and correlational studies have shown that severe life events predict the onset of clinical depression. Because the findings from correlational and analogue studies complement each other, this provides strong support for life event models of depression. The analogue studies of life stress provide the precision of an experiment (high internal validity), whereas correlational studies provide the ability to study very important influences that cannot be manipulated, like the influence of death and trauma (high external validity).

Harlow's famous analogue research examined the effects of early separation from the mother on infant monkeys. Even a cloth surrogate mother is better than isolation for preventing subsequent emotional distress and depression.

Quick Summary

Several types of analogues are commonly used in psychopathology research.

Analogue experiments rely on a milder version of a risk variable; the milder version of the risk variable is manipulated as the independent variable within the laboratory. Analogue experiments are helpful when a risk variable cannot be ethically manipulated.

Other types of analogue research rely on assessments of milder symptoms rather than full-blown diagnoses, or the use of animal models to understand human psychopathology.

Check Your Knowledge 4.4

Answer the questions.

1. A researcher decides to use an analogue experiment to study the effects of one hour of social separation on anxiety. What are the pros and cons of this type of analogue experiment as compared to a correlational study of the effects of maternal loss?

2. Which of the following are analogue studies? Circle all that apply.

   a. A researcher exposes dogs to uncontrollable stress as a way of understanding human depression

   b. A researcher conducts an online survey to assess how long the typical experience of sadness lasts

   c. A researcher asks participants about their most recent experience of sadness as a way to understand clinically diagnosable depression

   d. A researcher interviews 25 people each month for three years after their spouse dies to estimate the duration of bereavement.

Integrating the Findings of Multiple Studies

Understanding the pros and cons of different research designs should suggest a natural conclusion—there is no perfect research study. Rather, a body of research studies is needed to test a theory. After an important research finding emerges, dozens of studies may emerge on the same topic. Sometimes the results of different studies will be similar, but more often, differences will emerge across studies. Indeed, there has been growing attention throughout the scientific community, not just in psychology, about failures to replicate findings, and techniques for aggregating findings across multiple studies.

Replication

In a successful **replication**, findings from one research study hold up when that study is repeated a second time. Findings are considered *reproducible*, and hence more believable, when other researchers have independently replicated them, ideally more than once. Replication is a core aspect of the scientific method.

In recent years, a spotlight has been placed on replication failures across the sciences. In one report, Ioannidis identified 49 articles that were published in influential medical journals and had each been cited more than 1,000 times. Many of these studies described interventions that had been widely adopted by the medical community: for example, hormone replacement for menopausal women and vitamin E to reduce risk of cardiovascular disease. Ioannidis then identified 34 studies that attempted to replicate the original findings. In those replication studies, 20 percent of the interventions had not replicated at all, and another 20 percent had shown significantly smaller effects (Ioannidis, 2005a). Psychology has not been immune from problems with reproducibility. In one demonstration of these problems, researchers selected 100 publications from top-tier psychology journals and conducted new studies to see if those findings replicated. Only 39 percent of the findings were judged to have been replicated (Open Science Collaboration, 2015).

Obviously, lack of reproducibility is a major concern—after all, if we cannot believe the findings from our research, they are not of much value for advancing our understanding and improving treatments. Consistent failures to replicate reduce public trust and investment in science. Because many scientists build their work on previous findings, inaccurate publications also misguide the next wave of science.

Reproducibility may be overestimated when we rely only on published articles. Scientific journals tend to prioritize the publication of new and positive findings over negative results, which are regarded as uninteresting and difficult to interpret. There is always the possibility that methodological problems led to the negative finding—as an example, an effect for a given treatment might be observed with longer duration of treatment, more skilled therapists, or a better outcome measure. The tendency to publish only positive results is referred to as **publication bias**. Publication bias appears to be very widespread. In one study that tracked 221 experiments, positive findings were more than twice as likely to be published as were negative findings (Franco, Malhotra, & Simonovits, 2014). Publication bias may keep the scientific community unaware of replication failures.

There are many reasons why studies may fail to replicate. One simple explanation is fraud, but most believe that fraud is rare and does not explain the low rates of replication.

Another explanation is that statistical analyses rely on probability—earlier, we described how a finding is considered statistically significant when statistics indicate that there is 5 percent or less chance that the finding was obtained by chance alone (i.e., $p < .05$). This means that 5 percent of the time, purely by chance, a positive finding would not be expected to replicate in a second study. However, the estimates we describe here suggest that nonreplication happens much more than 5 percent of the time. Other factors must be involved.

Several issues in research methods can contribute to replication failures.

- Small samples, which are often used in clinical psychology, are more likely to yield unusual patterns of results (Ioannidis, 2005b). Findings are generally more believable when they come from studies with larger sample sizes.

- Findings are less likely to replicate if unreliable measures are used.

- Replication failures are more likely when the methods of the original research study are not described well.

- Differences in methods, such as measures or sample characteristics, between studies diminish the likelihood of replication (Gilbert, King, et al., 2016). For example, findings observed among people who are hospitalized may not generalize to outpatient or community samples. Findings are considered more generalizable when they can be replicated across a range of measures and samples.

In addition to these issues, several researchers have described **questionable research practices** that contribute to replication failures (Simmons, Nelson, & Simonsohn, 2011). Let's consider a hypothetical study of neuroticism and depression as an example of one form of questionable research practice. Imagine that the researchers collect two different measures of depression (a self-rating and an interviewer rating). After the data is collected, the researchers may decide to include either or both measures in their analyses. When the researchers examine the data, several participants have extremely high neuroticism scores; analyses could be conducted with or without these high scorers (doubling the number of potential analyses). Taken together, the investigators have the opportunity to conduct their analyses in six different ways depending upon the measures they include (self-rating, interview, or both measures of depression) and the participants they include (with or without the high scorers). Although the probability of a false positive finding is only 5 percent in each separate analysis, the probability of at least one false positive finding is much higher when the researchers conduct analyses six different ways. In other words, simply by taking a flexible approach to data analysis, the researchers can dramatically increase their chances of obtaining a positive result!

The situation gets even more complex if some of the six results are positive and others are negative, as often happens. This is partially because researchers tend to be biased to believe the findings that fit their hypotheses and to disregard the negative results, a phenomenon referred to as confirmation bias. Confirmation bias, along with awareness of publication bias, may tempt the researchers to report only the analyses that supported their hypotheses without acknowledging negative results. Researchers may also be motivated to continue to tweak their analyses or comb through their data until they arrive at a significant (and thus more publishable) result, a process known as **p-hacking.** The need to publish work for promotions and future grant funding is likely to intensify the temptation to search for and present only significant results. Some people, then, suggest that questionable research practices, as well as problematic systems that reward people for focusing on significant findings, are a major contributor to the lack of reproducibility in science (Ioannidis, 2005b).

Many people are working on policies to address these issues in replication, and optimism is high that these will improve the situation:

- Many scientists now *register* their hypotheses, measures, and analysis plan before conducting a study, to make the scientific process more transparent. This promotes a more honest presentation of which analyses did or did not support hypotheses. In one recent report, 44 percent of randomized clinical trials in psychology journals had been registered (Cybulski, Mayo-Wilson, & Grant, 2016). The National Institutes of Health now requires that clinical trials they fund be registered.

- Once a study is completed, many researchers now make their data publicly available (with all personally identifiable information about participants removed). The National Institute of Mental Health requires researchers to upload data funded by their agency into a repository that is accessible to other researchers. This will also make the scientific process more transparent.

- Some journals recommend that reviewers pay more attention to the quality of the study than to the specific findings—in a perfect world, scientists would value negative and positive findings from high-quality studies. To improve the odds that negative findings will be published, reviewers for these journals are asked to weight the rationale and methods of a study more heavily than the statistical results in evaluating a manuscript for potential publication, which removes rewards for p-hacking.

- Editors are now demanding that scientists use large sample sizes. There is a push to use parallel measures across studies, so that researchers can compile large integrated data sets. This type of aggregation has progressed rapidly in molecular genetic studies, where researchers now routinely use sample sizes in excess of 5,000 persons (although findings from these studies often still fail to replicate!).

- Consumers of science are advised to consider whether findings have been replicated. For example, the APA standards for empirically supported treatments, described above, specify that findings must be replicated. New APA guidelines are likely to weight not just whether a study has replicated but also whether negative findings have emerged for a given treatment (American Psychological Association, 2015).

On the whole, there is a growing acknowledgment of the importance of replicability in science. We hope that this awareness fosters change at the level of individual scientists, social systems guiding science, and among consumers of science.

Meta-Analysis

How does a researcher go about drawing conclusions from a series of investigations, especially when some findings are positive and others are negative? A simple way of drawing general conclusions is to read individual studies, mull them over, and decide what they mean overall. The disadvantage of this approach is that the researcher's biases and subjective impressions can play a significant role in determining what conclusion is drawn. It is common for two scientists to read the same set of studies and reach very different conclusions.

Meta-analysis was developed as a partial solution to this problem (Smith, Glass, & Miller, 1980). The first step in a meta-analysis is a thorough literature search, to identify all relevant studies. Because these studies have typically used different statistical tests, meta-analysis then puts all the results into a common scale, using a type of statistic called an *effect size*. For example, in treatment studies, the effect size offers a way of standardizing the differences in improvement between a therapy group and a control group so that the results of multiple studies can be averaged. **Figure 4.5** summarizes the steps in a meta-analysis.

As the effect sizes across studies are compiled, researchers also try to estimate publication bias—the tendency for negative findings not to be published. To do so, they can ask members of the research community to share unpublished findings. They also can examine the proportion of effect sizes that are barely above the threshold for statistical significance—if many effect sizes are in this range there is a stronger chance that there are unpublished findings that were not significant.

In their often-cited report, Smith and colleagues (1980) meta-analyzed 475 psychotherapy outcome studies involving more than 25,000 patients and 1,700 effect sizes; they came to conclusions that have attracted considerable attention and some controversy. Most importantly, they concluded that psychotherapies produce more improvement than does no treatment. Specifically, treated patients were found to be better off than almost 80 percent of untreated patients. Subsequent meta-analyses have confirmed that therapy appears to be effective (Lambert & Ogles, 2004).

Meta-analysis has been criticized primarily because researchers sometimes include studies that are of poor quality. For example, Smith and colleagues gave equal weight to all studies, so that a poorly controlled outcome study (such as one that did not evaluate what the therapists actually did in each session) received as much weight as a well-controlled one (such as a study in which therapists used a manual that specified what they did with each research participant). When Smith and colleagues attempted to address this problem by comparing the effect sizes of good versus poor studies and found no differences, they were further criticized for the criteria they employed in separating the good from the not so good (Rachman & Wilson, 1980). The ultimate problem is that someone has to make a judgment of good versus poor quality in research and others can find fault with that judgment. A good meta-analysis, though, will be clear about the criteria for including or excluding studies.

Table 4.8 provides another example of a meta-analysis. In this meta-analysis, researchers integrated the findings of 27 epidemiological studies conducted in Europe on the 12-month prevalence of psychological disorders (Wittchen & Jacobi, 2005). Across these studies, more than 155,000 participants were interviewed. Prevalence estimates from the different studies varied. Tallying the findings across studies should give a stronger estimate of how common the disorders are.

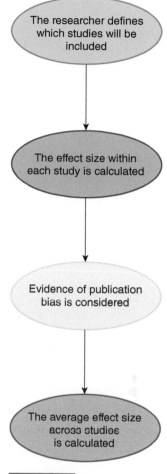

FIGURE 4.5 Steps in conducting a meta-analysis.

TABLE 4.8	An Example of a Meta-Analysis: One-Year Prevalence Rates for Psychological Disorders Across 27 European Studies			
DSM-IV Diagnosis	**Number of Studies**	**Combined N**	**12-Month Prevalence (percent) Across the Combined Sample**	**Range of Prevalence Estimates Within Different Studies**
Alcohol dependence	12	60,891	3.3	0.1–6.6
Illicit substance dependence	6	28,429	1.1	0.1–2.2
Psychotic disorders	6	27,291	0.9	0.2–2.6
Major depressive disorder	17	152,044	6.4	3.1–10.1
Bipolar I disorder	6	21,848	0.8	0.2–1.1
Anxiety disorders	12	53,597	1.6	0.7–3.1
Somatic symptom disorders	7	18,894	6.4	1.1–11
Eating disorders	5	19,761	4.8	0.2–0.7

Source: Adapted from Wittchen and Jacobi (2005).

Check Your Knowledge 4.5

Answer the questions.

1. In a recent project to examine reproducibility in psychological science, researchers had success with only __ percent of the psychological studies they attempted to replicate.

2. Describe approaches recommended to improve replicability.

Choose the best answer.

3. The step in meta-analysis that has received extensive criticism is:
   a. determining which studies should be included
   b. calculating the effect size of each study
   c. calculating the average effect size across studies
   d. none of the above

Summary

Science, Theory, and Hypotheses

- Science involves forming a Theory, and developing hypotheses based on that theory, and then systematically gathering data to test the hypotheses. Good science requires reliable and valid measures.

Research Designs in Psychopathology

- Common methods for studying psychopathology include case studies, correlational studies, and experimental studies. Each method has strengths and weaknesses.

Case Studies

- Case studies provide detailed descriptions of rare phenomena or novel procedures. Case studies also can disconfirm that a relationship is universal and can generate hypotheses to be tested through controlled research. Case studies, however, may be biased by the researcher's perspective, and they are of limited value in providing evidence to support a theory.

Correlational Research

- Correlational methods are the most common way to study the causes of psychological disorders, because we cannot manipulate most of the major risk factors in psychopathology, nor can we manipulate diagnosis.

- Cross-sectional correlational studies do not provide evidence for cause and effect because of the directionality problem. Longitudinal studies help address which variable came first but can still suffer from the third-variable problem.

- One form of correlational study, epidemiological research, involves gathering information about the prevalence and incidence of disorders in populations and about the correlates of disorders. Epidemiological studies avoid the sampling biases seen in studies of participants drawn from undergraduate psychology classes or from treatment clinics.

- Studies of behavior genetics typically rely on correlational techniques as well. The goal of behavior genetics is to understand the magnitude of genetic and environmental contributions, and the interaction of genetic and environmental contributions to disease and related risk variables. The most common behavior genetics methods include the family method, the twin method, and the adoptees method.

Experimental Research

- In the experimental method, the researcher randomly assigns people to an experimental group or a control group. The effects of the independent variable on a dependent variable are then tested. Treatment outcome studies and analogue studies are common types of experimental research in psychopathology. Single-case experimental designs can provide well-controlled data.

- Generally, experimental methods help enhance internal validity, but correlational methods sometimes offer greater external validity.

Treatment Outcome Research

- Research on the efficacy of various forms of psychological treatments has been conducted for many decades. Overall, this research suggests that about 80 percent of people gain some improvement from therapy. Therapy also seems to be more helpful than a placebo or the passage of time.

- Scientists have defined standards for research on psychotherapy trials. These standards typically include the need to use a treatment manual, to randomly assign participants to treatment or a control condition, to define the sample carefully, and to use reliable and valid outcome measures. Guidelines suggest that positive findings should be observed from more than one research team before a treatment is considered empirically-supported. Scientists have used these standards to identify empirically supported treatments (ESTs).

- Researchers are urged to evaluate whether treatments may cause harm.

- External validity is a concern in treatment research, in that many people are excluded from or will not take part in clinical trials. A growing number of studies, though, demonstrate that empirically supported psychotherapies are helpful for people from diverse ethnic and cultural backgrounds.

- A broader concern is that a gap exists between what happens in the research world and the real world. Efficacy research focuses on how well therapies work in carefully controlled experiments, whereas effectiveness research focuses on how well therapies work in the real world with a broader array of clients and therapists. Dissemination refers to the process of implementing empirically supported treatments in community settings.

Analogue Studies

- Analogue experiments allow the researcher to study a minor variant of a risk factor related to psychopathology, such as stressors. Although the stressor used in an analogue study is typically much milder than the types of stressors that might trigger psychopathology, the experimental method provides greater control. Analogue samples are comprised of people with mild symptoms. Animal studies can also provide an analogue to human disorders.

Integrating the Findings of Multiple Studies

- Replication refers to obtaining parallel findings when a study is repeated. There has been growing concern about a lack of reproducibility of scientific findings. Policy reforms are beginning to address these concerns.

- Meta-analysis is an important tool for reaching conclusions from a group of research studies. It entails putting the statistical comparisons from single studies into a common format—the effect size—so that scientists can average the results of many studies.

Answers to Check Your Knowledge Questions

4.1 1. F; 2. F; 3. F

4.2 1. a and b; 2. d; 3. c; 4. c; 5. d

4.3 1. RCT refers to randomized controlled trial—a form of treatment outcome study in which the active treatment is compared to at least one comparison condition (controlled), and people are assigned to treatments randomly; 2. Pro: Placebos allow for a control of the effects of treatment expectations, and research suggests that the placebo effect can be large; Con: Placebo trials involve withholding active treatment from people who may have serious symptoms and distress, which is an ethical concern. 3. Treatment manuals provide specific guidance to therapists, so that researchers can be more confident that therapists are providing the same type of intervention; 4 False (Explanation: Hundreds of trials have been conducted to test empirically supported treatments with minority individuals and those from differing ethnic and racial backgrounds); 5. b; 6. c; 7. a

4.4 1. Pro: the analogue study has the advantage of the experimental manipulation, which provides internal validity. Con: Brief periods of social separation may not invoke even minor temporary symptoms that are similar to losing one's mother, and so external validity may be limited; 2. a, c

4.5 1. 39 percent; 2. Registering study hypotheses, measures, and analyses before the study begins; making data available; placing more emphasis on the importance of hypotheses and the quality of study methods than the results of a study when reviewing a manuscript to consider potential publication; using larger samples; routinely considering whether a finding has been replicated; 3. a

Key Terms

ABAB design
adoptees method
analogue experiment
case study
clinical significance
concordance
control group
correlation
correlational method
correlation coefficient
cross-fostering
cross-sectional design
cultural competence
dependent variable
directionality problem
dissemination
dizygotic (DZ) twins
double-blind procedure

effectiveness
efficacy
empirically supported treatments (ESTs)
epidemiology
experiment
experimental effect
external validity
family method
high-risk method
hypothesis
incidence
independent variable
index case (proband)
internal validity
longitudinal design
meta-analysis
monozygotic (MZ) twins
p-hacking

placebo
placebo effect
prevalence
probands
publication bias
questionable research practices
random assignment
randomized controlled trials (RCTs)
replication
reversal (ABAB) design
single-case experimental design
statistical significance
theory
third-variable problem
treatment outcome research
twin method

CHAPTER 5

Mood Disorders

LEARNING GOALS

1. Describe the symptoms of depression, the diagnostic criteria for depressive disorders, and the epidemiology of depressive disorders.

2. Explain the symptoms of mania, the diagnostic criteria for bipolar disorders, and the epidemiology of bipolar disorders.

3. Discuss the genetic, neurobiological, social, and psychological factors that contribute to the mood disorders.

4. Describe the medication and psychological treatments of mood disorders as well as the current views of electroconvulsive therapy.

5. Explain the epidemiology of suicide, the risk factors for suicide, and methods for preventing suicide.

Clinical Case

Mary

Mary M., a 38-year-old mother of four children, had been deeply depressed for about 2 months when she first went to see a psychologist. Three years earlier, she had returned to work when health care bills made it hard for her family to get by on her husband's income as a high school teacher. About 7 months before her visit to the psychologist, she was laid off from her job as an administrative assistant, which was a serious blow to the family's finances. She felt guilty about the loss of her job and became preoccupied with signs of her overall incompetence. Each night, she struggled for more than an hour to fall asleep, only to wake up frequently throughout the night. She had little appetite and as a result had lost 10 pounds. She also had little energy for and no interest in activities that she had enjoyed in the past. Household chores felt impossible for her to complete and her husband began to complain. Their marriage had already been strained for 2 years, and her negativity and lack of energy contributed to further arguments. Finally, realizing that Mary's symptoms were serious, Mr. M. cajoled her into making an appointment with a psychologist. (You will read about the outcome of Mary's treatment later in this chapter.)

Mood disorders involve profound disturbances in emotion—from the deep sadness and disengagement of depression to the extreme elation and irritability of mania. In this chapter, we begin by discussing the clinical description and the epidemiology of the different mood disorders. Next, we consider various perspectives on the etiology of these disorders, and then we consider approaches to treating them. We conclude with an examination of suicide, an action far too often associated with mood disorders.

TABLE 5.1   Overview of the Major DSM-5 Mood Disorders

Unipolar Depressive Disorders	
DSM-5 Diagnoses	**Major Features**
Major depressive disorder	Five or more depressive symptoms, including sad mood or loss of pleasure, for 2 weeks
Persistent depressive disorder	Low mood and at least two other symptoms of depression at least half of the time for 2 years
Premenstrual dysphoric disorder	Mood symptoms in the week before menses
Disruptive mood dysregulation disorder	Severe recurrent temper outbursts and persistent negative mood for at least 1 year beginning before age 10
Bipolar Disorders:	
DSM-5 Diagnoses	**Major Features**
Bipolar I disorder	At least one lifetime manic episode
Bipolar II disorder	At least one lifetime hypomanic episode and one major depressive episode
Cyclothymia	Recurrent mood changes from high to low for at least 2 years, without hypomanic or depressive episodes

The DSM-5 recognizes two broad types of mood disorders: those that involve only depressive symptoms (unipolar depressive disorders) and those that involve manic symptoms (bipolar disorders). **Table 5.1** presents a summary of the symptoms of each of these disorders. We will begin by discussing the depressive disorders, and then we will turn to the bipolar disorders. Within each, we will describe the core signs, the formal criteria for the specific disorders, and then the epidemiology and consequences of these disorders.

Clinical Descriptions and Epidemiology of Depressive Disorders

The cardinal symptoms of depression include profound sadness and/or an inability to experience pleasure. Most of us experience sadness during our lives, and most of us say that we are "depressed" at one time or another. But most of these experiences do not have the intensity and duration to be diagnosable. The author William Styron (1992) wrote about his depression: "Like anyone else I have always had times when I felt deeply depressed, but this was something altogether new in my experience—a despairing, unchanging paralysis of the spirit beyond anything I had ever known or imagined could exist."

The symptoms of depression are varied. When people develop a depressive disorder, their heads may reverberate with self-recriminations. Like Mary, described in the Clinical Case, they may become focused on their flaws and deficits. Paying attention can be so exhausting that they have difficulty absorbing what they read and hear. They often view things in a very negative light, and they tend to lose hope. Initiative may disappear. Social withdrawal is common; many prefer to sit alone and be silent. Some people with depression neglect their appearance. When people become utterly dejected and hopeless, thoughts about suicide are common.

Physical symptoms of depression are also common, including fatigue and low energy as well as physical aches and pains. These symptoms can be profound enough to convince afflicted persons that they must be suffering from some serious medical condition, even though the symptoms have no apparent physical cause. Although people with depression typically feel exhausted, they may find it hard to fall asleep and may wake up frequently. Other people sleep throughout the day. They may find that

> ### DSM-5 Criteria for Major Depressive Disorder
>
> Sad mood or loss of pleasure in usual activities.
> At least five symptoms (counting sad mood and loss of pleasure):
>
> - Sleeping too much or too little
> - Psychomotor retardation or agitation
> - Weight loss or change in appetite
> - Loss of energy
>
> - Feelings of worthlessness or excessive guilt
> - Difficulty concentrating, thinking, or making decisions
> - Recurrent thoughts of death or suicide
>
> Symptoms are present nearly every day, most of the day, for at least 2 weeks. Symptoms are distinct and more severe than a normative response to significant loss.

food tastes bland or that their appetite is gone, or they may experience an increase in appetite. Sexual interest disappears. Some may find their limbs feel heavy. Thoughts and movements may slow for some (**psychomotor retardation**), but others cannot sit still—they pace, fidget, and wring their hands (**psychomotor agitation**).

The DSM-5 includes several depressive disorders. Here, we focus on major depressive disorder and persistent depressive disorder, because both diagnoses are well researched. We will briefly discuss a newly defined diagnosis specific to children and adolescents, **disruptive mood dysregulation disorder**, in **Focus on Discovery 13.3**. We will not discuss **premenstrual dysphoric disorder** because so little is known about it.

Major Depressive Disorder

The DSM-5 diagnosis of **major depressive disorder (MDD)** requires five depressive symptoms to be present for at least 2 weeks. These symptoms must include either depressed mood or loss of interest and pleasure. As shown in the DSM-5 criteria, additional symptoms must be present, such as changes in sleep, appetite, concentration, decision making, feelings of worthlessness, suicidality, or psychomotor agitation or retardation.

Even though episodes tend to dissipate over time, an untreated episode may stretch on for 6 months or even longer. MDD is an **episodic disorder**, because symptoms tend to be present for a period of time and then clear. Major depressive episodes often recur—once a given episode clears, a person is likely to experience another episode. To estimate the course of disorder, researchers have used representative community samples (rather than patient samples, which may have a more severe course of disorder). In one such study in which researchers conducted annual interviews of people who had experienced a first episode of MDD, about 15% of people reported depressive symptoms that persisted for 10 years. About 40–50% of people who recovered from a first episode of major depression experienced at least one more episode across the 10 years of follow-up (Eaton, Shao, et al., 2008).

Some people with depression have trouble falling asleep and staying asleep. Others find themselves sleeping for more than 10 hours but still feeling exhausted.

Persistent Depressive Disorder

People with **persistent depressive disorder** are chronically depressed—more than half of the time for at least 2 years, they feel blue or obtain little pleasure from activities and pastimes. In addition to these mood changes, they have at least two of the other symptoms of depression. The central feature of this diagnosis is the chronicity of symptoms, which is a stronger predictor of poor outcome than the number of symptoms. Among people who have experienced depressive symptoms for at least 2 years, those who do and do not have a history of major

© Shannon Fagan/Stone/Getty Images

DSM-5 Criteria for Persistent Depressive Disorder (Dysthymia)

Depressed mood for most of the day more than half of the time for 2 years (or 1 year for children and adolescents).
At least two of the following during that time:

- Poor appetite or overeating
- Sleeping too much or too little
- Low energy

- Poor self-esteem
- Trouble concentrating or making decisions
- Feelings of hopelessness

The symptoms do not clear for more than 2 months at a time. Bipolar disorders are not present.

---

depressive disorder appear similar in their treatment response (McCullough, Klein, et al., 2000). Persistent depressive disorder is similar to a DSM-IV-TR diagnosis of dysthymia.

Epidemiology and Consequences of Depressive Disorders

MDD is one of the most common psychological disorders. One large-scale epidemiological study estimated that 16.2 percent of people in the United States met the criteria for diagnosis of MDD at some point in their lives (Kessler, Berglund, et al., 2003). This may be an underestimate because researchers asked people to recall depressive episodes that happened anytime in their life, and people may forget episodes of depression that happened many years ago (Moffitt, Caspi, et al., 2010). About 5 percent of people report experiencing depressive episodes that persisted for more than 2 years (Murphy & Byrne, 2012).

MDD and persistent depressive disorder are both twice as common among women as among men (Seedat et al., 2009); see **Focus on Discovery 5.1** for a discussion of possible reasons for this gender difference. Socioeconomic status also matters—that is, MDD is three times as common among people who are impoverished compared with those who are not (Kessler, Birnbaum, et al., 2010).

The prevalence of depression varies considerably across cultures. In a major cross-cultural study using the same diagnostic criteria and structured interview in each country, the prevalence of MDD varied from a low of 6.5 percent in China to a high of 21 percent in France (Bromet, Andrade, et al., 2011). It is tempting to assume that differences in prevalence rates by country indicate a strong role for culture. It turns out that differences among countries in rates of depression may be fairly complex. As described in **Focus on Discovery 5.2**, one

Kirsten Dunst's personal experience with major depressive disorder (MDD) provided her with insight for her role as an actress in the award-winning film *Melancholia*. One out of every five women will experience an episode of depression during her lifetime.

Library/Alstar Picture Library/Alamy

Focus on Discovery 5.1

Gender Differences in Depression

Women are twice as likely as men are to experience major depression and persistent depressive disorder, and the gender ratio is observed in large scale studies around the world, even in countries with relatively more equitable gender roles (Salk, Hyde, & Abramson, 2017). The gender gap typically begins to emerge during early adolescence and is fully present by late adolescence (Avenevoli, Swendsen, et al., 2015). Some of you might wonder if these findings just reflect a tendency for men not to disclose symptoms. Evidence does not support that idea (Kessler, 2003). Several factors may help explain this gender difference (Hilt & Nolen-Hoeksema, 2014):

Biological Factors

- Fluctuations in gonadal hormones, experienced at puberty, premenstrually, postpartum, and at menopause, may increase

stress reactivity for some women. This may explain only a small portion of the gender difference, as hormone findings are mixed.

Social Factors

- Twice as many girls as boys are exposed to childhood sexual abuse.
- During adulthood, women are more likely than men to be exposed to chronic stressors such as poverty and caretaker responsibilities.
- Women tend to provide more support to others facing stress. This exposure to other's stress has been called "the cost of caring".

Stress Reactivity Factors

- Acceptance of traditional social roles among girls may intensify self-critical attitudes about appearance. Adolescent girls worry more than adolescent boys about their body image, and this worry is tied to depression (Hankin & Abramson, 2001).

- Exposure to childhood and chronic stressors, as well as the effects of female hormones, could change the reactivity of the hypothalamic-pituitary-adrenal (HPA) axis, a biological system guiding reactions to stress.

- A focus on gaining approval and closeness within interpersonal relationships, which is more commonly endorsed by women, may intensify reactions to interpersonal stressors (Hankin, Young, et al., 2015). Men are more likely than women to become depressed after life events involving financial or occupational stress, whereas women are more likely than men to become depressed after interpersonal life events (Kendler & Gardner, 2014).

- Social roles promote emotion-focused coping among women, which may then extend the

The gender difference in depression does not emerge until adolescence. At that time, young women encounter many stressors and more pressure concerning social roles and body image, and they tend to ruminate about the resulting negative feelings.

duration of sad moods after major stressors. More specifically, women tend to spend more time ruminating about sad moods or wondering about why unhappy events have occurred. Men tend to spend more time using distracting or action-focused coping, such as playing a sport or engaging in other activities that shake off the sad mood. As we discuss when we review cognitive factors in depression later in this chapter, a fair amount of research suggests that rumination prolongs sad moods and can predict the onset of MDD.

It's pretty clear that gender differences in depression are related to multiple factors. In considering these issues, bear in mind that men are more likely to demonstrate other types of disorders, such as alcohol and substance abuse as well as antisocial personality disorder (Seedat, et al., 2009). Hence, understanding gender differences in psychopathology is likely to require attending to many different risk factors and syndromes.

factor may be distance from the equator. Rates of winter depression, or **seasonal affective disorder**, are higher farther from the equator, where winter days are shorter. There is also a robust correlation of per capita fish consumption with depression; countries with more fish consumption, such as Japan and Iceland, have much lower rates of MDD and bipolar disorder (Hibbeln, Nieminen, et al., 2006). Income disparity also appears to be tied to a much higher prevalence of depression (Pickett & Wilkinson, 2010). Undoubtedly, other cultural factors, such as family cohesion and mental health stigma, play an important role in rates of depression as well.

The symptom profile of a depressive episode also varies across cultures, and one likely reason is the differences in cultural standards regarding expression of emotional distress.

Focus on Discovery 5.2

Seasonal Affective Disorder: The Winter Blues

The DSM-5 includes a specifier (subtype) to indicate that a person has a consistent seasonal pattern to their mood disorders. In the most common form of seasonal affective disorder, depressive episodes occur during the winter. These winter depressions appear to be much more common in northern than in southern climates; whereas less than 2 percent of people living in sunny Florida report these patterns, about 10 percent of people living in New Hampshire report seasonal affective disorder (Rosen, Targum, et al., 1990).

For mammals living in the wild, a slower metabolism in the winter could have been a lifesaver during periods of scarce food. For some unlucky humans, though, this same mechanism might contribute to seasonal affective disorder. It is believed that seasonal affective disorder is related to changes in the levels and timing of melatonin release in the brain. Melatonin is exquisitely sensitive to light and dark cycles and is only released during dark

periods. People with seasonal affective disorder show greater changes in nightly melatonin levels in the winter than do people without seasonal affective disorder (Wehr, Duncan, et al., 2001). Factors other than melatonin also are likely to contribute to seasonal mood shifts; for example, people with seasonal affective disorder show a change in their retinal sensitivity to light that appears to be genetically guided (Roecklein, Wong, et al., 2013).

Hibernation in animals typically involves sleeping long hours, along with lowered appetite and energy. This same profile of symptoms is shown in seasonal affective disorder. Indeed, even among those who do not develop seasonal affective disorder, sleep, appetite, and energy changes are very common responses to the shortened days of winter. Some people, though, respond to those physical changes self-critically. For example, faced with a lack of energy to tackle new projects, some people may be more prone to feeling guilt. Those who are self-critical and troubled by other forms of negative cognitions may be particularly likely to develop the full constellation of depressive symptoms in the face of the seasonal shifts in energy, sleep, and appetite (Whitcomb-Smith, Sigmon, et al., 2014).

Fortunately, several treatment options are available for seasonal affective disorder. Like other subtypes of depression, seasonal affective disorder responds to antidepressant medications and cognitive behavioral therapy (Rohan, Roecklein, et al., 2007). Winter blues, though, are as likely to remit with 30 minutes

of bright light each morning as with fluoxetine (Prozac) (Lam, Levitt, et al., 2006). Many high-quality studies support bright light as a treatment for seasonal affective disorder (Golden, Gaynes, et al., 2005), and it is the first-line recommendation in the American Psychiatric Association treatment guidelines for depression. Intriguingly, light therapy has been shown to help relieve depression even among those without a seasonal pattern to their depressions (Lam, Levitt, et al., 2016).

Media for Medical/UIG via Getty Images

This woman is having light therapy, which is an effective treatment for patients with seasonal depression.

Gilles Mingasson/Getty Images

Seasonal affective disorder is most common in regions far from the equator.

Among persons who are seeking treatment for depression, ethnic minorities in the United States, as well as people from Latin American and some Asian countries, tend to focus on their somatic symptoms, such as fatigue and pain (Bagayogo, Interian, & Escobar, 2013). There are many theories for these differences. Some cultures may place greater focus on mind–body connections. Some cultures may stigmatize psychological syndromes, such as depression, more than physical health concerns. Even though these theories may help explain the pattern, some have suggested that this profile may be specific to patient samples. When representative community samples from Eastern and Western countries are asked about each depressive symptom carefully, there are more parallels than distinctions in the way that people from different countries describe their depressive symptoms (Kim & López, 2014).

In most countries, the age of onset for MDD has decreased over the past 50 years (Kessler, Birnbaum, et al., 2010). **Figure 5.1** shows that the age of onset has become lower for each recent generation of people in the United States: Among people in their 60s, less than 5 percent reported that they had experienced an episode of MDD by age 20, whereas among people ages 18–29, almost 10 percent reported that they had experienced an episode of MDD by age 20. The median age of onset is now the late teens to early 20s, and depression is now all too present on college campuses (Auerbach, Alonso, et al., 2016).

There is a fair amount of overlap, or comorbidity, in diagnoses of persistent depressive disorder and MDD. Fifteen to 30 percent of those with MDD will have symptoms that persist for at least 2 years, so will then qualify for persistent depressive disorder (Murphy & Byrne, 2012; Eaton, et al., 2008). Most people with persistent depressive disorder will experience episodes of MDD (Vandeleur, Fassassi, et al., 2017).

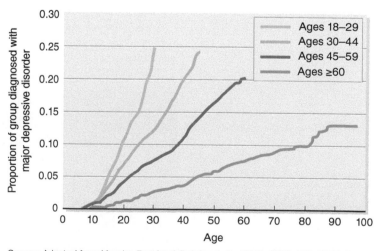

Source: Adapted from Kessler, Berglund, Demler et al., JAMA, 2003: 289, 3095–3105.

FIGURE 5.1 With each generation, the median age of onset for MDD gets younger.

Both MDD and persistent depressive disorder are often comorbid with other psychological disorders. About 60 percent of people who meet the criteria for diagnosis of MDD during their lifetime also will meet the criteria for diagnosis of an anxiety disorder at some point (Kessler, et al., 2010). See **Focus on Discovery 5.5** later in the chapter for more discussion of the overlap of anxiety disorders and depressive disorders. Other common comorbid conditions include substance-related disorders, sexual dysfunctions, and personality disorders.

Depression has many serious consequences. From the depths of a depression, getting to work may require overwhelming effort, parenting can feel like a burden, and suicide can seem like an option. As we will discuss later in this chapter, suicide is a real risk. MDD is also the third leading cause of disability worldwide (Vos, Allen, et al., 2016). In 2010, MDD was associated with more than $80 billion in treatment costs and lost productivity in the United States (Greenberg, Fournier, et al., 2015). MDD also has important effects for the next generation: Offspring who are exposed to a mother's MDD during early childhood are at high risk for developing depression (Hammen, Hazel, et al., 2012).

MDD is also related to a high risk of other health problems (Scott, et al., 2016), including death from medical diseases (Mykletun, Bjerkeset, et al., 2009). There is particularly strong evidence that depression is related to the onset and more severe course of cardiovascular disease (Carney & Freedland, 2017). Depression is related to a more than twofold increase in the risk of death from cardiovascular disease, even after controlling for baseline cardiovascular health (Meijer, Conradi, et al., 2011).

Although the diagnostic criteria for persistent depressive disorder include fewer symptoms than those for MDD do, do not make the mistake of thinking that persistent depressive disorder is a less severe disorder than MDD. Chronic depressive symptoms persist on average for 10 years (Klein & Kotov, 2016). The chronicity of these symptoms takes a toll. Indeed, a study following patients for 5 years found that people with chronic depressive symptoms were more likely to require hospitalization, to attempt suicide, and to be impaired in their functioning than were people with MDD (Klein, Schwartz, et al., 2000). Functioning declines as depressive symptoms persist for more years (Klein, Shankman, & Rose, 2006).

Quick Summary

The DSM-5 contains two broad types of mood disorders: depressive disorders and bipolar disorders.

Depressive disorders include major depressive disorder and persistent depressive disorder as well as two more recently recognized disorders: premenstrual dysphoric disorder and disruptive mood dysregulation disorder.

Major depression is characterized by severe episodes lasting at least 2 weeks, whereas persistent depressive disorder is characterized by symptoms that last at least 2 years.

MDD is one of the most common psychological disorders. MDD and persistent depressive disorder affect twice as many women as men. Forty to 50% of people with MDD will experience another episode within 10 years.

Check Your Knowledge 5.1
(Answers are at the end of the chapter.)

Fill in the blanks.

1. Major depressive disorder is diagnosed based on at least _____ symptoms lasting at least _____ weeks.

2. Approximately _____ percent of people will experience major depressive disorder during their lifetime.

Answer the question.

3. What is the key difference between the diagnostic criteria for major depressive disorder and persistent depressive disorder?

Clinical Descriptions and Epidemiology of Bipolar Disorders

The DSM-5 recognizes three forms of bipolar disorders: bipolar I disorder, bipolar II disorder, and cyclothymic disorder. Manic symptoms are the defining feature of each of these disorders. The bipolar disorders are differentiated by how severe and long-lasting the manic symptoms are.

These disorders are labeled "bipolar" because most people who experience mania will also experience depression during their lifetime (mania and depression are considered opposite poles). Contrary to what people may believe, an episode of depression is not required for a diagnosis of bipolar I (although most people with an episode of mania will experience an episode of depression; see Cuellar, Johnson, & Winters, 2005). Depression is required for a diagnosis of bipolar II disorder.

Mania is a state of intense elation or irritability, along with activation and other symptoms shown in the diagnostic criteria. During manic episodes, people will act and think in ways that are highly unusual compared to their typical selves. They may become louder and make an incessant stream of remarks, sometimes full of puns, jokes, rhymes, and interjections about nearby stimuli that attract their attention. They may be difficult to interrupt and may shift rapidly from topic to topic, reflecting an underlying **flight of ideas**. During mania, people may become sociable to the point of intrusiveness. They can also become excessively self-confident. They may stop sleeping even as they become incredibly energetic. Attempts by others to curb such excesses can quickly bring anger and even rage. Mania often comes on suddenly over a period of a day or two. For many, the boundless energy, bursts of joy, and incredible surge in goal pursuit are welcome, so that some fail to recognize the sudden changes as a sign of disorder. The passages in the clinical description by Kay Redfield Jamison illustrate some of the rapid shifts that can occur.

Demi Lovato, the highly successful singer, songwriter, and actress, has drawn from her own experiences with bipolar disorder to become a mental health advocate (Washington, 2017).

Clinical Case

Kay Redfield Jamison

The following passage from Kay Redfield Jamison describes some of the positive feelings that can accompany hypomanic states, and some of the concerns that can unfold as mania develops.

> When you're high it's tremendous. The ideas and feelings are fast and frequent like shooting stars, and you follow them until you find better and brighter ones. Shyness goes, the right words and gestures are suddenly there, the power to captivate others a felt certainty. There are interests found in uninteresting people. Sensuality is pervasive and the desire to seduce and be seduced irresistible. Feelings of ease, intensity, power, well-being, financial omnipotence, and euphoria pervade one's marrow. But, somewhere, this changes. The fast ideas are far too fast, and there are far too many; overwhelming confusion replaces clarity. Memory goes. Humor and absorption on friends' faces are replaced by fear and concern. (Jamison, 1993, pp. 67–68)

Unfortunately, people can be oblivious to the potentially disastrous consequences of their manic behavior, which can include risky sexual activities, overspending, and reckless driving. The following quote, also from Kay Redfield Jamison, illustrates some of the impulsivity of this state.

> When I am high I couldn't worry about money if I tried. So I don't. The money will come from somewhere; I am entitled; God will provide. . . So I bought twelve snakebite kits, with a sense of urgency and importance. I bought precious stones, elegant and unnecessary furniture, three watches within an hour of one another (in the Rolex rather than Timex class: champagne tastes bubble to the surface, are the surface, in mania), and totally inappropriate siren-like clothes. During one spree in London I spent several hundred pounds on books having titles or covers that somehow caught my fancy: books on the natural history of the mole, twenty sundry Penguin books because I thought it could be nice if the penguins could form a colony. Once I think I shoplifted a blouse because I could not wait a minute longer for the woman-with-molasses feet in front of me in line. Or maybe I just thought about shoplifting, I don't remember, I was totally confused. I imagine I must have spent far more than thirty thousand dollars during my two major manic episodes, and God only knows how much more during my frequent milder manias. But then back on lithium and rotating on the planet at the same pace as everyone else, you find your credit is decimated, your mortification complete. (Jamison, 1995, p. 75)

DSM-5 Criteria for Manic and Hypomanic Episodes

Distinctly elevated or irritable mood.
Abnormally increased activity or energy.
At least three of the following are noticeably changed from baseline (four if mood is irritable):

- Increase in goal-directed activity or psychomotor agitation

- Unusual talkativeness; rapid speech

- Flight of ideas or subjective impression that thoughts are racing

- Decreased need for sleep

- Increased self-esteem; belief that one has special talents, powers, or abilities

- Distractibility; attention easily diverted

- Excessive involvement in pleasurable activities that are likely to have painful consequences, such as reckless spending, sexual indiscretions, or unwise business investments
- Symptoms are present most of the day, nearly every day

For a manic episode:

- Symptoms last 1 week, require hospitalization, or include psychosis
- Symptoms cause significant distress or functional impairment

For a hypomanic episode:

- Symptoms last at least 4 days
- Clear changes in functioning are observable to others, but impairment is not marked
- No psychotic symptoms are present

The DSM-5 also includes criteria for **hypomania** (see diagnostic criteria for manic and hypomanic episodes). *Hypo-* comes from the Greek for "under"; hypomania is "under"—less extreme than—mania. Although mania involves significant impairment, hypomania does not. Rather, hypomania involves a change in functioning that does not cause serious problems. The person with hypomania may feel more social, energized, productive, and sexually alluring.

Bipolar I Disorder

In the DSM-5, the criteria for diagnosis of **bipolar I disorder** (formerly known as manic-depressive disorder) include at least one episode of mania during the course of a person's life. Note, then, that a person who is diagnosed with bipolar I disorder may or may not be experiencing current symptoms of mania. In fact, even someone who experienced only 1 week of manic symptoms years ago is still diagnosed with bipolar I disorder.

Bipolar II Disorder

The DSM-5 also includes a milder form of bipolar disorder, called **bipolar II disorder**. To be diagnosed with bipolar II disorder, a person must have experienced at least one major depressive episode and at least one episode of hypomania (and no lifetime episode of mania).

Cyclothymic Disorder

Catherine Zeta-Jones has discussed her diagnosis of bipolar II disorder (*Reuters*, 2013). As is common, her depression was recognized before the hypomanic episodes were.

Also called *cyclothymia*, **cyclothymic disorder** is a chronic mood disorder. Parallel to the diagnosis of persistent depressive disorder, the DSM-5 criteria require that symptoms be present for at least 2 years among adults. In cyclothymic disorder, the person has frequent but mild symptoms of depression, alternating with mild symptoms of mania. Although the symptoms do not reach the severity of full-blown hypomanic or depressive episodes, people with the disorder and those close to them typically notice the ups and downs.

DSM-5 Criteria for Cyclothymic Disorder

For at least 2 years (or 1 year in children or adolescents):

- Numerous periods with hypomanic symptoms that do not meet criteria for a hypomanic episode
- Numerous periods with depressive symptoms that do not meet criteria for a major depressive episode

The symptoms do not clear for more than 2 months at a time.

Criteria for a major depressive, manic, or hypomanic episode have never been met.

Symptoms cause significant distress or functional impairment.

Epidemiology and Consequences of Bipolar Disorders

Bipolar I disorder is much rarer than MDD. In the World Mental Health Survey, an epidemiological study that involved structured diagnostic interviews with a representative sample of 61,392 people across 11 countries, about 0.6 percent of people met the criteria for bipolar I disorder (Merikangas, Jin, et al., 2011). Rates of bipolar disorder appear to be higher in the United States than in other countries. In the United States, about 1 percent of people experience bipolar I disorder.

Less is known about the prevalence of milder forms of bipolar disorder. Findings of large-scale epidemiological studies suggest that bipolar II disorder affects somewhere between 0.4 percent and 2 percent of people (Merikangas, et al., 2011). It is estimated that about 4 percent of people experience cyclothymic disorder (Regeer, ten Have, et al. 2004).

Like depression, bipolar disorders are being seen with increasing frequency among children and adolescents (Kessler, Berglund, et al., 2005). More than half of those with bipolar spectrum disorders report onset before age 25 (Merikangas, et al., 2011). Although bipolar disorders occur equally often in men and women, women diagnosed with bipolar disorder experience more episodes of depression than do men with this diagnosis (Altshuler, Kupka, et al., 2010). Even more than episodes of MDD, bipolar episodes tend to recur. More than half of people with bipolar I disorder experience four or more episodes during their lifetimes (Goodwin & Jamison, 2007). Across the forms of bipolar disorder, a meta-analysis of eight studies ($N = 734$) found that rates of recurrence averaged 41% in the first year and 60% over the first four years after the first episode of bipolar disorder (Gignac, McGirr, et al., 2015). About two-thirds of people diagnosed with bipolar disorder meet diagnostic criteria for a comorbid anxiety disorder, and many report a history of substance abuse.

Bipolar I disorder is among the most severe forms of psychological disorders. In a large community sample, less than 15 percent of people with bipolar disorder had been employed full-time in the past year. Functional outcomes were particularly low for those with ongoing symptoms (Morgan, Mitchell, & Jablensky, 2005).

In the World Mental Health Survey, one in four persons diagnosed with bipolar I disorder reported a suicide attempt and more than half reported suicidal ideation within the past year (Merikangas, et al., 2011). In a national cohort of individuals who were followed for 36 years after psychiatric hospitalization, bipolar disorder was the psychiatric condition with the highest rate of suicide (Nordentoft, Mortensen, & Pedersen, 2011). Even in countries with accessible medical care for all, bipolar disorder has been found to relate to dying an average of 8.5 to 9 years earlier than those in the general population (Crump, Sundquist, et al., 2013). Increased risk of death from cardiovascular disease has been particularly well documented, with estimates that the risk of death from cardiovascular disease is twice as high for those with bipolar disorder compared with the general population. Risks, though, are not restricted to cardiovascular disease—large national cohort studies suggest higher mortality from a range of medical conditions (Westman, Hällgren, et al., 2013). These sad consequences of bipolar disorders are not offset by evidence that bipolar individuals and their family members possess heightened creativity (see **Focus on Discovery 5.3**).

People with cyclothymia are at elevated risk for developing episodes of mania and major depression. Even if full-blown manic episodes do not emerge, the chronicity of cyclothymic symptoms takes its toll.

Focus on Discovery 5.3

Creativity and Mood Disorders

In her book *Touched with Fire: Manic-Depressive Illness and the Artistic Temperament* (1993), Kay Redfield Jamison, an expert on bipolar disorders, and a longtime sufferer from bipolar I disorder, assembled evidence linking mood disorders, especially bipolar disorder, to artistic creativity. Of course, most people with mood disorders are not exceptionally creative, and most creative people do not have mood disorders—but the list of visual artists, composers, and writers who seem to have experienced mood disorders is impressive. The list includes Michelangelo, van Gogh, Tchaikovsky, Schumann, Gauguin, Tennyson, Shelley, Faulkner, Hemingway, F. Scott Fitzgerald, Whitman, and Robert Lowell. In recent years, many actors and actresses have also spoken out about their history of mania, including Stephen Fry, Carrie Fisher, and Linda Hamilton. The biographical findings dovetail with results from a population-based study of more than a million people in which those with bipolar disorder and their unaffected family members were overrepresented in creative occupations compared to the general population (Kyaga, Landen, et al., 2013). Some organizations, such as the Sean Costello Memorial Fund for Bipolar Research (http://www.seancostellofund.org) focus on this topic.

Many people assume that the manic state itself fosters creativity through elated mood, increased energy, rapid thoughts, and a heightened ability to make connections among seemingly unrelated events. Extreme mania, however, lowers creative output, and even if people produce more work during a manic period, the quality of that work might suffer, as seems to have been the case for the composer Robert Schumann (Weisberg, 1994). Moreover, studies have shown that people who have experienced episodes of mania tend to be less creative than those who have had the milder episodes of hypomania, and both groups tend to produce less creative output than do non-ill family members (Richards, Kinney, et al., 1988). Although many people with bipolar disorder worry that taking medications may limit their creativity, these findings suggest that reducing manic symptoms should help, rather than hurt, creativity.

Frank Sinatra is quoted as having said this about himself: "Being an 18-karat manic depressive, and having lived a life of violent emotional contradictions, I have an over-acute capacity for sadness as well as elation." (Summers & Swan, 2006, p. 218).

Mood disorders are common among artists and writers. Tchaikovsky was affected.

Quick Summary

Bipolar disorders include bipolar I disorder, bipolar II disorder, and cyclothymic disorder.

Bipolar I disorder is diagnosed on the basis of a single lifetime manic episode, and bipolar II disorder is diagnosed on the basis of hypomania and major depression. Cyclothymia is defined by frequent shifts between mild depressive and manic symptoms that last at least 2 years.

Bipolar I disorder affects 1 percent or less of the population.

About half of people with bipolar I disorder experience four or more episodes.

Check Your Knowledge 5.2

Fill in the blank.

1. Worldwide, approximately _____ out of every 1000 people will experience a manic episode during their lifetime.

Answer the question.

2. What is the key difference between the diagnostic criteria for bipolar I disorder and bipolar II disorder?

Etiology of Mood Disorders

When we think of the profound extremes embodied in the mood disorders, it is natural to ask why these extremes happen. How can we explain Mary sinking into the depths of depression? What factors combined to drive Kay into her racing thoughts and reckless shopping? Studies of etiology focus on why these disorders unfold. No single cause can explain mood disorders. A number of different factors combine to explain their onset.

Although the DSM includes several different depressive disorders and bipolar disorders, the research on etiology and treatment has tended to focus on major depressive disorder and bipolar I disorder. For simplicity, we refer to these conditions as *depression* and *bipolar disorder* through the remainder of this chapter.

We begin by discussing biological factors involved in depression and bipolar disorder. As **Table 5.2** shows, many different biological approaches have been applied to mood disorders, and we will describe genetic, neurotransmitter, brain-imaging, and neuroendocrine research. After describing these biological risk factors for depressive and bipolar disorders, we discuss psychosocial predictors of depression, and then turn to psychosocial models of bipolar disorder.

Genetic Factors

As described in Chapter 2, heritability can be interpreted as the proportion of the variance in depression (within the population) that is explained by genes. The most careful studies of heritability involve interviews with representative samples of twins selected from the community (rather than focusing only on people who seek treatment, who may have more severe cases of the disorder than those who are not treated). These more careful studies of MZ (identical) and DZ (fraternal) twins yield heritability estimates of .37 for MDD (Sullivan, Neale, & Kendler, 2000). Heritability estimates are higher when researchers study more severe samples (e.g., when the people in the study are recruited from inpatient hospitals rather than outpatient clinics).

Bipolar disorder is among the most heritable of disorders. One community-based twin sample that used structured interviews to verify diagnoses obtained a heritability estimate of .93 (Kieseppa, Partonen, et al., 2004). Adoption studies also confirm the importance of heritability in bipolar disorder (Wender, Kety, et al., 1986). Bipolar I and Bipolar II disorders are both highly heritable (Edvardsen, Torgersen, et al., 2008).

Molecular genetics research (see Chapter 2) aims to identify the specific genes involved in mood disorders. To place molecular genetics research in context, it is worth pausing to consider the incredible range of depressive and bipolar symptoms that a person might experience. Because mood disorders, and indeed most psychological disorders, are so complex and heterogeneous, it is highly unlikely that there is one single gene that explains these illnesses. Most researchers believe that these disorders will be related eventually to a large set of genes, with each gene accounting for a minute proportion of risk.

TABLE 5.2	Summary of Neurobiological Hypotheses About Major Depression and Bipolar Disorder	
Neurobiological Hypothesis	**Major Depression**	**Bipolar Disorder**
Genetic contribution	Moderate	High
Neurotransmitter (serotonin, dopamine) dysfunction	Mixed evidence	Mixed evidence
Changes in activation of regions in the brain in response to emotion stimuli	Present	Present
Activation of the striatum in response to reward	Diminished	Elevated
Cortisol awakening response	Elevated	Elevated among those with depression

Likely due to the very small effects of any one gene, genome-wide association studies (GWAS) with tens of thousands of participants have failed to identify specific genetic loci replicably associated with MDD (Ripke, Wray, et al., 2013). Researchers will likely need to consider more specific dimensions within MDD to identify molecular genetic profiles. Researchers have had more success when they consider how age of onset, recurrence, ethnic background, neuroticism, and symptom profiles influence the molecular genetic profile of MDD (Converge Consortium, 2015; Gale, Hagenaars, et al., 2016; Power, Tansey, et al., 2017). These findings suggest that it will be helpful to study genetic loci in more narrowly defined subgroups of those with MDD.

In a GWAS study of more than 24,000 participants, 56 single nucleotide polymorphisms (SNPs) related to bipolar disorder were identified (Mühleisen, Leber, et al., 2014). Copy number variants (CNVs) also have been identified in bipolar disorder. Many of the CNVs and SNPs related to bipolar disorder overlap with those involved in schizophrenia (CDGPGC, 2013; Green, Rees, et al., 2016).

One way to enhance statistical power is to examine a narrower set of genetic loci, focusing on those genetic loci that are most relevant for biological pathways involved in mood disorders rather than the broad set of more than a million loci typically examined in GWAS. Using this type of approach, MDD has been tied to genetic loci involved in serotonin and glutamate function (Smoller, 2016). Bipolar disorder has been related to genetic polymorphisms relevant to serotonin (Lasky-Su, Faraone, et al., 2005) and to multiple pathways that help regulate neurotransmitter function (Nurnberger, Koller, et al., 2014).

A different approach is to consider whether a given gene might increase risk of depression in the presence of environmental risk factors (a gene × environment interaction, as discussed in Chapter 2). This approach shows that a polymorphism of the **serotonin transporter gene** does appear to be related to MDD. In one study, a large sample of children in New Zealand was followed from the age of 5 until their mid-20s (Caspi, Sugden, et al., 2003). The researchers repeatedly assessed a number of variables, including early childhood maltreatment (abuse) and depression as an adult. They also measured a particular gene called the serotonin transporter gene. This gene has a polymorphism such that some people have two short alleles (short–short), some have two long alleles (long–long), and some have one short and one long allele (short–long). Caspi and colleagues found that those who had the short-short allele or the short-long allele combinations of the serotonin transporter gene were at risk for depression—but only if they also experienced childhood maltreatment (see **Figure 5.2**, panel A). Thus, having the gene was not a strong predictor of an episode of depression, nor was the presence

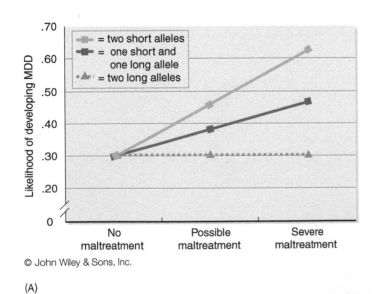

© John Wiley & Sons, Inc.

(A)

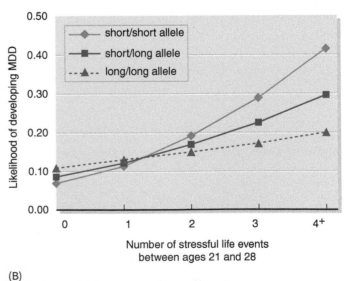

(B)

FIGURE 5.2 Childhood maltreatment (A) and adulthood life events (B) interact with the serotonin transporter gene to predict the likelihood of major depressive disorder. Source: Adapted from Caspi et al., Science, 2003, 388.

of childhood maltreatment. Rather, it was the specific combination of the gene configuration and environmental events that predicted depression. They found the same gene–environment interaction for having at least one short allele of the gene and reports of stressful life events. That is, those people who reported more severe stressful life events and had at least one short allele of the serotonin transporter gene were at greater risk of developing depression (see Figure 5.2, Panel B). In rhesus monkeys, the presence of at least one short allele in this gene is associated with poor serotonergic function. Thus, some people seem to inherit a propensity for a weaker serotonin system, which is then expressed as a greater likelihood to experience depression after childhood maltreatment or an adulthood severe stressor.

The Caspi findings have been replicated in other large-scale studies, particularly when the studies involved careful measurement of maltreatment and life stressors (Hankin, et al., 2015; Uher & McGuffin, 2010). When researchers did not use more careful measures of life stress and adversity, the findings have not been replicated (Culverhouse, Saccone, et al., 2017). This suggests that it is important to use careful measures of environmental factors if we hope to understand gene $\times$ environment effects.

Other researchers have extended these findings. In one large study, this genetic polymorphism appeared particularly likely to lead to the onset of depressive symptoms among those who encounter serious interpersonal stressors, but not those with non-interpersonal stressors (Vrshek-Schallhorn, Mineka, et al., 2013). Intriguingly, this polymorphism in the serotonin transporter gene has also been related to risk factors for depression that we will be discussing later in this chapter, including activity in key brain regions (e.g., the amygdala, described below; Caspi, Hariri, et al., 2010) and negative cognitive tendencies (e.g., biased attention to negative information; Gibb, Beevers, & McGeary, 2013). Similar findings have emerged for CRH1, a gene involved in guiding the reactivity of the cortisol system, which appears related to depression only among those with a history of child abuse (Smoller, et al., 2016). This type of work, then, suggests that we should be considering genes for depression in concert with environmental risk factors.

Neurotransmitters

Several neurotransmitters have been intensively studied in mood disorders: norepinephrine, dopamine, and serotonin. Each of these neurotransmitters is present in many different areas of the brain. **Figure 5.3** illustrates how widespread serotonin and dopamine pathways are in the brain. For decades, researchers studied the idea that mood disorders would be related to having too much or too little of a neurotransmitter, with mixed results. More recent models have focused on the idea that mood disorders might involve changes in receptors that respond to the presence of neurotransmitters in the synaptic cleft (see **Figure 5.4**). Because imaging methods are not well developed for norepinephrine, most of the studies that use PET or SPECT imaging to examine neurotransmitters focus on the function of the serotonin and dopamine pathways.

There are several reasons to think that serotonin would be involved in mood disorders. The most common forms of antidepressant medications (discussed below) target the serotonin system. This may not tell us about the cause of depression though—aspirin may be helpful for a sprained ankle, but no one believes that sprained ankles are caused by a deficit in aspirin. Beyond the effects of treatment, though, there is considerable evidence, discussed above, that the serotonin transporter polymorphism interacts with adversity to increase risk for depression.

Similarly, there are several reasons to think that dopamine may be important to understanding mood disorders. Dopamine plays a major role in the sensitivity of the **reward system** in the brain, which is believed to guide pleasure, motivation, and energy in the context of opportunities to obtain rewards (Depue & Iacono, 1989). At a conceptual level, diminished function of the dopamine system could help explain the deficits in

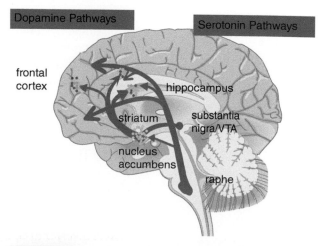

FIGURE 5.3 Serotonin and dopamine pathways are widespread in the brain.

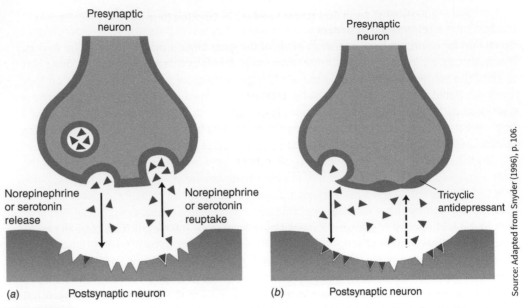

Presynaptic neuron

Presynaptic neuron

Norepinephrine or serotonin release

Norepinephrine or serotonin reuptake

Tricyclic antidepressant

(a) Postsynaptic neuron

(b) Postsynaptic neuron

Source: Adapted from Snyder (1996), p. 106.

FIGURE 5.4 (a) When neurotransmitters are released into a synapse, a pump-like reuptake mechanism begins to recapture some of the neurotransmitter before it reaches the postsynaptic neuron. (b) Tricyclic antidepressant drugs block this reuptake process so that more neurotransmitter reaches the receptor. Selective serotonin reuptake inhibitors, another form of antidepressant, act more selectively on serotonin.

pleasure, motivation, and energy in depression (Treadway & Zald, 2011), and similarly, heightened activity in this system could help explain the joy, goal-driven behavior, and energy seen in mania (Cousins, Butts, & Young, 2009).

Consistent with theory, there is some evidence from pharmacological studies that the functioning of the dopamine is disrupted in the mood disorders. People with depression are less responsive than other people are to drugs that increase dopamine levels (Pizzagalli, 2014). Among people with bipolar disorder, drugs that increase dopamine levels have been found to trigger manic symptoms (Anand, Verhoeff, et al., 2000; Burdick, Braga, et al., 2014).

Despite the pharmacological evidence, the findings of several dozen PET imaging studies have not consistently identified differences in the function of serotonin or dopamine pathways among people with MDD as compared to controls (Treadway & Pizzagalli, 2014). Given these gaps, many are considering more refined models of how neurotransmitters might relate to mood disorders. A growing body of research suggests that stress may lead to changes in the sensitivity of serotonin receptors (Maes, Leonard, et al., 2011). Perhaps those stress-related shifts could intensify the risk of depression. Testing this idea will require longitudinal studies (Treadway & Pizzagalli, 2014). Another possibility is that dopamine dysfunction is tied to specific symptoms in the mood disorders, such as lowered energy and motivation (Treadway & Pizzagalli, 2014). Hopefully, models of neurotransmitter dysfunction will be improved by considering the effects of stress and more specific symptom profiles (Pizzagalli, 2014).

Neural Regions Involved in Emotion and Reward Processing

Functional brain-imaging studies suggest that MDD is associated with changes in neural systems involved in experiencing and regulating emotion and in responding to rewards (Treadway & Pizzagalli, 2014). Many of these studies examine neural responses to stimuli that would likely induce emotion, such as pictures of positive or negative scenes, or to rewards, such as earning money. **Table 5.3** summarizes five primary brain structures that have been most studied in depression: the amygdala, the **anterior cingulate**, the **prefrontal cortex**,

TABLE 5.3	Activity of Brain Structures Involved in Emotion Responses Among People With Mood Disorders	
Brain Structure	**Level in Depression**	**Level in Mania**
Amygdala	Elevated	Elevated
Anterior cingulate	Elevated	Elevated
Regions of the prefrontal cortex	Diminished	Diminished
Hippocampus	Diminished	Diminished
Striatum	Diminished	Elevated

the hippocampus, and the **striatum** (see also **Figure 5.5**). Several different regions of the prefrontal cortex, including the medial prefrontal cortex, the orbitofrontal cortex, and the **dorsolateral prefrontal cortex**, are involved in the mood disorders. We will discuss each of these regions, beginning with the amygdala.

The amygdala is engaged when people perceive salient and emotionally important stimuli. For example, the amygdala responds when people are shown pictures of threatening stimuli. Animals with damage to the amygdala fail to react with fear to threatening stimuli and also fail to respond positively to food. Functional brain activation studies show

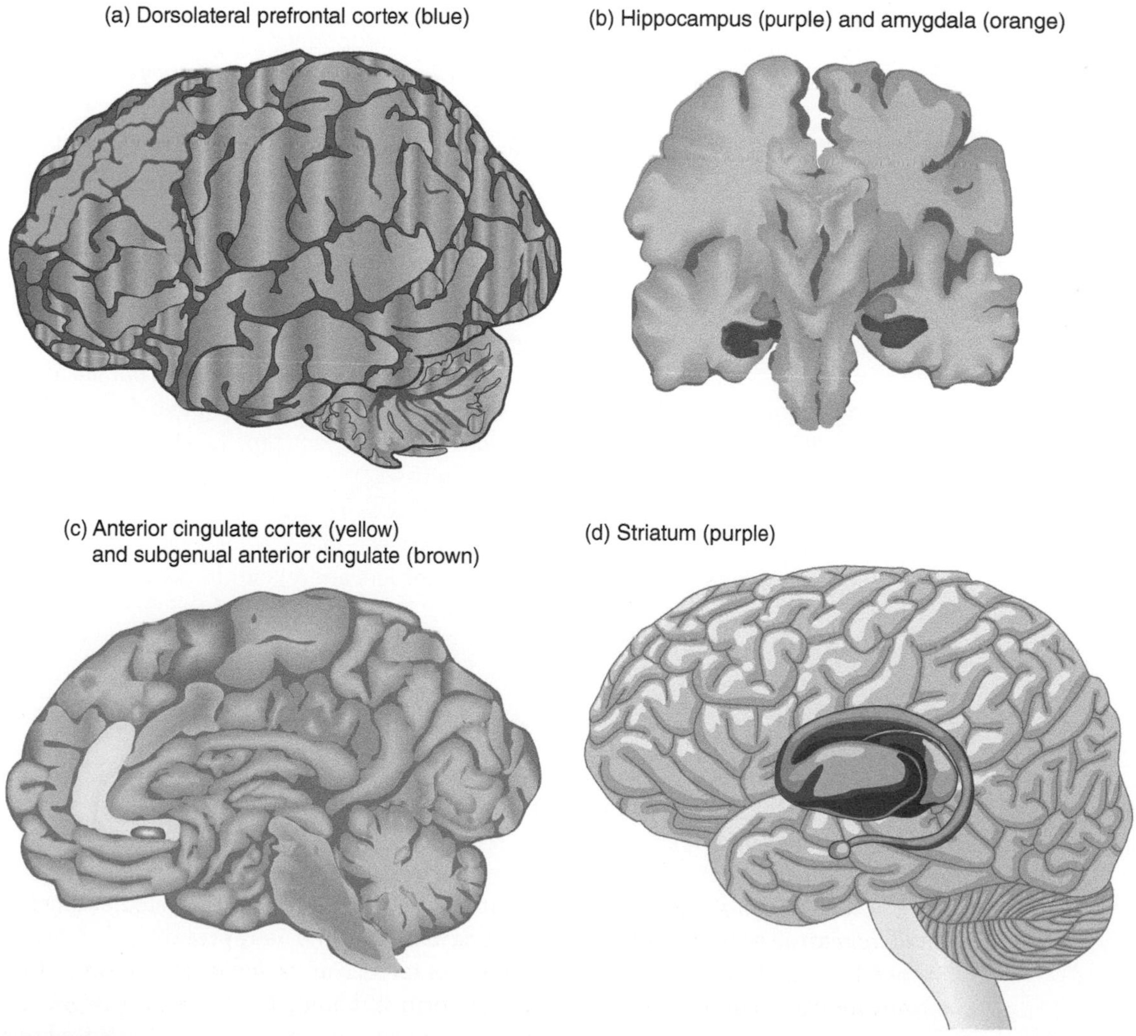

(a) Dorsolateral prefrontal cortex (blue)

(b) Hippocampus (purple) and amygdala (orange)

(c) Anterior cingulate cortex (yellow) and subgenual anterior cingulate (brown)

(d) Striatum (purple)

Source: Adapted from Davidson, *Annual Review of Psychology*, 53, 2002. Copyright 2002 by Annual Reviews, www.annualreviews.org.

FIGURE 5.5 Key brain regions involved in mood disorders.

elevated activity of the amygdala when processing emotion-relevant stimuli among people with MDD. For example, when shown negative words or pictures of sad or angry faces, people with current MDD show a more intense and sustained reaction in the amygdala than do people with no MDD (Treadway & Pizzagalli, 2014). Amygdala over-reactivity to emotional stimuli is also shown among relatives of people with depression who have no personal history of MDD, suggesting this might be part of the vulnerability to depression rather than just the aftermath of being depressed (Pilhatsch, Vetter, et al., 2014; Swartz, Williamson, & Hariri, 2015). Amygdala over-reactivity is also shown in other groups who are at risk for depression, such as those who have been exposed to recent stressful life events (Swartz, et al. 2015).

In addition to the amygdala, MDD is associated with greater activation of the anterior cingulate (Hamilton, Etkin, et al., 2012) and diminished activation of the hippocampus and several regions of the prefrontal cortex when viewing negative stimuli (Hamilton, et al., 2012; Treadway & Pizzagalli, 2014). Disturbances in these regions are believed to interfere with effective emotion regulation. In addition to changes in functional activation patterns to specific stimuli, an analysis of more than 8500 participants suggested that the size of the hippocampus was diminished among those with MDD, particularly among those with earlier onset and those with more previous episodes of depression (Schmaal, Veltman, et al., 2016).

How might these findings fit together? One theory is that the over-activity in the amygdala during depression is related to oversensitivity to emotionally relevant stimuli. At the same time, systems involved in regulating emotions are compromised (the anterior cingulate, the hippocampus, and regions of the dorsolateral prefrontal cortex).

In addition to these models of emotion reactivity and regulation, neural regions involved in responding and mobilizing to rewards may also be underactive. For example, people with depression demonstrate diminished activation of the striatum during exposure to emotional stimuli (Hamilton, et al., 2012), and particularly to reward stimuli, such as money (Treadway & Pizzagalli, 2014). A specific region of the striatum (called the nucleus accumbens) is a central component of the reward system in the brain and plays a key role in motivation to pursue rewards (Salamone & Correa, 2012). The lack of activity of the striatum in response to positive feedback, then, may help explain why people with depression feel less motivated by the positive events in their lives.

Many of the brain structures implicated in MDD also appear to be involved in bipolar disorder. Bipolar I disorder is associated with elevated activity of the amygdala and the anterior cingulate during emotion regulation tasks, and diminished activity of the hippocampus and dorsolateral prefrontal cortex (Phillips & Swartz, 2014). Although these patterns parallel those observed among people with MDD, one difference emerges. People with bipolar disorder tend to show high activation of the striatum in functional MRI studies (Chen, Suckling, et al., 2011), in contrast with the low activity observed for those with MDD.

Many researchers have begun to focus on how these regions interact, using connectivity analyses to examine the strength of connection between these regions, or neural circuits. A growing body of work suggests that the mood disorders are related to disruptions in the connectivity of these regions (Phillips & Swartz, 2014; Singh & Gotlib, 2014; Williams, 2017).

Cortisol Dysregulation

The HPA axis (hypothalamic–pituitary–adrenocortical axis; see Figure 2.10) may be overly active during episodes of MDD, which is consistent with the idea that stress reactivity is an important part of depression. As described above, there is evidence that the amygdala is overly reactive among people with MDD, and the amygdala sends signals that activate the HPA axis. The HPA axis triggers the release of cortisol, the main stress hormone. Cortisol is secreted at times of stress and increases the activity of the immune system to help the body prepare for threats.

Various findings link depression to high cortisol levels. For example, people with **Cushing syndrome**, which causes over-secretion of cortisol, frequently experience depressive symptoms. A second line of research with animals has shown that when chemicals that trigger cortisol release are injected into the brain, many of the classic symptoms of depression are produced, including decreased interest in sex, decreased appetite, and sleep disturbance (Gutman & Nemeroff, 2003). In animals and humans, then, too much cortisol seems to produce depressive symptoms.

Cortisol has very strong diurnal rhythms, and research suggests that this rhythm may be important to consider in depression. Cortisol levels increase sharply as people wake and then in the 30–40 minutes after waking, a pattern that is called the **cortisol awakening response (CAR)**. In a longitudinal study of 270 adolescents, a larger CAR at study baseline was related to higher risk of a major depressive episode over the next two and a half years. CAR predicted the onset of a first episode among those with no prior history, and a recurrence among those with a previous MDE (Vrshek-Schallhorn, Doane, et al., 2013). In a second study of 549 adults who had achieved remission from MDE, high CAR levels predicted recurrence of MDE (Hardeveld, Spijker, et al., 2014). CAR has also been found to be elevated among those with bipolar disorder, although it is more tied to depression than mania among those with bipolar disorder (Girshkin, Matheson, et al., 2014).

Although cortisol helps mobilize beneficial short-term stress responses, prolonged high levels of cortisol can cause harm to body systems. For example, long-term excesses of cortisol have been linked to damage to the hippocampus—this may help explain findings we noted above of smaller-than-normal hippocampus volume among people who have experienced depression for years. Cortisol is also related to the release of pro-inflammatory cytokines, and many studies have found elevated levels of pro-inflammatory cytokines in both MDD (Moylan, Maes, et al., 2013) and bipolar disorder (Modabbernia, Taslimi, et al., 2013). In sum, both bipolar depression and MDD are characterized by problems in the regulation of cortisol levels. Dysregulation in cortisol levels also predicts a more severe course of illness for MDD.

Social Factors in Depression: Childhood Adversity, Life Events, and Interpersonal Difficulties

Interpersonal problems are very common for those with depression, but showing cause and effect takes much more than just documenting this correlation. The depressive symptoms could easily contribute to interpersonal difficulties, as the person withdraws, begins to feel irritable, and finds no joy when engaging with others. To show that interpersonal concerns are not just an effect of the depressive symptoms, longitudinal studies showing that an interpersonal factor is present before onset are extremely important. Fortunately, many large longitudinal studies are available, and we will focus on social variables that have been shown to precede and predict the onset of depressive episodes, including childhood adversity, negative life events, lack of social support, and family criticism.

Childhood adversity, such as early parental death, physical abuse, or sexual abuse, increases the risk that depression will develop later, in adolescence or adulthood (Daley, Hammen, & Rao, 2000) and that those depressive symptoms will be chronic (Klein, Arnow, et al., 2009). One aspect of childhood adversity, child abuse, can set the stage for many of the other risk factors in depression, including a negative cognitive style (Lumley & Harkness, 2007), poorer marital relationship quality (DiLillo, Giuffre, et al., 2001), increased rates of life stress (Harkness, Bagby, & Kennedy, 2012), and altered activity in brain regions involved in depression (Hanson, Adluru, et al., 2013). Child abuse, though, is even more strongly tied to anxiety disorders than to depression (Kessler, McLaughlin, et al., 2010). This suggests that child abuse may increase the risk for several different disorders, whereas other factors may more uniquely contribute to depression.

Beyond childhood adversity, the role of recent stressful life events in triggering episodes of depression is well established. Prospective studies have shown that life events often precede a depressive episode. Even with a prospective study, though, it remains possible that some life events are caused by early symptoms of depression that have not yet developed into a full-blown disorder. Remember the case of Mary, who developed symptoms after she was laid off from her job. Maybe Mary lost her job because her trouble waking in the morning caused her to arrive at work late; disturbed sleep patterns can be an early sign of depression. Even when researchers exclude stressful life events that could have been caused by mild depressive symptoms, there is much evidence that stress can cause depression. In careful prospective studies, 42 to 67 percent of people report that they experienced a very serious life event that was not caused by symptoms in the year before their depression began. Common events include losing a job, a key friendship, or a romantic relationship (Brown & Harris, 1989).

Certain types of stressors, such as those involving interpersonal loss and humiliation, are particularly likely to trigger depressive episodes (Kendler, Hettema, et al., 2003; Vrshek-Schallhorn, Stroud, et al., 2015) and recurrences (Sheets & Craighead, 2014). As examples, the death of a close other or a breakup with one's partner both seem to triple the risk of a depressive episode within the next several months (Kendler et al., 2003). Animals also show depressive-type symptoms after loss. We discuss one model of the role of interpersonal loss and stress in provoking biological changes and depressive symptoms in **Focus on Discovery 5.4**.

Why do some people, but not others, become depressed after stressful life events? The obvious answer is that some people must be more vulnerable to stress than others. Disturbances in many of the neurobiological systems we described above could increase reactivity to stress. Neurobiological factors, then, may be diatheses (preexisting vulnerabilities) that increase risk for mood disorders in the context of other triggers or stressors. The serotonin transporter polymorphism provides one example of a potential diathesis, but social, psychological, and cognitive vulnerabilities also are important and could be diatheses. The most common models, then, consider both diatheses and stressors.

Focus on Discovery 5.4

Integrating Biological and Social Risk Factors for Depression: Cytokines

Depression rates are very high among people with medical conditions such as obesity, cardiovascular disorder, cancer, diabetes, and Alzheimer's disease (Scott, et al., 2016). For a long time, people thought that perhaps depression unfolded as a psychological response to the medical symptoms, but evidence suggests that this overlap in conditions may give us a clue about biological mechanisms in depression (Dantzer, O'Connor, et al., 2008).

The key to this model is that medical conditions often trigger elevations in cytokines. As described in Chapter 2, cytokines are proteins that are released as part of an immune response. One set of these cytokines, pro-inflammatory cytokines, play a vital role in wound healing and fighting off infection by triggering inflammation. In the short term, this inflammation is adaptive. Problems arise, though, when the inflammation becomes prolonged. Current theory is that people may vary in how well and quickly they recover from the influence of pro-inflammatory cytokines and that this prolonged response might be tied to depression.

Two of these pro-inflammatory cytokines, IL-1Beta and TNF-alpha, have been shown to cause a syndrome called sickness behavior, which includes many of the symptoms that are seen in depression: decreased motor activity, reduced food consumption, social withdrawal, changes in sleep patterns, and reduced interest in rewards (like sugar, in the case of rats). A wide range of studies support the idea that pro-inflammatory cytokines can cause sickness behavior. For example, experimental administration of these two cytokines to animals triggers the symptoms of sickness behavior, which can be relieved by administering antidepressant medications. In humans, drugs such as interferon, which are used

for severe medical conditions such as cancer, also increase levels of pro-inflammatory cytokines. Between a third and a half of patients treated with interferon develop the symptoms of MDD (Raison, Capuron, & Miller, 2006). In naturalistic studies without experimental manipulation, many people with MDD, and even those with no medical disorder, show elevated levels of pro-inflammatory cytokines (Raison, Capuron, & Miller, 2006). Researchers have found support for elevated expression of genes related to the pro-inflammatory cytokine IL-6 among those with current MDD as well (Jansen, Penninx, et al., 2016). Pro-inflammatory cytokines are more likely to be elevated in those with repeated episodes of depression (Moylan, et al., 2013). High levels of pro-inflammatory cytokines predict modest increases in depressive symptoms over time (Valkanova, Ebmeier, & Allan, 2013).

Although researchers do not think that all depressions are related to cytokines, cytokines may be important for understanding some of the triggers of depression. One theory is that pro-inflammatory cytokines might be the culprit among people who develop depression in the context of a major medical illness (Dantzer, et al., 2008). Others have argued that inflammation may play a role in how life events trigger symptoms (Slavich & Irwin, 2014). Major life stresses, and particularly interpersonal life stressors, can provoke increases in pro-inflammatory cytokines. In experimental studies, harsh social feedback has been shown to produce temporary increases in pro-inflammatory cytokines (Dickerson, Gruenewald, & Kemeny, 2009). The social stressors that commonly trigger depression may operate in part through this inflammatory mechanism (Slavich & Irwin, 2014). Researchers are testing whether reducing the activity of pro-inflammatory cytokines could help relieve depression (Kohler-Forsberg, Sylvia, et al., 2017; Rosenblat, Kakar, et al., 2016).

One diathesis may be a lack of social support. People who are depressed tend to have sparse social networks and to regard those networks as providing little support. Low social support may lessen a person's ability to handle stressful life events. One study showed that women experiencing a severely stressful life event without support from a confidant had a 40 percent risk of developing depression, whereas those with a confidant's support had only a 4 percent risk (Brown & Andrews, 1986). Social support, then, seems to buffer against the effects of severe stressors.

Family problems are another important interpersonal predictor of depression. A long line of research has focused on **expressed emotion (EE)**—defined as a family member's critical or hostile comments toward or emotional over-involvement with the person with depression. High EE strongly predicts relapse in depression. Indeed, one review of six studies found that 69.5 percent of patients in families with high EE relapsed within 1 year, compared to 30.5 percent of patient in families with low EE (Butzlaff & Hooley, 1998). Marital discord also can predict the onset of depression (Whisman & Bruce, 1999).

Clearly, interpersonal problems can trigger the onset of depressive symptoms, but it is also important to consider the flip side of the coin. Once depressive symptoms emerge, they can create interpersonal problems—that is, depressive symptoms often elicit negative reactions from others (Coyne, 1976). Taken together, it is clear that interpersonal loss, isolation, and relationship concerns can trigger depression, but it is good to be aware that the depression and the related vulnerability can also create challenges in interpersonal relationships.

Psychological Factors in Depression

Many different psychological factors play a role in depressive disorders. In this section, we discuss personality and cognitive factors that operate as diatheses to increase the risk of depression in the context of stress. Here again, we will focus on some of the longitudinal research documenting variables that predict increases in depressive symptoms over time.

Neuroticism   Several longitudinal studies suggest that **neuroticism**, a personality trait that involves the tendency to experience frequent and intense negative affect, predicts the onset of depression (Jorm, Christensen, et al., 2000). A large study of twins suggests that neuroticism explains at least part of the link of genetic vulnerability with depression (Fanous, Prescott, & Kendler, 2004). As you would expect, neuroticism also predicts the onset of anxiety (Zinbarg, Mineka, et al., 2016), an overlap we discuss in **Focus on Discovery 5.5**.

Focus on Discovery 5.5

Understanding the Overlap in Anxiety and Depression

There are several reasons to question whether anxiety disorders are separable from depressive disorders. Chief among these reasons is the high rate of comorbidity. At least 60 percent of people with an anxiety disorder will experience MDD during their lifetime, and vice versa—about 60 percent of those with depression will experience an anxiety disorder (Kessler, et al., 2003; Moffitt, Caspi, et al., 2007). Given the high rates of co-occurrence, many researchers have argued that we should consider depression and anxiety disorders conjointly in an over-arching category of internalizing disorders (Wright, Krueger, et al., 2013).

Beyond patterns of comorbidity, the etiology of anxiety and depression overlaps. The genetic risk for anxiety and depression overlaps substantially (Kendler, Aggen, et al., 2011). Many psychological and social risk factors are tied to both depressive disorders and anxiety disorders, such as neuroticism (Ormel, Jeronimus, et al., 2013) and childhood adversity (Kessler, McLaughlin, et al., 2010).

Rather than lumping the anxiety and depressive symptoms together, the DSM-5 includes a specifier (subtype) "with anxious distress" to be used when depressive episodes are accompanied by at least two anxiety symptoms. Many patients meet the criteria for this specifier. The presence of anxiety among people who are seeking treatment for depression predicts a poor response to antidepressant treatment (Saveanu, Etkin, et al., 2015), suggesting the need to understand much more about people who experience both depression and anxiety.

Cognitive Theories Pessimistic and self-critical thoughts can torture the person with depression. In cognitive theories, these negative thoughts and beliefs are seen not just as symptoms, but as major causes of depression. We will describe three cognitive theories. Beck's theory and hopelessness theory both emphasize these types of negative thoughts, although the theories differ in some important ways. Rumination theory emphasizes the tendency to dwell on negative moods and thoughts. These models are not incompatible with the interpersonal and life stress research discussed earlier; a person's negative thoughts may sometimes reflect genuinely stressful life circumstances. In cognitive models, though, cognitions are seen as the most important force driving depression.

Beck's Theory Aaron Beck (1967) argued that depression is associated with a **negative triad**: negative views of the self, the world, and the future. According to this model, in childhood, people with depression acquired negative schemas through experiences such as loss of a parent, the social rejection of peers, or the depressive attitudes of a parent. Schemas are different from conscious thoughts—they are an underlying set of beliefs that operate outside a person's awareness to shape the way a person makes sense of his or her experiences. The negative schema is activated whenever the person encounters situations similar to those that originally caused the schema to form. Once activated, negative schemas are believed to cause **information-processing biases**, or tendencies to process information in certain negative ways (Kendall & Ingram, 1989). That is, people with depression might attend to and remember even the smallest negative feedback about themselves, while at the same time failing to notice or remember positive feedback about themselves. People with a schema of ineptness might readily notice and remember signs that they are inept, while ignoring or forgetting signs that they are competent. Together, these cognitive errors in attention, interpretation, and recall lead people with depression to draw conclusions that are consistent with their underlying schema, which then maintains the schema (a vicious cycle shown in **Figure 5.6**).

How has Beck's theory been tested? One widely used instrument in studies of Beck's theory is a self-report scale called the Dysfunctional Attitudes Scale (DAS), which includes items concerning whether people would consider themselves worthwhile or lovable. Hundreds of studies have shown that people who are depressed endorse patterns of negative thinking on scales like the DAS (Haaga, Dyck, & Ernst, 1991). Large longitudinal studies suggest that people with negative cognitive styles are at elevated risk for developing a first episode of MDD (Carter & Garber, 2011) and depressive relapse (Segal, Kennedy, et al., 2006).

In studies of information processing, depression is associated with a tendency to stay focused on negative information once it is initially noticed (Gotlib & Joormann, 2010). For example, if shown pictures of negative and positive facial expressions, those with depression tend to look at the negative pictures longer than they look at the positive pictures. Depression also influences memory for negative and positive information. In a meta-analysis of 25 studies, Mathews and MacLeod (2002) described evidence that most people who are not depressed will remember more positive than negative information. For example, if presented with a list of 20 negative and 20 positive self-descriptive adjectives, most people will remember more of the positive than the negative words when queried later in a session. People with MDD, though, tend to remember about 10 percent more negative words than positive words. While nondepressed people seem to wear rose-colored glasses, those with depression tend to have a negative bias in the way that they attend to and recall information.

As with self-reports of negative thoughts, information-processing biases predict depression. In one study, 139 soldiers were tested before they went to the war in Iraq. Baseline tendencies to attend to sad faces were related to greater risk of developing depressive symptoms with exposure to the stresses of war (Beevers, Lee, et al., 2011). Taken together, support has been obtained for Beck's model using a range of measures.

Hopelessness Theory According to **hopelessness theory** (see **Figure 5.7**; Abramson, Metalsky, & Alloy, 1989), the most important trigger of depression is hopelessness, which is defined by the belief that desirable outcomes will not occur and that there is nothing a person can do to change this. The model places emphasis on two key dimensions of **attributions**—the explanations a person forms about why a stressor has occurred (Weiner,

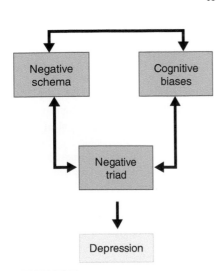

FIGURE 5.6 The interrelationships among different kinds of cognitions in Beck's theory of depression.

Frieze, et al., 1971):

- Stable (permanent) versus unstable (temporary) causes
- Global (relevant to many life domains) versus specific (limited to one area) causes.

Table 5.4 illustrates these dimensions by considering how different people might explain their low score on the Graduate Record Examination (GRE). People whose **attributional style** leads them to believe that negative life events are due to stable and global causes are likely to become hopeless, and this hopelessness will set the stage for depression.

Many studies have been conducted on the hopelessness model of depression. Those studies consistently show that people who are depressed tend to endorse making stable, global attributions for negative events. Among those who are not depressed at baseline, tendencies to make stable, global attributions predict increases in depressive symptoms and greater risk of depressive episodes over time among those who encounter life events (Liu, Kleiman, et al., 2015).

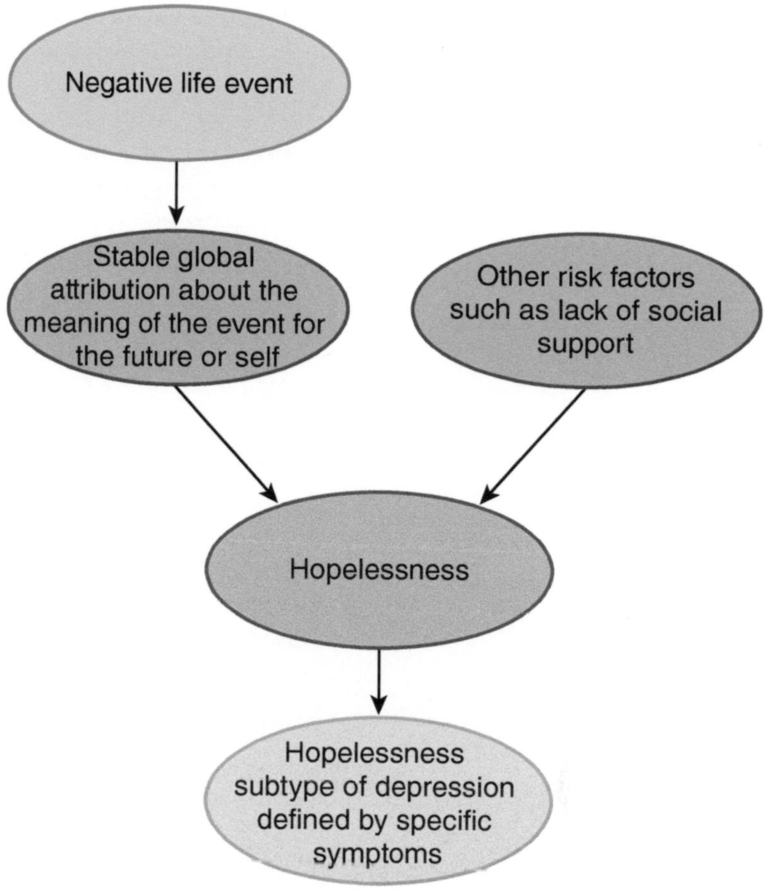

Rumination Theory While Beck's theory and the hopelessness model tend to focus on the nature of negative thoughts, Susan Nolen-Hoeksema (1991) suggested that a way of thinking called **rumination** may increase the risk of depression. Rumination is defined as a tendency to repetitively dwell on sad experiences and thoughts, or to chew on material again and again. The most detrimental form of rumination may be a tendency to brood regretfully about why a sad event happened (Treynor, Gonzalez, & Nolen-Hoeksema, 2003).

FIGURE 5.7 Major elements of the hopelessness theory of depression.

Tendencies to ruminate, as measured using self-report scales, have been found to predict the onset of major depressive episodes among initially nondepressed persons (Nolen-Hoeksema, 2000). As described in Focus on Discovery 5.1, one interesting aspect of this theory is that women tend to ruminate more than men do, perhaps because they are exposed to high levels of interpersonal stressors that can be difficult to solve (Hamilton, Stange, et al., 2015). The tendency for women to ruminate more may help explain the higher rates of depression among women as compared with men (Nolen-Hoeksema, 2000).

Dozens of experimental studies have been conducted to see how inducing rumination affects moods. Typically, in the rumination–induction condition, participants are exposed to stress and then asked to dwell on their current feelings and on themselves (e.g., "Think about the way you feel inside"), whereas in a distraction (control) condition, participants are asked to think about topics unrelated to their self or feelings (e.g., "Think about a fire darting round a log in a fireplace"). The findings of these experimental studies indicate that rumination increases negative moods, particularly when people focus on negative aspects of their mood and their self (Watkins, 2008).

TABLE 5.4 **An Example of Attributions: Why I Failed My GRE Math Exam**

	Stable	Unstable
Global	I lack intelligence.	I am exhausted.
Specific	I lack mathematical ability.	I am fed up with math right now.

If rumination leads to sustained negative moods and even depression, why might people do it? One model suggests that getting stuck on negative thoughts results from a basic inability to control the focus of thoughts. Research shows that people with depression do have a hard time ignoring irrelevant information to complete a task, particularly when they are asked to ignore negative information (Gotlib & Joormann, 2010).

Social and Psychological Factors in Bipolar Disorder

Most people who experience a manic episode during their lifetime will also experience a major depressive episode, but not everyone will. For this reason, researchers often study the triggers of manic and depressive episodes separately within bipolar disorder.

Depression in Bipolar Disorder The triggers of depressive episodes in bipolar disorder are similar to the triggers of major depressive episodes (Johnson, Cuellar, & Peckham, 2014). As in MDD, early adversity, negative life events, neuroticism, negative cognitive styles, family criticism, and lack of social support predict depressive symptoms in bipolar disorder. Not only do these variables predict bipolar depression, but sadly, people with bipolar disorder all too often experience early adversity, negative life events, and high levels of criticism from their loved ones (Johnson & Miklowitz, 2017).

Predictors of Mania Two factors have been found to predict increases in manic symptoms over time: reward sensitivity and sleep deprivation. Both of these models integrate psychological and biological facets of vulnerability to mania.

Reward Sensitivity One model suggests that mania reflects a disturbance in the reward system of the brain (Depue, Collins, & Luciano, 1996). Findings of many studies indicate that people with bipolar disorder tend to describe themselves as highly responsive to rewards on self-report scales (Johnson, Edge, et al., 2012). Being highly reward-sensitive has also been shown to predict the onset of bipolar disorder (Alloy, Abramson, et al., 2008) and a more severe course of mania after onset (Meyer, Johnson, & Winters, 2001). In addition, a particular kind of life event predicts increases in manic symptoms among people with bipolar I disorder—specifically, life events that involve attaining goals, such as gaining acceptance to graduate school or getting married. How could successes like these promote increases in symptoms? Researchers have proposed that life events involving success may trigger cognitive changes in confidence, which then spiral into excessive goal pursuit (Johnson, et al., 2012). This excessive goal pursuit may help trigger manic symptoms among people who are biologically vulnerable to bipolar disorder.

Sleep Deprivation A large body of work shows that people with bipolar disorder show problems in sleep and circadian rhythms, even during well periods (Ng, Chung, et al., 2015). Experimental studies indicate that sleep deprivation can trigger manic episodes. In one study, participants who were experiencing bipolar depression were asked to stay at a sleep center, where they were kept awake all night. By the next morning, about 10 percent were experiencing at least mild symptoms of mania (Colombo, Benedetti, et al., 1999). In naturalistic studies, people often report that they had experienced a life event that disrupted their sleep just before the onset of manic episodes (Malkoff-Schwartz, Frank, et al., 2000). Just as sleep deprivation can trigger manic symptoms, protecting sleep can reduce symptoms of bipolar disorder (Harvey, Soehner, et al., 2015). Sleep and circadian rhythm disruption are important aspects of mania risk.

Quick Summary

Bipolar disorder is highly heritable. Major depression is modestly heritable. GWAS findings have been difficult to replicate in MDD, but 56 genetic loci related to bipolar disorder have been identified in one major study. Some researchers have focused the search for genetic loci on biological pathways related to mood disorders, and those studies have suggested that mood disorders are tied to multiple genetic loci involved in neurotransmitter systems. A polymorphism of the serotonin transporter gene may increase risk for depression in the context of environmental adversity.

Neurotransmitter models have traditionally focused on serotonin, dopamine, and norepinephrine. Current imaging research focuses on the serotonin and dopamine systems. Findings of neurotransmitter imaging studies have been mixed, but responses to drugs that increase dopamine levels appear to be blunted for those with depression and heightened for those with bipolar disorder.

Neuroimaging studies suggest that depression and bipolar disorder are both associated with changes in regions of the brain that are involved in emotion. These changes are consistent with a greater emotional reactivity (heightened activity of the amygdala) but less ability to regulate emotion (diminished activity of the hippocampus and regions of the prefrontal cortex, and greater activity of the anterior cingulate). One neuro-imaging difference between depression and bipolar disorder is that depression is related to lower activity of the striatum, whereas striatum activity is high among those with bipolar disorder in response to reward cues.

Several lines of work suggest that cortisol is important to depression, and heightened cortisol awakening response (CAR) predicts the onset of depressive episodes. Heightened CAR is also related to depression within bipolar disorder. Cortisol dysregulation also predicts a more severe course of mood symptoms over time for those with depression.

Social research strongly suggests that childhood adversity and recent life events increase the risk for MDD. Because many people do not become depressed after a life event, researchers have studied diatheses that could explain vulnerability to life events. Social risk factors for depression include low social support, high expressed emotion, and marital discord.

Beyond social factors, psychological risk factors can help explain why some people become depressed in the face of life stressors. Evidence suggests that neuroticism, which involves frequent and intense negative affect, predicts the onset of depression. Several cognitive models have been proposed. Beck proposed that cognitive schemas guide information-processing errors in attention and memory that sustain the negative cognitive triad. Alloy and colleagues proposed that global and stable attributions for negative events guide hopelessness. Nolan-Hoeksema proposed that tendencies to ruminate about negative feelings contribute to depression and may help explain the gender difference in depression. Prospective evidence supports each of these cognitive models.

Many of the variables that predict MDD also predict depressive symptoms within bipolar disorder. Mania is predicted by sleep deprivation, by tendencies to be highly reward sensitive, and by life events involving goal attainment.

Check Your Knowledge 5.3

Answer the questions.

1. Estimates of heritability are approximately _____ for MDD and _____ for bipolar I disorder.
   - **a.** .60, .93
   - **b.** .20, 1.00
   - **c.** .37, .93
   - **d.** .10, .59

2. Depression is tied to which of the following indicators of HPA activity?
   - **a.** hypersensitivity of the pituitary gland
   - **b.** heightened cortisol awakening response
   - **c.** too little cortisol
   - **d.** elevated parasympathetic nervous system activity

3. One brain region that appears to be overly active in response to emotion stimuli among people with mood disorders is the:
   - **a.** hippocampus
   - **b.** prefrontal cortex
   - **c.** cerebellum
   - **d.** amygdala

4. What types of recent life events are most likely to trigger major depressive episodes?

5. Describe key elements of the three cognitive models of depression.

Treatment of Mood Disorders

Many episodes of depression end in a year or less, but the time may seem immeasurably longer to people with the disorder and to those close to them. With mania, even a few days of acute symptoms can create troubles for relationships and jobs. Moreover, suicide is a risk for people with mood disorders. Thus, it is important to treat mood disorders. Indeed, research suggests that it pays to treat depression. In one study, researchers ran a program at 16 large U.S. companies to identify depression, provide referrals for people with the condition, and offer therapy by phone (Wang, Simon, et al., 2007). Although the treatment cost several hundred dollars per worker, it saved about $1800 per employee in lost time at work, employee turnover, and other costs.

On one hand, more than 18.5 million prescriptions per year are filled for antidepressants in the United States (IMS Health, 2012), and about 25 percent of college students have tried antidepressant medication (Iarovici, 2014). On the other hand, community-based studies suggest that about half of people who meet diagnostic criteria for major depression do not receive care for their symptoms (Gonzalez, Vega, et al., 2010).

For those with bipolar disorder, receipt of appropriate treatment is often delayed by the failure to recognize the diagnosis. Because patients are more likely to seek treatment during depression than mania, and providers often do not ask about prior mania, it typically takes about 7 years after the first episode for those with bipolar disorder to receive the correct diagnosis (Mantere, Suominen, et al., 2004). Even once treatment begins to address bipolar disorder, more than half of people will discontinue that treatment (Merikangas, et al., 2011). Minorities may be particularly unlikely to receive good care for bipolar disorder. In one large epidemiological sample, none of the African American persons who were diagnosed with bipolar disorder were receiving adequate pharmacological treatment (Johnson & Johnson, 2014). With these concerns about treatment availability in mind, we turn to evidence concerning the best treatments for the mood disorders.

Psychological Treatment of Depression

Several different forms of psychological treatment have been shown to help relieve depression. These treatments are similar in being relatively brief (3–4 months of weekly sessions) and focused on the here and now. As with studies of etiology, most of the research has focused on MDD, but similar treatments can be helpful when depressive symptoms are chronic (Schramm, Kriston, et al., 2017).

Interpersonal Psychotherapy As we described in Chapter 2, interpersonal psychotherapy (IPT) builds on the idea that depression is closely tied to interpersonal problems (Klerman, Weissman, et al., 1984). The core of the therapy is to examine major interpersonal problems, such as role transitions, interpersonal conflicts, bereavement, and interpersonal isolation. Typically, the therapist and the patient focus on one or two such issues, with the goal of helping the person identify his or her feelings about these issues, make important decisions, and effect changes to resolve problems related to these issues. Techniques include discussing interpersonal problems, exploring negative feelings and encouraging their expression, improving communications, problem solving, and suggesting new and more satisfying modes of behavior.

IPT has fared well in a series of randomized controlled trials. Several studies have found that IPT is efficacious in relieving MDD as compared to placebo or usual care, and that IPT achieves results that are as powerful as those observed for cognitive therapy (van Hees, Rotter, et al., 2013). Research also indicates that IPT prevents relapse when continued after recovery (Frank, Kupfer, et al., 1990).

IPT also works well outside the confines of carefully controlled university studies. That is, in a dissemination trial, over 100 therapists in the Veterans Administration system were taught to administer IPT. Clients who received IPT treatment from those therapists showed large decreases in their depressive symptoms during the course of treatment (Stewart, Raffa, et al., 2014).

Cognitive Therapy In keeping with their theory that depression is caused by negative schema and information-processing biases, Beck and associates developed a cognitive therapy (CT) aimed at altering maladaptive thought patterns. To begin, the client is taught to understand how powerfully our thoughts can influence our moods and to see that the negative self-talk that they engage in day by day contributes to their low mood. To help increase awareness of the connection between thoughts and their mood, the client might be asked to complete daily monitoring homework that involves recording their negative thoughts throughout the week. The therapist then tries to help the person with depression to change his or her self beliefs. When a person states that he or she is worthless because "nothing goes right, and everything I do ends in a disaster," the therapist helps the person look for evidence that contradicts this overgeneralization, such as abilities that the person is overlooking or discounting. The therapist then teaches the person to challenge negative beliefs and to learn strategies that promote making realistic and positive assumptions. Often, the client is asked to practice challenging overly negative thoughts in his or her day-to-day life, recording an initially negative thought and then reconsidering whether this is the most accurate lens on the situation (see **Table 5.5** for an example of a thought-monitoring homework assignment). Beck's emphasis is on cognitive restructuring (i.e., persuading the person to think less negatively).

Beck also includes a behavioral technique in his therapy called behavioral activation (BA) in which people are encouraged to engage in pleasant activities that might bolster positive thoughts about one's self and life. For example, the therapist encourages patients to schedule positive events such as going for a walk and talking with friends.

More than 100 randomized controlled trials have provided support for the efficacy of CT for depression (Cuijpers, Berking, et al., 2013). The strategies that clients learn in CT help diminish the risk of relapse even after therapy ends; this is an important issue given how common relapse is in MDD (Vittengl, Clark, et al. 2007). As with IPT, the findings of a large-scale

TABLE 5.5 An Example of a Daily Thought-Monitoring Log, a Strategy Commonly Used in Cognitive Therapy

Date and Time	Situation *What was happening?*	Negative emotion *Note type of emotion (e.g., sad, nervous, angry) and the intensity of the emotion (0–100)*	Automatic negative thought	How much did you believe this initial thought (0–100)?	Alternative thought *Is there another view of the situation?*	Re-rate your belief in the initial thought	Outcome *Note type of emotion felt and emotion intensity (0–100) after considering the alternative*
Tuesday 9:30 A.M.	I made a mistake on a report at work.	Sad–90 Embarrassed–80	I always mess things up. I'm never going to be good at anything.	90	My boss didn't give me enough time to prepare the report. I could have done a better job with more time.	50	Relief–30 Sad–30
Wednesday 7 P.M.	Eating dinner at a restaurant. An old friend from high school was at the next table and didn't recognize me.	Sad–95	I'm a nobody.	100	I've changed my hair drastically since then. Many people don't recognize me but maybe she would have been happy to see me if I had reminded her of who I was.	25	Sad–25
Thursday 8:30 A.M.	My husband left for work without saying goodbye to me.	Sad–90	Even the people I love don't seem to notice me.	100	I know that he had a huge presentation and he gets stressed.	20	Sad–20

Clinical Case

An Example of Challenging a Negative Thought in Cognitive Therapy

The following dialogue is an example of one way that a therapist might begin to challenge a person's negative thoughts in CT, although it would take several sessions to help a client learn the cognitive model and to identify overly negative thoughts.

Therapist: You said that you are a "loser" because you and Roger got divorced. Now we already defined what it is to be a loser—not to achieve anything.

Patient: *Right. That sounds really extreme.*

Therapist: OK. Let's look at the evidence for and against the thought that you have achieved something. Draw a line down the center of the page. On the top, I'd like you to write, "I have achieved some things."

Patient: *[draws line and writes statement]*

Therapist: What is the evidence that you have achieved some things?

Patient: *I graduated from college, I raised my son, I worked at the office, I have some friends, and I exercise. I am reliable. I care about my friends.*

Therapist: OK. Let's write all that down. Now, in the right column let's write down evidence against the thought that you have achieved some things.

Patient: *Well, maybe it's irrational, but I would have to write down that I got divorced.*

Therapist: OK. Now, in looking at the evidence for and against your thought that you have achieved some things, how do you weigh it out? 50–50? Differently than 50–50?

Patient: *I'd have to say it's 95% in favor of the positive thought.*

Therapist: So, how much do you believe now that you have achieved some things?

Patient: *100%.*

Therapist: And how much do you believe that you are a failure because you got divorced?

Patient: *Maybe I'm not a failure, but the marriage failed. I'd give myself about 10%.*

(Quoted from Leahy, R.L., (2003) (2017) Cognitive Behavior Therapy Techniques: A Practitioner's Guide, p 46. 64-65, Published by Guilford Press.

Note: As is typical, this dialogue challenges some, but not all, negative thoughts. Future sessions are likely to examine other negative thoughts.

dissemination trial, in which therapists in the VA system were taught to administer CT, showed that clients who received CT experienced large reductions in their depressive symptoms (Karlin, Brown, et al., 2012).

Internet-administered versions of CT have been developed. More than a dozen randomized controlled trials provide evidence that Internet-based CT is effective compared with treatment as usual for patients with MDD (Andrews & Williams, 2015). Internet-based CT is more helpful when clinicians are available to review the material with the patient not only at baseline but throughout the treatment (Johansson & Andersson, 2012).

An adaptation of CT called **mindfulness-based cognitive therapy (MBCT)** focuses on preventing relapse after successful treatment for recurrent episodes of major depression (Segal, Williams, & Teasdale, 2001). MBCT is based on the assumption that a person becomes vulnerable to relapse because of repeated associations between sad mood and patterns of self-devaluing, hopeless thinking during major depressive episodes. As a result, when people who have recovered from depression become sad, they begin to think as negatively as they had when they were severely depressed. These reactivated patterns of thinking in turn intensify the sadness (Teasdale, 1988). Thus, in people with a history of MDD, sadness is more likely to escalate, which may contribute to the recurrence of depressive episodes.

The goal of MBCT is to teach people to recognize when they start to feel sad and to try adopting what can be called a "decentered" perspective—viewing their thoughts merely as "mental events" rather than as core aspects of the self or as accurate reflections of reality. For example, the person might say to himself or herself such things as "thoughts are not facts" and "I am not my thoughts" (Teasdale, et al., 2000, p. 616). In other words, using a wide array of strategies, including meditation, the person is taught over time to develop a detached relationship to depression-related thoughts and feelings. This perspective, it is believed, can prevent the escalation of negative thinking patterns that may cause depression.

Across six studies, MBCT has been more efficacious than treatment as usual in reducing the risk of relapse among people with three or more previous major depressive episodes

(Piet & Hougaard, 2011). MBCT also appears to be comparable to antidepressants in those with three or more episodes of MDD (Kuyken, Hayes, et al., 2015). Nonetheless, some randomized controlled trials have not supported the efficacy of mindfulness-based interventions (Hofmann, Sawyer, et al., 2010), and so researchers have tried to identify the predictors of response. MBCT has been found to be helpful for people with three or more episodes and a history of childhood trauma, but does not appear more helpful than treatment as usual when those risk factors are not present (Williams, Crane, et al., 2014). This treatment, then, seems most helpful for more vulnerable clients.

Behavioral Activation (BA) Therapy   Earlier we mentioned that BA is one component of Beck's therapy. BA was originally developed as a standalone treatment, and it is based on the idea that many of the risk factors for depression interfere with receiving positive reinforcement (Lewinsohn, 1974). That is, poverty, negative life events, low social support, marital distress, and individual differences in social skills, personality, and coping may all lead to low levels of positive reinforcement. As depression begins to unfold, inactivity, withdrawal, and inertia are common symptoms, and these symptoms diminish the already low levels of positive reinforcement even further. Consequently, the goal of BA is to increase participation in positively reinforcing activities so as to disrupt the spiral of depression, withdrawal, and avoidance (Martell, Addis, & Jacobson, 2001).

BA has received a great deal of attention after positive findings in a study designed to identify the most effective ingredients in Beck's therapy (Jacobson, Dobson, et al., 1996). The BA component of CT is more affordable to implement (Richards, Ekers, et al., 2016) and has been found to perform as well as the full package does in relieving MDD and preventing relapse over a 2-year follow-up period (Dobson, Hollon, et al., 2008). Group versions of BA also are efficacious (Chan, Sun, et al., 2017), and the treatment has now been successfully applied in many different settings for clients from a diverse range of backgrounds (Oei & Dingle, 2008). These findings challenge the notion that people must directly modify their negative thinking to alleviate depression and suggest instead that engaging in rewarding activities may be enough.

Behavioral Couples Therapy   Because depression is often tied to relationship problems, including marital distress, researchers have studied **behavioral couples therapy** as a treatment for depression. In this approach, researchers work with both members of a couple to improve communication and relationship satisfaction. When a person with depression is experiencing marital distress, behavioral couples therapy is as helpful in relieving depression as individual CT or antidepressant medication (Barbato & D'Avanzo, 2008). As you might expect, marital therapy has the advantage of relieving relationship distress more than does individual therapy.

Psychological Treatment of Bipolar Disorder

Medication is a necessary part of treatment for bipolar disorder, but psychological treatments can supplement medication to help address many of its associated social and psychological problems. These psychotherapies can also help reduce depressive symptoms and reduce the risk of hospitalization in bipolar disorder.

Educating people about their illness is a common component of treating many disorders, including bipolar disorder and schizophrenia. **Psychoeducational approaches** typically help people learn about the symptoms of the disorder, the expected time course of symptoms, the biological and psychological triggers for symptoms, and treatment strategies. Studies confirm that education about bipolar disorder can help people adhere to treatment with medications such as lithium (Colom, et al., 2003). This is an important goal because as many as half of people being treated for bipolar disorder do not take medication consistently (Merikangas, et al., 2011). Psychoeducation can help clients understand the rationale for taking these medications even after symptoms dissipate and can foster hope that the medications will help. Most importantly, psychoeducation lowers the risk of relapse (Bond & Anderson, 2015).

Several other types of therapy are used to build skills, reduce symptoms, and decrease the risk of relapse for those with bipolar disorder. Both CT and family-focused therapy (FFT) for bipolar disorder have received strong support across multiple randomized controlled trials. CT draws on the types of techniques that are used in MDD, with some additional content designed to address the early signs of manic episodes (Lam, et al., 2000). FFT aims to educate the family about the illness, enhance family communication, and develop problem-solving skills (Miklowitz & Goldstein, 1997).

In one large study, researchers recruited people who had bipolar disorder and who were depressed at treatment entry (Miklowitz, Otto, et al., 2007). All patients in the trial received intensive medication treatment because researchers were interested in whether adding psychotherapy to medication treatment for bipolar disorder is helpful. Patients were randomly assigned to receive either psychotherapy or three sessions of a control treatment called collaborative care (psychoeducation about bipolar disorder). The 163 patients in the psychotherapy condition were further assigned to receive CT, FFT, or IPT. Each type of psychotherapy helped relieve depression more than collaborative care did. There was no evidence that CT, FFT, or IPT differed in their effects on depression. These findings suggest that several types of psychotherapy are helpful for bipolar depression.

Biological Treatment of Mood Disorders

A variety of biological therapies are used to treat depression and mania. The two major biological treatments are electroconvulsive therapy and drugs. We will also briefly discuss transcranial magnetic stimulation, a technique that is FDA-approved for a small subset of people with MDD.

Electroconvulsive Therapy for Depression Perhaps the most controversial treatment for MDD is electroconvulsive therapy (ECT). For the most part now, ECT is only used to treat MDD that has not responded to medication. ECT entails deliberately inducing a momentary seizure by passing a 70- to 130-volt current through the patient's brain. Formerly, electrodes were placed on each side of the forehead, a method known as bilateral ECT. Today, *unilateral ECT*, in which the current passes only through the nondominant (typically the right) cerebral hemisphere, is often used because side effects are less pronounced than with bilateral ECT (McCall, Reboussin, et al., 2000). The patient is given a muscle relaxant before the current is applied so that they sleep through the procedure and the convulsive spasms of muscles are barely perceptible. The patient awakens a few minutes later remembering nothing about the treatment. Typically, patients receive between 6 and 12 treatments, spaced several days apart.

Inducing a seizure is drastic treatment. Why should anyone agree to undergo such radical therapy? The answer is simple. ECT is more powerful than antidepressant medications for the treatment of depression (UK ECT Review Group, 2003), particularly when psychotic features are present (Sackeim & Lisanby, 2001). Most professionals acknowledge that people undergoing ECT face some risks of short-term confusion and memory loss. It is fairly common for patients to have no memory of the period during which they received ECT and sometimes for the weeks surrounding the procedure. Even unilateral ECT is associated with some deficits in memory 6 months after treatment (Sackeim, Prudic, et al., 2007). Because of the concerns, clinicians typically resort to ECT only if less drastic treatments have failed. Given that suicide is a real possibility among people who are depressed, many experts regard the use of ECT after other treatments have failed as a responsible approach.

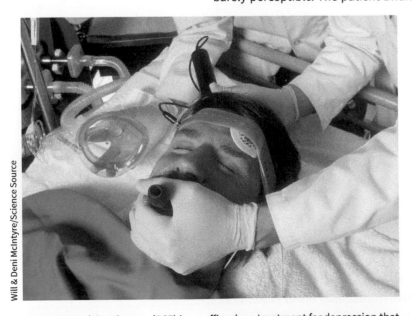

Will & Deni McIntyre/Science Source

Electroconvulsive therapy (ECT) is an efficacious treatment for depression that has not responded to medication. Using unilateral shock and muscle relaxants has reduced undesirable side effects.

TABLE 5.6   Medications for Treating Mood Disorders

Antidepressants		
Category	**Generic Name**	**Trade Name**
MAO inhibitors	tranylcypromine	Parnate
Tricyclic antidepressants	imipramine, amitriptyline	Tofranil, Elavil
Selective serotonin reuptake inhibitor (SSRI)	fluoxetine, sertraline	Prozac, Zoloft
Serotonin norepinephrine reuptake inhibitor (SNRI)	venlafaxine, duloxetine	Effexor, Cymbalta
Mood stabilizers		
Category	**Generic Name**	**Trade Name**
	lithium	Lithium
Anticonvulsants	divalproex sodium	Depakote
Antipsychotics	olanzapine	Zyprexa

Medications for Depressive Disorders

Drugs are the most commonly used and best-researched treatments—biological or otherwise—for depressive disorders (and, as we will see, for bipolar disorders as well). In the United States, about 75 percent of people receiving treatment for depression are prescribed antidepressant medications (Marcus & Olfson, 2010). As shown in **Table 5.6**, there are four major categories of **antidepressant** drugs: **monoamine oxidase inhibitors (MAOIs)**, **tricyclic antidepressants**, **selective serotonin reuptake inhibitors (SSRIs)**, and **serotonin norepinephrine reuptake inhibitors (SNRIs)** (see Figure 5.4 for more detail on tricyclic antidepressants and SSRIs). The clinical effectiveness of all classes of antidepressants is about the same (Depression Guidelines Panel, 1993; Gartlehner, Gaynes, et al., 2008). More than 150 double-blind studies have shown antidepressant medications to be efficacious in treating depressive disorders, with about 60 percent of people who complete treatment showing at least a 50% drop in symptom levels, and about 40 to 50 percent achieving remission of their symptoms (Gartlehner, et al., 2008).

Treatment guidelines recommend continuing antidepressant medications for at least 6 months after a depressive episode ends—and longer if a person has experienced several episodes. Continuing antidepressants after remission lowers the risk of recurrence from approximately 40 percent to about 20 percent (Geddes, Carney, et al., 2003). To prevent recurrence, medication doses should be as high as those offered during acute treatment.

In the past several years, a number of controversies have developed regarding antidepressants. One concern is that antidepressants do not appear to be more efficacious than placebos for relieving mild or moderate symptoms of MDD. Antidepressants do offer a clear advantage compared to placebos in the treatment of severe MDD (Fournier, et al., 2010) or persistent depressive disorder (Keller, McCullough, et al., 2000).

Beyond the evidence that these medications may not be helpful for those with mild depression, published studies may overestimate how many people respond well to antidepressant medications. When pharmaceutical companies apply for either initial approval to market a medication or a change in the use of a medication in the United States, their relevant data must be filed with the Food and Drug Administration (FDA). One research team examined what happened to the data from antidepressant studies conducted between 1987 and 2004 (Turner, Matthews, et al., 2008). Of the 74 studies conducted, the FDA rated 51 percent as having positive findings (i.e., supported the use of the antidepressant). All but one of the studies with positive findings were published. Of the studies that the FDA rated as having neutral or negative findings, less than half were published, and even in those reports, the published reports described the findings as positive despite the FDA ratings. Overall, then, the published reports are much more positive than the data in the FDA files.

If many people are still depressed after taking an antidepressant, will a different antidepressant be helpful for them? In an attempt to answer this type of question, the STAR-D

(Sequenced Treatment Alternatives to Relieve Depression) trial examined antidepressant response among 3671 patients (Rush, Trivedi, et al., 2006). In sharp contrast to the types of clean, non-comorbid depression histories reported in most medication trials, most of the patients enrolled in STAR-D suffered from chronic or recurrent depression, had comorbid psychiatric conditions, and had already received some (unsuccessful) treatment for the current episode. Patients were all started on citalopram (Celexa), an SSRI. If they did not respond to citalopram, they were offered (1) a choice of a different medication to replace the citalopram, (2) a chance to add a second medication to the citalopram, or (3) CT if they were willing to pay part of the cost. The researchers provided patients who did not respond to the second form of treatment with a third type of antidepressant, and if needed, even a fourth.

The findings were sobering. Only about one-third of patients achieved full symptom relief when treated with citalopram (Trivedi, Rush, et al., 2006). Among those who did not respond to citalopram, very few wanted to pay for CT and only 30.6 percent who received a second medication (either alone or as a supplement to citalopram) achieved remission. Even with the complex array of treatments offered, remission rates were low and relapse rates were high, so that only 43 percent of people achieved sustained recovery (Nelson, 2006). The findings from this study highlight the need to develop new treatments for depression.

Researchers are working to understand the predictors of treatment response for a given antidepressant or treatment approach. In one ambitious study of more than 1,000 participants, researchers are examining genetic, neuroimaging, and cognitive predictors of treatment response (Palmer, 2015). It is hoped that this type of work could help match clients to treatment.

Among patients who are prescribed an antidepressant, many stop taking the medication within the first month, most commonly because they have a hard time tolerating the side effects such as dizziness, headaches, erectile dysfunction, or gastrointestinal complaints (Gartlebner, et al., 2008). The MAOIs are the least used antidepressants because of their potentially life-threatening side effects if combined with certain foods or beverages. The SSRIs and SNRIs are the most commonly prescribed antidepressants because they tend to produce fewer side effects than the other classes of antidepressants, but about 60 percent of people who take these medications report at least one side effect (Gartlebner, et al., 2008). Although most of the side effects are minor, the FDA required manufacturers to include packaging information warning people that SSRIs have been associated with suicidality during the early phases of treatment or after increases in dosage among those younger than age 25 (Fergusson, Doucette, et al., 2005).

Transcranial Magnetic Stimulation for Depression

In 2008, the FDA approved **transcranial magnetic stimulation** (rTMS) for a subset of those with depression: patients who have failed to respond to a first antidepressant during the current episode. In the most typical rTMS approach, an electromagnetic coil is placed against the scalp, and intermittent pulses of magnetic energy are used to increase activity in the left dorsolateral prefrontal cortex. Typical treatment lasts 30 to 60 minutes, with daily doses delivered for 10 to 30 days. In most randomized controlled trials, researchers have compared the treatment with a sham treatment in which the device is placed against the scalp at enough of an angle that the magnetic pulse will not increase brain activity. Multiple randomized controlled trials suggest that rTMS can help relieve treatment-resistant depression compared with the sham treatment (Berlim, van den Eynde, et al., 2014). Treatment gains persist at one year after treatment (Dunner, Aaronson, et al., 2014).

Medications for Bipolar Disorder

Medications that reduce manic symptoms are called *mood-stabilizing medications*. Even though symptoms are usually decreased substantially with medications, most patients continue to experience at least mild manic and depressive symptoms. It is recommended that mood-stabilizing medications be used continually for the person's entire life (American Psychological Association [APA], 2002).

Lithium, a naturally occurring chemical element, was the first mood stabilizer identified. Up to 80 percent of people with bipolar I disorder experience at least mild benefit from taking this drug (Prien & Potter, 1993). Results of a meta-analysis indicated that 40 percent of people

Returning to Clinical Case

Treatment Decisions for Mary

Mary, the woman described at the beginning of this chapter, reported increasing problems because of her depression. Accordingly, her therapist referred her to a psychiatrist, who prescribed fluoxetine (Prozac). Both the psychologist and the psychiatrist agreed that medication might help by quickly relieving her symptoms. But after 2 weeks, Mary decided she did not want to continue taking Prozac because she found the side effects uncomfortable and did not like the idea of taking medication over the long term. She had not gotten much relief, maybe because her concerns about medication had led her to skip many doses.

With so many different types of treatment available, determining the best therapy for a given client can be a challenge. Mary had experienced a major life event and transition, suggesting that interpersonal psychotherapy might fit. But she was blaming herself for her job loss and other issues, suggesting that CT might

help. Marital conflicts suggested behavioral couples therapy could be appropriate. How does a therapist choose which approach to use? Sometimes this decision reflects the personal preferences and training of the therapist. Ideally, the approach incorporates the treatment preferences of the client as well.

Her therapist began CT, in the belief that Mary's tendency to blame herself excessively when things went wrong was contributing to her depression. CT helped her learn to identify and challenge irrationally negative cognitions about herself. Therapy began by helping her identify times in her day-to-day life when her sad moods could be explained by overly negative conclusions about small events. For example, when her children would misbehave, Mary would quickly assume this was evidence that she was a bad mother. Over time, Mary began to examine and challenge long-held beliefs about her lack of competence. By the end of 16 weeks of treatment, she had obtained relief from her depression.

relapsed while taking lithium as compared with 60 percent while taking a placebo (Geddes, Burgess, et al., 2004). Lithium also appears to decrease the severity of relapse. Because of possibly serious side effects, lithium must be prescribed and used very carefully. Lithium levels that are too high can be toxic, so patients taking lithium must have regular blood tests.

Two classes of medications other than lithium have been approved by the FDA for the treatment of acute mania: anticonvulsant (antiseizure) medications such as divalproex sodium (Depakote) and antipsychotic medications such as olanzapine (Zyprexa). These other treatments are recommended for people who are unable to tolerate lithium's side effects. Like lithium, these medications help reduce mania and, to some extent, depression.

Typically, lithium is used in combination with other medications. Because lithium takes effect gradually, therapy for acute mania often begins with both lithium and an antipsychotic medication, such as olanzapine, which has an immediate calming effect (Scherk, Pajonk, & Leucht, 2007).

The mood-stabilizing medications used to treat mania also help relieve depression. Nonetheless, many people continue to experience depression even when taking a mood-stabilizing medication such as lithium. For these people, an antidepressant medication is often added to the regimen, but two potential issues are associated with this practice. First, it is not clear whether antidepressants help reduce depression among persons who are already taking a mood stabilizer. Second, among people with bipolar disorder, antidepressants are related to a modest increase in the risk of a manic episode if taken without a mood stabilizer (Pacchiarotti, Bond, et al., 2013).

Comparing Medication and Psychotherapy for MDD Combining psychotherapy and antidepressant medication bolsters the odds of recovery from MDD by more than 10–20 percent compared with either psychotherapy or medication alone (Hollon, Thase, & Markowitz, 2002). One study found that even offering CT by telephone for those beginning antidepressants improved outcomes compared with medication alone (Simon, 2009). It may be particularly helpful to add psychotherapy to medication when a person has more severe depression (Hollon, DeRubeis, et al., 2014). Each treatment offers unique advantages. Antidepressants work more quickly than psychotherapy, thus providing immediate relief. Psychotherapy may help people learn skills that they can use after treatment is finished to protect against recurrent depressive episodes.

Many patients are interested in knowing whether medications or therapy will be more efficacious. In the most careful study to date comparing cognitive therapy to antidepressants, researchers focused on the treatment of severe depression. Two hundred forty patients with severe depression were randomly assigned to receive antidepressant medication, CT, or a placebo for four months. Those who recovered were followed for another 12 months. CT was as helpful as antidepressant medication for severe depression, and both treatments provided more symptom relief than placebo. CT had two advantages compared with medication: It was less expensive, and it helped protect against relapse after treatment was finished (Hollon, DeRubeis, et al., 2005).

Quick Summary

Many different treatments are available for depression. Cognitive therapy (CT), interpersonal psychotherapy (IPT), behavioral activation (BA) treatment, and behavioral couples therapy have all received support. ECT is efficacious, but there are concerns about cognitive side effects. The four forms of antidepressants are similarly efficacious; SSRIs and SNRIs have become more popular because they have fewer side effects than MAOIs and tricyclic antidepressants. CT is as powerful as antidepressant medication even in the treatment of severe MDD.

Medication treatment is the first line of defense against bipolar disorder. The best-researched mood stabilizer is lithium, but anticonvulsants and antipsychotic medications are also effective mood stabilizers. It is less clear whether antidepressant medication is helpful in bipolar disorder. Some psychological treatments may help when offered as supplements to medications for the treatment of bipolar disorder. The best-validated approaches include psychoeducation, CT, and family-focused therapy (FFT). IPT also fared well in the largest trial of psychological supplements to medications. These psychological treatments help improve adherence to medication regimens, relieve depressive symptoms within bipolar disorder, and reduce the risk of relapse.

Check Your Knowledge 5.4

Circle all answers that apply.

1. Which of the following psychotherapies have obtained randomized controlled trial support in the treatment of MDD?

    a. interpersonal psychotherapy

    b. behavioral activation

    c. psychoanalytic therapy

    d. cognitive therapy

2. The most efficacious treatment for MDD with psychotic features is:

    a. Prozac

    b. any antidepressant medication

    c. ECT

    d. psychotherapy

3. Selective serotonin reuptake inhibitors (SSRIs) and serotonin norepinephrine reuptake inhibitors (SNRIs) are more popular than other antidepressants because they:

    a. are more efficacious

    b. have fewer side effects

    c. are cheaper

Suicide

The effects of suicide on the surviving friends and relatives are profound. Survivors have an especially high mortality rate in the months after the suicide of a loved one (Mogensen, Möller, et al., 2016). In one population-based study of the offspring of more than 40,000 parents who

Clinical Case

Steven

"Shannon Neal can instantly tell you the best night of her life: Tuesday, December 23, 2003, the Hinsdale Academy debutante ball. Her father, Steven Neal, a 54-year-old political columnist for The Chicago Sun-Times, was in his tux, white gloves, and tie. 'My dad walked me down and took a little bow,' she said, and then the two of them goofed it up on the dance floor as they laughed and laughed. A few weeks later, Mr. Neal parked his car in his

garage, turned on the motor and waited until carbon monoxide filled the enclosed space and took his breath, and his life, away."

He had been under stress as he finished a book and had been hospitalized for heart problems. "Still, those who knew him were blindsided. 'If I had just 30 seconds with him now,' Ms. Neal said of her father, 'I would want all these answers.'"

(Cohen, 2008, p. 1)

died from suicide, researchers found that offspring who were younger than 18 at the time of the death showed a threefold greater risk of dying from suicide. The risk of suicide among offspring who were older, or whose parents died from causes other than suicide, was not significantly elevated compared with the general population (Niederkrotenthaler, Fu, et al., 2012). Suicide is a profoundly distressing event.

We will focus on quantitative research on suicide, but those who study suicide learn from many different sources. Many philosophers have written searchingly on the topic, including Descartes, Voltaire, Kant, Heidegger, and Camus. In addition, novelists such as Herman Melville and Leo Tolstoy have provided insights on suicide, as have writers who have killed themselves, such as Virginia Woolf and Sylvia Plath. Increasingly, those who have survived suicide attempts have joined public advocacy and support movements to help inform this field, and their perspectives may enhance our ability to understand factors that lead up to suicide attempts (see livethroughthis.org).

We begin by defining terms (see **Table 5.7**). Suicidal ideation refers to thoughts of killing oneself and is much more common than attempted or completed suicide. Suicide attempts involve behaviors that are intended to cause death. Most suicide attempts do not result in death. **Suicide** involves behaviors that are intended to cause death and do so. **Nonsuicidal self-injury** involves behaviors that are meant to cause immediate bodily harm but are not intended to cause death (see **Focus on Discovery 5.6**).

Epidemiology of Suicide and Suicide Attempts

Suicide rates may be grossly underestimated because the circumstances of some deaths are ambiguous; for example, a seemingly accidental death may have involved suicidal intentions. Nonetheless, worldwide, it is estimated that more than three-quarters of a million people die from suicide each year (WHO, 2012). In the United States, suicide is the 10th leading cause of death (Heron, 2016).

Studies on the epidemiology of suicidality suggest the following:

- Worldwide, about 9 percent of people report suicidal ideation at least once in their lives, and 2.5 percent have made at least one suicide attempt. The rate of suicide attempts in the United States is about twice the rate in other countries (Nock & Mendes, 2008)

TABLE 5.7	Key Terms in the Study of Suicidality
Suicidal ideation: thoughts of killing oneself	
Suicide attempt: behavior intended to kill oneself	
Suicide: death from deliberate self-injury	
Nonsuicidal self-injury (NSSI): behaviors intended to cause immediate injury to oneself without intent to cause death	

Writers who killed themselves, such as Sylvia Plath, have provided insights into the causes of suicide. In an act that could be related to the heritability of suicide or to social modeling, Sylvia Plath's son also killed himself.

Focus on Discovery 5.6

Nonsuicidal Self-Injury

Nonsuicidal self-injury (NSSI) is more common than previously thought, and contrary to previous thinking, it is practiced by many who do not have borderline personality disorder (Nock, 2010). Here we define this behavior and give some reasons it occurs.

There are two key issues to consider in defining NSSI. The first is that the person did not intend to cause death. The second is that the behavior is designed to cause immediate injury. Most commonly, people cut, hit, or burn their body (Franklin, Hessel, et al., 2010). When surveyed, anywhere from 12 to 24 percent of adolescents report having engaged in NSSI (Muehlenkamp, Claes, et al., 2012), but the higher estimates may be due to overly broad definitions. For example, some studies will include "scratching to the point of bleeding," without ruling out poison ivy or other reasons people might be scratching. Without a doubt, though, there is a group of people who engage in serious attempts to hurt themselves. NSSI is most common in early adolescence, and most who try NSSI do so less than 10 times (Nock, 2009). A subset of people persist in self-injury, sometimes reporting more than 50 incidents of self-injury per year, and it is this profile of persistent NSSI that researchers are working to understand (Nock & Prinstein, 2004). Persistent NSSI is a risk factor for suicidal ideation and behavior (Whitlock, Muehlenkamp, et al., 2013). Three domains are very important to consider in whether people engage in NSSI repeatedly: social factors, emotionality, and self-critical beliefs.

Many different social factors may be involved in the onset and perpetuation of NSSI. Social modeling may influence whether NSSI begins—in one longitudinal study, adolescent girls were more likely to try NSSI if their best friend had engaged in NSSI (Prinstein, Heilbron, et al., 2010). Among those who engage in NSSI, social stress may also trigger the behavior in the moment. People who engage in self-injury often report that it is hard for them to manage their relationships, and that they will engage in self-injury after experiencing interpersonal rejection (Nock, Prinstein, & Sterba, 2009). After NSSI occurs, some may receive reinforcement for engaging in the behavior—friends and family members may respond by offering support or by reducing aggression. Hence social factors may be important from initiation to maintenance of NSSI.

There are also many different psychological reasons for self-injury, but problems with emotion appear particularly important (Nock, 2010). For some, the injury seems to help quell negative emotions, such as anger. Several studies provide evidence that those who are prone to self-injury experience more intense emotions and more intense psychophysiological responses to stress than others do (Nock & Mendes, 2008).

Even when social and psychological risk factors are present, some wonder why people would want to inflict pain on themselves. Self-critical beliefs are an important part of this puzzle. Some report that self-injury satisfies a need for punishment that they believe they deserved. In a study in which people who engaged in NSSI were asked to record feelings, events, and NSSI incidents daily over time, feelings of self-hatred and of being rejected were common just before incidents of self-injury took place (Nock, Prinstein, & Sterba, 2009). These self-critical beliefs may help explain why people would engage in a behavior that involves pain. In one study, people who engage in NSSI were asked to take part in a laboratory experiment in which they were asked to place their finger in a device that created pain by applying pressure; participants could choose the level and duration of pressure. Those who engaged in NSSI selected settings involving more pressure, and they left their finger in the device for longer, than did those with no history of NSSI. Self-critical beliefs were highly related to this willingness to endure more pain (Glenn, Michel, et al., 2014). Hence, self-critical beliefs may provide a reason to engage in behaviors that cause pain, as a form of self-punishment. Consistent with this idea, when researchers provided a brief cognitive intervention designed to reduce self-critical beliefs, people who engage in NSSI became less willing to tolerate pain (Hooley & St. Germain, 2013).

Taken together, NSSI may be driven by social modeling and reinforcement, by difficulties in coping with emotions, and by self-critical beliefs. Researchers will need to consider social, emotional, and cognitive factors to fully understand this complex behavioral pattern. To foster more attention to this issue, the DSM-5 includes a NSSI diagnosis in the appendix as a condition for further study.

WireImage/Getty Images, Inc.

In an interview with the BBC, Princess Diana described reaching a point of such pain that she engaged in nonsuicidal self-injury.

- Suicide rates are higher in regions where more people own guns. Guns are by far the most common means of suicide in the United States, accounting for about 50 percent of all suicides (Kochanek, Murphy, et al., 2016). People who live in homes with guns have more than a threefold greater risk of death by suicide (Anglemyer, Horvath, & Rutherford, 2014).

- Worldwide, men are 1.7 times more likely than women to kill themselves (WHO, 2012). The gender ratio is larger in the United States (see Figure 5.8).

- Women are more likely than men are to make suicide attempts that do not result in death (Nock & Mendes, 2008).

- Men usually choose to shoot or hang themselves; women are more likely to use pills, a less lethal method, which may account for their lower rate of completed suicide.

- The highest rates of suicide in the United States are for white males over age 50 (Heron, 2016).

- The rates of suicide for adolescents and children in the United States are increasing dramatically but are still far below the rates of adults (see Figure 5.8). Some estimates suggest that at least 40 percent of children and adolescents experience suicidal ideation at least once. Because young people are less likely to die from other causes, suicide ranks as the second leading cause of death among those aged 10 to 24 (Heron, 2016).

- Being divorced or widowed elevates suicide risk four- or fivefold.

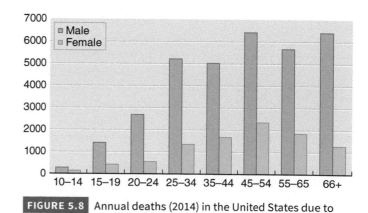

FIGURE 5.8 Annual deaths (2014) in the United States due to suicides.

Sources: Reported in Heron, 2016, and NCHS, 2016.

Risk Factors for Suicide

Suicide is such a complex and multifaceted act that no single model can hope to explain it. Even our best current models leave much unanswered (Franklin, Ribeiro, et al., 2017).

Psychological Disorders Psychological disorders are important in understanding suicide: as many as 90 percent of people who attempt suicide are suffering from a psychological disorder. Among those who have psychological symptoms severe enough to lead to hospitalization, about 6–8 percent of people diagnosed with MDD, with bipolar disorder, and with schizophrenia eventually die from suicide (Nordentoft, Mortensen, & Pedersen, 2011). Impulse control disorders, substance use disorders, PTSD, and borderline personality disorder are also each related to a higher risk of suicidal actions (Linehan, 1997; Nock & Mendes, 2008; Nock, et al., 2009).

With most of these disorders, though, suicides are most likely when a person is experiencing comorbid depression (Angst, Stassen, et al., 2002; Schmidt, et al., 2000). Suicide is discussed in this chapter because many persons with mood disorders have suicidal thoughts, and some engage in suicidal behaviors. More than half of those who try to kill themselves are depressed at the time of the act (Centers for Disease Control and Prevention, 2006). Although understanding the effects of psychological disorders on suicidality is extremely important, most people with psychological disorders, even those with depression, do not die from suicide.

Neurobiological Factors Twin studies suggest that heritability accounts for about 50 percent of whether a person will engage in a suicide attempt (Fiori, Ernst, & Turecki, 2014). That is, genes may explain about half of the variance in who will attempt suicide. Adoption studies also support the heritability of suicidality.

Just as with depression, major models focus on the role of serotonin, dopamine, and cortisol in understanding suicidality, and new work suggests that the neurotransmitter glutamate may be involved as well. Researchers have found suicidality to be tied to a polymorphism of the serotonin transporter gene (parallel with findings for mood disorders) (Fiori, et al., 2014). Persons who have attempted suicide also appear to have diminished function of dopamine, in that they show less response to drugs that would increase dopamine levels (Fiori, et al., 2014). In addition, multiple studies suggest that suicidality is related to a down-regulation of several types of glutamate receptors (Fiori, et al., 2014). Beyond the role of neurotransmitters, among patients with MDD, abnormal cortisol regulation has been related to increased risk of suicide over the next 18 years (Jokinen, Carlborg, et al., 2007). Neurotransmitter and cortisol dysregulation, then, are important predictors of suicidality.

J. Vespa/Wire Images/Getty Images

Robin Williams, a highly acclaimed actor and comedian, died from suicide in 2014 (Williams, 2016). Researchers have shown that suicide rates increase in the month after a celebrity dies from suicide. These findings provide evidence that the social environment is an influence on suicide. Guidelines have been developed for media reporting, to avoid glamorizing suicidality.

Social Factors Economic and social events have been shown to influence suicide rates. As one example, across the past 100 years, suicide rates have been shown to increase modestly during economic recessions (Luo, Florence, et al., 2011).

Some of the strongest evidence for the role of the social environment in suicide comes from the major effects of media reports of suicide (Jeong, Shin, et al., 2012). In one example of these effects, suicides rose 12 percent in the month after Marilyn Monroe's suicide (Phillips, 1985). A review of 293 studies found that media coverage of a celebrity suicide is much more likely to spark an increase in suicidality than coverage of a noncelebrity suicide (Stack, 2000). Media reports of natural deaths of famous people are not followed by increases in suicide, suggesting that it is not grief per se that is the influential factor (Phillips, 1974). Statistics suggest that sociocultural factors matter.

Social factors that are more directly relevant to the individual are also powerful predictors of suicidality. In a large-scale study, a history of multiple physical and sexual assaults was related to suicide attempts (Nock & Kessler, 2006). Joiner (2005) has suggested that suicidality is closely tied to two key issues: a perceived sense of burden to others and a lack of belongingness. In a comprehensive review, Van Orden and colleagues (2010) argue that a lack of social belonging is among the most powerful predictors of suicidal ideation and behavior. They maintain that the sensation of being alone, without others to turn to, is a major factor in the development of suicidality. Consistent with this idea, adolescents often describe social isolation, interpersonal conflict, and peer victimization as triggers of suicidal behavior, and peer ratings of interpersonal status have been found to predict the onset of suicidality over a 2-year period (Prinstein, et al., 2010). Taken together, social factors appear highly important to suicidality.

Psychological Factors Almost all individuals who have attempted suicide and yet lived to be interviewed describe wanting to escape from a sense of unbearable pain (Wenzel & Spokas, 2014). What factors lead a person to reach that point in which life seems so unbearable? After a suicide attempt, many people report that they were facing a problem that seemed inescapable.

For some, inability to engage in effective problem-solving may cause problems to seem inescapable. People who express suicidal ideation not only describe themselves as poor problem solvers, but they have more difficulty with solving puzzles presented to them in laboratory experiments (Wenzel & Spokas, 2014). Problem-solving deficits also predict suicide attempts prospectively (Dieserud, Roysamb, et al., 2003).

A person who has trouble resolving problems can be expected to be more vulnerable to hopelessness. Hopelessness—the expectation that life will be no better in the future than it is in the present—is strongly tied to suicidality. Findings from multiple longitudinal studies indicate that high levels of hopelessness are associated with at least a fourfold elevation in risk of suicide, and hopelessness is important even after controlling for depression levels and early trauma exposure (Wenzel & Spokas, 2014).

Although many people think about suicide, relatively few engage in suicidal actions. Additional variables predict the switch from thinking about suicide to acting on those thoughts (van Orden, Witte, et al., 2008). Among people who are experiencing suicidal thoughts, hundreds of studies demonstrate that people who are more impulsive are more likely to attempt suicide or to die from suicide (Brezo, Paris, & Turecki, 2006). A growing body of work also suggests that people with more intense fear of bodily harm and death are less likely to take suicidal action (Klonsky, May, & Saffer, 2016).

George C Beresford/Getty Images, Inc.

English novelist and critic Virginia Woolf (1882–1941).

On March 28, 1941, at the age of 59, Virginia Woolf drowned herself in the river near her Sussex home. Two suicide notes were found in the house, similar in content; one may have been written 10 days earlier, and it is possible that she may have made an unsuccessful attempt then, for she returned from a walk soaking wet, saying that she had fallen. The first was addressed to her sister Vanessa and the second to her husband, Leonard. To him, she wrote:

Dearest, I feel certain I am going mad again. I feel we can't go through another of those terrible times. And I shan't recover this time. I begin to hear voices, and I can't concentrate. So I am doing what seems the best thing to do. You have given me the greatest possible happiness. You have been in every way all that anyone could be. I don't think two people could have been happier till this terrible disease came. I can't fight it any longer. I know that I am spoiling your life, that without me you could work. And you will I know. You see I can't even write this properly. I can't read. What I want to say is I owe all the happiness of my life to you. You have been entirely patient with me and incredibly good. I want to say that—everybody knows it. If anybody could have saved me it would have been you. Everything has gone from me but the certainty of your goodness. I can't go on spoiling your life any longer. I don't think two people could have been happier than we have been. V.

Quoted from pp. 400–401, Briggs, J. (2005). Virginia Woolf: An Inner Life. Orlando, Fl: Harcourt, Inc.

Preventing Suicide

Many people worry that talking about suicide will make it more likely to happen. Rather, clinicians have learned that it is helpful to talk about suicide in an open and matter-of-fact manner. Most people who are contemplating suicide will discuss their intention, and giving a person permission to talk about suicide may relieve a sense of isolation. Most people are ambivalent about whether to engage in suicidal behavior, and talking can help them identify other ways to relieve the pain that is driving the suicidality. Among those who attempt suicide but do not die, 80 percent report within the next 2 days that they are either glad to be alive or ambivalent about whether they want to die (Henriques, Wenzel, et al., 2005).

Treating the Associated Psychological Disorder One approach to suicide prevention builds on our knowledge that most people who kill themselves are suffering from a psychological disorder. Thus, when Beck's cognitive approach successfully lessens a patient's depression, that patient's suicidal risk is also reduced. Marsha Linehan's dialectical behavior therapy for borderline personality disorder provides another example of a treatment that is designed for a specific disorder but also provides protection from suicide (see Chapter 15). Dialectical behavior therapy has been found to reduce suicidal or self-harm behaviors in four randomized controlled trials (Ward-Ciesielski & Linehan, 2014).

Studies have found that medications for mood disorders reduce the risk of suicidality three- to fourfold (Angst, et al., 2002). Specifically, lithium reduces suicidality among people with bipolar disorder (Cipriani, Pretty, et al., 2005). Among people who have been diagnosed with depressive disorders, ECT and antidepressants reduce suicidality (Bruce, ten Have, et al., 2004; Kellner, Fink, et al., 2005). Risperidone, an antipsychotic medication, reduces the risk of suicide attempts among people with schizophrenia (Meltzer, 2003).

Treating Suicidality Directly A large literature indicates that CBT can help reduce suicidality. In a meta-analysis of 28 treatment trials, adults who received CBT reported less hopelessness, suicidal ideation, and suicidal behavior than those who received no treatment or other forms of treatment (Tarrier, Taylor, & Gooding, 2008). CBT has been found to halve the risk of a future attempt among those who have tried to kill themselves compared with treatment as usually offered in the community (Brown, ten Have, et al., 2005). CBT also has been found to reduce NSSI (Hawton, Witt, et al., 2016).

CBT encompasses a set of strategies to prevent suicide. Therapists help clients understand the emotions and thoughts that trigger urges to commit suicide. Therapists work with clients to challenge their negative thoughts and to provide new ways to tolerate emotional distress. They also help clients solve problems they are facing. The goal is to improve problem solving and social support and thereby to reduce the feelings of hopelessness that often precede these episodes.

Professional organizations such as the American Psychiatric Association, the National Association of Social Workers, and the American Psychological Association charge their members with protecting people from suicide even if doing so requires breaking the confidentiality of the therapist–patient relationship. Therapists are expected to take reasonable precautions when they learn a patient is suicidal. One approach to keeping such patients alive is to hospitalize them as a short-term means of keeping them safe until they can begin to consider ways of improving their lives.

Broader Approaches to Suicide Prevention It is exceedingly difficult to do controlled research on suicide prevention because the base rates are so low. One approach to this issue has been to study suicide prevention within the military, where rates of suicide are much higher than in the general population, programs can be offered to the entire community, and

Granger Collection

After a broken engagement at age 31, Abraham Lincoln developed symptoms of depression that were so severe that his friends feared he would hurt himself, and they removed any sharp objects from his room. "I am now the most miserable man living," he confessed. "Whether I shall ever be better I cannot tell; I awfully forebode I shall not. To remain as I am is impossible; I must die or be better." (Cited in Goodwin, 2003.)

vicm / Getty Images

The Golden Gate Bridge is one of the most popular locations for suicide in the world, and more than 1600 people have jumped to their death from its heights. In 2017, drawing on evidence showing that means restriction programs can be highly effective, construction began on a suicide barrier for the bridge.

outcomes can be tracked carefully. In one study, researchers examined suicide rates in the Air Force before and after implementation of a comprehensive suicide prevention program. The program provided training for military leaders and for soldiers to encourage and destigmatize help seeking, to normalize the experience of distress, and to promote effective coping. Implementation of the program led to a 25 percent drop in rates of completed suicide (Knox, Pflanz, et al., 2010). It appears that prevention efforts can reduce suicide rates.

Beyond prevention programs that target high-risk individuals, **means restriction** approaches to suicide prevention involve making highly lethal methods less available. For decades, the most common ovens in England relied on coal gas. Coal gas was cheap and widely available, but before it was burned, it released levels of carbon monoxide that were so high as to be deadly if one put one's head into a coal gas oven for even a couple of minutes. By the late 1950s, about 2500 suicides per year (almost half of the suicides in Britain) were completed in this manner. The British government phased out coal gas, and by the 1970s, almost no coal gas ovens remained. Over the course of those years, the British suicide rate dropped by a third and has remained at this lower rate.

Public health researchers emphasize that most suicides are impulsive—people often make a suicide attempt very quickly without much forethought. In one study, researchers interviewed people within 3 days of a hospitalization for a suicide attempt. Participants were asked to think back to the suicidal thought that had started the episode. Half the participants reported that they had made their suicide attempt within 10 minutes after the suicidal thought entered their mind (Deisenhammer, Ing, et al., 2009). Given this evidence, any type of delay or barrier in gaining access to means may help save lives. For this reason, strategies such as erecting a barrier on a bridge, so that people cannot jump off the bridge on a moment's impulse, can be highly successful (Beautrais, Gibb, et al., 2009). Other examples of policies include reducing the availability of lethal poisons, and encouraging people to keep their guns in locked cabinets. The key to the means restriction approach is that often, intense suicidal urges really do last only a moment—anything that reduces access to lethal tools in that moment can be helpful (Barber & Miller, 2014).

Check Your Knowledge 5.5

True or false?

1. Men have higher rates of suicide than women.

2. Adolescents have higher rates of suicide than older adults do.

3. Suicide rates increase after media reports of both noncelebrity and celebrity suicides.

Answer the questions.

4. Which psychological disorder is most consistently present when people commit suicide?

5. What psychological factor seems to buffer against suicidal action among those who are experiencing suicidal ideation?

Summary

Clinical Descriptions and Epidemiology of Depressive Disorders

- Depressive disorders include major depression and persistent depressive disorder, along with the newer diagnoses of premenstrual dysphoric disorder and disruptive mood dysregulation disorder.

- Major depressive disorder is episodic, and recurrence is common.

- Persistent depressive disorder is characterized by low levels of symptoms that last at least 2 years.

- Major depression is one of the most common psychological disorders, affecting at least 16.2 percent of people during their lifetime.

Clinical Descriptions and Epidemiology of Bipolar Disorders

- Bipolar disorders include bipolar I disorder, bipolar II disorder, and cyclothymia. Bipolar I disorder is defined by mania. Bipolar II disorder is defined by hypomania and episodes of depression. Cyclothymic disorder is characterized by low levels of manic and depressive symptoms that last at least 2 years.

- Bipolar I disorder and bipolar II disorder are episodic. Recurrence is even more common in these disorders than it is in major depressive disorder.

- Bipolar I disorder affects less than 1 percent of the population. Estimates of the prevalence of bipolar II disorder are varied (.4 to 2 percent). Cyclothymic disorder may affect 4 percent of the population.

Etiology

- Bipolar disorder is strongly heritable, and depression is somewhat heritable. A polymorphism of the serotonin transporter gene is related to increased risk of depression when environmental adversity is also present.

- Neurotransmitter research has focused on the sensitivity of receptors rather than on the levels of various transmitters. People with depression show diminished sensitivity to drugs that increase dopamine levels, and those with mania show increased sensitivity to drugs that increase dopamine levels. Nonetheless, imaging research on neurotransmitters has provided conflicting findings regarding mood disorders.

- Bipolar disorders and unipolar disorders are tied to elevated activity of the amygdala and the anterior cingulate and to diminished activity in the hippocampus and regions of the prefrontal cortex during tasks that involve emotion and emotion regulation. Bipolar disorder is related to heightened activation of the striatum, but activity in this region is low among those with depression.

- The cortisol awakening response (CAR) is elevated in unipolar depression and bipolar depression.

- Socioenvironmental models focus on the role of childhood adversity, recent negative life events (and particularly negative interpersonal life events), lack of social support, marital discord, and expressed emotion as triggers for episodes.

- The personality trait that is most closely related to depression is neuroticism. Neuroticism predicts the onset of depression.

- Influential cognitive theories include Beck's cognitive theory, hopelessness theory, and rumination theory. All argue that depression can be caused by cognitive factors, but the nature of the cognitive factors differs across theories. Beck's theory focuses on the cognitive triad, negative schemas, and information-processing biases. According to hopelessness theory, beliefs that a life event will have long-term meaningful consequences can instill a sense of hopelessness, which in turn results in depression. Rumination theory focuses on the negative effects of repetitively dwelling on the reasons for a sad mood. Prospective evidence is available for each model.

- Psychological theories of depression in bipolar disorder are similar to those proposed for unipolar depression. Some researchers have proposed that manic symptoms arise because of dysregulation in the reward system in the brain. Mania can be triggered by life events involving goal attainment. Mania also can be triggered by sleep deprivation.

Treatment

- Several psychological therapies are effective for depression, including interpersonal psychotherapy, cognitive therapy, behavioral activation therapy, and behavioral couples therapy.

- Psychoeducation, family therapy, and cognitive therapy are helpful adjuncts to medication for bipolar disorder, with some support for interpersonal psychotherapy as well.

- Electroconvulsive shock and several antidepressant drugs (tricyclics, MAOIs, selective serotonin reuptake inhibitors, and serotonin norepinephrine reuptake inhibitors) have proved their worth in lifting depression. Transcranial magnetic stimulation is FDA-approved for people with antidepressant-resistant depression.

- Lithium is the best-researched treatment for bipolar disorder, but antipsychotic and anticonvulsant medications also help decrease manic symptoms. Antidepressant medications are controversial in the treatment of bipolar disorder.

Suicide

- Men, elderly people, and people who are divorced or widowed are at elevated risk for suicide. Most people who die from suicide meet diagnostic criteria for psychological disorders, with more than half experiencing depression. Suicide is at least partially heritable, and neurobiological models focus on serotonin, dopamine, glutamate, and overactivity in the HPA. Environmental factors are also important: sociocultural events such as celebrity suicides and economic recessions can influence rates of suicide in the population, and a lack of social belonging is a robust predictor of suicide. Psychological vulnerability factors for suicidal ideation include poor problem solving, hopelessness, and lack of reasons to live; among those with suicidal ideation, suicidal action appears to be related to impulsivity.

- Several approaches have been taken to suicide prevention. For people with a psychological disorder, medications and psychotherapies targeting those symptoms help reduce suicidality. Many people, however, believe it is important to address suicidality more directly. CBT can help reduce suicidal ideation and behavior. Research suggests that suicide prevention can work. Public health interventions reduce the available means for suicide.

Answers to Check Your Knowledge Questions

5.1 five (including mood), two; 2. 16.2; 3. Chronicity; MDD is diagnosed on the basis of five symptoms lasting at least 2 weeks; persistent depressive disorder requires only two symptoms, but they must be present for 2 years (or 1 year in children and adolescents).

5.2 1. Six; 2. Bipolar I disorder is diagnosed on the basis of manic episodes, which are more severe than the hypomanic episodes that are the core criterion for bipolar II disorder.

5.3 1. c; 2. b; 3. d; 4. Interpersonal; 5. Beck's model of cognitive schemas guiding information-processing errors in attention and memory that sustain the negative cognitive triad, Alloy's model of global and stable attributions guiding hopelessness, and rumination

5.4 1. a, b, d; 2. c; 3. b

5.5 1. T; 2. F; 3. F; 4. depression; 5. fear of bodily harm

Key Terms

anterior cingulate
antidepressant
attribution
attributional style
behavioral couples therapy
bipolar I disorder
bipolar II disorder
cortisol awakening response (CAR)
Cushing syndrome
cyclothymic disorder
disruptive mood dysregulation disorder
dorsolateral prefrontal cortex
episodic disorder
flight of ideas
hopelessness theory

hypomania
information-processing biases
lithium
major depressive disorder (MDD)
mania
means restriction
mindfulness-based cognitive therapy (MBCT)
monoamine oxidase inhibitors (MAOIs)
mood disorders
negative triad
neuroticism
nonsuicidal self-injury (NSSI)
persistent depressive disorder (dysthymia)
prefrontal cortex
psychoeducational approaches
psychomotor agitation

psychomotor retardation
reward system
rumination
seasonal affective disorder (SAD)
selective serotonin reuptake inhibitors (SSRIs)
serotonin–norepinephrine reuptake inhibitors (SNRIs)
serotonin transporter gene
striatum
suicidal ideation
suicide
suicide attempt
transcranial magnetic stimulation (rTMS)
tricyclic antidepressants

CHAPTER 6

Anxiety Disorders

LEARNING GOALS

1. Define the emotions of anxiety and fear and their adaptive benefits.

2. Describe the clinical features of the anxiety disorders, the prevalence of the anxiety disorders, and how the anxiety disorders co-occur with each other.

3. Discuss how gender and culture influence the prevalence of anxiety disorders.

4. Explain commonalities in etiology across the anxiety disorders.

5. Describe the factors that shape the expression of specific anxiety disorders.

6. Discuss psychological and medication treatment approaches that are common across the anxiety disorders and how psychological treatment approaches are modified for the specific anxiety disorders.

Clinical Case

Jenny

Jenny was a 23-year-old student completing her first year of medical school. The year had been a hard one, not only because of the long hours and academic challenges of medical school but also because her mother had been diagnosed with cancer. One day, while attending rounds, Jenny found herself feeling lightheaded and dizzy. During rounds, the attending physician would ask students to diagnose and explain a given case, and on that day Jenny became extremely worried about whether she would be able to answer these questions when her turn came. As she thought about all this, her heart began to pound and her palms began to sweat. Overwhelmed by a deep sense of fear that something was horribly wrong, she abruptly fled the room without explaining her departure.

Later in the day, she wanted to explain leaving rounds but could not think of a good way to describe the situation to the attending physician. That night, she could not sleep, wondering what had happened and worrying about whether it would happen again. She worried about how this would affect her ability

not only to take part in rounds but also to perform well in other roles, such as leading a small research group and meeting with other medical staff and clients. One week later, while driving to school, she experienced a sudden attack of similar symptoms, which forced her to pull off to the side of the road. She took the day off from school. Over the next several weeks, she began to avoid public situations as much as possible because she feared being humiliated by the return of these symptoms. She avoided study groups and going out with friends, and she turned down opportunities for training that involved public interviews of patients. She resigned from the choir that she had enjoyed being a part of for several years. Despite her withdrawal, she experienced three more attacks, each in unexpected situations. She began to think that maybe medical school was a poor choice for her because she had such deep fears about experiencing another attack during rounds. After she read about panic disorder in one of her textbooks, she decided to visit a psychologist. The psychologist confirmed that she was experiencing panic disorder, and they started cognitive behavioral treatment.

Very few of us go through even a week of our lives without experiencing anxiety or fear. In this chapter, we focus on a group of disorders called **anxiety disorders**. Both anxiety and fear play a significant role in these disorders, so we begin with a description of these two emotions. After discussing normative experiences of anxiety and fear, we turn to the core clinical features of anxiety disorders and their outcomes before discussing specific anxiety disorders. Then, we turn to the common themes in the etiology of anxiety disorders as a group. We then describe specific etiological factors that shape whether a specific anxiety disorder develops. As with most disorders, many different paradigms have helped shed light on anxiety disorders. Therefore, throughout our discussions of etiology we look at issues from various perspectives, with particular focus on genetic, neurobiological, personality, cognitive, and behavioral research. Finally, we consider the treatment of the anxiety disorders. We describe commonalities in the psychological treatment of various anxiety disorders, and then we describe how these general treatment principles are modified to address specific anxiety disorders. Finally, we discuss biological treatments of anxiety disorders.

Emotions of Anxiety and Fear

Anxiety is defined as apprehension over an anticipated problem. In contrast, **fear** is defined as a reaction to immediate danger. Psychologists focus on the "immediate" aspect of fear versus the "anticipated" aspect of anxiety—fear tends to be about a threat that is happening now, whereas anxiety tends to be about a future threat. Thus, a person facing a bear experiences fear, whereas a college student concerned about the possibility of unemployment after graduation experiences anxiety.

Both anxiety and fear can involve arousal, or sympathetic nervous system activity (see Focus on Discovery 2.1 for a brief overview of the sympathetic nervous system). Anxiety often involves moderate arousal, and fear involves higher arousal. At the low end, a person experiencing anxiety may feel no more than restless energy and physiological tension; at the high end, a person experiencing fear may sweat profusely, breathe rapidly, and feel an overpowering urge to run.

Anxiety and fear are not necessarily "bad"; in fact, both are adaptive. Fear is fundamental for "fight-or-flight" reactions—that is, fear triggers rapid changes in the sympathetic nervous system to prepare the body for escape or fighting. In the right circumstance, fear saves lives. (Imagine a person who faces a bear and doesn't marshal energy to run quickly!) In some anxiety disorders, though, the fear system seems to misfire—a person experiences fear even when no danger is present in the environment. This is most vividly seen in panic attacks, which we will discuss later in this chapter.

Anxiety is adaptive in helping us notice and plan for future threats—that is, to increase our preparedness, to help people avoid potentially dangerous situations, and to think through potential problems before they happen. In laboratory studies first conducted 100 years ago and since verified many times over, a small degree of anxiety has been found to improve performance on laboratory tasks (Yerkes & Dodson, 1908). Ask anyone with extreme test anxiety, though, and they will tell you that too much anxiety interferes with performance. Anxiety, then, provides a classic example of an inverse U-shaped curve with performance—an absence of anxiety is a problem, a little anxiety is adaptive, and a lot of anxiety is detrimental.

Quick Summary

Anxiety helps us notice and plan for future threats; it increases our preparedness, helps us to avoid potentially dangerous situations, and motivates us to think through potential problems before they happen. Both anxiety and fear play a significant role in anxiety disorders. Anxiety is defined as apprehension over an anticipated problem, and fear is defined as a reaction to immediate danger. They are also very costly to society and to people with the disorders. The anxiety disorders involve excessive amounts of anxiety and fear.

True/False

1. Both anxiety and fear play a significant role in anxiety disorders.
2. Fear often involves moderate arousal, and anxiety involves higher arousal.
3. Anxiety and fear are usually adaptive.

Clinical Descriptions of the Anxiety Disorders

In this chapter, we examine the major anxiety disorders included in DSM-5: specific phobias, social anxiety disorder, panic disorder, agoraphobia, and generalized anxiety disorder (see **Table 6.1** for key features of each of these). Obsessive-compulsive disorder and trauma-related disorders have a good deal in common with the anxiety disorders but are also distinct in some important ways. To recognize those distinctions, the DSM-5 places these conditions in chapters next to anxiety disorders. We will cover obsessive-compulsive and trauma-related disorders in Chapter 7. All of the anxiety disorders covered in this chapter involve excessive amounts of anxiety, and with the exception of generalized anxiety disorder, all involve tendencies to experience unusually intense fear (Kotov, Krueger et al., 2017).

Anxiety disorders as a group are the most common type of psychological disorder. For example, in the NCS-R study of over 8000 adults in the United States, about 28 percent of people endorsed having experienced symptoms at some point during their lives that met criteria for diagnosis of an anxiety disorder (Kessler, Petukhova, et al., 2012). See **Table 6.2** for the prevalence estimates for specific anxiety disorders. A prevalence estimate of more than a quarter of people may seem very high, but this may be an underestimate. In the NCS-R study, researchers conducted only one diagnostic interview in which they asked participants to describe anxiety that had happened at any time during their lives. As noted in Chapter 4, research calls into question whether people can accurately remember their anxiety symptoms for years, particularly if symptoms were short-lived (Moffitt, Caspi, et al., 2010). If people forget diagnosable experiences of anxiety when asked to reflect on their entire lifetime, prevalence estimates of 28 percent are likely too low.

As a group, anxiety disorders are very costly to society and to people with the disorders. Anxiety disorders were ranked as the ninth leading cause of disability worldwide in 2015 (Vos, Allen, et al., 2016). These disorders are related to an elevated risk of major medical conditions (Scott, Lim, et al., 2016; Stein, Aguilar-Gaxiola, et al., 2014) and marital discord (Whisman, 2007), and more than a fourfold increase in the risk of suicide attempts (Nock, Hwang, et al.,

TABLE 6.1   **Overview of the Major DSM-5 Anxiety Disorders**

Disorder	Description
Specific phobia	Fear of objects or situations that is out of proportion to any real danger
Social anxiety disorder	Fear of unfamiliar people or social scrutiny
Panic disorder	Anxiety about recurrent panic attacks
Agoraphobia	Anxiety about being in places where escaping or getting help would be difficult if anxiety symptoms occurred
Generalized anxiety disorder	Uncontrollable worry

TABLE 6.2	Percent of Adults Ages 18–64 in the General Population Who Meet Diagnostic Criteria for Anxiety Disorders in the Past Year and in Their Lifetime	
	12-Month Prevalence Estimate	Lifetime Prevalence Estimate
Anxiety Disorder		
Specific phobia	10.1	13.8
Social anxiety disorder	8.0	13.0
Panic disorder	3.1	5.2
Agoraphobia	1.7	2.6
Generalized anxiety disorder	2.9	6.2

Source: Kessler et al., 2012

2010) compared with the absence of a psychological diagnosis. The following quote illustrates some of the ways that anxiety can influence daily life.

> On ordinary days, doing ordinary things—reading a book, lying in bed, talking on the phone, sitting in a meeting, playing tennis—I have thousands of times been stricken by a pervasive sense of existential dread and been beset by nausea, vertigo, shaking, and a panoply of other physical symptoms. In these instances, I have sometimes been convinced that death, or something somehow worse, was imminent. (Stossel, 2014, p. 2)

For each anxiety disorder, several criteria must be met for a DSM-5 diagnosis to be made:

- Symptoms interfere with important areas of functioning or cause marked distress
- Symptoms are not caused by a drug or a medical condition
- Symptoms persist for at least 6 months, or at least 1 month for panic disorder
- The fears and anxieties are distinct from the symptoms of another anxiety disorder.

Each disorder, though, is defined by a different set of symptoms related to anxiety or fear (see Table 6.1 for a brief summary). In the next sections, we discuss the symptoms of the specific anxiety disorders.

Specific Phobias

Acrophobia, or phobia of heights, is common. People with this fear would find a glass elevator terrifying. Other specific phobias include fears of animals, injections, and enclosed spaces.

A **specific phobia** is a disproportionate fear caused by a specific object or situation, such as flying, snakes, or heights. The person recognizes that the fear is excessive but still goes to great lengths to avoid the feared object or situation. In addition to fear, the object of a phobia may elicit intense disgust (Olatunji, Etzel, et al., 2011). The names for these fears consist of a Greek word for the feared object or situation followed by the suffix *-phobia* (derived from the name of the Greek god Phobos, who frightened his enemies). Two of the more common phobias are claustrophobia (fear of closed spaces) and acrophobia (fear of heights). Specific phobias tend to cluster around a small number of feared objects and situations (see **Table 6.3**). A person with a specific phobia for one type of object or situation is very likely to have a specific phobia for a second object or situation—that is, specific phobias are highly comorbid (Kendler, Myers, & Prescott, 2002). The Clinical Case of Jan provides a glimpse of how specific phobias can interfere with important life goals.

DSM-5 Criteria for Specific Phobia

- Marked and disproportionate fear consistently triggered by specific objects or situations
- The object or situation is avoided or else endured with intense anxiety

TABLE 6.3   **Types of Specific Phobias**

Type of Phobia	Examples of the Feared Object	Associated Characteristics
Animal	Snakes, insects	Generally begins during childhood
Natural environment	Storms, heights, water	Generally begins during childhood
Blood, injection, injury	Blood, injury, injections, or other invasive medical procedures	Runs in families; profile of heart rate slowing and possible fainting when facing feared stimulus (LeBeau, Glenn, et al., 2010)
Situational	Public transportation, tunnels, bridges, elevators, flying, driving, closed spaces	Tends to begin either in childhood or in mid-20s
Other	Choking, contracting an illness, etc. Children's fears of loud sounds, clowns, etc.	

Clinical Case

Jan

Jan, a 42-year-old woman, had been offered a high-paying job in Florida. She was considering declining the offer because it would force her to live in an area known for having snakes. Before making this decision, she decided to see a therapist. During her first meeting with the therapist, she described a litany of ways she had avoided any contact with anything remotely resembling a snake. She had steered clear of outdoor activities, TV programs on nature, and even her children's books on nature. Although her fears had not interfered with meaningful life goals so far, the idea of living in an area with snakes had greatly increased her apprehension. Aside from her phobia, Jan reported that she had always been a bit of a nervous person, a trait she shared with her mother.

Getty Images/Cultura RF

One form of specific phobia is an intense fear of blood, injection, or injuries.

Social Anxiety Disorder

The core feature of **social anxiety disorder** is a persistent, unrealistically intense fear of social situations that might involve being scrutinized by, or even just exposed to, unfamiliar people. Although this disorder is labelled social phobia in the DSM-IV-TR, the term *social anxiety disorder* is used in the DSM-5 because it tends to cause more pervasive problems than other phobias do (Liebowitz, Heimberg, et al., 2000). In interpersonal interactions, people with social anxiety disorder are deeply concerned that they will do or say embarrassing things and that others will

---

DSM-5 Criteria for Social Anxiety Disorder

- Marked and disproportionate fear consistently triggered by exposure to potential social scrutiny
- Exposure to the trigger leads to intense anxiety about being evaluated negatively

- Trigger situations are avoided or else endured with intense anxiety

---

Spencer Grant/PhotoEdit

Social anxiety disorder typically begins in adolescence and interferes with developing friendships.

judge them harshly as a result. Although this may sound like shyness, people with social anxiety disorder experience intense feelings of shame and humiliation, and they experience these symptoms for longer periods of their lifetime than do people who are shy (Burstein, Ameli-Grillon, & Merikangas, 2011). Many fear that their anxiety will become apparent to others. The intense anxiety leads most such people to avoid social situations, as illustrated by Maureen in the next Clinical Case. The most common fears for those with social anxiety include public speaking, speaking in meetings or classes, meeting new people, and talking to people in authority (Ruscio, Brown, et al., 2008). Forced to engage in one of these feared activities, the person may spend days in advance thinking about all the possible ways things could go wrong, and then spend days after the event reliving the small moments that did go badly with a sense of shame.

The manifestations and outcomes of social anxiety disorder vary greatly. Social anxiety disorder can range in severity from a few specific fears to a generalized host of fears. For example, some people might be anxious about speaking in public but not about other social situations. In contrast, others fear most social situations. Those with a broader array of fears are more likely to experience comorbid depression and alcohol abuse (Acarturk, de Graaf, et al., 2008). Although many who suffer with social anxiety are withdrawn and submissive, people vary in how they cope with the threat of social rejection, and a small proportion respond with overtly hostile and aggressive behavior (Kashdan & McKnight, 2010). People with social anxiety disorder often work in occupations far below their talents because of their extreme social fears. Many would rather work in an unrewarding job with limited social demand than deal with social situations every day.

Among people with social anxiety disorder, at least a third also meet the criteria for a diagnosis of avoidant personality disorder (see Chapter 15). The symptoms of the two conditions overlap a great deal, as does the genetic vulnerability for the two conditions (Torvik, Welander-Vatn, et al., 2016). Avoidant personality disorder, though, is a more severe disorder with more pervasive symptoms.

Clinical Case

Maureen

Maureen, a 30-year-old accountant, sought psychotherapy after reading a newspaper notice advertising group therapy for people with difficulties in social situations. Maureen appeared nervous during the interview and described feeling intensely anxious in conversations with others. She described the anxiety as worsening over the years, to the point where she no longer interacted

socially with anyone other than her husband. She would not even go to the supermarket for fear of having to interact with people. Maureen deeply feared being perceived as stupid. This fear made her so nervous that she would often stammer or forget what she was going to say while talking to others, thus adding to her apprehension that others would see her as stupid and creating a vicious circle of ever-increasing fear.

Social anxiety disorder generally begins during adolescence, when peer relationships become particularly important. For some, however, the symptoms first emerge during childhood. Without treatment, social anxiety disorder tends to be chronic (Bruce, Yonkers, et al., 2005).

Panic Disorder

Panic disorder is characterized by recurrent panic attacks that are unrelated to specific situations and by worry about having more panic attacks (see the Clinical Case of Jenny at the beginning of this chapter). A **panic attack** is a sudden attack of intense apprehension, terror, and feelings of impending doom, accompanied by at least four other symptoms. Physical symptoms can include shortness of breath, heart palpitations, nausea, upset stomach, chest pain, feelings of choking and smothering, dizziness, lightheadedness, faintness, sweating, chills, heat sensations, numbness or tingling sensations, and trembling. Other symptoms that may occur during a panic attack include **depersonalization** (a feeling of being outside one's body); **derealization** (a feeling of the world not being real); and fears of losing control, of going crazy, or even of dying. Not surprisingly, people often report that they have an intense urge to flee whatever situation they are in when a panic attack occurs. The symptoms tend to come on very rapidly and reach a peak of intensity within 10 minutes. Many people seek emergency medical care when they first experience a panic attack because they are terrified that they are having a heart attack.

As noted above, we can think about a panic attack as a misfire of the fear system: physiologically, the person experiences a level of sympathetic nervous system arousal matching what most people might experience when faced with an immediate threat to life. Because the symptoms are inexplicable, the person tries to make sense of the experience. A person who begins to think that he or she is dying, losing control, or going crazy is likely to feel even more fear. Among people with panic disorder, 90 percent report just these types of beliefs when panic attacks occur.

The diagnostic criteria for panic disorder require more than the presence of recurrent panic attacks. According to the DSM criteria for panic disorder, a person must experience recurrent panic attacks that are unexpected. Panic attacks that are triggered by specific situations, such as seeing a snake, are typically related to a phobia and should not be considered in diagnosing panic disorder. Beyond the occurrence of unexpected panic attacks, DSM criteria also specify that the person must worry about the attacks or change his or her behavior because of the attacks for at least 1 month. Hence, in making this diagnosis, the response to panic attacks is as important as the attacks themselves.

Remember that the criteria for panic disorder specify that panic attacks must be recurrent. It is fairly common for people to experience a single panic attack—more than a quarter of people in the United States report that they have experienced at least one panic attack during their lifetime (Kessler, Chiu, et al., 2006). As Table 6.2 shows, though, many fewer people develop full-blown panic disorder. Among those who develop panic disorder, the onset is typically in adolescence. The symptoms of panic disorder tend to wax and wane over time (Nay, Brown, & Roberson-Nay, 2013). It can take a heavy toll; for example, as many as one-quarter of people with panic disorder are unemployed for more than 5 years (Leon, Portera, & Weissman, 1995).

Agoraphobia

Agoraphobia (from the Greek *agora*, meaning "marketplace") is defined by anxiety about situations in which it would be embarrassing or difficult to escape if anxiety symptoms occurred. Commonly feared situations include crowds and crowded places such as grocery stores, malls, and churches. Sometimes the

---

DSM-5 Criteria for Panic Disorder

- Recurrent unexpected panic attacks
- At least 1 month of concern or worry about the possibility of more attacks occurring or the consequences of an attack, or maladaptive behavioral changes because of the attacks

Emma Stone has described experiencing panic attacks when younger (Eells, 2017).

Kathy Hutchins/Shutterstock

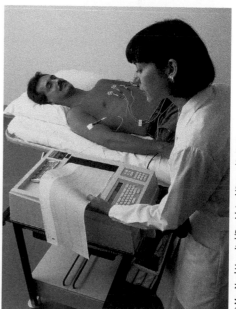

People with panic disorder often seek cardiac tests because they are frightened by changes in their heart rate.

© MacNeal Hospital/David Joel/Stone/Getty Images

DSM-5 Criteria for Agoraphobia

Disproportionate and marked fear or anxiety about at least two situations where it would be difficult to escape or receive help in the event of incapacitation, embarrassing symptoms, or panic-like symptoms, such as being outside the home alone; traveling on public transportation; being in open spaces such as parking lots and marketplaces; being in enclosed spaces such as shops, theaters, or cinemas; or standing in line or being in a crowd.

- These situations consistently provoke fear or anxiety
- These situations are avoided, require the presence of a companion, or are endured with intense fear or anxiety

---

situations are those that are difficult to escape from, such as trains, bridges, or long road trips. As a consequence of their fear of these situations, many people with agoraphobia are virtually unable to leave their house, and even those who can leave do so only with great distress.

About half of people with agoraphobia symptoms experience panic attacks (Andrews, Charney, et al., 2009). The effects of agoraphobia on quality of life are as severe as those observed for the other anxiety disorders (Wittchen, Gloster, et al., 2010).

Generalized Anxiety Disorder

The central feature of **generalized anxiety disorder** (GAD) is worry. Like Joe in the Clinical Case, people with GAD are persistently worried, often about minor things. The term *worry* refers to the cognitive tendency to chew on a problem and to be unable to let go of it (Mennin, Heimberg, & Turk, 2004). Often, worry continues because a person cannot settle on a solution to the problem. Most of us worry from time to time, but the worries of people with GAD are excessive, uncontrollable, and long-lasting. The worries of people with GAD center on the same types of threats that worry most of us: they worry about relationships, health, finances, and daily hassles—but they worry more about these issues, as illustrated by the following passage.

Mitchell Funk/Photographer's Choice/Getty Images

People with agoraphobia often find crowds very distressing because escape would be difficult if anxiety symptoms occurred.

I had graduated from college the year before, with honors. I had a prestigious job, loyal friends, a good apartment I shared with a bright and beautiful girlfriend, and as much money as I needed. Yet every day was torture. I slept fitfully, with recurring nightmares—tsunamis, feral animals, the violent deaths of loved ones. I had intestinal cramps and nausea and headaches. A sense of impending catastrophe colored every working moment. Worse, I had the distinct sense that catastrophe had already occurred. I had made the wrong decisions, gone down the wrong path, screwed up in a ruinous, irrevocable, epoch-making way. (Smith, 2012, pp. 3–4)

DSM-5 Criteria for Generalized Anxiety Disorder

- Excessive anxiety and worry at least 50 percent of days about a number of events or activities (e.g., family, health, finances, work, and school)
- The person finds it hard to control the worry
- The anxiety and worry are associated with at least three (or one in children) of the following:
  - restlessness or feeling keyed up or on edge

- easily fatigued
- difficulty concentrating or mind going blank
- irritability
- muscle tension
- sleep disturbance

Clinical Case

Joe

Joe, a 24-year-old mechanic, was referred for psychotherapy by his physician, whom he had consulted because of difficulty falling asleep. He was visibly distressed during the entire initial interview, with a furrowed brow and continuous fidgeting. Although he first described worries about his health, a picture of pervasive anxiety soon emerged. He reported that he nearly always felt tense and he seemed to worry about everything. He was apprehensive of disasters that could befall him as he interacted with people and worked, and he described worrying much of the time about his finances, his inability to establish a romantic relationship, and other issues. He reported a long history of difficulties relating to others, which had led to his being fired from several jobs. As he put it, "I really like people and try to get along with them, but I fly off the handle too easily. Little things upset me too much." Joe reported that he had always felt more nervous than other people but that his anxiety had become much worse after a romantic breakup 1 year ago.

Beyond the uncontrollable worries, other symptoms of GAD include difficulty concentrating, tiring easily, restlessness, irritability, and muscle tension. GAD is not diagnosed if a person worries only about concerns driven by another psychological disorder; for example, a person with claustrophobia who only worries about being in closed spaces would not meet the criteria for GAD.

GAD typically begins in adolescence (Ruscio, Hallion, et al., 2017). Once it develops, GAD is often chronic; in one study, about half of people with GAD at an initial interview reported ongoing symptoms 10 years later (Bruce et al., 2005). Perhaps because of the chronicity, GAD is more strongly related to marital distress than any other anxiety disorder (Whisman, 2007). People diagnosed with GAD report having few friendships (Whisman, Sheldon, & Goering, 2000) and experiencing difficulties in the workplace as well (Newman, Llera, et al., 2013).

Comorbidity in Anxiety Disorders

More than half of people with one anxiety disorder meet the criteria for another anxiety disorder during their lives (Wright, Krueger, et al., 2013). Anxiety disorders are also highly comorbid with other disorders: Three-quarters of people with an anxiety disorder meet the diagnostic criteria for at least one other psychological disorder (Kessler, Chiu, et al., 2005). More specifically, about 60 percent of people in treatment for anxiety disorders meet the diagnostic criteria for major depression. We discuss this overlap in Focus on Discovery 5.5. Obsessive compulsive disorder also commonly co-occurs with anxiety disorders (Wright et al., 2013). As with many disorders, comorbidity is associated with greater severity and poorer outcomes of the anxiety disorders (Bruce et al., 2005).

Quick Summary

As a group, anxiety disorders are the most common type of psychological disorder. Large-scale epidemiological studies suggest that 28 percent of people will experience an anxiety disorder during their lifetime, and some research suggests that this may be an underestimate.

Specific phobia is defined by an intense fear of an object or situation, social anxiety disorder by an intense fear of strangers or social scrutiny, panic disorder by anxiety about recurrent panic attacks, agoraphobia by a fear of places where escaping or getting help would be difficult if anxiety symptoms were to occur, and generalized anxiety disorder by worries lasting at least six months.

People with one anxiety disorder are very likely to experience a second anxiety disorder during their lives. About 60 percent of people with anxiety disorders will experience major depression during their lives.

For items 1–4, match the word to the definition.

1. fear
2. anxiety
3. worry
4. phobia

    a. an emotional response to immediate danger

    b. an excessive fear of a specific object or situation that causes distress or impairment

    c. a state of apprehension often accompanied by mild autonomic arousal

    d. thinking about potential problems, often without settling on a solution

Fill in the blank.

5. In epidemiological studies that conduct just one interview with people about whether they met diagnostic criteria for an anxiety disorder, the estimated lifetime prevalence of anxiety disorders is: _____.

6. The key symptom of GAD is: _____

Gender and Cultural Factors in the Anxiety Disorders

It is well known that gender and culture are closely tied to the risk for anxiety disorders and to the specific types of symptoms that a person develops. As you will see, however, there are still some puzzles about why these patterns exist.

Gender

Women are more vulnerable to anxiety disorders than are men, with several studies documenting a 2 to 1 gender ratio (Baxter, Scott, et al., 2013). When present, anxiety disorders also appear related to more functional impairment for women compared with men (McLean, Asnaani, et al., 2011). Many different theories have been proposed to explain these gender differences. First, women may be more likely to report their symptoms. Social factors, such as gender roles, are also likely to play a role. For example, men may experience more social pressure than women to face fears—as you will see below, facing fears is the basis for one of the most effective treatments available. Women may also experience different life circumstances than do men. For example, women are much more likely than men to be sexually assaulted during childhood and adulthood (Tolin & Foa, 2006). These traumatic events may interfere with developing a sense of control over one's environment, and, as we will see below, having less control over one's environment may set the stage for anxiety disorders. Men may be raised to believe more in their personal control over situations as well. It also appears that women show more biological reactivity to stress than do men (Olff, Langeland, et al., 2007), perhaps as a result of these cultural and psychological influences. Although the gender gap is not fully understood, it is an important phenomenon.

Culture

People in every culture seem to experience problems with anxiety disorders, but culture and environment influence what people come to fear (Kirmayer, 2001). "If you live near a volcano you're going to fear lava. If you live in the rainforest you're going to fear malaria" (Smith, 2012, p. 72).

Kayak-angst, a disorder that is similar to panic disorder, occurs among the Inuit people of western Greenland; seal hunters who are alone at sea may experience intense fear, disorientation, and concerns about drowning.

Several cultural concepts of distress (see Chapter 3) provide examples of how culture and environment may shape the expression of an anxiety disorder. For example, in Japan a syndrome called *taijin kyofusho* involves fear of displeasing or embarrassing others; people with this syndrome typically fear making direct eye contact, blushing, having body odor, or having a bodily deformity. The symptoms of this disorder overlap with those of social anxiety disorder, but the focus on others' feelings is distinct (Hofmann & Hinton, 2014). Perhaps this focus is related to characteristics of traditional Japanese culture that encourage deep concern for the feelings of others. Other syndromes, such as *koro* (a sudden fear that one's genitals will recede into the body—reported in southern and eastern Asia), *shenkui* (intense anxiety and somatic symptoms attributed to the loss of semen, as through masturbation or excessive sexual activity—reported in China and similar to other syndromes reported in India and Sri Lanka), and *susto* (fright-illness, the belief that a severe fright has caused the soul to leave the body—reported in Latin America and among Latinos in the United States), also involve symptoms similar to those of the anxiety disorders defined in the DSM. As with the Japanese syndrome *taijin kyofusho*, the objects of anxiety and fear in these syndromes relate to environmental challenges as well as to attitudes that are prevalent in the cultures where the syndromes occur.

Beyond cultural concepts of distress, the prevalence of anxiety disorders varies across cultures. This is not surprising given that cultures differ with regard to factors such as stress levels, the nature of family relationships, and the prevalence of poverty—all of which are known to play a role in the occurrence of anxiety disorders. Cultural attitudes may also guide how comfortable people are with disclosing psychological symptoms. In some countries, cultural concepts of distress related to anxiety may be more common than the anxiety disorders listed in the main body of the DSM, such that prevalence estimates may be misleading if they only cover DSM diagnoses (Steel, Silove, et al., 2009). Countries with recent war, revolution, or large-scale persecution have higher rates of anxiety disorders than do those without such conflicts (Baxter et al., 2013). Nonetheless, the prevalence of anxiety disorders is higher in Europe and the United States than in most other regions of the world (see Table 3.2).

Disorders with symptoms similar to panic attacks occur cross-culturally. Among the Inuit, kayak-angst is defined by intense fear in lone hunters.

B & C Alexander/Science Source

For some time, researchers have thought that people from different cultures express symptoms of psychological distress and anxiety in different ways. For example, many thought that those from some cultures, and particularly those with a strong belief in mind–body connections, would express their emotional concerns through somatic complaints, but it now seems that this conclusion might reflect sampling problems—that is, researchers often studied anxiety and depression in psychological clinics in the United States but in medical clinics in other cultures. One can imagine that a person seeing a medical doctor might be likely to emphasize somatic concerns! Indeed, many people, regardless of culture, tend to describe anxiety and depression initially in terms of bodily sensations when visiting a medical clinic. When researchers interview people in similar settings and ask specifically about psychological concerns, the ratio of somatic to psychological symptoms expressed appears to be much more similar across cultures (Kirmayer, 2001).

Quick Summary

Women are much more likely than men to report an anxiety disorder. Culture influences the focus of fears, the ways that symptoms are expressed, and even the prevalence of different anxiety disorders.

Common Risk Factors Across the Anxiety Disorders

As we consider risk factors associated with anxiety disorders, we begin by describing a set of factors that seem to increase risk for all of the anxiety disorders. The existence of such risk factors may help explain why people with one anxiety disorder are likely to develop a second one—that is, some risk factors increase the odds of having more than one anxiety disorder. For example, the factors that increase risk for social anxiety disorder may also increase risk for panic disorder.

Unlike the way we have organized most of the other chapters in this book, we have chosen to begin here with the behavioral model. We do this because classical conditioning of a fear response is at the heart of many anxiety disorders. Many of the other risk factors, including genes, neurobiological correlates, personality traits, and cognition, influence how readily a person can be conditioned to develop a new fear response. Taken together, the risk factors combine to create an increased sensitivity to threat (Craske, Rauch, et al., 2009). **Table 6.4** summarizes the general risk factors for anxiety disorders.

Fear Conditioning

Earlier we mentioned that most anxiety disorders involve fears that are more frequent or intense than what most people experience. Where do these fears come from? The behavioral theory of anxiety disorders focuses on conditioning. **Mowrer's two-factor model** of anxiety disorders, published in 1947, continues to influence thinking in this area. Mowrer's model suggests two steps in the development of an anxiety disorder (Mowrer, 1947):

1. Through *classical conditioning* (see Chapter 1), a person learns to fear a neutral stimulus (the conditioned stimulus, or CS) that is paired with an intrinsically aversive stimulus (the unconditioned stimulus, or UCS).

2. A person gains relief by avoiding the CS. Through *operant conditioning* (also discussed in Chapter 1), this avoidant response is maintained because it is reinforcing (it reduces fear).

Consider the example shown in **Figure 6.1**. Imagine that a man is bitten by a dog and then develops a phobia of dogs. Through classical conditioning, he has learned to associate dogs (the CS) with painful bites (the UCS). This corresponds to step 1 above. In step 2, the man reduces his fear by avoiding dogs as much as possible; the avoidant behavior is reinforced by the reduction in fear. This second step explains why the phobia isn't extinguished. With repeated exposure to dogs that don't bite, the man would have lost his fear of dogs, but by avoiding dogs, the man gets little or no such exposure.

We should note that Mowrer's early version of the two-factor model does not actually fit the evidence very well, for two reasons. First, many people who have anxiety disorders cannot remember any exposure to a threatening event that triggered their symptoms. Second, many people who do experience serious threats do not develop anxiety disorders. Several extensions of this model, which we look at next, have been developed that explain these gaps.

TABLE 6.4   Factors That Increase General Risk for Anxiety Disorders

Behavioral conditioning (classical and operant conditioning)

Genetic vulnerability

Disturbances in the activity in the fear circuit of the brain

Decreased functioning of gamma-aminobutyric acid (GABA) and serotonin; increased norepinephrine activity

Increased cortisol awakening response (CAR)

Behavioral inhibition

Neuroticism

Cognitive factors, including sustained negative beliefs, perceived lack of control, over-attention to cues of threat, and intolerance of uncertainty

We begin with an extension to the model to explain why some people with anxiety disorders do not remember any conditioning experience (Mineka & Zinbarg, 1998). According to this extension, classical conditioning could occur in different ways (Rachman, 1977), including:

- Direct experience (like the dog bite in the example above)
- Modeling (e.g., seeing a dog bite a man or watching a video of a vicious dog attack)
- Verbal instruction (e.g., hearing a parent warn that dogs are dangerous).

In any of these ways, a person could learn to associate a stimulus with fear.

The second major problem with Mowrer's model is that many people who are exposed to major threats (e.g., a dog bite) do not develop anxiety disorders. That is, some people are more vulnerable to developing anxiety disorders than others. Researchers have shown in carefully controlled tests in laboratory settings that people with anxiety disorders are more responsive to threats, and they have measured this in many different ways.

Most centrally, people with anxiety disorders seem to acquire fears more readily through classical conditioning, and those fears are more persistent once conditioned (Craske et al., 2009). Focusing on the persistence of conditioned fear, in one study, researchers conditioned people to fear a neutral picture of a Rorschach card (see Figure 3.11) by pairing the card with a shock six times (Michael, Blechert, et al., 2007). After receiving six shocks, most participants learned to fear the Rorschach card, as measured by skin conductance responses to seeing the card—even those without an anxiety disorder developed this conditioned response. However, participants with and without an anxiety disorder (in this study, panic disorder) differed in the extinction phase of the study, when the card was shown without any shock being provided. People who were not diagnosed with panic disorder showed a quick drop in their fear responses during the extinction phase, but people with panic disorder showed very little decrease in their fear response. Thus, a person with an anxiety disorder may find that once a fear is conditioned, that fear stubbornly persists and is difficult to unlearn in spite of evidence to the contrary. Findings from a meta-analysis of 20 studies suggest that anxiety disorders are related to an elevated propensity to develop fears through classical conditioning, and slowed extinction of fears (Lissek, Powers, et al., 2005). Research also suggests that the offspring of those with anxiety disorders show slow extinction of conditioned fears (Waters, Peters, et al. 2014). These findings help explain why some people

Courtesy Susan Mineka

When monkeys observe another monkey display fear of a snake, they also acquire the fear (Cook & Mineka, 1989). This finding supports the idea that modeling plays a role in the etiology of phobias.

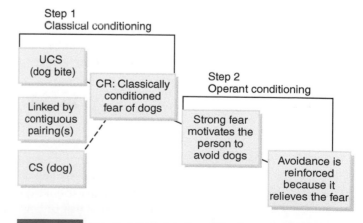

FIGURE 6.1 Two-factor model of conditioning as applied to dog phobia.

are more likely to develop an anxiety disorder after a threatening event, whereas other people seem not to do so.

People with anxiety disorders also appear to experience certain types of threats as particularly powerful. One body of research suggests that people with anxiety disorders are particularly sensitive to unpredictable, as compared with predictable, threats. Most people are more anxious about unpredictable threats. Imagine that you have to face a really angry person. Knowing when that conversation will occur reduces anxiety compared with being faced with the idea that the person could show up anytime, anyplace! Unpredictability leads to a prolonged state of threat. People with anxiety disorders, though, are particularly sensitive to this unpredictability.

In a careful experimental approach to testing responses to unpredictability, participants are assigned to undergo three different conditions of a behavioral task called the **neutral predictable unpredictable (NPU) threat task**: (1) a neutral condition in which they do not experience an aversive stimulus, (2) a predictable condition in which they experience an aversive stimulus and receive a warning beforehand, and (3) an unpredictable condition in which they experience an aversive stimulus without prior warning. The threat in the predictable and unpredictable threat condition is the same—for example, participants could receive identical electric shocks in both threat conditions. The difference is that in the predictable threat condition, it is clear when the threat will happen, but in the unpredictable threat condition, the timing of the threat is unclear. Response to the three conditions is usually measured by psychophysiological indices of arousal (Schmitz & Grillon, 2012). Of the three experimental conditions, anxiety disorders are specifically related to increased affective and psychophysiological response to the *unpredictable* threat condition compared with the predictable threat condition. That is, people with social anxiety disorder, specific phobias, panic disorder, and PTSD have been found to show particularly high psychophysiological arousal levels during the unpredictable threat condition compared with healthy controls (Gorka, Lieberman, et al., 2017; Grillon, Lissek, et al., 2008). This profile appears to be specific to anxiety disorders, in that people with major depressive disorder respond like healthy controls do to unpredictable threat (Gorka, et al., 2017). Unpredictable threats, then, seem to be key in anxiety disorders.

In sum, although Mowrer's two-factor model continues to shape our understanding of the processes through which anxiety disorders develop, clearly not everyone who is bitten by a dog will go on to develop a phobia. So, what factors seem to distinguish individuals with anxiety disorders from those without? People with anxiety disorders seem to be (1) more easily conditioned to fear stimuli, (2) to sustain conditioned fears longer, and (3) to respond more strongly to unpredictable, uncertain threats. How might this look in everyday life? Imagine a child who is bullied on the playground. Because it is hard to know when the bully will target the child, the threat is unpredictable. The child with an anxiety disorder might experience more fear of the bullying (an unpredictable threat), and they might more easily begin to fear stimuli related to the bullying (classical conditioning). Although most kids might feel safe again if they were able to play in that area without bullying happening (extinction), this process is slow for the child with an anxiety disorder.

As you can see, fear-conditioning models have begun to consider many different aspects of the process of how people learn fears and how those fears are sustained. Many of the risk factors we describe next could influence this sensitivity to fear conditioning.

Genetic Factors

A large-scale twin study suggested a heritability estimate of .5 to .6 percent for anxiety disorders (Kendler, Aggen, et al., 2011). This indicates that genes may explain about 50-60 percent of the risk for anxiety disorders in the population. Some genes may elevate risk for several different types of anxiety disorder. For example, having a family member with a phobia is related to increased risk of developing not only a phobia but also other anxiety disorders (Tambs, Czajkowsky, et al., 2009), perhaps because those genes increase the risk for neuroticism. Other genes may elevate risk for a specific type of anxiety disorder (Hettema, Prescott, et al., 2005).

Neurobiological Factors: The Fear Circuit and the Activity of Neurotransmitters

A set of brain structures is engaged when people feel anxious or fearful. This set of regions has been called the **fear circuit**, although it is important to note that these structures are also activated during processing of other types of salient stimuli (Feldman Barrett, 2017) and are also implicated in other disorders involving emotion disturbances, such as the mood disorders. Key regions of the fear circuit, shown in **Figure 6.2**, are related to anxiety disorders. One important part of the fear circuit is the amygdala. The amygdala is a small, almond-shaped structure in the temporal lobe that appears to be involved in assigning emotional significance to stimuli. In animals, the amygdala has been shown to be critical for the conditioning of fear. The amygdala sends signals to a range of different brain structures involved in the fear circuit, including other regions that also appear involved in responses to threat. Studies suggest that when shown pictures of angry faces (one signal of threat), people with several different anxiety disorders respond with greater activity in the amygdala than do people without anxiety disorders (Fox, Oler, et al., 2015). Hence, elevated activity in the amygdala, a core part of the fear circuit, may help explain many different anxiety disorders.

The **medial prefrontal cortex** helps to regulate amygdala activity—it is involved in extinguishing fears and is engaged when people are regulating their emotions (Indovina, Robbins, et al., 2011; Kim, Loucks, et al., 2011). The medial prefrontal cortex is involved in the conscious processing of anxiety and fear (LeDoux & Pine, 2016). Researchers have found that adults who meet diagnostic criteria for anxiety disorders display less activity in the medial prefrontal cortex when viewing and appraising threatening stimuli (Britton, Grillon, et al., 2013) and when asked to regulate their emotional responses to threatening stimuli (Goldin, Manber-Ball, et al., 2009). The pathway, or connectivity, linking the amygdala and the medial prefrontal cortex may be deficient among those with anxiety disorders (Kim et al., 2011). These deficits in connectivity between these two regions may interfere with the effective regulation and extinction of anxiety.

Although we focus on the amygdala and the medial prefrontal cortex here, other regions interface with the amygdala to process threat-related stimuli. The bed nucleus of the stria terminalis is also engaged by cues of threat (Shackman & Fox, 2016). The anterior cingulate cortex appears involved in the anticipation of threat, and the insula appears related to awareness of and processing of bodily cues, such as the high arousal invoked by threat. The hippocampus plays a role in encoding the context in which feared stimuli occur (Vervliet, Craske, & Hermans, 2013). We'll discuss the hippocampus more as we discuss PTSD in Chapter 7. We will discuss another part of the fear circuit, the locus coeruleus, when we discuss specific anxiety disorders.

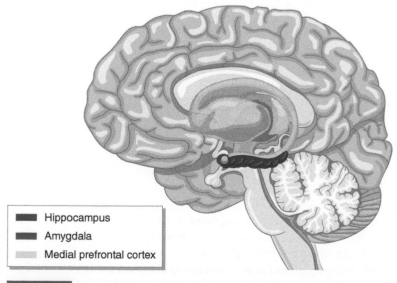

■ Hippocampus
■ Amygdala
▨ Medial prefrontal cortex

FIGURE 6.2 Fear and anxiety appear to be related to a set of structures in the brain called the fear circuit. The amygdala and medial prefrontal cortex are particularly involved in anxiety disorders.

Multiple neurotransmitters and neuropeptides are implicated in anxiety disorders, and many different techniques have been used to test their role. PET and SPECT imaging studies link anxiety disorders to disruptions in serotonin levels (Frick, Åhs, et al., 2015). Serotonin, which we discussed in Chapter 5 for its role in mood disorders, is believed to help modulate emotions (Carver, Johnson, & Joormann, 2008). PET and SPECT imaging studies also suggest changes in the function of the GABA system in the anxiety disorders (Bandelow, Baldwin, et al., 2016). GABA is widely distributed throughout the brain and is centrally involved in modulating activity in the amygdala and fear circuit (Nuss, 2015). Researchers have also used drug manipulation studies to show that anxiety disorders are related to increased levels of norepinephrine and changes in the sensitivity of norepinephrine receptors (Neumeister, Daher, & Charney, 2005). Norepinephrine is a key neurotransmitter in the activation of the sympathetic nervous system for "fight-or-flight" responses. In addition to human research, a huge body of animal research, using genetic paradigms and pharmacological manipulations, suggests that an array of neurotransmitters and neuropeptides are involved in the process of fear conditioning and extinction. Like the human research, this work supports the role of GABA, serotonin, and norepinephrine, as well as endogenous opioids (Bukalo, Pinard, & Holmes, 2014; Graeff, 2017).

Other research has focused on the HPA system (see Chapter 2). As mentioned in Chapter 5, cortisol has a strong diurnal rhythm, with a large increase as people awaken. In one study of adolescents who had no lifetime history of an anxiety disorder, the size of this early morning rise, called the cortisol awakening response (CAR), predicted the onset of anxiety disorders over the next 6 years (Adam, Vrshek-Schallhorn, et al., 2014).

Personality: Behavioral Inhibition and Neuroticism

Some infants show the trait of **behavioral inhibition**, a tendency to become agitated and cry when faced with novel toys, people, or other stimuli. This behavioral pattern, which has been described in infants as young as 4 months old, may be inherited and may set the stage for the later development of anxiety disorders. One study followed infants from 14 months through 7.5 years; 45 percent of those who showed elevated behavioral inhibition levels at 14 months showed symptoms of anxiety at age 7.5, compared with only 15 percent of those who had shown low behavioral inhibition levels (Kagan & Snidman, 1999). Behavioral inhibition is a particularly strong predictor of social anxiety disorder: infants showing elevated behavioral inhibition were 3.79 times as likely as those with low behavioral inhibition to develop social anxiety disorder by adolescence (Chronis-Tuscano, Degnan, et al., 2009).

Neuroticism is a personality trait defined by the tendency to experience frequent or intense negative affect. How does neuroticism relate to anxiety disorders? In studies involving more than 10,000 participants, neuroticism predicted the onset of both anxiety disorders and depression (Ormel, Jeronimus, et al., 2013). In one large study, people with high levels of neuroticism were more than twice as likely to develop an anxiety disorder as were those with low levels (de Graaf, Bijl, et al., 2002).

Cognitive Factors

Researchers have focused on several separate cognitive factors in anxiety disorders. Here, we concentrate on four: sustained negative beliefs about the future, a perceived lack of control, over-attention to signs of threat, and intolerance of uncertainty.

Sustained Negative Beliefs About the Future
People with anxiety disorders often report believing that bad things are likely to happen. For example, people with panic disorder might believe that they will die when their heart begins to pound, whereas people with social anxiety disorder might believe that they will suffer humiliating rejection if they blush. As pointed out by David Clark and colleagues (Clark, Salkovskis, et al., 1999), the key issue is not why people think so negatively initially but, rather, how these beliefs are sustained. For example, by the time a person survives 100 panic attacks, you might expect the belief "this attack means I am about to die" would fade. One reason these beliefs might be sustained is that people think and act in

ways that maintain these beliefs. That is, to protect against feared consequences, they engage in **safety behaviors**. For example, people who fear they will die from a fast heart rate stop all physical activity the minute they feel their heart race. They come to believe that only their safety behaviors have kept them alive. Hence, safety behaviors allow a person to maintain overly negative cognitions.

Perceived Lack of Control
People who report experiencing little sense of control over their surroundings are at risk for a broad range of anxiety disorders (Mineka & Zinbarg, 2006). Childhood experiences, such as traumatic events, punitive and restrictive parenting, or abuse, may promote a view that life is not controllable. Beyond childhood experiences, more recent life events can threaten the sense of control over one's life. Indeed, about half of people with anxiety disorders report a history of childhood physical or sexual abuse (Cougle, Timpano, et al., 2010), and more than 70 percent of people report a severe life event before the onset of an anxiety disorder (Finlay-Jones, 1989). Other life

Infants and toddlers showing behavioral inhibition—high anxiety about novel situations and people—are at greater risk of developing anxiety disorders during their lifetime.

experiences may shape the sense of control over the feared stimulus. For example, people who are used to dogs and feel comfortable about controlling dogs' behavior are much less likely to develop a phobia after a dog bite. On the whole, the degree to which a person experiences control over their environment can influence whether an anxiety disorder develops.

Animal studies have illustrated that a lack of control over the environment can promote anxiety. For example, Insel, Scanlan, et al. (1988) randomly assigned monkeys to one of two conditions. One group of monkeys grew up with the ability to choose whether and when they would receive treats. A second group of monkeys had no control over whether and when they received treats but received the same number of treats. In the third year of life, monkeys who had grown up without control behaved in ways that looked anxious when facing new situations and interacting with other monkeys; monkeys who had grown up with control showed less anxiety. In sum, animal and human studies both point toward the importance of perceived lack of control in the development of anxiety disorders.

Attention to Threat
A large body of research indicates that people with anxiety disorders pay more attention to negative cues in their environment than do people without anxiety disorders (Williams, Watts, et al., 1997). To test attention to threatening stimuli, researchers have used measures like the dot probe task (see **Figure 6.3**). In a meta-analysis of 172 studies, each of the specific anxiety disorders was associated with heightened attention to threatening stimuli on tasks such as the dot probe task (Bar-Haim, Lamy, et al., 2007). For example, people with social anxiety disorder have been found to selectively attend to negative faces (Bantin, Stevens, et al., 2016), whereas people with snake phobias selectively attend to cues related to snakes (Öhman, Flykt, & Esteves, 2001). Researchers have also shown that this heightened attention to threatening stimuli happens automatically and very quickly—before people are even consciously aware of the stimuli (Staugaard, 2010). Once a threatening object captures their attention, anxious people have a difficult time pulling their attention away from that object; they tend to stay focused on a threatening object longer than others do (Cisler & Koster, 2010). In sum, anxiety disorders are associated with selective attention to signs of threat.

In one line of experimental research, investigators have examined whether attention to anxiety-related information can be created, then whether this attention "bias" leads to more anxiety (MacLeod & Mathews, 2012). To train people to attend to threatening words, researchers used the dot probe task. To teach a negative bias, participants view hundreds of trials in which the dot is more likely to occur where the negative word was. For a control group, the dot is equally likely to appear where either the negative or neutral word was. People who were trained to attend to negative words reported a more anxious mood after training, especially when they were given a challenging task like an unsolvable puzzle to perform. The control group did not show an increase in anxious mood after training. The findings suggest that the way we focus our attention can foster an anxious mood.

First screen

Table   Death

Second screen

FIGURE 6.3 The computerized dot probe task is used to test biases in attention and, in some studies, to train attentional biases. On the first screen of each trial, participants see one neutral word and one negative word. On the second screen, a dot appears in the location where one of the two words was. The participant is asked to press a button as quickly as possible to indicate whether the dot appears on the left or right side of the screen. In the case shown here, a person who was looking at the word *death* will see the dot and respond more quickly than a person who was looking at the word *table*.

Eric Audras/Onoky/Getty Images

Could these types of trained biases help us understand diagnosable levels of anxiety? Researchers have examined this question by training people diagnosed with generalized anxiety disorder to attend to positive information (Amir, Beard, et al., 2009). To train a positive bias, the researchers used a version of the dot probe task in which dots appeared where the positive words had been. Participants in a control group completed an equivalent number of training sessions with a control version of the dot probe task. Participants completed 240 trials of training twice a week for four weeks. Anxiety levels did not change over the course of the study in the control group. Participants in the positive-bias training condition obtained lower anxiety scores on self-report and interview measures post-training, and these changes were large enough that half of the people who received positive-bias training no longer met the diagnostic criteria for GAD. Parallel benefits of positive attention training have been shown among adults with social anxiety and among children with clinically significant anxiety (MacLeod & Clarke, 2015). To date, more positive findings have been observed from programs focused on training positive rather than negative cognitive biases (Mogg, Waters, & Bradley, 2017).

Intolerance of Uncertainty People who have a hard time accepting ambiguity, that is, who find it intolerable to think that something bad *might* happen in the future, are more likely to develop anxiety disorders (Dugas, Marchand, & Ladouceur, 2005). This intolerance of uncertainty can predict increases in worry over time (Laugesen, Dugas, & Bukowski, 2003). People with anxiety disorders, but also those with major depressive disorder and obsessive-compulsive disorder tend to struggle when the future is uncertain (Gentes & Ruscio, 2011; McEvoy & Mahoney, 2012).

Quick Summary

Many risk factors set the stage for anxiety disorders generally, rather than for a specific anxiety disorder. Behavioral models of anxiety disorders build from Mowrer's two-factor model (classical conditioning followed by operant conditioning). These models have been extended to consider that the classical conditioning may be driven by direct exposure to an event, observation of someone else experiencing an event (modeling), or verbal instruction. It also appears that people with anxiety disorders acquire classically conditioned fears more quickly than others do, and find it harder to extinguish these fears. They are also more sensitive than others are to unpredictable threats.

Other risk factors may increase the propensity toward fear conditioning. Genes increase risk for anxiety disorders. Neurobiological research on anxiety focuses on the brain's fear circuit, including the connectivity of regions such as the amygdala and medial prefrontal cortex. Anxiety disorders also appear to involve poor functioning of the GABA, norepinephrine, and serotonin systems. The personality traits of behavioral inhibition and neuroticism are both related to the development of anxiety disorders. From the cognitive perspective, anxiety disorders are associated with negative expectations about the future, beliefs that life is uncontrollable, a bias to attend to negative information, and intolerance of uncertainty. The role of attentional bias has been supported using experimental designs.

Check Your Knowledge 6.4

Choose the best answer for each item.

1. Research suggests that genes can explain _____ percent of the variance in anxiety disorders.

   a. 0–20

   b. 20–40

   c. 40–60

   d. 60–80

2. _____ is a personality trait characterized by a tendency to experience frequent and intense negative affect.

   a. Extraversion

   b. Neurosis

   c. Neuroticism

   d. Psychosis

Circle all that apply.

3. Cognitive factors found to correlate with anxiety disorders include:
    a. low self-esteem
    b. attention to signs of threat
    c. hopelessness
    d. lack of perceived control

4. A key structure in the fear circuit is the:
    a. cerebellum
    b. amygdala
    c. occipital cortex
    d. inferior colliculi

Fill in the blanks.

5. The first step in Mowrer's two-factor model includes _____ conditioning, and the second step involves _____ conditioning.
    a. operant, operant
    b. classical, classical
    c. classical, operant
    d. operant, classical

Etiology of Specific Anxiety Disorders

So far, we have discussed factors that might set the stage for development of anxiety disorders in general. Here, we turn to the question of how each of the specific anxiety disorders arises. That is, why does one person develop a specific phobia while another person develops generalized anxiety disorder? Keep in mind the common etiological factors already described, and think about how these commonalities relate to and combine with the specifics described next.

Etiology of Specific Phobias

The dominant model of phobias is the two-factor model of behavioral conditioning described earlier. Here we elaborate on how this model can be applied to understanding phobias. We'll describe some of the research evidence, as well as several refinements of the model.

In the behavioral model, specific phobias are seen as a conditioned response that develops after a threatening experience and is sustained by avoidant behavior. In one of the first illustrations of this model, John Watson and his graduate student Rosalie Rayner published a case report in 1920 in which they demonstrated creating an intense fear of a rat (a phobia) in an infant, Little Albert, using classical conditioning (see photo). Little Albert was initially unafraid of the rat, but after repeatedly seeing the rat while a very loud noise was made, he began to cry when he saw the rat. Although this type of experiment would likely not be approved by modern ethics boards, the experiment provided important evidence that intense fears could be conditioned.

As already mentioned, behavioral theory suggests that phobias *could* be conditioned by direct trauma, modeling, or verbal instruction. But do most people with a phobia report one of these types of conditioning experiences? In one study, 1937 people were asked whether they had these types of conditioning experiences before

Little Albert, shown here with Rayner and Watson, was classically conditioned to develop a fear of a white rat (Watson & Raynor, 1920).

Courtesy of Benjamin Harris

The prepared learning model suggests that we have evolved to pay special attention to signs of danger, including angry people, threatening animals, and dangerous natural environments.

the onset of their phobias (Kendler, Myers, & Prescott, 2002). Although conditioning experiences were common, about half of the people in the study could not remember any such experiences. Obviously, if many phobias start without a conditioning experience, this is a big problem for the behavioral model. But proponents of the behavioral model argue that people may forget conditioning experiences (Mineka & Öhman, 2002). Because of memory gaps, simple surveys of how many people remember a conditioning experience do not provide accurate evidence about the behavioral model.

Even among those who have had a threatening experience, many do not develop a phobia. How might we understand this? To begin, the risk factors we have described, such as genetic vulnerability, neuroticism, negative cognition, and propensity toward fear conditioning, probably operate as diatheses—vulnerability factors that shape whether or not a phobia will develop in the context of a conditioning experience (Mineka & Sutton, 2006).

It also is believed that only certain kinds of stimuli and experiences will contribute to development of a phobia. Mowrer's original two-factor model suggests that people could be conditioned to be afraid of all types of stimuli. But people with phobias tend to fear certain types of stimuli. Typically, people do not develop phobias of flowers, lambs, or lamp shades! But phobias of insects or other animals, natural environments, and blood are common. As many as half of women report a fear of snakes; moreover, many different types of animals also fear snakes (Öhman & Mineka, 2003). Researchers have suggested that during the evolution of our species, people learned to react strongly to stimuli that could be life-threatening, such as heights, snakes, and angry humans (Seligman, 1971). That is, evolution may have "prepared" our fear circuit to learn fear of certain stimuli very quickly and automatically; hence, this type of learning is called **prepared learning**. In support of this idea of evolutionarily-adaptive fears, researchers have shown that monkeys can be conditioned to fear snakes and crocodiles but not flowers and rabbits (Cook & Mineka, 1989). As researchers have tested this model, some have discovered that people can be initially conditioned to fear many different types of stimuli (McNally, 1987). Fears of most types of stimuli fade quickly with ongoing exposure, though, whereas fears of naturally dangerous stimuli are sustained in most studies (Dawson, Schell, & Banis, 1986).

Etiology of Social Anxiety Disorder

In this section, we review behavioral and cognitive factors related to social anxiety disorder. The trait of behavioral inhibition may also be important in the development of social anxiety disorder.

Behavioral Factors: Conditioning of Social Anxiety Disorder As
with social anxiety disorder, behavioral perspectives on specific phobias are based on a two-factor conditioning model. That is, a person could have a negative social experience (directly, through modeling, or through verbal instruction) and become classically conditioned to fear similar situations, which the person then avoids. The next step involves operant conditioning: avoidance behavior is reinforced because it reduces the fear the person experiences. There are few opportunities for the conditioned fear to be extinguished because the person tends to avoid social situations. Even when the person interacts with others, he or she may show avoidant behavior in smaller ways that have been labeled as safety behaviors. Examples of safety behaviors in social anxiety disorder include avoiding eye contact, disengaging from conversation, and standing apart from others. Although these behaviors are used to avoid negative feedback, they create other problems. Other people tend to disapprove of these types of avoidant behaviors, which then intensifies the problem. (Think about how you might respond if you were trying to talk to someone who looks at the floor, fails to answer your questions, and leaves the room in the middle of the conversation.)

Cognitive Factors: Too Much Focus on Negative Self-Evaluations Theory focuses on several different ways in which cognitive processes might intensify social anxiety (Clark & Wells, 1995). First, people with social anxiety disorders appear to have unrealistically harsh views of their social behaviors and overly negative beliefs about the consequences of their social behaviors—for example, they may believe that others will reject them if they blush or pause while speaking. Second, they attend more to how they are doing in social situations and their own internal sensations than other people do. Instead of attending to their conversation partner, they are often thinking about how others might perceive them (e.g., "He must think I'm an idiot"). In one approach to understanding this type of cognition, researchers asked men to recount the thoughts that ran through their mind when they thought about introducing themselves to an attractive woman. Men with social anxiety were much more likely to verbalize thoughts about their own performance than were those without social anxiety (Zanov & Davison, 2010). Of course, good conversation requires a focus on the other person, so too much thinking about inner feelings and evaluation can foster social awkwardness. The resultant anxiety interferes with their ability to perform well socially, creating a vicious circle. For example, the socially anxious person doesn't pay enough attention to others, who then perceive the person as not interested in them.

The evidence is clear that people with social anxiety disorder are overly negative in evaluating their social performance, even when they are not socially awkward, and they form powerful visual images of being rejected (Hirsch, Meeten, et al., 2016). For example, in one study, researchers assessed blushing in people with and without social anxiety disorder. Participants were asked to estimate how much they would blush during different tasks, such as singing a children's song. Then they were asked to engage in these different tasks. Participants with social anxiety disorder overestimated how much they would blush (Gerlach, Wilhelm, et al., 2001). Similarly, one research team asked people with social anxiety disorder to rate videos of their performance in giving a short speech. Socially anxious people rated their speeches more negatively than objective raters did, whereas people who were not socially anxious were not harsh in rating their own performance (Ashbaugh, Antony, et al., 2005). The evidence is clear that people with social anxiety disorder are unfairly harsh in their self-evaluations.

Evidence also indicates that people with social anxiety disorder attend more to internal cues than to external (social) cues. For example, people with social anxiety disorder appear to spend more time than other people do monitoring for signs of their own anxiety. In one study, researchers gave participants a chance to watch their own heart rate displayed on a computer screen or to view faces. Many of the faces were threatening. People diagnosed with social anxiety disorder attended more closely to their own heart rate than did the people who were not diagnosed with social anxiety disorder (Pineles & Mineka, 2005). Hence, rather than keeping their eye on potential external threats, people with this disorder tend to be busy monitoring their own anxiety levels.

How might all these risk variables fit together when we consider a person with social anxiety disorder, like Maureen? Maureen is likely to have inherited some tendency to be anxious when faced with new people. As she grew up, her anxiety may have interfered with her chances to acquire social skills and to gain self-confidence. Her fear of other people's opinions and her own negative thoughts about her social abilities created a vicious circle in which her intolerable anxiety led her to avoid social situations, and then the avoidance led to increased anxiety. Even when she is in social situations, her focus on her performance and anxiety levels may interfere with being fully engaged in the interaction.

Kim Basinger, the Oscar-winning actress, describes her experiences of anxiety in the video *Panic Attacks: A Film About Coping*. She is reported to have suffered from panic disorder and social anxiety disorder.

Matthew Simmons/Getty Images News and Sport Services

Etiology of Panic Disorder

In this section, we look at current thinking about the etiology of panic disorder from neurobiological, behavioral, and cognitive perspectives. As you will see, all these perspectives focus on how people respond to somatic (bodily) changes like increased heart rate.

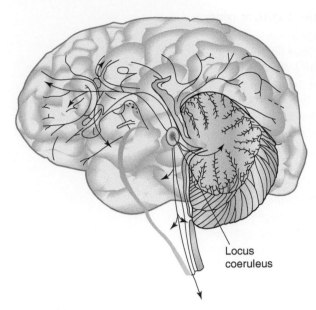

FIGURE 6.4 The locus coeruleus is the major source of norepinephrine. Surges in norepinephrine lead to a number of physiological shifts, including faster heart rate.

Source: J. H. Martin, *Neuroanatomy Text and Atlas*, 4th ed. (1996), copyright McGraw Hill Education LLC with permission.

Neurobiological Factors We have seen that the fear circuit appears to play an important role in many of the anxiety disorders. Now we will see that a particular part of the fear circuit is especially important in panic disorder: the **locus coeruleus** (see **Figure 6.4**). The locus coeruleus is the major source of the neurotransmitter norepinephrine in the brain. Surges in norepinephrine are a natural response to stress, and when these surges occur, they are associated with increased activity of the sympathetic nervous system, reflected in a faster heart rate and other psychophysiological responses that support the fight-or-flight response. People with panic disorder show a more dramatic biological response to drugs that trigger releases of norepinephrine (Neumeister et al., 2005). Drugs that increase activity in the locus coeruleus can trigger panic attacks, and some imaging research is consistent with a role of norepinephrine in panic disorder as well (Bandelow et al., 2017).

Behavioral Factors: Classical Conditioning The behavioral perspective on the etiology of panic disorder focuses on classical conditioning. This model draws from an interesting pattern—panic attacks are often triggered by internal bodily sensations of arousal. Theory suggests that panic attacks are classically conditioned responses to either the situations that trigger anxiety or the internal bodily sensations of arousal (Bouton, Mineka, & Barlow, 2001). Classical conditioning of panic attacks in response to bodily sensations has been called **interoceptive conditioning**: a person experiences somatic signs of anxiety, which are followed by the person's first panic attack; panic attacks then become a conditioned response to the somatic changes (see **Figure 6.5**).

Cognitive Factors Cognitive perspectives on panic disorder focus on catastrophic misinterpretations of somatic changes (Clark, 1996). According to this model, panic attacks develop when a person interprets bodily sensations as signs of impending doom (see **Figure 6.6**). For example, the person may interpret the sensation of an increase in heart rate as a sign of an

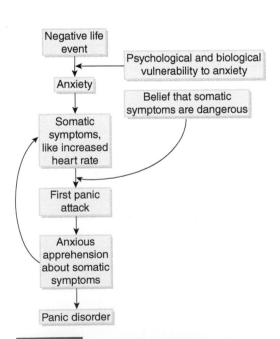

FIGURE 6.5 Interoceptive conditioning. After the first panic attack, the person is classically conditioned to fear somatic symptoms.

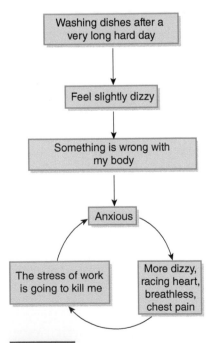

FIGURE 6.6 An example of catastrophic misinterpretation of bodily cues.

impending heart attack. Obviously, such thoughts will increase the person's anxiety, which produces more physical sensations, creating a vicious circle.

The evidence that these cognitive factors can contribute to panic attacks is quite strong. To understand the evidence, it is important to know that panic attacks can be experimentally induced in the laboratory. Research has focused on triggering panic attacks experimentally for more than 75 years. These studies suggest that an array of factors that create physiological sensations can trigger panic attacks among people with a history of panic attacks, including more than a dozen different medications (Swain, Koszycki, et al., 2003). Even drugs that have opposite physiological effects can set off panic attacks (Lindemann & Finesinger, 1938). Exercise alone, simple relaxation, or the physical sensations caused by an illness such as inner-ear disease also can induce panic attacks (Asmundson, Larsen, & Stein, 1998). Another commonly used procedure involves exposing people to air with high levels of carbon dioxide; in response to the diminished oxygen, breathing rate increases, and for some people this induces panic. In short, many different bodily sensations can trigger panic attacks (Barlow, 2004). Cognitive researchers have focused on how to differentiate the people who do and do not develop a panic attack in these experimental studies. People who develop panic attacks after being exposed to these agents seem to differ from those who do not develop panic attacks on only one characteristic—the extent to which they are frightened by the bodily changes (Margraf, Ehlers, & Roth, 1986).

To show the role of cognition as a predictor of panic attacks, researchers in one study used a paradigm described above, in which carbon dioxide levels are manipulated. Before breathing the carbon dioxide-manipulated air, some people were given a full explanation of the physical sensations they were likely to experience, and others were given no explanation. After breathing the air, those who had received a full explanation reported that they had fewer catastrophic interpretations of their bodily sensations, and they were much less likely to have a panic attack than those who did not receive an explanation (Rapee, Mattick, & Murrell, 1986). Catastrophic interpretations of bodily sensations, then, seem to be important in triggering panic attacks.

The propensity toward catastrophic interpretations can be detected before panic disorder develops, most commonly using a subscale of the **Anxiety Sensitivity Index**, which measures the extent to which people respond fearfully to their bodily sensations (Telch, Shermis, & Lucas, 1989). Sample items from this subscale include "Unusual body sensations scare me" and "When I notice that my heart is beating rapidly, I worry that I might have a heart attack." The Anxiety Sensitivity Index has predicted the onset of panic attacks and anxiety disorders in longitudinal studies (Schmidt, Zvolensky, & Maner, 2006). In analyses of two twin studies, high scores on the bodily concerns subscale of the Anxiety Sensitivity Index were related to the genetic risk for anxiety disorders (Brown, Waszczuk, et al., 2014). Taken together, it appears that the Anxiety Sensitivity Index captures an important part of the vulnerability to anxiety disorders.

Experiments demonstrate that panic attacks can be triggered by a variety of agents that change bodily sensations, including drugs and even exercise.

A large body of experimental research examines how high scores on the Anxiety Sensitivity Index might contribute to symptoms of panic disorder. In one study, college students with no history of panic attacks were divided into high and low scorers on the Anxiety Sensitivity Index (Telch & Harrington, 1992). Researchers then used the carbon dioxide manipulation described earlier to see who would develop panic attacks. As with the Rapee study just described, half of the participants were told that carbon dioxide would produce arousal symptoms, and half were not. When breathing carbon dioxide, panic attacks were most common among people who feared their bodily sensations, particularly if they were not warned about the physical effects of carbon dioxide on arousal. This result is exactly what the model predicts: unexplained physiological arousal in someone who is fearful of such sensations leads to panic attacks.

Etiology of Agoraphobia

Because agoraphobia was only recognized as a distinct disorder with the DSM-5, less is known about its etiology. As with other anxiety disorders, risk of agoraphobia appears to be related to genetic vulnerability and life events (Wittchen et al., 2010). One major model of how these symptoms evolves focuses on cognition.

The principal cognitive model for the etiology of agoraphobia is the **fear-of-fear hypothesis** (Goldstein & Chambless, 1978), which suggests that agoraphobia is driven by negative thoughts about the consequences of experiencing anxiety in public. Research findings indicate that people with agoraphobia tend to think the consequences of public anxiety would be horrible (Clark, 1997). They seem to have catastrophic beliefs that their anxiety will lead to socially unacceptable consequences (e.g., "I am going to go crazy"; Chambless, Caputo, et al., 1984).

Etiology of Generalized Anxiety Disorder

Generalized anxiety disorder (GAD) tends to co-occur with other anxiety disorders. Because the comorbidity is so high, researchers believe that many of the factors involved in predicting anxiety disorders in general are particularly important for understanding GAD. GAD, though, seems to differ from the other anxiety disorders in a few important ways. People who meet diagnostic criteria for GAD are much more likely to experience episodes of MDD than those with other anxiety disorders are. This suggests that some of the risk factors involved in MDD are also likely to be important in GAD. Here, we focus on a specific model of GAD though.

Worry is the core feature of GAD. Worry is associated with negative affect, and with modest increases in psychophysiological arousal. When instructed to worry, participants with and without GAD experience an increase in negative affect and small shifts in psychophysiological arousal—that is, they look distressed (Stapinski, Abbott, & Rapee, 2010). Worry is such an unpleasant experience that one might ask why anyone would worry a lot. The **contrast avoidance model** may help explain why some people worry more than others do (Newman & Llera, 2011). Core to this model is the finding that people diagnosed with GAD find it highly aversive to experience rapid shifts in emotions. According to this theory, to ward off sudden shifts in emotion, people with GAD find it preferable to sustain a chronic state of worry and distress: A worrier confronted with a stressor has less room for a large shift in mood and psychophysiological arousal. Consistent with this theory, when people with GAD are presented with a laboratory stressor, they show less of an increase in mood and psychophysiological arousal than do those without GAD (McTeague & Lang, 2012). The point isn't that worriers are happier or calmer during stress, but that they demonstrate less volatility. This is in contrast with other anxiety disorders, which tend to be related to very intense psychophysiological responses to threatening stimuli. Taken together, these findings suggest that worry could help a person sustain a more stable emotional state, even if it is an uncomfortable one!

Quick Summary

In addition to variables that increase the overall risk of developing a range of anxiety disorders, researchers have identified risk variables related to specific anxiety disorders.

Specific phobias are believed to reflect conditioning in response to a traumatic event. Many people report that they experienced traumatic conditioning experiences before developing specific phobias, but many people don't, perhaps because the conditioning experience has been forgotten. Prepared learning refers to the fact that people are likely to sustain conditioned responses to fear stimuli that are evolutionarily significant.

Social anxiety disorder appears to be related to conditioning and behavioral inhibition. Cognitive factors involved in social anxiety disorder include self-critical evaluations of social performance and tendencies to focus on internal thoughts and sensations.

Neurobiological research demonstrates that panic attacks are related to high activity in the locus coeruleus. Behavioral models emphasize the possibility that people could become classically conditioned to experience panic attacks in response to external situations or to internal somatic signs of arousal. Conditioning to somatic signs is called interoceptive conditioning. Cognitive perspectives focus on catastrophic misinterpretations of somatic symptoms, which can be measured with the Anxiety Sensitivity Index.

A cognitive model of agoraphobia focuses on "fear of fear," or overly negative beliefs about what will happen if one experiences anxiety.

One cognitive model, the contrast avoidance model, suggests that worry might protect people from sudden increases in negative moods, by sustaining a more chronically negative mood.

Check Your Knowledge 6.5

Match the theory to the model of etiology:

1. Panic disorder
2. GAD
3. Specific phobias
4. Agoraphobia
5. Social anxiety disorder

    a. anxiety sensitivity

    b. prepared learning

    c. avoidance of powerful changes in negative emotions

    d. too much of a focus on one's own flaws

    e. fear of fear

Treatments of the Anxiety Disorders

Most people who seek treatment for anxiety disorders will only visit a family doctor. Most commonly, people will be offered a medication: in 2011, more than 80 million prescriptions were written for a class of anti-anxiety medications called benzodiazepines (IMS Health, 2012). As we shall see in the next section, many other treatment options can be helpful for the anxiety disorders.

Commonalities Across Psychological Treatments

Effective psychological treatments for anxiety disorders share a common focus: exposure—that is, people must face what they deem too terrifying to face. Therapists from varying perspectives all agree that we must face up to the source of our fear or, as an ancient Chinese proverb puts it, "Go straight to the heart of danger, for there you will find safety." Even psychoanalysts, who believe that the unconscious sources of anxiety are buried in the past, eventually encourage confronting the source of fears (Zane, 1984).

Exposure is a core component of cognitive behavioral treatment (CBT). In a typical approach to exposure treatment, the therapist and the client make a list of triggers—situations and activities that might elicit anxiety or fear, and they create an "exposure hierarchy," a graded list of the difficulty of these triggers. Early sessions involve exposure to relatively less challenging triggers, and gradually, as the client learns that exposure will extinguish his or her anxiety, the more challenging triggers are faced. Findings from more than 100 randomized controlled studies of CBT for anxiety disorders (Norton & Price, 2007), dozens of which have included a control form of psychotherapy (Hofmann & Smits, 2008), suggest that CBT works well. Exposure treatment is effective for 70–90 percent of clients. Although much of the research has been conducted with samples of majority individuals, CBT also has been shown to be helpful for non-Latino white clients (Chavira, Golinelli, et al., 2014).

The effects of CBT endure when follow-up assessments are conducted 6 months after treatment (Hollon, Stewart, & Strunk, 2006) but in the years after treatment, many people experience some return of their anxiety symptoms. A couple of key principles appear important in protecting against relapse (Craske & Mystkowski, 2006). First, exposure should include as many features of the feared object as possible. For example, exposure for a person with a spider phobia might include exposure to different spiders, but also a focus on different features of those spiders such as the hairy legs and the beady eyes. Second, exposure should be conducted in as many different contexts as possible (Bouton & Waddell, 2007). As an example, it might be important to expose a person to a spider in an office and outside in nature. An elevator phobic might be urged to ride elevators in many different buildings.

The behavioral view of exposure is that it works by extinguishing the fear response. A good deal of work has focused on how extinction works at a neurobiological level and how this information might be used to refine exposure treatment (Vervliet, Craske, & Hermans, 2013). This work suggests that extinction does not work like an eraser. Let's take dog phobia as an example. Extinction will not erase the underlying fear of dogs altogether—the conditioned fear still resides deep inside the brain, and it can resurface over time or in certain contexts. Rather, extinction involves learning new associations to stimuli related to dogs. These newly learned associations inhibit activation of the fear. Thus, extinction involves learning, not forgetting.

A cognitive view of exposure treatment has also been proposed. According to this view, exposure helps people correct their mistaken beliefs that they are unable to cope with the stimulus. In this view, exposure relieves symptoms by allowing people to realize that, contrary to their beliefs, they can tolerate feared situations without loss of control (Foa & Meadows, 1997). Cognitive approaches to treatment of anxiety disorders typically focus on challenging people's beliefs about (1) the likelihood of negative outcomes if they face an anxiety-provoking object or situation, and (2) their ability to cope with the anxiety. Thus, cognitive treatments typically involve exposure in order to help people learn that they can cope with these situations. Because both behavioral and cognitive treatments involve exposure and learning to cope differently with fears, it is not surprising that most studies suggest that adding a cognitive therapy component to exposure therapy for anxiety disorders does not bolster results (Deacon & Abramowitz, 2004). Some very specific cognitive techniques, however, seem to help when added to exposure treatment, and we will discuss these as we review how treatment can be tailored for the specific anxiety disorders.

Virtual reality is sometimes used to simulate feared situations such as flying, heights, and even social interactions. Findings of small randomized controlled trials indicate that exposure to these simulated situations appears to be as effective as **in vivo** (real-life) **exposure** (Kampmann, Emmelkamp, & Morina, 2016; Morina, Ijntema, et al., 2015).

In addition to virtual reality programs, Internet-based programs have been developed to guide clients in CBT for the anxiety disorders. Internet CBT programs for social anxiety disorder, panic disorder, and GAD achieve large effects compared with control conditions, and these effects appear to be sustained when clients are reassessed 6 months after they finish the program (Andersson, 2016; Olthuis, Watt, et al., 2016). These programs seem to work best when at least some human contact is provided. For example, therapists might conduct the initial screening to ensure that a person is enrolled in the right type of program, they might help a person develop an appropriate exposure hierarchy, or they might review homework assignments (Marks & Cavanagh, 2009). Even with this type of support, these programs substantially reduce the amount of professional contact time required to provide exposure treatment.

Although exposure treatment is considered primary, several treatments have been developed to help people take a more reflective, less reactive stance toward their intense anxiety and other emotions. These treatments include components such as mindfulness meditation and skills to promote acceptance of emotions. Most typically, these are used in combination with other CBT techniques, such as exposure treatment. Although few randomized trials are available, mindfulness meditation and acceptance treatments appear to be more powerful in reducing anxiety symptoms than are placebos and have fared as well as CBT in the treatment of mixed anxiety disorders and GAD (Roemer, Williston, et al., 2013).

Psychological Treatments of Specific Anxiety Disorders

Exposure treatment is used with all anxiety disorders, but next, we look at how this psychotherapy can be tailored to specific anxiety disorders. Researchers have adapted exposure treatment to address the more specific content of specific anxiety disorders, and they have considered the best length and format of treatment for each of the specific anxiety disorders.

Psychological Treatment of Phobias
Many different types of exposure treatments have been developed for phobias. Exposure treatments often include in vivo (real-life) exposure to feared objects. For phobias involving fear of animals, injections, or dental work, very brief treatments lasting only a couple of hours have been found to be highly effective (Wolitzky-Taylor, Horowitz, et al., 2008).

Psychological Treatment of Social Anxiety Disorder
CBT of social anxiety has shown efficacy compared with wait list controls and supportive treatment (Mayo-Wilson, Dias, et al., 2014). CBT appears to be more cost effective than medications for the treatment of social anxiety (Mavranezouli, Mayo-Wilson, et al., 2015).

As with other anxiety disorders, exposure is a core aspect of CBT for social anxiety. To provide a graded hierarchy of exposure, such treatments often begin with role playing or practicing with the therapist or in small therapy groups before undergoing exposure in more public social situations. Social skills training, in which a therapist might provide extensive modeling of behavior, can help people with social anxiety disorder who may not know what to do or say in social situations. Remember that safety behaviors, like avoiding eye contact, are believed to interfere with the extinction of social anxiety. Consistent with this idea, the effects of exposure treatment seem to be enhanced when people with social anxiety disorder are taught to stop using safety behaviors (Kim, 2005). That is, not only are people asked to engage in social activities, but, while doing so, they are asked to make direct eye contact, to engage in conversation, and to be fully present. Doing so leads to immediate gains in how they are perceived by others, and it enhances the power of the exposure treatment (Taylor & Alden, 2011).

Virtual reality technology is sometimes used to facilitate exposure to feared stimuli.

Kim Kulish/Corbis/Getty Images

David Clark (1997) has developed a version of cognitive therapy for social anxiety disorder that expands on other treatments in a couple of ways. The therapist helps people learn not to focus their attention internally. The therapist also helps them combat their very negative images of how others will react to them. This cognitive therapy has been shown to be more effective than fluoxetine (Prozac) or than exposure treatment plus relaxation (Clark, Ehlers, et al., 2003; Clark, Ehlers, et al., 2006). In one study, people who had received cognitive therapy for social anxiety continued to show positive outcomes 5 years later (Mortberg, Clark, & Bejerot, 2011).

Psychological Treatment of Panic Disorder
Like the behavioral treatments for phobias already discussed, CBT for panic disorder focuses on exposure (Craske & Barlow, 2014). CBT for panic disorder is based on the tendency of people with this diagnosis to overreact to bodily sensations (Craske & Barlow, 2014). That is, the therapist uses exposure techniques—he or she persuades the client to deliberately elicit the bodily sensations associated with panic. For example, a person whose panic attacks begin with hyperventilation is asked to breathe rapidly for 3 minutes. Some examples of the techniques that can be used to provoke body sensations in this type of exposure therapy are shown in **Table 6.5**. When sensations such as dizziness, dry mouth, light-headedness, increased heart rate, and other somatic signs of panic begin, the person experiences them under safe conditions; in addition, the person practices coping tactics for dealing with somatic symptoms (e.g., breathing from the diaphragm to reduce hyperventilation). With practice and encouragement from the therapist, the person learns to stop seeing physical sensations as signals of loss of control and to see them instead

Social anxiety disorder is often treated in groups, which provide exposure to social threats and provide opportunities to practice new skills.

TABLE 6.5	Techniques for Provoking Somatic Symptoms During Exposure Treatment for Panic Disorder
Technique	**Body Sensation**
Rapid deep breathing for 90 seconds	Shortness of breath, sense of unreality
Attempt to swallow quickly five times in a row	Throat tightness, lump in throat
Run in place	Chest tightness, shortness of breath
Spin in chair	Dizziness

Source: Abramowitz, J. S., & Braddock, A. E. (2008). Psychological treatment of hypochondriasis and health anxiety: A biopsychosocial approach. Cambridge, MA: Hogrefe & Huber.

as intrinsically harmless and controllable sensations. The person's ability to create these physical sensations and then cope with them makes them seem more predictable and less frightening (Clark, 1996).

In cognitive treatment for panic disorder (Clark, 1996), the therapist helps the person identify and challenge the thoughts that make the physical sensations threatening (see **Figure 6.6** for an example of one patient's thoughts). For example, if a person with panic disorder imagines that he or she will collapse, the therapist might help the person examine the evidence for this belief and develop a different image of the consequences of a panic attack. This treatment has been shown to work well in at least seven studies and appears to be a helpful supplement to exposure treatment (Clark et al., 1999).

A psychodynamic treatment for panic disorder also has been developed. The treatment involves 24 sessions focused on identifying the emotions and meanings surrounding panic attacks. Therapists help clients gain insight into areas believed to relate to the panic attacks, such as issues involving separation, anger, and autonomy. Findings for psychodynamic treatment for panic disorder were mixed compared with CBT in one large trial (Milrod, Chambless, et al., 2015).

Psychological Treatment of Agoraphobia

CBT of agoraphobia also focuses on systematic exposure to feared situations. The person with agoraphobia may be coached to gradually tackle leaving home, then driving a couple of miles from home, then sitting in a movie theatre for 5 minutes, and then staying for the full duration of a movie in a crowded theater. Exposure treatment of agoraphobia can be enhanced by involving the patient's partner (Cerny, Barlow, et al., 1987). The partner without agoraphobia is taught that recovery rests upon exposure. Many will have sheltered the person from facing their fears, and through treatment, partners learn to foster exposure rather than avoidance.

Psychological Treatment of Generalized Anxiety Disorder

Multiple behavioral and cognitive treatment strategies for GAD have been developed. The most widely used behavioral technique involves relaxation training to promote calmness. Relaxation techniques can involve relaxing muscle groups one by one or generating calming mental images. With practice, clients typically learn to relax rapidly. Studies suggest that relaxation training is more effective than nondirective treatment or no treatment. Broader forms of CBT have also been developed, which include strategies to help improve problem solving and to address the thought patterns that contribute to GAD. One form of cognitive therapy includes strategies to help people tolerate uncertainty, as people with anxiety disorders seem to be distressed by uncertainty (Dugas, Brillon, et al., 2010). Other cognitive behavioral strategies used to target worry include asking people to worry only during scheduled times, asking people to test whether worry "works" by keeping a diary of the outcomes of worrying, helping people focus their thoughts on the present moment instead of worrying, and helping people address core fears (Borkovec, Alcaine, & Behar, 2004). A small number of studies indicate that broader CBT treatment is more helpful than is relaxation treatment alone (Cuijpers, Sijbrandij, et al., 2014).

Quick Summary

Exposure treatment is the most validated psychological treatment for anxiety disorders. Cognitive treatments supplement exposure with interventions to challenge negative beliefs about what will happen when a person faces his or her fears.

For specific phobias, exposure treatments can work quite quickly. For social anxiety disorder, cognitive strategies, such as teaching a person to focus less on internal thoughts and sensations, are a helpful addition to exposure treatment. The most effective treatments for panic disorder include exposure to somatic sensations, along with cognitive techniques to challenge catastrophic misinterpretations of those symptoms. Exposure treatment for agoraphobia may be enhanced by including partners. CBT of GAD can include relaxation training, strategies to help a person tolerate uncertainty and face core fears, and specific tools to combat tendencies to worry.

Medications That Reduce Anxiety

Drugs that reduce anxiety are referred to as **anxiolytics** (the suffix *-lytic* comes from a Greek word meaning "to loosen or dissolve"). Two types of medications are most commonly used for the treatment of anxiety disorders: **benzodiazepines** (e.g., Valium and Xanax) and antidepressants, including tricyclic antidepressants, selective serotonin reuptake inhibitors (SSRIs), and serotonin–norepinephrine reuptake inhibitors (SNRIs) (Hoffman & Mathew, 2008). Benzodiazepines are sometimes referred to as minor tranquilizers or sedatives. A large number of studies have confirmed that antidepressants provide more benefit than do placebos. Although few studies are available that compare benzodiazepenes to placebos, research does indicate that benzodiazepenes are more powerful than wait list controls for anxiety disorders (Bighelli, Trespidi, et al., 2016; Martin, Sainz-Pardo, et al., 2007; Mayo-Wilson et al., 2014). Beyond these medications that seem to help the range of anxiety disorders, certain drugs seem to be effective for specific anxiety disorders. For example, buspirone (BuSpar) has received approval from the Food and Drug Administration for generalized anxiety disorder (Hoffman & Mathew, 2008).

Given the many effective treatments for anxiety, how does one decide which one to use? Generally, antidepressants are preferred over benzodiazepines. This is because people may experience severe withdrawal symptoms when they try to stop using benzodiazepines—that is, they can be addictive. Benzodiazepines can have significant cognitive and motor side effects, such as memory lapses and drowsiness, and the side effects have been found to have real-world significance: benzodiazepines are related to an increased risk of car accidents (Baldwin, Aitchison, et al., 2013; Rapoport, Lanctot, et al., 2009). Antidepressants tend to have fewer side effects than benzodiazepines. Nonetheless, as many as half of people discontinue tricyclic antidepressants because of side effects such as jitteriness, weight gain, elevated heart rate, and high blood pressure (Taylor et al., 1990). Compared with tricyclic antidepressants, SSRIs and SNRIs tend to have fewer side effects. As a result, SSRIs and SNRIs are considered the first-choice medication treatments of most anxiety disorders. Some people, however, do experience side effects from SSRIs and SNRIs, including gastrointestinal distress, restlessness, insomnia, headache, and diminished sexual functioning (Bandelow, Sher, et al., 2012) Many people stop taking anxiolytic medications because of the side effects.

This discussion leads us to the key problem: most people relapse once they stop taking medications. In other words, medications are

In an interview with Oprah Winfrey (September 24, 2009), Barbra Streisand described social anxiety so intense that she was unable to perform in public for 27 years.

Ricky Williams, the Heisman Trophy winner who became a star for his incredible skills as a running back, obtained relief of his social anxiety symptoms from antidepressant treatment.

only effective during the time when they are taken. Because of this fact, and because exposure treatments and medications provide comparable levels of relief from anxiety symptoms (Cuijpers, Sijbrandij, et al., 2013), psychological treatments are considered the preferred treatment of most anxiety disorders, with the possible exception of GAD, where medication and psychological treatments are considered equivalent (Cuijpers et al., 2014).

Check Your Knowledge 6.6

Answer the questions.

1. What is the most common strategy used in CBT for anxiety disorders?
2. List two reasons psychological treatment is a better option than medication for anxiety disorders.
3. List two reasons that antidepressant medications are preferred to benzodiazepines for the treatment of anxiety disorders.

Summary

Emotions of Anxiety and Fear

- Anxiety is defined as apprehension over an anticipated problem.

- In contrast, fear is defined as a reaction to immediate danger.

- Both anxiety and fear can involve arousal, or sympathetic nervous system activity.

- Anxiety is adaptive in helping us notice and plan for future threats—that is, to increase our preparedness, to help people avoid potentially dangerous situations, and to think through potential problems before they happen.

Clinical Descriptions of the Anxiety Disorders

- As a group, anxiety disorders are the most common type of psychological disorder.

- The five major DSM-5 anxiety disorders are specific phobia, social anxiety disorder, panic disorder, agoraphobia, and generalized anxiety disorder. Anxiety is common to all the anxiety disorders, and fear is common in anxiety disorders other than generalized anxiety disorder.

- Phobias are intense, unreasonable fears that interfere with functioning. Specific phobias commonly include fears of animals; natural environments such as heights; blood, injury, or injections; and situations such as bridges or flying.

- Social anxiety disorder is defined by intense fear of possible social scrutiny.

- Panic disorder is defined by recurrent attacks of intense fear that occur out of the blue. Panic attacks alone are not sufficient for the diagnosis; a person must be worried about the potential of having another attack.

- Agoraphobia is defined by fear and avoidance of being in situations where escaping or getting help would be difficult if anxiety symptoms were to occur.

- The key feature of generalized anxiety disorder is worry that lasts at least 6 months.

Gender and Sociocultural Factors in the Anxiety Disorders

- Anxiety disorders are much more common among women than men.

- The focus of anxiety, the prevalence of anxiety disorders, and the specific symptoms expressed may be shaped by culture.

Common Risk Factors Across the Anxiety Disorders

- Mowrer's two-factor model suggests that anxiety disorders are related to two types of conditioning. The first stage involves classical conditioning, in which a formerly innocuous object is paired with a feared object. This can occur through direct exposure, modeling, or verbal instruction. The second stage involves operant conditioning, in which avoidance is reinforced because it reduces anxiety, and so the person does not gain the chance to have their fears extinguished. Many people do not develop an anxiety disorder after a major threat, though, and this is a challenge to the Mowrer model. The model has been extended to consider the idea that those with anxiety disorders may be particularly likely to develop classically conditioned fears, and slow to extinguish those fears; they also may be particularly responsive to unpredictable threats compared with other people. Many of the other risk factors may increase the propensity to develop and sustain conditioned fears.

- Genes increase risk for a broad range of anxiety disorders, and they account for about 50–60 percent of the variance in whether a person develops an anxiety disorder. Beyond this general risk for anxiety disorders, there may be more specific heritability for certain anxiety disorders. In addition to genetic diatheses, other biological factors that are involved in a range of anxiety disorders include disturbances in the activity in the fear circuit (including the amygdala and medial prefrontal cortex), poor functioning of the serotonin and GABA neurotransmitter systems, and increased norepinephrine activity.

- Cognitive factors include sustained negative beliefs about the future, lack of perceived control, a heightened attention to signs of potential danger, and intolerance of ambiguity.

- Personality risk factors include behavioral inhibition and neuroticism.

Etiology of Specific Anxiety Disorders

- Behavioral models of specific phobias build on the two-factor model of conditioning. The learned preparedness model suggests that fears of objects with evolutionary significance may be more sustained after conditioning. Because not all people with negative experiences develop phobias, diatheses must be important.

- The behavioral model of social anxiety disorder expands the two-factor conditioning model to consider the role of safety behaviors. Other key risk factors include behavioral inhibition and cognitive variables such as excessively critical self-evaluations and a focus on internal sensations rather than social cues.

- Neurobiological models of panic disorder have focused on the locus coeruleus, the brain region responsible for norepinephrine release. Behavioral theories of panic attacks have posited that the attacks are classically conditioned to internal bodily sensations. Cognitive theories suggest that such sensations are more frightening due to catastrophic misinterpretation of somatic cues. A polymorphism of the NPSR1 gene also appears to increase risk of panic disorder.

- Cognitive models of agoraphobia focus on "fear of fear"—overly negative beliefs about the negative consequences of anxiety.

- One model of GAD suggests that worry helps people avoid intense changes in negative emotions. People with GAD also seem to have difficulty tolerating ambiguity.

Psychological Treatment for the Anxiety Disorders

- Behavior therapists focus on exposure to what is feared. For some anxiety disorders, cognitive components may also be helpful in therapy.

- Exposure treatment for specific phobias tends to work quickly and well.

- Adding cognitive components to exposure treatment may help for social anxiety disorder.

- Treatment for panic disorder often involves exposure to physiological changes.

- Treatment for agoraphobia may be enhanced by including partners in the treatment process.

- Relaxation and cognitive behavioral approaches are helpful for GAD.

Medications to Relieve Anxiety

- Antidepressants and benzodiazepines are the most commonly used medications for anxiety disorders. Benzodiazepines can be addictive.

- Discontinuing medications usually leads to relapse. For this reason, cognitive behavior therapy is considered a more helpful approach than medication treatment for most anxiety disorders.

Answers to Check Your Knowledge Questions

6.1 1. True 2. False 3, True

6.2 1. a; 2. c; 3. d; 4. b; 5. 28 percent; 6. worry

6.3 1. 2 to 1; 2. the United States and European countries; 3. False

6.4 1. c; 2. c; 3. b, d; 4. b; 5. C

6.5 1. a; 2. c; 3. b; 4. e; 5. d

6.6 1. Exposure, sometimes supplemented with cognitive approaches; 2. Although efficacy of psychotherapy and medications is similar, medications have significant side effects, and relapse is common once medications are discontinued; 3. Side effects are more severe with benzodiazepines compared with antidepressant medications; there is a risk of addiction with benzodiazepines.

Key Terms

agoraphobia
anxiety
anxiety disorders
Anxiety Sensitivity Index
anxiolytics
behavioral inhibition
benzodiazepines
contrast avoidance model
depersonalization

derealization
fear
fear circuit
fear-of-fear hypothesis
generalized anxiety disorder (GAD)
interoceptive conditioning
in vivo exposure
locus coeruleus
medial prefrontal cortex

Mowrer's two-factor model
neutral predictable unpredictable (NPU) threat task
panic attack
panic disorder
prepared learning
safety behaviors
social anxiety disorder
specific phobia

CHAPTER 7

Obsessive-Compulsive-Related and Trauma-Related Disorders

LEARNING GOALS

1. Explain the symptoms and epidemiology of obsessive-compulsive and related disorders.

2. Describe the commonalities in the etiology of obsessive-compulsive and related disorders, as well as the factors that shape the expression of the specific disorders within this cluster.

3. Discuss the medication and psychological treatments for obsessive-compulsive and related disorders.

4. Define the symptoms and outcomes of the trauma-related disorders: acute stress disorder and posttraumatic stress disorder.

5. Summarize how the nature and severity of trauma, as well as biological and psychological risk factors, contribute to whether trauma-related disorders develop.

6. Describe the medication and psychological treatments for trauma-related disorders.

Clinical Case

Jacob

Jacob was a 28-year-old graduate student when he sought treatment. Shortly after starting graduate school 2 years earlier, Jacob had begun to experience intrusive images of running over animals with his car. Although he knew that he had not done so, the images were so vivid that he could not get them out of his mind. Several times a week, he would be so disturbed by the idea that he may have hit animals that he would feel compelled to turn his car around and drive his route again, looking for any signs of wounded or dead animals. If he spotted a wounded or dead animal, he would pull off the road and inspect his car for any signs that he might have been the person who hit the animal. Sometimes, when he finished his second trip, he would become concerned that he might have missed a wounded or dead animal, and he would feel the need to drive the route again. This

often made him late for work or appointments, but if he didn't get the chance to look for wounded or dead animals, he would ruminate about the possibility of injured animals throughout the day. He also felt compelled to engage in elaborate bathing rituals, to solve math problems again and again in his head, to chew his food a certain number of times, to flip his light switch on and off three times before he left his bedroom in the morning, and to tap his right elbow three times at the top of the hour. He knew these compulsive behaviors didn't make sense, but he still felt a terrible sense of anxiety if he didn't engage in them. The images occupied his mind and the behavioral rituals absorbed his time, such that his progress in graduate school had slowed to a crawl. He sought treatment after his advisor raised concerns about the slow progress of his thesis research.

In this chapter, we examine obsessive-compulsive-related and trauma-related disorders. Obsessive-compulsive and related disorders are defined by repetitive thoughts and behaviors that are so extreme that they interfere with everyday life. Trauma-related disorders include posttraumatic stress disorder and acute stress disorder, two conditions that are triggered by exposure to severely traumatic events.

As you will see, many people with obsessive-compulsive and related disorders, and those with trauma-related disorders report feeling anxious, and they often experience anxiety disorders as well. Many of the risk factors for anxiety disorders contribute to these disorders, and the treatment approaches overlap a good deal as well. Nonetheless, these disorders have some distinct causes compared with anxiety disorders. As you read this chapter, consider the parallels with the anxiety disorders described in Chapter 6.

We will begin by reviewing the clinical features of the obsessive-compulsive and related disorders, and then will discuss research on their epidemiology and etiology before turning to an overview of treatment approaches. Then, we will discuss the symptoms, etiology, and treatment of trauma-related disorders.

Clinical Descriptions and Epidemiology of Obsessive-Compulsive and Related Disorders

We will focus on three disorders in this section: obsessive-compulsive disorder (OCD), body dysmorphic disorder (BDD), and hoarding disorder (see **Table 7.1**). OCD, the prototypical disorder of this cluster, is defined by repetitive thoughts and urges (obsessions), as well as an irresistible need to engage in repetitive behaviors or mental acts (compulsions). BDD and hoarding disorder share symptoms of repetitive thoughts and behaviors. People with BDD spend hours a day thinking about their appearance and engage in compulsive behaviors designed to address concerns about their appearance. People with hoarding disorder spend a good deal of their time repetitively thinking about their current and potential future possessions. They also engage in intensive efforts to acquire new objects, and these efforts can resemble the compulsions observed in OCD. For the people with all three conditions, the repetitive thoughts and behaviors feel unstoppable and consume a considerable amount of time. Although these three disorders share the quality of repetitive thought as well as irresistible urges to engage repetitively in some behavior or mental act, you will see that the focus of thought and behavior takes a different form across the three conditions.

Obsessive-Compulsive Disorder

The diagnosis of **obsessive-compulsive disorder (OCD)** is based on the presence of obsessions or compulsions. Most people with OCD experience both obsessions and compulsions.

TABLE 7.1   **Diagnoses of Obsessive-Compulsive and Related Disorders**

Diagnoses	Key Features
Obsessive-compulsive disorder (OCD)	Repetitive, intrusive, uncontrollable thoughts or urges (obsessions)
	Repetitive behaviors or mental acts that a person feels compelled to perform (compulsions)
Body dysmorphic disorder (BDD)	Preoccupation with imagined flaw in one's appearance
	Excessive repetitive behaviors or acts regarding appearance (e.g., checking appearance, seeking reassurance)
Hoarding disorder	Acquisition of an excessive number of objects
	Inability to part with those objects

Although many think that the chief distinction here is of thoughts (obsessions) versus behaviors (compulsions), they are mistaken. Let's consider the technical definitions of obsessions and compulsions.

Obsessions are intrusive and persistently recurring thoughts, images, or impulses that are uncontrollable (i.e., the person cannot stop the thoughts) and that often appear irrational to the person experiencing them. With a moment's reflection, most of you can likely think of a time when you had a repetitive thought. At least 80 percent of people experience brief intrusive thoughts from time to time—a terrible song or image gets stuck in your head. And most of us also have thoughts now and then about behaving in ways that would be embarrassing or dangerous (Rachman & DeSilva, 1978). But few of us have thoughts or urges that are persistent and intrusive enough to qualify as obsessions. Like Jacob's images of animals (see the Clinical Case of Jacob), the obsessions of most people with OCD have such force and frequency that they interfere with normal activities. Typically, a person with OCD spends hours of every day immersed in these thoughts, images, or urges.

Obsessions often involve fear of contamination from germs or disease. Although most of us would like to avoid germs and disease, cues that are remotely related to disease can trigger the fears of a person with OCD. One man with OCD was frightened by all cues that reminded him of cancer. He described seeing a bald cashier and thinking that the man's baldness might have been the result of chemotherapy. In response to these thoughts, he stopped shopping at the store to avoid exposure to whatever toxins might have contributed to the man's cancer (Woody & Teachman, 2000). Others with contamination fears describe the need to change clothes and shower after being in a room with someone who has coughed, and then to wash the clothes as well as any part of their home that the contaminated clothes might have touched. The famous mathematician Gödel was so obsessed with the idea that tainted food could poison him that he would only eat food that his wife had first tasted. When she was unable to taste his food due to illness, he starved to death (Adam, 2014).

To understand how contamination could spread so drastically from an initial threatening stimulus, researchers asked people with OCD to consider the building where the research was taking place and to identify the most contaminated object in the building. Most chose a trash can or a toilet. In this regard, the people with OCD were similar to people with anxiety disorders and those with no disorder. With each participant, the researcher then removed a pencil from a new box of 12 pencils and rubbed the pencil against the contaminated object. The researcher then rubbed a second pencil against the first pencil, and then rubbed a third pencil against the second pencil, and so on, through the 12 pencils. Participants were asked to rate the contamination level for each of the 12 pencils. Those without OCD generally rated the sixth pencil as free of contamination. Those with OCD rated even the 12th pencil as highly contaminated (Tolin, Worhunsky, & Maltby, 2004).

Beyond contamination, other frequent foci of obsessions include sex and morality, violence, religion, symmetry/order, and responsibility for harm. We provide some examples of each of these in **Table 7.2**. Obsessions are extremely uncomfortable to experience, and those with OCD will often go to great lengths to avoid situations that might trigger their obsessions.

DSM-5 Criteria for Obsessive-Compulsive Disorder (OCD)

- Obsessions and/or compulsions

Obsessions are defined by
1. Recurrent, intrusive, persistent, unwanted thoughts, urges, or images
2. The attempt to ignore, suppress, or neutralize such thoughts, urges, or images

Compulsions are defined by
1. Repetitive behaviors or mental actions that a person feels compelled to perform to prevent distress or a dreaded event

2. The drive to perform repetitive behaviors or thoughts in response to obsessions or according to rigid rules

3. Acts that are excessive or unlikely to prevent the dreaded situation

- The thoughts or activities are time consuming (e.g., at least 1 hour per day) or cause clinically significant distress or impairment

TABLE 7.2 Common foci of obsessions in OCD

Foci of Obsession	Example
Contamination	What if the public toilet I used had the AIDS virus on it?
Responsibility for harm	What if I dropped my baby down the stairs by mistake?
Sex and morality	What if I could not resist the impulse to touch a stranger's breasts?
Violence	What if my husband was stabbed on his way to work today?
Religion	Inappropriate, disturbing sexual images of deities
Symmetry or order	The feeling that books, dishes, or other objects must be perfectly arranged on a shelf

Adapted from Abramowitz & Jacoby (2015).

Compulsions are repetitive, clearly excessive behaviors or mental acts that the person feels driven to perform to reduce the anxiety caused by obsessive thoughts (Abramowitz & Jacoby, 2015). Jacob's need to revisit his route, described in the Clinical Case, fits this definition. Samuel Johnson, one of the most famous authors of the eighteenth century, suffered from multiple compulsions. For example, he felt compelled "to touch every post in a street or step exactly in the center of every paving stone. If he perceived one of these acts to be inaccurate, his friends were obliged to wait, dumbfounded, while he went back to fix it" (Stephen, 1900, cited in Szechtman & Woody, 2004). Like Samuel Johnson, many people with OCD feel compelled to repeat a ritual if they did not execute it with precision. The sheer frequency with which those with OCD repeat their compulsions can be staggering. See **Table 7.3** for commonly reported compulsions.

We often hear people described as compulsive gamblers, compulsive eaters, and compulsive drinkers. Even though people may report irresistible urges to gamble, eat, and drink, these behaviors are not considered compulsions because they are often experienced as pleasurable. Rather than being motivated by pleasure, compulsions are motivated by the feeling that something dire will happen if the act is not performed. A person who experiences obsessions about contamination is likely to feel intense distress if prevented from engaging in cleaning rituals, even though they may recognize that the cleaning rituals are not warranted.

OCD begins before age 14 for most people affected, but at least a quarter of those affected report that symptoms began in early adulthood (Taylor, 2011). People with OCD tend to experience high levels of distress and self-doubt, and their distress is worsened as the symptoms of OCD interfere with occupational and relationship outcomes (Ruscio, Stein, et al., 2010). OCD also relates to premature mortality from medical conditions and from suicide (Meier, Mattheisen, et al., 2016). Obsessions and compulsions are observed across cultures, but cultural values may shape the prevalence of the disorder and the nature of obsessions and compulsions. For example, in cultures

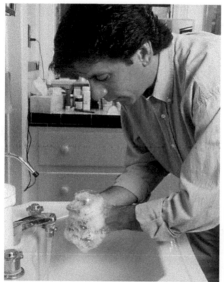

For people with obsessive-compulsive disorder (OCD), extreme fears of contamination can trigger abnormally frequent handwashing.

TABLE 7.3 Common compulsive rituals for those with OCD

Foci of Compulsion	Example
Decontamination	Showering for hours a day, wiping down all objects upon entering the house, or asking visitors to wash before they enter the house
Checking	Returning seven or eight times in a row to see that lights, stove burners, or faucets are turned off, windows fastened, and doors locked
Repeating routine activities	Touching a body part or repeating a word again and again
Ordering/arranging	Sorting all books and cereal boxes into alphabetical order
Mental rituals	Counting, solving a math problem, or repeating a phrase in one's mind until anxiety is relieved

Adapted from Abramowitz & Jacoby (2015).

where people consider uncleanliness sinful, washing compulsions are more common (Clark & González, 2014).

Body Dysmorphic Disorder

People with **body dysmorphic disorder (BDD)** are preoccupied with one or more imagined or exaggerated defects in their appearance, even when others would not share this perception. Although people with BDD may appear attractive to others, they perceive themselves as ugly or even "monstrous" in their appearance (Phillips, 2006). Women tend to be worry about perceived flaws in their skin, hair, facial features, hips, breasts, or legs, whereas men are more likely to worry about their height, penis size, body hair, small size, or insufficient muscularity (Perugi, Akiskal, et al., 1997).

In a somewhat obsessional manner, people with BDD find it very hard to stop thinking about their concerns. As one woman wrote: "It's always in the back of my mind. I can't push it away. It's always there, taunting and haunting me" (Phillips, 2005, p. 69). On average, people with BDD think about their appearance for 3 to 8 hours per day (Phillips, Wilhelm, et al., 2010). Also like people with OCD, people with BDD find themselves compelled to engage in certain behaviors to reduce the distress associated with these obsessional thoughts. The most common compulsive behaviors for those with BDD include checking their appearance in the mirror, comparing their appearance to that of other people, asking others for reassurance about their appearance, or using strategies to change their appearance or camouflage disliked body areas (grooming, tanning, exercising, changing clothes, and applying makeup) (Phillips et al., 2010). While many spend several hours a day checking their appearance, some try to avoid reminders of their perceived flaws by avoiding mirrors, reflective surfaces, or bright lights (Phillips, 2005). Although most of us do things to feel better about our appearance, people with this disorder spend an inordinate amount of time and energy on these endeavors.

The symptoms are extremely distressing. About a third of patients with BDD have little insight into their overly harsh views, and so they are convinced that others will see their flaws as grotesque (Phillips, Pinto, et al., 2012). As many as a fifth of them endure plastic surgery, and many withstand multiple surgeries (Phillips, 2005). Unfortunately, plastic surgery does little to allay their concerns, such that many report wanting to sue or hurt their physicians after the surgery (Bowyer, Krebs, et al., 2016). About a third of people with BDD report some history of suicidal ideation, and about 20 percent have attempted suicide (Buhlmann, Glaesmer, et al., 2010).

Howie Mandel describes his struggle with OCD in his book, *Here's the Deal: Don't Touch Me.* Deeply afraid of germs, he has been unable to shake hands with people, touch a glass, or use a handrail without feeling the intense urge to clean. At age 6, he had trouble learning to tie his shoes because he was afraid to touch his dirty shoelaces.

Dominic Chan/DC5 WENN Photos/Newscom

Clinical Case

Paul

After years of living with anxiety and shame over his appearance, Paul sought psychotherapy at age 33. He had first become "horrified" by his appearance during puberty, when he noticed that he was not developing the square jaw lines that many of his male friends had begun to show. In the past several years, his shame was focused on his nose, which he perceived as being too thin. He had sought surgery, but the surgeon refused to operate on his seemingly flawless nose. Over the past two decades, his preoccupation with his appearance had often interfered with socializing and altogether prevented dating. Even when he did venture out, he had to check his appearance repeatedly throughout the evening. Sometimes he was unable to go to work in his position as a physical therapist because he was overwhelmed by his anxiety. When he did go to work, he worried that his clients were too distracted by his physical flaws to attend to his instructions.

Drawn with permission from Wilhelm, Buhlmann, et al., 2010.

As is the case for Paul (see the Clinical Case), preoccupation with appearance can interfere with many aspects of occupational and social functioning. To cope with the intense shame they feel about their appearance, people with BDD may avoid contact with others. In one survey, about a third reported missing work or avoiding school in the past month because of concerns about their appearance (Phillips, 2005), and many take long breaks from work or interpersonal interactions to check their appearance or cope with the anxiety of being viewed by others. In another survey, about 40 percent of people with the disorder reported being unable to work (Didie, Menard, et al. 2008), and some even become housebound.

BDD typically begins in adolescence. Many people never receive treatment, in part because mental health professionals often do not ask about these symptoms, and in part because those with the disorder often feel too ashamed to raise their concerns (Phillips, 2005).

Social and cultural factors certainly play a role in how people decide whether they are attractive. Although many social factors are likely involved, a large body of cross-sectional and experimental research suggests that exposure to media images of a thin ideal can intensify body image concerns (Grabe, Ward, & Hyde, 2008). Most of these concerns, though, are not extreme enough to be characterized as psychological disorders. People with BDD experience agonizing distress over their perceived physical flaws.

Among those who develop BDD, case reports from around the world suggest that the symptoms and outcomes are similar across cultures (Phillips, 2005). The body part that becomes a focus of concern sometimes differs by culture, though. For example, eyelid concerns are more common in Japan than in Western countries. In addition, Japanese patients with BDD appear more concerned about offending others than are Western patients (Suzuki, Takei, et al., 2003).

Clinicians should take care to distinguish BDD from eating disorders. Most people with BDD are concerned about several different aspects of their appearance. When shape and weight concerns are the only foci, however, the symptoms are better explained by an eating disorder.

DSM-5 Criteria for Body Dysmorphic Disorder (BDD)
• Preoccupation with one or more perceived defects in appearance
• Others find the perceived defect(s) slight or unobservable
• Performance of repetitive behaviors or mental acts (e.g., mirror checking, seeking reassurance, or excessive grooming) in response to the appearance concerns
• Preoccupation is not restricted to concerns about weight or body fat

Hoarding Disorder

Collecting is a hobby for about a third of people in the United States (Frost & Steketee, 2010), and almost all children go through a phase of collecting objects, but these hobbies are distinctly different from hoarding. What distinguishes the common fascination with collections from the clinical disorder of hoarding? Undoubtedly, the desire to acquire and save objects varies along a continuum (Timpano, Broman-Fulks, et al., 2013). For people with **hoarding disorder**, the need to acquire is clearly excessive, and it is only part of the problem. The bigger problem is that they abhor parting with their objects, even when others cannot see any potential value in them. Most typically, as illustrated in the Clinical Case of Dena, the person acquires a huge range of different kinds of objects—they may gather collections of clothes, tools, or antiques along with old containers and bottle caps. People with hoarding disorder feel extremely attached to their possessions, and they are very resistant to efforts to get rid of them.

Clinical Case

Dena

Dena was referred for treatment after animal care officials received reports from neighbors. A home inspection revealed over 100 animals living in her 3-acre yard and inside her house, many of them suffering from malnutrition, overcrowding, and disease. When interviewed, she reported that she was running a rescue mission for animals and that she was "just a little behind" due to financial stress.

When the therapist visited her home, it became clear that her collections extended far beyond her animals. The rooms of her small home were so crowded that two of the doors to the outside had become unreachable. Heaps of clothes mixed with miscellaneous furniture parts brimmed to the ceiling of her living room. In the kitchen, a collection of theater memorabilia crowded out access to the stove and refrigerator. The dining room was covered with assorted items—bags of trash, piles of bills, stacks of old newspapers, and several sets of china she had purchased "at a bargain" at yard sales.

When the therapist offered to help Dena organize and neaten her home, Dena became enraged. She said that she had only allowed the therapist to visit to help her broker an arrangement with the animal control authorities and that she did not want to hear any comments about her home. She described years of fighting with her family over her housekeeping, and she said she had done everything in her power to escape from their uptight expectations. She denied needing the stove, stating that she wasn't about to start cooking hot meals as a single woman living alone. After the initial unsuccessful home visit, she refused any further contact with the therapist.

DSM-5 Criteria for Hoarding Disorder

- Persistent difficulty discarding or parting with possessions, regardless of their actual value
- Perceived need to save items
- Distress associated with discarding items

- The accumulation of possessions clutters active living spaces to the extent that their intended use is compromised unless others intervene

---

Hoarding captured the attention of the public in 1947, when the Collyer brothers were found dead, surrounded by 140 tons of objects, ranging from grand pianos to antique sculptures to a human skeleton, piled from floor to ceiling in their New York City brownstone.

Many people who hoard are unaware of the severity of their behavior (Steketee & Frost, 2015), but to those surrounding them, the consequences of hoarding are clear and sometimes quite severe. For those who do have insight, the difficulties of controlling one's home environment can have profound effects on self-esteem (Frost & Steketee, 2010). The accrual of objects can interfere with the ability to use the kitchen or bathroom of the home, or to have safe exits. Resultant poor hygiene, exposure to dirt, and difficulties with cooking can all contribute to poor physical health, such as respiratory problems. Many family members sever relationships, unable to understand the attachment to the objects. About three-quarters of people with hoarding disorder engage in excessive buying (Frost, Tolin, et al., 2009), and many are unable to work (Tolin, Frost, et al., 2008), making poverty all too common among people with this condition (Samuels, Bienvenu, et al., 2007). As the problem escalates, health officials often become involved to address safety and health concerns. An estimated 10 percent of persons with hoarding disorder are threatened with eviction at some point in their lives (Tolin et al., 2008). For some, the money spent on acquiring possessions leads to homelessness.

About one-third of people with hoarding disorder, much more often women than men, also engage in animal hoarding (Patronek & Nathanson, 2009). People who engage in animal hoarding sometimes view themselves as animal rescuers, but those who witness the problem see it differently—the accumulating number of animals often outstrips the person's ability to provide adequate care, shelter, and food. Animal hoarding is more associated with squalor than are other forms of hoarding. When animals are involved, animal protection agencies sometimes become involved.

Hoarding behavior usually begins in childhood or early adolescence (Grisham, Frost, et al., 2006). Because parents and a lack of income may control these early symptoms, severe impairment from hoarding typically does not surface until later in life. Animal hoarding often does not emerge until middle age or older (Patronek & Nathanson, 2009).

Prevalence and Comorbidity of Obsessive-Compulsive and Related Disorders

Although most of us have had a repetitive thought, have worried about our appearance, and have gone through a phase of collecting, these symptoms lead to the genuine distress or impairment required for a diagnosis in only a small proportion of people. Lifetime prevalence estimates are about 2 percent for OCD (Ruscio et al., 2010) and for BDD (Buhlmann et al., 2010), and 1.5 percent for hoarding disorder (Nordsletten, Reichenberg, et al., 2013). OCD and BDD are both slightly more common among women than men (Buhlmann et al., 2010; Torres, Prince, et al., 2006). Hoarding is equally common among men and women (Samuels et al., 2007), but men are less likely to seek treatment (Steketee & Frost, 2015). Once present, each of these disorders tends to be chronic (Eisen, Sibrava, et al., 2013; Phillips, Menard, et al., 2013).

OCD, BDD, and hoarding disorder often co-occur. For example, about a third of people with BDD and up to a quarter of people with hoarding disorder meet diagnostic criteria for OCD during their lifetime. About one-third of people with OCD experience at least some symptoms of hoarding (Weaton & Van Meter, 2015; Mancebo, Eisen, et al., 2011).

In addition to the high rates of comorbidity within these three syndromes, all three of these syndromes tend to co-occur with depression and anxiety disorders (Brakoulias, Starcevic, et al., 2011). OCD, BDD, and hoarding disorder are associated with somewhat elevated rates of substance use disorders (Frost, Steketee, & Tolin, 2011; Gustad & Phillips, 2003; Ruscio et al., 2010).

Krista Kennell/Shutterstock

Quick Summary

The obsessive-compulsive and related disorders include obsessive-compulsive disorder (OCD), body dysmorphic disorder (BDD), and hoarding disorder. OCD is defined by obsessions and/or compulsions. BDD is defined by a preoccupation with an imagined defect in appearance and by intensive behavioral attempts to cope with the imagined defect. Hoarding disorder is defined by excessive acquisition of objects and severe difficulties in discarding objects, even when they are objectively without value.

Lifetime prevalence estimates are 2 percent for OCD and for BDD, and 1.5 percent for hoarding disorder.

A third of people with BDD and a quarter of those with hoarding disorder have a history of OCD. Beyond this, obsessive-compulsive and related disorders are commonly comorbid with anxiety disorders, major depressive disorder, and substance use disorders.

Lena Dunham has described her childhood experiences of OCD and anxiety (Dunham, 2014). Many people with OCD experience comorbid anxiety.

Check Your Knowledge 7.1
(Answers are at the end of the chapter.)

Answer the questions.

1. Describe the most typical course of obsessive-compulsive and related disorders over time.

2. What is the chief difference between obsessions and compulsions?

Etiology of the Obsessive-Compulsive and Related Disorders

There is a moderate genetic contribution to OCD, hoarding, and BDD. Heritability accounts for 40 to 50 percent of the variance in whether each of these conditions develops (Monzani, Rijsdijk, et al., 2014).

OCD, BDD, and hoarding disorder share some overlap in genetic and neurobiological risk factors. For example, in a study of over 5,000 twins, OCD, BDD and hoarding disorder appeared to have some shared genetic vulnerability (Mozani et al., 2014). In regard to neurobiological risk, OCD, BDD, and hoarding disorder seem to involve **fronto-striatal circuits**. Brain-imaging studies indicate that three regions of the fronto-striatal circuits are unusually active in people with OCD (see **Figure 7.1**): the **orbitofrontal cortex** (an area of the medial prefrontal cortex located just above the eyes), the **caudate nucleus** (part of the basal ganglia), and the anterior cingulate (Menzies, Chamberlain, et al., 2008). When people with OCD are shown objects that tend to provoke symptoms (such as a soiled glove for a person who fears contamination), activity in these three areas increases (McGuire, Bench, et al., 1994). The functional connectivity, or synchronization of activity between these regions, when viewing objects that tend to provoke symptoms also appears to differentiate those with OCD from controls (Bandelow, Baldwin, et al., 2016). Successful treatment, whether through cognitive behavioral therapy or antidepressant medication,

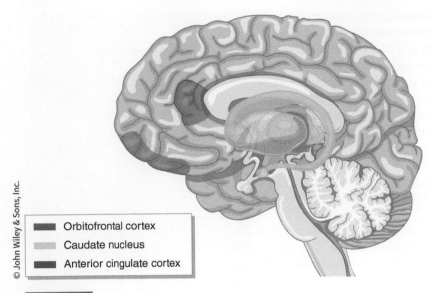

© John Wiley & Sons, Inc.

- ■ Orbitofrontal cortex
- ■ Caudate nucleus
- ■ Anterior cingulate cortex

FIGURE 7.1 Key brain regions in the obsessive-compulsive and related disorders: the orbitofrontal cortex, caudate nucleus, and anterior cingulate.

reduces activation of the orbitofrontal cortex and caudate nucleus (Ahmari & Dougherty, 2015).

These same fronto-striatal regions also are implicated in BDD and hoarding. When people with BDD observe pictures of their own face, hyperactivity of the orbitofrontal cortex and the caudate nucleus is observed (Feusner, Phillips, & Stein, 2010). When people with hoarding disorder are faced with decisions about whether to keep or discard their possessions such as old mail, hyperactivity in the orbitofrontal cortex (Tolin, Kiehl, et al., 2009) and the anterior cingulate is observed compared with a control group (Tolin, Stevens, et al., 2012).

While these genetic and neurobiological risk factors may set the stage for developing one of these disorders, why might one person develop OCD and another develop BDD? Cognitive behavioral models focus on factors that might promote one disorder as compared with the other.

Etiology of Obsessive-Compulsive Disorder

Cognitive behavioral models explain how a person might get stuck repeating obsessions and compulsions again and again. A narrower cognitive model focuses on why obsessions might persist.

Cognitive Behavioral Model of Obsessions and Compulsions In moderation, many of the thoughts and behaviors that disrupt the days of those with OCD, such as checking, cleaning, or reconsidering a thought, have adaptive value. Cleaning, for example, can help reduce the risk of contamination and germs. Even strange, intrusive thoughts are common. Most people report that they have had thoughts that made no sense, such as impulses to jump in front of a car or to engage in violence (Rachman & DeSilva, 1978). The question, then, is why these thoughts and behaviors become so persistent, often in inappropriate contexts, as to cause real distress or impairment.

The goal of cognitive behavioral theory is to understand why a person with OCD continues to show the behaviors or thoughts used to ward off an initial threat well after that threat is gone. To gather data on how people with OCD respond once a threat is gone, researchers conducted a two-phase experiment. In the first phase, they created a threat by placing electrodes on participants' wrists and then teaching participants that they would receive a shock (an unconditioned stimulus) when a certain shape (the conditioned stimulus) appeared on the computer screen. To avoid the shock, participants had to press a foot pedal (the conditioned response). In this first phase, participants with and without OCD learned equally well to press the foot pedal to avoid shock. In the key second phase of the study, researchers unhooked the wrist electrodes so the participants could see that the threat of shock was gone. Even though they knew the threat was removed and even showed little psychophysiological response to the stimulus, many people with OCD either pressed the foot pedal or felt a strong urge to press the foot pedal when the conditioned stimulus (the shape) appeared on the screen. In contrast, people without OCD quit pressing the foot pedal, and most didn't have an urge to press the foot pedal. The authors argue that for those with OCD, previously functional responses for reducing threat become habitual and therefore difficult to override after the threat was gone (Gillan, Morein-Zamir, et al., 2014). Consistent with this idea, other researchers have found that once someone with OCD develops a conditioned response to a stimulus, they are slower to change their response to that stimulus after it is no longer rewarded (Voon, Derbyshire, et al., 2015).

Thought Suppression: A Cognitive Model of Obsessions A different model focuses on obsessions. This model suggests that people with OCD may try harder to suppress their obsessions than other people do and, in the process, may make the situation worse (Salkovskis, 1996). Several types of evidence support this model.

Several researchers have shown that people with OCD tend to believe that (1) thinking about something is as morally wrong as engaging in the action, or (2) thinking about an event can make it more likely to occur. These types of beliefs have been labeled as **thought-action fusion**. People with OCD also tend to feel especially responsible for preventing harm. You can imagine how these types of thoughts lead to alarm when a negative thought or image intrudes (Clark & González, 2014). Because those with OCD tend to have these dysfunctional beliefs about their obsessions, the initial intrusive thought is distressing.

To rid themselves of these uncomfortable thoughts, people with OCD are more likely to attempt **thought suppression** (Amir, Cashman, & Foa, 1997). Unfortunately, it is hard to suppress thoughts. Consider the findings of one study in which researchers asked people to suppress a thought (Wegner, Schneider, et al., 1987). College students in an experimental group were asked not to think about a white bear, and a control group was asked to think about a white bear. Both groups were told to ring a bell every time they thought about a white bear. Attempts to avoid thinking about the white bear did not work—students in the experimental group thought about the bear more than once a minute when trying not to do so (more than the control group did). Beyond that, there was a rebound effect—after students tried to suppress thoughts about the bear for 5 minutes, they thought about the bear much more often during the next 5 minutes than the control group did. Trying to suppress a thought had the paradoxical effect of inducing preoccupation with it. Indeed, in one experimental study, suppressing thoughts even briefly led to more intrusions of that thought over the next four days (Trinder & Salkovaskis, 1994). Obviously, thought suppression is not a very good way to control obsessions.

According to this theory, the problem with OCD is not the initial intrusive thought but the response to that thought. To study this, one group of researchers assessed a group of people highly prone to intrusive disturbing thoughts—parents with 1-month-old babies. As expected, almost all parents reported thoughts of terrible events that could befall their baby (e.g., "What if I drop the baby?"). To test the idea that OCD might relate to thought-action fusion, researchers asked parents whether they believed that having thoughts or images could make an event more likely to occur. Those who endorsed such beliefs showed greater increases in OCD symptoms by the time their baby was 3 to 4 months old (Abramowitz, Nelson, et al., 2007). These findings illustrate that the presence of a disturbing, intrusive thought does not matter nearly as much as how people respond to that thought—consistent with thought-action fusion theory.

Etiology of Body Dysmorphic Disorder

Why would Paul (see the Clinical Case) look in the mirror, see a nose that others see as perfectly reasonable, and respond with horror? Cognitive models of BDD focus on what happens when a person with this syndrome looks at his or her body. People with BDD can accurately see and process their physical features without distortion. However, people with BDD are usually detail oriented, and this characteristic influences how they look at facial features (Feusner et al., 2010). Instead of considering the whole, they examine one feature at a time, which makes it more likely that they will become engrossed in considering a small flaw (Lambrou, Veale, & Wilson, 2011). They also consider attractiveness vastly more important than do control participants (Lambrou et al., 2011). Indeed, many people with BDD believe that their self-worth is exclusively dependent on their appearance (Veale, 2004).

Etiology of Hoarding Disorder

In considering hoarding, many take an evolutionary perspective (Zohar & Felz, 2001). Imagine you were a caveman with no access to grocery stores to replenish food reserves and no clothing stores to find warm clothes when the weather got cold. In those situations, it would be adaptive to store any resources you could find. The question, though, is how these basic instincts become so uncontrollable for some people. The cognitive behavioral model suggests several factors might be involved. According to this model, people with hoarding disorder have poor organizational abilities, unusual beliefs about possessions, and avoidance behaviors (Timpano, Muroff, & Steketee, 2016). Let's review each of these factors, considering how they might lead to excessive acquisition as well as difficulties getting rid of objects.

People with hoarding disorder have several different types of problems with cognitive organizational abilities. Problems with attention interfere with staying focused on the task at hand (Tolin & Villavicencio, 2011), and once they do focus on dealing with their possessions, they have difficulty categorizing their objects and making decisions (Samuels, 2009). When asked to sort objects into categories in laboratory studies, many people with hoarding disorder are slow, generate more categories than others do, and find the process highly anxiety-provoking (Wincze, Steketee, & Frost, 2007). These difficulties in paying attention, organizing objects, and making decisions influence almost every aspect of acquiring objects, organizing the home, and removing excessive acquisitions. Faced with decisions about which object is the better one to acquire, many will go ahead and get two, three, or more of the same type of object. Many patients find it excruciatingly hard to sort through their objects and figure out what to discard, even with a supportive therapist present (Frost & Steketee, 2010). They can spend hours per day churning through their possessions without being able to discard a single object.

Beyond these organizational difficulties, the cognitive model focuses on the unusual beliefs that people with hoarding disorder hold about their possessions. To begin with, they have the ability to see the potential in each of their objects. As examples, a stray cap to a pen could make a good game piece, and junk mail might have some important information to offer (Frost & Steketee, 2010). Almost by definition, people with hoarding disorder demonstrate an extreme emotional attachment to their possessions. They report feeling comforted by their objects, feeling frightened by the idea of losing an object, and seeing the objects as core to their sense of self and identity. They hold a deep sense of responsibility for taking care of those objects (Timpano et al., 2016). Many feel grief when forced to part with an object (Frost, Steketee, & Tolin, 2012). These attachments may be even stronger when animals are involved. People who hoard animals often describe their animals as their closest confidants (Patronek & Nathanson, 2009). These beliefs about the importance of each and every object interfere with any attempt to tackle the clutter.

In the face of the anxiety of all these decisions, avoidance is common. Many with this disorder find organizing their clutter so overwhelming that they delay tackling the chaos. This avoidance maintains the clutter.

Quick Summary

OCD, BDD, and hoarding disorder are moderately heritable. There is some overlap in the heritability of OCD, BDD, and hoarding disorder.

Obsessive-compulsive and related disorders appear related to dysfunction of fronto-striatal circuits. OCD is characterized by high activity in the orbitofrontal cortex, the caudate nucleus, and the anterior cingulate in response to symptom-provoking stimuli, and atypical connectivity of these neural regions. People with BDD show heightened activity of the orbitofrontal cortex and the caudate nucleus when viewing pictures of their own face. Hoarding disorder relates to heightened activity in the orbitofrontal cortex and the anterior cingulate when making decisions about possessions.

Cognitive behavioral models help explain why one might develop a specific disorder in the cluster of obsessive-compulsive and related disorders. A behavioral model of OCD suggests that people sustain conditioned responses as habits long after the contingencies that conditioned the initial behavior have shifted. Thought suppression may exacerbate tendencies toward obsessions.

The cognitive model of BDD focuses on a detail-oriented analytic style and tendencies to overvalue the meaning of appearance for self-worth.

Cognitive behavioral models of hoarding disorder focus on poor organizational abilities (difficulties with attention, categorization, and decision making), unusual beliefs about possessions, and avoidance behaviors.

Check Your Knowledge 7.2

Answer the questions.

1. How heritable are the obsessive compulsive and related disorders?
2. List four reasons to consider OCD, BDD, and hoarding as related conditions.

Treatment of the Obsessive-Compulsive and Related Disorders

Treatments that work for OCD, BDD and hoarding disorder are similar. Each of these disorders responds to antidepressant medications. The major psychological approach for each of these disorders is exposure and response prevention, although this treatment is tailored for the specific conditions. Even though good treatments are available, many people do not receive state-of-the-art care. As is all too common with many disorders, individuals from ethnic minority groups are less likely to receive treatment for OCD (de la Cruz, Llorens, et al., 2015)

Medications

Antidepressants are the most commonly used medications for obsessive-compulsive and related disorders. Although they were developed to treat depression, randomized controlled trials support their effectiveness in the treatment of OCD (Pittenger & Bloch, 2014) and BDD (Grant, Odlaug, & Schreiber, 2014). Clomipramine (Anafranil), a serotonin-norepinephrine reuptake inhibitor (SNRI) and selective serotonin reuptake inhibitors (SSRIs) are helpful. Because they have fewer side effects, SSRIs are recommended as a first-line treatment approach (Abramovitch, Elliott, et al., 2014).

Some caution is warranted. SSRIs may require more time (up to 12 weeks) and higher doses to treat OCD as compared with depression (Abramovitch et al., 2014). Most people with OCD continue to experience at least mild symptoms after antidepressant treatment.

Even more caution is warranted about medication treatment of hoarding disorder. Results of two small nonrandomized trials suggest that the symptoms of hoarding disorder decrease with antidepressant treatment (Saxena, 2015), but no randomized controlled trials of medications are available for hoarding disorder. Much of the research focuses on hoarding symptoms among OCD patients. Among patients with OCD, hoarding symptoms predict a poorer response to treatment; in a meta-analysis of 14 studies, patients with hoarding symptoms and OCD were about half as likely to respond to medication treatment as were those with OCD alone (Bloch, Bartley, et al., 2014).

Psychological Treatment

The most widely used psychological treatment for obsessive-compulsive and related disorders is **exposure and response prevention (ERP)**. Victor Meyer (1966) developed this approach for OCD by tailoring the exposure treatment discussed in Chapter 6 to address the compulsive rituals that people with OCD use to ward off threats. We'll describe this cognitive behavioral treatment (CBT) for OCD, and then how it has been adapted for BDD and hoarding disorder.

Obsessive-Compulsive Disorder   Many OCD sufferers hold an almost magical belief that their compulsive behavior will prevent awful things from happening. In the exposure component of ERP, clients expose themselves to situations that elicit obsessions and related anxiety. At the same time, for the response-prevention component of ERP, clients refrain from performing any compulsive ritual during the exposure. For instance, a client is asked to touch

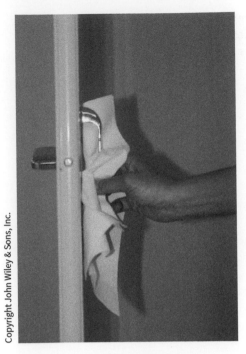

Exposure treatment for OCD involves confronting one's worst fears, such as contamination by dirty objects.

a dirty dish and then refrain from washing his or her hands. Not only does a client need to refrain from overt compulsive behaviors like hand washing, he or she must also refrain from compulsive thoughts, such as covertly counting to 10. The reasoning behind this approach goes like this:

1. Not performing the ritual exposes the person to the full force of the anxiety provoked by the stimulus.

2. The exposure promotes the extinction of the conditioned response (the anxiety).

The exposure component of ERP uses the exposure hierarchy approach that we discussed in Chapter 6, in which a client begins with tackling less threatening stimuli and progresses to completing exposure sessions focused on more threatening stimuli. As an example, a client with a focus on contamination might start by being in a dirty room and progress to placing their hands on a sticky, grimy floor. Throughout the exposure sessions, the therapist guides the client to avoid engaging in compulsions. Often, the therapist guides exposure to feared stimuli in the home, with help from family members (Franklin & Foa, 2014). Typically, ERP involves refraining from performing rituals during therapy sessions lasting up to 90 minutes as well as during home practice between sessions. Acute treatment typically requires up to 20 sessions. Researchers have varied in whether they offered sessions daily, twice a week, or weekly (Ponniah, Magiati, & Hollon, 2013). Clients are often offered booster sessions in the first 6 months after acute treatment (Abramovitch et al., 2014).

Randomized clinical trials indicate that ERP is more powerful than control conditions such as anxiety management and relaxation treatment, and as powerful as antidepressants in the treatment of OCD (Abramovitch et al., 2014; Romanelli, Wu, et al., 2014). It is effective for children and adolescents as well as adults (Franklin & Foa, 2011). About 69–75 percent of people who receive this treatment show significant improvement (Abramowitz & Jacoby, 2015), although mild symptoms often persist. Researchers have shown excellent outcomes for ERP offered by community therapists who do not specialize in OCD (Franklin & Foa, 2011). Although some people make gains using self-help resources, working with a therapist produces better outcomes (Abramovitch et al., 2014).

Despite the strong evidence to support ERP, it is a demanding therapy for the clients—refraining from performing a ritual is extremely unpleasant for people with OCD. (To get some idea of how unpleasant, try delaying for a minute or two before scratching an itch.) About a third of people diagnosed with OCD are not willing to begin ERP, and among those who do enroll, about a third drop out (Abramovitch et al., 2014). The challenging nature of this treatment may help explain why so few therapists offer it. In a survey of licensed psychologists, therapists were more likely to offer relaxation training (which appears to be fairly ineffective) than ERP to their OCD clients (Foa & McLean, 2016).

Cognitive approaches to OCD focus on challenging people's beliefs about what will happen if they do not engage in rituals (Clark, 2006). For example, a therapist may help the client reconsider thought-action fusion and inflated perceptions of responsibility. Eventually, to help test such beliefs, these approaches will use exposure at least briefly. Several studies suggest that cognitive approaches perform as well as ERP (Abramovitch et al., 2014).

Body Dysmorphic Disorder The basic principles of ERP are tailored in several ways to address the symptoms of BDD. For example, to provide exposure to the most feared activities, therapists might ask clients to interact with people who could be critical of their looks. For response prevention, therapists might ask clients to avoid activities they use to reassure themselves about their appearance, such as looking in mirrors. As illustrated in the Clinical Case of Paul, these behavioral techniques are supplemented with strategies to address the cognitive features of the disorder, such as excessively critical evaluations of physical features and the belief that self-worth depends on appearance.

Multiple trials have shown that ERP produces a major decrease in BDD symptoms compared with control conditions and that effects are maintained in the months after treatment ends (Harrison, Fernández de la Cruz, et al., 2016). Early evidence indicates that an Internet-based version of ERP can be helpful for BDD, with about half of those treated showing a symptom reduction that was sustained at 6-month follow-up (Enander, Andersson, et al., 2016). Caution is warranted, though, because many people continue to experience at least mild symptoms after treatment (Harrison et al., 2016), whether it is offered in person or online.

Returning to Clinical Case

CBT Treatment for Paul

Paul and his therapist agreed to work together using CBT. To begin, they reviewed childhood and current influences on Paul's symptoms. Paul described his parents' extremely high standards for appearance, along with his father's obsessive and perfectionistic style. Throughout his life, Paul had felt he could not live up to their standards.

He and the therapist then identified several cognitions (thoughts) that triggered anxiety, such as "Any flaw means I'm ugly" or "I know my client is thinking about how ugly my nose is." The therapist asked Paul to record his most negative thoughts each day, and taught him ways to evaluate whether these thoughts might be overly harsh. He began to consider alternative ways of thinking.

As Paul's thinking became more positive, the therapist began to target his avoidant behaviors. Paul tended to avoid social events, bright lights, and even eye contact with others, and he understood that these behaviors were interfering with his life. Treatment consisted of exposure, in which the therapist gradually coached Paul to make eye contact, to engage in social activities, and even to talk with others under bright light.

While Paul reduced his avoidant behaviors, the therapist introduced response prevention. Paul had been conducting a series of rituals to try to reduce his anxiety, including engaging in facial exercises, studying others' noses, and surfing plastic surgery websites. The therapist helped him understand that the rituals did not actually relieve his anxiety. Rituals were tackled using response prevention: Paul was asked to stop conducting the rituals and to monitor his mood and anxiety as he did so.

After five sessions of treatment, Paul's therapist introduced perceptual retraining. When people with BDD look in the mirror, they focus on small details of their worst feature, and they are overly evaluative. As daily homework, the therapist asked Paul to spend time looking in the mirror but focusing on the whole of his appearance. She also asked him to describe his nose using non-evaluative, objective language. The intense anxiety he initially experienced when completing this exercise diminished within a week. Soon, he was able to appreciate some of his features that he had previously ignored—for example, he noticed that he had nice eyes.

People with BDD often focus excessive attention on their own appearance. The therapist guided Paul to refocus his attention on people and events outside himself. For example, when Paul dined with a friend, she coached him to attend to the sound of his friend's voice, the flavor of the food, and the content of their conversation.

As Paul made gains, the therapist began to work on the more difficult and core aspects of cognitions—his deeply held beliefs about the meaning of his appearance. Paul described feeling that his physical flaws made him unlovable. The therapist helped him begin to consider his many positive qualities.

The tenth and final session consisted of reviewing the skills he had learned and discussing the strategies he would use if symptoms returned. Over the course of treatment, Paul's symptoms remitted so greatly that by the last session, he was no longer distressed about his nose.

Drawn with permission from Wilhelm et al., 2010.

Hoarding Disorder To address hoarding disorder symptoms, the exposure element of ERP focuses on the most feared situation for people with hoarding disorder—getting rid of their objects (Steketee & Frost, 2003). The response-prevention element of ERP centers on halting the rituals that people with hoarding disorder engage in to reduce their anxiety, such as counting or sorting their possessions. As with other exposure treatments, the client and the therapist work through a hierarchy, tackling increasingly difficult challenges as therapy progresses.

Despite the common elements with treatment of OCD, treatment for hoarding is tailored in many ways. As illustrated in the Clinical Case of Dena, many people with hoarding disorder don't recognize the gravity of problems created by their symptoms. Therapy cannot begin to address the hoarding symptoms until the person develops insight. To facilitate insight, therapists use motivational strategies to help clients consider reasons to change. Once people decide to change, therapists help them make decisions about their objects and can provide tools and strategies to help them organize and remove their clutter. Therapists often supplement their office sessions with in-home visits, which can help them gain a better sense of the degree of hoarding but also allow for in vivo exercises on de-cluttering (Tolin, Frost, et al., 2015).

Despite the evidence that removing possessions too rapidly tends to fail, the TV show *Hoarders* featured many people who were faced with ridding themselves of objects under dire threat of eviction or other contingencies, and so were forced to discard their collections immediately.

Early cognitive behavioral interventions focused on helping clients discard their objects as quickly as possible, hoping to avoid the quagmire of indecision and anxiety that is triggered when evaluating possessions. Unfortunately, patients tended to drop out of treatment, and few of those who did remain showed a good response (Abramowitz, Franklin, et al., 2003; Mataix-Cols, Marks, et al., 2002).

Findings of randomized controlled trials provide support for individual and group versions of ERP (Timpano et al., 2016). Self-help groups supplemented with structured readings also appear helpful and have the advantage of affordability (Muroff, Levis, & Bratiotis, 2014). Despite the evidence that ERP is helpful, about two-thirds of patients continue to show at least some hoarding symptoms after treatment—hoarding is very difficult to treat (Tolin et al., 2015).

Hoarding symptoms can profoundly damage family relationships. Relatives usually try various approaches to help clear the clutter, only to become more and more distressed as those attempts fail (Drury, Ajmi, et al., 2014). Many resort to coercive strategies, including removing the hoarder's possessions while the person is away—strategies that typically create mistrust and animosity. Family approaches to hoarding begin by building rapport around these difficult issues (Tompkins & Hartl, 2013). Rather than aiming for a total absence of clutter, therapists urge family members to identify the aspects of hoarding and clutter that are most dangerous, for example, lack of access to an emergency exit. Their concerns about these key issues can help set priorities with the person with hoarding disorder. Support groups and online communities for family members of those with hoarding disorder (e.g., Children of Hoarders) have become increasingly common.

Deep Brain Stimulation: A Treatment in Development for OCD

About 10 percent of those with OCD will not respond to multiple pharmacological treatments. For those patients, randomized controlled trials support the efficacy of deep brain stimulation, a treatment that involves implanting electrodes into the brain. For the treatment of OCD, electrodes are typically implanted into one of several regions in the basal ganglia. About half of patients treated with deep brain stimulation attain significant relief with a couple months of treatment (Hamani, Pilitsis, et al., 2014). Because of the limited data and the chance of severe side effects from electrode implantation, this treatment is considered only for those with severe OCD that has failed to respond to standard treatments, and only after a board carefully reviews the case history (Abramovitch et al., 2014). Nonetheless, the gains from this approach provide support for neurobiological models of OCD.

Quick Summary

Antidepressants are the most supported medication treatment for obsessive-compulsive and related disorders.

The major psychological treatment approach for obsessive-compulsive and related disorders is exposure and response prevention (ERP). ERP for hoarding disorder often involves motivational strategies to enhance insight and willingness to consider change.

Deep brain stimulation is an experimental treatment for OCD.

Check Your Knowledge 7.3

Answer the questions.

1. What class of medication is most recommended for the treatment of obsessive-compulsive and related disorders?

2. Describe the foci of the response-prevention component of ERP in OCD, BDD, and hoarding disorder.

Clinical Description and Epidemiology of Posttraumatic Stress Disorder and Acute Stress Disorder

Clinical Case

Ashley

Ashley, a 20-year-old college student, sought help at the college counseling center. Three months earlier, she had been raped by a man whom she had met at a party. She sought help when the ongoing terror and associated symptoms led her to fail her classes for the semester. Since the rape, she had felt as though she were on constant alert, scanning the environment for the man who had assaulted her. When she would see someone who looked even remotely like her attacker, her heart would pound, her knees would shake, and she would feel overwhelmed by terror. She had avoided social events because the thought of interacting with men frightened her. Most nights, she had tossed and turned for at least an hour before falling asleep, and then intense nightmares related to the event would wake her. Her sleep loss often left her too exhausted to attend class, and even when she did attend class, she felt distracted and unable to concentrate. As she developed a newly cynical attitude toward people, she withdrew from most of her friends. She lost her motivation to be a part of campus life, and she stopped attending the club meetings that had been an important part of her social life before the trauma. Although she had tried hard to stop thinking about the event, she faced almost daily reminders, as sexual assaults were a constant issue in the school newspapers, activist rallies, and conversations in the cafeteria. Each time she was reminded of the event, she would feel overwhelmed.

Trauma-related disorders are diagnosed only when a person develops symptoms after a traumatic event, such as the symptoms Ashley developed after being raped. Trauma-related diagnoses rest on the idea that horrific life experiences can trigger serious psychological symptoms. These diagnoses contrast with all other major DSM diagnoses, which are defined entirely by symptom profiles. No other major DSM diagnosis places emphasis squarely on the cause.

We will begin with a focus on posttraumatic stress disorder. Then, we will more briefly discuss the DSM diagnosis for acute stress disorder.

Posttraumatic stress disorder (PTSD) entails an extreme response to a severe stressor, including recurrent memories of the trauma, avoidance of stimuli associated with the trauma, negative emotions and thoughts, and symptoms of increased arousal. Although people have known for decades that the stresses of combat can have powerful adverse effects on soldiers, the aftermath of the Vietnam War spurred the development of this diagnosis.

The diagnostic criteria define serious trauma as an event that involves actual or threatened death, serious injury, or sexual violation. Even though the estimates vary widely, far too many people have experienced these types of traumas. In large-scale studies, at least 55 percent of people report at least one serious trauma during their lifetime (Creamer, Burgess, &

McFarlane, 2001). Whereas military trauma is the most common type of trauma preceding PTSD for men, rape is the most common type of trauma preceding PTSD for women (Creamer, Burgess, & McFarlane, 2001). An estimated one in every six women in the United States will be raped during their lifetime (Tjaden & Thoennes, 2006). A discouraging 30 percent of female college students report that they have experienced the use of physical force, threats, or harm after they refused sexual contact with a person, with 8.7 percent reporting that they had experienced physical harm (Struckman-Johnson, 1988).

Exposure to trauma, however, is only the first part of considering this diagnosis. In addition to trauma, the diagnosis of PTSD requires that a set of symptoms be present. The DSM-5 diagnostic criteria for PTSD consider four symptom clusters:

- *Intrusively reexperiencing* the traumatic event. Like Ashley (see Clinical Case), many people with PTSD have dreams or nightmares about themes related to the trauma night after night. Others are haunted by painful and intrusive memories, often evoked by small sensory cues. Sensory reminders of the event can bring on a wave of psychophysiological arousal. For example, a veteran may tremble when he hears the sound of a helicopter that reminds him of the battlefield; for months after the event, a woman who was raped in one area of a campus may find her heart pounds whenever she nears that area.

- *Avoidance* of stimuli associated with the event. Most people with PTSD strive to avoid thinking about the event, and some try to avoid all reminders of the event. For example, a Turkish earthquake survivor stopped sleeping indoors after he was buried alive at night (McNally, 2003). Although most say they try to avoid remembering and reliving the event, avoidance usually fails; most people with PTSD remember the event all too often (Rubin, Berntsen, & Bohni, 2008).

- Other signs of *negative mood and thought* that developed after the trauma. Many people with PTSD feel detached from friends and activities and find that nothing in life brings joy. As they wrestle with questions of blame about the event, many come to believe that they are bad, and others develop the belief that all people are untrustworthy.

- Symptoms of *increased arousal and reactivity*. The person with PTSD often feels continuously on guard, monitoring the environment for danger. Laboratory studies confirm that people with PTSD demonstrate heightened arousal, as measured by physiological responses to trauma-relevant images (Orr, Metzger, et al., 2003). This heightened arousal can manifest in jumpiness when startled, outbursts over small events, and trouble falling asleep or sleeping through the night.

The symptoms of PTSD may develop soon after the trauma but sometimes the full syndrome does not develop for years after the initial event. Once PTSD develops, symptoms can be relatively chronic. In one representative community-based study of people diagnosed with PTSD, about half continued to experience diagnosable symptoms when interviewed several years later (Perkonigg, Pfister, et al., 2005). Even 40 years after the Vietnam War, some veterans who served in the war zone continued to meet diagnostic criteria for PTSD (Marmar, Schlenger, et al., 2015).

PTSD is tied to a broad range of difficulties. Many with PTSD describe feeling less satisfied in their relationships, and rates of marital dissatisfaction and divorce are high compared with the general population (Bovin, Wells, et al., 2014). Unemployment is common as well (Bovin et al., 2014). Suicidal thoughts are common among people with PTSD (Bovin, Haro, et al., 2007), as are incidents of nonsuicidal self-injury (Weierich & Nock, 2008). People with PTSD also show high rates of medical illness (Scott, Lim, et al., 2016). In a study of 15,288 army veterans followed for 30 years after their military service, PTSD predicted an elevated risk of early death from medical illness, accidents, and suicides (Boscarino, 2006).

AFP/Getty Images

Rescue workers, such as this firefighter, could be vulnerable to PTSD.

DSM-5 Criteria for Posttraumatic Stress Disorder

A. Exposure to actual or threatened death, serious injury, or sexual violence, in one or more of the following ways: experiencing the event personally, witnessing the event in person, learning that a violent or accidental death or threat of death occurred to a close other, or experiencing repeated or extreme exposure to aversive details of the event(s) other than through the media

B. At least one of the following **intrusion** symptoms:

- Recurrent, involuntary, and intrusive distressing memories of the trauma(s), or in children, repetitive play regarding the trauma themes

- Recurrent distressing dreams related to the event(s)

- Dissociative reactions (e.g., flashbacks) in which the individual feels or acts as if the trauma(s) were recurring, or in children, reenactment of trauma during play

- Intense or prolonged distress or physiological reactivity in response to reminders of the trauma(s)

C. At least one of the following **avoidance** symptoms:

- Avoids internal reminders of the trauma(s)

- Avoids external reminders of the trauma(s)

D. At least two of the following **negative alterations in cognitions and mood** began after the event:

- Inability to remember an important aspect of the trauma(s)

- Persistent and exaggerated negative beliefs or expectations about one's self, others, or the world

- Persistently excessive blame of self or others about the trauma(s)

- Persistently negative emotional state, or in children younger than 7, more frequent negative emotions

- Markedly diminished interest or participation in significant activities

- Feeling of detachment or estrangement from others, or in children younger than 7, social withdrawal

- Persistent inability to experience positive emotions

E. At least two of the following changes in **arousal and reactivity:**

- Irritable or aggressive behavior

- Reckless or self-destructive behavior

- Hypervigilance

- Exaggerated startle response

- Poor concentration

- Sleep disturbance

F. The symptoms began or worsened after the trauma(s) and continued for at least 1 month

G. Among children younger than 7, diagnosis requires criteria A, B, E, and F, but only one symptom from either category C or D

It has been argued that prolonged exposure to trauma, such as repeated childhood abuse, might lead to a broader range of symptoms than those covered by the DSM criteria for PTSD. Some have proposed that this syndrome be referred to as complex PTSD (Herman, 1992). Authors differ in the symptom profiles they link to prolonged trauma, but most write about negative emotions, relationship disturbances, and negative self-concept (Cloitre, Courtois, et al., 2011). What does the research suggest about the effects of prolonged trauma? Comprehensive review suggests that prolonged trauma can lead to more severe PTSD symptoms but does not result in a distinct subtype with unique symptomatology (Resick, Bovin, et al., 2012). Given this, the DSM-5 does not include a diagnosis or a specifier for complex PTSD.

Like PTSD, the **acute stress disorder (ASD)** diagnosis is considered when symptoms occur after a trauma. The symptoms of ASD are similar to those of PTSD, but the duration is shorter; this diagnosis is only applicable when the symptoms last for 3 days to 1 month.

The ASD diagnosis is not as well accepted as the PTSD diagnosis. There are two major concerns about the ASD diagnosis. First, the diagnosis could stigmatize very common short-term reactions to serious traumas (Harvey & Bryant, 2002). For example, in the month after a rape, more than 90 percent of women report significant symptoms (Rothbaum, Foa, et al., 1992), and in the month after an assault, more than half of people show clinically significant symptoms (Riggs, Rothbaum, & Foa, 1995). Second, the diagnosis of ASD is not very predictive of who will develop PTSD. Less than half of people who experience ASD develop PTSD within 2 years. Conversely, about half of people who go on to develop PTSD do not experience ASD in the first month after the trauma (Bryant, Creamer, et al., 2015). Some argue that it may be inappropriate to diagnose normative posttrauma symptoms, particularly if those symptoms are not very predictive.

Despite concerns about the ASD diagnosis, the ASD diagnosis may encourage providers to identify people who could use more support after a trauma. When we consider treatments, we will describe evidence that treating ASD may help prevent the development of PTSD. Because less is known about ASD, we will focus on PTSD as we discuss epidemiology and etiology.

PTSD is usually comorbid with other conditions. In one study of a representative community sample, researchers conducted diagnostic assessments repeatedly from age 3 until age 26. Among people who had developed PTSD by age 26, almost all (93 percent) had been diagnosed with another psychological disorder before age 21. Two-thirds of those with PTSD at age 26 had experienced another anxiety disorder by age 21. The other common comorbid disorders are major depression, substance abuse, conduct disorder, and personality disorders (Koenen, Moffitt, et al., 2007; Pietrzak, Goldstein, et al., 2011).

Among people exposed to a trauma, women are 1.5 to 2 times as likely to develop PTSD as are men (Creamer et al., 2001). This finding is consistent with the gender ratio observed for most anxiety disorders. Some argue that this is due to differential life circumstances that women face. For example, women are much more likely than men to be sexually assaulted during childhood and adulthood (Tolin & Foa, 2006). In studies that control for history of sexual abuse and assault, men and women have comparable rates of PTSD (Tolin & Foa, 2006).

Culture may shape the risk for PTSD in several ways. In the World Mental Health Survey study, which used comparable diagnostic interviews with more than 50,000 persons, the prevalence of PTSD varied dramatically across the 20 countries studied. The prevalence of PTSD in the previous year was more than double in the United States and Northern Ireland compared with other countries (Karam, Friedman, et al., 2014). Some cultural groups may be exposed to higher rates of trauma and, as a consequence, manifest higher rates of PTSD. In Northern Ireland, where civil conflict has been long-standing, events related to that strife are the primary form of trauma preceding PTSD (Atwoli, Stein, et al., 2015). Minority populations in the United States also experience high rates of trauma exposure, and this contributes to the elevated rates of PTSD observed in African American individuals (Roberts, Gilman, et al., 2011). Culture also may shape the types of symptoms observed in PTSD. *Ataque de nervios*, originally identified in Puerto Rico, involves physical symptoms and fears of going crazy in the aftermath of severe stress and thus is similar to PTSD.

Quick Summary

Posttraumatic stress disorder (PTSD) and acute stress disorder (ASD) are both severe reactions to trauma. The symptoms of PTSD and ASD are similar, but ASD can be diagnosed only if symptoms have lasted less than 1 month. Most people who develop PTSD have a history of other psychological disorders, and two-thirds have a history of anxiety disorders.

Check Your Knowledge 7.4

Answer the questions

1. What is the major difference in the diagnostic criteria for PTSD and ASD?
2. Describe the four clusters of symptoms considered in the diagnosis of PTSD.
3. What are the major concerns about the ASD diagnosis?

Etiology of Posttraumatic Stress Disorder

Would any of us break if exposed to severe enough life circumstances? Are some people so resilient that they could withstand whatever horrors life directs at them? Who is most likely to be haunted in the months and years after a terrible event? We will consider these questions as we review the etiology of PTSD.

Earlier, we mentioned that two-thirds of people who develop PTSD have a history of an anxiety disorder. Not surprisingly, then, many of the risk factors for PTSD overlap with the risk factors for anxiety disorders that we described in Chapter 6 (see Table 6.4). For example, PTSD appears related to genetic risk for anxiety disorders (Tambs, Czajkowsky, et al., 2009), childhood exposure to trauma (Cougle, Timpano, et al., 2010), greater amygdala activation and diminished activation of regions of the medial prefrontal cortex in response to cues of threat (Patel, Spreng, et al., 2012), and greater emotional reactivity to cues of threat (DiGangi, Gomez, et al., 2013).

Also parallel with anxiety disorders, Mowrer's two-factor model of conditioning has been applied to PTSD (Keane, Zimering, & Caddell, 1985). In this model, the initial fear in PTSD is assumed to arise from classical conditioning. For example, a man may come to fear walking in the neighborhood (the conditioned stimulus) where he was assaulted (the unconditioned stimulus). Like those with anxiety disorders, those with PTSD show elevated tendencies to develop and sustain conditioned fears (Hayes, VanElzakker, & Shin, 2012). This classically conditioned fear is so intense that the man avoids the neighborhood as much as possible. Operant conditioning contributes to the maintenance of this avoidance behavior; the avoidance is reinforced by the reduction of fear that comes from not being in the presence of the conditioned stimulus. This avoidant behavior interferes with chances for the fear to extinguish.

Keeping these parallels in mind, in this section we focus on factors that are uniquely associated with PTSD. We begin by describing evidence that certain kinds of traumas may be more likely to trigger PTSD than other types. Even among people who experience serious traumas, though, not everyone develops PTSD. Thus, a great deal of research has been conducted on neurobiological and coping variables related to PTSD.

Nature of the Trauma: Severity and the Type of Trauma Matter

The severity of the trauma influences whether or not a person will develop PTSD. Consider the case of people exposed to war. Findings of the World Mental Health Survey, described earlier, indicate that simply living in a country at war does not increase the risk of PTSD, perhaps because many in these countries do not witness the violence; in contrast, those who directly witness atrocities are at a fourfold higher risk than the general population of developing PTSD (Liu, Petukhova, et al., 2017). Among soldiers serving in Afghanistan or Iraq, the U.S. Veterans Administration estimates that rates of PTSD are doubled among those with a second tour of duty as compared with those with one tour of duty. About 20 percent of American fighters wounded in Vietnam developed PTSD, contrasted with 50 percent of those who were prisoners of war there (Engdahl, Dikel, et al., 1997). During Operation Desert Storm (in the 1990–1991 conflict following the Iraqi invasion of Kuwait), among those assigned to collect, tag, and bury scattered body parts of the dead, 65 percent developed PTSD (Sutker, Uddo, et al., 1994). As shown in Figure 7.2, the number of World War II soldiers admitted for psychiatric care was closely related to how many casualties occurred in their battalions (Jones & Wessely, 2001). During World War II, doctors estimated that 98 percent of men with 60 days of continuous combat would develop psychiatric problems (Grossman, 1995).

Beyond severity, the nature of the trauma matters. Traumas caused by humans are more likely to cause PTSD than are natural disasters (Charuvastra & Cloitre, 2008). For example, rapes, combat experience, abuse, and assault all are associated with higher risk than are natural disasters (McMillan & Asmundson, 2016). Perhaps these events are more distressing because they challenge ideas about humans as benevolent.

Neurobiology: The Hippocampus

Earlier, we noted that PTSD appears related to dysregulation of the amygdala and prefrontal cortex, as with anxiety disorders discussed

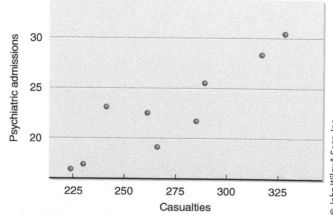

Drawn from Jones & Wessely (2001).

© John Wiley & Sons, Inc.

FIGURE 7.2 Percent of Canadian soldiers admitted for psychiatric care as a function of the number of casualties in their battalion during World War II.

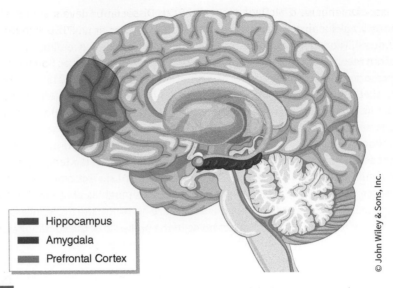

© John Wiley & Sons, Inc.

Legend:
- Hippocampus
- Amygdala
- Prefrontal Cortex

FIGURE 7.3 People with PTSD show heightened activation of the hippocampus when completing various tasks.

in Chapter 6. Beyond regions tied to anxiety disorders, PTSD appears uniquely related to function of the hippocampus, a brain region shown in **Figure 7.3** (Patel et al., 2012). People with PTSD show greater activation of the hippocampus during cognitive tasks than do those without PTSD. The hippocampus plays a central role in our ability to locate autobiographical memories in space, time, and context.

Biologically based difficulties in placing memories in context could set the stage for PTSD. People with PTSD can experience fear when they experience any reminder of their trauma, even out of context. For example, the soldier who witnessed bombs dropping from a plane may be frightened by all planes after he returns from the war. For those with PTSD, the cues that one is in a safe environment do not work; the fear remains as intense as it did in the moment of the trauma. Changes in the function of the hippocampus might increase the risk that a person will experience fear even in safe contexts (Maren, Phan, & Liberzon, 2013).

A growing body of research examines the functional connectivity of the hippocampus, amygdala, medial prefrontal cortex, and other key regions in PTSD (Stark, Parsons, et al., 2015). This work focuses on how these regions coordinate activity during various tasks.

AFP/Getty Images

Survivors of natural disasters, such as the Japanese earthquake in 2011, are at risk for PTSD, but their risk may not be as high as those who experience traumas caused by humans, such as assaults.

Coping

Several types of studies suggest that people who cope with a trauma by trying to avoid thinking about it are more likely than others to develop PTSD. Much of the work on avoidance coping focuses on symptoms of **dissociation** (such as feeling removed from one's body or emotions or being unable to remember the event). We discuss dissociation in more detail in Chapter 8. Dissociation may allow the person to avoid confronting memories of the trauma. People who have symptoms of dissociation during and immediately after the trauma are more likely to develop PTSD. For example, in one study, researchers interviewed women within 2 weeks of a rape about dissociation during the rape (e.g., "Did you feel numb?" and "Did you have moments of losing track of what was going on?"). Women with high levels of dissociation were much more likely to develop PTSD symptoms than were women with low levels of dissociation. Many studies now show that people who describe dissociation shortly after trauma are more likely to develop

PTSD (Carlson, Dalenberg, & McDade-Montez, 2012). Dissociation levels are usually at their highest in the weeks after the trauma and then dissipate over time. PTSD symptoms usually decline as dissociation improves (Carlson, Dalenberg, & McDade-Montez, 2012).

To encourage clinicians to consider these coping patterns, the DSM-5 includes a dissociative symptom specifier to denote when persistent or recurrent symptoms of dissociation are present for those with PTSD. About 15 percent of people meet the criteria for this specifier (Stein, Koenen, et al., 2013), and it is more common among people who have a history of childhood abuse (Wolf, Miller, et al., 2012).

Other protective factors may help a person cope with severe traumas more adaptively. Factors that are particularly important include cognitive ability (DiGangi et al., 2013) and strong social support (Brewin, Andrews, & Valentine, 2000). As an example, veterans returning from war who report a stronger sense of social support are less likely to develop PTSD (Vogt, Smith, et al., 2011). Having better intellectual ability to make sense of horrifying events, and more friends and family members to assist in that process, helps people avoid symptoms after traumatic events.

A surprisingly high proportion of people cope quite well with trauma. For some, trauma awakens an increased appreciation of life, renews a focus on life priorities, and provides an opportunity to understand one's strengths in overcoming adversity (Bonanno, 2004).

Quick Summary

Some of the general risk factors for anxiety disorders are involved in the development of PTSD. These general risk factors include genetic vulnerability, amygdala hyperactivity, diminished activity of the prefrontal cortex, childhood trauma exposure, and reactivity to threat. In addition, Mowrer's two-factor model of conditioning has been applied to PTSD.

Risk factors more specific to PTSD have been identified as well. The likelihood that a person will develop PTSD depends on the severity of the trauma. Neurobiological research has found that people with PTSD tend to show greater activation of the hippocampus when completing a broad range of tasks, and different patterns of connectivity of the hippocampus with other neural regions. After exposure to trauma, people who rely on dissociative coping strategies (i.e., who avoid thinking about the trauma) are more likely to develop PTSD than people who rely on other strategies. Other resources that might promote adaptive coping, such as higher cognitive ability and stronger social support, can protect against the development of PTSD.

Check Your Knowledge 7.5

Answer the questions.

1. List major risk factors that contribute specifically to PTSD (as opposed to increasing general risk for anxiety disorders).

2. Describe the types of dissociation that are most relevant to PTSD.

Treatment of Posttraumatic Stress Disorder and Acute Stress Disorder

A good deal of work has focused on treatment of PTSD using medication and psychological treatments. Less research is available on ASD.

Medication Treatment of PTSD

Randomized controlled trials indicate that two forms of antidepressants, SSRIs and SNRIs, both provide relief from PTSD symptoms as compared with placebos (Jonas, Cusack, et al.,

2013). Nonetheless, many patients relapse after medications are discontinued. Although many doctors prescribe benzodiazapines for PTSD, evidence from randomized controlled trials does not support this approach (Guina, Rossetter, et al., 2015).

Psychological Treatment of PTSD

Psychological treatments appear more powerful than medications are for the treatment of PTSD (Jonas et al., 2013). Parallel with the psychological treatment of anxiety disorders discussed in Chapter 6, exposure treatment is the primary psychological approach to treating PTSD. Randomized controlled trials suggest that exposure treatment provides more relief from the symptoms of PTSD than medication, supportive unstructured psychotherapy, or relaxation therapy (Powers, Halpern, et al., 2010; Taylor, Thordarson, et al., 2003). Exposure treatment has been found to be helpful across a broad range of cultural groups and treatment settings (Foa, Gillihan, & Bryant, 2013), and the benefits of exposure treatment have been found to persist over a 5-year period (Foa & McLean, 2016). Despite the success of this approach, we discuss a controversial version of exposure treatment in **Focus on Discovery 7.1**.

Focus on Discovery 7.1

Eye Movement Desensitization and Reprocessing

In 1989, Francine Shapiro began to promulgate an approach to trauma treatment called eye movement desensitization and reprocessing (EMDR). In this procedure, the client recalls a scene related to the trauma. Keeping the scene in mind, the client visually tracks the therapist's fingers as the therapist moves them back and forth about a foot in front of the person's eyes. This process continues for a minute or so, or until the client reports that the image is becoming less painful. At this point, the therapist tells the client to say whatever negative thoughts he or she is having, while continuing to track the therapist's fingers. Finally, the therapist tells the client to think a positive thought (e.g., "I can deal with this") and to hold this thought in mind, still tracking the therapist's fingers. This treatment, then, consists of classic imaginal exposure techniques, along with the extra technique of eye movement.

EMDR proponents argue that the eye movements promote rapid extinction of the conditioned fear and correction of mistaken beliefs about fear-provoking stimuli (Shapiro, 1999). The claims of dramatic efficacy have extended to disorders other than PTSD,

including attention-deficit/hyperactivity disorder, dissociative disorders, panic disorder, public-speaking fears, test anxiety, and specific phobias (Lohr, Tolin, & Lilienfeld, 1998). Because multiple randomized controlled trials indicate that EMDR is more helpful than control treatments for PTSD (Jonas et al., 2013), several national guidelines list EMDR as an efficacious approach to PTSD treatment.

Despite the claims about this approach, several studies have indicated that the eye movement component of treatment is not necessary. Findings from a series of studies indicate that this therapy is no more effective than traditional exposure treatment for PTSD (Seidler & Wagner, 2006). The theoretical explanations for the eye movement component are not supported either. Gerald Rosen made the following clever comparison. Imagine a practitioner begins to offer exposure treatment wearing a purple hat. We would hardly allow the "new" approach to merit labeling and marketing as "purple hat therapy" (Rosen & Davison, 2003). Given the lack of effective innovation in this approach, several authors have argued that therapists should not offer this approach (Goldstein, de Beurs, et al., 2000).

As with anxiety disorders, a therapist who is offering exposure therapy will ask the client to face his or her worst fears, most typically by working through an exposure hierarchy from less intense fears to the most intense fears. Typically, exposure treatment for PTSD involves 8 to 15 90-minute sessions, held once or twice per week (Foa & McLean, 2016). One goal of treatment is to extinguish the fear response, particularly the overgeneralized fear response; another goal is to help challenge the idea that the person could not cope with the anxiety and fear generated by those stimuli. As clients learn that they can deal with their anxiety, they are able to reduce their avoidance responses.

In PTSD, the focus of exposure treatment is on memories and reminders of the original trauma, with the person being encouraged to confront the trauma to gain mastery and extinguish the anxiety. Where possible, the person is exposed directly to reminders of the trauma in vivo—for example, by returning to the scene of the event. Often, it may not be feasible or safe to return to the scene of a horrible trauma, and therapists use **imaginal exposure**—that is, the person deliberately remembers the event. Therapists have also used virtual reality technology to treat PTSD. Exposure therapy is hard for both the patient and the therapist because it requires such intense focus on traumatizing events. For example, therapists might ask women who have developed PTSD after rape to recall the worst moments of the attack in vivid detail. More than a third of patients will drop out of treatments focused on discussion of their trauma (Imel, Laska, et al., 2013).

Treatment might be particularly hard and require more time when the client has experienced recurrent traumas during childhood, as repeated trauma exposure can interfere with learning to cope with emotions. In one randomized controlled trial, researchers examined whether teaching skills to regulate emotions would bolster the effects of exposure treatment for women who reported PTSD symptoms due to childhood abuse. The addition of emotion regulation skills led to several positive gains compared with standard exposure treatment, including diminished PTSD symptoms, improved emotion regulation, enhanced interpersonal functioning, and lower rates of posttreatment relapse (Cloitre, Stovall-McClough, et al., 2010).

Several cognitive strategies have been used to supplement exposure treatment for PTSD and have been shown to fare well in a series of randomized controlled trials. The goals of one form of cognitive therapy are to reduce overly negative interpretations about the trauma and its meaning and to help a person address their intrusive memories (Ehlers & Clark, 2008). One well-supported form of cognitive therapy is designed to bolster people's beliefs in their ability to cope with the initial trauma (Kulkarni, Barrad, & Cloitre, 2014). Cognitive processing therapy, designed to help victims of rape and childhood sexual abuse dispute tendencies toward self-blame, has also received empirical support (Tran, Moulton, et al., 2016) and appears particularly helpful in reducing guilt (Resick, Nishith, & Griffin, 2003) and dissociation (Resick, Suvak, et al., 2012).

Even with the clear evidence that exposure treatment (with or without cognitive intervention) is superior to other types of treatment, many psychologists do not provide exposure treatment for their clients with PTSD (Becker, Zayfert, & Anderson, 2004). To address this lack of dissemination, over 1,500 therapists at the Veterans Affairs Medical Center (VAMC) were taught how to administer either standard exposure treatment or cognitive processing therapy for PTSD (Karlin & Cross, 2014). Clients offered these treatments achieved more than double the level of symptom reduction observed among clients before the training occurred (Karlin, Ruzek, et al., 2010). Sadly, in the years after the training, less than 10 percent of veterans with PTSD have been receiving a full dose of these interventions; therapists in the VAMC system report not having the time available to provide this type of care (Chard, Ricksecker, et al., 2012; Shiner, D'Avolio, et al., 2013).

With the lack of dissemination of effective psychological treatments, a natural question is whether the Internet could make treatments more accessible for people. Although Internet-based CBT provides some acute relief, Internet-based therapies do not appear to provide the long-term relief from PTSD symptoms gained from receiving treatment with a therapist (Kuester, Niemeyer, & Knaevelsrud, 2016). Nonetheless, websites and support groups provide helpful social support and information for those recovering from traumatic experiences (**http://maketheconnection.net**).

Psychological Treatment of Acute Stress Disorder

Is it possible to prevent the development of PTSD by offering treatment to people who have developed ASD? Short-term (four- to six-session) exposure treatment appears to do so. Across five studies, risk of PTSD among those who received exposure therapy was reduced to 32 percent, as compared with 58 percent for those who were assigned to a control condition (Kornør, Winje, et al., 2008).

The positive effects of early exposure treatment appear to last for years. Researchers examined the long-term effect of treatment among adolescents who survived a devastating earthquake. Even 5 years after the earthquake, adolescents who had received cognitive behavioral intervention reported less severe PTSD symptoms than did those who had not received treatment (Goenjian, Walling, et al., 2005).

Exposure treatment appears more effective than cognitive restructuring in preventing the development of PTSD (Bryant, Mastrodomenico, et al., 2008). Unfortunately, not all approaches to prevention work as well as exposure treatment (see **Focus on Discovery 7.2**).

Focus on Discovery 7.2

Critical Incident Stress Debriefing

Critical incident stress debriefing (CISD) involves immediate treatment of trauma victims within 72 hours of the traumatic event (Mitchell & Everly, 2000). Unlike CBT, CISD is usually limited to one long group session and is given regardless of whether the person has developed symptoms. Therapists encourage people to remember the details of the trauma and to express their feelings as fully as they can. Therapists who practice this approach often visit disaster sites immediately after events, sometimes invited by local authorities and sometimes not; they offer therapy both to victims and to their families.

Like EMDR, CISD is highly controversial. A review of six studies, all of which included randomly assigning clients to receive CISD or no treatment, found that those who received CISD tended to fare worse (Litz, Gray, et al., 2002). No one is certain why harmful effects occur, but remember that many people who experience a trauma do not develop PTSD. Many experts are dubious about the idea of providing therapy for people who have not developed a disorder. Some researchers raise the objection to CISD that a person's natural coping strategies may work better than those recommended by someone else (Bonanno, Wortman, et al., 2002).

Check Your Knowledge 7.6

Answer the questions.

1. In conducting exposure treatment for PTSD, _____exposure is sometimes used because _____ exposure cannot be conducted for experiences as horrific as war and rape.

2. Cognitive therapy when added to exposure for PTSD is particularly helpful in addressing (choose the answer that best fits):

   a. suicidal tendencies

   b. risk of relapse

   c. insomnia

   d. guilt

3. Describe the findings for Internet-based psychotherapy for PTSD.

Summary

Obsessive-Compulsive and Related Disorders

- People with obsessive-compulsive disorder (OCD) have intrusive, unwanted thoughts and feel compelled to engage in rituals to avoid overwhelming anxiety. People with body dysmorphic disorder (BDD) experience persistent highly self-critical thoughts that they have a flawed appearance, and they engage in intensive efforts to cope with their appearance. Hoarding disorder is characterized by tendencies to acquire an excessive number of objects and extreme difficulties in ridding oneself of those objects.

- OCD, BDD, and hoarding disorder are each moderately heritable. There is some shared genetic risk across these three disorders.

- OCD has been linked to activity in the orbitofrontal cortex, the caudate nucleus, and the anterior cingulate during tasks that provoke symptoms. People with BDD also show hyperactivity in regions of the orbitofrontal cortex and the caudate nucleus when viewing photos of themselves. Hoarding disorder involves hyperactivity in the orbitofrontal cortex and the anterior cingulate during symptom-provocation tasks.

- Tendencies toward repetitive thought and behavior in OCD may be related to a tendency for conditioned responses to become habitual, such that they are sustained even after the threat is removed. Obsessions may be intensified by attempts to suppress unwanted thoughts, in part because people with OCD tend to believe that thinking about something is as bad as doing it, a tendency referred to as thought-action fusion.

- The cognitive model relates BDD to a detail-oriented analytic style and an overvaluing of the importance of appearance to self-worth.

- Cognitive behavioral risk factors for hoarding include poor organizational abilities, unusual beliefs about the importance of possessions and responsibility for those possessions, and avoidance behaviors.

- ERP is a well-validated approach for the treatment of OCD that involves exposure, along with strategies to prevent engaging in compulsive behaviors. ERP has been adapted for the treatment of BDD and hoarding. For the treatment of BDD, ERP is supplemented with cognitive strategies to challenge people's overly negative views of their appearance, their excessive focus on their appearance, and their beliefs that self-worth depends on their appearance. For hoarding disorder, therapists supplement ERP with strategies to increase insight and motivation.

- Antidepressants are the most commonly used medications for OCD, BDD, and hoarding disorder. Although these medications have received strong support for OCD and BDD, no randomized controlled trial has assessed medication treatment for hoarding disorder.

Trauma-Related Disorders

- Posttraumatic stress disorder (PTSD) is diagnosed only after a traumatic event. It is marked by symptoms of reexperiencing the trauma, avoidance of reminders of the trauma, negative alterations in cognitions and mood, and arousal. Acute stress disorder (ASD) is defined by similar symptoms with a duration of less than 1 month. PTSD is highly comorbid with other psychological disorders; about two-thirds of people who develop PTSD have a history of other anxiety disorders.

- Many of the risk factors involved in anxiety disorders are related to the development of PTSD, such as genetic vulnerability, hyperactivity of the amygdala and diminished function of the prefrontal cortex, childhood trauma exposure, neuroticism, reactivity to negative stimuli, and behavioral conditioning. Research and theory on the causes that are specific to PTSD focus on the severity and nature of the traumatic event, and on risk factors such as hippocampal activity, dissociation, and other factors that may enhance the ability to cope with stress, such as social support and intelligence.

- Antidepressants (SSRIs and SNRIs) are the most supported medication approach for PTSD.

- Psychological treatment of PTSD involves exposure, but often imaginal exposure is used. Exposure treatment for ASD can reduce the risk that PTSD will develop.

Answers to Check Your Knowledge Questions

7.1. 1. chronic; 2. Obsessions involve a repetitive and intrusive thought, urge, or image; compulsions involve either a thought or a behavior that the person feels the need to engage in to ward off threats or the anxiety associated with obsessions.

7.2. 1. 40–50 percent 2. (a) all share symptoms of uncontrollable repetitive thoughts and behavior; (b) the syndromes often co-occur; (c) the genetic vulnerability for these conditions overlaps; (d) fronto-striatal circuits are involved in all three syndromes.

7.3. 1. Antidepressants (and more specifically serotonin reuptake inhibitors [SSRIs]); 2. In OCD, the focus of response prevention is on compulsions; in BDD, the focus is on behaviors designed to seek reassurance or relieve anxiety about the appearance such as checking one's appearance in the mirror; in hoarding disorder, rituals like counting and sorting possessions are the focus.

7.4 1. The ASD diagnosis can be considered when symptoms have lasted less than 1 month, whereas the PTSD can be considered when symptoms have lasted at least 1 month; 2. Intrusion symptoms, avoidance symptoms, negative alterations in cognition and mood, and changes in arousal and reactivity. 3. Brief symptoms may be normative after severe trauma; ASD is not highly predictive of PTSD.

7.5. 1. any two of the following: greater activation of the hippocampus when completing a wide range of tasks; avoidant coping strategies that prevent processing the trauma, such as dissociation; low cognitive function; poor social support; 2. People with PTSD often report feeling removed from one's body or emotions or being unable to remember the traumatic event, either at the time of the trauma or after the trauma.

7.6 1. imaginal, in vivo; 2. d; 3. Internet CBT appears helpful initially, but gains are maintained for longer when psychotherapy is offered by a therapist.

Key Terms

acute stress disorder (ASD)
body dysmorphic disorder (BDD)
caudate nucleus
compulsion
dissociation

exposure and response prevention (ERP)
fronto-striatal circuits
hoarding disorder
imaginal exposure
obsession

obsessive-compulsive disorder (OCD)
orbitofrontal cortex
posttraumatic stress disorder (PTSD)
thought-action fusion
thought suppression

CHAPTER 8

Dissociative Disorders and Somatic Symptom-Related Disorders

LEARNING GOALS

1. Summarize the symptoms and epidemiology of the three major dissociative disorders.

2. Discuss current debate regarding the etiology of dissociative identity disorder.

3. Describe the available treatments for dissociative identity disorder.

4. Define the symptoms of the somatic symptom-related disorders.

5. Explain the etiological models of the somatic symptom-related disorders.

6. Describe the available treatments for somatic symptom-related disorders.

Clinical Case

Gina

In December 1965, a woman named Gina Rinaldi sought therapy with Dr. Robert Jeans. Gina, single and 31 years old, lived with another single woman and was working successfully as a writer at a large educational publishing firm. Her friends saw her as efficient, businesslike, and productive, but had observed that she was becoming forgetful and sometimes acted out of character. Gina reported that she had been sleepwalking since her early teens; her present roommate had told her that she sometimes screamed in her sleep.

The youngest of nine siblings, Gina described her 74-year-old mother as the most domineering woman she had ever known. She reported that as a child she had been a fearful and obedient daughter. At age 28 she had her first romantic relationship, with a former Jesuit priest, although it was not physical in nature. Then she became involved with T.C., a married man who assured her he would get a divorce and marry her. She indicated that she had been faithful to him since the start of their relationship. She became discouraged about their relationship when he did not come through with his promised divorce and stopped seeing Gina regularly.

After several sessions with Gina, Dr. Jeans noticed a second personality emerging. Mary Sunshine, as Gina and Dr. Jeans came to call her, was quite different from Gina. She seemed more childlike, more traditionally feminine, ebullient, and seductive. Gina felt that she walked like a coal miner, but Mary certainly did not. Some concrete incidents indicated Mary's existence. Sometimes while cleaning her home, Gina found cups that had had hot chocolate in them—neither Gina nor her roommate liked hot chocolate. There were large withdrawals from Gina's bank account that she could not remember making. She even discovered herself ordering a sewing machine on the telephone although she disliked sewing; some weeks later, she arrived at her therapy session wearing a new dress that Mary had sewn. At work, people were finding Gina more pleasant, and her colleagues took to consulting her on how to encourage people to work better with one another. All these phenomena were entirely alien to Gina. Jeans and Gina came to realize that sometimes Gina transformed into Mary.

More and more often, Jeans witnessed Gina turning into Mary in the consulting room. T.C. accompanied Gina to a session during which her posture and demeanor became more relaxed, her tone of voice warmer. Then Mary and Gina started having conversations with each other in front of Jeans.

A year after the start of therapy, a synthesis of Gina and Mary began to emerge. At first it seemed that Gina had taken over entirely, but then Dr. Jeans noticed that Gina was not as serious as before, particularly about "getting the job done," that is, working extremely hard on the therapy. Dr. Jeans encouraged Gina to talk with Mary. The following is that conversation:

I was lying in bed trying to go to sleep. Someone started to cry about T.C. I was sure that it was Mary. I started to talk to her. The person told me that she didn't have a name. Later she said that Mary called her Evelyn. I was suspicious at first that it was Mary pretending to be Evelyn. I changed my mind, however, because the person I talked to had too

much sense to be Mary. She said that she realized that T.C. was unreliable but she still loved him and was very lonely. She agreed that it would be best to find a reliable man. She told me that she comes out once a day for a very short time to get used to the world. She promised that she will come out to see you [Dr. Jeans] sometime when she is stronger. (Jeans, 1976, pp. 254–255)

Throughout that month, Evelyn appeared more and more often, and Dr. Jeans felt that his patient was improving rapidly. Within a few months, she seemed to be Evelyn all the time; soon thereafter, this woman married a physician. Years later, she had shown no recurrences of the other personalities.

(Drawn from Jeans, 1976)

In this chapter, we discuss the dissociative disorders and the somatic symptom-related disorders. We cover these disorders together because both are hypothesized to be triggered by stressful experiences yet do not involve direct expressions of anxiety. In the dissociative disorders, the person experiences disruptions of consciousness—he or she loses track of self-awareness, memory, and identity. In the somatic symptom-related disorders, the person complains of bodily symptoms that suggest a physical defect or dysfunction, sometimes dramatic in nature. For some of the somatic symptom-related disorders, no physiological basis can be found, and for others, the psychological reaction to the symptoms appears excessive.

Beyond the idea that both types of disorders are related to stress, dissociative disorders and somatic symptom-related disorders are often comorbid. Patients with dissociative disorders often meet the criteria for somatic symptom-related disorders, and vice versa; those with somatic symptom-related disorders are somewhat more likely than those in the general population to meet the diagnostic criteria for dissociative disorders (Akyüz, Gökalp, et al., 2017; Brown, Cardena, et al., 2007; Dell, 2006).

Clinical Descriptions and Epidemiology of the Dissociative Disorders

The DSM-5 includes three major **dissociative disorders**: depersonalization/derealization disorder, dissociative amnesia, and dissociative identity disorder (formerly known as multiple personality disorder). **Table 8.1** summarizes the key clinical features of the DSM-5 dissociative disorders. Dissociation, the core feature of each dissociative disorder, involves some aspect of emotion, memory, or experience being inaccessible consciously. Because dissociation is such a broad term, let's consider some of the different types of experience it encompasses.

TABLE 8.1   **Diagnoses of Somatic Symptom and Related Disorders**

DSM-5 Diagnosis	Description
Depersonalization/derealization disorder	Experience of detachment from the self and reality
Dissociative amnesia	Lack of conscious access to memory, typically of a stressful experience. The fugue subtype involves traveling or wandering coupled with loss of memory of one's identity or past.
Dissociative identity disorder	At least two distinct personalities that act independently of each other

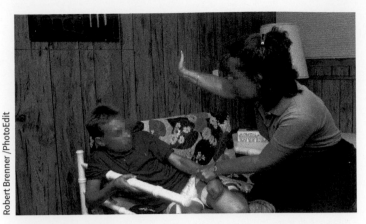

Physical or sexual abuse in childhood is regarded as a major factor in the development of dissociative disorders.

Some types of dissociation are common. Many of you will have had experiences of studying so hard for a test that you lost track of time and might not even have noticed people coming and going from the room where you were studying. Some of you may have missed a turn on the road home when thinking about problems. These types of dissociative experiences are usually a harmless sign that one has been so focused on some aspect of experience that other aspects of experience are lost from awareness.

In contrast to these common dissociative experiences, dissociative disorders are defined by more severe types of dissociation. Depersonalization/derealization involves a form of dissociation involving detachment, in which the person feels removed from the sense of self and surroundings. The person may feel "spaced out," numb, or as though in a dream (Holmes, Brown, et al., 2005). Dissociative amnesia and dissociative identity disorder involve a more dramatic form of dissociation, in which the person cannot access important aspects of memory. In dissociative identity disorder, the gaps in memory are so extensive that the person loses his or her sense of a unified identity.

What causes dissociation? Both psychodynamic and behavioral theorists consider pathological dissociation to be an avoidance response that protects the person from consciously experiencing stressful events. Consistent with the idea that this is a coping response, people undergoing very intense stressors, such as advanced military survival training, often report brief moments of mild dissociation (Morgan, Hazlett, et al., 2001). In addition to the idea of dissociation as a coping response, sleep disruptions may contribute to dissociation (Giesbrecht, Smeets, et al., 2013). Recent research jointly considers how trauma and sleep could contribute to dissociation. In one study of preschoolers, abuse led to sleep disturbance, and the sleep disturbance then predicted parental report of child dissociation (Hébert, Langevin, et al., 2016).

Researchers know less about dissociative disorders than about other disorders, and considerable controversy surrounds the risk factors for these disorders, as well as the best treatments. To some, this controversy may seem daunting. We find the process of discovery to be fascinating as researchers strive to untangle this complex puzzle.

Depersonalization/Derealization Disorder

As described earlier, **depersonalization/derealization disorder** involves a disconcerting and disruptive sense of detachment from one's self or surroundings. Depersonalization is defined by a sense of being detached from one's self (e.g., being an observer outside one's body). Derealization is defined by a sense of detachment from one's surroundings, such that the surroundings seem unreal. People with this disorder may have the impression that they are outside their bodies, viewing themselves from a distance or looking at the world through a fog. Sometimes they feel mechanical, as though they are robots. Although more than a third of college students report that they have experienced at least fleeting moments of depersonalization or derealization in the past year (Hunter, Sierra, & David, 2004), these mild and intermittent symptoms are rarely of concern. The DSM-5 criteria for depersonalization/derealization disorder specify that the symptoms must be persistent or recurrent. Unlike the other dissociative disorders, this disorder involves no disturbance of memory.

The following quote, drawn from a 1953 medical textbook, captures some of the experience of this disorder:

> The world appears strange, peculiar, foreign, dream-like. Objects appear at times strangely diminished in size, at times flat. Sounds appear to come from a distance.... The emotions likewise undergo marked alteration. Patients complain that they are capable of experiencing neither pain nor pleasure; love and hate have perished with

---

DSM-5 Criteria for Depersonalization/Derealization Disorder

- **Depersonalization:** Experiences of detachment from one's mental processes or body, or
- **Derealization:** Experiences of unreality of surroundings
- Symptoms are persistent or recurrent

- Reality testing remains intact
- Symptoms are not explained by substances, another dissociative disorder, another psychological disorder, or by a medical condition

---

them. They experience a fundamental change in their personality, and the climax is reached with their complaints that they have become strangers to themselves. It is as though they were dead, lifeless, mere automatons. (Schilder, 1953, pp. 304–305)

The symptoms of depersonalization and derealization are usually triggered by stress. Depersonalization/derealization disorder usually begins in adolescence, and it can start either abruptly or gradually. Most people who experience depersonalization also experience derealization, and the course of symptoms is similar for both symptoms. Symptoms are often continuously present for years (Simeon, 2009). Comorbid personality disorders are frequently present, and during their lifetime, about 90 percent of people with this disorder will experience anxiety disorders or depression (Simeon, Knutelska, et al., 2003). As in the Clinical Case of Mrs. A., childhood trauma is often reported (Michal, Adler, et al., 2016).

The DSM-5 diagnostic criteria for depersonalization/derealization disorder specify that the symptoms can co-occur with other disorders but should not be entirely explained by those disorders. It is important to rule out disorders that commonly involve these symptoms, including schizophrenia, posttraumatic stress disorder, and borderline personality disorder. Depersonalization is also relatively common during panic attacks and during marijuana intoxication.

Dissociative Amnesia

The person with **dissociative amnesia** is unable to recall important personal information, usually information about some traumatic experience. The holes in memory are too extensive to be ordinary forgetfulness. The episode of amnesia may last as briefly as several hours or for as long as several years. The amnesia usually disappears as suddenly as it began, with complete recovery of memory and only a small chance of recurrence.

Typically the memory loss of amnesia involves information about some part of a traumatic experience, such as witnessing the sudden death of a loved one. More rarely the amnesia is for entire events during a circumscribed period of stress. During the

John Springer Collection / Corbis Historical / Getty Images

In *Spellbound*, Gregory Peck played a man with amnesia. Dissociative amnesia is typically triggered by a stressful event, as it was in the film.

Clinical Case

Mrs. A.

Mrs. A was a 43-year-old woman who lived with her mother and son and worked in a clerical job. She had experienced symptoms of depersonalization several times per year for as long as she could remember. "It's as if the real me is taken out and put on a shelf or stored somewhere inside of me. Whatever makes me me is not

there. It is like an opaque curtain… like going through the motions…" She had found these symptoms to be extremely distressing. She had experienced panic attacks for one year when she was 35. She described a childhood trauma history that included nightly sexual abuse by her mother from her earliest memory to age 10. (Simeon, Gross, et al., 1997, p. 1109)

DSM-5 Criteria for Dissociative Amnesia

- Inability to remember important autobiographical information, usually of a traumatic or stressful nature, that is too extensive to be ordinary forgetfulness
- The amnesia is not explained by substances, or by other medical or psychological conditions

- Specify fugue subtype if the amnesia is associated with bewildered or apparently purposeful wandering

period of amnesia, the person's behavior is otherwise unremarkable, except that the memory loss may cause some disorientation. Procedural memory remains intact—the person remembers how to answer the phone, ride a bike, and execute other complex actions, even though he or she is unable to remember specific events.

In the **fugue subtype** of dissociative amnesia (from the Latin *fugere*, "to flee"), the memory loss is more extensive. The person typically disappears from home and work. Some people wander away from home in a bewildered manner. Others may take on a new name, a new home, a new job, and even a new set of personality characteristics. The person may even succeed in establishing a fairly complex social life. More often, however, the new life does not crystallize to this extent, and the fugue is more like the experience of Hannah Upp (see Clinical Case) in being of relatively brief duration, consisting of limited but apparently purposeful travel during which social contacts are minimal or absent. As in other forms of amnesia, recovery is usually complete, although it takes varying amounts of time; after recovery, people are fully able to remember the details of their life and experiences, except for those events that took place during the fugue.

In diagnosing dissociative amnesia, it is important to rule out other common causes of memory loss, such as substance abuse, brain injury, medication side effects, and dementia.

Clinical Case

Hannah

In 2008, Hannah Upp's family and friends mounted an intensive search for her through media and Internet outlets after she had been missing for four days. As reported in *The New York Times* (Marx & Ddiziulis, 2009), Hannah, a 23-year-old Spanish teacher living in New York City (see photo), had gone out for a run on the last day before the new school year began, leaving behind her ID and wallet. Almost 3 weeks later, she was rescued floating in the water about a mile southwest of Manhattan. She was suffering from dehydration and hypothermia, and she had large blisters on her heels. She had no memory of the events that occurred during those 3 weeks, and it is believed she suffered from an episode of dissociative amnesia, fugue subtype. When interviewed, Hannah could not identify any stressful trigger that would have provoked the episode—although her job was demanding, she loved teaching, and she was doing well in her pursuit of a master's degree. Some of the events from those three weeks could be retraced from public video footage and reports from people who had seen her wandering around on Riverside Drive, entering an Apple store, and attending a local gym. She appears to have suffered a relapse in 2013, when she disappeared again for two days (Marx, 2017).

It is believed that Hannah Upp's 3-week disappearance from home and work in 2008 could have resulted from an episode of dissociative amnesia, fugue subtype.

ASSOCIATED PRESS

Heavy drinking can cause blackouts, and medications such as the benzodiaze-pines used in the treatment of anxiety (e.g., Valium) and the sedative-hypnotics used in the treatment of insomnia (e.g., Ambien) can cause amnesia. Dementia can be distinguished from dissociative amnesia. In dementia, memory fails slowly over time, is not linked to stress, and is accompanied by an inability to learn new information.

We mentioned that dissociative amnesia typically occurs after severe stress. Nonetheless, not all amnesias immediately follow trauma (Hacking, 1998). In addition, dissociative amnesia is rare even among people who have experienced intense trauma, such as imprisonment in a concentration camp (Merckelbach, Dekkers, et al., 2003).

Dissociative amnesia raises fundamental questions about how memory works under stress. Psychodynamic theory suggests that in dissociative amnesia, trau-matic events are repressed. In this model, memories are forgotten (i.e., dissociated) because they are so aversive. There is considerable debate about whether repres-sion occurs. Cognitive scientists have questioned how repression could happen because research shows that stress usually enhances rather than impairs encoding of memories for the negative event. Not only has this been documented again and again in laboratory studies (Shields, Sazma, et al., 2017), but it has been observed among people who have experienced traumatic events. For example, survivors of a plane crash had extremely accurate, detailed memories of the experience (McKinnon, Palombo, et al., 2015). Among a sample of veterans, those with the most severe war experiences were most likely to provide consistent descriptions of combat memo-ries over time (Krinsley, Gallagher, et al., 2003). Norepinephrine, a neurotransmitter associated with heightened arousal, enhances memory consolidation and retrieval (Sara, 2009).

In moments of severe stress, people tend to focus on the most central element of threat. After a hold-up, the person who was attacked may remember details of the gun but be un-able to recall less threatening aspects of the situation, such as the clothes and appearance of the attacker.

The nature of attention and memory, however, does change during periods of intense stress. People under stress tend to focus on the central features of the threat-ening situation and to stop paying attention to peripheral features (McNally, 2003). As a conse-quence, people tend to remember emotionally relevant material more than the neutral details surrounding an event (Shields et al., 2017).

Given that the usual response to trauma is enhanced memory of the central features of the threat, how can we explain the stress-related memory loss of dissociative amnesia? One answer might be that dissociative amnesia involves unusual ways of responding to stress. For example, extremely high levels of stress hormones could interfere with memory forma-tion (Shields, Bonner, et al., 2015). Chronic stress, such as repeated abuse, might have more detrimental effects on memory than acute stress does (Reinhold & Markowitsch, 2009). Dissociative amnesia is considered an extreme outcome of this process. Debate continues about how to understand memory loss in the context of trauma and dissociation (see **Focus on Discovery 8.1**).

Focus on Discovery 8.1

Debates About Repression: Recovered Memories of Abuse in Childhood

Clearly, abuse happens all too often and exerts important effects on mental health and well-being. Here we focus on recovered memo-ries of childhood abuse—that is, on cases in which a person had no memory of being abused as a child but then "recovered" the mem-ory. Few issues are more hotly debated in psychology than whether these recovered memories are real. On one side, some argue that these recovered memories provide evidence for repression.

Repression, as initially defined by Freud, involved suppressing unacceptably painful memories from consciousness. In contrast to the idea that recovered memories provide evidence of repression, some question how valid the memories are.

What does the evidence say about repression? In laboratory studies of memory, researchers have asked people to forget infor-mation, such as a list of words, and have shown that people can do so (Anderson & Green, 2001). This demonstrates that people can deliberately forget material, but are people with recovered mem-ories better at forgetting than are others? Apparently not—people with recovered memories of child sexual abuse (CSA) do not show superior ability to forget words related to their trauma (McNally, Ristuccia, & Perlman, 2005). The word lists used in these studies, though, may not be painful enough to inspire repression.

To understand more about memories for highly painful events, some researchers have studied memory for traumas that occurred outside the laboratory setting. In one study of whether memories of abuse can be forgotten, 92 percent of people with documented childhood abuse still reported a memory of the abuse when they were asked about it almost 15 years later (Goodman, Ghetti, et al., 2003). Those with more severe abuse memories were more likely to remember and disclose their abuse. On the other hand, 8 percent of people reported that they had no memory of abuse.

Even for those 8 percent, the lack of reported recall might reflect many processes other than repression. People might not want to disclose such distressing events to a researcher. Some people might have been too young at the time of the abuse to be able to remember the events: People were less likely to report the memory at the 15-year follow-up if they had been younger than age 5 at the time the abuse occurred. Some of the traumas may have caused brain injury that could explain the gaps in memory. Thus, a failure to describe a memory may not be the same thing as repression.

Beyond the debate about whether repression occurs, how should we interpret it when someone develops a new memory? Where could recovered memories come from, if not from actual experiences? A leading researcher suggests a couple of possibilities (Loftus, 1993):

1. **Popular writings.** *The Courage to Heal* (Bass & Davis, 2008) is an extremely popular guide for victims of CSA. It suggests to readers that they were probably abused and offers as signs of abuse low self-esteem, feeling different from others, substance abuse, sexual dysfunction, and depression. The problem is that symptoms such as these can result from many factors other than CSA.

2. **Therapists' suggestions.** By their own accounts (Poole, Lindsay, et al., 1995), many therapists who genuinely believe that adult disorders result from abuse will suggest to their clients that they were probably sexually abused as children; sometimes the therapist does this with the assistance of hypnotic age regression and guided imagery (Legault & Laurence, 2007). Unfortunately, techniques such as hypnosis may actually create false memories (Lynn, Lock, et al., 2003). Guided imagery, in which a person closes his or her eyes and tries to imagine an event occurring, tends to increase confidence that

events of a false memory actually occurred. With three rounds of guided imagery, 70 percent of participants developed a false memory of committing a crime that led to police contact (Shaw & Porter, 2015). To examine the validity of memories recovered in therapy, one group of researchers studied three groups: persons who had continuous memories of CSA, those who had recovered memories without a therapist, and those who had recovered memories within the context of therapy. Striking differences emerged: Whereas about half of the continuous memories or those recalled outside therapy could be corroborated by another source, none of the 16 events recalled within therapy could be corroborated (Geraerts, Schooler, et al., 2007). Most clinical psychologists now express doubts about the validity of at least some memories recovered in therapy (Patihis, Ho, et al., 2014).

Not only do memory distortions occur, but once they do, they hold emotional power. In one study, researchers interviewed people who reported having been abducted by space aliens (presumably a false memory). While participants talked about the experience, the researchers recorded heart rate, sweating, and other signs of arousal. People describing their abduction demonstrated just as much arousal as others did when they recounted experiences of war or trauma (McNally, Lasko, et al., 2004). Even false memories, then, can be associated with a lot of pain!

Undoubtedly, abuse occurs. But we must be wary of uncritically accepting reports of abuse. This is an important issue because recovered memories of abuse have been used in hundreds of court cases (Pope, 1998). In a typical scenario, a woman recovers a memory during psychotherapy, accuses one of her parents of having abused her during childhood, and brings charges against the parent. For most crimes, plaintiffs must file suit within a certain number of years of a crime. In the 1980s, courts in more than 30 states increased the time allowed for filing suit in cases where plaintiffs claimed to have recovered memories of CSA (Brown, Scheflin, & Whitfield, 1999). By the late 1990s, however, the tide had turned, and many appellate courts refused to allow testimony based on recovered memories (Piper, Pope, & Borowiecki, 2000). More than 100 former patients have sued therapists for malpractice, claiming that the therapists implanted false memories of abuse (McNally, 2003).

Social scientists and the courts share a heavy responsibility in deciding whether a given recovered memory is an accurate reflection of a criminal event. Erring in either direction could result in an injustice to either the accused or the accuser.

Dissociative Identity Disorder

Consider what it would be like to have dissociative identity disorder (DID), as did Gina, the woman described at the opening of this chapter. People tell you about things you have done that are out of character and interactions of which you have no memory. How can you explain these events?

The diagnosis of **dissociative identity disorder (DID)**, formerly labeled multiple personality disorder, requires that a person have at least two separate personalities, or alters—different modes of being, thinking, feeling, and acting that exist independently of one another and that emerge at different times. Each determines the person's nature and activities when it is in command. The primary alter may be totally unaware that any other alter exists and may have no memory of what those other alters do and experience when they are in control.

DSM-5 Criteria for Dissociative Identity Disorder

- Disruption of identity characterized by two or more distinct personality states (alters) or an experience of possession. These disruptions lead to discontinuities in the sense of self or agency, as reflected in altered cognition, behavior, affect, perceptions, consciousness, memories, or sensory-motor functioning. This disruption may be observed by others or reported by the patient.
- Recurrent gaps in memory for events or important personal information that are beyond ordinary forgetting

- Symptoms are not part of a broadly accepted cultural or religious practice
- Symptoms are not due to drugs or a medical condition
- In children, symptoms are not better explained by an imaginary playmate or by fantasy play

---

According to case reports, there is typically one primary personality and this is usually the alter who seeks treatment. Most commonly, two to four alters are identified when the diagnosis is made, but over the course of treatment others may emerge. Each alter has its own behavior patterns, memories, and relationships. Usually, the personalities of the different alters are quite different from one another, even polar opposites. Case reports have described alters who have different handedness, like different foods, and have allergies to different substances (Boysen & VanBergen, 2014). The alters are aware of lost periods of time, and the voices of the others may sometimes echo in an alter's consciousness, even though the alter may not know to whom these voices belong. In some cultures, people value the experience of spirits who take control of the person's body (Seligman & Kirmayer, 2008); when experiences of possession are part of a broadly accepted spiritual or cultural practice, the diagnosis of DID is not appropriate.

DID is rarely diagnosed until adulthood, but after their diagnosis, patients often will recall symptoms dating back to childhood. It is more severe and extensive than the other dissociative disorders (Mueller-Pfeiffer, Rufibach, et al., 2012). DID is much more common in women than in men. Other diagnoses are often present, including posttraumatic stress disorder, major depressive disorder, somatic symptom disorders, and personality disorders (APA, 2013). DID is commonly accompanied by other symptoms such as headaches, hallucinations, suicide attempts, and self-injurious behavior, as well as by other dissociative symptoms such as amnesia and depersonalization.

The inclusion of DID as a diagnosis in DSM is controversial. For example, in a survey of psychiatrists, two-thirds reported reservations about the presence of DID in the DSM (Pope, Oliva, et al., 1999). Students and the public often ask, "Does DID exist?" Clinicians can describe DID reliably; it "exists" in this sense. As we will discuss later, though, controversy swirls about the reasons these symptoms occur.

The Epidemiology of Dissociative Disorders: Increases Over Time

We do not know how common dissociative disorders are. Only two studies assessed the lifetime prevalence of the dissociative disorders in community samples using face-to-face diagnostic interviews (Ross, 1991; Sar, Akyuz, & Dogan, 2007). Both studies relied on the Dissociative Disorders Interview Schedule (Ross, 1989), and the probes from this interview are vague. For example, the major probe to assess dissociative amnesia is, "Have you ever experienced sudden inability to recall important personal information or events that is too extensive to be explained by ordinary forgetfulness?" People vary in their definition of ordinary forgetfulness. Indeed, in one study, researchers found that twice as many cases were labeled as meeting dissociative amnesia with the Dissociative Disorders Interview Schedule as compared with a lengthier interview (Ross, Duffy, & Ellason, 2002). Bearing in mind that these are likely overestimates, then, the two available community studies found that about 2.5 percent of people endorsed the lifetime diagnostic criteria for depersonalization/derealization, about 7.5 percent for dissociative amnesia, and 1 to 3 percent for dissociative identity disorder (Ross, 1991; Sar et al., 2007).

Even if one considers that these may be inflated estimates, these figures are quite high comparatively—prevalence was earlier thought to be about one in a million. Although descriptions of anxiety, depression, and psychosis have abounded in literature since ancient times, there were almost no identified reports of DID or dissociative amnesia before 1800 (Pope, Poliakoff, et al., 2006). Reports of DID increased markedly in the 1970s, not only in the United States but also in countries such as Japan (Uchinuma & Sekine, 2000).

What has caused the ballooning rates of the DID diagnosis over time? It is possible that more people began to experience symptoms of DID. But there are other possible explanations for the surge. The case of Eve White, popularized in the book and film adaptation of *The Three Faces of Eve*, provided a highly detailed report of DID in 1957. The popular 1973 book *Sybil* presented a dramatic case with 16 personalities (Schreiber, 1973). The book sold more than 6 million copies in the first four years in print, and more than a fifth of all Americans watched a TV adaptation broadcast in 1976 (Nathan, 2011). A series of other case reports were published in the 1970s as well. DSM-III, which appeared in 1980, defined the diagnosis of DID for the first time (Putnam, 1996). The diagnostic criteria and growing literature may have increased detection and recognition of symptoms. Some critics hypothesize that the heightened professional and media attention to this diagnosis led some therapists to suggest strongly to clients that they had DID, sometimes using hypnosis to probe for alters.

As with DID, diagnoses of dissociative fugue may vary with cultural and professional attention to the condition. The first documented case of dissociative fugue appeared in the medical literature in 1887 in France of Albert Dadas, who traveled during his fugue states from France to Algeria, Moscow, and Constantinople (Hacking, 1998). The case received widespread attention at medical conferences, and a small epidemic of fugue cases were reported throughout Europe in the years that followed (Hacking, 1998).

Quick Summary

Dissociative disorders are defined on the basis of disruptions in consciousness, in which memories, self-awareness, or other aspects of cognition become inaccessible to the conscious mind. In depersonalization/derealization disorder, the person's perception of the self and surroundings is altered such that people may feel detached from their body or may perceive the world as seeming unreal. Dissociative amnesia is defined by inability to recall important personal experience(s), usually of a traumatic nature. In the fugue subtype of dissociative amnesia, the person not only is unable to recall important information but also leaves home and wanders without regard to work or social obligations. The person with dissociative identity disorder has two or more distinct personalities, each with unique memories, behavior patterns, and relationships.

The epidemiology of the dissociative disorders is not well researched. The number of diagnosed cases of DID surged during the 1970s, and some attribute this to the increased media and professional attention to the syndrome.

Check Your Knowledge 8.1
(Answers are at the end of the chapter.)

Answer the questions.

1. The key feature of the fugue subtype of dissociative amnesia is:

2. In the context of dissociative identity disorder, *alter* refers to:

3. Describe historical changes in rates of DID.

Etiology of DID

Because so little is known about dissociative disorders, we will focus on the etiology of one of these disorders, DID. There are two major theories for DID: the **posttraumatic model** and the **sociocognitive model**. Despite their different names, both theories suggest that severe physical or sexual abuse during childhood sets the stage for DID. It is widely acknowledged that child abuse has profoundly negative effects (Curran, Adamson, et al., 2016). Almost all patients in therapy for DID report severe childhood abuse (Dalenberg, Brand, et al., 2012). Since few people who are abused develop DID, both models focus on why only some people develop DID after abuse. As we will see, considerable debate has arisen between the proponents of these two approaches.

The Posttraumatic Model

The posttraumatic model proposes that some people are particularly likely to use dissociation to cope with trauma and that dissociation is the key reason people develop alters after trauma (Gleaves, 1996). Research supports two important tenets of this model (Dalenberg, Brand, et al., 2012). First, children who are abused are at risk for developing dissociative symptoms. Second, children who dissociate are more likely to develop psychological symptoms after trauma (Ensink, Berthelot, et al., 2017). But because DID is so rare, these studies have tended to focus on dissociative symptoms rather than diagnosable disorder, and no prospective studies have followed children from the time of trauma through the development of DID.

In the film version of *Sybil*, about a famous case of dissociative identity disorder, the title role was played by Sally Field. Later review of case notes suggested that "Sybil's personalities had not popped up spontaneously, but were provoked over many years of rogue treatment" (Nathan, 2011, p. xviii).

(c) NBC/Photofest

The Sociocognitive Model

According to the sociocognitive model, people who have been abused seek explanations for their symptoms and distress, and alters appear in response to suggestions by therapists, exposure to media reports of DID, or other cultural influences (Lilienfeld, Lynn, et al., 1999). Proponents of this model note that the prevalence of DID surged when media and professionals began to place more emphasis on the diagnosis. This model, then, implies that DID could be **iatrogenic** (created within treatment) in that the person often learns to role-play these symptoms within treatment. This does not mean, however, that DID is viewed as conscious deception; the issue is not whether DID is real but how it develops.

Many of the treatment manuals for DID recommend therapeutic techniques that reinforce clients' identification of different alters, such as interviewing clients about their identities after administering hypnosis or sodium pentothal (Nathan, 2011). The reinforcement and suggestive techniques might promote false memories and DID symptoms in vulnerable people (Lilienfeld et al., 1999). The famous case of Sybil is now widely cited as an example of how a therapist might elicit and reinforce stories of alters. It has been claimed that in Sybil's case, the alters were created by a therapist who gave substance to Sybil's different emotional states by giving them names, and who helped Sybil elaborate on her early childhood experiences while administering sodium pentothal, a drug that has been shown to contribute to false memories (Borch-Jacobsen, 1997; Nathan, 2011). As another example of troubling therapeutic techniques, the Clinical Case of Elizabeth provides an extreme example of a therapist who unwittingly encouraged her client to adopt a diagnosis of DID when it wasn't justified by the symptoms. All the symptoms Elizabeth described are common experiences; indeed, none of the symptoms listed are actual diagnostic criteria for DID.

We will never have experimental evidence for the sociocognitive model, since it would be unethical to intentionally reinforce dissociative symptoms. Given this reality, what kinds of evidence have researchers raised in support of the sociocognitive model?

DID Symptoms Can Be Role-Played   Across 20 studies, researchers have shown that people are capable of role-playing the symptoms of DID (Boysen & VanBergen, 2014). For example, in one study university students were hypnotized and instructed to let a second personality come forward. Most of the students endorsed having a second personality, and 81 percent of them even adopted a new name. Those who adopted a second personality were asked to take personality tests twice—once for each personality. The personality test results of the two personalities differed considerably. These findings indicate that people can

Clinical Case

Elizabeth

An Example of Unwarranted Diagnosis of DID

The book *Creating Hysteria: Women and Multiple Personality Disorder* provides a personal account of a person who received a false diagnosis of DID. Elizabeth Carlson, a 35-year-old married woman, was referred to a psychiatrist after being hospitalized for severe depression. Elizabeth reported that soon after treatment began, her psychiatrist suggested to her that perhaps her problem was the elusive, often undiagnosed condition of multiple personality disorder (MPD, now referred to as DID). Her psychiatrist reviewed

... certain telltale signs of MPD. Did Carlson ever "zone out" while driving and arrive at her destination without remembering how she got there? Why yes, Carlson said. Well, that was an alter taking over the driving and then vanishing again, leaving her, the "host" personality, to account for the blackout. Did Carlson ever have internal arguments—for example, telling herself, "Turn right" and then "No, turn left"? Yes, Carlson replied, that happened sometimes. Well, that was the alters fighting with each other inside her head. Carlson was amazed and embarrassed. All these years, she had done these things, never realizing that they were symptoms of a severe mental disorder. (Acocella, 1999, p. 1)

©AP/Wide World Photos

Ken Bianchi, a serial killer known as the Hillside strangler, unsuccessfully attempted an insanity defense, claiming that he suffered from DID. The jury decided that he was faking the symptoms of DID.

adeptly role-play DID. This evidence has been criticized though—people can mimic having a broken leg (and indeed many other symptoms), but this does not cast doubt on the reality of broken legs.

Some Therapists Reinforce DID Symptoms in Their Clients

Therapists who diagnose more people with DID tend to use hypnosis, to urge clients to try to unbury unremembered abuse experiences, or to name different alters (Powell & Gee, 2000). Consistent with the idea that treatment evokes the DID symptoms, most patients are unaware of having alters until after they begin treatment, and as treatment progresses, they report a rapid increase in the number of alters they can identify.

Alters Share Memories, Even When They Report Amnesia

One of the defining features of DID is the inability to recall information experienced by one alter when a different alter is present. One way to test whether alters share memory is to use implicit tests of memory (Huntjen, Postma, et al., 2003). In **explicit memory** tests, researchers might ask a person to remember words. In **implicit memory** tests, experimenters determine if the word lists have subtler effects on performance. For example, if persons are first shown a word list that included the word *lullaby*, they might be quicker on a second task to identify *lullaby* as a word that fills in the puzzle l_l_a_y. People with DID were taught the initial word list and were then asked to complete the implicit memory test when they returned to the second session as a different alter. Twenty-one of the participants diagnosed with DID claimed at the second testing session that they had no memory of the first session. On tests of implicit memory, however, these 21 people performed comparably to people without DID. That is, memories were transferred between alters. At least nine studies replicate this finding (Boysen & VanBergen, 2013). People with DID demonstrate more accurate memory than they tend to acknowledge.

Quick Summary

Little research is available concerning the causes of the dissociative disorders. DID is related to severe abuse, but considerable debate exists about the other causes of this disorder. The posttraumatic model suggests that DID is the result of using dissociation as a coping strategy to deal with the abuse. The sociocognitive model suggests that DID is caused by role-playing of symptoms among patients with a history of abuse. Proponents of the sociocognitive model note the dramatic shifts in diagnosis over time, the use of suggestive techniques among therapists who frequently diagnose DID, the increases in number of alters recognized after treatment begins, and the evidence that people can role-play symptoms of DID and that alters share more information than they acknowledge.

Check Your Knowledge 8.2

True or false?

1. Most patients with DID report childhood abuse.

Answer the question.

2. List the major sources of evidence for the sociocognitive model of DID.

Treatment of DID

There are no well-validated treatments available for DID. No randomized controlled trials have assessed psychological treatment. Medications have not been shown to relieve DID symptoms.

In the absence of strong evidence, expert clinicians agree on several principles in the treatment of dissociative identity disorder (International Society for the Study of Dissociation, 2011). These include the importance of an empathic and gentle stance. The goal of treatment should be to convince the person that splitting into different personalities is no longer necessary to deal with traumas. In addition, as DID is conceptualized as a means of escaping from severe stress, therapists can help teach the person more effective ways to cope with stress, such as adaptive emotion regulation strategies. Psychoeducation can help a person to understand why dissociation occurs and to begin to identify the triggers for dissociative responses in day-to-day life (Brand et al., 2012). Often, people with DID are hospitalized to help them avoid self-harm and to offer more intensive treatment.

Psychodynamic treatment is probably used more for DID and the other dissociative disorders than for any other psychological disorder. The goal of this treatment is to overcome repressions (MacGregor, 1996), as DID is believed to arise from traumatic events that the person is trying to block from consciousness. Unfortunately, some psychodynamic practitioners use hypnosis as a means of helping patients diagnosed with dissociative disorders to gain access to repressed material (International Society for the Study of Dissociation, 2011). Typically, the person is hypnotized and encouraged to go back in his or her mind to traumatic events in childhood—a technique called *age regression*. The hope is that accessing these traumatic memories will allow the person to realize that childhood threats are no longer present and that adult life need not be governed by these ghosts from the past (Grinker & Spiegel, 1944). Using hypnosis to promote age regression and recovered memories, though, can exacerbate DID symptoms (Lilienfeld, 2007). More than 100 patients have sued therapists for harm caused by treatment of DID (Hanson, 1998). Hypnotic techniques have become less popular as the problems have received more attention.

Quick Summary

There are no randomized controlled trials of psychological treatments for DID. There are no medications shown to reduce the symptoms of DID.

In the safe, supportive context of therapy, patients with DID are encouraged to learn new strategies for coping with emotions, to gain better control over tendencies to rely on dissociation. Hypnosis and age regression techniques to recover memories are contraindicated for DID.

Check Your Knowledge 8.3

Answer the questions.

1. How many randomized controlled trials are available to assess the efficacy of psychological treatments of DID?

2. Which medications reduce DID symptoms?

3. Which types of interventions for DID appear to be harmful?

Clinical Description of Somatic Symptom and Related Disorders

Somatic symptom and related disorders are defined by excessive concerns about physical symptoms or health. As shown in **Table 8.2**, the DSM-5 includes three major somatic symptom-related disorders: somatic symptom disorder, illness anxiety disorder, and conversion disorder. Many of us use the term *hypochondriasis* to describe chronic worries about developing a serious medical illness. Although hypochondriasis is not a DSM-5 diagnosis, both somatic symptom disorder and illness anxiety disorder overlap to some degree with hypochondriasis in that they involve high levels of distress and energy expenditure about a health concern. In somatic symptom disorder, the distress revolves around a somatic symptom that exists, whereas in illness anxiety disorder, the distress is about the potential for a medical illness in the absence of significant somatic symptoms. Conversion disorder involves neurological symptoms that are medically unexplained (labeled as functional neurological disorder in medical literature). Table 8.2 also lists malingering and factitious disorder, related disorders that we discuss in **Focus on Discovery 8.2**.

People with somatic symptom and related disorders tend to seek frequent medical treatment, sometimes at great expense. They often see several different physicians for a given health concern, and they may try many different medications. Hospitalization and even surgery are common experiences for them. Somatic symptom disorders lead to medical expenditures estimated at $256 billion per year in the United States (Barsky, Orav, & Bates, 2005). In the UK, the average cost of medical care for patients with high levels of health anxiety was £2,796 (roughly $4,622) for a 6-month period in 2009–2010 (Barrett, Tyrer, et al., 2012). Although people with these disorders seek medical care quite frequently, they are often dissatisfied when doctors cannot provide a medical explanation or cure. They often view their physicians as incompetent and uncaring (Persing, Stuart, et al., 2000). Despite their negative assessment of the medical profession, they will often continue extensive treatment-seeking, visiting new doctors and demanding new tests. Many patients become unable to work because of the severity of their concerns (van der Leeuw, Gerrits, et al., 2015). For patients for whom pain is a concern, dependency on painkillers is a risk.

The DSM-5 diagnoses of somatic symptom and related disorders can be reliably diagnosed, particularly if a semistructured clinical interview is conducted (Axelsson, Andersson, et al., 2016). Nonetheless, there are a couple important criticisms of the diagnostic criteria for somatic symptom and related disorders:

- These conditions are remarkably varied. For example, some people develop somatic symptoms in the context of anxiety and depressive disorders, whereas others do not (Lieb, Meinlschmidt, & Araya, 2007).

TABLE 8.2   **Diagnoses of Somatic Symptom and Related Disorders**

DSM-5 Diagnosis	Description
Somatic symptom disorder	Excessive thought, distress, and behavior related to somatic symptoms
Illness anxiety disorder	Unwarranted fears about a serious illness in the absence of any significant somatic symptoms
Conversion disorder	Neurological symptom(s) that cannot be explained by medical disease or culturally sanctioned behavior
Malingering	Intentionally faking psychological or somatic symptoms to gain from those symptoms
Factitious disorder	Falsification of psychological or physical symptoms, without evidence of gains from those symptoms

- Patients often find the diagnosis of somatic symptom and related disorders stigmatizing. This may interfere with applying diagnoses of somatic symptom disorders in clinical practice.

Because these disorders are defined differently than they were in DSM-IV-TR (where they were labeled as *somatoform disorders*), we don't have data on the epidemiology or course of the somatic symptom-related disorders. When the fears about a serious disease are accompanied by somatic symptoms, the appropriate DSM-5 diagnosis is somatic symptom disorder. Because so few people with intense fears about their health are free of somatic symptoms, somatic symptom disorder is estimated to be three times as common as illness anxiety disorder (Bailer, Kerstner, et al., 2016).

Somatic symptom disorder and illness anxiety disorder both involve health anxiety. Anxieties about health tend to develop early in adulthood (Cloninger, Martin, et al., 1986). Many experience these concerns throughout their lifetime. In longitudinal studies, less than half of those with somatic symptom-related disorders achieve remission within a 5-year period (olde Hartman, Borghuis, et al., 2009), although the severity of symptoms may wax and wane. Somatic symptom-related disorders tend to co-occur with anxiety disorders, mood disorders, and personality disorders (APA, 2013).

Symptoms of these disorders may begin or intensify after some conflict or stress. To an outside observer, it may seem that the person is using the health concern to avoid some unpleasant activity or to get attention and sympathy. People with somatic symptom and related disorders have no sense of this, however; they experience their symptoms as completely medical. Their distress over their symptoms is authentic.

Clinical Description of Somatic Symptom Disorder

The key feature of **somatic symptom disorder** is excessive anxiety, energy, or behavior focused on somatic symptoms that persists for at least 6 months. The person with this disorder is typically quite worried about his or her health and tends to view even small physical concerns as a sign of looming disease. Tormented by a broad range of somatic symptoms that were not solved by visiting 20 different doctors (Campbell & Matthews, 2005), Charles Darwin completed a log for 6 years of his bodily complaints, which was dominated by ratings of his flatulence and other gastrointestinal complaints. Although his symptoms were likely genuine, his extensive notes signal that he was spending too much energy monitoring his health (Dillon, 2010). As illustrated by the Clinical Case of Maria, some might experience a multitude of symptoms from many different body systems. Others experience pain as the major concern.

Somatic symptom disorder can be diagnosed regardless of whether symptoms can be explained medically. It is nearly impossible to determine whether some symptoms are biologically caused. Doctors often disagree on whether a symptom has a medical cause (Rief & Broadbent, 2007). Indeed, when asked about their physical symptoms, people receiving primary care report that two-thirds of their symptoms have not received a medical explanation (Steinbrecher et al., 2011). Some people might have a condition that defies diagnosis because of limits in medical knowledge and technology. As technology has improved, the medical profession now understands some conditions that were historically difficult to explain. As one example, complex regional pain syndrome was previously believed to be caused by psychological factors, but animal and human research now indicate that these symptoms result from inflammation secondary to autoimmune disorder (Cooper & Clark, 2013). Many common syndromes remain a focus for research because their etiology is not well understood, including irritable bowel syndrome, fibromyalgia, chronic fatigue, nonulcer dyspepsia, and some forms of chronic pain (Cooper & Clark, 2013). The presence of these syndromes is not a reason to diagnose somatic symptom disorders. When psychological factors exert a negative effect on medical symptoms, an alternative DSM diagnosis, labeled Psychological Factors Affecting Other Medical Conditions, may be appropriately considered.

DSM-5 Criteria for Somatic Symptom Disorder

- At least one somatic symptom that is distressing or disrupts daily life
- Excessive thought, distress, and behavior related to somatic symptom(s) or health concerns, as indicated by at least one of the following:

  1. health-related anxiety

  2. disproportionate and persistent concerns about the seriousness of symptoms

  3. excessive time and energy devoted to health concerns

- Duration of at least 6 months
- Specify if predominant pain

Clinical Description of Illness Anxiety Disorder

The main feature of **illness anxiety disorder** is a preoccupation with fears of having a serious disease despite having no significant somatic symptoms. To meet the DSM criteria for diagnosis, these fears must lead to excessive care seeking or maladaptive avoidance behaviors that persist for at least 6 months. People with this disorder are easily alarmed about their health, and they tend to worry about the possibility of cancer, heart attacks, AIDS, and strokes (Rachman, 2012). They may be haunted by powerful visual images of becoming ill or dying (Muse, McManus, et al., 2010). They may react with anxiety when they hear about illnesses in their friends or in the broader community. These fears are not easily calmed, and others may become frustrated when attempts to soothe worries fail.

Clinical Description of Conversion Disorder

In **conversion disorder**, the person suddenly develops neurological symptoms, such as blindness, seizures, or paralysis. The symptoms suggest an illness related to neurological damage, but medical tests indicate that the bodily organs and nervous system are fine. People may experience partial or complete paralysis of arms or legs; seizures; coordination disturbances; a sensation of prickling, tingling, or creeping on the skin; insensitivity to pain; or anesthesia—the

---

Clinical Case

Maria

Maria was 32 when her physician referred her to a psychologist after seeing her 23 times in 6 months for a range of complaints—general aches and pains, bouts of nausea, fatigue, irregular menstruation, and dizziness. Various tests, including complete blood workups, X-rays, and spinal taps, had not revealed any pathology.

On meeting her therapist, Maria let him know that she was a reluctant client: "I'm here only because I trust my doctor, and she urged me to come. I'm physically sick and don't see how a psychologist is going to help." But when the therapist asked Maria to describe the history of her physical problems, she quickly warmed to the task.

According to Maria, she had always been sick. As a child, she had had episodes of high fever, frequent respiratory infections, convulsions, and her first two operations—an appen-dectomy and a tonsillectomy. During her 20s, Maria had gone from one physician to another. She had suffered with unbearable periods of vomiting. She had seen several gynecologists for her menstrual irregularity and for pain during intercourse, and she had undergone dilation and curettage (scraping the lining of the uterus). She had been referred to neurologists for her headaches, dizziness, and fainting spells, and they had performed EEGs, spinal taps, and a CT scan. Other physicians had ordered EKGs for her chest pains. Maria seemed genuinely distressed by her health problems, and doctors responding to her desperate pleas for a cure had performed rectal and gallbladder surgery.

When the interview shifted away from Maria's medical history, it became clear that she was anxious in many situations, particularly those in which she feared others might evaluate her. Indeed, some of her physical symptoms were typical of those experienced by people diagnosed with anxiety disorders.

DSM-5 Criteria for Illness Anxiety Disorder

- Preoccupation with and high level of anxiety about having or acquiring a serious disease
- Excessive illness behavior (e.g., checking for signs of illness, seeking reassurance) or maladaptive avoidance (e.g., avoiding medical care)

- No more than mild somatic symptoms are present
- Not explained by other psychological disorders
- Preoccupation lasts at least 6 months

---

loss of sensation. Vision may be seriously impaired; the person may become partially or completely blind or have tunnel vision, in which the visual field is constricted as it would be if the person were peering through a tube. *Aphonia*, loss of the voice other than whispered speech, can also occur. Many people with conversion disorder do not connect their symptoms with their stressful situations.

The earliest writings on psychological disorders describe these symptoms. *Hysteria* was the term originally used to describe the disorder, which the Greek physician Hippocrates considered to be an affliction limited to women and brought on by the wandering of the uterus through the body. (The Greek word *hystera* means "womb"; the wandering uterus symbolized the longing of the woman's body to produce a child.) The term *conversion* originated with Sigmund Freud, who thought that anxiety and psychological conflict were converted into physical symptoms (see the Clinical Case of Anna O., an influential case for Freud's theory).

When a patient reports a neurological symptom, the clinician must be careful to assess whether that symptom has a true neurological basis. It is estimated that genuinely physical problems are misdiagnosed as conversion disorder about 4 percent of the time (Stone, Smyth, et al., 2005). Sometimes behavioral tests can help make this distinction. Nonepileptic seizure disorder, a common form of conversion disorder, is defined by seizure-like events that occur at the same time that a normal EEG pattern is recorded (Stone et al., 2010). In another example, arm tremors might disappear when the person is asked to move the arm rhythmically. Leg weakness might not be consistent when tested with resistance (Stone et al., 2010). Tunnel vision, another conversion disorder symptom, is incompatible with the biology of the visual system.

Some symptoms that might seem medically implausible have been shown to have a biological basis. Consider, for instance, the classic example of "glove anesthesia," in which the person experiences little or no sensation in the part of the hand and lower arm that would be covered by a glove. For years, this was considered a textbook illustration of anatomical nonsense because the nerves run continuously from the hand up the arm. Yet now it appears that carpal tunnel syndrome, a recognized medical condition, can produce symptoms like those of glove anesthesia. Nerves in the wrist run through a tunnel formed by the wrist bones and membranes. Swelling in this tunnel can pinch the nerves, leading to tingling, numbness, and pain in the hand. People who use computer keyboards for many hours a day are at risk for this condition. Beyond glove anesthesia, other symptoms that would intuitively seem difficult to explain medically, such as the perception of a burning sensation

---

DSM-5 Criteria for Conversion Disorder

- One or more symptoms affecting voluntary motor or sensory function
- The symptoms are incompatible with recognized medical disorder

- Symptoms cause significant distress or functional impairment or warrant medical evaluation

Clinical Case

Anna O.

As described in a case report, Anna O. was sitting at the bedside of her seriously ill father when she dropped off into a waking dream. She saw a black snake come toward her sick father to bite him. She tried to ward it off, but her arm had gone to sleep. When she looked at her hand, her fingers seemed to turn into little snakes with death's heads. The next day, when a bent branch recalled her waking dream of the snake, her right arm became rigidly extended. After that, whenever some object revived her hallucination, her arm responded in the same way—with rigid extension. Later, her symptoms extended to paralysis and anesthesia of her entire right side.

(Drawn from Breuer & Freud, 1982/1895)

when touching a cold object, have clear medical explanations (in this case, ciguatera, a disease caused by eating certain reef fish). To enhance the reliability of conversion disorder, the DSM-5 provides guidance to clinicians about how to assess whether symptoms might be medically unexplained.

Some, but not all, people with conversion disorder seem motivated to appear ill. When relevant neurological abilities are tested (e.g., visual tests for a person with a conversion disorder involving blindness), some with conversion disorders perform more poorly than what would be achieved by chance, and show evidence of little effort on the tests related to their deficit (Drane, Williamson, et al., 2006). Some with these disorders endorse multiple implausible and rare neurological symptoms (Benge, Wisdom, et al., 2012; Peck, Schroeder, et al., 2013). Some report a symptom, such as a tremor, much more continuously than is observed with objective measures, such as wristbands that monitor motion (Parees, Saifee, et al., 2012). Many people with conversion disorder, though, show no signs that they are amplifying their symptoms. When present, any amplification of symptoms may be outside conscious awareness. See **Focus on Discovery 8.2** for diagnoses to be considered when a person appears to be consciously producing symptoms.

Symptoms of conversion disorder usually develop in adolescence or early adulthood. Onset is usually rapid, with symptoms developing in less than one day (Carson & Lehn, 2016). Many patients with conversion disorder experience work-related disability (Carson & Lehn, 2016). An episode may end abruptly, but about 40 percent show symptoms when reassessed 5 years later (Gelauff, Stone, et al., 2013). Although there are no community-based studies using diagnostic interviews, the prevalence of conversion disorder is estimated to be less than 1 percent in the community but more common among patients visiting neurology clinics, where as many as 10 percent of patients have no medical explanation for their symptoms (Carson & Lehn, 2016). More women than men are given the diagnosis (Carson & Lehn, 2016). Patients with conversion disorder are highly likely to meet criteria for another somatic symptom disorder (Brown et al., 2007).

DSM-5 Criteria for Factitious Disorder

- Fabrication or induction of physical or psychological symptoms, injury, or disease
- Deceptive behavior is present in the absence of obvious external rewards

- In Factitious Disorder Imposed on Self, the person presents himself or herself to others as ill, impaired, or injured
- In Factitious Disorder Imposed on Another, the person fabricates or induces symptoms in another person and then presents that person to others as ill, impaired, or injured

Focus on Discovery 8.2

Malingering and Factitious Disorder

In evaluating somatic symptoms, clinicians must rule out factitious disorder and malingering. Both can involve somatic symptoms. In **malingering**, a person intentionally fakes a symptom to avoid a responsibility, such as work or military duty, or to achieve some reward, such as an insurance settlement. This contrasts with factitious disorder, where the sole goal is to adopt the patient role.

To distinguish between malingering and conversion disorder, clinicians try to determine whether the symptoms have been adopted consciously or unconsciously; in malingering, the symptoms are under voluntary control, which is not thought to be the case in conversion disorder. Insurance companies often go to great lengths to show that a person is faking symptoms and can function well outside of doctors' offices. When such detective work fails, though, it is often difficult, if not impossible, to know whether behavior is consciously or unconsciously motivated.

In **factitious disorder**, people intentionally produce symptoms to assume the role of a patient. Most of the symptoms are physical, but some produce psychological symptoms as well. They may make up symptoms—for example, reporting acute pain. Some will take extraordinary measures to make themselves ill. They may injure themselves, take damaging medications, or inject themselves with toxins.

In one of the most severe examples of factitious disorder reported, a woman named Miss Scott described being hospitalized at more than 600 hospitals and having 42 operations, nearly all of which were not needed (Grady, 1999). Some days she would leave one hospital and be admitted to a different hospital by nightfall. One doctor who examined the scars on her abdomen reported that "she looked as if she had lost a duel with Zorro." When asked about her treatment-seeking, she reported, "To begin with, it was just something I did when I needed someone to care about me. Then it became something I had to do. It was as if something took me over. I just had to be in the hospital. I had to."

She had grown up as an abused, lonely child, and one of her early positive memories was the care she received from a nurse after having her appendix removed. After that experience, she once walked into her local hospital feigning a stomachache, hoping that someone would care about her experience. She spent several days

Kathleen Bush was charged with child abuse and fraud for deliberately causing her child's illnesses.

there appreciating the attention that she received. Over the course of the next year, she began to seek care at a series of different hospitals. "Soon she was spending all her time hitchhiking from town to town, trying to get into the hospital (Grady, 1999, p. D5). For Miss Scott, being a patient became her chief way of gaining support and nurturance.

Factitious disorder may also be diagnosed in a parent who creates physical illness in a child; in this case, it is called *factitious disorder imposed on another* or *Munchausen syndrome by proxy.* In one extreme case, a 7-year-old girl was hospitalized more than 300 times and experienced 40 surgeries at a cost of over $2 million. Her mother, Kathleen Bush (see photo), had caused her illnesses by administering drugs and even contaminating her feeding tube with fecal material (Toufexis, Blackman, & Drummond, 1996). The motivation in a case such as this appears to be a need to be regarded as an excellent parent who is tireless in attending to the child's needs.

Quick Summary

The common feature of somatic symptom-related disorders is the excessive focus on physical symptoms. The nature of the concern, however, varies by disorder. The major somatic symptom-related disorders in the DSM-5 include somatic symptom disorder, illness anxiety disorder, and conversion disorder. Somatic symptom disorder is defined by excessive anxiety, worry, or behavior focused on somatic symptoms. Illness anxiety disorder is defined by fears of a severe disease in the absence of somatic symptoms. Conversion disorder is defined by sensory and motor dysfunctions that cannot be explained by medical tests. Somatic symptom-related disorders may arise suddenly in stressful situations. Health anxiety and conversion disorder often develop by early adulthood.

Check Your Knowledge 8.4

Match the case description to the disorder. Assume that the symptoms cause significant distress or impairment.

1. Paula, a 24-year-old librarian, sought psychological help on the advice of her sister because of her deep fears about her health. In daily phone calls with her sister, she would describe worries that she had cancer or a brain tumor. She had no somatic symptoms or signs of these conditions, but every time she saw an Internet report, a TV program, or a newspaper article on some new serious condition, she became worried she might have it. She had seen doctors frequently for years, but when they identified no disease, she became annoyed with them, criticized the insensitivity of their medical tests, and sought a new consultant.

2. John's surgeon referred him for psychological treatment because he seemed excessively nervous about his health. In the past 5 years, John, now 35 years old, had sought a stunning array of medical treatments and tests for stomach distress, itching, frequent urination, and any number of other complaints. He had received 10 MRIs and too many X-rays to count, and he had seen 15 different specialists. Each test had been negative. He genuinely seemed to experience physical symptoms, and there was no indication that he stood to gain from a medical diagnosis.

3. Thomas's ophthalmologist referred him for psychological treatment. Thomas reported that 2 weeks before, he had suddenly developed tunnel vision. Medical tests failed to reveal any reason for his tunnel vision, and there was no sign he was faking symptoms.

    a. somatic symptom disorder

    b. illness anxiety disorder

    c. malingering

    d. conversion disorder

Answer the question.

4. What is the major difference between somatic symptom disorder and illness anxiety disorder?

Etiology of Somatic Symptom-Related Disorders

Although one might expect somatic symptom-related disorders to be heritable, there is little concordance among twins for somatic symptom disorder (Torgersen, 1986) or conversion disorder (Slater, 1961). These disorders do not appear to be heritable.

Little is known about the etiology of the DSM-5 somatic symptom-related disorders because most researchers have used the DSM-IV-TR diagnoses, which differ considerably. The major features of somatic symptom disorder and illness anxiety disorder, though, include excessive attention to somatic symptoms and disproportionate anxiety about one's health. Neurobiological and cognitive behavioral models have focused on understanding these two tendencies, and we describe those models here. After discussing that research, we consider models of conversion disorder.

Neurobiological Factors That Increase Awareness of and Distress Over Somatic Symptoms

Everyone experiences occasional somatic symptoms. For example, we may feel muscle pain after a tough workout, small signs of an impending cold, or a faster heart rate as we exercise. In understanding somatic symptom disorders, then, the key issue is not whether people have some bodily sensation but rather why some people are more keenly aware of and distressed by these sensations.

Neurobiological models of somatic symptom-related disorders focus on brain regions activated by unpleasant body sensations. Pain and uncomfortable physical sensations, such as heat, increase activity in regions of the brain called the rostral anterior insula and the anterior cingulate cortex (ACC) (Price, Craggs, et al., 2009). These regions have strong connections with the somatosensory cortex, a region of the brain involved with processing bodily sensations (see **Figure 8.1**). Heightened activity in these regions is related to greater propensity for somatic symptoms (Landgrebe, Barta, et al., 2008) and more intense pain ratings in response to a standardized stimulus (Mayer, Berman, et al., 2005). Some people, then, may have hyperactive brain regions that are involved in evaluating the unpleasantness of body sensations (Bourke, Langford, & White 2015). This would help explain why they are more vulnerable to experiencing somatic symptoms and pain.

Pain and somatic symptoms can be increased by anxiety, depression, and stress hormones, and those with somatic symptom disorders show elevated rates of trauma, anxiety, and depression (Rief & Martin, 2014). Depression and anxiety also directly relate to activity in specific regions of the ACC (Shackman, Salomons, et al., 2011; Wiech & Tracey, 2009). Even briefer experiences of emotional pain, such as remembering a relationship breakup, can activate the ACC and the anterior insula. The involvement of these regions in experiences of physical and emotional pain may help explain why emotions and depression can intensify experiences of pain (Villemure & Bushnell, 2009).

In an interesting study, researchers studied whether learning to control ACC activity using real-time functional magnetic resonance imaging (fMRI) feedback could help reduce pain (deCharms, Maeda, et al., 2005).). In a first study, healthy individuals with no somatic symptom-related disorder completed brain-scanning sessions in which they viewed graphs showing the changing level of activity in key regions of the ACC as they were exposed to uncomfortable sensations (a heat bar was attached to their hand, and pulses of 116–120° heat were sent to the bar). They were told various strategies for manipulating activity in their ACC, such as attending toward or away from the heat, changing their thoughts about their heat (e.g., to consider it as neutral rather than tissue-damaging), and trying to think of it as high or low intensity. Within three sessions, most individuals did learn to control the activity in their ACC. The more that people learned to control their ACC, the more they could reduce their experiences of pain. The fMRI feedback training was more powerful in reducing pain than control conditions of false fMRI feedback or no fMRI feedback. In a second study, ACC feedback training was helpful for people who suffered from chronic pain. These findings, then, support the idea that the ACC is important in experiences of pain.

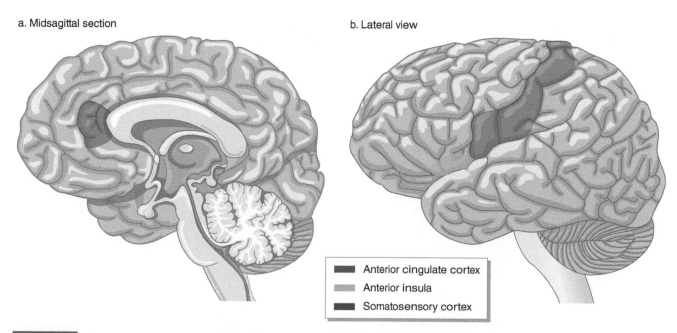

a. Midsagittal section

b. Lateral view

Anterior cingulate cortex
Anterior insula
Somatosensory cortex

FIGURE 8.1 People with somatic symptom-related disorders have increased activity in brain regions implicated in evaluating the unpleasantness of body sensations: the rostral anterior insula, the anterior cingulate, and the somatosensory cortex. The anterior cingulate is also involved in depression and anxiety.

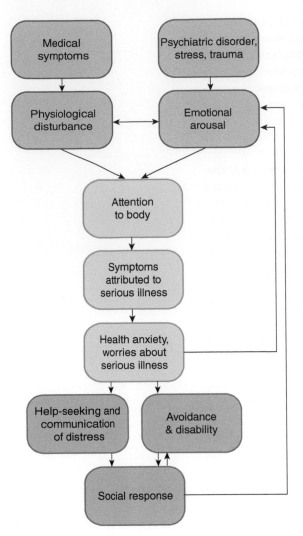

FIGURE 8.2 Mechanisms involved in somatic symptom-related disorders (Looper & Kirmayer, 2002).

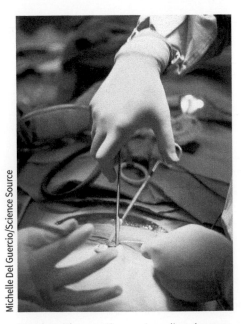

People with somatic symptom disorder may undergo unnecessary surgeries in hopes of finding a cure for their medical symptoms.

Michelle Del Guercio/Science Source

Cognitive Behavioral Factors That Increase Awareness of and Distress Over Somatic Symptoms

Like the neurobiological models of somatic symptom-related disorders, cognitive behavioral models focus on the mechanisms that could contribute to the excessive focus on and anxiety over health concerns. **Figure 8.2** illustrates one model of how these cognitive and behavioral risk factors could fit together. The orange boxes are relevant to understanding how a person might initially develop a somatic symptom. The blue boxes are relevant for understanding reactions to a somatic symptom. Once a somatic symptom develops, two cognitive variables are important: attention to body sensations and interpretation of those sensations.

People with health worries tend to be overly focused on their somatic symptoms, particularly when they are in a negative mood (Bogaerts et al., 2010). Once they attend to those somatic symptoms, they tend to interpret their physical symptoms in the worst possible way (Rief & Broadbent, 2007). They may interpret small physical symptoms as a sign of impending catastrophe. For example, one person might interpret a red blotch on the skin as a sign of cancer (Marcus, Gurley, et al., 2007). Another person might overestimate the odds that a symptom is a sign of a disease (Rief, Buhlmann et al., 2006). The exact form of the cognitive bias may vary, but once these negative thoughts begin, the resultant elevations of anxiety may exacerbate somatic symptoms and distress over those symptoms. Catastrophic thoughts about somatic symptoms are not only elevated among those with somatic symptom disorders, but they predict more severe pain and fatigue among those with medical conditions (Rief & Martin, 2014).

In Chapter 6, we described a very similar cognitive process as part of panic disorder. That is, people with panic disorder are likely to overreact to physiological symptoms. In panic disorder, the person often believes that the symptoms are a sign of an immediate threat (e.g., a heart attack), whereas in somatic symptom disorder, the person believes the symptoms are a sign of an underlying long-term disease (e.g., cancer or AIDS).

A growing body of experimental research shows how negative thoughts might even trigger the onset of some somatic symptoms. In one example of this work, researchers randomly assigned participants to watch a TV documentary about the effects of Wi–Fi exposure on somatic symptoms or to watch a control film (Witthoft & Rubin, 2013). After the films, experimenters falsely stated they would be exposing all participants to a new type of Wi–Fi signal for 15 minutes; in actuality no Wi–Fi signals were emitted during that time. Those who had seen the documentary reported significant increases in physical symptoms, including GI, head, and skin-tingling symptoms after the sham Wi–Fi exposure, and particularly so if they were more anxious at baseline. Those who saw the control film did not report these symptoms. This is exactly what theory would predict—beliefs predicted physical symptoms even when there was no medical explanation for those symptoms. These findings illustrate that worrying about possible symptoms can make them more likely to occur, and the effect of those worries may be particularly strong for those who are already anxious.

Fear of impending illness is likely to have behavioral consequences. The person may assume the role of being sick and avoid work, exercise, and social activities (Martin & Jacobi, 2006), and these avoidant behaviors in turn can intensify poor health. Some people are reinforced for disengagement from these key roles. For example, people receive disability payments based on how much symptoms interfere with their daily activities.

Beyond avoidance, many with health anxiety engage in "safety behaviors." As we discussed in Chapter 7, people use safety behaviors to try to reduce immediate anxiety. In health anxiety, safety behaviors involve seeking reassurance from doctors, family members, and the Internet, or taking other steps to protect health (e.g., conducting self-exams, disinfecting household surfaces). Safety behaviors may help quell anxiety briefly, and reassurance-seeking can elicit attention or sympathy. Nonetheless, safety behaviors are believed to be counterproductive for several reasons. Some may come to believe that they have warded off serious health problems only because they engaged in safety behaviors. Safety behaviors also prevent focused exposure to the initial somatic symptom and, as such, prevent the person from extinguishing their fear of that symptom. At the same time, safety behaviors may keep the person focused on potential health problems.

In an experiment designed to test whether safety behaviors intensify health anxiety, researchers randomly assigned undergraduates to a control condition or an experimental condition for 1 week. Those in the control condition were asked to monitor their use of health safety behaviors each day. Those in the experimental condition were asked to engage in health safety behaviors as many times per day as they could. To foster this, they were given diagrams of how to conduct breast or testicular self-exams, bottles of hand sanitizer to be carried at all times, disinfectant wipes to clean their office and home, tongue depressors to check their throats each day, and instructions for avoiding contamination. The experimental manipulation worked: Persons in the experimental group engaged in an average of 116 safety behaviors during the week compared with an average of 26 for the control participants. More importantly, after 1 week of engaging in safety behavior, the experimental group developed a set of new symptoms. They reported anxiety about their health, worries that they could have a serious illness, and a lack of willingness to approach a potentially contaminated object (e.g., a dirty tissue) in a lab task. The control group showed none of these changes. Taken together, the findings indicate that health safety behaviors can intensify health anxiety (at least until participants were debriefed). Of course, it would be unethical to conduct this experiment in a clinical population, and so caution is warranted in interpreting how well these effects generalize to those with diagnosable disorders (Olatunji, Etzel, et al., 2011).

Taken together, many different behavioral and cognitive factors can maintain and intensify health anxiety. We'll return to many of these factors when we discuss cognitive behavioral therapy for health anxiety.

Etiology of Conversion Disorder

We mentioned earlier that stress is a potential trigger of the somatic symptom and related disorders. To evaluate this idea, researchers have tested whether conversion disorder might be triggered by overwhelming stress and by difficulty coping with the resultant emotions. Although those with conversion disorder often report a history of trauma and life events, the rates are not distinct compared to other psychological disorders (van der Hoeven, Broersma, et al., 2015). Moreover, findings are inconsistent on the coping and emotion profiles of those with conversion disorder (Roberts & Reuber, 2014). In this section, then, we focus on the idea that conversion disorder symptoms can be produced unconsciously. Then we consider sociocultural factors.

Psychodynamic and Neuroscience Perspectives on the Unconscious in Conversion Disorder Conversion disorder occupies a central place in psychodynamic theories because the symptoms provide a clear example of the role of the unconscious. Consider trying to diagnose a woman who says that she awoke one morning with a paralyzed left arm. Assume that a series of neurological tests reveal no neurological disorder. Perhaps she has decided to fake paralysis to achieve some end—this would be an example of malingering (see Focus on Discovery 8.2). But what if you believe her? You would almost have to conclude that unconscious processes were operating. On a conscious level, she is telling the truth; she believes that her arm is paralyzed. On an unconscious level, some psychological factor is at work, making her unable to move her arm despite the absence of any physical cause. Psychodynamic theory suggests that the physical symptom is a response to an unconscious psychological conflict.

Neuroscience supports the idea that much of our perceptual processing may operate outside our conscious awareness. Take the example of unexplained blindness. The vision system relies on a set of brain regions. If these regions are not coordinated in an overarching conscious fashion, the brain may process some visual input such that the person can do well on certain visual tests yet still lack a conscious sense of "seeing" certain types of stimuli. In one neuroimaging case study, a person with a conversion disorder involving blindness showed activity in brain regions involved with processing low levels of visual stimuli (such as lines and squares) but showed diminished activity in higher-level visual cortex regions involved in integrating visual inputs into a consolidated whole (such as a house) (Becker, Scheele, et al., 2013). Because people may not be processing visual inputs at a higher level, they can truthfully claim that they cannot see, even when tests suggest that they can.

This idea of neural processing outside consciousness can be applied to motor symptoms in conversion disorder. Consider a medically inexplicable tremor. If monitoring systems in the brain do not process the initiation of motor movement, the person could experience the tremor as involuntary (Brown, 2016). Consistent with the idea that people could be unaware of their own initiation of tremors, some people with medically unexplained tremors show diminished activation of association cortices involved in conscious processing (Hallett, 2016). Although a growing number of small studies provides these types of illustrations that brain systems involved in awareness *could* be involved, neuroimaging findings remain mixed, and no central neural process has emerged that could explain the lack of conscious awareness across patients with DID (Aybek & Vuilleumier, 2016).

Social and Cultural Factors in Conversion Disorder Social and cultural factors shape the symptoms of conversion disorder. For example, symptoms of conversion disorder are more common among people from rural areas and people of lower socioeconomic status (Binzer & Kullgren, 1996). The influence of social factors is also supported by the many documented cases of "mass hysteria," in which a group of people with close contact, such as schoolmates or coworkers, develop inexplicable medical symptoms that would likely warrant a diagnosis of conversion disorder. Consider the outbreak of seizure-type symptoms (a relatively common conversion symptom) in a cotton-processing facility, described in 1787. "A girl . . . put a mouse into the breast of another girl who had great dread of mice. She was immediately thrown into a fit and continued in it with the most violent convulsions for 24 hours. On the following day, three more girls were seized in the same manner, and the day after, six more." Within 3 days, 24 girls were affected. "The alarm was so great, that the whole work . . . was totally stopped" (Dr. St. Clare, 1787, *Gentleman's Magazine*, p. 268). Incidents like this suggest that social factors, including modeling, shape how conversion symptoms unfold.

Quick Summary

Neurobiological models suggest that some people may have a propensity toward hyperactivity in those regions of the brain involved in processing the unpleasantness of somatic sensations, including the anterior cingulate and the rostral anterior insula. These brain regions are also implicated in negative emotions and depression. Cognitive behavioral models focus on attention to and interpretation of somatic symptoms. Behavioral responses to health concerns can include disengagement and isolation, as well as excessive safety and help-seeking behavior.

Psychodynamic theories of conversion disorder have focused on the idea that people can be unaware (unconscious) of their perceptions or their own control of a motor symptom like tremor. Social influences on conversion disorder seem important, particularly given that sometimes cases cluster within small groups of co-workers or schoolmates.

Check Your Knowledge 8.5

True or false?

1. Conversion disorder is highly heritable.
2. The psychodynamic model of conversion disorder emphasizes unconscious perceptions.
3. Somatic symptom disorder involves hyperactivation of the cerebellum.

Treatment of Somatic Symptom and Related Disorders

One of the major obstacles to treatment is that most people with somatic symptom-related disorders usually want medical care, not mental health care. Patients may resent mental health referrals from their physician because they interpret such a referral as a sign that the doctor thinks the illness is "all in their head." It is not a good idea for a provider to try to convince patients that psychological factors are causing the symptoms. Most somatic and pain concerns have both physical and psychological components, and so it is unwise for the physician to debate the source of these symptoms with the patient. For many patients, a gentle reminder of the mind–body connection can enhance their willingness to consider psychological treatment. With this as a backdrop, we consider interventions for those with the intense health anxiety of somatic symptom disorder and illness anxiety, and then consider novel evidence for cognitive behavioral treatment of conversion disorders.

Somatic Symptom Disorder and Illness Anxiety Disorder

Because most people with somatic symptom-related disorders seek treatment through general practitioners, one approach has been to teach primary care teams to tailor care for people with somatic symptom-related disorders. The goal is to establish a strong doctor–patient relationship that bolsters the patient's sense of trust and comfort, so that the patient will feel more reassured about his or her health. In one study, researchers randomly assigned patients with distressing and medically unexplained gastrointestinal symptoms to receive standard care or high levels of warmth, attention, and reassurance from doctors. Those who received high levels of support showed more improvement in symptoms and quality of life over the next 6 weeks compared to those who received standard care (Kaptchuk, Kelley, et al., 2008).

Other health care system interventions involve alerting physicians when a patient is an intensive user of health care services so as to minimize the use of diagnostic tests and medications. This type of intervention with physicians can reduce the use of costly health care services (Konnopka, Schaefert, et al., 2012).

In addition to interventions by medical providers, cognitive behavioral therapy (CBT) includes many different techniques to help people with somatic symptom-related disorders. As illustrated by our Clinical Case of Louis, these techniques include helping people (1) identify and change the emotions that trigger somatic concerns, (2) change cognitions regarding their somatic symptoms, and (3) change behaviors to improve social interactions (Looper & Kirmayer, 2002). Family interventions are also often applied. Let's review each of these.

As we discussed earlier, the negative emotions that accompany anxiety and depressive disorders often trigger physiological symptoms and intensify the distress about those somatic symptoms. It should be no surprise that treating anxiety and depression often reduces somatic symptoms, and that providers use many of the techniques that we discussed in Chapters 5 and 6 (Payne & Blanchard, 1995).

Therapists also use many different cognitive strategies to treat somatic symptom and related disorders. Some involve training people to pay less attention to their body. Alternatively, cognitive strategies might help people identify and challenge negative thoughts about their health (Warwick & Salkovskis, 2001). The person who struggles with thoughts such as "I cannot cope with this pain" might be taught to make more positive self-statements, such as "I've been able to manage bouts of pain on other days, and I'll get through this one as well" (Christensen, Frostholm, et al., 2015).

Behavioral techniques might help people reduce safety behaviors, resume healthy activities, and rebuild a lifestyle damaged by too much focus on illness-related concerns (Warwick & Salkovskis, 2001). Maria, the woman described earlier, revealed that she was extremely anxious about her shaky marriage and about situations in which other people might judge her. Couples therapy, assertiveness training, and social skills training—for example, coaching Maria in effective ways to approach and talk to people—could help her improve her social interactions. In general, it is advisable to focus less on what patients cannot do because of their pain and somatic symptoms and more on encouraging them to reengage in satisfying activities and to gain a greater sense of control.

Behavioral and family approaches could help change Maria's reliance on playing the role of a sick person (Warwick & Salkovskis, 2001). If Maria's family members have adjusted to her illness by reinforcing her avoidance of responsibilities, family therapy might help. A therapist might teach family members about operant conditioning to reduce the amount of attention (reinforcement) they give the person's somatic symptoms.

CBT is more efficacious in reducing health concerns, depression, and anxiety than standard medical care or psychodynamic treatment of somatic symptom-related disorders (Olatunji, Kauffman, et al., 2014). In one study, CBT was as effective as antidepressant treatment in reducing illness anxiety symptoms (Greeven, van Balkom, et al., 2007). In addition to reducing distress and anxiety, CBT produces reductions in the actual somatic symptoms compared to control treatment, but the effects are small (van Dessel, den Boeft, et al., 2014). That is, these interventions may do more to reduce the *distress* about somatic symptoms than they do to reduce the actual somatic symptoms.

Researchers have also examined several new approaches to treatment. One large-scale study found that Internet-based CBT was not potent enough to reduce health anxiety levels to a normative range (Tyrer, Tyrer, & Barrett, 2013). More positive effects were observed by teaching people to practice mindfulness meditation daily. Participants who learned mindfulness reported less health anxiety than control participants who took part in standard medical care (McManus, Surawy, et al., 2012). The improvements associated with mindfulness practice were sustained at a 1-year follow-up assessment.

When the focus of somatic symptom disorder is on pain, several techniques can be helpful. Low-dose antidepressants, CBT, hypnosis, and a variant of CBT called acceptance and commitment therapy (ACT) have each been found to be helpful in randomized controlled treatments (Ehde, Dillworth, & Turner, 2014; Fishbain, Cutler, et al., 2000; Jensen & Patterson, 2014; Veehof, Oskam, et al., 2011). In ACT, the therapist encourages the client to adopt a more accepting attitude toward pain, suffering, and moments of depression and anxiety, and to view these as a natural part of life. The person might be coached not to struggle so intensely to avoid these difficult moments (McCracken & Vowles, 2014). Although pain is harder to treat than is health anxiety (Rief & Martin, 2014), these treatments are preferred over opioid medications, which are highly addictive (Streltzer & Johansen, 2006).

Conversion Disorder

Two small randomized controlled trials indicate beneficial effects of CBT for specific forms of conversion disorder. In one trial, researchers randomly assigned 61 individuals who had medically unexplained gait disorders, such as limping or foot dragging, to immediate treatment or to a wait list control (Jordbru, Smedstad, et al., 2014). As a first step in treatment, therapists explained to patients and their family members that medical tests had not revealed an explanation for gait disturbance but disconnections in the interface of the nervous system and the body are common. Patients were then hospitalized for 3 weeks, so that they could take part in daily physical training. The CBT had two major components. First, patients were reinforced for taking part in the training. Second, to avoid reinforcing conversion symptoms, the treatment team ignored ongoing signs of gait disturbance. Patients showed large increases in their mobility, independence, and quality of life during the CBT intervention, and those gains were present one year later. In a second trial, researchers found that 12 sessions of outpatient CBT was more helpful than standard medical care in reducing the rate of non-epileptic seizures (Goldstein, Chalder, et al., 2010). Although these initial studies on the treatment of conversion disorder are promising, many patients with conversion disorder are not willing to take part in psychological treatments (Lehn, Gelauff, et al., 2016).

Clinical Case

Louis

Louis, a 66-year-old man, was referred to a psychiatrist by his cardiologist because of health anxiety. Although Louis acknowledged years of depressive and anxiety symptoms, he reported being much more concerned about his potential for heart problems. Several years before, he had developed intermittent symptoms of heart palpitations and chest pressure. Although extensive medical tests were within the normal range, he continued to seek additional tests. He had gathered a thick file of articles on cardiovascular conditions, had adopted strenuous diet and exercise routines, and had stopped all activities that might be too exciting and therefore challenging to his heart, such as travel and sex. He had even retired early from running his restaurant. By the time he sought treatment, he was measuring his blood pressure four times a day using two machines so that he could average the readings, and he was keeping extensive logs of his blood pressure readings.

Before treatment could begin, Louis had to understand that the way he was thinking about his physical symptoms was intensifying those physical symptoms as well as creating emotional distress. His therapist taught him a model of symptom amplification, in which initial physical symptoms are exacerbated by negative thoughts and emotions. The therapist used statements such as "A headache you believe is due to a brain tumor hurts much more than a headache you believe is due to eye strain." Once Louis understood that his thoughts and behavior might be increasing his medical concerns, treatment focused on four goals. First, the therapist coached Louis to identify one doctor with whom to routinely discuss health concerns and to stop seeking multiple medical opinions. Second, the therapist taught Louis to reduce the time spent engaging in illness-related safety behaviors, such as logging his blood pressure. His therapist showed him that these behaviors were actually increasing his anxiety rather than providing relief. Third, the therapist taught Louis to consider the negative and pessimistic thoughts he had in response to his

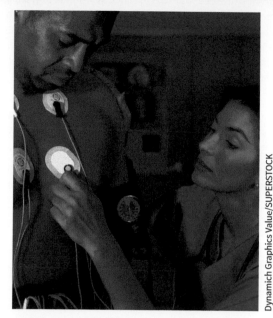

Dynamich Graphics Value/SUPERSTOCK

People with health anxiety are not easily reassured that they are well, even when extensive medical tests indicate no problems.

symptoms. For example, the therapist and Louis identified ways in which he tended to catastrophize harmless physical sensations by viewing them as evidence for heart disease. Louis began to consider more benign reasons for his physical symptoms. Finally, Louis was encouraged to build other aspects of his life to diminish the focus on physical symptoms, and in response, he began to consult for restaurants. Taken together, these interventions helped Louis reduce his anxiety, diminish his focus on and concern about his health, and begin to lead a more enjoyable life.

Adapted from Barsky, 2006.

Check Your Knowledge 8.6

1. Describe outcomes that have been shown to be improved using CBT with somatic symptom and related disorders.

2. Describe treatments to reduce pain in somatic symptom and related disorders.

Summary

Dissociative Disorders

- Dissociative disorders are defined by disruptions in the conscious awareness of experience, memory, or identity.

- As described in Table 8.1, the DSM-5 dissociative disorders include depersonalization/derealization disorder, dissociative amnesia, and dissociative identity disorder.

- Most of the writing about the causes of dissociative disorders focuses on dissociative identity disorder. People with dissociative identity disorder very often report severe physical or sexual abuse during childhood. One model, the posttraumatic model, suggests that extensive reliance on dissociation to fend off overwhelming feelings from abuse puts people at risk for developing dissociative identity disorder. The sociocognitive model, though, proposes that these symptoms are elicited by treatment. Proponents of the sociocognitive model point out that some therapists use strategies that suggest such symptoms to people, and that most people do not recognize the presence of any alters until after they see a therapist. Although one of the defining features of DID is the lack of shared memories among alters, evidence suggests that alters may share more memories than they report. DID can also be role-played effectively.

- Regardless of theoretical orientation, all clinicians focus their treatment efforts on helping clients cope with anxiety, face fears more directly, and operate in a manner that integrates their memory and consciousness.

- Psychodynamic treatment is perhaps the most commonly used treatment for dissociative disorders, but some of the techniques involved, such as hypnosis and age regression, may make symptoms worse.

Somatic Symptom and Related Disorders

- Somatic symptom and related disorders share a common focus on physical symptoms. As shown in Table 8.2, the major somatic symptom-related disorders include somatic symptom disorder, illness anxiety disorder, and conversion disorder.

- The somatic symptom-related disorders do not appear to be heritable.

- Neurobiological models suggest that key brain regions involved in processing the unpleasantness of bodily sensations may be hyperactive among people with somatic symptom-related disorders.

These regions include the anterior cingulate and the anterior insula. Cognitive variables are also important: Some people are overly attentive to physical concerns and make overly negative interpretations about these symptoms and their implications. Avoidance may lead to health declines, and behavioral reinforcement may maintain help-seeking behavior. Safety behaviors may prolong and intensify health anxiety.

- Early imaging data is consistent with the psychodynamic idea that people with conversion disorder may not be conscious of their perceptions (in the case of blindness) or their control of movements (in the case of movement symptoms). Sociocultural factors also appear important in conversion disorder.

- People with somatic symptom-related disorders often resent being referred for mental health care. Programs that involve primary care physicians in addressing these symptoms by providing warmth and reassurance while limiting medical tests have been shown to be helpful. Cognitive behavioral treatments of somatic symptoms, which are efficacious approaches to addressing the distress over somatic symptoms, try to relieve depressive and anxious symptoms, to reduce the excessive attention to bodily cues, to address the overly negative interpretations of physical symptoms, and to reinforce behavior that is not consistent with the sick role. Meditation may also help patients reduce their health focus and anxiety. When pain is a primary concern in somatic symptom disorder, CBT, hypnosis, ACT, and low doses of antidepressant medication may be helpful. Recent trials indicate that CBT may be helpful for conversion disorder, but many patients do not want to take part in this treatment.

Answers to Check Your Knowledge Questions

8.1 1. assumption of a new identity or bewildered wandering; 2. a distinct personality; 3. Before 1800, very few cases were recorded. There was a marked increase with media attention, and diagnostic criteria were introduced in the 1970s.

8.2 1. T; 2. Base rates of the disorder increased with media attention to the disorder; the therapists who see the most DID cases rely on techniques like hypnosis that could produce alters; most clients are unaware of alters until after they receive psychotherapy; DID can be role-played; most people with DID do share memories among alters when sophisticated memory tests are used.

8.3 1. 0; 2. None; 3. age repression and hypnosis

8.4 1. b; 2. a; 3. d; At least one somatic symptom is present in somatic symptom disorder, but no significant somatic symptoms are present in illness anxiety disorder.

8.5 1. F; 2. T; 3. F

8.6 1. Diminished health anxiety, lower anxiety and depression, slightly decreased pain and somatic symptoms in somatic symptom-related disorders, improved gait disturbance and lowered rate of non-epileptic seizures in conversion disorders; 2. CBT, hypnosis, ACT, and low-dose antidepressants

Key Terms

conversion disorder
depersonalization
depersonalization/derealization disorder
derealization
dissociation
dissociative amnesia
dissociative disorders

dissociative identity disorder (DID)
explicit memory
factitious disorder
fugue subtype
iatrogenic
illness anxiety disorder
implicit memory

malingering
posttraumatic model of DID
sociocognitive model of DID
somatic symptom disorder
somatic symptom and related disorders

CHAPTER 9

Schizophrenia

LEARNING GOALS

1. Describe the clinical symptoms of schizophrenia, including positive, negative, and disorganized symptoms.

2. Differentiate the genetic factors, both behavioral and molecular, in the etiology of schizophrenia.

3. Distinguish the medication treatments and psychological treatments for schizophrenia.

Clinical Case

A Woman With Schizophrenia

All of a sudden things weren't going so well. I began to lose control of my life and, most of all, myself. I couldn't concentrate on my schoolwork, I couldn't sleep, and when I did sleep, I had dreams about dying. I was afraid to go to class, imagined that people were talking about me, and on top of that I heard voices. I called my mother in Pittsburgh and asked for her advice. She told me to move off campus into an apartment with my sister.

After I moved in with my sister, things got worse. I was afraid to go outside, and when I looked out of the window, it seemed that everyone outside was yelling, "Kill her, kill her." My sister forced me to go to school. I would go out of the house until I knew she had gone to work; then I would return home. Things continued to get worse. I imagined that I had a foul body odor, and I sometimes took up to 6 showers a day. I recall going to the grocery store one day, and I imagined that the people in the store were saying, "Get saved, Jesus is the answer." Things worsened—I couldn't remember a thing. I had a notebook full of reminders telling me what to do on that particular day. I couldn't remember my schoolwork, and I would study from 6:00 p.m. until 4:00 a.m. but never had the courage to go to class on the following day. I tried to tell my sister about it, but she didn't understand. She suggested that I see a psychiatrist, but I was afraid to go out of the house to see him.

One day I decided that I couldn't take this trauma anymore, so I took an overdose of 35 Darvon pills. At the same moment, a voice inside me said, "What did you do that for? Now you won't go to heaven." At that instant, I realized that I didn't really want to die. I wanted to live, and I was afraid. I got on the phone and called the psychiatrist whom my sister had recommended. I told him I had taken an overdose of Darvon and that I was afraid. He told me to take a taxi to the hospital. When I arrived at the hospital, I began vomiting, but I didn't pass out. Somehow, I just couldn't accept the fact that I was really going to see a psychiatrist. I thought that psychiatrists were only for crazy people, and I definitely didn't think I was crazy. As a result, I did not admit myself right away. As a matter of fact, I left the hospital and ended up meeting my sister on the way home. She told me to turn right back around because I was definitely going to be admitted. We then called my mother, and she said she would fly down the following day. (Quoted in O'Neal, 1984, pp. 109–110)

Clinical Descriptions of Schizophrenia

The young woman described in this clinical case was diagnosed with schizophrenia. **Schizophrenia** is a disorder characterized by disordered thinking, in which ideas are not logically related; faulty perception and attention; a lack of emotional expressiveness; and disturbances in behavior, such as a disheveled appearance. People with schizophrenia may withdraw from other people and from everyday reality, often into a life of odd beliefs (delusions) and hallucinations. Given that schizophrenia is associated with such widespread disruptions in a person's life, it has been difficult to uncover the causes of the disorder and develop effective methods to treat it. We still have a long way to go before we fully understand the multiple factors that trigger schizophrenia and develop treatments that are both effective and free of unpleasant side effects.

The symptoms of schizophrenia invade every aspect of a person: the way someone thinks, feels, and behaves. Not surprisingly then, these symptoms can interfere with maintaining a job, living independently, and having close relationships with other people. They can also provoke ridicule and persecution. Substance use rates are high (Blanchard, Brown, et al., 2000), perhaps reflecting an attempt to achieve some relief from the symptoms (Blanchard, Squires, et al., 1999). Moreover, the suicide rate among people with schizophrenia is high. Indeed, they are 12 times more likely to die of suicide than people in the general population. People with schizophrenia are also more likely to die from any cause than people in the general population (Laursen, Nordentoft, & Mortensen, 2014; Olfson, Gerhard, et al., 2015; Saha, Chant, & McGrath, 2007), and their mortality rates are as high as or higher than the rates for people who smoke (Chesney, Goodwin, & Fazel, 2014).

The lifetime prevalence of schizophrenia is around 1 percent, and it affects men slightly more often than women (Kirkbride, Fearon, et al., 2006; Walker, Kestler, et al., 2004). Schizophrenia is diagnosed more frequently among some groups, such as African Americans, though this likely reflects a bias among clinicians (Kirkbride et al., 2006). Schizophrenia rarely begins in childhood; it usually appears in late adolescence or early adulthood, and usually somewhat earlier in men than in women. People with schizophrenia typically have several acute episodes of their symptoms and less severe but still debilitating symptoms between episodes.

The range of symptoms in the diagnosis of schizophrenia is extensive, although people with the disorder typically have only some of these symptoms at any given time (see the DSM-5 criteria box). Schizophrenia symptoms are often described in three broad domains: positive, negative, and disorganization. The distinction among these domains has been very useful in research on etiology and treatment of schizophrenia; **Table 9.1** shows the symptoms that comprise these domains.

In the following sections, we describe in some detail the individual symptoms that make up the positive, negative, and disorganized domains.

Positive Symptoms

Positive symptoms comprise excesses and distortions, and include hallucinations and delusions. For the most part, acute episodes of schizophrenia are characterized by positive symptoms.

Delusions   No doubt all of us at one time or another have been concerned because we believed that others thought ill of us. Some of the time this belief may be justified. After all, who

TABLE 9.1   **Summary of the Major Symptom Domains in Schizophrenia**

Positive Symptoms	Negative Symptoms	Disorganized Symptoms
Delusions, hallucinations	Avolition, alogia, anhedonia, blunted affect, asociality	Disorganized behavior, disorganized speech

is universally loved? Consider, though, the anguish you would feel if you were firmly convinced that many people did not like you—indeed, that they disliked you so much that they were plotting against you. Imagine that your persecutors have sophisticated listening devices that let them tune in on your most private conversations and gather evidence in a plot to discredit you. Those around you, including your loved ones, are unable to reassure you that people are not spying on you. Even your closest friends are gradually joining forces with your tormentor. Anxious and angry, you begin taking counteractions against your persecutors. You carefully check any new room you enter for listening devices. When you meet people for the first time, you question them at great length to determine whether they are part of the plot against you.

Such **delusions**, which are beliefs contrary to reality and firmly held despite disconfirming evidence, are common positive symptoms of schizophrenia. Delusions may take several forms, including the following:

Believing that others are taking special notice is a common paranoid delusion.

- A person may believe that thoughts that are not his or her own have been placed in his or her mind by an external source; this is called *thought insertion*. For example, a woman may believe that the government has inserted a computer chip in her brain so that thoughts can be inserted into her head.

- A person may believe that his or her thoughts are broadcast or transmitted, so that others know what he or she is thinking; this is called *thought broadcasting*. When walking down the street, a man may look suspiciously at passersby, thinking that they are able to hear what he is thinking even though he is not saying anything out loud.

- A person may believe that an external force controls his or her feelings or behaviors. For example, a person may believe that his or her behavior is being controlled by the signals emitted from cell phone towers.

- A person may have **grandiose delusions**, an exaggerated sense of his or her own importance, power, knowledge, or identity. For example, a woman may believe that she can cause the wind to change direction just by moving her hands.

- A person may have **ideas of reference**, incorporating unimportant events within a delusional framework and reading personal significance into the trivial activities of others. For instance, people with this symptom might think that overheard segments of conversations are about them, that the frequent appearance of the same person on a street where they customarily walk means that they are being watched, and that what they see on TV or read in magazines somehow refers to them.

Hallucinations

People with schizophrenia frequently report that the world seems somehow different or even unreal to them. As in the Clinical Case at the beginning of this chapter, some people report difficulties in paying attention to what is happening around them.

The most dramatic examples of this are **hallucinations**—sensory experiences in the absence of any relevant stimulation from the environment. They are more often auditory than visual.

Some people with schizophrenia report hearing their own thoughts spoken by another voice. Other people may claim that they hear voices arguing, and others hear voices commenting on their behavior. Many people with schizophrenia experience their hallucinations as frightening or annoying. In one study of nearly 200 people with schizophrenia, those whose hallucinations were longer, louder, more frequent, and experienced in the third person found the hallucinations unpleasant. Hallucinations that were believed to come from a known person were experienced more positively (Copolov, Mackinnon, & Trauer, 2004).

Some theorists propose that people who have auditory hallucinations misattribute their own voice as being someone else's voice. Behavioral studies have shown that people with hallucinations are more likely to misattribute recordings of their own speech to a different source than are people without hallucinations or healthy controls (Allen, Johns, et al., 2004). Neuroimaging studies have examined what happens in the brain during auditory hallucinations. These studies have found greater activity in Broca's area (an area of the frontal cortex that supports our ability to produce speech) and in Wernicke's area (an area of the temporal cortex that supports our ability to understand speech) when people with schizophrenia report hearing voices (Curcic-Blake, Liemburg, et al., 2013). These data suggest that there is a problem in the connections between the frontal lobe areas that enable the production of speech and the temporal lobe areas that enable the understanding of speech (Ford, Mathalon, et al., 2002). A meta-analysis of 10 neuroimaging studies found strongest activation in those areas of the brain associated with speech production (e.g., Broca's area), but it also found activation in areas associated with speech processing and understanding in the temporal lobes (Jardri, Pouchet, et al., 2011).

Although delusions and hallucinations are often considered the quintessential symptoms of schizophrenia, they are not specific to schizophrenia and can occur in other psychological disorders, including bipolar disorder, major depressive disorder, and substance use disorders, to name just a few. Someone presenting with these symptoms may be incorrectly given a diagnosis of schizophrenia. In **Focus on Discovery 9.1**, we discuss the case of a young woman who had these symptoms but who most definitely did not have schizophrenia. This case points to the importance of conducting thorough assessments, as we discussed in Chapter 3.

Focus on Discovery 9.1

An Example of Misdiagnosis

A successful young woman who is a reporter for a major city newspaper begins to feel inklings of paranoia. At first, it doesn't seem like paranoia, but more like jealousy. She looks through her boyfriend's drawers for evidence he is cheating on her—something not atypical for new relationships.

But later, she begins to think people are taking special notice of her, that she is receiving special messages from TV, that her family is plotting against her. People are talking about her, whispering her name. People are spying on her and trying to hurt her. When others don't take her concerns seriously, she erupts into rages and becomes very agitated, and then without warning, begins sobbing uncontrollably.

She reports that she sees bright colors; then she reports having visions and seeing things that are most definitely not observed by others. In short, she begins to have visual hallucinations.

She begins to feel like she is having an out-of-body experience, like she is looking down on herself from above, watching her every move. She writes down random musings in a journal, but the thoughts are not connected and are very disorganized. Then, she has a seizure.

What can account for these symptoms, including hallucinations, paranoid delusions, disorganized thinking and behavior; and rapidly changing moods? Is it schizophrenia? Bipolar disorder with psychotic features? A substance use disorder? A seizure disorder? All of these are plausible diagnoses for the symptoms this young woman presented with. Yet none of them was correct.

In her beautifully written book, *Brain on Fire: My Month of Madness,* Susannah Cahalan writes about her experience with these symptoms over the course of a month. She did not remember

Tom Gannam/AP Images

In her book *Brain on Fire: My Month of Madness,* Susannah Cahalan described her experiences with a rare condition with symptoms very similar to those of schizophrenia.

many of these experiences and instead had to piece together what happened to her based on reports from family and friends who cared for her as well as her records that were collected once she was hospitalized because she was considered a danger to herself.

When Susannah later watched these videotapes of her disorganized and bizarre behavior and ramblings, she did not recognize herself.

She was under the care of neurologists in the hospital who were concerned she had a seizure disorder or some other neurological condition. Yet they did not fully rule out a psychological disorder because her paranoia, hallucinations, and disorganization were so profound. And her MRIs and CT scans came back normal as did her blood tests, suggesting that she did not have an infection or a disease that had attacked the brain. The neurologists consulted psychiatrists who felt certain that she had some type of psychotic disorder. She was given antipsychotic medications. She began to develop motor symptoms that looked like catatonia. She wasn't getting any better.

Finally, the results of a second lumbar puncture (spinal tap) pointed to a possible clue. She had a very high number of white blood cells in her cerebrospinal fluid (CSF). Susannah's brain was quite literally inflamed or "on fire" as the title of her book describes. Further neuropsychological testing (see Chapter 3) revealed that she was experiencing left neglect, and this indicated that it was primarily the right side of her brain that was inflamed. Her immune system was not responding to an infection, instead it was attacking her healthy neurons as if they were infectious agents. Additional testing revealed that her immune system was attacking specific neurons with NMDA (N-methyl-D-aspartate acid) receptors. As we discuss later in this chapter, new treatments for schizophrenia are targeting NMDA receptors (if these receptors are blocked too much, psychotic symptoms can occur). Susannah was having what is called an "autoimmune" reaction, meaning the immune system was automatically going off for no identifiable reason and it was wreaking havoc on neurons with NMDA receptors, causing the paranoia, hallucinations, catatonia, and other symptoms. Her official diagnosis was "anti-NMDA-receptor-autoimmune encephalitis," an extremely rare condition that was only first identified in 2005 (Dalmau, Tüzün, et al., 2007; Vitaliani, Mason, et al., 2005).

At the time of her diagnosis, Susannah was just the 217th person to receive the diagnosis, and it took her doctors nearly a month to make the diagnosis. Cahalan poignantly wonders, "If it took so long for one of the best hospitals in the world to get to this step, how many other people were going untreated, diagnosed with a mental illness or condemned to a life in a nursing home or a psychiatric ward?" (Cahalan, 2012, p. 151).

Given that anti-NMDA-receptor-autoimmune encephalitis is so rare, it is not likely that a huge number of people with schizophrenia are misdiagnosed. In fact, recent research has found that some people early in the course of schizophrenia have the NMDA antibodies but not anti-NMDA-receptor-autoimmune encephalitis (Steiner, Walter, et al., 2013). Still, Cahalan presents an important cautionary tale about diagnosis of psychological disorders. Since we do not yet have a blood or brain test for schizophrenia, the diagnosis is made based on the set of observed behavioral symptoms. Yet, as we have seen, these symptoms can occur in other disorders besides the psychological disorders we cover in this book. Thus, mental health professionals would do well not to be too quick to make a diagnosis of schizophrenia or bipolar disorder or any psychological disorder and instead consider that other factors might be contributing to the symptoms.

In Susannah's case, she was successfully treated over the course of several months with a combination of steroids to reduce the brain inflammation, plasma exchange (taking blood out of the body, treating the plasma to get rid of anti-NMDA antibodies, and returning the blood), and an intravenous immunoglobulin treatment. She also attended several cognitive rehabilitation sessions to help restore cognitive functions like planning, memory, and attention that were disrupted by the inflammation in her brain. She returned to work 7 months after her hospitalization, and she wrote a newspaper article 8 months after her diagnosis. Her book was published 3 years later.

Negative Symptoms

The **negative symptoms** of schizophrenia consist of behavioral deficits in motivation, pleasure, social closeness, and emotion expression (Kirkpatrick, Fenton, et al., 2006). These symptoms tend to endure beyond an acute episode and have profound effects on the lives of people with schizophrenia. They are also important prognostically; the presence of many negative symptoms is a strong predictor of a poor quality of life (e.g., occupational impairment, few friends) 2 years following hospitalization (Ho, Nopoulos, et al., 1998; Milev, Ho, et al., 2005; Siegel, Irani, et al., 2006).

Avolition   Apathy, or **avolition**, refers to a lack of motivation and a seeming absence of interest in or an inability to persist in what are usually routine activities, including work or school, hobbies, or social activities. For example, people with avolition may not be motivated to go to a movie or hang out with friends. They may have difficulty persisting at work, school, or household chores and may spend much of their time sitting around doing nothing. One study examined the types of motivation deficits in schizophrenia by interviewing people with and without schizophrenia four times a day for 7 days about their daily goals using EMA (ecological momentary assessment; see Chapter 3). The researchers found that people with schizophrenia were less motivated by goals about autonomy (self-expression), gaining new knowledge or skills, or praise by others compared to people without schizophrenia but were more motivated by goals that had to do with reducing boredom (Gard, Sanchez, et al., 2014). People with schizophrenia were equally motivated, however, by goals that had to do with relatedness to others and with avoiding a negative outcome (e.g., criticism). Thus, it appears that people with schizophrenia may have trouble with motivation for certain life areas but not for others.

Asociality   Some people with schizophrenia have severe impairments in social relationships, referred to as **asociality**. They may have few friends, poor social skills, and very little interest in being with other people. They may not desire close relationships with family, friends, or romantic partners. Instead, they may wish to spend much of their time alone. When around others, people with this symptom may interact only superficially and briefly and may appear aloof or indifferent to the social interaction.

Blend Images/Superstock

ThinkStock/Superstock

People with schizophrenia who have blunted affect may not outwardly show happiness, but they will feel it as strongly as people who smile.

Anhedonia   A loss of interest in or a reported lessening of the experience of pleasure is called **anhedonia**. There are two types of pleasure experiences in the anhedonia construct. The first, called **consummatory pleasure**, refers to the amount of pleasure experienced in the moment or in the presence of something pleasurable. For example, the amount of pleasure you experience as you are eating a good meal is known as consummatory pleasure. The second type of pleasure, called **anticipatory pleasure**, refers to the amount of expected or anticipated pleasure from future events or activities. For example, the amount of pleasure you expect to receive after graduating from college is anticipatory pleasure. People with schizophrenia appear to have a deficit in anticipatory pleasure but not consummatory pleasure (Gard, Kring, et al., 2007; Kring & Caponigro, 2010). That is, when asked about expected future situations or activities that are pleasurable for most people (e.g., good food, recreational activities, social interactions) on an anhedonia questionnaire, people with schizophrenia report that they derive less pleasure from these sorts of activities than do people without schizophrenia (Gard et al., 2007; Horan, Kring, & Blanchard, 2006). However, when presented with actual pleasant activities, such as amusing films or tasty beverages, people with schizophrenia report experiencing as much pleasure as do people without schizophrenia (Gard et al., 2007). Thus, the anhedonia deficit in schizophrenia appears to be in anticipating pleasure, not experiencing pleasure in the presence of pleasurable things.

Blunted Affect   **Blunted affect** refers to a lack of outward expression of emotion. A person with this symptom may stare vacantly, the muscles of the face motionless, the eyes lifeless. When spoken to, the person may answer in a flat and toneless voice and not look at his or her conversational partner.

The concept of blunted affect refers only to the outward expression of emotion, not to the patient's inner experience, which is not impoverished at all. Over 20 different studies have shown that people with schizophrenia are much less facially expressive than are people without schizophrenia; this is true in daily life or in laboratory studies when emotionally evocative stimuli (films, pictures, foods) are presented. However, people with schizophrenia report experiencing the same amount or *even more* emotion than people without schizophrenia (Kring & Elis, 2013).

Alogia   **Alogia** refers to a significant reduction in the amount of speech. Simply put, people with this symptom do not talk much. A person may answer a question with one or two words and will not be likely to elaborate on an answer with additional detail. For example, if you ask a person with alogia to describe a happy life experience, the person might respond "getting married" and then fail to elaborate even when asked for additional information.

Although we have just described five different negative symptoms, research suggests that these symptoms can be understood more simply as representing two domains (Blanchard & Cohen, 2006; Kring, Gur, et al., 2013; Messinger, Tremeau, et al., 2011). The first domain, involving motivation, emotional experience, and sociality, is sometimes referred to as the *motivation and pleasure* domain. The second domain, involving outward expression of emotion and vocalization, is referred to as the *expression* domain.

Disorganized Symptoms

Disorganized symptoms include disorganized speech and disorganized behavior.

Disorganized Speech   Also known as *formal thought disorder*, **disorganized speech** refers to problems in organizing ideas and in speaking so that a listener can understand. The following excerpt illustrates the incoherence sometimes found in the conversation of people with schizophrenia as an interviewer tries to ask John, a person with schizophrenia, several questions.

Interviewer: Have you been nervous or tense lately?

John: No, I got a head of lettuce.

Interviewer: You got a head of lettuce? I don't understand.

John: Well, it's just a head of lettuce.

Interviewer: Tell me about lettuce. What do you mean?

John: Well . . . lettuce is a transformation of a dead cougar that suffered a relapse on the lion's toe. And he swallowed the lion and something happened. The . . . see, the . . . Gloria and Tommy, they're two heads and they're not whales. But they escaped with herds of vomit, and things like that.

Interviewer: Who are Tommy and Gloria?

John: Uh, . . . there's Joe DiMaggio, Tommy Henrich, Bill Dickey, Phil Rizzuto, John Esclavera, Del Crandell, Ted Williams, Mickey Mantle, Roy Mande, Ray Mantle, Bob Chance . . .

Interviewer: Who are they? Who are those people?

John: Dead people . . . they want to be fucked . . . by this outlaw.

Interviewer: What does all that mean?

John: Well, you see, I have to leave the hospital. I'm supposed to have an operation on my legs, you know. And it comes to be pretty sickly that I don't want to keep my legs. That's why I wish I could have an operation.

Interviewer: You want to have your legs taken off?

John: It's possible, you know.

Interviewer: Why would you want to do that?

John: I didn't have any legs to begin with. So I would imagine that if I was a fast runner, I'd be scared to be a wife, because I had a splinter inside of my head of lettuce. (Neale & Oltmanns, 1980, pp. 103–104)

Although John may make repeated references to central ideas or themes, the images and fragments of thought are not connected; it is difficult to understand what he is trying to tell the interviewer.

Speech may also be disorganized by what are called **loose associations**, or **derailment**, in which case the person may be more successful in communicating with a listener but has difficulty sticking to one topic. Steve Lopez, a reporter for the *Los Angeles Times*, befriended a man with schizophrenia named Nathaniel in the L.A. area who was a gifted musician (and also homeless). Lopez wrote about their friendship in the book *The Soloist* (see photo) (Lopez, 2008). Nathaniel often exhibited loose associations. For example, in response to a question about Beethoven, Nathaniel replied:

Cleveland doesn't have the Beethoven statue. That's a military-oriented city, occupied, preoccupied, with all the military figures of American history, the great soldiers and generals, but you don't see the musicians on parade, although you do have Severance Hall, Cleveland Music School Settlement, Ohio University Bobcats, Buckeyes of Ohio State. All the great soldiers are there from the United States Military, World War Two, Korean War, whereas in Los Angeles you have the LAPD, Los Angeles County Jail, Los Angeles Times, Mr. Steve Lopez. That's an army, right? (Quoted in Lopez, 2008, pp. 23–24)

© AF archive/Alamy

Jamie Foxx played Nathaniel in the movie version of *The Soloist* (2009).

As this quote illustrates, a person with this symptom seems to drift off on a train of associations evoked by an idea from the past.

Disorganized Behavior   People with the symptom of **disorganized behavior** may go into inexplicable bouts of agitation, dress in unusual clothes, act in a silly manner, hoard food, or collect garbage. They seem to lose the ability to organize their behavior and make it conform to community standards. They also have difficulty performing the tasks of everyday living.

In DSM-5, one manifestation of disorganized behavior is called **catatonia**. People with this symptom may gesture repeatedly, using peculiar and sometimes complex sequences of finger, hand, and arm movements, which often seem to be purposeful. Some people manifest an unusual increase in their overall level of activity, including much excitement, flailing of the limbs, and great expenditure of energy similar to that seen in mania. At the other end of the spectrum is immobility: people adopt unusual postures and maintain them for very long periods of time. Catatonia can also involve waxy flexibility—another person can move the person's limbs into positions that the person will then maintain for long periods of time.

Catatonia is seldom seen today in people with schizophrenia, perhaps because medications work effectively on these disturbed movements or postures. See **Focus on Discovery 9.2** for more details on the history of schizophrenia and its symptoms.

Focus on Discovery 9.2

History of the Concept of Schizophrenia

Two European psychiatrists, Emil Kraepelin and Eugen Bleuler (see photos), initially formulated the concept of schizophrenia. Kraepelin first described dementia praecox, his term for what we now call schizophrenia, in 1898. Although people with dementia praecox were symptomatically diverse, Kraepelin believed that they shared a common core. The term *dementia praecox* reflected what he believed was that core—an early-onset (praecox) and a progressive, inevitable intellectual deterioration (dementia). The dementia in dementia praecox is not the same as the dementias we discuss in the chapter on neurocognitive disorders (Chapter 14). Kraepelin's term referred to a general "mental enfeeblement."

Bleuler broke with Kraepelin's description on two major points: He believed that the disorder did not necessarily have an early onset, and he believed that it did not inevitably progress toward dementia. Thus, the label "dementia praecox" was no longer appropriate, and in 1908 Bleuler proposed his own term, *schizophrenia*, from the Greek words *schizein* ("to split") and *phren* ("mind"), capturing what he viewed as the essential nature of the condition.

Bleuler used a metaphor—the "breaking of associative threads" to describe the essential features of schizophrenia. For Bleuler, associative threads joined not only words but also thoughts. Thus, goal-directed, efficient thinking and communication were possible only when these hypothetical structures were intact. The notion that associative threads were disrupted in people with schizophrenia could then be used to account for the range of other symptoms.

Kraepelin had recognized that a small percentage of people with symptoms of dementia praecox did not deteriorate, but he preferred to limit this diagnostic category to people who had a poor prognosis. Bleuler's work, in contrast, led to a broader concept of the disorder. He diagnosed some people with a good prognosis as having schizophrenia, and he also diagnosed schizophrenia in many people who would have received different diagnoses from other clinicians.

Hulton Archive/Getty Images

Emil Kraepelin (1856–1926), a German psychiatrist, articulated descriptions of schizophrenia (then called dementia praecox) that have proved remarkably durable in light of contemporary research.

De Agostini Picture Library/Getty Images

Eugen Bleuler (1857–1939), a Swiss psychiatrist, contributed to our conceptions of schizophrenia and coined the term.

Other Schizophrenia Spectrum Disorders

Schizophrenia is part of the DSM-5 chapter entitled "Schizophrenia Spectrum and Other Psychotic Disorders." Two other brief psychotic disorders appearing in this chapter are **schizophreniform disorder** and **brief psychotic disorder**. The symptoms of schizophreniform disorder are the same as those of schizophrenia but last only 1 to 6 months. Brief psychotic disorder lasts from 1 day to 1 month and is often brought on by extreme stress, such as bereavement. **Schizoaffective disorder** comprises a mixture of symptoms of schizophrenia and mood disorders. The DSM-5 requires either a depressive or manic episode rather than simply mood disorder symptoms.

A person with **delusional disorder** is troubled by persistent delusions. These can be delusions of persecution or jealousy, such as the unfounded conviction that a spouse or lover is unfaithful. Other delusions seen in this disorder include grandiose delusions, delusions of erotomania (believing that one is loved by some other person, usually a complete stranger with a higher social status), and somatic delusions (e.g., delusions about body functions).

The DSM-5 added a new category to the "Conditions for Further Study" part of Section III called *attenuated psychosis syndrome.* We discuss this disorder in more detail in **Focus on Discovery 9.3**.

Focus on Discovery 9.3

Attenuated Psychosis Syndrome

When DSM-5 first considered adding a new disorder to the "Schizophrenia Spectrum and Other Psychotic Disorders" chapter called attenuated psychosis syndrome (APS), the proposal generated a good deal of discussion and debate in the field. Ultimately, APS was placed in Section III of DSM-5 that covers conditions in need of further research before being included In the DSM.

The idea for APS came from research over the past two decades that has sought to identify young people who are at risk for developing schizophrenia. These types of studies are called **clinical high-risk studies**, and the starting point for these prospective, longitudinal studies is the reliable identification of youth who present with mild positive symptoms that might later develop into schizophrenia (Miller, McGlashan, et al., 2002). Research has identified groups of young people who differ from people without these mild symptoms and from people who have a family history of schizophrenia (people studied in *familial high-risk* studies). Such people have been referred to as prodromal; the word *prodrome* refers to the early signs of a disease. Young people who show these mild symptoms differ from young people who do not in several domains, including their everyday functioning and their rate of conversion to schizophrenia spectrum disorders (Woods, Addington, et al., 2009). Between 10 and 30 percent of people meeting prodromal criteria develop a schizophrenia spectrum disorder compared with only 0.2 percent of the general population (Carpenter & van Os, 2011; Yung, Woods, et al., 2012).

What were some of the arguments in favor of adding this new category to DSM-5? First, identifying APS may help people get treatment who otherwise would go unnoticed by mental health professionals. Unfortunately, under the current health insurance system in the United States, people often cannot get treatment unless they have an official diagnosis. Second, the hope is that the identification and treatment of people with APS might prevent them from developing schizophrenia or other schizophrenia spectrum disorders.

However, there were also several arguments against adding this new category (Yung et al., 2012). First, the category itself does not yet have enough reliability and validity to support its inclusion in the DSM. Second, there is a high level of comorbidity with prodromal symptoms: over 60 percent of young people with the prodromal symptoms have a history of depression, raising the possibility that APS is really part of a mood disorder, not a schizophrenia spectrum disorder. Third, there is concern that applying a new diagnostic label, particularly to young people, might be stigmatizing or lead to discrimination. Because not all people with APS will develop schizophrenia, it may unnecessarily alarm young people and their families. Finally, although providing treatment for people with distressing or disabling attenuated positive symptoms is a laudable goal, the treatment may too closely resemble that for schizophrenia, further blurring the line between the two conditions. Indeed, there is not yet an effective treatment for APS (Carpenter & van Os, 2011).

Quick Summary

Schizophrenia is a very heterogeneous disorder. It affects men slightly more than women and typically begins in late adolescence or early adulthood. Symptoms can be distinguished as positive, negative, and disorganized. Positive symptoms include hallucinations and delusions; negative symptoms include avolition, alogia, blunted affect, anhedonia, and asociality. Together, the negative symptoms represent two domains: motivation/pleasure and expression. Disorganized symptoms include disorganized speech and disorganized behavior. Other schizophrenia spectrum disorders include schizophreniform disorder and brief psychotic disorder, which differ from schizophrenia in duration. Schizoaffective disorder involves symptoms of both schizophrenia and either a depressive or manic episode. Delusional disorder involves delusions but no other symptoms of schizophrenia. The category of attenuated psychosis syndrome, which involves positive symptoms in attenuated form that cause distress and have worsened in the past year, needs additional study.

Check Your Knowledge 9.1
(Answers are at the end of the chapter.)

List the symptom that each clinical vignette describes.

1. Charlie enjoyed going to the movies. He particularly liked to see horror movies because they made him feel really scared. His sister was surprised to learn this because when she went to the movies with Charlie, he didn't gasp out loud or show fear on his face.

2. Marlene was convinced that Christian Bale was sending her messages. In his movie *The Dark Knight*, his battles with the Joker were a signal that he was prepared to fight for them to be together. That he signed autographs at his movie opening also told her that he was trying to get in touch with her.

3. Sophia didn't want to go out to dinner with her family. She reasoned that these dinners were always the same food and conversation, so why bother? Later in the week, her mother mentioned that Sophia was not doing much around the house. Sophia said that nothing she could think of to do would be fun.

4. Jevon was talking with his doctor about the side effects of his medication. He talked about having dry mouth and then immediately began talking about cottonmouth snakes and jungle safaris and how hiking was good for your health but that Barack Obama was in better shape than George Bush.

Etiology of Schizophrenia

What can explain the scattering and disconnection of thoughts, delusions, hallucinations, and diminished motivation and emotion expression of people with schizophrenia? As we will see, many factors contribute to the cause of this complex disorder.

Genetic Factors

A good deal of research supports the idea that schizophrenia has a genetic component, as we discuss in the following sections on behavior genetics and molecular genetics research. The evidence is somewhat more convincing from behavior genetics studies, largely because they have been well replicated (see Chapter 4 on the importance of replication). Current evidence indicates that schizophrenia is genetically heterogeneous—that is, genetic factors may vary from case to case—mirroring the fact, noted earlier, that schizophrenia is symptomatically heterogeneous. As is the case for any gene or genes, they do their work via the environment, so gene–environment interaction studies are likely to help pinpoint the nature of the genetic contribution to schizophrenia (Walker, Mittal, & Tessner, 2008).

Behavior Genetics Research Family, twin, and adoption studies (described in Chapter 4) support the idea that genetic factors play a role in schizophrenia. Many behavior genetics studies of schizophrenia were conducted when the definition of schizophrenia was considerably broader than it is now. However, behavior genetics investigators collected extensive descriptive data on their samples, allowing the results to be reanalyzed later using newer diagnostic criteria.

Family Studies Table 9.2 presents a summary of the risk for schizophrenia in various relatives of people with schizophrenia. (In evaluating the figures, keep in mind that the risk for

TABLE 9.2 Summary of Major Family and Twin Studies of the Genetics of Schizophrenia

Relation to Person with Schizophrenia	Percentage with Schizophrenia
Spouse	1.00
Grandchildren	2.84
Nieces/nephews	2.65
Children	9.35
Siblings	7.30
DZ twins	12.08
MZ twins	44.30

Source: Gottesman, McGuffin, & Farmer (1987).

schizophrenia in the general population is a little less than 1 percent.) Quite clearly, relatives of people with schizophrenia are at increased risk, and the risk increases as the genetic relationship between the person with schizophrenia and the relative becomes closer (Kendler, Karkowski-Shuman, et al., 1996). Other studies have found that people with schizophrenia in their family histories have more negative symptoms than those whose families are free of schizophrenia (Malaspina, Goetz, et al., 2000); this finding suggests that negative symptoms may have a stronger genetic component.

A family study examined over 2 million people from Denmark from the Danish Civil Registration System (Gottesman, Laursen, et al., 2010). This system records all inpatient and outpatient admissions for health-related issues, including psychological disorders. The researchers examined the cumulative incidence of schizophrenia and bipolar disorder among people with one, two, or no biological parents who had been admitted for treatment for schizophrenia or bipolar disorder. They also examined the incidence of these disorders among children who had one parent admitted for schizophrenia and one parent admitted for bipolar disorder. The findings are presented in **Table 9.3**. As you might expect, the incidence of schizophrenia was highest for children who had two parents admitted for schizophrenia. The incidence of schizophrenia was also higher for people with one parent admitted for schizophrenia and one parent admitted for bipolar disorder compared with those people who had just one parent admitted for schizophrenia. These findings suggest that there may be some shared genetic vulnerability between schizophrenia and bipolar disorder; molecular genetics studies, which we turn to shortly, also suggest this link.

Family studies show that genes likely play a role in schizophrenia, but of course the relatives of a person with schizophrenia share not only genes but also common experiences. Therefore, the influence of the environment cannot be discounted in explaining the higher risks among relatives.

Twin Studies Table 9.2 also shows the risk for identical (MZ) and fraternal (DZ) twins of people with schizophrenia. The risk for MZ twins (44.3 percent), though greater than that for DZ twins (12.08 percent), is still much less than 100 percent. Similar results have been obtained in more recent studies (Cannon, Kaprio, et al., 1998; Cardno, Marshall, et al., 1999). The less-than-100-percent concordance in MZ twins is important: If genetic transmission alone accounted for schizophrenia and one identical twin had schizophrenia, the other twin would also have schizophrenia. Twin study research also suggests that negative symptoms may have a stronger genetic component than do positive symptoms (Dworkin, Lenzenwenger, & Moldin, 1987; Dworkin & Lenzenwenger, 1984).

© UK History/Alamy

Behavior genetics studies often focus on twins or, more rarely, triplets and quadruplets. In one rare case, all of the Genain quadruplet girls (not pictured), born in 1930, developed schizophrenia. Two of the still surviving sisters were recently evaluated at age 81, and both were still taking antipsychotic medication (Mirsky, Bieliauskas, et al., 2013).

TABLE 9.3   Summary of Gottesman and Colleagues (2010) Family Study

Psychopathology in Parents	Incidence of Schizophrenia
Both parents with schizophrenia	27.3%
One parent with schizophrenia	7.0%
No parent with schizophrenia	0.86%
One parent with schizophrenia and one parent with bipolar disorder	15.6%

As with family studies, of course, there is a critical problem in interpreting the results of twin studies. Common shared (e.g., child-rearing practices) and nonshared (e.g., peer relationships) environmental factors rather than common genetic factors could account for some portion of the increased risk.

A clever analysis supporting a genetic interpretation of the high risk found for identical twins was performed by Fischer (1971). She reasoned that if these rates indeed reflected a genetic effect, the twins without schizophrenia would presumably carry risk genes for schizophrenia, even though it was not expressed behaviorally, and thus might pass along an increased risk for the disorder to their children. Indeed, the rate of schizophrenia and schizophrenia-like psychoses in the children of the MZ twins without schizophrenia was 9.4 percent, while the rate among the children of the twins with schizophrenia was only slightly and nonsignificantly higher, 12.3 percent. Both rates are substantially higher than the 1 percent prevalence found in the general population, which lends further support to the importance of genetic factors in schizophrenia.

Adoption Studies   The study of children whose biological mothers had schizophrenia but who were reared from early infancy by adoptive parents without schizophrenia is another useful behavior genetics study method. Such studies eliminate the possible effects of being reared in an environment where a parent has schizophrenia.

In a now-classic study, Heston (1966) followed up 47 people born between 1915 and 1945 to women with schizophrenia who were raised by adoptive parents who did not have schizophrenia. Fifty control participants were selected from the same adoption agency that had placed the children of the women with schizophrenia. The follow-up assessment revealed that none of the controls was diagnosed with schizophrenia, versus 10.6 percent (five) of the offspring of women with schizophrenia.

Courtesy Sarnoff A. Mednick

Sarnoff Mednick, a psychologist at the University of Southern California, pioneered the use of the familial high-risk method for studying schizophrenia. He has also contributed to the hypothesis that a maternal viral infection is implicated in this disorder.

Another large study of adopted offspring of mothers with schizophrenia found similar results. In this study, the risk for developing schizophrenia or a related diagnosis among the 164 adoptees who had a biological mother with schizophrenia was 8.1 percent; the risk for the 197 control adoptees who did not have a biological parent with schizophrenia was significantly lower, at 2.3 percent (Tienari, Wynne, et al., 2000).

Familial High-Risk Studies   A different type of family study is called the **familial high-risk study**. This type of study begins with one or two biological parents with schizophrenia and follows their offspring longitudinally to identify how many of these children may develop schizophrenia and what types of childhood neurobiological and behavioral factors may predict the disorder's onset. The first familial high-risk study of schizophrenia was begun in the 1960s (Mednick & Schulsinger, 1968). The high-risk participants were 207 young people whose mothers had schizophrenia; the low-risk participants were similar in all respects to the high-risk group except that their mothers did not have schizophrenia. In 1972, the now-grown men and women were followed up with several measures, including a battery of diagnostic tests. Fifteen of the high-risk participants were diagnosed with schizophrenia; none of the control participants were so diagnosed.

In the wake of this pioneering study, other familial high-risk investigations were undertaken. The New England Family Study found that children of a parent (mother or father) with a schizophrenia spectrum disorder were six times more likely to develop a schizophrenia spectrum disorder by age 40 than children without a parent with schizophrenia (Goldstein, Buka, et al., 2010). This study also included a group of parents who had what they called "affective psychosis," including bipolar disorder or major depressive disorder with psychotic features. Children of parents with affective psychosis were not at greater risk for developing a schizophrenia spectrum disorder, but they were 14 times more likely to develop an affective psychosis than children of parents without any psychosis.

A meta-analysis of 33 familial high-risk studies that included offspring of parents with schizophrenia, bipolar disorder, or major depressive disorder found that the risk of developing schizophrenia was highest for offspring of a parent with schizophrenia. However, offspring of a parent with schizophrenia were also at nearly two times greater risk of developing any severe psychological disorder compared with offspring of parents with no psychological disorders (Rasic, Hajek, et al., 2014).

Molecular Genetics Research   Knowing that schizophrenia has a genetic component is in many ways just the starting point for research. Understanding exactly what constitutes the genetic predisposition is the challenge faced by molecular genetics researchers. As with nearly all disorders we cover in this book, the predisposition for schizophrenia is not transmitted by a single gene. Furthermore, recent molecular genetics research has found that there are multiple common genes associated with both schizophrenia and bipolar disorder (Cross-Disorder Group of the Psychiatric Genomics Consortium, 2013) suggesting that the predisposition may not even be specific to schizophrenia. Current molecular genetics research indicates that there is tremendous genetic heterogeneity associated with schizophrenia (Kim, Zerwas, et al., 2011).

Association studies try to narrow in on specific candidate genes associated with schizophrenia by establishing how often specific genes and a particular trait or behavior (i.e., phenotype) co-occur. Approximately 25 candidate genes have been identified over the past 20 years. However, the evidence for many of these candidate genes has not been replicated using newer genome-wide association studies (GWAS) that have much larger samples (Farrell, Werge, et al., 2015). Nevertheless, that several studies have found candidate genes associated with some of the behavior associated with schizophrenia suggests that researchers have identified part of the genetic puzzle to schizophrenia (Braff, 2015).

One candidate gene linked with schizophrenia that has been found in association studies and GWAS is called *DRD2* (Farrell et al., 2015). This gene encodes a specific type of dopamine receptor called D2. As we shall see in the next section when we discuss neurotransmitters, the dopamine D2 receptor has been implicated in the treatment of schizophrenia for many years.

Another candidate gene that has been linked to schizophrenia is called *COMT* and is associated with cognitive control processes that rely on the prefrontal cortex (reviewed by Goldberg & Weinberger, 2004). Many studies have demonstrated that people with schizophrenia have deficits in cognitive control processes, which include planning, working memory, and problem solving, and other studies have shown problems in the prefrontal cortex. This gene is in a region on chromosome 22 where rare mutations associated with schizophrenia have been found, as we discuss later. Although many association studies (Harrison & Weinberger, 2005; Owen, Williams, & O'Donovan, 2004) and at least one GWAS study (Sullivan, Lin, et al., 2013) have implicated the *COMT* gene in schizophrenia, it has not been found in the largest GWAS study to date (Farrell et al., 2015; Ripke, Neale, et al., 2014).

Recall from Chapter 2 that the GWAS technique allows researchers to identify rare mutations, such as CNVs (copy number variations), in genes rather than just known gene loci (locations). Mutations are changes in a gene that occur randomly and for unknown reasons. A CNV refers to an abnormal copy (a deletion or a duplication) of one or more sections of DNA in a gene (see Chapter 2). One GWAS found over 50 rare CNV mutations that were three times more common among people with schizophrenia than in people without schizophrenia across two different samples of people (Walsh, McClellan, et al., 2008). Some of the identified gene mutations are known to be associated with other presumed risk factors in the etiology of schizophrenia, including the neurotransmitter glutamate and proteins that promote the proper placement of

What do all the letters and numbers mean?

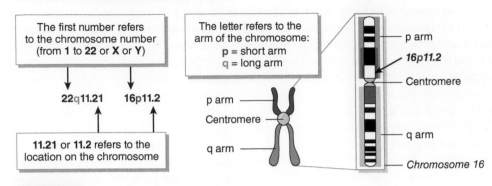

FIGURE 9.1 Decoding the language of genes.

neurons in the brain during brain development. However, even though the identified mutations were more common in people with schizophrenia than people without schizophrenia, they were identified in only about 20 percent of the people with schizophrenia.

Reviews of GWAS studies in schizophrenia have identified CNV deletions such as 22q11.21, 15q13.3, and 1q21 (see **Figure 9.1** for how to decode these tangles of letters and numbers), and these studies meet the stringent replication requirements of modern-day genetics research (Bassett, Scherer, & Brzustowicz, 2010; Kim et al., 2011). Interestingly, many observed CNVs in schizophrenia are also observed in other disorders, including autism spectrum disorder and intellectual disability, suggesting that these CNVs are not specific to schizophrenia (Fromer, Pocklington, et al., 2013).

GWAS studies of the sequence of genes have also been conducted. These studies seek to identify single nucleotide polymorphisms (SNPs; see Chapter 2) that are associated with schizophrenia. An intriguing finding from these studies is that some SNPs associated with schizophrenia are also associated with bipolar disorder. SNP studies, like the familial high-risk studies, suggest that there may be a common genetic vulnerability for both disorders (Owen, Craddock, & O'Donovan, 2010; Ruderfer, Fanous, et al., 2013; Sullivan, Daly, & O'Donovan, 2012).

Two key methodological requirements for any GWAS are (a) very large sample sizes, and (b) replication and rigorous statistical tests (see Chapter 4 for more on these topics). When looking at the entire genome—over 20,000 genes—and then comparing groups of people with and without a psychological disorder, the odds of finding a difference between groups by chance alone are large unless the sample size is very big. To address the sample size challenge, the Psychiatric Genomics Consortium (PGC) formed in 2007. The PGC includes over 800 researchers from around the world who work together by combing individual samples into very large samples for GWAS.

In 2014, the Schizophrenia Working Group of the PGC conducted the largest GWAS to date in schizophrenia, with over 36,000 people with schizophrenia and over 110,00 people without schizophrenia. They identified 108 different genetic loci containing SNPs that were associated with schizophrenia (Ripke et al., 2014). The statistical tests were very rigorous, and they conducted replication studies within this very large sample. That so many different locations were found supports the findings that schizophrenia is polygenic (involves many genes). Many of the genetic locations involved genes associated with dopamine and glutamate, two neurotransmitters associated with schizophrenia that we discuss later in the chapter. Follow-up studies from this landmark GWAS will work to identify the significance of these loci as well as their association with other disorders (Corvin & Sullivan, 2016).

We can make three important points about these GWAS findings:

(1) observed mutations are rare: CNVs account for less than 1 percent of genetic variance (Schwab & Wildenauer, 2013), and SNPs account for less than 25 percent of genetic variance (Ripke, Sanders, et al., 2011);

(2) only some people with these rare mutations have schizophrenia; and

(3) the mutations are not specific to schizophrenia.

Given that the genetic mutations are so rare, does this mean that these researchers are on the wrong track in identifying genetic vulnerability to schizophrenia? Not necessarily. These findings confirm the genetic heterogeneity of schizophrenia and the idea that people with the same disorder (schizophrenia) may not necessarily have the same genetic factors contributing to the disorder. Current genetics research supports the idea that the genetic vulnerability to schizophrenia may be made up of many rare mutations.

The Role of Neurotransmitters

Present research is examining several different neurotransmitters, such as serotonin and gluta-mate, to see what role they might play in the etiology of schizophrenia. The first neurotransmit-ter to receive substantial research attention was dopamine. This research has both helped and hindered efforts to identify causes and treatments for schizophrenia.

Indeed, it is has been challenging to pinpoint the ways in which neurotransmitters are involved in schizophrenia. This is in part because many neurotransmitter discoveries were based on finding out, quite serendipitously, that a medication alleviated the symptoms. Researchers then worked backwards to identify how the medication was influencing neurotransmitters. Translating the way a medication works into the cause of schizophrenia, however, is not that straightforward, as we illustrate next with the story of the dopamine theory.

Dopamine Theory   The theory that schizophrenia is related to excess activity of the neu-rotransmitter dopamine is based principally on the knowledge that drugs effective in treating schizophrenia reduce dopamine activity. Researchers have noted that antipsychotic drugs, in addition to being useful in treating some symptoms of schizophrenia, produce side effects resembling the symptoms of Parkinson's disease. Parkinson's disease is caused in part by low levels of dopamine in a particular area of the brain. Antipsychotic drugs fit into and thereby block a type of postsynaptic dopamine receptor called the D2 receptor (Seeman, 2013). From this knowledge about the action of the drugs that help people with schizophrenia, it was natu-ral to conjecture that schizophrenia resulted from excess activity in dopamine. Further indirect support for this dopamine theory of schizophrenia came from findings that amphetamines, which amplify dopamine activity, can produce a state that closely resembles schizophrenia in people who do not have the disorder; they can also exacerbate the symptoms of people with schizophrenia (Angrist, Lee, & Gershon, 1974).

However, as other studies progressed, this assumption turned out to be too simple to account for schizophrenia's wide range of symptoms. For example, an excess of dopamine receptors appears to be related mainly to positive and disorganization symptoms, and antipsy-chotic medications help these symptoms by blocking dopamine receptors in the mesolimbic pathway (see **Figure 9.2**), thereby lowering dopamine activity. But what about the negative symptoms? A revision to the dopamine theory hypothesized that dopamine abnormalities in the prefrontal cortex may account for negative symptoms (Davis, Kahn, et al., 1991), but evidence accumulated over the past 25 years does not strongly support this idea. However, research in the past few years has pointed to the important role of dopamine in reward and motivation in the striatum, and this has been linked with motivational deficits in schizophrenia that are part of the negative symptoms (Kring & Barch, 2014).

Nevertheless, the dopamine theory is not a complete theory of schizophrenia. Later revi-sions to the theory now suggest that the negative symptoms may be more clearly accounted for by other neurotransmitters (Howes & Kapur, 2009; Howes, McCutcheon, & Stone, 2015). In addition, it takes several weeks for antipsychotic medications to begin lessening the pos-itive symptoms of schizophrenia, although they begin blocking dopamine receptors rapidly (Davis, 1978). This disjunction between the behavioral and pharmacological effects of these medications is difficult to understand within the context of the theory. One possibility is that, although antipsychotics do indeed block D2 receptors (Yilmaz, Zai, et al., 2012), their ulti-mate therapeutic effect may result from the effect this blockade has on other brain areas and other neurotransmitter systems.

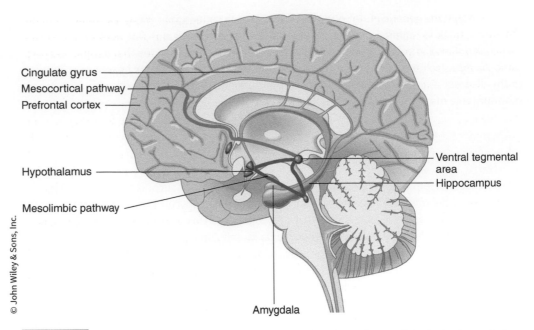

© John Wiley & Sons, Inc.

FIGURE 9.2 The brain and schizophrenia. The mesocortical pathway (in green) begins in the ventral tegmental area and projects to the prefrontal cortex. The mesolimbic pathway (in blue) also begins in the ventral tegmental area but projects to the hypothalamus, amygdala, hippocampus, and nucleus accumbens (not shown in the figure).

Because schizophrenia is a disorder with widespread symptoms covering perception, emotion, cognition, and social behavior, it is unlikely that a single neurotransmitter could account for all of them. Thus, schizophrenia researchers have cast a broader neurotransmitter net, moving away from an emphasis on dopamine.

Other Neurotransmitters   As we discuss later, newer drugs used in treating schizophrenia implicate other neurotransmitters, such as serotonin, in the disorder. These newer drugs partially block D2 receptors, but they also work by blocking the serotonin receptor 5HT2 (e.g., Burris, Molski, et al. 2002). Dopamine neurons generally modulate the activity of other neural systems; for example, in the prefrontal cortex they regulate gamma-aminobutyric acid (GABA) neurons. Thus, it is not surprising that GABA transmission is disrupted in the prefrontal cortex of people with schizophrenia (Volk, Austin, et al., 2000). Similarly, serotonin neurons regulate dopamine neurons in the mesolimbic pathway.

Glutamate, a neurotransmitter that is widespread in the human brain, may also play a role, though the evidence accumulated over the past 20 years remains suggestive and not definitive. Low levels of glutamate have been found in the cerebrospinal fluid of people with schizophrenia (Faustman, Bardgett, et al., 1999), and postmortem studies have revealed low levels of the enzyme needed to produce glutamate (Weickert, Fung, et al., 2013). Studies have found elevated levels of the amino acid homocysteine, a substance that is known to interact with the NMDA receptor among people with schizophrenia and, during their third trimester, in the blood of pregnant women whose offspring developed schizophrenia as adults (Brown, Bottiglieri, et al., 2007; Regland, Johansson, et al., 1995). The drugs PCP and ketamine can induce both positive and negative symptoms in people without schizophrenia by interfering with NMDA receptors that are part of the glutamate system (O'Donnell & Grace, 1998). Newer brain imaging methods, such as SPECT and a specialized form of MRI (see Chapter 2 for more on SPECT and MRI) called proton magnetic resonance spectroscopy, have found evidence for decreased NMDA receptor activity (Pilowsky, Bressan, et al., 2006) and lower levels of glutamate (Marsman, van den Heuvel, et al., 2013) in the prefrontal cortex. Additional evidence suggests that cognitive deficits in schizophrenia supported by the prefrontal cortex as well as symptoms of disorganization may be connected to deficits involving NMDA (Howes et al., 2015; MacDonald & Chafee, 2006).

Brain Structure and Function   Because schizophrenia affects so many domains (thought, emotion, and behavior), it makes sense that a single type of brain dysfunction cannot account for all of schizophrenia's symptoms. Among the most well-replicated findings of brain abnormalities in schizophrenia are enlargement of the ventricles and dysfunction in the prefrontal cortex and temporal cortex, as well as surrounding brain regions. Newer research has identified problems in how different areas of the brain are connected to one another (Crossley, Mechelli, et al., 2016). A recent longitudinal study of people with and without schizophrenia indicated faster aging in the brains of people with schizophrenia, suggesting that over time, the disorder (and unfortunately the medications used to treat it) takes a toll on the brain (Schnack, van Haren, et al., 2016).

Enlarged Ventricles   As discussed in Chapter 2, the brain has four ventricles, which are spaces in the brain filled with cerebrospinal fluid. Having larger fluid-filled spaces implies a loss of brain cells. Meta-analyses of several neuroimaging studies have revealed that some people with schizophrenia, even very early in the course of the illness and across the course of the illness, have enlarged ventricles (Chung, Haut, et al., 2017; Kempton, Stahl, et al., 2010; Olabi, Ellison-Wright, et al., 2011). Further evidence concerning enlarged ventricles comes from a meta-analysis of 69 studies that included over 2000 people with schizophrenia who had never taken antipsychotic medication (Haijma, Van Haren, et al., 2013). This is important because it helps to rule out the possibility that enlarged ventricles or other overall brain size reductions may be due to the side effects of medications.

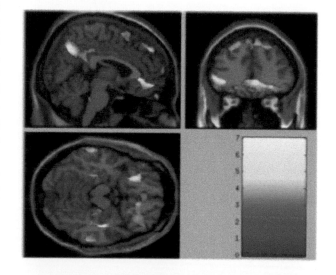

Large ventricles in people with schizophrenia are correlated with impaired performance on neuropsychological tests, poor functioning prior to the onset of the disorder, and poor response to medication treatment (Andreasen, Olsen, et al., 1982; Weinberger, Cannon-Spoor, et al., 1980). The extent to which the ventricles are enlarged, however, is modest, and many people with schizophrenia do not differ from people without schizophrenia in this respect. Furthermore, enlarged ventricles are not specific to schizophrenia, as they are also evident in the CT scans of people with other disorders, such as bipolar disorder with psychotic features (Rieder, Mann, et al., 1983). People with these disorders can show ventricular enlargement almost as great as that seen in schizophrenia (Elkis, Friedman, et al., 1995).[1]

Factors Involving the Prefrontal Cortex   A variety of evidence suggests that the prefrontal cortex is of particular importance in schizophrenia.

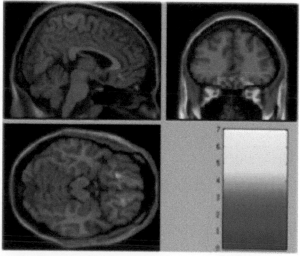

- The prefrontal cortex is known to play a role in behaviors such as speech, decision making, emotion, and goal-directed behavior, which are disrupted in schizophrenia.
- MRI studies have shown reductions in gray matter and overall volume (size) in the prefrontal cortex (Goodkind, Eikhoff, et al., 2015; Gupta, Calhoun, et al., 2014; Ohtani, Levitt, et al., 2014) even in people early in the course of the illness (Cannon, Chung, et al., 2015; Sun, Phillips, et al., 2009). Unfortunately, antipsychotic medications may contribute to some of this loss (Ho, Andreasen, et al., 2011; Torres, Portela-Oliveira, et al., 2013).

The pictures show brain activation from an fMRI study that involved maintaining pleasant emotional experience over a 12-second delay. The control group showed greater activation in areas of the frontal lobes compared with the schizophrenia group.

Courtesy of Ann Kring

---

[1]Other findings also suggest that perhaps schizophrenia and psychotic mood disorders should not be totally separate diagnostic categories. The disorders share some symptoms (notably, delusions) and some possible etiological factors (e.g., genetic factors, increased dopamine activity), and they respond similarly to medications. Researchers would be well served to focus some of their efforts on psychotic symptoms in other disorders as well as in schizophrenia.

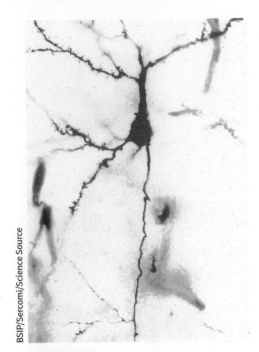

BSIP/Sercomi/Science Source

FIGURE 9.3 Micrograph of a neuron. The bumps on the dendrites are dendritic spines, which receive inputs from other neurons. Having fewer dendritic spines may impair connections among neurons and may be a factor in schizophrenia.

- People with schizophrenia perform more poorly than people without schizophrenia on neuropsychological tests designed to tap functions supported by the prefrontal region, including working memory or the ability to hold bits of information in memory (Barch, Csernansky, et al., 2002; Heinrichs & Zakzanis, 1998), with some evidence that performance on some of these tests declines from before disorder onset to when people are in their late 30s (Meier, Caspi, et al., 2014).

- PET brain-imaging studies find that people with schizophrenia show lower glucose metabolism in the prefrontal cortex when performing neuropsychological tests tapping prefrontal function (Buchsbaum, Kessler, et al., 1984). People with schizophrenia also show activation with fMRI during performance of these same types of tests (Barch, Carter, et al., 2001).

- Finally, less activation in the prefrontal cortex is related to more severe negative symptoms (O'Donnell & Grace, 1998; Ohtani et al., 2014; Potkin, Alva, et al., 2002; Weinberger, Berman, & Illowsky, 1988).

Despite the reduced volume of the gray matter in the prefrontal cortex, the number of neurons in this area does not appear to be reduced. More detailed studies indicate that what is lost may be what are called "dendritic spines" (Glausier & Lewis, 2013; Goldman-Rakic & Selemon, 1997; McGlashan & Hoffman, 2000). Dendritic spines are small projections on the shafts of dendrites where nerve impulses are received from other neurons at the synapse (see **Figure 9.3**). The loss of these dendritic spines means that communication among neurons (i.e., functioning of the synapses) is disrupted, resulting in what some have termed a "disconnection syndrome." One possible result of the failure of neural systems to communicate could be the speech and behavioral disorganization seen in schizophrenia. Research has linked these abnormalities in dendritic spines with the candidate genes and CNVs identified in schizophrenia, discussed in the earlier section on genetic factors (Copf, 2016; Pathania, Davenport, et al., 2014; Penzes, Cahill, et al., 2011).

Problems in the Temporal Cortex and Surrounding Regions Additional research has found that people with schizophrenia have structural and functional abnormalities in the temporal cortex, including areas such as the temporal gyrus, hippocampus, parts of the insula, fusiform gyrus, amygdala, and cingulate cortex. For example, research also shows a reduction in cortical gray matter in temporal as well as frontal brain regions (Gupta, Calhoun, et al., 2015) and reduced volume in the basal ganglia (e.g., the caudate nucleus), hippocampus, and limbic structures (Glahn, Laird, et al., 2008; Mathew, Gardin, et al., 2014). A twin study found reduced hippocampus volume among twins with schizophrenia but not among the twins without schizophrenia (van Erp, Saleh, Huttunen, et al., 2004). A meta-analysis of MRI studies conducted with people during their first episode of schizophrenia concluded that the volume of the hippocampus was significantly reduced compared to people without schizophrenia (Steen, Mull, et al., 2006).

An additional interesting piece of evidence regarding the hippocampus comes from a meta-analysis of nine studies assessing the brain volume of more than 400 first-degree relatives of people with schizophrenia and more than 600 first-degree relatives of people without schizophrenia (Boos, Aleman, et al., 2007). Relatives of people with schizophrenia had smaller hippocampal volumes than relatives of people without schizophrenia. These findings suggest that reduced hippocampal volume in people with schizophrenia may reflect a combination of genetic and environmental factors.

What makes these findings about the hippocampus all the more intriguing is the fact that the hypothalamic–pituitary–adrenal (HPA) axis is closely connected to this area of the brain. Chronic stress is associated with reductions in hippocampal volume in other disorders, such as posttraumatic stress disorder (see Chapter 7). Although people with schizophrenia do not necessarily experience more stress than people without schizophrenia, they are more reactive to stress. Other evidence indicates that the HPA axis is disrupted in schizophrenia, particularly very early in the course of the disorder (Walker et al. 2008; Walker, Trotman, et al., 2013). Taken together, stress reactivity and a disrupted HPA axis likely contribute to the reductions in hippocampal volume observed in people with schizophrenia (Walker et al., 2008).

Connectivity in the Brain

As we discussed in Chapter 2, current neuroimaging methods measure how different areas of the brain are connected to each other. Given the widespread involvement of brain dysfunction in schizophrenia, it is perhaps not surprising that the connections between areas are also problematic (Rapoport, Giedd, & Gogtay, 2012).

Studies have found that people with schizophrenia have less connectivity in brain white matter than people without schizophrenia in the frontal and temporal cortices (Ellison-Wright & Bullmore, 2009) and this is associated with the genetic diathesis for schizophrenia (Bohlken, Brouwer, et al., 2016). Like the other types of connectivity, research has found diminished effective connectivity in schizophrenia (Deserno, Sterzer, et al., 2012).

Brain connectivity research in schizophrenia has revealed that there is less connectivity between brain networks, including the frontoparietal and default-mode networks, and this diminished connectivity is correlated with poor performance on cognitive tests (Unschuld, Buchholz, et al., 2014). Research has also found diminished connectivity among healthy relatives of people with schizophrenia, suggesting that diminished connectivity might be part of the genetic diathesis for schizophrenia (Collin, Kahn, et al., 2014; Unschuld et al., 2014).

Measures of brain connectivity in schizophrenia have also been shown to be helpful in predicting who will respond well to antipsychotic medication treatment. In one study, researchers found that greater connectivity between the striatum, an area of the brain rich in dopamine, and other areas of the brain predicted a greater reduction in symptoms early in the course of a hospital stay (Sarpal, Argyelan, et al., 2016).

Environmental Factors Influencing the Developing Brain

Several different environmental factors have been studied as possible contributing factors to schizophrenia (Brown, 2011; van Os, Kenis, & Rutten, 2010). A possible cause of some of the observed brain abnormalities in schizophrenia is damage during gestation or birth. Many studies have shown high rates of delivery complications in people with schizophrenia (Brown, 2011; Walker et al., 2004); such complications could have resulted in a reduced supply of oxygen to the brain, resulting in loss of cortical gray matter (Cannon, van Erp, et al., 2002). These obstetrical complications do not raise the risk for schizophrenia in everyone who experiences them. Rather, the risk for schizophrenia is increased in those who experience complications and have a genetic diathesis (Cannon & Mednick, 1993).

Additional research suggests that maternal infections during pregnancy are associated with greater risk of their children developing schizophrenia when they become adults (Brown & Derkits, 2010). For example, one study found that maternal exposure to the parasite toxoplasma gondii was associated with a nearly 2.5 times greater risk of schizophrenia among the mothers' children when they became adults (Brown, Schaefer, et al., 2005; Pedersen, Stevens, et al., 2011). This is a common parasite, carried by many people with no ill effects.

If, as the findings we have just reviewed suggest, the development of the brains of people with schizophrenia goes awry very early, why does the disorder begin many years later, in adolescence or early adulthood? The prefrontal cortex is a brain structure that matures late, typically in adolescence or early adulthood. Thus, a problem in this area, even one that begins early in the course of development, may not show itself in the person's behavior until the period of development when the prefrontal cortex begins to play a larger role in behavior (Weinberger, 1987). Notably, dopamine activity also peaks in adolescence, which may further set the stage for the onset of schizophrenia symptoms (Walker et al., 2008). Adolescence is also typically a developmental period that is fraught with stress. Recall from our discussions in Chapter 2 that stress activates the HPA axis, causing cortisol to be secreted. Research in the past 20 years has demonstrated that cortisol increases dopamine activity, particularly in the mesolimbic pathway, perhaps increasing the likelihood of developing schizophrenia symptoms (Pruessner, Cullen, et al., 2017).

Another proposed explanation is that the development of symptoms in adolescence could reflect a loss of synapses due to excessive pruning, the elimination of synaptic connections. Pruning is a normal part of brain development that occurs at different rates in different areas of the brain. It is mostly complete in sensory areas by about age 2 but continues in the prefrontal cortex until mid-adolescence. If too extensive, pruning may result in the loss of necessary communication among neurons (McGlashan & Hoffman, 2000; Sekar, Bialas, et al., 2016).

An additional environmental factor that has been studied as a risk factor for schizophrenia among adolescents is cannabis (marijuana) use. Among people already diagnosed with schizophrenia, cannabis use is associated with a worsening of symptoms (Foti, Kotov, et al., 2010). But does cannabis use contribute to the onset of schizophrenia? A longitudinal study examining the prospective relationship between cannabis use in adolescence and the onset of schizophrenia in adolescence or adulthood indicated that the risk of developing schizophrenia symptoms was greater among those who used cannabis compared with those who did not (Arseneault, Cannon, et al., 2002), and a small meta-analysis of seven studies reported the same increased risk (Moore, Zammit, et al., 2007). Furthermore, more frequent use, higher-potency cannabis, and using more over time are associated with greater risk (Di Forti, Sallis, et al., 2013; Kelley, Wan, et al., 2016). However, recall from Chapter 4 that correlation does not mean causation. Other studies suggest that the linkage between cannabis use and risk of developing schizophrenia is observed only among those who are genetically vulnerable to schizophrenia (Shuckit, 2006). For example, Caspi and colleagues (2005) found a gene–environment interaction between a particular polymorphism in the *COMT* gene and cannabis use. The combination of cannabis use and one *COMT* polymorphism was associated with increased risk of schizophrenia, but neither alone was associated with increased risk for schizophrenia.

Psychological Factors

People with schizophrenia do not appear to experience more stress in daily life than people without schizophrenia (Phillips, Francey, et al., 2007; Walker et al., 2008). However, people with the disorder appear to be very reactive to the stressors we all encounter in daily living. In one study, people with psychotic disorders (92 percent with schizophrenia), their first-degree relatives, and people without any psychiatric disorder participated in a 6-day ecological momentary assessment study in which they recorded stress and mood several times each day. Daily life stress predicted greater decreases in positive moods in both people with schizophrenia and their relatives compared with controls. Stress also predicted greater increases in negative moods in the people with schizophrenia compared with both relatives and controls (Myin-Germeys, van Os, et al., 2001). Thus, people with schizophrenia were particularly vulnerable to daily stress. Research also shows that, as with many of the disorders we have discussed in this book, increases in life stress increase the likelihood of a relapse (Ventura, Neuchterlein, et al., 1989; Walker et al., 2008).

Additional research on psychological factors in the development and relapse of schizophrenia has focused on sociocultural factors, the family, and developmental factors.

Sociocultural Factors: Poverty, Urbanicity, and Migration
Three sociocultural factors that have been associated with schizophrenia are poverty (socioeconomic status), urbanicity (living in cities), and migration (moving from one country to another). These three variables can be related to one another, but each appears to be independently associated with a higher risk of developing schizophrenia.

For many years, we have known that the highest rates of schizophrenia are found in people with the highest poverty levels (Hollingshead & Redlich, 1958; Kohn, 1968). The correlation between poverty and schizophrenia is consistent but difficult to interpret in causal terms. Does the stress associated with poverty, such as low education, limited opportunities, and stigma from others of high status, contribute to the development of schizophrenia? Or is it the case that during the course of their developing illness, people with schizophrenia drift into poor neighborhoods because their illness impairs their earning power and they cannot afford to live elsewhere? Though it is difficult to sort out these two possibilities, the bulk of the evidence supports the notion that people with schizophrenia drift into poor neighborhoods as a consequence of the illness (Dohrenwend, Levav, et al., 1992).

Another sociocultural factor that has been linked with schizophrenia is urbanicity. That is, the likelihood of developing schizophrenia is higher for people living in urban areas (i.e., densely populated cities) compared with those in rural areas. A meta-analysis of 20 studies found that risk for developing schizophrenia was nearly three times as high for people living in urban versus those in rural areas (March, Hatch, et al., 2008). These effects were not the result of drift to urban areas in adolescence or adulthood (just prior to the onset of schizophrenia) but rather showed that people born and raised in urban areas had a greater risk of developing schizophrenia in adulthood.

What about living in densely populated cities might increase the risk for developing schizophrenia? The answer to this question is not fully known, but researchers have speculated that living in such areas may be more stressful or that exposure to infection or other environmental toxins may be more likely than in less densely populated areas (Tost, Champagne, & Meyer-Lindenberg, 2015).

A final sociocultural factor that is associated with a greater risk of developing schizophrenia is migration. By migration, we refer to people who were born in one country and moved to another (first-generation migrant) or a person whose parents (one or both) were born in a different country (second-generation migrant). A meta-analysis of 18 studies found that the risk for developing schizophrenia was three times as high among first-generation and four times as high among second-generation migrants compared to people who did not migrate to a different country (Cantor-Graae & Seleten, 2005). The risk was particularly high for people of color, which may reflect a bias in diagnostic practices, exposure to greater stress, less access to treatment, or likely some combination of these factors (Kirkbride, Barker, et al., 2008).

Family-Related Factors   Early theorists regarded family relationships, especially those between a mother and her son, as crucial in the development of schizophrenia. At one time, the view was so prevalent that the terms *schizophrenogenic mother* was coined for the supposedly cold and dominant, conflict-inducing parent who was said to produce schizophrenia in her offspring (Fromm-Reichmann, 1948). Controlled studies evaluating the schizophrenogenic mother theory have not supported it. The damage done to families by this theory, however, was significant. For generations, parents blamed themselves for their child's illness and, until the 1970s, psychiatrists often joined in this blame game.

How Do Families Influence Schizophrenia?   There is not much evidence for the role of the family in causing schizophrenia. However, studies have found differences in families of people with and without schizophrenia, and these differences may influence the course of the illness and certainly relationships among family members. For example, a few studies of families of people with schizophrenia have found that they communicate more vaguely with one another and have higher levels of conflict than families of people without schizophrenia. It is plausible that the conflict and unclear communication are a response to having a family member with schizophrenia.

Families and Relapse   A series of studies initiated in London found that the family can have an impact on the recovery of people with schizophrenia. In a pioneering study, investigators conducted a 9-month follow-up study of people with schizophrenia who returned to live with their families after being discharged from the hospital (Brown, Bone, et al., 1966). Interviews were conducted with parents or spouses before discharge and rated for the number of critical comments made about the family member with schizophrenia and for expressions of hostility toward and emotional overinvolvement with the ill relative. Combining these three characteristics—critical comments, hostility, and emotional overinvolvement—led to the creation of the construct called **expressed emotion (EE)**. Families in the original study were divided into two groups: those revealing a great deal of expressed emotion (high-EE families) and those

Lisette Le Bon/Superstock

Expressed emotion, which includes hostility, critical comments, and emotional overinvolvement, has been linked with relapse in schizophrenia.

revealing little (low-EE families). At the end of the follow-up period, only 10 percent of the people returning to low-EE homes had relapsed, but 58 percent of the people returning to high-EE homes had gone back to the hospital.

This research, which has since been replicated (see Butzlaff & Hooley, 1998, for a meta-analysis), indicates that the home environment of people with schizophrenia can influence how soon they relapse. Researchers have also found that negative symptoms of schizophrenia are most likely to elicit critical comments, and that the relatives who make the most critical comments are the most likely to view people with schizophrenia as being able to control their symptoms (Lopez, Nelson, et al., 1999; Weisman, Neuchterlein, et al., 1998).

There are also important cultural differences in EE. Lopez and colleagues (2009) found that Anglo American caregivers were higher in EE than recently immigrated Mexican American caregivers, and this was true for all aspects of EE (i.e., critical comments, hostility, and emotional overinvolvement). Nearly three-quarters of European American caregivers designated as high EE were so designated due to high hostility and critical comments; only 8 percent were designated as high EE based on emotional overinvolvement. By contrast, the Mexican American caregivers high in EE were fairly evenly divided between those who were high in hostility and critical comments and those who were high in emotional overinvolvement. These findings have important implications for developing and providing family interventions for schizophrenia, which we review a bit later in this chapter. Another study found that emotional overinvolvement specifically predicted relapse in Mexican Americans with schizophrenia, and that the linkage between EE and relapse was highest among Mexican Americans who had acculturated more to U.S. ways (Aguilera, Lopez, et al., 2010). However, the relationship between emotional overinvolvement and relapse in other European and Asian countries is not as robust as it is in North American countries (Singh, Harley, & Suhail, 2013). The different findings may be attributed either to the fact that emotional overinvolvement is measured differently across countries and cultures, or that emotional overinvolvement is more harmful in some cultures and countries than in others. This issue needs to be sorted out in future research.

What is not yet clear is exactly how to interpret the effects of EE. Is EE causal, or does it reflect a reaction to the ill relative's behavior? For example, if the condition of a person with schizophrenia begins to deteriorate, family concern and involvement may increase. Indeed, disorganized or dangerous behavior might seem to warrant familial efforts that could increase the level of EE. Research indicates that both interpretations of the operation of EE may be correct. In one study, people with schizophrenia and their high- or low-EE families were observed as they engaged in a discussion of a family problem. Two key findings emerged (Rosenfarb, Goldstein, et al., 1994).

1. The expression of unusual thoughts by the people with schizophrenia ("If that kid bites you, you'll get rabies") elicited a greater number of critical comments by family members who had previously been characterized as high in EE than by those characterized as low in EE.

2. In high-EE families, critical comments by family members led to increased expression of unusual thoughts by the people with schizophrenia.

Thus, this study found a bidirectional relationship in high-EE families: critical comments by family members elicited more unusual thoughts by relatives with schizophrenia, and unusual thoughts expressed by the relatives with schizophrenia led to increased critical comments.

How does stress, such as a high level of EE, increase the symptoms of schizophrenia and precipitate relapses? One answer to this question involves the effects of stress on the HPA axis and its link to dopamine (Walker et al., 2008). Stress activates the HPA axis, causing cortisol to be secreted, which can then increase dopamine activity (Walker et al., 2008). Furthermore, heightened dopamine activity itself can increase HPA activation, which may make a person overly sensitive to stress. Thus, there is a bidirectional relationship between HPA activation and dopamine activity.

Developmental Factors

What are people who develop schizophrenia like before their symptoms begin? This question has been addressed using retrospective and prospective studies.

Elaine Walker has conducted many studies on the development of schizophrenia.

Retrospective Studies
In the 1960s, researchers found that children who later developed schizophrenia had lower IQs and were more often delinquent and withdrawn than members of various control groups, usually comprising siblings and neighborhood peers (Albee, Lane, & Reuter, 1964; Berry, 1967; Lane & Albee, 1965). Other studies found that boys who later developed schizophrenia were rated by teachers as disagreeable, whereas girls who later developed schizophrenia were rated as passive (Watt, 1974; Watt, Stolorow, et al., 1970).

More recently, researchers have examined emotional and cognitive deficits that were present before the onset of schizophrenia. In one very clever study, Elaine Walker (see photo) and colleagues analyzed the home movies of children who later developed schizophrenia. The movies were made as part of normal family life and were made before the onset of schizophrenia (Walker, Davis, & Savoie, 1994; Walker, Grimes, et al., 1993). Compared with their siblings who did not later develop schizophrenia, the children who later developed schizophrenia as young adults showed poorer motor skills and more expressions of negative emotions. Other studies have examined past childhood assessments of the cognition and intellectual functioning of adults who had schizophrenia. These studies found that adults with schizophrenia scored lower on IQ and other cognitive tests as children compared with adults without schizophrenia (Davis, Malmberg, et al., 1997; Woodberry, Giuliano, & Seidman, 2008).

As intriguing as these findings are, these studies were not necessarily designed with the intention of predicting the development of schizophrenia from childhood behavior. Rather, they began with an adult sample of people with schizophrenia and then looked back at records and data collected from their childhoods to see if there were characteristics that distinguished them as young children.

Prospective Studies
A large prospective study identified childhood characteristics that were associated with the development of schizophrenia in early adulthood (Reichenberg, Avshalom, et al., 2010). In this study, a large sample of people from Dunedin, New Zealand, were assessed several times between the ages of 7 and 32. IQ tests were administered at ages 7, 9, 11, and 13; diagnostic assessments were conducted at ages 21, 26, and 32. The researchers found that lower scores on the IQ test in childhood predicted the onset of schizophrenia in young adulthood, even after they controlled for low socioeconomic status (which is associated with lower IQ scores; see Chapter 3). Thus, children who developed schizophrenia as adults had signs of a cognitive deficit beginning at age 7 that remained stable through adolescence.

These findings are broadly consistent with the idea that something goes awry in development that is associated with the onset of schizophrenia in late adolescence or early adulthood. Nevertheless, more specific information is required if developmental histories are to provide clear evidence regarding the etiology of schizophrenia.

One of the difficulties with the familial high-risk studies that we discussed earlier has to do with the large sample sizes that are required. As shown in Table 9.2, around 10 percent of children with a biological parent who has schizophrenia go on to develop schizophrenia. If a study begins with 200 high-risk children, only about 20 of them may go on to develop schizophrenia. In addition, it is not particularly easy to locate a large sample of women or men with schizophrenia who have had their own children.

Because of these difficulties, the **clinical high-risk study** has been used in more recent research. A clinical high-risk study is a design that identifies people with early, attenuated signs of schizophrenia, most often milder forms of hallucinations, delusions, or disorganization that nonetheless cause impairment (see Focus on Discovery 9.3). One such study followed people ages 14 to 30 in Australia who were referred to a mental health clinic in the mid-1990s (Yung, McGorry, et al., 1995). None of the participants had schizophrenia when they entered the study, but many later exhibited varying degrees of schizophrenia symptoms and some, but not all, had a biological relative with a psychotic disorder. These participants were deemed to be at "ultra-high risk" of developing schizophrenia or psychotic disorders. Since the study began, 41 of the original 104 participants have developed some type of psychotic disorder (Yung, Phillips, et al., 2004). An MRI study of 75 of the 104 participants found that those people who later developed a psychotic disorder had lower gray matter volumes than those who had not developed a psychotic disorder (Pantelis, Velakoulis, et al., 2003). Recall that reduced gray matter volume has been found in people with schizophrenia; the Pantelis et al. study suggests that this characteristic may predate the onset of schizophrenia and other psychotic disorders.

A similar longitudinal study, the North American Prodrome Longitudinal Study (NAPLS) was carried out at eight different centers in the United States and Canada. Participants were identified as clinical high-risk based on the Structured Interview for Prodromal Syndromes (see Focus on Discovery 9.3). In this study, 82 of the 291 clinical high-risk (CHR) participants who also had a family history of schizophrenia (familial high risk, or FHR) had developed schizophrenia or some type of psychotic disorder (Cannon, Cadenhead, et al., 2008). The researchers identified several factors that predicted a greater likelihood of developing a psychotic disorder, including having a biological relative with schizophrenia, a recent decline in functioning, high levels of positive symptoms, and high levels of social impairment. Later analyses from the NAPLS sample are broadly consistent with the retrospective studies of 50 years ago: social and academic difficulties in childhood predicted conversion to a psychotic disorder (Tarbox, Addington, et al., 2013).

The NAPLS-2 study builds upon the first study and includes many more participants. In this study, nearly 600 people were identified as CHR and are being followed longitudinally (Addington, Cadenhead, et al., 2012). In this larger study, impaired cognition, particularly attention and working memory, which are associated with the prefrontal cortex, were impaired among those at clinical high risk (Seidman, Shapiro, et al., 2016). The researchers have developed a risk calculator to help determine who among those at high risk will go on to develop schizophrenia (Cannon, Yu, et al., 2016). Based on clinical symptoms, cognitive functioning, and other individual characteristics, the risk calculator identified people at high risk who developed schizophrenia with about the same accuracy as risk calculators that predict who will develop cardiovascular disease. The risk calculator has been used successfully in another sample (Carrion, Cornblatt, et al., 2016), suggesting that this can be a very useful tool for researchers and clinicians.

Quick Summary

Given its complexity, several causal factors are likely to contribute to schizophrenia. The genetic evidence is strong, with much of it coming from family, twin, and adoption studies. Familial high-risk studies have found that children with a biological parent with schizophrenia are more likely to develop adult psychopathology, including schizophrenia, and have difficulties with attention and motor control, among other things. Molecular genetics studies include association studies and GWAS studies. Candidate genes from association studies include *DRD2* and *COMT*, but replication in GWAS is not always found. GWAS studies have pointed to copy number variations (CNVs) and single nucleotide polymorphisms (SNPs) that are associated with genetic vulnerability to schizophrenia.

Neurotransmitters play a role in schizophrenia. For years, dopamine was the single focus of study, but later findings led investigators to conclude that this one neurotransmitter could not fully account for schizophrenia. Other neurotransmitters are now also the focus of study, such as serotonin, GABA, and glutamate. Many different brain areas have been implicated in schizophrenia. One of the most widely replicated findings is that of enlarged ventricles. Other research supports the role of the prefrontal cortex, particularly reduced activation of this area, in schizophrenia. Dysfunction in the temporal cortex has also been documented.

Environmental factors, such as obstetric complications and prenatal infections, may impact the developing brain and increase the risk of schizophrenia. Cannabis use among adolescents has been associated with greater risk of schizophrenia, particularly among those who are genetically vulnerable to the disorder.

Research has examined the role of sociocultural risk factors including poverty, urbanicity, and migration. This work supports the idea that people with schizophrenia may drift into poverty as the illness develops, but that being born and raised in a densely populated urban area is a distinct risk factor. Furthermore, people who were born in one country but move to another are at greater risk for schizophrenia, particularly people of color.

Early theories blamed families, particularly mothers, for causing schizophrenia, but research does not support this view. Communication in families is important and could perhaps constitute the stress in the diathesis–stress theory of schizophrenia. Expressed emotion has also been found to predict relapse in schizophrenia, though there are important cultural differences in expressed emotion.

Retrospective developmental studies looked back at the childhood records of adults with schizophrenia and found that some adults with schizophrenia had lower IQs and were withdrawn as children. Other studies found that adults who later developed schizophrenia expressed a lot of negative emotion and had poor motor skills. A prospective study confirmed that lower IQ in childhood is a predictor of the later onset of schizophrenia and that the IQ deficits are stable across childhood. Clinical high-risk studies identify people who are showing early signs of schizophrenia.

Check Your Knowledge 9.2

Fill in the blanks.

1. _____ and _____ studies do not do such a good job of teasing out genetic and environmental effects; _____ studies do a better job.

2. _____ and _____ are two candidate genes that have been associated with schizophrenia.

3. Some studies showing the _____ area of the brain to be disrupted in schizophrenia also show that people with schizophrenia do poorly on tasks that rely on this area, such as planning and problem solving.

4. _____, _____, and _____ are the three components of expressed emotion.

5. _____, _____, and _____ are three sociocultural risk factors for schizophrenia.

Treatment of Schizophrenia

Treatments for schizophrenia may include a combination of short-term hospital stays (during the acute phases of the illness), medication, and psychosocial treatments. An issue with any kind of treatment is that some people with schizophrenia lack insight into their impaired condition and refuse any treatment at all (Amador, Flaum, et al., 1994). Results from one study suggest that gender (female) and age (older) are predictors of better insight among people in their first episode of the illness (McEvoy, Johnson, et al., 2006), and this may help account for why women with schizophrenia tend to respond better to treatment than men (Salem & Kring, 1998). Those who lack insight, and thus don't believe they have an illness, don't see the need for professional help, particularly when it includes hospitalization or drugs. Family members therefore face a major challenge in getting their relatives into treatment.

Medications

In the 1950s, several medications collectively referred to as **antipsychotic drugs** (also referred to as *neuroleptics* because they produce side effects similar to the symptoms of a neurological disease), were found to help with some of the symptoms of schizophrenia. For the first time, many people with schizophrenia did not need to stay in a hospital for long periods of time and could instead go home with a prescription. **Focus on Discovery 9.4** presents a brief history of the development of these drugs. As we discussed in Chapter 1 and return to in Chapter 16, the zeal to discharge people with schizophrenia from hospitals did not match the needs of all people with the disorder. Some people did and still do need treatment in a hospital, even if for a short time. Unfortunately, it is difficult to receive such treatment today due to the cost and limited availability of hospital beds for people with schizophrenia and other psychological disorders. Nevertheless, medications reduce symptoms for some people with schizophrenia. As we will see, however, medications have their own drawbacks.

Focus on Discovery 9.4

Stumbling Toward a Cure: The Development of Antipsychotic Medications

One of the more frequently prescribed antipsychotic drugs, phenothiazine, was first produced by a German chemist in the late nineteenth century. But it was not until the discovery of the antihistamines, which have a phenothiazine nucleus, in the 1940s, that phenothiazines received much attention.

Reaching beyond their use to treat the common cold and asthma, the French surgeon Henri Laborit pioneered the use of antihistamines to reduce surgical shock. He noticed that they made his patients somewhat sleepy and less fearful about the impending operation. Laborit's work encouraged pharmaceutical companies to reexamine antihistamines in light of their tranquilizing effects. Shortly thereafter, the French chemist Paul Charpentier prepared a new phenothiazine derivative, which he called chlorpromazine. This drug proved very effective in calming people with schizophrenia. Phenothiazines derive their therapeutic properties by blocking dopamine receptors in the brain, thus reducing the influence of dopamine on thought, emotion, and behavior.

Chlorpromazine (trade name Thorazine) was first used therapeutically in the United States in 1954 and rapidly became the preferred treatment for schizophrenia. By 1970, more than 85 percent of all people in treatment were receiving chlorpromazine or another phenothiazine.

First-Generation Antipsychotic Drugs and Their Side Effects The first-generation antipsychotic drugs are those broad classes of medications that were the first to be discovered. See **Table 9.4** for a summary of major drugs used to treat schizophrenia. These drugs can reduce the positive and disorganization symptoms of schizophrenia but have little or no effect on the negative symptoms. Despite the enthusiasm with which these drugs are prescribed, they are not a cure. About 30 percent of people with schizophrenia do not respond favorably to the first-generation antipsychotics, and about half the people who take any antipsychotic drug quit after 1 year and up to three-quarters quit before 2 years because the side effects are so unpleasant (Lieberman, Stroup, et al., 2005).

People who respond positively to the antipsychotics are typically kept on so-called maintenance doses of the drug, just enough to continue the therapeutic effect. Results from a meta-analysis of over 60 randomized controlled clinical trials comparing either first- or second-generation drugs with placebo found that maintenance dosages of both were equally effective at reducing relapse as compared with placebo (Leucht, Tardy, et al., 2012). Some people who are maintained on medication may still have difficulty with day-to-day functioning, however. For example, they may be unable to live independently or to hold down the kind of job for which they would otherwise be qualified, and their social relationships may be sparse. In short, some symptoms may go away, but lives are still not fulfilling for many people with schizophrenia.

The commonly reported side effects of all antipsychotics include sedation, dizziness, blurred vision, restlessness, and sexual dysfunction. In addition, some particularly disturbing side effects, termed *extrapyramidal side effects*, resemble the symptoms of Parkinson's disease. People taking antipsychotics may develop tremors of the fingers, a shuffling gait, and drooling. Other side effects can include dystonia, a state of muscular rigidity, and dyskinesia, an abnormal

TABLE 9.4   **Summary of Major Drugs Used in Treating Schizophrenia**

Drug Category	Generic Name	Trade Name
First-generation drugs	chlorpromazine	Thorazine
	fluphenazine decanoate	Prolixin
		Haldol
	haloperidol	Navane
	thiothixene	Stelazine
	trifluoperazine	
Second–generation drugs	clozapine	Clozaril
	aripiprazole	Abilify
	olanzapine	Zyprexa
	risperidone	Risperdal
	ziprasidone	Geodon
	quetiapine	Seroquel

motion of voluntary and involuntary muscles, producing chewing movements as well as other movements of the lips, fingers, and legs. Another side effect is akasthesia, an inability to remain still; some people on antipsychotics pace constantly and fidget.

In a rare muscular disturbance called *tardive dyskinesia*, the mouth muscles involuntarily make sucking, lip-smacking, and chin-wagging motions. In more severe cases, the whole body can be subject to involuntary motor movements.

Because of these serious side effects, some clinicians believe it is unwise to prescribe high doses of antipsychotics for extended periods of time. Current clinical practice guidelines from the American Psychiatric Association call for treating people with the smallest possible doses of drugs (APA, 2004). This situation puts the clinician in a bind: If medication is reduced, the chance of relapse increases, but if medication is continued, serious and untreatable side effects may develop.

Second-Generation Antipsychotic Drugs and Their Side Effects   In the decades following the introduction of the first-generation antipsychotic drugs, there was little interest in developing new drugs to treat schizophrenia. Nevertheless, it was clear that these drugs did not help everyone, and they also produced troubling side effects.

Drug companies thus began to search for other drugs that might be more effective than first-generation antipsychotics. These drugs are referred to as the **second-generation antipsychotic drugs** because their mechanism of action is not like that of the typical or first-generation antipsychotic medications. Examples are shown in **Table 9.5**. According to a meta-analysis comparing the second-generation drugs with one another, all of them work about the same, with some advantage in reducing positive symptoms observed for clozapine and olanzapine (Leucht, Komossa, et al., 2009).

Early research suggested that the second-generation antipsychotics were equally as effective as first-generation antipsychotics in reducing positive and disorganized symptoms (Conley & Mahmoud, 2001), particularly for people who have not responded to at least two other medications (Lewis, Barnes, et al., 2006). A meta-analysis of 124 studies comparing first- and second-generation antipsychotic drugs found that some, but not all, second-generation drugs were modestly more effective than the first-generation drugs in reducing negative symptoms and improving cognitive deficits (Davis, Chen, & Glick, 2003). However, a more recent study found no differences in relapse or adverse side effects between a long-acting (i.e., injectable) first- and second-generation drug (McEvoy, Byerly, et al., 2014).

Other research suggests that these medications may be more effective than the first-generation drugs in improving cognitive functioning (Harvey, Green, et al., 2004; Harvey, Green, et al., 2003;

Keefe, Bilder, et al., 2007). More generally, the second-generation antipsychotics may thus make possible more thoroughgoing changes in schizophrenia and its behavioral consequences than do drugs that do not help with these cognitive abilities. However, other evidence suggests that psychological treatments are also effective, perhaps more so, at alleviating cognitive deficits.

Although early evidence suggested that the second-generation medications held promise, additional research began to paint a bleaker picture. A comprehensive randomized controlled clinical trial (called Clinical Antipsychotic Trials of Intervention Effectiveness, or CATIE) compared four second-generation drugs (olanzapine, risperidone, ziprasidone, and quetiapine) and one first-generation drug (perphenazine) with one another (Lieberman et al., 2005). Close to 1500 people from all over the United States were in the study. What set this study apart from others included in the meta-analyses mentioned earlier in this chapter was that it was not sponsored by one of the drug companies that makes the drugs. Among the many findings from this study, three stand out. First, the second-generation drugs were not more effective than the older, first-generation drugs. Second, the second-generation drugs did not produce fewer unpleasant side effects. And third, nearly three-quarters of the people stopped taking the medications before the 18 months of the study design had ended. Similar results have been found in another large study (Jones, Barnes, et al., 2006).

In addition, other studies have revealed that second-generation antipsychotics have serious side effects of their own (Freedman, 2003). First, these drugs can and do also produce extrapyramidal side effects (Miller, Caroff, et al., 2008; Rummel-Kluge, Komossa, et al., 2010). Second, second-generation drugs cause weight gain (Rummel-Kluge et al., 2010), with one study finding that nearly half of the people taking these medications had significant weight gain (Young, Goey, et al., 2010). In addition to being unpleasant, weight gain is associated with other serious health problems, such as increased cholesterol and increases in blood glucose, which can cause type 2 diabetes. For example, clozapine and olanzapine have been related to the development of type 2 diabetes (Leslie & Rosenheck, 2004). However, it is not clear whether the medicine itself increases this risk, perhaps via the side effect of weight gain, or whether people taking the medications were predisposed to developing diabetes independent of their medication usage. By 2007, the drug company that produces olanzapine, Eli Lilly, settled more than 25,000 lawsuits, paying out over $1.2 billion to people taking the drug. The company was sued for failing to adequately warn people of these serious side effects. The drug's label now contains warnings about possible side effects, including weight gain and elevated blood sugar and cholesterol levels.

TABLE 9.5   **Side Effects Associated with First- and Second-Generation Antipsychotic drugs**

Side Effect	First-Generation	Second-Generation
Extrapyramidal signs	✓	✓
Drowsiness/sedation/fatigue	✓	✓
Blurred vision	✓	✓
Weight gain		✓
Restlessness	✓	
Dizziness		✓
Sexual dysfunction	✓	
Dry mouth	✓	
Tachycardia		✓
Constipation	✓	✓
Nausea		✓
Insomnia		✓
Headache		✓
Urinary incontinence		✓

Another disturbing aspect of the second-generation antipsychotic medications is that African Americans do not tend to receive them. Two different studies have found that African Americans were more likely to be prescribed first-generation than second-generation antipsychotic medications (Kreyenbuhl, Zito, et al., 2003; Valenti, Narendran, & Pristach, 2003). This is unfortunate for many reasons, but particularly because African Americans may experience more side effects than whites in response to the first-generation medications (Frackiewicz, Sramek, et al., 1997). More broadly, these results echo the findings of the Surgeon General's supplement to his landmark report on mental health in 2001 that elucidated several disparities in mental health treatment among members of racial and ethnic minority groups (U.S. Department of Health and Human Services, 2001). Compared with other disorders reviewed in this book, relatively less research has been done on schizophrenia across different ethnic groups. This must be a focus of future research.

Evaluation of Drug Treatments   At this point, antipsychotic drugs are an indispensable part of treatment for schizophrenia. A recent review of 60 years' worth of clinical trials with these drugs found that just over half of the people with schizophrenia had a minimal response compared with placebo, but only 23 percent had a good response (Leucht, Leucht, et al., 2017). Thus, even though these drugs work better than placebo, they do not work well for many people. Furthermore, the mixed success of second-generation antipsychotic drugs has stimulated a continued effort to find new and more effective drug therapies for schizophrenia. New drugs are currently being evaluated, but no significant breakthrough medications have yet been developed. Thus, the "third generation" is not soon forthcoming. Clearly, more work is needed to develop better medications for schizophrenia.

Second-generation antipsychotic drugs such as olanzapine may have different side effects than first-generation antipsychotic drugs, but they still have side effects.

Psychological Treatments

The limits of antipsychotic medications have spurred efforts to develop psychosocial treatments that can be used in addition to the medications. Indeed, the current treatment recommendations for schizophrenia as compiled by the schizophrenia Patient Outcomes Research Team (PORT) include psychosocial interventions in addition to medications (Kreyenbuhl, Buchanan, et al., 2010). The PORT recommendations are based on extensive reviews of treatment research recommendations and were updated to include different types of psychosocial treatments. Several psychosocial interventions, including skills training, cognitive behavior therapy, and family-based treatments, have a solid evidence base to support their use as an adjunctive treatment to medications (Dixon, Dickerson, et al., 2010). A review of 37 prospective studies of people after their first episode of schizophrenia found that the combination of medication and psychosocial treatment predicted the best outcome (Menezes, Arenovich, & Zipursky, 2006).

An example of the positive effects that come from combination treatments is found in a large (more than 1200 people) randomized controlled trial conducted in China that compared medication alone with medication plus a comprehensive psychosocial intervention that included family therapy, cognitive behavior therapy, psychoeducation, and skills training. People in both groups had a similar reduction in schizophrenia symptoms. However, people who received the combined treatment had lower rates of relapse and treatment discontinuation, as well as greater improvements in functioning (Guo, Zhai, et al., 2010). See **Focus on Discovery 9.5** for another example of a successful combination treatment approach.

Other treatments, such as cognitive remediation approaches, have a growing evidence base and are the focus of much current research. We turn to these psychosocial treatments next.

Social Skills Training **Social skills training** is designed to teach people with schizophrenia how to successfully manage a wide variety of interpersonal situations—discussing their medications with their psychiatrist, ordering meals in a restaurant, filling out job applications, interviewing for jobs, saying no to drug dealers on the street, and reading bus schedules. Most of us take these skills for granted and give little thought to them in our daily lives, but people with schizophrenia cannot consider them a given—they need to work hard to acquire or reacquire such skills (Heinssen, Liberman, & Kopelowicz, 2000; Liberman, Eckman, et al., 2000). Social skills training typically involves role-playing and other group exercises to practice skills, both in a therapy group and in actual social situations.

Research has shown that social skills training can help people with schizophrenia achieve fewer relapses, better social functioning, and a higher quality of life (Kopelowicz, Liberman, & Zarate, 2002). Some of the studies are noteworthy in demonstrating benefits over a 2-year period following treatment (Liberman, Wallace, et al., 1998; Marder, Wirshing, et al., 1999), though not all results are positive (Pilling, Bebbington, et al., 2002). Social skills training is usually a component of treatments for schizophrenia that go beyond the use of medications alone, including family therapies for lowering expressed emotion, which we discuss next. For example, social skills training that included family therapy was found to be more effective than treatment as usual (medication plus a 20-minute monthly meeting with a psychiatrist) in a randomized controlled trial conducted in Mexico (Valencia, Racon, et al., 2007). There is some evidence that social skills training may also be effective in reducing negative symptoms (Elis, Caponigro, & Kring, 2013).

Focus on Discovery 9.5

Living with Schizophrenia

A heartening example of one woman's struggles with and triumphs over schizophrenia is found in the 2007 book *The Center Cannot Hold: My Journey Through Madness*. This book was written by Elyn Saks (see photo), an endowed professor of law at the University of Southern California who also happens to have schizophrenia (Saks, 2007). In the book, she describes her lifelong experience with this illness. Prior to the publication of the book, only a few of Professor Saks's close friends even knew that she had schizophrenia. Why did she keep it a secret? Certainly, stigma is part of the reason. As we have discussed throughout this book, stigma toward people with psychological disorders is very much alive in the twenty-first century and can have seriously negative consequences for people with disorders such as schizophrenia.

What makes Professor Saks's life story particularly encouraging is that she has achieved exceptional professional and personal success in her life despite having such a serious psychological disorder. She grew up in a loving and supportive family; earned a bachelor's degree from Vanderbilt University, graduating as her class valedictorian; earned a prestigious Marshall fellowship to study philosophy at Oxford in the United Kingdom; graduated from Yale Law School as editor of the prestigious *Yale Law Review*; and is a tenured professor of law at a major university. How did she do it?

She believes that a combination of treatments (including psychoanalysis and medications), social support from family and friends, hard work, and acknowledgment of the seriousness of her illness have all helped her cope with schizophrenia and its sometimes unpredictable and frightening symptoms. Although psychoanalysis does not have a good deal of empirical support for its efficacy with schizophrenia, it was and remains a central part of Professor Saks's treatment regimen. Thus, even though some treatments may not be effective for a group of people, they can nonetheless be beneficial for individuals. One characteristic that appears to have been helpful for Professor Saks, from her early days in psychoanalysis as a Marshall scholar at Oxford University until the present, has been her ability to "be psychotic" when she is with her psychoanalyst. So much of her energy was spent trying to hide her symptoms and keep them from interfering with her life; psychoanalysis became a safe place for her to bring these symptoms more fully out into the open. The different analysts she has had over the years were also among the chief proponents of adding antipsychotic medication to her treatment, something that Professor Saks resisted for many years. Having the unwavering support of close friends and her husband has also been a tremendous help, particularly during her more symptomatic

Damian Dovarganes/AP Images

Elyn Saks, a law professor at USC, has schizophrenia.

periods. Her loved ones would not turn and run the other way when she was psychotic. Instead, they would support her and help her get additional treatment if it was needed.

Professor Saks still experiences symptoms, sometimes every day. Her symptoms include paranoid delusions, which she describes as very frightening (e.g., believing that her thoughts have killed people). She also experiences disorganization symptoms, which she eloquently describes in the book:

> Consciousness gradually loses its coherence. One's center gives way. The center cannot hold. The "me" becomes a haze, and the solid center from which one experiences reality breaks up like a bad radio signal. There is no longer a sturdy vantage point from which to look out, take things in, assess what's happening. No

> core holds things together, providing the lens through which to see the world, to make judgments and comprehend risk. (Saks, 2007, p. 13)

Even though she still experiences symptoms, she has come to terms with the fact that schizophrenia is a part of her life. Would she prefer not to have the illness? Sure. But she also recognizes that she has a wonderful life filled with friends, loved ones, and meaningful work. She is not defined by her illness, and she importantly notes that "the humanity we all share is more important than the mental illness we may not" (Saks, 2007, p. 336). Her life is an inspiration to all, not just those with psychological disorders. Her story reminds us that life is difficult, more so for some than others, but that it can be lived, and lived to the fullest.

Family Therapies   Many people with schizophrenia live with their families. Earlier we discussed research showing that high levels of expressed emotion (EE) within the family, including being hostile, critical, and emotionally overinvolved, have been linked to relapse. Based on this finding, a few family therapies have been developed. These therapies may differ in length, setting, and specific techniques, but they have several features in common:

- *Education about schizophrenia—specifically about the genetic or neurobiological factors that predispose some people to the illness, the cognitive problems associated with schizophrenia, the symptoms of schizophrenia, and the signs of impending relapse.* Knowing, for example, that neurobiology has a lot to do with having schizophrenia and that the illness involves problems in thinking clearly and rationally might help family members be more accepting and understanding of their relative's actions.

- *Information about antipsychotic medication.* Therapists impress on both the family and the ill relative the pros and cons of taking antipsychotic medication, becoming better informed about the intended effects and the side effects of the medication, taking responsibility for monitoring response to medication, and seeking medical consultation rather than discontinuing the medication if adverse side effects occur.

- *Blame avoidance and reduction.* Therapists encourage family members to blame neither themselves nor their relative for the illness and for the difficulties all may have in coping with it.

- *Communication and problem-solving skills within the family.* Therapists focus on teaching the family ways to express both positive and negative feelings in a constructive, empathic, nondemanding manner rather than in a finger-pointing, critical, or overprotective manner. They also focus on making personal conflicts less stressful by teaching family members ways to work together to solve everyday problems.

- *Social network expansion.* Therapists encourage people with schizophrenia and their families to expand their social contacts, especially their support networks.

- *Hope.* Therapists instill hope that things can improve, including the hope that the person with schizophrenia may not have to return to the hospital.

Therapists use various techniques to implement these strategies. Examples include identifying stressors that could trigger relapse, and training families in communication skills and problem solving (Penn & Mueser, 1996). Family psychoeducation is effective at reducing relapse in several countries (McFarlane, 2016). Compared with standard treatments (usually just medication), family therapy plus medication has typically lowered relapse over periods of 1 to 2 years. This positive finding is evident particularly in studies in which the treatment lasted for at least 9 months (Falloon, Boyd, et al., 1982, 1985; Hogarty, Anderson, et al., 1986, 1991; Kopelowicz & Liberman, 1998; McFarlane, Lukens, et al., 1995; Penn & Mueser, 1996).

Bruce Ayres/Stone/Getty Images

Family therapy can help educate people with schizophrenia and their families about schizophrenia and reduce expressed emotion.

Cognitive Behavior Therapy At one time, researchers assumed that it was futile to try to alter the cognitive distortions, including delusions, of people with schizophrenia. Now, however, a growing body of evidence demonstrates that the maladaptive beliefs of some people with schizophrenia can in fact benefit from cognitive behavior therapy (CBT) (Garety, Fowler, & Kuipers, 2000; Wykes, Steel, et al., 2008).

People with schizophrenia can be encouraged to test out their delusional beliefs in much the same way as people without schizophrenia test out their beliefs. Through collaborative discussions (and in the context of other modes of treatment, including antipsychotic drugs), some people with schizophrenia have been helped to attach a nonpsychotic meaning to paranoid symptoms and thereby reduce their intensity and aversive nature (Beck & Rector, 2000; Drury, Birchwood, et al., 1996; Haddock, Tarrier, et al., 1998). Researchers have found that CBT can also reduce negative symptoms, for example, by challenging belief structures tied to low expectations for success (avolition) and low expectations for pleasure (anticipatory pleasure deficit in anhedonia) (Grant, Huh, et al., 2012; Wykes et al., 2008).

Results from meta-analyses of over 50 studies of more than 2000 people with schizophrenia across eight countries found small to moderate effect sizes for positive symptoms, negative symptoms, mood, and general life functioning (Jauhar, McKenna, et al., 2014; Wykes et al., 2008). The results are less encouraging for negative symptoms, but CBT is currently the most effective treatment for these symptoms (Ellis et al., 2013). CBT has been used as an adjunctive treatment for schizophrenia in Great Britain for many years, and the results have been positive, even in community settings (Sensky, Turkington, et al., 2000; Turkington, Kingdom, & Turner, 2002; Wykes et al., 2008).

A newer therapy for schizophrenia combines two effective treatments; social skills training and cognitive behavior therapy (Granholm, McQuaid, & Holden, 2016). Termed cognitive-behavioral social skills training (CBSST), this treatment focuses on reducing symptoms and improving functioning. Randomized controlled clinical trials have shown it to be effective (Granholm, McQuaid, et al., 2005; Granholm, Holden, et al., 2014), and it has also shown promise among people early in the course of the disorder (Herman, Shireen, et al., 2016). CBSST is a group therapy and it lasts longer than some other treatments, but the length of treatment has been shown to be associated with better outcomes. For working on complex symptoms and skills, it may well take longer. How long? CBSST typically lasts for six to nine months. This may well be a good investment in time.

Another type of combined treatment that has shown promise for young people early in the course of schizophrenia is called NAVIGATE (Mueser, Penn, et al., 2015). This treatment involves medication, family psychoeducation, individual therapy, and help with employment and education. In a large randomized controlled clinical trial called the Recovery After an Initial Schizophrenia Episode (RAISE) Early Treatment Program, researchers found that this combined treatment was more effective than standard community care. This was particularly true for people who got into treatment sooner. That is, the longer psychosis was left untreated, the worse the outcome for participants (Kane, Robinson, et al., 2016).

We highlight two important aspects from this study that are true for any treatment for schizophrenia: (1) Combined and comprehensive treatments in community settings are important to develop and implement for people with schizophrenia, and (2) the earlier treatment begins, the better.

Cognitive Remediation Therapies Researchers and clinicians have been paying more attention to fundamental aspects of cognition that are disordered in schizophrenia to improve these functions and thereby favorably affect behavior. The fact that positive clinical outcomes from risperidone are associated with improvements in certain kinds of memory (Green, Marshall, et al., 1997) lends support to the more general notion that therapies directed at basic cognitive processes—the kind that nonclinical cognitive scientists study—hold promise for improving the social and emotional lives of people with schizophrenia. This general approach concentrates on trying to normalize such functions as attention and memory, which are known to be deficient in many people with schizophrenia and are associated with poor social adaptation (Green, Kern, et al., 2000).

Treatments that seek to enhance basic cognitive functions such as verbal learning ability are referred to as **cognitive remediation**, or more simply, *cognitive training*. These treatments, whether done individually or in groups, typically include hours of computer-based training in attention, memory, and problem solving. Groups also worked on such routine social-cognitive skills as reading and understanding newspaper editorials, solving social problems, and starting and maintaining conversations. Compared to other psychosocial treatments such as supportive therapy, cognitive enhancement therapy has shown promising results in randomized controlled trials (Eack, Greenwald, et al., 2010; Hogarty, Flesher, et al., 2004). These results indicate that this type of treatment can be effective in reducing symptoms and improving cognitive abilities, and it is linked to good functional outcomes, such as employment and social functioning.

Two meta-analyses of 26 (McGurk, Twamley, et al., 2007) and 40 studies of cognitive remediation interventions (Wykes, Huddy, et al., 2011) found small to medium effect sizes for overall cognitive functioning and specific cognitive domains, including attention, verbal memory, problem solving, verbal working memory, processing speed, and social cognition. Cognitive remediation was also associated with a reduction in symptoms and an improvement in everyday functioning, though the effect sizes for these two domains were small. Cognitive remediation was more likely to be associated with an improvement in functioning if another type of psychosocial treatment, such as social skills training, was added to the treatment program. As promising as these findings are, nearly all of the studies have been with white men; thus, their generalizability remains to be established.

A somewhat different cognitive remediation program has also shown promising results. This treatment also involves intensive (50 hours) computer training, but the task was developed based on neuroscience research showing that improving basic cognitive and perceptual processes (e.g., discriminating simple sounds) can then have an impact on higher-order cognitive processes (e.g., memory and problem solving). The cognitive remediation task in this training is an auditory task that gets progressively more difficult as people get better at it. They perform a series of tasks that require them to discriminate between complex speech sounds. In a randomized controlled trial, people with schizophrenia who received the intensive auditory computer training showed greater improvement in overall cognition as well as in specific domains (memory, attention, processing speed, working memory, and problem solving) compared with participants who played computer games for the same amount of time (Fisher, Holland, et al., 2009).

Psychoeducation

As we discussed in Chapter 5 about bipolar disorder, psychoeducation is an approach that seeks to educate people about their illness, including the symptoms of the disorder, the expected time course of symptoms, the biological and psychological triggers for symptoms, and treatment strategies. A meta-analysis of 44 studies of psychoeducation in schizophrenia found that, in combination with medication, it was effective in reducing relapse and rehospitalization and increasing medication compliance (Xia, Merinder, & Belgamwar, 2011).

Residential Treatment

Residential treatment homes are sometimes good alternatives for people who are not quite well enough to live on their own or even with their family. Here people live, take their meals, and gradually return to ordinary community life by holding a part-time job or going to school. As part of what is called *vocational rehabilitation*, residents learn marketable skills that can help them secure employment and thereby increase their chances of functioning well in the community. Living arrangements may be relatively unstructured; some houses set up moneymaking enterprises that help train and support the residents.

Depending on how well funded the residential treatment facility is, the staff may include psychiatrists or clinical psychologists, or both. The frontline staff members are often undergraduate psychology majors or graduate students in clinical psychology or social work, who live at the facility and act both as administrators and as friends to the residents. Group meetings, at which residents talk out their frustrations and learn to relate to others in honest and constructive ways, are often part of the routine. Many such programs across the United States have helped thousands of people with schizophrenia make substantial social adaptations.

The need in the United States for effective residential treatment cannot be underestimated, especially in light of the deinstitutionalization that involved discharging tens of thousands of people from hospitals (Torrey, 2014). People with schizophrenia almost always need follow-up community-based services, and these services are scarce. Indeed, today a large percentage of homeless people in the United States are mentally ill, including many people with schizophrenia. Social Security disability benefits are available to those with schizophrenia, but if they do not have an address, they often do not receive all the benefits to which they are entitled. Although good residential treatment programs are available, there simply are not enough of them.

Still, obtaining employment poses a major challenge because of the bias and stigma attached to people with schizophrenia. Although the Americans with Disabilities Act of 1990 prohibits employers from asking applicants if they have a history of serious psychological disorders, people with schizophrenia still have a difficult time obtaining regular employment. Their symptoms make negatively biased employers fearful of hiring them, and in addition, many employers are unwilling to give much leeway to people whose thinking, emotions, and behavior can be unconventional.

Given these difficulties, additional funding will be needed to create more residential treatment facilities, with the hope of reducing the number of people with schizophrenia in need of treatment.

Check Your Knowledge 9.3

True or false?

1. First-generation antipsychotics include medications like Haldol or prolixin; second-generation antipsychotics include clozapine and olanzapine.

2. Second-generation antipsychotics produce more motor side effects than first-generation antipsychotics.

3. Cognitive behavior therapy, but not cognitive remediation therapy, is effective for schizophrenia, if given along with medications.

4. One important focus of residential treatment programs is to help people with schizophrenia gain employment.

Summary

Clinical Description

- The symptoms of schizophrenia involve several areas, including thought, perception, and attention; motor behavior; emotion; and life functioning. Symptoms are typically divided into positive, negative, and disorganized categories. Positive symptoms include excesses and distortions, such as delusions and hallucinations. Negative symptoms are behavioral deficits, which include avolition, asociality, anhedonia, blunted affect, and alogia. Disorganized symptoms include disorganized speech and behavior.

- Other schizophrenia spectrum disorders in DSM-5 include schizophreniform disorder, brief psychotic disorder, schizoaffective disorder, and delusional disorder.

Etiology

- The evidence for genetic transmission of schizophrenia is impressive. Family and twin studies suggest a genetic component; adoption studies show a strong relationship between having a parent with schizophrenia and the likelihood of developing the disorder, typically in early adulthood. Familial high-risk studies have longitudinally studied the offspring of a parent with schizophrenia to determine if problems in childhood might predict the onset of the disorder. Molecular genetic studies indicate that genes such as *COMT* and *DRD2* are associated with schizophrenia. Genome-wide association studies (GWAS) have found rare genetic mutations called copy number variations (CNVs) and single nucleotide polymorphisms (SNPs) to be associated with schizophrenia.

- Neurotransmitters are also implicated in schizophrenia. It appears that increased sensitivity of dopamine receptors in the brain is related to the positive symptoms of schizophrenia. Other neurotransmitters, such as serotonin, glutamate, and GABA, are also involved.

- The brains of some people with schizophrenia have enlarged ventricles as well as problems with the prefrontal cortex, the temporal cortex, and connectivity between brain regions. Some of these structural abnormalities could result from maternal viral infection during the first trimester of pregnancy or from damage sustained during a difficult birth. The combination of brain development during adolescence, stress, and the HPA axis is important for understanding why symptoms typically emerge during late adolescence, even if a brain disturbance has been in place since gestation. Cannabis use in adolescence has been linked to a higher risk for developing schizophrenia, primarily for those who are genetically vulnerable to schizophrenia.

- Three sociocultural factors that have been associated with schizophrenia are poverty, urbanicity, and migration. High levels of expressed emotion in families, as well as increases in general life stress, have been shown to be important triggers of relapse.

- Retrospective developmental studies have identified problems in childhood that existed prior to the onset of schizophrenia. Because these studies were not designed to predict schizophrenia, however, it is difficult to interpret the findings. Clinical high-risk studies have identified young people with mild symptoms who are at higher risk for developing schizophrenia spectrum disorders.

Treatment

- Antipsychotic drugs are widely used to treat schizophrenia. The first-generation drugs are somewhat effective, but they can also produce serious side effects. Second-generation antipsychotic drugs are equally as effective as first-generation drugs, and they have their own set of side effects. Drugs alone are not a completely effective treatment, though, as people with schizophrenia may need support in dealing with the challenges of everyday life.

- Family therapy and psychoeducation has been shown to be valuable in preventing relapse. In addition, social skills training and various cognitive behavioral therapies (or their combination) have helped people with schizophrenia meet the inevitable stresses of family and community living. Recent efforts to change the thinking of people with schizophrenia using cognitive behavior therapy are showing promise as well. Cognitive remediation therapies focus on improving cognitive skills. These therapies help promote memory, attention, and problem-solving skills and improve daily functioning.

Answers to Check Your Knowledge Questions

9.1 1. blunted affect; 2. delusion or ideas of reference; 3. anhedonia (anticipatory); 4. disorganized thinking or derailment.

9.2 1. family, twin, adoption; 2. *COMT, DRD2;* 3. prefrontal; 4. hostility, critical comments, emotional overinvolvement; 5. poverty, urbanicity, migration

9.3 l. T; 2. F; 3. F; 4. T

Key Terms

alogia
anhedonia
anticipatory pleasure
antipsychotic drugs
asociality
avolition
blunted affect
brief psychotic disorder
catatonia
clinical high-risk study

cognitive remediation
consummatory pleasure
delusional disorder
delusions
disorganized behavior
disorganized speech
disorganized symptoms
expressed emotion (EE)
familial high-risk study
grandiose delusions

hallucinations
ideas of reference
loose associations (derailment)
negative symptoms
positive symptoms
schizoaffective disorder
schizophrenia
schizophreniform disorder
second-generation antipsychotic drugs
social skills training

CHAPTER 10

Substance Use Disorders

LEARNING GOALS

1. Describe substance use disorder and its symptoms.

2. Describe the epidemiology and symptoms associated with alcohol, tobacco, and marijuana use disorders.

3. Describe the epidemiology and symptoms associated with opioid, stimulant, and other drug use disorders.

4. Understand the major causal factors for substance use disorders, including genetic factors, neurobiological

factors, emotion regulation and expectancy effects, and sociocultural factors.

5. Describe the approaches to treating substance use disorders, including psychological treatments, medications, and drug substitution treatments.

6. Describe the major approaches to preventing substance use disorders.

People have used various substances in the hope of reducing pain or negative emotion, increasing positive emotion, or altering states of consciousness for centuries. The United States is a drug culture. Americans use drugs to wake up (coffee or tea), to stay alert throughout the day (soft drinks), to relax (alcohol), and to reduce pain (aspirin). The widespread availability and frequent use of drugs set the stage for the potential abuse of drugs, the topic of this chapter.

Overview: Substance Use and the DSM-5

How common is substance use? In 2015, more than 27 million people over the age of 12 in the United States reported having used an illicit drug in the past month [Substance Abuse and Mental Health Services Administration (SAMHSA, 2016)]. Marijuana was the most frequently used, with over 22 million people over the age of 12 reporting using it in the past month. As we discuss later, this drug is illegal according to the United States federal government but legal in eight states. Alcohol remains the most used substance, with more than 138 million Americans over the age of 12 reporting alcohol use of some kind, and 66.7 million Americans reported at least one episode of binge drinking (defined as having five or more drinks) in the last 30 days (Center for Behavioral Health Statistics and Quality, 2016; SAMHSA, 2016). Recent data on the frequency of use of several drugs, legal and illegal, are presented in **Tables 10.1** and **10.2**. These figures do not represent the frequency of substance use disorders but simply indicate the pervasiveness of drug and alcohol use in the United States. And for some drugs, like opioids, the numbers in 2015 do not capture the rapid increase in use over the past two years, a topic we return to later in the chapter.

TABLE 10.1   Percentage of U.S. Population Reporting Drug Use in Past Month (2015)

Substance	Percentage Reporting Use
Alcohol	51.7
Cigarettes	19.4
Marijuana	8.3
Psychotherapeutics (misuse)	2.4
Cocaine	0.7
Heroin	0.1
Hallucinogens including PCP	0.5
Inhalants	0.2

Data are percentages of people in the United States age 12 and over. Misuse of psychotherapeutics refers to the use of pain medicines (1.4%), tranquilizers (0.7%), stimulants (0.6%), or sedatives (0.2%) for a nonmedical, nonprescribed use.

Source: SAMHSA (2016).

TABLE 10.2   Number of People in the U.S. Who Reported Use in Past Year (2015)

Substance	Number of people
Alcohol	175.8 million
Cigarettes	61.8 million
Marijuana	36 million
Pain medications (misuse)	18.9 million
Cocaine	4.8 million
Heroin	828,000
Ecstasy	2.6 million
Inhalants	1.8 million
Methamphetamine	1.7 million

Source: Hughes, Williams, et al. (2016). Numbers include people age 12 and older.

Use of a substance is not the same thing as a substance use disorder. The DSM-5 includes **substance use disorder** (see below for criteria) for many specific substances, such as alcohol opioids, and tobacco. For the first time in the history of the DSM, a non-substance category was added to the Substance-Related and Addictive Disorders chapter: gambling disorder. We discuss this new disorder in **Focus on Discovery 10.1** The term *addiction* is not in the DSM, but it is a term we are all familiar with. It typically refers to a severe substance use disorder. **Table 10.3** lists the DSM-5 severity ratings for substance use disorders. In the DSM-5, meeting six or more of the diagnostic criteria constitutes a severe substance use disorder.

DSM-5 Criteria for Substance Use Disorder

Problematic pattern of use that impairs functioning. Two or more symptoms within a 1-year period:

- Failure to meet obligations
- Repeated use in situations where it is physically dangerous
- Repeated relationship problems
- Continued use despite problems caused by the substance
- Tolerance

- Withdrawal
- Substance taken for a longer time or in greater amounts than intended
- Efforts to reduce or control use do not work
- Much time spent trying to obtain the substance
- Social, hobbies, or work activities given up or reduced
- Craving to use the substance is strong

TABLE 10.3	Severity Ratings for Substance Use Disorders in DSM-5
Rating Number of Diagnostic	Criteria Met
Mild	2–3 criteria
Moderate	4–5 criteria
Severe	6 or more criteria

Two symptoms that often are part of a severe substance use disorder are tolerance and withdrawal. **Tolerance** is indicated by either (1) larger doses of the substance being needed to produce the desired effect or (2) the effects of the drug becoming markedly less if the usual amount is taken. **Withdrawal** refers to the negative physical and psychological effects that develop when a person stops taking the substance or reduces the amount. Substance withdrawal symptoms can include muscle pains and twitching, sweats, vomiting, diarrhea, and insomnia.

Clinical Descriptions: Alcohol, Tobacco, and Marijuana Use Disorders

Clinical Case

Alice

Alice was 54 and living alone when her family finally persuaded her to check into an alcohol rehabilitation clinic. She had taken a bad fall while drunk, and it may have been this event that finally got her to admit that something was wrong. Her drinking had been out of control for several years. She began each day with a drink, continued through the morning, and was totally intoxicated by the afternoon. She seldom had any memory for events after noon of any day. Since early adulthood she had drunk regularly, but rarely during the day and never to the point of drunkenness. The sudden death of her husband in an automobile accident 2 years earlier had triggered a quick increase in her drinking, and within 6 months she had slipped into a pattern of severe alcohol use. She had little desire to go out of her house and had cut back on social activities with family and friends. Repeated efforts by her family to get her to curtail her intake of alcohol had only led to angry confrontations.

In 2015, more than 20 million people in the United States met the diagnostic criteria for a substance use disorder. Of this large number of people, most (15.7 million) met the criteria for alcohol use disorder. More than 7 million met the criteria for a drug use disorder, and 2.7 million met the criteria for both drug and alcohol use disorders (SAMHSA, 2015).

Drug and alcohol use disorders are among the most stigmatized of disorders. Terms such as *addict* or *alcoholic* are tossed about carelessly, as if these words capture the essence of people, not the disorder from which they suffer. Historically, drug and alcohol problems have been viewed as moral lapses rather than as conditions in need of treatment. Unfortunately, such attitudes persist today. True, people make decisions about whether to try alcohol or drugs, but the ways in which these decisions and the substances involved interact with an individual's neurobiology, social setting, culture, and other environmental factors all conspire to create a substance use disorder. Thus, it is a mistake to consider substance use disorders as somehow being solely the result of moral failing or personal choice.

We turn now to an overview of some of the major substance use disorders, those involving alcohol, tobacco, marijuana, opioids, stimulants, and hallucinogens.

Focus on Discovery 10.1

Is Gambling the Same as Other Substance Use Disorders?

The DSM-5 now includes a non-substance condition—gambling disorder—in the chapter on Substance-Related and Addictive Disorders. Although the name is new and it is now explicitly considered alongside substance use disorders, it is not entirely new to the DSM. In fact, "pathological gambling" disorder was included in the DSM since 1980, but it was included in the chapter for Impulse Disorders Not Elsewhere Classified.

Although gambling may look like fun, for many people it becomes out of control, as in gambling disorder.

Symptoms of Gambling Disorder (4 or more needed to meet the diagnosis)

1. Gambling often occurs when feeling negative emotions
2. Efforts to stop or reduce gambling cause negative feelings and restlessness
3. Repeated reliance on other people to fix financial consequences of gambling
4. Continued gambling despite relationship, job, or school problems caused by it
5. Continued gambling even after losing to try to recoup losses
6. Lying to others about gambling
7. Gambling with more money is needed to get the desired good feelings
8. Efforts to reduce or control gambling do not work
9. Much time spent thinking about and planning gambling

Why was this disorder moved into the DSM-5 chapter that contains drug and alcohol use disorders? According to DSM-5, recent research discoveries warranted the inclusion of gambling disorder in the DSM-5, particularly studies that show that people who are unable to stop gambling have similar patterns of brain activation as do people with other substance use disorders (e.g., Holden, 2001). In addition, a large study that examined the criteria for substance use disorder alongside criteria for gambling disorder using a technique called *factor analysis* found that the criteria for both disorders were related to one another, suggesting that gambling is a part of the broader addiction concept (Blanco, Garcia-Anaya, et al., 2015).

Nevertheless, some mental health professionals worry that including gambling disorder in the DSM-5 chapter on substance-related disorders may create a "slippery slope" such that other types of behavioral "addictions" (shopping? exercise? sex?) will soon be added. In fact, Internet gaming disorder is included in the DSM-5 appendix as a condition in need of further study. Internet gaming disorder was not included as a formal disorder in the DSM-5 because there is not yet enough research to justify its inclusion. But it may well make it into the next revision of the DSM.

What are some of the similarities and differences between substance use disorders/addictions and behavioral addictions like gambling disorder? One difference is that gambling does not involve putting some type of substance into the body. Related to this is the difficulty in determining whether someone with gambling disorder can have withdrawal symptoms. Tolerance, however, is something that may be relevant for both types of addictive disorders. Other similarities include the consequences of the behavior. Whether people are gambling or ingesting a substance, there are significant consequences for work, school, and relationships.

Do people with gambling disorder participate in some types of gambling more often than those without a gambling disorder? It turns out that the answer to this question is no. Playing the lottery is the most common type of gambling for all people, whether they have a problem with gambling or not. However, those with gambling disorder are more likely to have participated in a wider variety of gambling activities (e.g., sports betting, casino gambling, Internet gambling, slot machines) than people who do not have problems with gambling (Kessler, Hwang, et al., 2008). Indeed, one of the characteristics that may put a person at higher risk for moving from social or recreational gambling to developing a gambling disorder is the frequency with which they gamble.

What distinguishes professional gamblers from people with gambling disorder? After all, professional gamblers gamble even more than people with gambling disorder (Weinstock, Massura, & Petry, 2013). One study compared 22 professional gamblers with 13 people in the now-obsolete pathological gambling disorder category and found some interesting similarities and several key differences. Card games were the most frequent type of gambling among both group, and both groups gambled at a pretty high frequency. However, professional gamblers won more money (about $125,000) than those with gambling disorder. In fact, people with gambling disorder had no income from their gambling. In addition, people with gambling disorder reported more stressful life events, less quality of life, more impulsivity, and more comorbid psychological disorders than professional gamblers.

Alcohol and nicotine are a frequent combination, although most people who smoke and drink in social situations do not have problems with these substances.

Alcohol Use Disorder

People who develop tolerance or withdrawal generally have more severe alcohol use disorder and would be considered "dependent" or addicted (Schuckit, Daeppen, et al., 1998). The effects of the abrupt withdrawal of alcohol in a person with severe alcohol use disorder may be rather dramatic because the body has become accustomed to alcohol. Specifically, a person may experience withdrawal symptoms that can include feeling anxious, depressed, weak, restless, and unable to sleep. He or she may have muscle tremors, especially of the fingers, face, eyelids, lips, and tongue, and pulse, blood pressure, and temperature may be elevated.

In relatively rare cases, a person who has been drinking heavily for several years may also experience **delirium tremens (DTs)** when the level of alcohol in the blood drops suddenly. The person becomes delirious as well as tremulous and has hallucinations that are primarily visual but may be tactile as well. Unpleasant and very active creatures—snakes, cockroaches, spiders, and the like—may appear to be crawling up the wall or over the person's body or to be filling the room. Feverish, disoriented, and terrified, the person may claw frantically at his or her skin to get rid of the creatures.

Alcohol use disorder is associated with other drug use (Grant, Goldstein, et al., 2015). It is estimated, for example, that 80 to 85 percent of people who abuse alcohol are smokers. This very high comorbidity may occur because alcohol and nicotine are cross-tolerant; that is, nicotine can induce tolerance for the rewarding effects of alcohol, and vice versa. Thus, consumption of both drugs may be increased to maintain their rewarding effects (Rose, Brauer, et al., 2004). Evidence from animal studies suggests that this may happen because nicotine influences the way alcohol works in the brain's dopamine pathways associated with reward (Doyon, Dong, et al., 2013), a topic we turn to later in this chapter.

Prevalence of Alcohol Use Disorder Results from the annual survey conducted by SAMHSA indicates that 15.7 million people in the United States age 12 or older met criteria for alcohol use disorder in 2015—more than the total state populations of North Carolina and Minnesota combined.

Alcohol use is especially frequent among college-age adults. This is true for binge drinking, defined, as noted earlier, as having five drinks in a short period of time (e.g., within an hour), and heavy-use drinking, defined as having five drinks on the same occasion five or more times in a 30-day period. Among full-time college students, binge and heavy-use prevalence rates were 39.4 percent and 12.5 percent, respectively in 2015, (SAMHSA, 2016), which is about the same as in 2012.

Binge drinking can have serious consequences. Estimates suggest that as many as 1800 college students die from alcohol-related incidents (e.g., driving under the influence, toxicity) each year. Close to 700,000 are assaulted by other students who have been drinking, and as many as 97,000 students are sexually assaulted (Hingson, Edwards, et al., 2009).

The prevalence of alcohol use disorder varies by gender, race, and education level, as is shown in **Table 10.4**. In 2015, significantly fewer men met criteria for alcohol use disorder than in 2014, a welcome piece of news. Historically, men have had more problems with alcohol than women, but this gender difference continues to shrink. In an analysis of studies from 1948 to 2014, researchers found that men born in the early to mid-1900s were three times as likely to have alcohol problems as women. However, men born after 1991 were only 1.2 times as likely as women to have alcohol problems (Slade, Chapman, et al., 2016). Two recent large epidemiological studies, one in the United States and one in Sweden, found that the risk of alcohol use disorder was significantly higher for never married or divorced men and women (Grant et al., 2015; Kendler, Lönn, et al., 2016). In the Swedish study of close to a million people, people who had a family history of alcohol problems were more likely to develop alcohol use disorder following a divorce, suggesting a gene-environment interaction.

TABLE 10.4	Prevalence of Alcohol Use Disorder by Gender, Race/Ethnicity, and Education Level (2015)	
Group		**Percentage**
Women		9.6
Men		12.3
Black or African American		7.5
Native American or Alaska Native		16.1
White		12.1
Hispanic or Latino		11.1
Asian		6.8
Two or more races		13.0
Less than high school		9.4
High school degree		9.4
College degree		13.4

Data are percentages of people in the United States ages 18–25.

Source: SAMHSA (2016).

Alcohol use disorders are comorbid with borderline and antisocial personality disorders, mood disorders, and anxiety disorders (Grant et al., 2015). In 2015, 19.1 percent of people ages 18–25 that met the criteria for alcohol use disorder also had at least one other psychological disorder (SAMHSA, 2016).

Short-Term Effects of Alcohol How does alcohol produce its short-term effects? After being swallowed and reaching the stomach, alcohol begins to be metabolized by enzymes. Most of it goes into the small intestine and from there it is absorbed into the blood. It is then broken down, primarily in the liver, which can metabolize about 1 ounce of 100-proof (50 percent alcohol) liquor per hour.

Figure 10.1 shows mean blood alcohol levels based on a person's weight and amount of alcohol consumption. Importantly, however, the effects of alcohol vary with its concentration in the bloodstream. Levels in the bloodstream depend on the amount ingested in a particular period of time, the presence of food in the stomach (food retains the alcohol and reduces its absorption rate), the weight and body fat of the person drinking, and the efficiency of the liver. Two ounces of alcohol will thus have a different effect on a 180-pound man who has just eaten than on a 110-pound woman with an empty stomach. However, women achieve higher blood alcohol concentrations even after adjustment for differences in body weight, perhaps due to differences in body water content between men and women.

It is also important to consider the question: What counts as a drink? A 12-ounce glass of beer, a 5-ounce glass of wine, and 1.5 ounces of "hard liquor" (like a shot of tequila) are all considered one drink. The size of the drink is not what matters. Rather, it is the alcohol content of the beverage (http://rethinkingdrinking.niaaa.nih.gov).

Alcohol produces its effects through its interactions with several neurotransmitters. It stimulates gamma-aminobutyric acid (GABA) receptors, which may account for its ability to reduce tension. (GABA is a major inhibitory neurotransmitter; the benzodiazepines, such as Xanax, have an effect on GABA receptors similar to that of alcohol.) Alcohol also increases levels of serotonin and dopamine, which may be the source of its ability to produce pleasurable effects. Finally, alcohol inhibits glutamate receptors, which may cause the cognitive effects of alcohol intoxication, such as slowed thinking and memory loss.

A novel study examined the effects of alcohol on both the brain and behavior. Participants were given different doses of alcohol while in an fMRI scanner performing a simulated driving test (Calhoun, Pekar, & Pearlson, 2004). The low dose (.04 blood alcohol content) led to just a

# OF DRINKS CONSUMED/SEX		WEIGHT							
		100	120	140	160	180	200	220	240
1	Male	.04	.04	.03	.03	.02	.02	.02	.02
	Female	.05	.04	.04	.03	.03	.03	.02	.02
2	Male	.09	.07	.06	.05	.05	.04	.04	.04
	Female	.10	.08	.07	.06	.06	.05	.05	.04
3	Male	.13	.11	.09	.08	.07	.07	.06	.05
	Female	.15	.13	.11	.10	.08	.08	.07	.06
4	Male	.17	.15	.13	.11	.10	.09	.08	.07
	Female	.20	.17	.15	.13	.11	.10	.09	.09
5	Male	.22	.18	.16	.14	.12	.11	.10	.09
	Female	.25	.21	.18	.16	.14	.13	.12	.11
6	Male	.26	.22	.19	.16	.15	.13	.12	.11
	Female	.30	.26	.22	.19	.17	.15	.14	.13
7	Male	.30	.25	.22	.19	.17	.15	.14	.13
	Female	.36	.30	.26	.22	.20	.18	.16	.15
8	Male	.35	.29	.25	.22	.19	.17	.16	.15
	Female	.41	.33	.29	.26	.23	.20	.18	.16
9	Male	.39	.35	.28	.25	.22	.20	.18	.16
	Female	.46	.38	.33	.29	.26	.23	.21	.19
10	Male	.39	.35	.28	.25	.22	.20	.18	.16
	Female	.51	.42	.36	.32	.28	.25	.23	.21
11	Male	.48	.40	.34	.30	.26	.24	.22	.20
	Female	.56	.46	.40	.35	.31	.27	.25	.23
12	Male	.53	.43	.37	.32	.29	.26	.24	.21
	Female	.61	.50	.43	.37	.33	.30	.28	.25
13	Male	.57	.47	.40	.35	.31	.29	.26	.23
	Female	.66	.55	.47	.40	.36	.32	.30	.27
14	Male	.62	.50	.43	.37	.34	.31	.28	.25
	Female	.71	.59	.51	.43	.39	.35	.32	.29
15	Male	.66	.54	.47	.40	.36	.34	.30	.27
	Female	.76	.63	.55	.46	.42	.37	.35	.32

Blood Alcohol Concentration Calculator

© John Wiley & Sons, Inc.

FIGURE 10.1 Blood alcohol concentration calculator. Note that values are just estimates. An actual BAC will vary depending on metabolism and amount of food in the stomach.

small impairment in motor functioning, but the high dose (.08 blood alcohol content) led to more significant motor impairment that interfered with driving ability. Furthermore, the effects of the alcohol in the brain were in areas associated with monitoring errors and making decisions (the anterior cingulate and orbitofrontal cortex). Based on this finding, the researchers suggested that people at the legal limit of alcohol may make poor decisions about driving and may not realize they are making mistakes.

Long-Term Effects of Prolonged Alcohol Abuse Prolonged consumption of alcohol adversely affects every tissue and organ of the body. For example, alcohol impairs the digestion of food and absorption of vitamins. In older people who have chronically abused alcohol, a deficiency of B-complex vitamins can cause a severe loss of memory for both recent and long-past events.

Prolonged alcohol use plus reduction in the intake of proteins contributes to the development of cirrhosis of the liver, a disease in which some liver cells become engorged with fat and protein, impeding their function. Some cells die, triggering an inflammatory process, and when scar tissue develops, blood flow is obstructed.

Other common changes to the body due to drinking include damage to the endocrine glands, brain, and pancreas, as well as heart failure, erectile dysfunction, hypertension, stroke, and capillary hemorrhages, which are responsible for the swelling and redness in the face, especially the nose, of people who chronically abuse alcohol.

Heavy alcohol consumption by a woman during pregnancy is the leading known cause of intellectual disability among children. The growth of the fetus is slowed, and cranial, facial, and limb anomalies can be produced, a condition known as **fetal alcohol syndrome (FAS)**. Even moderate drinking can produce undesirable, if less severe, effects on the fetus, leading the National Institute on Alcohol Abuse and Alcoholism to counsel total abstention during pregnancy as the safest course.

There has long been debate about whether alcohol in moderation might have some positive health benefits. For example, light to moderate drinking has been related to lower risk factors for coronary heart disease, such as higher levels of the so-called good cholesterol (HDL) levels (Brien, Ronksley, et al., 2011). Other evidence, however, suggests that even moderate drinking can have ill effects on health. For example, a prospective study with more than 500 people in the United Kingdom found that greater alcohol consumption predicted less gray matter density, particularly in the hippocampus, 30 years later (Topiwala, Allan, et al., 2017). Recall from Chapter 2 that gray matter refers to the neural tissue that constitutes the cortex and the hippocampus is an area of the brain that supports memory.

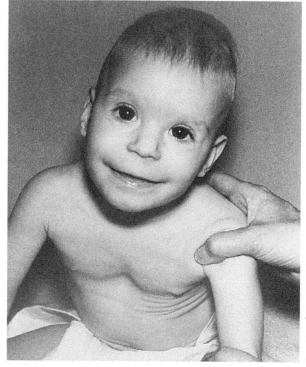

Heavy drinking during pregnancy can cause fetal alcohol syndrome. Children with this disorder can have facial abnormalities and intellectual developmental disorder.

Courtesy of James W. Hanson

Tobacco Use Disorder

Nicotine is the addicting agent of tobacco. The neural pathways that become activated stimulate the dopamine neurons in the mesolimbic area that seem to be involved in producing the reinforcing effects of most drugs (Stein, Pankiewicz, et al., 1998).

Prevalence and Health Consequences of Smoking For over 50 years, the threats to health posed by smoking have been documented convincingly by the Surgeon General of the United States. In 2014, the Surgeon General released a new report commemorating the 50th anniversary of its first groundbreaking report on the health consequences of smoking (http://www.surgeongeneral.gov/library/reports/50-years-of-progress/). Although more than 20 million Americans died from smoking between 1964 and 2014, another 45 million quit smoking, no doubt saving many lives. Unfortunately, the declines in smoking have not affected everyone equally. Smoking among people with a college degree declined by 83 percent, but it declined by only 39 percent among people with less than a high school degree. Worldwide, the number of people who smoke has declined by about a third from 1990 to 2015 (Reitsma, Fullman, et al., 2017). Although these trends are encouraging, smoking remains the single most preventable cause of premature death in the United States as well as in other parts of the world.

Among the other medical problems associated with, and almost certainly caused or exacerbated by, long-term cigarette smoking are emphysema; cancers of the larynx, esophagus, pancreas, bladder, cervix, and stomach; complications during pregnancy; sudden infant death syndrome; periodontitis; and a number of cardiovascular disorders [U.S. Department of Health

Children of mothers who smoke are at increased risk for respiratory infections, bronchitis, and inner-ear infections.

Image Source/Alamy Stock Photo

TABLE 10.5   **Use of Any Tobacco Product in 2015 by Gender and Race/Ethnicity**

Group	Percentage Who Used Tobacco in 2015
Women	35.6
Men	52.0
Black or African American	38.0
Native American or Alaska Native	61.5
White	49.9
Hispanic or Latino	35.8
Asian	24.1

Data are percentages of people in the United States ages 18–25 who used any tobacco product—cigarettes, smokeless tobacco, cigars, pipe tobacco—during the year 2015.

Source: SAMHSA (2016).

and Human Sources (USDHHS), 2014]. The most probable harmful components in the smoke from burning tobacco are nicotine, carbon monoxide, and tar, which consists primarily of certain hydrocarbons, many of which are known carcinogens. Results from a longitudinal study with close to 300,000 people found that people who smoked as little as one cigarette per day were more likely to die from any cause than people who never smoked (Inoue-Choi, Liao, et al., 2017).

In 2015, nearly 64 million people in the United States had used a tobacco product (cigarette, cigar, smokeless tobacco, pipe) at some point in their lives, with 58.5 million of these people smoking cigarettes (SAMHSA, 2016). The number of people who used any tobacco product in 2015 are nontrivial, as we show in **Table 10.5**. Encouragingly, cigarette smoking among youths ages 12 to 17 has decreased from 15.2 percent in 2002 to 8 percent in 2015. Smoking is more prevalent among people in the lower socioeconomic classes (Dwyer-Lindgren, Mokdad, et al., 2014), likely adding to the disparity in health between rich and poor in the United States.

Research demonstrates the significance of race and ethnicity in nicotine addiction as well as the intricate interplay among behavioral, social, and neurobiological factors. It has been known for years that African American cigarette smokers are less likely to quit and are more likely, if they continue to smoke, to get lung cancer. Why? It turns out that they retain nicotine in their blood longer than do European Americans; that is, they metabolize it more slowly (Mustonen, Spencer, et al., 2005). The type of cigarette smoked also matters. African Americans are more likely to smoke menthol cigarettes, largely due to extensive advertising of these types of cigarettes to this community beginning in the 1950s and continuing today (Kreslake, Wayne, & Connolly, 2008; Moreland-Russell, Harris, et al., 2013; USDHHS, 2014). Research shows that people who smoke menthol inhale more deeply and hold in the smoke for a longer time, thus providing more opportunity for deleterious effects (Celebucki, Wayne, et al., 2005). Given the additional health concerns associated with menthol cigarettes, the Food and Drug Administration (FDA) has proposed removing them from the market, but no action has been taken.

Research has also found that Chinese Americans metabolize less nicotine from cigarettes than do either European American or Latino smokers (Benowitz, Pérez-Stable, et al., 2002). In general,

WARNING: SMOKING CAUSES IMPOTENCE

California's Tobacco Education Media Campaign parodies tobacco ads to illustrate health risks associated with smoking and to attack pro-tobacco influences (see more at http://tobaccofreeca.com/resources/).

California Tobacco Control Program

lung cancer rates are lower among Asians than among European Americans or Latinos. The relatively lower metabolism of nicotine among Chinese Americans may help explain why lung cancer rates are lower in this group.

Parental smoking greatly increases the chances that children will begin to smoke.

Health Consequences of Secondhand Smoke As we have known for many years, the health hazards of smoking are not restricted to those who smoke. The smoke coming from the burning end of a cigarette, so-called **secondhand smoke**, or environmental tobacco smoke (ETS), contains higher concentrations of ammonia, carbon monoxide, nicotine, and tar than does the smoke inhaled by the smoker. In 2014, the Surgeon General updated its report detailing the health hazards of secondhand smoke. The National Institutes of Health has classified ETS as a known carcinogen, indicating that evidence has established a cause–effect relationship between ETS and cancer. The effects of ETS include the following:

- Nonsmokers can suffer lung damage, possibly permanent, from extended exposure to cigarette smoke. Those living with smokers are at greatest risk. Precancerous lung abnormalities have been observed in those living with smokers, and nonsmokers are at greater risk for developing cardiovascular disease and lung cancer. In addition, some nonsmokers have allergic reactions to the smoke from burning tobacco.
- Babies of women exposed to secondhand smoke during pregnancy are more likely to be born prematurely, to have lower birth weights, and to have birth defects.
- Children of smokers are more likely to have upper respiratory infections, asthma, bronchitis, and inner-ear infections than are their peers whose parents do not smoke.

The Surgeon General has stated that the best form of prevention for exposure to secondhand smoke is to promote smoke-free environments, since there is really no safe level of exposure to secondhand smoke (USDHHS, 2006, 2014). As of 2017, 26 states[1] plus the District of Columbia received an A grade from the American Lung Association for their strong smoke-free laws that ban smoking in nearly all public places, including restaurants and bars (http://www.lung.org/our-initiatives/tobacco/reports-resources/sotc/state-grades/state-rankings/smokefree-air-laws.html).

E-cigarettes are becoming more popular even though we do not yet know about the safety of these products.

E-Cigarettes Electronic cigarettes or e-cigarettes sometimes look like cigarettes, but they are made of plastic or metal and are filled with liquid nicotine that is mixed with other chemicals and often with flavors. They are battery operated and work by heating up the nicotine liquid concoction, and users inhale and exhale the vapor. The term *vaping* has come to mean smoking an e-cigarette. Some models include a light at the end of the tube to mimic a lit cigarette. Indeed, e-cigarettes are often not called cigarettes at all, but are instead called vape pipes, vaping pens, hookah pens, or e-hookahs. Although it is true that these devices do not always contain nicotine (many are sold with flavored water vapor), they can all be used to deliver liquid nicotine.

[1]Arizona, California, Colorado, Delaware, Hawaii, Illinois, Iowa, Kansas, Maine, Maryland, Massachusetts, Minnesota, Montana, Nebraska North Dakota, New Jersey, New Mexico, New York, Ohio, Oregon, Rhode Island, South Dakota, Utah, Vermont, Washington, and Wisconsin.

In a study of more than 100,000 college students in the United States, researchers reported that 30 percent of them had tried an e-cigarette at least once (Primack, Shensa, et al., 2013). In this large sample, twice as many students (16.8 percent) were using cigarettes as were using e-cigarettes (8.4 percent). In 2014, adults ages 18–24 used e-cigarettes more than adults 25 or older, suggesting that these were particularly popular for younger people (USDHHS, 2016a). Other data suggest that this trend may be reversing: Use of e-cigarettes among middle and high school students declined in 2016 compared with 2015 (Miech, Johnston, et al., 2017).

Some argue that e-cigarettes are safer alternatives to cigarettes containing tar and other carcinogens and that they may assist people who want to quit smoking or dissuade others from trying actual cigarettes. However, longitudinal studies now show that, at least among young people, those who vape are *more* likely to take up smoking old-fashioned tobacco cigarettes (Miech, Patrick, et al., 2017).

The Surgeon General issued a report in 2016 on e-cigarettes. Its findings on the health impact of e-cigarettes noted the hazards of nicotine and said that additional research is needed on the health impact of the aerosol products used in vape pipes and pens. However, the ingredients used to heat and convert nicotine to vapor are not always listed on packages, and the health impact of these ingredients are not yet known (Talih, Balhas, et al., 2015; Varlet, Farsalinos, et al., 2015).

The FDA finalized regulations for e-cigarettes in 2016. These regulations treat e-cigarettes like any other regulated tobacco product, thus making it illegal to sell them to children under the age of 18, requiring warning labels about nicotine's addictive properties, and calling for scientific evidence to support any claims about their safety relative to other tobacco products. Seven states plus the District of Columbia prohibit the use of e-cigarettes wherever smoking is prohibited. Another 24 states impose some prohibitions on e-cigarette use in public places (http://www.publichealthlawcenter.org/resources/us-e-cigarette-regulations-50-state-review).

Marijuana

Marijuana consists of the dried and crushed leaves and flowering tops of the hemp plant, *Cannabis sativa*. It is most often smoked, but it may be chewed, prepared as a tea, or eaten in baked goods. **Hashish**, much stronger than marijuana, is produced by removing and drying the resin exudate of the tops of cannabis plants. In DSM-5, cannabis use disorder is the category name that includes marijuana.

Synthetic marijuana contains artificially created chemicals similar to those contained in cannabis. These chemicals are typically sprayed onto inert plant materials and placed in small packages and sold under names such as Spice or K2. Synthetic marijuana was made illegal in 2011, and use among high school students declined from 11 percent to 3 percent from 2011 to 2016 (Johnston, O'Malley, et al., 2017).

Prevalence of Marijuana Use Although it is considered an illicit (illegal) drug by SAMHSA, marijuana is legal for all uses in 8 states and for medical use in 29 states. In 2015, over 22 million people reported using marijuana in the past month, and it is the most commonly used drug across all age groups (SAMHSA, 2016). (See **Figure 10.2** for data on usage from 2006 to 2015 among young adults.) Prevalence was higher among men (10.9 percent) than women (6.1 percent) ages 18 and older reporting use in the past month in 2015. However, marijuana use was roughly equivalent across racial and ethnic groups (SAMHSA, 2016). Daily use of marijuana increased from 5.1 million in 2007 to 7.6 million in 2012. This increase may reflect that fact that marijuana use among adults is currently legal for recreational use in eight states (Alaska, California, Colorado, Maine, Massachusetts, Nevada,

The Surgeon General's report from 2006 noted that no amount of secondhand smoke is safe.

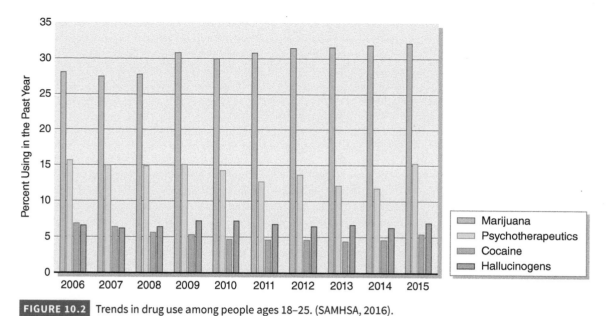

FIGURE 10.2 Trends in drug use among people ages 18–25. (SAMHSA, 2016).

Note: Annual survey questions in 2015 for hallucinogens and psychotherapeutics (and thus the 2015 numbers) are not directly comparable to prior years, according to SAMHSA. Psychotherapeutics refers to the misuse of pain relievers, tranquilizers, stimulants, or sedatives and do not include over-the-counter medications.

Oregon, Washington) and the District of Columbia. It is approved for medical use in many more states, a topic we return to later.

Effects of Marijuana As with most other drugs, legal or not, marijuana use has its risks. Generally, the more we learn about a drug, the less benign it turns out to be, at least for some people, and marijuana is no exception (see **Focus on Discovery 10.2**).

The major active chemical in marijuana is delta-9-tetrahydrocannabinol (THC). The amount of THC in marijuana is variable, but marijuana is more potent now than it was 20 years ago (Mehmedic, Chandra, et al., 2010). In addition, users smoke more now than in the past (e.g., a "blunt" contains more cannabis than a joint).

Psychological Effects The intoxicating effects of marijuana, like those of most drugs, depend in part on the potency and size of the dose. Smokers of marijuana find that it makes them feel relaxed and sociable. Large doses can bring rapid shifts in emotion, dull attention, fragment thoughts, impair memory, and give the sense that time is moving more slowly. Extremely heavy doses have sometimes induced hallucinations and other effects similar to those of hallucinogens, including extreme panic, sometimes arising from the belief that a frightening experience will never end. Dosage can be difficult to regulate because it may take up to half an hour after smoking marijuana for its effects to appear; many users thus get much higher than intended.

Focus on Discovery 10.2

Is Marijuana a Gateway Drug?

The so-called gateway hypothesis of marijuana use has been around for a long time. According to this view, marijuana is dangerous not only in itself but also because it is a first step for young people on the path to developing problems with other drugs, such as heroin.

Is there evidence that marijuana is indeed a gateway to more serious substance use? Overall, the answer to this question is no.

Most young people who use marijuana do *not* go on to use such drugs as heroin and cocaine (Hall & Lynskey, 2005). So, if by *gateway* we mean that escalation to a more serious drug is inevitable, then marijuana is not a gateway drug. However, we do know that many, but far from all, who use heroin and cocaine began their drug experimentation with marijuana. And some evidence suggests that users of marijuana are more likely than nonusers to experiment later with heroin and cocaine (Kandel & Kandel, 2015; Miller & Volk, 1996).

Most people who use marijuana do not go on to use heroin, but many heroin users do begin their drug use with marijuana.

Animal models have been developed to explain how the physiological effects of marijuana may alter the brain to influence the response to other drugs. However, translating these findings to people is challenging. Even though marijuana use often precedes other drug use, it does not appear to *cause* later drug use, as the term *gateway* implies (Hall & Lynskey, 2005). Rather, it may be that marijuana is the first drug to be tried because it is more socially acceptable than other drugs.

Has legalization of medical or recreational marijuana changed patterns of use? One analysis of the impact of medical marijuana laws found that high school students from states with legal medical marijuana were more likely to use it than students from states that do not have legal medical marijuana. However, use in states with medical marijuana did not increase after the law was passed. Time will tell whether legalization of recreational marijuana will increase the likelihood of other serious drug use, as some critics of legalization argue, or will instead be more like cigarettes and alcohol—legal drugs that are associated with other drug use but not necessarily a direct cause of their use.

Accumulated scientific evidence indicates that marijuana can interfere with cognitive functioning, including areas such as attention, planning, decision making, working memory, and problem solving (Broyd, van Hell, et al., 2016; Crean, Crane, & Mason, 2011). Does chronic use of marijuana affect cognitive functioning even when the person is not using the drug? Unfortunately, not many well-controlled studies have been conducted to address this question. One large longitudinal study of people from New Zealand assessed marijuana use at five time points from the ages of 18 to 38. Neuropsychological functioning was assessed at age 13 prior to initiation of marijuana use and again at age 38. The researchers found that those people who persistently met the criteria for what would now be called severe cannabis use disorder had reductions in IQ points and poorer performance on tests assessing working memory and processing compared with people who had never used marijuana or did so less persistently (Meier, Caspi, et al., 2012). This was particularly true for those who began using marijuana chronically as adolescents. Those people in the study who used marijuana but not regularly showed no decline in IQ or impairment on the neuropsychological tests.

Studies have also demonstrated that being high on marijuana can impair complex psychomotor skills necessary for driving (Romano & Voas, 2011; Sewell, Poling, & Sofuoglu, 2009). Poor performance after smoking one or two marijuana cigarettes containing 2 percent THC can persist for up to 8 hours after a person believes he or she is no longer high. This creates the danger that people will drive when they are not functioning adequately.

Physical Consequences The short-term effects of marijuana include bloodshot and itchy eyes, dry mouth and throat, increased appetite, reduced pressure within the eye, and somewhat raised blood pressure.

We know that the long-term use of marijuana can impair lung structure and function (Martinasek, McGrogan, et al., 2016). Even though marijuana users smoke far fewer cigarettes than do tobacco smokers, most inhale marijuana smoke more deeply and retain it in their lungs for much longer periods of time. Since marijuana has some of the same carcinogens found in tobacco, it too has harmful effects.

How does marijuana affect the brain? Researchers have identified two cannabinoid brain receptors, called CB1 and CB2 (Matsuda, Lolait, et al., 1990; Munro, Thomas, et al., 1993). CB1 receptors are found throughout the body and the brain, with a particularly high number in the hippocampus, an important region of the brain for learning and memory. Researchers have found that the cognitive problems associated with marijuana use are linked to the effects of marijuana on these receptors in the hippocampus (Ranganthan & D'Souza, 2006).

An fMRI study of people who did and did not regularly use marijuana found that regular users showed different patterns of connectivity (see Chapter 2) between the amygdala and frontal cortex while attempting to regulate negative emotions (Zimmerman, Walz, et al., 2017). These findings might help explain some of the psychological effects associated with marijuana use, including changes in emotion and attentional capabilities.

Marijuana users can develop tolerance, and withdrawal symptoms such as restlessness, depression, anxiety, tension, stomach pains, and insomnia can occur if marijuana is discontinued (Hasin, Keyes, et al., 2008).

Therapeutic Effects and Legalization Research since the 1970s has established a number of therapeutic uses for marijuana. These include reduction in the nausea and loss of appetite that accompany chemotherapy for some people with cancer, glaucoma, chronic pain, muscle spasms, seizures, and discomfort from AIDS.

The potential benefits of smoking marijuana were confirmed 20 years ago (National Institutes of Health, 1997; Institute of Medicine, 1999). The Institute of Medicine report recommended that people with "debilitating symptoms" or terminal illnesses be allowed to smoke marijuana under close medical supervision for up to 6 months; the rationale for smoking was based on findings that THC swallowed by mouth does not provide the same relief as does smoking. But the Institute of Medicine report also emphasized the dangers of smoking per se and urged the development of alternative delivery systems, such as inhalers.

California was the first state to pass a law legalizing medical use of marijuana, in 1996. Since then, 28 other states as well as the District of Columbia have approved the use of marijuana for

Demonstrators advocate the legalization of marijuana.

medical purposes.[2] As noted earlier, eight states have legalized all use of marijuana as of 2017, though several states are still working out regulations regarding sales. These state laws are currently in conflict with a federal law that makes any marijuana use illegal. Thus, state officials in these states will not prosecute people for using medical marijuana, even though federal officials may do so. The debate on this issue will likely continue for years to come as more states consider legalization of all uses of marijuana for adults.

One question that will inform this debate is whether state laws legalizing marijuana are associated with an increase in use, particularly among adolescents. One study addressed this question using data from the annual *Monitoring the Future Survey,* which collected data from more than 1 million eighth-, tenth-, and twelfth-grade students from 1991 to 2014 (Hasin, Wall, et al., 2015). They found that use among adolescents was higher in states that had legalized medical marijuana compared with states that had not done so. However, within those states that legalized medical marijuana, use did not increase after the law was passed—use among adolescents was already higher in these states. Therefore, it does not appear that medical marijuana legalization is associated with an increase in use among adolescents. Since so few states have legalized recreational use, it is difficult to ascertain the impact of these laws on adolescent use. One study looked at Colorado and Washington—the first two states to legalize recreational use—and found that usage increased in Washington, but not Colorado (Cerdá, Wall, et al., 2017). Additional studies will likely continue to address this question in the future.

[2]States that have approved medical marijuana use are: Alaska, Arizona, Arkansas, California, Colorado, Connecticut, Delaware, Florida, Hawaii, Illinois, Maine, Maryland, Massachusetts, Michigan, Minnesota, Montana, Nevada, New Hampshire, New Jersey, New Mexico, New York, North Dakota, Ohio, Oregon, Pennsylvania, Rhode Island, Vermont, Washington, and West Virginia.

Frances Roberts/Alamy

Quick Summary

Alcohol and drug use is common in the United States. The DSM-5 lists substance use disorders for alcohol and many other substances, with severity determined by the number of symptoms present.

Withdrawal from alcohol can involve hallucinations and delirium tremens (DT). People who use or have severe alcohol use disorder may use other drugs as well, particularly nicotine. Alcohol use is particularly high among college students; men are more likely to drink alcohol than women, though this difference continues to shrink, and differences in alcohol use disorder by race and ethnicity have been observed. Moderate drinking has been linked to cardiovascular health benefits but also problems during pregnancy and for brain health.

Smoking remains widespread, though it has been on the decline. Cigarette smoking causes several illnesses, including several cancers, heart disease, and other lung diseases. The ill effects of tobacco are greater for African Americans. Secondhand smoke, also called environmental tobacco smoke (ETS), is also linked to many serious health problems. E-cigarettes rapidly became popular among young people, though use may be declining. The ill effects of nicotine in these products are the same as in cigarettes; additional studies suggest that there may be negative effects on health from the aerosol products used in vape pipes.

Marijuana makes people feel relaxed and sociable, but it can also interfere with cognitive functioning. In addition, it has been linked to lung-related problems. It remains the most prevalently used drug, particularly among younger people. Men use it more than women. Users can develop tolerance to and suffer withdrawal symptoms from marijuana. Marijuana also has therapeutic benefits, including for those suffering from the side effects of chemotherapy and for those with AIDS, glaucoma, seizures, chronic pain, and muscle spasms.

Check Your Knowledge 10.1
(Answers are at the end of the chapter.)

True or false?

1. The diagnosis of a substance use disorder requires both tolerance and withdrawal.

2. Research suggests that nicotine can enhance the rewarding properties of alcohol.

3. Even moderate drinking by pregnant women can cause learning and attention problems in their children.

Fill in the blanks.

4. List three types of cancer that are caused by smoking.

5. Marijuana can have _____ effects on learning and memory; it is less clear if there are _____ effects.

6. List three of the therapeutic benefits of marijuana.

7. Describe two similarities and two differences between e-cigarettes and cigarettes.

Clinical Descriptions: Opioid, Stimulant, and Other Drug Use Disorders

Clinical Case

Brandon

Brandon played middle linebacker on his high school football team in a small town in Ohio. Impressed by his speed, agility, and strength, his coaches were talking about college scholarships.

During his junior year, Brandon injured his knee. He had surgery and was up and around the day after. He was prescribed Vicodin for pain, and this helped him recover with less pain and get the most out of his physical therapy. Brandon noticed that the medication was helpful not just for his pain, but it also helped him "even out" and feel better all around. He found that taking an extra pill here and there was helpful. With the pills, he would not get so upset by his girlfriend Brianna's complaints about him taking more and more pills or his parents' nagging about doing housework. At spring practice, he felt invincible. No matter how hard the hit, he could take it.

By summer, he was having a hard time getting by without pain pills. When he tried to stop, he felt awful, like he had the flu. He would sweat and have the chills, even shake. He couldn't eat, and this was bad for bulking up for the season. Even though his doctor continued to provide him with a new prescription, the supply that should have lasted a month was gone in a few days. He could buy more from a guy downtown, but he was running out of money. The pills cost $5 each, and he needed as many as 20 a day. He wondered if he had a problem, but he thought football was a contact sport and pain went with it. Other guys on the team were taking stuff too. Plus, his senior year was coming up and re-cruiters were going to be at the games.

The guy who sold him pain pills told him he could sell him heroin for a lot less than the Norco he was now taking. He thought heroin was for losers and guys who shot up in the poorest parts of the city. The guy gave him a small bag for free, and told him he could sniff it and not shoot it. It lasted for 3 days. He reasoned he would take it just until the season was over, and then he would stop for good.

Brianna was furious with him when she found out he was taking heroin, and she threatened to tell his parents. Brandon pleaded with her not to and that he would stop. He quit taking it but again felt horrible—the worst flu ever. He decided to drive downtown and get another bag, just to help him slowly stop.

The police found Brandon slumped over the front seat of his car. They tried reviving him with Narcan, but it was too late. He was pronounced dead at the scene. An autopsy revealed that he had fentanyl—a synthetic opioid—in his system. Brandon thought he was buying heroin, but his dealer had likely substituted fentanyl without telling him. Brandon was 17 years old.

Opioids

The **opioids** include opium and its derivatives: morphine, **heroin**, and codeine. Misuse of these drugs has exploded in the past several years. In moderate doses, they can relieve pain, which is of tremendous relief to many people. Unfortunately, prescription pain medications have become among the most abused of the drugs we discuss. In 2015, nearly 19 million people (7 percent of the U.S. population) misused prescription pain medications at least once (Hughes, Williams, et al., 2016). DSM-5 categories the misuse of such drugs as opioid use disorder.

There are many different pain medications that can be legally prescribed, including **hydrocodone** and **oxycodone**. Hydrocodone is most often combined with other drugs, such as acetaminophen (the active agent in Tylenol), to create prescription pain medicines such as Vicodin, Zydone, or Lortab. Oxycodone is found in medicines such as Percodan, Tylox, and OxyContin. Vicodin is one of the most commonly abused drugs containing hydrocodone, and OxyContin is one of the most commonly abused drugs containing oxycodone. Fentanyl is another prescription pain medicine that has also become a serious and deadly drug of abuse since 2015.

Prevalence of Opioid Use and Its Consequences More than 800,000 people over age 12 in the United States reported using heroin in 2015, a slight decline from 2014 but an increase of over 30 percent from 2013 (SAMHSA, 2016). More men than women use heroin, but both are using heroin most often after first taking prescription pain medicines (Cicero, Ellis, et al., 2014), as the Clinical Case of Brandon illustrates.

Prescription pain medicines used for nonprescribed purposes are the most commonly abused opioids. According to SAMHSA, 12 million people over the age of 12 in the United States misused pain medicines in 2015 (Hughes et al., 2016). Over 2 million people met criteria for opioid use disorder based on misuse of prescription pain medicines (SAMHSA, 2016). And the number of people seeking treatment for dependence on pain medications continues to increase, more than doubling from 2005 to 2012. Although more women than men used prescription pain medicines in 2015, slightly more men than women *misused* or abused them. Misuse is substantially higher among white Americans compared to any other ethnic or racial group (SAMHSA, 2015). **Table 10.6** lists some of the common pain medications.

TABLE 10.6 **Types of Prescription Pain Medications**

Category	Commonly prescribed examples
Oxycodone	OxyContin, Percocet, Percodan
Hydrocodone	Vicodin, Lortab, Norco
Morphine	Avinza, MS Contin
Fentanyl	Actiq, Fentora
Tramadol	Ultram, Ultracet
Oxymorphone	Opana
Hydromorphone	Dilaudid, Exalgo
Buprenorphine*	Suboxone
Methadone*	

*Buprenorphine and methadone are also used to treat opioid addiction.

Source: Adapted from Hughes et al. 2016 review of NSDUH 2015 survey results.

Heroin was synthesized from opium in 1874 and was soon added to a variety of medicines that could be purchased without prescription. This ad shows a teething remedy containing heroin. It probably worked.

Pharmaceutical companies encouraged use of prescription pain medicines, arguing that the risk of addiction was very low (Quinones, 2015). Once it became clear that addiction was not as rare as these companies promised in their sales materials, lawsuits were filed. Pharmaceutical companies then began to change practices. For example, medicines such as OxyContin or Opana came in a pill format with polymer coating that made it easy to dissolve or crush into a form that could then be injected or snorted. Companies replaced the polymer-coated pills with a newly developed extended-release formula that is not as susceptible to crushing for injection.

Unfortunately, users figured out a way to inject the new formula, which is also quite dangerous. As shown in **Figure 10.3b**, visits to hospital emergency rooms after overdoses of hydrocodone and oxycodone products tripled from 2004 to 2011 (SAMHSA, 2013). As shown in **Figure 10.3a**, emergency room visits for overdoses on all pain medications also rose. From 2005 to 2014, the number of ER visits doubled (Weiss, Bailey, et al., 2017). According to the CDC, nearly 91 people *a day* died from an opioid overdose in 2015 (see https://www.cdc.gov/drugoverdose/epidemic/index.html). That is more than the number of people who died in car crashes (NHTSA, 2015). An even larger number of deaths was expected in 2016 (Katz, 2017).

Psychological and Physical Effects Opioids produce euphoria, drowsiness, and sometimes a lack of coordination. Heroin and OxyContin also produce a "rush," a feeling of warm, suffusing ecstasy immediately after an intravenous injection. The user sheds worry and fear and has great self-confidence for 4 to 6 hours. However, the user then experiences a severe letdown, bordering on stupor.

Opioids produce their effects by stimulating neural receptors of the body's own opioid system (the body naturally produces opioids, called endorphins and enkephalins). Heroin, for example, is converted into morphine in the brain and then binds to opioid receptors, which are located throughout the brain. Some evidence suggests that a link between these receptors and the dopamine system is responsible for opioids' pleasurable effects. However, evidence from animal studies suggests that opioids may achieve their pleasurable effects via their action in the area of the brain called the nucleus accumbens (Wade, Kallupi, et al., 2017).

Opioids users develop tolerance and show withdrawal symptoms. Withdrawal from heroin may begin within 8 hours of the last injection in users who have built up high tolerance.

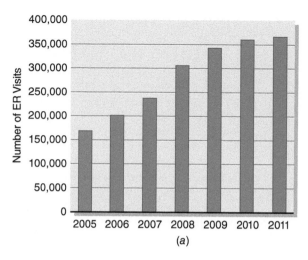

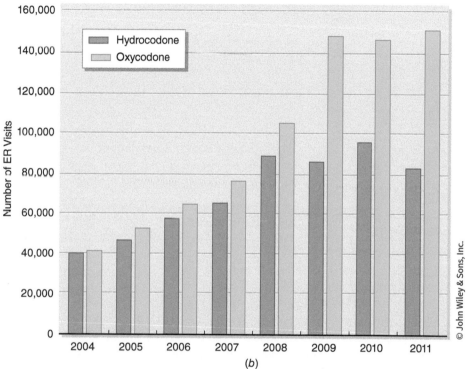

FIGURE 10.3 (a) The total number of emergency room visits for nonmedical uses of all pain medicines. (b) The total number of emergency room visits for just two drugs: hydrocodone and oxycodone (adapted from Crane, 2015.)

During the next few hours after withdrawal begins, the person typically experiences muscle pain, sneezing, and sweating; becomes tearful; and yawns a great deal. The symptoms resemble those of influenza. Within 36 hours, the withdrawal symptoms become more severe. There may be uncontrollable muscle twitching, cramps, chills alternating with excessive flushing and sweating, and a rise in heart rate and blood pressure. The person is unable to sleep, vomits, and has diarrhea. These symptoms typically persist for about 72 hours and then diminish gradually over a 5- to 10-day period.

An additional problem associated with intravenous drug use is exposure, through sharing needles, to infectious agents such as the human immunodeficiency virus (HIV), which causes AIDS. Notably, there is good consensus among scientists that needle exchange programs reduce needle sharing and the spread of infectious agents associated with intravenous drug use (Gibson, 2001; Yoast, Williams, et al., 2001). In 2009, the U.S. Congress lifted a 21-year ban on federal funding for needle exchange programs.

Clinical Case

James

James was a 27-year-old man who had been addicted to heroin for 7 years. He first tried heroin during his time in the Marine Corps. Unable to control his habit, he was dishonorably discharged from the Marines a year later. He lived with his family for a short time, but after stealing money and valuables to support his habit, he was asked to leave the house. He then began living on the street, panhandling for money to support his habit. He also donated blood platelets when he was physically able. Over the years, James lost a tremendous amount of weight and became quite malnourished. He was over 6 feet tall, but he weighed only 150 pounds. Food wasn't a priority on most days, though he was usually able to gather a meal of scraps from the local diner. James tried to get into several rehabilitation programs, but they required that he remain free of heroin for at least a week before

he could be admitted. James was able to resist for a day or two, but then withdrawal symptoms would begin, making it too painful to continue without the drug. A friend from the streets, formerly addicted to heroin, had recently helped James get to a methadone clinic. James tried methadone for a few weeks but was unable to tolerate the long waits outside the clinic each morning and the shame of being stared at by people passing on their way to work. Still, having been free of heroin for over a week, James gained admittance to a residential treatment program. One of the physicians at the program prescribed a newly approved medication called Suboxone that eased the discomfort of heroin withdrawal while replacing the cravings for heroin. James no longer needed to go to the methadone clinic, and he was getting job training at the treatment program. He was hopeful that he would shake his habit for good.

Stimulants

Stimulants act on the brain and the sympathetic nervous system to increase alertness and motor activity. Amphetamines are synthetic stimulants; cocaine is a natural stimulant extracted from the coca leaf. **Focus on Discovery 10.3** discusses a less risky and more prevalently used stimulant, caffeine.

Amphetamines Amphetamines such as Dexedrine and Adderall produce their effects by causing the release of norepinephrine and dopamine and blocking the reuptake of these neurotransmitters. **Amphetamines** are taken orally or intravenously and can be addicting. Amphetamines can heighten wakefulness, inhibit intestinal functions, and suppress appetite—hence their use in dieting. They can quicken heart rate and constrict blood vessels. A person becomes alert, euphoric, and outgoing and feels boundless energy and self-confidence. Larger doses can make a person nervous, agitated, and confused; other symptoms include palpitations, headaches, dizziness, and sleeplessness. Sometimes heavy users become extremely suspicious and hostile, to the extent that they can be dangerous to others.

Tolerance to amphetamines develops rapidly, so more and more of the drug is required to produce the stimulating effect. One study has demonstrated tolerance after just 6 days of repeated use (Comer, Hart, et al., 2001).

Focus on Discovery 10.3

Our Tastiest Addiction—Caffeine

What may be the world's most popular drug is seldom viewed as a drug at all, and yet it has strong effects. People can develop tolerance and experience withdrawal symptoms if they stop taking it (Hughes, Higgins, et al., 1991). Users and nonusers joke about it, and most readers of this book have probably had some this very day. We are, of course, referring to **caffeine**, a substance found in coffee, tea, cocoa, cola and other soft drinks, some cold remedies, and some diet pills.

A "grande" (160 ounces) cup of coffee from Starbucks contains 300 milligrams of caffeine. As little as 150 milligrams of caffeine can affect most people within half an hour. Metabolism, body temperature, and blood pressure all increase; urine production goes up; there may be hand tremors, appetite can diminish, and, most familiar of all, sleepiness is warded off. Extremely large doses of caffeine can cause headache, diarrhea, nervousness, severe agitation, even convulsions and death. Death, though, is very rare unless a person takes a very large amount of caffeine in a very short period of time because the drug is eliminated by the kidneys without much accumulation. Unfortunately, this is just what happened to a 16-year-old high school student in 2017. He consumed coffee, a soft drink, and an energy drink in 2 hours or less and subsequently died from cardiac arrest, probably caused by a heart arrhythmia triggered by the excessive caffeine. His heart was healthy; the caffeine was too much for it.

Although it has long been recognized that drinkers of very large amounts of caffeinated coffee daily can experience withdrawal symptoms when consumption ceases, people who drink no more than two cups of coffee a day can suffer from headaches, fatigue, and anxiety if caffeine is withdrawn from their daily diet (Ferré, 2008), and these symptoms can interfere with social and occupational functioning. These findings are important because two-thirds of Americans have at least one cup of coffee a day, and coffee drinkers report having close to three cups a day according to a 2015 Gallup poll (Saad, 2015). And although parents may prohibit coffee, they often allow their children to have caffeine-laden soft drinks, energy drinks, or hot chocolate and to eat chocolate. Thus, our addiction to caffeine can begin to develop as early as 6 months of age, the form of it changing as we move from childhood to adulthood.

Bloomberg via Getty Images

The caffeine found in coffee, tea, and soft drinks is probably the world's favorite drug.

Methamphetamine The most commonly abused stimulant drug is an amphetamine derivative called **methamphetamine**. The percentage of people over the age of 12 who reported ever using methamphetamine declined from 7.4 percent to 3 percent from 2002 to 2014 according to annual survey data from the National Survey on Drug Use and Health (SAMHSA, 2014). However, these may have been underestimates because the survey only asked about misuse of prescription methamphetamine. In fact, most methamphetamine comes from illicit sources, and in 2015 the annual survey questions were changed to ask about these uses (Center for Behavioral Health Statistics and Quality, 2015). In 2015, 5.4 percent (897,000 people) reported ever having used methamphetamine (SAMHSA, 2016).

Men are more likely to abuse methamphetamine than women, in contrast with abuse of other amphetamines, where few gender differences occur. Methamphetamine is used (and manufactured) in small towns in the United States as much as, if not more than, in big cities. The loss of manufacturing jobs in rural towns along with consolidation of the American food business into a few big conglomerates instead of many smaller family farms may have contributed to a rise in methamphetamine use (Redding, 2009).

Like other amphetamines, methamphetamine can be taken orally, intravenously, or intranasally (i.e., by snorting). In a clear crystal form, the drug is often referred to as "crystal meth" or "ice." Craving for methamphetamine is particularly strong, often lasting several years after use is discontinued. Craving is also a reliable predictor of later use (Hartz, Frederick-Osborne,

Clinical Case

Anton

Anton, a 37-year-old man, had just been arrested for a parole violation: stealing a package of string cheese from a convenience store. He was also found to be under the influence of methamphetamine. Two months earlier, he had been released from prison after serving time for petty theft and for purchasing methamphetamine. He was determined to remain out of prison, but his cravings for meth were so intense that he was unable to abide by the terms of his parole. He had been using meth since he was 26 years old and had been arrested numerous times for drug-related offenses, including prostitution (to get money to support his habit).

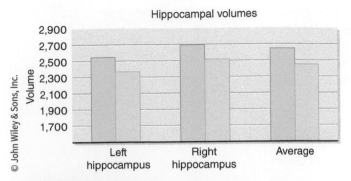

Hippocampal volumes

FIGURE 10.4 Results from an fMRI study showing that those who abused methamphetamine (green bars) had smaller hippocampal volume (size) than those in the control group (blue bars) who did not abuse methamphetamine. (Adapted from Thompson et al., 2004.)

& Galloway, 2001). As with other amphetamines, users get an immediate high, or rush, that can last for hours. This includes feelings of euphoria as well as changes to the body, such as increases in blood flow to the heart and other organs and an increase in body temperature. The high eventually levels off (the "shoulder"), and then it comes crashing down ("tweaking"). Not only do the good feelings crash, but the person also becomes very agitated. Physiological dependence on methamphetamine often includes both tolerance and withdrawal.

Several animal studies have indicated that chronic use of methamphetamine causes damage to the brain, affecting both the dopamine and the serotonin systems (Frost & Cadet, 2000). Neuroimaging studies have found that methamphetamine use is associated with reductions in brain volume (size) in areas in the temporal and frontal cortices (Hall, Alhassoon, et al., 2015; Mackey & Paulus, 2013). For example, one study of chronic meth users found damage to the hippocampus (see **Figure 10.4**). The volume of the hippocampus was smaller among chronic meth users, which correlated with poorer performance on a memory test (Thompson, Hayashi, et al., 2004).

Meta-analyses of brain imaging studies indicate that areas of the brain impacted by methamphetamine use involve areas associated with reward and decision making, such as the insula, areas of the frontal and temporal cortex, and striatum (Ersche, Williams, et al., 2013; Hall et al., 2015). One study found that lower activation in these regions during a decision-making task predicted relapse to methamphetamine use 1 year after treatment (Paulus, Tapert, & Schuckit, 2005). Although it may seem obvious that poor decision making might put one at higher risk for relapse, it is less clear whether the methamphetamine damaged these areas or whether these areas were damaged before methamphetamine use began.

A caveat should be noted here. One difficulty with conducting these types of studies is finding participants who use only the drug of interest (in this case, methamphetamine) so that any observed effects can be linked exclusively to that drug. However, it is difficult to find meth users who have not at some point used other substances, particularly alcohol and nicotine. For example, in one of the studies described earlier, the meth users did not differ from the control group in alcohol consumption, but they did smoke more (Thompson et al., 2004). Nevertheless, it seems clear that the deleterious effects of methamphetamine are many and serious.

Cocaine The drug **cocaine** comes from the leaves of the coca shrub. A form of cocaine, called **crack**, was developed in the mid-1980s and comes in a rock-crystal form that is then heated, melted, and smoked. The name *crack* comes from the crackling sound the rock makes when being heated. Crack is cheaper than cocaine and is used predominantly in urban areas.

Although very popular in the 1970s and 1980s, cocaine is used less frequently today. From 2006 to 2015, usage in the past year declined among people ages 18 to 25, from 6.9 to 5.4 percent (see Figure 10.2). In 2015, 1.9 million people over the age of 12 reported using cocaine in the past month, down from 2.4 million in 2006 (SAMHSA, 2016). Use of crack is also declining. The number of people using crack for the first time decreased from 2002 to 2015, from 337,000 to 37,000 (SAMHSA, 2016). Men use cocaine and crack more often than women do.

Cocaine can be sniffed (snorted), smoked in pipes or cigarettes, swallowed, or even injected into the veins; some heroin users mix the two drugs. It acts rapidly on the brain, blocking the reuptake of dopamine in mesolimbic areas. Cocaine yields pleasurable states because dopamine left in the synapse facilitates neural transmission. Self-reports of pleasure induced by cocaine are related to the extent to which cocaine has blocked dopamine reuptake (Volkow, Wang, et al., 1997). Cocaine can increase sexual desire and produce feelings of self-confidence, well-being, and stamina. An overdose may bring on chills, nausea, and insomnia, as well as strong paranoid

Crack use is highest in urban areas.

feelings and terrifying hallucinations of insects crawling beneath the skin. Chronic use can lead to heightened irritability, impaired social relationships, paranoid thinking, and disturbances in eating and sleeping. Some, but not all, users develop tolerance to cocaine, requiring a larger dose to achieve the same effect. Stopping cocaine use appears to cause severe withdrawal symptoms.

Cocaine is a vasoconstrictor, causing the blood vessels to narrow. As users take larger and larger doses of the purer forms of cocaine, they are more often rushed to emergency rooms and may die of an overdose, often from a heart attack. As shown in Figure 10.3, there were over 500,000 cocaine related visits to emergency rooms in 2001 (SAMHSA, 2013). Cocaine also increases a person's risk for stroke and causes cognitive impairments, such as difficulty paying attention and remembering.

Because of its strong vasoconstricting properties, cocaine poses special dangers in pregnancy, for the blood supply to the developing fetus may be compromised. An MRI study compared the gray matter (i.e., neural tissue of the brain) volume of adolescents who were exposed to cocaine prenatally with those who were not. Adolescents who had been exposed to cocaine prenatally were found to have lower volumes in areas of the frontal cortex and nearby regions that aid in cognitive control and emotion regulation compared with adolescents who were not prenatally exposed to cocaine (Rando, Chaplin, et al., 2013). However, the prenatally exposed adolescents were also more likely to have initiated their own substance use, so it is impossible to tell if the different brain sizes were the result of prenatal cocaine exposure or their own substance use. It is likely that both factors contributed.

A coca plant. The leaves contain about 1 percent cocaine.

Hallucinogens, Ecstasy, and PCP

LSD and Other Hallucinogens Hallucinogens include drugs such as LSD, psilocybin, and mescaline. The term **hallucinogen** refers to the main effects of such drugs, hallucinations. Unlike the hallucinations in schizophrenia, however, these are usually recognized by the person as being caused by the drug. More men than women use hallucinogens, and more European Americans use them compared with other racial and ethnic groups (SAMHSA, 2016).

LSD (lysergic acid diethylamide) was very popular in the 1960s but regular use generally declined over the next 50 years. However, the number of new users of LSD increased to 664,000 in 2015, up from 421,000 in 2012 (SAMHSA, 2016). There is no evidence of withdrawal symptoms, but tolerance appears to develop rapidly (Halberstadt, 2015).

Hallucinogens appear to exert their effects via the serotonin system and the 5-HT$_{2A}$ receptor (Halberstadt, 2015). In addition to hallucinations, LSD can alter a person's sense of time (it seems to go slowly). A person using LSD may have sharp mood swings but can also experience an expanded consciousness such that he or she seems to appreciate sights and sounds as never before. These effects take place within 30 minutes of taking LSD and can last for up to 12 hours (Schmid, Enzler, et al., 2015).

Cocaine can be smoked, swallowed, injected, or snorted as shown here.

Some users can feel anxious after taking LSD, in part because the perceptual experiences and hallucinations can provoke fears that they are "going crazy." The anxiety usually subsides as the drug is metabolized. Paradoxically, LSD has shown modest success for reducing anxiety in people diagnosed with life-threatening illnesses (Gasser, Holstein, et al., 2014).

Flashbacks are visual recurrences of perceptual experiences after the physiological effects of the drug have worn off. In DSM-5, the category hallucinogen persisting perception disorder involves re-experiences of flashbacks and other perceptual symptoms that occurred during hallucinogen use, even though the drug is no longer used.

Ecstasy and PCP The hallucinogen-like substance **Ecstasy** is made from **MDMA** (methylenedioxymethamphetamine). Not until the 1970s were the psychoactive properties of MDMA reported in the scientific literature. Ecstasy became illegal in 1985.

Clinical Case

Tamara

Tamara tried Ecstasy (X) for the first time when she was a freshman in college. She went to her first rave, and a friend gave her a pill she thought was a Sweet Tart. Within a short period of time, she began to feel almost magical, as if she was seeing everything around her in a new light. She felt incredibly close to her friends and even to men and women she had just met. Hugging and close dancing were intensely pleasurable in a completely new way. A few days after the party, she asked her friend about the "Sweet Tart" and found out how she could obtain more. But the next time she tried X, she was unable to achieve the same pleasurable feelings. Instead, she felt more subdued, even anxious. After several more times using X, she noticed that despite her enthusiasm and even craving for the effects, she found instead that she felt a little depressed and anxious, even several days after taking the drug.

Ecstasy is a popular party drug but, like many drugs, is not free of ill effects.

Ecstasy contains compounds from both the hallucinogen and amphetamine families, but it is currently classified in its own DSM-5 category: "other hallucinogen use disorder." Ecstasy remains popular on college campuses and in clubs; it became the mind-expanding drug of the 1990s that LSD was in the 1960s. **Focus on Discovery 10.4** discusses the use and effects of another club drug, nitrous oxide. MDMA can be taken in pill form but is often mixed with other substances (e.g., caffeine) or drugs (e.g., LSD, ketamine, talcum powder), making the effects vary dramatically. A purer powder version of Ecstasy is referred to as Molly. Whether it is actually purer requires a leap of faith, as powder can also be mixed with other substances. In 2015, over 2.5 million people age 12 or older reported using in Ecstasy during the past year (SAMHSA, 2016). The average age of first use is around 21, a statistic that has remained stable since 2002.

Ecstasy acts primarily by contributing to both the release and the subsequent reuptake of serotonin (Huether, Zhou, & Ruther, 1997; Liechti, Bauman, et al., 2000; Morgan, 2000). Whether Ecstasy causes harm is still a topic of scientific debate. A meta-analysis of 7 studies found that Ecstasy has neurotoxic effects on the serotonin system by reducing the availability of a transporter called SERT throughout the brain (Roberts, Jones, & Montgomery, 2016). It is difficult to say whether these toxic effects

Focus on Discovery 10.4

Nitrous Oxide—Not a Laughing Matter

Nitrous oxide is a colorless gas that has been available since the nineteenth century. Within seconds, it induces lightheadedness and a state of euphoria in most people; for some, important insights seem to flood the mind. Many people find otherwise mundane events and thoughts irresistibly funny, hence the nickname *laughing gas.*

Many people have received nitrous oxide at a dentist's office to facilitate relaxation and otherwise make a potentially uncomfortable and intimidating dental procedure more palatable. A major advantage of nitrous oxide over other analgesics and relaxants is that a person can return to a normal waking state within minutes of breathing enriched oxygen or normal air.

Nitrous oxide fits in the broader category of inhalants and has been used recreationally since it first became available, although it has been illegal for many years in most states except as administered by appropriate health professionals. As with the other drugs examined in this chapter, illegality has not prevented unsupervised use. It is one of the most commonly used inhalants among teens (sniffing glue, gasoline, and paint are more prevalent), with 684,000 teens ages 12 to 17 reporting use in 2015 (SAMHSA, 2016). Sometimes called "hippie crack" or "whippets," nitrous oxide balloons are often combined with the use of Ecstasy and other drugs at parties with bright laser lights and loud dance music (i.e., at raves).

Nitrous oxide is no laughing matter.

are directly due to drug use, since no studies in humans have assessed serotonin functioning both before and after Ecstasy use. One small study reported that serotonin system functioning appeared to revert to normal after use was discontinued (Selvaraj, Hoshi, et al., 2009).

Users report that Ecstasy enhances intimacy and insight, improves interpersonal relationships, elevates positive emotion and self-confidence, and promotes aesthetic awareness. It can also cause muscle tension, rapid eye movements, jaw clenching, nausea, faintness, chills or sweating, anxiety, depression, depersonalization, and confusion.

PCP, phencyclidine, often called *angel dust*, is coded as phencyclidine use disorder in DSM-5 and is in the chapter on hallucinogen-related disorders. The number of people trying PCP for the first time in 2015 was 42,000 down from 90,000 in 2012 (SAMHSA, 2016). Like most drugs, more men than women use PCP.

PCP generally causes serious negative reactions, including severe paranoia and violence. Coma and death are also possible. PCP affects multiple neurotransmitters in the brain, and chronic use is associated with a variety of neuropsychological deficits. People who abuse PCP are likely to have used other drugs either before or concurrently with PCP, so it is difficult to sort out whether neuropsychological impairments are due solely to PCP, to other drugs, or to the combination.

Quick Summary

Opioids include heroin and other pain medications such as hydrocodone and oxycodone. Abuse of prescription pain medications has risen dramatically, and overdoses are common. Initial effects of opioids include euphoria; later, users experience a letdown. Death by overdose from opioids is a severe problem. Other problems include exposure to HIV and other infectious agents via shared needles. Withdrawal is severe for opioids.

Amphetamines are stimulants that produce wakefulness, alertness, and euphoria. Men and women use these equally. Tolerance develops quickly. Methamphetamine is a synthesized amphetamine, and use increased dramatically in the 1990s but has leveled off in recent years. Methamphetamine can damage the brain, including the hippocampus. Cocaine can increase sexual desire, feelings of well-being, and alertness, but chronic use is associated with problems in relationships, paranoia, and trouble sleeping, among other things.

LSD was a popular hallucinogen in the 1960s, often thought of as a mind-expanding drug. The mind-expanding drug of the 1990s was Ecstasy. Although these drugs do not typically elicit withdrawal symptoms, tolerance can develop. A so-called purer form of Ecstasy called Molly is used, but its purity cannot be ascertained. PCP remains a problem, though use has declined in the past three years. This drug can cause severe paranoia and violence.

Check Your Knowledge 10.2

True or false?

1. Withdrawal from heroin begins slowly, days after use has been discontinued.

2. The use of OxyContin began in urban areas but quickly spread to rural areas.

3. Methamphetamine is a less potent form of amphetamine and so is less likely to be associated with brain impairment.

4. Ecstasy contains compounds associated with hallucinogens and amphetamines.

Etiology of Substance Use Disorders

As with all the disorders we have discussed in this book, several factors contribute to the etiology of substance use disorders. Of course, not all people who use a substance develop a substance use disorder. One of the key questions about the etiology of substance use disorders is why some people develop a disorder after substance use and others do not. In the following sections, we discuss genetic, neurobiological, psychological, and sociocultural factors associated with substance use disorders. Keep in mind that these factors are likely to be differently related to different substances. Genetic factors, for example, may play a role in alcohol use disorder but may be less important in hallucinogen use disorder.

Genetic Factors

Much research has addressed the possibility that there is a genetic contribution to drug and alcohol use disorders. Several studies have shown that relatives and children of problem drinkers have higher-than-expected rates of alcohol use disorder (e.g., Chassin, Pitts, et al., 1999). Stronger evidence for genetic factors comes from twin studies, which have revealed greater concordance in identical twins than in fraternal twins for alcohol use disorder (McGue, Pickens, & Svikis, 1992), smoking (Li, Cheng, et al., 2003), heavy use of marijuana (Kendler & Prescott, 1998), and drug use disorders in general (Tsuang, Lyons, et al., 1998). Other behavioral genetics studies indicate that the genetic and shared environmental risk factors (see Chapter 2) for illicit drug use disorders may be rather nonspecific (Kendler, Jacobsen, et al., 2003). That is, genetic and shared environmental risk factors appear to be the same no matter what the drug (marijuana, cocaine, opioids, hallucinogens, sedatives, stimulants), and this appears to be true for both men and women (Kendler, Prescott, et al., 2003).

Of course, genes do their work via the environment, and research has uncovered gene–environment relationships in alcohol and drug use disorders (Kendler, Chen, et al., 2012). Among adolescents, peers appear to be particularly important environmental variables. For example, a large twin study in Finland found that heritability for alcohol problems among adolescents was higher among those teens who had many peers who drank compared with those who had a smaller number of peers who drank (Dick, Pagan, et al., 2007). The environment in this case was peer-group drinking behavior. Another study found that heritability for both alcohol and smoking among adolescents was higher for those teens whose best friend also smoked and drank (Harden, Hill, et al., 2008). In this case, the environment was best-friend behavior. Another study found that heritability for smoking was greater for teens who went to schools where the "popular crowd" smoked compared with schools where the popular students did not smoke (Boardman, Saint Onge, et al., 2008).

The ability to tolerate large quantities of alcohol may be inherited for alcohol use disorder. That is, to become dependent on alcohol, a person usually must be able to drink a lot. Some ethnic groups, such as Asians, may have a low rate of alcohol problems because of physiological intolerance, which is caused by an inherited deficiency in the enzymes involved in alcohol metabolism, called *alcohol dehydrogenases* or ADH. Mutations in genes called ADH2 and ADH3 code proteins for the ADH enzymes, and these genes have been linked with alcohol use disorders generally as well as among some Asian populations specifically (Edenberg, Xuie, et al., 2006; Sher, Grekin, & Williams, 2005). About three-quarters of Asians experience unpleasant effects such as flushing (blood flow to the face) from small quantities of alcohol, which may protect them from becoming dependent on alcohol.

Research has also emerged on the mechanism through which genetics plays a role in smoking. Like most drugs, nicotine appears to stimulate dopamine release and inhibit its reuptake, and people who are more sensitive to these effects of nicotine are more likely to become regular smokers (Pomerleau, Collins, et al., 1993). Research has examined a link between smoking and a gene that regulates the reuptake of dopamine called SLC6A3 (also known as *DAT1*). One form of this gene has been related to a lower likelihood of smoking (Lerman, Caporaso, et al., 1999), a greater likelihood of quitting (Sabo, Nelson, et al., 1999; Stapleton, Sutherland, & O'Gara, 2007), and greater sensitivity to smoking cues (e.g., cigarette pack) (Wetherill, Jagannathan, et al., 2014).

Research has also found that genes, such as *CYP2A6*, which codes for an enzyme that metabolizes nicotine, may contribute to nicotine dependence (Furberg, Kim, et al., 2010). Slower nicotine metabolism means that nicotine stays in the brain longer. Evidence suggests that variants of this gene are linked to more smoking per day (Murphy, 2017); people who metabolize nicotine more quickly are likely to smoke more. In addition, a prospective study of smokers found that *CYP2A6* was associated with a greater risk of developing lung cancer even after controlling for other variables, such as amount of smoking (Park, Murphy, et al., 2017). Other evidence has found that people who show reduced activity in the *CYP2A6* gene smoke fewer cigarettes and are less likely to become dependent on nicotine (Audrain-McGovern & Tercyak, 2011). This is an interesting example of a gene polymorphism serving a protective function. GWAS studies have identified SNPs (single nucleotide polymorphisms; see Chapter 2) that are associated with nicotine dependence (Furberg et al., 2010; Kendler et al., 2012).

The role of genes in marijuana use has also been studied. In a large GWAS study of over 32,000 people, four different genes were associated with marijuana use, but none of the SNPs reached statistical significance at the genome-wide level, even with this large sample (Stringer, Minica, et al., 2016). Recall from earlier chapters that GWAS studies require very large sample sizes and rigorous statistical tests. In the search for SNPs associated with marijuana and other drug use, the sample sizes are not yet large enough to uncover the genetic complexity that may play a role in drug use.

Neurobiological Factors

You may have noticed that in our discussions of specific drugs, the neurotransmitter dopamine has almost always been mentioned. This is not surprising given that dopamine pathways in the brain are linked to pleasure and reward. Drug use typically results in rewarding or pleasurable feelings, and it is via the dopamine system that these feelings are produced. Research with both humans and animals shows that nearly all drugs, including alcohol, stimulate the dopamine systems in the brain (see **Figure 10.5**), particularly the mesolimbic pathway (Camí & Farré, 2003; Koob, 2008). Researchers have wondered, then, whether problems in the dopamine pathways in the brain might somehow account for why certain people become dependent on drugs.

It is difficult to tease out whether problems in the dopamine system increase the vulnerability of some people to becoming dependent on a substance, sometimes called the "vulnerability model," or whether problems in the dopamine system are the consequence of taking substances (the "toxic effect model"). For drugs such as cocaine, current research supports both views. This remains an important area to work out in future research.

Although people take drugs to feel good, they also take them to feel less bad. This is particularly true once a person becomes dependent on a substance, such as alcohol, methamphetamine, or heroin, whose withdrawal symptoms are excruciatingly unpleasant. In other

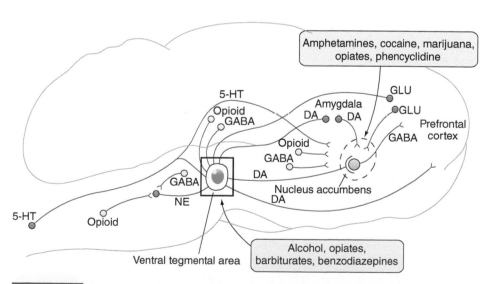

FIGURE 10.5 Reward pathways in the brain that are affected by different drugs. DA = dopamine; GABA = gamma-aminobutyric acid; GLU = glutamate; 5-HT = serotonin; NE = norepinephrine. (Adapted from Camí & Farré, 2003.)

words, people continue to take drugs to avoid the bad feelings associated with withdrawal. Moreover, they may be particularly sensitive to stress just after stopping a substance, and exposure to stress may then trigger a return to use (Kaye, Bradford, et al., 2017). A substantial body of research with animals supports this motivation for drug-taking behavior (Koob & Le Moal, 2008). Newer research supports this in humans as well. For example, one study found that people with alcohol use disorder who had recently stopped drinking exhibited larger physiological responses to unpredictable stress than did people who did not have alcohol use disorder (Moberg, Bradford, et al., 2017). This research helps to explain why relapse is so common.

Investigators have proposed a neurobiological theory to explain **cravings**, referred to as the *incentive-sensitization theory,* which considers both the craving ("wanting") for drugs and the pleasure that comes with taking the drug ("liking") (Robinson & Berridge, 1993, 2003). According to this theory, the dopamine system linked to pleasure, or liking, becomes supersensitive not just to the direct effects of drugs but also to the cues associated with drugs (e.g., needles, spoons, rolling paper). This sensitivity to cues induces craving, or wanting, and people go to extreme lengths to seek out and obtain drugs. Over time, the liking for drugs decreases, but the wanting remains very intense. These investigators argue that the transition from liking to powerful wanting, accomplished by the drug's effects on brain pathways involving dopamine, is what maintains the addiction.

Craving or wanting a substance is an important component of substance use disorders.

Many researchers study the neurobiology of cravings. A number of laboratory studies have shown that cues for a particular drug can elicit responses not altogether unlike those associated with actual use of the drug. For example, those who were dependent on cocaine showed changes in physiological arousal, increases in cravings and "high" feelings, and increases in negative emotions in response to cues of cocaine (which consisted of audio and video of people preparing to inject or snort cocaine), compared with people not dependent on cocaine (e.g., Robbins, Ehrman, et al., 2000). Brain-imaging studies have shown that cues for a drug, such as a needle or a cigarette, activate the reward and pleasure areas of the brain implicated in drug use. One study of smokers found that anticipating smoking by looking at a cigarette prior to a stressful task lessened physiological and self-report stress responses more than actually smoking prior to the task (Bradford, Curtin, & Piper, 2015).

What about the psychology of craving? Do people with stronger cravings for a substance actually use it more, even when they are trying to quit? The answer appears to be yes. In a longitudinal study of heavy drinkers, the more participants reported wanting (craving) and liking samples of alcohol (carefully presented to reduce expectancies about alcohol) at a baseline assessment, the more alcohol use disorder symptoms they had 6 years later (King, McNamara, et al., 2014).

An experience-sampling study (see Chapter 3) of people who were trying to quit smoking showed that more craving was associated with more smoking (Berkman, Falk, & Lieberman, 2011). People who had just started a smoking-cessation program were given text messages 8 times a day for 21 consecutive days. At each text prompt, they reported how many cigarettes they had smoked, how much they were craving a cigarette, and how they were feeling. Reports of more craving predicted a greater likelihood of smoking when the participants received their next text. These investigators also examined participants' brain activation using fMRI during a task called the "go/no-go task." In this task, people are presented with onscreen letters one at a time and are instructed to press a button when they see certain letters (e.g., L, V, T, N; the "go" part) but refrain from pressing the button when they see another letter (X; the "no-go" part). There are many more "go" trials than "no-go" trials, and thus it is challenging to keep from pressing the button during a "no-go" trial because people get into the habit of pressing the button many times in a row on the "go" trials. Areas of the brain that showed greater activation during "no-go" trials compared to "go" trials included the basal ganglia, inferofrontal gyrus, and pre-motor areas. People who showed greater activation in these areas during the task were better able to inhibit their button pressing; their brain was therefore likely doing a better job of providing the support for inhibiting a response when needed. In addition, greater activation in these brain regions was associated with less linkage between craving and smoking. That is, people who showed greater brain activation when inhibiting a button press were less likely to act on their cravings and begin to smoke again.

A large prospective study of heavy and light drinkers examined how wanting and liking during a lab session predicted actual drinking 2 years later. Heavy drinkers were people who had between 10 and 40 drinks a week and had more than one binge-drinking episode in most weeks; light drinkers were people who had between 1 and 5 drinks a week and had less than five binge-drinking episodes a year. The participants came to three lab sessions where they were given different amounts of alcohol and then rated wanting, liking, and sedation feelings. The researchers assessed participants' real-world drinking behavior 2 years later. Perhaps not surprisingly, they found that the heavy drinkers reported greater wanting and liking of alcohol during the laboratory sessions than did the light drinkers. By contrast, the light drinkers reported greater feelings of sedation than the heavy drinkers during the lab sessions. At follow-up, the heavy drinkers who reported greater wanting and liking for alcohol during the laboratory sessions were drinking more than the heavy drinkers who reported less liking and wanting during the lab sessions (King, de Wit, et al., 2011). Thus, even self-reports of wanting and liking are important for predicting drinking behavior.

Valuing the Short Term Over the Long Term A related psychological and neurobiological model emphasizes the distinction between the value people place on short-term (immediate) versus long-term (delayed) rewards. People with a substance use disorder often value the immediate, even impulsive, pleasure and reward that comes from taking a drug more than a delayed reward, such as a monthly paycheck from work.

Laboratory experiments to assess whether people value immediate or delayed rewards typically present people with choices of monetary rewards that are immediate but small (e.g., $1 now) or delayed but larger (e.g., $10 in a day). The extent to which people opt for the smaller, immediate reward can be calculated mathematically and is often called delay discounting. In other words, researchers can compute the extent to which people discount the value of larger, delayed rewards. People who are dependent on alcohol and drugs, such as opioids, nicotine, and cocaine, discount delayed rewards more steeply than do people not dependent on these substances (reviewed in Bickel, Koffarnus, et al., 2014). One longitudinal study found that the extent of delay discounting predicted smoking initiation in adolescents that continued into early adulthood (Audrain-McGovern, Rodriguez, et al., 2009).

At the level of the brain, valuing immediate versus delayed rewards recruits different brain regions. Researchers have hypothesized that these brain regions compete with one another when people are faced with a decision of whether to take a drug. In fMRI studies, valuing the delayed reward is associated with activation of the prefrontal cortex; valuing the immediate reward is associated with activation in amygdala and nucleus accumbens (Bechara, 2005; Bickel, Miller, et al., 2007).

Psychological Factors

In this section, we look at three other types of psychological factors that may contribute to the etiology of substance use disorders. First, we consider the effects of drugs (particularly alcohol and nicotine) on emotion regulation; we examine the situations in which a tension-reducing effect occurs and the role of cognition in this process. Second, we consider people's expectancies about the effects of substances on behavior, including beliefs about the prevalence with which a drug is used and about the health risks associated with using that drug. Third, we consider personality traits that may make it more likely for some people to use drugs heavily.

Emotion Regulation It is generally assumed that one of the main psychological motives for using drugs is to alter emotion—that is, drug use is reinforced because it enhances positive feelings or diminishes negative ones (Sayette, 2017). For example, most people believe that stress or negative emotion (e.g., because of a bad day at work) leads to increased alcohol consumption.

Unfortunately, people with substance use disorders may be less successful than people without substance use disorders in regulating negative emotion, at least when it comes to recruiting brain regions and networks that support regulation, such as the prefrontal cortex (Wilcox, Pommy, & Adinoff, 2016). Whether this is a cause or consequence of substance use is not entirely clear, but most studies that have examined emotion regulation in brain imaging studies have done so following at least 2 weeks of abstinence.

Laboratory studies have demonstrated that alcohol reduces self-reported and physiological indicators of anxiety, particularly when there is uncertainty about a negative event (e.g., having arrived home late after having drinks with friends, will you argue with your spouse?) (Bradford, Shapiro, & Curtin, 2013). In addition, research has found that alcohol lessens negative emotions such as stress and anxiety, but it also lessens positive emotions in response to anxiety-provoking situations (Curtin, Lang, et al., 1998; Stritzke, Patrick, & Lang, 1995). Longitudinal studies of stress and consumption have also provided support for this idea. For example, a longitudinal study of adolescent smokers found that increases in negative emotion and negative life events were associated with increases in smoking (Wills, Sandy, & Yaeger, 2002). Other studies have found that life stress precedes alcohol-related relapses (e.g., Brown, Beck, et al., 2000).

For many people, alcohol is consumed with other people, whether at a party, a ballgame, or dinner. Social situations can elicit a variety of emotions, including negative ones (anxiety, anger, sadness) and positive ones (love, happiness, contentment). Sayette and colleagues (Fairbairn & Sayette, 2014) have proposed that people may turn to alcohol as an emotion regulation tool in social situations because it can help people damp down thoughts of being rejected ("I must sound so stupid to these people") and focus instead on the pleasures of being around others ("This is so fun to laugh together!").

Studies of the emotion regulating properties of nicotine have yielded mixed findings, with some studies showing that nicotine reduces negative emotion and others not finding this effect (Kassel, Stroud, & Paronis, 2003). The reasons for the mixed findings may have to do with a failure to consider where people are in the course of their smoking behavior. Did they just start? Are they regular smokers? Have they tried to quit and failed? Research suggests that people experience a greater reduction of negative emotion when starting to smoke than when regularly smoking or when in relapse after treatment (Kassel et al., 2003; Shiffman & Waters, 2004). Why might this be? A laboratory study examined the types of situations associated with a reduction in negative emotion after smoking (Perkins, Karelitz, et al., 2010). Participants, who were regular smokers, had to give a speech, play a difficult computer game, abstain from smoking for 12 hours, and view disturbing pictures. The researchers found that people experienced the greatest reduction in negative emotion after the abstinence condition. That is, smoking, after not being able to smoke, provided more relief from negative emotion than it did after other stressful situations; thus, the situation is important to consider when thinking about whether smoking reduces negative emotion.

Other studies suggest that it is the sensory aspect of smoking (i.e., inhaling), not nicotine, that is associated with reducing negative emotion. In the study just described, participants experienced a reduction in negative emotion regardless of whether they were smoking cigarettes with or without nicotine (Perkins et al., 2010). Another experimental study randomly assigned smokers to have cigarettes with or without nicotine (indistinguishable by participants) after a negative or positive emotion was induced (Perkins, Ciccocioppo, et al., 2008). The researchers also manipulated smokers' expectancies. That is, some smokers expected and received a cigarette with nicotine, others expected nicotine but didn't get it, others expected no nicotine and didn't get it, and others expected no nicotine but received it anyway. Smoking reduced negative emotion for all smokers, regardless of what they expected and actually received to smoke (i.e., a cigarette with or without nicotine). Instead, the effects of inhaling, whether or not there was nicotine, had the greatest association with reducing negative emotion.

Subsequent research to examine why substances appear to reduce negative emotion in some situations but not others has focused on distraction, and several studies find that emotion effects are more likely to occur when distractions are present (Curtin et al., 1998; Fairbairn & Sayette, 2013; Josephs & Steele, 1990; Steele & Josephs, 1988). Why might this be? Alcohol impairs cognitive processing and narrows our attention to the most immediately available cues, resulting in "alcohol myopia" (Steele & Josephs, 1990). In other words, an intoxicated person has less cognitive capacity and tends to use that capacity to focus on the immediate situation, which may be a distraction from negative emotion, and thus negative emotions may decrease.

Research has also documented the added benefits of distraction for relieving anxiety with nicotine. Specifically, smokers who smoked during a distracting activity experienced a reduction in anxiety, whereas smokers who smoked without a distracting activity did not experience lessened anxiety (Kassel & Shiffman, 1997; Kassel & Unrod, 2000). However, alcohol and nicotine may increase negative emotion when no distractions are present. For example, a person drinking alone may focus all their limited cognitive capacity on unpleasant thoughts, begin brooding, and become increasingly tense and anxious, a situation reflected in the expression "crying in one's beer."

Some people smoke to reduce stress. But it does not always help.

Some people may use drugs to reduce negative emotion, whereas others may use them to increase positive emotion when they are bored (Cooper, Frone, et al., 1995). In this case, increased drug use results from a high need for stimulation combined with expectancies that drugs will promote increased positive emotion. These patterns have been found among people who abuse alcohol and cocaine (Cooper et al., 1995; Hussong, Hicks, et al., 2001).

Another reason people may opt to use substances is to increase positive emotion in social situations. In one study, participants were placed in groups of three unacquainted people to do assigned tasks and talk about whatever they wished. Some of these small groups were given alcohol to drink (cranberry juice and vodka); others were given cranberry juice. Other groups told they were drinking alcohol, but were actually given non-alcoholic beverages (tonic and cranberry juice with vodka on the outside of the glass for smell). The researchers found that the groups that drank alcohol smiled and bonded more than the other two groups (Sayette, Creswell, et al., 2012). In this study, the effects of alcohol were stronger than the expectations about alcohol. As we discuss in the next section, however, simply expecting to receive alcohol can have a profound impact on behavior.

Expectancies About Alcohol and Drug Effects

If substances don't always reduce negative emotion, why do so many people who drink or take drugs believe that it helps them unwind? Expectation may play a role here—that is, people may drink not because it actually reduces negative emotion but because they expect it to do so. In support of this idea, studies have shown that people who expect alcohol to reduce stress and anxiety are more likely to be frequent users (Rather, Goldman, et al., 1992; Sher, Walitzer, et al., 1991; Tran, Haaga, & Chambless, 1997). Furthermore, the expectation that drinking will reduce anxiety increases drinking, which in turn makes the positive expectancies even stronger (Sher, Wood, et al., 1996; Smith, Goldman, et al., 1995).

Other research has shown that expectancies about a drug's effects—for example, the beliefs that a drug will stimulate aggression and increase sexual responsiveness—predict increased drug use in general (Stacy, Newcomb, & Bentler, 1991). Similarly, people who believe (falsely) that alcohol will make them seem more socially skilled are likely to drink more heavily than those who accurately perceive that alcohol can interfere with social interactions. In now-classic experiments demonstrating the power of expectancies, participants who believe they are consuming a quantity of alcohol when they

Expectations about alcohol influence whether people will drink.

are actually consuming an alcohol-free beverage subsequently become more aggressive (Lang, Goeckner, et al., 1975). Alcohol consumption is associated with increased aggression, but expectancies about alcohol's effects can also play a role (Bushman & Cooper, 1990; Ito, Miller, & Pollock, 1996). Thus, as we have seen in other contexts, cognitions can have a powerful effect on behavior.

The extent to which a person believes a drug is harmful and the perceived prevalence of use by others are also factors related to use. In general, the greater the perceived risk of a drug, the less likely it will be used. For example, the most commonly used illegal drug among high school students is marijuana; it is also the drug with the lowest perceived risk of harm in this age group (Miech et al., 2017).

Personality Factors Personality factors that appear to be important in predicting the later onset of substance use disorders include high levels of negative affect, sometimes called *negative emotionality* or *neuroticism*; a persistent desire for arousal along with increased positive affect; and constraint, which refers to cautious behavior, harm avoidance, and conservative moral standards. One longitudinal study found that 18-year-olds who were low in constraint but high in negative emotionality were more likely to develop a substance use disorder as young adults (Krueger, 1999).

Another prospective longitudinal study investigated whether personality factors could predict the onset of substance use disorders in over 1000 male and female adolescents at age 17 and then again at age 20 (Elkins, King, et al., 2006). Low constraint and high negative emotionality predicted the onset of alcohol, nicotine, and illicit drug use disorders for both men and women.

A large meta-analysis of both cross-sectional and prospective studies assessing personality traits and psychopathology, including substance use disorders, found strong associations with low levels of agreeableness and conscientiousness, and high levels of disinhibition (i.e., low constraint), as well as moderate associations with neuroticism (Kotov, Gamez, et al., 2010). Current research is linking these personality factors with the neural circuits and genes that are associated with them (Belcher, Volkow, et al., 2014).

Sociocultural Factors

Sociocultural factors play a widely varying role in substance use disorders. People's interest in and access to drugs are influenced by peers, the media, and cultural norms about acceptable behavior.

At the broadest level, for example, we can look at great cross-national variation in substance consumption. Some research suggests that there are commonalities in substance use across countries. For example, a cross-national study of alcohol and drug use among high school students in 36 countries found that alcohol was the most common substance used across countries, despite great variation in the proportions of students who consumed alcohol, ranging from 32 percent in Zimbabwe to 99 percent in Wales (Smart & Ogburne, 2000). In all but two of the countries studied, marijuana was the next most commonly used drug. In those countries where marijuana was used most often (with more than 15 percent of high school students having ever used marijuana), there were also higher rates of use of amphetamines, Ecstasy, and cocaine.

Despite the commonalities across countries, other research documents cross-national differences in alcohol consumption. For example, high consumption rates have typically been found in wine-drinking societies, such as France, Spain, and Italy, where

Realimage/Alamy Limited

Alcohol dependence is more prevalent in countries in which alcohol use is heavy.

drinking alcohol regularly is widely accepted (deLint, 1978). Cultural attitudes and patterns of drinking thus influence the likelihood of drinking heavily and therefore of abusing alcohol. One finding that seems quite similar across different cultures is that men consume more alcohol than women. An analysis conducted by the International Research Group on Gender and Alcohol found that men drank more than women in Australia, Canada, the Czech Republic, Estonia, Finland, Israel, the Netherlands, Russia, Sweden, and the United States. Despite this consistency in gender differences, there was a large disparity across countries in the extent to which men drank more than women. For example, men drank three times more than women in Israel but only one and a half times more than women in the Netherlands (Wilsnack, Vogeltanz, et al., 2000). These findings suggest that cultural prescriptions about drinking by men and women are important to consider.

Family factors are important as well. For example, exposure to alcohol use by parents increases children's likelihood of drinking (Hawkins, Graham, et al., 1997). Unhappy marriages predicted the onset of alcohol use disorder in a study of nearly 2000 married couples (Whisman & Uebelacker, 2006). Parental support can also buffer against the negative effects of discrimination that is associated with greater drug use among minority youth (Gibbons, Gerrard, et al., 2004; Zapolski, Fisher, et al., 2016). Longitudinal studies have shown that a lack of parental monitoring leads to increased association with drug-abusing peers and subsequent higher use of drugs (Chassin, Curran, et al., 1996; Thomas, Reifman, et al., 2000). Acculturation into American society may interact with family factors for people of other cultural and ethnic backgrounds. For example, a study of 1000 Hispanic adolescents in four large U.S. cities found that substance use was related to acculturation gap stress, that is, the stress in the family associated with the gap between country of origin and the United States (Cardoso, Goldbach, et al, 2016).

The social setting in which a person operates can also affect substance use (Dimoff & Sayette, 2017; Fairbairn & Sayette, 2014). For example, studies of smokers in daily life show that they are more likely to smoke with other smokers than with nonsmokers. In addition, smoking was more likely to occur in or outside bars and restaurants, or at home, rather than in the workplace or in others' homes (Shiffman, Gwaltney, et al., 2002; Shiffman, Paty, et al., 2004).

Other studies showed that having friends who smoke predicts smoking. In longitudinal studies, peer-group identification in the 7th grade predicted smoking in the 8th grade (Sussman, Dent, et al., 1994) and increased drug use over a 3-year period (Chassin et al., 1996). Peer influences are also important in promoting alcohol (Hussong et al., 2001; Deutsch, Chernyavskiy, et al., 2015; Kelly, Chan, et al., 2012), e-cigarette (Pentz, Shin, et al., 2015), and polydrug (Chan, Kelly, et al., 2017) use.

These findings support the idea that social networks influence a person's drug or alcohol behavior. However, other evidence indicates that people who are inclined to develop substance use disorders may select social networks that conform to their own drinking or drug use patterns. Thus, we have two broad explanations for how the social environment is related to substance use disorders: a social influence model and a social selection model. A longitudinal study of over 1200 adults designed to test which model best accounted for drinking behavior found support for both models (Bullers, Cooper, & Russell, 2001). A person's social network predicted individual drinking, but individual drinking also predicted subsequent social network drinking. In fact, the social selection effects were stronger, indicating that people often choose social networks with drinking patterns like their own. No doubt the selected networks then support or reinforce their drinking.

Another variable to be considered is the media. Television commercials associate beer with attractive men and women having a good time. Billboards equate cigarettes with excitement, relaxation, and being in style. A review

Advertising is one way that expectancies develop.

Bill Aaron/PhotoEdit

of studies found that tobacco billboards were more than twice as common in primarily African American neighborhoods than they were in primarily European American neighborhoods (Primack, Bost, et al., 2007).

Does advertising change substance use patterns among young people? Some evidence indicates that it does. In a longitudinal study of nonsmoking adolescents, those who had a favorite cigarette ad were twice as likely to begin smoking subsequently or to be willing to do so (Pierce, Choi, et al., 1998). Advertising about the ill effects of smoking is also associated with a lower likelihood of becoming a smoker (Emery, Kim, et al., 2012).

As part of the 1998 settlement of a class action brought by 46 states that charged U.S. tobacco companies with manipulating nicotine levels to keep smokers addicted, several companies agreed to stop advertising and marketing efforts aimed at children. Despite these promises by tobacco companies, an analysis of internal documents of several of these companies (made public thanks to the lawsuit) by researchers at the Harvard School of Public Health revealed that they were still targeting their advertising toward young people (Kreslake, Wayne, et al., 2008). The tobacco companies' own research had found that cigarettes with mild menthol appealed more to young people, and thus they made efforts to market these milder menthol brands to young people. Between 2008 and 2010, over half of adolescent smokers chose menthol cigarettes (Giovino, Villanti, et al., 2013). Adolescents who begin smoking menthol cigarettes are more likely to continue smoking than those who do not begin with menthol cigarettes (Nonnemaker, Hersey, et al., 2013).

Quick Summary

Several, etiological factors have been proposed regarding substance use disorders. Genetic factors play a role in both alcohol and nicotine dependence. The ability to tolerate alcohol and metabolize nicotine may be what is heritable. Genes crucial to the operation of the dopamine system may be an important factor in explaining how genes influence substance dependence. Several studies show how genes interact with the environment to cause smoking and alcohol use disorders. The most-studied neurobiological factors are brain systems associated with dopamine pathways—the major reward pathways in the brain. The incentive-sensitization theory describes brain pathways involved in liking and wanting (i.e., craving) drugs. People with substance use problems also value immediate rewards more than delayed rewards.

Psychological factors have also been evaluated, and there is support for the idea that tension reduction plays a role, but only under certain circumstances, such as when distractions are present. Expectancies about the effects of drugs, such as reducing tension and increasing social skills, have been shown to predict drug and alcohol use. These expectancies are also powerful: The greater the perceived risk of a drug, the less likely it will be used. Studies of personality factors also help us understand why some people may be more prone to abuse drugs and alcohol.

Sociocultural factors play a role, including the culture, availability of a substance, family factors, social settings and networks, and advertising. Support exists for both a social influence model and a social selection model.

Check Your Knowledge 10.3

1. Which of the following is *not* one of the sociocultural factors implicated in the etiology of substance use disorders?

   a. the media

   b. gender

   c. availability of a substance

   d. social networks

2. Which of the following statements best captures the link between wanting, liking, and drinking according to a large prospective study?

   a. Wanting, but not liking, predicted more drinking among heavy drinkers.

   b. Wanting predicted more drinking for heavy drinkers; liking predicted more drinking for light drinkers.

    c. Wanting and liking predicted more drinking among heavy drinkers.

    d. Sedation predicted less drinking for all types of drinking.

3. Genetic research on substance dependence indicates that:

    a. Genetic factors may be the same for many drugs.

    b. Additional studies need to be done to determine heritability.

    c. The dopamine receptor DRD1 may be faulty.

    d. Twin studies show that the environment is just as important as genes.

Treatment of Substance Use Disorders

The chronicity of addiction is really a kind of fatalism writ large. If an addict knows in his heart he is going to use again, why not today? But if a thin reed of hope appears, the possibility that it will not always be so, things change. You live another day and then get up and do it again. Hope is oxygen to someone who is suffocating on despair. (Carr, 2008)

The challenges in treating people with substance use disorders are great, as illustrated by the quote above. Substance use disorders are typically chronic, and relapse occurs often. In view of these challenges, the field is constantly working to develop new and effective treatments, many of which we review in this section. The author of the quote, David Carr, was formerly addicted to cocaine, crack, and alcohol. He wrote about his experiences in a beautiful memoir while working as a media columnist for *The New York Times*. For him, residential treatment was successful.

    Many who work with those with alcohol or drug use disorders suggest that the first step to successful treatment is admitting there is a problem. To a certain extent, this makes sense. Why would someone get treatment for something that is not deemed a problem? Unfortunately, several treatment programs require people not only to admit a problem but also to demonstrate their commitment to treatment by stopping their use of alcohol or drugs before beginning treatment. This requirement can exclude many who desire and need treatment. For example, in the Clinical Case of James, he might not have been admitted to a residential program had he not been free of heroin for a week before trying to gain admission. Imagine if people with lung cancer were told they had to demonstrate their commitment to treatment by stopping smoking before the cancer could be treated.

    Unfortunately, many who need treatment for substance use disorders do not receive it. In 2015, over 21 million people needed treatment for a substance use problem (SAMHSA, 2015). The Surgeon General's report on addiction published in 2016 reported that only 1 out of 10 people who needed it received treatment (USDHHS, 2016b). We must do better.

    Whether treating an alcohol or drug problem, relapse prevention is a cognitive behavioral treatment that is useful as a stand-alone treatment or in addition to other treatments (Brandon, Vidrine, & Litvin, 2007; Hendershot, Witkiewitz, & Marlatt, 2011). Unfortunately, relapse is the norm when it comes to any substance use disorder. The relapse prevention approach developed by Marlatt and colleagues (Marlatt & Gordon, 1985; Witkiewitz & Marlatt, 2004) emphasizes that relapse should be regarded as a learning experience rather than as a sign that all is lost. Broadly, the goal is to help people avoid relapsing into problematic drinking or drug use.

Treatment of Alcohol Use Disorder

In 2015, 2.2 million people over the age of 12 received treatment for alcohol use disorder (SAMHSA, 2016). Unfortunately, more than 16 million people over the age of 12 were in need of treatment for alcohol problems in 2015 and did not receive it. A large epidemiological study found that only 24 percent of people who are physiologically dependent on alcohol ever receive treatment (Hasin, Stinson, et al., 2007). We have far to go in developing and providing effective treatments and making sure that people who need treatment can get it.

Detoxification is often the first step in treatment for alcohol use disorder.

Inpatient Hospital Treatment Often, the first step in treatment for substance use disorders is called **detoxification**, or detox for short. Withdrawal from substances, including alcohol, can be difficult, both physically and psychologically. Although detox does not have to occur in a hospital, it can be less unpleasant in such a supervised setting. Alice, the woman described in the earlier Clinical Case, would likely need hospital treatment, at least for detox.

Twenty years ago, many people received treatment beyond detox in an inpatient hospital, in part because such treatment was covered by both private insurance companies and the federal government (Holder, Longabaugh, et al., 1991). However, inpatient treatment is much more expensive than outpatient treatment, and even with the 2009 Affordable Care Act, most people receive outpatient treatment. In 2015, 2.6 million people received treatment for drug or alcohol use disorders at an outpatient facility, and 1.6 million received treatment in an inpatient rehabilitation or hospital setting (SAMHSA, 2016).

Alcoholics Anonymous The largest and most widely known self-help group in the world is Alcoholics Anonymous (AA), founded in 1935 by two men with alcohol problems. It has over 100,000 chapters and a membership numbering more than 2 million people around the world. In 2015, over half of the people who received treatment for alcohol or drug use disorders did so through a self-help program like AA (SAMHSA, 2016).

Each AA chapter runs regular and frequent meetings at which attendees announce that they are alcoholics and give testimonials relating the stories of their problems with alcohol and how their lives have improved with the help of AA. The group provides emotional support, understanding, and close counseling as well as a social network. Members are urged to call on one another around the clock when they need companionship and encouragement not to relapse. Programs modeled after AA are available for other substances, for example, Narcotics Anonymous, Cocaine Anonymous, and Marijuana Anonymous.

The AA program tries to instill in each member the belief that alcohol use disorder is a disease that can never be cured and that continuing vigilance is necessary to resist taking even a single drink, lest uncontrollable drinking begin all over again. AA's principles, which can include some spiritual aspects, are outlined in the 12 steps, shown in **Table 10.7**. Even if the person has not consumed any alcohol for 15 years or more, the designation "alcoholic" is still necessary according to the tenets of AA, since the person always has the disorder, even if it is currently under control.

Uncontrolled trials show that AA provides significant benefit to participants (Moos & Moos, 2006; Ouimette, Finney, & Moos, 1997; Timko, Moos, et al., 2001). A large prospective study of over 2,000 men with alcohol dependence found that participation in AA predicted a better outcome 2 years later (McKeller, Stewart, & Humphreys, 2003). A 16-year prospective study of over 400 people seeking treatment for the first time found that of the people who attended AA meetings for at least 27 weeks of the first year in the program, two-thirds were abstinent at the 16-year follow-up. Of the people who attended AA meetings for fewer than 27 weeks, only one-third were abstinent at follow-up (Moos & Moos, 2006). In addition, attending AA meetings early in treatment and staying involved for a longer period is associated with a better outcome 8 years after treatment began (Moos & Humphreys, 2004).

All of this sounds like good news for people participating in AA. However, a review of eight randomized controlled clinical trials found little benefit of AA over other types of treatment, including motivational

Alcoholics Anonymous is the largest self-help group in the world. At their regular meetings, attendees announce their addiction and receive advice and support from others.

TABLE 10.7	The 12 Steps of Alcoholics Anonymous

1. We admitted we were powerless over alcohol—that our lives had become unmanageable.

2. Came to believe that a power greater than ourselves could restore us to sanity.

3. Made a decision to turn our will and our lives over to the care of God as we understood Him.

4. Made a searching and fearless moral inventory of ourselves.

5. Admitted to God, to ourselves, and to another human being the exact nature of our wrongs.

6. Were entirely ready to have God remove all these defects of character.

7. Humbly asked Him to remove our shortcomings.

8. Made a list of all persons we had harmed, and became willing to make amends to them all.

9. Made direct amends to such people wherever possible, except when to do so would injure them or others.

10. Continued to take personal inventory and, when we were wrong, promptly admitted it.

11. Sought through prayer and meditation to improve our conscious contact with God as we understood Him, praying only for knowledge of His will for us and the power to carry that out.

12. Having had a spiritual awakening as the result of these steps, we tried to carry this message to alcoholics and to practice these principles in all our affairs.

Source: The Twelve Steps are reprinted with permission of Alcoholics Anonymous World Services, Inc. ("A.A.W.S.") Permission to reprint the Twelve Steps does not mean that A.A.W.S. has reviewed or approved the contents of this publication, or that A.A. necessarily agrees with the views expressed herein. A.A. is a program of recovery from alcoholism only - use of the Twelve Steps in connection with programs and activities which are patterned after A.A., but which address other problems, or in any other non-A.A., does not imply otherwise..

enhancement, inpatient treatment, couples therapy, or cognitive behavior therapy (Ferri, Amato, & Davoli, 2008). In addition, AA has very high dropout rates, and the dropouts are not always factored into the results of studies (Dodes & Dodes, 2014).

Couples Therapy

Behaviorally oriented couples therapy has been found to achieve some reduction in problem drinking as well as some improvement in couples' distress generally (McCrady, Epstein, et al., 2004; O'Farrell & Clements, 2012). This appears to be effective for straight, gay, and lesbian couples (Fals-Stewart, O'Farrell, & Lam, 2009). This treatment combines the skills covered in individual cognitive behavior therapy, with a focus on the couple's relationship and dealing with alcohol-related stressors together as a couple. A meta-analysis of 12 studies found that behaviorally oriented couples therapy was more effective than individual treatment approaches (Powers, Vedel, & Emmelkamp, 2008).

Motivational Interventions

As we described earlier, heavy drinking is particularly common among college students. One team of investigators designed a brief intervention to try to curb such heavy drinking in college (Carey, Carey, et al., 2006). The intervention contained two parts: (1) a comprehensive assessment that included the Timeline Follow Back (TLFB) interview (Sobell & Sobell, 1996), which carefully assesses drinking in the past 3 months, and (2) a brief motivational treatment that included individualized feedback about a person's drinking in relation to community and national averages, education about the effects of alcohol, and tips for reducing harm and moderating drinking. Results from the study showed that the TLFB alone decreased drinking behavior, but that the combination of the TLFB and motivational intervention was associated with a longer-lasting reduction in drinking behavior, up to 1 year after the interview and intervention.

Moderation in Drinking

At least since the advent of Alcoholics Anonymous, the popular belief has been that people with alcohol use disorder must abstain completely if they are to be successfully treated, for they presumably have no control over drinking once they take that first drink. This continues to be the belief of Alcoholics Anonymous, but as noted earlier, many people drop out of AA.

The term **controlled drinking** was introduced by Mark and Linda Sobell, who developed the *guided self-change* approach to treatment (Sobell & Sobell, 1993). The basic assumption is that people have more potential control over their drinking than they typically believe and that heightened awareness of the costs of drinking to excess as well as of the benefits of cutting

Courtesy of Teva Pharmaceuticals

Antabuse is used to treat alcohol dependence.

down can help. For example, getting the person to delay 20 minutes before taking a second or third drink can help him or her reflect on the costs versus the benefits of drinking to excess. Evidence supports the effectiveness of this approach in helping people moderate their intake and otherwise improve their lives (Sobell & Sobell, 1993). A randomized controlled clinical trial demonstrated that guided self-change was just as effective as an individual or group treatment (Sobell, Sobell, & Agrawal, 2009).

Medications Disulfiram, or **Antabuse** is a medication that discourages drinking by causing violent vomiting after drinking alcohol. As you can imagine, adherence to an Antabuse regimen is difficult, and the person using such treatment must already be strongly committed to change. However, in a large, multicenter study, Antabuse was not shown to have any benefit, and drop-out rates were as high as 80 percent (Fuller, 1988).

The opiate antagonist naltrexone blocks the activity of endorphins that are stimulated by alcohol, thus reducing the craving for it. Evidence is mixed regarding whether this drug is more effective than a placebo in reducing drinking when it is the only treatment offered (Krystal, Cramer, et al., 2001; Lobmaier, Kunøe, et al., 2011). But it does appear to add to overall treatment effectiveness when combined with cognitive behavioral therapy (Pettinati, Oslin, et al., 2010; Streeton & Whelan, 2001). In addition, it may help to dampen cravings for alcohol (Helstrom, Blow, et al., 2016).

The drug acamprosate has also been shown to be somewhat effective. Meta-analyses have found acamprosate more effective than placebo in reducing drinking and cravings (Donoghue, Elzerbi, et al., 2015; Rösner, Hackl-Herrwerth, et al., 2010). A meta-analysis comparing the effectiveness of acamprosate and naltrexone found them to be equally effective (Kranzler & van Kirk, 2001). Researchers believe that the drug impacts the glutamate systems and thereby reduces the cravings associated with withdrawal.

There is, of course, the more general question of whether it makes sense to treat a substance use disorder with another drug. Nevertheless, to the extent that medications are an effective treatment for substance use disorders, avoiding them due to concern over substituting one drug for another may be misguided if the medications are effective and can reduce the consequences of taking other substances.

Quick Summary

Inpatient hospital treatment for alcohol dependence is not as common today as it was in earlier years, primarily due to the cost. Detoxification from alcohol often takes place in hospitals, but other treatment is more commonly done in outpatient settings.

Alcoholics Anonymous is the most common form of treatment for alcohol use disorder. This group-based self-help treatment instills the notion that alcohol use disorder is always with you and abstinence is the only suitable outcome. Uncontrolled studies suggest that AA is effective, but randomized controlled trials do not. There is some evidence that behavioral couples therapy is an effective treatment. The guided self-change treatment approach emphasizes control over moderate drinking, the costs of drinking to excess, and the benefits of abstaining.

Medications for alcohol use disorder treatment include Antabuse, naltrexone, and acamprosate. Antabuse is not an effective treatment in the long run because noncompliance is common. Some evidence suggests that other medications are effective on their own, but they seem more beneficial in combination with other treatments.

Treatments for Smoking

The numerous laws that currently prohibit smoking in almost all public places are part of a social context that provides incentives and support to stop smoking. In addition, people are more likely to quit smoking if other people around them quit. A longitudinal study of over 12,000 people demonstrated that if people in one's social network quit smoking (spouses, siblings, friends, co-workers), the odds that a person will quit smoking are much greater (Christakis &

Fowler, 2008). For example, if a person's spouse stopped smoking, his or her chances of continued smoking decreased by nearly 70 percent. In short, peer pressure to quit smoking appears to be as effective as peer pressure to start smoking.

Some smokers who want to quit attend smoking clinics or consult with professionals for specialized smoking-reduction programs. Even so, it is estimated that only about half of those who go through smoking-cessation programs succeed in abstaining by the time the program is over; only a very small percentage of those who have succeeded in the short term remain nonsmoking after a year (Brandon et al., 2007).

Psychological Treatments

Probably the most widespread psychological treatment consists of a physician telling a person to stop smoking. Each year millions of smokers are given this advice—because of hypertension, heart disease, lung disease, or diabetes, or on general grounds of preserving or improving health. There is some evidence that a physician's advice can get some people to stop smoking, at least for a while, especially when the person also chews nicotine gum (Law & Tang, 1995). Motivational interviewing has been tried to help people quit smoking, but results from meta-analyses indicate that it is only modestly effective (Hettema & Hendricks, 2010; Lai, Cahill, et al., 2010).

Laws that have banned smoking in many places have probably increased the quit rate.

Should people quit smoking abruptly or gradually? For some people, quitting abruptly is too difficult. Gradually reducing the number of cigarettes smoked leading up to an ultimate "quit day" appears to be effective compared with stopping all at once (Lindson-Hawley, Aveyard, et al., 2012).

By age 18, about two-thirds of cigarette smokers regret having started smoking, one-half have already made an attempt to quit, and nearly 40 percent show interest in obtaining treatment to stop (Henningfield, Michaelides, & Sussman, 2000). Thus, much effort has been directed at getting young people to stop smoking. Unfortunately, many efforts have failed to show effectiveness beyond 6 months after treatment (Villanti, McKay, et al., 2010). One school-based program called Project EX appears to work and maintain the benefits up to a year post-treatment. The treatment includes training in coping skills and a psychoeducational component about the harmful effects of smoking. This program has been found to be effective in the United States (Sussman, Miyano, et al., 2007), China (Zheng, Sussman, et al., 2004), Spain (Espada, Gonzálvez, et al., 2015), and Russia (Idrisov, Sun, et al., 2013). It was translated and adapted for each culture. Cognitive behavioral approaches that focus on problem-solving and coping skills show some promise (Curry, Mermelstein, & Sporer, 2009).

Nicotine Replacement Treatments and Medications

Nicotine replacement therapy (NRT) substitutes a different delivery system for nicotine (in the form of gum, patches, inhalers, or e-cigarettes) to allay cravings while gradually reducing dosages, with the goal of eliminating reliance on nicotine. Although NRT is often intended to alleviate withdrawal symptoms, the severity of withdrawal is only minimally related to success in stopping smoking (Ferguson, Shiffman, & Gwaltney, 2006; Hughes, Higgins, et al., 1990).

The nicotine in nicotine gum, available over the counter, is absorbed much more slowly and steadily than that in tobacco. However, in hourly doses that deliver an amount of nicotine equivalent to one cigarette an hour, the gum causes cardiovascular changes, such as increased blood pressure, that can be dangerous to people with cardiovascular diseases. Although not everyone manages to completely wean themselves from using nicotine gum, some experts believe that even prolonged, continued use of the gum is healthier than obtaining nicotine by smoking because the carcinogens are avoided (de Wit & Zacny, 2000).

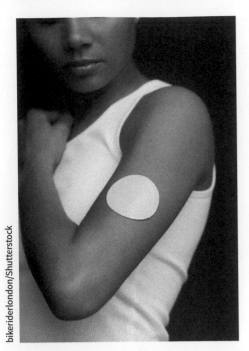

bikeriderlondon/Shutterstock

Nicotine patches are available over the counter to help relieve withdrawal symptoms.

Nicotine patches, also available over the counter, contain a polyethylene patch taped to the arm that slowly and steadily releases the drug into the bloodstream transdermally (through the skin), and then to the brain. An advantage of the patch over nicotine gum is that the person need only apply one patch each day and not remove it until applying the next patch, making compliance easier. Treatment can be effective after 8 weeks of use for most smokers (Stead, Perera, et al., 2012), with the dosage tapering down as treatment progresses. However, people who continue smoking while wearing the patch risk increasing the amount of nicotine in their body to dangerous levels.

Evidence suggests that the nicotine patch is superior to the placebo patch in terms of both abstinence and craving (Hughes et al., 1990). A meta-analysis of 117 trials of all types of nicotine replacement treatments (patch, gum, nasal spray, inhaler, tablets) found that NRT was more effective than placebo in smoking cessation (Stead et al., 2012). People who begin to stop smoking after wearing the patch but before dedicated cessation efforts begin are more likely to remain abstinent from smoking at the end of NRT (Rose, Herskovic, et al., 2009). However, NRT is not a panacea. Abstinence rates are only about 50 percent at 12-month follow-ups. The manufacturers state that the patch is to be used only as part of a psychological smoking-cessation program and then for not more than 3 months at a time. These types of NRT are not effective with adolescents (Curry et al., 2009).

NRT plus the antidepressant medication bupropion (trade name Wellbutrin) is not more effective than NRT alone but it may be more effective than bupropion alone (Stead et al., 2012). Another drug, varenicline (trade name Chantix), may be effective in combination with behavioral treatment (Cahill, Stead, & Lancaster, 2007; Tonstad, Tonnesen, et al., 2006). One randomized trial found that bupropion combined with varenicline was more effective than varenicline alone (Rose & Behm, 2014).

There is a current debate about whether e-cigarettes are an effective form of NRT. Results from one longitudinal study found that only 10 percent of people using e-cigarettes had quit smoking 1 year later (Grana, Popova, & Ling, 2014). An internet survey of over 400 people who used e-cigarettes found that 22 percent of people had stopped smoking after 1 month and 46 percent had stopped at the 1-year follow-up (Etter & Bullen, 2014). A randomized controlled clinical trial assigned people who wanted to quit smoking to either e-cigarettes, the nicotine patch, or placebo e-cigarettes. The numbers of people who quit smoking were very small in all three groups, so small in fact that the researchers did not have the statistical power to detect any significant differences between the groups (Bullen, Howe, et al., 2013). Clearly, more research is needed, but thus far, e-cigarettes do not appear to be more effective than other forms of NRT.

Treatment of Drug Use Disorders

Central to the treatment of people who use drugs such as opioids and cocaine is detoxification—withdrawal from the drug itself. Opioid withdrawal reactions range from relatively mild bouts of anxiety, nausea, and restlessness for several days to more severe and frightening bouts of delirium and panic. The cravings for the substance often remain even after the substance has been removed through detoxification.

Psychological Treatments Cognitive behavior therapy has been shown to be effective in treating drug use disorders. For example, in a study of people using cocaine (Carroll, Rounsaville, et al., 1994; Carroll, Rounsaville, et al., 1995), people learned how to avoid high-risk situations (e.g., being around people using cocaine), recognize the lure of the drug for them, and develop alternatives to using cocaine (e.g., recreational activities with nonusers). People also learned strategies for coping with the craving and for resisting the tendency to regard a slip as a catastrophe.

A more recent study of computer-based CBT compared to standard substance abuse counseling found that CBT was more effective in helping people remain abstinent from cocaine (Carroll, Kiluk, et al., 2014) for up to 6 months after treatment.

Contingency management involves teaching people and those close to them to reinforce behaviors inconsistent with drug use—for example, taking the drug methadone (discussed later in the chapter) and avoiding situations associated with drug use in the past. This treatment is based on the belief that environmental contingencies can play an important role in encouraging or discouraging drug use. Vouchers are provided for not using a substance (verified by urine samples), and are exchangeable for things that the person would like to have more of.

Contingency management with vouchers has shown promise for cocaine, heroin, and marijuana use disorders (Dallery, Silverman, et al., 2001; Katz, Gruber, et al., 2001; Petry, Alessi, et al., 2005; Silverman, Higgins, et al., 1996). For example, a randomized treatment trial for people with marijuana use disorder compared a voucher treatment, CBT, and CBT plus vouchers (Budney, Moore, et al., 2006). During the treatment, people who received the voucher treatment were more likely to remain abstinent than those in the CBT treatment or in the CBT plus vouchers treatment. After treatment was over, however, people who received CBT plus vouchers were most likely to remain abstinent. Thus, vouchers appear to work in the short term, but CBT appears to be an effective component of treatment for marijuana use disorder in the long term with respect to maintaining abstinence after treatment is over.

Group therapy in residential settings is frequently used to treat heroin addiction.

David Grossman/Science Source

Studies of contingency management for cocaine use disorder find that it is associated with a greater likelihood of abstinence and a better quality of life (Petry, Alessi, & Hanson, 2007). A meta-analysis of four randomized controlled clinical trials comparing contingency management, day treatment, or both treatments (combined condition) for cocaine use among homeless people found that the combined treatment and contingency management were both more effective than day treatment alone (Schumacher, Milby, et al., 2007).

Motivational enhancement therapy has also shown promise. This treatment involves a combination of CBT techniques and techniques associated with helping people generate solutions that work for themselves. A meta-analysis of this treatment found that it was effective for both alcohol and drug use disorders (Burke, Arkowitz, & Menchola, 2003). Another study found that motivational enhancement combined with CBT and contingency management was an effective treatment package for young people (ages 18–25) who were dependent on marijuana (Carroll, Easton, et al., 2006).

Self-help residential homes are another psychological approach to treating heroin and other types of drug use disorders. Daytop Village, Phoenix House, Odyssey House, and other drug-rehabilitation homes share the following features:

- Separation of people from previous social contacts, on the assumption that these relationships have been instrumental in maintaining the drug use disorder
- A comprehensive environment in which drugs are not available and continuing support is offered to ease the transition from regular drug use to a drug-free existence
- The presence of role models, people formerly with a drug use disorder who appear to be meeting life's challenges without drugs
- Direct, often intense, confrontation in group therapy, in which people are urged to accept responsibility for their problems and for their drug habits and are encouraged to take charge of their lives
- A setting in which people are respected as human beings rather than stigmatized as failures or criminals

There are several obstacles to evaluating the efficacy of residential drug-treatment programs. Because the dropout rate is high, those who remain cannot be regarded as representative of the population of people with substance use disorders; their motivation to stop using drugs is probably much stronger than that of people who don't volunteer for treatment or people who drop out. Any improvement participants in these programs make may reflect their strong motivation to quit more than the specific qualities of the treatment program.

Ninety percent of people who need treatment for substance use disorder do not get it. What happens? Many people end up going to prison; some for drug use and many for crimes associated with drug use (e.g., stealing to get money to buy drugs). Yet the cost of treating substance use problems is substantially less expensive than prison (Florence, Zhou, et al., 2016) and possibly more effective too.

All states have drug courts. Though these vary by state, the general idea behind them is to offer people the option of treatment instead of jail time for nonviolent drug offenses. For example, the program in California found that 4 out of 10 people completed the treatment program (failure to do so meant a return to jail). This number may seem low, but it is quite favorable in comparison to completion rates of other programs, particularly those to which offenders are referred by the criminal justice system (Longshore, Urada, et al., 2003, 2005; Urada, Evans, et al., 2009). This program also saved money. Prison would have cost four times more than treatment (Longshore, Hawken, et al., 2006). The news was not all good, however. Participants who went into treatment were more likely to be rearrested for drug offenses than people who had similar offenses before the California drug treatment diversion program was begun (Longshore et al., 2005; Urada et al., 2009).

Developing effective treatments for methamphetamine dependence remains a challenge for the field. People like Anton, described in the Clinical Case earlier, do not have many places to turn for treatment. The largest research effort to date is a randomized controlled clinical trial conducted across eight different sites referred to as the Methamphetamine Treatment Project (Rawson, Martinelli-Casey, et al., 2004). This study compared a multifaceted treatment called Matrix with treatment as usual. The Matrix treatment consisted of 16 CBT group sessions, 12 family education sessions, 4 individual therapy sessions, and 4 social support group sessions. Treatment as usual (TAU) consisted of the best available treatment currently offered at the eight outpatient clinics. This varied quite a bit across the sites, with some offering individual counseling and others offering group counseling, some offering 4 weeks of treatment and others offering 16 weeks. Results of the study are somewhat supportive of the Matrix treatment. Compared to those in TAU, those people receiving Matrix stayed in treatment longer and were less likely to use methamphetamine during treatment (confirmed with urine analysis). Unfortunately, at the end of treatment and at the 6-month follow-up, people who received Matrix were no less likely to have used methamphetamine than those in TAU. The good news is that all participants were less likely to use methamphetamine after 6 months, regardless of whether they received Matrix or TAU. Although these results are promising, additional work is clearly needed to develop effective treatments for methamphetamine problems.

Medications Medications are an effective treatment for opioid use disorders. Two widely used medications include *opioid substitutes*, drugs chemically similar to opioids that can replace the body's craving for it, and (2) *opioid antagonists*, drugs that prevent the user from experiencing the high. An antagonist is a drug that dampens the activity of neurotransmitters, and an agonist is a drug that stimulates neurotransmitters.

Opioid substitutes include methadone and buprenorphine (Suboxone). Since these drugs are themselves addicting, people often consider that this treatment means converting a person's dependence on one type of opioid into dependence on a different one. However, because these medications do not create the same high and they dampen the cravings, the problems associated with opioid use are diminished. Nevertheless, abrupt discontinuation of these medications can also cause withdrawal reactions, but they are less severe than those of heroin or prescription pain medications.

Methadone treatment typically involves going to a drug-treatment clinic and swallowing the drug in the presence of a staff member. There is some evidence that methadone maintenance can be carried out more simply and just as effectively by weekly visits to a physician (Fiellin, O'Connor, et al., 2001). The effectiveness of methadone treatment is improved if a high (80- to 100-milligram) dose is used as opposed to the more typical 40- to 50-milligram dose (Strain, Bigelow, et al., 1999) and if it is combined with regular psychological counseling (Ball & Ross, 1991). Drug treatment experts generally believe that treatment with methadone is best conducted in the context of a supportive social interaction, not merely as a medical encounter (Lilly, Quirk, et al., 2000).

Since methadone does not provide a euphoric high, many people will return to heroin if it becomes available to them. To improve outcomes, researchers have tried adding contingency management to the usual treatment at methadone clinics. In one randomized controlled trial (Pierce, Petry, et al., 2006), people receiving methadone from a clinic could draw for prizes each time they submitted a (carefully supervised and obtained) urine sample that had no trace of illegal drugs or alcohol. Prizes ranged from praise to televisions. People who were in the contingency management group were more likely to remain drug-free than those people who received only usual care from the methadone clinic.

Methadone is an opioid substitute. People come to clinics each day and swallow their dose.

Unfortunately, many people drop out of methadone programs, in part because of side effects such as insomnia, constipation, excessive sweating, and diminished sexual functioning. The stigma associated with going to methadone clinics is also linked to dropout rates, as illustrated in the Clinical Case of James described earlier.

One of the advantages of buprenorphine (Suboxone) is that it can be prescribed and taken at home, not a clinic. However, physicians must receive specialized training to receive a waiver from the Drug Enforcement Agency that allows them to prescribe it. Thus, many people, particularly those in rural areas, must still go to a clinic daily to receive it (Andrilla, Coulthard, & Larson, 2017).

Buprenorphine contains two agents: buprenorphine and naloxone. Buprenorphine is a partial opioid agonist, which means it does not have the same powerfully addicting properties as other opioids. Naloxone is an opioid antagonist, often used in emergency rooms for pain medication or heroin overdoses. This unique combination in Suboxone does not produce an intense high, is only mildly addictive, and lasts for as long as 3 days. Suboxone is effective at relieving withdrawal symptoms (Gowing, Ali, et al., 2009), something that researchers hope will reduce the likelihood of relapse. Still, some users may miss the more euphoric high associated with heroin or pain medications and return to those deadlier opioids. Indeed, unless treatment is continued for longer than 12 weeks or coupled with behavioral counseling, relapse is likely (Weiss, Potter, et al., 2011).

In May 2016, the FDA approved a longer acting type of buprenorphine. Specifically, an implanted version can last for up to 6 months. Because this will not require remembering (or complying) with taking a daily dose, relapse may be lower (Barnwal, Das, et al., 2017).

Treatment with the opioid antagonists involves a drug called naltrexone. First, people are gradually weaned from either heroin or pain medications. Then they receive increasing dosages of naltrexone, which prevents them from experiencing any high should they later take other opioids. Naltrexone works because it has great affinity for the receptors to which opioids usually bind; their molecules occupy the

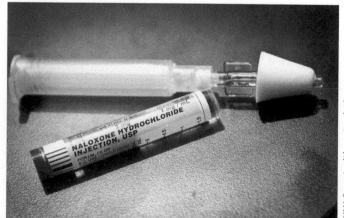

Opioid agonists such as naloxone can be helpful in treating opioid dependence.

receptors without stimulating them. This leaves heroin or pain medication molecules with no place to go, so these deadlier opioids do not have the usual effect. Like buprenorphine, naloxone can be prescribed. Giving people vouchers that they can exchange for food and clothing in return for taking naltrexone and having drug-free urine samples markedly improves effectiveness. One study compared two different naltrexone treatments: the daily pill naltrexone and surgically implanted naltrexone that was slowly released into the body over 30 days. People with implanted naltrexone used opioids less and reported fewer cravings compared with those who received oral dose naltrexone (Hulse, Ngo, & Tait, 2010).

What about medication treatment for other drug use disorders? Substitute medications do not appear to be an effective treatment for cocaine use disorder. A meta-analysis of nine randomized controlled clinical trials of stimulant medication as a treatment for cocaine revealed little evidence that this type of medication is effective (Castells, Casas, et al., 2007).

Researchers were hopeful that a vaccine to prevent the high associated with cocaine use would be effective. The vaccine contains tiny amounts of cocaine attached to otherwise harmless pathogens. The body's immune system responds to this invasion by developing antibodies that squelch the cocaine. It was hoped that with repeated exposure, the antibodies would be able to keep a good deal of the cocaine from reaching the brain. However, a randomized controlled clinical trial with over 100 people addicted to cocaine was not particularly promising (Martell, Orson, et al., 2009). First, for the vaccine to be effective, people needed to receive five shots, and only half of the sample followed through. Second, just over a third of people receiving all shots developed enough antibodies to keep cocaine from reaching the brain. And finally, although about half of the sample used cocaine less, the vaccine did not help stave off cravings for cocaine. Work on a new vaccine is currently underway.

Quick Summary

Psychological treatments have not been all that effective for smoking cessation. Nicotine gum appears to be somewhat effective, though users may never stop chewing the gum. Nicotine patches are more effective than placebo patches, but 9 months after the treatment, abstinence differences between those receiving the drug and those receiving a placebo disappear. Adding bupropion or therapy along with nicotine patches may be effective but not for adolescents. Early evidence about e-cigarettes as an effective treatment for stopping smoking is not promising but more work needs to be done.

Detoxification, or detox, is usually the first step in treatment for drug use disorders. There is some evidence that CBT is an effective treatment for cocaine dependence. Motivational interviewing has shown promise for the treatment of alcohol and other drug use disorders. Residential treatment homes have not been adequately evaluated for their efficacy, though they are a common form of treatment.

The use of heroin substitutes, such as methadone or naltrexone, is an effective treatment for heroin use disorder. Methadone can only be administered in a special clinic, and there is stigma associated with this type of treatment. A prescription drug called buprenorphine can be taken at home. Treating methamphetamine dependence remains a challenge.

Check Your Knowledge 10.4

Match the treatment approach to the type of substance(s).

Treatment

1. Suboxone

2. AA

3. couples therapy

4. opiate antagonist

5. antidepressant

6. patch

7. Matrix

Substance

    a. alcohol

    b. heroin

    c. cocaine

    d. nicotine

    e. methamphetamine

Prevention of Substance Use Disorders

Half of adult smokers began their habit before the age of 15, and nearly all before the age of 19 (USDHHS, 2014). Therefore, developing ways of discouraging young people from experimenting with tobacco has become a top priority among health researchers and politicians, with encouragement from the Surgeon General and funding from the National Cancer Institute, one of the National Institutes of Health. The Truth Initiative (formerly known as the American Legacy Foundation) is a nonprofit organization developed to prevent smoking among young people. It was funded in part from the settlement that followed the class action against tobacco companies in 1998. The group seeks to counter advertising and other efforts to encourage young people to smoke, and offers many informative online resources at https://truthinitiative.org.

A related initiative, the *truth* campaign also developed a website (www.thetruth.com) and radio and television ads to tell youth about the health and social consequences of smoking and the ways in which the tobacco industry targets them, so that they can make informed choices about smoking. This campaign has been well received among young people, and one study found that awareness of and agreement with the *truth* messages were associated with less smoking among teens (Niederdeppe, Farrelly, & Haviland, 2004).

The measures that hold promise for persuading young people to resist smoking may also be useful in dissuading them from trying other drugs and alcohol. Brief family interventions like the Strengthening Families Program and the five-session Preparing for the Drug Free Years Program have been found to forestall the onset of nicotine and alcohol use among teens (Spoth, Redmond, et al., 2004). For adolescents, family treatments may also have preventative effects. Research has shown that two different brief family interventions were associated with less initiation of alcohol use among teens (Spoth, Guyll, & Day, 2002).

Examples of the health warnings for cigarette packages proposed by the FDA. Tobacco companies sued to prevent the graphic images from being added to packages, and a federal judge and appeals panel ruled in their favor. Antismoking groups have now sued over the FDA's delay in developing new graphic labels.

Statewide comprehensive tobacco control programs, which include increasing taxes on cigarettes, restricting tobacco advertising, conducting public education campaigns, and creating smoke-free environments, appear to be an effective strategy for reducing teenage smoking (Wakefield & Chaloupka, 2000). In 2011, the FDA proposed new health warnings for cigarette packages that contained graphic images of the ill effects on health that smoking can have. Several tobacco companies sued to prevent these graphic images from appearing on cigarette packages, and they prevailed, at least for now. This is unfortunate because research has found that graphic warning labels are effective in preventing smoking and helping people to quit, largely because they make clear the health consequences of smoking (Hammond, 2011; Huang, Chaloupka, & Fong, 2014). The FDA is currently working on new health warnings for cigarette packages.

Summary

Clinical Descriptions

- DSM-5 includes substance use disorder instead of separate categories for substance abuse and substance dependence. The number of symptoms present determines severity.

- Alcohol has a variety of short-term and long-term effects on individuals, ranging from poor judgment and impaired motor coordination to chronic health problems.

- People can become physiologically dependent on nicotine, most often via smoking cigarettes. Medical problems associated with long-term cigarette smoking include many cancers, emphysema, and cardiovascular disease. Moreover, the health hazards of smoking are not restricted to those who smoke because second-hand (environmental) smoke can also cause lung damage and other problems. The 2016 Surgeon General's report noted the known hazards of nicotine in e-cigarettes and that additional research is needed on health impacts of the other ingredients in vape pipes.

- When used regularly, marijuana can damage the lungs and cardiovascular system and can lead to cognitive impairments. Tolerance to marijuana may develop. However, marijuana also has therapeutic effects, easing the nausea experienced by people undergoing chemotherapy and relieving the discomfort associated with AIDS, glaucoma, chronic pain, seizures, and muscle spasms.

- Opioids slow the activities of the body and, in moderate doses, are used to relieve pain and induce sleep. Heroin has been a focus of concern because usage is up and stronger varieties have become available. Dependence on prescription pain medication has skyrocketed in the past 20 years.

- Stimulants, which include amphetamines and cocaine, act on the brain and the sympathetic nervous system to increase alertness and motor activity. Tolerance and withdrawal are associated with all these drugs. Abuse of methamphetamine, a derivative of amphetamine, has declined since the 1990s but remains a problem.

- Hallucinogens such as LSD alter or expand consciousness. Use of the hallucinogen-like drug Ecstasy is associated with positive feelings. PCP use often leads to violence.

Etiology

- Several factors are related to the etiology of substance use disorders. Genetic factors have been studied most often with alcohol and tobacco use disorders.

- Specific genes have been identified, but the interaction of these genes with the environment is key for understanding genetic contributions.

- Neurobiological factors involving the brain's reward pathways appear to play a role in the use of some substances. Many substances are used to regulate emotion (e.g., to reduce negative or increase positive emotion), and people with certain personality traits, such as those high in negative affect or low in constraint, are especially likely to use drugs. Cognitive variables, such as the expectation that the drug will yield positive effects, are also important.

- Finally, sociocultural variables, such as attitudes toward the substance, peer pressure, and media portrayal of the substance, are all related to how frequently a substance is used.

Treatment

- Medications are effective for some drug use disorders more than others. For opioid use disorders, medications lessen the high and dampen cravings. Benefits have been observed for medications such as naltrexone, suboxone, and methadone.

- Nicotine replacement via gum, patches, or inhalers has met with some success in reducing cigarette smoking. It is less clear whether e-cigarettes can help people stop smoking.

- Psychological treatments that are effective in treating alcohol abuse include cognitive behavior therapy, couples therapy, motivational interviewing, and contingency management. Controlled studies do not find that Alcoholics Anonymous is effective, but it is a standard part of many treatment programs.

- Since it is easier to never begin using drugs than to stop using them, considerable effort has been expended to prevent drug and alcohol use using multimedia initiatives and in school programs.

Answers to Check Your Knowledge Questions

10.1 1. F; 2. T; 3. T; 4. lung, larynx, esophagus, pancreas, bladder, cervix, stomach; 5. short-term, long-term; 6. pain relief, reduction of nausea, increased appetite, relief from the discomfort from AIDS; 7. similarities: contain nicotine; regulated by the FDA; differences: more carcinogens in cigarettes; aerosol products are in vape pipes.

10.2 l. F; 2. F; 3. F; 4. T

10.3 l. b; 2. c; 3. a

10.4 1. b; 2. a; 3. a; 4. b; 5. a, c, d; 6. d; 7. e

Key Terms

amphetamines
Antabuse
caffeine
cocaine
controlled drinking
crack
delirium tremens (DTs)
detoxification
Ecstasy
fetal alcohol syndrome (FAS)

flashback
hallucinogen
hashish
heroin
hydrocodone
LSD
marijuana
MDMA
methamphetamine
nicotine

nitrous oxide
opioids
oxycodone
PCP
secondhand smoke
stimulants
substance use disorders
tolerance
withdrawal

CHAPTER 11

Eating Disorders

LEARNING GOALS

1. Distinguish the symptoms associated with anorexia, bulimia, and binge eating disorder and distinguish among the different eating disorders.

2. Describe the neurobiological, sociocultural, and psychological factors implicated in the etiology of eating disorders.

3. Discuss the issues surrounding the growing epidemic of obesity in the United States.

4. Describe the treatments for eating disorders and the evidence supporting their effectiveness.

Clinical Case

Lynne

Lynne, a 24-year-old white woman, was admitted to the psychiatric ward of a general hospital for treatment of anorexia nervosa. Although she didn't really think anything was wrong with her, her parents had consulted with a psychiatrist, and the three of them had confronted her with the choice to admit herself or be committed involuntarily.

At the time, Lynne stood 5 feet, 5 inches and weighed only 78 pounds. She hadn't menstruated for 3 years, and she had a variety of medical problems—hypotension, irregularities in her heartbeat, and abnormally low levels of potassium and calcium.

Lynne had experienced several episodes of dramatic weight loss, beginning at age 18 when she first left home for college. But none of the prior episodes had been this severe, and she had not sought treatment before. She had an intense fear of gaining weight, and although she had never really been overweight, she felt that her buttocks and abdomen were far too large. (This belief persisted even when she weighed 78 pounds.) During the periods of weight loss, she severely restricted food intake and used laxatives heavily. She had occasionally had episodes of binge eating, typically followed by self-induced vomiting so that she would not gain any weight.

Many cultures are preoccupied with food. In the United States today, new restaurants abound, and numerous blogs, websites, and TV shows are devoted to food and food preparation. Grocery stores in the United States are stocked with embarrassingly huge quantities of food, and food in the United States has never been cheaper. Dieting to lose weight is common, and the desire of many people, especially women, to be thinner has created a multibillion-dollar-a-year business.

In this chapter, we will discuss three DSM-5 eating disorders: anorexia nervosa, bulimia nervosa, and binge eating disorder. DSM-5 also includes disorders of early childhood such as pica (eating nonfood substances for extended periods), rumination disorder (repeated regurgitation of foods), and avoidant/restrictive food intake disorder (diminished interest in food based mostly on the sensory aspects of food).

Like many of the disorders we cover in this book, eating disorders are also likely to be stigmatized. In one study, college students were presented vignettes depicting fictional women with different disorders and were then asked to rate these fictional women on several dimensions (Wingfield, Kelly, et al., 2011). Participants rated the women depicted with eating disorders as self-destructive and responsible for their conditions. Men in the study were particularly likely to believe that eating disorders were easy to overcome. In another study (Roehrig & McLean, 2010), participants were randomly assigned to read a vignette about a woman with an eating disorder or a woman with depression. Participants who read about the woman with the eating disorder viewed her as more responsible, more fragile, and more likely to be trying to get attention with her disorder compared with participants who read about the woman with depression. These types of attitudes and beliefs are not consistent with the current research on eating disorders.

More broadly, there is stigma about body shape and weight, particularly for women. The cultural expectation for women is that they be thin, but some women are pushing back via social media. For example, the model Tess Holliday has written a book called *The Not So Subtle Art of Being a Fat Girl* and has posted many photos on Instagram proudly showcasing her size 22 body. Other hashtags, such as #bodypositive or #bodyacceptance appear on Instagram and Twitter with increasing frequency.

Tess Holliday celebrates her body size and is a successful model.

Cindy Ord/Getty Images

Clinical Descriptions of Eating Disorders

We begin by describing anorexia nervosa and bulimia nervosa. We then discuss binge eating disorder, which is a new diagnostic category in the DSM-5.

Anorexia Nervosa

Lynne, the woman described in the Clinical Case, had **anorexia nervosa**. The term *anorexia* refers to loss of appetite, and *nervosa* indicates that the loss is due to emotional reasons. The term is something of a misnomer because most people with anorexia nervosa do not lose their appetite or interest in food. On the contrary, while starving themselves, most people with the disorder become preoccupied with food; they may read cookbooks constantly and prepare gourmet meals for their families.

Lynne met all three features required for the diagnosis (see DSM-5 Criteria for Anorexia Nervosa):

1. *Restriction of behaviors that promote healthy body weight.* This is usually taken to mean that the person weighs much less than is considered normal (e.g., **body mass index [BMI]** less than 18.5 for adults; see **Table 11.1**) for that person's age and height. Weight loss is typically achieved through dieting, although purging (self-induced vomiting, heavy use of laxatives or diuretics) and excessive exercise can also be part of the picture.

2. *Intense fear of gaining weight or behavior that interferes with gaining weight.* This fear is not reduced by weight loss. There is no such thing as "too thin."

3. *Distorted body image or sense of body shape.* Even when emaciated, those with anorexia nervosa maintain that they are overweight and that certain parts of their bodies, particularly the abdomen, hips, and thighs, are too fat. To check on their body size, they typically weigh themselves frequently, measure the size of different parts of the body, and gaze critically at their reflections in mirrors. Their self-esteem is closely linked to maintaining thinness.

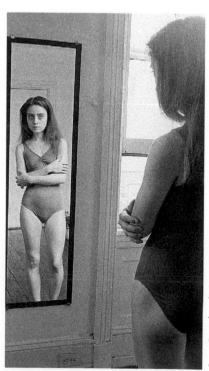

Despite being thin, women with anorexia believe that parts of their bodies are too fat, and they spend a lot of time critically examining themselves in front of mirrors.

Susan Rosenberg/Science Source

TABLE 11.1   Computing Your Body Mass Index (BMI)

WEIGHT lbs	100	105	110	115	120	125	130	135	140	145	150	155	160	165	170	175	180	185	190	195	200	205	210	215
kgs	45.5	47.7	50.0	52.3	54.5	56.8	59.1	61.4	63.6	65.9	68.2	70.5	72.7	75.0	77.3	79.5	81.8	84.1	86.4	88.6	90.9	93.2	95.5	97.7
HEIGHT in/cm	Underweight					Healthy								Overweight				Obese				Extremely obese		
5'0" – 152.4	19	20	21	22	23	24	25	26	27	28	29	30	31	32	33	34	35	36	37	38	39	40	41	42
5'1" – 154.9	18	19	20	21	22	23	24	25	26	27	28	29	30	31	32	33	34	35	36	36	37	38	39	40
5'2" – 157.4	18	19	20	21	22	22	23	24	25	26	27	28	29	30	31	32	33	33	34	35	36	37	38	39
5'3" – 160.0	17	18	19	20	21	22	23	24	24	25	26	27	28	29	30	31	32	32	33	34	35	36	37	38
5'4" – 162.5	17	18	18	19	20	21	22	23	24	24	25	26	27	28	29	30	31	31	32	33	34	35	36	37
5'5" – 165.1	16	17	18	19	20	20	21	22	23	24	25	26	27	28	29	30	30	31	32	33	34	35	35	35
5'6" – 167.6	16	17	17	18	19	20	21	21	22	23	24	25	25	26	27	28	29	29	30	31	32	33	34	34
5'7" – 170.1	15	16	17	18	18	19	20	21	22	22	23	24	25	25	26	27	28	29	29	30	31	32	33	33
5'8" – 172.7	15	16	16	17	18	19	19	20	21	22	22	23	24	25	25	26	27	28	28	29	30	31	32	32
5'9" – 175.2	14	15	16	17	17	18	19	20	20	21	22	22	23	24	25	25	26	27	28	28	29	30	31	31
5'10" – 177.8	14	15	15	16	17	18	18	19	20	20	21	22	23	23	24	25	25	26	27	28	28	29	30	30
5'11" – 180.3	14	14	15	16	16	17	18	18	19	20	21	21	22	23	23	24	25	25	26	27	28	28	29	30
6'0" – 182.8	13	14	14	15	16	17	17	18	19	19	20	21	21	22	23	23	24	25	25	26	27	27	28	29
6'1" – 185.4	13	13	14	15	15	16	17	17	18	19	19	20	21	21	22	23	23	24	25	25	26	27	27	28
6'2" – 187.9	12	13	14	14	15	16	16	17	18	18	19	19	20	21	21	22	23	23	24	25	25	26	27	27
6'3" – 190.5	12	13	13	14	15	15	16	16	17	18	18	19	20	20	21	21	22	23	23	24	25	25	26	26
6'4" – 193.0	12	12	13	14	14	15	15	16	17	17	18	18	19	20	20	21	22	22	23	23	24	25	25	26

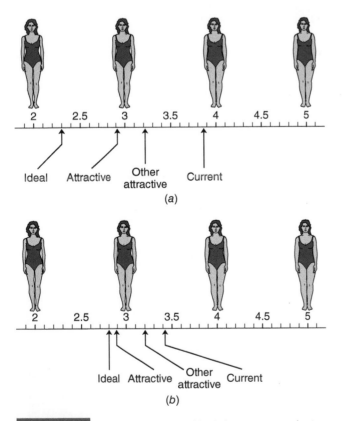

FIGURE 11.1   In this assessment of body image, respondents indicate their current shape, their ideal shape, and the shape they think is most attractive to the opposite sex. The figure rated as most attractive by members of the opposite sex is shown in both panels. Ratings of women who scored high on a measure of distorted attitudes toward eating are shown in (a); ratings of women who scored low are shown in (b). The high scorers overestimated their current size and ideally would be very thin (Zellner, Harner, & Adler, 1989).

For anorexia nervosa, the DSM-5 severity ratings (see **Table 11.2**) are based on BMI, which is consistent with the approach of the World Health Organization. The BMI is calculated by dividing weight in kilograms by height in meters squared and is considered a more valid estimate of body fat than many others. For women, a healthy weight BMI is between 20 and 25. To calculate your own BMI, see Table 11.1. The BMI is not a perfect measure. Many people have a higher or lower BMI for reasons that do not have to do with body fat. For example, someone who is very muscular will likely have a high BMI but will not be overweight or obese. By contrast, an elite runner may be very lean and have a low BMI but not have anorexia.

The body image disturbance that accompanies anorexia nervosa has been assessed in several ways, most frequently by a questionnaire such as the Eating Disorders Inventory (Garner, Olmsted, & Polivy, 1983). Some of the items on this questionnaire are presented in **Table 11.3**. In another type of assessment, people with anorexia nervosa are shown line drawings of women with varying body weights and asked to pick the one closest to their own and the one that represents their ideal shape (see **Figure 11.1**). People with anorexia overestimate their own body size and choose a thin figure as their ideal. Despite this distortion in body size, people with anorexia

TABLE 11.2   Severity Ratings for Anorexia Nervosa in DSM-5

Rating	BMI Range
Mild	≤ 17
Moderate	16–16.99
Severe	15–15.99
Extreme	< 15

DSM-5 Criteria for Anorexia Nervosa

- Restriction of food that leads to very low body weight; body weight is significantly below normal
- Intense fear of weight gain or repeated behaviors that interfere with weight gain

- Body image disturbance

---

nervosa are fairly accurate when reporting their actual weight (McCabe, McFarlane, et al., 2001), perhaps because they weigh themselves frequently.

DSM-5 includes two subtypes of anorexia nervosa, even though research calls into question the validity of these types. In the *restricting type*, weight loss is achieved by severely limiting food intake; in the *binge eating/purging type*, as illustrated in Lynne's case, the person has also regularly engaged in binge eating and purging. Longitudinal research, however, suggests that the distinction between subtypes may not be all that useful (Eddy, Keel, et al., 2002). Nearly two-thirds of women who initially met criteria for the restricting subtype had switched over to the binge eating/purging type 8 years later. A review of the subtype literature for the preparation of DSM-5 concluded that the subtypes had limited predictive validity even though clinicians found them useful (Peat, Mitchell, et al., 2009). One of the top priorities for the DSM-5 was to be useful to clinicians, which may explain why these subtypes were retained despite their limited validity.

Anorexia nervosa typically begins in the early to middle teenage years, often after an episode of dieting and the occurrence of a life stress. Lifetime prevalence of anorexia is less than

TABLE 11.3   Subscales and Illustrative Items from the Eating Disorders Inventory

Drive for thinness	I think about dieting.
	I feel extremely guilty after overeating.
	I am preoccupied with the desire to be thinner.
Bulimia	I stuff myself with food.
	I have gone on eating binges where I have felt that I could not stop.
	I have the thought of trying to vomit in order to lose weight.
Body dissatisfaction	I think that my thighs are too large.
	I think that my buttocks are too large.
	I think that my hips are too big.
Ineffectiveness	I feel inadequate.
	I have a low opinion of myself.
	I feel empty inside (emotionally).
Perfectionism	Only outstanding performance is good enough in my family.
	As a child, I tried hard to avoid disappointing my parents and teachers.
	I hate being less than best at things.
Interpersonal distrust	I have trouble expressing my emotions to others.
	I need to keep people at a certain distance (feel uncomfortable if someone tries to get too close).
Interoceptive awareness	I get confused about what emotion I am feeling.
	I don't know what's going on inside me.
	I get confused as to whether or not I am hungry.
Maturity fears	I wish that I could return to the security of childhood.
	I feel that people are happiest when they are children.
	The demands of adulthood are too great.

Note: Responses use a 6-point scale ranging from "always" to "never."
Source: From Garner, Olmsted, & Polivy (1983).

ABACAUSA/Polaris

Anorexia nervosa can be a life-threatening condition. It is especially prevalent among young women who are under intense pressure to keep their weight low. Brazilian model Ana Carolina Reston died from the condition in 2006 at age 21.

1 percent, and this rate has been stable for several decades. In short, the rates of anorexia are not rising or falling. Anorexia nervosa is at least three times more frequent in women than in men (Hudson, Hiripi, et al., 2007). When anorexia nervosa does occur in men, symptoms and other characteristics, such as reports of family difficulties, are generally similar to those reported by women with the disorder (Olivardia, Pope, et al., 1995). As we discuss more fully later in this chapter, the gender difference in the prevalence of anorexia most likely reflects the greater cultural emphasis on women's beauty, which has promoted a thin shape as the ideal over the past several decades. Even though rare in men, one study found higher mortality from the disorder for men than women in France (Gueguen, Godart, et al., 2012).

For both men and women, anorexia nervosa is frequently comorbid with depression, obsessive-compulsive disorder, specific phobias, panic disorder, and various personality disorders (Baker, Mitchell, et al., 2010; Hudson et al., 2007; Root, Pinheiro, et al., 2010; Steinhausen, 2002). Suicide rates are quite high for people with anorexia, with as many as 5 percent completing suicide and 20 percent attempting suicide (Franko & Keel, 2006).

Physical Consequences of Anorexia Nervosa Self-starvation and use of laxatives to lose weight produce numerous undesirable consequences in people with anorexia nervosa. Blood pressure often falls, heart rate slows, kidney and gastrointestinal problems develop, bone mass declines, the skin dries out, nails become brittle, hormone levels change, and mild anemia may occur. Some people lose hair from the scalp, and they may develop lanugo—a fine, soft hair—on their bodies. As in Lynne's case, levels of electrolytes, such as potassium and sodium, are altered. These ionized salts, present in various bodily fluids, are essential to neural transmission, and lowered levels can lead to tiredness, weakness, cardiac arrhythmias, and even sudden death.

Prognosis Fifty to seventy percent of people with anorexia eventually recover or at least significantly improve (Keel & Brown, 2010). However, recovery often takes 6 or 7 years, and relapses are common before a stable pattern of eating and weight maintenance is achieved (Steinhausen, 2002). One long-term study of over 100 women with anorexia found that nearly a third of the women had recovered 9 years after diagnosis and nearly two-thirds had recovered 22 years after diagnosis (Eddy, Tabri, et al., 2017). As we discuss later, changing peoples' distorted views of themselves is very difficult, particularly in cultures that value thinness.

Anorexia nervosa is a life-threatening illness; death rates are 10 times higher among people with the disorder than among the general population and twice as high as among people with other psychological disorders. A meta-analysis found that death from anorexia was higher than for either bulimia nervosa or binge eating disorder (Arcelus, Mitchell, et al., 2011). Mortality

Clinical Case

Jill

Jill was the second child born to her parents. Both she and her brother became intensely involved in athletics at an early age, Jill in gymnastics and her brother in Little League baseball. At age 4, Jill was enrolled in gymnastics school, where she excelled. By the time she was 9, her mother had decided that Jill had outgrown the coaching abilities of the local instructors and began driving her to a nationally recognized coach several times a week. Over the next few years, Jill's trophy case swelled and her aspirations for a place on the Olympic team grew. As she reached puberty, though, her thin frame began to

fill out, raising concerns about the effects of weight gain on her performance as a gymnast. She began to restrict her intake of food but found that after several days of semistarvation she would lose control and go on an eating binge. This pattern of dieting and bingeing lasted for several months, and Jill's fear of gaining weight seemed to increase during that time. At age 13, she hit on the solution of self-induced vomiting. She quickly fell into a pattern of episodes of bingeing and vomiting three or four times per week. Although she maintained this pattern in secret for a while, eventually her parents caught on and initiated treatment for her.

rates among women with anorexia range from 3 to 5 percent (Crow, Peterson, et al., 2009; Keel & Brown, 2010). Death most often results from physical complications of the illness—for example, congestive heart failure—and from suicide (Herzog, Greenwood, et al., 2000; Steinhausen, 2002). One longitudinal study found that death was more likely to occur among those who had had anorexia the longest (ranging from 7 to 25 years) (Franko, Keshaviah, et al., 2013).

Bulimia Nervosa

Jill's behavior illustrates the features of **bulimia nervosa**. *Bulimia* is from a Greek word meaning "ox hunger." This disorder involves episodes of rapid consumption of a large amount of food, followed by compensatory behavior such as vomiting, fasting, or excessive exercise to prevent weight gain. The DSM defines a *binge* as having two characteristics. First it involves eating an excessive amount of food, that is, much more than most people would eat, within a short period of time (e.g., 2 hours). Second, it involves a feeling of losing control over eating—as if one cannot stop. Bulimia nervosa is not diagnosed if the bingeing and purging occur only in the context of anorexia nervosa and its extreme weight loss; the diagnosis in such a case is anorexia nervosa, binge eating/purging type. The key difference between anorexia and bulimia is weight loss: People with anorexia nervosa lose a tremendous amount of weight, whereas people with bulimia nervosa do not.

In bulimia, binges typically occur in secret; they may be triggered by stress and negative emotions, and they continue until the person is uncomfortably full (Grilo, Shiffman, & Carter-Campbell, 1994). In the case of Jill, she was likely to binge after periods of stress associated with being an elite athlete. Foods that can be rapidly consumed, especially sweets such as ice cream and cake, are usually part of a binge. One study found that women with bulimia nervosa were more likely to binge while alone and during the morning or afternoon. In addition, avoiding a craved food on one day was associated with a binge episode with that food the next morning (Waters, Hill, & Waller, 2001). Other studies show that a binge is likely to occur after a negative social interaction—or at least, the perception of a negative social exchange (Steiger, Jabalpurwala, et al., 1999).

Research suggests that, although people with bulimia nervosa sometimes eat enormous quantities of food during binges, there is wide variation in the caloric content consumed (e.g., Rossiter & Agras, 1990). People report that they lose control during a binge, even to the point of experiencing something akin to what happens in addiction (Lowe, Arigo, et al., 2016; Smith & Robbins, 2013), even losing awareness of their behavior. They are usually ashamed of their binges and try to conceal them.

After the binge is over, feelings of discomfort, disgust, and fear of weight gain lead to the second step of bulimia nervosa—the inappropriate compensatory behavior (also known as purging) to attempt to undo the caloric effects of the binge. People with bulimia most often stick their fingers down their throats to cause gagging, but after a time many can induce vomiting at will without gagging themselves. Laxative and diuretic abuse (which do little to reduce body weight) as well as fasting and excessive exercise are also used to prevent weight gain.

Although many people binge occasionally and some people also purge, the DSM-5 diagnosis of bulimia nervosa requires that the episodes of bingeing and compensatory behavior occur at least once a week for 3 months. Is this frequency a well-established cutoff point? Probably not. DSM-5 severity ratings are based on the number of compensatory behaviors in a week (see **Table 11.4**).

DSM-5 Criteria for Bulimia Nervosa

- Recurrent episodes of binge eating
- Recurrent compensatory behaviors to prevent weight gain, for example, vomiting
- Body shape and weight are extremely important for self-evaluation

TABLE 11.4 **Severity Ratings for Bulimia Nervosa in DSM-5**

Rating	Number of Compensatory Behaviors
Mild	1–3 compensatory behaviors/week
Moderate	4–7
Severe	8–13
Extreme	14 or more

Like people with anorexia nervosa, people with bulimia nervosa depend heavily on maintaining normal weight to maintain self-esteem. Whereas people without eating disorders typically underreport their weight and say they are taller than they actually are, people with bulimia nervosa are more accurate in their report (Doll & Fairburn, 1998; McCabe et al., 2001). Yet people with bulimia nervosa are also likely to be highly dissatisfied with their bodies.

Bulimia nervosa typically begins in late adolescence or early adulthood. About 90 percent of people with bulimia are women, and prevalence among women is thought to be about 1 to 2 percent of the population (Hoek & van Hoeken, 2003). Many people with bulimia nervosa were somewhat overweight before the onset of the disorder, and the binge eating often started during an episode of dieting. Although both anorexia nervosa and bulimia nervosa among women begin in adolescence, they can persist into adulthood and middle age (Keel, Gravener, et al., 2010; Slevec & Tiggemann, 2011).

Bulimia nervosa is comorbid with other disorders, including depression, personality disorders, anxiety disorders, substance use disorders, and conduct disorder (Baker et al., 2010; Gadalla & Piran, 2007; Godart, Flament, et al., 2000; Godart, Flament, et al., 2002; Root et al., 2010; Stice, Burton, & Shaw, 2004; Striegel-Moore, Garvin, et al., 1999). Suicide rates are higher among people with bulimia nervosa than in the general population (Favaro & Santonastaso, 1997) but substantially lower than among people with anorexia (Arcelus et al., 2011; Franko & Keel, 2006).

Which comes first, bulimia nervosa or the comorbid disorders? A prospective study examined the relationship between bulimia and depression symptoms among adolescent girls (Stice et al., 2004). This study found that bulimia symptoms predicted the onset of depression symptoms. However, the converse was also true: depression symptoms predicted the onset of bulimia symptoms. Thus, it appears each disorder increases the risk for the other. With respect to substance use disorders, another prospective study of over 1200 twin pairs found that bulimia symptoms surfaced before substance use disorder symptoms (Baker et al., 2010).

Physical Consequences of Bulimia Nervosa

Bulimia nervosa, like anorexia, is a serious disorder with many unfortunate medical consequences (Mehler, 2011). For example, frequent purging can cause potassium depletion. Heavy use of laxatives induces diarrhea, which can also lead to changes in electrolytes and cause irregularities in the heartbeat. Recurrent vomiting may lead to tearing of tissue in the stomach and throat and to loss of dental enamel as stomach acids eat away at the teeth, which become ragged. The salivary glands may become swollen. Death from bulimia nervosa is less common than from anorexia nervosa (Herzog et al., 2000; Keel & Brown, 2010; Keel & Mitchell, 1997), but mortality rates are higher than for other disorders (Arcelus et al., 2011; Crow et al., 2009).

Prognosis Long-term follow-ups of people with bulimia nervosa reveal that 68 to 75 percent of them recover, although about 10 to 20 percent remain fully symptomatic (Eddy et al., 2017; Keel et al., 2010; Reas, Williamson, et al., 2000; Steinhausen & Weber, 2009). Intervening soon after a diagnosis is made (i.e., within the first few years) is linked with an even better prognosis (Reas et al., 2000). People with bulimia nervosa who binge and vomit more and who have comorbid substance use or a history of depression have a poorer prognosis than people without these factors (Wilson, Loeb, et al., 1999).

Clinical Case

Amy

Amy, a 27-year-old African American woman, described a life-long struggle with her weight. She was described as "chubby" as a child, and peers often called her "fatty." She went on several diets as a child, but none of them were successful. Currently, Amy is 5 feet, 4 inches tall and weighs 212 pounds (with a BMI of 35).

Amy had experienced several episodes of binge eating beginning at age 18, when she first left home for college. After being left out of a social group on campus, she retreated to her dorm room alone, where she ate two large pizzas and a bag of Doritos. After the binge, she felt very full and went to sleep. After

that first binge, she found herself doing this as often as twice a week throughout college. She was not always hungry when she binged, but even though she felt extremely full, she could not stop eating. Afterwards, she felt ashamed and angry at herself for having eaten so much. She gained 70 pounds during her college years.

Amy reported that she currently binges at least once a week, typically when she has had a very stressful day at work. She has recently confided in a friend about her troubled eating, and her friend recommended that she seek treatment at the local university mental health clinic.

Binge Eating Disorder

Binge eating disorder was first included as a diagnosis in DSM-5. This disorder includes recurrent binges (one time per week for at least 3 months), lack of control during the bingeing episode, and distress about bingeing, as well as other characteristics, such as rapid eating and eating alone. As with bulimia nervosa, binges often include sweets and other rapidly consumed foods. It is distinguished from bulimia, however, by the absence of compensatory behaviors (purging, fasting, or excessive exercise) and from anorexia by the absence of weight loss.

Most people with binge eating disorder are **obese**. A person with a BMI greater than 30 is considered obese. With the current explosion in the prevalence of obesity in the United States, it is perhaps not surprising that research on binge eating disorder continues to increase (Attia, Becker, et al., 2013). It is important to point out, however, that not all obese people meet criteria for binge eating disorder. Indeed, only those who have binge episodes and report feeling a loss of control over their eating will qualify, which amounts to anywhere from 2 to 25 percent of obese people (Wonderlich, Gordon, et al., 2009). For further discussion of obesity, **see Focus on Discovery 11.1**.

Focus on Discovery 11.1

Obesity: A Twenty-First Century Epidemic?

Obesity is not an eating disorder, though it is a serious public health problem, with estimated yearly health care costs of nearly $150 billion in the United States (Finkelstein, Trogdon, et al., 2009; Kim & Basu, 2016). The estimated lifetime health care costs for *each* 10-year-old child in the United States is $19,000, which added up among all 10-year-olds who are currently obese, comes to $14 billion (Finkelstein, Graham, & Malhotra, 2014). Why are the health care costs so high? Obesity is linked to many health problems, including diabetes, hypertension, cardiovascular disease, and several forms of cancer.

Recently, there was hopeful news about obesity in very young children ages 2 to 5, with one study finding that, although obesity rates increased from 1988 to 2004, to 14 percent, they have declined to 9 percent in 2014 (Ogden, Carroll, et al., 2016). However, another research team using different data found that obesity rates in children have remained consistent since 1999 (Skinner & Skelton, 2014). Among the most populated countries in the world, childhood obesity is greatest in the United States (GBD 2015 Obesity Collaborators, 2017).

Unfortunately, obesity rates are remaining steady and even growing among older children and adults (Flegal, Kruszon-Moran, et al., 2016; Ogden et al., 2016). In 2014, over a third of adults (37.7 percent) were obese (Ogden, Carroll, et al., 2015). Furthermore, 17.2 percent of older children and adolescents in the United States were obese in 2014. According to data collected by the Center for Disease Control and Prevention (https://www.cdc.gov/obesity/data/prevalence-maps.html), obesity rates are higher in some states than in others—the obesity rate was greater than 30 percent of adults in 19 states in 2015 (up from 13 states in 2012). Rates of obesity are much higher in the United States than in many other countries. Nevertheless, obesity is also increasing in other parts of the world, from Aborigines in Australia to children in Egypt, and in Siberia to Peru (Ng, Fleming, et al., 2014). Why are so many people overweight?

Several factors play a role, including the environment we live in. In the United States, the availability and amount of all food, not just fast food, have exponentially increased in the past decades. We pay far less for our food now, spending less than 10 percent of our income on food today compared to 25 percent of our income in the 1920s (Cohen, 2014). We can also buy food at any time of day or night, with most grocery stores featuring unhealthy items (with higher profit margins) more prominently than healthy items. At the same time, many people, including children, have become more sedentary, spending more time working or playing on the computer or smartphones and watching TV than ever before. Furthermore, physical education programs for children in schools have been declining (Critser, 2003). People eat in restaurants more than ever before (at least one third of total calories consumed by people in the United States, according to the FDA), and portion sizes of foods, both in restaurants and in grocery stores, are larger than ever.

In fact, most people do not know the portion size of most foods recommended by the U.S. Department of Agriculture, even though the Food and Drug Administration (FDA) now requires packaged foods to use new nutrition fact labels that more prominently display serving size and total calories. A 20-ounce bottle of soda is not one serving, but two and a half servings. The recommended serving of cheese is 1½ ounces, about the size of a 9-volt battery. In one study, researchers compared the depicted serving size on 158 different breakfast cereal boxes with the actual serving size listed in the nutrition facts box (Tal, Niemann, & Wansink, 2017). The depicted serving sizes were nearly two-thirds larger than the actual

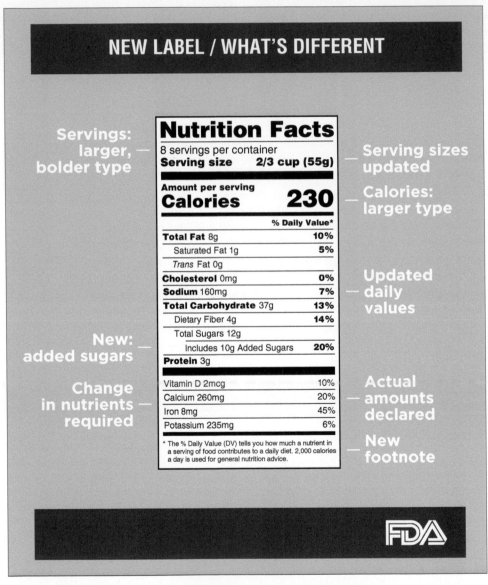

Nutrition facts labels approved in 2016 for packaged foods make it easier to see the serving size and total calories in foods.

serving size in the nutrition box. In a second study, college students poured more cereal into their bowls from boxes with larger depicted serving sizes, suggesting that a simple picture of large serving sizes can influence how much people (over)eat.

Americans today eat an average of 2700 calories daily compared with closer to 2200 calories a day 50 years ago. The ever-increasing portion sizes as well as the greater availability of

unhealthy foods impact the amount we eat. Even our cookbooks can influence what we eat. In an analysis of 18 recipes that have been in *The Joy of Cooking* since 1936, Wansink and Payne (2009) found that the calories in these recipes increased by a third between 1936 and 2006. The limited availability and greater expense of healthy foods in poorer neighborhoods also contributes to obesity. Research has shown that poorer neighborhoods have fewer grocery stores, more fast food restaurants, and fewer healthy food selections in their stores (Moreland et al., 2002). In addition, people in poorer neighborhoods may not have a means of transportation to and from grocery stores that carry more affordable, healthy food choices and that are farther away.

We are all subject to the continuing impact of advertisements, especially those promoting alluring high-calorie products such as snack foods, sodas, and meals at fast food restaurants. For example, Coke and Pepsi combined spent over $7 billion in advertising in 2013 (Bailey, 2014); all fast food restaurants combined spent over $4 billion in 2009 (Harris, Schwartz, et al., 2010). Compare this to the $6.5 *million* annual budget for *all operations* of the Center for Nutrition Policy and Promotion in the Department of Agriculture (Moss, 2010). A task force of the American Psychological Association concluded in 2004 that television advertisements of unhealthy foods (e.g., sugary cereals, soda) contribute to unhealthy eating habits of children under 8 years of age, largely because these children lack the requisite cognitive skills to discern truth from advertising (Kunkel, Wilcox, et al., 2004). Showing the direct effects of TV marketing, one study provided snacks to children as they watched a TV cartoon containing commercials for snack foods or a TV cartoon containing commercials for other products. Children randomly assigned to watch the show with the snack food commercials ate more snacks than children assigned to watch the cartoon with nonfood advertising (Harris, Bargh, & Brownell, 2009).

Along with the environment, heredity plays a role in obesity. In behavioral genetics terms, 25 to 40 percent of the variance in obesity is attributed to genetic factors (Brownell & Horgen, 2003). Of course, these factors have an impact only when they interact with environmental factors. Heredity could produce its effects by regulating metabolic rate, affecting the hypothalamus, or influencing the production of enzymes that make it easier to store fat and gain weight. Molecular genetics studies have identified several possible genes that might contribute to obesity, including genes that help regulate fatty acids, metabolism, and insulin (Locke, Kahali, et al., 2015; Shungin, Winkler, et al., 2015).

Related to genetics is the role of the neural pathways associated with reward. Recent prospective studies have found that brain activation in areas associated with reward (e.g., striatum, nucleus accumbens) in response to tasty, high-calorie foods or cues about food (e.g., pictures of food) predict weight gain (Stice & Yokum, 2016). Indeed, a meta-analysis of 45 food cue studies found medium effect sizes (see Chapter 4) for food cues predicting greater eating and weight gain (Boswell & Kober, 2016). Activation in these regions is linked to genes associated with the neurotransmitter dopamine, which is also part of our brain's reward system.

Although genetic and neural factors are part of the story, the environment also plays a critical role. For example, one study of over 500,000 women found that mothers' weight gain during pregnancy was more important in predicting high birth weight among babies than genetic factors (Ludwig & Currie, 2010).

In 2011, researchers published a study showing that many mammals, not just humans, have been gaining weight over the past decades (Klimentidis, Beasley, et al., 2011). The researchers examined different kinds of monkeys, as well as mice, rats, and marmosets, all of whom were raised in captivity, and found that these animals have all become heavier over the decades even though they were fed highly controlled diets that have not markedly changed over the years in quantity or quality. Clearly, animals are

BourreauScience Source

Obesity has become quite prevalent, particularly in the United States, in the past 30 years.

not gaining weight based on advertising or access to fast food or even limited exercise. The researchers' findings show that changes in the environment, such as chemicals that disrupt the endocrine system, bacteria or other infectious agents, and stress, are influencing the obesity epidemic in humans.

Indeed, stress and its associated negative moods can induce eating in some people (Arnow, Kenardy, & Agras, 1992; Heatherton & Baumeister, 1991), and research in rats shows that foods rich in fat and sugar may reduce stress in the short term, giving new meaning to the term *comfort food* (Dallman, Pecoraro, et al., 2003; Kessler, 2009). Unfortunately, research also shows that negative moods usually get worse after binge eating (Haedt-Matt & Keel, 2011). In addition, trying to suppress negative feelings is not effective in avoiding the tendency to eat when feeling bad. In one study, people who were asked to suppress their feelings of sadness after watching a sad film ate more ice cream than those who were asked to just watch the film (Vohs & Heatherton, 2000).

The stigma associated with being overweight remains a problem. Several reality TV shows are devoted to watching obese people struggle to lose weight, such as *The Biggest Loser*, where participants are subjected to a tough exercise and eating regimen, or *Dance Your Ass Off*, where overweight people lose weight through dancing. Obese people are now presented as entertainment: This does not seem to be an effective way to reduce stigma.

Stigma can also perpetuate the idea that obesity is simply a matter of personal responsibility—the belief that if people would just eat less and exercise more, obesity would not be a problem. But the science behind self-control tells another story. Given the multitude of factors contributing to obesity, such a simple solution is not reasonable. Despite the evidence that environmental factors, including the availability and relatively unhealthy nature of a lot of fast food, contribute to obesity, some argue that obesity is mostly a matter of personal responsibility. Of course, personal responsibility is important. People can and should make better choices about what and how much they eat. Nevertheless, other environmental factors, such as availability, cost, and transportation can sometimes make it harder to make good choices.

During President Obama's tenure, several legislative and policy changes were initiated to try to curb obesity. For example, First Lady Michelle Obama began the Let's Move! campaign to target childhood obesity by focusing on getting young people to eat healthy foods and to exercise. President Obama's Domestic Policy Council and White House Taskforce on Childhood Obesity included a pledge from 16 of the largest American food companies to reduce the calorie content of their products by 1.5 trillion calories by 2015. These companies exceeded their pledge by nearly 5 trillion calories (Ng, Slining, & Popkin, 2014). Many cities and states now require restaurants to post the calorie contents of their products, and the federal Food and Drug Administration (FDA) finalized a nationwide rule regarding the labeling of calorie content for chain restaurants with more than 20 locations (new labeling must be implemented by 2018). Still, much work needs to be done to help halt the obesity epidemic.

Binge eating disorder was added to DSM-5 based on a growing body of research supporting its validity as a diagnostic category (Attia et al., 2013; Striegel-Moore & Franco, 2008; Wonderlich et al., 2009). Severity ratings for this disorder are shown in **Table 11.5** and are based on the number of binges per week. Many people with binge eating disorder have a history of dieting (Kinzl, Traweger, et al., 1999; Pike, Dohm, et al., 2001). Binge eating disorder is comorbid with several disorders, including mood disorders, anxiety disorders, ADHD, conduct disorder, and substance use disorders (Kessler, Berglund, et al., 2013; Wonderlich et al., 2009). Risk factors for developing binge eating disorder include childhood obesity, critical comments about being overweight, weight-loss attempts in childhood, low self-concept, depression, and childhood physical or sexual abuse (Fairburn, Doll, et al., 1998; Rubinstein, McGinn, et al., 2010).

Binge eating disorder is more prevalent than either anorexia nervosa or bulimia nervosa (Hudson et al., 2007; Kessler et al., 2013; Stice, Marti, & Rohde, 2013). In one study of several countries, the lifetime prevalence ranged from 0.2 to 4.7 percent (Kessler et al., 2013). Binge eating disorder is more common in women than men, although the gender difference is not as great as it is in anorexia or bulimia (Kessler et al., 2013). Though only a few epidemiological studies have been done, binge eating disorder appears to be equally prevalent among European, African, Asian, and Hispanic Americans (Striegel-Moore & Franco, 2008).

Physical Consequences of Binge Eating Disorder

Like the other eating disorders, binge eating disorder has physical consequences. Many of the physical consequences are likely a function of associated obesity, including increased risk of type 2 diabetes, cardiovascular problems, chronic back pain, and headaches even after controlling for the independent effects of other comorbid disorders (Kessler et al., 2013). Other research shows that many physical problems are present among people with binge eating disorder that are independent from co-occurring obesity, including sleep problems, anxiety, depression, irritable bowel syndrome, and, for women, early onset of menstruation (Bulik & Reichborn-Kjennerud, 2003).

Prognosis

Perhaps because it is a relatively new diagnosis, fewer studies have assessed the prognosis of binge eating disorder. Research so far suggests that 25 to 82 percent of people recover (Keel & Brown, 2010; Striegel-Moore & Franco, 2008). One epidemiological study of binge eating disorder in several countries reported a duration of just over 4 years (Kessler et al., 2013).

DSM-5 Criteria for Binge Eating Disorder

- Recurrent binge eating episodes
- Binge eating episodes include at least three of the following:
  - eating more quickly than usual
  - eating until over full
- eating large amounts even if not hungry
- eating alone due to embarrassment about large food quantity
- feeling bad (e.g., disgusted, guilty, or depressed) after the binge
- No compensatory behavior is present

TABLE 11.5	Severity Ratings for Binge Eating Disorder in DSM-5
Rating	**Number of Binges**
Mild	1–3 binges/week
Moderate	4–7
Severe	8–13
Extreme	14 or more

Quick Summary

Anorexia nervosa has three characteristics: restriction of behaviors to promote a healthy body weight, an intense fear of gaining weight, and a distorted body image. Anorexia usually begins in the early teen years and is more common in women than men. Bodily changes that can occur after severe weight loss can be serious and life threatening. About 70 percent of women with anorexia eventually recover, but it can take many years.

Bulimia nervosa involves both bingeing and compensatory behavior. Bingeing often involves sweet foods and is more likely to occur when someone is alone, after a negative social encounter, and in the morning or afternoon. One striking difference between anorexia and bulimia is weight loss: People with anorexia nervosa lose a tremendous amount of weight, whereas people with bulimia nervosa do not lose weight. Bulimia typically begins in late adolescence and is more common in women than men. Depression often co-occurs with bulimia, and each condition appears to be a risk factor for the other. Dangerous changes to the body can also occur as a result of bulimia, such as menstrual problems, tearing in tissues of the stomach and throat, and swelling of the salivary glands.

Binge eating disorder is characterized by several binges, and most (but not all) people who suffer from it are obese (defined as having a BMI greater than 30). Not all obese people meet the criteria for binge eating disorder—only those who have binge episodes and report feeling a loss of control over their eating qualify. Binge eating disorder is more common than anorexia and bulimia and is more common in women than men, though the gender difference is not as great as it is in anorexia and bulimia. About 60 percent of people with binge eating disorder recover, but it may take even longer than recovery for anorexia or bulimia.

Check Your Knowledge 11.1
(Answers are at the end of the chapter.)

Answer the questions.

1. All the following are symptoms of anorexia *except*:
   a. fear of gaining weight
   b. unwillingness to maintain normal weight
   c. perfectionism
   d. distorted body image

2. Which statement is true regarding binge eating disorder?
   a. It is more common in men than women.
   b. It was not an eating disorder category in DSM-IV-TR.
   c. It is synonymous with obesity.
   d. It includes binges and purges.

3. Which of the following are characteristics of both anorexia and bulimia?
   a. They involve a good deal of weight loss.
   b. They are more common in women than men.
   c. They have physical side effects (e.g., menstrual irregularities).
   d. All the above but *a* are correct.

4. List three factors that contribute to obesity.

Etiology of Eating Disorders

As with other disorders, any single factor is unlikely to cause an eating disorder. Several areas of current research—genetics, neurobiology, cognitive behavioral factors, sociocultural pressures to be thin, personality, and the role of the family—suggest that eating disorders result when several influences converge in a person's life. The strongest evidence for causal factors is found from prospective studies. Prospective studies identify and measure causal factors *before* the onset of an eating disorder and demonstrate that the causal factors predict the onset of disorder (Stice, 2016). Prospective studies can come closer to identifying causes rather than consequences of eating disorders. Unfortunately, there are currently too few of these prospective studies.

Genetic Factors

Eating disorders run in families. First-degree relatives of women with anorexia nervosa are more than 10 times more likely than average to have the disorder themselves (Strober, Freeman, et al., 2000) Similar results are found for bulimia nervosa, where first-degree relatives of women with bulimia nervosa are about four times more likely than average to have the disorder (Strober et al., 2000). Heritability estimates for anorexia range from .48 to .74 and for bulimia from .55 to .62 (Yilmaz, Hardaway, & Bulik, 2015). Furthermore, first-degree relatives of women with eating disorders appear to be at higher risk for anorexia or bulimia (Lilenfeld, Kaye, et al., 1998; Strober, Lampert, et al., 1990, Strober et al. 2000). Although eating disorders are less frequent among men, one study found that first-degree relatives of men with anorexia nervosa were at greater risk for having anorexia nervosa (though not bulimia) than relatives of men without anorexia (Strober et al., 2000). One behavioral genetics study (Hudson, Lalonde, et al., 2006) found that relatives of people with binge eating disorder and obesity were more likely to have binge eating disorder themselves (20 percent) than were relatives of people who were obese but did not have binge eating disorder (9 percent).

Twin studies of eating disorders also suggest a genetic influence. Most studies of both anorexia and bulimia report higher MZ than DZ concordance rates (Bulik, Wade, & Kendler, 2000) and show that genes account for a portion of the variance among twins with eating disorders (Wade, Bulik, et al., 2000). On the other hand, research has shown that nonshared/unique environmental factors (see Chapter 2), such as different interactions with parents or different peer groups, also contribute to the development of eating disorders (Klump, McGue, & Iacono, 2002). For example, a study of more than 1200 twin pairs found that 42 percent of the variance in bulimia symptoms was attributable to genetic factors but 58 percent of the variance was attributable to unique environmental factors (Baker et al., 2010). Research also suggests that key features of the eating disorders, such as dissatisfaction with one's body, a strong desire to be thin, binge eating, and preoccupation with weight, are heritable (Klump, McGue, & Iacono, 2000). Additional evidence suggests that common genetic factors may account for the relationship between certain personality characteristics, such as negative emotionality and constraint with eating disorders (Klump, McGue, & Iacono, 2002). One GWAS study (see Chapter 2) included nearly 3000 people with anorexia nervosa and identified several single nucleotide polymorphisms (SNPs; see Chapter 2) that were associated with anorexia (Boraska, Franklin, et al., 2014). Even though this sample size sounds large, it was not large enough for the findings to hold up during replication, something that GWAS researchers frequently do to avoid reporting findings that could be due to chance. A more recent GWAS study included more than 3000 participants with anorexia by combining samples from several research groups. This study found a significant location on chromosome 12 that overlapped with six genes and was close to another six genes (Duncan, Yilmaz, et al., 2017). The results of all the genetic studies are consistent with the possibility that genes play a role in eating disorders, but studies showing how genetic factors interact with the environment are needed.

Neurobiological Factors

The hypothalamus is a key brain center for regulating hunger and eating. Research on animals with lesions to the lateral hypothalamus indicates that they lose weight and have no appetite

(Hoebel & Teitelbaum, 1966). Thus, it is not surprising that the hypothalamus has been proposed to play a role in anorexia. The level of some hormones regulated by the hypothalamus, such as cortisol, is indeed different in people with anorexia. Rather than causing the disorder, however, these hormonal differences occur as a result of self-starvation, and levels return to normal after weight gain (Doerr, Fichter, et al., 1980; Stoving, Hangaard, et al., 1999). Furthermore, the weight loss of animals with hypothalamic lesions does not parallel what we know about anorexia. These animals appear to have no hunger and to become indifferent to food, whereas people with anorexia continue to starve themselves despite being hungry and having an interest in food. Nor does the hypothalamic model account for body-image disturbance or fear of gaining weight. Thus, a dysfunctional hypothalamus does not seem a likely causal factor in anorexia nervosa.

Endogenous opioids are substances produced by the body that can reduce pain sensations, enhance mood, and suppress appetite. Opioids are released during starvation and have been hypothesized to play a role in anorexia, bulimia, and binge eating disorder. Starvation among people with anorexia may increase the levels of endogenous opioids, resulting in a positively reinforcing positive mood state (Marrazzi & Luby, 1986). Furthermore, the excessive exercise seen among some people with eating disorders would increase opioids and thus be reinforcing.

Some research supports the theory that endogenous opioids play a role in eating disorders. For example, two studies found low levels of the endogenous opioid beta-endorphin (see **Figure 11.2**) in people with bulimia (Brewerton, Lydiard, et al., 1992; Waller, Kiser, et al., 1986). In one of these studies, the researchers observed that the people with more severe cases of bulimia had the lowest levels of beta-endorphin (Waller et al., 1986). It is important to note, however, that these findings demonstrate that low levels of opioids are seen concurrently with bulimia, not that such levels are seen before onset of the disorder. In other words, we don't know if the low levels of opioids are a cause of bulimia or an effect of changes in food intake or purging. The same thing is true for binge eating disorder. Animal studies have shown that bingeing leads to changes in the opioid system (e.g., Bello et al., 2011) but not that changes In the opioid system lead to more bingeing. Additional research with animals has linked endogenous opioids to the rewarding aspects of food, which may be relevant for binge eating disorder in humans (Nathan & Bullmore, 2009).

Human brain imaging studies have examined areas of the brain associated with rewards in people with and without anorexia. These studies have found that people with anorexia display different patterns of activation when viewing pictures of food or tasting food compared to people without anorexia (Steinglass & Walsh, 2016). One recent fMRI study of 21 women hospitalized with anorexia and 21 women without anorexia examined brain activity when women made choices between two foods (Foerde, Steinglass, et al., 2015). Not surprisingly, women with anorexia chose high-fat foods less often than women without anorexia. Interestingly, however, both groups of women showed comparable brain activation in the ventral striatum, an area associated with reward, during the food choice task. Where the groups differed was in the dorsal striatum, an area of the brain linked with habitual choices and anxiety. These findings suggest that eating habits may be important in anorexia. That is, dieting or restrictive eating may become habitual, and these habits may themselves become rewarding (Walsh, 2013).

Finally, some research has focused on two neurotransmitters (Kaye, 2008): serotonin, which is related to eating and satiety (feeling full), and dopamine, which is related to the rewarding/pleasing aspects of food.

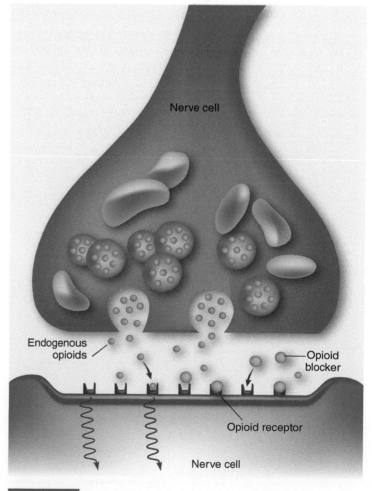

FIGURE 11.2 Endogenous opioid systems in the brain.

Animal research has shown that serotonin promotes feeling full. Therefore, the binges of people with bulimia or binge eating disorder could result from a serotonin deficit that prevents them from feeling full after they eat. Animal research has also shown that food restriction interferes with serotonin synthesis in the brain. Thus, among people with anorexia, severe food intake restrictions could interfere with the serotonin system.

Researchers have examined levels of serotonin metabolites among people with anorexia and bulimia. Several studies have found low levels of serotonin metabolites among people with anorexia (e.g., Kaye, Ebert, et al., 1984) and bulimia (e.g., Carrasco, Dyaz-Marsa, et al., 2000; Jimerson, Lesem, et al., 1992; Kaye, Greeno, et al., 1998). Lower levels of a neurotransmitter's metabolites are one indicator that the neurotransmitter activity is underactive. In addition, people with anorexia who have not been restored to a healthy weight show a poorer response to serotonin agonists (i.e., drugs that stimulate serotonin receptors) than those people who have regained a good portion of their weight, again suggesting an underactive serotonin system (Attia, Haiman, et al. 1998; Ferguson, La Via, et al., 1999). People with bulimia also show smaller responses to serotonin agonists (Jimerson, Wolfe, et al., 1997; Levitan, Kaplan, et al., 1997). The antidepressant drugs that can be effective treatments for some people with anorexia and bulimia (discussed later) are known to increase serotonin activity, adding to the possible importance of serotonin. Serotonin, though, more likely is linked to the comorbid depression often found in anorexia and bulimia.

Researchers have also examined the role of dopamine in eating behavior. Studies with animals have shown that dopamine is linked to the pleasurable aspects of food that compel an animal to go after food (e.g., Szczypka, Kwok, et al., 2001), and human brain-imaging studies have shown how dopamine is linked to the motivation to obtain food and other pleasurable or rewarding things. In one study, women with either anorexia or bulimia had greater expression of the dopamine transporter gene *DAT* (Frieling, Romer, et al., 2010). Recall from Chapter 2 that a gene is "turned on," or expressed, as it interacts with different aspects of the environment. The expression of *DAT* influences the release of a protein that regulates the reuptake of dopamine back into the synapse. A prospective study found that people with several genes that promote strong dopamine signals in the brain were more likely to have a higher BMI 2 years later (Yokum, Marti, et al. 2015). These findings point to the role of dopamine genes in eating disorders and weight gain and will need to be replicated in future studies. Newer research is studying the role of dopamine in binge eating disorder and obesity (see also Focus on Discovery 11.1). One theory about the role of dopamine comes from research on substance use disorders (discussed in Chapter 10). The *incentive-sensitization theory* considers both the cravings ("wanting") for food and the pleasure ("liking") that comes with eating foods, particularly tasty, high-calorie foods (Berridge, Ho, et al., 2010). In this model, dopamine plays a key role in the "liking" of food and the "wanting" or craving for food. Cravings for food can be triggered by cues in the environment, not just hunger. Cues about food (e.g., billboards, photos on food packaging) can elicit dopamine responses that in turn promote strong cravings for food that some people have a hard time resisting. You can probably remember a time when you saw an ad on TV for some food (e.g., Taco Bell) or even reading about a food (e.g., donuts) and then found yourself wanting that very food! The theory suggests that the cues can thus create cravings which can then promote (over) eating or bingeing. In support of this theory, brain imaging studies have found that people who show greater activation in areas of the brain associated with dopamine and reward during the presentation of food cues are more likely to subsequently gain weight (Stice & Yokum, 2016).

Although we can expect further neurotransmitter research in the future, keep in mind that much of this work focuses on brain mechanisms relevant

Cravings can be a powerful driver of behavior, including eating.

designs by Jack / Shutterstock

to hunger, eating, and satiety (and a lot of the research focuses on animals) but does little to account for other key features of eating disorders, in particular the intense fear of gaining weight. Furthermore, as suggested, much of the evidence so far does not show that brain changes come before the onset of eating disorders. Brain changes may happen because of under- or overeating, not the other way around. In other words, we know that brain activity or gene expression of certain dopamine genes is correlated with eating disorders, not that these things cause eating disorders.

Cognitive Behavioral Factors

Cognitive behavioral theories of eating disorders focus on understanding the thoughts, feelings, and behaviors that contribute to distorted body image, fear of weight gain, and loss of control over eating. People with eating disorders may have maladaptive schemata that narrow their attention toward thoughts and images related to weight, body shape, and food (Fairburn, Shafran, & Cooper, 1999).

Anorexia Nervosa Cognitive behavioral theories of anorexia nervosa emphasize body-image disturbance as the motivating factors that powerfully reinforce weight loss. Many people who develop anorexia symptoms report that the onset followed a period of weight loss and dieting. Behaviors that achieve or maintain thinness are negatively reinforced by the reduction of anxiety about gaining weight as well as positively reinforced by comments from others (*Did you lose weight? You look great!*). Dieting and weight loss may also be positively reinforced by the sense of mastery or self-control they create (Fairburn et al., 1999; Garner, Vitousek, & Pike, 1997). Some theories also include personality and sociocultural variables to explain how body-image disturbances develop. For example, perfectionism and a sense of personal inadequacy may lead a person to become especially concerned with his or her appearance, making dieting a potent reinforcer. Similarly, seeing portrayals in the media of thinness as an ideal, being overweight, and tending to compare oneself with especially attractive others all contribute to dissatisfaction with one's body (Stormer & Thompson, 1996).

Another important factor in producing a strong drive for thinness and a disturbed body image is criticism from peers and parents about being overweight. In one study supporting this conclusion, adolescent girls ages 10 to 15 were evaluated twice, with a 3-year interval between assessments. Obesity at the first assessment was related to being teased by peers, and at the second assessment it was linked to dissatisfaction with their bodies. Dissatisfaction was in turn related to symptoms of an eating disorder (Paxton, Schutz, et al., 1999).

People often binge when diets are broken (Polivy & Herman, 1985). Thus, when a person with anorexia nervosa experiences a lapse in her strict dieting, the lapse is likely to escalate into a binge. The purging after an episode of binge eating may be motivated by the fear of weight gain elicited by the binge.

Research has also examined the role of emotion in anorexia nervosa. Not surprisingly, people with anorexia experience many negative emotions. Surprisingly, though, people with anorexia also experience positive

The fear of weight gain, which is so important in eating disorders, is partly based on society's negative stereotypes of overweight people.

SERGIO MORAES/Reuters/Newscom

emotion, even though they may not distinguish among different positive emotional states all that well (Selby, Wonderlich, et al., 2013). In other words, people with anorexia may experience a positive emotion such as pride very intensely after losing weight or by avoiding eating a piece of cake at a party. This may in turn be indistinguishable from happiness or success and is referred to as low positive emotion differentiation. One study found that low positive emotion differentiation prospectively predicted eating disorder behaviors such as vomiting, checking weight, exercising excessively, and using laxatives in a group of 118 women with anorexia (Selby et al., 2013). Feeling stronger negative emotions also predicted these behaviors.

Bulimia Nervosa and Binge Eating Disorder People with bulimia nervosa are also thought to be overly concerned with weight gain and body appearance; indeed, they often view their self-worth in terms of their weight and shape. They may have low self-esteem, and because weight and shape are somewhat more controllable than are other features of the self, they tend to focus on weight and shape, hoping their efforts in this area will make them feel better generally. They try to follow a very rigid pattern of restrictive eating, with strict rules regarding how much to eat, what kinds of food to eat, and when to eat. These strict rules are inevitably broken, and the lapse escalates into a binge. After the binge, feelings of disgust and fear of becoming fat build up, leading to compensatory actions such as vomiting (Fairburn, 1997). Although purging temporarily reduces the anxiety from having eaten too much, this cycle lowers the person's self-esteem, which triggers still more bingeing and purging—a vicious cycle that maintains desired body weight but has serious medical consequences (see **Figure 11.3** for a summary of this theory).

People with bulimia nervosa or binge eating disorder typically binge when they encounter stress and experience negative emotions, as has been shown in several studies. In fact, the propensity to experience negative emotions has been shown to predict the onset of eating disorders (Culbert, Racine, & Klump, 2015). Using ecological momentary assessment (EMA; see Chapter 3), investigators show how specific binge-and-purge events are linked to changes in emotions and stress in the course of daily life (Smyth, Wonderlich, et al., 2007). A meta-analysis of 82 EMA studies found that negative emotion preceded the onset of a binge among people with bulimia or binge eating disorder, but the effect sizes (see Chapter 4) were stronger for binge eating disorder than for bulimia (Haedt-Matt & Keel, 2011). The binge may therefore function as a means of regulating negative emotion (Smyth et al., 2007; Stice & Agras, 1999). However, the meta-analysis of EMA studies also showed that people with bulimia or binge eating disorder experienced *more* negative emotion after the binge, so the use of bingeing as a way to regulate affect appears not to be very successful. Evidence also supports the idea that stress and negative emotion are relieved by purging. That is, negative emotion levels decline and positive emotion levels increase after a purge event, supporting the idea that purging is reinforced by negative affect reduction (Haedt-Matt & Keel, 2011; Jarrell, Johnson, & Williamson, 1986; Smyth et al., 2007).

Research methods from cognitive science have been used to study how attention, memory, and problem solving are affected in people with eating disorders. Research shows that people with anorexia and bulimia focus their attention on food-related words or images more than other images (Brooks, Prince, et al., 2011). People with anorexia nervosa and people who score high on restrained eating (Polivy, Herman, & Howard, 1988) remember food words better

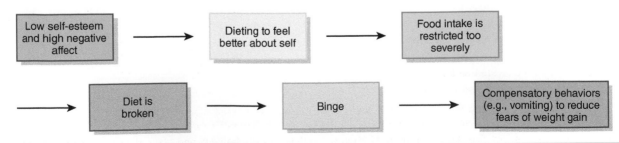

FIGURE 11.3 Schematic of cognitive behavioral theory of bulimia nervosa.

when they are full but not when they are hungry (Brooks et al., 2011). Other studies have found that college women with eating disorder symptoms pay attention to and better remember images depicting other people's body size more than images depicting emotion (Treat & Viken, 2010). Thus, women with eating disorders pay greater attention not only to their own bodies, food, and weight but also to other women's bodies, food, and shapes. This bias toward food and body image may make it harder for women with eating disorders to change their thinking patterns. As we shall see later, cognitive behavior therapy (CBT) devotes a good bit of time to teaching people with eating disorders to alter these memory and attention biases.

Sociocultural factors appear to play a role in the faulty perceptions and eating habits of those with eating disorders. We turn to these influences next.

Sociocultural Factors

Throughout history, the standards societies have set for the ideal body—especially the ideal female body—have varied greatly. Think of the famous nudes painted by Rubens in the seventeenth century: According to modern standards, these women are chubby. Over the past 60 years, the American cultural ideal has progressed steadily toward thinness.

Somewhat paradoxically, as cultural standards were moving in the direction of thinness over the latter part of the twentieth century, more and more people were becoming over-weight. The prevalence of obesity (see Focus on Discovery 11.1) has doubled since 1980 in 70 countries (GBD 2015 Obesity Collaborators, 2017). Currently, over two-thirds of Americans are overweight (and over a third are obese), setting the stage for greater conflict between the cultural ideal and reality.

As society has become more health conscious, dieting to lose weight has become more common; in results from a survey of over 4000 women ages 25 to 45, a third of the women reported spending more than half of their lifetime trying to lose weight (Reba-Harrelson, Von Holle et al., 2009). Diet crazes come and go. Are some diets more effective than others? A study in the *New England Journal of Medicine* reported that diets were equally effective, whether they cut carbs, fat, or protein (de Souza, Bray, et al., 2012; Sacks, Bray, et al., 2009). Research also indicates that the number of calories may not be as important as the type of calories when it comes to losing weight. People differ in body type and metabolism of different types of calories (Ludwig & Friedman, 2014). Procedures such as liposuction (vacuuming out fat deposits just under the skin) and bariatric surgery (surgically changing the stomach so that it cannot digest as much food) remain popular despite their risks (Brownell & Horgen, 2003).

Women are more likely than men to be dieters. The onset of eating disorders is typically preceded by dieting and other concerns about weight, supporting the idea that social standards stressing the importance of thinness play a role in the development of these disorders (Rubinstein et al., 2010; Stice, 2016).

It is likely that women who either are overweight or fear becoming so are also dissatisfied with their bodies. Not surprisingly, studies have found that women and adolescent girls with both a high BMI and body dissatisfaction are at higher risk for developing

© SuperStock /SuperStock

Photo by Lambert/Getty Images, Inc.

Photo by Frazer Harrison/Getty Images for Mercedes-Benz Fashion Week/Getty Images, Inc.

Cultural standards regarding the ideal feminine shape have changed over time. Even in the 1950s and 1960s, the feminine ideal was considerably heavier than what it has become in the 1970s through today.

eating disorders (Fairburn, 1997; Killen, Taylor, et al., 1996). Preoccupation with being thin or feeling pressure to be thin predicts an increase in body dissatisfaction among adolescent girls, which in turn predicts more dieting, eating pathology, and negative emotions (Stice, 2001); these factors were operating in the clinical case of Jill, presented earlier. Indeed, prospective studies indicate that body dissatisfaction, dieting, and desire to be thin all prospectively predict the onset of bulimia (Stice, 2016).

Finally, exposure to media portrayals of unrealistically thin models can influence reports of body dissatisfaction. One study reviewed results from 25 experiments that presented images of thin models to women and then asked the women to report on their body satisfaction. Perhaps not surprisingly, results from these studies showed that women reported a decline in body satisfaction after viewing these images (Groesz, Levine, & Murnen, 2002). Another study found that men's body dissatisfaction, as indexed by a greater discrepancy between the muscularity of the actual and ideal self, increased after viewing images of muscular men (Leit, Gray, & Pope, 2002).

The sociocultural ideal of thinness is a likely vehicle through which people learn to fear weight gain or even feeling fat, and this was probably influential in the Clinical Cases of both Lynne and Jill. In addition to creating an undesired physical shape, being overweight has negative connotations, such as being unsuccessful and having little self-control. Obese people are viewed by others as less smart and are stereotyped as lonely, shy, and greedy for the affection of others (DeJong & Kleck, 1986). Even more disturbing, health professionals who specialize in obesity have also exhibited beliefs that obese people are lazy, stupid, or worthless (Schwartz et al., 2003). Reducing the stigma associated with being overweight will be beneficial to those with eating disorders as well as those who are obese.

Not only does the fear of weight gain contribute to eating pathology, but the celebration of extreme thinness via websites, blogs, and magazines may also play a role. Websites that are "pro-ana" (short for anorexia) or "pro-mia" (short for bulimia) and other "thinsperation" websites and blogs have developed a following of women who seek support and encouragement for losing weight, often to a dangerously low level. These sites often post photos of female celebrities who are extremely thin as inspiration (hence, the term *thinsperation*). Some of these women have publicly discussed their struggles with eating disorders (e.g., the actress Jessica Alba), but others have not. Low BMI that goes along with extreme thinness has been shown to prospectively predict the onset of anorexia (Stice, 2016), and therefore sites that promote such low weight may nurture a risk factor for anorexia.

A review of the impact of these "pro–eating disorder" websites noted that women who visited these sites were more dissatisfied with their bodies, had more eating disorder symptoms, and experienced more prior hospitalizations for eating disorders (Rouleau & von Ranson, 2011). To tease apart causation from correlation, researchers have randomly assigned healthy women to view either pro–eating disorder, other health-related, or tourist websites (Jett, La Perte, & Wanchism, 2010), supposedly as part of a website evaluation survey. Women completed food diaries for 1 week before and 1 week after viewing these websites. Women assigned to the pro–eating disorder website condition restricted their eating more the following week than did the women assigned to the other website conditions. These results suggest that viewing these websites has the potential to cause unhealthful changes in eating behavior.

Gender Influences We have discussed the fact that eating disorders are more common in women than in men. One primary reason is likely the fact that Western cultural standards emphasize and reinforce the desirability of being thin more for women than for men. For men, magazines focus attention on the masculine ideal of normal body weight or on increased muscle mass (Mishkind, Rodin, et al., 1986). The risk for eating disorders among groups of women who might be expected to be particularly concerned with thinness and their weight—for example, models, dancers, and gymnasts, as in the case of Jill—appears to be especially high (Garner, Garfinkel, et al., 1980).

Another sociocultural factor, though, has remained remarkably resilient to change—namely, the objectification of women's bodies. Women's bodies are often viewed through a sexual lens; in effect, women are defined by their bodies, whereas men are esteemed more for their accomplishments. According to objectification theory (Fredrickson & Roberts, 1997), the prevalence of objectification messages in Western culture (in television, advertisements, and so forth) has led some women to "self-objectify," which means that they see their own bodies through the eyes of others. Research has shown that self-objectification causes women to feel more shame about their bodies. Shame is most often elicited in situations where an individual's ideal falls short of a cultural ideal or standard. Thus, women likely experience body shame when they observe a mismatch between their ideal self and the cultural (objectified) view of women. Research has also shown that both self-objectification and body shame are associated with disordered eating (Fredrickson & Levenson, 1998; McKinley & Hyde, 1996; Noll & Fredrickson, 1998).

Do eating disorders and weight concerns go away as women get older? A large, 20-year prospective study of over 600 men and women reported important differences in dieting and other eating disorder risk factors for men and women (Keel, Baxter, et al., 2007). The men and women were first surveyed about dieting, BMI, weight, body image, and eating disorder symptoms when they were in college. Follow-up surveys were completed 10 and 20 years after college. Thus, the men and women were around age 40 at the 20-year follow-up assessment. The researchers found that after 20 years, women dieted less and were less concerned about their weight and body image than they were in college, even though they weighed more now. In addition, eating disorder symptoms decreased over the 20 years for women, as did the risk factors for eating disorders (concern about body image, frequency of dieting). Changes in life roles—having a life partner, having a child—were also associated with decreases in eating disorder symptoms for women. By contrast, men were more concerned about their weight and were dieting more. Like women, they weighed more in their early 40s than when they were in college. Decreases in risk factors such as concern about body image and dieting frequency were also associated with decreases in eating disorder symptoms for men.

Gabourey Sidibe, the Oscar-nominated actress and author of the memoir *This Is Just My Face: Try Not to Stare*, had bariatric surgery to accomplish weight loss.

Cross-Cultural Studies Evidence for eating disorders across cultures depends on the disorder. Anorexia has been observed in several cultures and countries besides the United States; for example, in Hong Kong, China, Taiwan, England, Korea, Japan, Denmark, Nigeria, South Africa, Zimbabwe, Ethiopia, Iran, Malaysia, India, Pakistan, Australia, the Netherlands, and Egypt (Keel & Klump, 2003). Furthermore, cases of anorexia have been documented in cultures with very little Western cultural influence. An important caveat must be made, however. The anorexia observed in these diverse cultures does not always include the intense fear of gaining weight that is part of the DSM criteria, at least initially. Thus, intense fear of weight gain likely reflects an ideal more widely espoused in more Westernized cultures.

The variation in the clinical presentation of anorexia across cultures provides a window into the importance of culture in establishing realistic versus potentially disordered views of one's body. However, there is also evidence that cultural variation is diminishing when it comes to eating disorders. A 20-year study of eating disorders in Hong Kong found evidence of Western influence in both the prevalence and presentation of

Celebrities such as Christina Ricci and Lady Gaga have publicly discussed their struggles with eating disorders.

FilmMagic/Getty Images, Inc.

Jessica Alba has spoken openly about her eating disorder.

eating disorders (Lee, Ng, et al., 2010). First, both anorexia and bulimia were twice as common in 2007 than they were in 1987. Second, 25 percent more women reported body dissatisfaction and fear of fat in 2007 than in 1987. Thus, in a fairly short period of time, eating disorders in Hong Kong appear to have become more Western.

Bulimia nervosa appears to be more common in industrialized societies, such as the United States, Canada, Japan, Australia, and Europe, than in nonindustrialized nations. However, as cultures undergo social changes associated with adopting the practices of more Westernized cultures, particularly the United States (Watters, 2010), the incidence of bulimia appears to increase (Abou-Saleh, Younis, & Karim, 1998; Lee et al., 2010; Nasser, 1997). A comprehensive review of research on culture and eating disorders conducted nearly 10 years ago could not find evidence of bulimia outside a Westernized culture (Keel & Klump, 2003). It will be interesting to see if this changes in the next 10 years.

Racial and Ethnic Differences

There is a somewhat greater incidence of eating disturbances and body dissatisfaction among white women than black women (Grabe & Hyde, 2006; Perez & Joiner, 2003), but differences in actual eating disorders, particularly bulimia, do not appear to be as great (Wildes, Emery, & Simons, 2001). In addition, the greatest differences between white and black women in eating disorder pathology appear to be most pronounced in college student samples; fewer differences are observed in either high school or nonclinical community samples (Wildes et al., 2001). A meta-analysis found more similarities than differences in body dissatisfaction among ethnic groups in the United States (Grabe & Hyde, 2006). White women and Hispanic women reported greater body dissatisfaction than African American women, but no other ethnic differences were reliably found.

Differences have been observed in the United States in some areas, however. Studies show that white teenage girls diet more frequently than do African American teenage girls and are more likely to be dissatisfied with their bodies (Fitzgibbons, Spring, et al., 1998; Striegel-Moore, Schreiber, et al., 2000). The relationship between BMI and body dissatisfaction also differs by ethnicity. Compared with African American adolescents, white adolescents become more dissatisfied with their bodies as their BMI rises (Striegel-Moore et al., 2000). As already noted, both dieting and body dissatisfaction are related to an increased risk for developing an eating disorder. One study found that white women with binge eating disorder were more dissatisfied with their bodies than African American women with binge eating disorder, and that white women were more likely to have a history of bulimia nervosa than African American women (Pike et al., 2001).

Peter Horree / Alamy Stock Photo

Standards of beauty vary across cultures, as shown by Gauguin's painting of Tahitian women.

Little is known about the prevalence of eating disorders among Latina or Native American women, and this remains a much-needed research focus. Data from one epidemiological study of Latina women age 18 or older found that binge eating disorder was more prevalent than bulimia nervosa but that the prevalence rates for both disorders were comparable to prevalence rates in white women (Alegria, Woo, et al., 2007). The diagnosis of bulimia was more likely for women who had lived in the United States for several years than for women who had recently immigrated, indicating that acculturation may play a role. In contrast to other eating disorders, anorexia nervosa was very rare among Latina women (only 2 out of over 2,500 women had a lifetime history of anorexia).

Beyond the racial or ethnic differences in eating disorders, stereotyped beliefs about race and eating disorders may play a role. For example, one study found that college students who read a fictional case study about a woman with eating disorder symptoms were more likely to ascribe an eating disorder to the woman if she was described as white rather than African American or Hispanic (Gordon, Perez, & Joiner, 2002). Although it remains to be seen whether mental health professionals would exhibit the same stereotypes when making clinical judgments, it suggests that symptoms may be more easily overlooked among nonwhite women.

Socioeconomic status is also important to consider (Caldwell, Brownell, & Wilfley, 1997; French, Story, et al., 1997). The emphasis on thinness and dieting is found among all levels of socioeconomic status, as is the prevalence of eating disorder pathology (e.g., Story et al., 1995; Striegel-Moore et al., 2000).

Other Factors Contributing to the Etiology of Eating Disorders

Personality Influences We have already seen that neurobiological changes are associated with eating disorders. It is also important to keep in mind that the eating disorder itself can affect the personality. A study of semistarvation in male conscientious objectors conducted in the late 1940s supports the idea that the personality of people with eating disorders, particularly those with anorexia, is affected by their weight loss (Keys, Brozek, et al., 1950). For a period of 6 weeks, the men were given two meals a day, totaling 1500 calories, to simulate the meals in a concentration camp. On average, the men lost 25 percent of their body weight. They all soon became preoccupied with food; they also reported increased fatigue, poor concentration, lack of sexual interest, irritability, moodiness, and insomnia. Four became depressed, and one developed bipolar disorder. This research shows vividly how severe restriction of food intake can have powerful effects on personality and behavior, which we need to consider when evaluating the personalities of people with anorexia and bulimia.

In part as a response to these findings, some researchers have collected retrospective reports of personality before the onset of an eating disorder. This research describes people with anorexia as having been perfectionistic, shy, and compliant before the onset of the disorder. The description of people with bulimia includes the additional characteristics of histrionic features, affective instability, and an outgoing social disposition (Vitousek & Manke, 1994). It is important to remember, however, that retrospective reports in which people with an eating disorder and their families recall what the person was like before diagnosis can be inaccurate and biased by awareness of the person's current symptoms.

Prospective studies examine personality characteristics before an eating disorder is present. In one study, more than 2000 students in a suburban Minneapolis school district completed several tests, including measures of personality characteristics and the Eating Disorders Inventory, for 3 consecutive years. During year 1 of the study, cross-sectional predictors of disordered eating included body dissatisfaction; poor interoceptive awareness, which is the extent to which people can distinguish different biological states of their bodies (see Table 11.3 for items that assess interoceptive awareness); and a propensity to experience negative emotions (Leon, Fulkerson, et al., 1995). At year 3, these same variables were found to have prospectively predicted disordered eating (Leon, Fulkerson, et al., 1999). A prospective study found that perfectionism predicted the onset of anorexia in young adult women (Tyrka, Waldron, et al., 2002). Perfectionism combined with body dissatisfaction also predicts drive for thinness and concern about weight (Boone, Soenens, & Luyten, 2014).

Additional research has taken a closer look at the link between perfectionism and anorexia. Perfectionism is multifaceted and may be self-oriented (setting high standards for oneself), other-oriented (setting high standards for others), or socially oriented (trying to conform to the high standards imposed by others). A review of many studies concludes that perfectionism, no matter how it is measured, is higher among girls with anorexia than among girls without anorexia and that perfectionism remains high even after successful treatment for anorexia (Bardone-Cone, Wonderlich, et al., 2007). A multinational study found that people with anorexia scored higher

Severe food restriction can have profound effects on behavior and personality, as illustrated by the study of male conscientious objectors in the 1940s.

Penny Tweedie/Getty Images

People with eating disorders consistently report that their family life was high in conflict.

on self- and other-oriented types of perfectionism than people without anorexia (Halmi, Sunday, et al., 2000). Nevertheless, the evidence that perfectionism prospectively predicts the onset of anorexia is limited, largely because there are so few prospective studies (Stice, 2016).

Characteristics of Families Studies of the characteristics of families of people with eating disorders have yielded variable results. Some of the variation stems, in part, from the different methods used to collect the data and from the sources of the information. For example, self-reports of people with eating disorders reveal high levels of conflict in the family (Holtom-Viesel & Allan, 2014; Quiles Marcos, Quiles Sebastián, et al., 2013). Reports of parents, however, do not necessarily indicate high levels of family problems. Indeed, parent and child reports do not always agree when it comes to describing family characteristics in eating disorders.

To better understand the role of family functioning, it is necessary to study these families directly by observational measures rather than by self-reports alone. Although an adolescent's perception of his or her family's characteristics is important, we also need to know how much of reported family discord is perceived and how much is consistent with others' perceptions. In one of the few observational studies conducted thus far, parents of children with eating disorders did not appear to be very different from parents of children with no eating disorders. The two groups did not differ in the frequency of positive and negative messages given to their children, and the parents of children with eating disorders were more self-disclosing. The parents of children with eating disorders did lack some communication skills, however, such as the ability to request clarification of vague statements (van den Broucke, Vandereycken, & Vertommen, 1995). Observational studies such as this, coupled with data on perceived family characteristics, would help determine whether actual or perceived family characteristics are related to eating disorders.

Quick Summary

Sociocultural factors, including society's preoccupation with thinness, may play a role in eating disorders. This preoccupation is linked to dieting efforts, and dieting precedes the development of eating disorders among many people. In addition, a preoccupation with thinness, as well as media portrayals of thin women, predicts an increase in body dissatisfaction, which also precedes the development of eating disorders. Stigma associated with being overweight also contributes. Women are more likely to have eating disorders than men, and the ways in which women's bodies are objectified may lead some women to see their bodies as others do (self-objectify), which in turn may increase body dissatisfaction and eating pathology. Anorexia appears to occur in many cultures, whereas bulimia appears to be more common in industrialized and Westernized societies. Eating disorders are slightly more common among white women than women of color, with the difference being most pronounced in college student samples. Eating disorders used to be more common among women of higher socioeconomic status, but this is less true today.

Research on personality characteristics finds that perfectionism may play a role. Other personality characteristics that predicted disordered eating across 3 years include body dissatisfaction, the extent to which people can distinguish different biological states of their bodies, and a propensity to experience negative emotions. Troubled family relationships are fairly common among people with eating disorders, but this could be a result of the eating disorder, not necessarily a cause of it.

Genetic factors appear to play a role in both anorexia and bulimia. Both disorders tend to run in families, and twin studies support the role of genetics in the disorders and their characteristics, such as body dissatisfaction, preoccupation with thinness, and binge eating. The hypothalamus does not appear to be directly involved in eating disorders, and low levels of endogenous opioids are seen concurrently with bulimia, but not before the onset of the disorder. Thus, changes in food intake could affect the opioid system instead of changes in the opioid system affecting food intake. Research findings on the role of serotonin in anorexia are mixed. Serotonin may play a role in bulimia and binge eating disorders, with studies finding a decrease in serotonin metabolites and smaller responses to serotonin agonists. Research linking dopamine to the brain's reward system can help account for how the bingeing that is part of bulimia and binge eating disorder influences the dopamine system. The neurobiological factors do not do a particularly good job of accounting for some key features of anorexia and bulimia, in particular the intense fear of gaining weight.

Cognitive behavioral theories focus on body dissatisfaction, preoccupation with thinness, negative emotion, and attention and memory. People are more likely to binge when under stress or experiencing negative emotions. People with eating disorders pay greater attention to food and body-image-related things, and they tend to remember these better as well, suggesting that their attention and memory may be biased toward food and body image.

Check Your Knowledge 11.2

True or false?

1. The brain structure linked to the cause of eating disorders is the hypothalamus.

2. Dopamine has been studied in all the eating disorders.

3. Prospective studies of personality and eating disorders indicate that the tendency to experience negative emotions is related to disordered eating.

4. Anorexia appears to be specific to Western culture; bulimia is seen all over the world and is thus not culture specific.

5. Cognitive behavioral views of bulimia suggest that women judge their self-worth by their weight and shape.

Treatment of Eating Disorders

Hospitalization is frequently required to treat people with anorexia so that their ingestion of food can be gradually increased and carefully monitored. This was necessary for Lynne. Weight loss can be so severe that intravenous feeding is necessary to save the person's life. The medical complications of anorexia, such as electrolyte imbalances, also require treatment. For both anorexia and bulimia, both medications and psychological treatments have been used.

Medications

Because bulimia nervosa is often comorbid with depression, it has been treated with various antidepressants. Findings from most studies, including double-blind randomized controlled trials with placebo controls, confirm the efficacy of a variety of antidepressants in reducing purging and binge eating, even among people who had not responded to prior psychological treatment (Walsh, Agras, et al., 2000; Wilson & Fairburn, 1998; Wilson & Pike, 2001).

On the negative side, many people with bulimia stop taking medications (Fairburn, Agras, & Wilson, 1992). In contrast, in one study fewer than 5 percent of women dropped out of CBT (Agras, Rossiter, et al., 1992). Moreover, most people relapse when various kinds of antidepressant medications are stopped (Wilson & Pike, 2001). There is some evidence that this tendency to relapse is reduced if antidepressants are given in the context of CBT (Agras, Rossiter, et al., 1994).

Medications have also been used to treat anorexia nervosa with little success in improving weight or other core features of anorexia (Aigner, Treasure, et al., 2011; Attia et al., 1998; Frank & Shott, 2016; Sebaaly, Cox, et al., 2013). Medication treatment for binge eating disorder has not been as well studied. Limited evidence suggests that antidepressant medications are not effective in reducing binges or weight loss (Grilo, 2007). Clinical trials of anti-obesity drugs, such as sibutramine and atomoxetine, show some promise in binge eating disorder, but additional clinical trials are needed. A randomized controlled trial compared the antidepressant medication fluoxetine (Prozac) with CBT plus placebo, or CBT plus fluoxetine and found that that CBT plus placebo was more effective in reducing binge episodes than either condition including fluoxetine, and this remained the case at a 12-month follow-up (Grilo, Crosby, et al., 2012).

Psychological Treatment of Anorexia Nervosa

Little in the way of controlled research exists on psychological treatments for anorexia nervosa, but we will present the most promising of the psychotherapeutic approaches to this life-threatening disorder.

Therapy for anorexia is generally believed to be a two-tiered process. The immediate goal is to help the person gain weight to avoid medical complications and the possibility of death. The person is often so weak and physiological functioning so disturbed that hospital treatment is medically imperative (in addition to being needed to ensure that the patient ingests some food). Operant conditioning behavior therapy programs (e.g., providing reinforcers for weight gain) have been somewhat successful in achieving weight gain in the short term (Hsu, 1990). However, the second goal of treatment—long-term maintenance of weight gain—remains a challenge for the field.

Beyond immediate weight gain, psychological treatment for anorexia can also involve CBT. One study that combined hospital treatment with CBT found that reductions in many anorexia symptoms persisted up to 1 year after treatment (Bowers & Ansher, 2008). Other studies have found that CBT is effective after hospitalization in reducing the risk for relapse (Pike, Walsh, et al., 2003). A recent randomized controlled clinical trial compared CBT with supportive psychotherapy plus education about anorexia and found that both were equally effective for women with anorexia nervosa in reducing eating disorder symptoms and depression (Touyz, Le Grange, et al., 2013). Although BMI increased at the end of treatment and remained stable at the 12-month follow-up, the average BMIs for women in both treatment groups were still in the mild severity range (see Table 11.2). Additional analyses examined who might benefit the most from CBT, and the results indicated that women who were older and had more severe symptoms benefited the most from CBT (Le Grange, Fitzsimmons-Craft, et al., 2014).

Another randomized controlled clinical trial in Germany compared CBT to psychodynamic therapy and to "optimized treatment as usual," which included a good deal of support and referrals to psychotherapists (Zipfel, Wild, et al., 2014). All three treatments were equally effective in increasing BMI, but the increase was modest: only about 0.7 points at the 10-month follow-up treatment and another 0.4 points at the 12-month follow-up.

Family therapy is another form of psychological treatment for anorexia and is based on the notion that interactions among members of the patient's family can play a role in treating the disorder (Le Grange & Lock, 2005). A family-based therapy (FBT) developed in England focuses on helping parents restore their daughter to a healthy weight while at the same time building up family functioning in the context of adolescent development (Lock, Le Grange, et al., 2001; Loeb, Walsh, et al., 2007). A randomized controlled clinical trial compared FBT with individual therapy and found that both treatments were equally effective at the end of the 24-session treatment. However, more girls receiving FBT were in full remission (49 percent) 1 year after treatment than girls receiving individual therapy (23 percent) (Lock, Le Grange, et al., 2011). Another study of FBT found that the girls who had gained weight by session 4 were more likely to be in full remission at the end of treatment (Doyle, Le Grange, et al., 2010). Thus, early weight gain may be an important predictor of a good outcome. Although the findings are promising, additional work needs to be done to improve the outcomes for anorexia.

Psychological Treatment of Bulimia Nervosa

CBT is the best-validated and most current standard for the treatment of bulimia (Fairburn, Cooper, et al., 2009; Fairburn, Marcus, & Wilson, 1993; Wilson, Grilo, & Vitousek, 2007). In CBT, people with bulimia are encouraged to question society's standards for physical attractiveness.

People with bulimia must also uncover and then change beliefs that encourage them to starve themselves to avoid becoming overweight. They must be helped to see that healthy body weight can be maintained without severe dieting and that unrealistic restriction of food intake can often trigger a binge. They are taught that all is not lost with just one bite of high-calorie food and that snacking need not trigger a binge, which will be followed by induced vomiting or taking laxatives, which in turn will lead to still lower self-esteem and depression. Altering this all-or-nothing thinking can help people begin to eat more moderately. They also learn assertiveness skills, which help them cope with unreasonable demands placed on them by others, as well as more satisfying ways of relating to people.

Family therapy is a main form of treatment for anorexia nervosa.

The overall goal of treatment in bulimia nervosa is to develop more healthy eating patterns. People with bulimia need to learn to eat three meals a day and even some snacks between meals without sliding back into bingeing and purging. Regular meals control hunger and thereby, it is hoped, the urge to eat enormous amounts of food, the effects of which are counteracted by purging. To help people with bulimia develop less extreme beliefs about themselves, the cognitive behavior therapist gently but firmly challenges such beliefs as, "No one will respect me if I am a few pounds heavier than I am now" or "Eric loves me only because I weigh 112 pounds and would surely reject me if I ballooned to 120 pounds." Unrealistic demands and other cognitive distortions—such as the belief that eating a small amount of high-calorie food·means that the person is an utter failure and doomed never to improve—are continually challenged. The therapist works collaboratively with the person to identify events, thoughts, and feelings that trigger an urge to binge and then to learn more adaptive ways to cope with these situations.

In the case of Jill, she and her therapist discovered that bingeing often took place after she was criticized by her coach. Therapy included the following:

- Encouraging Jill to assert herself if the criticism is unwarranted
- Desensitizing her to social evaluation and encouraging her to question society's standards for ideal weight and the pressures on women to be thin—not an easy task by any means
- Teaching her that it is not a catastrophe to make a mistake and it is not necessary to be perfect, even if the coach's criticism is valid

Findings from several studies indicate that CBT is effective (Hay, 2013; Shapiro, Berkman, et al., 2007), and it often results in less frequent bingeing and purging, with reductions ranging from 70 to more than 90 percent. For example, a recent randomized controlled clinical trial compared 5 months of CBT with 2 years of psychoanalytic therapy and found that those who received CBT had far fewer bingeing and purging episodes, both at the end of 5 months and at the end of 2 years (Poulsen, Lunn, et al., 2014). Other studies find that therapeutic gains are maintained at 1-year follow-up (Agras, Crow, et al., 2000), nearly 6 years later (Fairburn, Norman, et al., 1995), and 10 years later (Keel, Mitchell, et al., 2002). But there are limitations to these positive outcomes, as we will see.

CBT alone is more effective than any available medication (Compas, Haaga, et al., 1998; Walsh, Wilson, et al., 1997), and a meta-analysis showed that CBT yielded better results than antidepressant medications (Whittal, Agras, & Gould, 1999). But are outcomes better when antidepressant medication is added to CBT? Evidence on this front is mixed. Adding antidepressant drugs, however, may be useful in helping to alleviate the depression that often occurs with bulimia (Keel et al., 2002; Wilson & Fairburn, 1998).

If, however, we focus on the people themselves rather than on the numbers of binges and purges across people, we find that at least half of those treated with CBT improve very little (Wilson & Pike, 2001). Clearly, while CBT may be the most effective treatment available for bulimia, it still has room for improvement.

Actress Mary-Kate Olsen has been treated for an eating disorder.

Some studies have examined whether adding exposure and response prevention (ERP) to CBT for bulimia might boost the treatment effects of CBT (recall that ERP is an aspect of the cognitive behavioral treatment of obsessive-compulsive disorder in Chapter 7). This ERP component involves discouraging the person from purging after eating foods that usually elicit an urge to vomit. In one study, the combination of ERP and CBT was more effective than CBT without ERP, at least in the short term (e.g., Fairburn et al., 1995). ERP may not continue to be an advantage over the long term, however. One study examined outcome 3 years after treatment for people with bulimia who had received CBT either with or without ERP. It found similar outcomes for the two groups (Carter, McIntosh, et al., 2003). That is, 85 percent of people with bulimia did not meet the criteria for bulimia 3 years after treatment, regardless of which treatment they had received. A review of studies combining CBT and ERP found that adding ERP does not appear to add much beyond CBT alone (Hay, Bacaltchuk, et al., 2009).

Another form of CBT, called guided self-help CBT, has also shown promise for some people (Hay, 2013; Steele, Bergin, & Wade, 2011). In this type of treatment, people receive self-help (book or on the internet) on topics such as perfectionism, body image, negative thinking, and food and health. Participants meet for a small number of sessions with a therapist who helps guide them through the self-help material. This appears to be an effective treatment compared to a wait-list control group and to traditional CBT for bulimia (Wilson & Zandberg, 2012). It may be more effective for binge eating disorder than bulimia, though additional research is needed. In the United Kingdom, guided self-help CBT is recommended as the first-line treatment for bulimia and binge eating disorder followed by individual CBT (National Collaborating Centre for Mental Health, 2017).

Interpersonal therapy (IPT) has also been used for bulimia, though it did not produce results as quickly as CBT (Fairburn, Jones, et al., 1991; Fairburn, Jones, et al., 1993). The two modes of intervention were equivalent at 1-year follow-up in effecting change in bingeing, purging, and maladaptive attitudes about body shape and weight (Wilson, 1995). This pattern—CBT superior to IPT immediately after treatment but IPT catching up at follow-up—was replicated in a later study (Agras et al., 2000). A small meta-analysis found that CBT had a slight advantage over IPT but long-term follow-ups were not included in most of the studies included in the meta-analysis (Cuijpers, Donker, et al., 2016).

Family therapy may also be effective for bulimia, though it has been studied less frequently than either CBT or IPT. A randomized clinical trial demonstrated that family-based therapy was superior to supportive psychotherapy for adolescents with bulimia with respect to decreasing bingeing and purging up to 6 months after treatment was completed (Le Grange, Crosby, et al., 2007).

Psychological Treatment of Binge Eating Disorder

Although not as extensively studied as with bulimia nervosa, CBT has been shown to be effective for binge eating disorder in several studies (Brownley, Berkman, et al., 2007; Grilo, 2007). CBT for binge eating disorder targets binges as well as emphasizing self-monitoring, self-control, and problem solving related to eating. Gains from CBT appear to last up to 1 year after treatment. CBT also appears to be more effective than treatment with fluoxetine (Grilo, 2007). Randomized controlled clinical trials have shown that IPT is as effective as CBT and guided self-help CBT for binge eating disorder (Wilfley, Welch, et al., 2002; Wilson, Wilfley, et al., 2010). These three treatments are more effective than behavioral weight-loss programs, which are often used to treat obesity. More specifically, CBT and IPT reduce binge eating (but not necessarily weight), whereas behavioral weight-loss programs may promote weight loss but do not curb binge eating.

One study compared three treatments for binge eating disorder: (1) therapist-led group CBT, (2) therapist-assisted group CBT, and (3) structured self-help group CBT with no therapist.

Peter Kramer/Getty Images News and Sport Services

Results showed that people in the therapist-led group CBT had the greatest reduction in binge eating at 6-month and 12-month follow-ups but that all groups had a greater reduction in binges than a group of people assigned to a wait-list control group (Peterson, Mitchell, et al., 2009). Fewer people dropped out of the therapist-led group as well. Thus, having a therapist lead a CBT group may help keep people in treatment and help reduce binges, but, importantly, people in the therapist-assisted and "therapist-free" groups also showed reductions in binges. Given that therapist cost and/or availability may limit treatment for some people, having options such as these available is promising.

Preventive Interventions for Eating Disorders

A different approach to treating eating disorders involves prevention. Intervening with children or adolescents before the onset of eating disorders may help to prevent these disorders from ever developing. Broadly speaking, three different types of preventive interventions have been developed and implemented:

1. *Psychoeducational approaches.* The focus is on educating children and adolescents about eating disorders to prevent them from developing the symptoms.

2. *Deemphasizing sociocultural influences.* The focus here is on helping children and adolescents resist or reject sociocultural pressures to be thin.

3. *Risk factor approach.* The focus here is on identifying people with known risk factors for developing eating disorders (e.g., weight and body-image concern, restricting food) and intervening to alter these factors.

Stice, Shaw, and Marti (2007) conducted a meta-analysis of all such prevention studies conducted between 1980 and 2006, and they found modest support for some of these prevention approaches. The most effective prevention programs are those that are interactive rather than didactic, include adolescents age 15 or older, include girls only, and involve multiple sessions rather than just one session. Some effects appear to last as long as 2 years.

One randomized trial found that two types of preventive interventions show promise for reducing eating disorder symptoms among adolescent girls (average age of 17). One program, called the Body Project, includes a dissonance reduction intervention, focused on deemphasizing sociocultural influences; the other, called Healthy Weight, targeted risk factors (Stice, Marti, et al., 2008). Both programs included just one 3-hour session. Specifically, girls in the Body Project intervention talked, wrote, and role-played with one another to challenge society's notions of beauty (i.e., the thin-ideal). Girls in the Healthy Weight intervention worked together on developing healthy weight and exercise programs for themselves. Participation in either program was associated with less negative affect, less body dissatisfaction, lower thin-ideal internalization, and lower risk of developing eating disorder symptoms 2 to 3 years after the session compared with girls who did not participate in a session. These interventions have been successfully implemented with other high school samples and college women in a sorority, with evidence suggesting that the Body Project may be more effective than Healthy Weight (Stice, Becker, & Yokum, 2013). An

Tony Freeman/PhotoEdit

Interactive prevention programs have been effective for girls with eating disorders.

online version of the Body Project (eBodyProject) also shows promise (Stice, Durant, et al., 2014; Stice, Rohde, et al., 2013). Furthermore, the Body Project is more effective than a video intervention whether it is delivered by mental health professionals, peers, or online (Stice, Rohde, et al., 2017).

Check Your Knowledge 11.3

Fill in the blanks.

1. Research suggests that _____ therapy is an effective treatment for bulimia, both in the short and long term.

2. For anorexia, _____ may be required to get the patient to gain weight. There are not many _____ that have been shown to be effective. The most common type of therapy used to treat anorexia is _____.

3. Research on prevention programs has shown that two programs show promise up to 3 years after the intervention: _____ and _____.

Summary

Clinical Descriptions

- The three DSM-5 eating disorders are anorexia nervosa, bulimia nervosa and binge eating disorder. The symptoms of anorexia nervosa include restriction of food that leads to very low body weight, an intense fear of weight gain, and a distorted sense of body shape. Anorexia typically begins in adolescence, is at least three times more frequent in women than in men, and is comorbid with several other disorders. Many people recover, but it can take years. It can also be life threatening.

- The symptoms of bulimia nervosa include episodes of binge eating followed by purging, and a distorted body image. Like anorexia, bulimia begins in adolescence; is much more frequent in women than in men; and is comorbid with other diagnoses, such as depression. Prognosis for this disorder is somewhat more favorable than for anorexia.

- The symptoms of binge eating disorder include episodes of bingeing and a feeling of losing control over eating but no compensatory purging. People with binge eating disorder are often obese, but not all obese people have binge eating disorder.

Etiology

- Evidence is consistent with possible genetic contributions. Endogenous opioids and serotonin, both of which play a role in mediating hunger and satiety, have been examined in eating disorders. Low levels of both have been found in people with eating disorders, but evidence that these cause eating disorders is limited. Dopamine is also involved with the rewarding aspects of eating, but the dopamine system may be altered because of eating disturbances and not cause them.

- Cognitive behavioral theories of eating disorders propose that fear of weight gain and body-image distortion make weight loss a powerful reinforcer. Among people with bulimia nervosa, negative affect and stress precipitate binges that create anxiety, which is then relieved by purging.

- As sociocultural standards changed to favor a thinner shape as the ideal for women, the frequency of eating disorders increased. The objectification of women's bodies also exerts pressure on women to see themselves through this sociocultural lens. The prevalence of eating disorders is higher in countries where the cultural pressure to be thin is strongest. White women tend to have more body dissatisfaction and general eating disturbances than African American women, though the prevalence rates for actual eating disorders are not markedly different between these two ethnic groups.

- Studies of personality have found that people with eating disorders are high in negative emotion and perfectionism and low in interoceptive awareness and positive emotion differentiation. Research on the characteristics of families has yielded different data depending on how the data were collected. Reports of people with eating disorders show high levels of conflict, but observations of the families do not find them especially troubled.

Treatment

- The main neurobiological treatment for eating disorders is the use of antidepressant medications. Although they are somewhat effective for bulimia, they are not effective for anorexia or binge eating disorder. Dropout rates from drug-treatment programs are high and relapse is common when people stop taking the medication. Treatment of anorexia often requires hospitalization to reduce the medical complications of the disorder. Cognitive behavioral treatment (CBT) has been shown to be somewhat effective for anorexia, and family-based treatments show promise but need further study.

- Cognitive behavioral treatment for bulimia focuses on questioning beliefs about physical attractiveness and food restriction, and on developing healthy eating patterns. Outcomes are good, both in the short and long term. Cognitive behavioral treatment for binge eating disorder focuses on reducing binges, and it also appears to be effective as does a guided self-help version of CBT.

- Prevention programs are effective, particularly those programs that include girls age 15 or older, involve more than one session, and are interactive rather than didactic (i.e., participatory rather than a lecture format).

Answers to Check Your Knowledge Questions

11.1 1. c; 2. b; 3. d; 4. Limited availability of healthy food; minimal awareness of portion size; abundance of food/cheap price; genetics; marketing/advertising

11.2 1. F; 2. T; 3, T; 4. F; 5. T

11.3 1. cognitive behavior; 2. hospitalization, medications, family therapy; 3. Body Project, Healthy Weight

Key Terms

anorexia nervosa
binge eating disorder

body mass index (BMI)
bulimia nervosa

obese

CHAPTER 12

Sexual Disorders

LEARNING GOALS

1. Describe the influence of culture and gender on sexual norms, and the sexual response cycle for men and women.

2. Explain the symptoms of the DSM-5 sexual dysfunction disorders, and discuss the prevalence of brief periods of sexual dysfunction.

3. Discuss the biological and psychosocial risk factors of sexual dysfunctions.

4. Describe psychological and medication treatments for sexual dysfunctions.

5. Discuss the symptoms of the DSM-5 paraphilic disorders.

6. Explain the risk factors for paraphilic disorders and limits in the knowledge concerning these risk factors.

7. Discuss common psychological and medication treatments for paraphilic disorders, the state of current evidence about treatment efficacy, and debates about community prevention programs.

Clinical Case

Anne

Anne was a 26-year-old, attractive woman who sought treatment after beginning her first "steady" sexual relationship. She reported that she and her partner, Colin, enjoyed their sexual life together. Nonetheless, Colin had begun to express concerns because she had been unable to achieve an orgasm. She sought therapy independently to talk about this concern. In therapy, she described that she had not really enjoyed sexual activities with her former partners and that she had rarely masturbated. Anne disclosed to the therapist that her brother had raped her when she was 12 years old, an event that she had not been able to disclose to anyone in the past. The therapist provided directed masturbation exercises (described as we review treatments) for Anne to begin to explore and enjoy her body independently, and in sessions they discussed her abuse history and her feelings about sexuality. With the use of a vibrator, Anne began to enjoy orgasms. As her comfort with her body and sexuality increased, Anne also learned to discuss her sexual preferences more openly with Colin.

Adapted from Graham, 2014.

Sexuality is one of the most personal areas of life. Each of us is a sexual being with preferences and fantasies that may surprise or even shock us from time to time. Usually, these are part of normal sexual functioning. But when our fantasies or desires begin to affect us or others in unwanted or harmful ways, they begin to qualify as abnormal.

For perspective, we begin by briefly describing norms and healthy sexual behavior. Then we consider two forms of sexual problems: sexual dysfunctions and paraphilic disorders. In the DSM, these are covered in separate chapters because they cover such distinct aspects of problems with sexuality. Sexual dysfunctions are defined as persistent disruptions in the ability to experience sexual arousal, desire, or orgasm, or as pain associated with intercourse. Paraphilic disorders are defined as persistent and troubling attractions to unusual sexual activities or objects.

Sexual Norms and Behavior

Definitions of what is normal or desirable in human sexual behavior vary with time and place. In contemporary Western worldviews, *inhibition* of sexual expression is seen as a problem. Contrast this with nineteenth- and early-twentieth-century views that *excess* was the culprit; in particular, excessive masturbation in childhood was widely believed to lead to sexual problems in adulthood. Von Krafft-Ebing (1902) postulated that early masturbation damaged the sexual organs and exhausted a finite reservoir of sexual energy, resulting in diminished ability to function sexually in adulthood. Even in adulthood, excessive sexual activity was thought to underlie problems such as erectile failure. The general Victorian view was that sexual appetite was dangerous and therefore had to be restrained. For example, to discourage children from handling their genitals, metal mittens were promoted; to distract adults from too much sex, outdoor exercise and a bland diet were recommended. In fact, Kellogg's Corn Flakes and graham crackers were developed as foods that would lessen sexual interest. They didn't.

More recent historical changes have influenced people's attitudes and experiences of sexuality. The availability of the birth control pill led to major shifts in attitudes toward premarital sex and contributed to the sexual revolution of the 1970s. The AIDS epidemic in the 1980s changed the perceived risks associated with sexual behavior. The number of people accessing sexual content on the Internet increased dramatically in the 1990s.

Aside from changes over time and across generations, culture influences attitudes and beliefs about sexuality. In some cultures, sexuality is viewed as an important part of well-being and pleasure, whereas in others, sexuality is seen as relevant only for procreation (Bhugra, Popelyuk, & McMullen, 2010). The level of acceptance of homosexual behavior differs by culture and time period. For example, among Sambians living in Papua New Guinea, Herdt wrote in 1984 about rituals in which pubescent males engage in oral sex with older men as a way of learning about their sexuality. In other cultures, it is common to stigmatize same-gender sexual behavior. In the United States, the DSM contained a diagnosis for homosexuality as recently as 1973.

What are the norms in our culture today? Conducting research on this question is difficult. To begin, samples must be representative of the population in terms of age, gender, ethnicity, socioeconomic status, and other key characteristics. Attaining such samples is difficult because many people decline to take part in surveys about sexuality. Nonetheless, we will discuss various representative surveys involving thousands of participants throughout this chapter.

Gathering a good sample is only one part of gaining a valid sense of sexual norms. How can one be certain that participants are honest in their responses, particularly when asking about stigmatized aspects of sexuality? When viewing data, we have to consider response biases that may differ by gender, age group, cohort, and culture. Let's consider **Table 12.1**, which shows responses from one of these large representative surveys (Herbenick, Reece, et al., 2010b). In this study, researchers gathered data over the Internet, reasoning that participants might feel most comfortable with this format. As shown in Table 12.1, elderly individuals were less likely to endorse engagement in several different sexual behaviors during their lifetime than were younger adults; is this because they genuinely had less sexual behavior, or does it reflect a discomfort of the elderly in describing these behaviors, particularly over the Internet?

Frederic Lewis/Getty Images

Norms about sexuality have fluctuated a great deal over time. In the early twentieth century, corn flakes were promoted as part of a bland diet designed to reduce sexual desire.

TABLE 12.1 Percent of People Who Self-Report Lifetime Participation in Selected Sexual Behaviors by Gender and Age Group

Age	Masturbated alone	Received oral from female	Received oral from male	Gave oral to female	Gave oral to male	Vaginal intercourse	Inserted penis into anus	Received penis in anus
Males (N = 2857)								
16–17	79	34	3	20	3	30	6	1
18–19	86	59	9	61	10	62	10	4
20–24	92	74	9	71	9	70	24	11
25–29	94	91	8	86	6	89	45	5
30–39	93	90	9	88	7	93	44	6
40–49	92	86	14	84	13	89	43	8
50–59	89	83	15	77	13	86	40	10
60–69	90	75	9	72	6	87	27	4
70+	80	58	8	62	5	88	14	5
Females (N = 2813)								
16–17	52	7	26	9	29	32		7
18–19	66	8	62	8	61	64		20
20–24	77	17	80	14	78	86		40
25–29	85	11	88	10	89	91		46
30–39	80	16	82	14	80	89		40
40–49	78	10	86	12	83	94		41
50–59	77	8	83	7	80	94		35
60–69	72	4	79	3	73	92		30
70+	58	2	47	2	43	89		21

(From Herbenick et al., 2010b.)

Returning to norms about homosexuality, Table 12.1 shows that many people have engaged in behavior involving same-sex partners. Fewer individuals describe themselves as sexual minorities, although rates appear to be increasing recently. **Figure 12.1** shows results of a U.S. telephone survey of more than 1.5 million people in which 4.1 percent of the

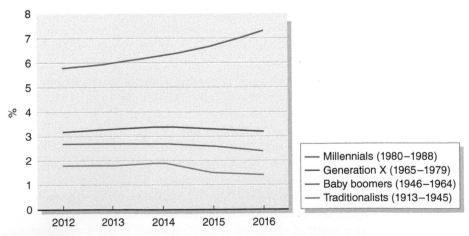

FIGURE 12.1 Percentage of U.S. Adults Identifying as Lesbian, Gay, Bisexual, or Transgender by Birth Cohort

(From Gates, 2017.)

respondents identified as lesbian, gay, bisexual, or transgender, with higher rates among millennials (those born from 1980 to 1998; Gates, 2017).

Clearly, we must keep varying cultural norms and response biases in mind as we study human sexual behavior. See **Focus on Discovery 12.1** for discussion of one of the most debated diagnoses in the DSM—gender dysphoria, a diagnosis that some argue reflects outdated cultural views.

Focus on Discovery 12.1

Debates About Gender Dysphoria

Gender identity refers to a person's inherent sense of being male or female, which is distinct from sexual orientation. Transgender people feel deep within themselves, usually from early childhood, that they are of the opposite sex. They are not persuaded by the presence of their genitals, nor by others' perceptions of their gender. A man can look at himself in a mirror, see the body of a biological man, and yet experience that body as belonging to a woman. Many children go through more temporary periods of cross-gender play, but only a small proportion of those develop and sustain the sense that their birth sex is not their true sex (Zucker, 2005). In a 2014 representative survey of more than 150,000 people in the United States, about one out of every 200 adults endorsed being transgender, with higher prevalence among younger age groups (Crissman, Berger, et al., 2017). Beyond the growing recognition of how many people are transgender, there has been increasing recognition that gender identity is not binary—some people do not feel that they fit entirely with the sense of being male or female.

Some people who desire to change their gender identity pursue hormonal treatments to change secondary sexual characteristics, and sex-reassignment surgery to alter the genitalia to be similar to those of the opposite sex. Surveys of hundreds of people 1 year after they have undergone such surgery indicate that about 90 percent of people are satisfied and do not regret the surgery (Gijs & Brewaeys, 2007). Sex-reassignment surgery is related to improvements in mental health, life satisfaction, social and partner relationships, and sexual satisfaction compared with pre-surgery levels (Monstrey, Vercruysse, et al., 2009).

The DSM-5 includes a diagnosis of gender dysphoria for people who experience a strong and persistent identification with the opposite sex. The DSM-5 diagnostic criteria for gender dysphoria specify that the desire to be a member of the opposite sex causes marked distress or functional impairment. Gender dysphoria is one of the most debated categories in the DSM (Vance, Cohen-Kettenis, et al., 2010). Clearly, there are many transgender people with the intense belief that they are a member of the opposite sex. But should this be labeled as a disorder? There are several reasons to think it should not be.

- Cross-gender behavior is universal. In countless species, biologically male animals will adopt behavior, courtship rituals, and

mating strategies that parallel those seen in female animals (Roughgarden, 2004). In humans, most children engage in some form of play that violates gender roles. It does not make sense to conceptualize such universal behavior as a disorder.

- The existence of this diagnosis implicitly contradicts the need for treatments to change the person's body to suit their gender identity. The psychological diagnosis of the desire to change one's gender is philosophically incongruent with the positive outcomes of sex-reassignment surgery.

- Rather than promoting mental health, diagnosing gender nonconformity might foster more stigma and social ostracism. Rates of victimization, including physical attacks and denial of employment attributed to transgender status, are far too common (Barboza, Dominguez, et al., 2016).

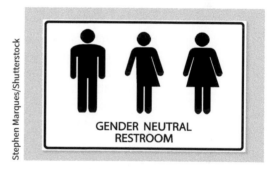

Debates about how to protect transgender youth reached the national level of politics after March 2016, when North Carolina passed a law requiring individuals to use the bathroom designated for the gender on their birth certificate. The White House, the Department of Justice, the NBA, the NCAA, and the chief executives of Apple, Google, Hilton, and Starbucks spoke out against the North Carolina law (Berman & Philips, 2017).

Although many oppose the diagnosis of gender dysphoria, others argue that for the time being, this diagnosis is warranted, because a diagnosis is a step in gaining insurance coverage for psychotherapy as well as gender reassignment medical procedures.

Gender and Sexuality

Throughout this chapter, we will see that gender shapes sexual disorders in a number of ways. Women are much more likely to report symptoms of sexual dysfunction than are men, but men are much more likely to meet diagnostic criteria for paraphilic disorder. We need research on gender differences in sexuality to understand why there are such major gender differences in sexual diagnoses. Few topics, though, raise as much debate as gender differences

As portrayed in the movie *Kinsey*, Alfred Kinsey (shown here) shocked people when he began to interview people to understand more about norms in sexual behavior.

in sexuality. Are reported gender differences based on cultural prohibitions regarding women's sexuality? Do they reflect gender differences in willingness to disclose sexual behavior? Are they based on biological differences? Are they tied to women's role in child-bearing?

On many dimensions, men and women may be more similar than stereotypes suggest. Take, for example, the commonly held idea that women, more than men, are motivated to have sex to promote relationship closeness. In a survey of more than 1000 women, many reported that their primary motivation for having sex was sexual attraction and physical gratification (Meston & Buss, 2009). It would be an exaggeration to claim that the sole reason women are having sex is to promote relationship closeness.

In one approach to studying gender differences, researchers compiled the findings on sexual behavior and attitudes from 834 surveys conducted in 87 different countries. Many gender differences in sexuality have decreased over time, and are less apparent in cultures with more empowered attitudes toward women (Petersen & Hyde, 2010). Nonetheless, in recent surveys across a broad range of countries, men continue to endorse engaging in more masturbation and using more pornography than women (Petersen & Hyde, 2010). Even with these two variables, there was a lot of overlap between the genders—about 67 percent of men and women were in the same range.

Is this gender difference in use of masturbation and pornography genuine, or could it reflect disclosure patterns? To examine this, researchers randomly assigned men and women to complete questionnaires about sexuality in one of three conditions: one in which the experimenter could view their responses, one in which the questionnaire was anonymous, and one (a sham) in which researchers applied physiological sensors and said they were administering a lie detector test (Alexander & Fisher, 2003). In the conditions without the lie detector, women reported less masturbation and use of pornography than men did, just as has been found in the large surveys. In the (sham) lie detector condition, men and women's level of reported masturbation and pornography did not differ. That is, some reported gender differences in sexual behavior could reflect respondents' attempts to match cultural expectations. Consider the potential for reporting biases to shape survey responses as we discuss sexual problems throughout this chapter.

The Sexual Response Cycle

Many researchers have focused on understanding the **sexual response cycle**. The Kinsey group made breakthroughs in the 1940s by interviewing people about their sexuality (Kinsey, Pomeroy, & Martin, 1948). Masters and Johnson created another revolution in research on human sexuality 50 years ago when they began to gather direct observations and physiological measurements of people masturbating and having sexual intercourse. Most contemporary conceptualizations of the sexual response cycle draw from proposals by Masters and Johnson (1966), which Kaplan developed further in 1974.

1. **Desire phase.** This phase, introduced by Kaplan (1974), refers to sexual interest or desire, often associated with sexually arousing fantasies or thoughts.

2. **Excitement phase.** During this phase, men and women experience increased blood flow to the genitalia (see **Figure 12.2** for the sexual anatomy of men and women). In men, this flow of blood into tissues produces an erection of the penis. In women, blood flow creates enlargement of the breasts and changes in the vagina, such as increased lubrication.

3. **Orgasm phase.** In this phase, sexual pleasure peaks in ways that have fascinated poets and the rest of us ordinary people for thousands of years. In men, ejaculation feels inevitable and indeed almost always occurs (in rare instances, men have an orgasm without ejaculating, and vice versa). In women, the outer walls of the vagina contract. In both sexes, there is general muscle tension.

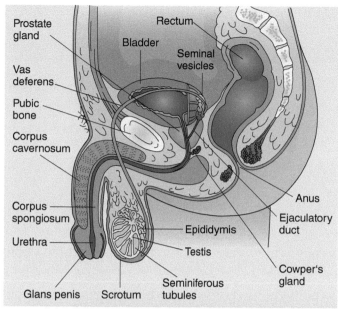

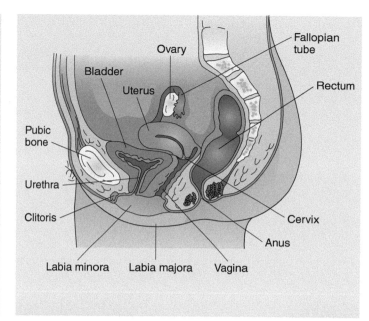

© John Wiley & Sons, Inc.

FIGURE 12.2 The male and female sexual anatomy.

4. **Resolution phase.** This last phase refers to the relaxation and sense of well-being that usually follow an orgasm. In men there is an associated refractory period during which further erection is not possible. The duration of the refractory period varies across men and even in the same man across occasions. Women are often able to respond again with sexual excitement almost immediately, a capability that permits multiple orgasms.

Data calls into question the validity of distinguishing the desire and excitement phases for women. Although the Kaplan model suggests that desire would precede excitement, many women report that their desire and excitement co-occur and are not distinct (Graham, 2010), and about a third of women report that their desire follows (rather than precedes) physiological arousal (Carvalheira, Brotto, & Leal, 2010).

Researchers also question the way in which Kaplan defined the excitement phase by relying on biological changes. Subjective excitement may not mirror biological excitement for women. Some of the research on this topic has used a device called a **vaginal plethysmograph** to measure women's physiological arousal (see **Figure 12.3**). When blood flow is measured by the vaginal plethysmograph, most women experience a rapid, automatic response to erotic stimuli. But the amount of blood flow to the vagina has little correlation with women's subjective level of desire or excitement (Basson, Brotto, et al., 2005). Indeed, many women report little or no subjective excitement when those biological changes happen (Chivers, Seto, et al., 2010). Biological and subjective excitement need to be considered separately for women, even though they are highly correlated for men.

Quick Summary

Sexuality is profoundly shaped by culture and experience. Attitudes about premarital sex, homosexuality, and gender roles in sexuality vary substantively across time and culture, and the attitudes prevalent for a given culture at a given time shape disclosure levels in survey research.

Kaplan described four phases of the sexual response cycle: desire, excitement, orgasm, and resolution. Over time, researchers have learned that the Kaplan phases do not fit the data for women in two ways: The desire and excitement phase may not be distinct stages, and the Kaplan definition of the excitement phase may be overly biological.

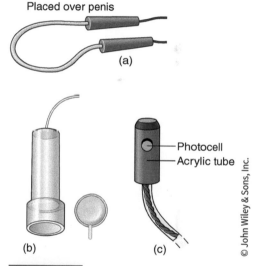

© John Wiley & Sons, Inc.

FIGURE 12.3 Behavioral researchers use genital devices for measuring biological sexual arousal. These devices are sensitive indicators of blood flow into the genitalia, a key physiological process in sexual arousal. For men, the penile plethysmograph measures changes in the size of the penis. (a) In one version of the penile plethysmograph, a very thin rubber tube is used. As the penis enlarges with blood, the tube stretches, changing its electrical resistance. (b) Less commonly, a rubber sheath is inserted over the penis, and then a chamber is placed over the penis. As the penis enlarges, the volume of air displaced is measured, providing a more accurate measure of change. (c) For women, biological sexual arousal can be measured by a vaginal plethysmograph. This tampon-shaped apparatus can be inserted into the vagina to measure increases in blood flow. Biological arousal may not be associated with subjective arousal or desire for women.

Answer the questions.

1. Describe the gender differences most currently observed in current survey research on sexuality.

2. List Kaplan's four phases of the sexual response cycle.

3. Describe the major challenges to the validity of the Kaplan sexual response cycle phases as applied to women.

Clinical Descriptions of Sexual Dysfunctions

At its best, sexuality provides a forum for closeness, connection, and shared pleasure. For better or for worse, our sexuality shapes at least part of our self-concept. Do we please the people we love, or, more simply, are we able to enjoy fulfilment from a pleasurable sexual experience?

We turn now to sexual problems that interfere with sexual enjoyment for many people at some time during their life. We begin by describing the different types of sexual dysfunctions described in the DSM-5. Then we discuss etiology and treatments for these problems.

The DSM-5 divides **sexual dysfunctions** into three categories: those involving sexual desire, arousal, and interest; orgasmic disorders; and a disorder involving sexual pain (see **Table 12.2**). Separate diagnoses are provided for men and women. The diagnostic criteria for all sexual dysfunctions specify that dysfunction should be persistent and recurrent and should cause clinically significant distress for the affected person. A diagnosis of sexual dysfunction is not appropriate if the problem is due entirely to a medical illness (such as advanced diabetes, which can cause erectile problems in men) or to another psychological disorder (such as major depression).

One might not expect people to be willing to report problems as personal as sexual dysfunction in community surveys. But many people do report these symptoms—the prevalence of occasional symptoms of sexual dysfunctions is quite high. **Table 12.3** presents data from a community survey of more than 20,000 men and women who were asked whether they had experienced various symptoms of sexual dysfunction for at least 2 of the past 12 months (Laumann, Nicolosi, et al., 2005). More women (43 percent) than men (31 percent) reported symptoms of sexual dysfunction (Laumann, Paik, & Rosen, 1999). Other studies have reported a very similar percentage of women who reported symptoms of sexual dysfunction (Peixoto & Nobre, 2015; Shifren, Monz, et al., 2008). Although these surveys indicate that many people have experienced these symptoms, clinical diagnoses are not made unless the symptoms cause distress or impairment. When asked whether they are distressed by these symptoms, less than 20 percent of women report experiencing both sexual symptoms and distress over the symptoms. Not only do most individuals cope well with temporary symptoms, most people who endorse periods of sexual dysfunction describe their partnerships as satisfying despite those symptoms (Rosen, Heiman, et al., 2016).

Time & Life Pictures/Getty Images, Inc.

The pioneering work of the sex therapists William H. Masters and Virginia Johnson helped launch a candid and scientific appraisal of human sexuality.

TABLE 12.2   **Diagnoses of Sexual Dysfunction in the DSM-5**

Category of Dysfunction	Diagnoses in Women	Diagnoses in Men
Sexual interest, desire, and arousal	Female sexual interest/arousal disorder	Male hypoactive sexual desire disorder
		Erectile disorder
Orgasmic disorder	Female orgasmic disorder	Premature ejaculation
		Delayed ejaculation
Sexual pain	Genito-pelvic pain/ penetration disorder	

TABLE 12.3	Self-Reported Rates of Experiencing Symptoms of Sexual Dysfunction for 2 of the Past 12 Months by Region Among 20,000 Sexually Active Adults Ages 40 to 80						
	Lacked Interest in Sex	Inability to Reach Orgasm	Orgasm Reached Too Quickly	Pain During Sex	Sex Not Pleasurable	Trouble Lubricating	Trouble Maintaining or Achieving an Erection
Women							
Northern Europe	25.6	17.7	7.7	9.0	17.1	18.4	NA
Southern Europe	29.6	24.2	11.5	11.9	22.1	16.1	NA
Non-European West	32.9	25.2	10.5	14.0	21.5	27.1	NA
Central/South America	28.1	22.4	18.3	16.6	19.5	22.5	NA
Middle East	43.4	23.0	10.0	21.0	31.0	23.0	NA
East Asia	34.8	32.3	17.6	31.6	29.7	37.9	NA
Southeast Asia	43.3	41.2	26.3	29.2	35.9	34.2	NA
Men							
Northern Europe	12.5	9.1	20.7	2.9	7.7	NA	13.3
Southern Europe	13.0	12.2	21.5	4.4	9.1	NA	12.9
Non-European West	17.6	14.5	27.4	3.6	12.1	NA	20.6
Central/South America	12.6	13.6	28.3	4.7	9.0	NA	13.7
Middle East	21.6	13.2	12.4	10.2	14.3	NA	14.1
East Asia	19.6	17.2	29.1	5.8	12.2	NA	27.1
Southeast Asia	28.0	21.1	30.5	12.0	17.4	NA	28.1

Note: Non-European West includes Australia, Canada, New Zealand, South Africa, and the United States.

Source: After Laumann et al., 2005.

DSM-5 criteria for sexual dysfunction disorders specify that symptoms must last at least 6 months, and no large-scale surveys assess how common it is for symptoms to last this long. It is common for people to have sexual symptoms for a month, but for most people, these symptoms will remit naturally over time (Mercer, Fenton, et al., 2003).

DSM-5 criteria for sexual dysfunctions are also clear regarding relationship distress. Sexual concerns that arise as a consequence of severe relationship distress, such as partner abuse, should not be diagnosed as sexual dysfunctions. For women in particular, sexuality has strong links with relationship satisfaction (Tiefer, Hall, & Tavris, 2002).

Although the diagnostic system for sexual dysfunction reflects the stages in the sexual cycle, the problems often don't break out so cleanly in real life. Many people with problems in one phase of a sexual cycle will report problems in another phase. Some of this may just be a vicious circle. For example, men who develop premature ejaculation may begin to worry about sex and then experience problems with sexual desire or sexual arousal (Wincze & Weisberg, 2015). Beyond the consequences for the individual, sexual problems in one person may lead to sexual problems in the partner (Kaya, Gunes, et al., 2015). Be aware of this potential for co-occurrence of diagnoses as we review the specific sexual dysfunction disorders defined in the DSM-5.

Disorders Involving Sexual Interest, Desire, and Arousal

The DSM-5 includes three disorders relevant to a lack of sexual interest, desire, or arousal. **Female sexual interest/arousal disorder** refers to persistent deficits in sexual interest (sexual fantasies or urges), biological arousal, or subjective arousal. For men, the DSM-5 diagnoses consider sexual interest and arousal separately. **Male hypoactive sexual desire disorder** refers to deficient or absent sexual fantasies and urges, and **erectile disorder** refers to failure to attain or maintain an erection through completion of the sexual activity. The Clinical Case of Robert provides an illustration of hypoactive sexual desire disorder.

DSM-5 Criteria for Female Sexual Interest/Arousal Disorder

Diminished, absent, or reduced frequency of at least three of the following:

- Interest in sexual activity
- Erotic thoughts or fantasies
- Initiation of sexual activity and responsiveness to partner's attempts to initiate

- Sexual excitement/pleasure during 75 percent of sexual encounters
- Sexual interest/arousal elicited by any internal or external erotic cues
- Genital or nongenital sensations during 75 percent of sexual encounters

DSM-5 Criteria for Male Hypoactive Sexual Desire Disorder

- Sexual fantasies and desires, as judged by the clinician, are deficient or absent

DSM-5 Criteria for Erectile Disorder

On at least 75 percent of sexual occasions:

- Inability to attain an erection, or
- Inability to maintain an erection for completion of sexual activity, or

- Marked decrease in erectile rigidity interferes with penetration or pleasure

Among people seeking treatment for sexual dysfunctions, more than half complain of low desire. As Table 12.3 shows, women are more likely than men to report at least occasional concerns about their level of sexual desire. Postmenopausal women are more likely than women in their 20s to report low sexual desire and low levels of arousal, but they are less likely to be distressed by these symptoms (Hendrickx, Gijs, & Enzlin, 2015). DSM-5 criteria for sexual interest/arousal disorder in women include biologically or subjectively low arousal or desire. Women tend to be more concerned by a lack of subjective desire than by a lack of biological arousal (Basson, Althof, et al., 2004). Most commonly, women with this disorder report that previously exciting stimuli, such as their partner's touch or a sensual dance, no longer trigger desire (Brotto & Luria, 2014). When studies are conducted using a vaginal plethysmograph, women who experience a subjective lack of desire often have normative levels of biological response to erotic stimuli (Graham, 2010). This again highlights the distinction between physiological and subjective measures of arousal in women.

Of all the DSM-5 diagnoses, the sexual interest and desire disorders, often colloquially referred to as low sex drive, are the most subjective. How often should a person want sex? And with what intensity? Often, one partner will encourage the other partner to see a clinician. The **female**

Clinical Case

Robert

Robert, a very bright 25-year-old graduate student in physics at a leading university, sought treatment for what he called "sexual diffidence" toward his fiancée. He said he loved his fiancée very much and felt compatible with her in every conceivable way except in bed. There, try as he might, and with understanding from his fiancée, he found himself uninterested in initiating or responding to sex. He and his fiancée had attributed these problems to the academic pressures he had faced for the past 2 years, but a discussion with the therapist revealed that Robert had had little interest in sex—either with men or with women—for as far back as he could remember, even when work pressures were not present. He asserted that he found his fiancée very attractive, but as with other women he had known, he did not feel passion for her.

He had masturbated very rarely in adolescence and did not begin dating until late in college, though he had had many female acquaintances. His general approach to life, including sex, was analytical and intellectual, and he described his problems in a very unemotional and detached way to the therapist. He freely admitted that he would not have contacted a therapist at all were it not for the quietly stated wishes of his fiancée, who worried that his lack of interest in sex would interfere with their future relationship.

After a few individual sessions, the therapist asked the young man to invite his fiancée to a therapy session, which the client readily agreed to do. During a joint session, the couple appeared to be in love and looking forward to a life together, despite the woman's concern about Robert's lack of sexual interest.

sexual interest/arousal and male hypoactive desire disorders may owe their existence to the high expectations some people have about being sexual, and those high expectations may be shaped by cultural norms about how much sex a person "should" want. Among women with low sexual desire in the last month, American women are more likely to report distress about the symptom than are European women (Hayes, Dennerstein, et al., 2007). Because ideals regarding how much sex one should have are so subjective, some object to labeling these individual differences as disorders (Segal, 2015).

Erectile disorder is distinct from low sex drive—many with erectile disorder report frequent desires for sex. In erectile disorder, the problem is physical arousal. As shown in Table 12.3, occasional inability to attain or sustain an erection is the most common sexual concern among men (Laumann et al., 2005). The prevalence of erectile disorder increases sharply with age, with as many as 50 percent of men age 60 and older reporting at least occasional erectile dysfunction (Rosen, Miner, & Wincze, 2014).

Orgasmic Disorders

The DSM-5 includes separate diagnoses for problems in achieving orgasm for women and men. **Female orgasmic disorder** refers to the persistent absence or reduced intensity of orgasm after sexual excitement. Women differ in their thresholds for orgasm. Although some women have orgasms quickly and without much clitoral stimulation, others need prolonged clitoral stimulation. Therefore, it is not surprising that about one-third of women report that they rarely or never experience orgasms during intercourse with their partners (Zietsch, Miller, et al., 2011). Women become more likely to have orgasms as they age, which may reflect a greater knowledge of their bodies and sexual needs (Wincze & Weisberg, 2015). They are also more likely to have orgasms in close relationships than they are in casual, short-term relationships (Armstrong, England, & Fogarty, 2009). Female orgasmic disorder is not diagnosed unless the absence of orgasms is persistent and troubling. For many women, enjoying a sense of emotional closeness to their partner is more important than achieving an orgasm. About two-thirds of women report that they have faked an orgasm, and most say that they did so to try to protect their partner's feelings (Muehlenhard & Shippee, 2010). Many men are unaware (or at least don't report) that their partners don't achieve orgasms (Herbenick, Reece, et al., 2010a).

Women's problems reaching orgasm are distinct from problems with sexual arousal. As with the clinical case of Anne described at the beginning of this chapter, many women with orgasmic disorder achieve sexual arousal and enjoy sexual contact, even though they have difficulty reaching orgasm. Indeed, laboratory research has shown that arousal levels while viewing erotic stimuli do not distinguish women with orgasmic disorder from those without orgasmic disorder (Meston & Gorzalka, 1995).

Clinical Case

Bill

Bill, age 42, and Mary, his girlfriend of 18 months, sought treatment due to concerns about premature ejaculation. Both were divorced with children, and they stayed together every other weekend. Bill had a history of hypertension, hyperlipidemia, and low total testosterone levels. Bill's symptom, though, began well before these medical issues—he reported that he had never been able to maintain an erection for more than a minute after insertion. Mary was his first partner to label this as premature ejaculation, and she often worried that it was an indicator that he did not find her attractive. Mary urged him to seek treatment for "his problem."

The therapist helped Bill and Mary understand that his rapid ejaculation was likely biologically based, and that he had developed "performance anxiety" as a result of this pattern. The therapist also encouraged Bill and Mary to put a premium on pleasure and intimacy rather than controlling the timing of his ejaculation. Mary was helped to understand that rather than a sign of lack of arousal, premature ejaculation could be viewed as a sign of intense arousal. The therapist also explained that their limited time together could intensify pressure, and they were encouraged to protect times between their weekends together to enjoy intimacy. With the pressures removed, Bill and Mary returned to an enjoyable sex life.

Adapted from Wincze and Weisberg, 2015.

DSM-5 Criteria for Female Orgasmic Disorder

On at least 75 percent of sexual occasions:

- Marked delay, infrequency, or absence of orgasm, or
- Markedly reduced intensity of orgasmic sensation

DSM-5 Criteria for Premature Ejaculation

- Tendency to ejaculate during partnered sexual activity within 1 minute of penile insertion on at least 75 percent of sexual occasions

DSM-5 Criteria for Delayed Ejaculation

- Marked delay, infrequency, or absence of orgasm on at least 75 percent of sexual occasions

DSM-5 Criteria for Genito-Pelvic Pain/Penetration Disorder

Persistent or recurrent difficulties with at least one of the following:

- Inability to have vaginal penetration during intercourse
- Marked vulvar, vaginal or pelvic pain during vaginal penetration or intercourse attempts
- Marked fear or anxiety about pain or penetration
- Marked tensing of the pelvic floor muscles during attempted vaginal penetration

The DSM-5 includes two orgasmic disorders of men: **premature (early) ejaculation**, defined by ejaculation that occurs too quickly, and **delayed ejaculation disorder**, defined by persistent difficulty in ejaculating. As experienced by Bill in the Clinical Case, the DSM-5 defines "premature" as less than 1 minute after the penis is inserted. One minute was chosen based on cross-national studies showing that the median time to ejaculation is 5 minutes after penis insertion (Waldinger, Quinn, et al., 2005). Many men who seek treatment concerned about premature ejaculation are well within the norms in the duration of their erections—in their case, psychoeducation can help them set realistic expectations (Wincze & Weisberg, 2015). As shown in Table 12.3, brief periods of premature ejaculation are fairly common, but less than 3 percent of men report symptoms of premature ejaculation lasting 6 months or more (Segraves, 2010).

Delayed ejaculation is the least common sexual dysfunction among men, reported by less than 1 percent of men (APA, 2013). Most men who seek treatment for delayed ejaculation report that the difficulty happens during intercourse but not when masturbating (Wincze & Weisberg, 2015).

Sexual Pain Disorder

The major symptom of **genito-pelvic pain/penetration disorder** is persistent or recurrent pain during intercourse. Although some men experience recurrent pain during sex, very few men seek treatment for it. For this reason, the DSM-5 criteria focus on women. Sexual pain is a very common concern heard by gynecologists (Nobre & Pinto-Gouveia, 2008). Women with this disorder often experience vaginismus, defined by involuntary muscle spasms of the outer third of the vagina to a degree that makes intercourse impossible (Binik, 2010). A first step in diagnosing genito-pelvic/penetration disorder is ensuring that the pain is not caused by a medical problem, such as an infection, or by a lack of vaginal lubrication due to low desire or postmenopausal changes. Without adequate treatment, one study found that half of women with genito-pelvic pain disorder had sustained symptoms across a 2-year follow-up, and another quarter had a fluctuating course of remission and relapse (Reed, Harlow, et al., 2016).

Most women diagnosed with this disorder experience sexual arousal and can have orgasms from manual or oral stimulation that does not involve penetration. Women who experience pain when attempting sexual intercourse show normative sexual arousal to films of oral sex, but, not surprisingly, their arousal declines when they watch a depiction of intercourse (Wouda, Hartman, et al., 1998).

Quick Summary

In the DSM-5, the sexual dysfunction disorders are divided as follows:

- Sexual interest, desire, and arousal disorders (female sexual interest/arousal disorder, male hypoactive sexual desire disorder and erectile disorder)
- Orgasmic disorders (female orgasmic disorder, premature ejaculation, and delayed ejaculation)
- Sexual pain disorder (genito-pelvic pain/penetration disorder)

Although there are no good estimates of how many people meet full diagnostic criteria for most of the sexual dysfunction disorders, in one major survey, 43 percent of women and 31 percent of men reported at least some symptoms of sexual dysfunction. People who experience one sexual dysfunction disorder often experience a comorbid sexual dysfunction disorder; for example, a man who is experiencing premature ejaculation may develop hypoactive sexual desire disorder.

True or false?

1. A person who experiences a brief problem with sexual arousal, orgasm, or desire is likely to meet the criteria for a sexual dysfunction.

2. People with one sexual dysfunction tend to have other comorbid sexual dysfunctions.

3. Relationships are usually unsatisfying when one person has a symptom of sexual dysfunction.

Answer the questions.

4. In the international survey conducted by Laumann and colleagues, which sexual dysfunction symptom did women most commonly report?

5. In the same survey, which sexual dysfunction symptom did men most commonly report?

Etiology of Sexual Dysfunctions

In their widely acclaimed book *Human Sexual Inadequacy*, Masters and Johnson (1970) drew on their case studies to publish a theory of why sexual dysfunctions develop. Masters and Johnson differentiated immediate and distal causes of sexual dysfunction. In their model, the two immediate causes are fears about performance and the adoption of a **spectator role**. Fears about performance involve concerns with how one is "performing" during sex. Spectator role refers to observing oneself rather than fully participating in a sexual experience. These two related concerns could both impede natural sexual responses. These immediate causes of sexual dysfunctions were hypothesized to have one or more distal antecedents, such as sociocultural influences, biological causes, or sexual abuse. Masters and Johnson emphasized that sexual functioning is complex, and that multiple factors usually combine to produce these symptoms in a given person. We now turn to research on the causes of sexual dysfunctions. **Table 12.4** summarizes key factors related to sexual dysfunctions.

TABLE 12.4   **Predictors of sexual dysfunction**

Domain	Predictors
Biological Factors	Heavy smoking
	Heavy drinking
	Cardiovascular disease
	Diabetes
	Neurological disease
	Hormone dysfunction
	SSRI medications
	Other medical illnesses and medications
Social Factors	Rape or sexual abuse
	Lack of opportunity to learn about sexuality
	Relationship difficulties
	Negative cultural attitudes toward sexuality
Psychological Factors	Depression and anxiety
	Low physiological arousal/exhaustion
	Negative cognitions and self-blame
	Spectator role and performance fears

Biological Factors

As noted earlier, a first step in making a diagnosis of sexual dysfunction is to rule out medical diseases as the cause. The DSM-5 includes separate diagnoses for sexual dysfunctions that are caused by medical illnesses. Some have criticized this division in the diagnoses because sexual dysfunctions often have both biological and psychological causes. Biological causes of sexual dysfunctions can include diseases such as diabetes, multiple sclerosis, and spinal cord injury; heavy alcohol use before sex; chronic alcohol use; and heavy cigarette smoking (Wincze & Weisberg, 2015). Laboratory tests of hormone levels are a routine part of assessment of sexual dysfunctions (Buvat, Maggi, et al., 2010) because sexual dysfunctions among men can be exacerbated by either low levels of testosterone or by the high levels induced by chronic use of anabolic steroids or testosterone supplements. Certain medications, such as selective serotonin reuptake inhibitor (SSRI) antidepressant drugs (e.g., Prozac and Zoloft), have effects on sexual function, including decreased arousal, and higher rates of orgasmic disorders (Kronstein, Ishida, et al., 2015).

Beyond these general biological contributions, some biological factors may be specific to certain sexual dysfunctions. As one example, some women who experience genito-pelvic pain/penetration disorder have a neurologically based supersensitivity to pain (van Lankveld, Granot, et al., 2010). There is some evidence that atypically low estradiol (Cappelletti & Wallen, 2016) and testosterone (Davis, Worsley, et al., 2016) can contribute to low sexual desire among women. Erectile symptoms are often related to an incipient vascular disorder (Rastrelli, Corona, et al., 2015). The effects of SSRI treatment on sexual sensitivity has led to a focus on abnormal serotonin receptors as the major explanation of premature ejaculation (Wincze & Weisberg, 2015).

Psychosocial Factors

Some sexual dysfunctions can be traced to rape, sexual abuse, or to an absence of positive sexual experiences. Childhood sexual abuse is associated with diminished arousal and desire; higher rates of genital pain; and, among men, with double the rate of premature ejaculation (Latthe, Mignini, et al., 2006; Laumann et al, 1999). See **Focus on Discovery 12.2** for a discussion of childhood sexual abuse and its repercussions. Beyond the role of traumatic experiences, positive experiences have important benefits—many people with sexual problems lack knowledge and skill because they have not had opportunities to learn about their sexuality.

Broader relationship problems often interfere with sexual arousal and pleasure (Burri & Spector, 2011). For women, concerns about a partner's affection are particularly likely to lower

---

Focus on Discovery 12.2

The Effects of Pedophilic Disorder: Outcomes After Childhood Sexual Abuse

It is hard to estimate the prevalence of childhood sexual abuse (CSA), as researchers vary in their definitions of abuse and of childhood, and they recruit participants from different sources. Nonetheless, it is clear that CSA happens far too often. In one major community survey, about 10 percent of adults reported some form of CSA, with CSA occurring three times as often to girls as to boys (Pérez-Fuentes, Olfson, et al., 2013).

A child abuser is usually not a stranger. He may be a father, an uncle, a brother, a teacher, a coach, a neighbor, or even a cleric. The abuser is often an adult whom the child knows and trusts. When the abuser is someone close to the child, the child is likely to feel torn on the one hand by allegiance to the abuser and, on the other hand, by fear, revulsion, and the knowledge that what is happening is wrong. The betrayal of this trust makes the crime

more abhorrent than it would be if no prior relationship existed between abuser and child. As with childhood incest, molestation or sexual harassment by an authority figure violates trust and respect. The victim, whatever their age, cannot give meaningful consent. The power differential is just too great.

Here, we consider two central questions. How does the all-too-common experience of CSA affect mental health during childhood and beyond? What can be done to help children heal from CSA?

Effects on the Child

After CSA, many children will develop symptoms, such as depression, low self-esteem, conduct disorder, and anxiety disorders like posttraumatic stress disorder (PTSD). On the other hand, many children do not exhibit immediate symptoms after CSA. What factors contribute to how CSA affects a child? Negative outcomes are more pronounced when the CSA involves sexual intercourse (Nelson, Heath, et al., 2002), violence (Dunn, Gilman, et al., 2012), or when the CSA started at an earlier age (Kaplow & Widom, 2007). Outcomes are better when the child has a supportive relationship with a non-abusive parent (Widom, 2014).

In adulthood, CSA is related to higher risk of many different psychological disorders. These effects are observed in large-scale representative community samples, as well as smaller longitudinal studies in which researchers have followed abused children over time (Widom, 2014). We have seen in previous chapters that a history of CSA is common among adults experiencing many different psychological disorders—notably, dissociative identity disorder, PTSD, eating disorders, borderline personality disorder, major depressive disorder, sexual dysfunctions, and substance abuse. CSA is also tied to lower self-esteem, less life satisfaction, and poorer romantic relationships during adulthood (Fergusson, McLeod, et al., 2013).

An issue in interpreting these correlations, though, is that families in which abuse occurs are often experiencing a broad array of problems, such as substance dependence in one or both parents, which may be entangled with other genetic and environmental risks for psychopathology. As a result, it is hard to isolate whether CSA is genuinely the factor that heightens the risk for a clinical disorder—most children exposed to child abuse also experience other forms of early adversity (Green, McLaughlin, et al., 2010). Twin studies provide a way to disentangle these effects, particularly when one twin but not the other has been abused, because the twin who was not abused shares genetic and at least some environmental risk factors. In one study of almost 2000 twin pairs, adults with a history of CSA had substantially increased risk of depression, suicide, conduct disorder, alcohol dependence, social anxiety, rape, and divorce compared to their nonabused twins (Nelson et al., 2002).

Dealing With the Problem

When they suspect that something is awry, parents must raise the issue with their children; unfortunately, many adults are uncomfortable doing so. Clinicians also need to be sensitive to signs of sexual abuse. The law requires health care professionals who suspect sexual or nonsexual child abuse to report their suspicions to the police or child protective agencies. Despite this, many crimes are not reported.

For a child, reporting sexual abuse can be extremely difficult. We tend to forget how helpless and dependent the child feels, and it is difficult to imagine how frightening it would be to tell one's parents that one had been fondled by a brother or grandfather. Most cases of sexual abuse do not leave any physical evidence, such as torn vaginal tissue. Furthermore, there is no behavioral sign or emotional syndrome that unequivocally indicates that abuse has occurred. Therefore, the child's own report is the primary source of information about whether CSA has occurred. The problem is that leading questions can produce some false reports (Larson, Cartwright, & Goodman, 2016). Great skill is required in questioning a child about possible sexual abuse to avoid biasing the youngster one way or the other.

Many children who have been abused need treatment. As with adult survivors of rape, PTSD can be a consequence. Many interventions are similar to those used for PTSD in adults; the emphasis is on exposure to memories of the trauma through discussion in a safe and supportive therapeutic atmosphere. As with rape, it is important to change the person's attribution of responsibility from "I was bad" to "he/she was bad." Such treatments have been shown to help abused children find relief from their symptoms and reduce their sense of shame (Cohen, Deblinger, et al., 2004).

---

sexual satisfaction (Nobre & Pinto-Gouveia, 2008). More than half of women with symptoms of sexual dysfunction believe those symptoms are caused by relationship problems (Nicholls, 2008). For people who are anxious about their relationships, sexual problems may exacerbate underlying worries about relationship security (Birnbaum, Reis, et al., 2006). As one might expect, people who are angry with their partners are less likely to want sex (Beck & Bozman, 1995). Even in couples who are satisfied with other realms of the relationship, poor communication can contribute to sexual dysfunction. For any number of reasons, including embarrassment, worry about the partner's feelings, or fear, one lover may not tell the other about preferences even if a partner is engaging in unstimulating or even aversive behaviors during sex.

Depression and anxiety increase the risk of sexual dysfunctions. People with a clinical diagnosis of mood disorder are more than three times as likely as those without a mood disorder to report a general dissatisfaction with their sexual life, and those with anxiety disorder are more than twice as likely to report sexual dissatisfaction (Vanwesenbeeck, Have, et al., 2014). Anxiety and depression are specifically comorbid with sexual pain (Meana, Binik, et al., 1998), lack of sexual desire or arousal (Forbes & Schniering, 2013; McCabe & Connaughton, 2014), and female orgasmic disorder (Leeners, Hengartner, et al., 2014).

Beyond the detrimental effects of depression and anxiety, several studies suggest that low general physiological arousal can interfere with specific sexual arousal. Meston and Gorzalka (1995) examined the role of arousal by assigning women to exercise or no-exercise conditions and then asking women to watch erotic films. Consistent with the positive role of higher arousal, exercise facilitated sexual arousal. No wonder, then, that exhausted couples, turning to sex after a full day of work, parenting, socializing, and other roles, can encounter problems with sexuality.

Negative cognitions, including worries about pregnancy or AIDS, negative attitudes about sex, or concerns about the partner, can interfere with sexual functioning (Wincze & Weisberg, 2015). Intrusive negative thoughts about their weight or appearance impinge on the enjoyment of sex for many women (Pujols, Seal, & Meston, 2010). But as Masters and Johnson first suggested, thoughts about sexual performance can be significant problems for both men and women (Carvalho & Nobre, 2010; Rowland, Adamski, et al., 2015). Consider the idea that variability in sexual performance is common; a stressful day, a distracting context, a relationship concern, or any number of other issues may diminish sexual responsiveness. The key issue may be how people think about their diminished physical response when it happens. One theory is that people who blame themselves for decreased sexual performance will be more likely to develop recurrent sexual problems.

In a test of the role of self-blame and erectile dysfunction, researchers asked male participants to watch erotic videos (Weisberg, Brown, et al., 2001). During the videos, their sexual arousal (penile circumference) was measured using a **penile plethysmograph** (see Figure 12.3). Regardless of their actual arousal, the men were given false feedback that the size of their erection was smaller than that typically measured among aroused men. Men were randomly assigned to receive two different explanations for this false feedback. In the first, they were told that the films were not working for most men (external explanation). In the second, they were told that the pattern of their responses on questionnaires about sexuality might help explain the low arousal (internal explanation). After receiving this feedback, the men were asked to watch one more film. The men who were given an internal explanation reported less arousal and also showed less physiological arousal during this film than those given an external explanation. These results, then, support the idea that people who blame themselves when their body doesn't perform will experience diminished subsequent arousal. Needless to say, men in this study were carefully debriefed after the experiment!

In considering the source of negative cognitions, Masters and Johnson found that many of their sex therapy patients had learned negative views of sexuality from their social and cultural surroundings. For example, some religions and cultures may discourage sexuality for the sake of pleasure, particularly outside marriage. Other cultures may disapprove of sexual initiative or behavior among women, other than for the sake of procreation. One female patient suffering from a lack of sexual desire, for example, had been taught as she was growing up not to look at herself naked in the mirror and that intercourse was reserved for marriage and then only to be endured for purposes of having children. Guilt about engaging in sexual behavior varies by cultural group and can inhibit sexual desire (Woo, Brotto, & Gorzalka, 2011).

Quick Summary

In diagnosing sexual dysfunction, it is important to consider potential medical and pharmacological explanations. If biological factors are central, separate diagnoses are applied. Key psychosocial etiological variables involved in sexual dysfunctions are sexual abuse or rape, lack of sexual knowledge, relationship problems, psychological disorders such as depression or anxiety, exhaustion, and negative cognitions and attitudes about sexuality.

Check Your Knowledge 12.3

Answer the questions.

1. Define the spectator role.
2. How large are the effects of depression and anxiety on sexual dissatisfaction?

Treatments of Sexual Dysfunctions

Given the complex matrix of factors that promote healthy sexual functioning, it is perhaps no surprise that therapists often draw on a rich array of strategies to help address sexual dysfunction. A therapist may choose only one technique for a given case, but the multifaceted nature of sexual dysfunctions often requires the use of a combination of techniques, as illustrated in the Clinical Case of Carol.

Clinical Case

Carol

Carol, a 52-year-old woman, sought treatment for her lack of interest in sex. Carol and Darren had been married for 11 years. Although they had engaged in sex once or twice per week in the early years of their marriage, her interest in sex had waned over the past 5 years, she began to refuse Darren's requests for sex 2 years ago, and they had not had intercourse for 9 months. Indeed, Carol tried to avoid any physical contact, including holding hands, as she did not want to send the signal that she was interested in sex. She also reported that she had stopped masturbating or having sexual fantasies.

Carol was raised in a devout Catholic family and had been taught that strong sex drives were immoral for women. In college, she had had sex with a few partners. She had been able to enjoy these experiences and sex with Darren during the early years of their relationship, even though she described feeling awkward about sex and uncomfortable describing her needs to a partner. The past several years had been very stressful for her, with care-taking for her ill mother and coping with budget cuts in her work place. As is typical with aging, she had also noticed more vaginal dryness, and this made sex more physically uncomfortable.

Darren reported feeling rejected and angry about their lack of sex, and Carol reported that she felt guilty, but that his anger only made her less interested in sex. In the context of her stress, Darren's requests for sex had begun to feel like one more demand in her life.

The clinical case of Carol illustrates how complicated sexual dysfunction can be. Carol describes beliefs that sex drive is shameful, difficulty communicating about sexual needs, significant life stress, normative changes in vaginal lubrication as she ages, and tension and lack of communication in her partnership. The therapist worked to address each of these concerns. To reduce the pressure and conflict around sex, the therapist banned the couple from having sex while they engaged in sensate focus exercises. Carol's shame and negative beliefs about her sexuality were tackled using cognitive approaches. Carol and Darren were coached in communication skills to improve their relationship and their sexual communication. Carol was encouraged to use a lubricant. Combining these different approaches restored their sexual intimacy and renewed their closeness.

Adapted from Wincze and Weisberg, 2015.

We will begin by considering interventions that are helpful across a broad range of sexual dysfunctions. Randomized controlled trials indicate that these interventions are more helpful than control treatments, and the evidence is particularly strong for female sexual interest/arousal disorder and female orgasmic disorder (Frühauf, Gerger, et al., 2013). After discussing approaches useful for addressing multiple sexual dysfunctions, we will describe interventions developed for specific sexual dysfunctions.

Psychoeducation

For many clients, the first step of treatment is to provide good information about how common sexual dysfunction is. By providing clear information about the sources of these types of issues, therapists can normalize the concern, reduce anxiety, model effective communication about sexuality, and eliminate blame (Wincze & Weisberg, 2015). For example, many men with premature ejaculation become focused on self-blame, and simply understanding that there is a likely biological basis for these symptoms can be a relief. Therapists often assign written materials and show clients explicit videos to help them understand more about the body and sexual techniques.

Couples Therapy

Some sexual dysfunctions are embedded in a distressed relationship, and in turn, sometimes sexual difficulties create problems between partners. Troubled couples often need training in nonsexual communication skills (Wincze & Weisberg, 2015). Some therapists focus on nonsexual issues, such as difficulties with in-laws or with child rearing—either in addition to or instead of interventions directly focused on sex. For some couples, planning romantic events together is recommended to restore closeness and intimacy (Wincze & Weisberg, 2015).

Encouraging partners to communicate their sexual likes and dislikes to each other can help a range of sexual dysfunctions (Wincze & Weisberg, 2015). Skills and communication training is particularly warranted when sexual dysfunction is specific to a given relationship and was not a concern with previous partners.

Cognitive Interventions

Cognitive interventions are often used to challenge the self-demanding, perfectionistic thoughts that often cause problems for people with sexual dysfunctions. A therapist might try to reduce the pressure a man with erectile dysfunction feels by challenging his belief that intercourse is the only true form of sexual activity. Therapists might coach women who are hypercritical of their appearance to consider more positive ways of viewing their bodies and their sexuality.

Sensate Focus

To help couples refocus on the sensual pleasure of their intimacy, many therapists prescribe sensate focus, a technique introduced by Masters and Johnson (1970). During sensate-focus exercises, the therapist instructs the couple not to have intercourse, and indeed, not even to touch each other's genitalia initially. Rather, the therapist instructs them to choose a time when both partners feel a sense of warmth and compatibility, and to undress and give each other pleasure by touching each other's bodies. Therapists appoint one partner to do the first pleasuring; the partner who is "getting" is simply to enjoy being touched. The one being touched is not required to feel a sexual response and is responsible for immediately telling the partner if something becomes uncomfortable. Then the roles are switched.

The sensate-focus assignment usually promotes contact, constituting a first step toward reestablishing sexual intimacy. Most of the time, partners begin to realize that their physical encounters could be intimate and pleasurable without necessarily being a prelude to sexual intercourse. Sensate focus often helps counter the destructive tendency to think about one's performance or attractiveness during sex, and helps a couple begin to communicate more constructively about their sexual preferences.

Treatments for Specific Sexual Dysfunctions

Therapists often use more specific techniques for female orgasmic disorder, genito-pelvic pain/penetration disorder, premature ejaculation, and erectile disorder, and we discuss these next. Many of these specific techniques are combined with the general treatments we already discussed.

Female Orgasmic Disorder Directed masturbation was devised by LoPiccolo and Lobitz (1972) to enhance women's comfort with and enjoyment of their sexuality. The first step is for the woman to carefully examine her nude body, including her genitals, and to identify various areas with the aid of diagrams. Next, she is instructed to touch her genitals and to find areas that produce pleasure. Then she increases the intensity of masturbation using erotic fantasies. If she does not achieve orgasm, she is to use a vibrator in her masturbation. Finally, her partner enters the picture, first watching her masturbate, then doing for her what she has been doing for herself, and finally having intercourse in a position that allows him to stimulate her genitals manually or with a vibrator. As illustrated in the Clinical Case of Anne in the beginning of this chapter, directed masturbation has been shown to help treat female orgasmic disorder, particularly when women have a lifelong inability to experience orgasm, with 60 to 90 percent of that subgroup achieving orgasm post-treatment (ter Kuile, Both, & van Lankveld, 2012).

Genito-Pelvic Pain/Penetration Disorder A woman with genito-pelvic pain/penetration disorder might be trained in relaxation, and then practice inserting her fingers or dilators into her vagina, starting with inserting smaller dilators and working up to larger ones. Such programs have been shown to help many women with sexual pain disorder (ter Kuile & Reissing, 2014).

Premature Ejaculation SSRI antidepressants have been found to help reduce premature ejaculation. The SSRI, dapoxetine, has been approved for the treatment of premature ejaculation in 50 countries. It is taken as needed in the hour before sex (Althof, McMahon, et al., 2014).

As a behavioral treatment of premature ejaculation, the squeeze technique is often used, in which a partner is trained to squeeze the penis in the area where the head and shaft meet to rapidly reduce arousal. This technique is practiced without insertion, and then during insertion, the penis is withdrawn and the squeeze is repeated as needed. In a similar approach, men are taught to withdraw their penis as needed during intercourse to reduce arousal. Behavioral techniques are not as powerful as antidepressant medication for premature ejaculation, but they are helpful as a supplement to medication (Cooper, Martyn-St James, et al., 2015). Psychotherapy can also help men regain confidence after experiences of these symptoms (Althof, 2014).

Erectile Disorder   The most common intervention for erectile disorder is a phosphodiesterase type 5 (PDE-5) inhibitor, such as sildenafil (Viagra), tadafil (Cialis), or vardenafil (Levitra). PDE-5 inhibitors relax smooth muscles and thereby allow blood to flow into the penis, creating an erection during sexual stimulation but not in its absence (Eardley et al., 2010). PDE-5 inhibitors can be taken daily, or one hour before sex (Burns, Rosen, et al., 2010). Although some men stop taking these medications due to side effects such as headaches and indigestion, most men will tolerate the side effects to gain relief from their sexual symptoms. Indeed, worldwide sales of PDE-5 medications have surpassed $5 billion (Wilson, 2011).

Across 27 treatment studies, about 83 percent of men who took sildenafil were able to successfully have intercourse compared with about 45 percent of men who took a placebo (Fink, Mac Donald, et al., 2002). Some men continue to experience intermittent erectile dysfunction on PDE-5 inhibitors, and so sex therapy is a helpful addition to medication treatment (Melnik, Soares, & Nasello, 2008). Several trials of PDE-5 inhibitors have been conducted for treatment of sexual dysfunction in women, but the results are not promising (Laan, Everaerd, & Both, 2005).

Quick Summary

Key cognitive behavioral treatments for sexual dysfunction include psychoeducation, couples therapy, cognitive interventions, and sensate focus. Directed masturbation is often used to treat female orgasmic disorder; relaxation coupled with use of dilators is used for pain disorder, SSRIs and variants of the squeeze technique are used for premature ejaculation, and PDE-5 inhibitors such as Viagra and Cialis are used for erectile disorder.

Check Your Knowledge 12.4

Answer the questions.

1. Describe the sensate focus technique.

Which is the most effective treatment for each of the following?

2. Female orgasmic disorder
3. Premature ejaculation
4. Erectile disorder

True or false?

5. Sex therapists may recommend that a woman who does not achieve orgasm practice masturbation without her partner present.

Clinical Descriptions of the Paraphilic Disorders

The DSM-5 defines the **paraphilic disorders** as recurrent sexual attraction to unusual objects or sexual activities lasting at least 6 months. In other words, there is a deviation *(para)* in what

TABLE 12.5 Paraphilic Disorders Included in DSM

DSM-5 Diagnosis	Object of Sexual Attraction
Fetishistic disorder	An inanimate object or nongenital body part
Transvestic disorder	Cross-dressing
Pedophilic disorder	Children
Voyeuristic disorder	Watching unsuspecting others undress or have sex
Exhibitionistic disorder	Exposing one's genitals to an unwilling stranger
Frotteuristic disorder	Sexual touching of an unsuspecting person
Sexual sadism disorder	Inflicting pain
Sexual masochism disorder	Receiving pain

the person is attracted to *(philia)*. DSM differentiates the paraphilic disorders based on the source of arousal; for example, it provides one diagnostic category for people whose sexual attractions are focused on causing pain and another diagnostic category for people whose attractions are focused on children (see **Table 12.5**). Large surveys have shown that many people occasionally fantasize about some of the activities we will be describing, and some engage in these behaviors. Voyeuristic attractions may be particularly common: More than 40 percent of people report fantasies of watching unsuspecting people undress, have sex, or be naked (Joyal & Carpentier, 2017). About 7.7 percent report that they had been aroused by spying on others having sex, 7 percent report that they had engaged in sadomasochistic sex at least once, 3.1 percent report that they had been aroused by exposing their genitalia to a stranger at least once during their lifetime, and 3.1 percent of adult men reported having fantasies or sexual interest in children ages 13 to 15 in the past year (although a smaller percent, 0.4 percent, endorsed an interest in children 12 and younger) (Långström & Seto, 2006; Vanwesenbeeck, Bakker, & Gesell, 2010; Santtila, Antfolk, et al., 2015). The website fetlife. com, a social network site for people interested in sadomasochistic and fetishistic sex, lists more than 5 million members. *Fifty Shades of Gray*, a book describing a sadomasochistic relationship, became one of the best-selling books of all time, with 125 million copies sold in the United States by 2015. Although many people are interested in or have tried these sexual activities, many fewer people report that these interests are sustained, uncontrollable, or distressing (Joyal & Carpentier, 2017).

As some of these behaviors and interests appear relatively common, considerable debate has emerged about whether it is appropriate to diagnose some of the paraphilias. In 2009, the Swedish National Board of Health and Welfare decided to remove some of the paraphilic diagnoses. Fetishistic disorder, sexual sadism disorder, sexual masochism disorder, and transvestic disorder are no longer included in their psychiatric classification system (Långström, 2010). The board reasoned that many people practice variant sexual behaviors safely with consenting adult partners and do not experience any distress or impairment as a result (Richters, De Visser, et al., 2008). The DSM-5 retains the labels, but the word *disorder* is added to the title of these diagnoses to emphasize that the clinician is to consider these diagnoses only if the sexual attractions cause marked distress or impairment or if the person engages in sexual activities with a nonconsenting person.

Impairment and engagement of nonconsenting others are important boundaries between normative and problematic sexual behavior. For some sexual behaviors, though, these dimensions rarely apply. For example, transvestic disorder does not typically involve nonconsenting others and rarely leads to impairment; the diagnosis of this disorder typically rests on the presence of distress. Diagnostic criteria that rely on distress about sexual desires and behaviors are somewhat illogical. The person who cross-dresses for sexual gratification and accepts the behavior won't meet the diagnostic criteria. In contrast, the person who feels guilty and ashamed because he or she has internalized stigma about this behavior is diagnosable.

Clinical Case

William

William and Nancy sought marital therapy after Nancy learned that William had a long history of voyeurism. Nancy had been startled to walk into their guest room and find him viewing the neighbor with binoculars while masturbating. Upon confrontation, William shared with his wife that he had felt intense and uncontrollable urges to watch strangers undress since his early adolescence.

William and Nancy reported that they had been married for 20 years, and that throughout the duration of their relationship, neither had found their sexual life very satisfying. Nancy was concerned that he rarely initiated sexual contact with her, and indeed, in an individual session, William reported that he preferred watching strangers to having sex with his wife. He had never found sex with a consenting partner as exciting as the forbidden. William had tried different strategies to gain control over his

voyeuristic urges, including reading self-help books and attending a support group, with no success. He reported that he came from an extremely strict family and had been teased relentlessly by his father. Although his desire to watch strangers haunted him, he had felt too ashamed to discuss his sexual preferences with anyone in the past. His sexual detachment was part of a broader pattern of emotional distance and lack of disclosure with others in his life.

In therapy, William began to explore the sense of social rejection that he had experienced since early childhood. As his wife learned of his past, they achieved a stronger emotional bond, which freed them to discuss their sexuality more openly. As their sex life improved, William reported that his desire to watch others undress faded.

Adapted from Kleinplatz, 2014.

Because transvestic behavior so rarely leads to impairment or involves nonconsenting others, we do not discuss transvestic disorder further here.

Accurate prevalence statistics are not available for the paraphilic disorders. Research is limited by the lack of structured diagnostic interviews to reliably assess paraphilic disorders (Krueger, 2010b) and even more by the reluctance of many people with paraphilias to reveal their proclivities. Because some persons with paraphilic disorders seek nonconsenting partners or otherwise violate people's rights in offensive ways (as we will see in exhibitionistic and pedophilic disorders), these disorders can have legal consequences. But statistics on arrests underestimate prevalence because so many crimes go unreported and some paraphilias (e.g., voyeuristic disorder) involve an unsuspecting victim. The data do indicate, however, that most people with paraphilic disorders are male and heterosexual; even with sexual masochism and voyeurism disorders, which occur in noticeable numbers of women, men vastly outnumber women (Richters, De Visser, et al., 2008). Onset for many of the paraphilic disorders, including fetishistic, voyeuristic, exhibitionistic, and pedophilic disorders, typically occurs during adolescence. The onset of sexual sadism disorder and sexual masochism disorder tends to occur by early adulthood (Balon, 2016; Grundmann, Krupp, et al., 2016). A person with one form of paraphilic interests is often aroused by other paraphilic stimuli—that is, tendencies to engage in exhibitionism, sexual sadism, sexual masochism, and voyeurism are correlated (Baur, Forsman, et al., 2016). Here we provide a clinical description of the paraphilic disorders.

DSM-5 Criteria for Fetishistic Disorder

- For at least 6 months, recurrent and intense sexually arousing fantasies, urges, or behaviors involving the use of nonliving objects or nongenital body parts
- Causes significant distress or impairment in functioning
- The sexually arousing objects are not limited to articles of clothing used in cross-dressing or to devices designed to provide tactile genital stimulation, such as a vibrator

Fetishistic Disorder

The key feature of **fetishistic disorder** is a reliance on an inanimate object or a nongenital part of the body for sexual arousal. A fetish refers to the object of these sexual urges, such as women's shoes or feet. The person with fetishistic disorder has recurrent and intense sexual urges toward these fetishes, and the presence of the fetish is strongly preferred or even necessary for sexual arousal. Clothing (especially underwear), leather, and articles related to feet (stockings, women's shoes) are common fetishes. Beyond nonliving objects, some people focus on nonsexual body parts, such as hair, nails, hands, or feet, for sexual arousal. Because there is no evidence of a difference in the etiology or consequences of a boot fetish compared to a foot fetish, the DSM-5 includes a reliance on nonsexual body parts for sexual arousal under the diagnosis of fetishistic disorder.

Clinical Case

Ruben

Ruben, a single, 32-year-old male photographer, sought treatment for his concern that he was more attracted to women's underwear than to the women themselves. Ruben remembered being excited by pictures of women in their underwear at age 7. At age 13 he reached orgasm by masturbating while imagining women in their underwear. He began to steal underwear from his sister to use while masturbating. As he grew older, he would sneak into women's rooms and steal their underwear. He began

to have intercourse at age 18, and his preferred partner was a prostitute whom he asked to wear underwear with the crotch removed while they had sex. He found that he preferred masturbating into stolen underwear more than sexual intercourse. He avoided dating because he feared the scorn that his focus on underwear might provoke. He had begun to experience significant depression over the ways in which his sexual behavior was limiting his social life.

Adapted from Spitzer, Gibbon, et al., 1994.

Like Ruben in the clinical case, the person with fetishistic disorder feels a compulsive attraction to the object; the attraction is experienced as involuntary and irresistible. The exclusive and very special status the object occupies as a sexual stimulant distinguishes fetishistic disorder from the ordinary attraction that, for example, high heels may hold for heterosexual men in Western cultures. The person with a boot fetish must see or touch a boot to become aroused, and the arousal is overwhelmingly strong when a boot is present. Some carry on their fetishism alone and in secret by fondling, kissing, smelling, gazing at the adored object, or using the fetish as they masturbate. Others can reach orgasm only if a partner dons the fetish.

Pedophilic Disorder and Incest

According to the DSM, **pedophilic disorder** (*pedes* is Greek for "child") is diagnosed when adults derive sexual gratification through sexual contact with prepubescent children, or in the absence of any actions, when their recurrent and intense desires for sexual contact with prepubescent children cause distress either for themselves or others. DSM-5 criteria specify that the offender be at least 16 years old and at least 5 years older than the child. As in most paraphilias, a strong attraction impels the behavior. Sometimes a man with pedophilic disorder is content to stroke the child's hair, but he may also manipulate the child's genitalia, encourage the child to manipulate his, and, less often, attempt penile insertion. The molestations may be repeated over a period of weeks, months, or years.

People with pedophilic disorder generally molest children whom they know, such as neighbors or friends of the family. Most with pedophilic disorder do not engage in violence other than the sexual act, although when they do become violent, it is often a focus of lurid stories in the media. Because overt physical force is seldom used in pedophilic disorder, the child molester often denies that he is forcing himself on his victim. Despite molesters' distorted beliefs, child sexual abuse inherently involves a betrayal of trust and other serious negative consequences (see **Focus on Discovery 12.2** for a discussion of these consequences).

What are the demographic characteristics of people who meet the criteria for pedophilic disorder? People with pedophilic disorder can be straight or gay, though most are heterosexual. Among those convicted of pedophilic offenses, about half have never been married (Seto & Eke, 2017).

Sexual arousal in response to pictures of young children can be measured by the penile plethysmograph. In large-scale studies, arousal as measured in this way discriminates those who have committed sexual offenses with children (Cantor & McPhail, 2015), and is one of the strongest predictors of repeated sexual offenses (Hanson & Bussiere, 1998). Nonetheless, arousal in response to pictures of children is not a perfect predictor of pedophilic disorder. Many men who are conventional in their sexual interests and behavior can be sexually aroused

DSM-5 Criteria for Pedophilic Disorder

- For at least 6 months, recurrent and intense sexually arousing fantasies, urges, or behaviors involving sexual contact with a prepubescent child

- Person has acted on these urges or the urges and fantasies cause marked distress or interpersonal problems

- Person is at least 16 years old and 5 years older than the child

Focus on Discovery 12.3

Rape

Rape is one of the most disturbing of human behaviors. It is typically defined as "attempted or completed vaginal, anal, or oral sexual intercourse obtained through force, through the threat of force, or when the victim is incapacitated and unable to give consent" (Abbey & McAuslan, 2004). The rapist is usually known to the victim.

Many more women than men are raped: In the United States, an estimated 19.3 percent of women and 1.7 percent of men have been raped during their lifetimes. For three-quarters of women who are raped, the rape occurs before the age of 25 (Zinzow & Thompson, 2015).

Rates of coercive sexual behavior, in which the person is pressured to engage in sexual contact, are even more common than rape. Coercive sexual behavior appears to be startlingly common. About 8 percent of male college students in the United States report that they have used force or the threat of force to engage in intercourse, anal sex, or oral sex (White & Smith, 2004). The high rates of rape and coercive sexual behavior have led many to suggest that sexual violence reflects a social and cultural problem (Gavey & Senn, 2014). This has led to policy efforts to provide education about the negative outcomes of rape and coercive sexual behavior, and to strengthen laws and response systems (DeMatteo, Galloway, et al., 2015).

Even with the consideration that this behavior must be viewed in a social context, it is only natural to ask questions about rapists. Who are the men who perpetrate these acts? Can treatment reduce the risk of recidivism?

Understanding the Etiology of Rape

Sexually aggressive men tend to show antisocial and impulsive personality traits, unusually high hostility toward women, and distorted beliefs about sexual coercion (e.g., women mean yes when they say no) (Zinzow & Thompson, 2015). It is also likely that there are different subgroups of rapists: some show more sadistic traits, some show more hypersexuality, and others show more impulsive traits (Krstic, Neumann, et al., 2017).

Data also suggests that exposure to violence may increase the likelihood of rape. That is, rapists are more likely than nonrapists to have been the victim of sexual and physical abuse (Knight & Sims-Knight, 2011). Even watching violence against women in films can lead men to view violence as more acceptable. At least eight experiments have been conducted in which men are asked to watch videos that contain sexual activities either with or without violence. After watching the videos that contained violence, men were significantly more likely to report that violence toward women was acceptable (Allen, D'Alessio, & Brezgel, 1995). This research suggests that rape may be encouraged by pornography that depicts violent sexual relations and more broadly highlights the importance of social factors.

Everett Collection, Inc.

This famous scene from *Gone With the Wind* illustrates one of the myths about rape—that despite initial resistance, women like to be "taken."

Treatment for Rapists

Treatment programs for rapists rely on the general approaches we describe for paraphilic disorders: motivational strategies, cognitive behavioral techniques, and pharmacological treatments. As with the research on treatment for paraphilic disorders, the evidence regarding the effectiveness of these approaches is remarkably slim—only 24 rapists have been studied in a randomized controlled trial (Marques, Wiederanders, et al., 2005). Outcomes of that study suggested that 20 percent of rapists assigned to cognitive behavioral treatment committed an offense during the 5-year follow-up period, compared with 29 percent in the no-treatment group. Although this may seem like a small gain from treatment, any gain is important with such a difficult problem.

by erotic pictures of children. In a study using both self-report and penile plethysmography, one-quarter of men drawn from a community sample showed or reported arousal when viewing sexually provocative pictures of children (Hall, Hirschman, & Oliver, 1995). The *relative* level of interest in children versus adults may be more telling. Pedophiles show more arousal to sexual stimuli involving children than to stimuli involving adults; nonpedophiles tend to show relatively more arousal to stimuli involving adults (Blanchard, Kuban, et al., 2009).

The diagnosis of pedophilia is not made on the basis of sexual attraction alone. Pedophilic disorder is diagnosed only when adults act on their sexual urges toward children, or when the urges reach the frequency or intensity to be distressing to the person or those close to them.

Incest is listed as a subtype of pedophilic disorder. **Incest** refers to sexual relations between close relatives for whom marriage is forbidden. It is most common between brother and sister. The next most common form, which is considered more pathological, is between father and daughter. Fathers who abuse their daughters tend to do so after the daughter achieves puberty.

The taboo against incest is virtually universal in human societies (Ford & Beach, 1951). The incest taboo makes sense according to present-day scientific knowledge. The offspring from a father–daughter or a brother–sister union have a greater probability of inheriting a pair of recessive genes, one from each parent. Many recessive genes have negative biological effects, such as serious birth defects. The incest taboo, then, has adaptive evolutionary significance.

Voyeuristic Disorder

The central feature of **voyeuristic disorder** is an intense and recurrent desire to obtain sexual gratification by watching unsuspecting others in a state of undress or having sexual relations. Voyeuristic fantasies are quite common in men, but as with the other paraphilic disorders, fantasies alone do not warrant a diagnosis. For some men with this disorder, voyeurism is their only sexual activity; for others, it is preferred but not absolutely essential for sexual arousal. As in the Clinical Case of William earlier in this chapter, the watching helps the person become sexually aroused and is sometimes essential for arousal. People with voyeuristic disorder achieve orgasm by masturbation, either while watching or later while remembering the peeping. Sometimes the person with voyeuristic disorder fantasizes about having sexual contact with the observed person, but it remains a fantasy; he or she seldom contacts the observed person. A true voyeur does not find it particularly exciting to watch someone undress for his benefit. The element of risk, and the threat of discovery, is important.

Exhibitionistic Disorder

The focus of sexual desire in **exhibitionistic disorder** is on exposing one's genitals to an unwilling stranger, sometimes a child. As with voyeuristic disorder, there is seldom an attempt to have other contact with the stranger. Many exhibitionists masturbate during the exposure. In most cases, there is a desire to shock or embarrass the observer. In one study, persons diagnosed with exhibitionistic disorder reported that they had been arrested for only 1 out of every 150 incidents (Abel et al., 1987).

Frotteuristic Disorder

The focus of sexual desire and urges in **frotteuristic disorder** is on touching an unsuspecting person. The person with this disorder may rub his penis against a woman's thighs or buttocks or fondle her breasts or genitals. These attacks typically occur in places such as a crowded bus or sidewalk that provide an easy means of escape. Most men who engage in frotteurism report doing so dozens of times (Abel, Becker, et al., 1987).

Sexual Sadism and Masochism Disorders

The focus of desire in **sexual sadism disorder** is on inflicting pain or psychological suffering (such as humiliation) on another, and the focus of desire in **sexual masochism disorder** is on being subjected to pain or humiliation. Sexual sadism and masochism can span a wide range of activities. Examples include physical bondage, blindfolding, spanking, whipping, electric shocks, cutting, humiliation (e.g., being urinated or defecated on, being forced to wear a collar and bark like a dog, or being put on display naked), and taking the role of slave and submitting to orders and commands. Most sadists establish relationships with masochists to derive mutual sexual gratification. Although many people are able to take both dominant and submissive roles, masochists outnumber sadists.

Sadistic and masochistic sexual behaviors have become more accepted over time. In major cities, clubs cater to members seeking sadomasochistic partnerships. Most people who engage in sadomasochistic behaviors are relatively comfortable with their sexual practices and would not meet the diagnostic criteria requiring that the desires lead to distress or impairment.

Because these disorders have become more common and are typically not related to impairment or distress, there was debate about whether these diagnoses should be retained in DSM-5 (Krueger, 2010b). These diagnostic labels were retained because some sadistic and masochistic practices can be dangerous. One particularly dangerous form of masochism, called asphyxiophilia, can result in death or brain damage; it involves sexual arousal by restricting breathing, which can be achieved using a noose, a plastic bag, or chest compression. More commonly, the diagnosis is applicable when the sadomasochistic urges and preferences lead to either personal or relationship distress.

There is some concern that the diagnosis of sexual sadism disorder is rarely applied in clinical settings. In an unpublished review of over 500 million visits to psychiatrists, gynecologists, urologists, and other physicians, no doctor recorded a diagnosis of sexual sadism disorder (Narrow, 2008, cited in Krueger, 2010a). Doctors in clinical settings may not use the diagnosis even when symptoms are present because of worries over stigma. The diagnosis, then, is applied almost entirely within forensic settings (Krueger, 2010a).

Many people experiment with sadomasochism and fetishes. Paraphilias are not diagnosed unless the sexual interests cause marked distress or impairment.

DSM-5 Criteria for Sexual Sadism Disorder

- For at least 6 months, recurrent, intense, and sexually arousing fantasies, urges, or behaviors involving the physical or psychological suffering of another person

- Causes clinically significant distress or impairment in functioning or the person has acted on these urges with a nonconsenting person

---

Quick Summary

Paraphilic disorders are defined as a sexual attraction to an unusual sexual object or activity that lasts at least 6 months and causes significant distress or impairment. The DSM diagnostic criteria for paraphilic disorders are distinguished based on the object of sexual attraction. The major DSM-5 diagnoses of paraphilias include fetishistic disorder, pedophilic disorder, voyeuristic disorder, exhibitionistic disorder, frotteuristic disorder, sexual sadism disorder, sexual masochism disorder, and transvestic disorder. (The last diagnosis is not discussed in this book.)

Researchers do not know the prevalence of these disorders. Few major studies are available on the etiology of paraphilic disorders, and the available studies largely focus on sexual offenders.

DSM-5 Criteria for Sexual Masochism Disorder

- For at least 6 months, recurrent, intense, and sexually arousing fantasies, urges, or behaviors involving the act of being humiliated, beaten, bound, or made to suffer

- Causes marked distress or impairment in functioning

Check Your Knowledge 12.5

Choose the diagnostic category that best fits each vignette. If not diagnosable, state so.

1. Joe is able to obtain sexual arousal only by rubbing his body against strangers. He has worked out a set of rituals to engage in this behavior; he knows which bus routes and times will be most crowded, chooses a bus that tends to have many women, and times his attacks so that he can leave the bus at a stop along with many other people.

2. Sam and Terry enjoy a good sexual relationship. They have mutually satisfying sex at least weekly. Occasionally, Terry likes to be tied down before sex, but she is able to enjoy sex without bondage as well. Most of their sex life involves no hint of pain or bondage.

3. Matt feels aroused only when he is able to cause pain to someone as part of engaging in sex. Most of the time, he indulges in these activities at a sadomasochism club. He has not been able to sustain a relationship with any of the women he has met in clubs. He is deeply distressed by his inability to enjoy other forms of sexuality.

4. Barry is a 40-year-old single man who has never had a sustained dating relationship or sexual partnership. Several times a week, Barry parks his car at the beach, masturbates, and then finds a way to lure a woman to his car, usually by asking for directions. He is unable to have an orgasm unless the woman notices his erection. He has been arrested three times for this behavior.

Etiology of the Paraphilic Disorders

Given that many people have interests in sexual sadism, masochism, or exhibitionism, why do some of these interests become difficult to control for some people, such that they reach a diagnosable level? As we consider possible causes of the paraphilic disorders, including neurobiological factors, early abuse, and psychological variables, keep in mind that there are many gaps in knowledge. Some research focuses on understanding paraphilic interests that do not lead to distress or impairment; this research indicates, for example, that people with paraphilic interests tend not to have histories of childhood sexual abuse or other risk factors (Långström & Seto, 2006; Richters et al., 2008). Such work does not tell us, though, why some people become unable to control their paraphilic interests and develop a paraphilic disorder. Because many people do not want to talk about their paraphilic disorders, researchers have few opportunities to understand their causes. Indeed, the vast majority of studies rely on samples of less than 25 persons (Kafka, 2010). Beyond the lack of research and the small sample sizes, most of the research focuses on men who are arrested for their sexual behavior; little is known about those whose sexual behavior does not lead to arrest. Hence, much of this literature is most relevant for understanding sexual offenders, who represent a more severe subset of those with paraphilic disorders.

Neurobiological Factors

Because the overwhelming majority of people with paraphilic disorders are men, there has been speculation that androgens (hormones like testosterone) play a role. Androgens regulate sexual desire, and sexual desire appears atypically high among some sexual offenders with paraphilic disorders. Nonetheless, men with paraphilic disorders do not appear to have high levels of testosterone or other androgens (Thibaut, De La Barra, et al., 2010).

Childhood Sexual Abuse

Childhood sexual abuse is relevant in understanding the most severe forms of paraphilic disorder. That is, across multiple studies, about 40 to 66 percent of adult sexual offenders reported a history of sexual abuse, rates that are substantially higher than the rates among those charged with nonsexual offenses or among those in the general population (Jespersen, Lalumiere, & Seto, 2009; Levenson & Grady, 2016). This suggests that sexual abuse is tied to sexual offending. Nonetheless, sexual abuse cannot be the whole story—large-scale follow-up studies of boys with confirmed sexual abuse have shown that fewer than 5 percent were charged with any type of sexual offense as adults (Ogloff, Cutajar, et al., 2012; Salter, McMillan, et al., 2003).

Psychological Factors

For some of the paraphilias, succumbing to the sexual urge can be thought of as an impulsive act, in which the person loses control over his behavior. Alcohol decreases the ability to inhibit impulses, and accordingly, many incidents of pedophilic disorder, voyeuristic disorder, and exhibitionistic disorder occur in the context of alcohol use. Others report that their sexual behaviors are more likely to happen in the context of negative moods, suggesting that sexual activity is being used to escape from negative affect.

What types of longer-term factors might set the stage for the loss of control? People with paraphilic disorders tend to show heightened impulsivity and poor emotion regulation (Ward & Beech, 2006). Men who engage in paraphilias that involve nonconsenting women or children may have hostile attitudes and a lack of empathy toward their sexual targets (Babchishin, Hanson, et al., 2015). See Focus on Discovery 12.3 for a discussion of rape.

A separate line of work focuses on pedophilia, and more specifically neurocognitive problems associated with pedophilia. On average, men with pedophilic disorder have a slightly lower IQ and higher rates of neurocognitive problems than the general population (Cantor, Blanchard, et al., 2005; Suchy, Eastvold, et al., 2014). Men with pedophilia also show minor physical anomalies related to atypical prenatal development more than those with other paraphilic sexual behaviors do (Dyshniku, Murray, et al., 2015).

Beyond the cognitive deficits related to pedophilia, there may be more than one psychological pathway to pedophilia (Knight & King, 2012). Some pedophiles show an intense preoccupation with sex, a sense of emotional compatibility with children, and a specific sexual preference for children. Other pedophiles demonstrate more general tendencies toward elevated impulsivity and psychopathy compared to the general population (Mann, Hanson, & Thornton, 2010).

Quick Summary

Neurobiological theory of paraphilic disorders has focused on excessively high levels of male hormones (testosterone), but the theory has not received strong support. Sexual offenders report higher rates of being sexually abused than do other offenders, but very few children who are abused grow up to engage in sexual offenses against others.

Alcohol use and negative affect are often immediate triggers of inappropriate sexual behaviors.

Psychological theories focus on impulsivity, poor emotion regulation, and when paraphilic behavior is directed at nonconsenting others, hostility and lack of empathy.

For pedophilia, there may be more than one pathway: some men are sexually preoccupied with children and experience a sense of emotional compatibility with children; other men have a profile of more general impulsive, psychopathic traits. Neurocognitive deficits, lower IQ, and signs of atypical prenatal development are sometimes observed in men diagnosed with pedophilic disorder.

Check Your Knowledge 12.6

Answer the questions.

1. Describe the major problems with the research literature on causes of paraphilic disorders.

2. What types of factors might contribute to the loss of control over sexual urges for those with paraphilic disorders?

Treatments and Community Prevention for the Paraphilic Disorders

We now describe motivational, cognitive behavioral, hormone, and SSRI treatments for the **paraphilic disorders**. After we discuss treatment approaches, we will turn to a discussion of issues in addressing the legal and public ramifications of sexual offending.

We know very little about the effectiveness of these treatments of paraphilic disorders. First, most of the available research on treatment focuses on men who have been charged with sexual offenses, so we know very little about treatment of those in the community. Second, very little long-term data is available. Third, because many researchers consider it unethical to withhold treatment when the consequences of sexual offenses are so severe, most studies have not randomly assigned people into control groups—very few randomized controlled trials (RCTs) are available. Indeed, no RCTs are available to consider the efficacy of SSRIs for paraphilic disorders (Balon, 2016).

What do the findings of the available RCTs indicate about treatment of paraphilic disorders? In the largest available RCT of cognitive behavioral therapy (CBT), no significant effects were observed on legal recidivism (Marques et al., 2005). RCTs show that hormone agents reduce arousal to deviant objects, as measured using penile plethysmography (Thibaut et al., 2010), but very little data is available on whether medications reduce sexual offending (Khan, Ferriter, et al., 2015).

Strategies to Enhance Motivation

Sex offenders often lack the motivation to change their illegal behavior. They may deny their problem or minimize the seriousness of their problem. Some blame the victim, even a child, for being overly seductive. Many refuse to take part in treatment, and even among those who begin treatment, many will drop out. To enhance motivation for treatment, a therapist can bolster the client's hope that he can gain control over his urges through treatment. The therapist can help the client focus on reasons for change, including the potential legal and other consequences of continued engagement in the same sexual behavior (Miller & Rollnick, 1991).

Cognitive Behavioral Treatment

In the earliest years of behavioral treatment, paraphilic disorders were narrowly viewed as attractions to inappropriate objects and activities. Looking to behavioral psychology for ways to reduce these attractions, researchers fixed on aversion therapy. Thus, a person with a boot fetish would be given a shock on the hands or a drug that produces nausea when looking at a boot, a person with pedophilic disorder when gazing at a photograph of a nude child, and so on. In the form of aversion therapy called *satiation*, men are coached to pair their paraphilic fantasies with another aversive stimulus: masturbating for 55 minutes after orgasm (Kaplan & Krueger, 2012). Over time, therapists began to use a broader array of techniques.

Cognitive interventions are often used to counter the distorted thinking of people with paraphilic disorders. For example, an exhibitionist might claim that the girls he exposes himself to are too young to be harmed by it. The therapist would counter this distortion by pointing out that the younger the victim, the worse the harm will be (Kaplan & Krueger, 2012).

Many other techniques have become common (Balon, 2016; Kaplan & Krueger, 2012). Therapists often offer social skills training, and teach sexual impulse control strategies such as distraction. As warranted, they might focus on early abuse experiences. Training in empathy toward others is another common technique; teaching the sex offender to consider how his or her behavior would affect someone else may lessen the tendency to engage in such activities. Relapse prevention, modeled after the work on substance abuse described in Chapter 10, is also an important component of many broader treatment programs. A therapist who uses relapse prevention techniques would help a person identify situations and emotions that might trigger symptomatic behavior.

Biological Treatments

A variety of biological interventions have been tried on sex offenders. Castration, or removal of the testes, was used a great deal until hormonal treatments (described next) became available (Balon, 2016). Surgical castration is not a common treatment today due to major ethical concerns.

On the other hand, several medications have been used to treat paraphilic disorders, particularly among sex offenders. Typically, these medications are used as a supplement to psychological treatment. Among men, sexual drive and functioning are regulated by androgens (such as testosterone). Hence, hormonal agents that reduce androgens have been used to treat paraphilic disorders, including medroxyprogesterone acetate (MPA, trade name Depo-Provera) and cyproterone acetate (CPA, Gyrostat; Khan et al., 2015). Ethical issues are raised about the indefinite use of hormonal agents. Long-term use of hormonal agents is associated with several negative side effects, including feminization, infertility, liver problems, osteoporosis, diabetes, and depression. Informed consent concerning these risks must be obtained, and many patients will not agree to use these drugs long term (Balon, 2016). Beyond drugs that influence hormones, SSRI antidepressants are commonly used despite the absence of evidence for this approach.

Balancing Efforts to Protect the Public Against Civil Liberties for Those with Paraphilias

Most people are frightened by sexual offenses, so balancing the protection of the public against the civil liberties of sexual offenders is not easy. Issues arise in multiple aspects of the legal process, including how diagnoses of paraphilic disorders can influence institutionalization, but also with laws concerning the public's "right to know" when a sex offender is released.

In the United States, it is generally unconstitutional to detain a person on the basis of his or her potential for *future* crimes. Nonetheless, the Supreme Court has ruled that a person deemed at high risk for a sex crime can be detained if the risk is related to a psychological disorder that diminishes the person's ability to control his or her sexual behavior. The diagnosis of paraphilia, then, has significant implications for civil liberties: receipt of this diagnosis can lead to placement in a psychiatric facility after a prison term is completed. In this context, it has been argued that particular care should be taken to ensure the validity of these diagnoses (Wakefield, 2011).

Legal statutes referred to as Megan's law allow police to publicize the whereabouts of registered sex offenders if they are considered a potential danger. Citizens can then use computerized police records to determine whether sex offenders are living in their neighborhoods. Megan's law and related statutes arose from public outrage at the brutal murder of a 2nd grader in New Jersey who was kidnapped while walking home from school. The person convicted of this crime was a twice-convicted child molester. The hope behind these laws is that they will protect against repeat offenses; to date, findings have been mixed about whether these programs are successful in reducing sexual crimes. One unintended consequence of these laws is that some have committed violent crimes toward sex offenders in their neighborhoods (Younglove & Vitello, 2003). Not surprisingly, civil liberties groups are challenging these laws. Navigating the tension between protecting the public and civil liberties for offenders is an ongoing process.

Check Your Knowledge 12.7

Answer the questions.

1. The most commonly used biological treatments to reduce sexual desire and paraphilic behaviors are:
    a. surgical castration
    b. hormonal agents and antidepressants
    c. anti-anxiety medications
    d. none of the above
2. Name four cognitive behavioral strategies used in the treatment of paraphilic disorders.
3. Describe the evidence base for the psychological and biological treatments of paraphilic disorders.

Summary

Sexual Norms

- Sexual behavior and attitudes are heavily influenced by culture, so any discussion of disorders in sexuality must be sensitive to the idea that norms are likely to change across time and place, and those norms will influence people's reports in surveys.

- Kaplan identified four phases in the sexual response cycle: desire, excitement, orgasm, and resolution. The validity of the Kaplan model for women has been criticized.

Sexual Dysfunctions

- The DSM-5 includes sexual dysfunction diagnoses relevant to arousal and desire (female sexual interest/arousal disorder, male hypoactive sexual desire disorder, erectile disorder), to orgasm (female orgasmic disorder, premature ejaculation, delayed ejaculation), and to pain (genito-pelvic pain/penetration disorder). Many people experience brief sexual symptoms, but these are not diagnosable unless they are recurrent, cause either distress or impairment, and are not explained by medical conditions.

- Research on the etiology of sexual dysfunctions is difficult to conduct, as surveys may be inaccurate and laboratory measures may be difficult to gather. Researchers have identified many different variables that contribute to sexual dysfunctions, including biological variables, previous sexual experiences, relationship issues, psychopathology, low arousal, and cognitions (for example, self-blame).

- Many effective cognitive behavioral interventions for sexual dysfunctions are available. Strategies include psychoeducation, couples therapy, cognitive interventions, sensate focus, and techniques to address more specific dysfunctions, such as directed masturbation for female orgasmic disorder, relaxation and use of dilators for genito-pelvic pain/penetration disorder, SSRIs and squeeze techniques for premature ejaculation, and PDE-5 inhibitors for erectile disorder.

Paraphilic Disorders

- The paraphilic disorders are defined by attractions and urges toward unusual sexual objects or behaviors that are persistent and lead to distress or impairment. The principal DSM-5 paraphilic disorders are fetishistic disorder, pedophilic disorder, voyeuristic disorder, exhibitionistic disorder, frotteuristic disorder, sexual sadism disorder, sexual masochism disorder, and transvestic disorder. (We do not discuss transvestic disorder.)

- Exposure to childhood sexual abuse may be a risk factor for paraphilic disorders. Alcohol use and negative affect may increase the odds of acting on sexual urges. Impulsivity and emotion dysregulation appear involved. Hostility and lack of empathy appear relevant when sexual behaviors are directed toward nonconsenting others.

- Pedophilia has been related to neurocognitive deficits and lower IQ. Some men with pedophilia are obsessed with sex and strongly attracted to children both emotionally and sexually; other men with pedophilia act out of a more general cluster of impulsive and antisocial traits.

- The research evidence regarding treatments for paraphilic disorders is limited. Treatment approaches must begin by engaging and motivating the client, which is often difficult to do. Early cognitive behavioral approaches focused on aversion therapy and cognitive techniques to challenge distorted beliefs about the consequences of sexual behaviors. Over time, cognitive behavioral therapists have also begun to use techniques to improve social skills, help people control impulses, increase empathy for potential victims, identify potential high-risk situations for the return of symptoms, and where relevant, address childhood experiences of sexual abuse. Research suggests that psychological treatments do not significantly reduce rates of legal offenses. Drugs that reduce testosterone levels have been found to reduce both sex drive and deviant sexual behaviors, but because of the side effects, there are ethical issues involved in the long-term use of these drugs. SSRI antidepressants are commonly prescribed to reduce the sexual drive of men with paraphilic disorders, but no RCTs are available.

- A diagnosis of paraphilic disorder has relevance for whether a person can be detained in a psychiatric facility for possible future crimes. Laws were passed that allowed the public to access information about where sexual offenders live, but some offenders have been victimized when such information became public.

Answers to Check Your Knowledge Questions

12.1 1. Men report higher frequency of masturbation and use of pornography than do women. 2. desire phase, excitement phase, orgasm phase, resolution phase; 3. Desire does not consistently precede the excitement phase for women, and although Kaplan relied on biological changes to define the excitement phase, biological changes do not closely mirror subjective arousal for women.

12.2 1. F (unless the problem is recurrent and leads to distress or impairment, it cannot be diagnosed); 2. T; 3. F; 4. lack of interest (or female hypoactive sexual desire/arousal disorder); 5. premature ejaculation

12.3 1. The spectator role refers to a problem in which a person becomes immersed in considering how they look and seem during a sexual encounter rather than enjoying the moment. 2. Depression is associated with a threefold increase in risk of sexual dissatisfaction and anxiety with a twofold increase.

12.4 1. The clients are instructed not to have intercourse. They are to focus on sensual touching, excluding genitals initially. They are to take turns pleasuring each other versus receiving.; 2. Directed masturbation; 3. SSRIs, and specifically dapoxetine; 4. PDE-5 inhibitors; 5. T

12.5. 1. frotteuristic disorder; 2. Not diagnosable as there is no evidence of distress or impairment; 3. Sexual sadism disorder; 4. Exhibitionistic disorder

12.6 1. Small samples comprised of sexual offenders, lack of well-validated diagnostic interviews, and few studies; 2 negative emotions, alcohol use, impulsivity, and poor emotion regulation

12.7 1. b; 2. Any 4 of the following: Covert sensitization, cognitive interventions to address maladaptive beliefs, social skills training, sexual impulse control training, therapy focused on early abuse, empathy training, relapse prevention; 3. The largest RCT for CBT showed little effect on repeat offending; hormone agents reduce sexual desire to deviant objects; no RCT is available for SSRIs; available trials typically focus on sexual offenders and little long-term data is available.

Key Terms

delayed ejaculation
desire phase
erectile disorder
excitement phase
exhibitionistic disorder
female orgasmic disorder
female sexual interest/arousal disorder
fetishistic disorder
frotteuristic disorder

genito-pelvic pain/penetration disorder
incest
male hypoactive sexual desire disorder
orgasm phase
paraphilic disorders
pedophilic disorder
penile plethysmograph
premature (early) ejaculation
resolution phase

sexual dysfunctions
sexual masochism disorder
sexual response cycle
sexual sadism disorder
spectator role
vaginal plethysmograph
voyeuristic disorder

CHAPTER 13

Disorders of Childhood

LEARNING GOALS

1. Describe the issues in the diagnosis of psychopathology in children.

2. Discuss the description, etiology, and treatments for externalizing problems, including ADHD and conduct disorder.

3. Discuss the description, etiology, and treatments for internalizing problems, including depression and anxiety disorders.

4. Understand the description, etiology, and treatments for dyslexia and intellectual disability.

5. Describe the symptoms, causes, and treatments for autism spectrum disorder.

Clinical Case

Eric

"Eric. Eric? Eric!" His teacher's voice and the laughter of his classmates roused the boy from his daydreaming. Glancing at the book of the girl sitting next to him, he noticed that the class was pages ahead of him. He was supposed to be answering a question about the Declaration of Independence, but he had been lost in thought, wondering about what seats he and his father would have for the baseball game they'd be attending that evening. A tall, lanky 12-year-old, Eric had just begun 7th grade. His history teacher had already warned him about being late to class and not paying attention, but Eric just couldn't seem to get from one class to the next without stopping for drinks of water or to investigate an altercation between classmates. In class, he was rarely prepared to answer when the teacher called on him, and he usually forgot to write down the homework assignment. He already had a reputation among his peers as an "airhead."

Eric's relief at the sound of the bell was quickly replaced by anxiety as he reached the field for baseball tryouts. Despite his speed and physical strength, Eric was always picked last for sports teams. During tryouts, the boys were assigned into two teams. His team was up to bat first, and Eric sat down to wait his

turn. Absorbed in studying a pile of pebbles at his feet, he failed to notice his team's third out and missed the change of innings. The other team had already come in from the outfield before Eric noticed that his team was out in the field—too late to avoid the irate yells of the coach to take his place at third base. Resolved to watch for his chance to field the ball, Eric nonetheless found himself without his glove on when a sharply hit ball rocketed his way; he had taken it off to toss it in the air in the middle of the pitch.

At home, Eric's father told him he had to finish his homework before they could go to the Giants game. He had only one page of math problems and was determined to finish them quickly. Thirty minutes later, his father emerged from the shower to find Eric building an elaborate Lego structure on the floor of his room; the math homework was only half done. In exasperation, Eric's father left for the game without him.

At bedtime, frustrated and discouraged, Eric was unable to sleep. He often lay awake for what seemed like hours, reviewing the disappointments of the day and berating himself for his failures. On this night, he ruminated about his lack of friends, the frustration of his teachers, and his parents' exhortations to pay attention and "get it together." Feeling hopeless about doing better, despite his daily resolve, Eric often found his thoughts turning to suicide. Tonight, he reviewed his fantasy of wandering out into the street in front of a passing car. Although Eric had never acted on his suicidal thoughts, he frequently replayed in his mind his parents' sorrow and remorse, his classmates' irritation with him, and the concern of his teachers.

Childhood disorders, like adult disorders, involve a combination of genetic, neurobiological, behavioral, cognitive, and social factors in their etiology and treatment. The number of children diagnosed with and treated for different psychological disorders has dramatically increased in the past decade, but not without controversy (see Focus on Discovery 13.3 later in this chapter). For example, the number of people who had received a diagnosis of ADHD (attention-deficit/hyperactivity disorder) in the United States increased 41 percent from 2003 to 2012 (Hinshaw & Scheffler, 2014)! Also controversial is the tremendous increase in medication prescribed for children. In fact, most antipsychotics prescribed for children are for "off label" uses; that is, they are intended to treat disorders or symptoms, such as ADHD and oppositional defiant disorder, that have not been approved by the FDA for these disorders (Harrison, Cluxton-Keller, & Gross, 2012; Olfson, Blanco, et al., 2012).

In this chapter we discuss several of the disorders that are most likely to arise in childhood and adolescence. We first consider disorders involving inattention, impulsivity, and disruptive behavior, followed by depression and anxiety disorders. Finally, we discuss disorders involving problems in the acquisition of cognitive, language, motor, or social skills. These include learning disorders, intellectual disability, and autism spectrum disorder (ASD).

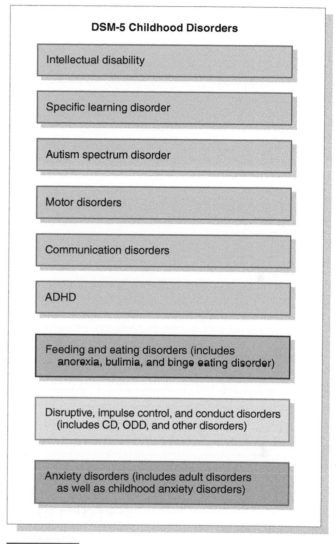

FIGURE 13.1 DSM-5 childhood disorders.

Classification and Diagnosis of Childhood Disorders

Before making a diagnosis of a disorder in children, clinicians must first consider what is typical for a particular age. Children who lie on the floor kicking and screaming when they don't get their way are assessed differently at age 2 than at age 7. The field of **developmental psychopathology** focuses on the disorders of childhood within the context of development over the life span, enabling us to identify behaviors that are considered appropriate at one stage but not at another. Childhood disorders are shown in **Figure 13.1**.

The more prevalent childhood disorders are often divided into two broad domains, externalizing disorders and internalizing disorders. **Externalizing disorders** are characterized by more outward-directed behaviors, such as aggressiveness, noncompliance, overactivity, and impulsiveness; the category includes attention-deficit/hyperactivity disorder, conduct disorder, and oppositional defiant disorder. **Internalizing disorders** are characterized by more inward-focused experiences and behaviors, such as depression, social withdrawal, and anxiety; the category includes childhood anxiety and mood disorders. Children and adolescents may exhibit symptoms from both domains, as described in the Clinical Case of Eric.

Focus on Discovery 13.1 discusses the possible role of culture in the prevalence childhood disorders.

Focus on Discovery 13.1

The Role of Culture in Internalizing and Externalizing Behaviors

The values of a culture may play a role in whether a certain pattern of child behavior develops or is considered a problem. Although studies have found that internalizing and externalizing problems are observed in children around the world (e.g., Rescorla, Achenbach, et al., 2011), there are more differences within a culture or society than there are among societies.

One study found that in Thailand, the children who were more commonly referred to mental health clinics for treatment were those with internalizing behavior problems such as fearfulness, whereas in the United States, the children referred for treatment were those with externalizing behavior problems such as aggressiveness and hyperactivity (Weisz, Suwanlert, et al., 1987). The researchers attributed these differences to the fact that Buddhism, which disapproves of and discourages aggression, is widely practiced in Thailand. In other words, cultural sanctions against acting out in aggressive ways may have kept these behaviors from developing at the rate that they do in the United States. One of the issues in this study was that the researchers only used assessment measures that were based on norms from U.S. samples, leaving open the possibility that behavior differences between the two cultures were missed because they were not validly assessed for both cultures (see Chapter 3 for more discussion of culture and assessment).

Indeed, follow-up studies suggest that the behavior problems described in the same terms may not really be the same across Thai and U.S. cultures (Weisz, Weiss, et al., 2003, 2006). The researchers compared specific behavior problems (e.g., somatic complaints, aggressive behavior) and the broad categories of internalizing and externalizing behaviors, using U.S. and Thai assessment measures. Internalizing and externalizing behaviors were the same in Thai and U.S. children, but more specific problems within those categories were not. Among boys, somatic complaints were seen consistently across cultures, but shyness was seen less consistently. Among girls, shyness was seen consistently across cultures but verbal aggressive behavior was not.

These studies point to the importance of studying psychopathology across cultures. It is dangerous to assume that the measures we develop to assess psychopathology in the United States will work as well in other cultures. As Weisz and colleagues point out, our theories about the causes of psychopathology should take into account cultural variation in factors such as parenting practices, beliefs, and values and the ways in which parents report on their child's behavior problems. This remains an urgent and important challenge for our field.

Thai teenagers serving as novices in a Buddhist temple. Buddhist culture may contribute to the relatively low prevalence of externalizing disorders in Thailand.

Bartosz Hadyniak/the Agency Collection/Getty Images

Externalizing Disorders: ADHD and Conduct Disorder

Attention-Deficit/Hyperactivity Disorder

The term *hyperactive* is familiar to most people, especially parents and teachers. The child who is constantly in motion—tapping fingers, jiggling legs, poking others for no apparent reason, talking out of turn, and fidgeting—is often called hyperactive. Often, these children also have difficulty concentrating on the task at hand for an appropriate period of time. When such problems are severe and persistent enough, these children may meet the criteria for diagnosis of **attention-deficit/hyperactivity disorder (ADHD)**.

Clinical Descriptions, Prevalence, and Prognosis of ADHD

Clinical Descriptions   What distinguishes the typical range of hyperactive behaviors from a diagnosable disorder? When these behaviors are extreme for a given developmental period, persistent across different situations, and linked to significant impairments in functioning, the diagnosis of ADHD may be appropriate (Hinshaw & Scheffler, 2014).

Children with ADHD seem to have more difficulty than others in controlling their activity in situations that call for sitting still, such as in the classroom or at mealtimes. When asked to be quiet, they appear unable to stop moving or talking. Their activities and movements may seem haphazard. They may quickly wear out their shoes and clothing, smash their toys, and exhaust their families and teachers.

Many children with ADHD struggle to get along with peers and to establish friendships (Blachman & Hinshaw, 2002; Hinshaw & Melnick, 1995), perhaps because their behavior can be aggressive and intrusive. Although these children are usually friendly and talkative, they often miss subtle social cues, such as noticing when other children are tiring of their constant jiggling. Unfortunately, children with ADHD often overestimate their ability to navigate social situations with peers (Hoza, Murray-Close, et al., 2010). A longitudinal study of children with and without ADHD who were followed up every year for 6 years found that poor social skills, aggressive behavior, and self-overestimation of performance in social situations all predicted problems with peers up to 6 years later. The researchers also found "vicious cycles" in the areas of poor social skills, aggressive behavior, and overestimation of one's social abilities, which predicted a decline in these abilities at the next follow-up, which in turn predicted greater problems with peers at the next follow-up (Murray-Close, Hoza, et al., 2010).

In another study, children were asked to instant-message (IM) other children in what appeared to be an online chat room (Mikami, Huang-Pollack, et al., 2007). In reality, the children were interacting with four computer-simulated peers in the chat room, and all children got the same IMs from the simulated peers. The researchers evaluated the participants' messages and their reported experiences of the chat elicited during subsequent interviews. Children with ADHD were more likely to IM statements that were hostile and off the topic than were children without ADHD, and children's chat room experiences were related to other measures of social skills difficulties, suggesting that the ability to interact even when not face-to-face is also impaired among children with ADHD.

DSM-5 Criteria for Attention-Deficit/Hyperactivity Disorder

- Either A or B:

  A. Six or more manifestations of inattention present for at least 6 months to a maladaptive degree and greater than what would be expected given a person's developmental level, e.g., careless mistakes, not listening well, not following instructions, easily distracted, forgetful in daily activities

  B. Six or more manifestations of hyperactivity-impulsivity present for at least 6 months to a maladaptive degree and greater than what would be expected given a person's developmental level, e.g., fidgeting, running about

inappropriately (in adults, restlessness), acting as if "driven by a motor," interrupting or intruding, incessant talking

- Several of the above present before age 12

- Present in two or more settings, e.g., at home, school, or, work

- Significant impairment in social, academic, or occupational functioning

- For people age 17 or older, only five signs of inattention and/or five signs of hyperactivity-impulsivity are needed to meet the diagnosis

---

Children with ADHD are often singled out very quickly and rejected or neglected by their peers. For example, in a study of previously unacquainted boys at a summer camp, boys with ADHD who exhibited a number of externalizing behaviors, such as overt aggression and noncompliance, were regarded quite negatively by their peers during the first day of camp, and these impressions remained unchanged throughout the 6-week camp period (Erhardt & CPPRG, 1994; Hinshaw, Zupan, et al., 1997).

ADHD in the DSM-5 and Comorbidities The DSM-5 includes three specifiers to indicate which symptoms predominate:

1. Predominantly inattentive presentation: children whose problems are primarily those of poor attention

2. Predominantly hyperactive-impulsive presentation: children whose difficulties result primarily from hyperactive/impulsive behavior

3. Combined presentation: children who have both sets of problems

Stephen Hinshaw, a renowned developmental psychopathology researcher and expert on mental illness stigma, is conducting one of the largest ongoing studies of girls with ADHD.

Most children with ADHD meet the criteria for the combined specifier. Children with the predominantly inattentive specifier have more difficulties with focused attention, perhaps associated with problems involving dopamine and the prefrontal cortex (Volkow, Wang, et al., 2009).

ADHD and conduct disorder (discussed later in this chapter) frequently co-occur and share some features in common (Beauchaine, Hinshaw, & Pang, 2010). There are some differences, however. ADHD is associated more with off-task behavior in school, cognitive and achievement deficits, and a better long-term prognosis.

When these two disorders occur in the same child, the worst features of each are manifest. Such children exhibit the most serious antisocial behavior, are most likely to be rejected by their peers, have the worst academic achievement, and have the poorest prognosis (Hinshaw & Lee, 2003). Girls with both ADHD and conduct disorder exhibit more antisocial behavior, other psychopathology, and risky sexual behavior than girls with only ADHD (Monuteaux, Faraone, et al., 2007).

Internalizing disorders, such as anxiety and depression, also frequently co-occur with ADHD. Estimates suggest that as many as 30 percent of children with ADHD may have comorbid internalizing disorders (e.g., Jensen, Martin, et al., 1997; MTA Cooperative Group, 1999b). A longitudinal study of girls with ADHD found that young women who had experienced childhood maltreatment were more likely to experience internalizing disorders as well as to attempt suicide and engage in self-harm compared with those who had not been maltreated as children (Guendelman, Owens, et al., 2016). In addition, about 15–30 percent of children with ADHD have a learning disorder (Barkley, DuPaul, & McMurray, 1990; Casey, Rourke, & Del Dotto, 1996).

Prevalence By some accounts, the prevalence of ADHD has risen dramatically in the past decade, ranging from 8 to 11 percent compared with older estimates of 3–7 percent (Merikangas, He, et al., 2010). A nationally representative study conducted by the Centers for Disease Control and Prevention (CDC) reported a prevalence rate of 11 percent in 2011 (Visser, Danielson, et al., 2014). By contrast, a study from one large health care system in California reported a prevalence rate of just over 3 percent (Getahun, Jacobsen, et al., 2013). Why the difference in rates? Several explanations are possible, suggesting that the increase is due to factors other than an actual increase in the disorder. For example, most children receive a diagnosis after a brief visit with a pediatrician, but correct diagnoses require careful and thorough assessments (Hinshaw & Scheffler, 2014). Thus, many children may be getting the diagnosis when it is not warranted.

Children in some states, such as North Carolina, are far more likely to get the diagnosis than children in other states, such as California, and this appears to be largely due to the education policies in the states (Hinshaw & Scheffler, 2014). Specifically, states like North Carolina that had school accountability standards in place prior to the national standards enacted in 2001 had strong incentives to remove children from the classroom (and thereby from classroom test score averages) that were disruptive and inattentive. Indeed, many children with ADHD are placed in special educational programs because of their difficulty in adjusting to a typical classroom environment (Barkley et al., 1990). Thus, these children's test scores would be counted as part of the overall school's performance statistics. As Hinshaw and Scheffler (2014) noted, "labels that produce mandated services tend to get used" (p. 77).

Sex Differences Evidence indicates that ADHD is three times more common in boys than in girls (Kessler, Avenevoli, et al., 2012; Merikangas et al., 2010), and for years ADHD studies focused mostly on boys. Two groups of researchers have conducted large and long-term prospective studies of ADHD in girls (Biederman & Faraone, 2004; Hinshaw, 2002). Here are some of the key findings at the initial and follow-up assessments as many as 16 years later (Biederman,

Petty, et al., 2010; Hinshaw, Carte, et al., 2002; Hinshaw, Owens, et al., 2006; Hinshaw, Owens, et al., 2012; Owens, Zalecki, et al., 2017):

- Girls with the DSM-IV-TR combined subtype (now a specifier in DSM-5) were more likely to have a comorbid diagnosis of conduct disorder or oppositional defiant disorder than girls without ADHD, and this difference remained 5 years after initial diagnosis.

- Girls with ADHD were viewed more negatively by peers than girls without ADHD. In early adulthood, girls with ADHD preferred online social interactions (e.g., Facebook) more than actual interactions but the quality of their online Facebook interactions were not as rich (e.g., fewer friends, less support from friends; Mikami, Szwedo, et al., 2015).

- Girls with ADHD were likely to have internalizing symptoms (anxiety, depression) than were girls without ADHD, and this remained true 16 years after initial diagnosis.

- Girls with ADHD exhibited several neuropsychological deficits, particularly in executive functioning (e.g., planning, solving problems), compared with girls without ADHD.

- By adolescence, girls with ADHD were more likely to have symptoms of an eating disorder and substance abuse than girls without ADHD (Mikami, Hinshaw, et al., 2010). Fortunately, problems with eating and substance abuse appeared to remit by early adulthood (Owens et al., 2017).

- By early adulthood, young women who continued to meet diagnostic criteria for ADHD were more likely to have internalizing and externalizing psychopathology than young women without ADHD or young women who no longer met criteria for ADHD.

Aggression is not uncommon among boys with ADHD, and it contributes to their being rejected by peers.

ADHD in Adulthood   At one time it was thought that ADHD simply went away as children entered adolescence. However, this belief has been challenged by numerous longitudinal studies (Barkley, Fischer, et al., 2002; Hinshaw et al., 2006; Lee, Lahey, et al., 2008; Owens et al., 2017; Weiss & Hechtman, 1993). Although some children show reduced severity of symptoms in adolescence and early adulthood, 65–80 percent of children with ADHD still have symptoms associated with impairments in adolescence (Biederman, Monuteaux, et al., 2006; Hinshaw et al., 2006; Lahey, Lee, et al., 2016). **Table 13.1** provides a sample of behaviors that are found

TABLE 13.1   Behaviors in Adolescents With and Without ADHD

Behavior	Percentage of Adolescents Who Show This Behavior	
	With ADHD	**Without ADHD**
Blurts out answers	65.0	10.6
Is easily distracted	82.1	15.2
Doesn't complete tasks before moving to another	77.2	16.7
Doesn't sustain attention	79.7	16.7
Doesn't follow instructions	83.7	12.1
Doesn't listen to others well	80.5	15.2
Engages in physically dangerous activities	37.4	3.0
Fidgets	73.2	10.6
Finds it hard to play quietly	39.8	7.6
Gets out of seat often	60.2	3.0
Interrupts others	65.9	10.6
Loses things needed for tasks	62.6	12.1
Talks a lot	43.9	6.1

Source: Adapted from Barkley et al. (1990).

more often among adolescents with ADHD than among adolescents without it. Many children with ADHD do not appear to take a "hit" with respect to academic achievement, however—many studies indicate that achievement is within the average range for both adolescent boys (Lee et al., 2008) and girls (Hinshaw et al., 2006).

In early adulthood, 60–74 percent of those diagnosed with ADHD as children continue to exhibit symptoms that are associated with impairment in several domains (Faraone, Biederman, & Mick, 2005; Hinshaw et al., 2012; Owens et al., 2017). For example, in a large prospective study of girls with ADHD, 57 percent of girls diagnosed with ADHD at ages 6–12 continue to meet diagnostic criteria 16 years later, and 74 percent of the girls continued to exhibit ADHD symptoms (Owens et al., 2017). Unfortunately, the young women who continued to meet ADHD diagnostic criteria in their mid-20s exhibited difficulties with work, educational achievement, and social functioning (Owens et al., 2017). Thus, ADHD symptoms may decline with age, but for many people they do not entirely go away, and these persistent symptoms are linked with difficulties in other areas of functioning.

Michael Phelps won more Olympic medals (28) than any other athlete in history. He won his medals (23 gold, three silver, two bronze) in swimming. He also struggled with ADHD as a child.

Etiology of ADHD

Genetic Factors Substantial evidence indicates that genetic factors play a role in ADHD (Thapar, Langley, et al., 2007). Adoption (Sprich, Biederman, et al., 2000) and twin studies (Burt, 2009a; Larsson, Chang, et al., 2014) indicate that ADHD has a genetic component, with heritability estimates as high as 70–80 percent (Sullivan, Daly, & O'Donovan, 2012). Molecular genetics studies that seek to discover the multiple genes linked to ADHD have revealed several candidate genes. Most notable are those genes associated with the neurotransmitter dopamine. Dopamine receptor genes have been implicated in ADHD, including *DRD4* and *DRD5*, and a dopamine transporter gene called *DAT1*; meta-analyses showed that these have modest effect sizes (Gizer, Ficks, & Waldman, 2009; Wu, Xia, et al., 2012). An additional gene, *SNAP-25*, that codes for a protein that promotes plasticity (i.e., adaptability) of neuron synapses has also been associated with ADHD (Forero, Arboleda, et al., 2009; Gizer et al., 2009). Even with these promising findings, most investigators agree that a single gene will not ultimately be found to account for ADHD (Nigg, 2013). Rather, several genes interacting with each other and with environmental factors will provide the most complete picture of the role of genes in ADHD. For example, studies have found that the *DRD4* or *DAT1* genes are associated with increased risk of ADHD only among those who also had environmental factors—namely, prenatal maternal nicotine or alcohol use (Brookes, Mill, et al., 2006; Neuman, Lobos, et al., 2007). In addition, polygene (i.e., multiple genes; see Chapter 2) scores derived from meta-analyses of genetic factors are higher in those with ADHD compared with those without ADHD (Hamshere, Langley, et al., 2013).

Neurobiological Factors Studies suggest that brain structure, function, and connectivity differ in children with and without ADHD, particularly in areas of the brain linked to the neurotransmitter dopamine. For example, studies of brain structure have found that dopaminergic areas of the brain, such as the caudate nucleus, globus pallidus, and frontal lobes, are smaller in children with ADHD than in children without ADHD (Castellanos, Lee, et al., 2002; Swanson, Kinsbourne, et al., 2007). A meta-analysis of 55 brain-imaging studies found that children with ADHD exhibit less activation in frontal areas of the brain (Cortese, Kelly, et al., 2012). Moreover, children with ADHD perform poorly on neuropsychological tests that rely on the frontal lobes, such as selective attention (i.e., selecting to focus on one thing and not another; Mueller, Hong, et al., 2017), working memory (i.e., how much you can hold in mind at any given time while doing a task; Fair, Bathula, et al., 2012), and inhibiting behavioral responses (Barkley, 1997). This evidence provides further support for the theory that a basic deficit in this part of the brain may be related to the disorder (Matthews, Nigg, & Fair, 2014; Nigg & Casey, 2005).

Perinatal and Prenatal Factors Other neurobiological risk factors for ADHD include a number of perinatal and prenatal complications. Low birth weight, for example, is a predictor of the development of ADHD (e.g., Bhutta, Cleves, et al., 2002). However, the impact of low birth weight on later symptoms of ADHD can be mitigated by greater maternal warmth (Tully, Arseneault, et al., 2004).

Environmental Toxins Research has found that elements of the diet, particularly additives, may influence ADHD symptoms for a subset of children. Two meta-analyses reported small effect sizes for artificial food coloring on hyperactive behavior among children with ADHD (Nigg, Lewis, et al., 2012; Schnab & Trinh, 2004). Thus, there is limited evidence that food additives impact hyperactive behavior. The popular view that refined sugar can cause ADHD has not been supported by careful research (Wolraich, Wilson, & White, 1995).

Some evidence suggests that higher blood levels of lead may be associated to a small degree with symptoms of ADHD (Braun, Kahn, et al., 2006). However, most children with higher blood levels of lead do not develop ADHD, and most children with ADHD do not show elevated blood levels. Nevertheless, given the unfortunate frequency with which children are exposed to low levels of lead, investigators continue to examine how lead exposure might play a role, perhaps by influencing other cognitive abilities.

Nicotine—specifically, maternal smoking—may play a role in the development of ADHD. A review of 24 studies examining the association between maternal smoking and ADHD found that exposure to tobacco in utero was associated with ADHD symptoms (Linnet, Dalsgaard, et al., 2003). However, an interesting study calls this linkage into question. Thapar and colleagues (2009) examined ADHD symptoms in the offspring of two groups of mothers who were regular smokers when pregnant. One group of smoking mothers delivered babies that were not genetically related to them (e.g., surrogate mother delivering a genetically unrelated baby for another family); the other group of mothers delivered babies that were genetically related. The researchers reasoned that if maternal smoking during pregnancy was an important factor in ADHD, smoking ought to be related to ADHD symptoms in the offspring from both groups of mothers. By contrast, if genetic factors were important, then the association between smoking and ADHD symptoms ought to be higher in the offspring of genetically related mothers. They found that ADHD symptoms were related to maternal smoking in both groups, but the association was significantly higher in children whose genetically related mothers smoked during pregnancy. These findings suggest that smoking might not be a causal factor by itself but that it is related to other maternal behavior and psychopathology that might increase the risk of ADHD.

Family Factors in ADHD Family factors are also important in ADHD, particularly in their interaction with neurobiological factors. For example, the parent–child relationship interacts with neurobiological factors in a complex way to contribute to ADHD symptom expression (Hinshaw et al., 1997). Just as parents of children with ADHD may give them more commands and have negative interactions with them (Anderson, Hinshaw, & Simmel, 1994; Heller, Baker, et al., 1996), so these children have been found to be less compliant and more negative in interactions with their parents (Barkley, Karlsson, & Pollard, 1985; Tallmadge & Barkley, 1983). Certainly, it must be difficult to parent a child who is impulsive, aggressive, noncompliant, and unable to follow instructions (Wells, Epstein, et al., 2000).

It is also important to consider a parent's own history of ADHD. As noted earlier, ADHD appears to have a substantial genetic component. Thus, it is not surprising that many parents of children with ADHD have ADHD themselves. In one study that examined couples' parenting practices with their ADHD children, fathers who had a diagnosis of ADHD were less effective parents, suggesting that parental psychopathology may make parenting more difficult (Arnold, O'Leary, & Edwards, 1997). Family characteristics may well contribute to maintaining or exacerbating the symptoms and consequences of ADHD; however, there is little evidence to suggest that families cause ADHD (Johnston & Marsh, 2001).

Treatment of ADHD ADHD is typically treated with medication and with behavioral therapies based on operant conditioning principles.

Children born to mothers who smoked cigarettes during pregnancy have an increased risk for ADHD.

Stimulant Medications Stimulant medications, such as methylphenidate, or Ritalin, have been prescribed for ADHD since the early 1960s. Other medications approved by the Food and Drug Administration (FDA) to treat ADHD include Adderall, Concerta, and Strattera. A report from a company that managed 90 million prescriptions in the United States found that more than 80 percent of children with ADHD had been given a prescription for stimulant medications, including almost 10 percent of all adolescent boys (Express Scripts Lab, 2014). The prescription of these medications often continues into adolescence and adulthood because of accumulating evidence that the symptoms of ADHD do not usually disappear with the passage of time. The number of adults taking stimulant medication increased more than 50 percent from 2008 to 2012 (Express Scripts Lab, 2014). In 2016, stimulant medications prescribed for "attention disorders" were in the top 15 of *all medications* prescribed from birth to age 54; they were the number one type of medication prescribed for children ages 0–19 (Express Scripts Lab, 2017).

The drugs used to treat ADHD reduce disruptive behavior and impulsivity and improve ability to focus attention (Hinshaw & Scheffler, 2014). Numerous controlled studies comparing stimulants with placebos in double-blind designs have shown short-term improvements in concentration, goal-directed activity, classroom behavior, and social interactions with parents, teachers, and peers, as well as reductions in aggressiveness and impulsivity in about 75 percent of children with ADHD (Spencer, Biederman, et al., 1996; Swanson, McBurnett, et al., 1995). These drugs appear to help in these domains by interacting with the dopamine system in the brain (Volkow, Wang, et al., 2011).

The Multimodal Treatment of Children with ADHD (MTA) study is an influential and well-designed randomized controlled trial of treatments for ADHD. Conducted at six different sites for 14 months with nearly 600 children with ADHD, the study compared standard community-based care with three other treatments: (1) medication alone, (2) medication plus intensive behavioral treatment involving both parents and teachers, and (3) intensive behavioral treatment alone. Over the 14-month period, children receiving medication alone had fewer ADHD symptoms than children receiving intensive behavioral treatment alone. The combined treatment was slightly superior to the medication alone and had the advantage of not requiring as high a dosage of Ritalin to reduce ADHD symptoms. In addition, the combined treatment yielded improved functioning in areas such as social skills more than did medication alone. The medication alone and the combined treatment were superior to community-based care, although behavioral treatment alone was not (MTA Cooperative Group, 1999a, 1999b).

Despite the initially promising findings from the MTA study, additional follow-ups from this study have not been quite as encouraging, at least where medication is concerned (Hinshaw & Arnold, 2015). Importantly, all the children maintained the gains made during the 14-month treatment, even as they all returned to receiving standard community care, and this was true at the 3-, 6-, and 8-year follow-ups. However, children in the medication alone or the combined treatment groups were no longer doing better than children who received intensive behavioral treatment or standard community care at the 3-year follow-up (Jensen, Arnold, et al., 2007) or the 6- and 8-year follow-ups (Molina, Hinshaw, et el., 2009). In other words, the relatively superior effects of medication that were observed in the combined treatment and medication alone groups did not persist beyond the study, at least for some of the children (Swanson, Hinshaw, et al., 2007).

Does this mean that medication does not work? Not necessarily. The MTA study demonstrated that carefully prescribed and managed stimulant medication is effective for children with ADHD. However, medication as it is administered in the community does not appear to offer any benefits above and beyond other forms of treatment, according to these MTA follow-up studies.

Additional randomized controlled trials have examined the efficacy of different doses. In a smaller study of 48 children with ADHD, Pelham and colleagues have found that children do well with about half the standard dose prescribed in the community in terms of their classroom and social behavior (Fabiano, Pelham, et al., 2007; Pelham, Burrows-MacLean, et al., 2014)

These findings are important in light of the side effects that stimulant medication can have, such as transient loss of appetite, weight loss, stomach pain, reduction in

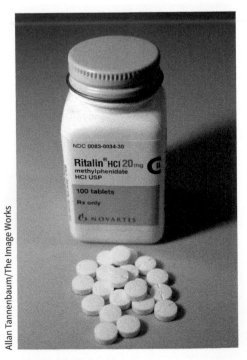

Ritalin is a commonly prescribed and effective drug treatment for ADHD.

Allan Tannenbaum/The Image Works

height, and sleep problems. In 2006 and again in 2011, the FDA recommended but did not mandate that a "black box" warning, the strongest possible safety warning the FDA can issue for medications, about cardiovascular risks (e.g., heart attack) be added to stimulant medications.

Psychological Treatment Other treatments for ADHD involve parent training and changes in classroom management (Chronis, Jones, & Raggi, 2006). These programs have demonstrated at least short-term success in improving both social and academic behavior. In these treatments, children's behavior is monitored at home and in school, and they are reinforced for behaving appropriately—for example, for remaining in their seats and working on assignments. Point systems and daily report cards (DRCs) are typical components of these programs. Children earn points or stars for behaving in certain ways; the children can then spend their earnings for rewards. The DRC also allows parents to see how their child is doing in school. The focus of these programs is on improving academic work, completing household tasks, or learning specific social skills rather than on reducing ADHD symptoms. Parent-training programs are also effective, although it is unclear whether they improve children's behavior beyond the effects of treatment with medication (MTA Cooperative Group, 1999a, 1999b).

Point systems and star charts, which are common in classrooms, are particularly useful in the treatment of ADHD.

Lew Merrim/Science Source

Findings from the MTA study indicate that intensive behavioral therapies can be very helpful to children with ADHD. In that study, some of the children participated in an intensive 8-week summer program that included several validated behavioral treatments. At the end of the summer program, children receiving the combined treatment had very few significant improvements compared with children receiving the intensive behavioral treatment alone (Arnold, et al., 2003; Pelham, Gnagy, Greiner, et al., 2000). This finding suggests that intensive behavioral therapy may be as effective as Ritalin combined with a less intensive behavioral therapy.

Conduct Disorder

Before discussing the externalizing disorder known as conduct disorder, we will briefly discuss two other related but less well-understood disorders.

Intermittent explosive disorder (IED) involves recurrent verbal or physical aggressive outbursts that are far out of proportion to the circumstances. What distinguishes IED from conduct disorder is that the aggression is impulsive and not preplanned toward other people (American Psychiatric Association, 2013). For example, a child with IED may have an aggressive outburst after not getting his or her way but would not plan aggressive retaliation.

There is some debate as to whether another DSM disorder, *oppositional defiant disorder* (ODD), is distinct from conduct disorder, a precursor to it, or an earlier and milder manifestation of it (Hinshaw & Lee, 2003; Lahey, McBurnett, & Loeber, 2000). ODD is diagnosed if a child does not meet the criteria for conduct disorder—most especially, extreme physical aggressiveness—but exhibits such behaviors as losing his or her temper, arguing with adults, repeatedly refusing to comply with requests from adults, deliberately doing things to annoy others, and being angry, spiteful, touchy, or vindictive. The National Comorbidity Study—Adolescent (NCS-A) interviewed

Conduct disorder is diagnosed among those who are aggressive, steal, lie, and vandalize property.

Ken Lax/Science Source

over 10,000 adolescents age13–17 and found the 12-month prevalence rate of ODD to be 8.3 percent (Kessler et al., 2012).

ODD and ADHD frequently occur together, but ODD is different from ADHD in that the defiant behavior is not thought to arise from attentional deficits or impulsiveness. One manifestation of difference is that children with ODD are more deliberate in their unruly behavior than children with ADHD. Although conduct disorder is three to four times more common among boys than among girls, research suggests that boys are only slightly more likely to have ODD, and some studies find no difference in prevalence rates for ODD between boys and girls (Loeber, Burke, et al., 2000; Merikangas et al., 2010).

Clinical Description, Prevalence, and Prognosis of Conduct Disorder

Perhaps more than any other childhood disorder, **conduct disorder** is defined by the impact of the child's behavior on people and surroundings.

Conduct Disorder in DSM-5 The DSM-5 criteria for conduct disorder focus on aggressive behaviors (e.g., physical cruelty to people or animals, serious rule violations (e.g., truancy), property destruction, and deceitfulness. Often the behavior is marked by callousness, viciousness, and lack of remorse.

DSM-5 includes a "limited prosocial emotions" diagnostic specifier for children who have what are referred to as callous and unemotional traits. These traits refer to characteristics such as a lack of remorse, empathy, and guilt, and shallow emotions. A longitudinal study found that children with high levels of conduct problems and high levels of callous and unemotional traits had more problems with symptoms, peers, and families compared with children with conduct problems but low levels of callous and unemotional traits (Fontaine, McCrory, et al., 2011). A comprehensive review of callous and unemotional traits in children and adolescence revealed that these traits are associated with a more severe course, more cognitive deficits, more antisocial behavior, poorer response to treatment, and perhaps distinct etiologies (Frick, Ray, et al., 2014).

Comorbidities and Longitudinal Course Many children with conduct disorder display other problems, such as substance abuse and internalizing disorders. Some research suggests that conduct disorder precedes substance use problems (Nock, Kazdin, et al., 2006), but other findings suggest that conduct disorder and substance use occur concomitantly, with the two conditions exacerbating each other (Loeber et al., 2000).

Anxiety and depression are common among children with conduct disorder, with comorbidity estimates varying from 15 to 45 percent (Loeber & Keenan, 1994; Loeber et al., 2000). Evidence suggests that conduct disorder precedes depression and most anxiety disorders, with the exceptions of specific phobias and social anxiety, which appear to precede conduct disorder (Nock et al., 2006).

How early does conduct disorder begin? Studies estimate that as many as 7 percent of preschool children exhibit the symptoms of conduct disorder (Egger & Angold, 2006). One longitudinal study assessed a group of preschool children at age 3 and again at age 6

DSM-5 Criteria for Conduct Disorder

- Repetitive and persistent behavior pattern that violates the basic rights of others or conventional social norms as manifested by the presence of three or more of the following in the previous 12 months and at least one of them in the previous 6 months:

  A. Aggression to people and animals, e.g., bullying, initiating physical fights, physical cruelty to people or animals, forcing someone into sexual activity

  B. Destruction of property, e.g., fire-setting, vandalism

  C. Deceitfulness or theft, e.g., breaking into another's house or car, conning, shoplifting

  D. Serious violation of rules, e.g., staying out at night before age 13 in defiance of parental rules, truancy before age 13

- Significant impairment in social, academic, or occupational functioning

(Rolon-Arroyo, Arnold, & Harvey, 2013). Parents were interviewed using diagnostic interviews at the two time points. The researchers found that conduct disorder symptoms at age 3 predicted conduct disorder symptoms at age 6, even when controlling for symptoms of ADHD and ODD. These findings suggest that assessing conduct disorder early is important because these symptoms are not just manifestations of typical developmentally disruptive behaviors.

Moffitt (1993) theorized that two different courses of conduct problems should be distinguished. Some people seem to show a life-course-persistent pattern of antisocial behavior, beginning to show conduct problems by age 3 and continuing to commit serious transgressions into adulthood. Others are adolescence-limited—they have typical childhoods, engage in high levels of antisocial

Children with the life-course-persistent type of conduct disorder continue to have trouble with the law into their mid-20s and beyond.

behavior during adolescence, and have typical, nonproblematic adulthoods. Moffitt proposed that the adolescence-limited form of antisocial behavior is the result of a maturity gap between the adolescent's physical maturation and his or her opportunity to assume adult responsibilities and obtain the rewards usually accorded such behavior.

Cumulative evidence supports this distinction (Moffitt, 2007). The original sample from which Moffitt and colleagues made the life-course-persistent and adolescence-limited distinction was a sample of over 1000 people from Dunedin, New Zealand, who were assessed every 2 or 3 years from age 3 to age 32. Both boys and girls with the life-course-persistent form of conduct disorder had an early onset of antisocial behavior that persisted through adolescence and into adulthood. As children they had a number of other problems, such as academic underachievement, neuropsychological deficits, and comorbid ADHD (Moffitt & Caspi, 2001). Other evidence supports the notion that children with the life-course-persistent type have more severe neuropsychological deficits and family psychopathology, and these findings have been replicated across cultures (Hinshaw & Lee, 2003).

Those who were classified as life-course-persistent continued to have the most severe problems, including psychopathology, poorer physical health, lower socioeconomic status, lower levels of education, partner and child abuse, and violent behavior at age 32; this was true for both men and women (Odgers, Moffitt, et al., 2008).

Interestingly, those classified as adolescence-limited, who were expected to "grow out" of their aggressive and antisocial behavior, continued to have troubles with substance use, impulsivity, crime, and overall mental health in their mid-20s (Moffitt, Caspi, et al., 2002). Moffitt and colleagues have since suggested that *adolescent onset* is the more appropriate term for this group of people, as the conduct problems are not entirely limited to adolescence (Odgers, Caspi, et al., 2007). By age 32, women with the adolescent-onset type were not having difficulties with violent behavior, but men still were. However, both men and women continued to have substance use problems, economic problems, and physical health problems (Odgers et al., 2008).

Prevalence Estimates suggest that conduct disorder is fairly common, with prevalence rates between 5 and 6 (Kessler et al., 2012; Merikangas et al., 2010). Like ADHD, conduct disorder is more common in boys than in girls. The life-course-persistent type is more common among boys (10.5 percent) than girls (7.5 percent); the adolescence-limited type is also more common among boys (19.6 percent) than girls (17.4 percent) (Odgers et al., 2008).

Prognosis The prognosis for children diagnosed with conduct disorder is mixed. Research results show that men and women with the life-course-persistent type of conduct disorder will likely continue to have all sorts of problems in adulthood, including violent and antisocial

Etiology of Conduct Disorder

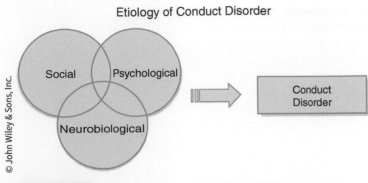

© John Wiley & Sons, Inc.

FIGURE 13.2 Neurobiological, psychological, and social factors all play a role in conduct disorder.

behavior. However, conduct disorder in childhood does not inevitably lead to antisocial behavior in adulthood. For example, a longitudinal study indicated that, although about half of boys with conduct disorder did not fully meet the criteria for the diagnosis at a later assessment (1 to 4 years later), almost all of them continued to demonstrate some conduct problems (Lahey, Loeber, et al., 2005).

Etiology of Conduct Disorder Multiple factors are involved in the etiology of conduct disorder, including genetic, neurobiological, psychological, and social factors that interact in a complex manner (**Figure 13.2**). A review concluded that the evidence favors an etiology that includes heritable temperamental characteristics that interact with other neurobiological difficulties (e.g., neuropsychological deficits) and with a host of environmental factors (e.g., parenting, school performance, peer influences) (Hinshaw & Lee, 2003).

Genetic Factors The evidence for genetic influences in conduct disorder is mixed, although heritability likely plays a part. Part of the reason for the mixed findings is that some of the genetic influences for conduct disorder are shared with other disorders, including ADHD and depression, and some of the genetic influences are specific to conduct disorder or antisocial behavior (Lahey, Van Hulle, et al., 2011; Lahey & Waldman, 2012; Rhee & Waldman, 2002).

Distinguishing types of conduct problems may help to clarify findings on the heritability of conduct disorder (Burt, 2012). Evidence from twin studies indicates that aggressive behavior (e.g., cruelty to animals, fighting, destroying property) is more heritable than other rule-breaking behavior (e.g., stealing, running away, truancy) (Burt, 2009b; Burt, Klump, et al., 2016). In an elegant study of twins ages 6–10, Burt and colleagues found that the genetic influence of rule-breaking behavior varied depending on the wealth of neighborhood (Burt et al., 2016). Specifically, genetics played more of a role in rule-breaking behavior for twins raised in wealthier neighborhoods compared with twins raised in poor neighborhoods. This finding reveals an important gene–environment interaction and underscores the impact that poverty can have on childhood misconduct.

Other evidence indicates that the combination of conduct problems and callous and unemotional traits is more highly heritable than conduct problems alone (Viding, Blair, et al., 2005). A clever longitudinal adoption study examined the development of callous emotional traits in very young children (Hyde, Waller, et al., 2016). In this study, callous and emotional behaviors were measured in over 500 adopted children at age 18 months and again at 27 months. The researchers also measure antisocial behaviors in biological mothers and adoptive mothers. Children of biological mothers who had exhibited severe antisocial behavior were more likely to exhibit callous and unemotional behaviors, but not if the adoptive mother gave a lot of positive reinforcement. In other words, parenting of the adoptive mother appeared to exert a buffer against the genetic propensity passed down from the biological mother. It will be important to see if these effects last as the children continue to develop.

Finally, evidence suggests that the age when antisocial and aggressive behavior problems begin is related to heritability. For example, aggressive and antisocial behaviors that begin in childhood, as in the case of Moffitt's life-course-persistent type, are more heritable than similar behaviors that begin in adolescence (Burt & Neiderhiser, 2009; Taylor, Iacono, & McGue, 2000).

Two candidate genes in the serotonin system have been linked to antisocial behavior: *MAOA* and *5HTTLPR*, and a meta-analysis confirmed the role of these genes, though the effect is small (Ficks & Waldman, 2014). Indeed, we know that individual genes are not likely to tell the genetic story for any psychological disorder, and we know that genes do their work via the environment.

Another gene–environment interaction study examined the *MAOA* gene, which is located on the X chromosome and releases an MAO enzyme, which metabolizes several neurotransmitters, including dopamine, serotonin, and norepinephrine (Caspi, McClay, et al., 2002). This gene varies in its activity, with some people having high and others low MAOA activity. Using a large sample of over 1000 children from Dunedin, New Zealand, the researchers measured MAOA activity and assessed the extent to which the children had been maltreated. Being maltreated as a child was not enough to predict later conduct disorder, nor was the presence of low MAOA activity. Rather, those children who were both maltreated and had low MAOA activity were more likely to develop conduct disorder than either children who were maltreated but had high MAOA activity or children who were not maltreated but had low MAOA activity. Thus, both environment and genes mattered. A meta-analysis of several such studies confirms these findings: Being maltreated was linked to later antisocial behavior only via genetics (Taylor & Kim-Cohen, 2007).

Brain Function, Autonomic Nervous System, and Neuropsychological Factors

Neuroimaging studies of children with conduct disorder have revealed deficits in regions of the brain that support emotion, particularly empathetic responses. For example, children with callous and unemotional traits have difficulty perceiving distress (fear, sadness, pain) and happiness on the face of others, but do not have trouble perceiving anger (Marsh & Blair, 2008). In addition, these children show reduced activation in brain regions associated with emotion and reward, such as the amygdala, ventral striatum, and prefrontal cortex (Alegria, Radua, & Rubia, 2016; Blair, 2013; Cardinale, Breeden, et al., 2017). Children with callous and unemotional traits also do not learn to associate their behavior with reward or punishment as easily as do other children, and this is associated with dysfunction in brain regions associated with emotion (e.g., amygdala) and reward (e.g., ventral striatum) (Blair, 2013).

Other studies indicate that autonomic nervous system abnormalities are associated with antisocial behavior in adolescents. Specifically, lower levels of resting skin conductance and heart rate are found among adolescents with conduct disorder, suggesting that they have lower arousal levels than adolescents without conduct disorder (Ortiz & Raine, 2004; Raine, Venebales, & Williams, 1990). Why does low arousal matter? Like the neuroimaging studies just discussed, these findings suggest that adolescents who exhibit antisocial behavior may not fear punishment as much as adolescents who don't exhibit such behavior. Thus, these children may be more likely to behave in antisocial ways without the fear that they will get caught.

Neuropsychological deficits have also been observed in children and adolescents with conduct disorder (Moffitt, Lynam, & Silvia, 1994; Pajer, Chung, et al., 2008; Raine, Moffitt, et al., 2005). These deficits include poor verbal skills, difficulty with executive functioning (the ability to anticipate, plan, use self-control, and solve problems), and problems with memory. In addition, children who develop conduct disorder at an earlier age (i.e., life-course-persistent type) have an IQ score of 1 standard deviation below age-matched peers without conduct disorder, and this IQ deficit is apparently not attributable to lower socioeconomic status or school failure (Lynam, Moffitt, & Stouthamer-Loeber, 1993; Moffitt & Silvia, 1988).

Psychological Factors

An important part of typical child development is the growth of social emotions and moral awareness—the acquisition of a sense of what is right and wrong and the ability, even desire, to abide by rules and norms. Most people refrain from hurting others not only because it is illegal but also because it would make them feel guilty. Children with conduct disorder, particularly those with callous and unemotional traits, seem to be deficient in this moral awareness, lacking remorse for their wrongdoing (Cimbora & McIntosh, 2003; Blair, 2013; Frick et al., 2014). In adulthood, these traits figure prominently in antisocial personality disorder and psychopathy (discussed in Chapter 15).

The work of Kenneth Dodge and colleagues provides a social-cognitive perspective on aggressive behavior (and, by extension, conduct disorder). In one of his early studies (Dodge & Frame, 1982), Dodge found that the social information processing of aggressive children had a hostile bias; these children interpreted ambiguous acts, such as being bumped in line, as evidence of hostile intent. Such perceptions may lead these children to retaliate aggressively for actions that may not have been intended as provocative. This can create a vicious cycle: Their peers, remembering these aggressive behaviors, may tend to be aggressive more often in return, further angering the already aggressive children (see **Figure 13.3**). Dodge and colleagues have linked deficits in social information processing to heart rate among adolescents who exhibit antisocial behavior. Specifically, low heart rate predicted antisocial behavior for

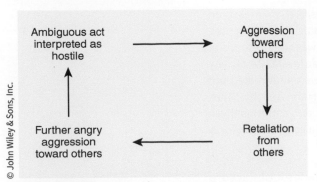

FIGURE 13.3 Dodge's cognitive theory of aggression. The interpretation of ambiguous acts as hostile is part of a vicious cycle that includes aggression toward and from others.

male adolescents independent from social information processing deficits, a finding consistent with studies reviewed earlier on low arousal and conduct problems. However, the link between low heart rate and antisocial behavior was accounted for by social information processing deficits for both male and female adolescents (Crozier, Dodge, et al., 2008).

Peer Influences Investigations of how peers influence aggressive and antisocial behavior in children have focused on two broad areas: (1) acceptance or rejection by peers and (2) affiliation with deviant peers. Studies have shown that being rejected by peers is causally related to aggressive behavior, particularly in combination with ADHD (Hinshaw & Melnick, 1995). Other studies have shown that being rejected by peers as early as 1st grade can predict later aggressive behavior, even after controlling for prior levels of aggressive behavior (Miller-Johnson, Coie, et al., 2002; Coie & Dodge, 1998). Additional longitudinal evidence suggests that children who are more prone to react negatively to situations are in turn more likely to be rejected by peers and subsequently more likely to engage in antisocial behavior (Buil, van Lier, et al., 2017).

Associating with other deviant peers also increases the likelihood of delinquent behavior (Forgatch, Patterson, et al., 2009), perhaps by modeling or even being coerced by peers (Dishion, Kim, & Tien, 2015). Do children with conduct disorder choose to associate with like-minded peers, thus continuing their path of antisocial behavior (i.e., a social selection view), or does simply being around deviant peers help initiate antisocial behavior (i.e., a social influence view)? Studies examining gene–environment interactions have shed light on this question, and the answer appears to be that both are correct. That is, we know that genetic factors are at play in conduct disorder, and these factors in turn play a role in encouraging children with conduct disorder to select more deviant peers to associate with. However, environmental influence, particularly neighborhood (e.g., poverty in the neighborhood) and family (e.g., parental monitoring) factors play a role in whether children associate with deviant peers, and this in turn influences and exacerbates conduct disorder (Kendler, Jacobson, et al., 2008).

Treatment of Conduct Disorder The treatment of conduct disorder appears to be most effective when it addresses the multiple systems involved in the life of a child (family, peers, school, neighborhood).

Family Interventions Some of the most promising approaches to treating conduct disorder involve intervening with the parents and families of the child. In addition, evidence suggests that intervening early, if even just briefly, can make an impact. An intervention called the family checkup (FCU) has been shown to have positive effects in preventing conduct problems and aggression in children. FCU involves three meetings to get to know, assess, and provide feedback to parents regarding their children and parenting practices. In the first randomized controlled trial (Shaw, Dishion, et al., 2006), FCU was offered to families with toddlers who were at high risk of developing conduct problems (based on the presence of conduct or substance abuse problems in parents or early signs of conduct behavior in the children). This brief, three-session intervention was associated with less disruptive behavior compared with no treatment, even 2 years after the intervention. Additional trials (Dishion, Shaw, et al., 2008) have confirmed the effectiveness of the FCU, showing that the preventive intervention is associated with less aggressive behavior and conduct problems in the early years of school (Dishion, Brennan, et al., 2014).

Gerald Patterson and colleagues developed a very successful behavioral program called **parent management training (PMT)**, in which parents are taught to modify their responses to their children so that prosocial rather than antisocial behavior is consistently rewarded. Parents are taught to use techniques such as positive reinforcement when the child exhibits positive behaviors and time-out and loss of privileges for aggressive or antisocial behaviors.

This treatment has been modified by others, but, in general, it is the most efficacious intervention for children with conduct disorder and oppositional defiant disorder. Both parents' and teachers' reports of children's behavior and direct observation of behavior at home and at school support the program's effectiveness (Kazdin, 2005; Patterson, 1982). PMT has been shown to alter parent–child interactions, which in turn is associated with a decrease in antisocial and aggressive behavior (Dishion & Andrews, 1995; Dishion, Patterson, & Kavanagh, 1992). PMT has been adapted for families in many different cultures and countries (Dishion, Forgatch, et al., 2016).

Parent and teacher training approaches have been incorporated into larger community-based programs, such as Head Start, and have been shown to reduce childhood conduct problems and increase positive parenting behaviors (Webster-Stratton, 1998; Webster-Stratton, Reid, & Hammond, 2001). (See **Focus on Discovery 13.2** for more information on Head Start.)

Parent management training can be effective in treating conduct disorder.

Focus on Discovery 13.2

Head Start: A Community-Based Prevention Program

Head Start is a federally funded program whose goal is to prepare children from low-income families to succeed in school. The core of the Head Start program is community-based preschool education, focusing on the early development of cognitive and social skills. Head Start contracts with professionals in the community to provide children with health and dental services, including vaccinations, hearing and vision testing, medical treatment, parent training, and nutrition information (http://www.acf.hhs.gov/programs/ohs). Mental health services are another important component of the Head Start program.

The National Head Start Impact study, mandated by Congress in 1998, was a randomized, controlled clinical trial of Head Start that included close to 5000 children in Head Start programs across the country. The study collected data from 2002 to 2006 to evaluate how Head Start impacts school readiness and what types of children benefit the most from the program. The final results showed that children reaped many intellectual, social, and behavioral benefits while in Head Start. Unfortunately, many of these gains did not seem to hold once children had completed 1st grade (U.S. Department of Health and Human Services, Administration for Children and Families, 2010) and 3rd grade (Puma, Bell, et al., 2012). Given the overall disappointing results, many changes to Head Start have been made, including more teacher and staff training and removal of programs that are not helping children, as well as other programs. Does this mean Head Start does not work? Not necessarily. That the children in Head Start were doing better than the children not in Head Start during preschool is encouraging. The challenge now is to help these positive effects last longer as the children go off to a variety of different school settings.

Multisystemic Treatment Another treatment for conduct disorder is **multisystemic treatment (MST)** (Henggeler, Schoenwald, et al., 2009). MST involves delivering intensive and comprehensive therapy services in the community, targeting the adolescent, the family, the school, and, in some cases, the peer group (**Figure 13.4**). The treatment is based on the view that conduct problems are influenced by multiple factors within the family as well as between the family and other social systems.

The strategies used by MST therapists are varied, incorporating behavioral, cognitive, family-systems, and case-management techniques. The therapy's uniqueness lies in emphasizing individual and family strengths, identifying the social context for the conduct problems, using present-focused and action-oriented interventions, and using interventions that require daily or weekly efforts by family members. Treatment is provided in homes, schools, or local recreational centers to maximize the chances that improvement will carry through into the regular daily lives of children and their families. MST has been shown to be effective in several studies around the world (Curtis, Ronan, & Bruin, 2004; Henggeler, 2011).

Prevention Programs It would be ideal if we could prevent conduct disorder from ever developing (see Focus on Discovery 13.2 for another type of prevention program, Head Start). Can this be done? One such prevention program that has been studied for over 25 years is called Fast Track. Findings from the Conduct Problems Prevention Research Group (CPPRG), the group of researchers who developed, implemented, and evaluated Fast Track, find impressive reductions in later psychopathology with just a brief intervention.

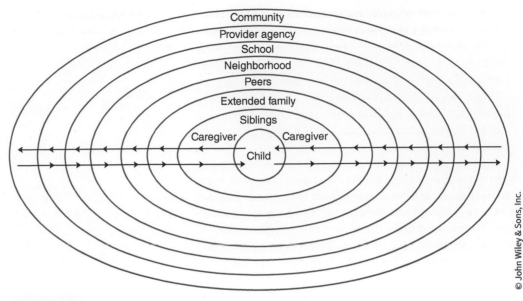

© John Wiley & Sons, Inc.

FIGURE 13.4 Multisystemic treatment (MST) includes consideration of many different factors when developing a child's treatment, including family, school, community, and peers.

The study evaluated 10,000 kindergarten children from four poor, high-crime regions in the United States, and nearly 900 children who were exhibiting conduct problems were randomly assigned to either the Fast Track intervention or a control intervention. The Fast Track intervention was designed to help children academically, socially, and behaviorally, focusing on areas that are problematic in conduct disorder, including peer relationships, aggressive and disruptive behavior, social information processing, and parent–child relationships. The intervention was delivered over the course of 10 years in groups and at individual families' homes, with a more intensive treatment in years 1 to 5 and less intensive in years 6 to 10.

Results from the study showed that children who received the Fast Track intervention benefited. Some of the benefits lasted for many years; others appeared to dwindle. For example, children who received Fast Track displayed fewer behavior problems and better social-information processing skills than children in the control condition at the end of 1st grade, but by 3rd grade some of the gains in social information processing were no longer evident, and even fewer gains were apparent by 4th and 5th grade (CPPRG, 2010a).

Nevertheless, the preventive intervention made a difference in other important domains. By 9th grade, the children who had the most severe problem behaviors at the baseline assessment in kindergarten and who received Fast Track exhibited fewer delinquent behaviors and were less likely to have a diagnosis of conduct disorder or any externalizing disorder compared to children in the control group (CPPRG, 2010a, 2011). Results from an additional analysis of outcomes in 9th grade revealed that the impact of Fast Track on reducing behavior problems was due, in part, to a decrease in the hostile attribution bias discussed earlier (Dodge & Godwin, 2013). By the end of high school, children who received Fast Track were less likely to have been arrested (CPPRG, 2010b) and receive a diagnosis of any externalizing disorder (CPPRG, 2011). By age 25, a full 8 years after the intervention ended, the young adults who received Fast Track were less likely to have externalizing or internalizing psychopathology, substance use problems, or antisocial personality disorder. In addition, the young people who had Fast Track were less likely to have been involved in violent crimes (Dodge, Bierman, et al., 2015). These are indeed impressive results, and they suggest that brief, intensive preventive interventions can make a positive impact in reducing later conduct disorder and antisocial behavior among children at risk.

Quick Summary

ADHD and conduct disorder are referred to as externalizing disorders. They appear across cultures, although there are also differences in the manifestation of externalizing symptoms in different cultures. Both disorders are more common in boys than girls. A number of factors work together to cause attention-deficit/

hyperactivity disorder (ADHD) and conduct disorder. Genetic factors play a particularly important role in ADHD but are also implicated in conduct disorder. Neurobiological research has implicated areas of the brain and neurotransmitters, such as dopamine, in ADHD and amygdala in conduct disorder; neuropsychological deficits are seen in both disorders. Other risk factors for ADHD include low birth weight and maternal smoking. Family and peer variables are also important factors to consider, especially in how they interact with genetic and neurobiological vulnerabilities. The most effective treatment for ADHD is a combination of stimulant medication and behavioral therapy. For conduct disorder, family-based treatments, such as parent management training (PMT), are effective, as are treatments that include multiple points for intervention, as in multisystemic treatment (MST). Prevention approaches, such as Fast Track, can also be helpful.

Check Your Knowledge 13.1
(Answers are at the end of the chapter.)

True or false?

1. The two broad categories of childhood psychopathology are internalizing disorders and externalizing disorders.

2. Adolescent girls with ADHD are more likely to have symptoms of an eating disorder and substance abuse than girls without ADHD.

3. Dopamine has been investigated in ADHD, with respect to both genes and the brain.

4. The most effective treatment for ADHD is behavioral treatment without medication.

Fill in the blanks.

5. Moffitt and colleagues have provided a good deal of evidence for two types of conduct disorder. The _____ type is associated with an early age of onset and continued problems into adolescence and adulthood. The _____ type begins in the teenage years and is hypothesized to remit by adulthood, though a recent follow-up study has not supported the idea that this type remits.

6. Comorbidity is common in conduct disorder. Other problems that co-occur with conduct disorder include: _____, _____, _____, and _____.

7. A successful treatment for conduct disorder that involves the family is called _____. Another successful community-focused treatment that works with the child, parents, peers, and schools is _____.

Internalizing Disorders: Depression and Anxiety Disorders

The internalizing disorders, which include depression and anxiety disorders, first begin in childhood or adolescence but are quite common in adults as well. Much richer descriptions of these disorders are presented in Chapter 5 (mood disorders) and Chapters 6 and 7 (anxiety disorders, obsessive-compulsive disorder, and trauma-related disorders). Here, we describe the ways in which the symptoms, etiology, and treatment of these disorders differ in children as compared with adults. We present the lifetime prevalence rates of these disorders in **Table 13.2**.

Depression

Clinical Descriptions, Prevalence, and Comorbidities of Depression in Childhood and Adolescence   There are both similarities and differences in the symptomatology of children and adults with major depressive disorder (Garber & Flynn, 2001). Children and adolescents ages 7–17 and adults show the following symptoms: depressed mood, inability to experience pleasure, fatigue, concentration problems, and suicidal ideation. Children and adolescents differ from adults in showing more guilt but lower rates of early-morning wakefulness, early-morning depression, loss of appetite, and weight loss. As in adults, depression in children is recurrent. Longitudinal studies have demonstrated that both children and adolescents with major depression are likely to continue to exhibit significant depressive symptoms when assessed even 4 to 8 years later (Garber, Kelly, & Martin, 2002; Lewinsohn, Rohde, et al., 2000).

Christian JACQUET/ Getty Images

Many of the symptoms of childhood depression are the same as adult depression, including sad mood.

	Lifetime Prevalence Rates of Mood and Anxiety Disorders in Adolescents
TABLE 13.2	

Disorder	Lifetime Prevalence Rate
Depression (or dysthymia)	11.7 %
Bipolar disorder (I or II)	2.9 %
Specific phobia	19.3 %
Social anxiety disorder	9.1 %
Separation anxiety disorder	7.6 %
Generalized anxiety disorder	2.2 %
Posttraumatic stress disorder	5.0 %

Source: Merikangas et al., 2010.

The prevalence among adolescent girls (15.9 percent) is almost twice that among adolescent boys (7.7 percent), just as we have seen with adult depression (Merikangas et al., 2010). Although adolescent girls experience depression more often than adolescent boys, there are few differences in the types of symptoms they experience (Lewinsohn, Petit, et al., 2003). Interestingly, the gender difference does not occur before age 12 (Hankin, Abramson, et al., 1998); depression occurs in 2–3 percent of school-age children under age 12 (Costello, Erkanli, & Angold, 2006).

As with adults, depression is comorbid with anxiety, particularly in adolescents (Cummings, Caporino, & Kendall, 2014). There is also evidence that comorbidity between depression and anxiety in adolescence may be caused in part by shared genetic vulnerabilities (Waszczuk, Zavos, et al., 2014).

Etiology of Depression in Childhood and Adolescence What causes a young person to become depressed? As with adults, evidence suggests that genetic factors play a role (Klein, Lewinsohn, et al., 2001). Indeed, the results of genetic studies with adults (see Chapter 5) also apply to children and adolescents because genetic influences are present from birth, though they may not be expressed right away. A child with a depressed parent has as much as four times the risk of developing depression as a child without a depressed parent (Hammen & Brennan, 2001). Of course, having a depressed parent confers risk via both genes and environment.

As has been found with older adults (see Chapter 5), gene–environment interactions predict the onset of depression in late adolescence and early adulthood. Results from the Northwestern–UCLA Youth Emotion Project, a large prospective study beginning with adolescents in their junior year of high school, are informative with respect to such interactions. In this study, those individuals who had a short allele of the serotonin transporter gene (short–short or short–long; see Chapter 5) *and* had experienced significant interpersonal stressful life events were more likely to have a major depressive disorder episode than either those people who had a short allele but no such stress or those people who experienced interpersonal stressful life events but had the long–long allele combination of the gene (Vrshek-Schallhorn, Mineka, et al., 2013). Other research shows that interpersonal factors seem to be particularly important in predicting the development of depression among adolescent girls (Hammen, 2009).

As with adults, other types of early adversity and negative life events also play a role (Garber, 2006). For example, one study found that early adversity (e.g., financial hardship, maternal depression, chronic illness as a child) predicted depression during ages 15–20, particularly among adolescents who had experienced a number of negative life events by age 15 (Hazel, Hamman, et al., 2008). Rejection by parents is modestly associated with depression in childhood, as confirmed by a meta-analysis of 45 studies (McLeod, Wood, & Weisz, 2007). The effect size for parental rejection was considered small across the studies, suggesting that factors other than parental rejection play a larger role in causing depression in childhood.

As we learned in Chapter 2, our bodies respond to stress via the HPA axis and the release of cortisol. Additional results from the Youth Emotion Project study indicate that cortisol levels upon awakening prospectively predicted the onset of a major depressive episode up to 2.5 years later (Vrshek-Schallhorn, Doane, et al., 2013). These results are consistent with findings from adults.

Recall from discussions in Chapters 5 that cortisol in people with depression is associated with smaller volumes (size) of the hippocampus. This may also be true for adolescents. A longitudinal study of adolescents at risk for developing depression found that the volume of the hippocampus grew more slowly between early and middle adolescence for those who developed an episode of depression compared with those who did not develop an episode (Whittle, Lichter, et al., 2014). Although these researchers did not measure stressful life events or cortisol, the evidence from the different studies reviewed here suggests that genes, stressful life events, cortisol, and the brain are all important when considering depression in adolescence.

Consistent with both Beck's theory and the hopelessness theory of depression (see Chapter 5), cognitive distortions and negative attributional styles are associated with depression in children and adolescents in ways similar to adults (Garber et al., 2002; Lewinsohn et al., 2000). For example, research on children with depression indicates that their outlook is more negative than those of children without depression and resemble those of adults with depression (Prieto, Cole, & Tageson, 1992). Negative thoughts and hopelessness also predict slower recovery from depression among adolescents (Rhode, Seeley, et al., 2006). Of course, depression can make children think more negatively (Cole, Martin, et al., 1998). Hence, it is important to consider longitudinal research.

A key question in the study of children with depression is, When do children develop stable attributional styles? That is, can young children have a stable way of thinking about themselves in the midst of such profound cognitive development? A longitudinal study examined the development of attributional style in children (Cole, Casella, et al., 2008). Specifically, the researchers prospectively studied three groups of children for 4 years each. At year 1 of the study, the three groups were (1) children in 2nd grade, (2) children in 4th grade, and (3) children in 6th grade. These three groups were followed yearly until the children were in grades 5, 7, and 9, respectively. The researchers found that attributional style didn't appear to be a stable style until children were early adolescents. In addition, attributional style did not interact with negative life events to predict depression (i.e., it was not a cognitive diathesis) for young children. It wasn't until the children were in 8th or 9th grade that support for attributional style as a cognitive diathesis emerged. Thus, results of this study suggest that attributional style becomes stable by early adolescence and serves as a cognitive diathesis for depression by the middle school years.

Treatment of Childhood and Adolescent Depression Results from a large randomized controlled trial called the Treatment for Adolescents with Depression Study (TADS) provide some support for the efficacy of antidepressants. In TADS, adolescents were randomized to receive either Prozac, cognitive behavioral therapy (CBT), or both combined. Results indicated that the combined treatment was the most effective through 12 weeks and that Prozac had modest advantages compared to CBT (March, Silva, et al., 2004), a pattern that remained true after 36 weeks (TADS team, 2007). A meta-analysis of 27 randomized controlled trials of antidepressant medication treatment for depression and anxiety disorders in children found that the medications were most effective for anxiety disorders other than obsessive-compulsive disorder (OCD) and less effective for OCD and depression (Bridge, Iyengar, et al., 2007).

However, several concerns have been raised about antidepressants (see **Focus on Discovery 13.3**). The side effects experienced by some children taking antidepressants include diarrhea, nausea, sleep problems, and agitation (Barber, 2008). More importantly, concerns with respect to suicidality prompted a series of hearings in the United States and the United Kingdom about the safety of antidepressants for children. In TADS (March et al., 2004), 7 out of 439 adolescents attempted suicide, of whom 6 were in the Prozac group and 1 was in the CBT group. (See Focus on Discovery 13.3 for more discussion of this complex issue.) In the meta-analysis by Bridge and colleagues (2007), the researchers looked at suicidality rates in the studies of depression. The risk of suicidal ideation was 3 percent for those children taking antidepressants and 2 percent for those taking placebo. It is important to note that this analysis shows that children taking medication were at risk for suicidal ideation, not that medication caused the suicide thoughts or attempts. There were no completed suicides in any of the 27 studies reviewed.

Focus on Discovery 13.3

Controversies in the Diagnosis and Treatment of Children with Psychopathology

The number of children diagnosed with psychological disorders continues to rise, sometimes dramatically, as has the number of children taking psychoactive medications. Here we briefly discuss some of the controversies and current evidence accumulated to address these questions.

Emotion Difficulties in Children: How Many Diagnoses Do We Need?

For years, professionals have struggled to distinguish problems with emotions and emotion regulation in children. Distinguishing bipolar disorder from ADHD in children is a challenge. DSM-5 introduced a new category, disruptive mood dysregulation disorder (DMDD) in part to distinguish episodic irritability seen in childhood bipolar disorder from more chronic irritability. Yet the new category is not all that different from the comorbid presentation of depression and oppositional defiant disorder (ODD). How many childhood diagnostic categories do we need?

One of the difficult diagnostic issues facing mental health professionals is distinguishing bipolar disorders from ADHD. Agitated behavior can be a sign of both, and only through careful and thorough assessments can the distinction be made. An early controversy was whether the diagnostic criteria for bipolar disorders in children should be the same as the criteria for bipolar disorders in adults. Some argued that the criteria for children should include explosive but brief outbursts of emotion and behavioral dysregulation (e.g., Biederman, Mick, et al., 2000), but these are fundamentally different from the current DSM criteria for bipolar I disorder (see Chapter 5), and emotion dysregulation is also present in ADHD (Carlson & Meyer, 2006; Dickstein & Leibenluft, 2006). Later research has confirmed that the adult criteria are applicable to children and adolescents (Youngstrom, Freeman, & Jenkins, 2009). The American Academy of Child and Adolescent Psychiatry recommends using the adult DSM-5 criteria for diagnosing bipolar disorder in children and adolescents (McClellan, Kowatch, & Findling, 2007). These guidelines also recommend that impairment be identified in two different settings (e.g., home, school), a requirement not found in the DSM.

The way mania presents in children can complicate diagnosis. The DSM-5 added a new category called *disruptive mood dysregulation disorder* (DMDD) in the hopes that this will help clinicians distinguish episodic irritability that is part of bipolar disorder from severe and chronic irritability, thus reducing the number of children receiving a diagnosis of bipolar disorder (Leibenluft, 2011). Indeed, the diagnoses of bipolar disorders in children increased dramatically over the past two decades. Yet it is unlikely that bipolar disorder among children was really increasing. In fact, bipolar disorder in children is much higher in the United States than in other countries, suggesting that the increase was specific to the United States (James, Hoang, et al., 2014; Van Meter, Moreira, & Youngstrom, 2011).

The criteria for DMDD include severe temper outbursts that tend to happen three times a week and in two different settings (e.g., home, school). The diagnosis is only for children ages 6–18, and it must be diagnosed prior to age 10. The symptoms need to have been present for at least a year. These criteria emphasize chronic and stable irritability—at least a year; for bipolar disorder, irritability must last for at least a week. The extent to which the DMDD criteria and symptoms are actually stable, however, is not clear. The evidence on this so far is mixed, with some longitudinal studies on symptoms (Mayes, Mathiowetz, et al., 2015) and the DMDD diagnosis (Dougherty, Smith, et al., 2016).

However, the introduction of DMDD has been controversial as there is not yet much evidence to support this category. The reliability of the diagnoses was quite low in the DSM-5 field trials (Regier, Narrow, et al., 2013), and recall from Chapter 3 that the question of validity cannot be addressed without first establishing reliability. Perhaps not surprisingly given the problems with reliability, prevalence rates vary widely, anywhere from 1 percent to over 30 percent (Copeland, Angold, et al., 2013; Dougherty et al., 2016; Freeman, Youngstrom, et al., 2016; Margulies, Weintraub, et al., 2012).

Other difficulties with DMDD include the high comorbidity with other disorders, including depression, ODD, and ADHD (Copeland et al., 2013; Mayes, Waxmonsky, et al., 2016). Thus, while the new category may decrease the number of children diagnosed with bipolar disorder (Margulies et al., 2012), it remains unclear if it is needed.

Even with these controversies, another reason DMDD was added to DSM-5 was based on the clinical reality of children who present with severe, unrelenting irritability who are in need of help. In a longitudinal study, Copeland and colleagues found that children ages 9–13 with DMDD were facing many challenges in young adulthood (ages 19–25; Copeland, Shanahan, et al., 2014). Compared with children with any psychological disorder, these young people had more psychopathology, health problems, and poorer overall functioning. Clearly, this group of young people could use early intervention. The debate over whether or not DMDD should remain in the DSM will continue.

Antidepressant Medications

Can antidepressant medications increase the likelihood of suicide in adolescents? This question was the focus of intense debate over 10 years ago, and the issue is still not fully resolved. Findings from the Treatment of Adolescent Depression Study (TADS) indicated that the most effective treatment was a combination of Prozac and cognitive behavioral therapy (March et al., 2004). However, the authors also reported that six adolescents taking Prozac attempted suicide (1.5 percent of the sample), whereas only one receiving cognitive behavioral therapy (CBT) attempted suicide. The participants in the study were randomly assigned to treatment conditions, so it is less likely that the adolescents taking Prozac were more seriously ill or suicidal than the ones receiving CBT.

Antidepressants can take as long as 3–4 weeks to start working (see Chapter 5), and one analysis of adolescent suicide attempts and antidepressant use found that the risk for suicide was highest in the first 3–4 weeks of treatment. Thus, it could be the case that the medications did not have sufficient time to begin working in the adolescents who attempted suicide. It may also be true that the combined treatment in TADS was most effective because CBT began working earlier in the course of treatment.

These findings prompted the FDA to hold a series of hearings on the safety of treating children and adolescents with antidepressant medications. The United Kingdom had already made a strong statement that the benefits of antidepressants for the treatment of adolescent depression were not greater than the risks. At the end of the FDA hearings, the panel mandated a "black box" warning to accompany information sent to physicians on the use of antidepressants with adolescents. This is the strongest safety warning the FDA can issue with medications. In the United Kingdom, the equivalent regulatory agency, the Medicines and Healthcare Products Regulatory Agency (MHRA), also recommended warnings for antidepressant labels. The 2014 U.K. guidelines for treating depression in young people suggest that the risks outweigh the benefits for antidepressants (https://www.gov.uk/government/publications/ssris-and-snris-use-and-safety/selective-serotonin-reuptake-inhibitors-ssris-and-serotonin-and-noradrenaline-reuptake-inhibitors-snris-use-and-safety). Following the warnings, the number of prescriptions for antidepressants initially declined in the United States and in the United Kingdom (Kurian, Ray, et al., 2007), but in the past 10 years, they have once again risen, doubling from 2006 to 2015 in the United Kingdom (Sarginson, Webb, et al., 2017).

Stimulant Medications

As discussed in the section on Treatment of ADHD, the number of children taking stimulant medications has risen dramatically since they were introduced in the sixties. Does the use of stimulant medications lead to increases in illicit drug use among children? Three prospective, longitudinal studies suggest that the answer to this question is no. In one study, two groups of children with ADHD were studied for 13 years (Barkley, Fischer, et al., 2003). One group of children had been treated with stimulant medication for 3½ years on average, and the other group had never received stimulant medication. At follow-up in young adulthood, those who had taken stimulant medication were not more likely to have used illicit drugs than those who had not been treated, with one exception—those who had taken stimulant medication were at greater risk for having tried cocaine. However, after controlling for the severity of conduct disorder symptoms, the relationship between stimulant medication use and trying cocaine disappeared. This suggests that having severe conduct disorder symptoms accounts for the link between stimulant medication and trying cocaine, not the use of stimulant medication per se.

The second study followed into adulthood a group of children with reading disorders who had been treated with stimulant medications for 12–18 weeks and compared them with a group of children with reading disorders who had not received stimulant medication. Sixteen years after the medication treatment, the two groups did not differ in their use of illicit drugs (Mannuzza, Klein, & Moulton, 2003).

The third study followed up children 8 years after they participated in the MTA treatment study (discussed earlier) when they were in middle to late adolescence (Molina, Hinshaw, et al., 2013). The children with ADHD, regardless of treatment type, were more likely to have used alcohol, tobacco, marijuana and other drugs in adolescence than the children without ADHD, a finding that is consistent with studies showing comorbidity between ADHD and substance use. However, there was no relationship between stimulant medication use and later drug use. Neither the total amount of medication taken, the dosage of medication, or initial MTA treatment group (medication alone, combined treatment), or continued use of medication after the MTA study was associated with later drug or alcohol use. Thus, children with ADHD are at a higher risk for substance use, but it is not because they have taken stimulant medication.

Autism Spectrum Disorder: Diagnosis and Causes

The number of cases of autism spectrum disorder (ASD) has increased dramatically since the turn of the century. As reported by the Centers for Disease Control and Prevention (CDC), the prevalence rate of ASD in the United States has risen from 1 in 150 children to 1 in 110 children to 1 in 68 children (CDC, 2009, 2014). Why has there been such an increase? Are there that many more children with autism, or have mental health professionals gotten better at making a diagnosis?

Autism wasn't formally recognized in the DSM until 1980, and the diagnostic criteria broadened quite a bit between the publication of DSM-III in 1980 and the release of DSM-IV in 1994. New prevalence rates for DSM-5 have not yet been calculated, but the rates could be even higher as DSM-5 combined three categories (autism, Asperger's disorder, pervasive developmental disorder NOS) into ASD. More children met the criteria for a diagnosis of autism under the broader criteria than they did under the narrower criteria (Gernsbacher, Dawson, & Goldsmith, 2005). Additionally, there is greater public awareness of ASD, and this may spur families to seek out mental health professionals for a formal psychological assessment. Indeed, the delay in or lack of language acquisition has become a widely recognized warning sign among parents and mental health professionals that ASD may be a possibility. In addition, public schools are mandated by law to provide services for children with ASD, and this may have helped families to seek a formal diagnosis. Indeed, the number of children classified as having ASD and thus qualifying for special education services increased between 2000 and 2011 by over 300,000 (U.S. Department of Education, 2013). However, the latest increases in ASD rates appear to be driven by children with ASD but no intellectual disability (CDC, 2014).

Although the rise in autism diagnoses may be accounted for in part by better diagnosis, awareness, and mandated services, most experts agree that there are indeed more cases today than there were 35 years ago.

What might be causing this increase? Based largely on celebrity proclamations, parents became particularly worried that vaccines routinely given to toddlers may cause ASD. The MMR vaccine (for measles, mumps, and rubella) is given to children around the same age when autism signs and symptoms begin to appear. A related concern is that the product used to preserve these vaccines—a substance called thimerosal, which contains mercury—may be responsible for autism.

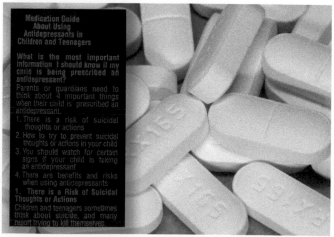

Scott Camazine/Medical Images

FDA required that black-box warnings be put on antidepressants for use with adolescents.

There is no evidence, however, linking autism with either the MMR vaccine or thimerosal (Wessel, 2017). Vaccines have not been stored in thimerosal for the past several years, and even those vaccines that were stored in thimerosal contained very small amounts of mercury. One study examined the number of ASD diagnoses reported to the California Department of Developmental Services between 1995 and 2007 (Schecter & Grether, 2008). By 2001, all but the smallest trace of thimerosal had been removed from childhood vaccines. If thimerosal was causing autism, the decline in its use in vaccines should correspond to a decrease in the number of new cases of autism. However, the study found no such association. In fact, the number of new cases of autism increased. The Institute of Medicine published the results of its comprehensive review of available evidence on the link between MMR and autism. This report concluded unequivocally that the MMR vaccines are not responsible for autism (Institute of Medicine, 2004). A meta-analysis including more than 1.2 million children found no link between autism and the vaccines (Taylor, Swerdfeger, & Eslick. 2014).

How long do the treatment effects studied last? A naturalistic follow-up of just under half the adolescents in TADS found that, although most (96 percent) participants had recovered 2 years after the study, close to half of those who recovered by the end of treatment had a recurrent episode of depression 5 years later (Curry, Silva, et al., 2011). Girls were more likely to have a recurrence than boys, as were adolescents who had a comorbid anxiety disorder. However, the rate of recurrence did not differ depending on the kind of treatment the adolescents received during TADS. In other words, the modest benefits of Prozac over cognitive behavior therapy reported in TADS did not seem to protect this group of adolescents from having a future episode of depression 5 years later.

CBT in school settings appears to be effective and is associated with more rapid reduction of symptoms than family or supportive therapy (Curry, 2001). About 63 percent of adolescents with depression treated with CBT show significant improvement at the end of treatment (Lewinsohn & Clarke, 1999). However, other evidence suggests that the benefits of CBT may not last long for young people (Weisz, McCarty, & Valeri, 2006). Some evidence shows that CBT is most beneficial for white adolescents, those adolescents with good coping skills at pretreatment, and adolescents with recurrent depression (Rhode et al., 2006). The Clinical Case of Sharon illustrates CBT techniques with an adolescent.

Clinical Case

Sharon

When initially seen, Sharon was extremely dysphoric, experienced recurrent suicidal ideation, and displayed numerous vegetative signs of depression. . . . [After being] placed on antidepressant medication . . . she was introduced to a cognitive behavioral approach to depression. . . . She was able to understand how her mood was affected by her thoughts and behavior and was able to engage in behavioral planning to increase the occurrence of pleasurable and mastery-oriented events. Sharon manifested extremely high standards for evaluating her performance in several areas, and it became clear that her parents also subscribed to these standards, so that family therapy sessions were held to encourage Sharon and her parents to reevaluate their standards.

Sharon had difficulty with the notion of changing her standards and noted that when she was not depressed she valued her perfectionism. At that point she resisted the therapy because she perceived it as trying to change something she valued in herself. With this in mind, we began to explore and identify those situations or domains in which her perfectionism worked for her and when and how it might work against her. She became increasingly comfortable with this perspective and decided she wanted to continue to set high standards regarding her performance in mathematical course work (which was a clear area of strength), but she did not need to be so demanding of herself regarding art or physical education.

Adapted from Braswell & Kendall, 1988, p. 194.

A good deal of work has focused on how to prevent the onset of depression in adolescents and children. A meta-analysis examined two types of preventive interventions for depression: selective and universal (Horowitz & Garber, 2006). Selective prevention programs target youth based on family risk factors (e.g., parents with depression), environmental factors (e.g., poverty), or personal factors (e.g., hopelessness). Universal programs are targeted toward large groups, typically in schools, and seek to provide education and information about depression. Results of the meta-analysis indicated that selective prevention programs were more effective than universal programs in preventing depression symptoms among adolescents.

A large randomized control clinical trial of a selective prevention program for at-risk adolescents, defined as having at least one parent with depression, showed promising results (Garber, Clarke, et al., 2009). Adolescents were randomly assigned to a group CBT intervention that focused on problem-solving skills and changing negative thoughts or to a usual care group (i.e., any mental health care they sought out on their own). The incidence of depression episodes was lower for adolescents in the CBT group than for those in the usual care group; therefore, the treatment may have had an effective preventative effect. Results from a 33-month follow-up of the sample indicated that the effects held: Those who received the prevention program had fewer depression episodes than those in the usual care group (Beardslee, Brent, et al., 2013).

As promising as the results are, there is still work to do. A more recent meta-analysis found selective prevention programs to be effective, though the effects were not as strong (Garber, Brunwasser, et al., 2016). And studies of group-based prevention programs in broad populations (e.g., schools) have yet to show results as encouraging as the randomized, controlled trials (Brunwasser & Garber, 2016).

Anxiety

Just about every child experiences fears and worries as part of the typical course of development. Common fears, most of which the child outgrows, include fear of the dark and of imaginary creatures and fear of being separated from parents. In general, as with adults, fears are reported more often for girls than for boys (Lichtenstein & Annas, 2000), though this sex difference may be due at least in part to social pressures on boys that make them reluctant to admit that they are afraid of things.

The seriousness of some childhood anxiety problems should not be underestimated. Not only do children suffer, as do adults, from the aversiveness of being anxious—simply put, anxiety doesn't feel good—but their anxiety may also work against their acquisition of skills appropriate to various stages of their development. For example, a child who is painfully shy and finds interacting with peers virtually intolerable is unlikely to learn important social skills. This deficit may persist as the child grows into adolescence and will form the foundation of social difficulties. Then, whether in the workplace or at college, the adolescent's worst fear—"people will dislike and reject me"—is likely to be realized as his or her awkward, even off-putting, behavior toward others may produce rejecting and aversive responses.

Clinical Descriptions and Prevalence of Anxiety in Childhood and Adolescence   For fears and worries to be classified as disorders according to DSM criteria, children's functioning must be impaired; unlike adults, however, children need not regard their fear as excessive or unreasonable, because children sometimes are unable to make such judgments. Based on these criteria, about 3–5 percent of children and adolescents would be diagnosed as having an anxiety disorder (Rapee, Schniering, & Hudson, 2009). Using data from the NCS-A sample, researchers found that 24.9 percent of the 10,000 adolescents ages 13–17 who were interviewed had a 12-month prevalence of an anxiety disorder. See Table 13.2 for the prevalence rates of the individual anxiety disorders.

Separation anxiety disorder is characterized by constant worry that some harm will befall their parents or themselves when they are away from their parents. When at home, such children shadow one or both of their parents. Since the beginning of school is often the first circumstance that requires lengthy and frequent separations of children from their parents, separation anxiety is often first observed when children begin school. Separation anxiety

Anxiety disorders in childhood and adolescence can interfere with other aspects of development.

disorder is associated with the development of other internalizing and externalizing disorders at later ages, and this is true in several countries around the world (Silove, Alonso, et al., 2015).

Children and adolescents also suffer from social anxiety disorder. Most classrooms include at least one or two children who are extremely quiet and shy. Often these children will play only with family members or familiar peers, avoiding strangers both young and old. Their social anxiety may prevent them from acquiring skills and participating in a variety of activities enjoyed by most of their peers, for they avoid playgrounds and stay out of games played by other children. Extremely shy children may refuse to speak at all in unfamiliar social circumstances, a condition called *selective mutism*.

Children who are exposed to traumas, such as chronic abuse, community violence, and natural disasters, may experience symptoms of posttraumatic stress disorder (PTSD) similar to those experienced by adults. For children older than 6, these symptoms are organized into the same four broad categories discussed in Chapter 7: (1) intrusively reexperiencing the traumatic event, as in nightmares, flashbacks, or intrusive thoughts; (2) avoiding trauma-related situations or information and experiencing a general numbing of responses, as in feelings of detachment or anhedonia; (3) negative changes in cognitions or mood related to the traumatic event; and (4) increased arousal and reactivity, which can include irritability, sleep problems, and hypervigilance.

DSM-5 Criteria for Separation Anxiety Disorder

Excessive anxiety that is not developmentally appropriate about being away from people to whom one is attached, with at least three symptoms that last for at least 4 weeks (for adults, symptoms must last for 6 months or more).

- Repeated and excessive distress when separated
- Excessive worry that something bad will happen to an attachment figure
- Refusal or reluctance to go to school, work, or elsewhere
- Refusal or reluctance to sleep away from home
- Nightmares about separation from attachment figure
- Repeated physical complaints (e.g., headache, stomachache) when separated from attachment figure

---

DSM-5 added separate criteria for PTSD in children age 6 and younger. The symptoms for these younger children fall into the same four broad categories just described, but they are presented in ways that are more developmentally appropriate for younger children. For example, extreme temper tantrums are an example of an increased reactivity symptom; intrusive thoughts about the trauma may be experienced as reenactment play. In addition, some of the symptom descriptors that don't apply to young children are removed from these criteria. For example, holding negative beliefs about oneself is part of the negative changes in cognitions or mood symptoms cluster that does not apply to very young children.

OCD is also found among children and adolescents, with prevalence estimates ranging from less than 1 to 4 percent (Rapee et al., 2009). The symptoms in childhood are similar to symptoms in adulthood: Both obsessions and compulsions are involved. The most common obsessions in childhood involve dirt or contamination as well as aggression; recurrent thoughts about sex or religion become more common in adolescence (Turner, 2006). OCD in children is more common in boys than girls, but by adulthood, OCD is slightly more common in women than men.

Etiology of Anxiety Disorders in Childhood and Adolescence As with adults, genetics plays a role in anxiety among children, with heritability estimates ranging from 29 to 50 percent in one study (Lau, Gregory, et al., 2007). However, genes do their work via the environment. For example, genetics play a role in separation anxiety in the context of more negative life events experienced by a child (Lau et al., 2007). Furthermore, shared environment factors (see Chapter 2) also play a significant role in childhood anxiety disorders (Burt, 2014).

Parenting practices play a small role in childhood anxiety. Specifically, parental control and overprotectiveness, more than parental rejection, is associated with childhood anxiety. However, parental control accounted for only 4 percent of the variance in childhood anxiety according to a meta-analysis of 47 studies (McLeod, Weisz, & Wood, 2007). Thus, 96 percent of the variance is accounted for by other factors. Other psychological factors that predict anxiety symptoms among children and adolescents include emotion-regulation problems and insecure attachment in infancy (Bosquet & Egeland, 2006). A more recent meta-analysis similarly found significant effects for parenting practices, including abuse, conflict between parents, warmth, and overinvolvement, but they only accounted for 2 percent of the variance in childhood anxiety (Yap & Jorm, 2015).

Another factor studied in childhood anxiety is the role of being bullied. Prospective studies have found that children who were bullied in childhood or early adolescence were more likely to develop an anxiety disorder or depression in early adulthood (Copeland, Wolke, et al., 2013; Stapinski, Bowes, et al., 2014).

Theories of the etiology of social anxiety in children are generally similar to theories of social anxiety in adults (Spence & Rapee, 2016). For example, research has shown that children with anxiety disorders overestimate danger in social situations and underestimate their ability to cope with social challenges (Boegels & Zigterman, 2000; Miers, Blöte, et al., 2009). The anxiety created by these thoughts then interferes with social interactions, causing the child to avoid social situations (Wong & Rapee, 2016) and thus not to get much practice at social skills. In adolescence, peer relationships are important (Spence & Rapee, 2016). One longitudinal study found that adolescents who perceived that their peers did not accept them were more likely to be socially anxious (Teachman & Allen, 2007). Other research points to behavioral inhibition as an important risk factor for developing social anxiety (also discussed in Chapter 6). Children who had high levels of behavioral inhibition at age 4 were 10 times as likely as children with lower levels to have social anxiety disorder by age 9 (Essex, Klein, et al., 2010).

Theories about the causes of PTSD are similar for children and adults. For both, there must be exposure to a trauma, either experienced or witnessed. Like adults, children who have a propensity to experience anxiety may be at more risk for developing PTSD after exposure to trauma. Specific risk factors for children may include level of family stress, coping styles of the family, and past experiences with trauma (Martini, Ryan, et al., 1990). Some theorists suggest that parental reactions to trauma can help to lessen children's distress; specifically, if parents appear to be in control and are calm in the face of stress, a child's reaction may be less severe (Davis & Siegal, 2000).

Separation anxiety disorder involves an intense fear of being away from parents or other attachment figures.

Treatment of Anxiety in Childhood and Adolescence Evidence from a meta-analysis of 48 randomized controlled trials indicates that cognitive behavior therapy can be helpful to many children with anxiety disorders (Reynolds, Wilson, et al., 2012). One of the more widely used treatments is a type of CBT called Coping Cat (Kendall, Aschenbrand, & Hudson, 2003). This treatment focuses on confrontation of fears, development of new ways to think about fears, exposure to feared situations, and relapse prevention. Parents are also included in a couple of sessions. Data from randomized controlled clinical trials have shown this treatment to be effective in the short term, 7 years later (Kendall, Flannery-Schroeder, et al., 1997; Kendall, Safford, et al., 2004), and 19 years later (Benjamin, Harrison, et al., 2013). Coping Cat treatment is a recommended treatment by the Children and Young People's Improving Access to Psychological Therapies Program in the United Kingdom for social anxiety, GAD, and separation anxiety disorder (Oldham-Cooper & Loades, 2017).

Another randomized controlled trial compared individual CBT, family CBT, and family psychoeducation for the treatment of childhood anxiety. Both individual and family CBT included the Coping Cat workbook, and both were more effective than family psychoeducation at reducing anxiety (Kendall, Hudson, et al., 2008), and the effects persisted after 1 year and 7 years (Benjamin et al., 2013). Family CBT was more effective than individual CBT when both parents had an anxiety disorder. This study points to the importance of considering not only the child's anxiety but also levels of parental anxiety when deciding on a treatment for childhood anxiety.

Another study examined the Coping Cat treatment alone and in combination with sertraline (Zoloft) for children with separation anxiety, general anxiety, and social anxiety and found that the combination treatment was more effective than either Coping Cat treatment or medication alone (Walkup, Albano, et al., 2008). Perhaps not surprisingly, given the characteristics of the Coping Cat treatment, follow-up analyses indicated that improvements in children's coping ability seemed to drive the change in both Coping Cat alone and the combined treatment groups (Kendall, Cummings, et al., 2016). Two- and 3-year follow-up studies of these children found that children assigned to Coping Cat treatment alone or medication alone continued to get better, such that these two conditions were as effective in reducing anxiety as the combination treatment (Vicentine, Bennett, et al., 2014). Thus, the combination treatment appears to provide the most immediate improvement, but over time the Coping Cat treatment (and medication alone) yielded the same benefits.

Behavior therapy and group cognitive behavior therapy have been found to be effective for social anxiety disorder in children (Davis & Whiting, 2011). CBT has been found to be effective for OCD in children and adolescents with effect sizes larger than those for medication (Watson & Rees, 2008). CBT is recommended as the first-line treatment for mild to moderate OCD according to the American Association of Child and Adolescent Psychiatry (AACP; Geller & March, 2012). Results from a recent randomized controlled trial suggest that CBT is also effective for young children (i.e., ages 5–8). In this study, participants were randomly assigned to receive either family-based CBT, which included exposure plus response prevention (see Chapter 7), or family-based relaxation therapy. At the end of the 14-week treatment, children who received CBT had fewer symptoms and better functioning compared with the children who received the relaxation training (Freeman, Sapyta, et al., 2014).

The AACP guidelines recommend medication plus CBT for severe OCD. In the Pediatric OCD Treatment Study, a combination of CBT and sertraline (Zoloft) was more effective than CBT alone for children and adolescents with severe OCD (Pediatric OCD Treatment Study [POTS] team, 2004). Results from the POTS II study indicated that CBT plus medication was more effective than medication alone or medication plus generic instructions about what CBT involves (Franklin, Sapyta, et al., 2011).

Other methods of providing treatment, including "bibliotherapy" and computer-assisted therapy, have shown promise as well. In bibliotherapy, parents are given written materials and perform the role of therapist with their children. Although this approach is effective in reducing childhood anxiety, it does not appear to be as effective as CBT group treatments (Rapee, Abbott, & Lyneham, 2006). Nevertheless, it will be important to develop these types of mobile treatments for people who live in areas where CBT therapists are not available or unaffordable.

Only a few studies have evaluated the efficacy of treatment of PTSD among children and adolescents, but the available research suggests that cognitive behavioral treatments, whether individual or group, are effective for children and adolescents with PTSD (Davis & Whiting, 2011).

Quick Summary

Anxiety disorders and depression in children are referred to as internalizing disorders. Depression in childhood and adolescence appears to be similar to depression in adulthood, although there are notable differences. In childhood, depression affects boys and girls equally, but in adolescence girls are affected almost twice as often as boys. Genetics and stressful life events play a role in depression in childhood. Research on cognitive factors in childhood depression supports the notion that attributional style also plays a role; however, this work must consider the developmental stage of the child. A randomized controlled trial found that a combination of medication and cognitive behavioral therapy (CBT) was the most effective treatment for depression, but concerns about the effect of medications on suicide risk need to be addressed.

Anxiety and fear are typical in childhood. When fears interfere with functioning, such as keeping a child from school, intervention is warranted. Theories about the causes of anxiety disorders in children are similar to theories about their causes in adulthood, though less research has been done with children on, for example, cognitive factors. Cognitive behavioral therapy is an effective intervention for a number of different anxiety disorders in childhood. Other problems, such as PTSD in childhood, require additional study.

Check Your Knowledge 13.2

Fill in the blanks.

1. _____ and _____ are the most common mood and anxiety disorders in children and adolescents.

2. Like research with adults, studies with children find the neurobiological factor of reduced volume of the _____ and the cognitive factor of _____ to be associated with depression.

3. Two broad types of depression prevention programs are _____ and _____, with _____ appearing to be the most effective.

4. The DSM-5 criteria for most anxiety disorders are similar for children and adults. For children age 6 and under, however, the criteria for _____ are different.

5. The _____ is a type of cognitive behavior therapy (CBT) that is effective for children with anxiety disorders.

Specific Learning Disorder and Intellectual Disability

Dyslexia: A Type of Specific Learning Disorder

Clinical Case

Marcus

Marcus was excited about his college major in psychology and dreamed of becoming a clinical psychologist. He eagerly signed up for as many courses as would fit into his schedule and had open seats. He sat in the front of the large lecture courses, raising his hand and contributing to the discussion whenever possible. When it came time to take the first exam, he carefully reviewed his notes and textbook. He also experienced that creeping anxiety that came whenever he took written exams. Even though he thought he studied as much if not more than the other students, he just did not do well on the exams. "He didn't test well" was what he told himself. But when he thought about it, he realized that when he was reading the textbook, the words and letters sometimes got scrambled in a way that made it difficult to remember the material.

When he received his grade on the first midterm, he was worried. It contained all sorts of marks from the grader indicating that his writing was indecipherable and that he had not covered all the concepts required for the correct answers. His graduate student instructor suggested that he go for testing at the campus clinic in charge of assessments for learning disorders.

After a comprehensive assessment from the campus clinic, Marcus received a diagnosis of specific learning disorder with the dyslexia specifier. Marcus was now going to get extra time for his exams and papers—not just in his psychology classes, but in all his classes. The following semester, Marcus's grade point average went up to 3.8, and he felt confident that he was closer to achieving his goal of attending graduate school in clinical psychology.

A **specific learning disorder** is a condition in which a person shows a problem in a specific area of academic, language, speech, or motor skills that is not due to intellectual disability or deficient educational opportunities. Children with a specific learning disorder are usually of average or above-average intelligence but have difficulty learning some specific skill in the affected area (e.g., math or reading), and thus their progress in school is impeded.

DSM-5 Criteria for Specific Learning Disorder

- Difficulties in learning basic academic skills (reading, mathematics, or writing) inconsistent with the person's age, schooling, and intelligence and persisting for at least 6 months

- Significant interference with academic achievement or activities of daily living

---

Clinical Description and Prevalence The DSM-5 includes several disorders in the areas of communication, learning, and motor development. These disorders are described briefly in **Table 13.3**. These disorders are often identified and treated within the school system rather than through mental health clinics.

Dyslexia is not named as a distinct disorder in DSM-5; instead, the category *specific learning disorder* is named with three different specifiers: (1) impairment in reading (dyslexia); (2) impairment in written expression; or (3) impairment in math (dyscalculia). Dyscalculia involves difficulty in producing or understanding numbers, quantities, or basic arithmetic operations. An impairment in written expression refers to problems in spelling, grammar, and the clarity and organization of written work.

Dyslexia involves significant difficulty with word recognition, reading fluency, and reading comprehension. An analysis of four large epidemiological samples indicates that dyslexia is

TABLE 13.3 **Specific Learning, Communication, and Motor Disorders in DSM-5**

DSM-5 Diagnoses	Major Features
Specific learning disorder	- Reading impairment (dyslexia) - Written expression impairment - Math impairment (dyscalculia)
Communication Disorders	
- Speech sound disorder	- Correct comprehension and sufficient vocabulary use, but unclear speech and improper articulation. For example, *blue* comes out *bu*, and *rabbit* sounds like *wabbit*. With speech therapy, complete recovery occurs in almost all cases, and milder cases may recover spontaneously by age 8.
- Childhood onset fluency disorder (stuttering)	- A disturbance in verbal fluency that is characterized by one or more of the following speech patterns: frequent repetitions or prolongations of sounds, long pauses between words, substituting easy words for those that are difficult to articulate (e.g., words beginning with certain consonants), and repeating whole words (e.g., saying "go-go-go-go" instead of just a single "go"). Up to 80 percent of people with stuttering recover, most of them without professional intervention, before the age of 16.
- Language disorder	- Problems in developing and using language.
- Social (pragmatic) communication disorder	- Difficulties in using verbal and nonverbal language in social communication.
Motor disorders	
- Tourette's disorder	- One or more vocal and multiple motor tics (sudden, rapid movement or vocalization) that start before age 18.
- Developmental coordination disorder	- Marked impairment in the development of motor coordination not explainable by intellectual disability or a disorder such as cerebral palsy.
- Stereotypic movement disorder	- Seemingly purposeless movements repeated over and over that interfere with functioning and could even cause self-injury.

more common in boys than in girls (Rutter, Caspi, et al., 2004). In general, dyslexia affects 5–15 percent of school-age children (Peterson & Pennington, 2015).

Etiology of Dyslexia Family and twin studies confirm that there is a heritable component to dyslexia (Fisher & DeFries, 2002). Furthermore, the genes that are associated with dyslexia are the same genes associated with typical reading abilities (Plomin & Kovas, 2005). Research has also examined gene–environment interactions in dyslexia, and here the evidence so far suggests that the heritability of reading problems varies depending on parental education. Genes play a bigger role in dyslexia among children whose parents have more education compared with children whose parents have less education (Friend, DeFries, et al., 2009; Kremen, Jacobson, et al., 2005). Homes with high parental education likely emphasize reading and provide a lot of opportunity for children to read. In this type of environment, a child's risk for developing dyslexia is more driven by heritable combinations of genes than by environment.

Evidence from psychological, neuropsychological, and neuroimaging studies suggests that dyslexia involves problems in language processing. Many of these processes fall under what is called *phonological awareness*, which is believed to be critical to the development of reading skills (Anthony & Lonigan, 2004; Lonigan, Schatschneider, et al., 2008; Snowling & Melby-Lervåg, 2016). Phonological awareness includes perceiving the sounds of spoken language and their relation to printed words, detecting syllables, and recognizing rhyme.

Early fMRI studies support the idea that children with dyslexia have poor phonological awareness. These studies show that areas in the left temporal, parietal, and occipital regions of the brain (see **Figure 13.5**) are important for phonological awareness, and these same regions are centrally involved in dyslexia (e.g., Shaywitz, Shaywitz, et al., 2002; Turkeltaub, Gareau, et al., 2003)

fMRI studies suggest that the problem might not be in areas of the brain that support phonological awareness per se, but in their connections to other areas of the brain that support the ability to produce speech (Boets, Op de Beeck, et al., 2013; Vandermosten, Boets, et al., 2012). These findings suggest the interesting possibility that children with dyslexia may have problems integrating phonological awareness with generating the ability to read (Ramus, 2014).

The fMRI studies involved participants in the United States who spoke English. A study examining Chinese children with dyslexia failed to find a problem with the temporoparietal area of the brain during reading tasks; instead, the left middle frontal gyrus showed less activation (Siok, Perfetti, et al., 2004). The investigators speculate that the differences between the English and Chinese written languages may account for the different brain regions involved. Reading English requires putting together letters that represent sounds. Reading Chinese, in contrast, requires putting together symbols that represent meanings. Indeed, reading Chinese requires mastery of nearly 6000 different symbols. Thus, Chinese relies more on visual processing, while English relies more on sound processing.

Keira Knightley, a highly successful actress, suffers from dyslexia.

DAVE M. BENETT/Getty Images, Inc.

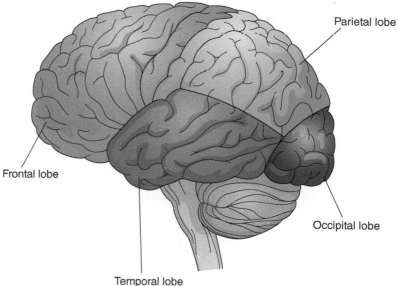

Parietal lobe

Frontal lobe

Occipital lobe

Temporal lobe

© John Wiley & Sons, Inc.

FIGURE 13.5 Areas of the brain implicated in dyslexia include parts of the frontal, parietal, and temporal lobes, at least for English language speakers.

Treatment of Dyslexia Several strategies are used to treat dyslexia, both in school programs and in private tutoring. In young children, readiness skills, such as letter discrimination, phonetic analysis, and learning letter–sound correspondences, may need to be taught before explicit instruction in reading is attempted. Phonological awareness training involves

Scholastic Studio 10/Getty Images, Inc.

Interventions for dyslexia have improved children's reading.

helping children master the task of converting sounds to words. Findings from the National Reading Panel, a comprehensive review of the research on teaching children to read, indicate that phonological awareness instruction is beneficial for children with reading difficulties (National Institute of Child Health and Human Development, 2000), and subsequent research has confirmed this recommendation (e.g., Snowling & Hulme, 2011). As in the Clinical Case of Marcus described earlier, people with dyslexia can often succeed in college with the aid of instructional supports, such as podcast or webcast lectures that can be replayed, tutors, and untimed tests. Colleges are required by law to provide special services to help such students, and public schools are now required to provide transitional vocational and career planning for older adolescents with learning disorders.

Intellectual Disability

Development of the DSM-5 criteria for **intellectual disability** was influenced by the guidelines of the American Association on Intellectual and Developmental Disabilities (AAIDD). The AAIDD's mission is to "promote progressive policies, sound research, effective practices, and universal human rights for people with intellectual and developmental disabilities" (www.aaidd.org). The current AAIDD guidelines are summarized in **Table 13.4**

Diagnosis and Assessment of Intellectual Disability The DSM-5 diagnostic criteria for intellectual disability include three criteria: (1) deficits in intellectual functioning, (2) deficits in adaptive functioning, and (3) onset during development (i.e., as a child).

DSM-5 Criteria for Intellectual Disability

- Intellectual deficits (e.g., in problem solving, reasoning, abstract thinking) determined by intelligence testing and broader clinical assessment
- Significant deficits in adaptive functioning relative to the person's age and cultural group in one or more of the following areas: communication; social participation, work or school; independence at home or in the community; requiring the need for support at school, work, or independent life
- Onset during child development

The first two of the DSM-5 criteria are consistent with the approach of the AAIDD. First, there is explicit recognition that an IQ score must be considered within the context of a more thorough assessment. Second, adaptive functioning must be assessed in a broad range of contexts.

TABLE 13.4 The AAIDD Definition of Intellectual Disability

Intellectual disability is characterized by significant limitations both in intellectual functioning and in adaptive behavior as expressed in conceptual, social, and practical adaptive skills.
    This disability begins before age 18.

Five Assumptions Essential to the Application of the Definition

1. Limitations in present functioning must be considered within the context of community environments typical of the individual's age, peers, and culture.
2. Valid assessment considers cultural and linguistic diversity as well as differences in communication, sensory, motor, and behavioral factors.
3. Within an individual, limitations often coexist with strengths.
4. An important purpose of describing limitations is to develop a profile of needed supports.
5. With appropriate personalized supports over a sustained period, the life functioning of the person with intellectual disability generally will improve.

Source: Adapted from Intellectual Disability: Definition, Classification, and Systems of Supports (11th Edition), © 2002 American Association on Intellectual and Developmental Disabilities.

Finally, the DSM-5 no longer distinguishes among mild, moderate, and severe intellectual disability based on IQ scores alone, as was done in DSM-IV-TR. The severity of intellectual disability is assessed in three areas: conceptual (which includes intellectual and other cognitive functioning), social, and practical.

The AAIDD approach encourages the identification of an individual's strengths and weaknesses in psychological, physical, and environmental dimensions with a view toward determining the kinds and degrees of support needed to enhance the person's functioning in various contexts. Consider Roger, a 24-year-old man with an IQ of 45 who has attended a special program for people with intellectual disability since he was 6. The AAIDD approach would emphasize what is needed to maximize Roger's functioning. Thus, a clinician might discover that Roger can use the bus system if he takes a route familiar to him, and therefore he might be able to go to a movie by himself from time to time. And although Roger cannot prepare complicated meals, he might be able to learn to prepare frozen entrées in a microwave oven. The assumption is that by building on what he can do, Roger will make more progress. We hope that the DSM-5 approach will also work like this.

In the schools, an individualized educational program (IEP) is based on the person's strengths and weaknesses and on the amount of instruction needed. Students are identified by the classroom environment they are judged to need. This approach can lessen the stigmatizing effects of having intellectual disability and may also encourage a focus on what can be done to improve the student's learning.

When assessing adaptive behavior, the cultural environment must be considered. A person living in a rural community may not need the same skills as those needed by someone living in New York City, and vice versa.

Etiology of Intellectual Disability
At this time, the primary cause of intellectual disability can be identified in only 25 percent of the people affected. The causes that can be identified are typically neurobiological.

Genetic or Chromosomal Abnormalities One chromosomal abnormality that has been linked with intellectual disability is *trisomy 21*, which refers to having an extra copy (i.e., three instead of two) of chromosome 21. This is also known as **Down syndrome (trisomy 21)**. It has been estimated that it occurs in about 1 out of every 850 live births in the United States (Shin, Besser, et al., 2009).

People with Down syndrome may have intellectual disability as well as some distinctive physical signs, such as short and stocky stature; oval, upward-slanting eyes; a prolongation of the fold of the upper eyelid over the inner corner of the eye; sparse, fine, straight hair; a wide and flat nasal bridge; square-shaped ears; a large, furrowed tongue, which may protrude because the mouth is small and its roof is low; and short, broad hands.

Another chromosomal abnormality that can cause intellectual disability is **fragile X syndrome**, which involves a mutation in the *fMR1* gene on the X chromosome (National Fragile X Foundation: www.fragilex.org). Physical symptoms associated with fragile X include large, underdeveloped ears and a long, thin face. Many people with fragile X syndrome have intellectual disability. Others may not have intellectual disability but may have a specific learning disorder, difficulties on neuropsychological

Child with Down syndrome.

tests, and mood swings. About a third of children with fragile X syndrome also exhibit autism spectrum behaviors, suggesting that the *fMR1* gene may be one of the many genes that contribute to autism spectrum disorder (Hagerman, 2006).

Recessive-Gene Diseases Several hundred recessive-gene diseases have been identified, and many of them can cause intellectual disability. Here we discuss one recessive-gene disease, phenylketonuria.

In **phenylketonuria (PKU)**, the infant, born without obvious signs of difficulty, soon begins to suffer from a deficiency of a liver enzyme, phenylalanine hydroxylase. Because of this enzyme deficiency, phenylalanine and its derivative, phenylpyruvic acid, are not broken down and instead build up in the body's fluids. This buildup can damage the brain because the unmetabolized amino acid interferes with the process of myelination, the sheathing of neuron axons, which is essential for neuronal function. Myelination supports the rapid transmittal of neuronal impulses. If not properly treated, intellectual disabilities can be profound.

Although PKU is rare, with an incidence of about 1 in 15,000 live births, it is estimated that 1 person in 70 is a carrier of the recessive gene. A blood test is available for prospective parents who have reason to suspect that they might be carriers. Pregnant women who carry the recessive gene must monitor their diet closely so that the fetus will not be exposed to toxic levels of phenylalanine. State laws require testing newborns for PKU. If the test is positive, the parents are taught to provide the infant a diet low in phenylalanine.

Infectious Diseases While in utero, the fetus is at increased risk of intellectual disabilities resulting from maternal infectious diseases, such as rubella, cytomegalovirus, toxoplasmosis, herpes simplex, and HIV. The consequences of these diseases are most serious during the first trimester of pregnancy, when the fetus has no detectable immunological response; that is, its immune system is not developed enough to ward off infection. The mother may experience slight or no symptoms from the infection, but the effects on the developing fetus can be devastating.

Infectious diseases can also affect a child's developing brain after birth. Encephalitis and meningococcal meningitis may cause brain damage and even death if contracted in infancy or early childhood. In adulthood, these infections are usually far less serious. There are several forms of childhood meningitis, a disease in which the protective membranes of the brain are acutely inflamed and fever is very high.

Environmental Hazards Several environmental pollutants are implicated in intellectual disability. One such pollutant is mercury, which may be ingested by eating affected fish. Another is lead, which is found in lead-based paints, smog, and even water pipes. The state of Michigan switched the water supply in the city of Flint in 2014, and because the new supply from the Flint River was not properly treated, lead from pipes carrying water to homes got into the water. Lead poisoning can cause kidney and brain damage as well as anemia, intellectual disabilities, seizures, and death. Lead-based paint is now prohibited in the United States, but it is still found in older homes, where children may eat pieces that flake off.

Treatment of Intellectual Disability

Residential Treatment Since the 1960s, serious and systematic attempts have been made to educate children with intellectual disability as fully as possible. Although many people can acquire

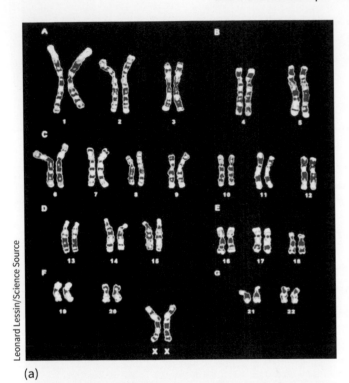

Leonard Lessin/Science Source

(a)

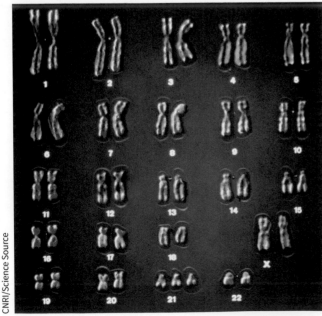

CNRI/Science Source

(a)

The normal complement of chromosomes is 23 pairs (a). In Down syndrome, there are three copies (a trisomy) of chromosome 21 (b).

the competence needed to function effectively in the community, some people need the extra support of a residential treatment program. Ideally, adults with intellectual disability in need of such support live in small to medium-size residences that are integrated into the community. Medical care is provided, and trained, live-in supervisors and aides help with residents' special needs around the clock. Residents are encouraged to participate in household routines to the best of their abilities.

Many adults with intellectual disability have jobs and are able to live independently in their own apartments. Others live semi-independently in apartments housing three to four adults; generally, a counselor provides aid in the evening.

Behavioral Treatments   Early-intervention programs using behavioral techniques have been developed to improve the level of functioning of people with intellectual disability. Specific behavioral objectives are defined, and children are taught skills in small, sequential steps (Carr, Horner, et al., 1999; Grey & Hastings, 2005).

To teach a child a routine, the therapist usually begins by dividing the targeted behavior, such as eating, into smaller components: pick up spoon, scoop food from plate onto spoon, bring spoon to mouth, remove food with lips, chew, and swallow food. Operant conditioning principles are then applied to teach the child these components of eating. For example, the child may be reinforced for successive approximations to picking up the spoon until he or she is able to do so. This operant approach, sometimes called *applied behavior analysis*, is also used to reduce inappropriate and self-injurious behavior.

Cognitive Treatments   Many children with intellectual disability have difficulty using strategies in solving problems, and when they do use strategies, they often do not use them effectively. Self-instructional training teaches these children to guide their problem-solving efforts through speech.

For example, one group of researchers taught high school students with intellectual disability to make their own buttered toast and clean up after themselves (Hughes, Hugo, & Blatt, 1996). A teacher would demonstrate and verbalize the steps involved in solving a problem, such as the toaster's being upside down or unplugged. The young people learned to talk themselves through the steps using simple verbal or signed instructions. For example, when the toaster was presented upside down, the person would be taught to first state the problem ("Won't go in"), then to state the response ("Turn it"), self-evaluate ("Fixed it"), and self-reinforce ("Good"). They were rewarded with praise and high-fives when they verbalized and solved the problem correctly. Several studies have demonstrated that even people with severe intellectual disability can learn self-instructional approaches to problem solving and then generalize the strategy to new tasks, including taking lunch orders at a cafeteria and performing janitorial duties (Hughes & Agran, 1993).

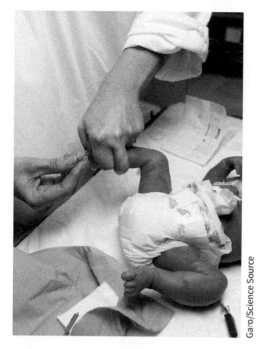

Garo/Science Source

States require that newborns be tested for PKU. If excess phenylalanine is found in the blood, a special diet is recommended for the baby.

Time & Life Pictures/Getty Images, Inc.

Although lead-based paint is now illegal, it can still be found in older homes. Eating these paint chips can cause lead poisoning, which can cause intellectual disability.

Robin Nelson/PhotoEdit

Computer-assisted instruction is well suited for applications in the treatment of intellectual disability.

Computer-Assisted Instruction Computer-assisted instruction is increasingly found in educational and treatment settings. This technology has also been useful in helping people with intellectual disability (Butcher & Jameson, 2016). The visual and auditory components of computers can help to maintain the attention of distractible students; the level of the material can be geared to the individual, ensuring successful experiences; and the computer can meet the need for numerous repetitions of material without becoming bored or impatient, as a human teacher might. For example, computers have been used to help people with intellectual disability learn to use an ATM (Davies, Stock, & Wehmeyer, 2003). Smartphones can be enormously helpful by serving as aids for reminders, directions, instructions, and daily tasks.

Quick Summary

Dyslexia is a specifier of the category specific learning disorder in DSM-5. Other specifiers include dyscalculia (impairment in math) and impairments in written expression. It affects 5–15 percent of children, and it is often identified and treated in schools. Dyslexia runs in families, and studies have found gene–environment interactions between risk genes and parental education. Problems in phonological awareness seem to contribute to dyslexia, and brain imaging studies have identified areas of the brain, including the temporoparietal area, that support the theory that phonological awareness is involved in dyslexia. Such studies suggest that dyslexia may also involve problems with the temporoparietal area's connections to other regions of the brain. Some of the brain imaging findings may not apply to all cultures. Treatments focus on building phonological awareness skills and then focusing on reading.

The DSM-5 category *intellectual disability* emphasizes the importance of assessing intellectual ability and adaptive functioning within a person's cultural group, consistent with the approach of the AAIDD. DSM-5 stresses the importance of identifying an individual's strengths and weaknesses. There are a number of known causes of intellectual disability, including genetic abnormalities, infections, and toxins.

Check Your Knowledge 13.3

Answer the questions.

1. Which of the following has not been discussed as part of the etiology of dyslexia?

   a. Family history.

   b. Early childhood trauma.

   c. Problems integrating phonological awareness with generating the ability to read.

   d. Phonological awareness.

2. A study examining children with dyslexia who spoke either Chinese or English found:

   a. The left middle frontal gyrus showed less activation during reading among Chinese-speaking children with dyslexia.

   b. The left temporoparietal cortex showed less activation during reading among Chinese-speaking children with dyslexia.

   c. The left middle frontal gyrus showed less activation during reading among English-speaking children with dyslexia.

   d. The left temporoparietal cortex showed more activation during reading among English-speaking children with dyslexia.

3. Which of the following has not been established as a cause for intellectual disability?

   a. chromosomal abnormalities such as trisomy 21

   b. PKU

   c. lead poisoning

   d. All the above have been found to cause intellectual disability.

4. Which of the following is not one of the DSM-5 criteria for intellectual disability?

   a. onset in childhood

   b. deficits in language acquisition

   c. deficits in intellectual functioning

   d. deficits in adaptive functioning

Autism Spectrum Disorder

Although autism was first described over 70 years ago (see **Focus on Discovery 13.4** for the history of autism), it was not formally included in the DSM until the third edition, published in 1980. As discussed in Focus on Discovery 13.3, the rates of **autism spectrum disorder (ASD)** have been rising over the past 20 years. With this increase in prevalence has come an increase in research on the causes of this disorder.

Focus on Discovery 13.4

A Brief History of Autism Spectrum Disorder

Autism was identified in 1943 by a psychiatrist at Johns Hopkins, Leo Kanner, who, in the course of his clinical work, noted 11 disturbed children who behaved in ways that were not common in children with intellectual disability or schizophrenia. He named the syndrome *early infantile autism* because he observed that "there is from the start an extreme autistic aloneness that, whenever possible, disregards, ignores, shuts out anything that comes to the child from the outside" (Kanner, 1943).

Kanner considered autistic aloneness to be the most fundamental symptom. He also learned that these 11 children had been unable from the beginning of life to relate to people in the ordinary way. They were severely limited in language and had a strong, obsessive desire for everything about them to remain unchanged. Despite its early description by Kanner and others (Rimland, 1964), the disorder was not accepted into official diagnostic nomenclature until the publication of DSM-III in 1980, where it was called autistic disorder.

Asperger's disorder was named after Hans Asperger, who in 1944 described the syndrome as being less severe and having fewer communication deficits than autism. It was first introduced to the DSM in 1994 in DSM-IV. Social relationships are poor and stereotyped behavior is intense and rigid, but language and intelligence are intact. Because research suggests that Asperger's disorder does not differ qualitatively from autistic disorder, these two categories will likely be combined in DSM-5. Nevertheless, more research has been conducted in the last 10 years on Asperger's disorder, perhaps due to the recognition of this condition among adults who for years wondered why they were different from others. Adults with the DSM-IV-TR diagnosis Asperger's disorder are now more frequently recognized and treated by mental health professionals (Gaus, 2007).

People formerly in the Asperger's disorder category but now under the broader domain of ASD will likely continue to seek and receive the support and help they need. Researchers, clinicians, and families have referred to the "autism spectrum" for years, so, in some ways, this change might not be so difficult to accommodate, at least in terms of the name. However, some worry that the stigma associated with the name *autism* might keep people from seeking help (see Focus on Discovery 3.3 on the underreporting of stigmatized behavior). On the other hand, some states, such as California and Texas, mandate services for children with autism but not Asperger's, and thus more people might get help.

Clinical Descriptions, Prevalence, and Prognosis of Autism Spectrum Disorder

In the next sections, we describe the clinical features of ASD, focusing on problems in social and emotional interactions and in communication as well as on repetitive or ritualistic behaviors.

Social and Emotional Disturbances
Children with ASD can have profound problems with the social world (Dawson, Toth, et al., 2004). They may rarely approach others and may look through or past people or turn their backs on them. For example, one study found that children with ASD rarely offered a spontaneous greeting or farewell (either verbally or through smiling, making eye contact, or gesturing) upon meeting or departing from an adult (Hobson & Lee, 1998). Few children with ASD initiate play with other children, and they can be unresponsive to anyone who approaches them.

Children with ASD sometimes make eye contact, but their gaze may have an unusual quality. Typically, children gaze to gain someone's attention or to direct the other person's attention to an object; children with ASD generally do not (Dawson et al., 2004). This is often referred to as a problem in **joint attention**. That is, interactions that require two people to pay attention to each other, whether speaking or communicating emotion nonverbally, are impaired in children with autism.

Heather Kuzmich, a finalist on the TV show *America's Next Top Model*, has what was called Asperger's disorder in DSM-IV-TR but is called autism spectrum disorder in DSM-5.

More fine-grained analyses of gaze involve measuring eye movements and looking time. In one study, 6-month old infants later diagnosed with ASD spent less time looking at videos of dynamic speaking faces, particularly in the eyes and mouth regions, compared to typically developing children (Shic, Macari, & Chawarska, 2014). A different study measured the eye movements of infants several different times between the ages of 2 months and 24 months (Jones & Klin, 2013). At 2 months, the eye movements of infants who later were diagnosed with ASD did not differ from typically developing infants, suggesting that children with ASD are not born with gaze deficits. However, from 2 months to 24 months, the pattern of gaze between the two groups of infants began to diverge. Overall, the time spent looking at faces declined in the group of infants with ASD, so much so that by 2 years of age, these children were looking at the faces 50 percent less than children without ASD. Infants who showed a faster decline in looking time, particularly in the eyes region, were the ones who later had more social deficits.

Consistent with the findings showing that children with ASD spend less time looking at other people's faces, fMRI studies have found that people with ASD do not show activation in the fusiform gyrus, other regions in the temporal lobes, and the amygdala, the areas of the brain most often associated with identifying faces and emotion, when completing face perception or identity tasks (Critchley, Daly, et al., 2001; Pierce, Haist, et al., 2004; Pierce, Muller, et al., 2001). Instead, other areas of the brain show activation during these tasks, suggesting perhaps a less efficient system for identifying faces.

Some researchers have proposed that children with ASD have a deficient "theory of mind" that is at the core of the kinds of social dysfunctions we have described here (Gopnik, Capps, & Meltzoff, 2000; Sigman, 1994). *Theory of mind* refers to a person's understanding that other people have desires, beliefs, intentions, and emotions that may be different from one's own. This ability is crucial for understanding and successfully engaging in social interactions. Theory of mind typically develops from the ages of 2½ to 5. Children with ASD seem not to undergo this developmental milestone and thus seem unable to understand others' perspectives and emotional reactions.

DSM-5 Criteria for Autism Spectrum Disorder

- Deficits in social communication and social interactions as exhibited by the following:
    1. Deficits in social or emotional reciprocity, such as not approaching others, not having a back-and-forth conversation, reduced sharing of interests and emotions
    2. Deficits in nonverbal behaviors, such as eye contact, facial expression, body language
    3. Deficit in development of peer relationships appropriate to developmental level
- Restricted, repetitive behavior patterns, interests, or activities exhibited by at least two of the following:
    1. Stereotyped or repetitive speech, motor movements, or use of objects

    2. Excessive adherence to routines, rituals in verbal or nonverbal behavior, or extreme resistance to change
    3. Very restricted interests that are abnormal in focus, such as preoccupation with parts of objects
    4. Hyper- or hyporeactivity to sensory input or unusual interest in sensory environment, such as fascination with lights or spinning objects
- Onset in early childhood
- Symptoms limit and impair functioning

Although some children with ASD can learn to understand emotional experiences, they have a good deal of difficulty with understanding others' feelings. Laboratory studies of children with ASD have found that they may recognize others' emotions without really understanding them (Capps, Rasco, et al., 1999; Capps, Yirmiya, & Sigman, 1991). For example, when asked to explain why someone was angry, a child with ASD responded "because he was yelling" (Capps, Losh, & Thurber, 2000).

Communication Deficits Even before they acquire language, some children with ASD show deficits in communication. By age 2, most typically developing children use words to represent objects in their surroundings and construct one- and two-word sentences to express more complex thoughts, such as "Mommy go" or "Me juice." In contrast, children with ASD lag well behind in these abilities and often show other language disturbances.

One such feature associated with ASD is echolalia, in which the child echoes, usually with remarkable fidelity, what he or she has heard another person say. The teacher may ask a child with ASD, "Do you want a cookie?" The child's response may be, "Do you want a cookie?" This is immediate echolalia. In delayed echolalia, the child may be in a room with the television on and appear to be completely uninterested. Several hours later or even the next day, the child may echo a word or phrase from the television program.

Another language abnormality common in the speech of children with ASD is *pronoun reversal*, in which children refer to themselves as "he," "she," or "you" (or even by their own name). For example:

Parent: *What are you doing, Johnny?*
Child: *He's here.*
Parent: *Are you having a good time?*
Child: *He knows it.*

Pronoun reversal is closely linked to echolalia—when children with ASD use echolalic speech, they refer to themselves as they have heard others speak of them and misapply pronouns. Children with ASD are very literal in their use of words. If a father provided positive reinforcement by putting his daughter on his shoulders when she learned to say the word *yes*, then the child might say *yes* to mean she wants to be lifted onto her father's shoulders. Or a child might say "do not drop the cat" to mean "no," because a parent had used these emphatic words when the child was about to drop the family feline.

Repetitive and Ritualistic Acts Children with ASD can become extremely upset over changes in their daily routines and surroundings. An offer of milk in a different drinking cup or a rearrangement of furniture may make them cry or may precipitate a temper tantrum.

Children with ASD may become focused and preoccupied on specific things. In their play, they may continually line up toys or construct intricate patterns with household objects. As they grow older, they may become preoccupied with train schedules, subway routes, and number sequences. Children with ASD are also likely to perform a more limited number of behaviors than children without ASD and are less likely to explore new surroundings.

Children with ASD may also display stereotypical behavior, peculiar ritualistic hand movements, and other rhythmic movements, such as endless body rocking, hand flapping, and walking on tiptoe. They may spin and twirl string, crayons, sticks, and plates; twiddle their fingers in front of their eyes; and stare at fans and other spinning things. Researchers often describe these as self-stimulatory activities. The children may become preoccupied with manipulating an object and may become very upset when interrupted.

Some children with ASD can become preoccupied with and form strong attachments to simple inanimate objects

Children with ASD do not often play or socially interact with other children.

People with ASD may engage in stereotyped behavior, such as ritualistic hand movements.

(e.g., keys, rocks, a wire-mesh basket, light switches, a large blanket) and to more complex mechanical objects (e.g., refrigerators and vacuum cleaners). If the object is something they can carry, they may walk around with it in their hands, and this may interfere with their learning to do more useful things.

Prevalence of Autism Spectrum Disorder ASD begins in early childhood and can be evident in the first months of life. It affects about 1 of every 68 children (CDC, 2014). About five times more boys than girls have ASD (CDC, 2014). It is found in all socioeconomic, ethnic, and racial groups. The diagnosis of ASD is very stable. In one study, only 1 out of 84 children diagnosed with ASD at age 2 no longer met the diagnostic criteria at age 9 (Lord, Risi, et al., 2006).

Comorbidity and ASD Many children with ASD also have intellectual disability. However, sensorimotor development is the area of greatest relative strength among these children. These children, who may show severe and profound deficits in cognitive abilities, can be quite graceful and adept at swinging, climbing, or balancing, whereas children with intellectual disability have far more difficulty in areas of gross motor development, such as learning to walk. Sometimes children with ASD may have isolated skills that reflect great talent, such as the ability to multiply two four-digit numbers rapidly in their heads. They may also have exceptional long-term memory, being able to recall the exact words of a song heard years earlier.

One study found that over a third of the children with ASD also have a specific learning disorder (Lichtenstein, Carlstrom, et al., 2010). In addition, ASD is also frequently comorbid with anxiety, including separation anxiety, social anxiety, general anxiety, and specific phobias (White, Oswald, et al., 2009).

Prognosis for Autism Spectrum Disorder What happens to children with ASD when they reach adulthood? Generally, children with higher IQs who learn to speak before age 6 have the best outcomes. For example, one longitudinal study of children with ASD from preschool to early adulthood found that IQ scores higher than 70 predicted more strengths and fewer weaknesses in adaptive functioning as the children grew older (McGovern & Sigman, 2005), and outcomes were better for those who had interacted and engaged more with their peers. Another large prospective study followed people from age 2 to age 19. Young adults with IQ scores over 70 at age 19 were doing better socially and on adaptive functioning; 25 percent no longer met criteria for ASD (Anderson, Liang, & Lord, 2014). Other studies of people with ASD who have higher IQ scores have indicated that most do not require residential care and some are able to attend college and support themselves through employment (Yirmiya & Sigman, 1991). Still, many independently functioning adults with ASD continue to show impairment in social relationships (Howlin, Goode, et al., 2004; Howlin, Mawhood, & Rutter, 2000). **Focus on Discovery 13.5** describes a woman with ASD whose adult life is remarkable for its professional distinction blended with the social and emotional deficits that are part of ASD.

Focus on Discovery 13.5

The Story of a Woman Living with Autism Spectrum Disorder

Temple Grandin has autism spectrum disorder. She also has a Ph.D. in animal science, runs her own business designing machinery for use with farm animals, and is on the faculty at Colorado State University. Four autobiographical books (Grandin 1986, 1995, 2008, 2013) and a profile by the late neurologist Oliver Sacks (1995) provide a moving and revealing portrait of the mysteries of ASD. A highly acclaimed HBO movie based on Grandin's 1995 book *Thinking*

in Pictures starred Clare Danes as Temple. Grandin has also written other books about her professional work with animals.

Lacking understanding of the complexities and subtleties of human social discourse, and deficient in the ability to empathize with others, Grandin sums up her relationship to the nonautistic world by saying, "Much of the time I feel like an anthropologist on Mars" (Sacks, 1995, p. 259).

Grandin was diagnosed with autism in 1950 at age 3. She had no speech at all, and doctors predicted that institutionalization would be her fate. However, with the help of a therapeutic nursery school, speech therapy, and the support of her family, she learned to speak by age 6 and began to make more contact with others. Still, as an adolescent she was mystified by the ability of other children to understand each other's needs and wishes, to empathize, and to communicate.

In her own writings, Grandin points out that many people with ASD are great fans of *Star Trek*, especially the characters of Spock and Data. Spock is a member of the Vulcan race, purely intellectual, logical beings who eschew any consideration of the emotional side of life. Data is an android, a highly sophisticated computer housed in a human body and, like Spock, lacking in emotion. (One of the dramatic themes involving both characters was, of course, their flirtation with the experience of human emotion, portrayed with particular poignancy by Data. This is a theme in Grandin's life as well.) As Grandin (1995) wrote at age 47:

> All my life I have been an observer, and I have always felt like someone who watches from the outside. I could not participate in the social interactions of high school life.
>
> Even today, personal relationships are something I don't really understand. I've remained celibate because doing so helps me avoid the many complicated situations that are too difficult for me to handle. [M]en who want to date often don't understand how to relate to a woman. They [and I myself] remind me of Data, the android on *Star Trek*. In one episode, Data's attempts at dating were a disaster. When he tried to be romantic [by effecting a change in a subroutine of his computer program], he complimented his date by using scientific terminology. Even very able adults with autism have such problems. (pp. 132–133)

Some of the difficulties of people with ASD make them charmingly honest and trustworthy. "Lying," wrote Grandin, "is very anxiety-provoking because it requires rapid interpretations of subtle social cues [of which I am incapable] to determine whether the other person is really being deceived" (Grandin, 1995, p. 135).

Grandin's professional career is impressive. She uses her remarkable powers of visualization and her empathy for farm animals to design machines that reduce suffering, such as a chute that leads cows to slaughter via a circular route, which protects them from the fear evoked by awareness of their fate until the moment of death.

Accounts from Grandin and others with ASD can provide insight into how people adapt to their own idiosyncrasies, using the seemingly peculiar gifts they have been given and working around the difficulties they experience. Sacks took note of Grandin's own words about how she has come to think of herself. "If I could snap my fingers and be nonautistic, I would not—because then I wouldn't be me. Autism is part of who I am" (quoted in Sacks, 1995, p. 291).

This type of sentiment was emphasized in Grandin's most recent book (2013) where she stated that there are many things *right* with the autistic brain. In other words, some of the difficulties experienced by people with autism can also be strengths. For example, one of the reasons that social interactions are difficult for her to decipher is that they require an integration of many things happening all at once (e.g., words, facial expressions, gestures, tone of voice). However, she is quite good at concentrating on one thing at a time, and she can bring a laser focus to small details. She credits her success with animals to this ability; she is able to see a small detail that might scare an animal that other people would ignore.

Temple Grandin, Ph.D., was diagnosed with autism in early childhood but has had a successful academic career.

Etiology of Autism Spectrum Disorder

The earliest theory about the etiology of ASD was that psychological factors, such as bad parenting, were responsible for its development. This narrow and faulty perspective has been replaced by theories based on evidence that genetic and neurological factors are important in the etiology. Despite the lack of empirical support for early psychological theories, they gained enough recognition to place a tremendous emotional burden on parents who were told that they were at fault for their child's ASD.

Genetic Factors Evidence suggests a strong genetic component for ASD, with heritability estimates between .50 and .80 (Gaugler, Klei, et al., 2014; Lichtenstein et al., 2010; Sullivan et al., 2012). The risk of ASD or language delay among siblings of people with the disorder is much higher than it is among siblings of people who do not have ASD (Constantino, Zhang, et al., 2010). Evidence for genetic transmission of ASD comes from twin studies, which have found 47–90 percent concordance for ASD between identical twins, compared with concordance rates of 0–20 percent between fraternal twins (Bailey, Le Couteur, et al., 1995; Le Couteur, Bailey, et al., 1996; Lichtenstein et al., 2010).

Even though genes play a big role in ASD, remember that genes do their work via the environment. Another twin study used the most current and well-validated method for diagnosing ASD rather than relying solely on medical records or parental reports, as other studies have done. This study found that shared environmental factors (e.g., common experiences in a family; see Chapter 2) accounted for over half the risk for developed autism (Hallmayer, Cleveland, et al., 2011).

Studies of twins and families with a member with ASD suggest that ASD is linked genetically to a broader spectrum of deficits in communication and social interaction. In families where more than one child had ASD or language delay, unaffected siblings also exhibited deficits in social communication and interactions (Constantino et al., 2010).

Molecular genetics studies try to pinpoint areas of the genome that may confer risk for ASD. Recall from Chapter 2 that genome-wide association studies (GWAS) look for candidate genes associated with a disorder as well as differences in gene sequence (single nucleotide polymorphisms, or SNPs) and gene structure (copy number variations, or CNVs). Evidence to date has indicated several genes are associated with ASD, including rare deletion CNVs and more common variation in genes (Gaugler et al., 2014). The deletion represents a genetic flaw—it was not supposed to be deleted—and although it is not clear why the flaw occurs, it is nonetheless associated with an increased risk of developing ASD (Sanders, He, et al., 2015). The largest GWAS study thus far of over 16,000 participants with ASD (Autism Spectrum Disorders Working Group of the Psychiatric Genomics Consortium, 2017) did not reveal genes that meet the strict statistical test thresholds required, but several genes were identified as possible markers, and, importantly, these genes had been found in other studies (Chaste, Klei, et al., 2015). We have a long way to go before we identify risk genes for ASD, but the pace of the research is rapid and promising.

Neurobiological Factors A number of studies examining the brain in ASD have been well replicated, allowing for a clearer picture of what may go wrong in the brain among people with ASD. What remains to be figured out is why the brain goes awry early in development.

Studies using magnetic resonance imaging (MRI) found that, overall, the brains of adults and children with ASD are larger than the brains of adults and children without ASD (Courchesne, Carnes, & Davis, 2001; Piven, Arndt, et al., 1995, 1996). What makes these findings more interesting and puzzling is that most children with ASD are born with brains of a relatively normal size; however, at ages 1–4, the brains of children with ASD become significantly larger (Courchesne, 2004). A longitudinal study of babies at high familial risk (i.e., someone else in the family had ASD) for ASD measured the trajectory of brain growth using MRI at 6, 12, and 24 months of age (Hazlett, Gu, et al., 2017). The researchers found that overall brain size growth rate was greater between 12 and 24 months, and that the surface area of the brain grew faster at 12–24 months for the high-risk babies. They also found that brain size at 24 months was positively correlated with ASD symptoms. These findings suggest that brain development during the first two years of life may be a critical period of brain development for children who develop ASD. Another longitudinal study assessed brain size using MRI when children with and without autism were 2 years old and again when they were 4 or 5 years old. The researchers found that the children with autism had larger brain size at age 2 but that it did not continue to increase at ages 4 or 5, thus suggesting that brain growth does not continue past the first few years of life (Hazlett, Poe, et al., 2011).

Having a larger-than-normal brain is not necessarily a good thing, as it might indicate that neurons are not being pruned correctly. The pruning of neurons is an important part of brain maturation; older children have fewer connections between neurons than do babies. Adding further to this puzzle, brain growth in ASD appears to slow abnormally in later childhood. We do not yet know how this pattern of brain growth is linked to the signs and symptoms of ASD. It is worth noting that the areas of the brain that are "overgrown" in ASD include the frontal, temporal, and cerebellar, which have been linked with language, social, and emotional functions.

Other areas of the brain are implicated in ASD as well. A meta-analysis of 46 studies found a large effect size for enlarged cerebellum (Stanfield, McIntosh, et al., 2008). Another study found that the commonly observed tendency of children with ASD to explore their surroundings less than other children do is correlated with a larger-than-normal cerebellum (Pierce & Courchesne, 2001).

Given that ASD is associated with social and emotional difficulties, and that the amygdalae are associated with social and emotional behavior, it stands to reason that the amygdalae might be involved in ASD. One study found that the amygdalae were larger among children with ASD (Munson, Dawson, et al., 2006) and that larger amygdalae at ages 3 or 4 predicted more difficulties in social behavior and communication at age 6. This finding is consistent with studies showing overgrowth of other brain areas. However, the other study found that *small* amygdalae size in ASD was correlated with difficulties in emotional face perception and less gaze in the eye region of faces during the perception task (Nacewicz, Dalton, et al., 2006). How can we make sense of these seemingly different findings? Participants in the study by Nacewicz and colleagues were older, suggesting that the brain changes that continue throughout in development may be differentially related to social and emotional impairments. A later meta-analysis confirmed that amygdala size was related to age, with older age being associated with smaller amygdala size (Stanfield et al., 2008).

Treatment of Autism Spectrum Disorder

Even though genetic and neurological factors in the etiology of ASD have much more empirical support than psychological factors, it is the psychological treatments that currently show the most promise, not medications.

Treatments for children with ASD are usually aimed at reducing their unusual behavior and improving their communication and social skills. In most cases, the earlier the intervention begins, the better the outcome. In a promising longitudinal study, children at high risk for developing ASD (parent or sibling with an ASD) were studied beginning at age 14 months. Even though these children did not yet have language, the researchers were able to identify deficits in joint attention and communication that allowed for an early provisional diagnosis of ASD (Landa, Holman, & Garrett-Mayer, 2007).

Behavioral Treatment Psychologist Ivar Lovaas developed a behavioral treatment consisting of intensive operant conditioning with young (under 4 years old) children with ASD (Lovaas, 1987). Therapy encompassed all aspects of the children's lives for more than 40 hours a week over a period of more than 2 years. Parents were also trained extensively so that treatment could continue during almost all the children's waking hours. Nineteen children receiving this intensive treatment were compared with 40 children who received a similar treatment for less than 10 hours per week. Both groups of children were rewarded for being less aggressive, more compliant, and more socially appropriate—for example, talking and playing with other children.

The results of this landmark study were dramatic and encouraging: children in the intensive-therapy group showed a larger increase in IQ scores in 1st grade, and more children in this group were advanced to 2nd grade than were children in the other group. A follow-up of these children 4 years later indicated that the intensive-treatment group maintained their gains in IQ score, adaptive behavior, and grade promotions in school (McEachin, Smith, & Lovaas, 1993). Although critics rightly pointed out weaknesses in the study's methodology and outcome measures (Schopler, Short, & Mesibov, 1989), this ambitious program demonstrated the benefits of intensive therapy with the heavy involvement of both professionals and parents in dealing with the challenges of ASD.

Ivar Lovaas, a behavior therapist, was noted for his operant conditioning treatment of children with autism.

A randomized controlled clinical trial examined the efficacy of intensive behavioral treatment on a broader scale. This study compared an intensive behavioral treatment (about 25 hours a week, instead of 40) with a treatment that consisted of parent training only (Smith, Groen, & Wynn, 2000). Although the behavioral treatment was more effective than parent training alone, the children in this study did not show the same gains as in the previous study discussed, perhaps because the treatment was implemented for fewer hours.

A meta-analysis of 22 studies using other types of intensive behavioral treatments, either in a clinic setting or with parents as the primary point of intervention, reported several noteworthy results. First, the average quality of these studies, rated on a 1 to 5 scale, with 5 being the best, was only 2.5. Few were randomized clinical trials, and many had very small sample sizes. With these limitations in mind, the overall effect sizes were large for changes in IQ score, language skills, overall communication, socialization, and daily living skills (Virués-Ortega, 2010). These results are encouraging, but it remains important to conduct more rigorous studies of these types of treatments.

Other interventions seek to improve children's problems in joint attention and communication. In a randomized controlled clinical trial, children ages 3 and 4 with ASD were randomly assigned to a joint attention (JA) intervention, a symbolic play (SP) intervention, or a control group (Kasari, Freeman, & Paparella, 2006). All children were already part of an early-intervention program; the JA and SP interventions were additional interventions provided to the children in 30-minute daily blocks for 6 weeks. Children in the JA and SP treatments showed more improvement than children in the control group, and at 6 and 12 months after the treatment, children in the JA and SP groups had greater expressive language skills than children in the control group (Kasari, Paparella, et al., 2008).

Medications Medication treatment of ASD is less effective than behavioral treatment. The most commonly used medications for treating problem behaviors in children with ASD are antipsychotic medications, such as haloperidol (trade name Haldol), aripiprazole (trade name Abilify), and risperidone (trade name Risperdol). Some controlled studies have shown that these drugs can reduce irritability or problem behaviors like aggression or self-injury (Fung, Mahajan, et al., 2016; Hellings, Arnold, et al., 2017; McCracken, McGough, et al., 2002). Many children do not respond positively to the medications however, and children may develop troubling side effects, such as weight gain, fatigue, or tremors (Masi, DeMayo, et al., 2017).

Check Your Knowledge 13.4

True or false?

1. All children with ASD also have intellectual disability.
2. Children with ASD have difficulty recognizing emotions in others.
3. Medication is an effective treatment for ASD.

Summary

Clinical Descriptions

- Childhood disorders are often organized into two domains: externalizing disorders and internalizing disorders. Externalizing disorders are characterized by such behaviors as aggressiveness, noncompliance, overactivity, and impulsiveness; they include attention-deficit/hyperactivity disorder, conduct disorder, and oppositional defiant disorder. Internalizing disorders are characterized by such behaviors as depression, social withdrawal, and anxiety; they include childhood anxiety and mood disorders.

- Attention-deficit/hyperactivity disorder (ADHD) is a persistent pattern of inattention and/or hyperactivity and impulsivity that is more frequent and more severe than what is typically observed in children of a given age. Conduct disorder is characterized by high and widespread levels of aggression, lying, theft, vandalism, cruelty to other people and to animals, and other acts that violate laws and social norms.

- Mood and anxiety disorders in children share similarities with the adult forms of these disorders. However, differences that reflect different stages of development are also important.

- Dyslexia is a type of specific learning disorder and it involves problems in reading. Phonological awareness appears to be a key deficit in dyslexia.

- The DSM-5 diagnostic criteria for intellectual disability include deficits in intellectual functioning and adaptive behavior, with childhood onset. Most professionals focus more on the strengths of people with intellectual disability. This shift in emphasis is associated with increased efforts to design psychological and educational interventions that make the most of individual abilities.

- Autism spectrum disorder begins early in life. The major symptoms are a failure to relate to other people; communication problems, consisting of either a failure to learn any language or speech irregularities, such as echolalia and pronoun reversal; and theory of mind problems.

Etiology

- There is strong evidence for genetic and neurobiological factors in the etiology of ADHD. Low birth weight and maternal smoking are also risk factors. Family factors interact with these genetic vulnerabilities.

- Among the apparent etiological and risk factors for conduct disorder are genes, inadequate learning of moral awareness and social emotions, dysfunction in brain areas including amygdala and prefrontal cortex, and negative peer influences.

- Etiological factors for mood and anxiety disorders in children are believed to be largely the same as in adulthood.

- There is mounting evidence that dyslexia has genetic and other neurobiological components. fMRI studies point to different areas of the brain impacted in dyslexia.

- Some forms of intellectual disability have a neurological basis, such as the chromosomal trisomy that causes Down syndrome. Certain infectious diseases in a pregnant mother, such as toxoplasmosis, HIV, and rubella, as well as illnesses that affect the child directly, such as encephalitis, can interfere with cognitive and social development. Environmental factors, such as lead paint, can also cause intellectual disability.

- Family, twin, and GWAS studies give compelling evidence for genetic factors in ASD. Abnormalities have been found in the brains of children with ASD, including an overgrowth of the brain by age 2 and abnormalities in the cerebellum.

Treatment

- A combined treatment including stimulant drugs, such as Adderall or Ritalin, and intensive behavioral treatment has shown effectiveness in reducing the symptoms of ADHD.

- The most promising approach to treating young people with conduct disorder involves intensive intervention in multiple systems, including the family, school, and peer systems.

- Cognitive behavior therapy is effective for mood and anxiety disorders. Medication is effective for depression among adolescents, though its use is not without controversy. Medication is also effective for anxiety when combined with cognitive behavior therapy.

- The most widespread interventions for dyslexia are educational.

- Behavioral treatments and self-instructional training have been used to successfully treat many of the behavioral problems of people with intellectual disability and to improve their problem-solving skills.

- The most effective treatments for ASD are psychological, involving intensive behavioral interventions and work with parents. Various drug treatments have been used but have proved less effective than behavioral interventions.

Answers to Check Your Knowledge Questions

13.1 1. T; 2. T; 3. T; 4. F; 5. life-course-persistent, adolescent-onset; 6. ADHD, substance abuse, depression, anxiety; 7. parent management training, multisystemic treatment.

13.2 1. Depression, Specific Phobia; 2. Hippocampus, attributional style; 3. Selective, Universal, Selective; 4. PTSD; 5. Coping Cat.

13.3 1. b; 2. a; 3. d; 4. b

13.4 1. F; 2. T; 3. F

Key Terms

attention-deficit/hyperactivity disorder (ADHD)
autism spectrum disorder
conduct disorder
developmental psychopathology
Down syndrome (trisomy 21)

dyslexia
externalizing disorders
fragile X syndrome
Intellectual disability
internalizing disorders
joint attention

multisystemic treatment (MST)
parent management training (PMT)
phenylketonuria (PKU)
separation anxiety disorder
specific learning disorder

CHAPTER 14

Late Life and Neurocognitive Disorders

LEARNING GOALS

1. Differentiate common misconceptions from established findings about age-related changes, and discuss methodological issues involved in conducting research on aging.

2. Describe the prevalence of psychological disorders in the elderly and issues involved in estimating the prevalence.

3. Discuss the symptoms, etiology, and treatment of differing forms of dementia.

4. List the symptoms, etiology, and treatment of delirium.

Clinical Case

Henry

Henry, a 56-year-old businessman, was hospitalized for cervical disc surgery. Henry drank heavily but did not appear to have problems from his drinking. Surgery went well, and in the first couple of days, recovery seemed normal. The third night after his operation, though, Henry could not sleep and became restless. The next day he appeared severely fatigued. The next night his restlessness worsened, and he became fearful. Later that night, he thought that he saw people hiding in his room, and just before dawn, he thought he saw strange little animals running around the room. By morning rounds, Henry was very frightened, lethargic, and incoherent. He knew who he was and where he was but did

not know the date or how many days it had been since his surgery. During that day his mental status fluctuated, but by nightfall he had become grossly disoriented and agitated.

A psychiatric consultant diagnosed Henry with delirium, probably due to several factors: alcohol withdrawal, use of strong analgesics, and the stress of the operation. The treatment consisted of a reduction in pain medications, the presence of a family member at all times, and administration of 50 mg of chlorpromazine (Thorazine) three times daily and 500 mg of chloral hydrate at bedtime. Treatment reversed his confusion within 2 days, and he was able to return home in a week with no symptoms. (Strub & Black, 1981, pp. 89–90).

In this chapter, we focus on psychological disorders in late life, with a focus on dementia and delirium. We begin by reviewing some general topics relevant to understanding late life. We describe common myths about aging, challenges faced by the elderly, and some remarkable strengths that come with growing older. Conducting research on aging, however, is complicated by some methodological issues. We discuss evidence that the prevalence of psychological disorders such as depression, anxiety, and substance abuse in the elderly is quite low, and we critique this evidence.

With this information as backdrop, we turn to the main focus of this chapter, the cognitive disorders of dementia and delirium. The elderly are vulnerable to both dementia and delirium. Dementia is defined by a deterioration of cognitive abilities, and delirium is a state of mental confusion and inability to focus attention. For dementia and delirium, we will consider the clinical description, causal factors, and treatment. Most elderly people do not have cognitive disorders. Indeed, the prevalence of cognitive impairment has declined among people over the age of 70 in the United States in the last 15 years, perhaps because of improvements in diet, medical care, and education levels over time (Langa, Larson, et al., 2008). Nonetheless, cognitive disorders account for more medical costs than any other geriatric condition (Zarit & Zarit, 2011).

Aging: Myths, Problems, and Methods

As we age, physiological changes are inevitable, and there may be emotional and mental changes as well. Many of these changes will influence social interactions. The social problems of aging may be especially severe for women. Even with the consciousness-raising of the past decades, our society does not readily accept women with wrinkles and sagging bodies. Although men with gray hair at the temples are seen as distinguished, signs of aging in women are not valued in most cultures. The cosmetics and plastic surgery industries make billions of dollars each year exploiting the fear inculcated in women about looking their age. These attitudes toward aging, though, are not universal. Some cultures respect and revere their elders. In Abkhazia, a region of the Caucasus known for the longevity of the villagers, there is no phrase for "old people"—after age 100, individuals are called "long-living people," and each year, villagers celebrate a holiday of the long-living people (Robbins, 2007).

The elderly are usually defined as people over the age of 65, an arbitrary point set largely by social policies rather than any physiological process. In less than 200 years, life expectancy has almost doubled in the Western world (Oeppen & Vaupel, 2002). At the time of the last census in 2010, people 65 and older comprised 12.4 percent (35 million) of the U.S. population. **Figure 14.1** shows the dramatic increase in the number of older Americans over time. As of 2009, there were 50,000 Americans at least 100 years old; by 2050, that number is expected to grow more than tenfold to over 800,000 (U.S. Bureau of the Census, 2010). The speed of population aging is more rapid in other parts of the world, including Europe and particularly Asia, than it is in

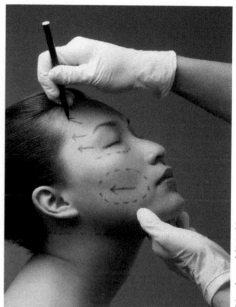

People spend billions of dollars per year on cosmetics and plastic surgery to reduce signs of aging.

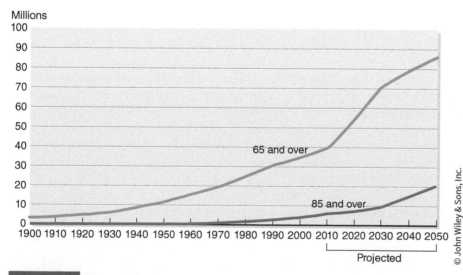

FIGURE 14.1 The number of elderly is on the rise. The number of elderly people and 85 and over, by decade of birth, 1900–2000, and projected, 2010–2050 in the United States (U.S. Bureau of the Census, 2010).

the United States (Bloomberg Data, 2012). In some countries, this has raised concerns about how to address the medical and financial needs of a growing group of retired individuals. Rapid increases in the population of elderly appear to be taking a toll—countries with a sharper rise in numbers of elderly hold more negative attitudes toward the elderly (North & Fiske, 2015). Worldwide, rates of elder abuse have been rising along with population aging (North & Fiske, 2015).

Given these statistics, it is not surprising that about 40 percent of practicing psychologists regularly conduct clinical work with older adults. A major concern, though, is that only 12 clinical psychology graduate programs provide a formal specialization in late-life issues (Institute of Medicine, 2012).

Myths About Late Life

The ethical principles of the American Psychological Association state that it is important for psychologists working with the elderly to examine their stereotypes about late life (APA, 2004). Most people in the United States cling to certain assumptions about old age. Common myths include the idea that we will become doddering and befuddled. We worry that we will be unhappy, cope poorly with troubles, become focused on our poor health, and lead a lonely life.

Each of these myths has been debunked. As we will see, severe cognitive problems do not occur for most people in late life. Although a mild decline in some facets of cognitive functioning is common, different facets of cognition peak at different ages. The speed of information processing tends to peak around age 18, and short-term memory around age 25, with slow declines after that point. In recent generations, though, people tend to be accruing knowledge later and later in their lives. In recent cohorts, many people show increases in their vocabulary through the mid-60s, and some show these increases even into their 80s (Hartshorne & Germine, 2015).

After a dip in middle age, happiness increases into late life in countries around the world (Blanchflower & Oswald, 2008). Although you might suspect that these findings are artifacts of a reluctance of older individuals to describe negative feelings to researchers, laboratory studies verify that the elderly are actually more skilled at regulating their emotions. For example, when shown positive and negative images, older people tend to pay more attention to the positive images (Isaacowitz, 2012) and to display less psychophysiological response to the negative images than do younger people (Kisley, Wood, & Burrows, 2007). When viewing negative images, they show more robust brain activation in regions implicated in emotion regulation than do younger people (Williams, Brown, et al., 2006). Many older people underreport somatic symptoms, perhaps because of beliefs that aches and pains are an inevitable part of aging. People in late life are less likely to meet criteria for somatic symptom disorders than are the young (Hilderink, Collard, et al., 2013).

Another myth, that older people are lonely, has received considerable attention. The truth is that the breadth of social activities that older people engage in is unrelated to their psychological well-being (Carstensen, 1996). As we age, our interests shift away from seeking new social interactions to cultivating a few social relationships that really matter to us, such as those with family and close friends. This phenomenon has been called **social selectivity.**

When we have less time ahead of us, we tend to place a higher value on emotional intimacy than on exploring the world. This preference applies not just to older people but also to younger people who see themselves as having limited time, such as those who are preparing to move far away from their home or who have a life-threatening illness (Frederickson & Carstensen, 1990). When we can't see a future without end, we prefer to spend our limited time with our closest ties rather than with casual acquaintances. Most older people do not report desiring more social contacts (York Cornwell & Waite, 2009). Those unfamiliar with these age-related changes could easily misinterpret social selectivity as harmful social withdrawal.

Many stereotypes we hold about the elderly are false, but considerable research suggests that the negative attitudes about the elderly learned early in life persist and become negative self-perceptions as people move into their later years (Levy, 2003). These negative self-perceptions have serious consequences. Even when stereotypes are cued outside conscious awareness, for example, by flashing words like *unable*

The quality of sleep diminishes as people age.

and *pitiful* on a screen for one tenth of a second, elderly participants who are reminded of these stereotypes reported less will to live than did those exposed to positive words (Marques, Lima, et al., 2014). The effects of stereotypes also appear to have long-term effects. Negative self-views about aging correlate with accelerated cellular aging (as assessed using telomere length) (Pietrzak, Zhu, et al., 2016) and predict biomarkers of dementia (Levy, Ferrucci, et al., 2016) and earlier death (Levy, Slade, & Kasl, 2002). Not only do we need to challenge our own negative stereotypes, but we also need to help older adults challenge those views.

The Problems Experienced in Late Life

As a group, no other people have more of these problems than the elderly. They have them all—physical decline and disabilities, sensory acuity deficits, loss of loved ones, the social stress of stigmatizing attitudes toward the elderly, and the cumulative effects of a lifetime of unfortunate experiences. By age 60, more than half of people have one medical condition that causes severe disability (Vos, Allen, et al., 2016). As people age, the quality and depth of sleep decline (Fetveit, 2009), which can worsen physical, psychological, and cognitive problems unless treated (Ancoli-Israel, 2000). As described by one author, "Late life would qualify as the Olympics of coping" (Fisher, 2011, p. 145).

Polypharmacy, the prescribing of multiple drugs to a person, has increased in the past decade, and about 40 percent of elderly persons are now prescribed at least five medications (Kantor, Rehm, et al., 2015). All too often, doctors do not check to see if the person is taking other medications or seeing other doctors. Many patients don't think to tell the doctor about over-the-counter medications, falsely assuming those wouldn't have side effects or interactions. Once a patient is taking a medication regularly, many doctors don't consider reducing or removing that medication when symptoms dissipate (Opondo, Eslami, et al., 2012). Polypharmacy increases the risk of adverse drug reactions such as side effects and toxicity. Often, physicians prescribe more medications to combat the side effects, thus amplifying the initial problem.

Further complicating the picture is the fact that most researchers test drugs on younger people. Gauging the appropriate dose for the less efficient metabolism of the kidneys and liver of the older person represents a challenge for the medical practitioner—side effects and toxicity are much more likely as people age. Many of those side effects, such as dizziness or cardiovascular symptoms, have particularly serious implications for the elderly. The Agency for Healthcare Research and Quality publishes a list of the many medications that are dangerous for elderly people (https://www.guideline.gov/summaries/summary/49933). A summary of 19 different studies indicates that more than one-fifth of elderly have been prescribed a medication deemed inappropriate for people over the age of 65 due to serious side effects (Opondo et al., 2012). The STOPP/START system is a screening tool designed to identify inappropriate medications for elderly patients and to suggest appropriate alternatives. Several randomized controlled trials indicate that implementing the STOPP/START system can reduce use of inappropriate medications, as well as falls, delirium, time spent in hospitals, and medical costs (Hill-Taylor, Walsh, et al., 2016).

Research Methods in the Study of Aging

Research on aging requires an understanding of several special issues. Because other factors associated with chronological age may influence findings, we must be cautious when we attribute differences between age groups solely to the effects of aging. In the field of aging, as in studies of childhood development, researchers distinguish among three kinds of effects (see **Table 14.1**):

- **Age effects** are the consequences of being a certain chronological age.
- **Cohort effects** are the consequences of growing up during a particular time period with its characteristic challenges and opportunities. For example, war and

As illustrated by John Glenn's space flight at age 77, advancing age need not lead to a curtailment of activities.

ROBERTO SCHMIDT/ AFP/Getty Images, Inc.

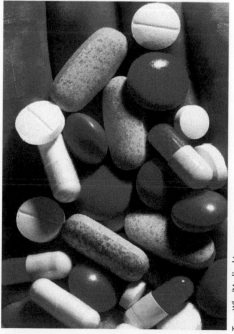

Polypharmacy is all too common in late life.

Tony Why/Medical Images

TABLE 14.1	Age, Cohort, and Time-of-Measurement Effects	
Age Effects	**Cohort Effects**	**Time-of-Measurement Effects**
The effects of being a certain age, e.g., being old enough to receive Social Security	The effects of having grown up during a particular time period; e.g., frugality may be increased among those who lived through the Great Depression of the 1930s	The effects of testing people at a particular time in history; e.g., people became franker during the 1990s in their responses to surveys about their sexual behavior, as media discussion of sexuality increased

famine shape attitudes and health for decades to follow. As another example, the expectations for marriage have changed drastically in the past century, at least in Western societies, from a focus on stability to a focus on happiness and personal fulfilment.

- **Time-of-measurement effects** are confounds that arise because events at a particular point in time can have a specific effect on a variable that is being studied. For example, people tested while anticipating a major hurricane might demonstrate elevated levels of anxiety.

Researchers use two major research designs to assess developmental change: cross-sectional and longitudinal. In cross-sectional studies, the investigator compares different age groups at the same moment in time on the variable. Suppose that in 1995 we took a poll in the United States and found that many interviewees over age 80 spoke with a European accent, whereas those in their 40s and 50s did not. Could we conclude that as people grow older, they develop European accents? Hardly! Cross-sectional studies do not examine the same people over time; consequently, they do not provide clear information about how people change as they age.

In longitudinal studies, the researcher periodically retests one group of people using the same measure over a number of years or decades. For example, the Baltimore Longitudinal Study of Aging is one of the longest-running studies of aging. Since 1958, researchers have been following 1400 men and women to see how their lifestyles, medical conditions, and psychological health change over time. In this study, a great deal has been learned about mental health and aging. For example, researchers were able to combat myths that people become unhappier over time. Rather, people who were happy at age 30 tended to be happy as they moved into late life (Costa, Metter, & McCrae, 1994). In general, longitudinal designs allow us to trace individual patterns of consistency or change over time. Although longitudinal studies offer fundamental advantages, results can be biased by attrition, in which participants drop out of the study due to death, immobility, or lack of interest. When people are no longer available for follow-up because of death, this is called **selective mortality**. Selective mortality results in a particular form of bias in that results obtained with the remaining sample are more relevant to drawing conclusions about relatively healthy people than about unhealthy people. Beyond attrition due to death, people with the most problems are likely to drop out from a study, whereas the people who remain are usually healthier than the general population. Later in this chapter, we will discuss how these issues of cohort effects and selective mortality might influence estimates of the prevalence of psychological disorder.

Cohort effects refer to the fact that people of the same chronological age may differ considerably depending on when they were born.

Quick Summary

As the number of older people in the United States burgeons, more and more mental health professionals are working with this population. Unfortunately, even mental health professionals tend to hold certain stereotypes about late life. In contrast with stereotypes, most people as they age tend to become more effective at regulating emotions, to downplay medical symptoms, and to focus on core relationships over superficial social acquaintances and activities. Even the elderly often hold negative stereotypes about aging, and the effects of such negative self-beliefs can be quite damaging. The challenges of late life do include declining health for many people. As increasing numbers of chronic health problems emerge, polypharmacy becomes an issue for many. Compounding the hazards of polypharmacy, people become more sensitive to medication side effects and toxicity as they age.

In research on aging, it is difficult to disentangle age effects, cohort effects, and time-of-measurement effects. Cross-sectional studies do not help distinguish age and cohort effects. Longitudinal studies provide more clarity about age and cohort effects, but attrition can challenge the validity of findings. One form of attrition, selective mortality, is particularly important to consider in studies of aging.

Check Your Knowledge 14.1
(Answers are at the end of the chapter.)

True or false?

1. The key to happiness in late life is to have many different types of social activities.

Answer the questions.

2. How do emotions and responses to emotion-relevant stimuli change as people age?

3. How do values about social relationships tend to change as people age?

Psychological Disorders in Late Life

The DSM criteria are the same for older and younger adults. Because medical conditions are more common in the elderly, it is particularly important to rule out such explanations. DSM criteria specify that a psychological disorder should not be diagnosed if the symptoms can be accounted for by a medical condition or medication side effects. Medical problems such as thyroid problems, Addison's disease, Cushing's disease, Parkinson's disease, Alzheimer's disease, hypoglycemia, anemia, testosterone deficits, and vitamin deficiencies can produce symptoms that mimic schizophrenia, depression, or anxiety. Age-related deterioration in the vestibular system (inner-ear control of one's sense of balance) can account for panic symptoms such as severe dizziness. Depression is also common after strokes or heart attacks (Carney & Freedland, 2017). Antihypertensive medication, corticosteroids, and antiparkinson medications may contribute to depression or anxiety. Cardiovascular problems can cause erectile problems. It is complex to disentangle medical and psychological concerns!

With this in mind, we next examine the prevalence of psychological disorders in late life. We begin by discussing the best available estimates, and then we address concerns about their accuracy. We then briefly note ways that treatments can be modified to address psychological disorders in the elderly.

Prevalence Estimates of Psychological Disorders in Late Life

The prevalence estimates for psychological disorders defy stereotypes of unhappiness and anxiety in late life. Findings indicate that persons over age 65 have the lowest prevalence of psychological disorders of all age groups. **Table 14.2** provides 12-month estimates from the National Comorbidity Survey–Replication (NCS–R) study, which involved a community representative sample of 9282 people living in the United States who completed extensive

TABLE 14.2 One-Year Prevalence Estimates for Psychological Disorders by Age Group

	18–44 Years	60–64 Years	65 Years and Older
Anxiety disorders			
Panic disorder	3.2 (0.3)	2.8 (0.4)	0.7 (0.2)
Agoraphobia without panic	0.8 (0.2)	1.1 (0.3)	0.4 (0.2)
Specific phobia	9.7 (0.5)	9.2 (0.7)	4.7 (0.6)
Social phobia	8.6 (0.5)	6.1 (0.5)	2.3 (0.4)
Generalized anxiety	2.8 (0.2)	3.2 (0.3)	1.2 (0.3)
Posttraumatic stress[a]	3.7 (0.4)	5.1 (0.6)	0.4 (0.1)
Any anxiety disorder[a]	20.7 (0.7)	18.7 (1.3)	7.0 (0.8)
Mood disorders			
Major depressive disorders	8.2 (0.4)	6.5 (0.5)	2.3 (0.3)
Dysthymia	1.5 (0.2)	1.9 (0.4)	0.5 (0.2)
Bipolar I and bipolar II disorders	1.9 (0.2)	1.2 (0.3)	0.2 (0.1)
Any mood disorder	10.2 (0.4)	8.0 (0.6)	2.6 (0.4)
Substance disorders[a]			
Alcohol abuse	2.6 (0.2)	0.9 (0.2)	0
Drug abuse	1.5 (0.2)	0.2 (0.01)	0
Any substance disorder	3.6 (0.3)	1.0 (0.2)	0
Any disorder			
Any disorder[a]			
At least one disorder	27.6 (0.8)	22.4 (1.5)	8.5 (0.9)

[a]5692 people completed interviews regarding these diagnoses.
Source: Drawn from the NCS–R study (Gum, King-Kallimanis, & Kohn, 2009).

diagnostic interviews (Gum, King-Kallimanis, & Kohn, 2009). As shown, every single disorder was less common in the elderly than in younger adults. None of those age 65 and older met criteria for a drug abuse or dependency disorder. Although not covered in the NCS–R study, rates of schizophrenia are also low among the elderly (Howard, Rabins, et al., 2000). Overall, only about 8.5 percent of elderly people who took part in the NCS–R survey reported symptoms in the year before the interview that were severe enough to diagnose. The elderly are also less likely to meet criteria for personality disorders compared with younger individuals (Balsis, Gleason, et al., 2007). Most people 65 years of age and older are free from serious psychopathology.

Beyond the prevalence rates of disorder, consider the incidence rates, or how many people are experiencing the onset of a new disorder. Most people who have an episode of a psychological disorder late in life are experiencing a recurrence of a disorder that started earlier in life rather than an initial onset. For example, 97 percent of older adults with generalized anxiety disorder report that their symptoms began before the age of 65 (Alwahhabi, 2003), and more than 90 percent of older adults with major depressive or agoraphobia report that their symptoms began earlier in life (Norton, Skoog, et al., 2006; Ritchie, Norton, et al., 2013). Late onset is also extremely rare for schizophrenia (Karon & VandenBos, 1998). In contrast, late onset is more common for drinking problems (Zarit & Zarit, 2011). Most people with psychological disorders in late life, though, are experiencing a continuation of symptoms that began earlier.

Why are rates of psychopathology so low in late life? There are several completely different answers to this question. Earlier, we described some of the ways that aging relates to more positive emotionality and more close-knit social circles. This should translate into a decrease in psychological disorders, and indeed some longitudinal studies suggest that many people who experience psychological disorders early in life grow out of those symptoms. In contrast, some have argued that methodological issues might be leading us to underestimate the prevalence of psychological disorders in late life. We turn to some of these methodological issues next.

Methodological Issues in Estimating the Prevalence of Psychopathology

Methodologically, older adults may be more uncomfortable acknowledging and discussing mental health or drug use problems than younger people are. In one study, researchers interviewed elderly people about depressive symptoms and then interviewed a family member about whether that elderly person was experiencing depressive symptoms. Among those elderly whom family members described as meeting the criteria for major depressive disorder, about one-quarter did not disclose depressive symptoms to the interviewer (Davison, McCabe, & Mellor, 2009). Discomfort discussing symptoms may minimize prevalence estimates.

In addition to reporting bias, there may be cohort effects. For example, many people who reached adulthood during the drug-oriented era of the 1960s continue to use drugs as they age (Zarit & Zarit, 2011). Their generation has more problems with substance abuse in late life than previous generations had. Although the 50-and-older age group accounted for only 6.6 percent of substance abuse admissions in the United States in 1992, by 2008 the same age group accounted for 12.2 percent of such admissions.

Beyond these explanations, people with psychological disorders are at risk for dying earlier—before age 65—for several different reasons. Heavy drinkers are at risk for premature mortality from cirrhosis. Cardiovascular disease and diabetes are more common among people with a history of anxiety disorders, depressive disorders, bipolar disorder, and alcohol use disorders (Scott, Lim, et al., 2016). Given the close ties between serious medical illness and these syndromes, it is perhaps not surprising that psychological disorders are associated with premature mortality (Lawrence, Kisely, & Pais, 2012). For example, Frojdh and colleagues (2003) conducted surveys with over 1200 elderly people. Compared to those with low scores, those who obtained high scores on a self-report measure of depression were 2.5 times as likely to die within the next 6 years. Because people with psychological disorders may die earlier, studies on aging may suffer from the issue of selective mortality.

These three methodological issues—response biases, cohort effects, and selective mortality—could help explain the low rates of psychological disorders in late life. Most researchers, however, believe that aging is also genuinely related to better mental health.

Treatment

Many of the pharmacological and psychological treatments that work in earlier life are efficacious for the elderly. Nonetheless, several issues require careful consideration. Many psychiatric medications, including benzodiazepines, antipsychotic medications, and some antidepressants, can cause serious side effects in the elderly (Mulsant & Pollock, 2015). Some psychotropic medications can be prescribed safely for elderly patients at lower doses. As with younger people, psychotherapy is the first-line approach for anxiety and has been shown to be helpful for other syndromes as well in late life. Therapists may need to adapt psychotherapies to adjust for vision or hearing loss, or to offer telephone sessions for elderly clients with limited mobility (Brenes, Danhauer, et al., 2015; Mavandadi, Benson, et al., 2015). When cognitive declines are present, including a caregiver in the therapy sessions and providing reminders of session content can be helpful (Smoski & Areán, 2015).

Quick Summary

When the elderly present with psychological disorders, it is critically important to evaluate potential medical causes. The elderly are particularly susceptible to the negative effects of medical conditions and medications, and these effects may mimic psychological conditions.

Studies suggest lower rates of psychological disorders among the elderly compared with other age groups. Although some methodological issues (cohort effects, selective mortality, and lack of disclosure) might explain part of this effect, it may be that people become more psychologically healthy as they age.

Medications and psychological treatments have shown efficacy in addressing psychological illnesses among the elderly. Those treatments may need to be tailored to consider medication sensitivity, sensory deficits, mobility, or memory loss.

Check Your Knowledge 14.2

True or false?

1. The DSM provides tailored criteria to evaluate diagnoses for those in late life.

Answer the questions.

2. Define selective mortality.

3. Discuss reasons that the elderly may not reveal psychological symptoms in interviews.

Dementia

Dementia is a descriptive term for the deterioration of cognitive abilities to the point that functioning becomes impaired. As we will discuss, there are many different causes for dementia, and the nature of symptoms depends on the type of dementia. The diagnosis of dementia is based on declines in cognitive abilities, including attention, executive function, learning, memory, language, perceptual-motor ability, abstract thinking, and social cognition. Of these, diminished memory, especially for recent events, is the most common symptom.

As dementia progresses, most people tend to develop neuropsychiatric symptoms—psychiatric symptoms that appear to be secondary to the neurological disease (Okura, Plassman, et al., 2010). The most common neuropsychiatric syndrome is depression, which affects about 50 percent of those with dementia, but other affective and motivational symptoms, such as apathy, anxiety, and irritability also can develop. Sleep disturbances are common. Delusions and hallucinations can occur (American Psychiatric Association, 2013). People with dementia may lose control of their impulses; they may use coarse language, tell inappropriate jokes, shoplift, and make sexually inappropriate remarks.

Most dementias develop very slowly over a period of years; subtle cognitive and behavioral deficits often emerge well before the person shows any noticeable impairment. The early signs of decline before functional impairment is present are labeled as **mild cognitive impairment (MCI)**.

Diagnostic criteria for dementia and MCI have been developed by a consensus panel of leading experts with support from the National Institute of Aging and the Alzheimer's Association (Albert, Dekosky, et al., 2011; McKhann, Knopman, et al., 2011). The DSM-5 system also provides parallel diagnoses like those for dementia and for MCI. See **Table 14.3** for an overview of the DSM-5 diagnoses. DSM mild neurocognitive disorders are similar to MCI, whereas DSM major neurocognitive disorders are similar to a diagnosis of dementia. Throughout this chapter, we use the terms *dementia* (rather than *major neurocognitive disorder*) and *mild cognitive impairment (MCI)* (rather than *mild neurocognitive disorder*).

TABLE 14.3   DSM-5 Neurocognitive Disorders
Delirium
Neurocognitive disorder: Specify mild or major
Neurocognitive disorder associated with Alzheimer's disease
Neurocognitive disorder associated with frontotemporal lobar degeneration
Neurocognitive disorder associated with vascular disease
Neurocognitive disorder associated with traumatic brain injury
Neurocognitive disorder associated with Lewy body disease
Neurocognitive disorder associated with Parkinson's disease
Neurocognitive disorder associated with HIV infection
Neurocognitive disorder associated with substance/medication use
Neurocognitive disorder associated with Huntington's disease
Neurocognitive disorder associated with prion disease
Neurocognitive disorder due to another medical condition
Neurocognitive disorder due to multiple etiologies

DSM-5 Criteria for Mild Neurocognitive Disorder

- Modest cognitive decline from previous levels in one or more domains based on both of the following:
1. Concerns of the patient, a close other, or a clinician
2. Modest neurocognitive decline (i.e., between the 3rd and 16th percentile) on formal testing or equivalent clinical evaluation

- The cognitive deficits do not interfere with independence in everyday activities (e.g., paying bills or managing medications), even though greater effort, compensatory strategies, or accommodation may be required to maintain independence
- The cognitive deficits do not occur exclusively in the context of delirium and are not due to another psychological disorder

DSM-5 Criteria for Major Neurocognitive Disorder

- Significant cognitive decline from previous levels in one or more domains based on both of the following:
1. Concerns of the patient, a close other, or a clinician
2. Substantial neurocognitive impairment (i.e., below the 3rd percentile on formal testing) or equivalent clinical evaluation

- The cognitive deficits interfere with independence in everyday activities
- The cognitive deficits do not occur exclusively in the context of delirium and are not due to another psychological disorder

There is some debate about how early to diagnose MCI. The DSM-5 criteria for mild neurocognitive disorder require a low score on only one cognitive test. There are problems with this approach. For one, some cognitive tests are more reliable and more relevant to dementia than others are, and the criteria do not address this. Second, the criteria suggest reliance on a single test, but using more than one test could improve reliability. Using a set of neuropsychological scores to define MCI drastically decreases the rates of MCI diagnosis, more accurately identifies people with early biological indicators of dementia, and is more predictive of the development of dementia (Bondi, Edmonds, et al., 2014). Overall, the current MCI criteria may not be very reliable and could lead to overdiagnosis.

When people experience declines in their cognitive function, all too often they assume that this is an expected part of aging. To the contrary, good clinical care involves a careful workup for problems that may be causing cognitive declines, such as infection, sleep loss, thyroid disease, or vitamin deficiencies. About 10 percent of the time, cognitive declines are tied to such factors and can be reversed. Treatments to reduce any cardiovascular disease can also reduce the odds that cognitive declines will progress to dementia (Langa & Levine, 2014).

Especially given the concerns about the current MCI criteria, caution is warranted in diagnosing these early signs of decline. Not all people with mild cognitive symptoms develop dementia. Estimates vary, but among adults with MCI, about 10 percent per year will develop dementia; among adults without MCI, about 1 percent per year will develop dementia (Mitchell & Shiri-Feshki, 2009). It is important to provide careful psychoeducation regarding these diagnoses so that patients and family members, like Mrs. J. in the clinical case, do not assume that symptoms will necessarily progress to dementia.

Clinical Case

Mrs. J.

Mrs. J., an 81-year-old woman, contacted a neurologist for evaluation, stating: "I am forgetting things I just heard." She and her husband reported that her memory problems had started about 18 months before the appointment and had slowly worsened since then. Her husband reported that she had developed other cognitive symptoms, such as less ability to problem solve, manage time, and take initiative, along with greater distractibility. Both noticed that she had trouble remembering recent conversations, more frequently misplaced her possessions, and had difficulty remembering directions to familiar places. With the cognitive changes, Mrs. J. became less interested in reading, she needed frequent reminders about how to use her computer and cell phone, her housekeeping declined, and she stopped cooking elaborate meals. She and her husband noted that her sleep and mood were fine, and they denied other mental health or behavioral symptoms. She was able to complete expected activities of daily living independently, and no medical cause of her cognitive symptoms was identified. After neuropsychological testing, Mrs. J. was diagnosed with mild cognitive impairment (MCI).

Source: Drawn from Langa & Levine, 2014

Worldwide prevalence estimates of dementia in 2010 were over 35 million. Although less than 2 percent of people develop dementia before age 65, the prevalence increases dramatically as people age, to more than a third of people in their 90s (Prince, Bryce, et al., 2013). The prevalence of dementia appears to be lower (2.07 percent) in sub-Saharan Africa, and higher in Latin America (8.5 percent) (Prince et al., 2013). The average age of onset for dementia is becoming slightly later over time in the United States and in Europe, perhaps because of improvements in diet, exercise, education, and general health (Satizabal, Beiser, et al., 2016; Wu, Fratiglioni, et al., 2016). Even with these gains, though, the number of cases of dementia in the world is expected to double by 2030 as the number of elderly grow (Prince et al., 2013).

There are many different types of dementia, and we discuss four types here: Alzheimer's disease, the most researched form; frontotemporal dementia, defined by the areas of the brain that are most affected; vascular dementia, caused by cerebrovascular disease; and Lewy body dementia, defined by the presence of Lewy bodies (a type of abnormal deposit that forms on neurons). Other than these four forms of dementia, other medical conditions, such as viruses, infections, toxins, or head trauma that affect brain tissue, can produce dementia. By far, the most common form of dementia is Alzheimer's disease, which accounts for more than half of dementias (Terry, 2006). We will discuss these forms of dementia separately; however, at autopsy, some show pathology of more than one form of dementia; for example, some with Alzheimer's disease also show vascular dementia (Kimchi & Lyketsos, 2015).

Alzheimer's Disease

In **Alzheimer's disease**, initially described by the German neurologist Alois Alzheimer in 1906, the brain tissue irreversibly deteriorates, and death usually occurs within 12 years after the onset of symptoms. Over 90,000 Americans die each year from this disease, and in 2014, it was the sixth leading cause of death in the United States (Heron, 2016). In 2015, the direct and indirect costs associated with Alzheimer's disease in the United States were estimated at $221 billion (Alzheimer's Association, 2016).

The most prominent symptom of Alzheimer's disease is memory loss. The illness may begin with absentmindedness and gaps in memory for new material, as described in the Clinical Case of Mary Ellen. The person may leave tasks unfinished and forgotten if interrupted. The person who had started to fill a teapot at the sink leaves the water running. It may be hard to find words. These shortcomings may be overlooked for several years but eventually interfere with daily living.

Memory loss is not the only symptom of Alzheimer's disease. Apathy is common even before the cognitive symptoms become noticeable (Balsis, Carpenter, & Storandt, 2005), and about a third of people develop full-blown depression as the illness worsens (Vinkers, Gussekloo, et al., 2004). As the disease develops, problems with language skills and word finding intensify.

Clinical Case

Ellen

"I am so glad you came," Ellen says when I greet her. She is sitting at the dining room table sipping juice, a slender, almost frail woman. But Ellen has presence. She has the posture of a dancer: shoulders back, neck elongated, head up, and the gaunt face of a once beautiful woman, with large milky hazel eyes and high patrician cheekbones. She smiles and reaches for my hand. "It is so nice of you to visit," she says.

Ellen is gracious and polite, but the truth is, she doesn't remember me. She doesn't remember that we've visited a half dozen times before, that a few days ago we had tea together, that just yesterday I sat on her bed for a

half hour massaging her hands with rosemary mint lotion. Ellen, like the 43 others living at this residential care facility, has Alzheimer's disease. Her short-term memory is shot, and her long-term memory is quirky and dreamlike, with images that are sometimes bright and lucid, and other times so out of focus that she can hardly make them out. Her life is like a puzzle someone took apart when she wasn't looking. She can see some of the pieces, but she can no longer see how they fit together. (Kessler, 2004, p. 1)

Source: Lauren Kessler, Finding Life in the Land of Alzheimer's (NY: Penguin. 2007) originally published in paperback as Dancing with Rose: Finding Life in the Land of Alzheimer's.

Clinical Case

Mary Ellen

Mary Ellen was a 62-year-old family therapist who loved her career in end-stage hospice work when she was first diagnosed with early-stage Alzheimer's disease.

All of a sudden—but it wasn't all of a sudden, of course—I began to realize that I wasn't the gal I used to be. It was different inside my head.

It was the very simple things. I would be talking with someone on the telephone, then hang up and ask myself, "Who was that? What did we talk about?" My husband

John says he knew something serious was going on when we returned from a vacation together and I told him, "I really had a great time in California. I'm so sorry you couldn't make it."

My message to people with Alzheimer's is this: Be gentle with yourself. This disease requires that you lower your expectations of yourself. That's a hard thing for most of us to do. The fear is losing yourself, knowing that you won't bring this self to the end stage of your life. —Mary Ellen Becklenberg (Park, 2010, p. 59)

Visual-spatial abilities decline, which can manifest in **disorientation** (confusion with respect to time, place, or identity). The person may easily become lost, even in familiar surroundings.

As the brain deterioration progresses, the range and severity of behavioral symptoms increase. People with the disorder are typically unaware of their cognitive problems initially, and they may blame others for lost objects even to the point of developing delusions of being persecuted. Memory continues to deteriorate, and the person becomes increasingly disoriented and agitated. As the dementia progresses, a parent is unable to remember the name of a daughter or son and later may not even recall that he or she has children or recognize them when they come to visit. The person may forget to bathe or dress adequately. Judgment may become faulty, and the person may have difficulty comprehending situations and making plans or decisions. In the terminal phase of the illness, personality loses its sparkle and integrity. Relatives and friends say that the person is just not himself or herself anymore. Social involvement with others keeps narrowing. Finally, the person is oblivious to his or her surroundings.

The brains of people with Alzheimer's disease have more **plaques** (small, round beta-amyloid protein deposits that are outside the neurons) and **neurofibrillary tangles** (twisted protein filaments composed largely of the protein tau in the axons of neurons) than would be expected for the person's age (see **Figure 14.2**). Some people produce excessive amounts of beta-amyloid, whereas others have deficiencies in the mechanisms for clearing

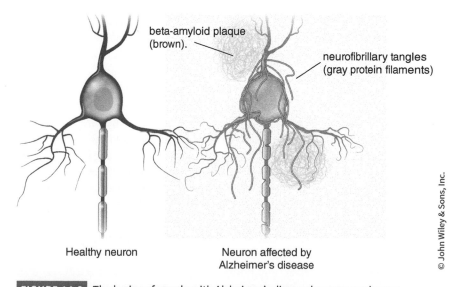

beta-amyloid plaque (brown).

neurofibrillary tangles (gray protein filaments)

Healthy neuron

Neuron affected by Alzheimer's disease

© John Wiley & Sons, Inc.

FIGURE 14.2 The brains of people with Alzheimer's disease have more plaques (small, round beta-amyloid protein deposits that are outside the neurons) and neurofibrillary tangles (twisted protein filaments composed largely of the protein tau in the axons of neurons) than would be expected for their age.

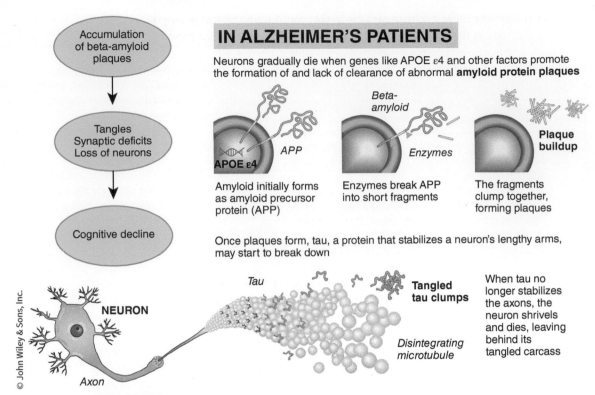

FIGURE 14.3 In Alzheimer's disease, risk factors such as the gene APOE ε4 lead to an increased deposition of beta-amyloid plaques. These plaques build up outside the neurons for decades before the cognitive symptoms are noticeable. Neurofibrillary tangles of tau form, and the neurons die.

beta-amyloid from the brain (Jack, Albert, et al., 2011). The beta-amyloid plaques are most densely present in the frontal cortex (Klunk, Engler, et al., 2004) and may be present for 20 to 30 years before the cognitive symptoms become noticeable (Jansen, Ossenkoppele, et al., 2015). A longer variant of beta-amyloid, beta-amyloid 42, is particularly prone to forming plaques and may be more strongly tied to disease progression (Kimchi & Lyketsos, 2015). Plaques can be measured using a PET scan. Tangles can be measured in cerebrospinal fluid or using a PET scan as well. Tangles are most densely present in the hippocampus, an area that is involved in memory. Over time, as the disease progresses, plaques and tangles spread through more of the brain (Klunk et al., 2004; Sperling, Aisen, et al., 2011).

Immune responses to plaques lead to inflammation (Gorelick, 2010), which then appear to trigger a series of brain changes over time, as shown in **Figure 14.3**. At early stages, there is a loss of synapses for acetylcholinergic (ACh) and glutamatergic neurons. Neurons also begin to die. As neurons die, the entorhinal cortex surrounding the hippocampus and then the hippocampus (see Figure 14.3) and other regions of the cerebral cortex shrink, and later the frontal, temporal, and parietal lobes shrink (see **Figure 14.4**). As this happens, the ventricles enlarge. The cerebellum, spinal cord, and motor and sensory areas of the cortex are less affected, which is why people with Alzheimer's do not appear to have anything physically wrong with them until late in the disease process. For some time, people with Alzheimer's are able to walk around normally, and their overlearned habits, such as making small talk, remain intact, so that in short encounters strangers may not notice anything amiss. About 25 percent of people with Alzheimer's disease eventually develop motor deficits.

The genetic contributions to Alzheimer's disease differ for those with early onset (before age 65) and those with later onset (65 or older). The vast majority of cases are late onset, and heritability estimates for late onset Alzheimer's disease range between 60 and 80 percent (Hollingworth & Williams, 2011). In GWAS research with more than 74,000 individuals, researchers have identified a set of 19 specific genetic loci. Most of the genes explain a very small amount of risk in the onset of Alzheimer's disease (Lambert, Ibrahim-Verbaas, et al., 2013).

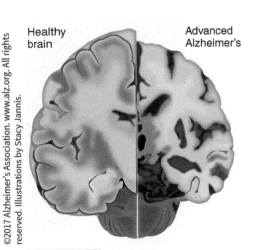

FIGURE 14.4 In Alzheimer's disease, neurons die; the entorhinal cortex, hippocampus, and other regions of the cerebral cortex shrink; and ventricles enlarge.

By far, the genetic polymorphism with the largest contribution to Alzheimer's disease is a polymorphism of a gene on chromosome 19, called the apolipoprotein ε4 or APOE ε4 allele (Lambert et al., 2013). Whereas having one ε4 allele increases the risk of Alzheimer's disease to about 20 percent, having two ε4 alleles brings the risk substantially higher. APOE ε4 appears more related to risk of disease among white and Japanese samples than among Hispanic or African-American samples (Hollingworth & Williams, 2011). Researchers are beginning to understand some of the ways that the ε4 may increase risk of the disorder. People with two of the ε4 alleles show overproduction of beta-amyloid plaques, less clearing of excess beta-amyloid from the brain, loss of neurons in the hippocampus, and low glucose metabolism in several regions of the cerebral cortex even before they develop symptoms of Alzheimer's disease (Bookheimer & Burggren, 2009).

Many of the genes that increase risk for Alzheimer's disease are related to immune function and cholesterol metabolism (Kimchi & Lyketsos, 2015). Immune processes and excessively high cholesterol can trigger inflammation, and accordingly conditions that involve immune and inflammatory processes appear related to a greater risk of Alzheimer's disease. For example, glycemia and diabetes, which have been tied to immune and inflammatory changes, are related to greater risk of developing Alzheimer's disease and other forms of dementia (Cooper, Sommerlad, et al., 2015; Crane, Walker, et al., 2013). Similarly, brain traumas from accidents or injuries can also increase the risk of Alzheimer's disease later in life.

Beyond genetic and medical risk factors, lifestyle variables play a role in Alzheimer's. For example, across large-scale representative samples, social isolation and insomnia are related to a greater risk of Alzheimer's disease, while fish consumption, a Mediterranean diet, exercise, education, and engagement in cognitive activities are related to a lower risk (Anstey, Cherbuin, et al., 2011; Beydoun, Beydoun, et al., 2014; Williams, Plassman, et al., 2010; Holth, Patel, et al., 2017). In one study of lifestyle effects, researchers enrolled 2509 elderly persons in a study during their 70s and then followed them for 8 years. Those with a high school education who exercised at least once a week, remained socially active, and did not smoke sustained their cognitive functioning without decline throughout the 8 years (Yaffe, Fiocco, et al., 2009). Of the various lifestyle factors, the effects for exercise and cognitive engagement have received a good deal of study, and so we focus on those here. We then turn to a discussion of depression findings which illustrate how complicated it is to understand risk factors in Alzheimer's disease.

Many large-scale longitudinal studies suggest that exercise may help prevent memory problems. Regular exercise predicts less decline in cognitive functions (Sofi, Valecchi, et al., 2011) and decreased risk of developing Alzheimer's disease over time (Beydoun et al., 2014). Exercise levels at mid-life are important, but so is sustained exercise in late life. Exercise has been related to lower levels of plaques in the brain, and particularly so for those with the APOE ε4 polymorphism (Head, Bugg, et al., 2012).

Engagement in intellectual activities also appears helpful, with some proposing a "use it or lose it" model of Alzheimer's. For example, regular reading of a newspaper is related to lower risk (Wilson, Scherr, et al., 2007). Findings of a meta-analysis including 29,000 persons drawn from 22 representative community samples suggested that frequent cognitive activity (for example, reading and puzzle solving) is related to a 46 percent decrease in risk of Alzheimer's disease compared to infrequent cognitive activity (Valenzuela & Sachdev, 2006). Parallel with the findings for exercise, engagement in intellectual activities protects against cognitive decline for those with the APOE ε4 polymorphism (Vemuri, Lesnick, et al., 2014).

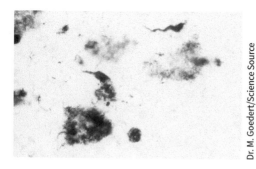

Light micrograph of a section of entorhinal cortex brain tissue affected by Alzheimer's disease showing amyloid plaques in brown and neurofibrillary tangles in grey. In Alzheimer's disease, neurons die in the entorhinal cortex, and then loss of neurons begins to occur in other regions of the brain.

Dr. M. Goedert/Science Source

Alzheimer's Disease

Normal Control

Positron emission tomography (PET) images of the brain after administration of Pittsburgh Compound B in a woman with Alzheimer's disease shows high levels of amyloid plaque (upper series). In contrast, low levels of amyloid plaque are seen in the PET images of a woman with no Alzheimer's symptoms (lower series).

Courtesy of Dr. Claudia Prada and Dr. Brian Bacskai

Exercise programs are of some help in reducing the severity of MCI.

© isitsharp/iStockphoto

Intriguingly, among people with similar levels of plaques and tangles in their brain, those with higher levels of intellectual activity show fewer cognitive symptoms. That is, intellectual activity seems to protect against the expression of underlying neurobiological disease (Wilson et al., 2007). This type of work has led to the concept of **cognitive reserve**, or the idea that some people may be able to compensate for the disease by using alternative brain networks or cognitive strategies such that cognitive symptoms are less pronounced.

Of concern, naturalistic studies cannot disentangle whether the people who engage in exercise or cognitive activities differ in some important way (on characteristics relevant to disease) from those who do not engage in these activities. We know that biological changes in the brain begin 20 years before the symptoms of Alzheimer's disease first emerge; it is plausible that those brain changes influence motivation to take part in exercise or cognitive activities. Intervention studies, described below, that randomly assign people to take part in exercise or cognitive training help address this methodological issue.

The complexity of trying to identify the direction of effects is illustrated by the relationship of depression and Alzheimer's disease. We mentioned earlier that depression can be a consequence of dementia. Vice versa, a lifetime history of depression predicts greater risk for Alzheimer's disease and other forms of dementia (Katon, Pedersen, et al., 2015). Remember, though, that biological changes begin to occur decades before the onset of Alzheimer's disease. Could those types of biological changes be causing even the depressive symptoms that precede dementia onset? To examine this, researchers plotted cognitive and depression scores of over 10,000 people for a 28-year period (Singh-Manoux, Dugravot, et al., 2017). Medical records were reviewed for diagnoses of dementia. As shown in **Figure 14.5**, among those who developed dementia, cognitive scores declined significantly 12 years before diagnosis, and their cognitive decline escalated in the years before diagnosis, while depressive symptoms began to increase significantly 10 years before the dementia diagnosis—that is, *after* cognitive declines had already begun. Depressive symptoms earlier in life were unrelated to the risk of dementia. These findings indicate that the depressive symptoms observed before dementia onset may be a manifestation of the neurological decline.

Frontotemporal Dementia

As suggested by the name, **frontotemporal dementia (FTD)** is caused by a loss of neurons in frontal and temporal regions of the brain. The neuronal deterioration of FTD occurs predominantly in the anterior temporal lobes and prefrontal cortex (Pressman & Miller, 2014). FTD typically begins in the late 50s, and it progresses rapidly; death usually occurs within 5 years of the diagnosis (Kimchi & Lyketsos, 2015). FTD is rare, affecting less than 1 percent of the population (Pressman & Miller, 2014).

Unlike Alzheimer's disease, memory is not severely impaired in FTD. There are multiple subtypes of FTD. The diagnostic criteria for behavioral variant FTD, the most common form, include deterioration in at least three of the following areas: empathy, executive function (cognitive capacity to plan and organize), ability to inhibit behavior, compulsive or perseverative behavior, tendencies to put nonfood objects in the mouth, and apathy (Rascovsky, Hodges, et al., 2011). In early stages, significant others may notice changes in personality and judgment. FTD strikes emotional processes more profoundly than Alzheimer's disease does, and in doing so, it can damage social relationships and marital satisfaction more than Alzheimer's disease does (Ascher, Sturm, et al., 2010). Particular deficits emerge in the ability to regulate emotions (Goodkind, Gyurak, et al., 2010). Socially inappropriate and impulsive behaviors, such as embarrassing or sexually inappropriate comments,

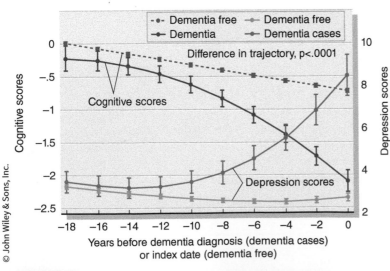

FIGURE 14.5 Cognitive scores begin to decline 12 years before the onset of dementia. Depression scores begin to increase a couple years later than cognitive scores, at 10 years before dementia onset (Singh-Manoux et al., 2017).

reckless spending, and criminal behaviors can emerge. Apathy and reduced sexual libido are often present, and many patients show a loss of sympathy and emotional responsiveness toward their friends and family members.

Because a person affected by this disorder might suddenly start to overeat, chain smoke, drink alcohol, or demonstrate other behavioral symptoms, FTD often is misdiagnosed as a midlife crisis or as a psychological disorder such as bipolar disorder or schizophrenia (Zhou & Seeley, 2014). The presence of apathy can result in a misdiagnosis of depression (Kimchi & Lyketsos, 2015).

FTD can be caused by many different molecular processes (Bang, Spina, et al., 2015). One of these is Pick's disease, characterized by the presence of Pick bodies (spherical inclusions) within neurons, but many other diseases or pathological processes can result in FTD. A third to a half of people with FTD show high levels of tau, the protein filaments that contribute to the neurofibrillary tangles observed in Alzheimer's disease. FTD has a strong genetic component (Bang et al., 2015).

Vascular Dementia

By definition, **vascular dementia** is caused by cerebrovascular disease. Most commonly, strokes cause a blood clot, which then impairs circulation and results in the death of neurons. About 7 percent of people will develop dementia in the year after a first stroke, and the risk of dementia increases with recurrent strokes (Pendlebury & Rothwell, 2009). Risk for vascular dementia involves the same risk factors as those for cardiovascular disease in general—for example, older age, a high level of "bad" (LDL) cholesterol, cigarette smoking, and elevated blood pressure (Moroney, Tang, et al., 1999). Strokes and vascular dementias are more common in African Americans than in whites (Froehlich, Bogardus, & Inouye, 2001). Because strokes and cardiovascular disease can strike different regions of the brain, the symptoms of vascular dementia vary a good deal. The onset of symptoms is usually more rapid in vascular dementia than in other forms of dementia.

Dementia with Lewy Bodies

In **dementia with Lewy bodies (DLB)**, protein deposits called Lewy bodies form in the brain and cause cognitive decline. As shown in **Figure 14.6**, the Lewy bodies are most often present in the olfactory bulb and the brain stem initially, and as they spread through the brain, the cognitive symptoms of DLB become noticeable. Lewy bodies are also implicated in Parkinson's disease. About 80 percent of people with Parkinson's disease will develop dementia, but some people without Parkinson's will develop DLB as well (Goedert, Spillantini, et al., 2013). DLB is rare, affecting one percent or less of elderly individuals. Among those with dementia, less than 10 percent have DLB (Hogan, Fiest, et al., 2016).

The symptoms associated with this type of dementia are often hard to distinguish from the symptoms of Parkinson's (such as the shuffling gait) and Alzheimer's disease (such as loss of memory). DLB is more likely than Alzheimer's disease to include prominent visual hallucinations and fluctuating cognitive symptoms (American Psychiatric Association, 2013). People with DLB are often extremely sensitive to the physical side effects of antipsychotic

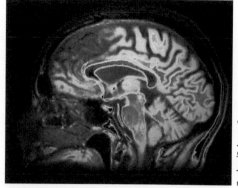
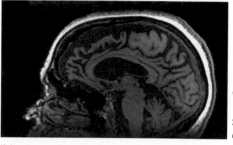

(a)

(b)

Zephyr/Science Source

Dr. Murray Grossman

Frontotemporal dementia. (a) A colored magnetic resonance imaging (MRI) scan of the brain of a 50-year-old with frontotemporal dementia. The front of the brain is at left. The frontal (left) and temporal (center) lobes have atrophied (shrunk). (b) An MRI scan of a healthy brain.

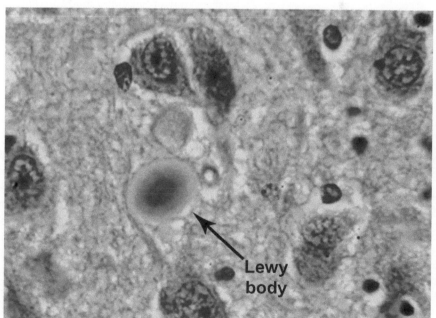

Lewy body

Courtesy Kondi Wong, Armed Forces Institute of Pathology website address: http://www.genome.gov/pressDisplay.cfm?photoID=10004

Dementia with Lewy bodies (DLB) is defined by the presence of abnormal deposits called Lewy bodies. The Lewy bodies are found throughout the brain.

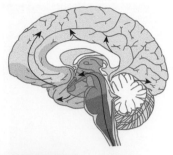

FIGURE 14.6 In dementia with Lewy bodies (DLB), the Lewy bodies usually are initially present in the olfactory bulb and the brain stem. Cognitive symptoms become noticeable as the Lewy bodies spread through the brain. Darker areas show the most common areas of denser concentrations of Lewy bodies (Goedert et al., 2013).

medications. Another distinct symptom of DLB is that people often experience intense dreams accompanied by levels of movement and vocalizing, as though they are "acting out their dreams" (McKeith, Dickson, et al., 2005).

Treatments for Dementia

Sadly, despite hundreds of attempts to create new medications since 2000 (Park, 2016), there is no cure for dementia. Some medications are used to delay symptom progression and to address related syndromes, but no medications have been shown to help address the cognitive symptoms of FTD (Bang et al., 2015). There are also some psychological and lifestyle approaches to dementia which are designed to slow cognitive decline, address related syndromes, and improve the well-being of caretakers.

Medications Much of the treatment research has focused on Alzheimer's disease and on memory decline. Medications help slow decline, but they do not restore memory function to previous levels (Brandt & Mansour, 2016). The most commonly used medications for dementia are the cholinesterase inhibitors (drugs that interfere with the breakdown of acetylcholine), including donepezil (Aricept) and rivastigmine (Exelon). Cholinesterase inhibitors have a slight effect in slowing memory decline compared to placebo for Alzheimer's disease and DLB (Boot, McDade, et al., 2013; Brandt & Mansour, 2016). In addition to cholinesterase inhibitors, memantine (Namenda), a drug that affects glutamate receptors involved in memory, has shown small effects in placebo-controlled trials for Alzheimer's disease (Brandt & Mansour, 2016). for Unfortunately, many people discontinue these drugs due to aversive side effects such as nausea (Maidment, Fox, & Boustani, 2006).

For those with vascular dementia, and for the many persons with Alzheimer's disease who have cardiovascular disease (Haynes, Seifan, et al., 2016), one goal is to improve cardiovascular health. For the treatment of vascular dementia, a key goal is to address high blood pressure when it is present and thus prevent further cognitive declines (O'Brien & Thomas, 2015). Although evidence is not entirely consistent, blood pressure management for those with hypertension may have some benefits in slowing the progression of Alzheimer's disease (National Academies of Sciences, 2017).

Medical treatments are used to address psychological symptoms, such as agitation that commonly co-occurs with dementia. Although antipsychotic medications may provide very modest relief for aggressive agitation (American Psychiatric Association Practice Guideline Group, 2016), they also increase the risk of death among elderly people with dementia (Maust, Kim, et al., 2015). Antidepressants have been shown to reduce agitation among those with dementia, although there is mixed evidence about whether antidepressants reduce the depressive symptoms that accompany dementia (Mulsant & Pollock, 2015).

Some of the disappointments in developing treatments to improve cognition have led to new ways of thinking about these disorders. For example, for some time, researchers were striving to find ways to remove plaques from the brains of people with Alzheimer's disease. Surprisingly, when researchers developed a medication that removed beta-amyloid plaques, they found that cognitive deficits continued and even worsened after the plaques were removed (Holmes, Boche, et al., 2008). Remember, though, that beta-amyloid plaques accumulate in the brain for years before symptoms are observable among people with Alzheimer's disease. By the time people had been diagnosed and had begun to receive the intervention, biological disease processes had already been occurring for years. Findings like these have led researchers to focus more on prevention. One way to do this is to study factors that reduce the chances that MCI will develop into full-blown dementia. Another way is to study people who have early biological markers indicating risk for Alzheimer's disease, such as signs of plaques, tangles, and neuronal death (Sperling et al., 2011). Researchers are testing a host of pharmacological and nutritional interventions to target the development of plaques and tangles, as well as the associated immune and inflammation processes

Nick Ut/ASSOCIATED PRESS/AP/Wide World Photos

Former President Ronald Reagan died from Alzheimer's disease. His daughter wrote the following about his disease: "The past is like the rudder of a ship. It keeps you moving through the present, steers you into the future. Without it, without memory, you are unmoored, a wind-tossed boat with no anchor. You learn this by watching someone you love drift away" (Davis, 2002).

(Brandt & Mansour, 2016). Other research is shedding light on the biology of memory among those with no signs of dementia or MCI. Researchers have shown that electrical stimulation from electrodes placed in the brain could help temporarily enhance memory encoding in some people undergoing surgery for epilepsy (Ezzyat, Kragel, et al., 2017). Although electrical stimulation cannot yet be used as a treatment in MCI or dementia, many are hopeful that pharmacological and basic research will yield novel treatments for dementia.

Psychological and Lifestyle Treatments Supportive psychotherapy can help families and patients deal with the effects of the disease. The therapist also provides accurate information about the illness, helps family members care for the person in the home, and encourages a realistic rather than a catastrophic attitude in dealing with the many specific challenges that this cognitive disorder presents. See **Focus on Discovery 14.1** for more detail on treatments offered to support caregivers.

Behavioral approaches have been shown to help compensate for memory loss and to reduce depression and disruptive behavior among people with early stages of Alzheimer's disease. For example, external memory aids such as shopping lists, calendars, phone lists, and labels can help when placed prominently as visual reminders (Buchanan, Christenson, et al., 2011). Music may help reduce agitation and disruptive behavior while it is being played (Galik, 2016). Findings of randomized controlled trials indicate that psychotherapy reduces depression among those with dementia (Orgeta, Qazi, et al., 2014),

John Keeble\John Keeble/Moment Mobile/Getty Images

Computerized training programs have been developed with the aim of enhancing cognitive skills. Companies producing these training programs report tens of millions of users, but the effects of these programs are modest.

Focus on Discovery 14.1

Support for Caregivers

For every person with severe dementia who is living in an institution, there are at least two living in the community, usually supported by a family. Caregiving is extremely stressful. Caregivers are at heightened risk for clinical depression and anxiety (Dura, Stukenberg, & Kiecolt-Glaser, 1991), physical illness (Vitaliano, Zhang, & Scanlan, 2003), and decreased immune functioning (Kiecolt-Glaser, Dura, et al., 1991) compared with noncaregivers.

Families can be helped to cope better with the daily stress of caregiving. For example, because people with Alzheimer's have difficulty placing new information into memory, they can engage in a reasonable conversation but forget the discussion within a few minutes. A caregiver may become impatient unless he or she understands that this impairment is an expected consequence of the brain damage. Family members can learn communication strategies to adapt to the memory loss. For example, families can ask questions that embed the answer. It is much easier to respond to "Was the person you just spoke to on the phone Harry or Tom?" than to "Who just called?" Family members and the patient can be encouraged to consider financial and legal planning.

It is also useful for caregivers to understand that patients do not always recognize their limitations and may try to engage in activities beyond their abilities. Caregivers must set limits regarding dangerous activities. For example, caregivers often need to tell a relative with Alzheimer's disease that driving is off limits (and then remove the car keys, as the relative is likely to forget the new rule).

Programs that teach coping strategies for the caregivers (e. g., increasing pleasant activities, exercise, or social support) have been shown to relieve caregiver burden and depression (Mittelman, Brodaty, et al., 2008). Because caregivers are so powerfully affected,

respite is highly recommended. To give the caretaker a break, sometimes the person with dementia is briefly admitted to a hospital or enrolled in an adult day-care center; sometimes a health care worker takes over long enough for the family to take a holiday. Programs lasting at least 6 weeks (Selwood, Johnson, et al., 2007) or offering multiple components (e. g., psychoeducation about dementia, case-management services, cognitive behavioral strategies, and respite) appear more helpful than briefer programs. Multicomponent programs have been found to improve quality of life and decrease medical costs for the person with memory loss, and to slow the timing of institutionalization (Samus, Johnston, et al., 2014).

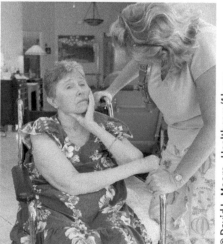

© David L. Moore - Healthcare/Alamy

Caring for a relative with Alzheimer's disease is a source of severe stress.

Providing memory aids is one way of compensating for memory loss.

RubberBall/SuperStock, Inc.

as does increasing pleasant and engaging activities (Logsdon, McCurry, & Teri, 2007). These behavioral interventions provide alternatives to medication approaches.

Exercise and cognitive training programs are used to prevent cognitive declines before dementia has begun. Findings are not strong regarding the use of these programs once dementia begins (Forbes, Forbes, et al., 2015), so these interventions are targeted at healthy elderly individuals and those with MCI.

Interventions to increase exercise have modest benefits in improving cognitive function. Meta-analyses of studies with hundreds of participants indicate that exercise programs improve cognitive functioning for healthy elderly (Smith, Blumenthal, et al., 2010) and for those with MCI (Heyn, Abreu, & Ottenbacher, 2004).

Cognitive training programs that focus on improving memory, reasoning, or cognitive processing speed have been shown to have modest benefits for healthy elderly persons. For example, the effects of 14 sessions of 60- to 75-minute reasoning and cognitive processing speed training were shown to have positive benefits at a 10-year follow-up. Of concern, these benefits are specific to the area involved in the training—for example, memory training might help enhance memory but doesn't help reasoning abilities (Rebok, Ball, et al., 2014). To help skills generalize more, researchers focus on how to teach "meta-cognitive" skills—that is, ways to think about thinking. As an example of the success of these meta-cognitive programs, teaching people strategies for enhancing memory improves performance across a range of tasks (Hertzog, Kramer, et al., 2009). Similarly, training in multitasking appeared to improve not just ability to multitask but also ability to hold items in memory and to sustain attention to a task (Anguera, Boccanfuso, et al., 2013). Although most of the work focuses on the healthy elderly, researchers have observed small benefits of cognitive training exercises for memory in three randomized controlled trials of those with MCI, with better results when training was offered for 60 sessions (Gates, Sachdev, et al., 2011).

To consider the effectiveness of addressing diet, exercise, and cognitive training, researchers randomly assigned 1260 elderly persons with MCI to an intensive program of diet, exercise, and cognitive training or to standard medical care and psychoeducation about healthy lifestyles. The intervention group showed gains in executive function at 1- and 2-year follow-up assessments compared to the control group. Although the effects were small, longer-term follow-up is planned to assess whether the intervention will help prevent dementia (Ngandu, Lehtisalo, et al., 2015).

Quick Summary

Dementia is a broad term to capture cognitive decline, most commonly a decline in memory for recent events. As the cognitive deficits become more widespread and profound, social and occupational functioning becomes more disturbed. Dementia affects approximately 1 to 2 percent of people in their 60s but a third of people over the age of 90.

There are many types of dementia, including Alzheimer's, frontotemporal, vascular, dementia with Lewy bodies (DLB), and dementia from other medical causes. Alzheimer's disease is characterized by plaques and tangles in the brain. Memory loss is a key symptom of Alzheimer's disease, but apathy may be present long before cognitive symptoms are observable. Risk of developing the disease is higher among those with at least one APOE ε4 allele. Immune and inflammation processes may increase vulnerability to Alzheimer's disease. Lifestyle and psychological factors, such as exercise and cognitive engagement, appear to be involved as well. Frontotemporal dementia (FTD) is characterized by neuronal deterioration in the frontal and temporal lobes. Pick's disease is one form of FTD. The primary symptoms of FTD include marked changes in social and emotional behavior, including problems with empathy, executive function, disinhibition, compulsive behavior, hyperorality, and apathy. Vascular dementia often occurs after a stroke. The symptoms of vascular dementia depend on the brain regions that are influenced by the cerebrovascular disease. DLB is characterized by visual hallucinations, fluctuations in cognitive functioning, supersensitivity to side effects of antipsychotic medications, and intense dreams during which the person moves and talks. It is common among people diagnosed with Parkinson's disease.

The cholinesterase inhibitors and memantine are the major medical treatments for Alzheimer's disease, and the cholinesterase inhibitors are also used for DLB, but these medications offer modest effects. Exercise appears to improve cognitive functioning for people with MCI. Cognitive training programs that teach meta-cognitive skills, such as general strategies for enhancing memory, may generalize across tasks. Behavioral treatments can help relieve comorbid symptoms of depression. Antipsychotic medications can reduce agitation for those with dementia but also increase the risk of death; antidepressant medication and behavioral treatments can safely reduce agitation. Multicomponent programs help address caregivers' needs.

Check Your Knowledge 14.3

Choose the best answer.

1. A plaque is:

   a. a small, round beta-amyloid protein deposit

   b. a filament composed of the protein tau

   c. a buildup of the myelin sheath surrounding neurons in the hippocampus

   d. a small white spot on a brain scan

2. A neurofibrillary tangle is:

   a. a small, round beta-amyloid protein deposit

   b. a filament composed of the protein tau

   c. a buildup of the myelin sheath surrounding neurons in the hippocampus

   d. a small white spot on a brain scan

3. FTD involves profound changes in:

   a. memory

   b. social and emotional behavior

   c. motor control

   d. attention

Answer the questions.

4. Which neurotransmitters are most involved in Alzheimer's disease?

5. Describe the efficacy of current medical treatments for dementia.

6. What is the most prominent symptom of Alzheimer's disease?

Delirium

The term **delirium** (derived from the Latin words *de,* meaning "out of," and *lira,* meaning "track") implies a deviation from the usual state. Extreme trouble focusing attention is the hallmark symptom (Saczynski & Inouye, 2015). As illustrated in the Clinical Case of Henry at the beginning of this chapter, delirium is described typically as a clouded state of consciousness. Patients, sometimes rather suddenly, have so much trouble focusing attention that they cannot maintain a coherent stream of thought. They may have trouble answering questions because their mind wanders. As the sleep/wake cycle becomes disturbed, patients become drowsy during the day yet awake and agitated at night. Vivid dreams and nightmares are common. People with delirium may be impossible to engage in conversation because of their wandering attention and fragmented thinking. In severe delirium, speech is rambling and incoherent. Bewildered and confused, some people with delirium may become so disoriented that they are unclear about what day it is, where they are, and even who they are. Memory impairment, especially for recent events, is common.

Perceptual disturbances are frequent in delirium. People mistake the unfamiliar for the familiar; for example, they may state that they are at home instead of in a hospital. Although

DSM-5 Criteria for Delirium

- Disturbance in attention and awareness
- A change in cognition, such as disturbance in orientation, language, memory, perception, or visuospatial ability, not better accounted for by a dementia

- Rapid onset (usually within hours or days) and fluctuation during the course of a day
- Symptoms are caused by a medical condition, substance intoxication or withdrawal, or toxin

visual hallucinations are common, they are not always present. Delusions—beliefs contrary to reality—have been noted in about 25 percent of older adults with delirium (Camus, Burtin, et al., 2000). These delusions tend to be fleeting and changeable.

Swings in activity and mood accompany these disordered thoughts and perceptions. People with delirium can be erratic, ripping their clothes one moment and sitting lethargically the next. They may also shift rapidly from one emotion to another, fluctuating between depression, anxiety, fright, anger, euphoria, and irritability. In the course of a 24-hour period, people with delirium have lucid intervals in which they become alert and coherent. Symptoms are usually worse during sleepless nights. These daily fluctuations help distinguish delirium from other syndromes, especially Alzheimer's disease.

People of any age are subject to delirium, but it is more common among children and older adults. Among older adults, it is particularly common in nursing homes and hospitals. It is the most common complication of hospitalization in elderly patients (Saczynski & Inouye, 2015)

Unfortunately, delirium is often misdiagnosed. For example, among hospitalized older adults with clear symptoms of delirium, hospital notes did not indicate delirium for 75 percent or more (Han, Zimmerman, et al., 2009). Physicians are particularly unlikely to detect delirium when lethargy or dementia are present (Saczynski & Inouye, 2015). **Table 14.4** compares the features of dementia and delirium. Consider this suggestion for distinguishing delirium from dementia:

The clinical "feel" of talking with a person with delirium is rather like talking to someone who is acutely intoxicated or in an acute psychotic episode. Whereas the demented patient may not remember the name of the place where she or he is, the delirious patient may believe it is a different sort of place altogether, perhaps mistaking a psychiatric ward for a used car lot. (Knight, 1996, pp. 96–97)

Detecting and treating delirium is of fundamental importance. Untreated, the mortality rate for delirium is high; multiple studies indicate that delirium is a predictor of death within the next 6 months (Saczynski & Inouye, 2015). Beyond the risk of death, elderly adults who develop delirium in the hospital are at an increased risk of

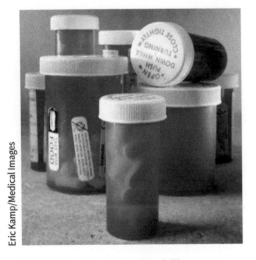

Eric Kamp/Medical Images

Medication misuse, whether deliberate or inadvertent, can be a serious problem among older people and can cause delirium.

TABLE 14.4 **Comparative Features of Dementia and Delirium**

Dementia	Delirium
Gradual deterioration of abilities	Rapid onset
Most commonly, deficits in memory for recent events	Trouble concentrating and staying with a train of thought
Caused by brain disease processes	Secondary to another medical condition
Usually progressive and nonreversible	Symptoms fluctuate over the course of a day
Treatment offers only minimal benefit	Usually reversible by treating underlying condition but potentially fatal if cause—e g., infection or malnutrition—not treated
Prevalence increases with age	Prevalence is highest in the very young as well as the old

further cognitive decline (Saczynski & Inouye, 2015). It is not clear why delirium predicts such bad outcomes; some believe that delirium may be an indicator of an underlying frailty that becomes apparent in the face of medical conditions.

Etiology of Delirium

As noted in the diagnostic criteria, several causes of delirium have been identified. Drug intoxications and drug-withdrawal reactions are the most common triggers, but other common triggers include metabolic and nutritional imbalances (as in diabetes, thyroid dysfunction, kidney or liver failure, congestive heart failure, or malnutrition), dehydration, infections (like pneumonia or urinary tract infections), neurological disorders (like dementia, head trauma, or seizures), and the stress of major surgery (Zarit & Zarit, 2011). Physical immobility, and more so physical restraints, are key risk factors (Saczynski & Inouye, 2015). As in the case of Henry at the start of this chapter, however, delirium usually has more than one cause.

Why are older adults so vulnerable to delirium? Many explanations have been offered: notably, the physical declines of late life, the increased susceptibility to chronic diseases, the many medications prescribed for older people, and the greater sensitivity to drugs.

Treatment of Delirium

Complete recovery from delirium is possible if doctors are able to promptly treat the underlying cause. Physicians must consider all possible reversible causes of the disorder and then treat any of the conditions identified. Beyond treating underlying medical conditions, the most common treatment is atypical antipsychotic medication, although side effects of the atypical antipsychotic medications may outweigh the gains (Saczynski & Inouye, 2015). It usually takes 1 to 4 weeks for the condition to clear; it takes longer in older people than in younger people.

Because of the high rates of delirium in hospitalized older adults, preventive strategies are recommended to keep delirium from starting. The goal is to reduce common risk factors for delirium within the hospital setting, such as sleep deprivation, immobility, dehydration, and visual and hearing impairment. It may help patients to stay oriented if clocks are placed within their field of vision, shades are open during the day and lights are turned off at night, and disruptions to sleep are minimized. Patients can be helped to resume walking soon after surgery, nursing staff can make sure that patients hydrate and consume enough calories, and patients' glasses and hearing aids should be returned as soon as possible after medical procedures. Family members are encouraged to be present. There is robust evidence that training nurses and hospital volunteers to implement these principles reduces the risks for delirium substantially (Inouye, Baker, et al., 2006).

The high risk of delirium among people with dementia raises another set of prevention issues. The family of a person with dementia should learn the symptoms of delirium and know about its reversible nature so that they do not interpret the onset of delirium as a new stage of a progressive dementia. With proper diagnosis and treatment, the person can usually return to the earlier state.

Check Your Knowledge 14. 4

Choose the best answer.

1. What is the most common symptom of delirium?
   a. anxiety
   b. memory loss
   c. inability to concentrate or attend
   d. sad mood

2. Mary, a 70-year-old woman, was hospitalized for hip surgery. Although there were no immediate complications from the surgery, her son became concerned when he visited her that night because she was

not making any sense. She thanked him for checking her into the Ritz-Carlton and laughed giddily when he told her that she was in the hospital. Half an hour later, she began sobbing. Although she seemed fine the next morning, symptoms of acute confusion reemerged by lunchtime. Which diagnosis is most likely for Mary?

    a. Alzheimer's disease

    b. frontotemporal dementia

    c. mania

    d. delirium

Summary

Aging: Issues and Methods

- As life expectancy continues to improve, it will become even more important to learn about the disorders suffered by some older people and the most effective means of treating them.

- Several stereotypes about aging are false. Generally, people in late life report low levels of negative emotion, are not inappropriately concerned with their health, and are not lonely. On the other hand, stigma, bereavement, physical disease, polypharmacy, medication sensitivity, and sleep disruption are common challenges for people as they age.

- In research studies, differences between a younger and an older group could reflect either cohort effects or effects of chronological age. Longitudinal studies are more helpful for making this distinction than cross-sectional studies are.

Psychological Disorders in Late Life

- Data indicate that persons over age 65 have the lowest overall rates of psychological disorders of all age groups. When older people do experience psychological disorders, the symptoms are often a recurrence of a disorder that first emerged earlier in life. It is important to rule out medical causes of psychological symptoms occurring during late life.

Neurocognitive Disorders in Late Life

- Serious cognitive disorders affect a small minority of older people. Two principal disorders have been distinguished: dementia and delirium.

- In dementia, the person's intellectual functioning declines and memory, abstract thinking, and judgment deteriorate. As the dementia progresses, the person may become oblivious to his or her surroundings. A variety of diseases can cause this deterioration. The most common is Alzheimer's disease. Genes play a major role in the etiology of Alzheimer's disease. Lifestyle factors, such as exercise and cognitive engagement, appear to be protective.

- Other forms of dementia include frontotemporal dementia (FTD), vascular dementia, dementia with Lewy bodies (DLB), and dementia due to other medical conditions.

- Cholinesterase inhibitors and memantine can be prescribed to slow memory decline but their effects are minimal. Antidepressant medication can address agitation, and psychological treatments can help diminish depression. The person and the family affected by the disease can be counseled on how to make the remaining time manageable and even rewarding. Exercise programs for people with MCI may help improve cognitive functioning.

- Delirium is defined by a sudden onset of inability to sustain attention; a clouding of consciousness; and symptoms such as fragmented and undirected thought, incoherent speech, hallucinations, disorientation, lethargy or hyperactivity, and mood swings. Symptoms tend to vary throughout the day. Delirium is most likely to affect children and older adults. The condition is reversible, provided that the underlying cause is adequately treated. Causes include drug effects and withdrawal, infection of brain tissue, high fevers, malnutrition, dehydration, endocrine disorders, head trauma, cerebrovascular problems, and surgery. Delirium is often undetected.

Answers to Check Your Knowledge Questions

14.1 1. F; 2. People report less negative emotion, tend to attend and react more to positive information, and are less reactive to negative information.; 3. People place more emphasis on close ties rather than broader social networks.

14.2 1. F; 2. Selective mortality refers to death of participants in longitudinal studies that is systematically related to risk factors and outcomes, such as people with depression being more likely to die in a long-term study of mental health.; 3. Stigma and attitudes toward mental health problems have shifted over time, and older people may feel more embarrassed about discussing mental health symptoms.

14.3 1. a; 2. b; 3. b; 4. Acetylcholine and glutamate; 5. Medications might slow decline but do not cure dementia; 6. memory loss

14.4 1. c; 2. d

Key Terms

age effects
Alzheimer's disease
cognitive reserve
cohort effects
delirium
dementia

dementia with Lewy bodies (DLB)
disorientation
frontotemporal dementia (FTD)
mild cognitive impairment (MCI)
neurofibrillary tangles
plaques

selective mortality
social selectivity
time-of-measurement effects
vascular dementia

CHAPTER **15**

Personality Disorders

LEARNING GOALS

1. Explain the DSM-5 approach to classifying personality disorders, and key concerns with this approach.

2. Describe the DSM-5 alternative approach to personality diagnosis.

3. Discuss commonalities in the risk factors across personality disorders.

4. Define the key features of each of the personality disorders in the odd/eccentric cluster, as well as

biological, social, and psychological risk factors that contribute to the odd/eccentric personality disorders.

5. Describe the key features and risk factors of each of the personality disorders in the dramatic/erratic cluster.

6. Define the key features and risk factors of each of the personality disorders in the anxious/fearful cluster.

7. Describe the available psychological treatments for the DSM-5 personality disorders.

Clinical Case

Mary

Mary was single and 26 years old when she was first admitted to a psychiatric hospital. She had been in outpatient treatment with a psychologist for several months when her persistent thoughts of cutting, burning, and killing herself led her therapist to conclude that she needed more than outpatient treatment.

Mary's first experience with psychotherapy occurred when she was an adolescent. In the 11th grade, her grades declined sharply; she began to miss curfews and occasionally to stay out all night. She often skipped school. Family therapy was started, and it seemed to go well at first. Mary was enthusiastic about the therapist and asked for additional private sessions with him.

During individual sessions, Mary revealed she had used drugs extensively and had traded sex for drug money. Her relationships with her peers were in chronic turmoil. There was a constant parade of new friends, whom Mary at first viewed as the greatest ever but whom she soon cast aside in unpleasant ways after they disappointed her.

After several weeks of family therapy, Mary's parents noticed that Mary was angry and abusive toward the therapist. After a few more weeks had passed, Mary refused to attend any more sessions. In a subsequent conversation with the therapist, Mary's father learned that she had behaved seductively toward the therapist during their private sessions and that her changed attitude coincided with his rejection of her advances despite the therapist's attempt to mix firmness with warmth and empathy.

Mary managed to graduate from high school and enrolled in a local community college, but the old patterns returned. Poor grades, continuing drug use, and lack of interest in her studies finally led her to quit college shortly into her second year. After leaving school, Mary held a series of low-paying jobs. Most of them didn't last long, as her relationships with co-workers paralleled her relationships with her peers in high school. When Mary started a new job, she would find someone she really liked, but something would come between them, and the relationship would end angrily. She was often suspicious of her co-workers and reported that she heard them plotting how to prevent her from getting ahead on the job. She was quick to find hidden meanings in their behavior, as when she interpreted being the last person asked to sign a birthday card to mean that she was the least-liked person in the office. She indicated that she "received vibrations" from others and could tell when they really didn't like her even in the absence of any direct evidence.

Mary's frequent mood swings, with periods of depression and extreme irritability, led her to seek therapy several times. But after initial enthusiasm, her relationships with therapists always deteriorated, resulting in premature termination of therapy. By the time of her hospitalization, she had seen six therapists.

Personality disorders are defined by enduring problems with forming a stable positive identity and with sustaining close and constructive relationships. Although all these disorders are defined by extreme and inflexible traits, the 10 **personality disorders** cover a broad range of symptom profiles. As examples of that heterogeneity, paranoid personality disorder is defined by chronic tendencies to be mistrustful and suspicious, antisocial personality disorder by patterns of irresponsibility and callous disregard for the rights of others, and dependent personality disorder by an overreliance on others. From time to time, we all behave, think, and feel in ways that are similar to symptoms of personality disorders, but an actual personality disorder is defined by the persistent, pervasive, and maladaptive ways in which these traits are expressed.

Our personalities shape almost every domain of our lives—our career choices, the quality of our relationships, the size of our social network, our favorite pastimes and preferred level of activity, our approach to tackling everyday problems, our willingness to break rules, and our typical level of well-being (Ozer & Benet-Martinez, 2006). Given how many areas of our life are shaped by personality traits, it stands to reason that the extreme and inflexible traits found in personality disorders create problems in multiple domains. People with personality disorders experience difficulties with their identity and their relationships, and these problems are sustained for years. Across a review of 127 studies, personality disorders were tied to problems in friendships and family relationships (Wilson, Stroud, et al., 2017). Some of the relationship problems can become quite severe. In a study of over 20,000 individuals, women with personality disorders were three times as likely to experience physical assault by a partner, sexual assault, or stalking as those without a personality disorder (Walsh, Hasin, et al., 2016). Personality disorders also predict poorer physical health even when comorbid psychological syndromes are accounted for, in both cross-sectional and longitudinal research (Quirk, Berk, et al., 2016).

In this chapter we begin by considering the DSM-5 approach to classifying personality disorders and the assessment of the personality disorders. We will note some concerns about the DSM-5 approach to personality disorders, and we will then discuss an alternative system of personality classification that has been placed after the main body of the DSM-5 manual, in section III. After considering these broad issues in the classification of personality disorders, we describe factors that increase the risk of personality disorders in general. Then, we discuss specific personality disorders, including clinical descriptions and risk factors. We conclude with discussion of treatment of personality disorders.

The DSM-5 Approach to Classification

DSM-5 provides criteria for personality disorder in general as well as specific criteria for the 10 personality disorders. As shown, the general personality disorder criteria highlight that personality disorders involve problems in thinking, affect, impulse control, and interpersonal functioning that persist for years and influence many domains of life. The 10 different personality disorders are classified in three clusters, reflecting the idea that these disorders are characterized by odd or eccentric behavior (cluster A); dramatic, emotional, or erratic behavior (cluster B); or anxious or fearful behavior (cluster C). These clusters form a useful organizational framework for our discussions in this chapter. **Table 15.1** presents the personality disorders, their key features, and their grouping in clusters.

TABLE 15.1 **Key Features of the DSM-5 Personality Disorders**

	Key Features	Included in the Alternative DSM-5 Model for Personality Disorders?
Cluster A (odd/eccentric)		
Paranoid	Distrust and suspiciousness of others	No
Schizoid	Detachment from social relationships and restricted range of emotional expression	No
Schizotypal	Lack of capacity for close relationships, cognitive distortions, and eccentric behavior	Yes
Cluster B (dramatic/erratic)		
Antisocial	Disregard for and violation of the rights of others	Yes
Borderline	Instability of interpersonal relationships, self-image, and affect, as well as marked impulsivity	Yes
Histrionic	Excessive emotionally and attention seeking	No
Narcissistic	Grandiosity, need for admiration, and lack of empathy	Yes
Cluster C (anxious/fearful)		
Avoidant	Social inhibition, feelings of inadequacy, and hypersensitivity to negative evaluation	Yes
Dependent	Excessive need to be taken care of, submissive behavior, and fears of separation	No
Obsessive-compulsive	Preoccupation with order, perfection, and control	Yes

About 1 out of every 10 people meet the diagnostic criteria for a personality disorder (Sansone & Sansone, 2011). With rates this high, it is likely you know people who would meet the diagnostic criteria for a personality disorder.

The DSM criteria for personality disorder specify that clinicians should be sensitive to whether patterns of behavior are unusual for the person's cultural background. For example, cultures vary in the degree to which self-promotion is considered appropriate, and this is relevant to the evaluation of narcissism. Cultural attitudes toward emotion expression are relevant to evaluating the cluster C personality disorders, which involve dramatic expressions of emotion. To date, researchers have considered differences in the prevalence of personality disorders between some countries (Jani, Johnson, et al., 2016), but less is known about how cultural values help explain any of the cross-national differences in prevalence that have been observed (Ryder, Dere, et al., 2014).

Personality disorders tend to co-occur with psychological disorders. For example, mood and anxiety disorders have high rates of comorbidity with cluster C personality disorders, and mood disorders are also tied to cluster B disorders (Friborg, Martinsen, et al., 2014; Friborg,

---

DSM-5 Criteria for General Personality Disorder

- An inflexible pattern of inner experience and behavior that is distinct from cultural expectations, and influences at least two of the following:
  1. cognition about the self and others
  2. affect
  3. interpersonal functioning
  4. impulse control.
- The pattern

1. causes significant distress or impairment
2. is inflexible
3. is pervasive across situations
- Onset by early adulthood and persistence for a long duration
- Not explained by another mental disorder, by a substance, or by a medical condition

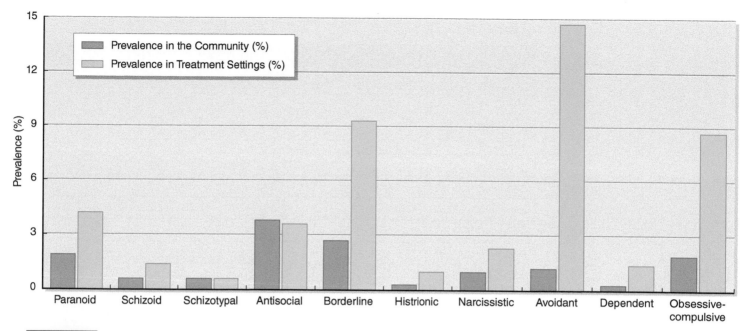

FIGURE 15.1   Rates of DSM personality disorders in the community and in treatment settings. Prevalence estimates for community settings are drawn from Trull, Jahng, et al. (2010); Samuels, Eaton, et al. (2002). Prevalence estimates for treatment settings are drawn from Zimmerman, Rothschild, & Chelminski (2005).

Martinussen, et al., 2013; Grant, Chou, et al., 2008). Antisocial personality disorder is highly comorbid with externalizing disorders such as substance use disorders (Krueger, Markon, et al., 2005). As a result of these high levels of comorbidity, personality disorders are commonly encountered in treatment settings, with as many as 40 percent of outpatients meeting the diagnostic criteria for a personality disorder (Newton-Howes, Tyrer, et al., 2010). See **Figure 15.1** for rates of specific personality disorders in the general community as compared with treatment settings.

When personality disorders are comorbid with other psychological syndromes, they are associated with more severe symptoms, poorer social functioning, and worse treatment outcome for those psychological disorders (Ansell, Pinto, et al., 2011; Newton-Howes, Tyrer, & Johnson, 2006). Similarly, when those with personality disorders have conditions like anxiety or depression, personality disorder symptoms are more likely to last for several years (Zanarini, Frankenburg, et al., 2004).

The accurate diagnosis of personality disorders requires care. When experienced clinicians use structured interviews to cover the personality disorder criteria, inter-rater reliability is adequate or good for most of the diagnoses, with one exception—experts often disagree about whether schizoid personality disorder is present. See **Table 15.2** for inter-rater reliability of personality disorder diagnoses when experts use structured diagnostic interviews. Of concern, most clinicians do not use structured interviews to assess personality. Unstructured clinical interviews are not reliable (Regier, Kuhl, & Kupfer, 2013), tend to miss as many as half of personality disorder diagnoses (Zimmerman & Mattia, 1999), and are less predictive than structured interviews of long-term outcomes (Samuel, Sanislow, et al., 2013).

Problems with the DSM-5 Approach to Personality Disorders

There are some major concerns about the DSM-5 approach to personality disorders. Here we focus on two of these concerns: These disorders are not as stable as the definition implies, and there are extremely high rates of comorbidity among the personality disorders.

TABLE 15.2 Inter-Rater Reliability for the Personality Disorders as Assessed by Structured Interview

Diagnosis	Inter-Rater Reliability (Correlation)
Paranoid	.86
Schizoid	.69
Schizotypal	.91
Antisocial	.97
Borderline	.90
Histrionic	.83
Narcissistic	.88
Avoidant	.79
Dependent	.87
Obsessive-compulsive	.85

Source: Structured interview estimates from Zanarini, Skodol, et al. (2000).

Personality Disorders Are Not Stable Over Time Although the very defini-tion of personality disorders suggests that they should be stable over time, **Figure 15.2** shows that about half of the people diagnosed with a personality disorder at one point in time had achieved remission (i.e., did not meet the criteria for the same diagnosis) when they were interviewed two years later (McGlashan, Grilo, et al., 2005). Even among patients diagnosed with severe personality disorder, 99 percent of personality disorder diagnoses remitted when reassessed after 16 years (Zanarini, Frankenburg, et al., 2011). Personality disorders appear to increase into adolescence and then decline over time, with even more declines by late life (Ullrich & Coid, 2009). These results, then, indicate that many of the personality disorders may not be as enduring as the DSM asserts.

Even though these symptoms are not as persistent as the definition of personality disor-der implies, many people still have some symp-toms after remission, and many will relapse as the symptoms of personality disorders wax and wane over time (Zanarini et al., 2011). Baseline diagnoses of personality disorders predict lower functioning and more depression even 10 to 15 years later (Morey, Hopwood, et al., 2012). Hence, even after remission, a diagnosis of per-sonality disorder can predict ongoing difficulty in achieving a truly satisfying lifestyle.

Personality Disorders Are Highly Comorbid A second major problem in clas-sifying personality disorders arises from their comorbidity with each other. The Clinical Case of Mary illustrates this issue: Mary met the diag-nostic criteria not only for borderline personality disorder but also for paranoid personality disor-der. More than 50 percent of people diagnosed with a personality disorder meet the diagnostic criteria for another personality disorder (Lenzen-weger, Lane, et al., 2007). Some of the personality disorders involve similar types of concerns. For

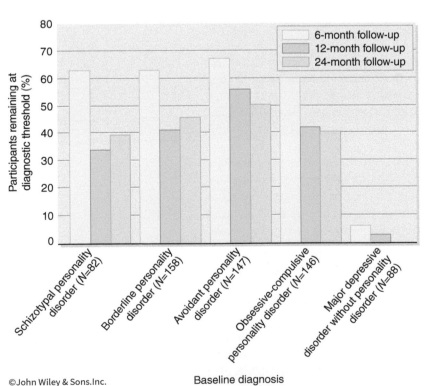

©John Wiley & Sons.Inc.

FIGURE 15.2 Test–retest stability for personality disorders and major depressive disorder across 6-, 12-, and 24-month follow-up interviews.

Drawn from Grilo, Shea, et al., 2004; Shea, Stout, et al., 2002.

example, as we will see, the diagnostic criteria for schizotypal, avoidant, and paranoid personality disorders all emphasize difficulty in forming close relationships, and so it is not surprising that these diagnoses often co-occur. The high rates of overlap among the personality disorders is discouraging when we try to interpret the results of research that compares people who have a specific personality disorder with some control group. If, for example, we find that people with borderline personality disorder differ from healthy people, is our finding related to borderline personality disorder or to personality disorders in general?

Quick Summary

Personality disorders are defined by long-standing and pervasive ways of being that cause distress and impairment through their obstructive influence on forming and sustaining a positive self-identity and constructive relationships.

Many people with personality disorders also meet the diagnostic criteria for comorbid conditions such as depressive, anxiety, and substance use disorders.

In DSM-5, 10 personality disorders are classified in three clusters: cluster A personality disorders are characterized by odd or eccentric behavior; cluster B by dramatic, emotional, or erratic behavior; and cluster C by anxious or fearful behavior.

Most personality disorders can be reliably assessed with structured clinical interviews, but unstructured clinical interviews are not reliable or sensitive and have less predictive validity.

Most diagnoses of personality disorders remit over time, and so personality disorders are not as stable as the DSM suggests. Nonetheless, even after a personality disorder remits, milder symptoms are often present and relapse is common, so that an initial personality disorder diagnosis can predict lower functioning even 15 years later.

Personality disorders co-occur. More than half of people who meet the diagnostic criteria for one personality disorder meet the criteria for at least one other personality disorder.

Check Your Knowledge 15.1
(Answers are at the end of the chapter.)

Answer the following questions.

1. Describe the level of inter-rater reliability obtained for the DSM-5 personality disorders with structured diagnostic interviews and with unstructured diagnostic interviews.

2. List two primary concerns about the DSM-5 approach to personality disorders.

Alternative DSM-5 Model for Personality Disorders

As we have discussed, the personality disorder diagnoses show poor test–retest stability and high rates of comorbidity. These types of concerns led the DSM-5 Committee on Personality and Personality Disorders to suggest a bold overhaul. They recommended reducing the number of personality disorders, and diagnosing personality disorders based on extreme scores on personality trait measures. The American Psychological Association Board of Trustees decided to retain the personality disorder system that was in place in DSM-IV-TR but included the alternative approach in section III of the DSM-5 manual. Although the approach to personality disorders that appears in the main text dominates clinical practice, let's consider the merits of the alternative approach.

As shown in Table 15.1, the alternative DSM-5 Model for Personality Disorders includes only six of the 10 DSM-5 personality disorders. The alternative system excludes schizoid, histrionic, and dependent personality disorders because they rarely occur, and paranoid personality disorder because it usually co-occurs with other personality disorders. Much less research is available on these four personality disorders. As shown in Table 15.2, inter-rater reliability is adequate for each of the six personality disorders included in the alternative system when assessed with a structured diagnostic interview.

In the alternative DSM-5 model, personality disorder diagnoses are considered when a person shows persistent and pervasive impairments in functioning from early adulthood. If this long-term dysfunction appears to be present, the clinician considers how personality traits explain those difficulties in functioning. The system includes two types of dimensional personality scores: 5 **personality trait domains** and 25 more specific **personality trait facets**, as shown in **Table 15.3**. These personality trait domains and facets are closely related to a very influential model of personality called the five-factor model (Watson, Stasik, et al., 2013). Each dimension can be evaluated using self-report items (Krueger, Derringer, et al., 2012). The profile of extreme scores on these dimensions is used to decide which personality disorder might best fit. For example, obsessive-compulsive personality disorder is defined by high scores on rigid perfectionism, along with high scores on at least two of the three dimensions of perseveration, intimacy avoidance, and restricted affectivity.

Some of the key strengths of the focus on personality traits include the following.

- Personality trait ratings are more stable over time than are personality disorder diagnoses (McGlashan et al., 2005).

- Those who meet the criteria for a given personality disorder can vary a good deal from one another in their symptoms. In the alternative system, clinicians can specify which personality

TABLE 15.3	The Five Personality Trait Domains and 25 Facets in the Alternative DSM-5 Model of Personality Disorders
Personality Trait Domain	**Facet**
I. Negative Affectivity (vs. Emotional Stability)	1. Anxiousness 2. Emotional lability 3. Hostility 4. Perseveration 5. Separation insecurity 6. Submissiveness
II. Detachment (vs. Extraversion)	7. Anhedonia 8. Depressivity 9. Intimacy avoidance 10. Suspiciousness 11. Withdrawal 12. Restricted affectivity
III. Antagonism (vs. Agreeableness)	13. Attention seeking 14. Callousness 15. Deceitfulness 16. Grandiosity 17. Manipulativeness
IV. Disinhibition (vs. Conscientiousness)	18. Distractibility 19. Impulsivity 20. Irresponsibility 21. (Lack of) rigid perfectionism 22. Risk taking
V. Psychoticism	23. Eccentricity 24. Cognitive perceptual dysregulation 25. Unusual beliefs and experiences

traits are of most concern for a given client. The 25 dimensional scores provide richer detail than do the personality disorder diagnoses.

- Personality traits are related to many psychological disorders: Anxiety and depression are related to negative affectivity, thought disorders are related to psychoticism, and externalizing disorders to disinhibition and antagonism (Morey, Krueger, et al., 2013).

- Personality traits robustly predict important outcomes such as the quality of friendships and partnerships, performance in one's career, health behaviors, happiness, and even life expectancy (Hopwood & Zanarini, 2010; Ozer & Benet-Martinez, 2006; Roberts, Kuncel, et al., 2007).

- Clinicians rate the alternative system as more descriptive of clinical problems, and more easily used to give clinical feedback and to plan treatment, compared to the system retained in the body of the DSM (Morey, Skodol, et al., 2014).

As the research base grows, some expect that the alternative model may become the major approach to classifying personality disorders in the future. For now, though, we will focus on the approach to personality disorders that appears in the main body of the DSM. Because so little is known about the four personality disorders excluded from the alternative model of DSM-5, though, we will not discuss the etiology of these disorders.

Quick Summary

The DSM-5 includes an alternative model for diagnosing personality problems, which was designed to address two concerns about the traditional personality disorder approach: Personality disorders are not stable over time, and they overlap substantially.

The alternative model includes only six personality disorders. The alternative model also provides a dimensional system for evaluating five personality trait domains and 25 more specific personality facets. These traits predict psychological syndromes and key life outcomes, and clinicians find them useful.

The alternative model is placed in section III of the DSM-5.

Check Your Knowledge 15.2

Answer the following question.

1. List two ways in which the alternative DSM-5 approach to personality differs from the approach that appears in the main body of the DSM manual.

Common Risk Factors Across the Personality Disorders

Theorists over the past 100 years have tried to understand why the chronic, wide-ranging symptoms of personality disorders develop. Although psychoanalytic and behavioral theory placed emphasis on parenting and early developmental influences, genetic work provides evidence for a strong biological component to these syndromes as well (Sharp, Wright, et al., 2015).

Several studies have examined the heritability of personality disorders. Not only do personality disorders often co-occur, but many of the personality disorders share genetic vulnerability—those at high genetic risk for one personality disorder are also at high genetic risk for other personality disorders (Kendler, Aggen, et al., 2008). One possibility is that genetic vulnerability contributes to personality traits like neuroticism or impulsivity, which then increase the risk for many different personality disorders (Sharp et al., 2015).

One genetic study is unusual in that the authors recruited a representative sample of twins through the Norwegian birth registry; this contrasts with a large amount of research that has focused on more severe patient samples. To improve diagnostic reliability, the researchers combined self-ratings with interview-based ratings of personality disorder severity. Heritability estimates for all the personality disorders were at least moderately high (see **Table 15.4** for estimates for the six personality disorders we focus on).

Beyond biological factors, environmental factors are also important. Let's consider the Children in the Community Study, one of the largest studies designed to assess the links between childhood adversity and personality disorders. In this study, researchers recruited a representative sample of 639 families with children ages 1–11. Families and children were interviewed initially in 1975, again during the period of 1983–1985, for a third time during the period of 1991–1993, and then the offspring were interviewed when they reached age 33. Child protective services documented childhood maltreatment for 31 of the children, and the children reported another 50 cases of abuse during their assessments. In the assessments conducted in the seventies and eighties, researchers conducted interviews with the parents and children to assess two aspects of parenting style: aversive parental behavior (e.g., harsh punishment, loud arguments) and lack of parental affection (e.g., little time together, poor supervision, poor communication). At the third and fourth interviews, the researchers conducted interviews to assess child neglect and conducted structured diagnostic interviews to assess personality disorders with the young adults. Offspring who experienced childhood abuse or neglect were compared with a control group matched on age, parental education, and parental psychiatric disorders. Researchers controlled for childhood behavioral problems and parental psychiatric disorders in considering the role of early adversity.

Findings of this study suggest that personality disorders are strongly related to early adversity. As shown in Table 15.4, childhood abuse or neglect related to significantly higher risk of four of the six personality disorders shown. Children who experienced abuse or neglect were 18 times as likely to develop narcissistic personality disorder and more than seven times as likely to develop borderline personality disorder compared with those with no history of abuse or neglect (Johnson, Cohen, et al., 1999). Parenting style also predicted the onset of each of the six alternative-model DSM-5 personality disorders. Offspring who had experienced aversive or unaffectionate parental styles were several times more likely to develop a personality disorder than were those who had not experienced those parental styles (Johnson, Cohen, et al., 2006). Clearly, many people with personality disorders have had difficult experiences during their childhood.

How can we integrate the findings regarding genetic and environmental risk factors? The magnitude of the genetic influence on personality disorders suggests that we should be cautious as we think about parenting and early environment—many parents of those with personality disorders are likely to experience at least mild personality problems themselves. We will discuss the idea that correlation may not mean causation later in this chapter, as we

TABLE 15.4 Estimated Heritability of the Personality Disorders

Disorder	Estimated Heritability	Odds Ratio of Personality Disorder After Child Abuse or Neglect
Schizotypal	.72	Not significantly related
Antisocial	.69	4.97
Borderline	.67	7.73
Narcissistic	.71	18.21
Avoidant	.64	Only neglect was related
Obsessive-compulsive	.78	Too few cases

Sources: Heritability estimates from Gjerde, Czajkowski, et al. (2012); Kendler, Myers, et al. (2007); Torgersen, Lygren, et al. (2000); Torgersen, Myers, et al. (2012). Child abuse or neglect drawn from Johnson et al. (1999).

consider research that jointly considers the genetic and environmental contributions to borderline personality disorder.

We now turn to the specific personality disorders. We'll consider the clinical description, and the risk factors that shape the development of these specific personality disorders. As we consider specific risk factors, keep in mind that these more general risk factors of genes and early adversity likely combine with the specific risk factors to produce symptoms.

Quick Summary

Considering the six personality disorders listed in the alternative DSM-5 model, all are at least moderately heritable and are predicted by aversive or unaffectionate parenting. Four are tied to abuse or neglect during childhood.

Check Your Knowledge 15.3

Answer the following.

1. What is the level of heritability for personality disorders?

2. Describe the magnitude of the effect of childhood adversity on the risk for personality disorders observed in the Children in the Community Study.

Clinical Description and Etiology of the Odd/Eccentric Cluster

The odd/eccentric cluster of personality disorders includes paranoid personality disorder, schizoid personality disorder, and schizotypal personality disorder. The symptoms of these three disorders bear some similarity to the types of bizarre thinking and experiences seen in schizophrenia. In the cluster A personality disorders, though, the bizarre thinking and functional impairments are less severe than they are in schizophrenia, and hallucinations are not present. The cluster A personality disorders are distinct from delusional disorders because full-blown delusions are not present.

Paranoid Personality Disorder

People with **paranoid personality disorder** (see the Clinical Case of Danielle) are suspicious of others, including strangers, casual acquaintances, and even family members. They expect

---

DSM-5 Criteria for Paranoid Personality Disorder

Presence of 4 or more of the following signs of distrust and suspiciousness from early adulthood across many contexts:

- Unjustified suspiciousness of being harmed, deceived, or exploited
- Unwarranted doubts about the loyalty or trustworthiness of friends or associates
- Reluctance to confide in others because of suspiciousness

- The tendency to read hidden meanings into the benign actions of others
- Bears grudges for perceived wrongs
- Angry reactions to perceived attacks on character or reputation
- Unwarranted suspiciousness of the partner's fidelity

DSM-5 Criteria for Schizoid Personality Disorder

Presence of 4 or more of the following signs of aloofness and flat affect from early adulthood across many contexts:

- Lack of desire for or enjoyment of close relationships
- Almost always prefers solitude to companionship
- Little interest in sex

- Few or no pleasurable activities
- Lack of friends
- Indifference to praise or criticism
- Flat affect, emotional detachment, or coldness

---

to be mistreated or exploited and thus are secretive and continually on the lookout for signs of trickery and abuse. They are often hostile and angry in response to perceived insults. Co-workers tend to see them as difficult and critical. Their social worlds are usually filled with conflict, and conflicts can be quite long-lasting. Sadly, the conflicts tend to perpetuate their paranoia—their frequent battles provide evidence that people just cannot be trusted. Many become extremely isolated.

Schizoid Personality Disorder

People with **schizoid personality disorder** do not desire or enjoy social relationships, and they usually have no close friends. When interacting with people, they appear aloof and show no warm, tender feelings. They rarely experience strong emotions, are not interested in sex, and enjoy few activities. Indifferent to praise or criticism, people with this disorder are loners who pursue solitary interests.

Schizotypal Personality Disorder

The defining features of **schizotypal personality disorder** include eccentric thoughts and behavior, interpersonal detachment, and suspiciousness. Like Emily in the Clinical Case, people with this disorder might have odd beliefs or magical thinking—for instance, the belief that they can read other people's minds and see into the future. It is also common for them to have ideas of reference (the belief that events have a particular and unusual meaning for them personally). For example, they might feel that a TV program conveys a special message designed for them. They are often suspicious of others and concerned that others might hurt them. They might also have recurrent illusions (inaccurate sensory perceptions), such as sensing

---

Clinical Case

Danielle

Danielle and her partner sought marital therapy because their day-to-day life was filled with acrimonious quarrels. At the first session, it became clear that Danielle was often angry with her partner over small daily incidents. For instance, she thought that he chewed loudly as a way of upsetting her and that he rolled over in bed to deliberately wake her up at night. At a deeper level, she intermittently became fearful that he was having an affair, and despite his protestations to the contrary, her fears were very difficult to calm.

In an individual interview, it became clear that her husband was only one of many sources of worry and annoyance

for Danielle. Danielle worried that the neighbors played their stereo loudly just to get at her and that her boss assigned her challenging jobs because he wanted to see her squirm. She had long since stopped using banks as she felt that the management might scheme to keep her money. Although bright and witty, she was unable to identify women whom she could trust, leaving her friendless. Indeed, every relationship in her life seemed colored by her worries that the other person could harm her in some way. Although Danielle felt extremely stressed by her social troubles, she did not believe that she had contributed to any of the conflicts, and she felt highly victimized by these difficult interpersonal circumstances.

DSM-5 Criteria for Schizotypal Personality Disorder

Presence of 5 or more of the following signs of unusual thinking, eccentric behavior, and interpersonal deficits from early adulthood across many contexts:

- Ideas of reference
- Odd beliefs or magical thinking, e.g., belief in extrasensory perception
- Unusual perceptions

- Odd thought and speech
- Suspiciousness or paranoia
- Inappropriate or restricted affect
- Odd or eccentric behavior or appearance
- Lack of close friends
- Social anxiety and interpersonal fears that do not diminish with familiarity

---

the presence of a force or a person that is not actually there. In their speech, they might use words in an unusual and unclear fashion—for example, they might say "not a very talkable person" to mean a person who is not easy to talk to. Their behavior and appearance might also be eccentric—for example, they might talk to themselves or wear dirty and disheveled clothing. Their affect is flat, and they are aloof from others. Although most do not develop delusions (convictions in patently absurd beliefs) or schizophrenia, some people diagnosed with schizotypal personality disorder develop more severe psychotic symptoms over time, and a small proportion do develop schizophrenia over time (Raine, 2006).

A fair amount of research has focused on the causes of the odd thinking, bizarre behavior, and interpersonal difficulties of schizotypal personality disorder. As noted earlier, genetic factors and childhood adversity are likely both involved. Beyond this, the biological vulnerability for schizotypal personality disorder appears to overlap with the genetic vulnerability for schizophrenia. That is, family studies and adoption studies have shown that the relatives of people with schizophrenia are at increased risk for schizotypal personality disorder (Nigg & Goldsmith, 1994; Tienari, Wynne, et al., 2003). Studies also have consistently shown that people with schizotypal personality disorder have deficits in cognitive and neuropsychological functioning

Clinical Case

Emily

Emily, a 40-year-old single woman, was referred to her employment counseling center by her boss. Her boss stated that she had always completed her clerical duties in a timely and careful manner, but was worried that her relationships with the other women who shared her office space were difficult. He himself said that he found it hard to relate to her, as she was a bit eccentric and expressed herself poorly at times.

At the interview with the counselor, Emily was slightly disheveled and extremely reserved, and had difficulty making eye contact. Emily reported that she did indeed feel very uncomfortable around others in the workplace, but that she had done her best to be polite toward her coworkers. Nonetheless, her social interactions had been a little strained from the time she started her position a couple months ago, and they had become worse after a difficult interaction in the lunch room. Since that time, she had felt frightened around her co-workers, and she found it difficult to say anything to them, even when they attended joint meetings.

When the therapist asked, Emily described the incident that seemed to intensify her co-worker problems. When several

of her co-workers had been making fun of people who believe in ESP, Emily had explained to them that she did have a keen sixth sense of when things were about to happen. She had described knowing in advance about a car accident that happened on her block one day, and occasionally being able to read minds. The more she tried to explain these experiences, the quieter the others became, and her co-workers quit making even basic greetings in the mornings that followed. As she described this incident, Emily's speech was occasionally hard to understand—her sentences became a bit disjointed, and she pronounced words in such an unusual way that the counselor had to ask her to explain what she meant a couple different times.

When the counselor asked about other areas of her life, Emily described a quiet, friendless existence. She spent most evenings and weekends alone at home. She said she was used to being alone, as she had been a lonely and teased child. She frequently thought she heard a voice saying her name, but then could find no one in the apartment that could have made the vocalization. Other times she felt as though there was a spiritual presence in her apartment, but she was not sure if that could be the case. She denied frank hallucinations. Her brother had schizophrenia, and Emily had long worried that she could develop the same disease.

that are similar to but milder than those seen in schizophrenia (Lenzenweger, 2015). Furthermore, people with schizotypal personality disorder have enlarged ventricles, less temporal lobe gray matter, and neurotransmitter dysregulation that are like those observed in schizophrenia but are less severe (Lenzenweger, 2015).

Quick Summary and cognitive

The odd/eccentric cluster of personality disorders (cluster A) includes paranoid personality disorder, schizoid personality disorder, and schizotypal personality disorder.

People with paranoid personality disorder are suspicious of others, people with schizoid personality disorder are socially aloof, and people with schizotypal personality disorder are eccentric in their thoughts and behavior.

Biological studies indicate that schizotypal personality disorder and schizophrenia are related.

Check Your Knowledge 15.4

Answer the questions.

1. Which personality disorder is most related to schizophrenia in family history studies?
2. Which personality disorder is most centrally characterized by an aloof interpersonal style?

Clinical Description and Etiology of the Dramatic/Erratic Cluster

The disorders in the dramatic/erratic cluster—antisocial personality disorder, borderline personality disorder, histrionic personality disorder, and narcissistic personality disorder—are characterized by symptoms that range from highly inconsistent behavior to inflated self-esteem, rule-breaking behavior, and exaggerated emotional displays, including anger outbursts. Antisocial and borderline personality disorders are major foci of research.

Antisocial Personality Disorder and Psychopathy

Informally, the lay public often uses the terms *antisocial personality disorder* and *psychopathy* interchangeably. Antisocial behavior, such as law breaking, is a core component of both, but the two syndromes differ in important ways. One difference is that antisocial personality disorder is included in the DSM, whereas psychopathy is not.

Antisocial Personality Disorder: Clinical Description The core feature of **antisocial personality disorder (APD)** is a pervasive pattern of disregard for the rights of others (as described in the Clinical Case of Alec). The person with APD is distinguished by aggressive, impulsive, and callous traits. DSM-5 criteria specify the presence of conduct disorder before age 15: People with APD often report a history of such symptoms as truancy, running away from home, frequent lying, theft, arson, and deliberate destruction of property by early adolescence. Adolescents who endorse symptoms of antisocial personality disorder are more likely to engage in a range of violent and criminal behaviors (Baskin-Sommers, Baskin, et al., 2016). As adults, people with APD show irresponsible behavior such as working inconsistently, breaking laws, being irritable and physically aggressive, defaulting on debts, being reckless and impulsive, and neglecting to plan ahead. They show little regard for truth and little remorse for their misdeeds, even when those actions hurt family and friends.

DSM-5 Criteria for Antisocial Personality Disorder

- Age at least 18
- Evidence of conduct disorder before age 15
- Pervasive pattern of disregard for the rights of others since the age of 15 as shown by at least three of the following:

  1. Repeated law breaking
  2. Deceitfulness, lying

3. Impulsivity
4. Irritability and aggressiveness
5. Reckless disregard for own safety and that of others
6. Irresponsibility as seen in unreliable employment or financial history
7. Lack of remorse

Men are about five times more likely than are women to meet criteria for APD (Oltmanns & Powers, 2012). About three-quarters of people with APD meet the diagnostic criteria for another disorder, with substance abuse being very common (Lenzenweger et al., 2007). More than half of prison inmates meet the diagnostic criteria for APD (Edens, Kelley, et al., 2015).

Psychopathy: Clinical Description The concept of **psychopathy** predates the DSM diagnosis of antisocial personality disorder. In his book *The Mask of Sanity*, Hervey Cleckley (1976) drew on his clinical experience to formulate diagnostic criteria for psychopathy. The criteria for psychopathy focus on the person's thoughts and feelings. One of the key characteristics of psychopathy is poverty of emotions, both positive and negative: Psychopathic people have no sense of shame, and their seemingly positive feelings for others are merely an act. They are superficially charming and use that charm to manipulate others for personal gain. Their lack of anxiety might make it impossible for them to learn from their mistakes, and their lack of remorse leads them to behave irresponsibly and often cruelly toward others. The rule-breaking behavior of a person with psychopathy is performed impulsively, as much for thrills as for financial gain.

The most commonly used scale to assess psychopathy is the Psychopathy Checklist–Revised (PCL-R; Hare, 2003). Ratings on this 20-item scale are based on an interview and review of criminal records and mental health charts. Many self-report scales have been developed as well. These scales differ a bit in the traits they cover, and there is debate about the underlying core traits that drive psychopathy. Some researchers have argued that three core traits underpin these different symptoms: boldness, meanness, and impulsivity (Patrick & Drislane, 2015). There is some evidence that meanness and impulsivity might be more core to the negative outcomes of psychopathy (Miller, Lamkin, et al., 2016; Miller & Lynam, 2012), while boldness may help explain the social poise and calm demeanor of some psychopaths (Lilienfeld, Patrick, et al., 2012).

There are two chief differences between the criteria for APD and the definition of psychopathy as reflected on the PCL-R. First, even though the PCL-R covers many of the criteria for APD, the scale differs from the DSM-5 criteria for APD in including more affective symptoms, such as shallow affect and lack of empathy. Second, the DSM-5 criteria for antisocial personality

Clinical Case

Alec

Alec, a 40-year-old man, was court-ordered to take part in a psychological assessment after being charged with manufacturing counterfeit bills. He described his history of three divorces with no remorse. His first marriage had ended in a rancorous divorce after he was discovered having two simultaneous extramarital affairs. His second marriage ended within 3 months, and he bragged about emptying her large savings account, stating, "A fool and her money are easily parted." His third wife divorced him after discovering that he had been trafficking in stolen furniture. He had a long history of petty financial and drug-related crimes, and despite his frequent drug dealing, he was deeply in debt. He was estranged from all family members, and his friends consisted of the regulars at his neighborhood bar.

Focus on Discovery 15.1

Media Images of Psychopathy: Will the Real Psychopath Please Stand Up?

Media images of psychopathy vary considerably, ranging from portrayals of ruthless murderers to charming business tycoons to white-collar criminals. The media is quick to label psychopathy in mass murderers and other ruthless, violent offenders. At the same time, the idea that people with psychopathy use their charm, boldness, and lack of empathy to climb their way into the boardroom, where they are influencing the culture of current business practice, also has become quite widespread in the media. Stories abound, such as the one featured in the film *The Wolf of Wall Street*, of remorseless capitalists who bilk their customers of money through white-collar crime (Smith & Lilienfeld, 2013).

Data is available regarding each of these stereotypes. Some, but certainly not all, people with high levels of psychopathy engage in violence as a means of achieving their goals (Reidy, Shelley-Tremblay, & Lilienfeld, 2011). Regarding corporate success, a widely cited study did suggest that employees in a large corporate management training program obtained PCL-R scores that were somewhat higher than the general population, but only 3 percent of the employees scored above the PCL-R threshold for psychopathy (Babiak, Neumann, & Hare, 2010). Moreover, psychopathy scores were not elevated in one sample of white-collar criminals (Ragatz, Fremouw, & Baker, 2012). It is not safe to presume that someone is psychopathic just because he or she engages in violent or unethical behavior, or is highly ambitious and successful. Careful diagnosis depends on evaluating whether an entire syndrome is present.

---

disorder differ from psychopathy criteria in the requirement that a person develop symptoms before age 15. Although psychopathy is highly correlated with antisocial behavior (Neumann, Hare, et al., 2015), the differences in definition lead to considerable divergence between the two syndromes. Many people diagnosed with DSM APD do not obtain high scores on the PCL-R, and vice versa (Few, Lynam, et al., 2015).

Etiology of Antisocial Personality Disorder and Psychopathy

As we review research on the etiology of ASP and psychopathy, keep in mind two issues that make findings a little hard to integrate. First, research has been conducted on persons diagnosed in different ways—some with APD and some with psychopathy. There may be important differences in vulnerability to APD versus psychopathy (Baskin-Sommers, 2016; Hyde, Shaw, et al., 2016; Venables, Hall, et al., 2015). Second, most research on APD and psychopathy has been conducted on persons who have been convicted as criminals. Thus, the results of this research might not be applicable to those with APD who are not criminals or who avoid arrest. Indeed, among people with high psychopathy levels, cognitive and psychophysiological deficits are more likely among people who have been convicted than those who have not been caught (Ishikawa, Raine, et al., 2001).

Many prison inmates meet the DSM criteria for antisocial personality disorder.

More than any other area of personality disorder research, the work on APD often conjointly considers biology with social and psychological risk factors. In this section, we will see this in two ways. First, in considering the social correlates of APD, we will describe how genes and social risk factors work together. Second, as we discuss psychological models of APD, we will note several studies that have used brain imaging to test these models. To capture these integrated models, we will deviate from our organizational approach in other sections of the book, where we tend to separate neurobiological and psychological models.

Interactions of Genes and the Social Environment

The social environment is a key factor in the development of APD. Above, we described one of the many studies showing that parenting qualities can predict antisocial behavior. Substantial prospective research also shows that broader social factors, including poverty and exposure to violence, predict antisocial behavior (Loeber & Hay, 1997). For example, among adolescents with conduct disorder, those who are impoverished are twice as likely to develop APD as are those from higher socioeconomic status backgrounds (Lahey, Loeber, et al., 2005). There is little question that childhood adversity can set the stage for the development of APD.

The effects of early adversity might be particularly negative for those who are genetically vulnerable to APD. Across multiple studies, a polymorphism of the *MAO-A* gene predicts psychopathy among males who had experienced childhood physical or sexual abuse or maternal rejection (Byrd & Manuck, 2014). The effects of growing up in a difficult environment on APD may be amplified by genetic factors.

Adoption research has also shown that genetic, behavioral, and family influences are very hard to disentangle (Ge, Conger, et al., 1996). That is, the genetically influenced antisocial behavior of the child can provoke harsh discipline and lack of warmth, even in adoptive parents, and these parental characteristics in turn exacerbate the child's antisocial tendencies. Nonetheless, the findings of many studies indicate that social influences such as harsh discipline and poverty robustly predict APD even after controlling for genetic risk (Jaffee, Strait, & Odgers, 2012).

Psychological Risk: Insensitivity to Threat and to Others' Emotions, and Too Much Focus on Goals People with psychopathy seem unable to learn from experience; they often repeat misconduct that has been harshly punished, even if it resulted in jail time. They seem immune to the anxiety that keeps most of us from breaking the law, lying, or injuring others. Cleckley argued that people with psychopathy do not learn to avoid trouble because they are insensitive to threats.

A large body of work relates psychopathy to deficits in the experience of fear and threat. At rest, people with psychopathy have lower-than-normal levels of skin conductance, and their skin conductance is less reactive when they are confronted with or anticipate an aversive stimulus (Lorber, 2004). This low skin conductance reactivity to aversive stimuli (loud tones) at age 3 predicted psychopathy scores at age 28 (Glenn, Raine, et al., 2007). In addition to skin conductance, those with psychopathy show blunted neural responsivity to aversive stimuli (Baskin-Sommers, 2016).

The lack of response to negative stimuli appears to shape difficulty learning from aversive feedback—that is, those with high psychopathy show diminished classical conditioning when aversive stimuli such as electric shock or loud blasts of noise (the unconditioned stimulus) are repeatedly paired with a conditioned stimulus (Smith & Lilienfeld, 2015). In an interesting test of classical conditioning deficits, researchers used brain activity to examine what happens when an unconditioned stimulus (painful pressure) was repeatedly paired with neutral pictures (the conditioned stimuli). To assess responses to the conditioned stimulus after these repeated pairings, the researchers measured the activity of the amygdala and other brain regions involved in emotion (Birbaumer, Veit, et al., 2005). The amygdala is a brain region that is strongly implicated in emotion reactivity (see Chapter 6, Figure 6.2), and activity of this region has been found to be heightened in several disorders that involve intense emotionality, including mood disorders and anxiety disorders. After conditioning, healthy control participants showed increases in amygdala activity when viewing the neutral pictures. People with high psychopathy scores, though, did not show this expected increase in amygdala activity. Weakened classical conditioning could help explain why people with psychopathy are slow to learn from punishment.

Beyond their general lack of response to threat, the person with psychopathy might become even more unresponsive to threats when trying to gain a reward, such as money or other resources, or when pursuing other rewards. In an early study demonstrating this phenomenon, participants played a computerized card game in which they earned 5¢ for each face card that appeared; if a nonface card appeared, the participant lost 5¢ (Newman, Patterson, & Kosson, 1987). Participants could quit the game anytime they wanted. The game was rigged so that over time, the probability of losing increased. People with high psychopathy scores continued to play the game much longer than did people with low psychopathy, even when they were being punished. Since the time of this study, researchers have conducted dozens of studies on this phenomenon. They have found evidence that psychopaths have poor attention to threats, but also to other peripheral information, once they are immersed in the pursuit of a goal (Smith & Lilienfeld, 2015). In parallel with the attention deficits, imaging research shows that antisocial behavior is associated with deficits in regions of the prefrontal cortex that are involved in attending to negative information during goal pursuit (Ermer, Cope, et al., 2012). This behavioral and neural pattern could help explain why those with antisocial behavior break rules and violate conventions when they are pursuing their goals. Across a large literature, though, the problems that those with antisocial behavior show in attending to context tend to be small and the size of deficit varies depending on the tasks and the measures of psychopathy, suggesting that there is a need to refine this model (Smith & Lilienfeld, 2015).

In contrast to a general insensitivity to threat, psychopathy might be particularly tied to a more specific insensitivity to threats experienced by other people (Blair, 2005). According to this model, a lack of empathy, defined by the capacity to share emotional reactions of others, could be the central deficit driving the callous exploitation of others observed in psychopathy. Several types of research provide support for this theory. When asked to identify the emotion conveyed in videos of strangers, men with psychopathy do very poorly in recognizing others' fear, even though they recognize other emotions well (Brook & Kosson, 2013). Those with antisocial symptoms show diminished amygdala response (presumably reflecting less emotional response) when imagining others' pain as compared to imagining their own pain (Marsh, Finger, et al., 2013).

Borderline Personality Disorder

Borderline personality disorder (BPD) has been a major focus of interest for several reasons: It is very common in clinical settings, very hard to treat, and associated with recurrent periods of suicidality. The core features of **borderline personality disorder** are impulsivity and instability in relationships and mood. For example, people with this disorder may shift from blissful happiness to outraged explosions in the blink of an eye. As in the Clinical Case of Mary, which opened this chapter, the intense anger of people with BPD often damages relationships.

Researchers have used experience sampling, in which a person reports on their feelings or behavior several times per day for weeks, to understand these emotional and interpersonal responses. That work shows that emotions can change drastically and very quickly (Trull, Solhan, et al., 2008). Research with experience sampling also has shown that people with BPD are overly sensitive to small signs of rejection in others, and in response to those signals, they are more prone to anger and aggression (Scott, Wright, et al., 2017).

People with borderline personality disorder exhibit high levels of impulsivity, particularly in response to emotion states (Few, Lynam, & Miller, 2015). Their unpredictable, impulsive, and potentially self-damaging behavior might include gambling, reckless spending, indiscriminate sexual activity, and substance abuse. Their symptoms also lead to high levels of stress, such as relationship conflicts and financial crises (Powers, Gleason, et al., 2013). Of the different personality disorders, borderline personality disorder is the one most tied to distress in romantic relationships (Wilson, Stroud, & Durbin, 2017).

People with BPD often have not developed a clear and coherent sense of self—they experience major swings in such basic aspects of identity as their values, loyalties, and career choices. One month, they might consider a career in the business world, complete with the wardrobe and polished demeanor of a professional salesperson; the next month, they might decide to try acting, trading in their business apparel for colorful artistic garb, accompanied by a new set of interests in the arts. They cannot bear to be alone, have fears of abandonment, and experience chronic feelings of depression and emptiness. They may experience transient psychotic and dissociative symptoms when stressed.

Suicidal behavior is all too common in BPD. Many people with this disorder make multiple suicide attempts during their lifetime (Boisseau, Yen, et al., 2013). In one 20-year follow-up study, about 7.5 percent of people with BPD died from suicide (Linehan & Heard, 1999). People with BPD are also particularly likely to engage in nonsuicidal self-injury. For example, they might slice their legs with a razor blade or burn their arms with cigarettes—behaviors that are harmful but unlikely to cause death. At least two-thirds of people with BPD will engage in self-mutilation at some point during their lives (Stone, 1993).

A colorful account by Jonathan Kellerman, a clinical psychologist and successful mystery writer, gives a good sense of what people with BPD are like.

> *Their egos are as fragile as spun sugar, their psyches irretrievably fragmented, like a jigsaw puzzle with crucial pieces missing. They play roles with alacrity, excel at being anyone but themselves, crave intimacy but repel it when they find it. Some of them gravitate toward stage or screen; others do their acting in more subtle ways. . . . Borderlines go from therapist to therapist, hoping to find a magic bullet for the crushing feelings of emptiness. They turn to chemical bullets, gobble tranquilizers and antidepressants, alcohol and cocaine. (Kellerman, 1989, pp. 113–114)*

After he was diagnosed with borderline personality disorder in 2010, Brandon Marshall, the highly successful wide receiver for the Chicago Bears, created the Brandon Marshall Foundation to help improve awareness of mental health, to reduce stigma, and to provide funding for treatment.

Tasos Katopodis/Getty Images for Child Mind Institute

Fortunately, research on new treatments for BPD, discussed later in the chapter, supports a more positive outlook than Kellerman offers.

Etiology of Borderline Personality Disorder
Researchers have considered many different risk factors for BPD. We will begin by considering the neural correlates of BPD. The literature on BPD, though, is very sophisticated in considering integrated models of how early adversity and abuse interface with other risk factors. Remember that earlier in this chapter, we described findings from the Children in the Community Study that childhood abuse and poor parenting styles both predict the onset of BPD. The links of early adversity in BPD have been shown again and again. For example, despite some nonreplications (Stepp, Lazarus, et al., 2016), longitudinal studies suggest that BPD symptoms can be predicted by difficult parental relationships, even when objective raters evaluate the quality of parenting (Belsky, Caspi, et al., 2012; Carlson, Egeland, & Sroufe, 2009; Lyons-Ruth, Bureau, et al., 2013). Work in BPD now tries to place these correlations of abuse and parenting into a framework that integrates other variables.

DSM-5 Criteria for Borderline Personality Disorder

Presence of five or more of the following signs of instability in relationships, self-image, and impulsivity from early adulthood across many contexts:

- Frantic efforts to avoid abandonment
- Unstable interpersonal relationships in which others are either idealized or devalued
- Unstable sense of self
- Self-damaging, impulsive behaviors in at least two areas, such as spending, sex, substance abuse, reckless driving, and binge eating

- Recurrent suicidal behavior, gestures, or self-injurious behavior (e.g., cutting self)
- Marked mood reactivity
- Chronic feelings of emptiness
- Recurrent bouts of intense or poorly controlled anger
- During stress, a tendency to experience transient paranoid thoughts and dissociative symptoms

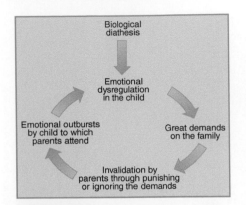

FIGURE 15.3 Marsha Linehan's diathesis–stress theory of borderline personality disorder.

Here, we will provide two illustrations of this integrative work. First, we will discuss Linehan's model of how parenting style may interact with a child's emotionality and behavior. Second, we will consider research findings that indicate that the experiences of abuse may even be explained by genetic vulnerability. Both types of findings highlight how important it is to consider the matrix of risk factors conjointly in trying to understand BPD.

Neurobiological Factors Core features of BPD involve the heightened emotionality and impulsivity. Relatedly, neurobiological research suggests the importance of regulatory control regions (such as regions of the prefrontal cortex and anterior cingulate cortex) and regions implicated in emotion response (such as the amygdala). Several studies link BPD to diminished connectivity of brain regions involved in emotion experience and those involved in regulatory control. These neurobiological patterns could help explain their poor control over emotions, and their impulsivity when emotions are present (Mancke, Herpertz, et al., 2015).

Parenting Interacts with Child Vulnerability Marsha Linehan (1987) proposes that we need to consider how parenting could amplify the vulnerabilities of some children. She argues that BPD develops when people who have difficulty controlling their emotions because of a biological diathesis (possibly genetic) are raised in a family environment that is invalidating. That is, a diathesis of emotional dysregulation interacts with experiences of invalidation to promote the development of BPD. In an invalidating environment, the person's feelings are discounted and disrespected—that is, the person's efforts to communicate feelings are disregarded or even punished.

The two main hypothesized factors—emotional dysregulation and invalidation—interact with each other in a dynamic fashion (see **Figure 15.3**). For example, the emotionally dysregulated child makes enormous demands on his or her family. The exasperated parents ignore or even punish the child's outbursts, which leads the child to suppress his or her emotions. The suppressed emotions build up to an explosion, which then gets the attention of the parents. Thus, the parents end up reinforcing the very behaviors that they find aversive. Many other patterns are possible, of course, but what they have in common is a constant back-and-forth between dysregulation and invalidation.

Research supports the dynamic nature of these interactions between children and their parents in the development of BPD. In one study, researchers assessed 2228 girls and their mothers annually from ages 5 to 14. Poor self-control (e.g., "cannot control temper outbursts") predicted increases over time in harsh parenting, and vice versa, harsh parenting predicted worse self-control during childhood. The childhood problems with self-control predicted more BPD symptoms as the girls reached age 14 (Hallquist, Hipwell, et al., 2015). These findings illustrate the importance of considering the dynamic interaction between child behavior and parenting.

Genetic Vulnerability and Abuse Other work considers abuse and adversity in the context of the genetic vulnerability to BPD. To consider whether genetic vulnerability and abuse are independent of each other in their effects on BPD, researchers studied 197 MZ twin pairs in

---

DSM-5 Criteria for Histrionic Personality Disorder

Presence of five or more of the following signs of excessive emotionality and attention seeking from early adulthood across many contexts:

- Strong need to be the center of attention
- Inappropriate sexually seductive behavior
- Rapidly shifting and shallow expression of emotions

- Use of physical appearance to draw attention to self
- Speech that is excessively impressionistic and lacking in detail
- Exaggerated, theatrical emotional expression
- Overly suggestible
- Misreads relationships as more intimate than they are

which one twin, but not the other, reported childhood abuse (Bornovalova, Huibregtse, et al., 2013). If abuse, rather than genetic vulnerability, is driving BPD, twins who experienced abuse should have a higher rate of BPD than their co-twins who were not abused. This was not the case. The twin pairs had similar levels of BPD. That is, childhood abuse did not predict BPD after genetic risk was controlled. In a second twin study, childhood traumatic experiences accounted for less than 1 percent in the variance in who developed BPD after accounting for family characteristics (Berenz, Amstadter, et al., 2013).

Even though a history of abuse is common for those with BPD, these findings indicate that abuse may not be the driving force that sets this personality disorder in motion. How can we make sense of the high rates of abuse among those with BPD, then? Researchers are still working on this puzzle, but consider the idea that abuse often happens against a background of many different problems. Genetically driven impulsivity, emotionality, or risk-seeking in the parents could increase the risk that both abuse and BPD will occur. Findings highlight the complexity of abuse, as it often occurs within a matrix of risk factors. Although much remains unknown, common sense still holds—child abuse has many deleterious effects. The damaging effects of child abuse have been well-documented, even in other studies of twins discordant for abuse (Nelson, Heath, et al., 2002). Nonetheless, researchers will need to conduct studies that integrate genetic vulnerability, early adversity, and child characteristics to understand how BPD develops.

Histrionic Personality Disorder

The key feature of **histrionic personality disorder** is overly dramatic and attention-seeking behavior. People with this disorder often use their physical appearance, such as unusual clothes, makeup, or hair color, to draw attention to themselves. Despite their expressions of extravagant and intense emotions, they seem emotionally shallow. For example, someone with this disorder might gush about and call a person his or her best friend, only to have trouble remembering a conversation with that person the next day. They are self-centered, overly concerned with their physical attractiveness, and uncomfortable when not the center of attention. They can be inappropriately sexually provocative and seductive, and they are easily influenced by others. Their speech is often impressionistic and lacking in detail. For example, they might state a strong opinion yet be completely unable to support it. (Patient: "She was absolutely the greatest." Interviewer: "What did you like best about her?" Patient: "Gosh, I'm not sure I could describe that.").

Narcissistic Personality Disorder

People with **narcissistic personality disorder** have a grandiose view of their qualities and are preoccupied with fantasies of great success (as demonstrated by Bob in the Clinical

Clinical Case

Bob

Bob, a 50-year-old college professor, sought treatment only after urging from his wife. During the interview, Bob's wife noted that he seemed so focused on himself and his own advancement that he often belittled others. Bob was dismissive of these concerns, stating that he had never been the sort of person to tolerate idiots, and he could see no reason why he should begin offering such tolerance now—in rapid fire, he described his supervisor, his students, his parents, and a set of former friends as lacking the intelligence to merit his friendship. He willingly acknowledged working long hours but stated that his research had the potential to change people's lives and that other activities could not be allowed to interfere with his success. The therapist's gentle questioning of whether his expressions of superiority might provoke some interpersonal tension was met with a scathing rebuke.

Case). They are more than a little self-centered—they require almost constant attention. Their interpersonal relationships are disturbed by their lack of empathy, by their arrogance coupled with feelings of envy, by their habit of taking advantage of others, and by their feelings of entitlement and expectations that others will do special favors for them.

People with narcissistic personality disorder view themselves as superior to others, and they overestimate their attractiveness to others and their contributions to group activities. ("Others must be jealous of me; I've been responsible for the lion's share of our progress here today."). In some studies, researchers have provided people with feedback that they were successful on a task (regardless of their actual performance) and then asked participants to rate the reasons why they were successful. In these types of studies, people with narcissistic personality disorder attribute successes to their abilities rather than to chance or luck to a greater extent than do those without personality disorder (Morf & Rhodewalt, 2001).

When people with narcissistic personality disorder interact with others, their primary goal is to bolster their own self-esteem (Morf & Rhodewalt, 2001). Indeed, they value being admired more than they do gaining or maintaining closeness (Campbell, Bosson, et al., 2007). They do a lot to gain the admiration of others. They often pursue fame and wealth. In one study, independent observers were able to make snap judgments of narcissism with some accuracy from photographs, most typically by noticing the expensive clothes and overinvestment in appearance of those with narcissistic traits (Vazire, Naumann, et al., 2008). People with narcissistic personality disorder work hard in contexts in which there is a chance for recognition (Roberts, Woodman, & Sedikides, 2017). They also tend to brag a lot.

There is a darker, aggressive side to the narcissistic pursuit of recognition. When someone else performs better than they do on a task that is relevant to self-esteem, they will denigrate the other person, even to that person's face (Roberts et al., 2017). People with narcissistic personality disorder are highly likely to be vindictive and aggressive when faced with a competitive threat or a put-down (Bushman & Thomaes, 2011). Although their ability to present their strengths and project confidence is often perceived positively in brief initial interactions, their aggressive, competitive tendencies tend to wear thin over time, and others tend to rate them more negatively after just a few sessions of working together (Leckelt, Küfner, et al., 2015).

Narcissism also tends to predict problems in romantic partnerships. People with narcissistic personality disorder tend to seek out high-status partners whom they idealize and proudly show off, only to change partners if given an opportunity to be with a person of higher status. In a study of newlyweds, high levels of narcissistic traits among wives predicted steep declines in marital satisfaction for both the husbands and wives over a 4-year period (Lavner, Lamkin, et al., 2016).

Given the associated tendencies toward confidence and ambition, could a small amount of narcissism be adaptive? In one study, 121 scholars with expertise in American leaders rated the degree of (subclinical) narcissism of the U.S. presidents. Presidents

Bettmann / Getty Images

Frank Lloyd Wright, one of the most influential American architects, displayed at least some narcissistic traits. He is quoted as saying "Early in life, I had to choose between honest arrogance and hypocritical humility. I chose honest arrogance and have seen no reason to change."

DSM-5 Criteria for Narcissistic Personality Disorder

Presence of five or more of the following signs of grandiosity, need for admiration, and lack of empathy from early adulthood across many contexts:

- Grandiose view of one's importance
- Preoccupation with one's success, brilliance, beauty
- Belief that one is special and can be understood only by other high-status people

- Extreme need for admiration
- Strong sense of entitlement
- Tendency to exploit others
- Lack of empathy
- Envious of others
- Arrogant behavior or attitudes

who were rated as relatively more narcissistic were more likely to be persuasive, won more of the popular vote, and initiated more legislation. On the other hand, they were also likely to get in trouble for unethical behavior (Watts, Lilienfeld, et al., 2013).

Etiology of Narcissistic Personality Disorder

In this section, we consider theory and research on how some people develop narcissistic personality traits. We begin by discussing parenting, and then consider models of fragile self-esteem.

Parenting In one prominent account of how parenting might influence the development of narcissism, Millon (1996) hypothesized that parents who are overly indulgent promote children's beliefs that they are special (and even more special than other children), and that behavioral expressions of their specialness will be tolerated by others. Several studies indicate that people with high self-rated levels of narcissism do report experiencing overindulgence from their parents (Horton, 2011). More importantly, independent ratings confirm this profile. Researchers assessed 565 children ages 7–11 and their parents twice a year for 2 years. Consistent with theory, parental tendencies to see their children as highly superior to others predicted increases at each time point in their children's narcissistic traits (Brummelman, Thomaes, et al., 2015).

Fragile Self-Esteem In his two books, *The Analysis of the Self* (1971) and *The Restoration of the Self* (1977), Heinz Kohut developed a model of narcissism based on self-psychology, a variant of psychodynamic theory. He started from the clinical observation that the person with narcissistic personality disorder projects self-importance, self-absorption, and fantasies of limitless success on the surface. Kohut theorized that these characteristics mask a very fragile self-esteem. People with narcissistic personality disorder strive to bolster their sense of self-worth through unending quests for respect from others. Inflated self-worth and denigration of others, then, are defenses against feelings of shame. Research does support the idea that people diagnosed with narcissistic personality disorder experience shame more frequently than do those without personality disorder (Ritter, Vater, et al., 2014).

The idea that narcissism is tied to fragile self-esteem has also shaped cognitive behavioral theory and research. To assess whether people with narcissistic personality disorder have fragile self-esteem, many researchers have examined how much their self-esteem depends on external feedback (Morf & Rhodewalt, 2001). For example, when falsely told they have done poorly on an IQ test, they show much more reactivity than others do; similarly, they show more reactivity to hearing they have succeeded at something.

In one study, researchers used fMRI to examine vulnerability to feedback, in the form of social rejection during a cyberball game. Participants were falsely led to believe that they were playing the game with two other people (Cascio, Konrath, et al., 2015). During one block of the game, the (sham) participants did not toss the ball to the participant. As expected, social exclusion activated neural regions associated with processing social and other forms of pain (such as the anterior insula and anterior cingulate). Narcissistic traits led to even more activation of those pain-relevant neural regions. That is, those with narcissistic tendencies were particularly sensitive to negative social interactions.

Narcissistic personality disorder draws its name from the Greek mythological figure Narcissus, who fell in love with his own reflection, was consumed by his own desire, and was transformed into a flower.

Peter Paul Rubens. 1577–1640/Flemish). *Narcissus*. Museum Bojimans Van Beuningen, Rotterdam, Netherlands.

There is some debate about whether fragile self-esteem is core to the diagnosis of narcissistic personality disorder (Pincus & Lukowitsky, 2010) or present only for a subset of those with this disorder (Miller, Lynam, et al., 2017). The more people show fragile self-worth, though, the higher their levels of neuroticism and depression (Orth, Robins, et al., 2016), and the more likely they are to seek treatment (Miller et al., 2017).

Quick Summary

The dramatic/erratic cluster (cluster B) includes antisocial personality disorder (APD), borderline personality disorder (BPD), histrionic personality disorder, and narcissistic personality disorder. The key features of APD include violation of rules and a disregard for others' feeling and social norms. Psychopathy is related to antisocial personality disorder but is not defined in the DSM. Psychopathy criteria focus on internal experiences (such as a poverty of emotion). BPD is defined by intense emotionality, unstable sense of identity, and impulsivity. Histrionic personality disorder is characterized by exaggerated emotional displays. Narcissistic personality disorder is characterized by highly inflated self-esteem but a deep need for admiration.

A harsh family environment and poverty play a role in the development of APD, and these social risk factors may be particularly important for those who are at higher genetic risk for the disorder. Psychopathy is related to blunted responses to threat and, as a consequence, to difficulty learning from punishment. This insensitivity to threat may be especially present during goal pursuit, or when viewing threats that are occurring to other people.

Consistent with their emotionality and impulsivity, people with BPD demonstrate diminished connectivity of the brain regions involved in emotionality and those involved in regulation. Abuse and negative parenting styles can predict the onset of BPD symptoms, but some of the abuse may be tied to parental genetic vulnerability. Linehan's model integrates the high rates of parental invalidation reported by people with BPD with the biological diathesis for emotional dysregulation.

Across studies, those with narcissistic personality disorder report that their parents were overly indulgent, and many show fragile self-esteem.

Check Your Knowledge 15.5

Answer the questions.

1. Which personality disorder is most common in clinical settings?
2. Which two of the cluster B personality disorders are strongly related to impulsivity?
3. Which personality disorder is most common in forensic settings?

Clinical Description and Etiology of the Anxious/Fearful Cluster

The anxious/fearful cluster includes avoidant personality disorder, dependent personality disorder, and obsessive-compulsive personality disorder. People with these disorders are prone to worry and distress.

Avoidant Personality Disorder

People with **avoidant personality disorder** are so fearful of criticism, rejection, and disapproval that they will avoid jobs or relationships to protect themselves from negative feedback. In social situations, they are restrained and timid because of an extreme fear of saying

People with avoidant personality disorder often avoid interpersonal interactions, as they find them so stressful.

DSM-5 Criteria for Avoidant Personality Disorder

A pervasive pattern of social inhibition, feelings of inadequacy, and hypersensitivity to criticism as shown by four or more of the following from early adulthood across many contexts:

- Avoidance of occupational activities that involve significant interpersonal contact, because of fears of criticism or disapproval
- Unwilling to get involved with people unless certain of being liked
- Restrained in intimate relationships because of the fear of being shamed or ridiculed

- Preoccupation with being criticized or rejected
- Inhibited in new interpersonal situations because of feelings of inadequacy
- Views self as socially inept, unappealing, or inferior
- Unusually reluctant to try new activities because they may prove embarrassing

---

something foolish, being embarrassed, blushing, or showing other signs of anxiety. They believe they are incompetent and inferior to others, and like Leon in the clinical case, they are reluctant to take risks or try new activities. Even though they would like to form close relationships, their fears often make it difficult for them to do so.

Avoidant personality disorder often co-occurs with social anxiety disorder (see Chapter 6), probably because the diagnostic criteria for these two disorders are so similar. The genetic vulnerability for avoidant personality disorder and social anxiety disorder appears to overlap (Torvik, Welander-Vatn, et al., 2016). Etiological variables, then, might overlap with those of social anxiety, discussed in Chapter 6.

Dependent Personality Disorder

The core feature of **dependent personality disorder** is an excessive reliance on others. People with dependent personality disorder have an intense need to be taken care of, which often leads them to feel uncomfortable with being alone. They subordinate their own needs to ensure that they do not threaten the protective relationships they have established. For example, people with dependent personality disorder may repeatedly end dating relationships to appease parents who are overly critical of potential partners. When a close relationship ends, they urgently seek another relationship to replace it. They see themselves as weak, and they turn to others for support and decision making. People with this disorder particularly fear being alone. Perhaps because of their insecurity when their partnerships are threatened, men with higher levels of dependency are at elevated risk of perpetrating domestic violence (Bornstein, 2006). People with dependent personality disorder are likely to develop depression after interpersonal losses (Hammen, Burge, et al., 1995).

Clinical Case

Leon

Leon, a 45-year-old man, sought treatment for depression. During the interview, Leon described feeling depressed and uncomfortable socially for as long as he could remember. By age 5, he would experience intense anxiety when he was with other children, and his mind would "go blank" if he had to speak in front of others. He grew up dreading birthday parties, teachers' classroom questions, and meeting new children. Although he was able to play with some of the children in his neighborhood, he had never asked a woman out on a date or developed a "best friend." He took a job at the post office after graduation because it involved little social interaction. (Adapted from Spitzer, Gibbon, et al., 1994.)

DSM-5 Criteria for Dependent Personality Disorder

An excessive need to be taken care of, as shown by the presence of at least five of the following from early adulthood across many contexts:

- Difficulty making decisions without excessive advice and reassurance from others
- Need for others to take responsibility for most major areas of life
- Difficulty disagreeing with others for fear of losing their support
- Difficulty doing things on own or starting projects because of lack of self-confidence
- Doing unpleasant things to obtain the approval and support of others
- Feelings of helplessness when alone because of fears of being unable to care for self
- Urgently seeking new relationship when one ends
- Preoccupation with fears of having to take care of self

For the person with obsessive-compulsive personality disorder, the overly perfectionistic quest for order may interfere with being productive.

Dan Saelinger/Getty Images, Inc.

Obsessive-Compulsive Personality Disorder

The person with **obsessive-compulsive personality disorder** is a perfectionist, preoccupied with details, rules, and schedules. Although order and perfectionism have their adaptive sides, particularly in fostering success in complex occupational goals, people with this disorder often pay so much attention to detail that they fail to finish projects (as illustrated in the Clinical Case of Sarah). They are more oriented toward work than pleasure, and social relationships often suffer as the pursuit of perfection in the workplace takes time away from family and friends. They have inordinate difficulty making decisions (lest they err) and allocating time (lest they focus on the wrong thing). Their interpersonal relationships are often troubled because they demand that everything be done the right way—their way. Generally, they are serious, rigid, formal, and inflexible, especially regarding moral issues. They are unable to discard worn-out and useless objects, even those with no sentimental value, and they are likely to be excessively frugal. Those with obsessive-compulsive personality disorder seem to have less interpersonal difficulty than do those with other personality disorders. Across studies, this personality disorder is not tied to major difficulties in friendships, family relationships, or romantic relationships, regardless of whether their own report or another's report is used to evaluate those relationships (Wilson et al., 2017).

Obsessive-compulsive personality disorder is distinct from obsessive-compulsive disorder, despite the similarity in names. The personality disorder does not include the obsessions and compulsions that define the latter. Nonetheless, the two conditions often co-occur (Skodol, Oldham, et al., 1995) and have some overlapping genetic vulnerability (Taylor, Asmundson, & Jang, 2011).

DSM-5 Criteria for Obsessive-Compulsive Personality Disorder

Intense need for order, perfection, and control, as shown by the presence of at least four of the following from early adulthood across many contexts:

- Preoccupation with rules, details, and organization to the extent that the point of an activity is lost
- Extreme perfectionism interferes with task completion
- Excessive devotion to work to the exclusion of leisure and friendships
- Inflexibility about morals and values
- Difficulty discarding worthless items
- Reluctance to delegate unless others conform to one's standards
- Miserliness
- Rigidity and stubbornness

Clinical Case

Sarah

Sarah, a 22-year-old woman, was ecstatic to attain a research assistant position with a highly accomplished scientist just after graduation. She was planning to pursue a career in science, and the position fit perfectly with her long-held interests. Despite Sarah's initial enthusiasm, things soon soured with her new boss. When asked to collect data using methods that she already knew well, she began by creating large spreadsheets of the planned process, and then shifted gears and invested in elaborate software for project management. No matter how hard she tried, she could not move from project planning into actual data collection. When faced with writing a project description for the university ethics board review, she wrote over 50 pages of detailed notes on potentially relevant issues but then could not find a way to describe the study in the one page allowed on the form. Although she was asked to manage eight undergraduate volunteers who worked with the team, she could not delegate tasks to them because she was so worried that they might make mistakes. Even though she worked 15-hour days, her boss asked her to resign at the end of the 3-month probation period because she had accomplished less than her predecessor who had worked only 20 hours a week. She was disillusioned by the experience, and she sought therapy with a sense that this was just one in a series of events in which she had gotten herself into trouble by losing sight of the forest for the trees.

Quick Summary

The anxious or fearful cluster of personality disorders (cluster C) includes avoidant personality disorder, dependent personality disorder, and obsessive-compulsive personality disorder. People with avoidant personality disorder are timid and often feel inadequate. Those with dependent personality disorder are overly reliant on others, to the extent that they are vulnerable to depression after interpersonal losses. Those with obsessive-compulsive disorder are intensely focused on the details of maintaining order, perfection, and control.

Avoidant personality disorder may be genetically related to social anxiety disorder. Obsessive-compulsive personality disorder and obsessive-compulsive disorder are often comorbid and share some genetic vulnerability.

Check Your Knowledge 15.6

You are the director of human resources for a large corporation. You are asked to review a set of situations in which employees had interpersonal and task-focused problems that were severe and persistent enough to raise concerns in the workplace. Name the most likely personality disorder for each of the following.

1. Mariana refuses to meet with customers. She states that she is terrified that they will see that she does not know much. It turns out that she has called in sick the last three times her boss scheduled an appointment with her, and her colleagues barely know her name. When asked, she says that meeting with any of these people makes her feel horribly nervous about potential rejection of her ideas. She asks for a position that would involve little social contact.

2. Sheila has had three subordinate employees request transfers from her department. They each stated that she was too controlling, picked on small mistakes, and would not listen to any new ideas for solving problems. At the interview, she brought in a typed, 15-page chart of the goals she would like to execute for the company. Despite having an inordinate number of goals, she has failed to complete a single project during her first year with the company.

3. Police contact you to let you know that they have arrested Sam, one of your employees. He was caught at a bank trying to cash a $10,000 company check on which he had forged the signature. You learn that Sam had previously defrauded three other companies. When you meet with Sam, he does not seem the least bit sorry.

Treatment of Personality Disorders

Many people with personality disorders enter treatment for a condition other than their personality disorder. For example, a person with antisocial personality disorder might seek treatment for substance abuse, and a patient with dependent personality disorder might seek help for depression. Clinicians are encouraged to consider whether personality disorders are present because their presence predicts slower improvement in psychotherapy. Often, addressing those conditions can lead to improvements in personality function as well.

Psychotherapy is the treatment of choice for personality disorders. You might think that it would be impossible to change personality, but there is evidence that personality traits do change in psychotherapy. Across 207 studies, psychotherapy and other interventions led to significant changes in personality traits such as neuroticism, and often did so within 6 weeks (Roberts, Luo, et al., 2017). Indeed, even with full-blown personality disorders, dozens of studies show that psychotherapy provides small but positive effects compared with treatment as usual (Budge, Moore, et al., 2013).

Psychotherapy is often supplemented with medications. For example, antidepressants are used to quell some of the depressive or impulsive symptoms that accompany personality disorders (Tyrer & Bateman, 2004). Medications, though, have not been shown to address the full spectrum of personality disorder symptoms (Perez-Rodriguez & Siever, 2015).

People with serious symptoms of personality disorders might attend weekly psychotherapy sessions, or they might attend a day treatment program that offers psychotherapy in both group and individual formats for several hours per day. The length of treatment programs varies, but some day treatment programs last for months and individual therapy for a year or longer.

Psychodynamic theory suggests that childhood problems are at the root of personality disorders, and so the aim of psychodynamic therapy is to help patients reconsider those early experiences, become more aware of how those experiences drive their current behaviors, and then reconsider their beliefs and responses to those early events. For example, a psychodynamic therapist might guide a man with obsessive-compulsive personality disorder to realize that his need to be perfect is based on a childhood quest to win his parents' love, and that this quest does not need be carried into adulthood—that others will love him even with his imperfections.

Cognitive theory suggests that negative cognitive beliefs, such as those shown in **Table 15.5**, are at the heart of the personality disorders (Beck & Freeman, 1990). The aim of cognitive therapy, then, is to help a person become more aware of those beliefs and then to challenge maladaptive cognitions. For example, cognitive therapy for a perfectionistic person with obsessive-compulsive personality disorder entails first persuading the patient to accept the essence of the cognitive model—that feelings and behaviors are primarily a function of thoughts. Biases in thinking are explored, such as when the patient concludes that he or she cannot do anything right because of a trivial failure. The therapist also looks for dysfunctional assumptions or schemas that might underlie the person's thoughts and feelings—for example, the belief that it is critical for every decision to be correct. Beyond challenging cognitions, Beck's approach to personality disorders incorporates a variety of other cognitive behavioral techniques.

Here, we focus on treatments for three specific personality disorders. Less is known about the specific treatment of the other personality disorders because treatment outcome studies often focus on a broad range of different personality disorders.

TABLE 15.5	Examples of Maladaptive Cognitions Hypothesized to Be Associated with Each Personality Disorder
Personality Disorder	**Maladaptive Cognitions**
Avoidant	If people get to know the real me, they will reject me.
Obsessive-compulsive	If things get disorganized, horrible mistakes will happen.
Antisocial	People ask for exploitation—they let down their guard.
Narcissistic	I am better than others, and people who can't understand that don't deserve my time.

Source: Adapted from Beck & Freeman (1990).

Treatment of Schizotypal Personality Disorder and Avoidant Personality Disorder

Remember that schizotypal personality disorder shares a good deal of overlap with the etiology with schizophrenia, and that avoidant personality disorder shares a good deal of overlap with the etiology of social anxiety disorder. Treatments for these two personality disorders draw on their overlap with other conditions.

More specifically, antipsychotic drugs (e.g., risperidone, trade name Risperdal) have shown effectiveness with schizotypal personality disorder (Raine, 2006). These medications seem particularly helpful for reducing unusual thinking.

The symptoms of avoidant personality disorder respond to the same treatments that are effective for those with social anxiety disorder: that is, antidepressant medications as well as cognitive behavioral treatment (Reich, 2000). Cognitive behavioral treatment might involve helping a person challenge his or her negative beliefs about social interactions by teaching behavioral strategies for dealing with difficult social situations and by exposure treatment, in which the person gradually takes part in feared social situations. Cognitive behavioral treatment lasting 20 sessions has been found to be more helpful than psychodynamic treatment for avoidant personality disorder (Emmelkamp, Benner, et al., 2006). Group versions of cognitive behavioral treatment have been found to be helpful and can provide chances to practice constructive social interactions in a safe environment (Alden, 1989).

Treatment of Borderline Personality Disorder

Clients with BPD tend to show their interpersonal problems in the therapeutic relationship as much as they do in other relationships. Because these clients find it inordinately difficult to trust others, therapists find it challenging to develop and maintain the therapeutic relationship. Patients alternately idealize and vilify the therapist, demanding special attention and consideration one moment—such as therapy sessions at odd hours and countless phone calls during crisis periods—and refusing to keep appointments the next; they beg the therapist for understanding and support but insist that certain topics are off-limits.

Suicide is always a serious risk, but it is often difficult for the therapist to judge whether a frantic phone call at 2:00 A.M. from a BPD patient is a call for help or a manipulative gesture designed to test how special the patient is to the therapist. As in the case of Mary (see the Clinical Case at the beginning of this chapter), hospitalization is sometimes needed to protect against the threat of suicide. Because of the risk of dangerous behavior and the difficulties of managing the therapeutic relationship, therapists working with BPD clients often endorse feeling overwhelmed, inadequate, and at the same time overly involved (Colli, Tanzilli, et al., 2014). To combat their stress, many therapists regularly consult with another therapist for advice and support as they cope with the extraordinary challenges of helping BPD clients.

Fortunately, more than three dozen randomized controlled trials have provided a strong evidence base concerning the treatment of borderline personality disorder (Cristea, Gentili, et al., 2017). Dialectical behavior therapy (DBT) is the most well-validated treatment, but multiple randomized controlled trials indicate that DBT and psychodynamic therapy are both more efficacious than control treatments such as treatment as usual. Both types of treatment reduce borderline symptoms, suicidality, and the risk of self-harm, and the benefits of both types of treatment have been sustained at follow-up assessments. Although encouraging, many researchers are working to improve these treatments because effects have tended to be small to moderate.

Both DBT and psychodynamic therapies for borderline personality disorder include techniques to help understand and reduce self-destructive and dangerous behaviors. Therapists examine the triggers for self-harm and other risky behaviors, and they provide the client with tools to manage and reduce those impulses.

Two forms of psychodynamic treatment of borderline personality disorder, called **transference-focused therapy** and **mentalization therapy**, have shown positive results. Transference-focused therapy places emphasis on the relationship with the therapist, and on the powerful feelings that clients with borderline personality disorder sometimes develop toward their therapists. The therapist helps clients consider parallels between their response to the therapist and their experiences in other relationships, as a way of helping clients understand and manage their relationships in a healthier manner (Clarkin, Foelsch, et al., 2001). Because many people with borderline personality disorder tend to respond quickly and impulsively to emotions, mentalization therapy focuses on helping the client to be more reflective about their own feelings, and those of other people, to avoid acting automatically without thinking when emotions or interpersonal stressors occur (Bateman & Fonagy, 2004).

Dialectical behavior therapy (DBT) combines empathy and acceptance with cognitive behavioral problem solving, emotion-regulation techniques, and social skills training (Linehan, 1987). The concept of dialectics refers to a constant tension between any phenomenon (any idea, event, etc., called the *thesis*) and its opposite (the *antithesis*), which is resolved by creating a new phenomenon (the *synthesis*). We discuss the dialectical tension between accepting clients as they are and yet helping them change in **Focus on Discovery 15.2**.

DBT therapists use group and individual therapy sessions to cover specific cognitive behavioral techniques in four stages. In the first stage, therapy addresses dangerously impulsive behaviors such as suicidal actions. In the second stage, the focus is on modulating the extreme emotionality and coaching the client to tolerate emotional distress. In this stage, clients are taught to mindfully notice their emotions in a nonjudgmental manner, without rushing into impulsive actions. Stage three focuses on improving relationships and self-esteem. Stage four is designed to promote connectedness and happiness. Throughout, clients learn more effective and socially acceptable ways of handling their day-to-day problems.

Focus on Discovery 15.2

Drawing from Personal Experience to Promote Acceptance and Change

Marsha Linehan (see photo) developed dialectical behavior therapy to treat BPD, now considered the best validated approach. In a brave move, Linehan decided to speak publicly about her own experiences of BPD (Carey, 2011). Hospitalized at age 17 for her severe suicidality, she found ways to injure herself even when the staff confined her to a seclusion chamber—left alone with no objects, she banged her head against the wall and floor. She remained hospitalized for 26 months. Failed treatments continued for several years, until she found a way out of the struggles on her own—through radical acceptance. She earned a Ph.D. in clinical psychology, and she drew on her own personal experiences to help others, in the process becoming one of the most productive researchers in the field of clinical psychology.

Linehan (1987) argues that a therapist must work for change while at the same time accepting the real possibility that no changes are going to occur. Linehan's reasoning is that people with BPD are so sensitive to rejection and criticism that even gentle encouragement to behave or think differently can be misinterpreted as a serious rebuke, leading to extreme emotional reactions. When this happens, the therapist, who may have been revered a moment earlier, is suddenly vilified. Thus, while observing limits—"I would be very sad if you killed yourself, so I hope very much that you won't"—the therapist must convey to the patient that he or she is fully accepted. This is hard to do if the patient is threatening suicide, showing uncontrolled anger, or railing against imagined rebukes from the therapist. Completely accepting the patient does not mean approving of everything the patient does; rather, it means that the therapist must accept the situation for what it is.

Linehan's approach also emphasizes that clients, too, must accept who they are and what they have been through. Clients are asked to accept that their childhood is now unchangeable, that their behaviors might have caused relationships to end, and that they feel emotions more intensely than others do. This approach, it is hoped, will provide a basis for understanding the self and promoting growth.

Courtesy Marsha M. Linehan

Marsha Linehan created dialectical behavior therapy, which combines cognitive behavioral therapy with acceptance.

Check Your Knowledge 15.7

Answer the questions.

1. What type of medication is used in the treatment of schizotypal personality disorder?

2. What types of treatments have been shown to be more helpful than treatment as usual for borderline personality disorder?

3. What are the four stages of treatment in DBT?

True or false?

4. Personality dimensions cannot be changed.

Summary

- Personality disorders are defined as enduring patterns of behavior and inner experience that disrupt functioning.

- The DSM-5 model includes 10 personality disorders; the alternative DSM-5 includes six personality disorders, along with dimensional personality domain and facet ratings.

- Personality disorders are usually comorbid with other disorders such as depression and anxiety disorders, and they predict poorer outcomes for these disorders.

- Most personality disorders appear at least moderately heritable when careful research methods are used. High rates of child abuse/neglect, aversive parental behavior, and lack of parental affection are observed across many of the personality disorders.

Odd/Eccentric Cluster

- Specific diagnoses in the odd/eccentric cluster include paranoid, schizoid, and schizotypal personality disorders.

- The major symptom of paranoid personality disorder is suspiciousness and mistrust; that of schizoid personality disorder, interpersonal detachment; and that of schizotypal personality disorder, unusual thought and behavior.

- Genetic, neurobiological, and cognitive research supports the idea that schizotypal personality disorder is related to schizophrenia.

Dramatic/Erratic Cluster

- The dramatic/erratic cluster includes antisocial, borderline, histrionic, and narcissistic personality disorders.

- Antisocial personality disorder and psychopathy overlap a great deal but are not equivalent. The assessment of psychopathy emphasizes emotional deficits more than the criteria for antisocial personality disorder do. The major symptom of borderline personality disorder (BPD) is unstable, highly changeable emotion and behavior; that of histrionic personality disorder, exaggerated emotional displays; and that of narcissistic personality disorder, highly inflated self-esteem.

- Psychopathy and antisocial behavior are related to family environment and poverty, and genes may amplify the effects of these social variables.

- Psychopathy is related to lack of response to punishment, lack of attention to cues of punishment or other information during goal pursuit, and lack of responsivity to other people's pain.

- BPD is related to diminished connectivity of neural regions involved in emotion and those involved in regulation.

- People with BPD report extremely high rates of child abuse compared with the general population, but the genetic vulnerability to the disorder may increase the risk of abuse.

- Linehan's cognitive behavioral theory of BPD proposes an interaction between emotional dysregulation and an invalidating family environment.

- Narcissism appears related to overindulgent parenting and fragile self-esteem.

Anxious/Fearful Cluster

- The anxious/fearful cluster includes avoidant, dependent, and obsessive-compulsive personality disorders.

- The major symptom of avoidant personality disorder is fear of rejection or criticism; that of dependent personality disorder, excessive reliance on others; and that of obsessive-compulsive personality disorder, a perfectionistic, detail-oriented style.

- Avoidant personality disorder might be a more severe variant of social anxiety disorder. Obsessive-compulsive personality disorder may be genetically related to obsessive compulsive disorder.

Treatment of Personality Disorders

- Psychodynamic, cognitive behavioral, and pharmacological treatments are all used for personality disorders. Relatively little research has been conducted regarding the treatment of some personality disorders.

- Treatment of schizotypal personality disorder is parallel with the treatment of schizophrenia; antipsychotic medication can be helpful.

- Treatment of avoidant personality disorder is parallel with the treatment of social anxiety disorder; antidepressants and cognitive behavioral treatment can be helpful.

- Dialectical behavior therapy and psychodynamic therapy have been well-validated as treatments for BPD.

Answers to Check Your Knowledge Questions

15.1 1. Most personality disorders can be reliably assessed when structured diagnostic interviews are used: Inter-rater reliability correlations have been .79 or higher, with the exception of schizoid personality disorder, where agreement is more modest. Inter-rater reliability when clinicians use unstructured interviews is not adequate for personality disorders; 2. Personality disorders are not as stable as the definition implies, and they are highly comorbid with each other.

15.2 1. Six personality disorders instead of 10, and the use of personality trait domains and facets (dimensional scores)

15.3 1. Moderately high, with estimates for the six specific personality disorders ranging from .64 to .78; 2. Children who experienced abuse or neglect were 18 times as likely to develop narcissistic personality disorder, more than seven times as likely to develop borderline personality disorder, and about five times as likely to develop antisocial personality disorder compared with those

with no history of abuse or neglect. Parental neglect also increased the risk of avoidant personality disorder.

15.4 1. Schizotypal personality disorder; 2. schizoid personality disorder

15.5 1. Borderline personality disorder; 2. antisocial personality disorder and borderline personality disorder; 3. antisocial personality disorder

15.6 1. avoidant personality disorder; 2. obsessive-compulsive personality disorder; 3. antisocial personality disorder

15.7 1. Antipsychotic medication; 2. Dialectical behavior therapy (DBT) and two forms of psychodynamic therapy (transference-focused therapy and mentalization therapy); 3. Phase 1: Address dangerous behaviors, Phase 2: Teach emotion regulation skills such as mindfulness, Phase 3: Improve relationships and self-esteem, Phase 4: Promote connectedness and happiness; 4. F

Key Terms

antisocial personality disorder (APD)
avoidant personality disorder
borderline personality disorder
dependent personality disorder
dialectical behavior therapy (DBT)
histrionic personality disorder

mentalization therapy
narcissistic personality disorder
obsessive-compulsive personality disorder
paranoid personality disorder
personality disorder
personality trait domains

personality trait facets
psychopathy
schizoid personality disorder
schizotypal personality disorder
transference-focused therapy

CHAPTER 16

Legal and Ethical Issues

LEARNING GOALS

1. Differentiate the legal concepts of insanity and the various standards for the insanity defense.

2. Describe the issues surrounding competency to stand trial.

3. Describe the conditions under which a person can be committed to a hospital under civil law.

4. Discuss the difficulties associated with predicting dangerousness and the issues surrounding the rights to receive and refuse treatment.

5. Describe the ethics surrounding psychological research and therapy.

Amendment I Congress shall make no law respecting an establishment of religion, or prohibiting the free exercise thereof; or abridging the freedom of speech, or of the press; or the right of the people peaceably to assemble, and to petition the Government for a redress of grievances.

Amendment IV The right of the people to be secure in their persons, houses, papers, and effects, against unreasonable searches and seizures, shall not be violated ...

Amendment V No person ... shall be compelled in any criminal case to be a witness against himself, nor be deprived of life, liberty, or property, without due process of law ...

Amendment VI In all criminal prosecutions, the accused shall enjoy the right to a speedy and public trial ... to be confronted with the witnesses against him; to have compulsory process for obtaining witnesses in his favor, and to have the Assistance of Counsel for his defense.

Amendment VIII Excessive bail shall not be required, nor excessive fines imposed, nor cruel and unusual punishment inflicted.

Amendment XIII ... Neither slavery nor involuntary servitude, except as a punishment for crime whereof the party shall have been duly convicted, shall exist within the United States, or any place subject to their jurisdiction ...

Amendment XIV ... No State shall ... deprive any person of life, liberty, or property, without due process of law; nor deny to any person within its jurisdiction the equal protection of the laws.

Amendment XV ... The right of citizens of the United States to vote shall not be denied or abridged by the United States or by any State on account of race, color, or previous condition of servitude.

Clinical Case

David

David had been hearing voices for several days. Unable to drown them out with music or talking, he became more and more troubled. The voices were telling him that he was the one chosen by God to rid the world of evil. David went to the emergency room of the local hospital seeking relief. Instead of being admitted, David was given a prescription for Haldol and sent on his way. Two days later, David took a loaded gun into a busy train station and began shooting. He killed two people and injured four others. When he was arrested, David told the police he was answering to God. His speaking was disorganized and hard to follow, and he expressed a number of paranoid beliefs.

David was found competent to stand trial because he understood that he was charged with murder and he was able to help his attorney with his defense. At trial, David entered a plea of "not guilty by reason of insanity." His defense lawyer arranged for David to be evaluated by a psychologist. The psychologist concluded that David had schizophrenia and that at the time of the crime he was unable to discern right from wrong (he thought his behavior was the right thing to do since God was directing him) and unable to conform his behavior to the requirements of the law. The prosecution did not dispute these findings, and the case

was settled before going to trial. David was committed to the local forensic hospital for an indeterminate period of time. He was to remain there until he was no longer dangerous and mentally ill. Periodic evaluations would be conducted to see if David could be transferred to a less secure hospital.

After 7 years in the hospital, David had done very well. He took his prescribed medication (Zyprexa), was never in a physical altercation with other people, participated in individual and group therapy, worked in the hospital machine shop, and served as a team leader for the unit he was living in. David felt horribly remorseful for the crimes he had committed, and he recognized that he had schizophrenia that would require treatment for the rest of his life. The treatment team on the unit all agreed that David was no longer dangerous and that his schizophrenia was under control with the medication. They recommended that he be transferred to a less secure psychiatric hospital. David's attorney presented the case before a judge in the courtroom that was part of the hospital. The attorneys for the state objected to David's release, arguing that David could stop taking his medications and become violent again. The judge agreed that release was premature at this time and ordered that David remain in the forensic hospital for another year before being evaluated again.

These eloquent statements describe and protect some of the rights of U.S. citizens and others residing in the United States. We open our final chapter in this way because the legal and mental health systems collaborate continually, although often subtly, to deny a substantial proportion of the U.S. population their basic civil rights. With the best of intentions, judges, legislatures, legal associations, and professional mental health groups have worked over the years to balance the need to protect individual rights guaranteed in the Constitution (i.e., the rights of a person with a psychological disorder) with the need to protect society from the actions of people with a psychological disorder and considered dangerous to themselves or to others. This balance is not always easy to achieve, as we shall see in this chapter.

People with a psychological disorder who have broken the law or who are alleged to have done so are subject to **criminal commitment**, a procedure that confines a person in a mental or forensic hospital (see Focus on Discovery 1.2 for discussion of types of hospitals) either for determination of competency to stand trial or after acquittal by reason of insanity, as in the Clinical Case of David. **Civil commitment** is a set of procedures by which a person who has a psychological disorder and is dangerous but who has not broken a law can be placed in a hospital even if he or she does not want to go. In this chapter we look at these legal procedures in depth. Then we turn to an examination of some important ethical issues as they relate to treatment and research.

Criminal Commitment

What happens when someone with a psychological disorder commits a crime? Will that person enter an insanity plea? What is insanity? Insanity is a legal concept, not a psychological one. As such, its definition comes from court proceedings. In today's courts, judges and lawyers call on psychiatrists and clinical psychologists for assistance in determining whether a person meets the legal criteria for insanity. Although the insanity defense was developed to protect people's rights, in practice, it often results in a greater denial of liberties than people would otherwise experience.

The Insanity Defense

The **insanity defense** is the legal argument that a defendant should not be held responsible for an illegal act if it is attributable to a psychological disorder or intellectual disability that interferes with rationality or that results from some other excusing circumstance, such as not knowing right from wrong. A staggering amount of material has been written on the insanity defense, even though it is pleaded in less than 1 percent of all cases that reach trial, and even when pleaded is rarely successful (Steadman 1979; Steadman, McGreevy, et al., 1993).

Because an insanity defense is based on the accused's mental condition at the time the crime was committed, retrospective, often speculative, judgment on the part of attorneys, judges, jurors, and mental health professionals is required. And disagreement between defense and prosecution psychiatrists and psychologists is the rule.

It is critically important to understand that psychological disorders and crime do not go hand in hand. That is, a person can have a diagnosis of a psychological disorder and be held fully responsible for a crime. For example, David Tarloff, a New York man with a confirmed diagnosis of schizophrenia, killed his psychologist in 2008; he was found guilty of this crime in 2014 and sentenced to life in prison without parole (his insanity defense was unsuccessful). However, someone who has no psychological disorder at all can commit the most heinous or bizarre crime, despite our tendency to think someone must have been "crazy" to commit such an act.

Landmark Cases and Laws Several court rulings and established principles bear on the problems of legal responsibility and psychological disorders. **Table 16.1** summarizes these rulings and principles (for more on these issues, see Frederick, Mrad, & DeMier, 2007). Even though some of these cases are over a century old, they still form the basis for insanity defenses today.

TABLE 16.1	Landmark Cases and Laws Regarding the Insanity Defense
Irresistible impulse (1834)	A pathological impulse or drive that the person could not control compelled that person to commit a criminal act.
M'Naghten rule (1843)	The person did not know the nature and quality of the criminal act in which he or she engaged, or, if the person did know it, the person did not know what he or she was doing was wrong.
Durham test (1954)	The person's criminal act is the product of mental disease or defect.
American Law Institute guidelines (1962)	1. The person's criminal act is a result of "mental disease or defect" that results in the person's not appreciating the wrongfulness of the act or in the person's inability to behave according to the law (combination of M'Naghten rule and irresistible impulse).
	2. "[T]he terms 'mental disease or defect' do not include an abnormality manifested only by repeated criminal or otherwise antisocial conduct" (American Law Institute, 1962).
Insanity Defense Reform Act (1984)	1. The person's criminal act is a result of severe mental illness or defect that prevents the person from understanding the nature of his or her crime.
	2. The burden of proof is shifted from the prosecution to the defense. The defense must prove that the person is insane.
	3. The person is released from the forensic or prison hospital only after being judged to be no longer dangerous and to have recovered from mental illness. This could be longer than he or she would have been imprisoned if convicted.
Guilty but mentally ill (1975)	The person can be found legally guilty of a crime—thus maximizing the chances of incarceration—and the person's mental illness plays a role in how he or she is dealt with. Thus, even a seriously ill person can be held morally and legally responsible but can then be committed to a prison hospital or other suitable facility for psychiatric treatment rather than to a regular prison for punishment.

Daniel M'Naghten had a mental disorder when he tried to kill the prime minister. His case helped to establish a legal definition for the insanity defense.

Irresistible Impulse The **irresistible-impulse** concept was formulated in 1834 in a case in Ohio. According to this concept, if a pathological impulse or uncontrollable drive compelled the person to commit the criminal act, an insanity defense is legitimate. The irresistible-impulse test was confirmed in two subsequent court cases, *Parsons v. State* and *Davis v. United States.*[1]

The M'Naghten Rule The **M'Naghten rule** was formulated in the aftermath of a murder trial in England in 1843. The defendant, Daniel M'Naghten (see photo), had set out to kill the British prime minister, Sir Robert Peel, but had mistaken Peel's secretary for Peel. M'Naghten claimed that he had been instructed to kill Lord Peel by the "voice of God." The judges ruled that

to establish a defense of insanity, it must be clearly proved that, at the time of the committing of the act, the party accused was labouring under such a defect of reason, from disease of the mind, as not to know the nature and quality of the act he was doing; or if he did know it, that he did not know he was doing what was wrong.

The Durham Test A 1954 ruling (*Durham v. United States*[2]) established that a person is not responsible for a crime if it was the "the product of mental disease or mental defect." The definition of what constitutes a mental disease or defect was left open to jurisdictions and mental health professionals to decide. The only state using the Durham standard for its insanity defense today is New Hampshire, likely because the defense is so vague. Yet concepts of mental disease or defect remain in later insanity defense standards, albeit more clearly defined.

American Law Institute Guidelines In 1962, the American Law Institute (ALI) proposed its own guidelines, which were intended to be more specific and informative to lay jurors than were other tests. The **American Law Institute guidelines**, sometimes referred to as the "model penal code test," state the following:

1. A person is not responsible for criminal conduct if at the time of such conduct as a result of mental disease or defect he lacks substantial capacity either to appreciate the criminality (wrongfulness) of his conduct or conform his conduct to the requirements of law.
2. As used in the article, the terms "mental disease or defect" do not include an abnormality manifested only by repeated criminal or otherwise antisocial conduct (American Law Institute, 1962, p. 66).

The first ALI guideline combines the M'Naghten rule and the concept of irresistible impulse. The phrase "substantial capacity" in the first guideline is designed to limit an insanity defense to those with the most serious psychological disorders. The second guideline concerns those who are repeatedly in trouble with the law; repetitive criminal behavior and psychopathy are not evidence for insanity.

Insanity Defense Reform Act In a highly publicized trial in March 1981, John Hinckley Jr. (see photo) was found not guilty by reason of insanity (NGRI) for his assassination attempt against President Ronald Reagan. After the verdict, the court received a flood of mail from citizens outraged that a would-be assassin of a U.S. president had not been held criminally responsible and had "only" been committed to an indefinite stay in a mental hospital. The outrage reflects the public's misperceptions about the insanity defense. The public often believes that a person is "getting away" with a crime when found not guilty by reason of insanity and that he or she will be released from the hospital in short order. In reality, many people who are committed to a mental hospital stay there longer than they would have stayed in prison had

[1]*Parsons v. State*, 2 So. 854, 866–67 (Ala.1887); *Davis v. United States*, 165 U.S. 373, 378 (1897).

[2]*Durham v. United States*, 214 F.2d 862, 876 (D.C. Cir. 1954).

they been given a sentence (as vividly illustrated in the Clinical Case of Michael Jones). With respect to John Hinckley, he was committed to St. Elizabeth's Hospital, a public mental hospital in Washington, D.C., for over three decades. Although he could have been released whenever his mental health was deemed adequate and he was no longer considered dangerous, this did not yet happen. In 2016, some 35 years after the shooting, he was released and allowed to live with his mother full time. His release included many conditions, including mandated appointments with treatment providers, restriction on travel, and a requirement to carry a GPS-enabled mobile phone, and the Secret Service still monitors him.

Following the Hinckley verdict, the political pressures to "get tough" on criminals pushed Congress to enact the Insanity Defense Reform Act in October 1984, addressing the insanity defense for the first time at the federal level. This law, which has been adopted in all federal courts, contains several provisions designed to make it more difficult to enter an insanity plea.

John Hinckley, President Reagan's assailant, was found not guilty by reason of insanity.

Evan Vucci/ASSOCIATEDPRESS/AP/Wide World Photos

- It eliminated the irresistible-impulse component of the ALI rules.
- It changed the ALI's "lacks substantial capacity … to appreciate" to "unable to appreciate," thus making the criterion for impaired judgment more stringent.
- The act also stipulated that the mental disease or defect must be "severe." Mitigating circumstances such as extreme passion or "temporary insanity" do not count.
- It shifted the burden of proof from the prosecution to the defense. Instead of the prosecution's having to prove that the person was sane beyond a reasonable doubt at the time of the crime (the most stringent criterion, consistent with the constitutional requirement that people are considered innocent until proved guilty), the defense must prove that the defendant was not sane and must do so with "clear and convincing evidence" (a less stringent but still demanding standard of proof). **Table 16.2** shows the different standards of proof used in U.S. courts.

Current Insanity Pleas

The two most common insanity pleas used in state and federal courts in the United States have been crafted from the legal definitions and precedents we have reviewed here. With the **not guilty by reason of insanity (NGRI)** plea, there is no dispute over whether the person actually committed the crime—both sides agree that the person committed the crime. However, due to the person's insanity at the time of the crime, the defense attorney argues that the person should not be held responsible for and thus should be acquitted of the crime. A successful NGRI plea means the person is not held responsible for the crime due to his or her psychological disorder. People acquitted with the NGRI plea are committed indefinitely to a forensic hospital. That is, they are released from forensic hospitals only if they are deemed no longer dangerous and no longer mentally ill (we discuss the difficulties in making these determinations later in the chapter).

A forensic hospital looks very much like a regular hospital except that the perimeter of the grounds is secured with gates, barbed wires, or electric fences. Inside the hospital, doors to the different units may be locked, and bars may be placed on windows on the lower floors. People do not stay in jail cells, however, but in either individual or shared rooms. Security

TABLE 16.2   **Standards of Proof**

Standard	Certainty Needed to Convict (%)
Beyond a reasonable doubt	95
Clear and convincing evidence	75
Beyond a preponderance of the evidence	51

Focus on Discovery 16.1

Insanity versus Psychological Disorder

People charged with crimes rarely enter an insanity plea—less than 1 percent of all felony cases by some estimates (Cirincione, Steadman, & McGreevy, 1995). And when such a plea is entered, it is rarely successful.

Here we briefly present two recent cases to illustrate the difficult path to a successful insanity defense (see Focus on Discovery 16.2 for an example of an ultimately successful insanity defense). These cases show the difficulty of mounting a successful insanity defense and are vivid examples of the critical difference between a psychological disorder and insanity. Even though a person has a psychological disorder, this does not necessarily mean the person meets the legal definition of insanity. Indeed, the juries believed that the defendants knew right from wrong even though they had a psychological disorder and thus did not meet the state's legal definition of insanity.

James Holmes

In the early hours of July 20, 2012, James Holmes entered a movie theater in Aurora, Colorado, during a midnight showing of *The Dark Knight* and opened fire. He killed 12 and injured 70 others.

Three years later his trial was held. It lasted for over 10 weeks and included hours of testimony from victims as well as from mental health professionals. The defense argued that he was mentally ill at the time of the murders—two psychiatrists testified for the defense arguing he met the legal definition of insanity, pointing to over 200 hours of interviews, his notebook showing incoherent and delusional thinking, and his seeking treatment from a psychiatrist prior to the killings. Two psychiatrists for the prosecution argued he did not meet the legal definition of insanity, noting that he was able to judge right from wrong and planned the attacks carefully ahead of time, demonstrating that he could control his behavior. In

Colorado, the burden of proof rests with the prosecution: They must convince the jury that an accused person was legally sane, defined in Colorado to include both the M'Naghten rule and irresistible-impulse standards, at the time of a crime. The jury was persuaded by the prosecution's arguments; they rejected the insanity defense and instead found him guilty. He was sentenced to prison for life without the possibility of parole.

Eddie Ray Routh

Eddie Ray Routh served in the United States Marine Corps during the Iraq and Afghanistan wars, and he was honorably discharged in 2011. He was diagnosed with post-traumatic stress disorder (PTSD) and prescribed antipsychotic medications even though such medications are not typically used to treat PTSD. Review of his medical records indicated delusions and other psychotic symptoms, suggesting that he was misdiagnosed. He continued to display psychotic symptoms, including paranoia and delusions of reference (see Chapter 9). In January 2013, he was hospitalized after exhibiting psychotic symptoms while holding his girlfriend at knifepoint. He was transferred to a VA hospital two days later, and the VA hospital subsequently discharged him. Less than 2 weeks later, Routh shot and killed former Marine sniper Chris Kyle (portrayed by Bradley Cooper in the film *American Sniper*) and his friend Chad Littlefield. Kyle had taken Routh out shooting to provide support, as he had been doing for several fellow Marines.

At his trial in Texas two years later, Routh entered a plea of not guilty by reason of insanity. In Texas, the burden of proof is on the defense to demonstrate that the defendant was legally insane at the time of the crime. The defense team argued that Routh had schizophrenia at the time of the killings but many of the records of his prior mental health treatment were not presented at the trial. The jury took less than 3 hours to deliberate and rejected the insanity defense, finding Routh guilty. He was sentenced to life in prison without the possibility of parole.

professionals are on hand to keep people safe. They typically do not carry weapons of any sort, and they may be dressed in regular clothing rather than uniforms.

The second insanity plea is **guilty but mentally ill (GBMI)**. A GBMI plea allows an accused person to be found legally guilty of a crime—thus maximizing the chances of incarceration—but also allows for a mental health professional to offer an opinion on how to deal with the convicted person if he or she had a psychological disorder when the act was committed. Thus, a person can be held morally and legally responsible for a crime but can then, in theory, be committed to a prison hospital or other facility for treatment rather than to a regular prison for punishment. In reality, however, people judged GBMI are usually put in the general prison population, where they may or may not receive treatment. If the person is still considered to be dangerous or mentally ill after serving the imposed prison sentence, he or she may be committed to a mental hospital under civil law proceedings.

One of the more famous cases involving something like the GBMI verdict was the 1992 conviction of Jeffrey Dahmer in Milwaukee, Wisconsin. He had been accused of and had admitted to butchering, cannibalizing, and having sex with the corpses of 15 boys and young men. Dahmer entered a plea of guilty but then his attorneys argued that his psychological disorder be considered when it came time to imposing a sentence. His sanity was the sole focus of an unusual trial that had jurors listening to conflicting testimony from mental health experts about his state of mind during the killings to which he had confessed. They had to decide whether he

Clinical Case

Michael Jones

To illustrate the predicament that a person can get into by raising insanity as a condition for a criminal act, we consider a celebrated—some would call it infamous—Supreme Court case.[3]

Michael Jones was arrested, unarmed, on September 19, 1975, for attempting to steal a jacket from a department store in Washington, D.C. He was charged the next day with attempted petty larceny, a misdemeanor punishable by a maximum prison sentence of 1 year. The court ordered that he be committed to St. Elizabeth's Hospital for a determination of his competency to stand trial.

On March 2, 1976, almost 6 months after the alleged crime, a hospital psychologist reported to the court that Jones was competent to stand trial, even though he had schizophrenia. The psychologist also reported that the alleged crime resulted from his schizophrenia. This comment is noteworthy because the psychologist was not asked to offer an opinion on Jones's state of mind during the crime, only on whether Jones was competent to stand trial. Jones then pleaded not guilty by reason of insanity

(NGRI). Ten days later, on March 12, the court found him NGRI and formally committed him to St. Elizabeth's Hospital for treatment of his schizophrenia.

On May 25, 1976, a customary 50-day hearing was held to determine whether Jones should remain in the hospital any longer. A psychologist from the hospital testified that Jones still suffered from schizophrenia and was a danger to himself and to others. A second hearing was held on February 22, 1977, 17 months after Jones's commitment to St. Elizabeth's, for determination of competency. The defendant demanded release since he had already been hospitalized longer than the 1-year maximum sentence he would have served had he been found guilty of the theft of the jacket. The court denied the request and returned him to St. Elizabeth's.

Ultimately, in November 1982, more than 7 years after his hospitalization, Jones's appeal to the Supreme Court was heard. On June 29, 1983, by a 5–4 decision, the Court affirmed the earlier decision: Jones was to remain at St. Elizabeth's. He was fully released from St. Elizabeth's in August 2004, 28 years after the crime!

---

had had a mental disease that prevented him from knowing right from wrong or from being able to control his actions. Even though there was no disagreement that he was mentally ill, with a diagnosis of a type of paraphilia (see Chapter 12), Dahmer was deemed sane and therefore legally responsible for the grisly murders. The judge sentenced him to 15 consecutive life terms. Later, another inmate in prison killed him.

Critics of the GBMI verdict argue that it does not benefit criminal defendants with psychological disorders and does not result in appropriate treatment for those convicted (Woodmansee, 1996). A South Carolina Supreme Court case[4] found that South Carolina's GBMI statute did provide some benefit because it mandated that convicted people with psychological disorders receive mental health evaluations before being placed in the general prison population. Unfortunately, these assessments have not been shown to lead to better treatment. Other critics of the GBMI verdict note that the verdict is confusing and even deceiving to jurors. Jurors believe that GBMI is not as "tough" as a guilty verdict, but in reality people receiving a GBMI verdict often spend more time incarcerated than if they had been found guilty (Melville & Naimark, 2002).

Table 16.3 compares these two insanity pleas. Only a few states allow for some of or all the GBMI provisions. Four states—Idaho, Montana, Kansas, and Utah—do not allow for any insanity

TABLE 16.3 Comparing NGRI and GBMI

	NGRI	GBMI
Responsibility for crime	Not responsible	Responsible
Where committed	Forensic hospital	Prison
Given sentence?	No	Yes
When released	When no longer dangerous and mentally ill	End of sentence, but could then be committed civilly if dangerous and mentally ill
Treatment given?	Yes	Possibly

---

[3]*Jones v. United States*, 463 U.S. 354 (1983).

[4]*South Carolina v. Hornsby*, 484 S.E.2d 869 (S.C. Sup. Ct. 1997).

defense, though three of them (Idaho, Montana, Utah) will consider mental state at the time of the crime in some form or fashion. The remaining states have some version of NGRI available. Taking a cue from the Insanity Defense Reform Act, 39 states require that the burden of proof rests with the defendant.

Quick Summary

Insanity is a legal term, not a mental health term. Meeting the legal definition is not necessarily the same thing as having a diagnosable psychological disorder. The insanity defense is the legal argument that a defendant should not be held responsible for an illegal act if it is attributable to a psychological disorder that interferes with rationality or that results from some other excusing circumstance, such as not knowing right from wrong.

The irresistible-impulse standard suggested that an impulse or drive that the person could not control compelled that person to commit the criminal act. The M'Naghten rule specified that a person could not distinguish right from wrong at the time of the crime because of the person's psychological disorder. The Durham test specified that a person not be held responsible if the crime was the product of a mental disease or defect. The first part of the American Law Institute guidelines combines the M'Naghten rule and the concept of irresistible impulse. The second concerns those who are repeatedly in trouble with the law; they are not to be deemed mentally ill only because they keep committing crimes. The Insanity Defense Reform Act shifted the burden of proof from the prosecution to the defense, removed the irresistible impulse component, changed wording regarding substantial capacity, and specified that the psychological disorder must be severe. The Jones case illustrates a number of the complexities associated with the insanity defense.

The not guilty by reason of insanity (NGRI) plea means that an accused person should not be held responsible for the crime due to his or her psychological disorder. The guilty but mentally ill (GBMI) plea means that an accused person is legally guilty of a crime but can then, in theory, be committed to a prison hospital or other suitable facility for psychiatric treatment rather than to a regular prison for punishment.

Check Your Knowledge 16.1
(Answers are at the end of the chapter.)

Match the statement with the correct insanity standard.

1. can't control behavior
2. found guilty
3. doesn't know right from wrong
4. affirmative defense

a. GBMI
b. NGRI
c. irresistible impulse
d. M'Naghten rule

Competency to Stand Trial

The insanity defense concerns the accused person's mental state at the time of the crime. An important consideration before deciding what kind of defense to adopt is whether the accused person is competent to stand trial at all. In the U.S. criminal justice system, **competency to stand trial** must be decided before it can be determined whether a person is responsible for the crime of which he or she is accused. It is possible for a person to be judged competent to stand trial and then be judged NGRI.

The legal standard for being competent to stand trial has not changed since it was articulated by a 1960 U.S. Supreme Court decision:[5] "The test [is] whether [the defendant] has sufficient present ability to consult with his lawyer with a reasonable degree of rational understanding, and whether he has a rational as well as a factual understanding of the proceedings against him."

With the 1966 Supreme Court case *Pate v. Robinson*[6] as precedent, the defense attorney, prosecutor, or judge may raise the question of psychological disorder whenever there is reason

[5]*Dusky v. United States*, 362 U.S. 402 (1960).
[6]*Pate v. Robinson*, 383 U.S. 375 (1996).

to believe that the accused person's mental condition might interfere with his or her upcoming trial. If, after examination, the person is deemed unable to participate meaningfully in a trial because of a psychological disorder, the trial is delayed, and the accused person is placed in a hospital with the hope that competence can be restored.

Focus on Discovery 16.2

Andrea Yates: An example of a Successful Insanity Plea

On June 20, 2001, believing that her five children, ranging in age from 6 months to 7 years, were condemned to eternal damnation, 37-year-old Andrea Yates (see photo), who lived with her husband and children in Houston, Texas, systematically drowned each child in a bathtub. As recounted on the CNN website:

> when the police reached [the] modest brick home on Beachcomber Lane in suburban Houston, they found Andrea drenched with bathwater, her flowery blouse and brown leather sandals soaking wet. She had turned on the bathroom faucet to fill the porcelain tub and moved aside the shaggy mat to give herself traction for kneeling on the floor. It took a bit of work for her to chase down the last of the children; toward the end, she had a scuffle in the family room, sliding around on wet tile…. She dripped watery footprints from the tub to her bedroom, where she straightened the blankets around the kids in their pajamas once she was done with them. She called 911 and then her husband. "It's time. I finally did it," she said before telling him to come home and hanging up.

The nation was horrified by her actions, and in the months following the murders, information became known about Yates's frequent bouts of depression, especially after giving birth, as well as her several suicide attempts and hospitalizations for severe depression.

Eight months later her trial was held. The defense argued that she was mentally ill at the time of the murders—and for many periods of time preceding the events—and that she was unable to distinguish right from wrong when she put her children to death. The prosecution argued that she had known right from wrong and therefore should be found guilty. The defense and the prosecution agreed on two points: (1) she had murdered her children, and (2) she was mentally ill at the time of the murder. Where they disagreed was on the crucial question as to whether her psychological disorder entailed not being able to distinguish right or wrong, the familiar M'Naghten principle of criminal responsibility.

No one disagreed that she was severely depressed, probably psychotic, when she killed her five small children. But, as we have seen, a psychological disorder is not the same as legal insanity. Employing the right–wrong principle, the jury deliberated for only 3 hours and 40 minutes on March 12, 2002, and delivered a verdict of guilty. They had rejected the defense's contention that Yates could not distinguish right from wrong at the time of the crime. On March 15, the jury decided to spare her life and recommended to the presiding judge that she get life in prison, not being eligible for parole for 40 years.

The trial and the guilty verdict provoked impassioned discussion in the media and among thousands of people. How could the

Andrea Yates, who drowned her five children, pled not guilty by reason of insanity (NGRI). Although she was suffering from a psychological disorder, her initial plea was unsuccessful because she was judged capable of knowing right from wrong. After the initial verdict was thrown out, her NGRI plea was successful in the second trial.

jury *not* have considered her insane? If such a person is not insane, who could be judged to be so? Should the right–wrong M'Naghten principle be dropped from the laws of half the states in the United States? Didn't her phoning 911 to report what she had done prove that she knew she had done something very wrong? Didn't the careful and systematic way she killed her children reflect a mind that, despite her deep depression and delusional thinking, could formulate a complex plan and execute it successfully? Had she received proper treatment from psychiatrists, especially from the one who had recently taken her off the antidepressant medication that had been helping her and had sent her home without adequate follow-up?

As it turns out, these questions were addressed in the Yates case after all. In January 2005, an appeals court overturned Yates's murder conviction because the jury had heard false testimony from one of the expert witnesses that may have unduly influenced their decision. A new trial was conducted, and on July 26, 2006, after 3 days of deliberations, the new jury found Yates not guilty by reason of insanity (NGRI). She was placed in a maximum-security forensic hospital in Texas. In 2007, she was transferred to a minimum-security hospital in Texas, where she remains today.

As with the insanity defense, having a psychological disorder does not necessarily mean that a person is incompetent to stand trial; a person with schizophrenia, for example, may still understand legal proceedings and be able to assist in his or her defense. In **Focus on Discovery 16.2**, we consider the case of Andrea Yates, who was found competent to stand trial despite clear agreement that she had a psychological disorder.

Being judged incompetent to stand trial can have severe consequences for a person. Bail is automatically denied, even if it would be routinely granted had the question of incompetency not been raised. The person is usually kept in a hospital for the pretrial examination. During this period the accused person is supposed to receive treatment to render him or her competent to stand trial.[7] In the meantime, the person may lose employment and undergo the stress of being separated from family and friends and from familiar surroundings for months or even years, perhaps making his or her psychological state even worse and thus making it all the more difficult to show competency to stand trial.

A 1972 Supreme Court case, *Jackson v. Indiana*,[8] forced the states to a speedier determination of incompetency. The case concerned a deaf and mute man with intellectual disability who was deemed not only incompetent to stand trial but unlikely ever to become competent. The Court ruled that the length of pretrial confinement must be limited to the time it takes to determine whether treatment during this detainment is likely to render the defendant competent to stand trial. If the defendant is unlikely ever to become competent, the state must, after this period, either institute civil commitment proceedings or release the defendant. Federal

---

Clinical Case

Yolanda

Yolanda, a 51-year-old African American woman, was arrested after taking a box of doughnuts from the local Quick Mart. At the time of her arrest, she claimed she needed the doughnuts to feed the seven babies growing inside her. She said that Malcolm X was the father of her soon-to-be-born children and that she would soon assume the position of Queen of the New Cities. When asked what the New Cities were, she responded this was a new world order that would be in place following the alignment of the clouds with the planets Jupiter, Saturn, and Venus. Yolanda's public defender immediately realized that Yolanda was not ready for trial; she asked for a competency hearing and arranged for a psychologist to conduct an evaluation. Yolanda was diagnosed with schizophrenia, and her thought disturbance was found to be so profound that she was not able to understand that she had been charged with a crime. Furthermore, she was unable to help her attorney prepare a defense. Instead, Yolanda viewed her attorney as a threat to her unborn babies (she was not pregnant) and feared the attorney would keep her from assuming her rightful position as queen. At her competency hearing, the judge declared that Yolanda was not competent to stand trial and that she be committed to the local forensic hospital for a period of 3 months, after which another competency evaluation would be held.

At the hospital, Yolanda was prescribed Olanzapine, and her thinking became more coherent and organized after 2 months. One of the unit's psychologists worked with Yolanda, teaching her about the criminal justice system. She worked to help Yolanda understand what the charge of theft meant and what a defense attorney, prosecuting attorney, judge, and jury were. At the end of 3 months, a different psychologist evaluated Yolanda and recommended that she now be considered competent to stand trial. Yolanda's public defender came to the hospital and met with her to discuss the case. Yolanda was able to help her attorney by telling her about her past hospitalizations and treatment history for schizophrenia. Yolanda realized she was not pregnant but still held onto beliefs about the New Cities. Still, Yolanda understood that she had stolen the doughnuts and this was why she had to go to court. At her next competency hearing, Yolanda was deemed competent to stand trial. Two months later, she went to court again. This time, she entered a plea of not guilty by reason of insanity (NGRI). After a short trial, the judge accepted her NGRI plea and she returned to the forensic hospital. The treatment goals were now focused on helping Yolanda recover from schizophrenia, not on restoring her competency to stand trial.

---

[7]*United States v. Sherman,* 912 F.2d 907 (7th Cir. 1990).

[8]*Jackson v. Indiana,* 406 U.S. 715 (1972).

Focus on Discovery 16.3

Dissociative Identity Disorder and the Insanity Defense

Imagine that as you are having a cup of coffee one morning, you hear pounding at the front door. There, you find two police officers. One of them asks, "Are you Jane Smith?" "Yes," you reply. "Well, ma'am, you are under arrest for grand theft and for the murder of John Doe." The officer then reads you your Miranda rights against self-incrimination, handcuffs you, and takes you to the police station, where you are permitted to call your lawyer.

This would be a scary situation for anybody. What is particularly frightening and puzzling to you and your lawyer is that you have absolutely no recollection of having committed the crime. You simply cannot account for the time period when the murder was committed—in fact, your memory is startlingly blank for that entire time. And, as if this were not bizarre enough, the detective shows you a tape in which you are clearly firing a gun at a bank teller during a holdup. "Is that you in the videotape?" asks the detective. You confer with your lawyer, saying that it certainly looks like you, including the clothes, but you are advised not to admit anything one way or the other.

Let's move forward in time now to your trial some months later. Witnesses have come forward and identified you beyond a reasonable doubt. There is no one you know who can testify that you were somewhere other than at the bank on the afternoon of the robbery and the murder. But did you murder the teller in the bank? You can assert honestly to yourself and to the jury that you did not. And yet even you have been persuaded that the person in the videotape is you—and that that person committed the robbery and the murder.

Your lawyer arranged prior to the trial to have you interviewed by a psychiatrist and a clinical psychologist, both well-known experts in forensics. Through extensive questioning, they have determined that you have dissociative identity disorder (DID, formerly called multiple personality disorder) and that the crimes were committed not by you, Jane Smith, but by your rather violent alter, Laura. Indeed, during one of the interviews, Laura emerged and boasted about the crime, even chuckling over the fact that you, Jane, would be imprisoned for it.

Can DID be an excusing condition for a criminal act? Should Jane Smith be held responsible for a crime committed by her alter, Laura?

Elyn Saks, a renowned legal scholar at the University of Southern California Law Center argued that DID should be regarded as a special case in mental health law and that a new legal principle should be established. Her argument takes issue with legal practice that would hold a person with DID responsible for a crime as long as the personality acting at the time of the crime intended to commit it (Saks, 1997).

What is intriguing about Saks's argument is that she devotes a major portion of it to defining personhood. What is a person? Is a person the body we inhabit? Well, most of the time our sense of who we are as persons does not conflict with the bodies we have come to know as our own or, rather, as us. But in DID there is a discrepancy.

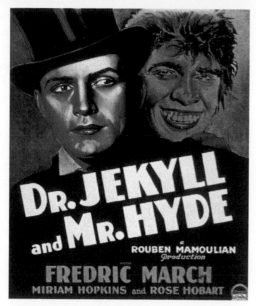

Poster for the classic film about Jekyll and Hyde.

Paramount Pictures/Photofest

The body that committed the crimes at the bank was Jane Smith. But it was her alter, Laura, who committed the crimes. Saks argues that, peculiar as it may sound, the law should be interested in the body only as a container for the person. It is the person who may or may not be blameworthy, not the body. Nearly all the time they are one and the same, but in the case of DID they are not. In a sense, Laura committed the murder by using Jane's body.

Then is Jane blameworthy? The person Jane did not commit the crime; she did not even know about it. For the judge to sentence Jane—or, more specifically, the body in the courtroom who usually goes by that name—would be unjust, argues Saks, for Jane is descriptively innocent. To be sure, sending Jane to prison would punish Laura, for whenever Laura would emerge, she would find herself imprisoned. But what of Jane? Saks concludes that it is unjust to imprison Jane because she is not blameworthy. Rather, we must find her not guilty by reason of dissociative identity disorder and remand her for treatment of the disorder.

DID would not, however, be a justification for a verdict of not guilty by reason of insanity (NGRI) if the alter who did not commit the crime was aware of the other alter's criminal intent and did not do anything to prevent the criminal act. Under these circumstances, argues Saks, the first alter would be complicit in the crime and would therefore be somewhat blameworthy. A comparison Saks draws is to Robert Louis Stevenson's fictional character of Dr. Jekyll and Mr. Hyde. Jekyll made the potion that caused the emergence of Mr. Hyde, his alter, with the foreknowledge that Hyde would do evil. So even though Jekyll was not present when Hyde was in charge, he would nonetheless be blameworthy because of his prior knowledge of what Hyde would do—not to mention that he, Jekyll, had concocted the potion that created his alter, Hyde.

and most state laws define more precisely the minimal requirements for competency to stand trial. Defendants cannot be committed for determination of competency for a period longer than the maximum possible sentence they face.[9] Most people are deemed competent to stand trial in about 6 months. As illustrated in the Clinical Case of Yolanda, she could understand the charges against her and assist her attorney in her defense after about 5 months of treatment. People who have intellectual disabilities or a serious psychological disorder such as schizophrenia that has required longer hospitalization are least likely to ever be deemed competent to stand trial (Zapf & Roesch, 2011).

Medication has had an impact on the competency issue. On the one hand, if a drug, such as Zyprexa, temporarily produces a bit of rationality in an otherwise incompetent person, the trial may proceed. The likelihood that the defendant will again become incompetent to stand trial if the drug is withdrawn does not disqualify the person from going to court.[10] On the other hand, the individual rights of the person should be protected against forced medication, because there is no guarantee that such treatment would render the person competent to stand trial, and there is a chance that it might cause harm.

Supreme Court rulings[11] held that a criminal defendant generally couldn't be forced to take medication in an effort to render him or her competent to stand trial and that the defendant's civil rights are protected, even when a drug might restore legal competency to stand trial.[12] The Supreme Court also ruled that forced medication could be used only if alternative treatments had failed, medication is likely to be effective, medication won't interfere with a person's right to defend themselves at trial, and there is an important government interest in trying the defendant for a serious crime.

It turns out, however, that medications are often the most effective means of restoring competency. Research has shown that the more medications reduce a person's symptoms, the more likely they are to be able to be deemed competent. Though more research is needed, education about the legal proceedings seems to help competency restoration, but it appears that education without medication is not as effective (Zapf & Roesch, 2011).

Even if a person with a psychological disorder is found competent to stand trial, that person may not be able to serve as his or her own defense attorney. A U.S. Supreme Court decision[13] held that a judge may deny the right of self-representation if it is clear that the defendant would not receive a fair trial. **Focus on Discovery 16.3** discusses the unusual challenge posed by dissociative identity disorder in criminal commitments.

Insanity, Intellectual Disability, and Capital Punishment

As we have just seen, an accused person's mental state can be taken into consideration to determine whether he or she is competent to stand trial and/or should be held legally responsible for a criminal act. On very rare occasions, the sanity or mental capacity of a person also becomes an issue after conviction. The question is, must a person who is sentenced to be put to death (i.e., capital punishment) by the state be legally sane at the time of the execution? Furthermore, what if the person has intellectual disability (formerly called mental retardation) and thus does not understand what is about to happen to him or her? The Clinical Cases of Horace Kelly and Scott Panetti illustrate the difficulties with capital punishment cases that involve a person with a psychological disorder.

[9]*United States v. DeBellis*, 649 F.2d 1 (1st Cir. 1981); State v. Moore, 467 N.W. 2d 201 (Wis. Ct. App. 1991).

[10]*State* v. *Hampton*, 218 So.2d 311 (La. 1969); *State v. Stacy*, no. 446 (Crim. App., Knoxville, Tenn., August 4, 1977); *United States v. Hayes*, 589 F.2d 811 (1979).

[11]*Riggins v. Nevada*, 504 U.S. 127 (1992).

[12]*United States v. Waddell*, 687 F. Supp. 208 (1988).

[13]*Indiana v. Edwards*, 554 U.S. 164 (2008).

Clinical Cases

Horace Kelly and Scott Panetti

The question of insanity and capital punishment arose in the case of Horace Kelly (see photo), a 39-year-old man who had been found guilty of the rape and murder of two women and the slaying of an 11-year-old boy in 1984. Although Kelly's mental state had not been an issue at the time of his trial, his lawyers argued—12 years later and just days before his scheduled execution by lethal injection—that his mental health had deteriorated during his imprisonment on death row to such an extent that one of his defense attorneys referred to him as a "walking vegetable." They made reference to a 1986 Supreme Court ruling[14] stating that it is a violation of the Eighth Amendment (which prohibits cruel and unusual punishment) for an insane individual to be executed.

Evidence of a psychological disorder during Kelly's imprisonment included psychiatrists' reports of delusions, hallucinations, and inappropriate affect. He was also described by fellow inmates and by guards as hoarding his feces and smearing them on the walls of his prison cell. By 1995, after 10 years on death row, one court-appointed psychiatrist had concluded that Kelly was legally insane. On the other hand, another psychiatrist reported that when asked what being executed would mean for him, Kelly had given the rational reply that he would not be able to have a family; he was also able to name two of his victims and beat the psychiatrist in several games of tic-tac-toe. A federal judge decided in June 1998 and the U.S. Supreme Court concurred in April 1999 to stay (delay) Kelly's execution and allow his lawyers to argue, among other things, that he should not be put to death because he was insane. After these arguments, Kelly's execution was permanently stayed.

In 2007, the U.S. Supreme Court overturned another death sentence in the case of Scott Panetti.[15] Panetti shot and killed his estranged wife's parents in 1992. He had been diagnosed with schizophrenia and had been hospitalized numerous times prior

Horace Kelly was sentenced to death, but this sentence was not carried out because the courts ruled that the insane cannot be executed.

to the murders. At his trial, Panetti served as his own attorney, dressed up as a cowboy (he had narrowly been deemed competent to stand trial). The court transcripts are filled with incoherent ramblings from him. For example, he tried to subpoena Jesus Christ. In his closing arguments, he said:

> *The ability to reason correctly. Common sense, the common sense, the horse sense. This is Texas and we're not talking loopholes and if we're talking—well, let's talk a lariat. Let's talk a catch rope . . .*

A Texas court sentenced him to death, and an appeals court upheld this sentence. The U.S. Supreme Court ruled, however, that Panetti could not understand why he was to be put to death given his mental state and returned the case for further evaluation of insanity by a Texas lower court. That court ruled that Panetti was competent to be executed, but just hours before his scheduled execution in 2014, an appeals court stayed the execution.

The question of intellectual disability and capital punishment arose in the case of Daryl Atkins who in 1996 was convicted and sentenced to death in Virginia for a kidnapping and murder. He had an IQ score of 59, which would likely place him in the category of what is today called intellectual disability but was then called moderate mental retardation. His defense attorney argued that his intellectual limitations rendered capital punishment unconstitutional because he lacked understanding of the consequences of his actions and was therefore not as morally culpable for his acts as a person of normal intelligence.

In 2002, the U.S. Supreme Court ruled in a 6–3 decision in the case *of Atkins v. Virginia*[16] that capital punishment of those with intellectual disability constitutes cruel and unusual punishment, which is prohibited by the Eighth Amendment. The Supreme Court left open the question of what constitutes intellectual disability, however, leaving it up to the states to decide how to remain within the requirements of the Eighth Amendment.

[14]*Ford v. Wainright,* 477 U.S. 399 (1986).
[15]*Panetti v. Quarterman,* 551 U.S. (2007).
[16]*Atkins v. Virgina,* 536 U.S. 304 (2002).

In 2005, a Virginia jury decided that Daryl Atkins did not meet Virginia's definition of intellectual disability. Thus, even though the *Atkins* case effectively abolished the practice of executing people with intellectual disabilities, Daryl Atkins could have been put to death in Virginia because the state jury's decision paved the way for the original death sentence to be carried out. However, in 2008 a Virginia judge changed Atkins's death sentence to life imprisonment. The reason for this change was not due to any rethinking of Atkins's mental capacity. Rather, it was due to prosecutorial misconduct (improper witness coaching) that was revealed by one of the attorneys.

In 2014, the Supreme Court revised its decision to leave determination of what constitutes intellectual disability up to the states with the case of Freddie Lee Hall, a Florida man with an IQ score of around 70 who was convicted of murder and sentenced to death. The Court ruled that intellectual disability cannot be determined solely on the basis of an IQ score (which can vary from testing occasion to testing occasion) but must also include assessments of adaptive functioning over the lifetime.[17] In 2016, the Florida Supreme Court ruled that Lee should not be executed and instead receive a life sentence in prison.[18]

In 2017, the Supreme Court again revised its decision to leave things up to states with the case of Bobby J. Moore,[19] a Texas man with an IQ score of 69–79, based on multiple tests. Texas had argued that Moore met the criteria the state had established, but the Supreme Court argued that those criteria were not consistent with the 2002 *Atkins* ruling.

Check Your Knowledge 16.2

True or false?

1. The Jackson case established that people who will not be restored to competency should be found NGRI.

2. To be competent to stand trial, a person must be able to understand the charges and assist his or her attorney.

3. The Supreme Court ruled that executing prisoners with a psychological disorder constitutes cruel and unusual punishment.

Civil Commitment

Historically, governments have had a duty to protect their citizens from harm. We take for granted the right and duty of government to set limits on our freedom for the sake of protecting us. Few drivers, for example, question the legitimacy of the state's imposing limits on them by requiring seat belts or by providing traffic signals that often make them stop when they would rather go. Government has a long-established right as well as an obligation to protect us both from ourselves and from others. Civil commitment is one further exercise of these powers.

In virtually all states, a person can be committed to a hospital against his or her will if a judgment is made that he or she (1) has a psychological disorder and (2) is a danger to self—that is, the person is suicidal or unable to provide for the basic physical needs of food, clothing, and shelter—or to others. Civil commitment is supposed to last for only as long as the person remains dangerous.[20] Civil commitment affects far more people than criminal commitment.

Civil commitment procedures generally fit into one of two categories, formal and informal. Formal (or judicial) commitment is by order of a court. Any responsible citizen—usually the police, a relative, or a friend—can request it. If a judge believes that there is a good reason to

---

[17]*Hall v. Florida,* 572 U.S. (2014).
[18]*Hall v. Florida,* SC10-1335 (2016).
[19]*Moore v. Texas,* 581 U.S. No. 15-797 (2017).
[20]*United States v. Debellis,* 649 F.2d 1 (1st Cir. 1981).

pursue the matter, he or she will order a mental health examination. The person has the right to object to these attempts to "certify" him or her, and a court hearing can be scheduled to allow the person to present evidence against commitment.

Informal, emergency commitment of people with a psychological disorder can be accomplished without initially involving the courts. The police may take any person acting in an out-of-control or dangerous manner immediately to a psychiatric hospital. Perhaps the most common informal commitment procedure is the PC, or physician's certificate. In most states, a physician, not necessarily a psychiatrist, can sign a certificate that allows a person to be hospitalized for some period of time, ranging from 24 hours to as long as 20 days. Detainment beyond this period requires formal judicial commitment.

Preventive Detention and Problems in the Prediction of Dangerousness

Based on news reports, it would seem that violence is rampant among those with psychological disorders. This is not the case (Bonta, Law, & Hanson, 1998; Monahan, 1992). Only about 3 percent of the violence in the United States is clearly linked to psychological disorders (Swanson, Holzer, et al., 1990). Moreover, about 90 percent of people diagnosed with psychotic disorders (primarily schizophrenia) are not violent (Swanson et al., 1990). People with psychological disorders are more likely to be the victim of violence than the perpetrator. Violent offenses are more likely to be committed by people who are in their teens and 20s, are male, abuse drugs or alcohol, and are poor (Corrigan & Watson, 2005; Douglas, Guy, & Hart, 2009; Fazel, Gulati, et al., 2009). The MacArthur Violence Risk Assessment Study, a large prospective study of violent behavior among persons recently discharged from psychiatric hospitals, found that people with psychological disorders who did not also abuse substances were no more likely to engage in violence than are people without psychological disorders and substance abuse (Steadman, Mulvey, et al., 1998). A reanalysis of these data, however, found a correlation between particular delusions and violence. Specifically, delusions that elicited anger were associated with violence. People who had delusions that others were out to get them and who felt very angry about this were more likely to be violent (Ulrich, Keers, & Coid, 2014).

When people with psychological disorders do act aggressively, it is usually against family members or friends, and the incidents tend to occur at home (Steadman et al., 1998). Indeed, stranger homicide by people with a psychological disorder is extremely rare (Nielssen, Bourget, et al., 2011). Two meta-analyses of violence and psychological disorders focusing mostly on disorders that involve psychosis (schizophrenia spectrum disorders, bipolar disorder, depression with psychotic features) found that people with some type of psychotic disorder were slightly more likely to be aggressive, but this was particularly true when a person had the positive or disorganization symptoms of schizophrenia (see Chapter 9) or was also abusing drugs (Douglas, Guy, & Hart, 2009; Fazel et al., 2009). Importantly, the increased risk for violence in people who also had a comorbid substance use disorder was similar to that found in people with a substance use disorder and no psychotic disorder. This suggests that issues of substance abuse rather than psychotic disorders are the main contributory factors to violence. By and large, then, the general public is seldom affected by violence from people with psychological disorders, even though certain people with certain disorders can and will be violent.

People with a psychological disorder are not necessarily more likely to be violent than people without a psychological disorder, contrary to the way movies often portray people with a psychological disorder.

The Prediction of Dangerousness A person's likelihood to commit a dangerous act is central to civil commitment, but can mental health

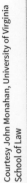

John Monahan is an expert on predicting dangerousness.

professionals predict dangerousness? Mental health professionals use empirically supported methods for assessing and predicting violence to identify and measure violence risk factors based on clinical judgment (e.g., Historical-Clinical-Risk Management-20, or HCR-20; Webster, Douglas, et al., 1997) or a combination of clinical judgment and statistical algorithms (e.g., Violence Risk Appraisal Guide [VRAG]; Quincey, Harris, et al., 2006). These measures seem to work equally well, but even with these improved measures, accurately predicting future dangerousness remains a challenge (Skeem & Monahan, 2011).

Research suggests that violence prediction is most accurate under the following conditions (Campbell, Stefan, & Loder, 1994; Monahan, 1984; Monahan & Steadman, 1994; Steadman et al., 1998):

- If a person has been repeatedly violent in the recent past, it is reasonable to predict that he or she will be violent in the near future unless there have been major changes in the person's mental health or environment.

- If violence is in the person's distant past, and if it was a single but very serious act, and if that person has been incarcerated for a period of time, then violence can be expected on release if there is reason to believe that the person's predetention mental state and physical abilities have not changed and if the person is going to return to the same environment in which he or she was previously violent.

- Even with no history of violence, violence can be predicted if the person is judged to be on the brink of a violent act, for example, if the person is pointing a loaded gun at an occupied building.

Violence among people with a psychological disorder is more likely when they do not receive treatment, whether due to lack of availability or noncompliance (Monahan, 1992; Keers, Ullrich, et al., 2014; Steadman et al., 1998). Outpatient commitment or **assisted outpatient treatment (AOT)** is one way of increasing medication compliance. It is an arrangement whereby a person is mandated by the court to receive treatment on an outpatient basis (i.e., not in the hospital); 45 states have laws covering this type of treatment (Torrey, 2014). To the extent that AOT increases compliance with medication regimens and other mental health treatment—and evidence indicates that it does (Munetz, Grande, et al., 1996; Torrey, 2014)—we can expect violence to be reduced. For a discussion of mental health professionals' responsibilities to predict dangerousness, see **Focus on Discovery 16.4**.

Protection of the Rights of People with Psychological Disorders

Several court decisions have been rendered to protect people from formal or informal civil commitment unless absolutely necessary. However, many rights of people with a psychological disorder are still curtailed. For example, an analysis of mental health–related bills introduced in state legislatures (Corrigan, Watson, et al., 2005) found that 75 percent of these bills took away liberties of people with a psychological disorder (e.g., allowing involuntary medication) and 33 percent took away privacy rights (e.g., sharing mental health records in the interest of public safety).

Being hospitalized against one's wishes is less likely today, in large part due to changes in health care that emphasize outpatient over inpatient care. In fact, today it is increasingly difficult to hospitalize a person who is in real need of at least a short hospital stay, and this is also problematic. People with a psychological disorder such as schizophrenia or bipolar disorder may need to spend time in a hospital when symptoms become severe. Yet people in need of hospitalization are more likely to be sent to a nursing home or board and care facility, which may offer little or substandard care. Worse, people with psychological disorders in need of a

Focus on Discovery 16.4

The *Tarasoff* Case—The Duty to Warn and to Protect

A person's right to privileged communication—the legal right to have the content of the therapy relationship remain confidential—is an important protection, but it is not absolute. Society has long stipulated certain conditions in which confidentiality in a relationship should not be maintained because of the harm that can befall others. A famous California court ruling in 1974[a] described circumstances in which a therapist not only may but also *must* breach the sanctity of a person's communication. First, we describe the facts of the case.

Clinical Case

In the fall of 1968, Prosenjit Poddar, a graduate student from India studying at the University of California at Berkeley, met Tatiana (Tanya) Tarasoff at a folk dancing class. They saw each other weekly during the fall, and on New Year's Eve she kissed him. Poddar interpreted this act as a sign of formal engagement (as it might have been in India, where he was a member of the Harijan, or "untouchable," caste). But Tanya told him that she was involved with other men and indicated that she did not wish to have an intimate relationship with him.

Poddar was unhappy because of the rebuff, but he saw Tanya a few times during the spring (occasionally tape-recording their conversations to understand why she did not love him). Tanya left for Brazil in the summer, and Poddar, at the urging of a friend, went to the student health facility, where a psychiatrist referred him to a psychologist for therapy. When Tanya returned in October 1969, Poddar discontinued therapy. Based in part on Poddar's stated intention to purchase a gun, the psychologist notified the campus police, both orally and in writing, that Poddar was dangerous and should be taken to a community mental health center for psychiatric commitment.

The campus police interviewed Poddar, who seemed rational and promised to stay away from Tanya. They released him and notified the student health facility. No further efforts at commitment were made because the supervising psychiatrist apparently decided that there was no need and, as a matter of confidentiality, requested that the letter to the police as well as certain therapy records be destroyed.

On October 27, Poddar went to Tanya's home armed with a pellet gun and a kitchen knife. She refused to speak to him. He shot her with the pellet gun. She ran from the house; he pursued, caught, and repeatedly and fatally stabbed her. Poddar was found guilty of voluntary manslaughter rather than first- or second-degree murder.

Under the privileged communication statute of California, the counseling center psychologist properly breached the confidentiality of the professional relationship and took steps to have Poddar civilly committed, for he judged Poddar to be an imminent danger. Poddar had stated that he intended to purchase a gun, and by his other words and actions he had convinced the therapist that he was desperate enough to harm Tarasoff. What the psychologist did not do, and what the court decided he should have done, was to warn the likely victim, Tanya Tarasoff, that her former friend had bought a gun and might use it against her. As stated by the California Supreme Court in *Tarasoff*: "Once a therapist does in fact determine, or under applicable professional standards reasonably should have determined, that a patient poses a serious danger of violence to others, he bears a duty to exercise reasonable care to protect the foreseeable victims of that danger." The *Tarasoff* ruling

Prosenjit Poddar was convicted of manslaughter in the death of Tatiana Tarasoff. The court ruled that his therapist, who had become convinced Poddar might harm Tarasoff, should have warned her of the impending danger.

requires clinicians, in deciding when to violate confidentiality, to use the very imperfect skill of predicting dangerousness. Since the original ruling, it has been extended in several ways.

Extending Protections from the *Tarasoff* Ruling

Since the original *Tarasoff* ruling, several other court cases have extended its protections. For example, the concept of "foreseeable victims" was extended to include close others of an identifiable victim,[b] such that all foreseeable victims must also be warned, even if a person had never made an explicit threat against them to the therapist,[c] as long as sufficient history of violence existed to suggest that a close other might also be harmed.

This broadening of the duty to warn and protect has placed mental health professionals in an even more difficult predicament, for the potentially violent person need not even mention the specific person they may harm. It is up to therapists to deduce the possible victims, based on what they can learn of their patient's past and present circumstances.

Other rulings extend the duty to warn and protect to foreseeable victims of child abuse even if the possible victims are as yet unknown.[d] Further, the duty to warn was also extended to include property damage.[f] The court's conclusion about property arose in a case of arson, where injury to people could have happened. Thus, the therapist's extended duty to warn was based on reasoning that arson is a violent act and therefore a lethal threat to people who may be in the vicinity of the fire.

Other rulings mandate that a therapist must warn a possible victim if the threat is reported by a member of the patient's family.[e] The court ruled that a close family member is, in essence, a part of the patient, and thus a therapist does have a duty to warn potential victims if notified by a close family member of a patient.

---

[a] *Tarasoff v. Regents of the University of California,* 529 P.2d 553 (Cal. 1974), vacated, reheard in bank, and affirmed, 131 Cal. Rptr. 14, 551 P.2d 334 (1976). The 1976 California Supreme Court ruling was by a 4–3 majority.
[b] *Hedlund v. Superior Court,* 34 Cal.3d 695 (1983).
[c] *Jablonski by Pahls v. United States,* 712 F.2d 391 (1983).
[d] *Almonte v. New York Medical College,* 851 F. Supp. 34, 40 (D. Conn. 1994) (denying motion for summary judgment).
[e] *Ewing v. Goldstein,* Cal. App. 4th B163112.2d. (2004).
[f] *Peck v. Counseling Service of Addison County,* 499 A.2d 422 (Vt. 1985).

hospital stay are now more likely to be sent to jails and prisons than to a hospital, a topic we return to later.

We turn now to a discussion of several issues and trends that revolve around the protections provided to those with psychological disorders: the principle of the least restrictive alternative; the right to treatment; the right to refuse treatment; and, finally, the way in which these several themes conflict in efforts to provide humane mental health treatment while respecting individual rights.

Least Restrictive Alternative

As noted earlier, civil commitment in most states rests on presumed dangerousness. The **least restrictive alternative** to freedom is to be provided when treating people with psychological disorders and protecting them from harming themselves and others. A number of court rulings require that only those people who cannot be adequately looked after in less restrictive settings be placed in hospitals.[21] In general terms, mental health professionals have to provide the treatment that restricts the person's liberty to the least possible degree while remaining workable.[22] It is unconstitutional to confine a person with a psychological disorder who is nondangerous and who is capable of living on his or her own or with the help of willing and responsible family or friends.[23] Of course, this principle has meaning only if society provides suitable residences and treatments, which unfortunately does not happen as much as it needs to.

Right to Treatment

Another aspect of civil commitment that has come to the attention of the courts is the so-called right to treatment. If a person is deprived of liberty because he or she is mentally ill and is a danger to self or others, is the state not required to provide treatment to alleviate these problems?

The right to treatment was extended to all people committed under civil law in a landmark 1972 case, *Wyatt v. Stickney.*[24] In that case, an Alabama federal court ruled that treatment is the only justification for the civil commitment of people with a psychological disorder to a psychiatric hospital. This ruling, upheld on appeal, is frequently cited as ensuring the protection of people confined by civil commitment, at least to the extent that the state cannot simply "put them away" without meeting minimal standards of care. In fact, when people with intellectual disability (as opposed to those deemed to be mentally ill) are released from an institution, health officials are not relieved of their constitutional duty to provide reasonable care and safety as well as appropriate training.[25]

The *Wyatt* ruling was also significant because it set forth very specific requirements for mental hospitals—for example, they must be a certain size and provide certain types of privacy and limit physical restraints except in emergency situations. The ruling also specified how many mental health professionals ought to be working in the hospital.

In another celebrated case, *O'Connor v. Donaldson,*[26] a civilly committed man sued two hospital doctors for his release and for monetary damages on the grounds that he had been kept against his will for 14 years without being treated and without being dangerous to himself or to others. In January 1957, at the age of 49, Kenneth Donaldson was committed to the Florida State Hospital in Chattahoochee on petition of his father, who felt that his son was delusional. At a brief court hearing, a county judge found that Donaldson had schizophrenia and committed him for "care, maintenance, and treatment."

Unfortunately, Donaldson did not receive treatment and he was not allowed to leave the hospital despite many requests to be discharged. Finally, the Supreme Court[27] ruled that "a

[21]*Lake v. Cameron,* 267 F. Supp 155 (D.C. Cir. 1967); Lessard, 349 F. Supp. at 1078.

[22]*In Re: Tarpley,* 556 N.E.2d, superseded by 581 N.E.2d 1251 (1991).

[23]*Project Release v. Prevost,* 722 F.2d 960 (2d Cir. 1983).

[24]*Wyatt v. Stickney,* 325 F.Supp. 781 (M.D. Ala. 1971), enforced in 334 F.Supp. 1341 (M.D. Ala. 1971), 344 F.Supp. 373, 379. (M.D. Ala.1972), *aff'd sub nom Wyatt v. Anderholt,* 503 F.2d 1305 (5th Cir. 1974).

[25]*Thomas S. v. Flaherty,* 902 F.2d 250, cert. denied, 111 S.Ct. 373 (1990).

[26]*O'Connor v. Donaldson,* 95 S.Ct. 2486 (1975).

[27]*O'Connor v. Donaldson,* 422, U.S. 563 (1975).

State cannot constitutionally confine . . . a nondangerous individual who is capable of surviving safely in freedom by himself or with the help of willing and responsible family members or friends." Because of this decision, a civilly committed person's status must be periodically reviewed, for the grounds on which the person was committed cannot be assumed to continue to be in effect forever.

Right to Refuse Treatment

Does a person committed under civil law have the right to refuse treatment or a particular kind of treatment? The answer is yes, but with qualifications.

The right of committed people to refuse medication is still debated. Some argue that because many people with a psychological disorder have no insight into their condition, they believe they do not need any treatment and thus subject themselves and their loved ones to sometimes desperate and frightening situations by refusing medication or other modes of therapy, most of which involve hospitalization. Failure to consider the costs of untreated psychological disorders, which are substantial, are often overlooked (Torrey, 2014).

On the other hand, there are many arguments against forcing a person to take medications. The side effects of most antipsychotic drugs are often aversive and are sometimes harmful and irreversible in the long run. Notably, one-third or more of people who take medications do not benefit from them.

Although there is inconsistency across jurisdictions, there is a trend toward granting even involuntarily committed people certain rights to refuse medication, based on the constitutional protections of freedom from physical invasion, freedom of thought, and the right to privacy. In an extension of the least-restrictive-treatment principle, the Supreme Court ruled that the government cannot force antipsychotic drugs on a person only on the supposition that at some future time he or she might become dangerous.[28] The threat to public safety has to be clear and imminent to justify the risks and restrictions that such medications pose, and it must be shown that less intrusive intervention will not likely reduce impending danger to others.

Deinstitutionalization, Civil Liberties, and Mental Health

Beginning in the 1950s, many states embarked on a policy referred to as *deinstitutionalization*, discharging as many people as possible from hospitals and discouraging admissions. Indeed, civil commitment is more difficult to achieve now than it was then, even though some people with psychological disorders very much need short stays in a hospital.

By 2010, there were approximately 14 psychiatric hospital beds for every 100,000 people in the United States; in 1955 there were 350 psychiatric hospital beds for every 100,000 people (Torrey, 2014). By some estimates, we need at least 50 hospital beds for every 100,000 people in the United States to meet the needs of people with psychological disorders—nearly four times what we currently have (Torrey, 2014). The maxim "Treat them in the community" has been in place for over 50 years, with the (incorrect) assumption being that virtually anything is preferable to institutionalization.

Kenneth Donaldson, displaying a copy of the Supreme Court opinion stating that nondangerous people with psychological disorders cannot be confined against their will under civil commitment.

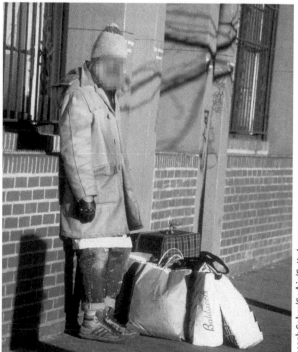

Civil commitment supposedly requires that the person be dangerous. But in actual practice, the decision to commit can be based on a judgment of severe disability, as in the case of some people who are homeless.

Joseph Sohm/Corbis/Getty Images

© AP/Wide World Photos

[28]*United States v. Charters,* 863, F.2d 302.

Unfortunately, there are woefully inadequate resources for treatment in the community. Some effective programs are described in Chapter 9, but these are very much the exception, not the rule. Rates of homelessness have soared among those with psychological disorders, and homeless persons do not have fixed addresses and need help in establishing eligibility and residency to receive benefits.

Deinstitutionalization may be a misnomer. *Trans-institutionalization* may be more apt, for declines in the number of psychiatric hospital beds have occasioned increases in the presence of people with psychological disorders in nursing homes; the mental health departments of nonpsychiatric hospitals; and, most sadly, prisons (Kiesler, 1991; Torrey, 2014). These settings are by and large not equipped to handle the needs of people with psychological disorders.

Indeed, jails and prisons have become the new "hospitals" for people with psychological disorders in the twenty-first century. In the 1970s, about 5 percent of people in prisons had a serious psychological disorder; by 2007, between 17 and 30 percent of people in prisons had a serious psychological disorder (Steadman, Osher, et al., 2009; Torrey, 2014). A 2014 report by the Treatment Advocacy Center notes that 44 of the 50 states have more people with psychological disorders in prison than in the remaining psychiatric hospitals in those states (Torrey, Zdano-wicz, et al., 2014). The lives of people with psychological disorders in prison is often "horrific," according to Federal Judge Lawrence Karlton, who ruled unconstitutional the ways in which California corrections officials were interacting with inmates (pepper spray, solitary confine-ment, forcing them out of their cells) with psychological disorders (Steinberg, Mills, et al., 2015).

In a cruel twist, some states are investigating whether shuttered former mental hospitals can be reopened and repurposed to house prisoners who have a serious psychological disorder (Torrey, 2014). Other states are repurposing closed hospitals as tourist attractions for people interested in ghost hunting (Searles, 2013). Have we come that far from the days of the abysmal institutions that we discussed in Chapter 1? Clearly, we must do more.

Police officers are now called on to do the work of mental health professionals. They are often the first to come into contact with a person with a psychological disorder and can make decisions as to whether a person should be taken to a hospital or jail. In several cities, men-tal health professionals have teamed up with police officers to form mobile crisis units (Lamb, Weinberger, & DeCuir, 2002). These units consist of trained mental health professionals who work in conjunction with local police to find the best option for people in the community with a psychological disorder. Because police officers are increasingly called on to work with such people, communities are recognizing the need for the police to receive proper training. Laws passed in the past 15 years—including America's Law Enforcement and Mental Health Project Act (2000) and the later extension of this law, called the Mentally Ill Offender Treatment and Crime Reduction Act (2004)—provide funding for such training. These laws also provide funds to set up so-called mental health courts in local communities. The idea is that people with psychological disorders who commit crimes may be better served by courts that can monitor treatment availability and adherence. So far, the evidence suggests that this is the case. A lon-gitudinal study found that people with a psychological disorder who went through a mental health court instead of traditional court went for a longer period of time after release without reoffending or committing a violent act (McNiel & Binder, 2007).

The approach of building partnerships between mental health professionals and law enforcement led to the creation of the Consensus Project (https://csgjusticecenter.org/mental-health-projects/report-of-the-consensus-project/). The Council of State Governments coordi-nated collaboration among criminal justice, mental health, and local and national lawmakers. A report entitled *Criminal Justice/Mental Health Consensus Project*, released in 2002, has been influential in increasing awareness of the large numbers of people with psychological disorders who are now housed in jails rather than in treatment facilities. The report outlines a number of policy ideas, all aimed at increasing cooperation between mental health and criminal justice and ultimately benefiting those with psychological disorders who are in the criminal justice system or who are at risk of becoming involved (e.g., sent to jail rather than treatment following a public outburst that reflects an exacerbation of illness). Over a decade later, however, few of these policy recommendations have been implemented to reduce the number of people with psychological disorders in prison even as they have helped to better the chances of receiving treatment while in prison.

Quick Summary

The legal standard for competency to stand trial requires that the accused understand the charges against them and be able to assist their attorney in the defense. Someone who is judged incompetent to stand trial receives treatment to restore competence, and then returns to face charges. The *Jackson* case specified that the pretrial period could be no longer than it takes to determine whether a person will ever become competent to stand trial. The use of medication to restore competency to stand trial can be used in limited circumstances.

The U.S. Supreme Court has ruled that it is unconstitutional (a violation of the Eighth Amendment, which prohibits cruel and unusual punishment) to execute people who are deemed legally insane or have intellectual disabilities. Individual states can determine what constitutes intellectual disability and insanity.

A person can be civilly committed to a hospital against his or her wishes if the person is mentally ill and a danger to self or others. Formal commitment requires a court order; informal commitment does not. People with psychological disorders who do not abuse substances are not necessarily more likely to engage in violence than are people who do not have psychological disorders.

Early studies on the prediction of dangerousness had several flaws. Later research has shown that violence can be more accurately predicted if any of these conditions apply: repeated acts of violence, a single serious violent act, being on the brink of violence, or medication noncompliance.

Court cases have tried to balance a person's rights with the rights of society to be protected. The least restrictive alternative to freedom is to be provided when treating people with mental disorders and protecting them from harming themselves and others. A series of court cases have generally supported the notion that those people committed to a hospital have the right to receive treatment. People with psychological disorders have the right to refuse treatment as well, except when doing so poses a danger to self or others.

Beginning in the 1950s, large numbers of people were released from mental hospitals in what has been called deinstitutionalization. Unfortunately, not enough treatment options are available in the community. Jails and prisons are now the new "hospitals" for people with psychological disorders. Police officers are called on to do the work once reserved for mental health professionals. Partnerships among police, courts, and community mental health providers are promising for helping people with psychological disorders.

Check Your Knowledge 16.3

True or false?

1. People with schizophrenia who have negative symptoms are more likely to be violent than those without negative symptoms.

2. Past violence is a predictor of future violence.

3. Court decisions have determined that hospitalized people do not have a right to treatment unless they are dangerous.

4. A person with schizophrenia who has many symptoms can refuse treatment if the person does not pose an imminent threat.

Ethical Dilemmas in Therapy and Research

The issues reviewed thus far place legal limits on the activities of mental health professionals. These legal constraints are important, for laws are one of society's strongest means of encouraging all of us to behave in certain ways. Mental health professionals also have ethical constraints. Ethics statements are designed to provide an ideal, to review moral issues of right and wrong that may or may not be reflected in the law. These ethics guidelines describe how mental health professionals ought to behave in their professions. Courts have also ruled on some of these questions. Most of the time what we believe is unethical is also illegal, but sometimes existing laws are in conflict with our moral sense of right and wrong. The American Psychological Association (APA) publishes a *Code of Ethics* that includes the ethical standards that constrain research and practice in psychology (American Psychological Association, 2002; http://www.apa.org/ethics). Unfortunately, the APA itself behaved in an ethically questionable manner when it sanctioned the use of torture during the United States wars in Iraq and Afghanistan. Following an extensive independent report completed in 2015 (Hoffman, Carter, et al. 2015), the APA revised its ethics code to explicitly state that "psychologists do not participate in, facilitate, assist or otherwise engage in torture."

We now examine the ethics of making psychological inquiries into and interventions in the lives of other human beings. In **Focus on Discovery 16.5**, we discuss the ethical issue of whether mental health professionals should offer opinions and diagnoses of public figures.

Ethical Restraints on Research

The training of scientists equips them to pose interesting questions, sometimes even important ones, and to design research that is as free of confounds as possible. Scientists have no special qualifications, however, for deciding whether a particular line of research with people should be followed. Society needs knowledge, and in a democracy a scientist has a right to seek that knowledge. However, the ordinary citizens who participate in experiments must be protected from unnecessary harm, risk, humiliation, and invasion of privacy.

Perhaps the most reprehensible ethical insensitivity was evidenced in the brutal experiments conducted by German physicians on concentration camp prisoners during World War II. One experiment, for example, investigated how long people lived when their heads were bashed repeatedly with a heavy stick. Clearly, such actions violate our sense of decency and morality. The Nuremberg Trials, conducted by the Allies following the war, brought these and other barbarisms to light and handed out severe punishment (including the death penalty) to some of the soldiers, physicians, and Nazi officials who had engaged in or contributed to such actions, even when they claimed that they had merely been following orders.

Focus on Discovery 16.5

Should Mental Health Professionals Diagnose Public Figures?

In 1964, several thousand psychiatrists offered their opinions on psychological disorder diagnoses for presidential candidate Barry Goldwater in response to a request from the now defunct *Fact* magazine. About half of the psychiatrists who responded believed Goldwater was unfit for office. Although Goldwater lost the election, he won a libel lawsuit against the magazine.

The American Psychiatric Association did not have any involvement with the article or the psychiatrists' decisions to participate, but they nevertheless considered the issue and subsequently decided that rendering such opinions about the mental health of public figures was a breach of professional ethics. In 1973, the American Psychiatric Association adopted a new ethics rule, formally known as section 7.3 of the ethics code but colloquially referred to as the "Goldwater Rule." The rule specifies: "On occasion psychiatrists are asked for an opinion about an individual who is in the light of public attention or who has disclosed information about himself/herself through public media. In such circumstances, a psychiatrist may share with the public his or her expertise about

psychiatric issues in general. However, it is unethical for a psychiatrist to offer a professional opinion unless he or she has conducted an examination and has been granted proper authorization for such a statement (retrieved from https://www.psychiatry.org/news-room/apa-blogs/apa-blog/2016/08/the-goldwater-rule.)"

Although the American Psychological Association does not have such a rule in its own code of ethics, psychologists are strongly discouraged from offering diagnoses or other mental health opinions about public figures. A major reason that psychologists are discouraged from offering such opinions is because they would not have established a professional relationship with the public figure and would thus be unable to do a thorough psychological assessment (see Chapter 3).

Following the 2016 presidential election in the United States, the issue was raised again, with mental health professionals being asked for their opinions on the mental health and fitness of public figures, most notably politicians. The American Psychiatric Association reaffirmed its ethical rule in 2017, noting that the profession was tarnished following the Goldwater lawsuit and that it need not go down that road again.

It would be reassuring to be able to say that such gross violations of human decency take place only during uniquely cruel epochs such as World War II, but unfortunately this is not the case. Spurred on by a blind enthusiasm for their work, researchers in the United States and other countries have sometimes dealt with human participants in unethical ways.

Following Pulitzer Prize–winning investigative journalism by Eileen Welsome in 1994, the United States Energy Department began to publicize numerous experiments conducted in the 1950s through the 1970s that had exposed hundreds of people—usually without their informed consent or prior knowledge—to harmful doses of radiation. Particular concern was expressed over the fact that the overwhelming majority were people of low socioeconomic status, members of ethnic minorities,

Defendants at the Nuremberg Trials.

people with intellectual disabilities, nursing home patients, or prisoners. The scientists, for the most part supported in their research with federal funds, understood that the risks were great, even though relatively little was known about the harmful effects of radiation at the time.

Responding to the many instances of harm inflicted on research participants, several international codes of ethics for the conduct of scientific research have been developed—the Nuremberg Code formulated in 1947 in the aftermath of the Nazi war-crime trials, the 1964 Declaration of Helsinki, and statements from the British Medical Research Council. In 1974, the U.S. Department of Health, Education, and Welfare began to issue guidelines and regulations governing scientific research that employs human and animal participants. In addition, a blue-ribbon panel, the National Commission for the Protection of Human Subjects of Biomedical and Behavioral Research, issued a report in 1979 (the Belmont Report) that arose from hearings and inquiries into restrictions that the U.S. government might impose on research performed with prisoners, children, and people in psychiatric hospitals. The U.S. Department of Health and Human Services issued regulations as well (45 CFR part 46; https://www.hhs.gov/ohrp/regulations-and-policy/regulations/45-cfr-46/index.html) that have come to be known as "The Common Rule." These various codes and principles are continually being reevaluated and revised as new challenges are posed to the research community. The Common Rule was revised most recently in 2017 (Menikoff, Kaneshiro, & Pritchard, 2017) and can be read here: https://www.gpo.gov/fdsys/pkg/FR-2017-01-19/pdf/2017-01058.pdf.

For more than four decades, the proposals of behavioral researchers, many of whom conduct experiments related to psychopathology, have been reviewed for safety and general ethical propriety by institutional review boards in hospitals, universities, and research institutes. Such committees—and this is significant—comprise not only behavioral scientists but also citizens from the community. They are able to block any research proposal, and they can require questionable aspects to be modified if, in their collective judgment, the research would put participants at too great a risk. Beginning in 2000, universities and other research institutions have been required to certify researchers on the basis of special coursework and examinations concerning research ethics. Researchers who receive funds from federal agencies, such as the National Institute of Mental Health, are also required to receive specialized training in research ethics.

Informed Consent

A core component of ethical research is **informed consent**. The investigator must provide enough information to enable people to decide whether they want to be in a study. Researchers must describe the study clearly, including any risks involved. Researchers should disclose even minor risks that could occur from a study, including emotional distress from answering personal questions or side effects from drugs. There must be no coercion in obtaining informed consent.

Informed consent must be obtained for research.

What people tell their therapist is confidential, although in certain situations confidentiality may be broken.

Participants must understand that they have every right not to take part in the study or to withdraw from the study at any point without penalty.

A central issue is that potential participants must be able to understand the study and associated risks. What if the prospective participant is a person with intellectual disability, unable to understand fully what is being asked? In clinical and research settings, researchers must ascertain that people are not having trouble understanding the study.

Still, as with the right to refuse treatment, there is recognition that people with a psychological disorder are not necessarily incapable of giving informed consent (Appelbaum & Gutheil, 1991). For example, although people with schizophrenia may do more poorly than people without schizophrenia on tests designed to assess decision-making skills, people with schizophrenia can give informed consent if a more detailed procedure describing a study is included—for example, one that describes what they will be asked to do and what they will see and explains that their participation is voluntary and that it in no way will impact their treatment (Carpenter, Gold, et al., 2000; Wirshing, Wirshing, et al., 1998).

The issue of informed consent is also of concern to researchers and clinicians who work with people with Alzheimer's disease. As with schizophrenia, having an Alzheimer's diagnosis does not necessarily mean a person cannot provide informed consent (Marson, Huthwaite, & Hebert, 2004). Measures have been developed to assess capacity for consent in this population (Marson, 2001); as the number of people over age 65 continues to increase, this will continue to be an area of active research.

These results point to the importance of examining each person individually for ability to give informed consent rather than assuming that a person hospitalized for schizophrenia or Alzheimer's disease is unable to do so.

Confidentiality and Privileged Communication

When people consult a psychiatrist or clinical psychologist, they are assured by professional ethics codes that what goes on in the session will remain confidential. **Confidentiality** means that nothing will be revealed to a third party except for other professionals and those intimately involved in the treatment, such as a nurse or medical secretary.

A **privileged communication** goes even further. It is communication between parties in a confidential relationship that is protected by law. The recipient of such a communication cannot legally be compelled to disclose it as a witness. The right of privileged communication is a major exception to the courts' access to evidence in judicial proceedings. Society believes that in the long term the interests of people are best served if some communications remain off limits to the prying eyes and ears of the police, judges, and prosecutors. The privilege applies to such relationships as those between husband and wife, physician and patient, pastor and penitent, attorney and client, and psychologist and patient. The legal expression is that the patient or client "holds the privilege," which means that only he or she may release the other person to disclose confidential information in a legal proceeding.

There are important limits to a person's right of privileged communication, however. For example, this right is eliminated for any of the following reasons in some states:

• A person has accused a therapist of malpractice. In such a case, the therapist can divulge information about the therapy to defend himself or herself in any legal action initiated by the person.

- The person is younger than 16, and the therapist has reason to believe that the child has been a victim of a crime such as child abuse. In fact, the psychologist is required to report to the police or to a child welfare agency within 36 hours any suspicion he or she has that the child has been physically or sexually abused.
- The person initiated therapy in hopes of evading the law for having committed a crime or for planning to do so.
- The therapist judges that the person is a danger to self or others and disclosure of information is necessary to ward off such danger (see Focus on Discovery 16.3 on *Tarasoff*).

Summary

- Some civil liberties can be set aside when mental health professionals and the courts judge that a psychological disorder has played a decisive role in determining an individual's behavior. This may occur through criminal or civil commitment.

- There is an important difference between a psychological disorder and insanity. Insanity is a legal concept. A person can be diagnosed as mentally ill and yet be deemed sane enough both to stand trial and to be found guilty of a crime.

- Criminal commitment can send a person to a hospital either before a trial for an alleged crime, because the person is deemed incompetent to stand trial, or after an acquittal by reason of insanity.

- Under civil commitment, a person who is considered mentally ill and dangerous to self and to others can be civilly committed to a hospital even if they did not commit a crime.

- Several landmark cases and principles in law address the conditions under which a person who has committed a crime might be excused from legal responsibility for it—that is, not guilty by reason of insanity. These involve the presence of an irresistible impulse and the notion that some people may not be able to

distinguish between right and wrong (the M'Naghten rule) or both (the ALI rule). The Insanity Defense Reform Act of 1984 made it harder for accused people to argue insanity as a defense.

- Two insanity pleas used today are not guilty by reason of insanity (NGRI) and guilty but mentally ill. They differ in terms of whether a person is responsible for their criminal actions, where the person receives treatment, and how long the person remains committed.

- Court rulings have provided greater protection to people with psychological disorders, particularly those under civil commitment. They have the right to the least restrictive treatment setting; the right to be treated; and, in most circumstances, the right to refuse treatment, particularly any procedure that entails considerable risk.

- Ethical issues concerning research include restraints on what kinds of research are allowable and the duty of scientists to obtain informed consent from prospective human participants.

- In the area of therapy, ethical issues concern the right of people to confidentiality.

Answers to Check Your Knowledge Questions

16.1 1. c; 2. a; 3. d; 4. b

16.2 1. F; 2. T; 3. T

16.3 1. F; 2. T; 3. F; 4. T

Key Terms

American Law Institute guidelines
assisted outpatient treatment
civil commitment
competency to stand trial
confidentiality

criminal commitment
guilty but mentally ill (GBMI)
informed consent
insanity defense
irresistible impulse

least restrictive alternative
M'Naghten rule
not guilty by reason of insanity (NGRI)
privileged communication

DSM-5 Diagnoses

Neurodevelopmental Disorders

Intellectual Disability

Intellectual Disability (Intellectual Development Disorder)

Communication Disorders

Language Disorder/Social (Pragmatic) Communication Disorder/Speech Sound Disorder/Childhood Onset Fluency Disorder (Stuttering)

Autism Spectrum Disorder

Autism Spectrum Disorder

Attention-Deficit/Hyperactivity Disorder

Attention-Deficit/Hyperactivity Disorder

Specific Learning Disorder
Motor Disorders

Developmental Coordination Disorder/Stereotypic Movement Disorder/Tourette's Disorder/Persistent (Chronic) Motor or Vocal Tic Disorder/Provisional Tic Disorder

Schizophrenia Spectrum Disorders

Schizophrenia/Schizotypal (Personality) Disorder/ Schizophreniform Disorder/Brief Psychotic Disorder/ Delusional Disorder/Schizoaffective Disorder

Bipolar and Related Disorders

Bipolar I Disorder/Bipolar II Disorder/Cyclothymic Disorder

Depressive Disorders

Disruptive Mood Dysregulation Disorder/Major Depressive Disorder/Persistent Depressive Disorder (Dysthymia)/ Premenstrual Dysphoric Disorder

Anxiety Disorders

Panic Disorder/Agoraphobia/Specific Phobia/Social Anxiety Disorder (Social Phobia)/Generalized Anxiety Disorder/Separation Anxiety Disorder/Selective Mutism

Obsessive-Compulsive and Related Disorders

Obsessive-Compulsive Disorder/Body Dysmorphic Disorder/Hoarding Disorder/Trichotillomania (Hair-Pulling Disorder)/Excoriation (Skin-Picking Disorder)

Trauma- and Stressor-Related Disorders

Reactive Attachment Disorder/Disinhibited Social Engagement Disorder/Acute Stress Disorder/Posttraumatic Stress Disorder/Adjustment Disorders

Dissociative Disorders

Depersonalization-Derealization Disorder/Dissociative Amnesia/Dissociative Identity Disorder

Somatic Symptom and Related Disorders

Somatic Symptom Disorder/Illness Anxiety Disorder/ Conversion Disorder/Psychological Factors Affecting Other Medical Conditions/Factitious Disorder

Feeding and Eating Disorders

Pica/Rumination Disorder/Avoidant/Restrictive Food Intake Disorder/Anorexia Nervosa/Bulimia Nervosa/Binge Eating Disorder

Elimination Disorders

Enuresis/Encopresis

Sleep-Wake Disorders

Insomnia Disorder/Hypersomnolence Disorder/Narcolepsy/Obstructive Sleep Apnea Hypopnea/Central Sleep Apnea/Sleep-Related Hypoventilation/Circadian Rhythm Sleep-Wake Disorders/Nightmare Disorder/Rapid Eye Movement Sleep Behavior Disorder/Restless Legs Syndrome/Non-Rapid Eye Movement Sleep Arousal Disorders

Sexual Dysfunctions

Erectile Disorder/Female Orgasmic Disorder/Delayed Ejaculation/Early Ejaculation/Female Sexual Interest/Arousal Disorder/Male Hypoactive Sexual Desire Disorder/Genito-Pelvic Pain/Penetration Disorder

Gender Dysphoria

Gender Dysphoria in Children, in Adolescents, or Adults

Disruptive, Impulse-Control, and Conduct Disorders

Oppositional Defiant Disorder/Intermittent Explosive Disorder/Conduct Disorder

Substance Use and Addictive Disorders

Alcohol Use Disorder/Amphetamine Use Disorder/Cannabis Use Disorder/Stimulant Use Disorder/Other Hallucinogen Use Disorder/Inhalant Use Disorder/Nicotine Use Disorder/Opioid Use Disorder/Phencyclidine Use Disorder/Sedative, Hypnotic, or Anxiolytic Use Disorders/Tobacco Use Disorder/Gambling Disorder

Neurocognitive Disorders

Delirium/Mild Neurocognitive Disorder/Major Neurocognitive Disorder

Personality Disorders

Antisocial Personality Disorder/Avoidant Personality Disorder/Borderline Personality Disorder/Narcissistic Personality Disorder/Obsessive-Compulsive Personality Disorder/Schizotypal Personality Disorder/Dependent Personality Disorder/Schizoid Personality Disorder/Paranoid Personality Disorder/Histrionic Personality Disorder

Paraphilic Disorders

Exhibitionistic Disorder/Fetishistic Disorder/Frotteuristic Disorder/Pedophilic Disorder/Sexual Masochism Disorder/Sexual Sadism Disorder/Transvestic Disorder/Voyeuristic Disorder

Conditions for Further Study

Attenuated Psychosis Syndrome/Depressive Episodes with Short-Duration Hypomania/Persistent Complex Bereavement Disorder/Caffeine Use Disorder/Internet Gaming Disorder/Neurobehavioral Disorder Associated with Prenatal Alcohol Exposure/Suicidal Behavior Disorder/Non-Suicidal Self Injury

DSM-5 Classification System

Neurodevelopmental Disorders

Schizophrenia Spectrum and Other Psychotic Disorders

Bipolar and Related Disorders

Depressive Disorders

Anxiety Disorders

Obsessive-Compulsive and Related Disorders

Trauma- and Stressor-Related Disorders

Dissociative Disorders

Somatic Symptom and Related Disorders

Feeding and Eating Disorders

Elimination Disorders

Sleep-Wake Disorders

Sexual Dysfunctions

Gender Dysphoria

Disruptive, Impulse-Control, and Conduct Disorders

Substance-Related and Addictive Disorders

Neurocognitive Disorders

Personality Disorders

Paraphilic Disorders

Other Mental Disorders

Medication-Induced Movement Disorders and Other Adverse Effects of Medication

Other Conditions That May Be a Focus of Clinical Attention

ABAB design. An experimental design in which behavior is measured during a baseline period (A), during a period when a treatment is introduced (B), during the reinstatement of the conditions that prevailed in the baseline period (A), and finally during a reintroduction of the treatment (B); commonly used in operant research to isolate cause–effect relationships.

acute stress disorder (ASD). A short-lived anxiety reaction to a traumatic event; if it lasts more than a month, it is diagnosed as posttraumatic stress disorder.

adoptees method. Research method that studies children who were adopted and reared completely apart from their parents, thereby eliminating the influence of being raised by disordered parents.

age effects. The consequences of being a given chronological age. Compare *cohort effects.*

agoraphobia. Anxiety disorder in which the person fears situations in which it would be embarrassing or difficult to escape if panic symptoms occurred; most commonly diagnosed in some individuals with panic disorder.

allele. Any of the various forms of a particular gene.

alogia. A negative symptom in schizophrenia, marked by diminished speaking.

alternate-form reliability See *reliability.*

Alzheimer's disease. A dementia involving a progressive atrophy of cortical tissue and marked by memory impairment, intellectual deterioration, and loss of motivation. See also *plaques* and *neurofibrillary tangles.*

American Law Institute guidelines. Rules proposing that insanity is a legitimate defense plea if, during criminal conduct, an individual could not judge right from wrong or control his or her behavior as required by law. Repetitive criminal acts are disavowed as a sole criterion. Compare *M'Naghten rule* and *irresistible impulse.*

amphetamines. A group of stimulating drugs that produce heightened levels of energy and, in large doses, nervousness, sleeplessness, and paranoid delusions.

amygdala. A subcortical structure of the temporal lobe involved in attention to emotionally salient stimuli and memory of emotionally relevant events.

analogue experiment. An experimental study of a phenomenon different from but related to the actual interests of the investigator; for example, animal research used to study human disorders or research on mild symptoms used as a bridge to clinical disorders.

anhedonia. A negative symptom in schizophrenia or a symptom in depression in which the individual experiences a loss of interest and pleasure. See also *anticipatory pleasure* and *consummatory pleasure.*

anorexia nervosa. A disorder in which a person restricts food that results in extreme weight loss, fears gaining weight, and has a distorted body image.

Antabuse. A drug that makes the drinking of alcohol produce nausea and other unpleasant effects; trade name for disulfiram.

anterior cingulate. In the subcortical region of the brain, the anterior portion of the cingulate gyrus, stretching about the corpus callosum.

anticipatory pleasure. Expected or anticipated pleasure for events, people, or activities in the future. See also *consummatory pleasure.*

antidepressant. Any drug that alleviates depression; also widely used to treat anxiety disorders.

antipsychotic drugs. Psychoactive drugs, such as thorazine or olanzapine, that reduce psychotic symptoms but have long-term side effects resembling symptoms of neurological diseases.

antisocial personality disorder (APD). Personality disorder defined by the absence of concern for others' feelings or social norms and a pervasive pattern of rule breaking.

anxiety. An unpleasant feeling of fear and apprehension accompanied by increased physiological arousal. Anxiety can be assessed by self-report, by measuring physiological arousal, and by observing overt behavior.

anxiety disorders. Disorders in which fear or anxiety is overriding and the primary disturbance; include phobic disorders, social anxiety disorder, panic disorder, generalized anxiety disorder, and agoraphobia.

Anxiety Sensitivity Index. A test that measures the extent to which people respond fearfully to their bodily sensations; predicts the degree to which unexplained physiological arousal leads to panic attacks.

anxiolytics. Minor tranquilizers or benzodiazepines used to treat anxiety disorders.

asociality. A negative symptom of schizophrenia marked by an inability to form close relationships and to feel intimacy.

assisted outpatient treatment. A form of civil commitment consistent with the principle of least restrictive alternative, whereby the person is not hospitalized but rather is allowed to remain free in the community under legal/medical constraints that ensure, for example, that prescribed medication is taken and other measures are observed.

asylums. Refuges established in western Europe in the fifteenth century to confine and provide for the mentally ill; forerunners of the mental hospital.

attachment theory. The type or style of an infant's attachment to his or her caregivers can set the stage for psychological health or problems later in development.

attention-deficit/hyperactivity disorder (ADHD). A disorder in children marked by difficulties in focusing adaptively on the task at hand, inappropriate fidgeting and antisocial behavior, and excessive non-goal-directed behavior.

attributional style. Trait-like tendencies to make a certain type of attribution for life events.

attribution. The explanation a person has for why an event or behavior has occurred.

autism spectrum disorder. A disorder beginning in childhood that involves deficits in social communication and social interactions, restricted and repetitive behaviors, and in some cases severe deficits in speech. DSM-5 combined Asperger's disorder, pervasive developmental disorder not otherwise specified, and childhood disintegrative disorder into the category of autism spectrum disorder.

autonomic nervous system (ANS). The division of the nervous system that regulates involuntary functions; innervates endocrine glands, smooth muscle, and heart muscle; and initiates the physiological changes that are part of the expression of emotion. See also *sympathetic* and *parasympathetic nervous systems.*

avoidant personality disorder. Personality disorder defined by aloofness and extreme sensitivity to potential rejection, despite an intense desire for affiliation and affection.

avolition. A negative symptom in schizophrenia in which the individual lacks interest and drive.

behavioral activation (BA) therapy. Clinical approach to depression that seeks to increase participation in positively reinforcing activities.

behavioral couples therapy. Clinical approach to depression in which a couple works to improve communication and satisfaction; more likely to relieve relationship distress than individual cognitive therapy.

behavioral inhibition. The tendency to exhibit anxiety or to freeze when facing threat. In infants, it manifests as a tendency to become agitated and cry when faced with novel stimuli and may be a heritable predisposition for the development of anxiety disorders.

behavior genetics. The study of individual differences in behavior that are attributable to differences in genetic makeup.

behaviorism. The school of psychology originally associated with John B. Watson, who proposed that observable behavior, not consciousness, is the proper subject matter of psychology. Contemporary behaviorists do use mediational concepts, provided they are firmly anchored to observables.

benzodiazepines. Any of several drugs commonly used to treat anxiety, such as Valium and Xanax.

Big Five Inventory-2 (BFI-2) A personality inventory that assesses the five broad domains of personality: openness, conscientiousness, agreeableness, extraversion, and neuroticism.

binge eating disorder. Included as a disorder in DSM-5; includes recurrent episodes of unrestrained eating.

bipolar I disorder. A diagnosis defined on the basis of at least one lifetime episode of mania. Most people with this disorder also experience episodes of major depression.

bipolar II disorder. A form of bipolar disorder, diagnosed in those who have experienced at least one major depressive episode and at least one episode of hypomania.

blunted affect. A negative symptom of schizophrenia that involves a lack of outward expression of emotion.

body dysmorphic disorder (BDD). A disorder marked by preoccupation with an imagined or exaggerated defect in appearance—for example, facial wrinkles or excess facial or body hair.

body mass index (BMI). Measure of body fat calculated by dividing weight in kilograms by height in meters squared; considered a more valid estimate of body fat than many others.

BOLD (blood oxygenation level dependent) The signal detected by functional MRI studies of the brain; measures blood flow and thus neural activity in any given region.

borderline personality disorder. Personality disorder defined by impulsiveness and unpredictability, an uncertain self-image, intense and unstable social relationships, and extreme swings of mood.

brain networks. Clusters of brain regions that are connected to one another as indicated by correlations between activation in these regions when people perform certain types of tasks or are at rest.

brief psychotic disorder. A disorder in which a person has a sudden onset of psychotic symptoms—incoherence, loose associations, delusions, hallucinations—immediately after a severely disturbing event; the symptoms last more than 1 day but no more than 1 month. Compare *schizophreniform disorder.*

bulimia nervosa. A disorder characterized by episodic, uncontrollable eating binges followed by purging either by vomiting or by taking laxatives.

caffeine. Perhaps the world's most popular drug; a generalized stimulant of body systems, including the sympathetic nervous system. Though seldom viewed as a drug, caffeine is addictive, produces tolerance, and induces withdrawal symptoms in habitual users upon cessation of use.

case study. The collection of historical or biographical information on a single individual, often including experiences in therapy.

catatonia. Constellation of schizophrenia symptoms including repetitive, peculiar, complex gestures and, in some cases, an almost manic increase in overall activity level. It can also manifest itself as immobility, with a fixity of posture maintained for long periods, with accompanying muscular rigidity, trancelike state of consciousness, and waxy flexibility.

categorical classification An approach to assessment in which a person is or is not a member of a discrete grouping. Compare *dimensional classification.*

cathartic method. A therapeutic procedure to relieve emotional suffering introduced by Breuer and developed further by Freud in the late nineteenth century, whereby a patient recalls and relives an earlier emotional catastrophe and reexperiences the tension and unhappiness.

caudate nucleus. A nucleus within the basal ganglia involved in learning and memory that is implicated in body dysmorphic disorder and obsessive-compulsive disorder.

civil commitment. A procedure whereby a person can be legally certified as mentally ill and hospitalized, even against his or her will. Compare *criminal commitment* and *assisted outpatient commitment.*

classical conditioning. A basic form of learning, sometimes referred to as Pavlovian conditioning, in which a neutral stimulus is repeatedly paired with another stimulus (called the unconditioned stimulus, UCS) that naturally elicits a certain desired response (called the unconditioned response, UCR). After repeated trials, the neutral stimulus becomes a conditioned stimulus (CS) and evokes the same or a similar response, now called the conditioned response (CR). Compare *operant conditioning.*

clinical high-risk study. A study that identifies people who show subtle or early clinical signs of a disorder, such as schizophrenia, and then follows them over time to determine who might be at risk for developing the disorder.

clinical interview General term for conversation between a clinician and a patient that is aimed at determining diagnosis, history, causes of problems, and possible treatment options. In a semistructured clinical interview, the clinician uses a standardized set of questions.

clinical psychologist. An individual who has earned a Ph.D. degree in psychology or a Psy.D. and whose training has included an internship in a mental hospital or clinic.

clinical significance. The degree to which effect size is large enough to be meaningful in predicting or treating a clinical disorder. Compare *statistical significance.*

cocaine. A pain-reducing, stimulating, and addictive alkaloid obtained from coca leaves that can increase attention, produce euphoria, heighten sexual desire, and in large doses cause paranoia and hallucinations.

cognition. The process of knowing; the thinking, judging, reasoning, and planning activities of the human mind. Behavior is now often explained as depending on these processes.

cognitive behavioral paradigm. General view that people can best be understood by studying how they perceive and structure their experiences and how this influences behavior.

cognitive behavior therapy (CBT). Behavior therapy that incorporates theory and research on cognitive processes such as thoughts, perceptions, judgments, self-statements, and tacit assumptions; a blend of both the cognitive and behavioral paradigms.

cognitive remediation. Also known as cognitive training, treatment that seeks to improve basic cognitive functions such as verbal learning ability in people with schizophrenia while also reducing symptoms.

cognitive reserve. Intellectual capacity that allows a person to continue to think and function well despite high levels of amyloid, plaques, or other dementia-related pathology in the brain.

cognitive restructuring. Any behavior therapy procedure that attempts to alter the manner in which a client thinks about life so that he or she changes overt behavior and emotions.

cohort effects. The consequences of having been born in a given year and having grown up during a particular time period with characteristic pressures, problems, challenges, and opportunities. Compare *age effects.*

comorbidity The co-occurrence of two disorders, as when a person has depression and social phobia.

competency to stand trial. A legal decision as to whether a person can participate meaningfully in his or her own defense.

compulsion. The irresistible impulse to repeat an irrational act or thought over and over. Compare *obsession.*

concordance. As applied in behavior genetics, the similarity in psychiatric diagnosis or in other traits within a pair of twins.

conditioned response (CR). See *classical conditioning.*

conditioned stimulus (CS). See *classical conditioning.*

conduct disorder. Pattern of extreme disobedience in youngsters, including theft, vandalism, lying, and early drug use.

confidentiality. A principle observed by lawyers, doctors, pastors, psychologists, and psychiatrists which dictates that the contents of a professional and private relationship are not to be divulged to anyone else. See also *privileged communication.*

connectivity The ways in which different brain regions are connected to one another and form networks. Structural connectivity refers to how different structures of the brain are connected via white matter. Functional connectivity refers to correlations between brain areas' blood oxygen level dependent (BOLD) signal measured with fMRI.

construct validity The extent to which scores or ratings on an assessment instrument relate to other variables or behaviors according to some theory or hypothesis.

consummatory pleasure. Pleasure experienced in the moment or in the presence of a pleasurable stimulus. See also *anticipatory pleasure*.

content validity See *validity*.

contrast avoidance model. The theory that the chronic worry of GAD provides a functional advantage in reducing the volatility of negative emotions and arousal in response to severe stress.

control group. Those for whom the active condition of the independent variable is not administered, thus forming a baseline against which the effects of the active condition of the independent variable can be evaluated.

controlled drinking. A pattern of alcohol consumption that is moderate, avoiding the extremes of total abstinence and of inebriation.

conversion disorder. A disorder in which sensory or motor function is impaired, even though there is no detectable neurological explanation for the deficits.

copy number variation (CNV). Refers to variation in gene structure involving copy number changes in a defined chromosomal region; could be in the form of a deletion where a copy is deleted or an addition (duplication) where an extra copy is added.

correlational method. The research strategy used to establish whether two or more variables are related without manipulating the independent variable. Relationships may be positive—as values for one variable increase, those for the other do also—or negative—as values for one variable increase, those for the other decrease. Compare *experiment*.

correlation coefficient. A statistic that provides an index of the strength and direction of a linear relationship between two variables; a correlation coefficient of 0 indicates no relationship, 1 indicates a perfect positive relationship, and –1 indicates a perfect negative relationship.

correlation. The tendency for two variables, such as height and weight, to covary.

cortisol. A "stress hormone" secreted by the adrenal cortices; helps the body prepare to face threats.

cortisol awakening response (CAR). An increase in cortisol levels that occurs in the first 30 minutes after awakening; about a 50% increase occurs on average, though levels vary across individuals. It has been related to the onset of anxiety and depressive disorders.

crack. A rock-crystal form of cocaine that is heated, melted, and smoked; more often used in poorer urban areas than conventional cocaine.

criminal commitment. A procedure whereby a person is confined in a mental hospital either for determination of competency to stand trial or after acquittal by reason of insanity. Compare *civil commitment*.

cross-fostering. Research method that studies offspring who were adopted and reared completely apart from their biological parents, where the adoptive parent has a particular disorder but the biological parent does not,

thereby introducing the influence of being raised by disordered parents.

cross-sectional design. Studies in which different age groups are compared at the same time. Compare *longitudinal design*.

CT or CAT scan Refers to computerized axial tomography, a method of diagnosis in which X-rays are taken from different angles and then analyzed by computer to produce a representation of the part of the body in cross section.

cultural competence. The capacity of a therapist to understand the patient's cultural framework and its implications for therapeutic work.

cultural concepts of distress Psychological syndromes that have been observed in specific cultural groups. Nine well-studied cultural concepts of distress are described in the appendix to DSM-5.

Cushing syndrome. An endocrine disorder usually affecting young women, produced by oversecretion of cortisone and marked by mood swings, irritability, agitation, and physical disfigurement.

cyclothymic disorder. A form of bipolar disorder characterized by swings between elation and depression over at least a 2-year period, but with moods not so severe as manic or major depressive episodes.

defense mechanisms. In psychoanalytic theory, reality-distorting strategies unconsciously adopted to protect the ego from anxiety.

delayed ejaculation. A disorder in men involving persistent delay in reaching orgasm or inability to reach orgasm.

delirium. A state of great mental confusion in which consciousness is clouded, attention cannot be sustained, and the stream of thought and speech is incoherent. The person is probably disoriented; emotionally erratic; restless or lethargic; and often has illusions, delusions, and hallucinations.

delirium tremens (DTs). One of the withdrawal symptoms that sometimes occurs when a period of heavy alcohol consumption is terminated; marked by fever, sweating, trembling, cognitive impairment, and hallucinations.

delusional disorder. A disorder in which the individual has persistent delusions and is very often contentious but has no disorganized thinking or hallucinations.

delusions. Beliefs contrary to reality, firmly held despite evidence to the contrary and common in paranoid disorders: of control, belief that one is being manipulated by some external force such as radar, TV, or a creature from outer space; of grandeur, belief that one is an especially important or powerful person; of persecution, belief that one is being plotted against or oppressed by others.

dementia. Deterioration of cognitive abilities, such as memory, judgment, abstract thought, control of impulses, intellectual ability, that impairs functioning. See *Alzheimer's disease*.

dementia with Lewy bodies (DLB). Form of dementia that often co-occurs with Parkinson's disease; characterized by shuffling gait, memory loss, and hallucinations and delusions.

dependent personality disorder. A personality disorder in which people are overly concerned about maintaining relationships. People with this disorder often allow others to make decisions for them and are reluctant to make demands that could challenge relationships.

dependent variable. In a psychological experiment, the behavior that is measured and is expected to change with manipulation of the independent variable.

depersonalization. An alteration in perception of the self in which the individual loses a sense of reality and feels estranged from the self and perhaps separated from the body; may be a temporary reaction to stress and fatigue or part of panic disorder, depersonalization disorder, or schizophrenia.

depersonalization/derealization disorder. A DSM-5 disorder defined by the sustained presence of depersonalization (detachment from sense of self) or derealization (detachment from the sense of reality).

Derealization. Experiences of extreme psychological detachment from surroundings.

derealization. Loss of the sense that the surroundings are real; present in several psychological disorders, such as panic disorder, depersonalization disorder, and schizophrenia.

desire phase. The first stage of the sexual response cycle, characterized by sexual interest or desire, often associated with sexually arousing fantasies.

detoxification. The initial stage in weaning an addicted person from a drug; involves medical supervision of the sometimes painful withdrawal.

developmental psychopathology. The field that studies disorders of childhood within the context of normal development over the life span.

diagnosis The determination that the set of symptoms or problems of a patient indicates a particular disorder.

Diagnostic and Statistical Manual of Mental Disorders Currently in its 5th edition (May 2013), the *Diagnostic and Statistical Manual of Mental Disorders* provides the major diagnostic guidelines for mental health syndromes in the United States. Published by the American Psychiatric Association.

dialectical behavior therapy (DBT). A therapeutic approach to borderline personality disorder that combines client-centered empathy and acceptance with behavioral problem solving, social skills training, and limit setting.

diathesis. Predisposition toward a disorder.

diathesis–stress. As applied in psychopathology, a view that assumes that individuals predisposed toward a particular psychological disorder will be particularly affected by stress and will then manifest abnormal behavior.

dimensional diagnostic system A diagnostic system that describes the degree of an entity that is present (e.g., a 1-to-10 scale of anxiety, where 1 represents minimal and 10, extremely severe).

directionality problem. A difficulty that arises in the correlational method of research when it is known that two variables are related but it is unclear which is causing the other.

disorganized behavior. Symptom of schizophrenia that is marked by odd behaviors that do not appear organized, such as bouts of agitation; unusual dress; or childlike, silly behavior.

disorganized speech. Speech found in schizophrenia patients that is marked by poorly organized ideas and speech that is difficult for others to understand; also known as formal thought disorder.

disorganized symptoms. Broad category of symptoms in schizophrenia that includes disorganized speech, disorganized thinking, and disorganized behavior.

disorientation. A state of mental confusion with respect to time; place; and identity of self, other persons, and objects.

disruptive mood dysregulation disorder. A DSM-5 disorder defined by severe temper outbursts and observably irritable mood between outbursts in youth older than age 6.

dissemination. The process of facilitating adoption of efficacious treatments in the community, most typically by offering clinicians guidelines about the best available treatments along with training on how to conduct those treatments.

dissociation. A symptom in which some aspect of emotion, memory, or experience is inaccessible consciously.

dissociative amnesia. A dissociative disorder in which the person suddenly becomes unable to recall important personal information to an extent that cannot be explained by ordinary forgetfulness.

dissociative disorders. Disorders in which the normal integration of consciousness, memory, or identity is suddenly and temporarily altered; include dissociative amnesia, dissociative identity disorder (multiple personality), and depersonalization/derealization disorder.

dissociative identity disorder (DID). A rare dissociative disorder (formerly called multiple personality disorder, or MPD) in which two or more distinct and separate personalities are present within the same individual, each with his or her own memories, relationships, and behavior patterns, with only one of them dominant at any given time.

dizygotic (DZ) twins. Birth partners who developed from separate fertilized eggs and who are only 50 percent alike genetically, just as siblings born from different pregnancies involving the same father; also called fraternal twins. Compare *monozygotic twins*.

dopamine. Central nervous system neurotransmitter, a catecholamine that is also a precursor of norepinephrine and apparently figures in schizophrenia and Parkinson's disease.

dorsolateral prefrontal cortex. A region of the prefrontal cortex involved in working memory, motor planning, organization, and regulation, which is implicated in many psychopathologies.

double-blind procedure. A method for reducing the biasing effects of the expectations of research participant and experimenter; neither is allowed to know whether the independent variable of the experiment is being applied to the participant.

Down syndrome (trisomy 21). A form of intellectual disability caused by a third copy of chromosome 21; involves an IQ score usually lower than 50 as well as distinctive physical characteristics.

dyslexia. A learning disorder involving significant difficulty with word recognition, reading comprehension, and (typically) spelling.

ecological momentary assessment (EMA) Form of self-observation involving collection of data in real time (e.g., diaries) regarding thoughts, moods, and stressors.

Ecstasy. A relatively new hallucinogen, chemically similar to mescaline and the amphetamines.

effectiveness. How well a therapeutic treatment works in the real world with broader samples seen by nonacademic, less supervised therapists. Compare *efficacy*.

efficacy. How well a therapeutic treatment works under rarified, academic research conditions. Compare *effectiveness*.

ego. In psychoanalytic theory, the predominantly conscious part of the personality, responsible for decision making and for dealing with reality.

electrocardiogram (EKG) A recording of the electrical activity of the heart, made with an electrocardiograph.

electroconvulsive therapy (ECT). A treatment that produces a convulsion by passing electric current through the brain; despite public concerns about this treatment, it can be useful in alleviating profound depression.

electrodermal responding A recording of the minute electrical activity of the sweat glands on the skin, allowing inference of an emotional state.

emotion. The expression, experience, and physiology that guide responses to problems and challenges in the environment.

empirically supported treatments (ESTs). Approaches whose efficacy has been demonstrated and documented through research that meets standards for research on psychotherapy.

epidemiology. The study of the frequency and distribution of illness in a population.

epigenetics. The study of changes in gene expression that are caused by something other than changes in the DNA (gene) sequence or structure, such as DNA methylation.

episodic disorder. A condition, such as major depressive disorder, whose symptoms dissipate but that tends to recur.

erectile disorder. A disorder involving recurrent and persistent inability to attain an erection or maintain it until completion of sexual activity.

excitement phase. As applied by Masters and Johnson, the second stage of the sexual response cycle, characterized by pleasure associated with increased blood flow to the genitalia.

exhibitionistic disorder. Marked preference for obtaining sexual gratification by exposing one's genitals to an unwilling observer.

exorcism. The casting out of evil spirits by ritualistic chanting or torture.

experimental effect. A statistically significant difference between two groups experiencing different manipulations of the independent variable.

experiment. The most powerful research technique for determining causal relationships; involves the manipulation of an independent variable, the measurement of a dependent variable, and the random assignment of participants to the several different conditions being investigated. Compare *correlational method*.

explicit memory. Memory involving the conscious recall of experiences; the area of deficits typically seen in dissociative amnesia. Compare *implicit memory*.

exposure and response prevention (ERP). The most widely used and accepted treatment of obsessive-compulsive disorder, in which the sufferer is prevented from engaging in compulsive ritual activity and instead faces the anxiety provoked by the stimulus, leading eventually to extinction of the conditioned response (anxiety).

exposure. Real-life (in vivo) or imaginal confrontation of a feared object or situation, especially as a component of systematic desensitization.

expressed emotion (EE). Hostility, criticism, and emotional overinvolvement directed from other people toward the patient, usually within a family.

externalizing disorders. Childhood disorders characterized by outward-directed behaviors, such as aggressiveness, noncompliance, excessive activity, and impulsiveness; the category includes attention-deficit/hyperactivity disorder, conduct disorder, and oppositional defiant disorder. Compare *internalizing disorders*.

external validity. The extent to which the results of a study can be considered generalizable.

extinction. The elimination of a classically conditioned response by the omission of the unconditioned stimulus. In operant conditioning, the elimination of the conditioned response by the omission of reinforcement.

factitious disorder. Disorder in which the individual's physical or psychological symptoms appear under voluntary control and are adopted merely to assume the role of a sick person; called factitious disorder by proxy or Munchausen syndrome when a parent produces a physical illness in a child.

familial high-risk study. A study involving the offspring of people with a disorder, such as schizophrenia, who have a high probability of later developing a disorder.

family method. A research strategy in behavior genetics in which the frequency of a trait or of abnormal behavior is determined in relatives who have varying percentages of shared genetic background.

fear. A reaction to real or perceived immediate danger in the present; can involve arousal, or sympathetic nervous system activity.

fear circuit. Set of brain structures, including the amygdala, that tend to be activated when the individual is feeling anxious or fearful; especially active among people with anxiety disorders.

fear-of-fear hypothesis. A cognitive model for the etiology of agoraphobia; suggests the condition is driven by negative thoughts about the consequences of having a panic attack in public.

female orgasmic disorder. A recurrent and persistent delay or absence of orgasm in a woman during sexual activity adequate in focus, intensity, and duration; in many instances the woman may experience considerable sexual excitement.

female sexual interest/arousal disorder. A DSM disorder defined by prolonged absence of sexual desire, subjective arousal, or biological arousal.

fetal alcohol syndrome (FAS). Retarded growth of the developing fetus and infant involving cranial, facial, and limb anomalies as well as intellectual disabilities; caused by heavy consumption of alcohol by the mother during pregnancy.

fetishistic disorder. A paraphilic disorder that involves reliance on an inanimate object for sexual arousal, to an extent that causes distress or social difficulties.

flashback. An unpredictable recurrence of experiences from an earlier drug high.

flight of ideas. A symptom of mania that involves a rapid shift in conversation from one subject to another with only superficial associative connections.

fragile X syndrome. Malformation (or even breakage) of the X chromosome, associated with intellectual disability; symptoms include large, underdeveloped ears; a long, thin face; a broad nasal root; enlarged testicles in males; and, in many cases, attention deficits and hyperactivity.

fronto-striatal circuits. Neural pathways that connect regions of the frontal cortex and areas of the basal ganglia; these pathways are implicated in obsessive-compulsive disorder.

frontotemporal dementia (FTD). Dementia that begins typically in the mid- to late 50s, characterized by deficits in executive functions such as planning, problem solving, and goal-directed behavior as well as recognition and comprehension of emotions in others. Compare *Alzheimer's disease.*

frotteuristic disorder. A disorder in which the person gains sexual gratification by sexually touching of an unsuspecting person, typically in public places that provide an easy means of escape.

fugue subtype. Subtype of dissociative amnesia disorder in which the person experiences total amnesia, moves, and establishes a new identity.

functional magnetic resonance imaging (fMRI) Modification of *magnetic resonance imaging (MRI)* that allows researchers to take pictures of the brain so quickly that metabolic changes can be measured, resulting in a picture of the brain at work rather than of its structure alone.

gamma-aminobutyric acid (GABA). Inhibitory neurotransmitter that may be involved in the anxiety disorders.

gene–environment interaction. The influence of genetics on an individual's sensitivity or reaction to an environmental event.

gene expression. The switching on and off of the reading (transcription and translation) of genes into their products (usually proteins) and thus their associated phenotypes.

generalized anxiety disorder (GAD). Disorder characterized by chronic, persistent anxiety and worry.

gene. The smallest portion of DNA within a chromosome that functions as a piece of functional hereditary information.

genetic paradigm. The approach to human behavior that focuses on both heritability of traits and complex interactions between genes and environment.

genito-pelvic pain/penetration disorder. A disorder in which the woman persistently experiences pain or vaginal muscle spasms when intercourse is attempted.

genome-wide association studies (GWAS). Studies of variations in the entire human genome to identify associations of genetic variants with particular behaviors, traits, or disorders. Large sample sizes are needed for these types of studies.

genotype. An individual's unobservable, genetic constitution, that is, the totality of genes present in the cells of an individual; often applied to the genes contributing to a single trait. Compare *phenotype.*

grandiose delusions. Found in paranoid schizophrenia, delusional disorder, and mania, an exaggerated sense of one's importance, power, knowledge, or identity. See also *delusions.*

gray matter. The neural tissue—made up largely of nerve cell bodies—that constitutes the cortex covering the cerebral hemisphere, the nuclei in lower brain areas, columns of the spinal cord, and the ganglia of the autonomic nervous system. Compare *white matter.*

guilty but mentally ill (GBMI). Insanity plea in which a mentally ill person can be held morally and legally responsible for a crime but can then, in theory, be sent to a prison hospital or other suitable facility for psychiatric treatment rather than to a regular prison for punishment. In reality, however, people judged GBMI are usually put in the general prison population, where they may or may not receive treatment. Compare *not guilty by reason of insanity.*

hallucinations. Perceptions in any sensory modality without relevant and adequate external stimuli.

hallucinogen. A drug or chemical, such as LSD, psilocybin, or mescaline, whose effects include hallucinations; often called a psychedelic.

hashish. The dried resin of the cannabis plant, stronger in its effects than the dried leaves and stems that constitute marijuana.

heritability. The extent to which variability in a behavior/disorder within a population can be attributed to genetic factors.

heroin. An extremely addictive narcotic drug derived from morphine.

high-risk method. A research technique involving the intensive examination of people, such as the offspring of people with schizophrenia, who have a high probability of later developing a disorder.

hippocampus. In the subcortical region of the brain, the long, tubelike structure that stretches from the septal area into the temporal lobe.

histrionic personality disorder. A personality disorder defined by overly dramatic behavior, emotional excess, and sexually provocative behavior.

hoarding disorder. A disorder in which the person has a compulsive need to acquire objects and extreme difficulty in disposing of those objects.

hopelessness theory. Cognitive theory of depression that began with learned helplessness theory, was modified to incorporate attributions, and has been modified again to emphasize hopelessness—an expectation that desirable outcomes will not occur and that no available responses can change the situation.

HPA axis. The neuroendocrine connections among hypothalamus, pituitary gland, and adrenal cortex, central to the body's response to stress.

hydrocodone. An opiate combined with other drugs such as acetaminophen to produce prescription pain medications, including the commonly abused drug Vicodin. See also *oxycodone.*

hypomania. An extremely happy or irritable mood accompanied by symptoms such as increased energy and decreased need for sleep, but without the significant functional impairment associated with mania.

hypothalamus. In the subcortical region of the brain, the structure that regulates many visceral processes, including metabolism, temperature, perspiration, blood pressure, sleeping, and appetite.

hypothesis. Specific expectation or prediction about what should occur or be found if a theory is true or valid.

iatrogenic. Inadvertently induced by treatment.

ideas of reference. Delusional thinking that reads personal significance into seemingly trivial remarks or activities of others and completely unrelated events.

id. In psychoanalytic theory, that part of the personality present at birth, comprising all the energy of the psyche and expressed as biological urges that strive continually for gratification.

illness anxiety disorder. A disorder defined by excessive concern and help-seeking about health concerns in the absence of major physical symptoms.

imaginal exposure. Treatment for anxiety disorders that involves visualizing feared scenes for extended periods of time. Frequently used in the treatment of posttraumatic stress disorder when in vivo exposure to the initial trauma cannot be conducted.

implicit memory. Memory that underlies behavior but is based on experiences that cannot be consciously recalled; typically not compromised in cases of dissociative amnesia. Compare *explicit memory*.

incest. Sexual relations between close relatives, most often between daughter and father or between brother and sister.

incidence. In epidemiological studies of a particular disorder, the rate at which new cases occur in a given place at a given time. Compare *prevalence*.

independent variable. In a psychological experiment, the factor, experience, or treatment that is under the control of the experimenter and that is expected to have an effect on the dependent variable.

index case. The person who in a genetic investigation bears the diagnosis or trait in which the investigator is interested.

information-processing biases. Tendencies to perceive events in a negative manner, for example, by attending to or remembering negative information more than positive information; hypothesized to be driven by underlying negative schemas.

informed consent. The agreement of a person to serve as a research participant or to enter therapy after being told the possible outcomes, both benefits and risks.

insanity defense. The legal argument that a defendant should not be held responsible for an illegal act if the conduct is attributable to mental illness. See also *not guilty by reason of insanity* and *guilty but mentally ill*.

intellectual disability. A disorder identified in early childhood characterized by below-average intellectual functioning associated with impairment in adaptive behavior.

intelligence test A standardized means of assessing a person's current mental ability, for example, the Stanford–Binet test or the Wechsler Adult Intelligence Scale.

internal consistency reliability See *reliability*.

internalizing disorders. Childhood disorders characterized by inward-focused experiences and behaviors, such as depression, social withdrawal, and anxiety; the category includes childhood anxiety and mood disorders. Compare *externalizing disorders*.

internal validity. The extent to which the experimental effect can be attributed confidently to the independent variable.

interoceptive conditioning. Classical conditioning of panic attacks in response to internal bodily sensations of arousal (as opposed to the external situations that trigger anxiety).

interpersonal psychotherapy (IPT). A short-term, here-and-now focused psychological treatment initially developed for depression and influenced by the psychodynamic emphasis on relationships.

inter-rater reliability See *reliability*.

in vivo exposure. As applied in exposure treatment, taking place in a real-life situation.

irresistible impulse. The term used in an 1834 Ohio court ruling on criminal responsibility which determined that an insanity defense can be established by proving that the accused had an uncontrollable urge to perform the act.

joint attention. Interactions between two people require paying attention to each other, whether speaking or communicating emotion nonverbally. This is impaired in children with autism spectrum disorder.

law of effect. A principle of learning that holds that behavior is acquired by virtue of its consequences.

least restrictive alternative. The legal principle according to which a hospitalized patient must be treated in a setting that imposes as few restrictions as possible on his or her freedom.

lithium. A drug useful in treating both mania and depression in bipolar disorder.

locus coeruleus. The brain region in the fear circuit that is especially important in panic disorder; the major source in the brain of norepinephrine, which helps trigger sympathetic nervous system activity.

longitudinal design. Investigation that collects information on the same individuals repeatedly over time, perhaps over many years, in an effort to determine how phenomena change. Compare *cross-sectional design*.

loose associations (derailment). In schizophrenia, an aspect of disorganized thinking wherein the patient has difficulty sticking to one topic and drifts off on a train of associations evoked by an idea from the past.

LSD. *d*-lysergic acid diethylamide, a drug synthesized in 1938 and discovered by accident to be a hallucinogen in 1943.

magnetic resonance imaging (MRI) A technique for measuring the structure (or, in the case of *functional magnetic resonance imaging*, the activity) of the living brain or body. The person is placed inside a large circular magnet that causes hydrogen atoms to move; the return of the atoms to their original positions when the current to the magnet is turned off is translated by a computer into pictures of brain tissue.

major depressive disorder (MDD). A disorder of individuals who have experienced episodes of depression but not of mania. Depression episodes are marked by sadness or loss of pleasure, accompanied by symptoms such as feelings of worthlessness and guilt; withdrawal from others; loss of sleep, appetite, or sexual desire; and either lethargy or agitation.

male hypoactive sexual desire disorder. A sexual dysfunction disorder defined by persistent absence of or deficiency in sexual fantasies and urges in men; for women, see *female sexual interest/arousal disorder*.

malingering. Faking a physical or psychological incapacity to avoid a responsibility or gain an end, where the goal is readily recognized from the individual's circumstances; distinct from conversion disorder, in which the incapacity is assumed to be beyond voluntary control.

mania. Intense elation or irritability, accompanied by symptoms such as excessive talkativeness, rapid thoughts, distractibility, grandiose plans, heightened activity, and insensitivity to the negative consequences of actions.

marijuana. A drug derived from the dried and ground leaves and stems of the female hemp plant *Cannabis sativa*.

MDMA. Methylenedioxymethamphetamine, a chemical component of Ecstasy; initially used as an appetite suppressant for World War I soldiers and derived from precursors found in nutmeg, dill, saffron, and sassafras.

means restriction. An approach to suicide prevention in which access to lethal methods is reduced. Examples include keeping guns locked in cabinets, reducing the unrestricted sale of poisons, and erecting suicide barriers on bridges.

medial prefrontal cortex. A region of the cortex in the anterior frontal lobes involved in executive function and emotion regulation that is implicated in mood and anxiety disorders.

mentalization therapy. A psychodynamic therapy, empirically validated for the treatment of borderline personality disorder, in which clients are taught to take a reflective stance in responding to their emotions and interpersonal difficulties.

meta-analysis. A quantitative method of analyzing the results of a set of studies on a topic, by standardizing the results.

metabolite A chemical breakdown product of an endogenous molecule, such as a neurotransmitter, or of an exogenous drug; used to gauge current or recent level of its precursor.

methamphetamine. An amphetamine derivative whose abuse skyrocketed in the 1990s.

mild cognitive impairment (MCI). Decline in cognitive ability that is not severe enough to cause functional impairment or to interfere with activities of daily living.

mindfulness-based cognitive therapy (MBCT). Recent adaptation of cognitive therapy/restructuring that focuses on relapse prevention after successful treatment for recurrent episodes of major depression; aims to "decenter" the person's perspective in order to break the cycle between sadness and thinking patterns.

Minnesota Multiphasic Personality Inventory-2 (MMPI-2) A lengthy personality inventory that identifies individuals with states such as anxiety, depression, masculinity–femininity, and paranoia, through their true or false replies to groups of statements.

M'Naghten rule. An 1843 British court decision stating that an insanity defense can be established by proving that the defendant did not know what he or she was doing or did not realize that it was wrong.

modeling. Learning by observing and imitating the behavior of others or teaching by demonstrating and providing opportunities for imitation.

molecular genetics. Studies that seek to determine the components of a trait that are heritable by identifying relevant genes and their functions.

monoamine oxidase inhibitors (MAOIs). A group of antidepressant drugs that prevent the enzyme monoamine oxidase from deactivating catecholamines and indolamines.

monozygotic (MZ) twins. Genetically identical twins who have developed from a single fertilized egg. Compare *dizygotic twins.*

mood disorders. Disorders, such as depressive disorders or mania, in which there are disabling disturbances in emotion.

moral treatment. A therapeutic regimen, introduced by Philippe Pinel during the French Revolution, whereby mentally ill patients were released from their restraints and were treated with compassion and dignity rather than with contempt and denigration.

Mowrer's two-factor model. Mowrer's theory of avoidance learning according to which (1) fear is attached to a neutral stimulus by pairing it with a noxious unconditioned stimulus, and (2) a person learns to escape the fear elicited by the conditioned stimulus, thereby avoiding the unconditioned stimulus.

multisystemic treatment (MST). Treatment for conduct disorder that involves delivering intensive and comprehensive therapy services in the community, targeting the adolescent, the family, the school, and, in some cases, the peer group, in ecologically valid settings and using varied techniques.

narcissistic personality disorder. Personality disorder defined by extreme selfishness and self-centeredness; a grandiose view of one's uniqueness, achievements, and talents; an insatiable craving for admiration and approval from others; willingness to exploit others to achieve goals; and expectation of much more from others than one is willing to give in return.

negative reinforcement. The strengthening of a tendency to exhibit desired behavior by rewarding responses in that situation with the removal of an aversive stimulus.

negative symptoms. Behavioral deficits in schizophrenia, which include flat affect, anhedonia, asociality, alogia, and avolition. Compare *positive symptoms.*

negative triad. In Beck's theory of depression, a person's negative views of the self, the world, and the future, in a reciprocal causal relationship with pessimistic assumptions (schemas) and cognitive biases such as selective abstraction.

neurofibrillary tangles. Abnormal protein filaments present in the cell bodies of brain cells in patients with Alzheimer's disease.

neuron. A single nerve cell.

neuropsychological tests Psychological tests, such as the Luria–Nebraska, which can detect impairment in different parts of the brain.

neuroscience paradigm. A broad theoretical view that holds that psychological disorders are caused in part by some aberrant process directed by the brain.

neuroticism. The tendency to react to events with more frequent or greater-than-average negative affect; a strong predictor of onset of anxiety disorders and depression.

neurotransmitters. Chemical substances important in transferring a nerve impulse from one neuron to another, for example, serotonin and norepinephrine.

neutral predictable unpredictable (NPU) threat task. A laboratory task designed to test sensitivity to unpredictable versus predictable threats. Participants are exposed to threat conditions in which they could receive a shock. In the predictable threat condition, there is a cue warning when the shock will occur. In the unpredictable threat condition, there is no cue warning when the shock will occur.

nicotine. The principal alkaloid of tobacco (an addicting agent).

nitrous oxide. A gas that, when inhaled, produces euphoria and sometimes giddiness.

nonshared environment. Factors distinct among family members, such as relationships with friends or specific experiences unique to a person. Compare *shared environment.*

nonsuicidal self-injury (NSSI). Behaviors that are meant to cause immediate bodily harm but are not intended to cause death.

norepinephrine. A catecholamine neurotransmitter, disturbances of which have been related to mania, depression, and particularly to anxiety disorders. It is also a sympathetic nervous system neurotransmitter, a hormone released in addition to epinephrine and similar in action, and a strong vasoconstrictor.

not guilty by reason of insanity (NGRI). Insanity plea that specifies an individual is not to be held legally responsible for the crime because the person had a mental illness at the time of the crime. Different states and federal law have different standards for defining mental illness and what must be demonstrated by the defense. In most cases, the defense must show that because of the mental illness,

the accused person could not conform his or her behavior to the law and did not know right from wrong when the crime was committed. Compare *guilty but mentally ill.*

obese. Currently defined as exhibiting a body mass index (BMI) greater than 30.

object relations theory. Variant of psychoanalytic theory that focuses on the way children internalize (*introject*) images of the people who are important to them (e.g., their parents), such that these internalized images (*object representations*) become part of the ego and influence how the person reacts to the world.

obsession. An intrusive and recurring thought that seems irrational and uncontrollable to the person experiencing it. Compare *compulsion.*

obsessive-compulsive disorder (OCD). An anxiety disorder involving persistent and uncontrollable thoughts or the performance of certain acts again and again, causing significant distress and interference with everyday functioning.

obsessive-compulsive personality disorder. Personality disorder defined by inordinate difficulty with making decisions, extreme concern with details and efficiency, and poor relations with others due to demands that things be done just so, as well as the person's unduly conventional, serious, formal, and stingy emotions.

operant conditioning. The acquisition or elimination of a response as a function of the environmental contingencies of reinforcement and punishment. Compare *classical conditioning.*

opioids. A group of addictive sedatives that in moderate doses relieve pain and induce sleep.

orbitofrontal cortex. The portion of the frontal lobe located just above the eyes; one of the brain regions that is unusually active in individuals with obsessive-compulsive disorder when symptoms are induced during functional neuroimaging.

orgasm phase. The third stage of the sexual response cycle, characterized by a peak of sexual pleasure, generally including ejaculation in men and contraction of the outer vaginal walls in women.

oxycodone. An opiate combined with other drugs to produce prescription pain medications, including the commonly abused drug OxyContin. See also *hydrocodone.*

panic attack. A sudden attack of intense apprehension, terror, and impending doom, accompanied by symptoms such as labored breathing, nausea, chest pain, feelings of choking and smothering, heart palpitations, dizziness, sweating, and trembling.

panic disorder. An anxiety disorder in which the individual has sudden, inexplicable, and frequent panic attacks, and then fears the possibility of another panic attack. See also *panic attack.*

paradigm. A set of basic assumptions that outlines the universe of scientific inquiry, specifying both the concepts regarded as legitimate and the methods to be used in collecting and interpreting data.

paranoid personality disorder. A personality disorder defined by expectation of mistreatment at the hands of others, suspicion, secretiveness, jealousy, argumentativeness, unwillingness to accept blame, and cold and unemotional affect.

paraphilic disorder. Sexual attraction to unusual objects or unusual sexual activities that leads to social difficulties or distress.

parasympathetic nervous system. The division of the autonomic nervous system that is involved with maintenance; controls many of the internal organs and is active primarily when the organism is not aroused. Compare *sympathetic nervous system.*

parent management training (PMT). Behavioral program in which parents are taught to modify their responses to their children so that prosocial rather than antisocial behavior is consistently rewarded.

PCP. Phencyclidine, also known by street names such as angel dust and zombie. This very powerful and hazardous drug causes profound disorientation; agitated and often violent behavior; and even seizures, coma, and death.

pedophilic disorder. A paraphilic disorder defined by a sexual attraction to prepubescent children; the person has either acted on the urges or the urges create distress or dysfunction.

penile plethysmograph. A device for detecting blood flow and thus for recording changes in the size of the penis.

persistent depressive disorder (dysthymia). A DSM-5 disorder defined by depressive symptoms that last at least 2 years.

personality disorder. A group of disorders involving long-standing, inflexible, and maladaptive personality traits that impair functioning

personality inventory A self-report questionnaire comprised of statements assessing habitual behavioral and affective tendencies.

personality trait domains. Five personality dimensions included in section III of the DSM-5 manual to help supplement diagnoses of personality disorders: negative affectivity, detachment, antagonism, disinhibition, and psychoticism.

PET scan Computer-generated picture of the living brain, created by analysis of emissions from radioactive isotopes injected into the bloodstream.

p-hacking. A problematic research practice in which researchers run multiple types of analyses in their quest to identify a significant result.

phenotype. The totality of physical characteristics and behavioral traits of an individual or of a particular trait exhibited by an individual; the product of interactions between genetics and the environment over the course of development. Compare *genotype.*

phenylketonuria (PKU). A genetic deficiency in a liver enzyme, phenylalanine hydroxylase, that causes severe intellectual disability unless phenylalanine can be largely restricted from the diet.

placebo. Any inactive therapy or chemical agent, or any attribute or component of such a therapy or chemical, that affects a person's behavior for reasons related to his or her expectation of change.

placebo effect. The action of a drug or psychological treatment that is not attributable to any specific operations of the agent. For example, a tranquilizer can reduce anxiety both because of its special biochemical action and because the recipient expects relief. See also *placebo.*

plaques. Small, round areas composed of remnants of lost neurons and beta-amyloid, a waxy protein deposit; present in the brains of patients with Alzheimer's disease.

polygenic. As applied to psychopathology or any other trait, caused by multiple genes contributing their effects, typically during multiple stages of development.

polymorphism. Any specific difference in DNA sequence that exists within a population.

positive reinforcement. The strengthening of a tendency to exhibit desired behavior by rewarding responses in that situation with a desired reward.

positive symptoms. Behavioral excesses in schizophrenia, such as hallucinations and delusions. Compare *negative symptoms.*

posttraumatic model (of DID). Etiological model of dissociative identity disorder that assumes the condition begins in childhood as a result of severe physical or sexual abuse. Compare *sociocognitive model (of DID).*

posttraumatic stress disorder (PTSD). An anxiety disorder in which a particularly stressful event, such as military combat, rape, or a natural disaster, brings in its aftermath intrusive reexperiencing of the trauma, a desire to avoid reminders of the event, changes in emotions and thought patterns, and indicators of heightened arousal.

prefrontal cortex. The region of the frontal lobe of the brain that helps maintain an image of threats and rewards faced, and also helps maintain focus and make plans relevant to those threats and rewards.

premature (early) ejaculation. Inability of the male to inhibit his orgasm long enough for mutually satisfying sexual relations.

prepared learning. In classical conditioning theory, a biological predisposition to associate evolutionarily-relevant stimuli (such as dangerous animals) readily with unconditioned stimuli.

prevalence. In epidemiological studies of a disorder, the percentage of a population that has the disorder at a given time. Compare *incidence.*

privileged communication. The communication between parties in a confidential relationship that is protected by statute, which a spouse, doctor, lawyer, pastor, psychologist, or psychiatrist thus cannot be forced to disclose, except under unusual circumstances.

proband. The person who in a genetic investigation bears the diagnosis or trait in which the investigator is interested.

projective test A psychological assessment device, such as the Rorschach series of inkblots, employing a set of standard but vague stimuli, on the assumption that unstructured material will allow unconscious motivations and fears to be uncovered.

pruning. In neural development, the selective loss of synaptic connections, especially in the

fine-tuning of brain regions devoted to sensory processing.

psychiatric nurse. A nurse, typically with a bachelor's degree, who receives specialized training in mental illness. A nurse practitioner may prescribe psychiatric medications.

psychiatrist. A physician (M.D.) who has taken specialized postdoctoral training, called a residency, in the diagnosis, treatment, and prevention of psychological disorders.

psychoanalysis. Primarily the therapy procedures pioneered by Freud, entailing free association, dream analysis, and working through the transference neurosis. More recently the term has come to encompass the numerous variations on basic Freudian therapy.

psychoanalytic theory. Theory originating with Freud that psychopathology results from unconscious conflicts in the individual.

psychoeducational approaches. Especially with bipolar disorder and schizophrenia, interventions that helps people learn about symptoms, expected time course, triggers for symptoms, and treatment strategies.

psychological disorder. The DSM defines psychological disorder as a clinically significant behavioral or psychological syndrome or patterns. The definition includes a number of key features, including distress, disability or impaired functioning, violation of social norms, and dysfunction.

psychomotor agitation. A symptom characterized by pacing, restlessness, and inability to sit still.

psychomotor retardation. A symptom commonly observed in major depressive disorder in which the person moves his or her limbs and body slowly.

psychopathology. The field concerned with the nature and development of psychological disorders.

psychopathy. A personality syndrome related to antisocial personality disorder but defined by an absence of emotion, impulsivity, manipulativeness, and irresponsibility.

psychophysiology The discipline concerned with the bodily changes that accompany psychological events.

psychotherapy. A primarily verbal means of helping troubled individuals change their thoughts, feelings, and behavior to reduce distress and to achieve greater life satisfaction.

publication bias. The tendency not to publish findings that do not support hypotheses.

questionable research practices. Selective presentation of analyses that support one's hypotheses while not disclosing analyses that fail to confirm hypotheses. Believed to contribute to nonreproducibility of findings.

random assignment. A method of assigning people to groups by chance (e.g., using a flip of a coin). The procedure helps to ensure that groups are comparable before the experimental manipulation begins.

randomized controlled trials (RCTs). Studies in which clients are randomly assigned to receive either active treatment or a comparison (a placebo condition involving no treatment or an active-treatment control group that receives another treatment); experimental treatment studies, where the independent variable is the treatment type and the dependent variable is client outcome.

reliability The extent to which a test, measurement, or classification system produces the same scientific observation each time it is applied. Reliability types include *test–retest*, the relationship between the scores that a person achieves when he or she takes the same test twice; *inter-rater*, the relationship between the judgments that at least two raters make independently about a phenomenon; split-half, the relationship between two halves of an assessment instrument that have been determined to be equivalent; alternate-form, the relationship between scores achieved by people when they complete two versions of a test that are judged to be equivalent; and internal consistency, the degree to which different items of an assessment are related to one another.

replication. A research study that duplicates the findings of a previous study.

research domain criteria (RDoc) A long-term project by the National Institute of Mental Health to develop new ways of classifying psychological disorders based on dimensions of observable behavior and neurobiological measures.

resolution phase. The fourth and final stage of the sexual response cycle, characterized by an abatement of muscle tension, relaxation, and a sense of well-being.

reuptake. Cellular process by which released neurotransmitters are taken back into the presynaptic cell, terminating their present postsynaptic effect but making them available for subsequent modulation of nerve impulse transmission.

reversal (ABAB) design. See *ABAB design*.

reward system. System of brain structures involved in the motivation to pursue rewards. Believed to be involved in depression, mania, schizophrenia, and substance use disorders.

rumination. Repetitive thought about why a person is experiencing a negative mood.

safety behaviors. Behaviors used to avoid experiencing anxiety in feared situations, such as the tendency of people with social phobia to avoid looking at other people (so as to avoid perceiving negative feedback) or the tendency of people with panic disorder to avoid exercise (so as to avoid somatic arousal that could trigger a panic attack).

schema. A mental structure for organizing information about the world.

schizoaffective disorder. Diagnosis applied when a patient has symptoms of both mood disorder and either schizophreniform disorder or schizophrenia.

schizoid personality disorder. A personality disorder defined by emotional aloofness; indifference to the praise, criticism, and feelings of others; maintenance of few, if any, close friendships; and solitary interests.

schizophrenia. A disorder characterized by disturbances in thought, emotion, and behavior; disordered thinking in which ideas are not logically related; delusional beliefs; faulty perception, such as hallucinations; disturbances in attention; disturbances in motor activity; blunted expression of emotion; reduced desire for interpersonal relations and withdrawal from people; diminished motivation and anticipatory pleasure. See also *schizoaffective disorder*, *schizophreniform disorder*, and *brief psychotic disorder*.

schizophreniform disorder. Diagnosis given to people who have all the symptoms of schizophrenia for more than 2 weeks but less than 6 months. Compare *brief psychotic disorder*.

schizotypal personality disorder. Personality disorder defined by eccentricity, oddities of thought and perception (magical thinking, illusions, depersonalization, derealization), digressive speech involving overelaborations, and social isolation; under stress, behavior may appear psychotic.

seasonal affective disorder (SAD). A subtype of mood disorders in which episodes consistently occur at the same time of year; in the most common form, major depressive episodes consistently occur in the winter.

second-generation antipsychotic drugs. Any of several drugs, such as clozapine, used to treat schizophrenia that produce fewer motor side effects than traditional antipsychotics while reducing positive and disorganized symptoms at least as effectively; may, however, be associated with increased and serious side effects of other varieties.

secondhand smoke. Also referred to as environmental tobacco smoke (ETS), the smoke from the burning end of a cigarette; contains higher concentrations of ammonia, carbon monoxide, nicotine, and tar than the smoke inhaled by the smoker.

selective mortality. The tendency for less healthy individuals to die more quickly, which leads to biased samples in long-term follow-up studies.

selective serotonin reuptake inhibitors (SSRIs). A specific form of serotonin reuptake inhibitors (SRIs) with less effect on dopamine and norepinephrine levels; SSRIs inhibit the reuptake of serotonin into the presynaptic neuron, so that serotonin levels in the cleft are sustained for a longer period.

separation anxiety disorder. A disorder in which the child feels intense fear and distress when away from someone on whom he or she is very dependent.

serotonin. A neurotransmitter of the central nervous system whose disturbances apparently figure in depression.

serotonin–norepinephrine reuptake inhibitors (SNRIs). Any of various drugs that inhibit the presynaptic reuptake of serotonin and norepinephrine, such that both neurotransmitters will have more prolonged effects on postsynaptic neurons.

serotonin transporter gene. A particular gene critical to the gene–environment interac-

tions that apparently contribute to the development of depression.

sexual dysfunctions. DSM-5 disorders involving problems with sexual arousal, desire, orgasm, or pain.

sexual masochism disorder. A paraphilic disorder defined by a sexual attraction to causing pain or humiliation.

sexual response cycle. The general pattern of sexual physical processes and feelings, made up of four phases: desire, excitement, orgasm, and resolution.

sexual sadism disorder. A paraphilic disorder defined by a sexual attraction to inflicting pain or humiliation on another person.

shared environment. Factors that family members have in common, such as income level, child-rearing practices, and parental marital status and quality. Compare *nonshared environment*.

shenjing shuairuo A common diagnosis in China, a syndrome characterized by weakness, mental fatigue, negative emotions, increased recollections, and sleep problems

single-case experimental design. A design for an experiment conducted with a single subject. Typically, behavior is measured within a baseline condition, then during an experimental or treatment condition, and finally within the baseline condition again.

single nucleotide polymorphism (SNP). A variation in gene sequence. Specifically, differences between people in a single nucleotide (A, T, G, or C) in the DNA sequence of a particular gene.

social anxiety disorder (social phobia). A collection of fears linked to the presence of other people.

social selectivity. The late-life shift in interest away from seeking new social interactions and toward cultivating those few social relationships that matter most, such as with family and close friends.

social skills training. Behavior therapy procedures, such as modeling and behavior rehearsal, for teaching individuals how to meet others, talk to them and maintain eye contact, give and receive criticism, offer and accept compliments, make requests and express feelings, and otherwise improve their relations with other people.

social worker. A mental health professional who holds a master of social work (M.S.W.) degree.

sociocognitive model (of DID). Etiological model of dissociative identity disorder that considers the condition to be the result of learning to enact social roles, though not through conscious deception, but in response to suggestion. Compare *posttraumatic model (of DID)*.

somatic symptom and related disorders. DSM-5 disorders defined by concerns about physical symptoms. See *conversion disorder*, *illness anxiety disorder, and somatic symptom disorder*.

somatic symptom disorder. A DSM-5 diagnosis defined by excessive concern and help-seeking regarding physical symptoms.

specific learning disorders. A set of developmental disorders encompassing dyslexia and dyscalculia; characterized by failure to develop in a specific academic area to the degree expected by the child's intellectual level.

specific phobia. An unwarranted fear and avoidance of a specific object or circumstance, for example, fear of nonpoisonous snakes or fear of heights.

SPECT Single photon emission computed tomography. This type of scan is particularly useful for viewing neurotransmitter activity.

spectator role. As applied by Masters and Johnson, a pattern of behavior in which the individual's focus on and concern with sexual performance causes him or her to be an observer rather than a participant, thus impeding natural sexual responses.

standardization The process of constructing a normed assessment procedure that meets the various psychometric criteria for reliability and validity.

statistical significance. A result that has a low probability of having occurred by chance alone and is by convention regarded as important. Compare *clinical significance*.

stigma. The pernicious beliefs and attitudes held by a society about groups considered deviant in some manner, such as people with mental illness.

stimulant. A drug, such as cocaine, that increases alertness and motor activity and at the same time reduces fatigue, allowing an individual to remain awake for an extended period of time.

stress State of an organism subjected to a stressor; can take the form of increased autonomic activity and in the long term can cause breakdown of an organ or development of a psychological disorder.

striatum. A neural region involved in motor action and responses to reward.

structured interview An interview in which the questions are set out in a prescribed fashion for the interviewer; assists professionals in making diagnostic decisions based on standardized criteria.

substance use disorders. Disorders in which drugs such as alcohol and cocaine are abused to such an extent that behavior becomes maladaptive, social and occupational functioning are impaired, and control or abstinence becomes impossible. Dependence on the drug may be physiological and produce tolerance and withdrawal.

suicidal ideation. Thoughts about intentionally taking one's own life.

suicide attempt. An act intended to cause one's own death.

suicide. The intentional taking of one's own life.

superego. In psychoanalytic theory, the part of the personality that acts as the conscience and reflects society's moral standards as learned from parents and teachers.

sympathetic nervous system. The division of the autonomic nervous system that acts on bodily systems—for example, contracting the blood vessels, reducing activity of the intestines, and increasing the heartbeat—to prepare the organism for exertion, emotional stress, or extreme cold. Compare *parasympathetic nervous system*.

synapse. Small gap between two neurons where the nerve signal passes electrically or chemically from the axon of the first to the dendrites, cell body, or axon of the second.

systematic desensitization. A major behavior therapy procedure that has a fearful person, while deeply relaxed, imagine a series of progressively more fearsome situations, such that fear is dispelled as a response incompatible with relaxation; useful for treating psychological problems in which anxiety is the principal difficulty.

taijin kyofusho A fear of offending others that has been observed in Japan and other cultures that place an emphasis on social hierarchy and appropriateness.

test–retest reliability See *reliability*.

theory. A formally stated and coherent set of propositions that explain and logically order a range of phenomena, generating testable predictions or hypotheses.

third-variable problem. The difficulty in the correlational method of research whereby the relationship between two variables may be attributable to a third factor.

thought-action fusion. The tendency to believe that thinking about something is as morally wrong as engaging in the action or can make the imagined event more likely to occur. Believed to contribute to the persistence of obsessions.

thought suppression. An attempt to stop a certain thought that has the paradoxical effect of inducing preoccupation with that thought; considered to intensify obsessions.

time-of-measurement effects. A possible confound in longitudinal studies whereby social context at a given point in time can have a specific effect on a variable that is being studied over time.

time-out. An operant conditioning procedure in which, after bad behavior, the person is temporarily removed from a setting where reinforcers can be obtained and placed in a less desirable setting, for example, in a boring room.

tolerance. A physiological process in which greater and greater amounts of an addictive drug are required to produce the same effect.

transcranial magnetic stimulation. A noninvasive technique in which pulsing magnets are used to intensify or diminish brain activity in a given region.

transference-focused therapy. A psychodynamic therapy that has been found to be more helpful than treatment as usual for those with borderline personality disorder, in which a focus is placed on the client's responses to the therapist and how those might shed light on experiences and expectations in the client's other relationships.

transference. The venting of the analysand's emotions, either positive or negative, by treating the psychoanalyst as the symbolic representative of someone important in the past.

treatment outcome research. Studies designed to assess whether medical or psychological approaches are efficacious in relieving symptoms of a disorder. See also *randomized controlled trials*.

tricyclic antidepressants. A group of antidepressants with molecular structures characterized by three fused rings; they interfere with the reuptake of norepinephrine and serotonin.

twin method. Research strategy in behavior genetics in which concordance rates of monozygotic and dizygotic twins are compared.

unconditioned response (UCR). See *classical conditioning*.

unconditioned stimulus (UCS). See *classical conditioning*.

unconscious. A state of unawareness without sensation or thought; in psychoanalytic theory, the part of the personality, in particular the id impulses or energy, of which the ego is unaware.

vaginal plethysmograph. A device for measuring physiological signs of sexual arousal in women; the device is shaped like a tampon and is inserted into the vagina to measure increases in blood flow.

validity In research, includes internal, the extent to which results can be confidently attributed to the manipulation of the independent variable, and external, the extent to which results can be generalized to other populations and settings. Validity as applied to psychiatric diagnoses includes concurrent, the extent to which previously undiscovered features are found among patients with the same diagnosis, and predictive, the extent to which predictions can be made about the future behavior of patients with the same diagnosis. Validity as applied to psychological and psychiatric measures includes content validity, the extent to which a measure adequately samples the domain of interest, and criterion, the extent to which a measure is associated in an expected way with some other measure (the criterion). See also *construct validity*.

vascular dementia. A form of dementia caused by cerebrovascular disease, most commonly occurring after strokes. Because the areas of the brain affected by disease can vary, the symptoms of vascular dementia vary as well.

ventricles. Cavities deep within the brain, filled with cerebrospinal fluid, that connect to the spinal cord.

voyeuristic disorder. A disorder defined by a sexual attraction to watching others in a state of undress or having sexual relations.

white matter. Neural tissue, particularly of the brain and spinal cord, consisting of tracts or bundles of myelinated (sheathed) nerve fibers. Compare *gray matter*.

withdrawal. Negative physiological and psychological reactions evidenced when a person suddenly stops taking an addictive drug; reactions include cramps, restlessness, and even death.

References

Abbey, A., & McAuslan, P. (2004). A longitudinal examination of male college students' perpetration of sexual assault. *Journal of Consulting and Clinical Psychology, 72*, 747–756. doi:10.1037/0022-006X.72.5.747

Abel, G. G., Becker, J. V., Mittelman, M., Cunningham-Rathner, J., Rouleau, J. L., & Murphy, W. D. (1987). Self-reported sex crimes of nonincarcerated paraphiliacs. *Journal of Interpersonal Violence, 2*, 3–25.

Abou-Saleh, M. T., Younis, Y., & Karim, L. (1998). Anorexia nervosa in an Arab culture. *International Journal of Eating Disorders, 23*, 207–212.

Abramovitch, A., Elliott, C. M., Wilhelm, S., Steketee, G., & Wilson, A. C. (2014). Obsessive-compulsive disorder: Assessment and treatment *The Wiley handbook of anxiety disorders* (pp. 1111–1144): John Wiley & Sons, Ltd.

Abramowitz, J. S., Franklin, M. E., Schwartz, S. A., & Furr, J. M. (2003). Symptom presentation and outcome of cognitive-behavioral therapy for obsessive-compulsive disorder. *Journal of Consulting and Clinical Psychology, 71*, 1049–1057.

Abramowitz, J. S., & Jacoby, R. J. (2015). Obsessive-compulsive and related disorders: A critical review of the new diagnostic class. *Annual Review of Clinical Psychology, 11*, 165–186. doi:10.1146/annurev-clinpsy-032813-153713

Abramowitz, J. S., Nelson, C. A., Rygwall, R., & Khandker, M. (2007). The cognitive mediation of obsessive-compulsive symptoms: A longitudinal study. *Journal of Anxiety Disorders, 21*, 91–104.

Abramson, L. Y., Metalsky, G. I., & Alloy, L. B. (1989). Hopelessness depression: A theory-based subtype of depression. *Psychological Review, 96*, 358–372.

Acarturk, C., de Graaf, R., van Straten, A., Have, M. T., & Cuijpers, P. (2008). Social phobia and number of social fears, and their association with comorbidity, health-related quality of life and help seeking: A population-based study. *Social Psychiatry and Psychiatric Epidemiology, 43*, 273–279.

Acocella, J. (1999). *Creating hysteria: Women and multiple personality disorder.* San Francisco, CA: Jossey-Bass.

Adam, D. (2014). The man who couldn't stop: OCD and the story of a life lost in thought. New York, NY: Sarah Crichton Books.

Adam, E. K., Vrshek-Schallhorn, S., Kendall, A. D., Mineka, S., Zinbarg, R. E., & Craske, M. G. (2014). Prospective associations between the cortisol awakening response and first onsets of anxiety disorders over a six-year follow-up; 2013 Curt Richter Award winner. *Psychoneuroendocrinology, 44*, 47–59. doi:10.1016/j.psyneuen.2014.02.014

Addington, J., Cadenhead, K. S., Cornblatt, B. A., Mathalon, D. H., McGlashan, T. H., Perkins, D. O., et al. (2012). North American Prodrome Longitudinal Study (NAPLS 2): Overview and recruitment. *Schizophrenia Research, 142*, 77–82.

Adler, A. (1930). *Guiding the child on the principles of individual psychology.* New York, NY: Greenberg.

Agras, W. S., Crow, S. J., Halmi, K. A., Mitchell, J. E., Wilson, G. T., & Kraemer, H. C. (2000). Outcome predictors for the cognitive-behavioral treatment of bulimia nervosa: Data from a multisite study. *American Journal of Psychiatry, 157*, 1302–1308.

Agras, W. S., Rossiter, E. M., Arnow, B., et al. (1994). One-year follow-up of psychosocial and pharmacologic treatments for bulimia nervosa. *Journal of Clinical Psychiatry, 55*, 179–183.

Agras, W. S., Rossiter, E. M., Arnow, B., Schneider, J. A., Telch, C. F., Raeburn, S. D., Bruce, B., Perl, M., & Koran, L. M. (1992). Pharmacologic and cognitive-behavioral treatment for bulimia nervosa: A controlled comparison. *American Journal of Psychiatry, 149*, 82–87.

Aguilera, A., Lopez, S. R., Breitborde, N. J., Kopelowicz, A., & Zarate, R. (2010). Expressed emotion and sociocultural moderation in the course of schizophrenia. *Journal of Abnormal Psychology, 119*, 875–885.

Ahmari, S. E., & Dougherty, D. D. (2015). Dissecting OCD circuits: From animal models to targeted treatments. *Depression and Anxiety, 32*(8), 550–562. doi:10.1002/da.22367

Aigner, M., Treasure, J., Kaye, W., Kasper, S., The WFSBP Task Force on Eating Disorders. (2011). World Federation of Societies of Biological Psychiatry (WFSBP) guidelines for the pharmacological treatment of eating disorders. *World Journal of Biological Psychiatry, 12*(6), 400–443. http://doi.org/10.3109/15622975.2011.602720

Ainsworth, M. S., Blehar, M. C., Waters, E., & Wall, S. (1978). *Patterns of attachment: A psychological study of the strange situation.* Oxford, UK: Erlbaum.

Akyüz, F., Gökalp, P. G., Erdiman, S., Oflaz, S., & Karşidağ, Ç. (2017). Conversion disorder comorbidity and childhood trauma. *Archives of Neuropsychiatry, 54*, 15–20. doi:10.5152/npa.2017.19184

Alarcon, R. D., Becker, A. E., Lewis-Fernandez, R., Like, R. C., Desai, P., Foulks, E., et al. for the Cultural Psychiatry Committee of the Group for the Advancement of Psychiatry. (2009). Issues for DSM-V: The role of culture in psychiatric diagnosis. *Journal of Nervous and Mental Disease, 197*, 559–560.

Albee, G. W., Lane, E. A., & Reuter, J. M. (1964). Childhood intelligence of future schizophrenics and neighborhood peers. *Journal of Psychology, 58*, 141–144.

Albert, M. S., Dekosky, S. T., Dickson, D., Dubois, B., Feldman, H. H., Fox, N. C., et al. (2011). The diagnosis of mild cognitive impairment due to Alzheimer's disease: Recommendations from the National Institute on Aging–Alzheimer's Association workgroups on diagnostic guidelines for Alzheimer's disease. *Alzheimer's and Dementia: The Journal of the Alzheimer's Association, 7*, 270–279.

Alden, L. E. (1989). Short-term structured treatment for avoidant personality disorder. *Journal of Consulting and Clinical Psychology, 57*, 756–764.

Alegria, A. A., Radua, J., & Rubia, K. (2016). Meta-analysis of fMRI studies of disruptive behavior disorders. *American Journal of Psychiatry, 173*, 1119–1130. http://doi.org/10.1176/appi.ajp.2016.15081089

Alegria, M., Canino, G., Shrout, P. E., Woo, M., Duan, N., & Vila, D. (2008). Prevalence of mental illness in immigrant and non-immigrant U.S. Latino groups. *American Journal of Psychiatry, 165*, 359–369.

Alegria, M., Woo, M., Cao, Z., Torres, M., Meng, X-L., & Striegel-Moore, R. (2007). Prevalence and correlates of eating disorders among Latinos in the United States. *International Journal of Eating Disorders, 40*, s15–s21.

Alexander, M. G., & Fisher, T. D. (2003). Truth and consequences: Using the bogus pipeline to examine sex differences in self-reported sexuality. *Journal of Sex Research, 40*, 27–35. doi:10.1080/00224490309552164

Alldderidge, P. (1979). Hospitals, mad houses, and asylums: Cycles in the care of the insane. *British Journal of Psychiatry, 134*, 321–324.

Allen, M., D'Alessio, D., & Brezgel, K. (1995). A meta-analysis summarizing the effects of pornography: II. Aggression after exposure. *Human Communication Research, 22*, 258–283.

Allen, P., Johns, L. C., Fu, C. H. Y., Broome, M. R., Vythelingum, G. N., & McGuire, P. K. (2004). Misattribution of external speech in patients with hallucinations and delusions. *Schizophrenia Research, 69*, 277–287.

Alloy, L. B., Abramson, L. Y., Walshaw, P. D., Cogswell, A., Grandin, L. D., Hughes, M. E., et al. (2008). Behavioral approach system and behavioral inhibition system sensitivities and bipolar spectrum disorders: Prospective prediction of bipolar mood episodes. *Bipolar Disorders, 10*, 310–322.

Alonso J., Angermeyer, M. C., Bernert, S., Bruffaerts, R., Brugha, T. S., Bryson, H., et al. (2004). Prevalence of mental disorders in Europe: results from the European Study of the Epidemiology of Mental Disorders (ESEMeD) project. *Acta Psychiatrica Scandinavica Supplement, 420*, 21–27.

Althof, S. E. (2014). Treatment of premature ejaculation: Psychotherapy, pharmacotherapy, and combined therapy. In Y. M. Binik & K. S. K. Hall (Eds.), *Principles and practice of sex therapy* (5th ed., pp. 112–137). New York, NY: Guilford Press.

Althof, S. E., McMahon, C. G., Waldinger, M. D., Serefoglu, E. C., Shindel, A. W., Adaikan, P. G., et al. (2014). An update of the International Society of Sexual Medicine's guidelines for the diagnosis and treatment of premature ejaculation (PE). *Sexual Medicine, 2*, 60–90. doi:10.1002/sm2.28

Altman, D. (1991). Weighted kappa. *Practical statistics for medical research*, 406–407.

Altshuler, L. L., Kupka, R. W., Hellemann, G., Frye, M. A., Sugar, C. A., McElroy, S. L., et al. (2010). Gender and depressive symptoms in 711 patients with bipolar disorder evaluated prospectively in the Stanley Foundation Bipolar Treatment Outcome Network. *American Journal of Psychiatry, 167*, 708–715.

Alwahhabi, F. (2003). Anxiety symptoms and generalized anxiety disorder in the elderly: A review. *Harvard Review of Psychiatry, 11*, 180–193.

Alzheimer's Association. (2016). 2016 Alzheimer's disease facts and figures. *Alzheimer's and Dementia: The Journal of the Alzheimer's Association, 12*, 459–509.

Amador, X. F., Flaum, M., Andreasen, N. C., Strauss, D. H., Yale, S. A., et al. (1994). Awareness of illness in schizophrenia and schizoaffective and mood disorder. *Archives of General Psychiatry, 51*, 826–836.

American Law Institute. (1962). *Model penal code: Proposed official draft*. Philadelphia, PA: Author.

American Psychiatric Association. (2002). *Practice Guideline for the Treatment of Patients with Bipolar Disorder* (2nd ed.). American Psychiatric Association Publishing. Retrieved from http://psychiatryonline.org/pb/assets/raw/sitewide/practice_guidelines/guidelines/bipolar.pdf

American Psychiatric Association. (2004). Practice guidelines for the treatment of patients with schizophrenia (2nd ed.) Available online at http://www.psych.org.

American Psychiatric Association. (2013). *Diagnostic and Statistical Manual of Mental Disorders 5th edition (DSM-5)*. Arlington, VA: American Psychiatric Press.

American Psychiatric Association Practice Guideline Group. (2016). *The American Psychiatric Association Practice Guideline on the use of antipsychotics to treat agitation or psychosis in patients with dementia*. Retrieved from http://psychiatryonline.org/doi/abs/10.5555/appi.books.9780890426807.ap00pre

American Psychological Association. (2004). Guidelines for psychological practice with older adults. *American Psychologist, 59*, 236–260.

American Psychological Association. (2015). Professional practice guidelines: Guidance for developers and users. *American Psychologist, 70*, 823–831. doi:10.1037/a0039644

Amir, N., Beard, C., Burns, M., & Bomyea, J. (2009). Attention modification program in individuals with generalized anxiety disorder. *Journal of Abnormal Psychology, 118*, 28–33.

Amir, N., Cashman, L., & Foa, E. B. (1997). Strategies of thought control in obsessive-compulsive disorder. *Behaviour Research and Therapy, 35*, 775–777.

Amir, N., Foa, E. B., & Coles, M. E. (1998). Negative interpretation bias in social phobia. *Behaviour Research and Therapy, 36*, 945–957.

Anand, A., Verhoeff, P., Seneca, N., Zoghbi, S. S., Seibyl, J. P., Charney, D. S., et al. (2000). Brain SPECT imaging of amphetamine-induced dopamine release in euthymic bipolar disorder patients. *American Journal of Psychiatry, 157*, 1109–1114.

Ancoli-Israel, S. (2000). Insomnia in the elderly: A review for the primary care practitioner. *Sleep, 23(Suppl 1)*, S23–30; discussion S36–28.

Andersen, S. M., Reznik, I., & Manzella, L. M. (1996). Eliciting transient affect, motivation, and expectancies in transference: Significant-other representations and the self in social relations. *Journal of Personality and Social Psychology, 71*, 1108–1129.

Anderson, C. A., Hinshaw, S. P., & Simmel, C. (1994). Mother–child interactions in ADHD and comparison boys: Relationships to overt and covert externalizing behavior. *Journal of Abnormal Child Psychology, 22*, 247–265.

Anderson, D. K., Liang, J. W., & Lord, C. (2014). Predicting young adult outcome among more and less cognitively able individuals with autism spectrum disorders. *Journal of Child Psychology and Psychiatry, 55*, 485–494.

Anderson, M. C., & Green, C. (2001). Suppressing unwanted memories by executive control. *Nature, 410*, 366–369.

Andersson, G. (2016). Internet-delivered psychological treatments. *Annual Review of Clinical Psychology, 12*(1), 157–179. doi:10.1146/annurev-clinpsy-021815-093006

Andreasen, N. C., Olsen, S. A., Dennert, J. W., & Smith, M. R. (1982). Ventricular enlargement in schizophrenia: Relationship to positive and negative symptoms. *American Journal of Psychiatry, 139*, 297–302.

Andrews, G., Charney, D. S., Sirovatka, P. J., & Regier, D. A. (Eds.). (2009). *Stress-induced and fear circuitry disorders*. Arlington, VA: American Psychiatric Association.

Andrews, G., & Williams, A. D. (2015). Up-scaling clinician assisted internet cognitive behavioural therapy (ICBT) for depression: A model for dissemination into primary care. *Clinical Psychology Review, 41*, 40–48. doi:http://dx.doi.org/10.1016/j.cpr.2014.05.006

Andrilla, C. H. A., Coulthard, C., & Larson, E. H. (2017). Barriers rural physicians face prescribing buprenorphine for opioid use disorder. *Annals of Family Medicine, 15*, 359–362. http://doi.org/10.1370/afm.2099

Anglemyer, A., Horvath, T., & Rutherford, G. (2014). The accessibility of firearms and risk for suicide and homicide victimization among household members: A systematic review and meta-analysis. *Annals of Internal Medicine, 160*(2), 101–110. doi:10.7326/M13–1301

Angrist, B., Lee, H. K., & Gershon, S. (1974). The antagonism of amphetamine-induced symptomatology by a neuroleptic. *American Journal of Psychiatry, 131*, 817–819.

Angst, F., Stassen, H. H., Clayton, P. J., & Angst, J. (2002). Mortality of patients with mood disorders: Follow-up over 34–38 years. *Journal of Affective Disorders, 68*, 167–181.

Anguera, J. A., Boccanfuso, J., Rintoul, J. L., Al-Hashimi, O., Faraji, F., Janowich, J., et al. (2013). Video game training enhances cognitive control in older adults. *Nature, 501*, 97–101.

Ansell, E. B., Pinto, A., Edelen, M. O., Markowitz, J. C., Sanislow, C. A., Yen, S., et al. (2011). The association of personality disorders with the prospective 7-year course of anxiety disorders. *Psychological Medicine, 41*, 1019–1028.

Anstey, K. J., Cherbuin, N., Budge, M., & Young, J. (2011). Body mass index in midlife and late-life as a risk factor for dementia: A meta-analysis of prospective studies. *Obesity Reviews, 12*, e426–e437. doi:10.1111/j.1467-789X.2010.00825.x

Anthony, J. L., & Lonigan, C. L. (2004). The nature of phonological awareness: Converging evidence from four studies of preschool and early grade school children. *Journal of Educational Psychology, 96*, 43–55.

Appelbaum, P. S., & Gutheil, T. (1991). *Clinical handbook of psychiatry and the law*. Baltimore, MD: Williams & Wilkins.

Appignannesi, L. (2008). *Mad, bad, and sad: Women and the mind doctors*. New York, NY: W. W. Norton.

Arbisi, P. A., Ben-Porath, Y. S., & McNulty, J. (2002). A comparison of MMPI-2 validity in African American and Caucasian psychiatric patients. *Psychological Assessment, 14*, 3–15.

Arcelus, J., Mitchell, A. J., Wales, J., et al. (2011). Mortality rates in patients with anorexia nervosa and other eating disorders. *Archives of General Psychiatry, 68*(7), 724–731. http://doi.org/10.1001/archgenpsychiatry.2011.74

Armstrong, E. A., England, P., & Fogarty, A. C. K. (2009). Orgasm in college hookups and relationships. In B. J. Risman (Ed.), *Families as they really are* (pp. 362–377). New York, NY: Norton.

Arnett, J. J. (2008). The neglected 95%: Why American psychology needs to become less American. *American Psychologist, 63*, 602–614.

Arnold, E. H., O'Leary, S. G., & Edwards, G. H. (1997). Father involvement and self-reported parenting of children with attention deficit hyperactivity disorder. *Journal of Consulting and Clinical Psychology, 65*, 337–342.

Arnold, L. E., Elliott, M., Sachs, L., Kraemer, H. C., Wells, K. C., Abikoff, H. B., et al. (2003). Effects of ethnicity on treatment attendance, stimulant response/dose, and 14-month outcome in ADHD. *Journal of Consulting and Clinical Psychology, 71*, 713–727.

Arnold, L. M., Keck, P. E., Jr., Collins J., Wilson, R., Fleck, D. E., Corey, K. B., Amicone, J., Adebimpe, V. R., & Strakowski, S. M. (2004). Ethnicity and first-rank symptoms in patients with psychosis. *Schizophrenia Research, 67*, 207–212.

Arnow, B., Kenardy, J., & Agras, W. S. (1992). Binge eating among the obese. *Journal of Behavioral Medicine, 15*, 155–170.

Arseneault, L., Cannon, M., Poulton, R., Murray, R., Caspi, A., & Moffitt, T. E. (2002). *Cannabis* use in adolescence and risk for adult psychosis: Longitudinal prospective study. *British Medical Journal, 325*, 1212–1213.

Ascher, E. A., Sturm, V. E., Seider, B. H., Holley, S. R., Miller, B. L., & Levenson, R. W. (2010). Relationship satisfaction and emotional language in frontotemporal dementia and Alzheimer's disease patients and spousal caregivers. *Alzheimer's Disease and Associated Disorders, 24,* 49–55.

Ashbaugh, A. R., Antony, M. M., McCabe, R. E., Schmidt, L. A., & Swinson, R. P. (2005). Self-evaluative biases in social anxiety. *Cognitive Therapy and Research, 29,* 387–398.

Asmundson, G. J., Larsen, D. K., & Stein, M. B. (1998). Panic disorder and vestibular disturbance: An overview of empirical findings and clinical implications. *Journal of Psychosomatic Research, 44,* 107–120.

Attia, E., Becker, A. E., Bryant-Waugh, R., Hoek, H. W., Kreipe, R. E., Marcus, M. D., et al. (2013). Feeding and eating disorders in DSM-5. *American Journal of Psychiatry, 170,* 1237–1239.

Attia, E., Haiman, C., Walsh, B. T., & Flater, S. R. (1998). Does fluoxetine augment the inpatient treatment of anorexia nervosa? *American Journal of Psychiatry, 155,* 548–551.

Atwoli, L., Stein, D. J., Koenen, K. C., & McLaughlin, K. A. (2015). Epidemiology of posttraumatic stress disorder: Prevalence, correlates and consequences. *Current Opinion in Psychiatry, 28*(4), 307–311. doi:10.1097/yco.0000000000000167

Audrain-McGovern, J., Rodriguez, D., Epstein, L. H., Cuevas, J., Rodgers, K., & Wiley, E. P. (2009). Does delay discounting play an etiological role in smoking or is it a consequence of smoking? *Drug and Alcohol Dependence, 103,* 99–106.

Audrain-McGovern, J., & Tercyak, K. P. (2011). Genes, environment, and adolescent smoking: Implications for prevention. In K. S. Kendler, S. R. Jaffee, & D. Romer (Eds.), *The dynamic genome and mental health* (pp. 294–321). New York, NY: Oxford University Press.

Auerbach, R. P., Alonso, J., Axinn, W. G., Cuijpers, P., Ebert, D. D., Green, J. G., et al. (2016). Mental disorders among college students in the World Health Organization World Mental Health Surveys. *Psychological Medicine, 46*(14), 2955–2970. doi:10.1017/S0033291716001665

Autism Spectrum Disorders Working Group of the Psychiatric Genomics Consortium. (2017). Meta-analysis of GWAS of over 16,000 individuals with autism spectrum disorder highlights a novel locus at 10q24.32 and a significant overlap with schizophrenia. *Molecular Autism, 8*(1), 21.

Avenevoli, S., Swendsen, J., He, J.-P., Burstein, M., & Merikangas, K. R. (2015). Major depression in the national comorbidity survey adolescent supplement: Prevalence, correlates, and treatment. *Journal of the American Academy of Child & Adolescent Psychiatry, 54*(1), 37–44.e32. doi:10.1016/j.jaac.2014.10.010

Aviv, R. (2017, April 3, 2017). The apathetic: Why are refugee children falling unconscious? *The New Yorker,* 68–77.

Axelsson, E., Andersson, E., Ljótsson, B., Wallhed Finn, D., & Hedman, E. (2016). The health preoccupation diagnostic interview: Inter-rater reliability of a structured interview for diagnostic assessment of DSM-5 somatic symptom disorder and illness anxiety disorder. *Cognitive Behaviour Therapy, 45,* 259–269. doi:10.1080/16506073.2016.1161663

Aybek, S., & Vuilleumier, P. (2016). Imaging studies of functional neurologic disorders. *Handbook of Clinical Neurology, 139,* 73–84. doi:http://dx.doi.org/10.1016/B978-0-12-801772-2.00007-2

Babchishin, K. M., Hanson, R. K., & VanZuylen, H. (2015). Online child pornography offenders are different: A meta-analysis of the characteristics of online and offline sex offenders against children. *Archives of Sexual Behavior, 44,* 45–66. doi:10.1007/s10508-014-0270-x

Babiak, P., Neumann, C. S., & Hare, R. D. (2010). Corporate psychopathy: Talking the walk. *Behavioral Sciences and the Law, 28,* 174–193.

Baer, R. A., & Sekirnjak, G. (1997). Detection of underreporting on the MMPI-II in a clinical population. Effects of information about validity scales. *Journal of Personality Assessment, 69,* 555–567.

Bagayogo, I. P., Interian, A., & Escobar, J. I. (2013). Transcultural aspects of somatic symptoms in the context of depressive disorders. *Advances in Psychosomatic Medicine, 33,* 64–74. doi:10.1159/000350057

Bagby, M. R., Nicholson, R. A., Bacchionchi, J. R., et al. (2002). The predictive capacity of the MMPI-2 and PAI validity scales and indexes to detect coached and uncoached feigning. *Journal of Personality Assessment, 78,* 69–86.

Bailer, J., Kerstner, T., Witthöft, M., Diener, C., Mier, D., & Rist, F. (2016). Health anxiety and hypochondriasis in the light of DSM-5. *Anxiety, Stress, & Coping, 29,* 219–239. doi:10.1080/10615806.2015.1036243

Bailey, A., Le Couteur, A., Gottesman, I., Bolton, P., Simonoff, E., Yuzda, E., & Rutter, M. (1995). Autism as a strongly genetic disorder: Evidence from a British twin study. *Psychological Medicine, 25,* 63–77.

Bailey, S. (2014). The role of branding and advertising in the soft drink industry. *Market Realist.* Retrieved from http://marketrealist.com/2014/11/role-branding-advertising-soft-drink-industry/

Baillargeon, J., Binswanger, I. A., Penn, J. V., Williams, B. A., & Murray, O. J. (2009). Psychiatric disorders and repeat incarcerations: The revolving prison door. *American Journal of Psychiatry, 166*(1), 103–109.

Baker, J. H., Mitchell, K. S., Neale, M. C., & Kendler, K. S. (2010). Eating disorder symptomatology and substance use disorders: Prevalence and shared risk in a population based twin sample. *International Journal of Eating Disorders, 43,* 648–658.

Baldwin, D. S., Aitchison, K., Bateson, A., Curran, H. V., Davies, S., Leonard, B., et al. (2013). Benzodiazepines: Risks and benefits. A reconsideration. *Journal of Psychopharmacology, 27*(11), 967–971. doi:10.1177/0269881113503509

Ball, J. C., & Ross, A. (1991). *The effectiveness of methadone maintenance treatment.* New York, NY: Springer-Verlag.

Balon, R. (2016). *Practical guide to paraphilia and paraphilic disorders.* Charm, Switzerland: Springer.

Balsis, S., Carpenter, B. D., & Storandt, M. (2005). Personality change precedes clinical diagnosis of dementia of the Alzheimer type. *Journal of Gerontology, 60B,* 98–101.

Balsis, S., Gleason, M. E., Woods, C. M., & Oltmanns, T. F. (2007). An item response theory analysis of DSM-IV personality disorder criteria across younger and older age groups. *Psychology and Aging, 22,* 171–185.

Bandelow, B., Baldwin, D., Abelli, M., Altamura, C., Dell'Osso, B., Domschke, K., et al. (2016). Biological markers for anxiety disorders, OCD and PTSD—a consensus statement. Part I: Neuroimaging and genetics. *The World Journal of Biological Psychiatry, 17*(5), 321–365.

Bandelow, B., Baldwin, D., Abelli, M., Bolea-Alamanac, B., Bourin, M., Chamberlain, S. R., et al. (2017). Biological markers for anxiety disorders, OCD and PTSD: A consensus statement. Part II: Neurochemistry, neurophysiology and neurocognition. *The World Journal of Biological Psychiatry, 18*(3), 162–214. doi:10.1080/15622975.2016.1190867

Bandelow, B., Sher, L., Bunevicius, R., Hollander, E., Kasper, S., Zohar, J., et al. (2012). Guidelines for the pharmacological treatment of anxiety disorders, obsessive-compulsive disorder and posttraumatic stress disorder in primary care. *International Journal of Psychiatry and Clinical Practice, 16*(2), 77–84. doi:10.3109/13651501.2012.667114

Bandura, A., & Menlove, F. L. (1968). Factors determining vicarious extinction of avoidance behavior through symbolic modeling. *Journal of Personality and Social Psychology, 8,* 99–108.

Bang, J., Spina, S., & Miller, B. L. (2015). Frontotemporal dementia. *The Lancet, 386,* 1672–1682. doi:10.1016/S0140-6736(15)00461-4

Bantin, T., Stevens, S., Gerlach, A. L., & Hermann, C. (2016). What does the facial dot-probe task tell us about attentional processes in social anxiety? A systematic review. *Journal of Behavior Therapy and Experimental Psychiatry, 50,* 40–51. doi:http://doi.org/10.1016/j.jbtep.2015.04.009

Barbato, A., & D'Avanzo, B. (2008). Efficacy of couple therapy as a treatment for depression: A meta-analysis. *Psychiatric Quarterly, 79,* 121–132.

Barber, C. (2008). *Comfortably numb.* New York, NY: Pantheon Books.

Barber, C. (2008). *Comfortably numb.* New York: Pantheon Books.

Barber, C. W., & Miller, M. J. (2014). Reducing a suicidal person's access to lethal means of suicide: A research agenda. *American Journal of Preventive Medicine, 47*(3, Supplement 2), S264–S272. doi:http://doi.org/10.1016/j.amepre.2014.05.028

Barboza, G. E., Dominguez, S., & Chance, E. (2016). Physical victimization, gender identity and suicide risk among transgender men and women. *Preventive Medicine Reports, 4,* 385–390. doi:10.1016/j.pmedr.2016.08.003

Barch, D. M., Carter, C. S., Braver, T. S., et al. (2001). Selective deficits in prefrontal cortex function in medication-naïve patients with schizophrenia. *Archives of General Psychiatry, 58,* 280–288.

Barch, D. M., Csernansky, J. G., Conturo, T., & Snyder, A. Z. (2002). Working and long-term memory deficits in schizophrenia: Is there a common prefrontal mechanism? *Journal of Abnormal Psychology, 111*, 478–494.

Bardone-Cone, A. M., Wonderlich, S. A., Frost, R. O., Bulik, C. M., Mitchell, J., et al. (2007). Perfectionism and eating disorders: Current status and future directions. *Clinical Psychology Review, 27*, 384–405.

Bar-Haim, Y., Lamy, D., Pergamin, L., Bakermans-Kranenburg, M. J., & van Ijzendoorn, M. H. (2007). Threat-related attentional bias in anxious and nonanxious individuals: A meta-analytic study. *Psychological Bulletin, 133*, 1–24.

Barkley, R. A. (1981). *Hyperactive children: A handbook for diagnosis and treatment.* New York, NY: Guilford Press.

Barkley, R. A. (1997) Behavioral inhibition, sustained attention, and executive functions: Constructing a unifying theory of ADHD. *Psychological Bulletin, 121*, 65–94.

Barkley, R. A., DuPaul, G. J., & McMurray, M. B. (1990). A comprehensive evaluation of attention deficit disorder with and without hyperactivity defined by research criteria. *Journal of Consulting and Clinical Psychology, 58*, 775–789.

Barkley, R. A., Fischer, M., Smallish, L., & Fletcher, K. (2002). The persistence of attention-deficit hyperactivity disorder into young adulthood as a function of reporting source and definition of disorder. *Journal of Abnormal Psychology, 111*, 279–289.

Barkley, R. A., Fischer, M., Smallish, L., & Fletcher, K. (2003). Does the treatment of attention-deficit/hyperactivity disorder with stimulants contribute to drug use/abuse? A 13 year prospective study. *Pediatrics, 111*, 97–109.

Barkley, R. A., Karlsson, J., & Pollard, S. (1985). Effects of age on the mother-child interactions of hyperactive children. *Journal of Abnormal Child Psychology, 13*, 631–638.

Barlow, D. H. (2004). *Anxiety and its disorders: The nature and treatment of anxiety and panic.* New York: Guilford Press.

Barnwal, P., Das, S., Mondal, S., Ramasamy, A., Maiti, T., & Saha, A. (2017). Probuphine® (buprenorphine implant): A promising candidate in opioid dependence. *Therapeutic Advances in Psychopharmacology, 7*, 119–134. http://doi.org/10.1177/2045125316681984

Barrett, B., Tyrer, P., Tyrer, H., Cooper, S., Crawford, M. J., & Byford, S. (2012). An examination of the factors that influence costs in medical patients with health anxiety. *Journal of Psychosomatic Research, 73*, 59–62.

Barrett, L. F. (2003). So you want to be a social neuroscientist? *APS Observer, 16*, 5–7.

Barsky, A. (2006). "Doctor, are you sure my heart is okay?" Cognitive-behavioral treatment of hypochondriasis. In R. L. Spitzer, M. B. W. First, J. B. Williams, & M. Gibbon (Eds.), *DSM-IV-TR® casebook, volume 2: Experts tell how they treated their own patients* (pp. 251–261). Washington, DC: American Psychiatric Association.

Barsky, A. J., Orav, E. J., & Bates, D. W. (2005). Somatization increases medical utilization and costs independent of psychiatric and medical comorbidity. *Archives of General Psychiatry, 62*, 903–910.

Baskin-Sommers, A. R. (2016). Dissecting antisocial behavior. *Clinical Psychological Science, 4*, 500–510. doi:10.1177/2167702615626904

Baskin-Sommers, A. R., Baskin, D. R., Sommers, I., Casados, A. T., Crossman, M. K., & Javdani, S. (2016). The impact of psychopathology, race, and environmental context on violent offending in a male adolescent sample. *Personality Disorders: Theory, Research, and Treatment, 7*, 354–362. doi:10.1037/per0000168

Baskin-Sommers, A. R., Brazil, I. A., Ryan, J., Kohlenberg, N. J., Neumann, C. S., & Newman, J. P. (2015). Mapping the association of global executive functioning onto diverse measures of psychopathic traits. *Personality Disorders: Theory, Research, and Treatment, 6*, 336–346. doi:10.1037/per0000125

Bass, E., & Davis, L. (2008). *The courage to heal: A guide for women survivors of child sexual abuse* (4th ed.). New York, NY: HarperCollins.

Bassett, A. S., Scherer, S. W., & Brzustowicz, L. M. (2010). Copy number variations in schizophrenia: Critical review and new perspectives on concepts genetics and disease. *American Journal of Psychiatry, 167*, 899–914.

Basson, R., Althof, S. A., Davis, S., Fugl-Meyer, K., Goldstein, I., Leiblum, S., et al. (2004). Summary of the recommendations on sexual dysfunctions in women. *Journal of Sexual Medicine, 1*, 24–34.

Basson, R., Brotto, L. A., Laan, E., Redmond, G., & Utian, W. H. (2005). Assessment and management of women's sexual dysfunctions: Problematic desire and arousal. *Journal of Sexual Medicine, 2*, 291–300.

Bateman, A. W., & Fonagy, P. (2004). Mentalization-based treatment of BPD. *Journal of Personality Disorders, 18*, 36–51. doi:10.1521/pedi.18.1.36.32772

Baur, E., Forsman, M., Santtila, P., Johansson, A., Sandnabba, K., & Langstrom, N. (2016). Paraphilic sexual interests and sexually coercive behavior: A population-based twin study. *Archives of Sexual Behavior, 45*, 1163–1172. doi:10.1007/s10508-015-0674-2

Baxter, A. J., Scott, K. M., Vos, T., & Whiteford, H. A. (2013). Global prevalence of anxiety disorders: A systematic review and meta-regression. *Psychological Medicine, 43*(5), 897–910. doi:10.1017/s003329171200147x

Baxter, L. R., Ackermann, R. F., Swerdlow, N. R., Brody, A., Saxena, S., Schwartz, J. M., et al. (2000). Specific brain system mediation of obsessive-compulsive disorder responsive to either medication or behavior therapy. In W. K. Goodman, M. V. Rudorfer, & J. D. Maser (Eds.), *Obsessive-compulsive disorder: Contemporary issues in treatment* (pp. 573–610). Mahwah, NJ: Lawrence Erlbaum.

Beardslee, W. R., Brent, D. A., Weersing, V. R., Clarke, G. N., Porta, G., Hollon, S. D., et al. (2013). Prevention of depression in at-risk adolescents. *JAMA Psychiatry, 70*(11), 1161–1170. http://doi.org/10.1001/jamapsychiatry.2013.295

Beauchaine, T. P., Hinshaw, S. P., & Pang, K. L. (2010). Comorbidity of attention-deficit/hyperactivity disorder and early-onset conduct disorder: Biological, environmental, and developmental mechanisms. *Clinical Psychology: Science and Practice, 17*, 327–336.

Beautrais, A. L., Gibb, S. J., Fergusson, D., Horwood, L. J., & Larkin, G. L. (2009). Removing bridge barriers stimulates suicides: An unfortunate natural experiment. *Australian and New Zealand Journal of Psychiatry, 43*, 495–497.

Bechara, A. (2005). Decision making, impulse control and loss of willpower to resist drugs: A neurocognitive perspective. *Nature Neuroscience, 8*, 1458–1463.

Beck, A. T. (1967). *Depression: Clinical, experimental and theoretical aspects.* New York, NY: Harper & Row.

Beck, A. T. (1976). *Cognitive therapy and the emotional disorders.* New York, NY: International Universities Press.

Beck, A. T., & Freeman, A. (1990). *Cognitive therapy for personality disorders.* New York, NY: Guilford Press.

Beck, A. T., & Rector, N. A. (2000). Cognitive therapy of schizophrenia: A new therapy for the new millennium. *American Journal of Psychotherapy, 54*, 291–300.

Becker, B., Scheele, D., Moessner, R., Maier, W., & Hurlemann, R. (2013). Deciphering the neural signature of conversion blindness. *American Journal of Psychiatry, 170*, 121–122.

Becker, C. B., Zayfert, C., & Anderson, E. (2004). A survey of psychologists' attitudes towards and utilization of exposure therapy for PTSD. *Behaviour Research and Therapy, 42*(3), 277–292. doi:10.1016/s0005-7967(03)00138-4

Beck, J. G., & Bozman, A. (1995). Gender differences in sexual desire: The effects of anger and anxiety. *Archives of Sexual Behavior, 24*, 595–612.

Beevers, C. G., Lee, H. J., Wells, T. T., Ellis, A. J., & Telch, M. J. (2011). Association of predeployment gaze bias for emotion stimuli with later symptoms of PTSD and depression in soldiers deployed in Iraq. *American Journal of Psychiatry, 168*, 735–741.

Belcher, A. M., Volkow, N. D., Moeller, F. G., & Ferre, S. (2014). Personality traits and vulnerability or resilience to substance use disorders. *Trends in Cognitive Sciences, 18*, 211–217.

Belsky, D. W., Caspi, A., Arseneault, L., Bleidorn, W., Fonagy, P., Goodman, M., et al. (2012). Etiological features of borderline personality related characteristics in a birth cohort of 12-year-old children. *Development and Psychopathology, 24*, 251–265. doi:10.1017/s0954579411000812

Benge, J. F., Wisdom, N. M., Collins, R. L., Franks, R., LeMaire, A., & Chen, D. K. (2012). Diagnostic utility of the Structured Inventory of Malingered Symptomatology for identifying psychogenic non-epileptic events. *Epilepsy & Behavior, 24*, 439–444. doi:https://doi.org/10.1016/j.yebeh.2012.05.007

Benjamin, C. L., Harrison, J. P., Settipani, C. A., Brodman, D. M., & Kendall, P. C. (2013). Anxiety and related outcomes in young adults 7 to 19 years after receiving treatment for child anxiety. *Journal of Consulting and Clinical Psychology, 81*(5), 865–876.

Benowitz, N., Pérez-Stable, E., Herrera, B., & Jacob, P. (2002). Slower metabolism and reduced intake of nicotine from cigarette smoking in Chinese-Americans. *Journal of the National Cancer Institute, 94,* 108–115.

Berenz, E. C., Amstadter, A. B., Aggen, S. H., Knudsen, G. P., Reichborn-Kjennerud, T., Gardner, C. O., et al. (2013). Childhood trauma and personality disorder criterion counts: A co-twin control analysis. *Journal of Abnormal Psychology, 122,* 1070–1076.

Berkman, E. T., Falk, E. M., & Lieberman, M. D. (2011). In the trenches of real-world self-control: Neural correlates of breaking the link between craving and smoking. *Psychological Science, 22,* 498–506.

Berlim, M. T., van den Eynde, F., Tovar-Perdomo, S., & Daskalakis, Z. J. (2014). Response, remission and drop-out rates following high-frequency repetitive transcranial magnetic stimulation (RTMS) for treating major depression: A systematic review and meta-analysis of randomized, double-blind and sham-controlled trials. *Psychological Medicine, 44*(2), 225–239. doi:10.1017/s0033291713000512

Berman, M., & Philips, A. (2017, March 30). North Carolina governor signs bill repealing and replacing transgender bathroom law amid criticism. *Washington Post.*

Bernal, M., Haro, J. M., Bernert, S., Brugha, T., de Graaf, R., Bruffaerts, R., et al. (2007). Risk factors for suicidality in Europe: Results from the ESEMED study. *Journal of Affective Disorders, 101,* 27–34.

Berridge, K. C., Ho, C. Y., Richard, J. M., & DiFeliceantonio, A. G. (2010). The tempted brain eats: Pleasure and desire circuits in obesity and eating disorders. *Brain Research, 1350,* 43–64. http://dx.doi.org/10.1016/j.brainres.2010.04.003

Berry, J. C. (1967). *Antecedents of schizophrenia, impulsive character and alcoholism in males.* Paper presented at the 75th Annual Convention of the American Psychological Association, Washington, DC.

Beydoun, M. A., Beydoun, H. A., Gamaldo, A. A., Teel, A., Zonderman, A. B., & Wang, Y. (2014). Epidemiologic studies of modifiable factors associated with cognition and dementia: Systematic review and meta-analysis. *BMC Public Health, 14,* 643. doi:10.1186/1471-2458-14-643

Bhugra, D., Popelyuk, D., & McMullen, I. (2010). Paraphilias across cultures: Contexts and controversies. *Journal of Sex Research, 47,* 242–256.

Bhutta, A. T., Cleves, M. A., Casey, P. H., Cradock, M. M., & Anand, K. J. (2002). Cognitive and behavioral outcomes of school-aged children who were born preterm: A meta-analysis. *Journal of the American Medical Association, 288,* 728–737.

Bickel, W. K., Koffarnus, M. N., Moody, L., & Wilson, A. G. (2014). The behavioral- and neuro-economic process of temporal discounting: A candidate behavioral marker of addiction. *Neuropharmacology, 76, Part B,* 518–527.

Bickel, W. K., Miller, M. L., Yi, R., Kowal, B. P., Lindquist, D. M., & Pitcock, J. A. (2007). Behavioral and neuroeconomics of drug addiction: Competing neural systems and temporal discounting processes. *Drug and Alcohol Dependence, 90,* S85–S91.

Biederman, J., & Faraone, S. (2004). The Massachusetts General Hospital studies of gender influences on attention-deficit/hyperactivity disorder in youth and relatives. *Psychiatric Clinics of North America, 27,* 215–224.

Biederman, J., Mick, E., Spencer, T., Wilens, T. E., Wozniak, J., et al. (2000). Pediatric mania: A developmental subtype of bipolar disorder? *Biological Psychiatry, 48,* 458–466.

Biederman, J., Monuteaux, M. C., Mick, E., Spencer, T., Wilens, T. E., Silva, J. M., et al. (2006). Young adult outcome of attention deficit hyperactivity disorder: A controlled 10-year follow-up study. *Psychological Medicine, 36,* 167–179.

Biederman, J., Petty, C. R., Monuteaux, M. C., Fried, R., Byrne, D., Mirto, T., et al. (2010). Adult psychiatric outcomes of girls with attention deficit hyperactivity disorder: 11-year follow-up in a longitudinal case-control study. *American Journal of Psychiatry, 167,* 409–417.

Bighelli, I., Trespidi, C., Castellazzi, M., Cipriani, A., Furukawa, T. A., Girlanda, F., et al. (2016). Antidepressants and benzodiazepines for panic disorder in adults. *Cochrane Database of Systematic Reviews* (9). doi:10.1002/14651858.CD011567.pub2

Binik, Y. M. (2010). The DSM diagnostic criteria for vaginismus. *Archives of Sexual Behavior, 39,* 278–291.

Binzer, M., & Kullgren, G. (1996). Conversion symptoms: What can we learn from previous studies? *Nordic Journal of Psychiatry, 50,* 143–152.

Birbaumer, N., Veit, R., Lotze, M., Erb, M., Hermann, C., Grodd, W., et al. (2005). Deficient fear conditioning in psychopathy: A functional magnetic resonance imaging study. *Archives of General Psychiatry, 62,* 799–805.

Birnbaum, G. E., Reis, H. T., Mikulincer, M., Gillath, O., & Orpaz, A. (2006). When sex is more than just sex: Attachment orientations, sexual experience, and relationship quality. *Journal of Personality and Social Psychology, 91,* 929–943.

Blachman, D. R., & Hinshaw, S. P. (2002). Patterns of friendship among girls with and without attention-deficit/hyperactivity disorder. *Journal of Abnormal Child Psychology, 30,* 625–640.

Blair, R. J. (2013). The neurobiology of psychopathic traits in youths. *Nature Reviews Neuroscience, 14*(11), 786–799.

Blair, R. J. R. (2005). Responding to the emotions of others: Dissociating forms of empathy through the study of typical and psychiatric populations. *Consciousness and Cognition, 14,* 698–718.

Blanchard, J. J., Brown, S. A., Horan, W. P., & Sherwood, A. R. (2000). Substance use disorders in schizophrenia: Review, integration, and a proposed model. *Clinical Psychology Review, 20,* 207–234.

Blanchard, J. J., & Brown, S. B. (1998). Structured diagnostic interviews. In C. R. Reynolds (Ed.), *Comprehensive clinical psychology, Volume 3, assessment* (pp. 97–130). New York, NY: Elsevier.

Blanchard, J. J., & Cohen, A. S. (2006). The structure of negative symptoms within schizophrenia: Implications for assessment. *Schizophrenia Bulletin, 32,* 238–245.

Blanchard, J. J., Squires, D., Henry, T., Horan, W. P., Bogenschutz, M., et al. (1999). Examining an affect regulation model of substance abuse in schizophrenia: The role of traits and coping. *Journal of Nervous and Mental Disease, 187,* 72–79.

Blanchard, R., Kuban, M. E., Blak, T., Cantor, J. M., Klassen, P. E., & Dickey, R. (2009). Absolute versus relative ascertainment of pedophilia in men. *Sex Abuse, 21,* 431–441. doi:10.1177/1079063209347906

Blanchflower, D. G., & Oswald, A. J. (2008). Is well-being U-shaped over the life cycle? *Social Science & Medicine, 66,* 1733–1749. https://doi.org/10.1016/j.socscimed.2008.01.030

Blanco, C., Garcia-Anaya, M., Wall, M., de Los Cobos, J. C. P., Swierad, E., Wang, S., & Petry, N. M. (2015). Should pathological gambling and obesity be considered addictive disorders? A factor analytic study in a nationally representative sample. *Drug and Alcohol Dependence, 150,* 129–134. doi:10.1016/j.drugalcdep.2015.02.018

Bloch, M. H., Bartley, C. A., Zipperer, L., Jakubovski, E., Landeros-Weisenberger, A., Pittenger, C., & Leckman, J. F. (2014). Meta-analysis: Hoarding symptoms associated with poor treatment outcome in obsessive-compulsive disorder. *Molecular Psychiatry, 19*(9), 1025–1030. doi:10.1038/mp.2014.50

Bloomberg Data. (2012). Most rapidly aging countries. *Data adapted from United Nations Population Division, International Labor Division.* Retrieved from http://www.bloomberg.com/visual-data/best-and-worst/most-rapidly-aging-countries

Boardman, J. D., Saint Onge, J. M., Haberstick, B. C., Timberlake, D. S., & Hewitt, J. K. (2008). Do schools moderate the genetic determinants of smoking? *Behavioral Genetics, 28,* 234–246.

Bockhoven, J. (1963). *Moral treatment in American psychiatry.* New York, NY: Springer-Verlag.

Boegels, S. M., & Zigterman, D. (2000). Dysfunctional cognitions in children with social phobia, separation anxiety disorder, and generalized anxiety disorder. *Journal of Abnormal Child Psychology, 28,* 205–211.

Boets, B., Op de Beeck, H. P., Vandermosten, M., Scott, S. K., Gillebert, C. R., Mantini, D., et al. (2013). Intact but less accessible phonetic representations in adults with dyslexia. *Science, 342*(6163), 1251–1254.

Bohlken, M. M., Brouwer, R. M., Mandl, R. C. W., van den Heuvel, M. P., Hedman, A. M., De Hert, M., et al. (2016). Structural brain connectivity as a genetic marker for schizophrenia. *JAMA Psychiatry, 73,* 11–19. http://doi.org/10.1001/jamapsychiatry.2015.1925

Boiger, M., & Mesquita, B. (2012). The construction of emotion in interactions, relationships, and cultures. *Emotion Review, 4,* 221–229.

Boisseau, C. L., Yen, S., Markowitz, J. C., Grilo, C. M., Sanislow, C. A., Shea, M. T., et al. (2013). Individuals with single versus multiple suicide attempts over 10 years of prospective follow-up. *Comprehensive Psychiatry, 54*, 238–242.

Bonanno, G. A. (2004). Loss, trauma, and human resilience: Have we underestimated the human capacity to thrive after extremely aversive events? *American Psychologist, 59*, 20–28.

Bondi, M. W., Edmonds, E. C., Jak, A. J., Clark, L. R., Delano-Wood, L., McDonald, C. R., et al. (2014). Neuropsychological criteria for mild cognitive impairment improves diagnostic precision, biomarker associations, and progression rates. *Journal of Alzheimers Disease, 42*, 275–289. doi:10.3233/jad-140276

Bond, K., & Anderson, I. M. (2015). Psychoeducation for relapse prevention in bipolar disorder: a systematic review of efficacy in randomized controlled trials. *Bipolar Disorders, 17*, 349–362. doi: 10.1111/bdi.12287

Bonta, J., Law, M., & Hanson, K. (1998). The prediction of criminal and violent recidivism among mentally disordered offenders. *Psychological Bulletin, 123*, 123–142.

Bookheimer, S., & Burggren, A. (2009). APOE ε4 genotype and neurophysiological vulnerability to Alzheimer's and cognitive aging. *Annual Review of Clinical Psychology, 5*, 343–362.

Boone, L., Soenens, B., & Luyten, P. (2014). When or why does perfectionism translate into eating disorder pathology? A longitudinal examination of the moderating and mediating role of body dissatisfaction. *Journal of Abnormal Psychology, 123*, 412–418.

Boos, H. B., Aleman, A., Cahn, W., Hulshoff, H., & Kahn, R. S. (2007). Brain volumes in relatives of patients with schizophrenia: A meta-analysis. *Archives of General Psychiatry, 64*, 297–304.

Boot, B. P., McDade, E. M., McGinnis, S. M., & Boeve, B. F. (2013). Treatment of dementia with Lewy bodies. *Current Treatment Options in Neurology, 15*, 738–764. doi:10.1007/s11940-013-0261-6

Boraska, V., Franklin, C. S., Floyd, J. A., Thornton, L. M., Huckins, L. M., Southam, L., et al. (2014). A genome-wide association study of anorexia nervosa. *Molecular Psychiatry, 19*, 1085–1094.

Borch-Jacobsen, M. (1997, April 24). Sybil: The making of a disease? An interview with Dr. Herbert Spiegel. *New York Review of Books, 44*(7), 60.

Borkovec, T. D., Alcaine, O. M., & Behar, E. (2004). Clinical presentation and diagnostic features. In R. G. Heimberg, C. L. Turk & D. S. Mennin (Eds.), *Generalized anxiety disorder* (pp. 77–108). New York: Guilford Press.

Bornovalova, M. A., Huibregtse, B. M., Hicks, B. M., Keyes, M., McGue, M., & Iacono, W. (2013). Tests of a direct effect of childhood abuse on adult borderline personality disorder traits: A longitudinal discordant twin design. *Journal of Abnormal Psychology, 122*, 180–194.

Bornstein, R. F. (2006). The complex relationship between dependency and domestic violence: Converging psychological factors and social forces. *American Psychologist, 61*, 595–606.

Boscarino, J. A. (2006). Posttraumatic stress disorder and mortality among U.S. Army veterans 30 years after military service. *Annals of Epidemiology, 16*, 248–256.

Bosquet, M., & Egeland, B. (2006). The development and maintenance of anxiety symptoms from infancy through adolescence in a longitudinal sample. *Development and Psychopathology, 18*, 517–550.

Boswell, R. G., & Kober, H. (2016). Food cue reactivity and craving predict eating and weight gain: A meta-analytic review. *Obesity Reviews, 17*, 159–177. doi:10.1111/obr.12354

Bourke, J. H., Langford, R. M., & White, P. D. (2015). The common link between functional somatic syndromes may be central sensitisation. *Journal of Psychosomatic Research, 78*, 228–236. doi:10.1016/j.jpsychores.2015.01.003

Bouton, M. E., Mineka, S., & Barlow, D. H. (2001). A modern learning theory perspective on the etiology of panic disorder. *Psychological Review, 108*, 4–32.

Bouton, M. E., & Waddell, J. (2007). Some biobehavioral insights into persistent effects of emotional trauma. In L. J. Kirmayer, R. Lemelson & M. Barad (Eds.), *Understanding trauma: Integrating biological, clinical, and cultural perspectives* (pp. 41–59). New York: Cambridge University Press.

Bovin, M. J., Wells, S. Y., Rasmusson, A. M., Hayes, J. P., & Resick, P. A. (2014). In P. Emmelkamp & T. Ehring (Eds.), *The Wiley handbook of anxiety disorders*. New York, NY: John Wiley & Sons, Ltd.

Bowers, W. A., & Ansher, L. S. (2008). The effectiveness of cognitive behavioral therapy on changing eating disorder symptoms and psychopathy of 32 anorexia nervosa patients at hospital discharge and one year follow-up. *Annals of Clinical Psychiatry, 20*, 79–86.

Bowyer, L., Krebs, G., Mataix-Cols, D., Veale, D., & Monzani, B. (2016). A critical review of cosmetic treatment outcomes in body dysmorphic disorder. *Body Image, 19*, 1–8. doi:10.1016/j.bodyim.2016.07.001

Boysen, G. A., & VanBergen, A. (2013). A review of published research on adult dissociative identity disorder: 2000–2010. *Journal of Nervous and Mental Disease, 201*, 5–11.

Boysen, G. A., & VanBergen, A. (2014). Simulation of multiple personalities: A review of research comparing diagnosed and simulated dissociative identity disorder. *Clinical Psychology Review, 34*, 14–28. doi:https://doi.org/10.1016/j.cpr.2013.10.008

Bradford, D. E., Curtin, J. J., & Piper, M. E. (2015). Anticipation of smoking sufficiently dampens stress reactivity in nicotine-deprived smokers. *Journal of Abnormal Psychology, 124*, 128–136. http://doi.org/10.1037/abn0000007

Bradford, D. E., Shapiro, B. L., & Curtin, J. J. (2013). How bad could it be? Alcohol dampens stress responses to threat of uncertain intensity. *Psychological Science, 24*, 2541–2549.

Braff, D. L. (2015). The importance of endophenotypes in schizophrenia research. *Schizophrenia Research, 163*, 108.

Brakoulias, V., Starcevic, V., Sammut, P., Berle, D., Milicevic, D., Moses, K., et al. (2011). Obsessive-compulsive spectrum disorders: A comorbidity and family history perspective. *Australasian Psychiatry, 19*, 151–155.

Brandon, T. H., Vidrine, J. I., & Litvin, E. B. (2007). Relapse and relapse prevention. *Annual Review of Clinical Psychology, 3*, 257–284.

Brandt, N. J., & Mansour, D. Z. (2016). Treatment of dementia: Pharmacological approaches. In M. Boltz & J. E. Galvin (Eds.), *Dementia Care: An Evidence-Based Approach* (pp. 73–95). Cham, Switzerland: Springer International Publishing.

Bransford, J. D., & Johnson, M. K. (1973). Considerations of some problems of comprehension. In W. G. Chase (Ed.), *Visual Information Processing*. New York, NY: Academic Press.

Braswell, L., & Kendall, P. C. (1988). Cognitive-behavioral methods with children. In K. S. Dobson (Ed.), *Handbook of Cognitive-Behavioral Therapies*. New York, NY: Guilford.

Braun, J. M., Kahn, R. S., Froehlich, T., Auinger, P., Lanphear, B. (2006). Exposures to environmental toxicants and attention deficit hyperactivity disorder in U.S. children. *Environmental Health Perspectives, 114*, 1904–1909.

Braun, K., & Champagne, F. A. (2014). Paternal influences on offspring development: Behavioral and epigenetic pathways. *Journal of Neuroendocrinology, 26*, 697–706.

Brenes, G. A., Danhauer, S. C., Lyles, M. F., Hogan, P. E., & Miller, M. E. (2015). Telephone-delivered cognitive behavioral therapy and telephone-delivered nondirective supportive therapy for rural older adults with generalized anxiety disorder: A randomized clinical trial. *JAMA Psychiatry, 72*, 1012–1020. doi:10.1001/jamapsychiatry.2015.1154

Breslau, N., Lucia, V., & Alvarado, G. F. (2006). Intelligence and other predisposing factors in exposure to trauma and posttraumatic stress disorder: A follow-up study at age 17 years. *Archives of General Psychiatry, 63*, 1238–1245.

Breuer, J., & Freud, S. (1982). *Studies in hysteria*. (J. Strachey, Trans. and Ed., with the collaboration of A. Freud). New York, NY: Basic Books. (Original work published 1895).

Brewerton, T. D., Lydiard, B. R., Laraia, M. T., Shook, J. E., & Ballenger, J. C. (1992). CSF beta-endorphin and dynorphin in bulimia nervosa. *American Journal of Psychiatry, 149*, 1086–1090.

Brezo, J., Paris, J., & Turecki, G. (2006). Personality traits as correlates of suicidal ideation, suicide attempts, and suicide completions: A systematic review. *Acta Psychiatrica Scandinavica, 113*, 180–206.

Brickman, A. S., McManus, M., Grapentine, W. L., & Alessi, N. (1984). Neuropsychological assessment of seriously delinquent adolescents. *Journal of the American Academy of Child Psychiatry, 23*, 453–457.

Bridge, J. A., Iyengar, S., Salary, C. B., Barbe, R. P., Birmaher, B., Pincus, H. A., et al. (2007). Clinical response and risk for reported suicidal ideation and suicide attempts in pediatric antidepressant treatment: A meta-analysis of randomized controlled trials. *Journal of the American Medical Association, 297*, 1683–1696.

Brien, S. E., Ronksley, P. E., Turner, B. J., Mukamal, K. J., & Ghali, W. A. (2011). Effect of alcohol consumption on biological markers associated with risk of coronary heart disease: Systematic review and meta-analysis of interventional studies. *British Medical Journal, 342*, d636–d636. http://doi.org/10.1136/bmj.d636

Britton, J., Grillon, C., Lissek, S., Norcross, M. A., Szuhany, K. L., Chen, G., et al. (2013). Response to learned threat: An fMRI study in adolescent and adult anxiety. *American Journal of Psychiatry, 170* 1195–1204.

Bromet, E., Andrade, L. H., Hwang, I., Sampson, N. A., Alonso, J., de Girolamo, G., et al. (2011). Cross-national epidemiology of DSM-IV major depressive episode. *BMC Medicine, 9*, 90.

Brookes, K., Mill, J., Guindalini, C., Curran, S., Xu, X., Knight, J., et al. (2006). A common haplotype of the dopamine transporter gene associated with attention-deficit/hyperactivity disorder and interacting with maternal use of alcohol during pregnancy. *Archives of General Psychiatry, 63*, 74–81.

Brook, M., & Kosson, D. S. (2013). Impaired cognitive empathy in criminal psychopathy: Evidence from a laboratory measure of empathic accuracy. *Journal of Abnormal Psychology, 122*, 156–166.

Brooks, M. (2004). *Extreme measures: The dark visions and bright ideas of Francis Galton*. London: Bloomsbury.

Brooks, S., Prince, A., Stahl, D., Campbell, I. C., & Treasure, J. (2011). A systematic review and meta-analysis of cognitive bias to food stimuli in people with disordered eating behaviour. *Clinical Psychology Review, 31*, 37–51.

Brosh, A. (2013). *Hyperbole and a half: Unfortunate situations, flawed coping mechanisms, mayhem, and other things that happened*. New York, NY: Simon and Schuster.

Brotto, L. A., & Luria, M. (2014). Sexual interest/arousal disorder in women. In Y. M. Binik & K. S. K. Hall (Eds.), *Principles and practice of sex therapy* (5th ed., pp. 17–41). New York, NY: Guilford Press.

Brown, A. S. (2011). The environment and susceptibility to schizophrenia. *Progress in Neurobiology, 93*, 23–58.

Brown, A. S., Bottiglieri, T., Schaefer, C. A., Quesenberry, C. P., Jr., Liu, L., Bresnahan, M., & Susser, E. S. (2007). Elevated prenatal homocysteine levels as a risk factor for schizophrenia. *Archives of General Psychiatry, 64*, 31–39.

Brown, A. S., & Derkits, E. J. (2010). Prenatal infections and schizophrenia: A review of epidemiologic and translational studies. *American Journal of Psychiatry, 167*, 261–280.

Brown, A. S., Schaefer, C. A., Quesenberry, C. P., Jr., Liu, L., Babulas, V. P., & Susser, E. S. (2005). Maternal exposure to toxoplasmosis and risk of schizophrenia in adult offspring. *American Journal of Psychiatry, 162*, 767–773.

Brown, D., Scheflin, A. W., & Whitfield, C. L. (1999). Recovered memories: The current weight of the evidence in science and in the courts. *Journal of Psychiatry and the Law, 27*, 5–156.

Brownell, K. D., & Horgen, K. B. (2003). *Food fight: The inside story of the food industry, America's obesity crisis, and what we can do about it*. Chicago, IL: Contemporary Books.

Brown, G. K., Beck, A. T., Steer, R. A., & Grisham, J. R. (2000). Risk factors for suicide in psychiatric outpatients: A 20-year prospective study. *Journal of Consulting and Clinical Psychology, 68*, 371–377.

Brown, G. K., Ten Have, T., Henriques, G. R., Xie, S. X., Hollander, J. E., & Beck, A. T. (2005). Cognitive therapy for the prevention of suicide attempts. *Journal of the American Medical Association, 294*, 563–570.

Brown, G. W., & Andrews, B. (1986). Social support and depression. In R. Trumbull & M. H. Appley (Eds.), *Dynamics of stress: Physiological, psychological, and social perspectives* (pp. 257–282). New York, NY: Plenum.

Brown, G. W., Bone, M., Dalison, B., & Wing, J. K. (1966). *Schizophrenia and social care*. London: Oxford University Press.

Brown, G. W., & Harris, T. O. (1978). *The Bedford College life events and difficulty schedule: Directory of contextual threat of events*. London, UK: Bedford College University of London.

Brown, G. W., & Harris, T. O. (1989). Depression. In T. O. Harris & G. W. Brown (Eds.), *Life events and illness* (pp. 49–93). New York, NY: Guilford Press.

Brown, H. M., Waszczuk, M. A., Zavos, H. M. S., Trzaskowski, M., Gregory, A. M., & Eley, T. C. (2014). Cognitive content specificity in anxiety and depressive disorder symptoms: A twin study of cross-sectional associations with anxiety sensitivity dimensions across development. *Psychological Medicine, 44*(16), 3469–3480. doi:10.1017/S0033291714000828

Brownley, K. A., Berkman, N. D., Sedway, J. A., Lohr, K. N., & Bulik, C. M. (2007). Binge eating disorder treatment: A systematic review of randomized controlled trials. *International Journal of Eating Disorders, 40*(4), 337–348.

Brown, R. J., Cardena, E., Nijenhuis, E., Sar, V., & Van der Hart, O. (2007). Should conversion disorder be reclassified as dissociative disorder in DSM-5? *Psychosomatics, 48*, 369–378.

Broyd, S. J., van Hell, H. H., Beale, C., Yücel, M., & Solowij, N. (2016). Acute and chronic effects of cannabinoids on human cognition—A systematic review. *Biological Psychiatry, 79*, 557–567.

Bruce, M. L., Ten Have, T. R., Reynolds III, C. F., Katz, I. I., Schulberg, H. C., Mulsant, B. H., et al. (2004). Reducing suicidal ideation and depressive symptoms in depressed older primary care patients. *Journal of the American Medical Association, 291*, 1081–1091.

Bruce, S. E., Yonkers, K. A., Otto, M. W., Eisen, J. L., Weisberg, R. B., Pagano, M., et al. (2005). Influence of psychiatric comorbidity on recovery and recurrence in generalized anxiety disorder, social phobia, and panic disorder: A 12-year prospective study. *American Journal of Psychiatry, 162*(6), 1179–1187. doi:10.1176/appi.ajp.162.6.1179

Brummelman, E., Thomaes, S., Nelemans, S. A., Orobio de Castro, B., Overbeek, G., & Bushman, B. J. (2015). Origins of narcissism in children. *Proceedings of the National Academy of Sciences, 112*, 3659–3662. doi:10.1073/pnas.1420870112

Brunwasser, S. M., & Garber, J. (2016). Programs for the prevention of youth depression: Evaluation of efficacy, effectiveness, and readiness for dissemination. *Journal of Clinical Child & Adolescent Psychology, 45*(6), 763–783. http://doi.org/10.1080/15374416.2015.1020541

Bryant, R. A., Creamer, M., O'Donnell, M., Silove, D., McFarlane, A. C., & Forbes, D. (2015). A comparison of the capacity of DSM-IV and DSM-5 acute stress disorder definitions to predict posttraumatic stress disorder and related disorders. *The Journal of Clinical Psychiatry, 76*(4), 391–397. doi:10.4088/jcp.13m08731

Bryant, R. A., Mastrodomenico, J., Felmingham, K. L., Hopwood, S., Kenny, L., Kandris, E., et al. (2008). Treatment of acute stress disorder: A randomized controlled trial. *Archives of General Psychiatry, 65*, 659–667.

Buchanan, J. A., Christenson, A., Houlihan, D., & Ostrom, C. (2011). The role of behavior analysis in the rehabilitation of persons with dementia. *Behavior Therapy, 42*, 9–21.

Buchsbaum, M. S., Kessler, R., King, A., Johnson, J., & Cappelletti, J. (1984). Simultaneous cerebral glucography with positron emission tomography and topographic electroencephalography. In G. Pfurtscheller, E. J. Jonkman, & F. H. L. d. Silva (Eds.), *Brain ischemia: Quantitative EEG and imaging techniques*. Amsterdam: Elsevier.

Budge, S. L., Moore, J. T., Del Re, A. C., Wampold, B. E., Baardseth, T. P., & Nienhuis, J. B. (2013). The effectiveness of evidence-based treatments for personality disorders when comparing treatment-as-usual and bona fide treatments. *Clinical Psychology Review, 33*, 1057–1066.

Budney, A. J., Moore, B. A., Rocha, H. L., & Higgens, S. T. (2006). Clinical trial of abstinence-based vouchers and cognitive behavior therapy for *Cannabis* dependence. *Journal of Consulting and Clinical Psychology, 74*, 307–316.

Buhlmann, U., Glaesmer, H., Mewes, R., Fama, J. M., Wilhelm, S., Brähler, E., et al. (2010). Updates on the prevalence of body dysmorphic disorder: A population-based survey. *Psychiatry Research, 178*, 171–175.

Buil, J. M., van Lier, P. A. C., Brendgen, M. R., Koot, H. M., & Vitaro, F. (2017). Developmental pathways linking childhood temperament with antisocial behavior and substance use in adolescence: Explanatory mechanisms in the peer environment. *Journal of Personality and Social Psychology, 112*(6), 948–966. http://doi.org/10.1037/pspp0000132

Bukalo, O., Pinard, C., & Holmes, A. (2014). Mechanisms to medicines: Elucidating neural and molecular substrates of fear extinction to identify novel treatments for anxiety disorders. *British Journal of Pharmacology, 171*(20), 4690–4718. doi: 10.1111/bph.12779

Bulik, C. M., & Reichborn-Kjennerud, T. (2003). *Medical morbidity in binge eating disorder.* Retrieved from http://www.interscience.wiley.com

Bulik, C. M., Wade, T. D., & Kendler, K. S. (2000). Characteristics of monozygotic twins discordant for bulimia nervosa. *International Journal of Eating Disorders, 29,* 1–10.

Bullen, C., Howe, C., Laugesen, M., McRobbie, H., Parag, V., Williman, J., & Walker, N. (2013). Electronic cigarettes for smoking cessation: A randomised controlled trial. *Lancet, 382,* 1629–1637.

Bullers, S., Cooper, M. L., & Russell, M. (2001). Social network drinking and adult alcohol involvement: A longitudinal exploration of the direction of influence. *Addictive Behaviors, 26,* 181–199.

Burdick, K. E., Braga, R. J., Gopin, C. B., Malhotra, A. K. (2014). Dopaminergic influences on emotional decision making in euthymic bipolar patients. *Neuropsychopharmacology, 39*(2), 274–282. doi: 10.1038/npp.2013.177.

Burke, B. L., Arkowitz, H., & Menchola, M. (2003). The efficacy of motivational interviewing: A meta-analysis of controlled clinical trials. *Journal of Consulting and Clinical Psychology, 71,* 843–861.

Burns, P. R., Rosen, R. C., Dunn, M., Baygani, S. K., & Perelman, M. A. (2010). Treatment satisfaction of men and partners following switch from on-demand phosphodiesterase type 5 inhibitor therapy to Tadalafil once daily. *Journal of Sexual Medicine, 12,* 720–727. doi:10.1111/jsm.12818

Burri, A., & Spector, T. (2011). Recent and lifelong sexual dysfunction in a female UK population sample: Prevalence and risk factors. *Journal of Sexual Medicine, 8,* 2420–2430.

Burris, K. D., Molski, T. F., Xu, C., Ryan, E., Tottori, K., Kikuchi, T., Yocca F. D., & Molinoff, P. B. (2002). Aripiprazole, a novel antipsychotic, is a high-affinity partial agonist at human dopamine D2 receptors. *Journal of Pharmacology and Experimental Therapeutics, 302,* 381–389.

Burstein, M., Ameli-Grillon, L., & Merikangas, K. R. (2011). Shyness versus social phobia in US youth. *Pediatrics, 128*(5), 917–925. doi:10.1542/peds.2011-1434

Burt, S. A. (2009a). Rethinking environmental contributions to child and adolescent psychopathology: A meta-analysis of shared environmental influences. *Psychological Bulletin, 135,* 608–637. doi:10.1037/a0015702.

Burt, S. A. (2009b). Are there meaningful etiological differences within antisocial behavior? Results of a meta-analysis. *Clinical Psychology Review, 29*(2), 163–178.

Burt, S. A. (2009). Rethinking environmental contributions to child and adolescent psychopathology: A meta-analysis of shared environmental influences. *Psychological Bulletin, 135,* 608–637. doi:http://dx.doi.org/10.1037/a0015702.

Burt, S. A. (2012). How do we optimally conceptualize the heterogeneity within antisocial behavior? An argument for aggressive versus non-aggressive behavioral dimensions. *Clinical Psychology Review, 32,* 263–279.

Burt, S. A. (2014). Research review: The shared environment as a key source of variability in child and adolescent psychopathology. *Journal of Child Psychology and Psychiatry, 55*(4), 304–312. http://doi.org/10.1111/jcpp.12173

Burt, S. A. (2014). Research review: The shared environment as a key source of variability in child and adolescent psychopathology. *Journal of Child Psychology and Psychiatry, 55*(4), 304–312. http://doi.org/10.1111/jcpp.12173

Burt, S. A., Klahr, A. M., & Klump, K. L. (2015). Do non-shared environmental influences persist over time? An examination of days and minutes. *Behavior Genetics, 45,* 24–34. http://doi.org/10.1007/s10519-014-9682-6

Burt, S. A., Klump, K. L., Gorman-Smith, D., & Neiderhiser, J. M. (2016). Neighborhood disadvantage alters the origins of children's non-aggressive conduct problems. *Clinical Psychological Science, 4,* 511–526. doi:10.1177/2167702615618164

Burt, S. A., & Neiderhiser, J. M. (2009). Aggressive versus nonaggressive antisocial behavior: Distinctive etiological moderation by age. *Devevlopmental Psychology, 45,* 1164–1176. doi:10.1037/a0016130

Bushman, B. J., & Cooper, H. M. (1990). Effects of alcohol on human aggression: An integrative research review. *Psychological Bulletin, 107,* 341–354.

Bushman, B. J., & Thomaes, S. (2011). When the narcissistic ego deflates, narcissistic aggression inflates. In W. K. Campbell & J. D. Miller (Eds.), *The handbook of narcissism and narcissistic personality disorder: Theoretical approaches, empirical findings, and treatments* (pp. 319–329). Hoboken, NJ: Wiley Press.

Butcher, J. N., Dahlstrom, W. G., Graham, J. R., Tellegen, A., & Kraemer, B. (1989). *Minnesota Multiphasic Personality Inventory-2: Manual for administration and scoring.* Minneapolis, MN: University of Minnesota Press.

Butcher, K. R., & Jameson, M. (2016). Computer-based Instruction (CBI) within special education. In J. K. Luiselli & A. J. Fischer (Eds.), *Computer-assisted and web-based innovations in psychology, special education, and health* (pp. 211–254). San Diego, CA: Elsevier Academic Press

Butzlaff, R. L., & Hooley, J. M. (1998). Expressed emotion and psychiatric relapse: A meta-analysis. *Archives of General Psychiatry, 55,* 547–553.

Butzlaff, R. L., & Hooley, J. M. (1998). Expressed emotion and psychiatric relapse: A meta-analysis. *Archives of General Psychiatry, 55,* 547–553.

Buvat, J., Maggi, M., Gooren, L., Guay, A. T., Kaufman, J., Morgentaler, A., et al. (2010). Endocrine aspects of male sexual dysfunctions. *Journal of Sexual Medicine, 7,* 1627–1656.

Byrd, A. L., & Manuck, S. B. (2014). MAOA, childhood maltreatment, and antisocial behavior: Meta-analysis of a gene-environment interaction. *Biological Psychiatry, 75,* 9–17.

Cadoret, R. J., Yates, W. R., Troughton, E., Woodworth, G., & Stewart, M. A. (1995). Adoption study demonstrating two genetic pathways to drug abuse. *Archives of General Psychiatry, 52,* 42–52.

Cahalan, S. (2012). *Brain on fire: My month of madness.* New York, NY: Free Press.

Cahill, K., Stead, L., & Lancaster, T. (2007). Nicotine receptor partial agonists for smoking cessation. *Cochrane Database of Systematic Reviews,* CD006103.

Caldwell, M. B., Brownell, K. D., & Wilfley, D. (1997). Relationship of weight, body dissatisfaction, and self-esteem in African American and white female dieters. *International Journal of Eating Disorders, 22,* 127–130.

Calhoun, V. D., Pekar, J. J., & Pearlson, G. D. (2004). Alcohol intoxication effects on simulated driving: Exploring alcohol-dose effects on brain activation using functional MRI. *Neuropsychopharmacology, 29,* 2197–2107.

Camí, J., & Farré, M. (2003). Drug addiction. *New England Journal of Medicine, 349,* 975–986.

Campbell, A. K., & Matthews, S. B. (2005). Darwin's illness revealed. *Postgrad Medical Journal, 81,* 248–251. doi: 10.1136/pgmj.2004.025569

Campbell, J., Stefan, S., & Loder, A. (1994). Putting violence in context. *Hospital and Community Psychiatry, 45,* 633.

Campbell, W. K., Bosson, J. K., Goheen, T. W., Lakey, C. E., & Kernis, M. H. (2007). Do narcissists dislike themselves "deep down inside"? *Psychological Science, 18,* 227–229.

Camus, V., Burtin, B., Simeone, I., Schwed, P., Gonthier, R., & Dubos, G. (2000). Factor analysis supports the evidence of existing hyperactive and hypoactive subtypes of delirium. *International Journal of Geriatric Psychiatry, 15,* 313–316.

Canivez, G. L., & Watkins, M. W. (1998). Long-term stability of the Wechsler Intelligence Scale for Children (3rd ed.). *Psychological Assessment, 10,* 285–291.

Cannon, T. D., Cadenhead, K., Cornblatt, B., Woods, S. W., Addington, J., Walker, E. F, Seidman, L. J., Perkins, D., Tsuang, M., McGlashan, T., & Heinssen, R. (2008). Prediction of psychosis in youth at high clinical risk: A multisite longitudinal study in North America. *Archives of General Psychiatry, 65,* 28–37.

Cannon, T. D., Chung, Y., He, G., Sun, D., Jacobson, A., van Erp, T. G. M., et al. (2015). Progressive reduction in cortical thickness as psychosis develops: A multisite longitudinal neuroimaging study of youth at elevated clinical risk. *Biological Psychiatry, 77,* 147–157. http://doi.org/10.1016/j.biopsych.2014.05.023

Cannon, T. D., Kaprio, J., Lonnqvist, J., Huttunen, M., & Koskenvuo, M. (1998). The genetic epidemiology of schizophrenia in a Finnish twin cohort: A population-based modeling study. *Archives of General Psychiatry, 55,* 67–74.

Cannon, T. D., & Mednick, S. A. (1993). The schizophrenia high-risk project in Copenhagen: Three decades of progress. *Acta Psychiatrica Scandanavica, 87,* 33–47.

Cannon, T. D., van Erp, T. G., Rosso, I. M., et al. (2002). Fetal hypoxia and structural brain abnormalities in schizophrenic patients, their siblings, and controls. *Archives of General Psychiatry, 59*, 35–42.

Cannon, T. D., Yu, C., Addington, J., Bearden, C. E., Cadenhead, K. S., Cornblatt, B. A., et al. (2016). An individualized risk calculator for research in prodromal psychosis. *American Journal of Psychiatry, 173*, 980–988. http://doi.org/10.1176/appi.ajp.2016.15070890

Cantor-Graae, E., & Selten, J.-P. (2005). Schizophrenia and migration: A meta-analysis and review. *The American Journal of Psychiatry, 162*, 12–24. http://doi.org/10.1176/appi.ajp.162.1.12

Cantor, J. M., Blanchard, R., Robichaud, L. K., & Christensen, B. K. (2005). Quantitative reanalysis of aggregate data on IQ in sexual offenders. *Psychological Bulletin, 131*, 555–568.

Cantor, J. M., & McPhail, I. V. (2015). Sensitivity and specificity of the phallometric test for hebephilia. *Journal of Sexual Medicine, 12*, 1940–1950. doi:10.1111/jsm.12970

Cappelletti, M., & Wallen, K. (2016). Increasing women's sexual desire: The comparative effectiveness of estrogens and androgens. *Hormones and Behavior, 78*, 178–193. doi:https://doi.org/10.1016/j.yhbeh.2015.11.003

Capps, L., Losh, M., & Thurber, C. (2000). "The frog ate the bug and made his mouth sad": Narrative competence in children with autism. *Journal of Abnormal Child Psychology, 28*, 193–204.

Capps, L., Rasco, L., Losh, M., & Heerey, E. (1999). *Understanding of self-conscious emotions in high-functioning children with autism.* Paper presented at the Biennial Meeting of the Society for Research in Child Development, Albuquerque, NM.

Capps, L., Yirmiya, N., & Sigman, M. (1992). Understanding of simple and complex emotion in high-functioning children with autism. *Journal of Child Psychology and Psychiatry, 33*, 1169–1182.

Cardinale, E. M., Breeden, A. L., Robertson, E. L., Lozier, L. M., Vanmeter, J. W., & Marsh, A. A. (2017). Externalizing behavior severity in youths with callous-unemotional traits corresponds to patterns of amygdala activity and connectivity during judgments of causing fear. *Development and Psychopathology,* 1–11. http://doi.org/10.1017/S0954579417000566

Cardno, A. G., Marshall, E. J., Coid, B., Macdonald, A. M., Ribchester, T. R., et al. (1999). Heritability estimates for psychotic disorders: The Maudsley twin psychosis series. *Archives of General Psychiatry, 56*, 162–170.

Cardoso, J. B., Goldbach, J. T., Cervantes, R. C., & Swank, P. (2016). Stress and multiple substance use behaviors among Hispanic adolescents. *Prevention Science, 17*, 208–217. http://doi.org/10.1007/s11121-015-0603-6

Carey, B. (2011, June 23). Expert on mental illness reveals her own fight, *The New York Times.*

Carey, B. (2017, July 24). England's mental health experiment: No-cost talk therapy. *New York Times.* Downloaded from https://www.nytimes.com/2017/07/24/health/england-mental-health-treatment-therapy.html?_r50 on July 28, 2017.

Carey, K. B., Carey, M. P., Maisto, S. A., & Henson, J. M. (2006). Brief motivational interventions for heavy college drinkers: A randomized controlled trial. *Journal of Consulting and Clinical Psychology, 74*, 943–954.

Carlson, E. A., Egeland, B., & Sroufe, L. A. (2009). A prospective investigation of the development of borderline personality symptoms. *Development and Psychopathology, 21*, 1311–1334. doi:10.1017/S0954579409990174

Carlson, E. B., Dalenberg, C., & McDade-Montez, E. (2012). Dissociation in posttraumatic stress disorder part I: Definitions and review of research. *Psychological Trauma: Theory, Research, Practice, and Policy, 4*(5), 479–489. doi:10.1037/a0027748

Carlson, G. A., & Meyer, S. E. (2006). Phenomenology and diagnosis of bipolar disorder in children, adolescents, and adults: Complexities and developmental issues. *Development and Psychopathology 18*, 939–969.

Carney, R. M., & Freedland, K. E. (2017). Depression and coronary heart disease. *Nature Reviews Cardiology, 14*(3), 145–155. doi:10.1038/nrcardio.2016.181

Carpenter, W. T., Gold, J. M., Lahti, A. C., Queern, C. A., Conley, R. R., Bartko, J. J., et al. (2000). Decisional capacity for informed consent in schizophrenia research. *Archives of General Psychiatry, 57*, 533–538.

Carpenter, W. T., & van Os, J. (2011). Should attenuated psychosis syndrome be a DSM-5 diagnosis? *American Journal of Psychiatry, 168*, 460–463.

Carrasco, J. L., Dyaz-Marsa, M., Hollander, E., Cesar, J., & Saiz-Ruiz, J. (2000). Decreased monoamine oxidase activity in female bulimia. *European Neuropsychopharmacology, 10*, 113–117.

Carr, D. (2008). *The night of the gun: A reporter investigates the darkest story of his life. His own.* New York, NY: Simon & Schuster Adult Publishing Group.

Carr, E. G., Horner R. H., Turnbull A. P., Marquis J. G., Magito-McLaughlin D., McAtee, M. L., et al. (1999a) *Positive behavior support for people with developmental disabilities: A research synthesis.* American Association on Mental Retardation Monograph Series, Washington, D.C.

Carrion, R. E., Cornblatt, B. A., Burton, C. Z., Tso, I. F., Auther, A. M., Adelsheim, S., et al. (2016). Personalized prediction of psychosis: External validation of the NAPLS-2 psychosis risk calculator with the EDIPPP project. *American Journal of Psychiatry, 173*, 989–996. http://doi.org/10.1176/appi.ajp.2016.15121565

Carroll, K. M., Ball, S. A., Nich, C., et al. (2001). Targeting behavioral therapies to enhance naltrexone treatment of opioid dependence: Efficacy of contingency management and significant other involvement. *Archives of General Psychiatry, 58*, 755–761.

Carroll, K. M., Easton, C. J., Nich, C., Hunkele, K. A., Neavins, T. M., et al. (2006). The use of contingency management and motivational/skills-building therapy to treat young adults with marijuana dependence. *Journal of Consulting and Clinical Psychology, 74*, 955–966.

Carroll, K. M., Kiluk, B. D., Nich, C., Gordon, M. A., Portnoy, G. A., Marino, D. R., & Ball, S. A. (2014). Computer-assisted delivery of cognitive-behavioral therapy: Efficacy and durability of CBT4CBT among cocaine-dependent individuals maintained on methadone. *American Journal of Psychiatry, 171*, 436–444.

Carroll, K. M., Rounsaville, B. J., Gordon, L. T., Nich, C., Jatlow, P., Bisighini, R. M., & Gawin, F. H. (1994). Psychotherapy and pharmacotherapy for ambulatory cocaine abusers. *Archives of General Psychiatry, 51*, 177–187.

Carroll, K. M., Rounsaville, B. J., Nich, C., Gordon, L. T., & Gawin, F. (1995). Integrating psychotherapy and pharmacotherapy for cocaine dependence: Results from a randomized clinical trial. In L. S. Onken, J. D. Blaine, & J. J. Boren (Eds.), *Integrating behavioral therapies with medications in the treatment of drug dependence* (pp. 19–36). Rockville, MD: National Institute on Drug Abuse.

Carson, A., & Lehn, A. (2016). Epidemiology. *Handbook of Clinical Neurology, 139*, 47–60. doi:http://dx.doi.org/10.1016/B978-0-12-801772-2.00005-9

Carstensen, L. L. (1996). Evidence for a life-span theory of socioemotional selectivity. *Current Directions in Psychological Science, 4*, 151–156.

Carter, F. A., McIntosh, V. V. W., Joyce, P. R., Sullivan, P. F., & Bulik, C. M. (2003). Role of exposure with response prevention in cognitive-behavioral therapy for bulimia nervosa: Three-year follow–up results. *International Journal of Eating Disorders, 33*, 127–135.

Carter, J. S., & Garber, J. (2011). Predictors of the first onset of a major depressive episode and changes in depressive symptoms across adolescence: Stress and negative cognitions. *Journal of Abnormal Psychology, 120*, 779–796.

Carvalheira, A. A., Brotto, L. A., & Leal, I. (2010). Women's motivations for sex: Exploring the *Diagnostic and Statistical Manual*, fourth edition, text revision criteria for hypoactive sexual desire and female sexual arousal disorders. *Journal of Sexual Medicine, 7*, 1454–1463.

Carvalho, J., & Nobre, P. (2010). Biopsychosocial determinants of men's sexual desire: Testing an integrative model. *Journal of Sexual Medicine, 8*, 754–763.

Carver, C. S., Johnson, S. L., & Joormann, J. (2008). Serotonergic function, two-mode models of self-regulation, and vulnerability to depression: What depression has in common with impulsive aggression. *Psychological Bulletin, 134*, 912–943.

Cascio, C. N., Konrath, S. H., & Falk, E. B. (2015). Narcissists' social pain seen only in the brain. *Social Cognitive and Affective Neuroscience, 10*, 335–341. doi:10.1093/scan/nsu072

Casey, J. E., Rourke, B. P., & Del Dotto, J. E. (1996). Learning disabilities in children with attention deficit disorder with and without hyperactivity. *Child Neuropsychology, 2*, 83–98.

Caspi, A., Hariri, A. R., Holmes, A., Uher, R., & Moffitt, T. E. (2010). Genetic sensitivity to the environment: The case of the serotonin transporter gene and its implications for studying complex diseases and traits. *American Journal of Psychiatry, 167*, 509–527.

Caspi, A., Houts, R. M., Belsky, D. W., Goldman-Mellor, S. J., Harrington, H., Israel, S., et al. (2014). The p Factor: One general psychopathology factor in the structure of psychiatric disorders? *Clinical Psychological Science, 2*, 119–137. doi:10.1177/2167702613497473

Caspi, A., McClay, J., Moffitt, T. E., Mill, J., Martin, J., Craig, I. W., et al. (2002). Role of genotype in the cycle of violence in maltreated children. *Science, 297*, 851–854.

Caspi, A., Moffitt, T. E., Cannon, M., McClay, J., Murray, R., Harrington, H., Taylor, A., Arseneault, L., Williams, B., Braithwaite, A., Pulton, R., & Craig, I. W. (2005). Moderation of the effect of adolescent-onset *Cannabis* use on adult psychosis by a functional polymorphism in the catechol-O-methyltransferase gene: Longitudinal evidence of a gene–environment interaction. *Biological Psychiatry, 57*, 1117–1127.

Caspi, A., Sugden, K., Moffitt, T. E., Taylor, A., Craig, I. W., Harrington, H., et al. (2003). Influence of life stress on depression: Moderation by a polymorphism in the 5-HTT gene. *Science, 301*, 386–389.

Castellanos, F. X., Lee, P. P., Sharp, W., Jeffries, N. O., Greenstein, D. K., et al. (2002). Developmental trajectories of brain volume abnormalities in children and adolescents with attention-deficit/hyperactivity disorder. *Journal of the American Medical Association, 288*, 1740–1748.

Castells, X., Casas, M., Vidal, X., Bosch, R., Roncero, C., Ramos-Quiroga, J. A., et al. (2007). Efficacy of central nervous system stimulant treatment for cocaine dependence. A systematic review and meta-analysis of randomized controlled clinical trials, *Addiction, 102*, 1871-1887.

Celebucki, C. C., Wayne, G. F., Connolly, G. N., Pankow, J. F., & Chang, E. I. (2005). Characterization of measured menthol in 48 U.S. cigarette sub-brands. *Nicotine and Tobacco Research, 7*, 523–531.

Center for Behavioral Health Statistics and Quality. (2015). Behavioral health trends in the United States: Results from the 2014 National Survey on Drug Use and Health (HHS Publication No. SMA 15-4927, NSDUH Series H-50). Retrieved from http://www.samhsa.gov/data/

Center for Behavioral Health Statistics and Quality. (2015). *National Survey on Drug Use and Health: 2014 and 2015 Redesign Changes.* Substance Abuse and Mental Health Services Administration, Rockville, MD.

Center for Behavioral Health Statistics and Quality (2016). Key substance use and mental health indicators in the United States: Results from the 2015 National Survey on Drug Use and Health (HHS Publication No. SMA 16-4984, NSDUH Series H-51). Retrieved online July 2017 from http://www.samhsa.gov/data/

Centers for Disease Control and Prevention (CDC). (2009). Prevalence of autism spectrum disorders—Autism and developmental disabilities monitoring network, 2006. *Morbitity and Mortality Weekly Report, 58*, 1–20.

Centers for Disease Control and Prevention (CDC). (2014). Prevalence of autism spectrum disorder among children aged 8 years—Autism and developmental disabilities monitoring network, 11 sites, United States, 2010. *Morbitity and Mortality Weekly Report, 63*(SS02), 1–21.

Cerdá, M., Wall, M., Feng, T., Keyes, K. M., Sarvet, A., Schulenberg, J., et al. (2017). Association of state recreational marijuana laws with adolescent marijuana use. *JAMA Pediatrics, 171*, 142–149. http://doi.org/10.1001/jamapediatrics.2016.3624

Cerny, J. A., Barlow, D. H., Craske, M. G., & Himadi, W. G. (1987). Couples treatment of agoraphobia: A two-year follow-up. *Behavior Therapy, 18*, 401–415.

Chabris, C. F., Lee, J. J., Benjamin, D. J., Beauchamp, J. P., Glaeser, E. L., Borst, G., et al. (2013). Why it is hard to find genes associated with social science traits: Theoretical and empirical considerations. *American Journal of Public Health, 103* Suppl 1, S152–S166.

Chambless, D. L., Caputo, G. C., Bright, P., & Gallagher, R. (1984). Assessment of fear in agoraphobics: The Body Sensations Questionnaire and the Agoraphobic Cognitions Questionnaire. *Journal of Consulting and Clinical Psychology, 52*, 1090–1097.

Champagne, F. A. (2016). Epigenetic legacy of parental experiences: Dynamic and interactive pathways to inheritance. *Development and Psychopathology, 28*, 1219–1228. http://doi.org/10.1017/S0954579416000808

Chan, A. T., Sun, G. Y., Tam, W. W., Tsoi, K. K., & Wong, S. Y. (2017). The effectiveness of group-based behavioral activation in the treatment of depression: An updated meta-analysis of randomized controlled trial. *Journal of Affective Disorders, 208*, 345–354. doi:10.1016/j.jad.2016.08.026

Chan, G. C. K., Kelly, A. B., Carroll, A., & Williams, J. W. (2017). Peer drug use and adolescent polysubstance use: Do parenting and school factors moderate this association? *Addictive Behaviors, 64*, 78–81.

Chard, K. M., Ricksecker, E. G., Healy, E. T., Karlin, B. E., & Resick, P. A. (2012). Dissemination and experience with cognitive processing therapy. *Journal of Rehabilitation Research and Development, 49*(5), 667–678.

Charuvastra, A., & Cloitre, M. (2008). Social bonds and posttraumatic stress disorder. *Annual Review of Psychology, 59*, 301–328.

Chassin, L., Curran, P. J., Hussong, A. M., & Colder, C. R. (1996). The relation of parent alcoholism to adolescent substance abuse: A longitudinal follow-up. *Journal of Abnormal Psychology, 105*, 70–80.

Chassin, L., Pitts, S. C., DeLucia, C., & Todd, M. (1999). A longitudinal study of children of alcoholics: Predicting young adult substance use disorders, anxiety, and depression. *Journal of Abnormal Psychology, 108*, 106–119.

Chaste, P., Klei, L., Sanders, S. J., Hus, V., Murtha, M. T., Lowe, J. K., et al. (2015). A genome-wide association study of autism using the Simons Simplex Collection: Does reducing phenotypic heterogeneity in autism increase genetic homogeneity? *Biological Psychiatry, 77*(9), 775–784. http://doi.org/10.1016/j.biopsych.2014.09.017

Chavira, D. A., Golinelli, D., Sherbourne, C., Stein, M. B., Sullivan, G., Bystritsky, A., et al. (2014). Treatment engagement and response to CBT among Latinos with anxiety disorders in primary care. *Journal of Consulting and Clinical Psychology, 82*(3), 392–403. doi:10.1037/a0036365

Chen, C. H., Suckling, J., Lennox, B. R., Ooi, C., & Bullmore, E. T. (2011). A quantitative meta-analysis of fMRI studies in bipolar disorder. *Bipolar Disorders, 13*, 1–15.

Chen, S., Boucher, H. C., Andersen, S. M., & Saribay, S. A. (2013). *Transference and the relational self.* New York, NY: Oxford University Press.

Chen, S., Boucher, H. C., & Parker Tapias, M. (2006). The relational self revealed: Integrative conceptualization and implications for interpersonal life. *Psychological Bulletin, 132*, 151–179.

Chesney, E., Goodwin, G. M., & Fazel, S. (2014). Risks of all-cause and suicide mortality in mental disorders: A meta review. *World Psychiatry, 13*, 153–160.

Chivers, M. L., Seto, M. C., Lalumiere, M. L., Laan, E., & Grimbos, T. (2010). Agreement of self-reported and genital measures of sexual arousal in men and women: A meta-analysis. *Archives of Sexual Behavior, 39*, 5–56.

Chorpita, B. F., Brown, T. A., & Barlow, D. H. (1998). Perceived control as a mediator of family environment in etiological models of childhood anxiety. *Behavior Therapy, 29*, 457–476.

Chorpita, B. F., Vitali, A. E., & Barlow, D. H. (1997). Behavioral treatment of choking phobia in an adolescent: An experimental analysis. *Journal of Behavior Therapy and Experimental Psychiatry, 28*, 307–315.

Christakis, N., & Fowler, J. (2008). The collective dynamics of smoking in a large social network. *New England Journal of Medicine, 358*, 2249–2258.

Christensen, S. S., Frostholm, L., Ørnbøl, E., & Schröder, A. (2015). Changes in illness perceptions mediated the effect of cognitive behavioural therapy in severe functional somatic syndromes. *Journal of Psychosomatic Research, 78*, 363–370. doi:10.1016/j.jpsychores.2014.12.005

Chronis, A. M., Jones, H. A., & Raggi, V. L. (2006). Evidence-based psychosocial treatments for children and adolescents with attention-deficit/hyperactivity disorder. *Clinical Psychology Review, 26*, 486–502.

Chronis-Tuscano, A., Degnan, K. A., Pine, D. S., Perez-Edgar, K., Henderson, H. A., Diaz, Y., et al. (2009). Stable early maternal report of behavioral inhibition predicts lifetime social anxiety disorder in adolescence. *Journal of the American Academy of Child and Adolescent Psychiatry, 48*, 928–935.

Chung, Y., Haut, K. M., He, G., van Erp, T. G. M., McEwen, S., Addington, J., et al. (2017). Ventricular enlargement and progressive reduction of cortical gray matter are linked in prodromal youth who develop psychosis. *Schizophrenia Research.* http://doi.org/10.1016/j.schres.2017.02.014

Cicero, T. J., Ellis, M. S., Surratt, H. L., & Kurtz, S. P. (2014). The changing face of heroin use in the United States: A retrospective analysisof the past 50 years. *Journal of the American Medical Association,Psychiatry, 71*, 821–826.

Cimbora, D. M., & McIntosh, D. N. (2003). Emotional responses to antisocial acts in adolescent males with conduct disorder: A link to affective morality. *Journal of Clinical Child and Adolescent Psychology, 32*, 296–301.

Cipriani, A., Pretty, H., Hawton, K., & Geddes, J. R. (2005). Lithium in the prevention of suicidal behavior and all-cause mortality in patients with mood disorders: A systematic review of randomized trials. *American Journal of Psychiatry, 162*, 1805–1819.

Cirincione, C., Steadman, H. J., & McGreevy, M. A. (1995). Rates of insanity acquittals and the factors associated with successful insanity pleas. *Bulletin of the American Academy of Psychiatry and Law, 23*, 399–409.

Cisler, J. M., & Koster, E. H. (2010). Mechanisms of attentional biases towards threat in anxiety disorders: An integrative review. *Clinical Psychology Review, 30*, 203–216.

Clark, D. A. (1997). Twenty years of cognitive assessment: Current status and future directions. *Journal of Consulting and Clinical Psychology, 65*, 996–1000.

Clark, D. A. (2006). *Cognitive-Behavioral Therapy for OCD*. York, NY: Guilford Press.

Clark, D. A., & González, A. d. P. (2014). Obsessive-compulsive disorder *The Wiley handbook of anxiety disorders* (pp. 497–534): John Wiley & Sons, Ltd.

Clark, D. M. (1996). Panic disorder: From theory to therapy. In P. M. Salkovskis (Ed.), *Frontiers of cognitive therapy* (pp. 318–344). New York: Guilford Press.

Clark, D. M., Ehlers, A., Hackmann, A., McManus, F., Fennell, M., Grey, N., et al. (2006). Cognitive therapy versus exposure and applied relaxation in social phobia: A randomized controlled trial. *Journal of Consulting and Clinical Psychology, 74*, 568–578.

Clark, D. M., Ehlers, A., McManus, F., Hackmann, A., Fennell, M., Campbell, H., et al. (2003). Cognitive therapy versus fluoxetine in generalized social phobia: A randomized control trial. *Journal of Consulting and Clinical Psychology, 71*, 1058–1067.

Clark, D. M., Salkovskis, P. M., Hackmann, A., Wells, A., Ludgate, J., & Gelder, M. (1999). Brief cognitive therapy for panic disorder: A randomized controlled trial. *Journal of Consulting and Clinical Psychology, 67*, 583–589.

Clark, D. M., & Wells, A. (1995). A cognitive model of social phobia. In R. Heimberg, M. R. Liebowitz, D. A. Hope & F. R. Schneier (Eds.), *Social phobia: Diagnosis, assessment and treatment* (pp. 69–93). New York, NY: Guilford Press.

Clarkin, J. F., Foelsch, P. A., Levy, K. N., Hull, J. W., Delaney, J. C., & Kernberg, O. F. (2001). The development of a psychodynamic treatment for patients with borderline personality disorder: A preliminary study of behavioral change. *Journal of Personality Disorders, 15*, 487–495. doi:10.1521/pedi.15.6.487.19190

Cloitre, M., Courtois, C. A., Charuvastra, A., Carapezza, R., Stolbach, B. C., & Green, B. L. (2011). Treatment of complex PTSD: Results of the ISTSS expert clinician survey on best practices. New York, NY: *Journal of Traumatic Stress, 24*, 615–627.

Cloitre, M., Stovall-McClough, K. C., Nooner, K., Zorbas, P., Cherry, S., Jackson, C. L., et al. (2010). Treatment for PTSD related to childhood abuse: A randomized controlled trial. *American Journal of Psychiatry, 167*, 915–924.

Cloninger, R. C., Martin, R. L., Guze, S. B., & Clayton, P. L. (1986). A prospective follow-up and family study of somatization in men and women. *American Journal of Psychiatry, 143*, 713–714.

Cohen, D. (2014). *A big fat crisis: The hidden forces behind the obesity epidemic and how we can end it.* New York, NY: Nation Books.

Cohen, J. A., Deblinger, E., Mannarino, A. P., & Steer, R. (2004). A multi-site, randomized controlled trial for children with abuse-related PTSD symptoms. *Journal of the American Academy of Child and Adolescent Psychiatry, 43*, 393–402.

Cohen, P. (2008, February 21). Midlife suicide rises, puzzling researchers, *New York Times*, pp. 1–4.

Cohen, S., Frank, E., Doyle, W. J., Rabin, B. S., et al. (1998). Types of stressors that increase susceptibility to the common cold in healthy adults. *Health Psychology, 17*, 214–223.

Coie, J. D., & Dodge, K. A. (1998). Aggression and antisocial behavior. In W. Damon & N. Eisenberg (Eds.), *Handbook of child psychology: Volume 3: Social, emotional and personality development* (pp. 779–862). New York, NY: John Wiley & Sons.

Cole, D. A., Ciesla, J. A., Dallaire, D. H., et al. (2008). Emergence of attributional style and its relations to depressive symptoms. *Journal of Abnormal Psychology, 117*, 16–31.

Cole, D. A., Martin, J. M., Peeke, L. G., Seroczynski, A. D., & Hoffman, K. (1998). Are cognitive errors of underestimation predictive or reflective of depressive symptoms in children? A longitudinal study. *Journal of Abnormal Psychology, 107*, 481–496.

Colli, A., Tanzilli, A., Dimaggio, G., & Lingiardi, V. (2014). Patient personality and therapist response: An empirical investigation. *American Journal of Psychiatry, 171*, 102–108. doi:10.1176/appi.ajp.2013.13020224

Collin, G., Kahn, R. S., de Reus, M. A., Cahn, W., & van den Heuvel, M. P. (2014). Impaired rich club connectivity in unaffected siblings of schizophrenia patients. *Schizophrenia Bulletin, 40*, 438–448.

Colombo, C., Benedetti, F., Barbini, B., Campori, E., & Smeraldi, E. (1999). Rate of switch from depression into mania after therapeutic sleep deprivation in bipolar depression. *Psychiatry Research, 86*, 267–270.

Colom, F., Vieta, E., Reinares, M., Martinez-Aran, A., Torrent, C., Goikolea, J. M., & Gasto, C. (2003). Psychoeducation efficacy in bipolar disorders: Beyond compliance enhancement. *Journal of Clinical Psychiatry, 64*, 1101–1105.

Comer, S. D., Hart, C. L., Ward, A. S., Haney, M., Foltin, R. W., & Fischman, M. W. (2001). Effects of repeated oral methamphetamine administration in humans. *Psychopharmacology, 155*, 397–404.

Compas, B. E., Haaga, D. A. F., Keefe, F. J., Leitenberg, H., & Williams, D. A. (1998). Sampling of empirically supported psychological treatments from health psychology: Smoking, chronic pain, cancer, and bulimia nervosa. *Journal of Consulting and Clinical Psychology, 66*, 89–112.

Conduct Problems Prevention Research Group (CPPRG). (2010a). The difficulty of maintaining positive intervention effects: A look at disruptive behavior, deviant peer relations, and social skills during the middle school years. *Journal of Early Adolescence, 30*(4).

Conduct Problems Prevention Research Group (CPPRG). (2010b). Fast track intervention effects on youth arrests and delinquency. *Journal of Experimental Criminology, 6*(2), 131–157.

Conduct Problems Prevention Research Group (CPPRG). (2011). The effects of the fast track preventive intervention on the development of conduct disorder across childhood. *Child Development, 82*(1), 331–345.

Conley, R. R., & Mahmoud, R. (2001). A randomized double-blind study of risperidone and olanzapine in the treatment of schizophrenia or schizoaffective disorder. *American Journal of Psychiatry, 158*, 765–774.

Constantino, J. N., Zhang, Z., Frazier, T., Abbachi, A. M., & Law, P. (2010). Sibling recurrence and the genetic epidemiology of autism. *American Journal of Psychiatry, 167*, 1349–1356.

Converge Consortium. (2015). Sparse whole-genome sequencing identifies two loci for major depressive disorder. *Nature, 523*(7562), 588–591. doi:10.1038/nature14659

Cook, M., & Mineka, S. (1989). Observational conditioning of fear to fear-relevant versus fear-irrelevant stimuli in rhesus monkeys. *Journal of Abnormal Psychology, 98*, 448–459.

Cooper, C., Sommerlad, A., Lyketsos, C. G., & Livingston, G. (2015). Modifiable predictors of dementia in mild cognitive impairment: A systematic review and meta-analysis. *American Journal of Psychiatry, 172*, 323–334. doi:10.1176/appi.ajp.2014.14070878

Cooper, K., Martyn-St James, M., Kaltenthaler, E., Dickinson, K., Cantrell, A., Wylie, K., et al. (2015). Behavioral therapies for management of premature ejaculation: A systematic review. *Sexual Medicine, 3*, 174–188. doi:10.1002/sm2.65

Cooper, M. L., Frone, M. R., Russell, M., & Mudar, P. (1995). Drinking to regulate positive and negative emotion: A motivational model of alcoholism. *Journal of Personality and Social Psychology, 69*, 961–974.

Cooper, M. S., & Clark, V. P. (2013). Neuroinflammation, neuroautoimmunity, and the co-morbidities of complex regional pain syndrome. *Journal of Neuroimmune Pharmacology, 8*, 452–469.

Copeland, W. E., Angold, A., Costello, E. J., & Egger, H. (2013). Prevalence, comorbidity, and correlates of DSM-5 proposed disruptive mood dysregulation disorder. *American Journal of Psychiatry, 170*(2), 173–179.

Copeland, W. E., Shanahan, L., Egger, H., Angold, A., & Costello, E. J. (2014). Adult diagnostic and functional outcomes of DSM-5 disruptive mood dysregulation disorder. *American Journal of Psychiatry, 171*(6), 668–674. http://doi.org/10.1176/appi.ajp.2014.13091213

Copeland, W. E., Wolke, D., Angold, A., & Costello, E. J. (2013). Adult psychiatric outcomes of bullying and being bullied by peers in childhood and adolescence. *JAMA Psychiatry, 70*(4), 419–426. http://doi.org/10.1001/jamapsychiatry.2013.504

Copf, T. (2016). Impairments in dendrite morphogenesis as etiology for neurodevelopmental disorders and implications for therapeutic treatments. *Neuroscience & Biobehavioral Reviews, 68*, 946–978. http://doi.org/10.1016/j.neubiorev.2016.04.008

Copolov, D. L., Mackinnon, A., & Trauer, T. (2004). Correlates of the affective impact of auditory hallucinations in psychotic disorders. *Schizophrenia Bulletin, 30*, 163–171.

Corrigan, P. W. (2015). Challenging the stigma of mental illness: Different agendas, different goals. *Psychiatric Services, 66*, 1347–1349. http://doi.org/10.1176/appi.ps.201500107.

Corrigan, P. W., Morris, S. B., Michaels, P. J., Rafacz, J. D., & Rüsch, N. (2012). Challenging the public stigma of mental illness: A meta-analysis of outcome studies. *Psychiatric Services, 63*, 963–973. http://doi.org/10.1176/appi.ps.201100529

Corrigan, P. W., & Watson, A. C. (2005). Findings from the National Comorbidity Survey on the frequency of violent behavior in individuals with psychiatric disorders. *Psychiatry Research, 136*, 153–162.

Corrigan, P. W., Watson, A. C., Heyrman, J. D., Warpinski, A., Gracia, G., Slopen, N., et al. (2005). Structural stigma in state legislatures. *Psychiatric Services, 56*, 557–563.

Cortese, S., Kelly, C., Chabernaud, C., Proal, E., Di Martino, A., Milham, M. P., & Castellanos, F. X. (2012). Toward systems neuroscience of ADHD: A meta-analysis of 55 fMRI studies. *American Journal of Psychiatry, 169*(10), 1038–1055.

Corvin, A., & Sullivan, P. F. (2016). What next in schizophrenia genetics for the Psychiatric Genomics Consortium? *Schizophrenia Bulletin, 42*, 538-541.

Costa, P. T., Metter, E. J., & McCrae, R. R. (1994). Personality stability and its contribution to successful aging. *Journal of Geriatric Psychiatry, 27*, 41–59.

Costello, J. E., Erkanli, A., & Angold, A. (2006). Is there an epidemic of child or adolescent depression? *Journal of Child Psychology and Psychiatry, 47*(12), 1263–1271.

Cougle, J. R., Timpano, K. R., Sachs-Ericsson, N., Keough, M. E., & Riccardi, C. J. (2010). Examining the unique relationships between anxiety disorders and childhood physical and sexual abuse in the national comorbidity survey-replication. *Psychiatry Research, 177*(1–2), 150–155. doi:http://doi.org/10.1016/j.psychres.2009.03.008

Courchesne, E. (2004). Brain development in autism: Early overgrowth followed by premature arrests of growth. *Mental Retardation and Developmental Disabilities Research Reviews, 10*, 106–111.

Courchesne, E., Carnes, B. S., & Davis, H. R. (2001). Unusual brain growth patterns in early life in patients with autistic disorder: An MRI study. *Neurology, 57*, 245–254.

Cousins, D. A., Butts, K., & Young, A. H. (2009). The role of dopamine in bipolar disorder. *Bipolar Disorders, 11*(8), 787–806. doi:10.1111/j.1399-5618.2009.00760.x

Coyne, J. C. (1976). Depression and the response of others. *Journal of Abnormal Psychology, 85*, 186–193.

Crane, E. H. (2015). *The CBHSQ report: Emergency department visits involving narcotic pain relievers.* Rockville, MD: Substance Abuse and Mental Health Services Administration, Center for Behavioral Health Statistics and Quality.

Crane, P. K., Walker, R., Hubbard, R. A., Li, G., Nathan, D. M., Zheng, H., et al. (2013). Glucose levels and risk of dementia. *New England Journal of Medicine, 369*, 540–548. doi:10.1056/NEJMoa1215740

Craske, M. G., & Barlow, D. (2014). In panic disorder and agoraphobia. D. Barlow (Ed.), *Clinical handbook of psychological disorders: A step-by-step treatment manual* (pp. 768). New York, NY: Guilford.

Craske, M. G., & Mystkowski, J. (2006). Exposure therapy and extinction: Clinical studies. In M. G. Craske, D. Hermans, & D. Vansteenwegen (Eds.), *Fear and learning from basic processes to clinical implications* (pp. 217–233). Washington DC: American Psychological Association.

Craske, M. G., Rauch, S. L., Ursano, R., Prenoveau, J., Pine, D. S., & Zinbarg, R. E. (2009). What is an anxiety disorder? *Depression and Anxiety, 26*, 1066–1085.

Creamer, M., Burgess, P., & McFarlane, A. C. (2001). Posttraumatic stress disorder: Findings from the Australian National Survey of Mental Health and Well-being. *Psychological Medicine, 31*, 1237–1247.

Crean, R. D., Crane, N. A., & Mason, B. J. (2011). An evidence based review of acute and long-term effects of *Cannabis* use on executive cognitive functions. *Journal of Addictive Medicines, 5*, 1–8.

Crissman, H. P., Berger, M. B., Graham, L. F., & Dalton, V. K. (2017). Transgender demographics: A household probability sample of U.S. adults, 2014. *American Journal of Public Health, 107*, 213–215. doi:10.2105/ajph.2016.303571

Cristea, I. A., Gentili, C., Cotet, C. D., Palomba, D., Barbui, C., & Cuijpers, P. (2017). Efficacy of psychotherapies for borderline personality disorder: A systematic review and meta-analysis. *JAMA Psychiatry, 74*, 319–328. doi:10.1001/jamapsychiatry.2016.4287

Critchley, H. D., Daly, E. M., Bullmore, E. T., Williams, S. C. R., Van Amelsvoort, T., Robertson, et al. (2001). The functional neuroanatomy of social behaviour: Changes in cerebral blood flow when people with autistic disorder process facial expressions. *Brain, 123*, 2203–2212.

Crits-Christoph, P., Chambless, D. L., Frank, E., Brody, C., et al. (1995). Training in empirically validated treatments: What are clinical psychology students learning? *Professional Psychology: Research and Practice, 26*, 514–522.

Critser, G. (2003). *Fatland: How Americans became the fattest people in the world.* Boston, MA: Houghton Mifflin.

Cronbach, L. J., & Meehl, P. E. (1955). Construct validity in psychological tests. *Psychological Bulletin, 52*, 281–302.

Cross-Disorder Group of the Psychiatric Genomics Consortium. (2013). Identification of risk loci with shared effects on five major psychiatric disorders: A genome-wide analysis. *The Lancet, 381*(9875), 1371–1379.

Crossley, N. A., Mechelli, A., Ginestet, C., Rubinov, M., Bullmore, E. T., & McGuire, P. (2016). Altered hub functioning and compensatory activations in the connectome: A meta-analysis of functional neuroimaging studies in schizophrenia. *Schizophrenia Bulletin, 42*, 434–442. http://doi.org/10.1093/schbul/sbv146

Crow, S. J., Peterson, C. B., Swanson, S. A., Raymond, N. C., Specker, S., Eckert, E. D., et al. (2009). Increased mortality in bulimia nervosa and other eating disorders. *American Journal of Psychiatry, 166*, 1342–1346.

Crozier, J. C., Dodge, K. A., Griffith, R. Lansford, J. E., Bates, J. E., Pettit, G. S., et al. (2008). Social information processing and cardiac predictors of adolescent antisocial behavior. *Journal of Abnormal Psychology, 117*, 253–267.

Crump, C., Sundquist, K., Winkleby, M. A., & Sundquist, J. (2013). Comorbidities and mortality in bipolar disorder: A Swedish national cohort study. *JAMA Psychiatry, 70*(9), 931–939. doi:10.1001/jamapsychiatry.2013.1394

Cuellar, A. K., Johnson, S. L., & Winters, R. (2005). Distinctions between bipolar and unipolar depression. *Clinical Psychology Review, 25*, 307–339.

Cuijpers, P., Berking, M., Andersson, G., Quigley, L., Kleiboer, A., & Dobson, K. S. (2013). A meta-analysis of cognitive-behavioural therapy for adult depression, alone and in comparison with other treatments. *Canadian Journal of Psychiatry, 58*(7), 376–385. doi:10.1177/070674371305800702

Cuijpers, P., Donker, T., Weissman, M. M., Ravitz, P., & Cristea, I. A. (2016). Interpersonal psychotherapy for mental health problems: A comprehensive meta-analysis. *American Journal of Psychiatry, 173*, 680–687. http://doi.org/10.1176/appi.ajp.2015.15091141

Cuijpers, P., Sijbrandij, M., Koole, S., Huibers, M., Berking, M., & Andersson, G. (2014). Psychological treatment of generalized anxiety disorder: A meta-analysis. *Clinical Psychology Review, 34*(2), 130–140. doi:http://doi.org/10.1016/j.cpr.2014.01.002

Cuijpers, P., Sijbrandij, M., Koole, S. L., Andersson, G., Beekman, A. T., & Reynolds, C. F. (2013). The efficacy of psychotherapy and pharmacotherapy in treating depressive and anxiety disorders: A meta-analysis of direct comparisons. *World Psychiatry, 12*, 137–148.

Culbert, K. M., Racine, S. E., & Klump, K. L. (2015). Research review: What we have learned about the causes of eating disorders—A synthesis of sociocultural, psychological, and biological research. *Journal of Child Psychology and Psychiatry, 56*(11), 1141–1164. http://doi.org/10.1111/jcpp.12441

Culverhouse, R. C., Saccone, N. L., Horton, A. C., Ma, Y., Anstey, K. J., Banaschewski, T., et al. (2017). Collaborative meta-analysis finds no evidence of a strong interaction between stress and 5-httlpr genotype contributing to the development of depression. *Molecular Psychiatry.* doi:10.1038/mp.2017.44

Cummings, C. M., Caporino, N. E., & Kendall, P. C. (2014). Comorbidity of anxiety and depression in children and adolescents: 20 years after. *Psychological Bulletin, 140*(3), 816–845.

Curcic-Blake, B., Liemburg, E., Vercammen, A., Swart, M., Knegtering, H., Bruggeman, R., & Aleman, A. (2013). When Broca goes uninformed: Reduced information flow to Broca's area in schizophrenia patients with auditory hallucinations. *Schizophrenia Bulletin, 39*, 1087–1095.

Curran, E., Adamson, G., Stringer, M., Rosato, M., & Leavey, G. (2016). Severity of mental illness as a result of multiple childhood adversities: US National Epidemiologic Survey. *Social Psychiatry and Psychiatric Epidemiology, 51*, 647–657. doi:10.1007/s00127-016-1198-3

Curry, J. F. (2001). Specific psychotherapies for childhood and adolescent depression. *Biological Psychiatry, 49*, 1091–1100.

Curry, J., Silva, S., Rohde, P., Ginsburg, G., Kratochvil, C., Simons, A., et al. (2011). Recovery and recurrence following treatment for adolescent major depression. *Archives of General Psychiatry, 68*, 263–270.

Curry, S. J., Mermelstein, R. J., & Sporer, A. K. (2009). Therapy for specific problems: Youth tobacco cessation. *Annual Review of Psychology, 60*, 229–255.

Curtin, J. J., Lang, A. R., Patrick, C. J., & Strizke, W. G. K. (1998). Alcohol and fear-potentiated startle: The role of competing cognitive demands in the stress-reducing effects of intoxication. *Journal of Abnormal Psychology, 107*, 547–557.

Curtis, N. M., Ronan, K. R., & Borduin, C. M. (2004). Multisystemic treatment: A meta-analysis of outcome studies. *Journal of Family Psychology, 18*(3), 411–419. doi:http://dx.doi.org/10.1037/0893-3200.18.3.411

Cybulski, L., Mayo-Wilson, E., & Grant, S. (2016). Improving transparency and reproducibility through registration: The status of intervention trials published in clinical psychology journals. *Journal of Consulting and Clinical Psychology, 84*(9), 753–767. doi:10.1037/ccp0000115

Dalenberg, C. J., Brand, B. L., Gleaves, D. H., Dorahy, M. J., Loewenstein, R. J., Cardeña, E., et al. (2012). Evaluation of the evidence for the trauma and fantasy models of dissociation. *Psychological Bulletin, 138*, 550–588. doi:10.1037/a0027447

Daley, S. E., Hammen, C., & Rao, U. (2000). Predictors of first onset and recurrence of major depression in young women during the 5 years following high school graduation. *Journal of Abnormal Psychology 109*, 525–533.

Dallery, J., Silverman, K., Chutuape, M. A., Bigelow, G. E., & Stitzer, M. (2001). Voucher-based reinforcement of opiate plus cocaine abstinence in treatment-resistant methadone patients: Effects of reinforcer magnitude. *Experimental and Clinical Psychopharmacology, 9*, 317–325.

Dallman, M. F., Pecoraro, N., Akana, S. F., La Fleur, S. E., Gomez, F., Houshyar, H., et al. (2003). Chronic stress and obesity: A new view of comfort food. *Proceedings of the National Academy of Sciences, 100*, 11696–11701.

Dalmau, J., Tüzün, E., Wu, H. Y., Masjuan, J., Rossi, J. E., Voloschin, A., et al. (2007). Paraneoplastic anti-N-methyl-D-aspartate receptor encephalitis associated with ovarian teratoma. *Annals of Neurology, 61*, 25–36.

Dantzer, R., O'Connor, J. C., Freund, G. G., Johnson, R. W., & Kelley, K. W. (2008). From inflammation to sickness and depression: When the immune system subjugates the brain. *Nature Reviews Neuroscience, 9*, 46–56.

Davidson, R. J., Pizzagalli, D., Nitschke, J. B., & Putnam, K. (2002). Depression: Perspectives from affective neuroscience. *Annual Review of Psychology, 53*(1), 545–574.

Davies, D. K., Stock, S. E., & Wehmeyer, M. (2003). Application of computer simulation to teach ATM access to individuals with intellectual disabilities. *Education and Training in Developmental Disabilities, 38*, 451–456.

Davis A. S., Malmberg, A., Brandt, L., Allebeck, P., & & Lewis, G. (1997). IQ and risk for schizophrenia: A population-based cohort study. *Psychological Medicine, 27*, 1311–1323.

Davis, J. M. (1978). Dopamine theory of schizophrenia: A two-factor theory. In L. C. Wynne, R. L. Cromwell, & S. Matthysse (Eds.), *The nature of schizophrenia.* New York, NY: John Wiley & Sons.

Davis, J. M., Chen, N., & Glick, I. D. (2003). A meta-analysis of the efficacy of second-generation antipsychotics. *Archives of General Psychiatry, 60*, 553–564.

Davis, K. L., Kahn, R. S., Ko, G., & Davidson, M. (1991). Dopamine and schizophrenia: A review and reconceptualization. *American Journal of Psychiatry, 148*, 1474–1486.

Davis, L., & Siegel, L. J. (2000). Posttraumatic stress disorder in children and adolescents: A review and analysis. *Clinical Child and Family Psychology Review, 3*, 135–153.

Davison, T. E., McCabe, M., & Mellor, D. (2009). An examination of the "gold standard" diagnosis of major depression in aged-care settings. *American Journal of Geriatric Psychiatry, 17*, 359–367.

Davis, S. R., Worsley, R., Miller, K. K., Parish, S. J., & Santoro, N. (2016). Androgens and female sexual function and dysfunction: Findings from the Fourth International Consultation of Sexual Medicine. *Journal of Sexual Medicine, 13*, 168–178. doi:10.1016/j.jsxm.2015.12.033

Davis, T. E., May, A., & Whiting, S. E. (2011). Evidence-based treatment of anxiety and phobia in children and adolescents: Current status and effects on the emotional response. *Clinical Psychology Review, 31*, 592–602.

Dawson, G., Toth, K., Abbott, R., Osterling, J., Munson, J., Estes, A., & Liaw, J. (2004). Early social attention impairments in autism: Social orienting, joint attention, and attention to distress. *Developmental Psychology, 40*, 271–283.

Dawson, M. E., Schell, A. M., & Banis, H. T. (1986). Greater resistance to extinction of electrodermal responses conditioned to potentially phobic CSs: A noncognitive process? *Psychophysiology, 23*, 552–561.

Deacon, B. J., & Abramowitz, J. S. (2004). Cognitive and behavioral treatments for anxiety disorders: A review of meta-analytic findings. *Journal of Clinical Psychology, 60*, 429–441.

Deary, I. J., & Johnson, W. (2010). Intelligence and education: Causal perceptions drive analytic processes and therefore conclusions. *International Journal of Epidemiology, 39*, 1362–1369.

deCharms, R. C., Maeda, F., Glover, G. H., Ludlow, D., Pauly, J. M., Soneji, D., et al. (2005). Control over brain activation and pain learned by using real-time functional MRI. *Proceedings of the National Academy of Sciences of the United States of America, 102*, 18626–18631.

de Graaf, R., Bijl, R. V., Ravelli, A., Smit, F., & Vollenbergh, W. A. M. (2002). Predictors of first incidence of DSM-III-R psychiatric disorders in the general population: Findings from the Netherlands mental health survey and incidence study. *Acta Psychiatrica Scandinavica, 106*, 303–313.

Deisenhammer, E. A., Ing, C. M., Strauss, R., Kemmler, G., Hinterhuber, H., & Weiss, E. M. (2009). The duration of the suicidal process: How much time is left for intervention between consideration and accomplishment of a suicide attempt? *Journal of Clinical Psychiatry, 70*(1), 19–24.

DeJong, W., & Kleck, R. E. (1986). The social psychological effects of overweight. In C. P. Herman, M. P. Zanna, & E. T. Higgins (Eds.), *Physical appearance, stigma, and social behavior.* Hillside, NJ: Lawrence Erlbaum.

de la Cruz, L. F., Llorens, M., Jassi, A., Krebs, G., Vidal-Ribas, P., Radua, J., . . . Mataix-Cols, D. (2015). Ethnic inequalities in the use of secondary and tertiary mental health services among patients with obsessive-compulsive disorder. *British Journal of Psychiatry, 207*(6), 530–535. doi:10.1192/bjp.bp.114.154062

deLint, J. (1978). Alcohol consumption and alcohol problems from an epidemiological perspective. *British Journal of Alcohol and Alcoholism, 17*, 109–116.

Dell, P. F. (2006). A new model of dissociative identity disorder. *Psychiatric Clinics of North America, 29*, 1–26, vii.

DeMatteo, D., Galloway, M., Arnold, S., & Patel, U. (2015). Sexual assault on college campuses: A 50-state survey of criminal sexual assault statutes and their relevance to campus sexual assault. *Psychology, Public Policy, and Law, 21*, 227–238. doi:10.1037/law0000055

Demyttenaere, K., Bruffaerts, R., Posada-Villa, J., Gasquet, I., Kovess, V., Lepine, J. P., et al. (2004). Prevalence, severity, and unmet need for treatment of mental disorders in the World Health Organization World Mental Health Surveys. *JAMA: The Journal of the American Medical Association, 291*, 2581–2590. doi:10.1001/jama.291.21.2581

Depression Guidelines Panel. (1993). Depression in primary care: Treatment of major depression. Clinical practice guideline No. 5. (Vol. 2). Rockville, MD: U.S. Department of Health and Human Services, Public Health Service, Agency for Health Care Policy and Research.

Depue, R. A., Collins, P. F., & Luciano, M. (1996). A model of neurobiology: Environment interaction in developmental psychopathology. In M. F. Lenzenweger & J. J. Haugaard (Eds.), *Frontiers of developmental psychopathology* (pp. 44–76). New York, NY: Oxford University Press.

Depue, R. A., & Iacono, W. G. (1989). Neurobehavioral aspects of affective disorders. *Annual Review of Psychology, 40*, 457–492.

Deserno, L., Sterzer, P., Wustenberg, T., Heinz, A., & Schlagenhauf, F. (2012). Reduced prefrontal-parietal effective connectivity and working memory deficits in schizophrenia. *Journal of Neuroscience, 32*, 12–20.

de Souza, R. J., Bray, G. A., Carey, V. J., Hall, K. D., LeBoff, M. S., Loria, C. M., et al. (2012). Effects of 4 weight-loss diets differing in fat, protein, and carbohydrate on fat mass, lean mass, visceral adipose tissue, and hepatic fat: Results from the POUNDS LOST trial. *American Journal of Clinical Nutrition, 95*, 614–625. http://doi.org/10.3945/ajcn.111.026328

Deutsch, A. R., Chernyavskiy, P., Steinley, D., & Slutske, W. S. (2015). Measuring peer socialization for adolescent substance use: A comparison of perceived and actual friends' substance use effects. *Journal of Studies on Alcohol and Drugs, 76*, 267–277. http://dx.doi.org/10.15288/jsad.2015.76.267

de Wit, H., & Zacny, J. (2000). Abuse potential of nicotine replacement therapies. In K. J. Palmer (Ed.), *Smoking Cessation* (pp. 79–92). Kwai Chung, Hong Kong: Adis International Publications.

Dick, D. M., Pagan, J. L., Viken, R., Purcell, S., Kaprio, J., Pulkinnen, L., et al. (2007). Changing environmental influences on substance use across development. *Twin Research and Human Genetics, 10*, 315–326.

Dickerson, S. S., Gruenewald, T. L., & Kemeny, M. E. (2009). Psychobiological responses to social self threat: Functional or detrimental? *Self and Identity, 8*, 270–285.

Dickerson, S. S., & Kemeny, M. E. (2004). Acute stressors and cortisol responses: A theoretical integration and synthesis of laboratory research. *Psychological Bulletin, 130*, 355–391.

Dickstein, D. P., & Leibenluft, E. (2006). Emotion regulation in children and adolescents: Boundaries between normalcy and bipolar disorder. *Development and Psychopathology, 18*, 1105–1131.

Didie, E. R., Menard, W., Stern, A. P., & Phillips, K. A. (2008). Occupational functioning and impairment in adults with body dysmorphic disorder. *Comprehensive Psychiatry, 49*, 561–569.

Dieserud, G., Roysamb, E., Braverman, M. T., Dalgard, O. S., & Ekeberg, O. (2003). Predicating repetition of suicide attempt: A prospective study of 50 suicide attempters. *Archives of Suicide Research, 7*, 1–15.

Di Forti, M., Sallis H., Allegri, F., Trotta, A., Ferraro L., Stilo, S. A., et al. (2013). Daily use, especially of high-potency *Cannabis*, drives the earlier onset of psychosis in *Cannabis* users. *Schizophrenia Bulletin*, doi: 10.1093/schbul/sbt181

DiGangi, J. A., Gomez, D., Mendoza, L., Jason, L. A., Keys, C. B., & Koenen, K. C. (2013). Pretrauma risk factors for posttraumatic stress disorder: A systematic review of the literature. *Clinical Psychology Review, 33*(6), 728–744. doi:https://doi.org/10.1016/j.cpr.2013.05.002

DiLillo, D., Giuffre, D., Tremblay, G. C., & Peterson, L. (2001). A closer look at the nature of intimate partner violence reported by women with a history of child sexual abuse. *Journal of Interpersonal Violence, 16*, 116–132.

Dillon, B. (2010). The hypochondriacs: Nine tormented lives. London, England: Faber & Faber.

Dimidjian, S., Barrera, M., Martell, C., Muñoz, R. F., & Lewinsohn, P. M. (2011). The origins and current status of behavioral activation treatments for depression. *Annual Review of Clinical Psychology, 7*, 1–38.

Dimoff, J. D., & Sayette, M. A. (2017) The case for investigating social context in laboratory studies of smoking. *Addiction, 12*, 388–395. doi:10.1111/add.13503.

Dishion, T., Forgatch, M., Chamberlain, P., & Pelham, W. E. (2016). The Oregon model of behavior family therapy: From intervention design to promoting large-scale system change. *Special 50th Anniversary Issue: Honoring the Past and Looking to the Future: Updates on Seminal Behavior Therapy Publications on Current Therapies and Future Directions, Part II, 47*(6), 812–837.

Dishion, T. J., & Andrews, D. W. (1995). Preventing escalation in problem behaviors with high-risk young adolescents: Immediate and 1-year outcomes. *Journal of Consulting and Clinical Psychology, 63*, 538–548.

Dishion, T. J., Brennan, L. M., Shaw, D. S., McEachern, A. D., Wilson, M. N., & Jo, B. (2014). Prevention of problem behavior through annual family check-ups in early childhood: Intervention effects from home to early elementary school. *Journal of Abnormal Child Psychology, 42*, 343–354. doi:10.1007/s10802-013-9768-2.

Dishion, T. J., Kim, H., & Tein, J.-Y. (2015). Friendship and adolescent problem behavior: Deviancy training and coercive joining as dynamic mediators. In T. P. Beauchaine & S. P. Hinshaw (Eds.), *The Oxford handbook of externalizing spectrum disorders* (pp. 303–311). New York, NY: Oxford University Press.

Dishion, T. J., Patterson, G. R., & Kavanagh, K. A. (1992). An experimental test of the coercion model: Linking theory, measurement, and intervention. In J. McCord & R. E. Tremblay (Eds.), *Preventing antisocial behavior.* (pp. 253–282). New York, NY: Guilford Press.

Dishion, T. J., Shaw, D., Connell, A., Gardner, F., Weaver, C., & Wilson, M. (2008). The family check-up with high-risk indigent families: Preventing problem behavior by increasing parents' positive behavior support in early childhood. *Child Development, 79*(5), 1395–1414. http://dx.doi.org/10.1111/j.1467-8624.2008.01195.x

Dixon, L. B., Dickerson, F., Bellack, A. S., Bennett, M., Dickinson, D., Goldberg, R. W., et al. (2010). The 2009 schizophrenia PORT psychosocial treatment recommendations and summary statements. *Schizophrenia Bulletin, 36*, 48–70.

Dobson, K. S., Hollon, S. D., Dimidjian, S., Schmaling, K. B., Kohlenberg, R. J., Gallop, R., et al. (2008). Randomized trial of behavioral activation, cognitive therapy, and antidepressant medication in the prevention of relapse and recurrence in major depression. *Journal of Consulting and Clinical Psychology, 76*, 468–477.

Dodes, L., & Dodes, Z. (2014). *The sober truth: Debunking the bad science behind 12-step programs and the rehab industry.* New York, NY: Beacon Press.

Dodge, K. A., Bierman, K. L., Coie, J. D., Greenberg, M. T., Lochman, J. E., McMahon, R. J., et al. (2015). Impact of early intervention on psychopathology, crime, and well-being at age 25. *American Journal of Psychiatry, 172*(1), 59–70. http://doi.org/10.1176/appi.ajp.2014.13060786

Dodge, K. A., & Frame, C. L. (1982). Social cognitive biases and deficits in aggressive boys. *Child Development, 53*, 620–635.

Dodge, K. A., & Godwin, J. (2013). Social-information-processing patterns mediate the impact of preventive intervention on adolescent antisocial behavior. *Psychological Science, 24*(4), 456–465.

Doerr, P., Fichter, M., Pirke, K. M., & Lund, R. (1980). Relationship between weight gain and hypothalamic pituitary adrenal function in patients with anorexia nervosa. *Journal of Steroid Biochemistry, 13*, 529–537.

Dohrenwend, B. P., & Dohrenwend, B. S. (1974). Social and cultural influences on psychopathology. *Annual Review of Psychology, 25*, 417–452.

Dohrenwend, B. P., Levav, P. E., Schwartz, S., Naveh, G., Link, B. G., Skodol, A. E., & Stueve, A. (1992). Socioeconomic status and psychiatric disorders: The causation–selection issue. *Science, 255*, 946–952.

Doll, H. A., & Fairburn, C. G. (1998). Heightened accuracy of self-reported weight in bulimia nervosa: A useful cognitive "distortion." *International Journal of Eating Disorders, 24*, 267–273.

Donoghue, K., Elzerbi, C., Saunders, R., Whittington, C., Pilling, S., & Drummond, C. (2015). The efficacy of acamprosate and naltrexone in the treatment of alcohol dependence, Europe versus the rest of the world: A meta-analysis. *Addiction, 110*, 920–930. doi:10.1111/add.12875.

Dougherty, L., Smith, V., Bufferd, S., Kessel, E., Carlson, G., & Klein, D. (2016). Disruptive mood dysregulation disorder at the age of 6 years and clinical and functional outcomes 3 years later. *Psychological Medicine, 46*(5), 1103–1114. doi:10.1017/S0033291715002809

Douglas, K. S., Guy, L. S., & Hart, S. D. (2009). Psychosis as a risk factor for violence to others: A meta-analysis. *Psychological Bulletin, 135*, 679–706.

Doyle, P. M., Le Grange, D., Loeb, K., Doyle, A. C., & Crosby, R. D. (2010). Early response to family-based treatment for adolescent anorexia nervosa. *International Journal of Eating Disorders, 43*, 659–662.

Doyon, W. M., Dong, Y., Ostroumov, A., Thomas, A. M., Zhang, T. A., & Dani, J. A. (2013). Nicotine decreases ethanol-induced dopamine signaling and increases self-administration via stress hormones. *Neuron, 79*, 530–540.

Drane, D. L., Williamson, D. J., Stroup, E. S., Holmes, M. D., Jung, M., Koerner, E., et al. (2006). Cognitive impairment is not equal in patients with epileptic and psychogenic nonepileptic seizures. *Epilepsia, 47*, 1879–1886. doi:10.1111/j.1528-1167.2006.00611.x

Drury, H., Ajmi, S., Fernández de la Cruz, L., Nordsletten, A. E., & Mataix-Cols, D. (2014). Caregiver burden, family accommodation, health, and well-being in relatives of individuals with hoarding disorder. *Journal of Affective Disorders, 159*, 7–14. doi:10.1016/j.jad.2014.01.023

Drury, V., Birchwood, M., Cochrane, R., & Macmillan, R. (1996). Cognitive therapy and recovery from acute psychosis: A controlled trial. *British Journal of Psychiatry, 169*, 593–601.

Dugas, M. J., Brillon, P., Savard, P., Turcotte, J., Gaudet, A., Ladouceur, R., et al. (2010). A randomized clinical trial of cognitive-behavioral therapy and applied relaxation for adults with generalized anxiety disorder. *Behavior therapy, 41*(1), 46–58. doi:10.1016/j.beth.2008.12.004

Dugas, M. J., Marchand, A., & Ladouceur, R. (2005). Further validation of a cognitive-behavioral model of generalized anxiety disorder: Diagnostic and symptom specificity. *Journal of Anxiety Disorders, 19*, 329–343.

Duncan, L. E., & Keller, M. C. (2011). A critical review of the first 10 years of candidate gene-by-environment interaction research in psychiatry. *American Journal of Psychiatry, 168*(10), 1041–1049.

Duncan, L., Yilmaz, Z., Gaspar, H., Walters, R., Goldstein, J., Anttila, V., et al. (2017). Significant locus and metabolic genetic correlations revealed in genome-wide association study of anorexia nervosa. *American Journal of Psychiatry, 174*, 850–858. appiajp201716121402. http://doi.org/10.1176/appi.ajp.2017.16121402

Dunham, L. (2014, September 1). Difficult girl growing up, with help. *The New Yorker.*

Dunn, E. C., Gilman, S. E., Willett, J. B., Slopen, N. B., & Molnar, B. E. (2012). The impact of exposure to interpersonal violence on gender differences in adolescent-onset major depression: Results from the National Comorbidity Survey Replication (NCS-R). *Depression and Anxiety, 29*, 392–399. doi:10.1002/da.21916

Dunner, D. L., Aaronson, S. T., Sackeim, H. A., Janicak, P. G., Carpenter, L. L., Boyadjis, T., et al. (2014). A multisite, naturalistic, observational study of transcranial magnetic stimulation for patients with pharmacoresistant major depressive disorder: Durability of benefit over a 1-year follow-up period. *Journal of Clinical Psychiatry, 75*(12), 1394–1401. doi:10.4088/JCP.13m08977

Dura, J. R., Stukenberg, K. W., & Kiecolt-Glaser, J. K. (1991). Anxiety and depressive disorders in adult children caring for demented parents. *Psychology and Aging, 6*, 467–473.

Dworkin, R. H., & Lenzenwenger, M. F. (1984). Symptoms and the genetics of schizophrenia: Implications for diagnosis. *American Journal of Psychiatry, 141*, 1541–1546.

Dworkin, R. H., Lenzenwenger, M. F., & Moldin, S. O. (1987). Genetics and the phenomenology of schizophrenia. In P. D. Harvey & E. F. Walker (Eds.), *Positive and negative symptoms of psychosis*. Hillsdale, NJ: Lawrence Erlbaum.

Dwyer-Lindgren, L., Mokdad, A. H., Srebotnjak, T., Flaxman, A. D., Hansen, G. M., & Murray, C. J. (2014). Cigarette smoking prevalence in US counties: 1996–2012. *Population Health Metrics, 12*, 5.

Dyshniku, F., Murray, M. E., Fazio, R. L., Lykins, A. D., & Cantor, J. M. (2015). Minor physical anomalies as a window into the prenatal origins of pedophilia. *Archives of Sexual Behavior, 44*, 2151–2159. doi:10.1007/s10508-015-0564-7

Eack, S. M., Greenwald, D. P., Hogarty, S. S., & Keshavan, M. S. (2010). One-year durability of the effects of cognitive enhancement therapy on functional outcome in early schizophrenia. *Schizophrenia Research, 120*, 210–216.

Eardley, I., Donatucci, C., Corbin, J., El-Meliegy, A., Hatzimouratidis, K., McVary, K., et al. (2010). Pharmacotherapy for erectile dysfunction. *Journal of Sexual Medicine, 7*, 524–540.

Eaton, W. W., Shao, H., Nestadt, G., Lee, H. B., Bienvenu, O. J., & Zandi, P. (2008). Population-based study of first onset and chronicity in major depressive disorder. *Archives of General Psychiatry, 65*(5), 513–520. doi:10.1001/archpsyc.65.5.513

Eddy, K. T., Keel, P. K., Dorer, D. J., Delinksy, S. S., Franko, D. L., & Herzog, D. B. (2002). Longitudinal comparison of anorexia nervosa subtypes. *International Journal of Eating Disorders, 31*, 191–201.

Eddy, K. T., Tabri, N., Thomas, J. J., Murray, H. B., Keshaviah, A., Hastings, E., et al. (2017). Recovery from anorexia nervosa and bulimia nervosa at 22-year follow-up. *The Journal of Clinical Psychiatry, 78*(2), 184–189. http://doi.org/10.4088/JCP.15m10393

Edenberg, H. J., Xuie, X., Chen, H-J., Tian, H., Weatherill, L. F., Dick, D. M., et al. (2006). Association of alcohol dehydrogenase genes with alcohol dependence: A comprehensive analysis. *Human Molecular Genetics, 15*, 1539–1549.

Edens, J. F., Kelley, S. E., Lilienfeld, S. O., Skeem, J. L., & Douglas, K. S. (2015). DSM-5 antisocial personality disorder: Predictive validity in a prison sample. *Law and Human Behavior, 39*, 123–129. doi:10.1037/lhb0000105

Edvardsen, J., Torgersen, S., Roysamb, E., Lygren, S., Skre, I., Onstad, S., et al. (2008). Heritability of bipolar spectrum disorders. Unity or heterogeneity? *Journal of Affective Disorders, 106*, 229–240.

Eells, J. (2017, June 15). Emma Stone talks 'Irrational Man,' the Sony hack and keeping her personal life private. *WSJ Magazine.*

Egger, H. L., & Angold, A. (2006). Common emotional and behavioral disorders in preschool children: Presentation, nosology, and epidemiology. *Journal of Child Psychology and Psychiatry, 47*(3–4), 313–337.

Ehde, D. M., Dillworth, T. M., & Turner, J. A. (2014). Cognitive-behavioral therapy for individuals with chronic pain: Efficacy, innovations, and directions for research. *American Psychologist, 69*, 153–166.

Ehlers, A., & Clark, D. M. (2008). Posttraumatic stress disorder: The development of effective psychological treatments. *Nordic Journal of Psychiatry, 62*(Suppl 47), 11–18. doi:10.1080/08039480802315608

Eisen, J. L., Sibrava, N. J., Boisseau, C. L., Mancebo, M. C., Stout, R. L., Pinto, A., et al. (2013). Five-year course of obsessive-compulsive disorder: Predictors of remission and relapse. *Journal of Clinical Psychiatry, 74*, 233–239.

Elis, O., Caponigro, J. M., & Kring, A. M. (2013). Psychosocial treatments for negative symptoms in schizophrenia: Current practices and future directions. *Clinical Psychology Review, 33*, 914–928.

Elkins, I. J., King, S. M., McGue, M., & Iacono, W. G. (2006). Personality traits and the development of nicotine, alcohol, and illicit drug disorders: Prospective links from adolescence to young adulthood. *Journal of Abnormal Psychology, 115*, 26–39. http://doi.org/10.1037/0021-843X.115.1.26

Elkis, H., Friedman, L., Wise, A., & Meltzer, H. T. (1995). Meta-analysis of studies of ventricular enlargement and cortical sulcal prominence in mood disorders. *Archives of General Psychiatry, 52*, 735–746.

Ellenberger, H. F. (1972). The story of "Anna O": A critical review with new data. *Journal of the History of the Behavioral Sciences, 8*, 267–279.

Ellis, A. (1993). Changing rational-emotive therapy (RET) to rational emotive behavior therapy (REBT). *The Behavior Therapist, 16*, 257–258.

Ellis, A. (1995). Changing rational-emotive therapy (RET) to rational emotive behavior therapy (REBT). *Journal of Rational-Emotive and Cognitive Behavior Therapy, 13*, 85–89.

Ellison-Wright, I., & Bullmore, E. (2009). Meta-analysis of diffusion tensor imaging studies in schizophrenia. *Schizophrenia Research, 108*, 3–10.

Emery, S., Kim, Y., Choi, Y. K., Szczypka, G., Wakefield, M., & Chaloupka, F. J. (2012). The effects of smoking-related television advertising on smoking and intentions to quit among adults in the United States: 1999–2007. *American Journal of Public Health, 102*, 751–757.

Emmelkamp, P. M. G., Benner, A., Kuipers, A., Feiertag, G. A., Koster, H. C., & van Apeldoorn, F. J. (2006). Comparison of brief dynamic and cognitive-behavioural therapies in avoidant personality disorder. *British Journal of Psychiatry, 189*, 60–64.

Enander, J., Andersson, E., Mataix-Cols, D., Lichtenstein, L., Alström, K., Andersson, G., . . . Rück, C. (2016). Therapist guided internet based cognitive behavioural therapy for body dysmorphic disorder: Single blind randomised controlled trial. *British Medical Journal, 352.* doi:10.1136/bmj.i241

Engdahl, B., Dikel, T. N., Eberly, R., & Blank, A. (1997). Posttraumatic stress disorder in a community group of former prisoners of war: A normative response to severe trauma. *American Journal of Psychiatry, 154,* 1576–1581.

Ensink, K., Berthelot, N., Bégin, M., Maheux, J., & Normandin, L. (2017). Dissociation mediates the relationship between sexual abuse and child psychological difficulties. *Child Abuse & Neglect, 69,* 116–124. doi:https://doi.org/10.1016/j.chiabu.2017.04.017

Erhardt, D., & Hinshaw, S. P. (1994). Initial sociometric impressions of attention-deficit hyperactivity disorder and comparison boys: Predictions from social behaviors and nonverbal behaviors. *Journal of Consulting and Clinical Psychology, 62,* 833–842.

Ermer, E., Cope, L. M., Nyalakanti, P. K., Calhoun, V. D., & Kiehl, K. A. (2012). Aberrant paralimbic gray matter in criminal psychopathy. *Journal of Abnormal Psychology, 121,* 649–658.

Ersche, K. D., Williams, G. B., Robbins, T. W., & Bullmore, E. T. (2013). Meta-analysis of structural brain abnormalities associated with stimulant drug dependence and neuroimaging of addiction vulnerability and resilience. *Addiction, 23,* 615–624.

Espada, J. P., Gonzálvez, M. T., Orgilés, M., Guillén-Riquelme, A., Soto, D., & Sussman, S. (2015). Pilot clinic study of project EX for smoking cessation with Spanish adolescents. *Addictive Behaviors, 45,* 226. Retrieved from https://search.proquest.com/docview/1666836700?accountid514496

Essex, M. J., Klein, M. H., Slattey, M. J., Goldsmith, H. H., & Kalin, N. H. (2010). Early risk factors and developmental pathways to chronic high inhibition and social anxiety disorder in adolescence. *American Journal of Psychiatry, 167,* 40–46.

Etter, J. F., & Bullen, C. (2014). A longitudinal study of electronic cigarette users. *Addictive Behaviors, 39,* 491–494.

Evans-Lacko, S., Brohan, E., Mojtabai, R., & Thornicroft, G. (2011). Association between public views of mental illness and self-stigma among individuals with mental illness in 14 European countries. *Psychological Medicine, 42,* 1741–1752. doi:10.1017/S0033291711002558

Exner, J. E. (1978). *The Rorschach: A comprehensive system: Volume 2.* Current research and advanced interpretation. New York, NY: John Wiley & Sons.

Exner, J. E. (1986). *The Rorschach: A comprehensive system: Volume 1. Basic foundations* (2nd ed.). New York, NY: John Wiley & Sons.

Express Scripts Lab. (2014). *Turning attention to ADHD report: An Express Scripts report on U.S. medication trends for attention deficit hyperactivity disorder.* http://lab.express-scripts.com/lab/insights/industry-updates/report-turning-attention-to-adhd

Express Scripts Lab. (2017). *2016 Drug trend report.* http://lab.express-scripts.com/lab/drug-trend-report).

Ezzyat, Y., Kragel, J. E., Burke, J. F., Levy, D. F., Lyalenko, A., Wanda, P., et al. (2017). Direct brain stimulation modulates encoding states and memory performance in humans. *Current Biology, 27,* 1251–1258. doi:10.1016/j.cub.2017.03.028

Fabiano, G. A., Pelham, W. E., Gnagy, E. M., Burrows-MacLean, L., Coles, E. K., Chacko, A., et al. (2007). The single and combined effects of multiple intensities of behavior modification and multiple intensities of methylphenidate in a classroom setting. *School Psychology Review, 36,* 195–216.

Fairbairn, C. E., & Sayette, M. A. (2013). The effect of alcohol on emotional inertia: A test of alcohol myopia. *Journal of Abnormal Psychology, 122,* 770–781. http://doi.org/10.1037/a0032980

Fairbairn, C.E. & Sayette, M. A. (2014). A social-attributional analysis of alcohol response. *Psychological Bulletin, 140,* 1361–1382.

Fairburn, C. G. (1997). Eating disorders. In D. M. Clark & C. G. Fairburn (Eds.), *Science and practice of cognitive behavior therapy* (pp. 209–243). New York, NY: Oxford University Press.

Fairburn, C. G., Agras, W. S., & Wilson, G. T. (1992). The research on the treatment of bulimia nervosa: Practical and theoretical implications. In G. H. Anderson & S. H. Kennedy (Eds.), *The biology of feast and famine: Relevance to eating disorders* (pp. 317-340). New York, NY: Academic Press.

Fairburn, C. G., Cooper, A., Doll, H. A., O'Connor, M. E., Bohn, K., Hawker, D. M., et al. (2009). Transdiagnostic cognitive-behavioral therapy for patients with eating disorders: A two-site trial with 60-week follow-up. *American Journal of Psychiatry, 166,* 311–319.

Fairburn, C. G., Doll, H. A., Welch, S. L., Hay, P. J., Davies, B. A., & O'Connor, M. E. (1998). Risk factors for binge eating disorder. *Archives of General Psychiatry, 55,* 425–432.

Fairburn, C. G., Jones, R., Peveler, R. C., Carr, S. J., Solomon, R. A., O'Connor, M. E., Burton, J., & Hope, R. A. (1991). Three psychological treatments for bulimia nervosa. *Archives of General Psychiatry, 48,* 463–469.

Fairburn, C. G., Jones, R., Peveler, R. C., Hope, R. A., & O'Connor, M. E. (1993). Psychotherapy and bulimia nervosa: The longer-term effects of interpersonal psychotherapy, behavior therapy, and cognitive therapy. *Archives of General Psychiatry, 50,* 419–428.

Fairburn, C. G., Marcus, M. D., & Wilson, G. T. (1993). Cognitive behaviour therapy for binge eating and bulimia nervosa: A comprehensive treatment manual. In C. G. Fairburn & G. T. Wilson (Eds.), *Binge eating: Nature, assessment, and treatment.* New York, NY: Guilford Press.

Fairburn, C. G., Norman, P. A., Welch, S. L., O'Connor, M. E., Doll, H. A., & Peveler, R. C. (1995). A prospective study of outcome in bulimia nervosa and the long-term effects of three psychological treatments. *Archives of General Psychiatry, 52,* 304–312.

Fairburn, C. G., Shafran, R., & Cooper, Z. (1999). A cognitive behavioural theory of anorexia nervosa. *Behaviour Research and Therapy, 37,* 1–13.

Fairburn, C. G., Stice, E., Cooper, Z., Doll, H. A., Norman, P. A., & O'Connor, M. E. (2003). Understanding persistence in bulimia nervosa: A 5-year naturalistic study. *Journal of Consulting and Clinical Psychology, 71,* 103–109.

Fair, D. A., Bathula, D., Nikolas, M. A., & Nigg, J. T. (2012). Distinct neuropsychological subgroups in typically developing youth inform heterogeneity in children with ADHD. *Proceedings of the National Academy of Sciences, 109*(17), 6769–6774.

Falloon, I. R. H., Boyd, J. L., McGill, C. W., Razani, J., Moss, H. B., & Gilderman, A. N. (1982). Family management in the prevention of exacerbation of schizophrenia: A controlled study. *New England Journal of Medicine, 306,* 1437–1440.

Fals-Stewart, W., O'Farrell, T. J., & Lam, W. K. K. (2009). Behavioral couple therapy for gay and lesbian couples with alcohol use disorders. *Journal of Substance Abuse Treatment, 37,* 379–387.

Fanous, A. H., Prescott, C. A., & Kendler, K. S. (2004). The prediction of thoughts of death or self-harm in a population-based sample of female twins. *Psychological Medicine, 34,* 301–312.

Faraone, S. V., Biederman, J., & Mick, E. (2005). The age-dependent decline of attention deficit hyperactivity disorder: A meta-analysis of follow-up studies. *Psychological Medicine, 36,* 159–165.

Farina, A. (1976). *Abnormal psychology.* Englewood Cliffs, NJ: Prentice-Hall.

Farrell, M., Werge, T., Sklar, P., Owen, M. J., Ophoff, R., O'Donovan, M., et al. (2015). Evaluating historical candidate genes for schizophrenia. *Molecular Psychiatry, 20,* 555–562.

Faustman, W. O., Bardgett, M., Faull, K. F., Pfefferman, A., & Cseransky, J. G. (1999). Cerebrospinal fluid glutamate inversely correlates with positive symptom severity in unmedicated male schizophrenic/schizoaffective patients. *Biological Psychiatry, 45,* 68–75.

Favaro, A., & Santonastaso, P. (1997). Suicidality in eating disorders: Clinical and psychological correlates. *Acta Psychiatrica Scandinavica, 95,* 508–514.

Fazel, S., Gulati, G., Linsell, L., Geddes, J. R., & Grann, M. (2009). Schizophrenia and violence: Systematic review and meta-analysis. *PLOS Medicine.* http://www.plosmedicine.org/article/info%3Adoi%2F10.1371%2Fjournal.pmed.100012.

Feldman Barrett, L. (2017). *How emotions are made.* Boston, MA: Houghton Mifflin Harcourt.

Ferguson, C. P., La Via, M. C., Crossan, P. J., & Kaye, W. H. (1999). Are selective reuptake inhibitors effective in underweight anorexia nervosa? *International Journal of Eating Disorders, 25,* 11–17.

Ferguson, S. B., Shiffman, S., & Gwaltney, C. J. (2006). Does reducing withdrawal severity mediate nicotine patch efficacy? A randomized clinical trial. *Journal of Consulting and Clinical Psychology, 74*, 1153–1161.

Fergusson, D., Doucette, S., Glass, K. C., Shapiro, S., Healy, D., Hebert, P., et al. (2005). Association between suicide attempts and selective serotonin reuptake inhibitors: Systematic review of randomised controlled trials. *British Medical Journal, 330*(7488), 396. doi:10.1136/bmj.330.7488.396

Fergusson, D. M., McLeod, G. F. H., & Horwood, L. J. (2013). Childhood sexual abuse and adult developmental outcomes: Findings from a 30-year longitudinal study in New Zealand. *Child Abuse & Neglect, 37*, 664–674. doi:http://dx.doi.org/10.1016/j.chiabu.2013.03.013

Ferré, S. (2008), An update on the mechanisms of the psychostimulant effects of caffeine. *Journal of Neurochemistry, 105*, 1067–1079. doi:10.1111/j.1471-4159.2007.05196.x

Ferri, M., Amato, L., & Davoli, M. (2008). Alcoholics anonymous and other 12 step programmes for alcohol dependence (review). *Cochrane Database of Systematic Reviews, 3*, CD005032.

Fetveit, A. (2009). Late-life insomnia: A review. *Geriatrics and Gerontology International, 9*, 220–234.

Feusner, J. D., Phillips, K. A., & Stein, D. J. (2010). Olfactory reference syndrome: Issues for DSM-V. *Depression and Anxiety, 27*, 592–599.

Few, L. R., Lynam, D. R., Maples, J. L., MacKillop, J., & Miller, J. D. (2015). Comparing the utility of DSM-5 Section II and III antisocial personality disorder diagnostic approaches for capturing psychopathic traits. *Personality Disorders: Theory, Research, and Treatment, 6*, 64–74. doi:10.1037/per0000096

Few, L. R., Lynam, D. R., & Miller, J. D. (2015). Impulsivity-related traits and their relation to DSM–5 section II and III personality disorders. *Personality Disorders: Theory, Research, and Treatment, 6*, 261–266. http://dx.doi.org/10.1037/per0000120

Ficks, C. A., & Waldman, I. D. (2014). Candidate genes for aggression and antisocial behavior: A meta-analysis of association studies of the 5HTTLPR and MAOA-uVNTR. *Behavior Genetics, 44*(5), 427–444.

Fiellin, D. A., O'Connor, P. G., Chawarski, M., Pakes, J. P., Pantalon, M. V., & Schottenfeld, R. S. (2001). Methadone maintenance in primary care: A randomized controlled trial. *Journal of the American Medical Association, 286*, 1724–1731.

Fineberg, A. M., & Ellman, L. M. (2013). Inflammatory cytokines and neurological and neurocognitive alterations in the course of schizophrenia. *Biological Psychiatry, 73*(10), 951–966. http://doi.org/10.1016/j.biopsych.2013.01.001

Finkelstein, E. A., Graham, W. C., & Malhotra, R. (2014). Lifetime direct medical costs of childhood obesity. *Pediatrics, 133*, 854–862. doi:10.1542/peds.2014-0063

Finkelstein, E. A., Trogdon, J. G., Cohen, J. W., & Dietz, W. (2009). Annual medical spending attributable to obesity: Payer- and service-specific estimates. *Health Affairs, 28*, w822–w831.

Fink, H. A., Mac Donald, R., Rutks, I. R., Nelson, D. B., & Wilt, T. J. (2002). Sildenafil for male erectile dysfunction: A systematic review and meta-analysis. *Archives of Internal Medicine, 162*, 1349–1360.

Finlay-Jones, R. (1989). Anxiety. In G. W. Brown & T. O. Harris (Eds.), *Life events and illness* (pp. 95–112). New York: Guilford Press.

Fiori, L. M., Ernst, C., & Turecki, G. (2014). In M. K. Nock (Ed.), *The Oxford handbook of suicide and self-injury.* New York, NY: Oxford University Press.

First, M. B, Williams, J. B. W, Karg, R. S., & Spitzer R. L. (2015). *Structured Clinical Interview For DSM-5 Disorders, Clinician Version* (SCID-5-CV). Arlington, VA: American Psychiatric Association.

Fischer, M. (1971). Psychoses in the offspring of schizophrenic monozygotic twins and their normal cotwins. *British Journal of Psychiatry, 118*, 43–52.

Fishbain, D. A., Cutler, R., Rosomoff, H. L., & Rosomoff, R. S. (2000). Evidence-based data from animal and human experimental studies on pain relief with antidepressants: A structured review. *Pain Medicine, 1*, 310–316.

Fisher, J. E. (2011). Understanding behavioral health in late life: Why age matters. *Behavior Therapy, 42*, 143–149.

Fisher, M., Holland, C., Merzenich, M. M., & Vinogradov, S. (2009). Using neuroplasticity-based auditory training to improve verbal memory in schizophrenia. *American Journal of Psychiatry, 166*, 805–811.

Fisher, S. E., & DeFries, J. C. (2002). Developmental dyslexia: Genetic dissection of a complex cognitive trait. *Nature Reviews Neuroscience, 3*(10), 767–780. http://doi.org/10.1038/nrn936

Fitzgibbons, M. L., Spring, B., Avellone, M. E., Blackman, L. R., Pingitore, R., & Stolley, M. R. (1998). Correlates of binge eating in Hispanic, black, and white women. *International Journal of Eating Disorders, 24*, 43–52.

Flegal, K. M., Kruszon-Moran, D., Carroll, M. D., Fryar, C. D., & Ogden, C. L. (2016). Trends in obesity among adults in the United States, 2005 to 2014. *Journal of the American Medical Association, 315*, 2284–2291. http://doi.org/10.1001/jama.2016.6458

Florence, C. S., Zhou, C., Luo, F., & Xu, L. (2016). The economic burden of prescription opioid overdose, abuse, and dependence in the United States, 2013. *Medical Care, 54*, 901–916.

Foa, E. B., Gillihan, S. J., & Bryant, R. A. (2013). Challenges and successes in dissemination of evidence-based treatments for posttraumatic stress: Lessons learned from prolonged exposure therapy for PTSD. *Psychological Science in the Public Interest, 14*(2), 65–111. doi:10.1177/1529100612468841

Foa, E. B., Gillihan, S. J., & Bryant, R. A. (2013). Challenges and successes in dissemination of evidence-based treatments for posttraumatic stress: Lessons learned from prolonged exposure therapy for PTSD. *Psychological Science Public Interest, 14*(2), 65–111. doi:10.1177/1529100612468841

Foa, E. B., & McLean, C. P. (2016). The efficacy of exposure therapy for anxiety-related disorders and its underlying mechanisms: The case of OCD and PTSD. *Annual Review of Clinical Psychology, 12*(1), 1–28. doi:10.1146/annurev-clinpsy-021815-093533

Foa, E. B., & Meadows, E. A. (1997). Psychosocial treatments for post-traumatic stress disorder: A critical review. *Annual Review of Psychology, 48*, 449–480.

Foa, E. B., Riggs, D. S., Marsie, E. D., & Yarczower, M. (1995). The impact of fear activation and anger on the efficacy of exposure treatment for posttraumatic stress disorder. *Behavior Therapy, 26*, 487–499.

Foerde, K., Steinglass, J. E., Shohamy, D., & Walsh, B. T. (2015). Neural mechanisms supporting maladaptive food choices in anorexia nervosa. *Nature Neuroscience, 18*, 1571–1573. http://doi.org/10.1038/nn.4136

Fontaine, N. M. G., McCrory, E. J. P., Boivin, M., Moffitt, T. E., & Viding, E. (2011). Predictors and outcomes of joint trajectories of callous-unemotional traits and conduct problems in childhood. *Journal of Abnormal Psychology, 120*, 730–742.

Forbes, D., Forbes, S. C., Blake, C. M., Thiessen, E. J., & Forbes, S. (2015). Exercise programs for people with dementia. *Cochrane Database of Systematic Reviews.* doi:10.1002/14651858.CD006489.pub4

Forbes, M. K., & Schniering, C. A. (2013). Are sexual problems a form of internalizing psychopathology? A structural equation modeling analysis. *Archives of Sexual Behavior, 42*, 23–34.

Ford, C. S., & Beach, F. A. (1951). *Patterns of sexual behavior.* New York, NY: Harper and Brothers.

Ford, J. M., Mathalon, D. H., Whitfield, S., Faustman, W. O., & Roth, W. T. (2002). Reduced communication between frontal and temporal lobes during talking in schizophrenia. *Biological Psychiatry, 51*, 485–492.

Forero, D. A., Arboleda, G. H., Vasquez, R., & Arboleda, H. (2009). Candidate genes involved in neural plasticity and the risk for attention-deficit hyperactivity disorder: A meta-analysis of 8 common variants. *Journal of Psychiatry and Neuroscience, 34*(5), 361–366.

Forgatch, M. S., Patterson, G. R., Degarmo, D. S., & Beldavs, Z. G. (2009). Testing the Oregon delinquency model with 9-year follow-up of the Oregon Divorce Study. *Development and Psychopathology, 21*, 637–660. http://dx.doi.org/10.1017/S0954579409000340

Foti, D. J., Kotov, R., Guey, L. T., & Bromet, E. J. (2010). *Cannabis* use and the course of schizophrenia: 10-year follow-up after first hospitalization. *American Journal of Psychiatry, 167*, 987–993.

Fournier, J. C., DeRubeis, R. J., Hollon, S. D., Dimidjian, S., Amsterdam, J. D., Shelton, R. C., et al. (2010). Antidepressant drug effects and depression severity: A patient-level meta-analysis. *Journal of the American Medical Association, 303*, 47–53.

Fox, A. S., Oler, J. A., Tromp, D. P. M., Fudge, J. L., & Kalin, N. H. (2015). Extending the amygdala in theories of threat processing. *Trends in Neurosciences, 38*(5), 319–329. doi:10.1016/j.tins.2015.03.002

Frackiewicz, E. J., Sramek, J. J., Herrera, J. M., Kurtz, N. M., & Cutler, N. R. (1997). Ethnicity and antipsychotic response. *Annals of Pharmacotherapy, 31,* 1360–1369.

Fraley, R. C., & Shaver, P. R. (2000). Adult romantic attachment: Theoretical developments, emerging controversies, and unanswered questions. *Review of General Psychology, 4,* 132–154.

Franco, A., Malhotra, N., & Simonovits, G. (2014). Publication bias in the social sciences: Unlocking the file drawer. *Science, 345*(6203), 1502–1505. doi:10.1126/science.1255484

Frank, E., Kupfer, D. J., Perel, J. M., Cornes, C., Jarrett, D. B., Mallinger, A. G., et al. (1990). Three-year outcomes for maintenance therapies in recurrent depression. *Archives of General Psychiatry, 47*(12), 1093–1099.

Frank, G. K. W., & Shott, M. E. (2016). The role of psychotropic medications in the management of anorexia nervosa: Rationale, evidence and future prospects. *CNS Drugs, 30*(5), 419–442. http://doi.org/10.1007/s40263-016-0335-6

Franklin, J. C., Hessel, E. T., Aaron, R. V., Arthur, M. S., Heilbron, N., & Prinstein, M. J. (2010). The functions of nonsuicidal self-injury: Support for cognitive-affective regulation and opponent processes from a novel psychophysiological paradigm. *Journal of Abnormal Psychology, 119,* 850–862.

Franklin, J. C., Ribeiro, J. D., Fox, K. R., Bentley, K. H., Kleiman, E. M., Huang, X., et al. (2017). Risk factors for suicidal thoughts and behaviors: A meta-analysis of 50 years of research. *Psychological Bulletin, 143*(2), 187–232. doi:10.1037/bul0000084

Franklin, M. E., & Foa, E. B. (2011). Treatment of obsessive compulsive disorder. *Annual Review of Clinical Psychology, 7,* 229–243.

Franklin, M. E., & Foa, E. B. (2014). Obsessive-compulsive disorder. In D. H. Barlow (Ed.), *Clinical handbook of psychological disorders* (5th ed., pp. 155–205). New York, NY: Guilford Press.

Franklin, M. E., Sapyta, J., Freeman, J. B., Khanna, M., Compton, S., Almirall, D., et al. (2011). Cognitive behavior therapy augmentation of pharmacotherapy in pediatric obsessive-compulsive disorder: The Pediatric OCD Treatment Study II (POTS II) randomized controlled trial. *Journal of the American Medical Association, 306*(11), 1224–1232.

Franko, D. L., & Keel, P. K. (2006). Suicidality in eating disorders: Occurrence, correlates, and clinical implications. *Clinical Psychology Review, 26,* 769–782.

Franko, D. L., Keshaviah, A., Eddy, K. T., Krishna, M., Davis, M. C., Keel, P. K., & Herzog, D. B. (2013). A longitudinal investigation of mortality in anorexia nervosa and bulimia nervosa. *American Journal of Psychiatry, 170*(8), 917–925.

Frederick, R. I., Mrad, D. F., & DeMier, R. L. (2007). *Examinations of criminal responsibility: Foundations in mental health case law.* Sarasota, FL: Professional Resource Press.

Frederickson, B. L., & Carstensen, L. L. (1990). Choosing social partners: How old age and anticipated endings make people more selective. *Psychology and Aging, 5,* 335–347.

Fredrickson, B. L., & Levenson, R. W. (1998). Positive emotions speed recovery from the cardiovascular sequelae of negative emotions. *Cognition and Emotion, 12,* 191–200.

Fredrickson, B. L., & Roberts, T. A. (1997). Objectification theory: Toward understanding women's lived experience and mental health risks. *Psychology of Women Quarterly, 21,* 173–206.

Freedman, R. (2003). Schizophrenia. *New England Journal of Medicine, 349,* 1738–1749.

Freeman, A. J., Youngstrom, E. A., Youngstrom, J. K., & Findling, R. L. (2016). Disruptive mood dysregulation disorder in a community mental health clinic: Prevalence, comorbidity and correlates. *Journal of Child and Adolescent Psychopharmacology, 26*(2), 123–130. http://doi.org/10.1089/cap.2015.0061

Freeman, J., Sapyta, J., Garcia, A., Compton, S., Khanna, M., Flessner, C., et al. (2014). Family-based treatment of early childhood obsessive-compulsive disorder: The Pediatric Obsessive-Compulsive Disorder Treatment Study for Young Children (POTS Jr)—A randomized clinical trial. *JAMA Psychiatry, 71*(6), 689–698. http://doi.org/10.1001/jamapsychiatry.2014.170

French, S. A., Story, M., Neumark-Sztainer, D., Downes, B., Resnick, M., et al. (1997). Ethnic differences in psychosocial and health behavior correlates of dieting, purging, and binge eating in a population-based sample of adolescent females. *International Journal of Eating Disorders, 22,* 315–322.

Freud, A. (1946/1966). *The ego and mechanisms of defense.* New York, NY: International Universities Press.

Friborg, O., Martinsen, E. W., Martinussen, M., Kaiser, S., Øvergård, K. T., & Rosenvinge, J. H. (2014). Comorbidity of personality disorders in mood disorders: A meta-analytic review of 122 studies from 1988 to 2010. *Journal of Affective Disorders, 152,* 1–11. http://dx.doi.org/10.1016/j.jad.2013.08.023

Friborg, O., Martinussen, M., Kaiser, S., Overgard, K. T., & Rosenvinge, J. H. (2013). Comorbidity of personality disorders in anxiety disorders: A meta-analysis of 30 years of research. *Journal of Affective Disorders, 145,* 143–155. doi:10.1016/j.jad.2012.07.004

Frick, A., Åhs, F., Engman, J., Jonasson, M., Alaie, I., Björkstrand, J., et al. (2015). Serotonin synthesis and reuptake in social anxiety disorder: A positron emission tomography study. *JAMA Psychiatry, 72*(8), 794–802. doi:10.1001/jamapsychiatry.2015.0125

Frick, P. J., Ray, J. V., Thornton, L. C., & Kahn, R. E. (2014). Can callous-unemotional traits enhance the understanding, diagnosis, and treatment of serious conduct problems in children and adolescents? A comprehensive review. *Psychological Bulletin, 140,* 1–57.

Frieling, H., Romer, K. D., Scholz, S., Mittelbach, F., Wilhelm, J., De Zwaan, M., et al. (2010). Epigenetic dysregulation of dopaminergic genes in eating disorders. *International Journal of Eating Disorders, 43,* 577–583.

Friend, A., DeFries, J. C., Olson, R. K., & Pennington, B. F. (2009). Heritability of high reading ability and its interaction with parental education. *Behavior Genetics, 39,* 427–436.

Friston, K. J. (1994). Functional and effective connectivity in neuroimaging: A synthesis. *Human Brain Mapping, 2,* 56–78.

Froehlich, T. E., Bogardus, S. T., & Inouye, S. K. (2001). Dementia and race: Are there differences between African Americans and Caucasians? *Journal of the American Gerontological Society, 49,* 477–484.

Frojdh, K., Hakansson, A., Karlsson, I., & Molarius, A. (2003). Deceased, disabled or depressed—A population-based 6-year follow-up study of elderly people with depression. *Social Psychiatry and Psychiatric Epidemiology, 38,* 557–562.

Fromer, M., Pocklington, A. J., Kavanagh, D. H., Williams, H. J., Dwyer, S., Gormley, P., et al. (2013). De novo mutations in schizophrenia implicate synaptic networks. *Nature, 506,* 179–184. http://doi.org/10.1038/nature12929

Fromm-Reichmann, F. (1948). Notes on the development of treatment of schizophrenics by psychoanalytic psychotherapy. *Psychiatry, 11,* 263–273.

Frost, D. O., & Cadet, J.-L. (2000). Effects of methamphetamine-induced toxicity on the development of neural circuitry: A hypothesis. *Brain Research Reviews, 34,* 103–118.

Frost, R. O., & Steketee, G. (2010). *Stuff: Compulsive hoarding and the meaning of things.* New York, NY: Houghton Mifflin Harcourt.

Frost, R. O., Steketee, G., & Tolin, D. F. (2011). Comorbidity in hoarding disorder. *Depression and Anxiety, 28,* 876–884.

Frost, R. O., Steketee, G., & Tolin, D. F. (2012). Diagnosis and assessment of hoarding disorder. *Annual Review of Clinical Psychology, 8,* 219–242.

Frühauf, S., Gerger, H., Schmidt, H. M., Munder, T., & Barth, J. (2013). Efficacy of psychological interventions for sexual dysfunction: A systematic review and meta-analysis. *Archives of Sexual Behavior, 42,* 915–933.

Fuller, R. K. (1988). Disulfiram treatment of alcoholism. In R. M. Rose & J. E. Barrett (Eds.), *Alcoholism: Origins and outcome* (pp. 237–250). New York, NY: Raven Press.

Fung, L. K., Mahajan, R., Nozzolillo, A., Bernal, P., Krasner, A., Jo, B., et al. (2016). Pharmacologic treatment of severe irritability and problem behaviors in autism: A systematic review and meta-analysis. *Pediatrics, 137(Suppl),* S124–S135. http://doi.org/10.1542/peds.2015-2851K

Furberg, H., Kim, Y., Dackor, J., Boerwinkle, E., Franceschini, N., Ardissino, D., et al. (2010). Genome-wide meta-analyses identify multiple loci associated with smoking behavior. *Nature Genetics, 42,* 441–447. http://doi.org/10.1038/ng.571

Gadalla, T., & Piran, N. (2007). Co-occurrence of eating disorders and alcohol use disorders in women: A meta analysis. *Archives of Women's Mental Health, 10,* 133–140.

Gale, C. R., Hagenaars, S. P., Davies, G., Hill, W. D., Liewald, D. C. M., Cullen, B., et al. (2016). Pleiotropy between neuroticism and physical and mental health: Findings from 108038 men and women in UK biobank. *Translational Psychiatry, 6*(4), e791. doi:10.1038/tp.2016.56

Galik, E. (2016). Treatment of dementia: Non-pharmacological approaches. In J. E. G. M. Boltz (Ed.), *Dementia Care: An Evidence-Based Approach* (pp. 97–112). Cham, Switzerland: Springer International.

Garber, J. (2006). Depression in children and adolescents: Linking risk research and prevention. *American Journal of Preventative Medicine, 31,* 5104–5125.

Garber, J., Brunwasser, S. M., Zerr, A. A., Schwartz, K. T. G., Sova, K., & Weersing, V. R. (2016). Treatment and prevention of depression and anxiety in youth: Test of cross-over effects. *Depression and Anxiety, 33*(10), 939–959. http://doi.org/10.1002/da.22519

Garber, J., Clarke, G. N., Weersing, V. R., Beardslee, W. R., Brent, D. A., Gladstone, T. R., et al. (2009). Prevention of depression in at-risk adolescents: A randomized controlled trial. *Journal of the American Medical Association, 301,* 2215–2224.

Garber, J., & Flynn, C. (2001). Vulnerability to depression in childhood and adolescence. In R. M. Ingram & J. M. Price (Eds.), *Vulnerability to psychopathology: Risk across the lifespan* (pp. 175–225). New York, NY: Guilford Press.

Garber, J., Kelly, M. K., & Martin, N. C. (2002). Developmental trajectories of adolescents' depressive symptoms: Predictors of change. *Journal of Consulting and Clinical Psychology, 70,* 79–95.

Garb, H. N. (2005). Clinical judgment and decision making. *Annual Review of Clinical Psychology, 1,* 67–89.

Gard, D. E., Kring, A. M., Germans Gard, M., Horan, W. P., & Green, M. F. (2007). Anhedonia in schizophrenia: Distinctions between anticipatory and consummatory pleasure. *Schizophrenia Research, 93,* 253–260.

Gard, D. E., Sanchez, A. H., Starr, J., Cooper, S., Fisher, M., Rowlands, A., & Vinogradov, S. (2014). Using self-determination theory to understand motivation deficits in schizophrenia: The "why" of motivated behavior. *Schizophrenia Research, 156,* 217–222.

Garety, P. A., Fowler, D., & Kuipers, E. (2000). Cognitive behavioral therapy for medication-resistant symptoms. *Schizophrenia Bulletin, 26,* 73–86.

Garfield, R. L., Zuvekas, S. H., Lave, J. R., & Donohue, J. M. (2011). The impact of national health care reform on adults with several mental disorders. *American Journal of Psychiatry, 168,* 486–494.

Garner, D. M., Garfinkel, P. E., Schwartz, D., & Thompson, M. (1980). Cultural expectation of thinness in women. *Psychological Reports, 47,* 483–491.

Garner, D. M., Olmsted, M. P., & Polivy, J. (1983). Development and validation of a multi-dimensional eating disorder inventory for anorexia nervosa and bulimia. *International Journal of Eating Disorders, 2,* 15–34.

Garner, D. M., Vitousek, K. M., & Pike, K. M. (1997). Cognitive-behavioral therapy for anorexia nervosa. In D. M. Garner & P. E. Garfinkel (Eds.), *Handbook of treatment for eating disorders.* (pp. 94–144). New York, NY: Guilford Press.

Gartlehner, G., Gaynes, B. N., Hansen, R. A., Thieda, P., DeVeaugh-Geiss, A., Krebs, E. E., et al. (2008). Comparative benefits and harms of second-generation antidepressants: Background paper for the American College of Physicians. *Annals of Internal Medicine, 149*(10), 734–750.

Gasser, P., Holstein, D., Michel, Y., Doblin, R., Yazar-Klosinski, B., Passie, T., & Brenneisen, R. (2014). Safety and efficacy of lysergic acid diethylamide-assisted psychotherapy for anxiety associated with life-threatening diseases. *Journal of Nervous and Mental Disease, 202,* 513–520.

Gates, G. J. (2017, November 1). In US, more adults identifying as LGBT. Gallup. Retrieved from http://www.gallup.com/poll/201731/lgbt-identification-rises.aspx

Gates, N. J., Sachdev, P. S., Fiatarone Singh, M. A., & Valenzuela, M. (2011). Cognitive and memory training in adults at risk of dementia: A systematic review. *BMC Geriatrics, 11,* 55. doi:10.1186/1471-2318-11-55

Gaugler, T., Klei, L., Sanders, S. J., Bodea, C. A., Goldberg, A. P., Lee, A. B., et al. (2014.). Most genetic risk for autism resides with common variation, *46*(8), 881–885. http://doi.org/10.1038/ng.3039

Gaus, V. L. (2007). *Cognitive behavior therapy for adults with Asperger's syndrome.* New York, NY: Guilford Press.

Gavey, N., & Senn, C. Y. (2014). Sexuality and sexual violence. In D. L. Tolman, L. M. Diamond, J. A. Bauermeister, W. H. George, J. G. Pfaus, & L. M. Ward (Eds.), *APA handbook of sexuality and psychology, Vol. 1: Person-based approaches* (pp. 339–382). Washington, DC: American Psychological Association.

GBD 2015 Obesity Collaborators. (2017). Health effects of overweight and obesity in 195 countries over 25 years. *New England Journal of Medicine,* NEJMoa1614362. http://doi.org/10.1056/NEJMoa1614362

Geddes, J. R., Burgess, S., Hawton, K., Jamison, K., & Goodwin, G. M. (2004). Long-term lithium therapy for bipolar disorder: Systematic review and meta-analysis of randomized controlled trials. *American Journal of Psychiatry, 161,* 217–222.

Geddes, J. R., Carney, S. M., Davies, C., Furukawa, T. A., Frank, E., Kupfer, D. J., et al. (2003). Relapse prevention with antidepressant drug treatment in depressive disorders: A systematic review. *The Lancet, 361,* 653–661.

Gelauff, J., Stone, J., Edwards, M., & Carson, A. (2013). The prognosis of functional (psychogenic) motor symptoms: A systematic review. *Journal of Neurology, Neurosurgery and Psychiatry.* doi:10.1136/jnnp-2013-305321

Geller, D. A., & March, J. (2012). Practice parameter for the assessment and treatment of children and adolescents with obsessive-compulsive disorder. *Journal of the American Academy of Child & Adolescent Psychiatry, 51*(1), 98–113.

Gentes, E. L., & Ruscio, A. M. (2011). A meta-analysis of the relation of intolerance of uncertainty to symptoms of generalized anxiety disorder, major depressive disorder, and obsessive-compulsive disorder. *Clinical Psychology Review, 31,* 923–933.

Geraerts, E., Schooler, J. W., Merckelbach, H., Jelicic, M., Hauer, B. J. A., & Ambadar, Z. (2007). The reality of recovered memories: Corroborating continuous and discontinuous memories of childhood sexual abuse. *Psychological Science, 18,* 564–568.

Gerlach, A. L., Wilhelm, F. H., Gruber, K., & Roth, W. T. (2001). Blushing and physiological arousability in social phobia. *Journal of Abnormal Psychology, 110,* 247–258.

Gernsbacher, M. A., Dawson, M., & Goldsmith, H. H. (2005). Three reasons not to believe in an autism epidemic. *Current Directions in Psychological Science, 14,* 55–58.

Getahun, D., Jacobsen, S. J., Fassett, M. J., Chen, W., Demissie, K., & Rhoads, G. G. (2013). Recent trends in childhood attention-deficit/hyperactivity disorder. *JAMA Pediatrics, 167*(3), 282–288.

Ge, X., Conger, R. D., Cadoret, R. J., Neiderhiser, J. M., Yates, W., Troughton, E., et al. (1996). The developmental interface between nature and nurture: A mutual influence model of child antisocial behavior and parent behaviors. *Developmental Psychology, 32,* 574–589.

Gibb, B. E., Beevers, C. G., & McGeary, J. E. (2013). Toward an integration of cognitive and genetic models of risk for depression. *Cognition and Emotion, 27*(2), 193–216. doi:10.1080/02699931.2012.712950

Gibbons, F. X., Gerrard, M., Cleveland, M. J., Wills, T. A., & Brody, G. (2004). Perceived discrimination and substance use in African American parents and their children: A panel study. *Journal of Personality and Social Psychology, 86,* 517–529. http://dx.doi.org/10.1037/0022-3514.86.4.517

Gibson, D. R. (2001). Effectiveness of syringe exchange programs in reducing HIV risk behavior and seroconversion among injecting drug users. *AIDS, 15,* 1329–1341.

Giesbrecht, T., Smeets, T., Leppink, J., Jelicic, M., & Merckelbach, H. (2013). Acute dissociation after 1 night of sleep loss. *Psychology of Consciousness: Theory, Research, and Practice, 1,* 150–159.

Gignac, A., McGirr, A., Lam, R. W., & Yatham, L. N. (2015). Recovery and recurrence following a first episode of mania: A systematic review and meta-analysis of prospectively characterized cohorts. *Journal of Clinical Psychiatry, 76*(9), 1241–1248. doi:10.4088/JCP.14r09245

Gijs, L. & Brewaeys, A. (2007). Surgical treatment of gender dysphoria in adults and adolescents: Recent developments, effectiveness, and challenges. *Annual Review of Sex Research, 18,* 178–224.

Gilbert, D. T., King, G., Pettigrew, S., & Wilson, T. D. (2016). Comment on "estimating the reproducibility of psychological science." *Science, 351*(6277), 1037. doi:10.1126/science.aad7243

Gillan, C. M., Morein-Zamir, S., Urcelay, G. P., Sule, A., Voon, V., Apergis-Schoute, A. M., et al. (2014). Enhanced avoidance habits in obsessive-compulsive disorder. *Biological Psychiatry, 75*, 631–638.

Giovino, G. A., Villanti, A. C., Mowery, P. D., Sevilimedu, V., Niaura, R. S., Vallone, D. M., & Abrams, D. B. (2013). Differential trends in cigarette smoking in the USA: Is menthol slowing progress? *Tobacco Control 24*, 28–37. doi:10.1136/tobaccocontrol-2013-051159

Girshkin, L., Matheson, S. L., Shepherd, A. M., & Green, M. J. (2014). Morning cortisol levels in schizophrenia and bipolar disorder: A meta-analysis. *Psychoneuroendocrinology, 49*, 187–206. doi:10.1016/j.psyneuen.2014.07.013

Gizer, I. R., Ficks, C., & Waldman, I. D. (2009). Candidate gene studies of ADHD: A meta-analytic review. *Human Genetics, 126*(1), 51–90.

Gjerde, L. C., Czajkowski, N., Røysamb, E., Ørstavik, R. E., Knudsen, G. P., Østby, K., et al. (2012). The heritability of avoidant and dependent personality disorder assessed by personal interview and questionnaire. *Acta Psychiatrica Scandinavica, 126*, 448–457. doi:10.1111/j.1600-0447.2012.01862.x

Glahn, D. C., Laird, A. R., Ellison-Wright, I., Thelen, S. M., Robinson, J. L., Lancaster, J. L., et al. (2008). Meta-analysis of gray matter anomalies in schizophrenia: Application of anatomic likelihood estimation and network analysis. *Biological Psychiatry, 64*, 774–781. http://doi.org/10.1016/j.biopsych.2008.03.031

Glass, C. R., & Arnkoff, D. B. (1997). Questionnaire methods of cognitive self-statement assessment. *Journal of Consulting and Clinical Psychology, 65*, 911–927.

Glausier, J. R., & Lewis, D. A. (2013). Dendritic spine pathology in schizophrenia. *Neuroscience, 251*, 90–107.

Gleaves, D. H. (1996). The sociocognitive model of dissociative identity disorder: A reexamination of the evidence. *Psychological Bulletin, 120*, 42–59.

Glenn, A. L., Raine, A., Venables, P. H., & Mednick, S. A. (2007). Early temperamental and psychophysiological precursors of adult psychopathic personality. *Journal of Abnormal Psychology, 116*, 508–518.

Glenn, J. J., Michel, B. D., Franklin, J. C., Hooley, J. M., & Nock, M. K. (2014). Pain analgesia among adolescent self-injurers. *Psychiatry Research, 220*(3), 921–926. doi:10.1016/j.psychres.2014.08.016

Godart, N. T., Flament, M. F., Lecrubier, Y., & Jeammet, P. (2000). Anxiety disorders in anorexia nervosa and bulimia nervosa: Co-morbidity and chronology of appearance. *European Psychiatry, 15*, 38–45.

Godart, N. T., Flament, M., Perdereau, F., & Jeammet, P. (2002). Comorbidity between eating disorders and anxiety disorders: A review. *International Journal of Eating Disorders, 32*, 253–270.

Goedert, M., Spillantini, M. G., Del Tredici, K., & Braak, H. (2013). 100 years of Lewy pathology. *Nature Reviews Neurology, 9*, 13–24.

Goenjian, A. K., Walling, D., Steinberg, A. M., Karayan, I., Najarian, L. M., & Pynoos, R. (2005). A prospective study of posttraumatic stress and depressive reactions among treated and untreated adolescents 5 years after a catastrophic disaster. *American Journal of Psychiatry, 162*, 2302–2308.

Goldberg, T. E., & Weinberger, D. R. (2004). Genes and the parsing of cognitive processes. *Trends in Cognitive Sciences, 8*, 325–335.

Golden, C. J., Hammeke, T., & Purisch, A. (1978). Diagnostic validity of a standardized neuropsychological battery derived from Luria's neuropsychological tests. *Journal of Consulting and Clinical Psychology, 46*, 1258–1265.

Golden, R. N., Gaynes, B. N., Ekstrom, R. D., Hamer, R. M., Jacobsen, F. M., Suppes, T., et al. (2005). The efficacy of light therapy in the treatment of mood disorders: A review and meta-analysis of the evidence. *American Journal of Psychiatry, 162*, 656–662.

Goldin, P. R., Manber-Ball, T., Werner, K., Heimberg, R., & Gross, J. J. (2009). Neural mechanisms of cognitive reappraisal of negative self-beliefs in social anxiety disorder. *Biological Psychiatry, 66*, 1091–1099.

Goldman-Rakic, P. S., & Selemon, L. D. (1997). Functional and anatomical aspects of prefrontal pathology in schizophrenia. *Schizophrenia Bulletin, 23*, 437–458.

Goldstein, A. J., & Chambless, D. L. (1978). A reanalysis of agoraphobic behavior. *Behavior Therapy, 9*, 47–59.

Goldstein, A. J., de Beurs, E., Chambless, D. L., & Wilson, K. A. (2000). EMDR for panic disorder with agoraphobia: Comparison with waiting list and credible attention-placebo control conditions. *Journal of Consulting and Clinical Psychology, 68*, 947–956.

Goldstein, J. M., Buka, S. L., Seidman, L. J., & Tsuang, M. T. (2010). Specificity of familial transmission of schizophrenia psychosis spectrum and affective psychoses in the New England Family Study's high-risk design. *Archives of General Psychiatry, 67*, 458–467.

Goldstein, L. H., Chalder, T., Chigwedere, C., Khondoker, M. R., Moriarty, J., Toone, B. K., & Mellers, J. D. (2010). Cognitive-behavioral therapy for psychogenic nonepileptic seizures: A pilot RCT. *Neurology, 74*, 1986–1994. doi:10.1212/WNL.0b013e3181e39658

Gonzalez, H. M., Vega, W. A., Williams, D. R., Tarraf, W., West, B. T., & Neighbors, H. W. (2010). Depression care in the United States: Too little for too few. *Archives of General Psychiatry, 67*, 37–46.

Goodkind, M., Eickhoff, S. B., Oathes, D. J., Jiang, Y., Chang, A., Jones-Hagata, L. B., et al. (2015). Identification of a common neurobiological substrate for mental illness. *JAMA Psychiatry, 72*, 305–315. http://doi.org/10.1001/jamapsychiatry.2014.2206

Goodkind, M. S., Gyurak, A., McCarthy, M., Miller, B. L., & Levenson, R. W. (2010). Emotion regulation deficits in frontotemporal lobar degeneration and Alzheimer's disease. *Psychological Aging, 25*, 30–37.

Goodman, G. S., Ghetti, S., Quas, J. A., Edelstein, R. S., Alexander, K. W., Redlich, A. D., et al. (2003). A prospective study of memory for child sexual abuse: New findings relevant to the repressed-memory controversy. *Psychological Science, 14*, 113–118.

Goodwin, D. K. (2003). Team of rivals: The political genius of Abraham Lincoln. New York, NY: Simon & Schuster.

Goodwin, F., & Jamison, K. (2007). *Manic-depressive illness: Bipolar disorders and recurrent depression* (2nd ed.). New York, NY: Oxford University Press.

Gopnik, A., Capps, L., & Meltzoff, A. N. (2000). Early theories of mind: What the theory can tell us about autism. In S. Baren-Cohen, H. Tager-Flusberg & D. Cohen (Eds.), *Understanding other minds* (2nd ed., pp. 50–72). Oxford, UK: Oxford University Press.

Gordon, K. H., Perez, M., & Joiner, T. E. (2002). The impact of racial stereotypes on eating disorder recognition. *International Journal of Eating Disorders, 32*, 219–224.

Gorelick, P. B. (2010). Role of inflammation in cognitive impairment: Results of observational epidemiological studies and clinical trials. *Annals of the New York Academy of Sciences, 1207*, 155–162.

Gorka, S. M., Lieberman, L., Shankman, S. A., & Phan, K. L. (2017). Startle potentiation to uncertain threat as a psychophysiological indicator of fear-based psychopathology: An examination across multiple internalizing disorders. *Journal of Abnormal Psychology, 126*(1), 8–18. doi:10.1037/abn0000233

Gotlib, H., & Joormann, J. (2010). Cognition and depression: Current status and future directions. *Annual Review of Clinical Psychology, 6*, 285–312.

Gottesman, I. I., Laursen, T. M., Bertelsen, A., & Mortensen, P. B. (2010). Severe mental disorders in offspring with 2 psychiatrically ill parents. *Archives of General Psychiatry, 67*, 252–257.

Gowing, L., Ali, R., & White, J. M. (2009). Buprenorphine for the management of opioid withdrawal. *Cochrane Database of Systematic Reviews, 3*, CD002025. http://doi.org/10.1002/14651858.CD002025.pub4

Grabe, S., & Hyde, J. S. (2006). Ethnicity and body dissatisfaction among women in the United States: A meta-analyis. *Psychological Bulletin, 132*, 622–640.

Grabe, S., Ward, L. M., & Hyde, J. S. (2008). The role of the media in body image concerns among women: A meta-analysis of experimental and correlational studies. *Psychological Bulletin, 134*(3), 460–476. doi:10.1037/0033-2909.134.3.460

Grady, D. (July 20, 1999). A great pretender now faces the truth of illness, *The New York Times*.

Graeff, F. G. (2017). Translational approach to the pathophysiology of panic disorder: Focus on serotonin and endogenous opioids. *Neuroscience & Biobehavioral Reviews 76*(Pt A):48–55. doi:http://doi.org/10.1016/j.neubiorev.2016.10.013

Graham, C. A. (2010). The DSM diagnostic criteria for female sexual arousal disorder. *Archives of Sexual Behavior, 39*, 240–255.

Graham, J. (2011). *MMPI-2: Assessing personality and psychopathology*, (5th ed.). New York, NY: Oxford University Press.

Grana, R. A., Popova, L., & Ling, P. M. (2014). A longitudinal analysis of electronic cigarette use and smoking cessation. *Journal of the American Medical Association, Internal Medicine, 174,* 812–813.

Grandin, T. (1986). *Emergence: Labeled autistic.* Novato, CA: Arena Press.

Grandin, T. (1995). *Thinking in pictures.* New York, NY: Doubleday.

Grandin, T. (2008). *The way I see it: A personal look at autism and Asperger's.* Arlington, TX: Future Horizons.

Grandin, T. (2013). *The autistic brain.* New York, NY: Houghton Mifflin Harcourt.

Granholm E., Holden J. L., Link P., & McQuaid J. R.(2014). Randomized clinical trial of cognitive behavioral social skills training for schizophrenia: Improvement in functioning and experiential negative symptoms. *Journal of Consulting and Clinical Psychology, 82,* 1173–1185.

Granholm, E., McQuaid. J.R., & Holden, J. (2016). *Cognitive Behavioral Social Skills Training for Schizophrenia: A Practical Treatment Guide.* New York, NY: Guilford Press.

Granholm E., McQuaid J. R., McClure F. S., Auslander, L. A., Perivoliotis, D., Paola Pedrelli, M. S., et al. (2005). A randomized, controlled trial for cognitive behavioral social skills training for middle-aged and older outpatients with chronic schizophrenia. *American Journal of Psychiatry, 162,* 520–529.

Grant, B. F., Chou, S. P., Goldstein, R. B., Huang, B., Stinson, F. S., Saha, T. D., et al. (2008). Prevalence, correlates, disability, and comorbidity of DSM-IV borderline personality disorder: Results from the Wave 2 National Epidemiologic Survey on Alcohol and Related Conditions. *Journal of Clinical Psychiatry, 69,* 533–545.

Grant, B. F., Goldstein, R. B., Saha, T. D., Chou, S. P., Jung, J., Zhang, H., et al. (2015). Epidemiology of DSM-5 alcohol use disorder: Results from the National Epidemiologic Survey on Alcohol and Related Conditions III. *JAMA Psychiatry, 72,* 757–766. http://doi.org/10.1001/jamapsychiatry.2015.0584

Grant, J. E., Odlaug, B. L., & Schreiber, L. R. N. (2014). Pharmacotherapy for obsessive-compulsive and related disorders among adults. In E. A. Storch & D. McKay (Eds.), *Obsessive-compulsive disorder and its spectrum: A life span approach.* Washington DC: American Psychological Association.

Grant, P. M., Huh, G., Perivoliotis, D., Stolar, N., & Beck, A. T. (2012). Randomized trial to evaluate the efficacy of cognitive therapy for low-functioning patients with schizophrenia. *Archives of General Psychiatry, 69,* 121–127.

Gravel, S., Henn, B. M., Gutenkunst, R. N., Indap, A. R., Marth, G. T., Clark, A. G., et al. (2011). Demographic history and rare allele sharing among human populations. *Proceedings of the National Academy of Sciences. 108,* 11983–11988.

Greenberg, P. E., Fournier, A. A., Sisitsky, T., Pike, C. T., & Kessler, R. C. (2015). The economic burden of adults with major depressive disorder in the United States (2005 and 2010). *Journal of Clinical Psychiatry, 76*(2), 155–162. doi:10.4088/JCP.14m09298

Green, E. K., Rees, E., Walters, J. T. R., Smith, K. G., Forty, L., Grozeva, D., et al. (2016). Copy number variation in bipolar disorder. *Molecular Psychiatry, 21*(1), 89–93. doi:10.1038/mp.2014.174

Green, J. G., McLaughlin, K. A., Berglund, P. A., Gruber, M. J., Sampson, N. A., Zaslavsky, A. M., et al. (2010). Childhood adversities and adult psychiatric disorders in the National Comorbidity Survey Replication: Associations with first onset of DSM-IV disorders. *Archives of General Psychiatry, 67,* 113–123.

Green, M. F., Kern, R. S., Braff, D. L., & Mintz, J. (2000). Neurocognitive deficits and functional outcome in schizophrenia: Are we measuring the "right stuff"? *Schizophrenia Bulletin, 26,* 119–136.

Green, M. F., Marshall, B. D., Wirshing, W. C., Ames, D., Marder, S. R., McGurk, S., Kern, R. S., & Mintz, J. (1997). Does risperidone improve verbal working memory in treatment-resistant schizophrenia? *American Journal of Psychiatry, 154,* 799–804.

Greeven, A., van Balkom, A. J. L. M., Visser, S., Merkelbach, J. W., van Rood, Y. R., van Dyck, R., et al. (2007). Cognitive behavior therapy and paroxetine in the treatment of hypochondriasis: A randomized controlled trial. *American Journal of Psychiatry, 164,* 91–99.

Grey, I. M., & Hastings, R. P. (2005). Evidence-based practices in intellectual disability and behaviour disorders. *Current Opinion in Psychiatry, 18,* 469–475. http://dx.doi.org/10.1097/01.yco.0000179482.54767.cf

Griffith, J. W., Zinbarg, R. E., Craske, M. G., Mineka, S., Rose, R. D., Waters, A. M., et al. (2009). Neuroticism as a common dimension in the internalizing disorders. *Psychological Medicine, 40,* 1125–1136. doi:10.1017/S0033291709991449

Griffiths, T. L. (2015). Manifesto for a new (computational) cognitive revolution. *Cognition, 135,* 21–23. http://doi.org/10.1016/j.cognition.2014.11.026

Grillon, C., Lissek, S., Rabin, S., McDowell, D., Dvir, S., & Pine, D. S. (2008). Increased anxiety during anticipation of unpredictable but not predictable aversive stimuli as a psychophysiologic marker of panic disorder. *The American Journal of Psychiatry, 165*(7), 898–904. doi:10.1176/appi.ajp.2007.07101581

Grilo, C. M. (2007). Treatment of binge eating disorder. In S. Wonderlich, J. E. Mitchell, M. D. Zwaan, & H. Steiger (Eds.), *Annual review of eating disorders* (pp. 23–34). Oxford, UK: Radcliffe.

Grilo, C. M., Crosby, R. D., Wilson, G. T., & Masheb, R. M. (2012). 12-month follow-up of fluoxetine and cognitive behavioral therapy for binge eating disorder. *Journal of Consulting and Clinical Psychology, 80,* 1108–1113.

Grilo, C. M., Sanislow, C. A., Gunderson, J. G., Pagano, M. E., Yen, S., Zanarini, M. C., et al. (2004). Two-year stability and change of schizotypal, borderline, avoidant, and obsessive-compulsive personality disorders. *Journal of Consulting and Clinical Psychology, 72,* 767–775.

Grilo, C. M., Shiffman, S., & Carter-Campbell, J. T. (1994). Binge eating antecedents in normal weight nonpurging females: Is there consistency? *International Journal of Eating Disorders, 16,* 239–249.

Griner, D., & Smith, T. B. (2006). Culturally adapted mental health intervention: A meta-analytic review. *Psychotherapy, 43,* 531–548.

Grinker, R. R., & Spiegel, J. P. (1944). *Management of neuropsychiatric casualties in the zone of combat: Manual of military neuropsychiatry.* Philadelphia, PA: W.B. Saunders.

Grisham, J. R., Frost, R. O., Steketee, G., Kim, H. J., & Hood, S. (2006). Age of onset of compulsive hoarding. *Journal of Anxiety Disorders, 20,* 675–686.

Groesz, L. M., Levine, M. P., & Murnen, S. K. (2002). The effect of experimental presentation of thin media images on body dissatisfaction: A meta-analytic review. *International Journal of Eating Disorders, 31,* 1–16.

Grossman, D. (1995). *On killing: The psychological cost of learning to kill in war and society.* Boston, MA: Little, Brown.

Grundmann, D., Krupp, J., Scherner, G., Amelung, T., & Beier, K. M. (2016). Stability of self-reported arousal to sexual fantasies involving children in a clinical sample of pedophiles and hebephiles. *Archives of Sexual Behavior, 45,* 1153–1162. doi:10.1007/s10508-016-0729-z

Gueguen, J., Godart, N., Chambry, J., Brun-Eberentz, A., Foulon, C., Divac, S. M., et al. (2012). Severe anorexia nervosa in men: Comparison with severe AN in women and analysis of mortality. *International Journal of Eating Disorders, 45*(4), 537–545.

Guendelman, M., Owens, E. B., Galan, C., Gard, A., & Hinshaw, S. P. (2016). Early adult correlates of maltreatment in girls with ADHD: Increased risk for internalizing problems and suicidality. *Development and Psychopathology, 28,* 1–14.

Guina, J., Rossetter, S. R., De, R. B., Nahhas, R. W., & Welton, R. S. (2015). Benzodiazepines for PTSD: A systematic review and meta-analysis. *Journal of Psychiatric Practice, 21*(4), 281–303. doi:10.1097/pra.0000000000000091

Gum, A. M., King-Kallimanis, B., & Kohn, R. (2009). Prevalence of mood, anxiety, and substance-abuse disorders for older Americans in the National Comorbidity Survey-Replication. *American Journal of Psychiatry, 17,* 769–781.

Guo, X., Zhai, J., Liu, Z., Fang, M., Wang, B., Wang, C., Hu, B., Sun, X., et al. (2010). Effect of antipsychotic medication alone vs. combined with psychosocial intervention on outcomes of early-stage schizophrenia. *Archives of General Psychiatry, 67,* 895–904.

Gupta, C. N., Calhoun, V. D., Rachakonda, S., Chen, J., Patel, V., Liu, J., et al. (2015). Patterns of gray matter abnormalities in schizophrenia based on an international mega-analysis. *Schizophrenia Bulletin, 41,* 1133–1142. http://doi.org/10.1093/schbul/sbu177

Gustad, J., & Phillips, K. A. (2003). Axis I comorbidity in body dysmorphic disorder. *Comprehensive Psychiatry, 44,* 270–276.

Gutman, D. A., & Nemeroff, C. B. (2003). Persistent central nervous system effects of an adverse early environment: Clinical and preclinical studies. *Physiology and Behavior, 79,* 471–478

Haaga, D. A. F., Dyck, M. J., & Ernst, D. (1991). Empirical status of cognitive theory of depression. *Psychological Bulletin, 110,* 215–236.

Hacking, I. (1998). *Mad travelers: Reflections on the reality of transient mental illness.* Charlottesville, VA: University Press of Virginia.

Haddock, G., Tarrier, N., Spaulding, W., Yusupoff, L. K., & McCarthy, E. (1998). Individual cognitive-behavior therapy in the treatment of hallucinations and delusions: A review. *Clinical Psychology Review, 18,* 821–838.

Haedt-Matt, A. A., & Keel, P. K. (2011). Revisiting the affect regulation model of binge eating: A meta-analysis of studies using ecological momentary assessment. *Psychological Bulletin, 137,* 660–681.

Hagerman, R. (2006). Lessons from fragile X regarding neurobiology, autism, and neurodegeneration. *Developmental and Behavioral Pediatrics, 27,* 63–74.

Haijma, S. V., Van Haren, N., Cahn, W., Koolschijn, P. C., Hulshoff Pol, H. E., & Kahn, R. S. (2013). Brain volumes in schizophrenia: A meta-analysis in over 18 000 subjects. *Schizophrenia Bulletin, 39*(5), 1129–1138.

Halberstadt, A. L. (2015). Recent advances in the neuropsychopharmacology of serotonergic hallucinogens. *Special Issue: Serotonin, 277,* 99–120.

Hallett, M. (2016). Neurophysiologic studies of functional neurologic disorders. *Handbook of Clinical Neurology, 139,* 61–71. doi:http://dx.doi.org/10.1016/B978-0-12-801772-2.00006-0

Hall, G. C., Hirschman, R., & Oliver, L. L. (1995). Sexual arousal and arousability to pedophilic stimuli in a community sample of normal men. *Behavior Therapy, 26,* 681–694.

Hallmayer, J., Cleveland, S., Torres, A., Phillips, J., Cohen, B., Torigoe, T., Miller, J., Fedele, A., et al. (2011). Genetic heritability and shared environmental factors among twin pairs with autism. *Archives of General Psychiatry, 68,* 1095–1102.

Hall, M. G., Alhassoon, O. M., Stern, M. J., Wollman, S. C., Kimmel, C. L., Perez-Figueroa, A., & Radua, J. (2015). Gray matter abnormalities in cocaine versus methamphetamine-dependent patients: A neuroimaging meta-analysis. *American Journal of Drug and Alcohol Abuse, 41,* 290–299. http://doi.org/10.3109/00952990.2015.1044607

Hallquist, M. N., Hipwell, A. E., & Stepp, S. D. (2015). Poor self-control and harsh punishment in childhood prospectively predict borderline personality symptoms in adolescent girls. *Journal of Abnormal Psychology, 124,* 549–564. doi:10.1037/abn0000058

Hall, W. D., & Lynskey, M. (2005). Is cannabis a gateway drug? Testing hypotheses about the relationship between cannabis use and the use of other illicit drugs. *Drug and Alcohol Review, 24,* 39–48.

Halmi, K. A., Sunday, S. R., Strober, M., Kaplan, A., Woodside, D. B., Fichter, N., Treasure, J., Berrettini, W. H., & Kaye, W. (2000). Perfectionism in anorexia nervosa: Variation by clinical subtype, obsessionality, and pathological eating behavior. *American Journal of Psychiatry, 157,* 1799–1805.

Hamani, C., Pilitsis, J., Rughani, A. I., Rosenow, J. M., Patil, P. G., Slavin, K. S., et al. (2014). Deep brain stimulation for obsessive-compulsive disorder: Systematic review and evidence-based guideline sponsored by the American Society for Stereotactic and Functional Neurosurgery and the Congress of Neurological Surgeons (CNS) and endorsed by the CNS and American Association of Neurological Surgeons. *Neurosurgery, 75*(4), 327–333. doi:10.1227/neu.0000000000000499

Hamilton, J. L., Stange, J. P., Abramson, L. Y., & Alloy, L. B. (2015). Stress and the development of cognitive vulnerabilities to depression explain sex differences in depressive symptoms during adolescence. *Clinical Psychological Science, 3*(5), 702–714. doi:10.1177/2167702614545479

Hamilton, J. P., Etkin, A., Furman, D. J., Lemus, M. G., Johnson, R. F., & Gotlib, I. H. (2012). Functional neuroimaging of major depressive disorder: A meta-analysis and new integration of baseline activation and neural response data. *American Journal of Psychiatry, 169,* 693–703.

Hammen, C. (2009). Adolescent depression: Stressful interpersonal contexts and risk for recurrence. *Current Directions in Psychological Science, 18,* 200–204.

Hammen, C., & Brennan, P. (2001). Depressed adolescents of depressed and nondepressed mothers: Tests of an interpersonal impairment hypothesis. *Journal of Consulting and Clinical Psychology, 69,* 284–294.

Hammen, C., Hazel, N. A., Brennan, P. A., & Najman, J. (2012). Intergenerational transmission and continuity of stress and depression: Depressed women and their offspring in 20 years of follow-up. *Psychological Medicine, 42,* 931–942.

Hammen, C. L., Burge, D., Daley, S. E., Davila, J., Paley, B., & Rudolph, K. D. (1995). Interpersonal attachment cognitions and prediction of symptomatic responses to interpersonal stress. *Journal of Abnormal Psychology, 104,* 436–443.

Hammond, D. (2011). Health warning messages on tobacco products: Review. *Tobacco Control, 20,* 327–337.

Hamshere, M. L., Langley, K., Martin, J., Agha, S. S., Stergiakouli, E., Anney, R. J., et al. (2013). High loading of polygenic risk for ADHD in children with comorbid aggression. *American Journal of Psychiatry, 170*(8), 909–916.

Hanel, P. H., & Vione, K. C. (2016). Do student samples provide an accurate estimate of the general public? *PLOS ONE, 11*(12), e0168354. doi:10.1371/journal.pone.0168354

Han, J. H., Zimmerman, E. E., Cutler, N., Schnelle, J., Morandi, A., Dittus, R. S., et al. (2009). Delirium in older emergency department patients: Recognition, risk factors, and psychomotor subtypes. *Academic Emergency Medicine, 16,* 193–200. doi:10.1111/j.1553-2712.2008.00339.x

Hankin, B. J., Abramson, L. Y., Moffitt, T. E., Silva, P. A., McGee, R., et al. (1998). Development of depression from preadolescence to young adulthood: Emerging gender differences in a 10-year longitudinal study. *Journal of Abnormal Psychology, 107,* 128–140.

Hankin, B. L., & Abramson, L. Y. (2001). Development of gender differences in depression: An elaborated cognitive vulnerability-transactional stress theory. *Psychological Bulletin, 127,* 773–796.

Hankin, B. L., Young, J. F., Abela, J. R. Z., Smolen, A., Jenness, J. L., Gulley, L. D., et al. (2015). Depression from childhood into late adolescence: Influence of gender, development, genetic susceptibility, and peer stress. *Journal of Abnormal Psychology, 124,* 803–816. doi:10.1037/abn0000089

Hanson, C. (1998, November 30). *Dangerous therapy: The story of Patricia Burgus and multiple personality disorder.* Chicago Magazine. Downloaded from http://www.chicagomag.com/Chicago-Magazine/June-1998/Dangerous-Therapy-The-Story-of-Patricia-Burgus-and-Multiple-Personality-Disorder/

Hanson, J. L., Adluru, N., Chung, M. K., Alexander, A. L., Davidson, R. J., & Pollak, S. D. (2013). Early neglect is associated with alterations in white matter integrity and cognitive functioning. *Child Development, 84,* 1566–1578.

Hanson, R. K., & Bussiere, M. T. (1998). Predicting relapse: A meta-analysis of sexual offender recidivism studies. *Journal of Consulting and Clinical Psychology, 66,* 348–362.

Hanson, R. K., Hunsley, J., & Parker, K. C. (1988). The relationship between WAIS subtest reliability, "g" loadings, and meta-analytically derived validity estimates. *Journal of Clinical Psychology, 44*(4), 557–563.

Harden, K. P., Hill, J. E., Turkheimer, E., & Emery, R. E. (2008). Gene–environment correlation and interaction in peer effects on adolescent alcohol and tobacco use. *Behavior Genetics, 38,* 339–347.

Hardeveld, F., Spijker, J., Vreeburg, S. A., Graaf, R. D., Hendriks, S. M., Licht, C. M. M., et al. (2014). Increased cortisol awakening response was associated with time to recurrence of major depressive disorder. *Psychoneuroendocrinology, 50,* 62–71. doi:http://dx.doi.org/10.1016/j.psyneuen.2014.07.027

Hare, R. D. (2003). *The Hare psychopathy checklist* (Rev. ed.). Toronto, Canada: Multi-Health System.

Harkness, K. L., Bagby, R. M., & Kennedy, S. H. (2012). Childhood maltreatment and differential treatment response and recurrence in adult major depressive disorder. *Journal of Consulting and Clinical Psychology, 80,* 342–353.

Harkness, K. L., & Monroe, S. M. (2016). The assessment and measurement of adult life stress: Basic premises, operational principles, and design requirements. *Journal of Abnormal Psychology, 125,* 727–745. doi:10.1037/abn0000178

Harrington, A. (2008). *The cure within: A history of mind-body medicine.* New York, NY: W. W. Norton.

Harris, J. L., Bargh, J. A., & Brownell, K. D. (2009). Priming effects of television food advertising on eating behavior. *Health Psychology, 28,* 404–413.

Harris, J. L., Schwartz, M. B., Brownell, K. D., et al. (2010). *Evaluating fast food nutrition and marketing to youth.* New Haven, CT: Yale Rudd Center for Food Policy and Obesity.

Harrison, A., Fernández de la Cruz, L., Enander, J., Radua, J., & Mataix-Cols, D. (2016). Cognitive-behavioral therapy for body dysmorphic disorder: A systematic review and meta-analysis of randomized controlled trials. *Clinical Psychology Review, 48,* 43–51. doi:https://doi.org/10.1016/j.cpr.2016.05.007

Harrison, J. N., Cluxton-Keller, F., & Gross, D. (2012). Antipsychotic medication prescribing trends in children and adolescents. *Journal of Pediatric Health Care, 26*(2), 139–145.

Harrison, P. J., & Weinberger, D. R. (2005). Schizophrenia genes, gene expression, and neuropathology: On the matter of their convergence. *Molecular Psychiatry, 10,* 40–68.

Harris, V. L. (2000). Insanity acquittees and rearrest: The past 24 years. *Journal of the American Academy of Psychiatry and the Law, 28,* 225–231.

Hartshorne, J. K., & Germine, L. T. (2015). When does cognitive functioning peak? The asynchronous rise and fall of different cognitive abilities across the life span. *Psychological Science, 26,* 433–443. doi:doi:10.1177/0956797614567339

Hartz, D. T., Fredrick-Osborne, S. L., & Galloway, G. P. (2001). Craving predicts use during treatment for methamphetamine dependence: A prospective repeated measures, within-subjects analysis. *Drug and Alcohol Dependence, 63,* 269–276.

Harvey, A. G., & Bryant, R. A. (2002). Acute stress disorder: A synthesis and critique. *Psychological Bulletin, 128,* 886–902.

Harvey, A. G., Soehner, A. M., Kaplan, K. A., Hein, K., Lee, J., Kanady, J., et al. (2015). Treating insomnia improves mood state, sleep, and functioning in bipolar disorder: A pilot randomized controlled trial. *Journal of Consulting and Clinical Psychology, 83*(3), 564–577. doi:10.1037/a0038655

Harvey, A. G., Watkins, E., Mansell, W., & Shafran, R. (2004). *Cognitive behavioural processes across psychological disorders: A transdiagnostic approach to research and treatment.* Oxford, UK: Oxford University Press.

Harvey, P. D., Green, M. F., Keefe, R. S. I., & Velligan, D. (2004). Cognitive functioning in schizophrenia: A consensus statement on its role in the definition and evaluation of effective treatments for the illness. *Journal of Clinical Psychiatry, 65,* 361–372.

Harvey, P. D., Green, M. F., McGurk, S., & Meltzer, H. Y. (2003). Changes in cognitive functioning with risperidone and olanzapine treatment: A large-scale, doubleblind, randomized study. *Psychopharmacology, 169,* 404–411.

Hasin, D. S., Keyes, K. M., Alderson, D., Wang, S., Aharonovich, E., & Grant, B. F. (2008). Cannabis withdrawal in the United States: Results from NESARC. *Journal of Clinical Psychiatry, 69,* 1354–1363.

Hasin, D. S., Stinson, F. S., Ogburn, E., & Grant, B. F. (2007). Prevalence, correlates, disability, and comorbidity of DSM-IV alcohol abuse and dependence in the United States: Results from the National Epidemiologic Survey on Alcohol and Related Conditions. *Archives of General Psychiatry, 64,* 830–842.

Hasin, D. S., Wall, M., Keyes, K. M., Cerdá, M., Schulenberg, J., O'Malley, P. M., et al. (2015). Medical marijuana laws and adolescent marijuana use in the USA from 1991 to 2014: Results from annual, repeated cross-sectional surveys. *Lancet. Psychiatry, 2,* 601–608. http://doi.org/10.1016/S2215-0366(15)00217-5

Hathaway, S. R., & McKinley, J. C. (1943). *MMPI manual.* New York, NY: Psychological Corporation.

Hawkins, J. D., Graham, J. W., Maguin, E., Abbott, R., et al. (1997). Exploring the effects of age of alcohol use initiation and psychosocial risk factors on subsequent alcohol misuse. *Journal of Studies on Alcohol, 58,* 280–290.

Hawton, K., Witt, K. G., Taylor Salisbury, T. L., Arensman, E., Gunnell, D., Hazell, P., et al. (2016). Psychosocial interventions for self-harm in adults. *Cochrane Database Syst Rev*(5), Cd012189. doi:10.1002/14651858.cd012189

Hayes, J., VanElzakker, M., & Shin, L. (2012). Emotion and cognition interactions in PTSD: A review of neurocognitive and neuroimaging studies. *Frontiers in Integrative Neuroscience, 6*(89). doi:10.3389/fnint.2012.00089

Hayes, R. D., Dennerstein, L., Bennett, C. M., Koochaki, P. E., Leiblum, S. R., & Graziottin, A. (2007). Relationship between hypoactive sexual desire disorder and aging. *Fertility and Sterility, 87,* 107–112. doi:10.1016/j.fertnstert.2006.05.071

Hayes, S. C. (2005). *Get out of your mind and into your life: The new acceptance and commitment therapy.* Oakland, CA: New Harbinger Publications.

Haynes, N., Seifan, A., & Isaacson, R. S. (2016). Prevention of dementia. In J. E. G. M. Boltz (Ed.), *Dementia care: An evidence-based approach* (pp. 97–112). Switzerland: Springer International.

Hay, P. (2013). A systematic review of evidence for psychological treatments in eating disorders: 2005–2012. *International Journal of Eating Disorders, 46,* 462–469. http://doi.org/10.1002/eat.22103

Hay, P. P., Bacaltchuk, J., Stefano, S., & Kashyap, P. (2009). Psychological treatments for bulimia nervosa and binging. *Cochrane Database of Systematic Reviews, 4.* http://doi.org/10.1002/14651858.CD000562.pub3

Hazel, N. A., Hamman, C., Brennan, P. A., Najman, J. (2008). Early childhood adversity and adolescent depression: The mediating role of continued stress. *Psychological Medicine, 38,* 581–589.

Hazlett, H. C., Gu, H., Munsell, B. C., Kim, S. H., Styner, M., Wolff, J. J., et al. (2017). Early brain development in infants at high risk for autism spectrum disorder. *Nature, 542*(7641), 348–351. http://doi.org/10.1038/nature21369

Hazlett, H. C., Poe, M. D., Gerig, G., Styner, M., Chappell, C., Smith, R. G., et al. (2011). Early brain overgrowth in autism associated with an increase in cortical surface area before age 2 years. *Archives of General Psychiatry, 68,* 467–476.

Head, D., Bugg, J. M., Goate, A. M., Fagan, A. M., Mintun, M. A., Benzinger, T., et al. (2012). Exercise engagement as a moderator of the effects of APOE ε genotype on amyloid deposition. *Archives of Neurology, 69,* 636–643.

Heatherton, T. F., & Baumeister, R. F. (1991). Binge eating as escape from self-awareness. *Psychological Bulletin, 110,* 86–108.

Hébert, M., Langevin, R., Guidi, E., Bernard-Bonnin, A. C., & Allard-Dansereau, C. (2016). Sleep problems and dissociation in preschool victims of sexual abuse. *Journal of Trauma & Dissociation, 1–15.* doi: 10.1080/15299732.2016.1240739

Heinrichs, R. W., & Zakzanis, K. K. (1998). Neurocognitive deficits in schizophrenia: A quantitative review of the evidence. *Neuropsychology, 12,* 426–445.

Heinssen, R. K., Liberman, R. P., & Kopelowicz, A. (2000). Psychosocial skills training for schizophrenia: Lessons from the laboratory. *Schizophrenia Bulletin, 26,* 21–46.

Heller, T. L., Baker, B. L., Henker, B., & Hinshaw, S. P. (1996). Externalizing behavior and cognitive functioning from preschool to first grade: Stability and predictors. *Journal of Clinical Child Psychology, 25,* 376–387.

Hellings, J. A., Arnold, L. E., & Han, J. C. (2017). Dopamine antagonists for treatment resistance in autism spectrum disorders: Review and focus on BDNF stimulators loxapine and amitriptyline. *Expert Opinion on Pharmacotherapy, 18*(6), 581–588. http://doi.org/10.1080/14656566.2017.1308483

Helmuth, L. (2003). In sickness or in health? *Science, 302,* 808–810.

Helstrom, A. W., Blow, F. C., Slaymaker, V., Kranzler, H. R., Leong, S., & Oslin, D. (2016). Reductions in alcohol craving following naltrexone treatment for heavy drinking. *Alcohol and Alcoholism, 51,* 562–566. http://dx.doi.org/10.1093/alcalc/agw038

Hendrickx, L., Gijs, L., & Enzlin, P. (2015). Age-related prevalence rates of sexual difficulties, sexual dysfunctions, and sexual distress in heterosexual women: Results from an online survey in Flanders. *Journal of Sexual Medicine, 12,* 424–435. doi:10.1111/jsm.12725

Henggeler, S. W. (2011). Efficacy studies to large-scale transport: The development and validation of multisystemic therapy programs. *Annual Review of Clinical Psychology, 7,* 351–381. http://doi.org/10.1146/annurev-clinpsy-032210-104615

Henggeler, S. W., Schoenwald, S. K., Borduin, C. M., Rowland, M. D., & Cunningham, P. B. (2009). *Multisystemic therapy for antisocial behavior in children and adolescents*. New York, NY: Guilford.

Henningfield, J. E., Michaelides, T., & Sussman, S. (2000). Developing treatment for tobacco addicted youth—issues and challenges. *Journal of Child and Adolescent Substance Abuse, 9*, 5–26.

Henriques, G., Wenzel, A., Brown, G. K., & Beck, A. T. (2005). Suicide attempter's reaction to survival as a risk factor for eventual suicide. *American Journal of Psychiatry, 162*, 2180–2182.

Herbenick, D., Reece, M., Schick, V., Sanders, S. A., Dodge, B., & Fortenberry, J. D. (2010a). Sexual behaviors, relationships, and perceived health status among adult women in the United States: Results from a national probability sample. *Journal of Sexual Medicine, 7 Suppl 5*, 277–290.

Herbenick, D., Reece, M., Schick, V., Sanders, S. A., Dodge, B., & Fortenberry, J. D. (2010b). Sexual behavior in the United States: Results from a national probability sample of men and women ages 14–94. *Journal of Sexual Medicine, 7*, 255–265. doi:10.1111/j.1743-6109.2010.02012.x

Herman, J. L. (1992). *Trauma and recovery*. New York: Basic Books.

Herman, Y., Shireen, H., Bromley, S., Yiu, N. and Granholm, E. (2016). Cognitive-behavioural social skills training for first-episode psychosis: A feasibility study. *Early Intervention in Psychiatry*. doi:10.1111/eip.12379

Heron, M. (2016). Deaths: Final data for 2014. *National Vital Statistics Reports, 65*(5). Hyattsville, MD: National Center for Health Statistics.

Heron, M. (2016). Deaths: Leading causes for 2014. *National Vital Statistics Reports, 65*(5). Retrieved from https://www.cdc.gov/nchs/data/nvsr/nvsr65/nvsr65_05.pdf

Hertzog, C., Kramer, A., Wilson, R. S., & Lindenberger, U. (2009). Enrichment effects on adult cognitive development: Can the functional capacity of older adults be preserved and enhanced? *Psychological Science in the Public Interest, 9*. 1–65.

Herzog, D. B., Greenwood, D. N., Dorer, D. J., Flores, A. T., Ekeblad, E. R., Richards, A., et al. (2000). Mortality in eating disorders: A descriptive study. *International Journal of Eating Disorders, 28*, 20–26.

Heston, L. L. (1966). Psychiatric disorders in foster home reared children of schizophrenic mothers. *British Journal of Psychiatry, 112*, 819–825.

Hettema, J. E., & Hendricks, P. S. (2010). Motivational interviewing for smoking cessation: A meta-analytic review. *Journal of Consulting and Clinical Psychology, 78*, 868–884.

Hettema, J. M., Prescott, C. A., Myers, J. M., Neale, M. C., & Kendler, K. S. (2005). The structure of genetic and environmental risk factors for anxiety disorders in men and women. *Archives of General Psychiatry, 62*, 182–189.

Heyn, P., Abreu, B. C., & Ottenbacher, K. J. (2004). The effects of exercise training on elderly persons with cognitive impairment and dementias: A meta-analysis. *Archives of Physical Medicine and Rehabilitation, 85*, 1694–1704.

Hibbeln, J. R., Nieminen, L. R. G., Blasbalg, T. L., Riggs, J. A., & Lands, W. E. M. (2006). Healthy intakes of n-3 and n-6 fatty acids: Estimations considering worldwide diversity. *Journal of Clinical Nutrition, 83*, 1483S–1493S.

Hilderink, P. H., Collard, R., Rosmalen, J. G., & Oude Voshaar, R. C. (2013). Prevalence of somatoform disorders and medically unexplained symptoms in old age populations in comparison with younger age groups: A systematic review. *Ageing Research Reviews, 12*, 151–156. doi:10.1016/j.arr.2012.04.004

Hill-Taylor, B., Walsh, K. A., Stewart, S., Hayden, J., Byrne, S., & Sketris, I. S. (2016). Effectiveness of the STOPP/START (Screening Tool of Older Persons' potentially inappropriate Prescriptions/Screening Tool to Alert doctors to the Right Treatment) criteria: Systematic review and meta-analysis of randomized controlled studies. *Journal of Clinical Pharmacy and Therapeutics, 41*, 158–169. doi:10.1111/jcpt.12372

Hilt, L. M., & Nolen-Hoeksema, S. (2014). Gender differences in depression. In I. H. Gotlib & C. L. Hammen (Eds.), *Handbook of depression* (3rd ed.). New York, NY: Guilford Press.

Hingson, R. W., Edwards, E. M., Heeren, T., & Rosenbloom, D. (2009). Age of drinking onset and injuries, motor vehicle crashes, and physical fights after drinking and when not drinking. *Alcoholism, Clinical and Experimental Research, 33*, 783–790.

Hinshaw, S. P. (2002). Preadolescent girls with attention-deficit/hyperactivity disorder: I. Background characteristics, comorbidity, cognitive and social functioning, and parenting practices. *Journal of Consulting and Clinical Psychology, 70*, 1086–1098.

Hinshaw, S. P. (2007). *The mark of shame: The stigma of mental illness and an agenda for change*. New York, NY: Oxford University Press.

Hinshaw, S. P., & Arnold, L. E. (2015). Attention-deficit hyperactivity disorder, multimodal treatment, and longitudinal outcome: Evidence, paradox, and challenge. *WIREs Cognitive Science, 6*, 39–52. doi:10.1002/wcs.1324

Hinshaw, S. P., Carte, E. T., Sami, N., Treuting, J. J., & Zupan, B. A. (2002). Preadolescent girls with attention-deficit/hyperactivity disorder: II. Neuropsychological performance in relation to subtypes and individual classification. *Journal of Consulting and Clinical Psychology, 70*, 1099–1111.

Hinshaw, S. P., & Lee, S. S. (2003). Oppositional defiant and conduct disorders. In E. J. Mash & R. A. Barkley (Eds.), *Child Psychopathology* (2nd ed., pp. 144–198). New York, NY: Guilford Press.

Hinshaw, S. P., & Melnick, S. M. (1995). Peer relationships in boys with attention-deficit hyperactivity disorder with and without comorbid aggression. *Development and Psychopathology, 7*, 627–647.

Hinshaw, S. P., Owens, E. B., Sami, N., & Fargeon, S. (2006). Prospective follow-up of girls with attention-deficit/hyperactivity disorder into adolescence: Evidence for continuing cross-domain impairment. *Journal of Consulting and Clinical Psychology, 74*, 489–499.

Hinshaw, S. P., Owens, E. B., Zalecki, C., Huggins, S. P., Montenegro-Nevado, A. J., Schrodek, E., & Swanson, E. N. (2012). Prospective follow-up of girls with attention-deficit/hyperactivity disorder into early adulthood: Continuing impairment includes elevated risk for suicide attempts and self-injury. *Journal of Consulting and Clinical Psychology, 80*(6), 1041–1051.

Hinshaw, S. P., & Scheffler, R. M. (2014). *The ADHD explosion: Myths, medication, money, and today's push for performance*. New York, NY: Oxford University Press.

Hinshaw, S. P., Zupan, B. A., Simmel, C., Nigg, J. T., & Melnick, S. (1997). Peer status in boys with and without attention-deficit hyperactivity disorder: Predictions from overt and covert antisocial behavior, social isolation, and authoritative parenting beliefs. *Child Development, 68*, 880–896.

Hinton, D. E., Pich, V., Marques, L., Nickerson, A., & Pollack, M. H. (2010). Khyâl attacks: A key idiom of distress among traumatized Cambodia refugees. *Culture, Medicine, and Psychiatry, 34*, 244–278. doi:10.1007/s11013-010-9174-y

Hirsch, C. R., Meeten, F., Krahe, C., & Reeder, C. (2016). Resolving ambiguity in emotional disorders: The nature and role of interpretation biases. *Annual Review of Clinical Psychology, 12*, 281–305. doi:10.1146/annurev-clinpsy-021815-093436

Ho, B.-C., Andreasen, N. C., Ziebell, S., Pierson, R., & Magnotta, V. (2011). Long-term antipsychotic treatment and brain volumes: A longitudinal study of first-episode schizophrenia. *Archives of General Psychiatry, 68*, 128–137. http://doi.org/10.1001/archgenpsychiatry.2010.199

Ho, B. C., Nopoulos, P., Flaum, M., Arndt, S., & Andreasen, N. C. (1998). Two-year outcome in first-episode schizophrenia: Predictive value of symptoms for quality of life. *American Journal of Psychiatry, 155*, 1196–1201.

Hobson, R. P., & Lee, A. (1998). Hello and goodbye: A study of social engagement in autism. *Journal of Autism and Developmental Disorders, 28*, 117–127.

Hoebel, B. G., & Teitelbaum, P. (1966). Weight regulation in normal and hypothalamic hyperphagic rats. *Journal of Comparative and Physiological Psychology, 61*, 189–193.

Hoek, H. W., & van Hoeken, D. (2003). Review of the prevalence and incidence of eating disorders. *International Journal of Eating Disorders, 34*, 383–396.

Hoffman, D. H., Carter, D. J., Lopez, C. R.V., Benzmiller, H. L., Guo, A. X., Latifi, S. Y., & Craig, D. C. (2015, July 2). Report to the Special Committee of the Board of Directors of the American Psychological Association: Independent review relating to APA Ethics Guidelines, national security interrogations, and torture. Chicago, IL: Sidley Austin LLP. Retrieved from http://www.apa.org/independent-review/APA-FINAL-Report-7.2.15.pdf

Hoffman, E. J., & Mathew, S. J. (2008). Anxiety disorders: A comprehensive review of pharmacotherapies. *Mount Sinai Journal of Medicine, 75,* 248–262.

Hofmann, S. G., & Hinton, D. E. (2014). Cross-cultural aspects of anxiety disorders. *Current psychiatry reports, 16*(6), 450. doi:10.1007/s11920-014-0450-3

Hofmann, S. G., Sawyer, A. T., Witt, A. A., & Oh, D. (2010). The effect of mindfulness-based therapy on anxiety and depression: A meta-analytic review. *Journal of Consulting and Clinical Psychology, 78,* 169–183.

Hofmann, S. G., & Smits, J. A. (2008). Cognitive-behavioral therapy for adult anxiety disorders: A meta-analysis of randomized placebo-controlled trials. *The Journal of Clinical Psychiatry, 69,* 621–632.

Hogan, D. B., Fiest, K. M., Roberts, J. I., Maxwell, C. J., Dykeman, J., Pringsheim, T., et al. (2016). The prevalence and incidence of dementia with Lewy bodies: A systematic review. *Canadian Journal of Neurological Sciences, 43(Suppl 1),* S83–95. doi:10.1017/cjn.2016.2

Hogarty, G. E., Anderson, C. M., Reiss, D. J., Kornblith, S. J., Greenwald, D. P., et al. (1986). Family psychoeducation, social skills training, and maintenance chemotherapy in the aftercare treatment of schizophrenia: 1. One-year effects of a controlled study on relapse and expressed emotion. *Archives of General Psychiatry, 43,* 633–642.

Hogarty, G. E., Anderson, C. M., Reiss, D. J., Kornblith, S. J., Greenwald, D. P., Ulrich, R. F., Carter, M., et al. The Environmental-Personal Indicators in the Course of Schizophrenia (EPICS) Research Group. (1991). Family psychoeducation, social skills training, and maintenance chemotherapy in the aftercare treatment of schizophrenia. *Archives of General Psychiatry, 48,* 340–347.

Hogarty, G. E., Flesher, S., Ulrich, R., et al. (2004). Cognitive enhancement therapy for schizophrenia: Effects of a 2-year randomized trial on cognition and behavior. *Archives of General Psychiatry, 61,* 866–876.

Holden C. (2001). "Behavioral" addictions: Do they exist? *Science, 294,* 980–982.

Holder, H. D., Longabaugh, R., Miller, W. R., & Rubonis, A. V. (1991). The cost effectiveness of treatment for alcoholism: A first approximation. *Journal of Studies on Alcohol, 52,* 517–540.

Hollingshead, A. B., & Redlich, F. C. (1958). *Social class and mental illness: A community study.* New York, NY: John Wiley & Sons.

Hollingworth, P., & Williams, J. (2011). Genetic risk factors for dementia *The handbook of Alzheimer's disease and other dementias* (pp. 195–234). Wiley-Blackwell. Hoboken, NJ.

Hollon, S. D., DeRubeis, R. J., Fawcett, J., Amsterdam, J.D. Shelton, C., Zajecka, D., et al. (2014). Effect of cognitive therapy with antidepressant medications vs. antidepressants alone on the rate of recovery in major depressive disorder: A randomized clinical trial. *JAMA Psychiatry, 71*(10), 1157–1164. doi:10.1001/jamapsychiatry.2014.1054

Hollon, S. D., DeRubeis, R. J., Shelton, R. C., Amsterdam, J. D., Salomon, R. M., & O'Reardon, J. P. (2005). Prevention of relapse following cognitive therapy vs medications in moderate to severe depression. *Archives of General Psychiatry, 62,* 417–422.

Hollon, S. D., Stewart, M. O., & Strunk, D. (2006). Enduring effects for cognitive behavior therapy in the treatment of depression and anxiety. *Annual Review of Psychology, 57,* 285–315.

Hollon, S. D., Thase, M. E., & Markowitz, J. C. (2002). Treatment and prevention of depression. *Psychological Science in the Public Interest, 3,* 39–77.

Holmes, C., Boche, D., Wilkinson, D., Yadegarfar, G., Hopkins, V., Bayer, A., et al. (2008). Long-term effects of Abeta42 immunization in Alzheimer's disease: Follow-up of a randomised, placebo-controlled phase I trial. *The Lancet, 372,* 216–223.

Holmes, E. A., Brown, R. J., Mansell, W., Fearon, R. P., Hunter, E. C., Frasquilho, F., et al. (2005). Are there two qualitatively distinct forms of dissociation? A review and some clinical implications. *Clinical Psychology Review, 25,* 1–23.

Holth, J., Patel, T., & Holtzman, D. M. (2017). Sleep in Alzheimer's disease: Beyond amyloid. *Neurobiology of Sleep and Circadian Rhythms, 2,* 4–14. doi:10.1016/j.nbscr.2016.08.002

Holtom-Viesel, A., & Allan, S. (2014). A systematic review of the literature on family functioning across all eating disorder diagnoses in comparison to control families. *Clinical Psychology Review, 34,* 29–43.

Hong, S., Walton, E., Tamaki, E., & Sabin, J. A. (2014). Lifetime prevalence of mental disorders among Asian Americans: Nativity, gender, and sociodemographic correlates. *Asian American Journal of Psychology, 5*(4), 353–363. doi:10.1037/a0035680

Hooley, J. M., & St. Germain, S. A. (2013). Nonsuicidal self-injury, pain, and self-criticism. *Clinical Psychological Science, 2*(3), 297–305. doi:10.1177/2167702613509372

Hopwood, C. J., & Zanarini, M. C. (2010). Borderline personality traits and disorder: Predicting prospective patient functioning. *Journal of Consulting and Clinical Psychology, 78,* 585–589.

Horan, W. P., Kring, A. M., & Blanchard, J. J. (2006). Anhedonia in schizophrenia: A review of assessment strategies. *Schizophrenia Bulletin, 32,* 259–273.

Horowitz, J. L., & Garber, J. (2006). The prevention of depressive symptoms in children and adolescents: A meta-analytic review. *Journal of Consulting and Clinical Psychology, 74,* 401–415.

Horton, A. M. J. (2008). The Halstead-Reitan Neuropsychological Test Battery: Past, present, and future. In A. M. Horton & D. Wedding (Eds.), *The Neuropsychology Handbook* (3rd ed.) (pp. 251–278). New York, NY: Springer Publishing.

Horton, R. S. (2011). Parenting as a cause of narcissism: Empirical support for psychodynamic and social learning theories. In W. K. Campbell & J. D. Miller (Eds.), *The handbook of narcissism and narcissistic personality disorder: Theoretical approaches, empirical findings, and treatments* (pp. 181–190). Hoboken, NJ: John Wiley & Sons.

Howard, R., Rabins, P. V., Seeman, M. V., & Jeste, D. V. (2000). Late-onset schizophrenia and very-late-onset schizophrenia-like psychosis: An international consensus. The International Late-Onset Schizophrenia Group. *American Journal of Psychiatry, 157,* 172–178.

Howes, O. D., & Kapur, S. (2009). The dopamine hypothesis of schizophrenia: Version III—The final common pathway. *Schizophrenia Bulletin, 35,* 549–562. http://doi.org/10.1093/schbul/sbp006

Howes, O., McCutcheon, R., & Stone, J. (2015). Glutamate and dopamine in schizophrenia: An update for the 21st century. *Journal of Psychopharmacology, 29,* 97–115. http://doi.org/10.1177/0269881114563634

Howlin, P., Goode, S., Hutton, J., & Rutter, M. (2004). Adult outcome for children with autism. *Journal of Child Psychology and Psychiatry, 45,* 212–229.

Howlin, P., Mawhood, L., & Rutter, M. (2000). Autism and developmental receptive language disorder—A follow-up comparison in early adult life. II. Social, behavioral, and psychiatric outcomes. *Journal of Child Psychiatry and Psychology, 41,* 561–578.

Hoza, B., Murray-Close, D., Arnold, L. E., Hinshaw, S. P., Hechtmen, L., & The MTA Cooperative Group. (2010). Time-dependent changes in positive illusory self-perceptions of children with attention-deficit/hyperactivity disorder: A developmental psychopathology perspective. *Developmental and Psychopathology, 22,* 375–390.

Hsu, L. K. G. (1990). *Eating disorders.* New York, NY: Guilford Press.

Huang, J., Chaloupka, F. J., & Fong, G. T. (2014). Cigarette graphic warning labels and smoking prevalence in Canada: A critical examination and reformulation of the FDA regulatory impact analysis. *Tobacco Control, 23 Suppl 1,* i7–12.

Hudson, J. I., Hiripi, E., Pope, H. G., & Kessler, R. C. (2007). The prevalence and correlates of eating disorders in the National Comorbidity Survey Replication. *Biological Psychology, 61,* 348–358.

Hudson, J. I., Lalonde, J. K., Berry, J. M., Pindyck, L. J., & Bulick, C. (2006). Binge-eating disorder as a distinct familial phenotype in obese individuals. *Archives of General Psychology, 63,* 3138–3319.

Huether, G., Zhou, D., & Ruther, E. (1997). Causes and consequences of the loss of serotonergic presynapses elicited by the consumption of 3, 4methylenedioxymethamphetamine (MDMA, "Ecstasy") and its congeners. *Journal of Neural Transmission, 104,* 771–794.

Huey, S. J., Jr., Tilley, J. L., Jones, E. O., & Smith, C. A. (2014). The contribution of cultural competence to evidence-based care for ethnically diverse populations. *Annual Review of Clinical Psychology, 10,* 305–338. doi:10.1146/annurev-clinpsy-032813-153729

Hughes, A., Williams, M. R., Lipari, R. N., Bose, J., Copello, E. A. P., & Kroutil, L. A. (2016, September). Prescription drug use and misuse in the United States: Results from the 2015 National Survey on Drug Use and Health. NSDUH Data Review. Retrieved from http://www.samhsa.gov/data/

Hughes, C., & Agran, M. (1993). Teaching persons with severe disabilities to use self-instruction in community settings: An analysis of applications. *Journal of the Association for Persons with Severe Handicaps, 18*, 261–274.

Hughes, C., Hugo, K., & Blatt, J. (1996). Self-instructional intervention for teaching generalized problem-solving within a functional task sequence. *American Journal on Mental Retardation, 100*, 565–579.

Hughes, J. R., Higgins, S. T., Bickel, W. K., Hunt, W. K., & Fenwick, J. W. (1991). Caffeine self-administration, withdrawal, and adverse effects among coffee drinkers. *Archives of General Psychiatry, 48*, 611–617.

Hughes, J. R., Higgins, S. T., & Hatsukami, D. K. (1990). Effects of abstinence from tobacco: A critical review. In L. T. Kozlowski, H. Annis, H. D. Cappell, F. Glaser, M. Goodstadt, Y. Israel, H. Kalant, E. M. Sellers, & J. Vingilis (Eds.), *Research advances in alcohol and drug problems*. New York, NY: Plenum.

Hulse, G. K., Ngo, H. T., & Tait, R. J. (2010). Risk factors for craving and relapse in heroin users treated with oral or implant naltrexone. *Biological Psychiatry, 68*, 296–302.

Human Genome Project. (2008). How many genes are in the human genome? Accessed online at http://www.ornl.gov/sci/techresources/ Human_Genome/faq/genenumber.shtml

Hunsley, J., & Bailey, J. M. (1999). The clinical utility of the Rorschach: Unfulfilled promises and an uncertain future. *Psychological Assessment, 11*, 266–277.

Hunter, E. C., Sierra, M., & David, A. S. (2004). The epidemiology of depersonalisation and derealisation. A systematic review. *Social Psychiatry and Psychiatric Epidemiology, 39*, 9–18.

Huntjen, R. J. C., Postma, A., Peters, M. L., Woertman, L., & van der Hart, O. (2003). Interidentity amnesia for neutral, episodic information in dissociative identity disorder. *Journal of Abnormal Psychology, 112*, 290–297.

Hussong, A. M., Hicks, R. E., Levy, S. A., & Curran, P. J. (2001). Specifying the relations between affect and heavy alcohol use among young adults. *Journal of Abnormal Psychology, 110*, 449–461.

Hustvedt, A. (2011). *Medical muses: Hysteria in nineteenth-century Paris*. New York, NY: W. W. Norton.

Hyde, L. W., Shaw, D. S., Murray, L., Gard, A., Hariri, A. R., & Forbes, E. E. (2016). Dissecting the role of amygdala reactivity in antisocial behavior in a sample of young, low-income, urban men. *Clinical Psychological Science, 4*, 527–544. doi:10.1177/2167702615614511

Hyde, L. W., Waller, R., Trentacosta, C. J., Shaw, D. S., Neiderhiser, J. M., Ganiban, J. M., et al. (2016). Heritable and nonheritable pathways to early callous-unemotional behaviors. *American Journal of Psychiatry, 173*, 903–910. http://doi.org/10.1176/appi.ajp.2016.15111381

Hyman, S. E. (2010). The diagnosis of mental disorders: The problem of reification. *Annual Review of Clinical Psychology, 6*, 155–179.

Iarovici, D. (2014). *Mental health issues and the university student*. Baltimore, MD: Johns Hopkins University Press.

Idrisov, B., Sun, P., Akhmadeeva, L., Arpawong, T. E., Kukhareva, P., & Sussman, S. (2013). Immediate and six-month effects of project EX Russia: A smoking cessation intervention pilot program. *Addictive Behaviors, 38*, 2402–2408. http://dx.doi.org/10.1016/j.addbeh.2013.03.013

Imel, Z. E., Laska, K., Jakupcak, M., & Simpson, T. L. (2013). Meta-analysis of dropout in treatments for posttraumatic stress disorder. *Journal of Consulting and Clinical Psychology, 81*, 394–404. doi:10.1037/a0031474

IMS Health. (2012). IMS national prescription audit PlusTM. (2011). Downloaded June 2014 from http://www.imshealth.com/portal/site/ imshealth.

IMS Health. (2014). Medicine use and shifting costs of healthcare: A review of the use of medicines in the United States in 2013. Retrieved April 28, 2014, at http://www.imshealth.com/cds/imshealth/Global/Content/ Corporate/IMS Health Institute/Reports/Secure/IIHI_US_Use_of_Meds_ for_2013.pdf

Indovina, I., Robbins, T. W., Nunez-Elizalde, A. O., Dunn, B. D., & Bishop, S. J. (2011). Fear-conditioning mechanisms associated with trait vulnerability to anxiety in humans. *Neuron, 69*, 563–571.

Inoue-Choi, M., Liao, L. M., Reyes-Guzman, C., Hartge, P., Caporaso, N., & Freedman, N. D. (2017). Association of long-term, low-intensity smoking with all-cause and cause-specific mortality in the National Institutes of Health–AARP Diet and Health Study. *JAMA Internal Medicine, 177*, 87–95. http://doi.org/10.1001/jamainternmed.2016.7511

Inouye, S. K., Baker, D. I., Fugal, P., & Bradley, E. H. (2006). Dissemination of the hospital elder life program: Implementation adaptation, and successes. *Journal of the American Geriatric Society, 54*, 1492–1499. doi:10.1111/j.1532-5415.2006.00869.x

Insel, T. R. (2014). The NIMH Research Domain Criteria (RDoC) Project: Precision medicine for psychiatry. *American Journal of Psychiatry, 171*, 395–397.

Insel, T. R. (2015). The NIMH experimental medicine initiative. *World Psychiatry, 14*(2), 151–153. doi:10.1002/wps.20227

Insel, T. R., Scanlan, J., Champoux, M., & Suomi, S. J. (1988). Rearing paradigm in a nonhuman primate affects response to B-CCE challenge. *Psychopharmacology, 96*, 81–86.

Institute of Medicine. (1999). *Marijuana and medicine: Assessing the science base*. Washington, DC: National Academy Press.

Institute of Medicine. (2004). *Immunization safety review: Vaccines and autism*. Immunization Safety Review Board on Health Promotion and Disease Prevention. Washington, DC: National Academies Press.

Institute of Medicine. (2012). The mental health and substance use workforce for older adults: In whose hands? Retrieved from: http:// www. iom. edu/Reports/2012/The-Mental-Health-and-Substance-Use- Workforce-for-Older-Adults. aspx

International Society for the Study of Dissociation. (2011). Guidelines for treating dissociative identity disorder in adults, third revision: Summary version. *Journal of Trauma and Dissociation, 12*, 188–212.

International Test Commission. (2010). *Guidelines for translating and adapting tests*. Retrieved from http://www.intestcom.org

Ioannidis, J. (2005a). Contradicted and initially stronger effects in highly cited clinical research. *JAMA: The Journal of the American Medical Association, 294*(2), 218–228. doi:10.1001/jama.294.2.218

Ioannidis, J. (2005b). Why most published research findings are false. *PLOS Medicine, 2*(8), e124. doi:10.1371/journal.pmed.0020124

Isaacowitz, D. M. (2012). Mood regulation in real time: Age differences in the role of looking. *Current Directions in Psychological Science, 21*, 237–242.

Ishikawa, S. S., Raine, A., Lencz, T., Bihrle, S., & Lacasse, L. (2001). Autonomic stress reactivity and executive functions in successful and unsuccessful criminal psychopaths from the community. *Journal of Abnormal Psychology, 110*, 423–432.

Ito, T., Miller, N. & Pollock, V. (1996). Alcohol and aggression: A meta-analysis on the moderating effects of inhibitory cues, triggering events, and self-focused attention. *Psychological Bulletin, 120*, 60–82.

Jack, C. R., Jr., Albert, M. S., Knopman, D. S., McKhann, G. M., Sperling, R. A., Carrillo, M. C., et al. (2011). Introduction to the recommendations from the National Institute on Aging-Alzheimer's Association workgroups on diagnostic guidelines for Alzheimer's disease. *Alzheimer's and Dementia: The Journal of the Alzheimer's Association, 7*, 257–262.

Jacobson, N. S., Dobson, K. S., Truax, P. A., Addis, M. E., Koerner, K., Gollan, J. K., et al. (1996). A component analysis of cognitive-behavioral treatment for depression. *Journal of Consulting and Clinical Psychology, 64*(2), 295–304.

Jacobson, N. S., Roberts, L. J., Berns, S. B., & McGlinchey, J. B. (1999). Methods for defining and determining the clinical significance of treatment effects: Description, application, and alternatives. *Journal of Consulting and Clinical Psychology, 67*, 300–307.

Jaffee, S. R., Strait, L. B., & Odgers, C. L. (2012). From correlates to causes: Can quasi-experimental studies and statistical innovations bring us closer to identifying the causes of antisocial behavior? *Psychological Bulletin, 138*, 272–295.

James, A., Hoang, U., Seagroatt, V., Clacey, J., Goldacre, M., & Leibenluft, E. (2014). A comparison of American and English hospital discharge rates for pediatric bipolar disorder, 2000 to 2010. *Journal of the American Academy of Child and Adolescent Psychiatry, 53*(6), 614–624.

James, D. J., & Glaze, L. E. (2006). Mental health problems of prison and jail inmates. *NCJ 213600*. Retrieved from http://www.bjs.gov/content/ pub/pdf/mhppji.pdf website: http://www.bjs.gov/content/pub/pdf/ mhppji.pdf

Jamison, K. R. (1993). *Touched with fire: Manic-depressive illness and the artistic temperament*. New York, NY: Simon & Schuster.

Jamison, K. R. (1995). *The unquiet mind: A memoir of moods and madness*. New York, NY: Vintage Books.

Jani, S., Johnson, R. S., Banu, S., & Shah, A. (2016). Cross-cultural bias in the diagnosis of borderline personality disorder. *Bulletin of the Menninger Clinic, 80*, 146–165. http://dx.doi.org/10.1521/bumc.2016.80.2.146

Jansen, R., Penninx, B. W., Madar, V., Xia, K., Milaneschi, Y., Hottenga, J. J., et al. (2016). Gene expression in major depressive disorder. *Molecular Psychiatry, 21*(3), 339–347. doi:10.1038/mp.2015.57

Jansen, W. J., Ossenkoppele, R., Knol, D. L., et al. (2015). Prevalence of cerebral amyloid pathology in persons without dementia: A meta-analysis. *Journal of the American Medical Association, 313*, 1924–1938. doi:10.1001/jama.2015.4668

Jardri, R., Pouchet, A., Pins, D., & Thomas, P. (2011). Cortical activation during auditory verbal hallucinations in schizophrenia: A coordinate-based meta-analysis. *American Journal of Psychiatry, 168*, 73–81.

Jarrell, M. P., Johnson, W. G., & Williamson, D. A. (1986). *Insulin and glucose response in the binge purge episode of bulimic women.* Paper presented at the annual convention of the Association for Advancement of Behavior Therapy, Chicago.

Jauhar, S., McKenna, P., Radua, J., E., F., R., S., & Laws, K. R. (2014). Cognitive-behavioural therapy for the symptoms of schizophrenia: Systematic review and meta-analysis with examination of potential bias. *British Journal of Psychiatry, 204*, 20–29.

Jeans, R. F. I. (1976). An independently validated case of multiple personality. *Journal of Abnormal Psychology, 85*, 249–255.

Jensen, M. P., & Patterson, D. R. (2014). Hypnotic approaches for chronic pain management: Clinical implications of recent research findings. *American Psychologist, 69*, 167–177.

Jensen, P. S., Arnold, L. E., Swanson, J. M., et al. (2007). 3-year follow-up of the NIMH MTA study. *Journal of the American Academy of Child and Adolescent Psychiatry, 46*, 989–1002.

Jensen, P. S., Martin, D., & Cantwell, D. P. (1997). Comorbidity in ADHD: Implications for research, practice, and DSM-V. *Journal of the American Academy of Child and Adolescent Psychiatry, 36*, 1065–1079.

Jeong, J., Shin, S. D., Kim, H., Hong, Y. C., Hwang, S. S., & Lee, E. J. (2012). The effects of celebrity suicide on copycat suicide attempt: A multi-center observational study. *Social Psychiatry and Psychiatric Epidemiology, 47*(6), 957–965. doi:10.1007/s00127-011-0403-7

Jespersen, A. F., Lalumiere, M. L., & Seto, M. C. (2009). Sexual abuse history among adult sex offenders and non-sex offenders: A meta-analysis. *Child Abuse and Neglect, 33*, 179–192.

Jett, D., LaPorte, D. J., & Wanchism, J. (2010). Impact of exposure to pro-eating disorder websites on eating behaviour in college women. *European Eating Disorders Review, 18*, 410–416.

Jimerson, D. C., Lesem, M. D., Kate, W. H., & Brewerton, T. D. (1992). Low serotonin and dopamine metabolite concentrations in cerebrospinal fluid from bulimic patients with frequent binge episodes. *Archives of General Psychiatry, 49*, 132–138.

Jimerson, D. C., Wolfe, B. E., Metzger, E. D., Finkelstein, D. M., Cooper, T. B., et al. (1997). Decreased serotonin function in bulimia nervosa. *Archives of General Psychiatry, 54*, 529–536.

Johansson, R., & Andersson, G. (2012). Internet-based psychological treatments for depression. *Expert Review of Neurotherapeutics, 12*(7), 861–869; quiz 870. doi:10.1586/ern.12.63

John, O. P., Naumann, L. P., & Soto, C. J. (2008). Paradigm shift to the integrative big-five trait taxonomy: History measurement, and conceptual issues. In O. P. John, R. W. Robins, & L. A. Pervin (Eds.), *Handbook of personality: Theory and research* (pp. 114–158). New York, NY: Guilford Press.

Johnson, J. G., Cohen, P., Brown, J., Smailes, E. M., & Bernstein, D. P. (1999). Childhood maltreatment increases risk for personality disorders during early adulthood. *Archives of General Psychiatry, 56*, 600–606.

Johnson, J. G., Cohen, P., Chen, H., Kasen, S., & Brook, J. S. (2006). Parenting behaviors associated with risk for offspring personality disorder during adulthood. *Archives of General Psychiatry, 63*, 579–583.

Johnson, K. R. & S. L. Johnson. (2014). Inadequate treatment of Black Americans with bipolar disorder. *Psychiatric Services, 65*(2), 255–258. doi:10.1176/appi.ps.201200590

Johnson, S. L., Cuellar, A. K., & Peckham, A. D. (2014). Risk factors for bipolar disorder. In I. H. Gotlib and C. Hammen (Eds.), *Handbook of depression* (3rd ed.). New York, NY: Guilford Press.

Johnson, S. L., Edge, M. D., Holmes, M. K., Carver, C. S., & NolenHoeksema, S. (2012). The behavioral activation system and mania. *Annual Review of Clinical Psychology, 8*, 243–267. doi:10.1146/annurev-clinpsy-032511-143148

Johnson, S. L. & Miklowitz, D. J. (2017). Bipolar and related disorders. In D. Beidel (Eds.), *Adult psychopathology and diagnosis (8th ed.).* New York, NY: Wiley and Sons.

Johnston, C., & Marsh, E. J. (2001). Families of children with attention-deficit/hyperactivity disorder: Review and recommendations for future research. *Clinical Child and Family Psychology Review, 4*, 183–207.

Johnston, L. D., O'Malley, P. M., Miech, R. A., Bachman, J. G., & Schulenberg, J. E. (2017). Monitoring the future: National survey results on drug use, 1975–2016: Overview, key findings on adolescent drug use. Ann Arbor, MI: Institute for Social Research, The University of Michigan.

Joiner, T. E. (2005). *Why people die by suicide.* Cambridge, MA: Harvard University Press.

Jokinen, J., Carlborg, A., Mårtensson, B., Forslund, K., Nordström, A.-L., & Nordström, P. (2007). DST non-suppression predicts suicide after attempted suicide. *Psychiatry Research, 150*(3), 297–303. doi:10.1016/j.psychres.2006.12.001

Jonas, B. S., Gu, Q., & Albertorio-Diaz, J. R. (2013). Psychotropic medication use among adolescents: United States, 2005–2010. *NCHS Data Brief*, no 135.

Jonas, D., Cusack, K., Forneris, C., et al. (2013). *Psychological and pharmacological treatments for adults with posttraumatic stress disorder (PTSD).* Rockville, MD: Agency for Healthcare Research and Quality. Retrieved from: https://www.ncbi.nlm.nih.gov/books/NBK137702/

Jones, E., & Wessely, S. (2001). Psychiatric battle casualties: An intra- and interwar comparison. *British Journal of Psychiatry, 178*, 242–247.

Jones, P. B., Barnes, T. R. E., Davies, L., Dunn, G., Lloyd, H., et al. (2006). Randomized controlled trial of the effect on quality of life of second- vs. first-generation antipsychotic drugs in schizophrenia: Cost utility of the latest antipsychotic drugs in schizophrenia study (CUt-LASS 1). *Archives of General Psychiatry, 63*, 1079–1087.

Jones, W., & Klin, A. (2013). Attention to eyes is present but in decline in 2–6-month-old infants later diagnosed with autism. *Nature, 504*(7480), 427–431.

Jordbru, A. A., Smedstad, L. M., Klungsoyr, O., & Martinsen, E. W. (2014). Psychogenic gait disorder: A randomized controlled trial of physical rehabilitation with one-year follow-up. *Journal of Rehabilitation Medicine, 46*, 181–187. doi:10.2340/16501977-1246

Jorm, A. F., Christensen, H., Henderson, A. S., Jacomb, P. A., Korten, A. E., & Rodgers, B. (2000). Predicting anxiety and depression from personality: Is there a synergistic effect of neuroticism and extraversion? *Journal of Abnormal Psychology, 109*, 145–149.

Josephs, R. A., & Steele, C. M. (1990). The two faces of alcohol myopia: Attentional mediation of psychological stress. *Journal of Abnormal Psychology, 99*, 115–126.

Joyal, C. C., & Carpentier, J. (2017). The prevalence of paraphilic interests and behaviors in the general population: A provincial survey. *Journal of Sex Research, 54*, 161–171. doi:10.1080/00224499.2016.1139034

Kafka, M. P. (2010). The DSM diagnostic criteria for fetishism. *Archives of Sexual Behavior, 39*, 357–362.

Kagan, J., & Snidman, N. (1999). Early childhood predictors of adult anxiety disorders. *Biological Psychiatry, 46*, 1536–1541.

Kampmann, I. L., Emmelkamp, P. M. G., & Morina, N. (2016). Meta-analysis of technology-assisted interventions for social anxiety disorder. *Journal of Anxiety Disorders, 42*, 71–84. doi:http://doi.org/10.1016/j.janxdis.2016.06.007

Kandel, D., & Kandel, E. (2015). The Gateway Hypothesis of substance abuse: Developmental, biological and societal perspectives. *Acta Paediatrica, 104*, 130–137. http://doi.org/10.1111/apa.12851

Kane, J. M., Robinson, D. G., Schooler, N. R., Mueser, K. T., Penn, D. L., Rosenheck, R. A., et al. (2016). Comprehensive versus usual community care for first-episode psychosis: 2-year outcomes from the NIMH RAISE early treatment program. *American Journal of Psychiatry, 173*, 362–372. http://doi.org/10.1176/appi.ajp.2015.15050632

Kanner, L. (1943). Autistic disturbances of affective contact. *Nervous Child, 2*, 217–250.

Kantor, E. D., Rehm, C. D., Haas, J. S., Chan, A. T., & Giovannucci, E. L. (2015). Trends in prescription drug use among adults in the United State from 1999–2012. *Journal of the American Medical Association, 314,* 1818–1830. doi:10.1001/jama.2015.13766

Kaplan, H. S. (1974). *The new sex therapy.* New York, NY: Brunner/Mazel.

Kaplan, M. S., & Krueger, R. B. (2012). Cognitive-behavioral treatment of the paraphilias. *Israel Journal of Psychiatry Related Sciences, 49,* 291–296.

Kaplow, J. B., & Widom, C. S. (2007). Age of onset of child maltreatment predicts long-term mental health outcomes. *Journal of Abnormal Psychology, 116,* 176–187.

Kaptchuk, T. J., Kelley, J. M., Conboy, L. A., Davis, R. B., Kerr, C. E., Jacobson, E. E., et al. (2008). Components of placebo effect: Randomised controlled trial in patients with irritable bowel syndrome. *British Medical Journal, 336,* 999–1003.

Karam, E. G., Friedman, M. J., Hill, E. D., Kessler, R. C., McLaughlin, K. A., Petukhova, M., et al. (2014). Cumulative traumas and risk thresholds: 12-month PTSD in the World Mental Health (WMH) surveys. *Depression and Anxiety, 31*(2), 130–142. doi:10.1002/da.22169

Karg, K., Burmeister, M., Shedden, K., & Sen, S. (2011). The serotonin transporter promoter variant (5-HTTLPR), stress, and depression meta-analysis revisited: Evidence of genetic moderation. *Archives of General Psychiatry, 68,* 444–454.

Karlin, B. E., & Cross, G. (2014). From the laboratory to the therapy room: National dissemination and implementation of evidence-based psychotherapies in the U.S. Department of Veterans Affairs health care system. *American Psychologist, 69*(1), 19–33. doi:10.1037/a0033888

Karlin, B. E., Ruzek, J. I., Chard, K. M., Eftekhari, A., Monson, C. M., Hembree, E. A., et al. (2010). Dissemination of evidence-based psychological treatments for posttraumatic stress disorder in the Veterans Health Administration. *Journal of Traumatic Stress, 23*(6), 663–673. doi:10.1002/jts.20588

Karon, B. P., & VandenBos, G. R. (1998). Schizophrenia and psychosis in elderly populations. In I. H. Nordhus, G. R. VandenBos, S. Berg, & P. Fromholt (Eds.), *Clinical geropsychology* (pp. 219–227). Washington, DC: American Psychological Association.

Kasari, C., Freeman, S., & Paparella, T. (2006). Joint attention and symbolic play in young children with autism: A randomized controlled intervention study. *Journal of Child Psychology and Psychiatry, 47,* 611–620.

Kasari, C., Paparella, T., Freeman, S., & Jahromi, L. B. (2008). Language outcome in autism: Randomized comparison of joint attention and play interventions. *Journal of Consulting and Clinical Psychology, 76,* 125–137.

Kashdan, T. B., & McKnight, P. E. (2010). The darker side of social anxiety: When aggressive impulsivity prevails over shy inhibition. *Current Directions in Psychological Science, 19,* 47–50.

Kashden, J., & Franzen, M. D. (1996). An interrater reliability study of the Luria-Nebraska Neuropsychological Battery Form-II quantitative scoring system. *Archives of Clinical Neuropsychology, 11,* 155–163.

Kassel, J. D., & Shiffman, S. (1997). Attentional mediation of cigarette smoking's effect on anxiety. *Health Psychology, 16,* 359–368.

Kassel, J. D., Stroud, L. R., & Paronis, C. A. (2003). Smoking, stress, and negative affect: Correlation, causation, and context across stages of smoking. *Psychological Bulletin, 129,* 270–304.

Kassel, J. D., & Unrod, M. (2000). Smoking, anxiety, and attention: Support for the role of nicotine in attentionally mediated anxiolysis. *Journal of Abnormal Psychology, 109,* 161–166.

Katon, W., Pedersen, H. S., Ribe, A. R., Fenger-Gron, M., Davydow, D., Waldorff, F. B., & Vestergaard, M. (2015). Effect of depression and diabetes mellitus on the risk for dementia: A national population-based cohort study. *JAMA Psychiatry, 72,* 612–619. doi:10.1001/jamapsychiatry.2015.0082

Katz, E. C., Gruber, K., Chutuape, M. A., & Stitzer, M. L. (2001). Reinforcement-based outpatient treatment for opiate and cocaine abusers. *Journal of Substance Abuse Treatment, 20,* 93–98.

Katz, J. (2017). Drug deaths in America are rising faster than ever. *New York Times,* June 5, 2017. Retrieved from https://www.nytimes.com/interactive/2017/06/05/upshot/opioid-epidemic-drug-overdose-deaths-are-rising-faster-than-ever.html

Kaya, C., Gunes, M., Gokce, A. M., & Kalkan, S. (2015). Is sexual function in female partners of men with premature ejaculation compromised? *Journal of Sex & Marital Therapy, 41,* 379–383. doi:http://dx.doi.org/10.1080/0092623X.2014.915905

Kaye, J. T., Bradford, D. E., Magruder, K. P., & Curtin, J. J. (2017). Probing for neuroadaptations to unpredictable stressors in addiction: Translational methods and emerging evidence. *Journal of Studies on Alcohol and Drugs, 78,* 353–371. http://doi.org/10.15288/jsad.2017.78.353

Kaye, W. H. (2008). Neurobiology of anorexia and bulimia nervosa. *Physiology and Behavior, 94,* 121–135.

Kaye, W. H., Ebert, M. H., Raleigh, M., & Lake, R. (1984). Abnormalities in CNS monoamine metabolism in anorexia nervosa. *Archives of General Psychiatry, 41,* 350–355.

Kaye, W. H., Greeno, C. G., Moss, H., Fernstrom, J., Lilenfeld, L. R., Wahlund, B., et al. (1998). Alterations in serotonin activity and platelet monoamine oxidase and psychiatric symptoms after recovery from bulimia nervosa. *Archives of General Psychiatry, 55,* 927–935.

Kazdin, A. (2011). *Single-case research designs: Methods for clinical and applied* settings (2nd ed.) New York, NY: Oxford University Press.

Kazdin, A. E. (2005). *Parent management training: Treatment for oppositional, aggressive, and antisocial behavior in children and adolescents.* New York, NY: Oxford University Press.

Kazdin, A. E., & Weisz, J. R. (1998). Identifying and developing empirically supported child and adolescent treatments. *Journal of Consulting and Clinical Psychology, 66,* 19–36.

Keane, T. M., Zimering, R. T., & Caddell, J. (1985). A behavioral formulation of posttraumatic stress disorder in Vietnam veterans. *The Behavior Therapist, 8,* 9–12.

Keefe, R. S. E., Bilder, R. M., Davis, S. M., Harvey, P. D., Palmer, B. W., et al. (2007). Neurocognitive effects of antipsychotic medications in patients with chronic schizophrenia in the CATIE trial. *Archives of General Psychiatry, 64,* 633–647.

Keel, P. K., Baxter, M. G., Heatherton, T. F., & Joiner, T. E. (2007). A 20-year longitudinal study of body weight, dieting, and eating disorder symptoms. *Journal of Abnormal Psychology, 116,* 422–432.

Keel, P. K., & Brown, T. A. (2010). Update on course and outcome in eating disorders. *International Journal of Eating Disorders, 43,* 195–204.

Keel, P. K., Gravener, J. A., Joiner, T. E., Jr., & Haedt, A. A. (2010). Twenty-year follow-up of bulimia nervosa and related eating disorders not otherwise specified. *International Journal of Eating Disorders, 43,* 492–497.

Keel, P. K., & Klump, K. L. (2003). Are eating disorders culture-bound syndromes? Implications for conceptualizing their etiology. *Psychological Bulletin, 129,* 747–769.

Keel, P. K., & Mitchell, J. E. (1997). Outcome in bulimia nervosa. *American Journal of Psychiatry, 154,* 313–321.

Keel, P. K., Mitchell, J. E., Davis, T. L., & Crow, S. J. (2002). Long-term impact of treatment in women diagnosed with bulimia nervosa. *International Journal of Eating Disorders, 31,* 151–158.

Keers, R., Ullrich, S., DeStavola, B. L., & Coid, J. W. (2014). Association of violence with emergence of persecutory delusions in untreated schizophrenia. *American Journal of Psychiatry, 171,* 332–339.

Kellerman, J. (1989). *Silent partner.* New York, NY: Bantam Books.

Keller, M. B., McCullough, J. P., Klein, D. N., Arnow, B., Dunner, D. L., Gelenberg, A. J., et al. (2000). A comparison of nefazodone, the cognitive behavioral-analysis system of psychotherapy, and their combination for the treatment of chronic depression. *The New England Journal of Medicine, 342,* 1462–1470.

Kelley, M. E., Wan, C. R., Broussard, B., Crisafio, A., Cristofaro, S., Johnson, S., et al. (2016). Marijuana use in the immediate 5-year premorbid period is associated with increased risk of onset of schizophrenia and related psychotic disorders. *Schizophrenia Research, 171,* 62–67.

Kellner, C. H., Fink, M., Knapp, R., Petrides, G., Husain, M., Rummans, T., et al. (2005). Relief of expressed suicidal intent by ECT: A consortium for research in ECT study. *American Journal of Psychiatry, 162,* 977–982.

Kelly, A. B., Chan, G. C. K., Toumbourou, J. W., O'Flaherty, M., Homel, R., Patton, G. C. & Williams, J. W. (2012). Very young adolescents and alcohol: Evidence of a unique susceptibility to peer alcohol use. *Addictive Behaviors, 37,* 414–419.

Kempton, M. J., Stahl, D., Williams, S. C., & DeLisi, L. E. (2010). Progressive lateral ventricular enlargement in schizophrenia: A meta-analysis of longitudinal MRI studies. *Schizophrenia Research, 120,* 54–62.

Kendall, P. C., Aschenbrand, S. G., & Hudson, J. L. (2003). Child-focused treatment of anxiety. In A. E. Kazdin & J. R. Weisz (Eds.), *Evidence-based psychotherapies for children and adolescents* (pp. 81–100). New York, NY: Guilford Press.

Kendall, P. C., & Beidas, R. S. (2007). Trial for dissemination of evidence-based practices for youth: Flexibility within fidelity. *Professional Psychology: Research and Practice, 38*, 13–20.

Kendall, P. C., Cummings, C. M., Villabø, M. A., Narayanan, M. K., Treadwell, K., Birmaher, B., et al. (2016). Mediators of change in the Child/Adolescent Anxiety Multimodal Treatment Study. *Journal of Consulting and Clinical Psychology, 84*(1), 1–14. http://dx.doi.org/10.1037/a0039773

Kendall, P. C., Flannery-Schroeder, E. C., Panichelli-Mindel, S., Southam-Gerow, M., Henin, A., & Warman, M. (1997). Therapy for youths with anxiety disorders: A second randomized clinical trial. *Journal of Consulting and Clinical Psychology, 65*, 366–380.

Kendall, P. C., Hudson, J. L. Gosch, E., Flannery-Schroeder, E., & Suveg, C. (2008). Cognitive–behavioral therapy for anxiety disordered youth: A randomized clinical trial evaluating child and family modalities. *Journal of Consulting and Clinical Psychology, 76*, 282–297.

Kendall, P. C., & Ingram, R. E. (1989). Cognitive-behavioral perspectives: Theory and research on depression and anxiety. In D. Watson & P. C. Kendall (Eds.), *Personality, psychopathology, and psychotherapy* (pp. 27–53). San Diego, CA: Academic Press.

Kendall, P. C., Safford, S., Flannery-Schroeder, E., & Webb, A. (2004). Child anxiety treatment: Outcomes in adolescence and impact on substance use and depression at 7.4-year follow-up. *Journal of Consulting and Clinical Psychology, 72*, 276–287.

Kendler, K. S., Aggen, S. H., Czajkowski, N., et al. (2008). The structure of genetic and environmental risk factors for DSM-IV personality disorders: A multivariate twin study. *Archives of General Psychiatry, 65*, 1438–1446. doi:10.1001/archpsyc.65.12.1438

Kendler, K. S., Aggen, S. H., Knudsen, G. P., Røysamb, E., Neale, M. C., & Reichborn-Kjennerud, T. (2011). The structure of genetic and environmental risk factors for syndromal and subsyndromal common DSM-IV Axis I and all Axis II disorders. *The American Journal of Psychiatry, 168*(1), 29–39. doi:10.1176/appi.ajp.2010.10030340

Kendler, K. S., Chen, X., Dick, D., Maes, H., Gillespie, N., Neale, M. C., & Riley, B. (2012). Recent advances in the genetic epidemiology and molecular genetics of substance use disorders. *Nature Neuroscience, 15*, 181–189.

Kendler, K. S., & Gardner, C. O. (2014). Sex differences in the pathways to major depression: A study of opposite-sex twin pairs. *American Journal of Psychiatry, 171*(4), 426–435. doi:10.1176/appi.ajp.2013.13101375

Kendler, K. S., Hettema, J. M., Butera, F., Gardner, C. O., & Prescott, C. A. (2003). Life event dimensions of loss, humiliation, entrapment, and danger in the prediction of onsets of major depression and generalized anxiety. *Archives of General Psychiatry, 60*, 789–796.

Kendler, K. S., Jacobson, K. C., Prescott, C. A., & Neale, M. C. (2003). Specificity of genetic and environmental risk factors for use and abuse/dependence of *Cannabis*, cocaine, hallucinogens, sedatives, stimulants, and opiates in male twins. *American Journal of Psychiatry, 160*, 687–695.

Kendler, K. S., Jacobson, K., Myers, J. M., & Eaves L. J. (2008). A genetically informative developmental study of the relationship between conduct disorder and peer deviance in males. *Psychological Medicine, 38*, 1001–1011.

Kendler, K. S., Karkowski-Shuman, L., & Walsh, D. (1996). Age of onset in schizophrenia and risk of illness in relatives. *British Journal of Psychiatry, 169*, 213–218.

Kendler, K. S., Lönn, S. L., Salvatore, J., Sundquist, J., & Sundquist, K. (2016). Effect of marriage on risk for onset of alcohol use disorder: A longitudinal and co-relative analysis in a Swedish national sample. *American Journal of Psychiatry, 173*, 911–918. http://doi.org/10.1176/appi.ajp.2016.15111373

Kendler, K. S., Myers, J., & Prescott, C. A. (2002). The etiology of phobias: An evaluation of the stress-diathesis model. *Archives of General Psychiatry, 59*, 242–249.

Kendler, K. S., Myers, J., Torgersen, S., Neale, M. C., & Reichborn-Kjennerud, T. (2007). The heritability of cluster A personality disorders assessed by both personal interview and questionnaire. *Psychological Medicine, 37*, 655–665. doi:10.1017/s0033291706009755

Kendler, K. S., & Prescott, C. A. (1998). *Cannabis* use, abuse, and dependence in a population-based sample of female twins. *American Journal of Psychiatry, 155*, 1016–1022.

Kendler, K. S., Prescott, C. A., Myers, J., & Neale, M. C. (2003). The structure of genetic and environmental risk factors for common psychiatric and substance use disorders in men and women. *Archives of General Psychiatry, 60*, 929–937.

Kessler, D. A. (2009). *The end of overeating*. Emmaus, PA: Rodale.

Kessler, L. (2004, August 22). Dancing with Rose: A strangely beautiful encounter with Alzheimer's patients provides insights that challenge the way we view the disease. *Los Angeles Times Magazine*.

Kessler, R. C. (2003). Epidemiology of women and depression. *Journal of Affective Disorders, 74*, 5–13.

Kessler, R. C., Aguilar-Gaxiola, S., Alonso, J., Chatterji, S., Lee, S., Ormel, J., et al. (2009). The global burden of mental disorders: An update from the WHO World Mental Health (WMH) Surveys. *Epidemiologia e Psichiatria Sociale, 18*, 23–33.

Kessler, R. C., Angermeyer, M., Anthony, J. C., de Graaf, R., Demyttenaere, K., Gasquet, I., et al. (2007). Lifetime prevalence and age-of-onset distributions of mental disorders in the World Health Organization's World Mental Health Survey Initiative. *World Psychiatry, 6*. 168–176.

Kessler, R. C., Avenevoli, S., Costello, E. J., Georgiades, K., Green, J. G., Gruber, M. J., et al. (2012). Prevalence, persistence, and socio-demographic correlates of DSM-IV disorders in the National Comorbidity Survey Replication Adolescent Supplement. *Archives of General Psychiatry, 69*(4), 372–380. http://doi.org/10.1001/archgenpsychiatry.2011.160

Kessler, R. C., Berglund, P. A., Chiu, W. T., Deitz, A. C., Hudson, J. I., Shahly, V., et al. (2013). The prevalence and correlates of binge eating disorder in the World Health Organization World Mental Health Surveys. *Biological Psychiatry, 73*(9), 904–914.

Kessler, R. C., Berglund, P., Demler, O., Jin, R., Koretz, D., Merikangas, K. R., et al. (2003). The epidemiology of major depressive disorder: Results from the National Comorbidity Survey Replication (NCS-R). *Journal of the American Medical Association, 289*, 3095–3105.

Kessler, R. C., Berglund, P., Demler, O., Jin, R., Merikangas, K. R., & Walters, E. E. (2005). Lifetime prevalence and age-of-onset distributions of DSM-IV disorders in the National Comorbidity Survey Replication. *Archives of General Psychiatry, 62 (6)*, 593–602.

Kessler, R. C., Birnbaum, H. G., Shahly, V., Bromet, E., Hwang, I., McLaughlin, K. A., et al. (2010). Age differences in the prevalence and co-morbidity of DSM-IV major depressive episodes: Results from the WHO World Mental Health Survey Initiative. *Depression and Anxiety, 27*, 351–364.

Kessler, R. C., Chiu, W. T., Demler, O., & Walters, E. E. (2005). Prevalence, severity, and comorbidity of 12-month DSM-IV disorders in the National Comorbidity Survey replication. *Archives of General Psychiatry, 62*, 617–627.

Kessler, R. C., Chiu, W. T., Jin, R., Ruscio, A. M., Shear, K., & Walters, E. E. (2006). The epidemiology of panic attacks, panic disorder, and agoraphobia in the National Comorbidity Survey replication. *Archives of General Psychiatry, 63*, 415–424.

Kessler, R. C., Crum, R. M., Warner, L. A., Nelson, C. B., Schulenberg, J., & Anthony, J. C. (1997). Lifetime co-occurrence of DSM-IIIR alcohol dependence with other psychiatric disorders in the National Comorbidity Study. *Archives of General Psychiatry, 54*, 313–321.

Kessler, R. C., Heeringa, S., Lakoma, M. D., Petukhova, M., Rupp, A. E., Schoenbaum, M., et al. (2008). Individual and society effects of mental disorders on earnings in the United States: Results from the National Comorbidity Survey Replication. *American Journal of Psychiatry, 165*, 703–711.

Kessler, R. C., Hwang, I., LaBrie, R., Petukhova, M., Sampson, N. A., Winters, K. C., & Shaffer, H. J. (2008). The prevalence and correlates of DSM-IV pathological gambling in the National Comorbidity Survey Replication. *Psychological Medicine, 38*, 1351–1360.

Kessler, R. C., McLaughlin, K. A., Green, J. G., Gruber, M. J., Sampson, N. A., Zaslavsky, A. M., et al. (2010). Childhood adversities and adult psychopathology in the WHO World Mental Health Surveys. *British Journal of Psychiatry, 197*, 378–385.

Kessler, R. C., Petukhova, M., Sampson, N. A., Zaslavsky, A. M., & Wittchen, H. U. (2012). Twelve-month and lifetime prevalence and lifetime morbid risk of anxiety and mood disorders in the United States. *International Journal of Methods in Psychiatric Research, 21*, 169–184.

Keys, A., Brozek, J., Hsu, L. K. G., McConoha, C. E., & Bolton, B. (1950). *The biology of human starvation.* Minneapolis, MN: University of Minnesota Press.

Khan, O., Ferriter, M., Huband, N., Powney, M. J., Dennis, J. A., & Duggan, C. (2015). Pharmacological interventions for those who have sexually offended or are at risk of offending. *Cochrane Database of Systematic Reviews,* CD007989. doi:10.1002/14651858.CD007989.pub2

Kiecolt-Glaser, J. K., Dura, J. R., Speicher, C. E., & Trask, O. (1991). Spousal caregivers of dementia victims: Longitudinal changes in immunity and health. *Psychosomatic Medicine, 54*, 345–362.

Kiecolt-Glaser, J. K., & Glaser, R. (2002). Depression and immune function: Central pathways to morbidity and mortality. *Journal of Psychosomatic Research, 53*, 873–876.

Kieseppa, T., Partonen, T., Haukka, J., Kaprio, J., & Lonnqvist, J. (2004). High concordance of bipolar I disorder in a nationwide sample of twins. *American Journal of Psychiatry, 161*, 1814–1821.

Kiesler, C. A. (1991). Changes in general hospital psychiatric care. *American Psychologist, 46*, 416–421.

Killen, J. D., Taylor, C. B., Hayward, C., Haydel, K. F., Wilson, D. M., Hammer, L., et al. (1996). Weight concerns influence the development of eating disorders: A 4-year prospective study. *Journal of Consulting and Clinical Psychology, 64*, 936–940.

Kimchi, E. Z., & Lyketsos, C. G. (2015). Dementia and mild neurocognitive disorders. In D. C. Steffens, D. G. Blazer, & M. E. Thakur (Eds.), *The American Psychiatric Publishing Textbook of Geriatric Psychiatry.* Washington, DC: APA.

Kim, D. D., & Basu, A. (2016). Estimating the medical care costs of obesity in the United States: Systematic review, meta-analysis, and empirical analysis. *Value in Health, 19*, 602–613.

Kim, E. (2005). The effect of the decreased safety behaviors on anxiety and negative thoughts in social phobics. *Journal of Anxiety Disorders, 19*, 69–86.

Kim, J. M., & López, S. R. (2014). The expression of depression in Asian Americans and European Americans. *Journal of Abnormal Psychology, 123*, 754–763. doi:10.1037/a0038114

Kim, M. J., Loucks, R. A., Palmer, A. L., Brown, A. C., Solomon, K. M., Marchante, A. N., et al. (2011). The structural and functional connectivity of the amygdala: From normal emotion to pathological anxiety. *Behavioural Brain Research, 223*, 403–410.

Kim, Y., Zerwas, S., Trace, S. E., & Sullivan, P. F. (2011). Schizophrenia genetics: Where next? *Schizophrenia Bulletin, 37*, 456–463.

King, A. C., de Wit, H., McNamara, P. J., & Cao, D. (2011). Rewarding, stimulant, and sedative alcohol responses and relationship to future binge drinking. *Archives of General Psychiatry, 68*, 389–399.

King, A. C., McNamara, P. J., Hasin, D. S., & Cao, D. (2014). Alcohol challenge responses predict future alcohol use disorder symptoms: A 6-year prospective study. *Biological Psychiatry, 75*, 798–806.

Kinsey, A. C., Pomeroy, W. B., & Martin, C. E. (1948). *Sexual behavior in the human male.* Philadelphia, PA: Saunders.

Kinzl, J. F., Traweger, C., Trefalt, E., Mangweth, B., & Biebl, W. (1999). Binge eating disorder in females: A population based investigation. *International Journal of Eating Disorders, 25*, 287–292.

Kirkbride, J. B., Barker, D., Cowden, F., Stamps, R., Yang, M., Jones, P. B., & Coid, J. W. (2008). Psychoses, ethnicity and socio-economic status. *The British Journal of Psychiatry, 193*, 18–24. http://doi.org/10.1192/bjp.bp.107.041566

Kirkbride, J. B., Fearon, P., Morgan, C., Dazzon, P., Morgan, K. et al. (2006). Heterogeneity in the incidence of schizophrenia and other psychotic illnesses: Results from the 3-center Aesop study. *Archives of General Psychiatry, 63*, 250–258.

Kirkpatrick, B., Fenton, W., Carpenter, W.T., & Marder, S.R. (2006). The NIMH-MATRICS consensus statement on negative symptoms. *Schizophrenia Bulletin, 32*, 296–303.

Kirmayer, L. J. (2001). Cultural variations in the clinical presentation of depression and anxiety: Implications for diagnosis and treatment. *Journal of Clinical Psychiatry, 62 (Suppl. 13)*, 22–28.

Kisley, M. A., Wood, S., & Burrows, C. L. (2007). Looking at the sunny side of life: Age-related change in an event-related potential measure of the negativity bias. *Psychological Science, 18*, 838.

Kitayama, S., & Uskul, A. K. (2011). Culture, mind, and the brain: Current evidence and future directions. *Annual Review of Psychology, 62*, 419–449.

Klein, D. N., Arnow, B. A., Barkin, J. L., Dowling, F., Kocsis, J. H., Leon, A. C., et al. (2009). Early adversity in chronic depression: Clinical correlates and response to pharmacotherapy. *Depression and Anxiety, 26*, 701–710.

Klein, D. N., & Kotov, R. (2016). Course of depression in a 10-year prospective study: Evidence for qualitatively distinct subgroups. *Journal of Abnormal Psychology, 125*(3), 337–348. doi:10.1037/abn0000147

Klein, D. N., Lewinsohn, P. M., Seeley, J. R., & Rohde, P. A. (2001). A family study of major depressive disorder in a community sample of adolescents. *Archives of General Psychiatry, 58*, 13–20.

Klein, D. N., Schwartz, J. E., Rose, S., & Leader, J. B. (2000). Five-year course and outcome of dysthymic disorder: A prospective, naturalistic follow-up study. *American Journal of Psychiatry, 157*, 931–939.

Klein, D. N., Shankman, S. A. M. A., & Rose, S. M. A. (2006). Ten-year prospective follow-up study of the naturalistic course of dysthymic disorder and double depression. *American Journal of Psychiatry, 163*, 872–880.

Kleinman, A. (1986). *Social origins of distress and disease: Depression, neurasthenia, and pain in modern China.* New Haven, CT: Yale University Press.

Kleinplatz, P. J. (2014). The paraphilias: An experiential approach to "dangerous" desires. In Y. M. Binik & K. S. K. Hall (Eds.), *Principles and practice of sex therapy* (5th ed.). New York, NY: Guilford Press.

Klerman, G. L., Weissman, M. M., Rounsaville, B. J., & Chevron, E. S. (1984). *Interpersonal psychotherapy of depression.* New York, NY: Basic Books.

Klimentidis, Y. C., Beasley, T. M., Lin, H. Y., Murati, G., Glass, G. E., Guyton, M., et al. (2011). Canaries in the coal mine: A cross-species analysis of the plurality of obesity epidemics. *Proceedings of the Royal Society B: Biological Sciences, 278*, 1626–1632.

Klonsky, E. D., May, A. M., & Saffer, B. Y. (2016). Suicide, suicide attempts, and suicidal ideation. *Annual Review of Clinical Psychology, 12*, 307–330. doi:10.1146/annurev-clinpsy-021815-093204

Klump, K. L., McGue, M., & Iacono, W. G. (2002). Genetic relationships between personality and eating attitudes and behaviors. *Journal of Abnormal Psychology, 111*, 380–389.

Klunk, W. E., Engler, H., Nordberg, A., Wang, Y., Blomqvist, G., & Holt, D. P. (2004). Imaging brain amyloid in Alzheimer's disease with Pittsburgh Compound-B. *Annals of Neurology, 55*, 306–319.

Knight, B. G. (1996). *Psychotherapy with older adults* (2nd ed.). Thousand Oaks, CA: Sage.

Knight, R. A., & King, M. (2012). Typologies for child molesters: The generation of a new structural model. In B. K. Schwartz (Ed.), *The sexual offender.* Kingston, NJ: Civic Research Institute.

Knight, R. A., & Sims-Knight, J. (2011). Risk factors for sexual violence. In J. White, M. Koss, & A. E. Kazdin (Eds.), *Violence against women and children, Volume 1: Mapping the terrain.* Washington DC: American Psychological Association.

Knox, K. L., Pflanz, S., Talcott, G. W., Campise, R. L., Lavigne, J. E., Bajorska, A., et al. (2010). The US Air Force suicide prevention program: Implications for public health policy. *American Journal of Public Health, 100*, 2457–2463.

Kochanek, K. D., Murphy, S. L., Xu, J., & Tejada-Vera, B. (2016). *Deaths: Final data for 2014.* National Vital Statistics Reports. Retrieved from https://www.cdc.gov/nchs/data/nvsr/nvsr65/nvsr65_04.pdf.

Koenen, K. C., Moffitt, T. E., Poulton, R., Martin, J., & Caspi, A. (2007). Early childhood factors associated with the development of posttraumatic stress disorder: Results from a longitudinal birth cohort. *Psychological Medicine, 37*, 181–192.

Kohler-Forsberg, O., Sylvia, L., Thase, M., Calabrese, J. R., Deckersbach, T., Tohen, M., et al. (2017). Nonsteroidal anti-inflammatory drugs (NSAIDs) and paracetamol do not affect 6-month mood-stabilizing treatment outcome among 482 patients with bipolar disorder. *Depression and Anxiety, 34*(3), 281–290. doi:10.1002/da.22601

Kohn, L. P., Oden, T., Munoz, R. F., Robinson, A., & Leavitt, D. (2002). Adapted cognitive behavioral group therapy for depressed low-income African American women. *Community Mental Health Journal, 38*(6), 497–504.

Kohn, M. L. (1968). Social class and schizophrenia: A critical review. In D. Rosenthal & S. S. Kety (Eds.), *The transmission of schizophrenia*. Elmsford, NY: Pergamon Press.

Kohut, H. (1971). *The analysis of the self*. New York, NY: International Universities Press.

Konnopka, A., Schaefert, R., Heinrich, S., Kaufmann, C., Luppa, M., Herzog, W., et al. (2012). Economics of medically unexplained symptoms: A systematic review of the literature. *Psychotherapy and Psychosomatics, 81*, 265–275.

Koob, G. F., & Le Moal. (2008). Addiction and the brain antireward system. *Annual Review of Psychology, 59*, 29–53.

Kopelowicz, A., & Liberman, R. P. (1998). Psychosocial treatments for schizophrenia. In P. E. Nathan & J. M. Gorman (Eds.), *A guide to treatments that work* (pp. 190–211). New York, NY: Oxford University Press.

Kopelowicz, A., Liberman, R. P., & Zarate, R. (2002). Psychosocial treatments for schizophrenia. In P. E. Nathan & J. M. Gorman (Eds.), *A guide to treatments that work*, 2nd ed. (pp. 201–229). New York, NY: Oxford University Press.

Kornør, H., Winje, D., Ekeberg, Ø., Weisæth, L., Kirkehei, I., Johansen, K., et al. (2008). Early trauma-focused cognitive-behavioural therapy to prevent chronic post-traumatic stress disorder and related symptoms: A systematic review and meta-analysis. *Biological Medical Central Psychiatry, 8*, 1–8.

Kotov, R., Gamez, W., Schmidt, F., & Watson, D. (2010). Linking "big" personality traits to anxiety, depressive, and substance use disorders: A meta-analysis. *Psychological Bulletin, 136*, 768–821.

Kotov, R., Krueger, R. F., Watson, D., Achenbach, T. M., Althoff, R. R., Bagby, R. M., et al. (2017, in press). The hierarchical taxonomy of psychopathology (HiTOP): A dimensional alternative to traditional nosologies. *Journal of Abnormal Psychology*. doi:10.1037/abn0000258

Kraemer, H. C. (2014). The reliability of clinical diagnoses: State of the art. *Annual Review of Clinical Psychology, 10*, 111–130. doi:10.1146/annurev-clinpsy-032813-153739

Kranzler, H. R., & van Kirk, J. (2001). Efficacy of naltrexone and acamprosate for alcoholism treatment: A meta analysis. *Alcoholism: Clinical and Experimental Research, 25*, 1335–1341.

Kremen, W. S., Jacobson, K. C., Xian, H., Eisen, S. A., Waterman, B., Toomey, R., et al. (2005). Heritability of word recognition in middle-aged men varies as a function of parental education. *Behavior Genetics, 35*, 417–433.

Kreslake, J. M., Wayne, G. F., Alpert, H. R., Koh, H. K., & Connolly, G. N. (2008). Tobacco industry control of menthol in cigarettes and targeting of adolescents and young adults. *American Journal of Public Health, 98*, 1685–1692.

Kreslake, J., Wayne, G. F., & Connolly, G. (2008). The menthol smoker: Tobacco industry research on consumer sensory perception of menthol cigarettes and its role in smoking behavior. *Nicotine & Tobacco Research, 10*, 705–715. http://doi.org/10.1080/14622200801979134

Kreyenbuhl, J., Buchanan, R. W., Dickerson, F. B., & Dixon, L. B. (2010). The Schizophrenia Patient Outcomes Research Team (PORT): Updated treatment recommendations 2009. *Schizophrenia Bulletin, 36*, 94–103.

Kreyenbuhl, J., Zito, J. M., Buchanan, R. W., Soeken, K. L., & Lehman, A. F. (2003). Racial disparity in the pharmacological management of schizophrenia. *Schizophrenia Bulletin, 29*, 183–193.

Kring, A. M., & Barch, D. M. (2014). The motivation and pleasure dimension of negative symptoms: Neural substrates and behavioral outputs. *European Neuropsychopharmacology, 24*, 725–736.

Kring, A. M., & Caponigro, J. M. (2010). Emotion in schizophrenia: Where feeling meets thinking. *Current Directions in Psychological Science, 19*, 255–259.

Kring, A. M., & Elis O. (2013). Emotion deficits in people with schizophrenia. *Annual Review of Clinical Psychology, 9*, 409–433.

Kring, A. M., Gur, R. E., Blanchard, J. J., Horan, W. P., & Reise, S. P. (2013). The Clinical Assessment Interview for Negative Symptoms (CAINS): Final development and validation. *American Journal of Psychiatry, 170*, 165–172.

Krinsley, K. E., Gallagher, J., Weathers, F. W., Kutter, C. J., & Kaloupek, D. G. (2003). Consistency of retrospective reporting about exposure to traumatic events. *Journal of Traumatic Stress, 16*, 399–409.

Kronstein, P. D., Ishida, E., Khin, N. A., Chang, E., Hung, H. M., Temple, R. J., & Yang, P. (2015). Summary of findings from the FDA regulatory science forum on measuring sexual dysfunction in depression trials. *Journal of Clinical Psychiatry, 76*, 1050–1059. doi:10.4088/JCP.14r09699

Krstic, S., Neumann, C. S., Roy, S., Robertson, C. A., Knight, R. A., & Hare, R. D. (2017). Using latent variable- and person-centered approaches to examine the role of psychopathic traits in sex offenders. *Personal Disord.* doi:10.1037/per0000249

Krueger (1999). The structure of common mental disorders. *Archives of General Psychiatry, 56*, 921–926.

Krueger, R. B. (2010a). The DSM diagnostic criteria for sexual masochism. *Archives of Sexual Behavior, 39*, 346–356.

Krueger, R. B. (2010b). The DSM diagnostic criteria for sexual sadism. *Archives of Sexual Behavior, 39*, 325–345.

Krueger, R. F., Derringer, J., Markon, K. E., Watson, D., & Skodol, A. E. (2012). Initial construction of a maladaptive personality trait model and inventory for DSM-5. *Psychological Medicine, 42*, 1879–1890.

Krueger, R. F., Markon, K. E., Patrick, C. J., & Iacono, W. G. (2005). Externalizing psychopathology in adulthood: A dimensional-spectrum conceptualization and its implications for DSM-V. *Journal of Abnormal Psychology, 114*, 537–550. doi:10.1037/0021-843X.114.4.537

Krystal, J. H., Cramer, J. A., Krol, W. F., et al. (2001). Naltrexone in the treatment of alcohol dependence. *New England Journal of Medicine, 345*, 1734–1739.

Kuester, A., Niemeyer, H., & Knaevelsrud, C. (2016). Internet-based interventions for posttraumatic stress: A meta-analysis of randomized controlled trials. *Clinical Psychology Review, 43*, 1–16. doi:https://doi.org/10.1016/j.cpr.2015.11.004

Kuhn, T. S. (1962/1970). *The structure of scientific revolutions*. Chicago, IL: University of Chicago Press.

Kulkarni, M., Barrad, A., & Cloitre, M. (2014). In P. Emmelkamp & T. Ehring (Eds.), *The Wiley handbook of anxiety disorders*. New York, NY: John Wiley & Sons, Ltd.

Kunkel, D., Wilcox, B. L., Cantor, J., Palmer, E., Linn, S., & Dowrick, P. (2004, February 20). Report of the APA Task Force on advertising and children. Washington, DC: American Psychological Association.

Kunst-Wilson, W. R., & Zajonc, R. B. (1980). Affective discrimination of stimuli that cannot be recognized. *Science, 207*, 557–558.

Kurian, B. T., Ray, W. A., Arbogast, P. G., Fuchs, D. C., Dudley, J. A., & Cooper, W. O. (2007). Effect of regulatory warnings on antidepressant prescribing for children and adolescents. *Archives of General Psychiatry, 161*, 690–696.

Kuyken, W., Hayes, R., Barrett, B., Byng, R., Dalgleish, T., Kessler, D., et al. (2015). Effectiveness and cost-effectiveness of mindfulness-based cognitive therapy compared with maintenance antidepressant treatment in the prevention of depressive relapse or recurrence (prevent): A randomised controlled trial. *The Lancet, 386*(9988), 63–73. doi:10.1016/S0140-6736(14)62222-4

Kwok, W. (2014). Is there evidence that social class at birth increases risk of psychosis? A systematic review. *International Journal of Social Psychiatry, 60*, 801–808.

Kyaga, S., Landen, M., Boman, M., Hultman, C. M., Langstrom, N., & Lichtenstein, P. (2013). Mental illness, suicide and creativity: 40-year prospective total population study. *Journal of Psychiatric Research, 47*(1), 83–90. doi:10.1016/j.jpsychires.2012.09.010

Laan, E., Everaerd, W., & Both, S. (2005). Female sexual arousal. In R. Balon & R. T. Segraves (Eds.), *Handbook of sexual dysfunctions and paraphilias*. Boca Raton, FL: Taylor and Francis Group.

Lahey, B. B., Lee, S. S., Sibley, M. H., Applegate, B., Molina, B. S. G., & Pelham, W. E. (2016). Predictors of adolescent outcomes among 4–6-year-old children with attention-deficit/hyperactivity disorder. *Journal of Abnormal Psychology, 125*(2), 168–181. http://dx.doi.org/10.1037/abn0000086

Lahey, B. B., Loeber, R., Burke, J. D., & Applegate, B. (2005). Predicting future antisocial personality disorder in males from a clinical assessment in childhood. *Journal of Consulting and Clinical Psychology, 73*, 389–399.

Lahey, B. B., McBurnett, K., & Loeber, R. (2000). Are attention-deficit/hyperactivity disorder and oppositional defiant disorder developmental precursors to conduct disorder? In A. J. Sameroff, M. Lewis, et al. (Eds.), *Handbook of developmental psychology* (2nd ed., pp. 431–446). New York, NY: Kluwer Academic/Plenum.

Lahey, B. B., Van Hulle, C. A., Singh, A. L., Waldman, I. D., & Rathouz, P. J. (2011). Higher-order genetic and environmental structure of prevalent forms of child and adolescent psychopathology. *Archives of General Psychiatry, 68*(2), 181–189.

Lahey, B. B., & Waldman, I. D. (2012). Phenotypic and causal structure of conduct disorder in the broader context of prevalent forms of psychopathology. *Journal of Child Psychology and Psychiatry, 53*, 536–557.

Lai, D. T., Cahill, K., Qin, Y., & Tang, J. L. (2010). Motivational interviewing for smoking cessation. *Cochrane Database of Systematic Reviews, 1*, CD006936.

Lambert, J. C., Ibrahim-Verbaas, C. A., Harold, D., Naj, A. C., Sims, R., Bellenguez, C., et al. (2013). Meta-analysis of 74,046 individuals identifies 11 new susceptibility loci for Alzheimer's disease. *Nature Genetics, 45*, 1452–1458. doi:10.1038/ng.2802

Lambert, M. J. (2004). Psychotherapeutically speaking—updates from the Division of Psychotherapy (29). Downloaded from http://www.divisionofpsychotherapy.org/updates.php

Lambert, M. J., & Ogles, B. M. (2004). The efficacy and effectiveness of psychotherapy. In M. J. Lambert (Ed.), *Bergin and Garfield's handbook of psychotherapy and behavior change* (5th ed., pp. 139–193). Hoboken, NJ: John Wiley & Sons.

Lamb, H. R., Weinberger, L. E., & DeCuir, W. J. (2002). The police and mental health. *Psychiatry Services, 53*, 1266–1271.

Lambrou, C., Veale, D., & Wilson, G. (2011). The role of aesthetic sensitivity in body dysmorphic disorder. *Journal of Abnormal Psychology, 120*, 443–453.

Lam, R. W., Levitt, A. J., Levitan, R. D., Enns, M. W., Morehouse, R., Michalak, E. E., et al. (2006). The Can-SAD study: A randomized controlled trial of the effectiveness of light therapy and fluoxetine in patients with winter seasonal affective disorder. *American Journal of Psychiatry, 163*, 805–812.

Lam, R. W., Levitt, A. J., Levitan, R. D., et al. (2016). Efficacy of bright light treatment, fluoxetine, and the combination in patients with nonseasonal major depressive disorder: A randomized clinical trial. *JAMA Psychiatry, 73*(1), 56–63. doi:10.1001/jamapsychiatry.2015.2235

Landa, R. J., Holman, K. C., & Garrett-Mayer, E. (2007). Social and communication development in toddlers with early and later diagnosis of autism spectrum disorders. *Archives of General Psychiatry, 64*, 853–864.

Landgrebe, M., Barta, W., Rosengarth, K., Frick, U., Hauser, S., Langguth, B., et al. (2008). Neuronal correlates of symptom formation in functional somatic syndromes: A fMRI study. *NeuroImage, 41*, 1336–1344.

Lane, E. A., & Albee, G. W. (1965). Childhood intellectual differences between schizophrenic adults and their siblings. *American Journal of Orthopsychiatry, 35*, 747–753.

Langa, K. M., Larson, E. B., Karlawish, J. H., Cutler, D. M., Kabeto, M. U., Kim, S. Y., et al. (2008). Trends in the prevalence and mortality of cognitive impairment in the United States: Is there evidence of a compression of cognitive morbidity? *Alzheimer's and Dementia: The Journal of the Alzheimer's Association, 4*, 134–144.

Langa, K. M., & Levine, D. A. (2014). The diagnosis and management of mild cognitive impairment: A clinical review. *Journal of the American Medical Association, 312*, 2551–2561. doi:10.1001/jama.2014.13806

Lang, A. R., Goeckner, D. J., Adessor, V. J., & Marlatt, G. A. (1975). Effects of alcohol on aggression in male social drinkers. *Journal of Abnormal Psychology, 84*, 508–518.

Långström, N. (2010). The DSM diagnostic criteria for exhibitionism, voyeurism, and frotteurism. *Archives of Sexual Behavior, 39*, 317–324.

Långström, N., & Seto, M. C. (2006). Exhibitionistic and voyeuristic behavior in a Swedish national population survey. *Archives of Sexual Behavior, 35*, 427–435. doi:10.1007/s10508-006-9042-6

Larson, R. P., Cartwright, A. E., & Goodman, G. S. (Eds.). (2016). Understanding and evaluating the testimony of child victims and witnesses in the legal system. *Behavioral Sciences & the Law, 34*, 1–245.

Larsson, H., Chang, Z., D'Onofrio, B. M., & Lichtenstein, P. (2014). The heritability of clinically diagnosed attention deficit hyperactivity disorder across the lifespan. *Psychological Medicine, 44*(10), 2223–2229. http://doi.org/10.1017/S0033291713002493

Lasky-Su, J. A., Faraone, S. V., Glatt, S. J., & Tsuang, M. T. (2005). Meta-analysis of the association between two polymorphisms in the serotonin transporter gene and affective disorders. *American Journal of Medical Genetics Part B: Neuropsychiatric Genetics, 133*(1), 110–115.

Latthe, P., Mignini, L., Gray, R., Hills, R., & Khan, K. (2006). Factors predisposing women to chronic pelvic pain: Systematic review. *British Medical Journal, 332*, 749–755. doi:10.1136/bmj.38748.697465.55

Laugesen, N., Dugas, M. J., & Bukowski, W. M. (2003). Understanding adolescent worry: The application of a cognitive model. *Journal of Abnormal Child Psychology, 31*, 55–64.

Lau, J. Y. F., Gregory, A. M., Goldwin, M. A., Pine, D. S., & Eley, T. C. (2007). Assessing gene–environment interactions on anxiety symptom subtypes across childhood and adolescence. *Development and Psychopathology, 19*, 1129–1146.

Laumann, E. O., Nicolosi, A., Glasser, D. B., Paik, A., Gingell, C., Moreira, E., et al. (2005). Sexual problems among women and men aged 40–80 years: Prevalence and correlates identified in the Global Study of Sexual Attitudes and Behaviors. *International Journal of Impotence Research, 17*, 39–57.

Laumann, E. O., Paik, A., & Rosen, R. C. (1999). Sexual dysfunction in the United States: Prevalence and predictors. *Journal of the American Medical Association, 281*, 537–544.

Laursen, T. M., Nordentoft, M., & Mortensen, P. B. (2014). Excess early mortality in schizophrenia. *Annual Review of Clinical Psychology, 10*, 425–448. http://doi.org/10.1146/annurev-clinpsy-032813-153657

Lavner, J. A., Lamkin, J., Miller, J. D., Campbell, W. K., & Karney, B. R. (2016). Narcissism and newlywed marriage: Partner characteristics and marital trajectories. *Personality Disorders, 7*, 169–179. doi:10.1037/per0000137

Law, M., & Tang, J. L. (1995). An analysis of the effectiveness of interventions intended to help people stop smoking. *Archives of Internal Medicine, 155*, 1933–1941.

Lawrence, D., Kisely, S., & Pais, J. (2012). The epidemiology of excess mortality in people with mental illness. *Canadian Journal of Psychiatry, 12*, 752–760.

Leahy, R. L. (2003). *Cognitive therapy techniques: A practitioner's guide.* New York, NY: Guilford Press

Leahy, R. L. (2017). *Cognitive therapy techniques: A practitioner's guide.* New York, NY: Guilford Press.

Leckelt, M., Küfner, A. C. P., Nestler, S., & Back, M. D. (2015). Behavioral processes underlying the decline of narcissists' popularity over time. *Journal of Personality and Social Psychology: Personality Processes and Individual Differences, 109*, 856–871. http://dx.doi.org/10.1037/pspp0000057

Le Couteur, A., Bailey, A., Goode, S., Pickles, A., Robertson, S., Gottesman, I., & Rutter, M. (1996). A broader phenotype of autism: The clinical spectrum in twins. *Journal of Child Psychology and Psychiatry and Allied Disciplines, 37*, 785–801.

LeDoux, J. E., & Pine, D. S. (2016). Using neuroscience to help understand fear and anxiety: A two-system framework. *American Journal of Psychiatry, 173*(11), 1083–1093. doi:10.1176/appi.ajp.2016.16030353

Leeners, B., Hengartner, M. P., Rössler, W., Ajdacic-Gross, V., & Angst, J. (2014). The role of psychopathological and personality covariates in orgasmic difficulties: A prospective longitudinal evaluation in a cohort of women from age 30 to 50. *Journal of Sexual Medicine, 11*, 2928–2937. doi:10.1111/jsm.12709

Lee, S., Ng, K. L., Kwok, K., & Fung, C. (2010). The changing profile of eating disorders at a tertiary psychiatric clinic in Hong Kong (1987–2007). *International Journal of Eating Disorders, 43*, 307–314.

Lee, S. S., Lahey, B., Owens, E. B., & Hinshaw, S. P. (2008). Few preschool boys and girls with ADHD are well-adjusted during adolescence. *Journal of Abnormal Child Psychology, 36*, 373–383.

Legault, E., & Laurence, J. P. (2007). Recovered memories of childhood sexual abuse: Social worker, psychologist, and psychiatrist reports of beliefs, practices, and cases. *Australian Journal of Clinical and Experimental Hypnosis, 35*, 111–133.

Le Grange, D., Crosby, R. D., Rathouz, P. J., & Leventhal, B. L. (2007). A randomized controlled comparison of family-based treatment and supportive psychotherapy for adolescent bulimia nervosa. *Archives of General Psychiatry, 64*, 1049–1056.

Le Grange, D., Fitzsimmons-Craft, E. E., Crosby, R. D., Hay, P., Lacey, H., Bamford, B., et al. (2014). Predictors and moderators of outcome for severe and enduring anorexia nervosa. *Behaviour Research and Therapy, 56*, 91–98.

Le Grange, D., & Lock, J. A. (2005). The dearth of psychological treatment studies for anorexia nervosa. *International Journal of Eating Disorders, 37*, 79–91.

Lehn, A., Gelauff, J., Hoeritzauer, I., Ludwig, L., McWhirter, L., Williams, S., et al. (2016). Functional neurological disorders: Mechanisms and treatment. *Journal of Neurology, 263*, 611–620. doi:10.1007/s00415-015-7893-2

Leibenluft, E. (2011). Severe mood dysregulation, irritability, and the diagnostic boundaries of bipolar disorder in youths. *American Journal of Psychiatry, 168*(2), 129–142.

Leit, R. A., Gray, J. J., & Pope, H. G. (2002). The media's presentation of the ideal male body: A cause for muscle dysmorphia? *International Journal of Eating Disorders, 31*, 334–338.

Lenzenweger, M. (2015). Schizotypic psychopathology: Theory evidence, and future directions In P. Blaney, R. B. Krueger, & T. Millon (Eds.), *Oxford textbook of psychopathology* (pp. 729–767). New York, NY: Oxford University Press.

Lenzenweger, M. F., Lane, M. C., Loranger, A. W., & Kessler, R. C. (2007). DSM-IV personality disorders in the National Comorbidity Survey Replication. *Biological Psychiatry, 62*, 553–564.

Leon, A. C., Portera, L., & Weissman, M. M. (1995). The social costs of anxiety disorders. *British Journal of Psychiatry, 166*(Suppl. 27), 19–22.

Leon, G. R., Fulkerson, J. A., Perry, C. L., & Early-Zald, M. B. (1995). Prospective analysis of personality and behavioral vulnerabilities and gender influences in the later development of disordered eating. *Journal of Abnormal Psychology, 104*, 140–149.

Leon, G. R., Fulkerson, J. A., Perry, C. L., Peel, P. K., & Klump, K. L. (1999). Three to four year prospective evaluation of personality and behavioral risk factors for later disordered eating in adolescent girls and boys. *Journal of Youth and Adolescence, 28*, 181–196.

Lerman, C., Caporaso, N. E., Audrain, J., Main, D., Bowman, E. D., et al. (1999). Evidence suggesting the role of specific genetic factors in cigarette smoking. *Health Psychology, 18*, 14–20.

Leslie, D. L., & Rosenheck, R. A. (2004). Incidence of newly diagnosed diabetes attributable to atypical antipsychotic medications. *American Journal of Psychiatry, 161*, 1709–1711.

Leucht, S., Komossa, K., Rummel-Kluge, C., Corves, C., Hunger, H., Schmid, F., Lobos, C. A., Schwarz, S., & Davis, J. M. (2009). A meta-analysis of head-to-head comparisons of second-generation antipsychotics in the treatment of schizophrenia. *American Journal of Psychiatry, 166*, 152–163.

Leucht, S., Leucht, C., Huhn, M., Chaimani, A., Mavridis, D., Helfer, B., et al. (2017). Sixty years of placebo-controlled antipsychotic drug trials in acute schizophrenia: Systematic review, Bayesian meta-analysis, and meta-regression of efficacy predictors. *The American Journal of Psychiatry*, appiajp201716121358. http://doi.org/10.1176/appi.ajp.2017.16121358

Leucht, S., Tardy, M., Komossa, K., Heres, S., Kissling, W., & Davis, J. M. (2012). Maintenance treatment with antipsychotic drugs for schizophrenia. Cochrane Database of Systematic Review, (5). http://doi.org/10.1002/14651858.CD008016.pub2

Levenson, J. S., & Grady, M. D. (2016). The influence of childhood trauma on sexual violence and sexual deviance in adulthood. *Traumatology, 22*, 94–103. doi:10.1037/trm0000067

Levitan, R. D., Kaplan, A. S., Joffe, R. T., Levitt, A. J., & Brown, G. M. (1997). Hormonal and subjective responses to intravenous meta-chlorophenylpiperazine in bulimia nervosa. *Archives of General Psychiatry, 54*, 521–528.

Levy, B. R. (2003). Mind matters: Cognitive and physical effects of aging self-stereotypes. *Journal of Gerontology: Psychological Sciences, 58B*, 203–211.

Levy, B. R., Ferrucci, L., Zonderman, A. B., Slade, M. D., Troncoso, J., & Resnick, S. M. (2016). A culture–brain link: Negative age stereotypes predict Alzheimer's disease biomarkers. *Psychology and Aging, 31*, 82–88. doi:http://dx.doi.org/10.1037/pag0000062

Levy, B. R., Slade, M. D., & Kasl, S. V. (2002). Longitudinal benefit of positive self-perceptions of aging on functional health. *Journal of Gerontology: Psychological Sciences, 57B*, 409–417.

Lewinsohn, P. M., & Clarke, G. N. (1999). Psychosocial treatments for adolescent depression. *Clinical Psychology Review, 19*, 329–342.

Lewinsohn, P. M. (Ed.). (1974). *A behavioral approach to depression*. New York, NY: Springer Publishing.

Lewinsohn, P. M., Petit, J. W., Joiner, T. E., & Seeley, J. R. (2003). The symptomatic expression of major depressive disorder in adolescents and young adults. *Journal of Abnormal Psychology, 112*, 244–252.

Lewinsohn, P. M., Rohde, P., Seeley, J. R., Klein, D. N., & Gotlib, I. H. (2000). Natural course of adolescent major depressive disorder in a community sample: Predictors of recurrence in young adults. *American Journal of Psychiatry, 157*, 1584–1591.

Lewis-Fernandez, R., & Aggarwal, N. K. (2013). Culture and psychiatric diagnosis. *Advances in Psychosomatic Medicine, 33*, 15–30. doi:10.1159/000348725

Lewis, S. W., Barnes, T. R. E., Davies, L., Murray, R. M., Dunn, G., et al. (2006). Randomized controlled trial of effect of quality of life of prescription of clozapine vs. other second-generation antipsychotic drugs in resistant schizophrenia. *Schizophrenia Bulletin, 32*, 715–723.

Liberman, R. P., Eckman, T. A., Kopelowicz, A., & Stolar, D. (2000). *Friendship and intimacy module*. Camarillo, CA: Psychiatric Rehabilitation Consultants.

Liberman, R. P., Wallace, C. J., Blackwell, G., Kopelowicz, J. V., et al. (1998). Skills training versus psychosocial occupational therapy for persons with persistent schizophrenia. *The American Journal of Psychiatry, 155*, 1087–1091.

Lichtenstein, P., & Annas, P. (2000). Heritability and prevalence of specific fears and phobias in childhood. *Journal of Child Psychology and Psychiatry and Allied Disciplines, 41*, 927–937.

Lichtenstein, P., Carlstrom, E., Ramstam, M., Gillberg, C., & Anckarsater, H. (2010). The genetics of autism spectrum disorders and related neuropsychiatric disorders in childhood. *American Journal of Psychiatry, 167*, 1357–1363.

Lieberman, J. A., Stroup, T. S., McEvoy, J. P. Swartz, M. S., Rosenheck, R. A., Perkins, D. O., et al. (2005). Effectiveness of antipsychotic drugs in patients with chronic schizophrenia. *New England Journal of Medicine, 353*, 1209–1223.

Liebowitz, M. R., Heimberg, R. G., Fresco, D. M., Travers, J., & Stein, M. B. (2000). Social phobia or social anxiety disorder: What's in a name? *Archives of General Psychiatry, 57*, 191–192.

Lieb, R., Meinlschmidt, G., & Araya, R. (2007). Epidemiology of the association between somatoform disorders and anxiety and depressive disorders: An update. *Psychosomatic Medicine, 69*, 860–863.

Liechti, M. E., Baumann, C., Gamma, A., & Vollenweider, F. X. (2000). Acute psychological effects of 3, 4methylenedioxymethamphetamine (MDMA, "Ecstasy") are attenuated by the serotonin uptake inhibitor citalopram. *Neuropsychopharmacology, 22*, 513–521.

Lilenfeld, L. R., Kaye, W. H., Greeno, C. G., Merikangas, K. R., Plotnicov, K., et al. (1998). A controlled family study of anorexia nervosa and bulimia nervosa: Psychiatric disorders in first-degree relatives and effects of proband comorbidity. *Archives of General Psychiatry, 55*, 603–610.

Lilienfeld, S. O. (2007). Psychological treatments that cause harm. *Perspectives on Psychological Science, 2*, 53–70.

Lilienfeld, S. O., Lynn, S. J., Kirsch, I., Chaves, J. F., Sarbin, T. R., & Ganaway, G. K. (1999). Dissociative identity disorder and the sociogenic model: Recalling lessons from the past. *Psychological Bulletin, 125*, 507–523.

Lilienfeld, S. O., Lynn, S. J., Ruscio, J., & Beyerstein, B. L. (2010). Sad, mad, and bad: Myths about mental illness. In S. O. Lilienfeld, S. J. Lynn, J. Ruscio & B. L. Beyerstein (Eds.), *50 great myths of popular psychology: Shattering widespread misconceptions about human behavior* (pp. 181–208). Hoboken, NJ: John Wiley & Sons.

Lilienfeld, S. O., Patrick, C. J., Benning, S. D., Berg, J., Sellbom, M., & Edens, J. F. (2012). The role of fearless dominance in psychopathy:

Confusions, controversies, and clarifications. *Personality Disorders: Theory, Research, and Treatment, 3*, 327–340. http://dx.doi.org/10.1037/a0026987

Lilienfeld, S. O., Wood, J. M., & Garb, H. N. (2000). The scientific status of projective techniques. *Psychological Science in the Public Interest, 1*, 27–66.

Lilly, R., Quirk, A., Rhodes, T., & Stimson, G. V. (2000). Sociality in methadone treatment: Understanding methadone treatment and service delivery as a social process. *Drugs: Education, Prevention and Policy, 7*, 163–178.

Li, M. D., Cheng, R., Ma, J. Z., & Swan, G. E. (2003). A meta-analysis of estimated genetic and environmental effects on smoking behavior in male and female adult twins. *Addiction, 98*, 23–31.

Lim, R. F. (2015). *Clinical Manual of Cultural Psychiatry* (2nd ed.). Washington, DC: American Psychiatric Association.

Lindemann, E., & Finesinger, I. E. (1938). The effect of adrenalin and mecholyl in states of anxiety in psychoneurotic patients. *American Journal of Psychiatry, 95*, 353–370.

Lindson-Hawley, N., Aveyard, P., Hughes, J.R. (2012). Reduction versus abrupt cessation in smokers who want to quit. *Cochrane Database of Systematic Reviews, 11*, CD008033. doi:10.1002/14651858.CD008033.pub3.

Linehan, M. M. (1987). Dialectical behavior therapy for borderline personality disorder. *Bulletin of the Menninger Clinic, 51*, 261–276.

Linehan, M. M., Comtois, K., Murray, A. M., Brown, M. A., Gallop, R. J., Heard, H. L., et al. (2006). Two-year randomized controlled trial and follow-up of dialectical behavior therapy vs. therapy by experts for suicidal behaviors and borderline personality disorder. *Archives of General Psychiatry, 63*(7), 757–766. doi:10.1001/archpsyc.63.7.757

Linehan, M. M., & Heard, H. L. (1999). Borderline personality disorder: Costs, course, and treatment outcomes. In N. E. Miller & K. M. Magruder (Eds.), *Cost-effectiveness of psychotherapy: A guide for practitioners, researchers, and policymakers* (pp. 291–305). London: Oxford Univeristy Press.

Linnet, K. M., Dalsgaard, S., Obel, C., et al. (2003). Maternal lifestyle factors in pregnancy risk of attention deficit hyperactivity disorder and associated behaviors: Review of the current evidence. *American Journal of Psychiatry, 160*, 1028–1040.

Lissek, S., Powers, A. S., McClure, E. B., Phelps, E. A., Woldehawariat, G., Grillon, C., et al. (2005). Classical fear conditioning in the anxiety disorders: A meta-analysis. *Behaviour Research and Therapy, 43*, 1391–1424.

Liu, H., Petukhova, M. V., Sampson, N. A., et al. (2017). Association of DSM-IV posttraumatic stress disorder with traumatic experience type and history in the World Health Organization World Mental Health Surveys. *JAMA Psychiatry, 74*, 270–281. doi:10.1001/jamapsychiatry.2016.3783

Liu, R. T., Kleiman, E. M., Nestor, B. A., & Cheek, S. M. (2015). The hopelessness theory of depression: A quarter century in review. *Clinical psychology: A publication of the Division of Clinical Psychology of the American Psychological Association, 22*(4), 345–365. doi:10.1111/cpsp.12125

Lobmaier, P. P., Kunøe, N., Gossop, M. and Waal, H. (2011), Naltrexone depot formulations for opioid and alcohol dependence: A systematic review. *CNS Neuroscience & Therapeutics, 17*, 629–636. doi:10.1111/j.1755-5949.2010.00194.x

Locke, A. E., Kahali, B., Berndt, S. I., Justice, A. E., Pers, T. H., Day, F. R., et al. (2015). Genetic studies of body mass index yield new insights for obesity biology. *Nature, 518*, 197–206. http://doi.org/10.1038/nature14177

Lock, J., Le Grange, D., Agras, S., Moye, A., Bryson, S. W., & Jo, B. (2011). Randomized clinical trial comparing family-based treatment with adolescent-focused individual therapy for adolescents with anorexia nervosa. *Archives of General Psychiatry, 67*, 1025–1032.

Lock, J., Le Grange, D., Agras, W. S., & Dare, C. (2001). *Treatment manual for anorexia nervosa: A family-based approach.* New York, NY: Guilford Press.

Loeber, R., Burke, J. D., Lahey, B. B., Winters, A., & Zera, M. (2000). Oppositional defiant and conduct disorder: A review of the past 10 years, Part I. *Journal of the American Academy of Child and Adolescent Psychiatry, 39*, 1468–1484.

Loeber, R., & Hay, D. (1997). Key issues in the development of aggression and violence from childhood to early adulthood. *Annual Review of Psychology, 48*, 371–410.

Loeber, R., & Keenan, K. (1994). Interaction between conduct disorder and its comorbid conditions: Effects of age and gender. *Clinical Psychology Review, 14*, 497–523.

Loeb, K. L., Walsh, B. T., Lock, J., le Grange, D., Jones, J., Marcus, S., et al. (2007). Open trial of family-based treatment for full and partial anorexia nervosa in adolescence: Evidence of successful dissemination. *Journal of the American Academy of Child and Adolescent Psychiatry, 46*, 792–800.

Loftus, E. F. (1993). The reality of repressed memories. *American Psychologist, 48*, 518–537.

Logsdon, R. G., McCurry, S. M., & Teri, L. (2007). Evidence-based psychological treatments for disruptive behaviors in individuals with dementia. *Psychology and Aging, 22*, 28–36.

Lohr, J., Tolin, D. F., & Lilienfeld, S. O. (1998). Efficacy of eye movement desensitization and reprocessing: Implications for behavior therapy. *Behavior Therapy, 29*, 123–156.

Longshore, D., Hawken, A., Urada, D., & Anglin, M. (2006). Evaluation of the Substance Abuse and Crime Prevention Act: SACPA cost-analysis report (first and second years). Retrieved from http://www.uclaisap.org/prop36/html/reports.html.

Longshore, D., Urada, D., Evans, E., Hser, Y. I., Prendergast, M., & Hawken, A. (2005). Evaluation of the Substance Abuse and Crime Prevention Act: 2004 report. Sacramento, CA: Department of Alcohol and Drug Programs, California Health and Human Services Agency.

Longshore, D., Urada, D., Evans, E., Hser, Y. I., Prendergast, M., Hawken, A., Bunch, T., & Ettner, S. (2003). Evaluation of the Substance Abuse and Crime Prevention Act. Retrieved from http://www.uclaisap.org/prop36/html/reports.html.

Lonigan, C. J., Schatschnieder, C., Westberg, L., & Smith, L. S. (2008). Impact of code-focused interventions on young children's early literacy skills. In *Developing early literacy: Report of the National Early Literacy Panel* (pp. 107–151). Washington, DC: National Institute for Literacy.

Looper, K. J., & Kirmayer, L. J. (2002). Behavioral medicine approaches to somatoform disorders. *Journal of Consulting and Clinical Psychology, 70*, 810–827.

Lopez-Ibor, J. J., Jr. (2003). Cultural adaptations of current psychiatric classifications: Are they the solution? *Psychopathology, 36*, 114–119.

Lopez, S. (2008). *The soloist: A lost dream, an unlikely friendship, and the redemptive power of music.* New York, NY: Putnam.

Lopez, S. R. (1989). Patient variable biases in clinical judgment: Conceptual overview and methodological considerations. *Psychological Bulletin, 106*, 184–203.

Lopez, S. R. (1994). Latinos and the expression of psychopathology: A call for direct assessment of cultural influences. In C. Telles & M. Karno (Eds.), *Latino mental health: Current research and policy perspectives.* Los Angeles, CA: UCLA.

Lopez, S. R. (1996). Testing ethnic minority children. In B. B. Wolman (Ed.), *The encyclopedia of psychology, psychiatry, and psychoanalysis.* New York, NY: Holt.

Lopez, S. R. (2002). Teaching culturally informed psychological assessment: Conceptual issues and demonstrations. *Journal of Personality Assessment, 79*, 226–234.

Lopez, S. R., Barrio, C., Kopelowicz, A., & Vega, W. A. (2012). From documenting to eliminating disparities in mental health care for Latinos. *American Psychologist, 67*, 511–523.

Lopez, S. R., Lopez, A. A., & Fong, K. T. (1991). Mexican Americans' initial preferences for counselors: The role of ethnic factors. *Journal of Counseling Psychology, 38*, 487–496.

Lopez, S. R., Nelson, K. A., Snyder, K. S., & Mintz, J. (1999). Attributions and affective reactions of family members and course of schizophrenia. *Journal of Abnormal Psychology, 108*, 307–314.

LoPiccolo, J., & Lobitz, W. C. (1972). The role of masturbation in the treatment of orgasmic dysfunction. *Archives of Sexual Behavior, 2*, 163–171.

Lorber, M. F. (2004). Psychophysiology of aggression, psychopathy, and conduct problems: A meta-analysis. *Psychological Bulletin, 130*, 531–552.

Lord, C., Risi, S., DiLavore, P. S., Shulman, C. Thurm, A., & Pickles, A. (2006). Autism from 2 to 9 years of age. *Archives of General Psychiatry, 63,* 694–701.

Lovaas, O. I. (1987). Behavioral treatment and normal educational and intellectual functioning in young autistic children. *Journal of Consulting and Clinical Psychology, 55,* 3–9.

Lowe, M. R., Arigo, D., Butryn, M. L., Gilbert, J. R., Sarwer, D., & Stice, E. (2016). Hedonic hunger prospectively predicts onset and maintenance of loss of control eating among college women. *Health Psychology, 35,* 238–244. doi:http://dx.doi.org/10.1037/hea0000291

Ludwig, D. S., & Currie, J. (2010). The association between pregnancy weight gain and birthweight: A within-family comparison. *The Lancet, 376,* 984–990.

Ludwig, D. S., & Friedman, M. I. (2014). Increasing adiposity. *Journal of the American Medical Association, 311,* 2167–2168. http://doi.org/10.1001/jama.2014.4133

Luhrmann, T. M., Padmavati, R., Tharoor, H., & Osei, A. (2015). Differences in voice-hearing experiences of people with psychosis in the USA, India and Ghana: Interview-based study. *The British Journal of Psychiatry, 206,* 41–44. http://doi.org/10.1192/bjp.bp.113.139048

Lumley, M. N., & Harkness, K. L. (2007). Specificity in the relations among childhood adversity, early maladaptive schemas, and symptom profiles in adolescent depression. *Cognitive Therapy and Research, 31,* 639–657.

Luo, F., Florence, C. S., Quispe-Agnoli, M., Ouyang, L., & Crosby, A. E. (2011). Impact of business cycles on US suicide rates, 1928–2007. *American Journal of Public Health, 101,* 1139–1146.

Lynam, D., Moffitt, T. E., & Stouthamer-Loeber, M. (1993). Explaining the relation between IQ and delinquency: Race, class, test motivation, school failure, or self-control. *Journal of Abnormal Psychology, 102,* 187–196.

Lynn, S. J., Lock, T., Loftus, E. F., Krackow, E., & Lilienfeld, S. O. (2003). The remembrance of things past: Problematic memory recovery techniques in psychotherapy. In S. J. Lynn & S. O. Lilienfeld (Eds.), *Science and pseudoscience in clinical psychology* (pp. 205–239). New York, NY: Guilford Press.

Lyons-Ruth, K., Bureau, J.-F., Easterbrooks, M. A., Obsuth, I., & Hennighausen, K. (2013). Parsing the construct of maternal insensitivity: Distinct longitudinal pathways associated with early maternal withdrawal. *Attachment and Human Development, 15.* doi:10.1080/14616734.2013.841051

MacDonald, A. W., III, & Chafee, D. (2006). Translational and developmental perspective on N-methyl-D-aspartate synaptic deficits in schizophrenia. *Development and Psychopathology, 18,* 853–876.

MacGregor, M. W. (1996). Multiple personality disorder: Etiology, treatment, and techniques from a psychodynamic perspective. *Psychoanalytic Psychology, 13,* 389–402.

Mackey, S., & Paulus, M. (2013). Are there volumetric brain differences associated with the use of cocaine and amphetamine-type stimulants? *Neuroscience & Biobehavioral Reviews, 37,* 300–316.

MacLeod, C., & Clarke, P. J. F. (2015). The attentional bias modification approach to anxiety intervention. *Clinical Psychological Science, 3*(1), 58–78. doi:doi:10.1177/2167702614560749

MacLeod, C., & Mathews, A. (2012). Cognitive bias modification approaches to anxiety. *Annual Review of Clinical Psychology, 8,* 189–217.

Maes, M., Leonard, B. E., Myint, A. M., Kubera, M., & Verkerk, R. (2011). The new '5-ht' hypothesis of depression: Cell-mediated immune activation induces indoleamine 2,3-dioxygenase, which leads to lower plasma tryptophan and an increased synthesis of detrimental tryptophan catabolites (trycats), both of which contribute to the onset of depression. *Progress in Neuro-Psychopharmacology and Biological Psychiatry, 35*(3), 702–721. doi:http://dx.doi.org/10.1016/j.pnpbp.2010.12.017

Maidment, I., Fox, C., & Boustani, M. (2006). Cholinesterase inhibitors for Parkinson's disease dementia. *Cochrane Database of Systematic Reviews, 1,* CD004747.

Main, M., Kaplan, K., & Cassidy, J. (1985). Security in infancy, childhood, and adulthood: A move to the level of representation. *Monographs of the Society for Research in Child Development, 50,* (1–2, Serial No. 209).

Malaspina, D., Goetz, R. R., Yale, S., et al. (2000). Relation of familial schizophrenia to negative symptoms but not to the deficit syndrome. *The American Journal of Psychiatry, 157,* 994–1003.

Malkoff-Schwartz, S., Frank, E., Anderson, B. P., Hlastala, S. A., Luther, J. F., Sherrill, J. T., et al. (2000). Social rhythm disruption and stressful life events in the onset of bipolar and unipolar episodes. *Psychological Medicine, 30,* 1005–1016.

Mancebo, M. C., Eisen, J. L., Sibrava, N. J., Dyck, I. R., & Rasmussen, S. A. (2011). Patient utilization of cognitive-behavioral therapy for OCD. *Behavior Therapy, 42,* 399–412.

Mancke, F., Herpertz, S. C., & Bertsch, K. (2015). Aggression in borderline personality disorder: A multidimensional model. *Personality Disorders: Theory, Research, and Treatment, 6,* 278–291. http://dx.doi.org/10.1037/per0000098

Mann, R. E., Hanson, R. K., & Thornton, D. (2010). Assessing risk for sexual recidivism: Some proposals on the nature of psychologically meaningful risk factors. *Sexual Abuse: A Journal of Research and Treatment, 22,* 191–217.

Mantere, O., Suominen, K., Leppämäki, S., Valtonen, H., Arvilommi, P., & Isometsä, E. (2004). The clinical characteristics of DSM-IV bipolar I and II disorders: Baseline findings from the Jorvi Bipolar Study (JOBS). *Bipolar Disorders, 6*(5), 395–405. doi:10.1111/j.1399-5618.2004.00140.x

Maramba, G. G., & Nagayama-Hall, G. C. (2002). Meta-analyses of ethnic match as a predictor of dropout, utilization, and level of functioning. *Cultural Diversity and Ethnic Minority Psychology, 8,* 290–297.

March, D., Hatch, S. L., Morgan, C., Kirkbride, J. B., Bresnahan, M., Fearon, P., & Susser, E. (2008). Psychosis and place. *Epidemiologic Reviews, 30,* 84–100. http://doi.org/10.1093/epirev/mxn006

March, J., Silva, S., Petrycki, S., et al. (2004). Fluoxetine, cognitive-behavioral therapy, and their combination for adolescents with depression: Treatment for adolescents with depression study (TADS) randomized controlled trial. *Journal of the American Medical Association, 292,* 807–820.

Marcus, D. K., Gurley, J. R., Marchi, M. M., & Bauer, C. (2007). Cognitive and perceptual variables in hypolchondriasis and health anxiety: A systematic review. *Clinical Psychology Review, 27,* 127–139.

Marcus, S. C., & Olfson, M. (2010). National trends in the treatment for depression from 1998 to 2007. *Archives of General Psychiatry, 67*(12), 1265–1273. doi:10.1001/archgenpsychiatry.2010.151

Marder, S. R., Wirshing, W. C., Glynn, S. M., Wirshing, D. A., Mintz, J., & Liberman, R. P. (1999). Risperidone and haloperidol in maintenance treatment: Interactions with psychosocial treatments. *Schizophrenia Research, 36,* 288.

Margraf, J., Ehlers, A., & Roth, W. T. (1986). Sodium lactate infusions and panic attacks: A review and critique. *Psychosomatic Medicine, 48,* 23–51.

Margulies, D. M., Weintraub, S., Basile, J., Grover, P. J., & Carlson, G. A. (2012). Will disruptive mood dysregulation disorder reduce false diagnosis of bipolar disorder in children? *Bipolar Disorders, 14*(5), 488–496. http://doi.org/10.1111/j.1399-5618.2012.01029.x

Marks, I. M., & Cavanagh, K. (2009). Computer-aided psychological treatments: Evolving issues. *Annual Review of Clinical Psychology, 5,* 121–141.

Marlatt, G. A., & Gordon, J. R. (Eds.). (1985). *Relapse prevention: Maintenance strategies in the treatment of addictive behaviors.* New York, NY: Guilford Press.

Marmar, C. R., Schlenger, W., Henn-Haase, C., et al. (2015). Course of posttraumatic stress disorder 40 years after the Vietnam War: Findings from the National Vietnam Veterans Longitudinal Study. *JAMA Psychiatry, 72*(9), 875–881. doi:10.1001/jamapsychiatry.2015.0803

Marques, J. K., Wiederanders, M., Day, D. M., Nelson, C., & van Ommeren, A. (2005). Effects of a relapse prevention program on sexual recidivism: Final results from California's Sex Offender Treatment and Evaluation Project (SOTEP). *Sexual Abuse: A Journal of Research and Treatment, 17,* 79–107.

Marques, S., Lima, M. L., Abrams, D., & Swift, H. (2014). Will to live in older people's medical decisions: Immediate and delayed effects of aging stereotypes. *Journal of Applied Social Psychology, 44,* 399–408. doi:10.1111/jasp.12231

Marrazzi, M. A., & Luby, E. D. (1986). An auto-addiction model of chronic anorexia nervosa. *International Journal of Eating Disorders, 5,* 191–208.

Marsh, A. A., & Blair, R. J. (2008). Deficits in facial affect recognition among antisocial populations: A meta-analysis. *Neuroscience and Biobehavioral Reviews, 32*(3), 454–465.

Marsh, A. A., Finger, E. C., Fowler, K. A., Adalio, C. J., Jurkowitz, I. T. N., Schechter, J. C., et al. (2013). Empathic responsiveness in amygdala and anterior cingulate cortex in youths with psychopathic traits. *Journal of Child Psychology and Psychiatry, 54*, 900–910. doi:10.1111/jcpp.12063

Marsman, A., van den Heuvel, M. P., Klomp, D. W. J., Kahn, R. S., Luijten, P. R., & Hulshoff Pol, H. E. (2013). Glutamate in schizophrenia: A focused review and meta-analysis of (1)H-MRS studies. *Schizophrenia Bulletin, 39*, 120–129. http://doi.org/10.1093/schbul/sbr069

Marson, D. C. (2001). Loss of competency in Alzheimer's disease: Conceptual and psychometric approaches. *International Journal of Law and Psychiatry, 24*, 267–283.

Marson, D. C., Huthwaite, J. S., & Hebert, K. (2004). Testamentary capacity and undue influence in the elderly: A jurisprudent therapy perspective. *Law and Psychology Review, 28*, 71–96.

Martell, B. A., Orson, F. M., Poling, J., Mitchell, E., Rossen, R. D., Gardner, T., & Kosten, T. R. (2009). Cocaine vaccine for the treatment of cocaine dependence in methadone-maintained patients: A randomized, double-blind, placebo-controlled efficacy trial. *Archives of General Psychiatry, 66*, 1116–1123.

Martell, C. R., Addis, M. E., & Jacobson, N. S. (2001). *Ending depression one step at a time: The new behavioral activation approach to getting your life back.* New York, NY: Oxford University Press.

Martin, A., & Jacobi, F. (2006). Features of hypochondriasis and illness worry in the general population in Germany. *Psychosomatic Medicine, 68*, 770–777.

Martinasek, M. P., McGrogan, J. B., & Maysonet, A. (2016). A Systematic review of the respiratory effects of inhalational marijuana. *Respiratory Care, 61*, 1543–1551. http://doi.org/10.4187/respcare.04846

Martini, D. R., Ryan, C., Nakayama, D., & Ramenofsky, M. (1990). Psychiatric sequelae after traumatic injury: The Pittsburgh regatta accident. *Journal of the American Academy of Child and Adolescent Psychiatry, 29*, 70–75.

Martin, J. L. R., Sainz-Pardo, M., Furukawa, T. A., Martin-Sanchez, E., Seoane, T., & Galan, C. (2007). Review: Benzodiazepines in generalized anxiety disorder: Heterogeneity of outcomes based on a systematic review and meta-analysis of clinical trials. *Journal of Psychopharmacology, 21*(7), 774–782. doi:doi:10.1177/0269881107077355

Marx, R. F., & Didziulis, V. (2009, February 27). A life, interrupted, *The New York Times.* http://www.nytimes.com/2009/03/01/nyregion/thecity/01miss.html?mcubz=0

Marx, R. F. (September 29, 2017). A Teacher Vanishes Again. This Time, in the Virgin Islands. https://www.nytimes.com/2017/09/29/nyregion/missing-teachervirgin-islands.html

Masi, A., DeMayo, M. M., Glozier, N., & Guastella, A. J. (2017). An overview of autism spectrum disorder, heterogeneity and treatment options. *Neuroscience Bulletin, 33*(2), 183–193.

Masters, W. H., & Johnson, V. E. (1966). *Human sexual response.* Boston, MA: Little, Brown.

Masters, W. H., & Johnson, V. E. (1970). *Human sexual inadequacy.* Boston, MA: Little, Brown.

Mataix-Cols, D., Marks, I. M., Greist, J. H., Kobak, K. A., & Baer, L. (2002). Obsessive-compulsive symptom dimensions as predictors of compliance with and response to behaviour therapy: Results from a controlled trial. *Psychotherapy and Psychosomatics, 71*, 255–262.

Mathew, I., Gardin, T. M., Tandon, N., Eack, S., Francis, A. N., Seidman, L. J., et al. (2014). Medial temporal lobe structures and hippocampal subfields in psychotic disorders: Findings from the Bipolar-Schizophrenia Network on Intermediate Phenotypes (B-SNIP) study. *Journal of the American Medical Association, Psychiatry, 71*, 769–777.

Mathews, A., & MacLeod, C. (2002). Induced processing biases have causal effects on anxiety. *Cognition and Emotion, 16*, 331–354.

Matsuda, L. A., Lolait, S. J., Brownstein, M. J., Young, A. C., & Bonner, T. I. (1990). Structure of a cannabinoid receptor and functional expression of the cloned cDNA. *Nature, 346*, 561–564.

Matthews, M., Nigg, J. T., & Fair, D. A. (2014). Attention deficit hyperactivity disorder. *Current Topics in Behavioral Neurosciences, 16*, 235–266.

Maust, D. T., Kim, H., Seyfried, L. S., Kavanagh, J., Schneider L. S., & Kales H. C. (2015). Antipsychotics, other psychotropics, and the risk of death in patients with dementia: Number needed to harm. *JAMA Psychiatry, 72*, 438–445. doi:10.1001/jamapsychiatry.2014.3018

Mavandadi, S., Benson, A., DiFilippo, S., Streim, J. E., & Oslin, D. (2015). A telephone-based program to provide symptom monitoring alone vs. symptom monitoring plus care management for late-life depression and anxiety: A randomized clinical trial. *JAMA Psychiatry, 72*, 1211–1218. doi:10.1001/jamapsychiatry.2015.2157

Mavranezouli, I., Mayo-Wilson, E., Dias, S., Kew, K., Clark, D. M., Ades, A. E., & Pilling, S. (2015). The cost effectiveness of psychological and pharmacological interventions for social anxiety disorder: A model-based economic analysis. *PloS one, 10*(10), e0140704. doi:10.1371/journal.pone.0140704

Mayer, E. A., Berman, S., Suyenobu, B., Labus, J., Mandelkern, M. A., Naliboff, B. D., et al. (2005). Differences in brain responses to visceral pain between patients with irritable bowel syndrome and ulcerative colitis. *Pain, 115*, 398–409.

Mayes, S. D., Mathiowetz, C., Kokotovich, C., Waxmonsky, J., Baweja, R., Calhoun, S. L., & Bixler, E. O. (2015). Stability of disruptive mood dysregulation disorder symptoms (irritable-angry mood and temper outbursts) throughout childhood and adolescence in a general population sample. *Journal of Abnormal Child Psychology, 43*(8), 1543–1549.

Mayes, S. D., Waxmonsky, J. D., Calhoun, S. L., & Bixler, E. O. (2016). Disruptive mood dysregulation disorder symptoms and association with oppositional defiant and other disorders in a general population child sample. *Journal of Child and Adolescent Psychopharmacology, 26*(2), 101–106. http://doi.org/10.1089/cap.2015.0074

Mayo-Wilson, E., Dias, S., Mavranezouli, I., Kew, K., Clark, D. M., Ades, A. E., & Pilling, S. (2014). Psychological and pharmacological interventions for social anxiety disorder in adults: A systematic review and network meta-analysis. *The Lancet Psychiatry, 1*(5), 368–376. doi:http://doi.org/10.1016/S2215-0366(14)70329-3

McCabe, R. E., McFarlane, T., Polivy, J., & Olmsted, M. (2001). Eating disorders, dieting, and the accuracy of self-reported weight. *International Journal of Eating Disorders, 29*, 59–64.

McCall, W. V., Reboussin, D. M., Weiner, R. D., & Sackeim, H. A. (2000). Titrated moderately suprathreshold vs fixed high-dose right unilateral electroconvulsive therapy: Acute antidepressant and cognitive effects. *Archives of General Psychiatry, 57*, 438–444.

McClellan, J., Kowatch, R., & Findling, R. L. (2007). Practice parameter for the assessment and treatment of children and adolescents with bipolar disorder. *Journal of the American Academy of Child and Adolescent Psychiatry, 46*, 107–125.

McCracken, J. T., McGough, J., Shah, B., Cronin, P., Hong, D., Aman, M. G., et al. (2002). Risperidone in children with autism and serious behavioral problems. *New England Journal of Medicine, 347*(5), 314–321.

McCracken, L. M., & Vowles, K. E. (2014). Acceptance and commitment therapy and mindfulness for chronic pain: Model, process, and progress. *American Psychologist, 69*, 178–187.

McCrady, B. S., Epstein, E. E., & Kahler, C. W. (2004). Alcoholics Anonymous and relapse prevention as maintenance strategies after conjoint behavioral alcohol treatment for men: 18-month outcomes. *Journal of Consulting and Clinical Psychology, 72*, 870–878. http://doi.org/10.1037/0022-006X.72.5.870

McCullough, J. P., Klein, D. N., Keller, M. B., Holzer, C. E., Davis, S. M., Korenstein, S. G., et al. (2000). Comparison of DSM-III major depression and major depression superimposed on dysthymia (double depression): Validity of the distinction. *Journal of Abnormal Psychology, 109*, 419–427.

McEachin, J. J., Smith, T., & Lovaas, O. I. (1993). Longterm outcome for children with autism who received early intensive behavioral treatment. *American Journal on Mental Retardation, 97*, 359–372.

McEvoy, J. P., Byerly, M., Hamer, R. M., Dominik, R., Swartz, M. S., Rosenheck, R. A., et al. (2014). Effectiveness of paliperidone palmitate vs haloperidol decanoate for maintenance treatment of schizophrenia: A randomized clinical trial. *Journal of the American Medical Association, 311*, 1978–1987.

McEvoy, J. P., Johnson, J., Perkins, D., Lieberman, J. A., Hamer, R. M., Keefe, R. S. E., et al. (2006). Insight in first episode psychosis. *Psychological Medicine, 36*, 1385–1393.

McEvoy, P. M., & Mahoney, A. E. J. (2012). To be sure, to be sure: Intolerance of uncertainty mediates symptoms of various anxiety disorders and depression. *Behavior Therapy, 43*(3), 533–545. doi:http://doi.org/10.1016/j.beth.2011.02.007

McFarlane, W. R. (2016). Family interventions for schizophrenia and the psychoses: A review. *Family Process, 55*, 460–482. doi:http://dx.doi.org/10.1111/famp.12235

McFarlane, W. R., Lukens, E., Link, B., Dushay, R., Deakins, S., Newmark, M., Dunne, E. J., Horen, B., & Toran, J. (1995). Multiple-family groups and psychoeducation in the treatment of schizophrenia. *Archives of General Psychiatry, 52*, 679–687.

McGlashan, T. H., & Hoffman, R. E. (2000). Schizophrenia as a disorder of developmentally reduced synaptic connectivity. *Archives of General Psychiatry, 57*, 637–648.

McGovern, C. W., & Sigman, M. (2005). Continuity and change from early childhood to adolescence in autism. *Journal of Child Psychology and Psychiatry, 46*, 401–408.

McGue, M., Pickens, R. W., & Svikis, D. S. (1992). Sex and age effects on the inheritance of alcohol problems: A twin study. *Journal of Abnormal Psychology, 101*, 3–17.

McGuire, P. K., Bench, C. J., Frith, C. D., & Marks, I. M. (1994). Functional anatomy of obsessive-compulsive phenomena. *British Journal of Psychiatry, 164*, 459–468.

McGurk, S. R., Twamley, E. W., Sitzer, D. I., McHugo, G. J., & Mueser, K. T. (2007). A meta-analysis of cognitive remediation in schizophrenia. *American Journal of Psychiatry, 164*, 1791–1802.

McHugh, R. K., & Barlow, D. H. (2010). The dissemination and implementation of evidence-based psychological treatments. A review of current efforts. *American Psychologist, 65*, 73–84.

McHugh, R. K., Whitton, S. W., Peckham, A. D., Welge, J. A., & Otto, M. W. (2013). Patient preference for psychological vs. pharmacological treatment of psychiatric disorders: A meta-analytic review. *Journal of Clinical Psychiatry, 74*, 595–602. doi:10.4088/JCP.12r07757.

McKeith, I. G., Dickson, D. W., Lowe, J., Emre, M., O'Brien, J. T., Feldman, H., et al. (2005). Diagnosis and management of dementia with Lewy bodies: Third report of the DLB consortium. *Neurology, 65*, 1863–1872.

McKeller, J., Stewart, E., & Humphreys, K. (2003). Alcoholics Anonymous involvement and positive alcohol related outcomes: Cause, consequence, or just a correlate? A prospective 2-year study of 2,319 alcohol dependent men. *Journal of Consulting and Clinical Psychology, 71*, 302–308.

McKhann, G. M., Knopman, D. S., Chertkow, H., Hyman, B. T., Jack, C. R., Jr., Kawas, C. H., et al. (2011). The diagnosis of dementia due to Alzheimer's disease: Recommendations from the National Institute on Aging–Alzheimer's Association workgroups on diagnostic guidelines for Alzheimer's disease. *Alzheimer's & Dementia: The Journal of the Alzheimer's Association, 7*, 263–269.

McKinley, N. M., & Hyde, J. S. (1996). The objectified body consciousness scale: Development and validation. *Psychology of Women Quarterly, 20*, 181–216.

McKinnon, M. C., Palombo, D. J., Nazarov, A., Kumar, N., Khuu, W., & Levine, B. (2015). Threat of death and autobiographical memory. *Clinical Psychological Science, 3*, 487–502. doi:doi:10.1177/2167702614542280

McKown, C., & Weinstein, R. S. (2003). The development and consequences of stereotype consciousness in middle childhood. *Child Development, 74*, 498–515.

McLean, C. P., Asnaani, A., Litz, B. T., & Hofmann, S. G. (2011). Gender differences in anxiety disorders: Prevalence, course of illness, comorbidity and burden of illness. *Journal of Psychiatric Research, 45*(8), 1027–1035. doi:10.1016/j.jpsychires.2011.03.006

McLeod, B. D., Weisz, J. R., & Wood, J. J. (2007). Examining the association between parenting and childhood anxiety: A meta-analysis. *Clinical Psychology Review, 27*, 155–172.

McManus, F., Surawy, C., Muse, K., Vazquez-Montes, M., & Williams, J. M. (2012). A randomized clinical trial of mindfulness-based cognitive therapy versus unrestricted services for health anxiety (hypochondriasis). *Journal of Consulting and Clinical Psychology, 80*, 817–828.

McMillan, K. A., & Asmundson, G. J. G. (2016). PTSD, social anxiety disorder, and trauma: An examination of the influence of trauma type on comorbidity using a nationally representative sample. *Psychiatry Research, 246*, 561–567. doi:https://doi.org/10.1016/j.psychres.2016.10.036

McNally, R. J. (1987). Preparedness and phobias: A review. *Psychological Bulletin, 101*, 283–303.

McNally, R. J. (2003). *Remembering trauma.* Cambridge, MA: Belknap Press of Harvard University Press.

McNally, R. J., Lasko, N. B., Clancy, S. A., Macklin, M. L., Pitman, R. K., & Orr, S. P. (2004). Psychophysiological responding during script-driven imagery in people reporting abduction by space aliens. *Psychological Science, 15*, 493–497.

McNally, R. J., Ristuccia, C. S., & Perlman, C. A. (2005). Forgetting trauma cues in adults reporting continuous or recovered memories of childhood sexual abuse. *Psychological Science, 16*, 336–340.

McNiel, D. E., & Binder, R. L. (2007). Effectiveness of a mental health court in reducing criminal recidivism and violence. *American Journal of Psychiatry, 164*, 1395–1403.

McTeague, L. M., & Lang, P. J. (2012). The anxiety spectrum and the reflex physiology of defense: From circumscribed fear to broad distress. *Depression and Anxiety, 29*, 264–281.

Meana, M., Binik, I., Khalife, S., & Cohen, D. (1998). Affect and marital adjustment in women's ratings of dyspareunic pain. *Canadian Journal of Psychiatry, 43*, 381–385.

Mednick, S. A., & Schulsinger, F. (1968). Some premorbid characteristics related to breakdown in children with schizophrenic mothers. In D. Rosenthal & S. S. Kety (Eds.), *The transmission of schizophrenia.* Elmsford, NY: Pergamon Press.

Mehler, P. S. (2011). Medical complications of bulimia nervosa and their treatments. *International Journal of Eating Disorders, 44*, 95–104.

Mehmedic, Z., Chandra, S., Slade, D., et al. (2010). Potency trends of D9-THC and other cannabinoids in confiscated cannabis preparations from 1993 to 2008. *Journal of Forensic Science, 55*, 1209–1217. doi:10.1111/j.1556-4029.2010.01441.x.

Meier, M. H., Caspi, A., Ambler, A., Harrington, H., Houts, R., Keefe, R. S. E., et al. (2012). Persistent cannabis users show neuropsychological decline from childhood to midlife. *Proceedings of the National Academy of Sciences, 109*, E2657–E2664.

Meier, M. H., Caspi, A., Reichenberg, A., Keefe, R. S., Fisher, H. L., Harrington, H., et al. (2014). Neuropsychological decline in schizophrenia from the premorbid to the postonset period: Evidence from a population-representative longitudinal study. *American Journal of Psychiatry, 171*, 91–101.

Meier, S. M., Mattheisen, M., Mors, O., Schendel, D. E., Mortensen, P. B., & Plessen, K. J. (2016). Mortality among persons with obsessive-compulsive disorder in Denmark. *JAMA Psychiatry, 73*(3), 268–274. doi:10.1001/jamapsychiatry.2015.3105

Meijer, A., Conradi, H. J., Bos, E. H., Thombs, B. D., van Melle, J. P., & de Jonge, P. (2011). Prognostic association of depression following myocardial infarction with mortality and cardiovascular events: A meta-analysis of 25 years of research. *General Hospital Psychiatry, 33*(3), 203–216. doi:10.1016/j.genhosppsych.2011.02.007

Melnik, T., Soares, B. G. O., & Nasello, A. G. (2008). The effectiveness of psychological interventions for the treatment of erectile dysfunction: Systematic review and meta-analysis, including comparisons to sildenafil treatment, intracavernosal injection, and vacuum devices. *Journal of Sexual Medicine, 5*, 2562–2574.

Meltzer, H. Y. (2003). Suicide in schizophrenia. *Journal of Clinical Psychiatry, 64*, 1122–1125.

Melville, J. D., & Naimark, D. (2002). Punishing the insane: The verdict of guilty but mentally ill. *Journal of the American Academy of Psychiatry and the Law, 30*, 553–555.

Menezes, N. M., Arenovich, T., & Zipursky, R. B. (2006). A systematic review of longitudinal outcome studies of first-episode psychosis. *Psychological Medicine, 36*, 1349–1362.

Menikoff, J., Kaneshiro, J., & Pritchard, I. (2017). The common rule, updated. *New England Journal of Medicine, 376*, 613–615.

Mennin, D. S., Heimberg, R. G., & Turk, C. L. (2004). Clinical presentation and diagnostic features. In R. G. Heimberg, C. L. Turk, & D. S. Mennin (Eds.), *Generalized anxiety disorder* (pp. 3–28). New York, NY: Guilford Press.

Menzies, L., Chamberlain, S. R., Laird, A. R., Thelen, S. M., Sahakian, B. J., & Bullmore, E. T. (2008). Integrating evidence from neuroimaging and neuropsychological studies of obsessive-compulsive disorder: The orbitofronto-striatal model revisited. *Neuroscience and Biobehavioral Reviews, 32*, 525–549.

Mercer, C. H., Fenton, K. A., Johnson, A. M., Wellings, K., Macdowall, W., McManus, S., et al. (2003). Sexual function problems and help seeking behaviour in Britain: National probability sample survey. *British Medical Journal, 327*, 426–427.

Merckelbach, H., Dekkers, T., Wessel, I., & Roefs, A. (2003). Dissociative symptoms and amnesia in Dutch concentration camp survivors. *Comprehensive Psychiatry, 44*, 65–69.

Merikangas, K. R., He, J.-P., Burstein, M., Swanson, S. A., Avenevoli, S., Cui, L., et al. (2010). Lifetime prevalence of mental disorders in U.S. adolescents: Results from the National Comorbidity Survey Replication–Adolescent Supplement (NCS-A). *Journal of the American Academy of Child & Adolescent Psychiatry, 49*(10), 980–989.

Merikangas, K. R., Jin, R., He, J., Kessler, R. C., Lee, S., Sampson, N. A., et al. (2011). Prevalence and correlates of bipolar spectrum disorder in the World Mental Health Survey Initiative. *Archives of General Psychiatry, 68*, 241–251.

Messinger, J. W., Tremeau, F., Antonius, D., Mendelsohn, E., Prudent, V., Stanfore, A. D., & Malaspina, D. (2011). Avolition and expressive deficits capture negative symptom phenomoenology: Implications for the DSM-5 and schizophrenia research. *Clinical Psychology Review, 31*, 161–168.

Meston, C. M., & Buss, D. (2009). *Why women have sex: Women reveal the truth about their sex lives, from adventure to revenge (and everything in between)*. New York, NY: St. Martin's Press.

Meston, C. M., & Gorzalka, B. B. (1995). The effects of sympathetic activation on physiological and subjective sexual arousal in women. *Behaviour Research and Therapy, 33*, 651–664.

Meyer, B., Johnson, S. L., & Winters, R. (2001). Responsiveness to threat and incentive in bipolar disorder: Relations of the BIS/BAS scales with symptoms. *Journal of Psychopathology and Behavioral Assessment, 23*, 133–143.

Meyer, G. J., & Archer, R. P. (2001). The hard science of Rorschach research: "What do we know and where do we go?" *Psychological Assessment, 13*, 486–502.

Meyer, V. (1966). Modification of expectations in cases with obsessional rituals. *Behaviour Research and Therapy, 4*, 273–280.

Micale, V., Kucerova, J., & Sulcova, A. (2013). Leading compounds for the validation of animal models of psychopathology. *Cell and Tissue Research, 354*(1), 309–330. doi:10.1007/s00441-013-1692-9

Michael, T., Blechert, J., Vriends, N., Margraf, J., & Wilhelm, F. H. (2007). Fear conditioning in panic disorder: Enhanced resistance to extinction. *Journal of Abnormal Psychology, 116*, 612–617.

Michal, M., Adler, J., Wiltink, J., Reiner, I., Tschan, R., Wölfling, K., et al. (2016). A case series of 223 patients with depersonalization-derealization syndrome. *BMC Psychiatry, 16*, 11.

Miech, R. A., Johnston, L. D., O'Malley, P. M., Bachman, J. G., Schulenberg, J. E., & Patrick, M. E. (2017). Monitoring the future: National survey results on drug use, 1975–2016: Volume I, Secondary school students. Ann Arbor, MI: Institute for Social Research, The University of Michigan. Retrieved from http://monitoringthefuture.org/pubs.html#monographs

Miech, R., Patrick, M. E., O'Malley, P. M., & Johnston, L. D. (2017). E-cigarette use as a predictor of cigarette smoking: Results from a 1-year follow-up of a national sample of 12th grade students. *Tob Control*, tobaccocontrol–2016–053291. http://doi.org/10.1136/tobaccocontrol-2016-053291

Miers, A. C., Blöte, A. W., Bokhorst, C. L., Westenberg, M. (2009). Negative self-evaluations and the relation to performance level in socially anxious children and adolescents. *Behaviour Research and Therapy, 47*, 1043–1049.

Mikami, A. Y., Hinshaw, S. P., Arnold, L. E., Hoza, B., Hechtman, L., Newcorn, J. H., et al. (2010). Bulimia nervosa symptoms in the multimodal treatment study of children with ADHD. *International Journal of Eating Disorders, 43*, 248–259.

Mikami, A. Y., Huang-Pollack, C. L., Pfiffner, L. J., McBurnett, K., & Hangai, D. (2007). Social skills differences among attention-deficit/hyperactivity disorder types in a chat room assessment task. *Journal of Abnormal Child Psychology, 35*, 509–521.

Mikami, A. Y., Szwedo, D. E., Ahmad, S. I., Samuels, A. S., & Hinshaw, S. P. (2015). Online social communication patterns among emerging adult women with histories of childhood attention-deficit/hyperactivity disorder *Journal of Abnormal Psychology, 124*(3), 576–588. http://dx.doi.org/10.1037/abn0000053

Miklowitz, D. J., George, E. L., Richards, J. A., Simoneau, T. L., & Suddath, R. L. (2003). A randomized study of family-focused psychoeducation and pharmacotherapy in the outpatient management of bipolar disorder. *Archives of General Psychiatry, 60*, 904–912.

Miklowitz, D. J., & Goldstein, M. J. (1997). *Bipolar disorder: A family-focused treatment approach* (2nd ed.). New York, NY: Guilford Press.

Miklowitz, D. J., Otto, M. W., Frank, E., Reilly-Harrington, N. A., Wisniewski, S. R., Kogan, J. N., et al. (2007). Psychosocial treatments for bipolar depression: A 1-year randomized trial from the systematic treatment enhancement program. *Archives of General Psychiatry, 64*, 419–427.

Miklowitz, D. J., & Taylor, D.O. (2005). Family-focused treatment of the suicidal bipolar patient. Unpublished manuscript.

Milev, P., Ho, B. C., Arndt, S., & Andreasen, N. C. (2005). Predictive values of neurocognition and negative symptoms on functional outcome in schizophrenia: A longitudinal first-episode study with 7-year follow-up. *American Journal of Psychiatry, 162*, 495–506.

Miller, D. D., Caroff, S. N., Davis, S. M., et al. (2008). Extrapyramidal side-effects of antipsychotics in a randomised trial. *British Journal of Psychiatry, 193*, 279–288.

Miller, J. D., Lamkin, J., Maples-Keller, J. L., & Lynam, D. R. (2016). Viewing the triarchic model of psychopathy through general personality and expert-based lenses. *Personality Disorders: Theory, Research, and Treatment, 7*, 247–258. http://dx.doi.org/10.1037/per0000155

Miller, J. D., & Lynam, D. R. (2012). An examination of the Psychopathic Personality Inventory's nomological network: A meta-analytic review. *Personality Disorders: Theory, Research, and Treatment, 3*, 305–326. http://dx.doi.org/10.1037/a0024567

Miller, J. D., Lynam, D. R., Hyatt, C. S., & Campbell, W. K. (2017). Controversies in narcissism. *Annual Review of Clinical Psychology, 13*, 291–315. doi:10.1146/annurev-clinpsy-032816-045244

Miller-Johnson, S., Coie, J. D., Maumary-Gremaud, A., & Bierman, K. (2002). Peer rejection and aggression and early starter models of conduct disorder. *Journal of Abnormal Child Psychology, 30*(3), 217–230.

Miller, T. J., McGlashan, T. H., Rosen, J. L., et al. (2002). Prospective diagnosis of the initial prodrome for schizophrenia based on the Structured Interview for Prodromal Syndromes: Preliminary evidence of interrater reliability and predictive validity. *American Journal of Psychiatry, 159*, 863–865.

Miller, T. Q., & Volk, R. J. (1996). Weekly marijuana use as a risk factor for initial cocaine use: Results from a six wave national survey. *Journal of Child and Adolescent Substance Abuse, 5*, 55–78.

Miller, W. R., & Rollnick, S. (Eds.). (1991). *Motivational interviewing: Preparing people to change addictive behavior*. New York, NY: Guilford Press.

Millon, T. (1996). *Disorders of personality: DSM-IV and beyond* (2nd ed.). New York, NY: John Wiley & Sons.

Milrod, B., Chambless, D. L., Gallop, R., Busch, F. N., Schwalberg, M., McCarthy, K. S., . . . Barber, J. P. (2015). Psychotherapies for panic disorder: A tale of two sites. *The Journal of Clinical Psychiatry.* doi:10.4088/jcp.14m09507

Mineka, S., & Öhman, A. (2002). Born to fear: Nonassociative vs. associative factors in the etiology of phobias. *Behaviour Research and Therapy, 40*, 173–184.

Mineka, S., & Sutton, J. (2006). Contemporary learning theory perspectives on the etology of fear and phobias. In M. G. Craske, D. Hermans, & D. Vansteenwegen (Eds.), *Fear and learning: From basic processes to Clinical implications* (pp. 75–97). Washington DC: American Psychological Association.

Mineka, S., & Zinbarg, R. (1998). Experimental approaches to the anxiety and mood disorders. In J. G. Adair, D. Belanger, & K. L. Dion (Eds.), *Advances in psychological science, Volume 1: Social personal and cultural aspects* (pp. 429–454). Hove, UK: Psychology Press.

Mineka, S., & Zinbarg, R. (2006). A contemporary learning theory perspective on the etiology of anxiety disorders: It's not what you thought it was. *The American Psychologist, 61*, 10–26.

Mishkind, M. E., Rodin, J., Silberstein, L. R., & Striegel-Moore, R. H. (1986). The embodiment of masculinity: Cultural, psychological, and behavioral dimensions. *American Behavioral Scientist, 29*, 545–562.

Mitchell, A. J., & Shiri-Feshki, M. (2009). Rate of progression of mild cognitive impairment to dementia—Meta-analysis of 41 robust inception cohort studies. *Acta Psychiatrica Scandinavica, 119,* 252–265. doi:10.1111/j.1600-0447.2008.01326.x

Mittelman, M. S., Brodaty, H., Wallen, A. S., & Burns, A. (2008). A three-country randomized controlled trial of a psychosocial intervention for caregivers combined with pharmacological treatment for patients with Alzheimer disease: Effects on caregiver depression. *American Journal of Geriatric Psychiatry, 16,* 893–904.

Moberg, C. A., Bradford, D. E., Kaye, J. T., & Curtin, J. J. (2017). Increased startle potentiation to unpredictable stressors in alcohol dependence: Possible stress neuroadaptation in humans. *Journal of Abnormal Psychology, 126,* 441–453. http://dx.doi.org/10.1037/abn0000265

Modabbernia, A., Taslimi, S., Brietzke, E., & Ashrafi, M. (2013). Cytokine alterations in bipolar disorder: A meta-analysis of 30 studies. *Biological Psychiatry, 74*(1), 15–25. doi:10.1016/j.biopsych.2013.01.007

Moffitt, T. E. (1993). Adolescence-limited and life-course-persistent antisocial behavior: A developmental taxonomy. *Psychological Review, 100,* 674–701.

Moffitt, T. E. (2007). A review of research on the taxonomy of life-course persistent versus adolescence-limited antisocial behavior. In D. J. Flannery, A. T. Vazsonyi, & I. D. Waldman (Eds.), *The Cambridge handbook of violent behavior and aggression* (pp. 49–74). New York, NY: Cambridge University Press.

Moffitt, T. E., & Caspi, A. (2001). Childhood predictors differentiate life-course persistent and adolescence-limited antisocial pathways among males and females. *Development and Psychopathology, 13*(2), 355–375.

Moffitt, T. E., Caspi, A., Harrington, H., & Milne, B. J. (2002). Males on the life-course persistent and adolescence-limited antisocial pathways: Follow-up at age 26. *Development and Psychopathology, 14,* 179–207.

Moffitt, T. E., Caspi, A., Harrington, H., Milne, B. J., Melchior, M., Goldberg, D., et al. (2007). Generalized anxiety disorder and depression: Childhood risk factors in a birth cohort followed to age 32. *Psychological Medicine, 37,* 441–452.

Moffitt, T. E., Caspi, A., Taylor, A., Kokaua, J., Milne, B. J., Polanczyk, G., & Poulton, R. (2010). How common are common mental disorders? Evidence that lifetime prevalence rates are doubled by prospective versus retrospective ascertainment. *Psychological Medicine, 40*(6), 899–909. doi:10.1017/S0033291709991036

Moffitt, T. E., Lynam, D., & Silva, P. A. (1994). Neuropsychological tests predict persistent male delinquency. *Criminology, 32,* 101–124.

Moffitt, T. E., & Silvia, P. A. (1988). IQ and delinquency: A direct test of the differential detection hypothesis. *Journal of Abnormal Psychology, 97,* 330–333.

Mogensen, H., Möller, J., Hultin, H., & Mittendorfer-Rutz, E. (2016). Death of a close relative and the risk of suicide in Sweden—a large scale register-based case-crossover study. *PloS one, 11*(10), e0164274. doi:10.1371/journal.pone.0164274

Mogg, K., Waters, A. M., & Bradley, B. P. (2017). Attention bias modification (ABM): Review of effects of multisession ABM training on anxiety and threat-related attention in high anxious individuals. *Clinical Psychological Science, 5,* 698–717.

Molina, B. S. G., Hinshaw, S. P., Swanson, J. M., Arnold, L. E., Vitiello, B., Jensen, P. S., et al. (2009). The MTA at 8 years: Prospective follow-up of children treated for combined-type ADHD in a multisite study. *Journal of the American Academy of Child and Adolescent Psychiatry, 48,* 484–500.

Molina, B. S., Hinshaw, S. P., Eugene Arnold, L., Swanson, J. M., Pelham, W. E., Hechtman, L., et al. (2013). Adolescent substance use in the multimodal treatment study of attention-deficit/hyperactivity disorder (ADHD) (MTA) as a function of childhood ADHD, random assignment to childhood treatments, and subsequent medication. *Journal of the American Academy of Child and Adolescent Psychiatry, 52*(3), 250–263.

Monahan, J. (1984). The prediction of violent behavior: Toward a second generation of theory and policy. *American Journal of Psychiatry, 141,* 10–15.

Monahan, J. (1992). Mental disorder and violent behavior: Perceptions and evidence. *American Psychologist, 47,* 511–521.

Monahan, J., & Steadman, H. (1994). Toward a rejuvenation of risk assessment research. In J. Monahan & H. Steadman (Eds.), *Violence and mental disorder: Developments in risk assessment.* Chicago, IL: University of Chicago Press.

Moniz, E. (1936). *Tentatives operatoires dans le traitement de certaines psychoses.* Paris: Mason.

Monstrey, S., Vercruysse, H., & De Cuypere, G. (2009). Is gender reassignment surgery evidence based? Recommendation for the seventh version of the WPATH Standards of Care. *International Journal of Transgenderism, 11,* 206–214. doi:10.1080/15532730903383799

Monuteaux, M., Faraone, S. V., Gross, L., & Biederman, J. (2007). Predictors, clinical characteristics, and outcome of conduct disorder in girls with attention-deficit/hyperactivity disorder: A longitudinal study. *Psychological Medicine, 37,* 1731–1741.

Monzani, B., Rijsdijk, F., Harris, J., & Mataix-Cols, D. (2014). The structure of genetic and environmental risk factors for dimensional representations of DSM-5 obsessive-compulsive spectrum disorders. *JAMA Psychiatry, 71*(2), 182–189. doi:10.1001/jamapsychiatry.2013.3524

Moore, T. H. M., Zammit, S., Lingford-Hughes, A., Barnes, T. R. E., Jones, P. B., Burke, M., & Lewis, G. (2007). Cannabis use and risk of psychotic or affective mental health outcomes: A systematic review. *The Lancet, 370,* 319–328.

Moore, T. J., & Mattison D. R. (2017). Adult utilization of psychiatric drugs and differences by sex, age, and race. *JAMA: Internal Medicine, 177,* 274–285. doi:10.1001/jamainternmed.2016.7507.

Moos, R. H., & Humphreys, K. (2004). Long-term influence of duration and frequency of participation in Alcoholics Anonymous on individuals with alcohol use disorders. *Journal of Consulting and Clinical Psychology, 72,* 81–90.

Moos, R. H., & Moos, B. S. (2006). Participation in treatment and Alcoholics Anonymous: A 16-year follow-up of initially untreated individuals. *Journal of Clinical Psychology, 62,* 735–750.

Moreland, K., Wing, S., Diez Roux, A., & Poole, C. (2002). Neighborhood characteristics associated with the location of food stores and food services places. *American Journal of Preventive Medicine, 22,* 23–29.

Moreland-Russell, S., Harris, J., Snider, D., Walsh, H., Cyr, J., & Barnoya, J. (2013). Disparities and menthol marketing: Additional evidence in support of point of sale policies. *International Journal of Environmental Research and Public Health, 10,* 4571–4583. http://doi.org/10.3390/ijerph10104571

Morey, L. C., Hopwood, C. J., Markowitz, J. C., Gunderson, J. G., Grilo, C. M., McGlashan, T. H., et al. (2012). Comparison of alternative models for personality disorders, II: 6-, 8- and 10-year follow-up. *Psychological Medicine, 42,* 1705–1713.

Morey, L. C., Krueger, R. F., & Skodol, A. E. (2013). The hierarchical structure of clinician ratings of proposed DSM–5 pathological personality traits. *Journal of Abnormal Psychology, 122,* 836–841. http://dx.doi.org/10.1037/a0034003

Morey, L. C., Skodol, A. E., & Oldham, J. M. (2014). Clinician judgments of clinical utility: A comparison of DSM-IV-TR personality disorders and the alternative model for DSM-5 personality disorders. *Journal of Abnormal Psychology, 123,* 398–405. http://dx.doi.org/10.1037/a0036481

Morf, C. C., & Rhodewalt, F. (2001). Unraveling the paradoxes of narcissism: A dynamic self-regulatory processing model. *Psychological Inquiry, 12,* 177–196.

Morgan, C. A. I., Hazlett, G., Wang, S., Richardson, E. G. J., Schnurr, P., & Southwick, S. M. (2001). Symptoms of dissociation in humans experiencing acute, uncontrollable stress: A prospective investigation. *American Journal of Psychiatry, 158,* 1239–1247.

Morgan, M. J. (2000). Ecstasy (MDMA): A review of its possible persistent psychological effects. *Psychopharmacology, 152,* 230–248.

Morgan, V. A., Mitchell, P. B., & Jablensky, A. V. (2005). The epidemiology of bipolar disorder: Sociodemographic, disability and service utilization data from the Australian National Study of low prevalence (psychotic) disorders. *Bipolar Disorders, 7*(4), 326–337. doi:10.1111/j.1399-5618.2005.00229.x

Morina, N., Ijntema, H., Meyerbröker, K., & Emmelkamp, P. M. G. (2015). Can virtual reality exposure therapy gains be generalized to real-life? A meta-analysis of studies applying behavioral assessments. *Behaviour Research and Therapy, 74,* 18–24. doi:http://doi.org/10.1016/j.brat.2015.08.010

Moroney, J. T., Tang, M. X., Berglund, L., Small, S., Merchant, C., Bell, K., et al. (1999). Low-density lipoprotein cholesterol and the risk of dementia with stroke. *Journal of American Medical Association, 282,* 254–260.

Mortberg, E., Clark, D. M., & Bejerot, S. (2011). Intensive group cognitive therapy and individual cognitive therapy for social phobia: Sustained improvement at 5-year follow-up. *Journal of Anxiety Disorders, 25,* 994–1000.

Moses, J. A., Schefft, B. A., Wong, J. L., & Berg, R. A. (1992). Interrater reliability analyses of the Luria–Nebraska neuropsychological battery, form II. *Archives of Clinical Neurology, 7,* 251–269.

Moss, M. (2010, November). While warning about fat, U.S. pushes cheese sales. *The New York Times,* p. A1.

Mowrer, O. H. (1947). On the dual nature of learning: A reinterpretation of "conditioning" and "problem-solving." *Harvard Educational Review, 17,* 102–148.

Moylan, S., Maes, M., Wray, N. R., & Berk, M. (2013). The neuroprogressive nature of major depressive disorder: Pathways to disease evolution and resistance, and therapeutic implications. *Molecular Psychiatry, 18*(5), 595–606. doi:10.1038/mp.2012.33

MTA Cooperative Group. (1999a). A 14-month randomized clinical trial of treatment strategies for attention-deficit/hyperactivity disorder. *Archives of General Psychiatry, 56,* 1073–1086.

MTA Cooperative Group. (1999b). Moderators and mediators of treatment response for children with attention-deficit/hyperactivity disorder. *Archives of General Psychiatry, 56,* 1088–1096.

Muehlenhard, C. L., & Shippee, S. K. (2010). Men's and women's reports of pretending orgasm. *Journal of Sex Research, 47,* 552–567.

Muehlenkamp, J. J., Claes, L., Havertape, L., & Plener, P. L. (2012). International prevalence of adolescent non-suicidal self-injury and deliberate self-harm. *Child and Adolescent Psychiatry and Mental Health, 6,* 10–10. doi:10.1186/1753-2000-6-10

Mueller, A., Hong, D. S., Shepard, S., & Moore, T. (2017). Linking ADHD to the neural circuitry of attention. *Trends in Cognitive Sciences, 21*(6), 474–488.

Mueller-Pfeiffer, C., Rufibach, K., Perron, N., Wyss, D., Kuenzler, C., Prezewowsky, C., et al. (2012). Global functioning and disability in dissociative disorders. *Psychiatry Research, 200,* 475–481.

Mueser, K. T., Penn, D. L., Addington, J., Brunette, M. F., Gingerich, S., Glynn, S. M., et al. (2015). The NAVIGATE program for first-episode psychosis: Rationale, overview, and description of psychosocial components. *Psychiatric Services, 66,* 680–690. http://doi.org/10.1176/appi.ps.201400413

Mühleisen, T. W., Leber, M., Schulze, T. G., Strohmaier, J., Degenhardt, F., Treutlein, J., et al. (2014). Genome-wide association study reveals two new risk loci for bipolar disorder. *Nature Communications, 5,* 3339. doi:10.1038/ncomms4339

Mukherjee, S. (2016). *The gene: An intimate history.* New York, NY: Scribner.

Mulsant, B. H., & Pollock, B. G. (2015). Psychopharmacology. In D. C. Steffens, D. G. Blazer, & M. E. Thakur (Eds.), *The American Psychiatric Publishing Textbook of Geriatric Psychiatry.* Washington, DC: APA.

Munetz, M. R., Grande, T., Kleist, J., & Peterson, G. A. (1996). The effectiveness of outpatient civil commitment. *Psychiatric Services, 47,* 1251–1253.

Munro, S., Thomas, K. L., & Abu-Shaar, M. (1993). Molecular characterization of a peripheral receptor for cannabinoids. *Nature, 365,* 61–65.

Munson, J., Dawson, G., Abbott, R., et al. (2006). Amygdalar volume and behavioral development in autism. *Archives of General Psychiatry, 63,* 686–693.

Muroff, J., Levis, M. E., & Bratiotis, C. (2014). Hoarding disorder. In E. A. Storch & D. McKay (Eds.), *Obsessive-compulsive disorder and its spectrum: A life-span approach* (pp. 117–140). Washington, DC: American Psychological Association.

Murphy, J. (1976). Psychiatric labeling in cross-cultural perspective. *Science, 191,* 1019–1028.

Murphy, J. A., & Byrne, G. J. (2012). Prevalence and correlates of the proposed DSM-5 diagnosis of chronic depressive disorder. *Journal of Affective Disorders, 139*(2), 172–180. doi:10.1016/j.jad.2012.01.033

Murphy, S. E. (2017). Nicotine metabolism and smoking: Ethnic differences in the role of P450 2A6. *Chemical Research in Toxicology, 30,* 410–419. http://doi.org/10.1021/acs.chemrestox.6b00387

Murray-Close, D., Hoza, B., Hinshaw, S. P., Arnold, L. E., Swanson, J., Jensen, P. S., Hechtman, L., & Wells, K. (2010). Developmental processes in peer problems of children with attention-deficit/hyperactivity disorder in the Multimodal Treatment Study of Children with ADHD: Developmental cascades and vicious cycles. *Developmental and Psychopathology, 22,* 785–802.

Muse, K., McManus, F., Hackmann, A., & Williams, M. (2010). Intrusive imagery in severe health anxiety: Prevalence, nature and links with memories and maintenance cycles. *Behaviour Research and Therapy, 48,* 792–798.

Mustonen, T. K., Spencer, S. M., Hoskinson, R. A., Sachs, D. P. L., & Garvey, A. J. (2005). The influence of gender, race, and menthol content on tobacco exposure measures. *Nicotine and Tobacco Research, 7,* 581–590.

Myin-Germeys, I., van Os, J., Schwartz, J. E., et al. (2001). Emotional reactivity to daily life stress in schizophrenia. *Archives of General Psychiatry, 58,* 1137–1144.

Mykletun, A., Bjerkeset, O., Overland, S., Prince, M., Dewey, M., & Stewart, R. (2009). Levels of anxiety and depression as predictors of mortality: The HUNT study. *British Journal of Psychiatry, 195,* 118–125.

Nacewicz, B. M., Dalton, K. M., Johnstone, T., et al. (2006). Amygdala volume and nonverbal social impairment in adolescent and adult males with autism. *Archives of General Psychiatry, 63,* 1417–1448.

Narrow, W. E., Clarke, D. E., Kuramoto, S. J., Kraemer, H. C., Kupfer, D. J., Greiner, L., et al. (2013). DSM-5 field trials in the United States and Canada, Part III: Development and reliability testing of a cross-cutting symptom assessment for DSM-5. *American Journal of Psychiatry, 170*(1), 71–82.

Nathan, D. (2011). *Sybil exposed: The extraordinary story behind the famous multiple personality case.* New York, NY: Free Press.

Nathan, P. E., & Gorman, J. M. (2015). Challenges to implementing evidence-based treatments. In P. E. Nathan & J. M. Gorman (Eds.), *A guide to treatments that work* (4th ed.). New York, NY: Oxford University Press.

Nathan, P. J., & Bullmore, E. T. (2009). From taste hedonics to motivational drive: Central m-opioid receptors and binge-eating behaviour. *International Journal of Neuropsychopharmacology, 12*(07), 995–1008. http://doi.org/10.1017/S146114570900039X

National Academies of Sciences, Engineering, and Medicine. (2017). Preventing Cognitive Decline and Dementia: A Way Forward. Washington, DC: The National Academies Press. https://doi.org/10.17226/24782

National Collaborating Centre for Mental Health. (2017). Eating disorders: Recognition and treatment. Retrieved from https://www.nice.org.uk/guidance/ng69

National Highway and Transportation Agency (NHTSA) (2015). Traffic safety facts 2015: A compilation of motor vehicle crash data from the fatality analysis reporting system and the general estimates system. Retrieved from https://crashstats.nhtsa.dot.gov/Api/Public/ViewPublication/812384

National Institute of Child Health and Human Development. (2000). Report of the National Reading Panel. Teaching children to read: An evidence-based assessment of the scientific research literature on reading and its implications for reading instruction. Retrieved from https://www.nichd.nih.gov/publications/pubs/nrp/Documents/report.pdf

National Institutes of Health. (1997, August). The Ad Hoc Group of Experts. *Workshop on the medical utility of marijuana: Report to the director.*

Nay, W., Brown, R., & Roberson-Nay, R. (2013). Longitudinal course of panic disorder with and without agoraphobia using the National Epidemiologic Survey on Alcohol and Related Conditions (NESARC). *Psychiatry Research, 208,* 54–61.

Neale, J. M., & Liebert, R. M. (1986). *Science and behavior: An introduction to methods of research* (3rd ed.). Englewood Cliffs, NJ: Prentice-Hall.

Neale, J. M., & Oltmanns, T. (1980). *Schizophrenia.* New York, NY: John Wiley & Sons.

Neisser, U. (1976). *Cognition and reality.* San Francisco, CA: Freeman.

Nelson, E. C., Heath, A. C., Madden, P. A. F., Cooper, M. L., Dinwiddie, S. H., Bucholz, K. K., et al. (2002). Association between self-reported childhood sexual abuse and adverse psychosocial outcomes: Results from a twin study. *Archives of General Psychiatry, 59,* 139–145.

Nelson, E. C., Heath, A. C., Madden, P. A. F., Cooper, M. L., Dinwiddie, S. H., Bucholz, K. K., et al. (2002). Association between self-reported childhood sexual abuse and adverse psychosocial outcomes: Results from a twin study. *Archives of General Psychiatry, 59,* 139–145.

Nelson, J. C. (2006). The STAR*D study: A four-course meal that leaves us wanting more. *American Journal of Psychiatry, 163,* 1864–1866.

Neugebauer, R. (1979). Mediaeval and early modern theories of mental illness. *Archives of General Psychiatry, 36,* 477–484.

Neumann, C. S., Hare, R. D., & Pardini, D. A. (2015). Antisociality and the construct of psychopathy: Data from across the globe. *Journal of Personality, 83,* 678–692. doi:10.1111/jopy.12127

Neuman, R. J., Lobos, E., Reich, W., Henderson, C. A., Sun, L. W., & Todd, R. D. (2007). Prenatal smoking exposure and dopaminergic genotypes interact to cause a severe ADHD subtype. *Biological Psychiatry, 61,* 1320–1328.

Neumeister, A., Daher, R. J., & Charney, D. S. (2005). Anxiety disorders: Noradrenergic neurotransmission. *Handbook of Experimental Pharmacology, 169,* 205–223.

Newman, J. P., Patterson, C. M., & Kosson, D. S. (1987). Response perseveration in psychopaths. *Journal of Abnormal Psychology, 96,* 145–149.

Newman, M. G., & Llera, S. J. (2011). A novel theory of experiential avoidance in generalized anxiety disorder: A review and synthesis of research supporting a contrast avoidance model of worry. *Clinical Psychology Review, 31*(3), 371–382. doi:http://doi.org/10.1016/j.cpr.2011.01.008

Newman, M. G., Llera, S. J., Erickson, T. M., Przeworski, A., & Castonguay, L. G. (2013). Worry and generalized anxiety disorder: A review and theoretical synthesis of evidence on nature, etiology, mechanisms, and treatment. *Annual Review of Clinical Psychology, 9,* 275–297. doi:10.1146/annurev-clinpsy-050212-185544

Newton-Howes, G., Tyrer, P., Anagnostakis, K., Cooper, S., Bowden-Jones, O., & Weaver, T. (2010). The prevalence of personality disorder, its comorbidity with mental state disorders, and its clinical significance in community mental health teams. *Social Psychiatry and Psychiatric Epidemiology, 45,* 453–460.

Newton-Howes, G., Tyrer, P., & Johnson, T. (2006). Personality disorder and the outcome of depression: Meta-analysis of published studies. *British Journal of Psychiatry, 188,* 13–20.

Ngandu, T., Lehtisalo, J., Solomon, A., Levälahti, E., Ahtiluoto, S., Antikainen, R., et al. (2015). A 2 year multidomain intervention of diet, exercise, cognitive training, and vascular risk monitoring versus control to prevent cognitive decline in at-risk elderly people (FINGER): A randomised controlled trial. *The Lancet, 385,* 2255–2263. doi:10.1016/S0140-6736(15)60461-5

Ng, M., Fleming, T., Robinson, M., Thomson, B., Graetz, N., Margono, C., et al. (2014). Global, regional, and national prevalence of overweight and obesity in children and adults during 1980–2013: A systematic analysis for the Global Burden of Disease Study 2013. *The Lancet.* doi:http://dx.doi.org/10.1016/S0140-6736(14)60460-8

Ng, S. W., Slining, M. M., & Popkin, B. M. (2014). The healthy weight commitment foundation pledge. *American Journal of Preventive Medicine, 47,* 508–519.

Ng, T. H., Chung, K.-F., Ho, F. Y.-Y., Yeung, W.-F., Yung, K.-P., & Lam, T.-H. (2015). Sleep–wake disturbance in interepisode bipolar disorder and high-risk individuals: A systematic review and meta-analysis. *Sleep Medicine Reviews, 20,* 46–58. doi:http://dx.doi.org/10.1016/j.smrv.2014.06.006

Nicholls, L. (2008). Putting the New View Classification Scheme to an empirical test. *Feminism and Psychology, 18,* 515–526.

Niederdeppe, J., Farrelly, M. C., & Haviland, M. L. (2004). Confirming "truth": More evidence of a successful tobacco countermarketing campaign in Florida. *American Journal of Public Health, 94,* 255–257.

Niederkrotenthaler, T., Fu, K.-W., Yip, P. S. F., Fong, D. Y. T., Stack, S., Cheng, Q., & Pirkis, J. (2012). Changes in suicide rates following media reports on celebrity suicide: A meta-analysis. *Journal of Epidemiology and Community Health, 66*(11), 1037–1042. doi:10.1136/jech-2011-200707

Nielssen, O., Bourget, D., Laajasalo, T., Liem, M., Labelle, A., Hakkanen-Nyholm, H., et al. (2011). Homicide of strangers by people with a psychotic illness. *Schizophrenia Bulletin, 37,* 572–579.

Nigg, J. T. (2013). Attention deficits and hyperactivity-impulsivity: What have we learned, what next? *Development and Psychopathology, 25*(4 Pt 2), 1489–1503.

Nigg, J. T., & Casey, B. J. (2005). An integrative theory of attention-deficit/hyperactivity disorder based on the cognitive and affective neurosciences. *Development and Psychopathology, 17,* 785–806.

Nigg, J. T., & Goldsmith, H. H. (1994). Genetics of personality disorders: Perspectives from personality and psychopathology research. *Psychological Bulletin, 115,* 346–380.

Nigg, J. T., Lewis, K., Edinger, T., & Falk, M. (2012). Meta-analysis of attention-deficit/hyperactivity disorder or attention-deficit/hyperactivity disorder symptoms, restriction diet, and synthetic food color additives. *Journal of the American Academy of Child & Adolescent Psychiatry, 51*(1), 86–97.e8. http://doi.org/10.1016/j.jaac.2011.10.015

Nobre, P. J., & Pinto-Gouveia, J. (2008). Cognitions, emotions, and sexual response: Analysis of the relationship among automatic thoughts, emotional responses, and sexual arousal. *Archives of Sexual Behavior, 37,* 652–661.

Nock, M. K. (2009). Why do people hurt themselves? New insights into the nature and function of self-injury. *Current Directions in Psychological Science, 18,* 78–83.

Nock, M. K. (2010). Self-injury. *Annual Review of Clinical Psychology, 6,* 339–363.

Nock, M. K., Hwang, I., Sampson, N. A., & Kessler, R. C. (2010). Mental disorders, comorbidity and suicidal behavior: Results from the National Comorbidity Survey Replication. *Molecular Psychiatry, 15*(8), 868–876.

Nock, M. K., Kazdin, A. E., Hiripi, E., & Kessler, R. C. (2006). Prevalence, subtypes, and correlates of DSM-IV conduct disorder in the National Comorbidity Survey Replication. *Psychological Medicine, 36,* 699–710.

Nock, M. K., & Kessler, R. C. (2006). Prevalence of and risk factors for suicide attempts versus suicide gestures: Analysis of the national Comorbidity Survey. *Journal of Abnormal Psychology, 115*(3), 616–623. doi:http://dx.doi.org/10.1037/0021-843X.115.3.616

Nock, M. K., & Mendes, W. B. (2008). Physiological arousal, distress tolerance, and social problem-solving deficits among adolescent self-injurers. *Journal of Consulting and Clinical Psychology, 76,* 28–38.

Nock, M. K., & Prinstein, M. J. (2004). A functional approach to the assessment of self-mutilative behavior. *Journal of Consulting and Clinical Psychology, 72,* 885–890.

Nock, M. K., Prinstein, M. J., & Sterba, S. K. (2009). Revealing the form and functions of self-injurious thoughts and behaviors: A real-time ecological assessment study among adolescents and young adults. *Journal of Abnormal Psychology, 118,* 816–827.

Nolen-Hoeksema, S. (1991). Responses to depression and their effects on the duration of depressive episodes. *Journal of Abnormal Psychology, 100,* 569–582.

Nolen-Hoeksema, S. (2000). The role of rumination in depressive disorders and mixed anxiety/depressive symptoms. *Journal of Abnormal Psychology, 109,* 504–511.

Noll, S. M., & Fredrickson, B. L. (1998). A mediational model linking self-objectification, body shame, and disordered eating. *Psychology of Women Quarterly, 22,* 623–636.

Nonnemaker, J., Hersey, J., Homsi, G., Busey, A., Allen, J., & Vallone, D. (2013). Initiation with menthol cigarettes and youth smoking uptake. *Addiction, 108,* 171–178.

Nordentoft, M., Mortensen, P., & Pedersen, C. (2011). Absolute risk of suicide after first hospital contact in mental disorder. *Archives of General Psychiatry, 68*(10), 1058–1064. doi:10.1001/archgenpsychiatry.2011.113

Nordsletten, A. E., Reichenberg, A., Hatch, S. L., de la Cruz, L. F., Pertusa, A., Hotopf, M., et al. (2013). Epidemiology of hoarding disorder. *British Journal of Psychiatry, 203,* 445–452.

North, M. S., & Fiske, S. T. (2015). Modern attitudes toward older adults in the aging world: A cross-cultural meta-analysis. *Psychological Bulletin, 141,* 993–1021. doi:10.1037/a0039469

Norton, M. C., Skoog, I., Toone, L., Corcoran, C., Tschanz, J. T., Lisota, R. D., et al. (2006). Three-year incidence of first-onset depressive syndrome in a population sample of older adults: The Cache County Study. *American Journal of Geriatric Psychiatry, 14,* 237–245.

Norton, P. J., & Price, E. C. (2007). A meta-analytic review of adult cognitive-behavioral treatment outcome across the anxiety disorders. *Journal of Nervous and Mental Disease, 195,* 521–531.

Nurnberger, J. I., Jr., Koller, D. L., Jung, J., Edenberg, H. J., Foroud, T., Guella, I., et al. (2014). Identification of pathways for bipolar disorder: A meta-analysis. *JAMA Psychiatry, 71*(6), 657–664. doi:10.1001/jamapsychiatry.2014.176

Nuss, P. (2015). Anxiety disorders and GABA neurotransmission: A disturbance of modulation. *Neuropsychiatric Disorders and Treatment 11*, 165–175. doi:10.2147/ndt.s58841

O'Brien, J. T., & Thomas, A. (2015). Vascular dementia. *The Lancet, 386*, 1698–1706. doi:10.1016/S0140-6736(15)00463-8

O'Brien, W. H., & Haynes, S. N. (1995). Behavioral assessment. In L. A. Heiden & M. Hersen (Eds.), *Introduction to clinical psychology* (pp. 103–139). New York, NY: Plenum.

Odgers, C. L., Caspi, A., Broadbent, J. M., Dickson, N., Hancox, R. J., Harrington, H., Poulton, R., Sears, M. R., Thomson, W. M., & Moffitt, T. E. (2007). Prediction of differential adult health burden by conduct problem subtypes in males. *Archives of General Psychiatry, 64*, 476–484.

Odgers, C. L., Moffitt, T. E., Broadbent, J. M., Dickson, N., Hancox, R. J., Harrington, H., Poulton, R., Sears, M. R., Thomson, W. M., & Caspi, A. (2008). Female and male antisocial trajectories: From childhood origins to adult outcomes. *Developmental and Psychopathology, 20*, 673–716.

O'Donnell, P., & Grace, A. A. (1998). Dysfunctions in multiple interrelated systems as the neurobiological bases of schizophrenic symptom clusters. *Schizophrenia Bulletin, 24*, 267–283.

Oei, T. P. S., & Dingle, G. (2008). The effectiveness of group cognitive behavior therapy for unipolar depressive disorders. *Journal of Affective Disorders, 107*, 5–21.

Oeppen, J., & Vaupel, J. W. (2002). Broken limits to life expectancy. *Science, 296*, 1029–1031. doi:10.1126/science.1069675

O'Farrell, T. J., & Clements, K. (2012). Review of outcome research on marital and family therapy in treatment for alcoholism. *Journal of Marital and Family Therapy, 38*, 122–144. http://doi.org/10.1111/j.1752-0606.2011.00242.x

Ogden, C. L., Carroll, M. D., Fryar, C. D., & Flegal, K. M. (2015). Prevalence of obesity among adults and youth: United States, 2011–2014. NCHS Data Brief, No. 219. Hyattsville, MD: National Center for Health Statistics.

Ogden, C. L., Carroll, M. D., Lawman, H. G., Fryar, C. D., Kruszon-Moran, D., Kit, B. K., & Flegal, K. M. (2016). Trends in obesity prevalence among children and adolescents in the United States, 1988–1994 Central 2013-2014. *Journal of the American Medical Association, 315*(21), 2292–2299. http://doi.org/10.1001/jama.2016.6361

Ogloff, J. R. P., Cutajar, M. C., Mann, E., & Mullen, P. (2012). Child sexual abuse and subsequent offending and victimisation: A 45-year follow-up study. *Trends and Issues in Crime and Criminal Justice, 440, 1–6.*

Öhman, A., Flykt, A., & Esteves, F. (2001). Emotion drives attention: Detecting the snake in the grass. *Journal of Experimental Psychology: General, 137*, 466–478.

Öhman, A., & Öhman, A. (2003). The malicious serpent: Snakes as a prototypical stimulus for an evolved module of fear. *Current Directions in Psychological Science, 12*, 5–9.

Ohtani, T., Levitt, J. J., Nestor, P. G., Kawashima, T., Asami, T., Shenton, M. E., et al. (2014). Prefrontal cortex volume deficit in schizophrenia: A new look using 3T MRI with manual parcellation. *Schizophrenia Research, 152*, 184–190.

Okura, T., Plassman, B. L., Steffens, D. C., Llewellyn, D. J., Potter, G. G., & Langa, K. M. (2010). Prevalence of neuropsychiatric symptoms and their association with functional limitations in older adults in the United States: The aging, demographics, and memory study. *Journal of the American Geriatrics Society, 58*, 330–337. doi:10.1111/j.1532-5415.2009.02680.x

Olabi, B., Ellison-Wright, I., McIntosh, A. M., Wood, S. J., Bullmore, E., & Lawrie, S. M. (2011). Are there progressive brain changes in schizophrenia? A meta-analysis of structural magnetic resonance imaging studies. *Biological Psychiatry, 70*, 88–96.

Olatunji, B. O., Etzel, E. N., Tomarken, A. J., Ciesielski, B. G., & Deacon, B. (2011). The effects of safety behaviors on health anxiety: An experimental investigation. *Behavior Research and Therapy, 49*, 719–728. doi:10.1016/j.brat.2011.07.008

Olatunji, B. O., Kauffman, B. Y., Meltzer, S., Davis, M. L., Smits, J. A. J., & Powers, M. B. (2014). Cognitive-behavioral therapy for hypochondriasis/health anxiety: A meta-analysis of treatment outcome and moderators. *Behavior Research and Therapy, 58*, 65–74. doi:https://doi.org/10.1016/j.brat.2014.05.002

olde Hartman, T. C., Borghuis, M. S., Lucassen, P. L., van de Laar, F. A., Speckens, A. E., & van Weel, C. (2009). Medically unexplained symptoms, somatisation disorder and hypochondriasis: Course and prognosis. A systematic review. *Journal of Psychosomatic Research, 66*, 363–377. doi:10.1016/j.jpsychores.2008.09.018

Oldham-Cooper, R., & Loades, M. (2017). Disorder-specific versus generic cognitive-behavioral treatment of anxiety disorders in children and young people: A systematic narrative review of evidence for the effectiveness of disorder-specific CBT compared with the disorder-generic treatment, Coping Cat. *Journal of Child and Adolescent Psychiatric Nursing, 30*(1), 6–17. http://doi.org/10.1111/jcap.12165

Olff, M., Langeland, W. L., Draijer, N., & Gersons, B. P. R. (2007). Gender differences in posttraumatic stress disorder. *Psychological Bulletin, 133*, 183–204.

Olfson, M., Blanco, C., Liu, S., Wang, S., & Correll, C. U. (2012). National trends in the office-based treatment of children, adolescents, and adults with antipsychotics. *Archives of General Psychiatry, 69*(12), 1247–1256.

Olfson, M., Gerhard, T., Huang, C., Crystal, S., & Stroup, T. S. (2015). Premature mortality among adults with schizophrenia in the United States. *JAMA Psychiatry, 72*, 1172–1181. http://doi.org/10.1001/jamapsychiatry.2015.1737

Olivardia, R., Pope, H. G., Mangweth, B., & Hudson, J. I. (1995). Eating disorders in college men. *American Journal of Psychiatry, 152*, 1279–1284.

Olthuis, J. V., Watt, M. C., Bailey, K., Hayden, J. A., & Stewart, S. H. (2016). Therapist-supported internet cognitive behavioural therapy for anxiety disorders in adults. *Cochrane Database of Systematic Reviews* (3). doi:10.1002/14651858.CD011565.pub2

Oltmanns, T. F., & Powers, A. D. (2012). Gender and personality disorder. In T. A. Widiger (Ed.), *The Oxford handbook of personality disorders* (1st ed.). New York, NY: Oxford University Press.

O'Neal, J. M. (1984). First person account: Finding myself and loving it. *Schizophrenia Bulletin, 10*, 109–110.

Open Science Collaboration. (2015). Estimating the reproducibility of psychological science. *Science, 349*(6251). doi:10.1126/science.aac4716

Opondo, D., Eslami, S., Visscher, S., de Rooij, S. E., Verheij, R., Korevaar, J. C., & Abu-Hanna, A. (2012). Inappropriateness of medication prescriptions to elderly patients in the primary care setting: A systematic review. *PLOS ONE, 7*, e43617. doi:10.1371/journal.pone.0043617

Orgeta, V., Qazi, A., Spector, A. E., & Orrell, M. (2014). Psychological treatments for depression and anxiety in dementia and mild cognitive impairment. *Cochrane Database of Systematic Reviews.* doi:10.1002/14651858.CD009125.pub2

Ormel, J., Jeronimus, B. F., Kotov, R., Riese, H., Bos, E. H., Hankin, B., et al. (2013). Neuroticism and common mental disorders: Meaning and utility of a complex relationship. *Clinical Psychology Review, 33*(5), 686–697. doi:10.1016/j.cpr.2013.04.003

Ormel, J., Jeronimus, B. F., Kotov, R., Riese, H., Bos, E. H., Hankin, B., et al. (2013). Neuroticism and common mental disorders: Meaning and utility of a complex relationship. *Clinical Psychology Review, 33*(5), 686–697. doi:10.1016/j.cpr.2013.04.003

Orr, S. P., Metzger, L. J., Lasko, N. B., Macklin, M. L., Hu, F. B., Shalev, A. Y., et al. (2003). Physiologic responses to sudden, loud tones in monozygotic twins discordant for combat exposure: Association with posttraumatic stress disorder. *Archives of General Psychiatry, 60*, 283–288.

Orth, U., Robins, R. W., Meier, L. L., & Conger, R. D. (2016). Refining the vulnerability model of low self-esteem and depression: Disentangling the effects of genuine self-esteem and narcissism. *Journal of Personality and Social Psychology: Personality Processes and Individual Differences, 110*, 133–149. http://dx.doi.org/10.1037/pspp0000038

Ortiz, J., & Raine, A. (2004). Heart rate level and antisocial behavior in children and adolescents: A meta-analysis. *Journal of the American Academy of Child and Adolescent Psychiatry, 43*, 154–162.

Ouimette, P. C., Finney, J. W., & Moos, R. H. (1997). Twelve-step and cognitive-behavioral treatment for substance abuse: A comparison of treatment effectiveness. *Journal of Consulting and Clinical Psychology, 65*, 230–240.

Owen, M. J., Craddock, N., & O'Donovan, M. C. (2010). Suggestion of roles for both common and rare risk variants in genome-wide studies of schizophrenia. *Archives of General Psychiatry, 67*, 667–673.

Owen, M. J., Williams, N. M., & O'Donovan, M. C. (2004). The molecular genetics of schizophrenia: New findings promise new insights. *Molecular Psychiatry, 9*, 14–27.

Owens, E. B., Zalecki, C., Gillette, P., & Hinshaw, S. P. (2017). Girls with childhood ADHD as adults: Cross-domain outcomes by diagnostic persistence. *Journal of Consulting and Clinical Psychology*, http://dx.doi.org/10.1037/ccp0000217

Ozer, D. J., & Benet-Martinez, V. (2006). Personality and the prediction of consequential outcomes. *Annual Review of Psychology, 57*, 401–421.

Pacchiarotti, I., Bond, D. J., Baldessarini, R. J., Nolen, W. A., Grunze, H., Licht, R. W., et al. (2013). The International Society for Bipolar Disorders (ISBD) task force report on antidepressant use in bipolar disorders. *American Journal of Psychiatry, 170*, 1249–1262.

Pajer, K., Chung, J., Leininger, L., Wang, W., Gardner, W., & Yeates, K. (2008). Neuropsychological function in adolescent girls with conduct disorder. *Journal of the American Academy of Child and Adolescent Psychiatry, 47*(4), 416–425. http://dx.doi.org/10.1097/CHI.0b013e3181640828

Palmer, D. M. (2015). Biomarkers for antidepressant selection: iSPOT-D study. *Current Behavioral Neuroscience Reports, 2*(3), 137–145. doi:10.1007/s40473-015-0046-1

Pantelis, C., Velakoulis, D., McGorry, P. D., et al. (2003). Neuroanatomical abnormalities before and after onset of psychosis: A cross-sectional and longitudinal MRI comparison. *The Lancet, 361*, 281–288.

Parees, I., Saifee, T. A., Kassavetis, P., Kojovic, M., Rubio-Agusti, I., Rothwell, J. C., et al. (2012). Believing is perceiving: Mismatch between self-report and actigraphy in psychogenic tremor. *Brain, 135*, 117–123. doi:10.1093/brain/awr292

Park, A. (2010, October 31). New research on understanding Alzheimer's. *Time*.

Park, A. (2016, Feb 16, 2016). Alzheimer's from a new angle. *Time*.

Park, S. L., Murphy, S. E., Wilkens, L. R., Stram, D. O., Hecht, S. S., & Le Marchand, L. (2017). Association of CYP2A6 activity with lung cancer incidence in smokers: The multiethnic cohort study. *PLOS ONE, 12*, e0178435. http://doi.org/10.1371/journal.pone.0178435

Patel, R., Spreng, R. N., Shin, L. M., & Girard, T. A. (2012). Neurocircuitry models of posttraumatic stress disorder and beyond: A meta-analysis of functional neuroimaging studies. *Neuroscience & Biobehavioral Reviews, 36*(9), 2130–2142. doi:https://doi.org/10.1016/j.neubiorev.2012.06.003

Patel, V., Chisholm, D., Parikh, R., Charlson, F. J., Degenhardt, L., Dua, T., et al. (2016). Addressing the burden of mental, neurological, and substance use disorders: Key messages from Disease Control Priorities. *The Lancet, 387*(10028), 1672–1685.

Pathania, M., Davenport, E. C., Muir, J., Sheehan, D. F., Lopez-Domenech, G., & Kittler, J. T. (2014). The autism and schizophrenia associated gene CYFIP1 is critical for the maintenance of dendritic complexity and the stabilization of mature spines. *Translational Psychiatry, 4*, e374.

Patihis, L., Ho, L. Y., Tingen, I. W., Lilienfeld, S. O., & Loftus, E. F. (2014). Are the "memory wars" over? A scientist-practitioner gap in beliefs about repressed memory. *Psychological Science, 25*(2), 519–530. doi: 10.1177/0956797613510718.

Patrick, C. J., & Drislane, L. E. (2015). Triarchic model of psychopathy: Origins, operationalizations, and observed linkages with personality and general psychopathology. *Journal of Personality, 83*, 627–643. doi:10.1111/jopy.12119

Patronek, G. J., & Nathanson, J. N. (2009). A theoretical perspective to inform assessment and treatment strategies for animal hoarders. *Clinical Psychology Review, 29*, 274–281.

Patterson, G. R. (1982). *Coercive family process.* Eugene, OR: Castilia.

Paulus, M. P., Tapert, S. F. & Schuckit, M. A. (2005). Neural activation patterns of methamphetamine-dependent subjects during decision making predict relapse. *Archives of General Psychiatry, 62*, 761–768.

Paxton, S. J., Schutz, H. K., Wertheim, E. H., & Muir, S. L. (1999). Friendship clique and peer influences on body image concerns, dietary restraint, extreme weight-loss behaviors, and binge eating in adolescent girls. *Journal of Abnormal Psychology, 108*, 255–264.

Payne, A., & Blanchard, E. B. (1995). A controlled comparison of cognitive therapy and self-help support groups in the treatment of irritable bowel syndrome. *Journal of Consulting and Clinical Psychology, 63*, 779–786.

Peat, C., Mitchell, J. E., Hoek, H. W., & Wonderlich, S. A. (2009). Validity and utility of subtyping anorexia nervosa. *International Journal of Eating Disorders, 42*, 590–594.

Peck, C. P., Schroeder, R. W., Heinrichs, R. J., Vondran, E. J., Brockman, C. J., Webster, B. K., & Baade, L. E. (2013). Differences in MMPI-2 FBS and RBS scores in brain injury, probable malingering, and conversion disorder groups: A preliminary study. *Clinical Neuropsychologist, 27*, 693–707. doi:10.1080/13854046.2013.779032

Pedersen, M. G., Stevens, H., Pedersen, C. B., Nørgaard-Pedersen, B., & Mortensen, P. B. (2011). Toxoplasma infection and later development of schizophrenia in mothers. *American Journal of Psychiatry, 168*, 814–821. http://doi.org/10.1176/appi.ajp.2011.10091351

Pediatric OCD Treatment Study (POTS) Team. (2004). Cognitive-behavior therapy, setraline, and their combination for children and adolescents with obsessive-compulsive disorder: The pediatric OCD treatment study (POTS) randomized controlled trial. *Journal of the American Medical Association, 292*, 1969–1976.

Peixoto, M. M., & Nobre, P. (2015). Prevalence and sociodemographic predictors of sexual problems in Portugal: A population-based study with women aged 18 to 79 years. *Journal of Sex & Marital Therapy, 41*, 169–180. doi:10.1080/0092623X.2013.842195

Pelham, W. E., Burrows-MacLean, L., Gnagy, E. M., Fabiano, G. A., Coles, E. K., Wymbs, B. T., et al. (2014). A dose-ranging study of behavioral and pharmacological treatment in social settings for children with ADHD. *Journal of Abnormal Child Psychology, 42*(6), 1019–1031.

Pelham, W. E., Gnagy, E. M., Greiner, A. R., Hoza, B., Hinshaw, S. P., Swanson, J. M., Simpson, S., Shapiro, C., Bukstein, O., Baron-Myak, C., & McBurnett, K. (2000). Behavioral versus behavioral plus pharmacological treatment for ADHD children attending a summer treatment program. *Journal of Abnormal Child Psychology, 28*, 507–525.

Pendlebury, S. T., & Rothwell, P. M. (2009). Risk of recurrent stroke, other vascular events and dementia after transient ischaemic attack and stroke. *Cerebrovascular Diseases, 27*(Suppl 3), 1–11.

Penn, D. L., & Mueser, K. T. (1996). Research update on the psychosocial treatment of schizophrenia. *American Journal of Psychiatry, 153*, 607–617.

Pentz, M. A., Shin, H., Riggs, N., Unger, J. B., Collison, K. L., & Chou, C. (2015). Parent, peer, and executive function relationships to early adolescent e-cigarette use: A substance use pathway? *Addictive Behaviors, 42*, 73–78. doi:http://dx.doi.org/10.1016/j.addbeh.2014.10.040

Penzes, P., Cahill, M. E., Jones, K. A., VanLeeuwen, J. E., & Woolfrey, K. M. (2011). Dendritic spine pathology in neuropsychiatric disorders. *Nature Neuroscience, 14*, 285–293.

Pérez-Fuentes, G., Olfson, M., Villegas, L., Morcillo, C., Wang, S., & Blanco, C. (2013). Prevalence and correlates of child sexual abuse: A national study. *Comprehensive Psychiatry, 54*, 16–27. doi:10.1016/j.comppsych.2012.05.010

Perez, M., & Joiner, T. E. (2003). Body image dissatisfaction and disordered eating in black and white women. *International Journal of Eating Disorders, 33*, 342–350.

Perez-Rodriguez, M. M., & Siever, L. J. (2015). Psychopharmacological treatment of personality disorders. New York, NY: Oxford University Press.

Perkins, K. A., Ciccocioppo, M., Conklin, C. A., Milanek, M. E., Grottenthaler, A., & Sayette, M. A. (2008). Mood influences on acute smoking responses are independent of nicotine intake and dose expectancy. *Journal of Abnormal Psychology, 117*, 79–93.

Perkins, K. A., Karelitz, J. L., Conklin, C. A., Sayette, M. A., & Giedgowd, G. E. (2010). Acute negative affect relief from smoking depends on the affect situation and measure but not on nicotine. *Biological Psychiatry, 67*, 707–714.

Perkonigg, A., Pfister, H., Stein, M. B., Hofler, M., Lieb, R., Maercker, A., et al. (2005). Longitudinal course of posttraumatic stress disorder and posttramatic stress. *American Journal of Psychiatry, 162*, 1320–1327.

Persing, J. S., Stuart, S. P., Noyes, R., & Happel, R. L. (2000). Hypochondriasis: The patient's perspective. *International Journal of Psychiatry in Medicine, 30*, 329–342.

Perugi, G., Akiskal, H. S., Giannotti, D., Frare, F., Di Vaio, S., & Cassano, G. B. (1997). Gender-related differences in body dysmorphic disorder. *Journal of Nervous and Mental Disease, 185*, 578–582.

Pescosolido, B. A., Martin, J. K., Long, J. S., Medina, T. R., Phelan, J. C., & Link, B. G. (2010). "A disease like any other?" A decade of change in public relations to schizophrenia, depression and alcohol dependence. *American Journal of Psychiatry, 167*, 1321–1330.

Petersen, J. L., & Hyde, J. S. (2010). A meta-analytic review of research on gender differences in sexuality, 1993–2007. *Psychological Bulletin, 136*, 21–38. doi:http://dx.doi.org/10.1037/a0017504

Peterson, C. B., Mitchell, J. E., Crow, S. J., Crosby, R. D., & Wonderlich, S. A. (2009). The efficacy of self-help group treatment and therapist-led group treatment for binge eating disorder. *American Journal of Psychiatry, 166*, 1347–1354.

Peterson, R. L., & Pennington, B. F. (2015). Developmental dyslexia. *Annual Review of Clinical Psychology, 11*, 283–307. http://doi.org/10.1146/annurev-clinpsy-032814-112842

Petry, N. M., Alessi, S. M., & Hanson, T. (2007). Contingency management improves abstinence and quality of life in cocaine abusers. *Journal of Consulting and Clinical Psychology, 75*, 307–315.

Petry, N. M., Alessi, S. M., Marx, J., Austin, M., & Tardif, M. (2005). Vouchers versus prizes: Contingency management treatment of substance abusers in community settings. *Journal of Consulting and Clinical Psychology, 73*, 1005–1014.

Pettersson-Yeo, W., Allen, P., Benetti, S., McGuire, P., & Mechelli, A. (2011). Dysconnectivity in schizophrenia: Where are we now? *Neuroscience Biobehavoral Reviews, 35*, 1110–1124.

Pettinati, H. M., Oslin, D. W., Kampman, K. M., Dundon, W. D., Xie, H., Gallis, T. L., et al. (2010). A double-blind, placebo-controlled trial combining sertraline and naltrexone for treating co-occuring depression and alcohol dependence. *American Journal of Psychiatry, 167*, 668–675.

Phillips, D. P. (1974). The influence of suggestion on suicide: Substantive and theoretical implications of the Werther effect. *American Sociological Review, 39*, 340–354.

Phillips, D. P. (1985). The Werther effect. *The Sciences, 25*, 33–39.

Phillips, K. A. (2005). *The broken mirror: Understanding and treating body dysmorphic disorder.* New York, NY: Oxford University Press.

Phillips, K. A. (2006). "I look like a monster": Pharmacotherapy and cognitive-behavioral therapy for body dysmorphic disorder. In R. L. Spitzer, M. B. First, J. B. W. Williams, & M. Gibbon (Eds.), *DSM-IV-TR Case Book* (Vol. 2) *Experts tell how they treated their own patients* (pp. 263–276). Washington, DC: American Psychiatric Publishing.

Phillips, K. A., Menard, W., Quinn, E., Didie, E. R., & Stout, R. L. (2013). A 4-year prospective observational follow-up study of course and predictors of course in body dysmorphic disorder. *Psychological Medicine, 43*, 1109–1117.

Phillips, K. A., Pinto, A., Hart, A. S., Coles, M. E., Eisen, J. L., Menard, W., et al. (2012). A comparison of insight in body dysmorphic disorder and obsessive-compulsive disorder. *Journal of Psychiatric Research, 46*, 1293–1299.

Phillips, K. A., Wilhelm, S., Koran, L. M., Didie, E. R., Fallon, B. A., Feusner, J., et al. (2010). Body dysmorphic disorder: Some key issues for DSM-V. *Depression and Anxiety, 27*, 573–591.

Phillips, L. J., Francey, S. M., Edwards, J., & McMurray, N. (2007). Stress and psychosis: Towards the development of new models of investigation. *Clinical Psychology Review, 27*, 307–317.

Phillips, M. L., & Swartz, H. A. (2014). A critical appraisal of neuroimaging studies of bipolar disorder: Toward a new conceptualization of underlying neural circuitry and a road map for future research. *The American Journal of Psychiatry, 171*(8), 829–843. doi:10.1176/appi.ajp.2014.13081008

Piacentini, J., Bennett, S., Compton, S. N., Kendall, P. C., Birmaher, B., Albano, A. M., et al. (2014). 24- and 36-week outcomes for the Child/Adolescent Anxiety Multimodal Study (CAMS). *Journal of the American Academy of Child and Adolescent Psychiatry, 53*(3), 297–310.

Pickett, K. E., & Wilkinson, R. G. (2010). Inequality: An underacknowledged source of mental illness and distress. *The British Journal of Psychiatry, 197*(6), 426–428. doi:10.1192/bjp.bp.109.072066

Pierce, J. M., Petry, N. M., Stitzer, M. L., Blaine, J., Kellog, S., et al. (2006). Effects of lower-cost incentives on stimulant abstinence in methadone maintenance treatment. *Archives of General Psychiatry, 63*, 201–208.

Pierce, J. P., Choi, W. S., Gilpin, E. A., Farkas, A. J., & Berry, C. C. (1998). Tobacco ads, promotional items linked with teen smoking. *Journal of the American Medical Association, 279*, 511–515.

Pierce, K., & Courchesne, E. (2001). Evidence for a cerebellar role in reduced exploration and stereotyped behavior in autism. *Biological Psychiatry, 49*, 655–664.

Pierce, K., Haist, F., Sedaghadt, F., & Courchesne, E. (2004). The brain response to personally familiar faces in autism: Findings of fusiform activity and beyond. *Brain, 127*, 1–14.

Pierce, K., Muller, R. A., Ambrose, J., Allen, G., & Courchesne, E. (2001). Face processing occurs outside the fusiform "face area" in autism: Evidence from functional MRI. *Brain, 124*, 2059–2073.

Piet, J., & Hougaard, E. (2011). The effect of mindfulness-based cognitive therapy for prevention of relapse in recurrent major depressive disorder: A systematic review and meta-analysis. *Clinical Psychology Review, 31*(6), 1032–1040. doi:http://dx.doi.org/10.1016/j.cpr.2011.05.002

Pietromonaco, P. R., & Barrett, L. F. (1997). Working models of attachment and daily social interactions. *Journal of Personality and Social Psychology, 73*, 1409–1423.

Pietrzak, R. H., Goldstein, R. B., Southwick, S. M., & Grant, B. F. (2011). Personality disorders associated with full and partial posttraumatic stress disorder in the U.S. population: Results from wave 2 of the National Epidemiologic Survey on Alcohol and Related Conditions. *Journal of Psychiatric Research, 45*(5), 678–686. doi:10.1016/j.jpsychires.2010.09.013

Pietrzak, R. H., Zhu, Y., Slade, M. D., Qi, Q., Krystal, J. H., Southwick, S. M., & Levy, B. R. (2016). Association between negative age stereotypes and accelerated cellular aging: Evidence from two cohorts of older adults. *Journal of the American Geriatrics Society, 64*, e228–e230. doi:10.1111/jgs.14452

Pike, K. M., Dohm, F., Striegel-Moore, R. H., Wilfley, D. E., & Fairburn, C. M. (2001). A comparison of black and white women with binge eating disorder. *American Journal of Psychiatry, 158*, 1455–1460.

Pike, K. M., Walsh, B. T., Vitousek, K., Wilson, G. T., & Bauer, J. (2003). Cognitive behavior therapy in the posthospitalization treatment of anorexia nervosa. *American Journal of Psychiatry, 160*, 2046–2049.

Pilhatsch, M., Vetter, N. C., Hubner, T., Ripke, S., Muller, K. U., Marxen, M., et al. (2014). Amygdala-function perturbations in healthy mid-adolescents with familial liability for depression. *Journal of the American Academy of Child & Adolescent Psychiatry, 53*, 559–558.

Pilling, S., Bebbington, P., Kuipers, E., Garety, P., Geddes, L., Martindale, B., et al. (2002). Psychological treatments in schizophrenia: II. Meta-analyses of randomized controlled trials of social skills training and cognitive remediation. *Psychological Medicine, 32*, 783–791.

Pilowsky, L. S., Bressan, R. A., Stone, J. M., Erlandsson, K., Mulligan, R. S., Krystal, J. H., et al. (2006). First in vivo evidence of an NMDA receptor deficit in medication-free schizophrenic patients. *Molecular Psychiatry, 11*, 118–119. http://doi.org/10.1038/sj.mp.4001751

Pincus, A. L., & Lukowitsky, M. R. (2010). Pathological narcissism and narcissistic personality disorder. *Annual Review of Clinical Psychology, 6*, 421–446. doi:10.1146/annurev.clinpsy.121208.131215

Pineles, S. L., & Mineka, S. (2005). Attentional biases to internal and external sources of potential threat in social anxiety. *Journal of Abnormal Psychology, 114*, 314–318.

Piper, A., Jr., Pope, H. G., Jr., & Borowiecki, J. J. I. (2000). Custer's last stand: Brown, Scheflin, and Whitfiled's latest attempt to salvage "dissociative amnesia." *Journal of Psychiatry and the Law, 28*, 149–213.

Pittenger, C., & Bloch, M. H. (2014). Pharmacological treatment of obsessive-compulsive disorder. *The Psychiatric clinics of North America, 37*(3), 375–391. doi:10.1016/j.psc.2014.05.006

Piven, J., Arndt, S., Bailey, J., & Andreasen, N. (1996). Regional brain enlargement in autism: A magnetic resonance imaging study. *Journal of the American Academy of Child and Adolescent Psychiatry, 35*, 530–536.

Piven, J., Arndt, S., Bailey, J., Havercamp, S., Andreasen, N. C., & Palmer, P. (1995). An MRI study of brain size in autism. *American Journal of Psychiatry, 152*, 1145–1149.

Pizzagalli, D. A. (2014). Depression, stress, and anhedonia: Toward a synthesis and integrated model. *Annual Reviews of Clinical Psychology, 10*, 393–423. doi:10.1146/annurev-clinpsy-050212-185606.

Plomin, R. (1999). Genetics and general cognitive ability. *Nature, 402,* C25–C29.

Plomin, R., DeFries, J. C., Craig, I. W., & McGuffin, P. (2003). *Behavioral genetics in the postgenomic era.* Washington, DC: APA Books.

Plomin, R., & Kovas, Y. (2005). Generalist genes and learning disabilities. *Psychological Bulletin, 131,* 592–617.

Polivy, J., & Herman, C. P. (1985). Dieting and binging: A causal analysis. *American Psychologist, 40,* 193–201.

Polivy, J., Herman, C. P., & Howard, K. (1988). The restraint scale: Assessment of dieting. In M. Hersen & A. S. Bellack (Eds.), *Dictionary of behavioral assessment techniques* (pp. 377-380). Elmsford, NY: Pergamon Press.

Pomerleau, O. F., Collins, A. C., Shiffman, S., & Pomerleau, C. S. (1993). Why some people smoke and others do not: New perspectives. *Journal of Consulting and Clinical Psychology, 61,* 723–731.

Ponniah, K., Magiati, I., & Hollon, S. D. (2013). An update on the efficacy of psychological treatments for obsessive-compulsive disorder in adults. *Journal of Obsessive-Compulsive and Related Disorders, 2*(2), 207–218. doi:https://doi.org/10.1016/j.jocrd.2013.02.005

Poole, D. A., Lindsay, D. S., Memon, A., & Bull, R. (1995). Psychotherapy and the recovery of memories of childhood sexual abuse: U.S. and British practitioners' opinions, practices and experiences. *Journal of Consulting and Clinical Psychology, 63,* 426–437.

Pope, H. G. J., Oliva, P. S., Hudson, J. I., Bodkin, J. A., & Gruber, A. J. (1999). Attitudes toward DSM-IV dissociative disorders diagnoses among board-certified American psychiatrists. *American Journal of Psychiatry, 156,* 321–323.

Pope, H. G. J., Poliakoff, M. B., Parker, M. P., Boynes, M., & Hudson, J. J. (2006). Is dissociative amnesia a culture-bound syndrome? Findings from a survey of historical literature. *Psychological Medicine, 37,* 1067–1068.

Pope, K. S. (1998). Pseudoscience, cross-examination, and scientific evidence in the recovered memory controversy. *Psychology, Public Policy, and Law, 4,* 1160–1181.

Potkin, S. G., Alva, G., Fleming, K., Anand, R., Keator, D., Carreon, D., et al. (2002). A PET study of the pathophysiology of negative symptoms in schizophrenia. *The American Journal of Psychiatry, 159,* 227–237.

Poulsen, S., Lunn, S., Daniel, S. I., Folke, S., Mathiesen, B. B., Katznelson, H., & Fairburn, C. G. (2014). A randomized controlled trial of psychoanalytic psychotherapy or cognitive-behavioral therapy for bulimia nervosa. *American Journal of Psychiatry, 171*(1), 109–116.

Powell, R. A., & Gee, T. L. (2000). "The effects of hypnosis on dissociative identity disorder: A reexamination of the evidence": Reply. *Canadian Journal of Psychiatry, 45,* 848–849.

Power, R. A., Tansey, K. E., Buttenschøn, H. N., Cohen-Woods, S., Bigdeli, T., Hall, L. S., et al. (2017). Genome-wide association for major depression through age at onset stratification: Major depressive disorder working group of the Psychiatric Genomics Consortium. *Biological Psychiatry, 81*(4), 325–335. doi:10.1016/j.biopsych.2016.05.010

Powers, A. D., Gleason, M. E., & Oltmanns, T. F. (2013). Symptoms of borderline personality disorder predict interpersonal (but not independent) stressful life events in a community sample of older adults. *Journal of Abnormal Psychology, 122,* 469–474. doi:10.1037/a0032363

Powers, M. B., Halpern, J. M., Ferenschak, M. P., Gillihan, S. J., & Foa, E. B. (2010). A meta-analytic review of prolonged exposure for posttraumatic stress disorder. *Clinical Psychology Review, 30,* 635–641.

Powers, M. B., Vedel, E., & Emmelkamp, P. M. G. (2008). Behavioral couples therapy (BCT) for alcohol and drug use disorders: A meta-analysis. *Clinical Psychology Review, 28,* 952–962.

Powers, R. (2017). *No one cares about crazy people: The chaos and heartbreak of mental health in America.* New York, NY: Hachette Books.

Pressman, P. S., & Miller, B. L. (2014). Diagnosis and management of behavioral variant frontotemporal dementia. *Biological Psychiatry, 75,* 574–581.

Price, D. D., Craggs, J. G., Zhou, Q., Verne, G. N., Perlstein, W. M., & Robinson, M. E. (2009). Widespread hyperalgesia in irritable bowel syndrome is dynamically maintained by tonic visceral impulse input and placebo/nocebo factors: Evidence from human psychophysics, animal models, and neuroimaging. *NeuroImage, 47,* 995–1001.

Prien, R. F., & Potter, W. Z. (1993). Maintenance treatment for mood disorders. In D. L. Dunner (Ed.), *Current psychiatric therapy.* Philadelphia, PA: Saunders.

Prieto, S. L., Cole, D. A., & Tageson, C. W. (1992). Depressive self-schemas in clinic and nonclinic children. *Cognitive Therapy and Research, 16,* 521–534.

Primack, B. A., Bost, J. E., Land, S. R., & Fine, M. J. (2007). Volume of tobacco advertising in African American markets: Systematic review and meta-analysis. *Public Health Reports, 122,* 607–615.

Primack, B. A., Shensa, A., Kim, K. H., Carroll, M. V., Hoban, M. T., Leino, E. V., et al. (2013). Waterpipe smoking among U.S. university students. *Nicotine and Tobacco Research, 15,* 29–35.

Prince, M., Bryce, R., Albanese, E., Wimo, A., Ribeiro, W., & Ferri, C. P. (2013). The global prevalence of dementia: A systematic review and metaanalysis. *Alzheimer's and Dementia: The Journal of the Alzheimer's Association, 9,* 63–75.e62. doi:http://dx.doi.org/10.1016/j.jalz.2012.11.007

Prinstein, M. J., Heilbron, N., Guerry, J. D., Franklin, J. C., Rancourt, D., Simon, V., & Spirito, A. (2010). Peer influence and nonsuicidal self injury: Longitudinal results in community and clinically-referred adolescent samples. *Journal of Abnormal Child Psychology, 38*(5), 669–682. doi:10.1007/s10802-010-9423-0

Pruessner, M., Cullen, A. E., Aas, M., & Walker, E. F. (2017). The neural diathesis-stress model of schizophrenia revisited: An update on recent findings considering illness stage and neurobiological and methodological complexities. *Neuroscience & Biobehavioral Reviews, 73,* 191–218.

Przeworski, A., & Newman, M. G. (2006). Efficacy and utility of computer-assisted cognitive behavioural therapy for anxiety disorders. *The Clinical Psychologist, 10,* 43–53.

Pujols, Y., Seal, B. N., & Meston, C. M. (2010). The association between sexual satisfaction and body image in women. *Journal of Sexual Medicine, 7,* 905–916.

Puma, M., Bell, S., Cook, R., Heid, C., Broene, P., Jenkins, F., et al. (2012). Third grade follow-up to the Head Start Impact Study Final Report *OPRE Report # 2012-45.* Washington, DC: U.S. Department of Health and Human Services.

Putnam, F. W. (1996). A brief history of multiple personality disorder. *Child and Adolescent Psychiatric Clinics of North America, 5,* 263–271.

Quiles Marcos, Y., Quiles Sebastián, M. J., Pamies Aubalat, L., Botella Ausina, J., & Treasure, J. (2013). Peer and family influence in eating disorders: A meta-analysis. *European Psychiatry, 28*(4), 199–206.

Quinones, S. (2015). *Dreamland: The true tale of America's opiate epidemic.* New York, NY: Bloomsbury Press.

Quinsey, V. L., Harris, G. T., Rice, M. E., & Cormier, C. A. (2006). *Violent offenders: Appraising and managing risk* (2nd ed.). Washington, DC: American Psychological Association.

Quirk, S. E., Berk, M., Chanen, A. M., Koivumaa-Honkanen, H., Brennan-Olsen, S. L., Pasco, J. A., & Williams, L. J. (2016). Population prevalence of personality disorder and associations with physical health comorbidities and health care service utilization: A review. *Personality Disorders: Theory, Research, and Treatment, 7,* 136–146. doi:10.1037/per0000148

Rachman, S. (2012). Health anxiety disorders: A cognitive construal. *Behaviour Research and Therapy, 50,* 502–512.

Rachman, S. J. (1977). The conditioning theory of fear acquisition: A critical examination. *Behaviour Research and Therapy, 15,* 375–387.

Rachman, S. J., & DeSilva, P. (1978). Abnormal and normal obsessions. *Behaviour Research and Therapy, 16,* 233–248.

Rachman, S. J., & Wilson, G. T. (1980). *The effects of psychological therapy* (2nd ed.). Elmsford, NY: Pergamon Press.

Ragatz, L. L., Fremouw, W., & Baker, E. (2012). The psychological profile of white-collar offenders: Demographics, criminal thinking, psychopathic traits, and psychopathology. *Criminal Justice and Behavior, 39,* 978–997.

Raine, A. (2006). Schizotypal personality: Neurodevelopmental and psychosocial trajectories. *Annual Review of Clinical Psychology, 2,* 291–326.

Raine, A., Moffitt, T. E., Caspi, A., Loeber, R., Stouthamer-Loeber, M., & Lynam, D. (2005). Neurocognitive impairments in boys on the life-course persistent antisocial path. *Journal of Abnormal Psychology, 114*(1), 38–49. http://dx.doi.org/10.1037/0021-843X.114.1.38

Raine, A., Venables, P. H., & Williams, M. (1990). Relationships between central and autonomic measures of arousal at age 15 years and criminality at age 24 years. *Archives of General Psychiatry, 47*, 1003–1007.

Raison, C. L., Capuron, L., & Miller, A. H. (2006). Cytokines sing the blues: Inflammation and the pathogenesis of depression. *Trends in Immunology, 27*, 24–31.

Ramus, F. (2014). Neuroimaging sheds new light on the phonological deficit in dyslexia. *Trends in Cognitive Sciences, 18*(6), 274–275.

Rando, K., Chaplin, T. M., Potenza, M. N., Mayes, L., & Sinha, R. (2013). Prenatal cocaine exposure and gray matter volume in adolescent boys and girls: Relationship to substance use initiation. *Biological Psychiatry, 74*, 482–489.

Ranganathan, M., & D'Souza, D. C. (2006). The acute effects of cannabinoids on memory in humans: A review. *Psychopharmacology, 188*, 425–444. http://doi.org/10.1007/s00213-006-0508-y

Rapee, R. M., Abbott, M., & Lyneham, H. (2006). Bibliotherapy for children with anxiety disorders using written materials for parents: A randomized controlled trial. *Journal of Consulting and Clinical Psychology, 74*, 436–444.

Rapee, R., Mattick, R., & Murrell, E. (1986). Cognitive mediation in the affective component of spontaneous panic attacks. *Journal of Behavior Therapy and Experimental Psychiatry, 17*, 245–253.

Rapee, R. M., Schniering, C. A., & Hudson, J. L. (2009). Anxiety disorders during childhood adolescence: Origins and treatment. *Annual Review of Clinical Psychology, 5*, 311–341.

Rapoport, J. L., Giedd, J., & Gogtay, N. (2012). Neurodevelopmental model of schizophrenia: Update 2012. *Molecular Psychiatry, 17*, 1228–1238.

Rapoport, M. J., Lanctot, K. L., Streiner, D. L., Bedard, M., Vingilis, E., Murray, B., et al. (2009). Benzodiazepine use and driving: A meta-analysis. *Journal of Clinical Psychiatry, 70*, 663–673.

Rascovsky, K., Hodges, J. R., Knopman, D., Mendez, M. F., Kramer, J. H., Neuhaus, J., et al. (2011). Sensitivity of revised diagnostic criteria for the behavioural variant of frontotemporal dementia. *Brain: A Journal of Neurology, 134*, 2456–2477.

Rasic, D., Hajek, T., Alda, M., & Uher, R. (2014). Risk of mental illness in offspring of parents with schizophrenia, bipolar disorder, and major depressive disorder: A meta-analysis of family high-risk studies. *Schizophrenia Bulletin, 40*, 28–38.

Rastrelli, G., Corona, G., Mannucci, E., & Maggi, M. (2015). Vascular and chronological age in subjects with erectile dysfunction: A cross-sectional study. *Journal of Sexual Medicine, 12*, 2303–2312. doi:http://dx.doi.org/10.1111/jsm.13044

Rather, B. C., Goldman, M. S., Roehrich, L., & Brannick, M. (1992). Empirical modeling of an alcohol expectancy memory network using multidimensional scaling. *Journal of Abnormal Psychology, 101*, 174–183.

Rawson, R. A., Martinelli-Casey, P., Anglin, M. D., et al. (2004). A multi-site comparison of psychosocial approaches for the treatment of methamphetamine dependence. *Addiction, 99*, 708–717.

Reas, D. L., Williamson, D. A., Martin, C. K., & Zucker, N. L. (2000). Duration of illness predicts outcome for bulimia nervosa: A long-term follow-up study. *International Journal of Eating Disorders, 27*, 428–434.

Reba-Harrelson, L., Von Holle, A., Hamer, R. M., Swann, R., Reyes, M. L., & Bulik, C. M. (2009). Patterns and prevalence of disordered eating and weight control behaviors in women ages 25–45. *Eating and Weight Disorders, 14*(4), e190–198.

Rebok, G. W., Ball, K., Guey, L. T., Jones, R. N., Kim, H. -Y., King, J. W., et al. (2014). Ten-year effects of the advanced cognitive training for Independent and Vital Elderly Cognitive Training Trial on cognition and everyday functioning in older adults. *Journal of the American Geriatrics Society, 62*, 16–24.

Redding, N. (2009). *Methland: The death and life of an American small town.* New York, NY: Bloomsbury USA.

Reed, B. D., Harlow, S. D., Plegue, M. A., & Sen, A. (2016). Remission, relapse, and persistence of vulvodynia: A longitudinal population-based study. *Journal of Women's Health, 25*, 276–283. doi:10.1089/jwh.2015.5397

Regeer, E. J., Ten Have, M., Rosso, M. L., van Roijen, L. H., Vollebergh, W., & Nolen, W. A. (2004). Prevalence of bipolar disorder in the general population: A reappraisal study of the Netherlands Mental Health Survey and Incidence Study. *Acta Psychiatrica Scandinavica, 110*, 374–382.

Regier, D. A., Kuhl, E. A., & Kupfer, D. J. (2013). The DSM-5: Classification and criteria changes. *World Psychiatry, 12*, 92–98.

Regier, D. A., Narrow, W. E., Clarke, D. E., Kraemer, H. C., Kuramoto, S. J., Kuhl, E. A., & Kupfer, D. J. (2013). DSM-5 field trials in the United States and Canada, Part II: Test-retest reliability of selected categorical diagnoses. *American Journal of Psychiatry, 170*, 59–70.

Regland, B., Johansson, B. V., Grenfeldt, B., Hjelmgren, L. T., & Medhus, M. (1995). Homocysteinemia is a common feature of schizophrenia. *Journal of Neural Transmission: General Section, 100*, 165–169.

Reichenberg, A., Avshalom, C., Harrington, H, Houts, R., Keefe, R. S. E., Murray, R. M., Poulton, R., & Moffitt, T. E. (2010). Static and dynamic cognitive deficits in childhood preceding adult schizophrenia: A 30-year study. *American Journal of Psychiatry, 167*, 160–169.

Reich, J. (2000). The relationship of social phobia to avoidant personality disorder: A proposal to reclassify avoidant personality disorder based on clinical empirical findings. *European Psychiatry, 15*, 151–159.

Reidy, D. E., Shelley-Tremblay, J. F., & Lilienfeld, S. O. (2011). Psychopathy, reactive aggression, and precarious proclamations: A review of behavioral, cognitive, and biological research. *Aggression and Violent Behavior, 16*, 512–524.

Reinhold, N., & Markowitsch, H. J. (2009). Retrograde episodic memory and emotion: A perspective from patients with dissociative amnesia. *Neuropsychologia, 47*, 2197–2206.

Reitsma, M. B., Fullman, N., Ng, M., Salama, J. S., Abajobir, A., Abate, K. H., et al. (2017). Smoking prevalence and attributable disease burden in 195 countries and territories, 1990–2015: A systematic analysis from the Global Burden of Disease Study 2015. *Lancet, 389*, 1885–1906.

Rescorla, L. A., Achenbach, T. M., Ivanova, M. Y., Harder, V. S., Otten, L., Bilenberg, N., et al. (2011). International comparisons of behavioral and emotional problems in preschool children: Parents' reports from 24 societies. *Journal of Clinical Child & Adolescent Psychology, 40*(3), 456–467. http://doi.org/10.1080/15374416.2011.563472

Resick, P. A., Bovin, M. J., Calloway, A. L., Dick, A. M., King, M. W., Mitchell, K. S., et al. (2012). A critical evaluation of the complex PTSD literature: Implications for DSM-5. *Journal of Traumatic Stress, 25*, 241–251.

Resick, P. A., Nishith, P., & Griffin, M. G. (2003). How well does cognitive-behavioral therapy treat symptoms of complex PTSD? An examination of child sexual abuse survivors within a clinical trial. *CNS Spectrums, 8*, 351–355.

Resick, P. A., Suvak, M. K., Johnides, B. D., Mitchell, K. S., & Iverson, K. M. (2012). The impact of dissociation on PTSD treatment with cognitive processing therapy. *Depression and Anxiety, 29*, 718–730.

Reuters. (2014, April 30). Catherine Zeta-Jones in treatment for bipolar disorder. *Telegraph.* Downloaded from http://www.telegraph.co.uk/news/celebritynews/10026834/Catherine-Zeta-Jones-in-treatment-for-bipolar-disorder.html on July 24, 2017.

Reynolds, C. R., Chastain, R. L., Kaufman, A. S., & McLean, J. E. (1997). Demographic characteristics and IQ among adults: Analysis of the WAIS-R standardization sample as a function of the stratification variables. *Journal of School Psychology, 25*, 323–342.

Reynolds, S., Wilson, C., Austin, J., & Hooper, L. (2012). Effects of psychotherapy for anxiety in children and adolescents: A meta-analytic review. *Clinical Psychology Review, 32*(4), 251–262.

Rhee, S. H., & Waldman, I. D. (2002). Genetic and environmental influences on antisocial behavior: A meta-analysis of twin and adoption studies. *Psychological Bulletin, 128*, 490–529.

Rhode, P., Seeley, J. R., Kaufman, N. K, Clarke, G. N., & Stice, E. (2006). Predicting time to recovery among depressed adolescents treated in two psychosocial group interventions. *Journal of Consulting and Clinical Psychology, 74*, 80–88.

Richards, D. A., Ekers, D., McMillan, D., Taylor, R. S., Byford, S., Warren, F. C., et al. (2016). Cost and outcome of behavioural activation versus cognitive behavioural therapy for depression (COBRA): A randomised, controlled, non-inferiority trial. *The Lancet, 388*(10047), 871–880. doi:10.1016/S0140-6736(16)31140-0

Richards, R. L., Kinney, D. K., Lunde, I., Benet, M., & Merzel, A. (1988). Creativity in manic-depressives, cyclothymes, their normal relatives, and control subjects. *Journal of Abnormal Psychology, 97*, 281–288.

Richters, J., De Visser, R. O., Rissel, C. E., Grulich, A. E., & Smith, A. M. A. (2008). Demographic and psychosocial features of participants in bondage and discipline, "sadomasochism" or dominance and submission (BDSM): Data from a national survey. *Journal of Sexual Medicine, 5*, 1660–1668. doi:10.1111/j.1743-6109.2008.00795.x

Ridley, M. (2003). *Nature via nurture: Genes, experience, and what makes us human.* Great Britain: HarperCollins.

Rieder, R. O., Mann, L. S., Weinberger, D. R., van Kammen, D. P., & Post, R. M. (1983). Computer tomographic scans in patients with schizophrenia, schizoaffective, and bipolar affective disorder. *Archives of General Psychiatry, 40*, 735–739.

Rief, W., & Broadbent, E. (2007). Explaining medically unexplained symptoms—models and mechanisms. *Clinical Psychology Review, 27*, 821–841.

Rief, W., Buhlmann, U., Wilhelm, S., Borkenhagen, A., & Brähler, E. (2006). The prevalence of body dysmorphic disorder: A population-based survey. *Psychological Medicine, 36*, 877–885.

Rief, W., & Martin, A. (2014). How to use the new DSM-5 somatic symptom disorder diagnosis in research and practice: A critical evaluation and a proposal for modifications. *Annual Review of Clinical Psychology, 10*, 339–367. doi:10.1146/annurev-clinpsy-032813-153745

Riggs, D. S., Rothbaum, B. O., & Foa, E. B. (1995). A prospective examination of symptoms of posttraumatic stress disorder in victims of nonsexual assault. *Journal of Interpersonal Violence, 10*(2), 201–214. doi:10.1177/0886260595010002005

Rimland, B. (1964). *Infantile autism.* New York, NY: Appleton-Century-Crofts.

Rios, J. A. & Sireci, S. G. (2014). Guidelines versus practices in cross-lingual assessment: A disconcerting disconnect. *International Journal of Testing, 14*, 289–312, doi:10.1080/15305058.2014.924006

Ripke, S., Neale, B. M., Corvin, A., Walters, J. T. R., Farh, K.-H., Holmans, P. A., et al. (2014). Biological insights from 108 schizophrenia-associated genetic loci. *Nature, 511*, 421–427. http://doi.org/10.1038/nature13595

Ripke, S., Sanders, A. R., Kendler, K. S., Levinson, D. F., Sklar, P., Holmans, P. A., et al. (2011). Genome-wide association study identifies five new schizophrenia loci. *Nature Genetics, 43*, 969–976. http://doi.org/10.1038/ng.940

Ripke, S., Wray, N. R., Lewis, C. M., Hamilton, S. P., Weissman, M. M., Breen, G., et al. (2013). A mega-analysis of genome-wide association studies for major depressive disorder. *Molecular Psychiatry, 18*(4), 497–511. doi:10.1038/mp.2012.21

Ritchie, K., Norton, J., Mann, A., Carriere, I., & Ancelin, M. L. (2013). Late-onset agoraphobia: General population incidence and evidence for a clinical subtype. *American Journal of Psychiatry, 170*, 790–798.

Ritter, K., Vater, A., Rusch, N., Schroder-Abe, M., Schutz, A., Fydrich, T., et al. (2014). Shame in patients with narcissistic personality disorder. *Psychiatry Research, 215*, 429–437.

Robbins, J. (2007). *Healthy at 100.* New York, NY: Ballantine Books.

Robbins, S. J., Ehrman, R. N., Childress, A. R., Cornish, J. W., & O'Brien, C. P. (2000). Mood state and recent cocaine use are not associated with levels of cocaine cue reactivity. *Drug and Alcohol Dependence, 59*, 33–42.

Roberts, A. L., Gilman, S. E., Breslau, J., Breslau, N., & Koenen, K. C. (2011). Race/ethnic differences in exposure to traumatic events, development of post-traumatic stress disorder, and treatment-seeking for post-traumatic stress disorder in the United States. *Psychological Medicine, 41*, 71–83. http://doi.org/10.1017/S0033291710000401

Roberts, B. W., Kuncel, N. R., Shiner, R., Caspi, A., & Goldberg, L. R. (2007). The power of personality: The comparative validity of personality traits, socioeconomic status, and cognitive ability for predicting important life outcomes. *Perspectives on Psychological Science, 2*, 313–345.

Roberts, B. W., Luo, J., Briley, D. A., Chow, P. I., Su, R., & Hill, P. L. (2017). A systematic review of personality trait change through intervention. *Psychological Bulletin, 143*, 117–141. doi:10.1037/bul0000088

Roberts, C. A., Jones, A., & Montgomery, C. (2016). Meta-analysis of molecular imaging of serotonin transporters in ecstasy/polydrug users. *Neuroscience & Biobehavioral Reviews, 63* 158–167.

Roberts, N. A., & Reuber, M. (2014). Alterations of consciousness in psychogenic nonepileptic seizures: Emotion, emotion regulation and dissociation. *Epilepsy & Behavior, 30*, 43–49. doi:10.1016/j.yebeh.2013.09.035

Roberts, R., Woodman, T., & Sedikides, C. (2017). Pass me the ball: Narcissism in performance settings. *International Review of Sport and Exercise Psychology*, 1–24. doi:10.1080/1750984X.2017.1290815

Robinson, T. E., & Berridge, K. C. (1993). The neural basis of drug craving: An incentive sensitization theory of addiction. *Brain Research Reviews, 18*, 247–191.

Robinson, T. E., & Berridge, K. C. (2003). Addiction. *Annual Review of Psychology, 54*, 25–53.

Rodriguez-Seijas, C., Eaton, N. R., & Krueger, R. F. (2015). How transdiagnostic factors of personality and psychopathology can inform clinical assessment and intervention. *Journal of Personality Assessment, 97*, 425–435. doi:10.1080/00223891.2015.1055752

Roecklein, K. A., Wong, P. M., Miller, M. A., Donofry, S. D., Kamarck, M. L., & Brainard, G. C. (2013). Melanopsin, photosensitive ganglion cells, and seasonal affective disorder. *Neuroscience & Biobehavioral Reviews, 37*(3), 229–239. doi:http://dx.doi.org/10.1016/j.neubiorev.2012.12.009

Roehrig, J. P., & McLean, C. P. (2010). A comparison of stigma toward eating disorders versus depression. *International Journal of Eating Disorders, 43*, 671–674.

Roemer, L., Williston, S. K., Eustis, E. H., & Orsillo, S. M. (2013). Mindfulness and acceptance-based behavioral therapies for anxiety disorders. *Current Psychiatry Reports, 15*(11), 410. doi:10.1007/s11920-013-0410-3

Rogler, L. H., & Hollingshead, A. B. (1985). *Trapped: Families and schizophrenia* (3rd ed.). Maplewood, NJ: Waterfront Press.

Rohan, K. J., Roecklein, K. A., Tierney Lindsey, K., Johnson, L. G., Lippy, R. D., Lacy, T. J., et al. (2007). A randomized controlled trial of cognitive-behavioral therapy, light therapy, and their combination for seasonal affective disorder. *Journal of Consulting and Clinical Psychology, 75*, 489–500.

Rolon-Arroyo, B., Arnold, D. H., & Harvey, E. A. (2013). The predictive utility of conduct disorder symptoms in preschool children: A 3-year follow-up study. *Child Psychiatry and Human Development 45*, 329–337.

Romanelli, R. J., Wu, F. M., Gamba, R., Mojtabai, R., & Segal, J. B. (2014). Behavioral therapy and serotonin reuptake inhibitor pharmacotherapy in the treatment of obsessive-compulsive disorder: A systematic review and meta-analysis of head-to-head randomized controlled trials. *Depression and Anxiety, 31*(8), 641–652. doi:10.1002/da.22232

Romano, E., & Voas, R. B. (2011). Drug and alcohol involvement in four types of fatal crashes. *Journal of Studies on Alcohol and Drugs, 72*, 567–576.

Root, T. L., Pinheiro, A. P., Thornton, L., Strober, M., Fernandez-Aranda, F., Brandt, H., et al. (2010). Substance use disorders in women with anorexia nervosa. *International Journal of Eating Disorders, 43*, 14–21.

Rose, J. E., & Behm, F. M. (2014). Combination treatment with varenicline and bupropion in an adaptive smoking cessation paradigm. *American Journal of Psychiatry, 171*, 1199–1205.

Rose, J., E., Brauer, L. H., Behm, F. M., Cramblett, M. Calkins, K., & Lawhon, D. (2004). Psychopharmacological interactions between nicotine and ethanol. *Nicotine & Tobacco Research, 6*, 133–144.

Rose, J. E., Herskovic, J. E., Behm, F. M., & Westman, E. C. (2009). Precessation treatment with nicotine patch significantly increases abstinence rates relative to conventional treatment. *Nicotine and Tobacco Research, 11*, 1067–1075.

Rosenblat, J. D., Kakar, R., Berk, M., Kessing, L. V., Vinberg, M., Baune, B. T., et al. (2016). Anti-inflammatory agents in the treatment of bipolar depression: A systematic review and meta-analysis. *Bipolar Disorders, 18*(2), 89–101. doi:10.1111/bdi.12373

Rosenfarb, I. S., Goldstein, M. J., Mintz, J., & Neuchterlein, K. H. (1994). Expressed emotion and subclinical psychopathology observable within transactions between schizophrenics and their family members. *Journal of Abnormal Psychology, 104*, 259–267.

Rosen, G. M., & Davison, G. C. (2003). Psychology should list empirically supported principles of change (ESPs) and not credential trademarked therapies or other treatment packages. *Behavior Modification, 27*, 300–312.

Rosen, L. N., Targum, S. D., Terman, M., Bryant, M. J., Hoffman, H., Kasper, S. F., et al. (1990). Prevalence of seasonal affective disorder at four latitudes. *Psychiatry Research, 31*, 131–144.

Rosen, R. C., Heiman, J. R., Long, J. S., Fisher, W. A., & Sand, M. S. (2016). Men with sexual problems and their partners: Findings from the International Survey of Relationships. *Archives of Sexual Behavior, 45*, 159–173. doi:10.1007/s10508-015-0568-3

Rosen, R. C., Miner, M. M., & Wincze, J. P. (2014). Erectile dysfunction: Integration of medical and psychological approaches. In Y. M. Binik & K. S. K. Hall (Eds.), *Principles and practice of sex therapy* (5 ed., pp. 61–88). New York, NY: Guilford Press.

Rösner, S., Hackl-Herrwerth, A., Leucht, S., Lehert, P., Vecchi, S., & Soyka, M. (2010). Acamprosate for alcohol dependence. *Cochrane Database of Systematic Reviews, 9*, CD004332. http://doi.org/10.1002/14651858.CD004332.pub2

Ross, C. A. (1989). *Multiple personality disorder: Diagnosis, clinical features, and treatment.* New York, NY: John Wiley & Sons.

Ross, C. A. (1991). Epidemiology of multiple personality disorder and dissociation. *Psychiatric Clinics of North America, 14*, 503–517.

Ross, C. A., Duffy, C. M. M., & Ellason, J. W. (2002). Prevalence, reliability and validity of dissociative disorders in an inpatient setting. *Journal of Trauma and Dissociation, 3*, 7–17.

Rossello, J., Bernal, G., & Rivera-Medina, C. (2008). Individual and group CBT and IPT for Puerto Rican adolescents with depressive symptoms. *Cultural Diversity and Ethnic Minority Psychology, 14*, 234–245.

Rossiter, E. M., & Agras, W. S. (1990). An empirical test of the DSM-IIIR definition of binge. *International Journal of Eating Disorders, 9*, 513–518.

Rothbaum, B. O., Foa, E. B., Murdock, T., Riggs, D. S., & Walsh, W. (1992). A prospective examination of posttraumatic stress disorder in rape victims. *Journal of Traumatic Stress, 5*, 455–475.

Roughgarden, J. (2004). Evolution's rainbow: Diversity, gender and sexuality in nature and people. Oakland, CA: University of California Press.

Rouleau, C. R., & von Ranson, K. M. (2011). Potential risks of pro-eating disorder websites. *Clinical Psychology Review, 31*, 525–531.

Rowland, D. L., Adamski, B. A., Neal, C. J., Myers, A. L., & Burnett, A. L. (2015). Self-efficacy as a relevant construct in understanding sexual response and dysfunction. *Journal of Sex & Marital Therapy, 41*, 60–71. doi:10.1080/0092623X.2013.811453

Rubin, D. C., Berntsen, D., & Bohni, M. K. (2008). A memory-based model of posttraumatic stress disorder: Evaluating basic assumptions underlying the PTSD diagnosis. *Psychological Review, 115*, 985–1011.

Rubinstein, T. B., McGinn, A. P., Wildman, R. P., & Wylie-Rosett, J. (2010). Disordered eating in adulthood is associated with reported weight loss attempts in childhood. *International Journal of Eating Disorders, 43*, 663–666.

Ruderfer, D. M., Fanous, A. H., Ripke, S., McQuillin, A., Amdur, R. L., Gejman, P. V., et al. (2013). Polygenic dissection of diagnosis and clinical dimensions of bipolar disorder and schizophrenia. *Molecular Psychiatry, 19*, 1017–1024. doi: 10.1038/mp.2013.138

Rummel-Kluge, C., Komossa, K., Schwarz, S., Hunger, H., Schmid, F., Lobos, C. A., et al. (2010). Head-to-head comparisons of metabolic side effects of second generation antipsychotics in the treatment of schizophrenia: A systematic review and meta-analysis. *Schizophrenia Research, 123*, 225–233.

Ruscio, A. M., Brown, T. A., Chiu, W. T., Sareen, J., Stein, M. B., & Kessler, R. C. (2008). Social fears and social phobia in the USA: Results from the National Comorbidity Survey Replication. *Psychological Medicine, 38*, 15–28.

Ruscio, A. M., Hallion, L. S., Lim, C. C., Aguilar-Gaxiola, S., Al-Hamzawi, A., Alonso, J., et al. (2017). Cross-sectional comparison of the epidemiology of DSM-5 generalized anxiety disorder across the globe. *JAMA Psychiatry.* doi:10.1001/jamapsychiatry.2017.0056

Ruscio, A. M., Stein, D. J., Chiu, W. T., & Kessler, R. C. (2010). The epidemiology of obsessive-compulsive disorder in the national comorbidity survey replication. *Molecular Psychiatry, 15*(1), 53–63.

Rush, A. J., Trivedi, M., Wisniewski, S. R., Nierenberg, A. A., Stewart, J. W., Warden, D., et al. (2006). Acute and longer-term outcomes in depressed outpatients requiring one or several treatment steps: A STAR-D report. *American Journal of Psychiatry, 163*, 1905–1917.

Rush, A. J., Trivedi, M., Wisniewski, S. R., Nierenberg, A. A., Stewart, J. W., Warden, D., et al. (2006). Acute and longer-term outcomes in depressed outpatients requiring one or several treatment steps: A STAR*D report. *American Journal of Psychiatry, 163*, 1905–1917.

Rutter, M., Caspi, A., Fergusson, D., Horwood, L. J., Goodman, R., Maughan, B., Moffitt, T. E., Meltzer, H., & Carroll, J. (2004). Sex differences in developmental reading disability: New findings from 4 epidemiological studies. *Journal of the American Medical Association, 291*, 2007–2012.

Rutter, M., & Silberg, J. (2002). Gene-environment interplay in relation to emotional and behavioral disturbance. *Annual Review of Psychology, 53*, 463–490.

Ryder, A. G., Dere, J., Sun, J., & Chentsova-Dutton, Y. E. (2014). The cultural shaping of personality disorder. In F. T. L. Leong, L. Comas-Díaz, G. C. Nagayama Hall, V. C. McLoyd, & J. E. Trimble (Eds.), *APA handbook of multicultural psychology, vol. 2: Applications and training* (pp. 307–328. Washington, DC: American Psychological Association.

Saad, L. (2015, July 29). Americans' coffee consumption is steady, few want to cut back. Retrieved from http://www.gallup.com/poll/184388/americans-coffee-consumption-steady-few-cut-back.aspx)

Sabo, S. Z., Nelson, M. L., Fisher, C., Gunzerath, L., Brody, C. L., et al. (1999). A genetic association for cigarette smoking behavior. *Health Psychology, 18*, 7–13.

Sackeim, H. A., & Lisanby, S. H. (Eds.). (2001). *Physical treatments in psychiatry: Advances in electroconvulsive therapy, transcranial magnetic stimulation, and vagus nerve stimulation.* Washington, DC: American Psychiatric Publishing.

Sackeim, H. A., Prudic, J., Fuller, R., Keilp, J., Lavori, P. W., & Olfson, M. (2007). The cognitive effects of electroconvulsive therapy in community settings. *Neuropsychopharmacology, 32*, 244–254.

Sacks, F. M., Bray, G. A., Carey, V. J., Smith, S. R., Ryan, D. H., Anton, S. D., et al. (2009). Comparison of weight-loss diets with different compositions of fat, protein, and carbohydrates. *New England Journal of Medicine, 360*, 859–873.

Sacks, O. (1995). *An anthropologist on Mars.* New York, NY: Knopf.

Saczynski, J. S. D., & Inouye, S. K. (2015). Delirium. In D. C. Steffens, D. G. Blazer, & M. E. Thakur (Eds.), *The American Psychiatric Publishing Textbook of Geriatric Psychiatry.* Washington, DC: APA.

Saha, S., Chant, D., & McGrath, J. (2007). A systematic review of mortality in schizophrenia: Is the differential mortality gap worsening over time? *Archives of General Psychiatry, 64*, 1123–1131.

Sakel, M. (1938). The pharmacological shock treatment of schizophrenia. *Nervous and Mental Disease Monograph, 62.*

Saks, E. R. (1997). *Jekyll on trial: Multiple personality disorder and criminal law.* New York, NY: New York University Press.

Saks, E. R. (2007). *The center cannot hold: My journey through madness.* New York, NY: Hyperion.

Salamone, J. D. (2000). A critique of recent studies on placebo effects of antidepressants: Importance of research on active placebos. *Psychopharmacology, 152*, 1–6.

Salamone, J. D., & Correa, M. (2012). The mysterious motivational functions of mesolimbic dopamine. *Neuron, 76*, 470–485.

Salem, J. E., & Kring, A. M. (1998). The role of gender differences in the reduction of etiologic heterogeneity in schizophrenia. *Clinical Psychology Review, 18*, 795–819.

Salkovskis, P. M. (1996). Cognitive-behavioral approaches to understanding obsessional problems. In R. M. Rapee (Ed.), *Current controversies in anxiety disorders.* New York, NY: Guilford Press.

Salter, D., McMillan, D., Richards, M., Talbot, T., Hodges, J., Bentovim, A., et al. (2003). Development of sexually abusive behaviour in sexually victimised males: A longitudinal study. *Lancet, 361*, 471–476.

Samuel, D. B., Sanislow, C. A., Hopwood, C. J., Shea, M. T., Skodol, A. E., Morey, L. C., et al. (2013). Convergent and incremental predictive validity of clinician, self-report, and structured interview diagnoses for personality disorders over 5 years. *Journal of Consulting and Clinical Psychology, 81*, 650–659.

Samuels, J., Eaton, W. W., Bienvenu, O. J., 3rd, Brown, C. H., Costa, P. T., Jr, & Nestadt, G. (2002). Prevalence and correlates of personality disorders in a community sample. *British Journal of Psychiatry, 180*, 536–542.

Samuels, J. F. (2009). Recent advances in the genetics of obsessive-compulsive disorder. *Current Psychiatry Reports, 11*, 277–282.

Samuels, J. F., Bienvenu, O. J., 3rd, Pinto, A., Fyer, A. J., McCracken, J. T., Rauch, S. L., et al. (2007). Hoarding in obsessive-compulsive disorder: Results from the OCD Collaborative Genetics Study. *Behaviour Research and Therapy, 45*, 673–686.

Samus, Q. M., Johnston, D., Black, B. S., Hess, E., Lyman, C., Vavilikolanu, A., et al. (2014). A multidimensional home-based care coordination intervention for elders with memory disorders: The maximizing independence at home (MIND) pilot randomized trial. *American Journal of Geriatric Psychiatry, 22*, 398–414. doi:10.1016/j.jagp.2013.12.175

Sanders, S. J., He, X., Willsey, A. J., Ercan-Sencicek, A. G., Samocha, K. E., Cicek, A. E., et al. (2015). Insights into autism spectrum disorder genomic architecture and biology from 71 risk loci. *Neuron, 87*(6), 1215–1233. http://doi.org/10.1016/j.neuron.2015.09.016

Sansone, R. A., & Sansone, L. A. (2011). Personality disorders: A nation-based perspective on prevalence. *Innovations in Clinical Neuroscience, 8*, 13–18.

Santtila, P., Antfolk, J., Räfså, A., Hartwig, M., Sariola, H., Sandnabba, N. K., & Mokros, A. (2015). Men's sexual interest in children: One-year incidence and correlates in a population-based sample of Finnish male twins. *Journal of Child Sexual Abuse, 24*, 115–134. doi:10.1080/10538712.2015.997410

Sara, S. J. (2009). The locus coeruleus and noradrenergic modulation of cognition. *Nature Reviews Neuroscience, 10*, 211–223.

Sarginson, J., Webb, R. T., Stocks, S. J., Esmail, A., Garg, S., & Ashcroft, D. M. (2017). Temporal trends in antidepressant prescribing to children in UK primary care, 2000–2015. *Journal of Affective Disorders, 210*, 312–318.

Sarpal, D. K., Argyelan, M., Robinson, D. G., Szeszko, P. R., Karlsgodt, K. H., John, M., et al. (2016). Baseline striatal functional connectivity as a predictor of response to antipsychotic drug treatment. *American Journal of Psychiatry, 173*, 69–77.http://doi.org/10.1176/appi.ajp.2015.14121571

Sartorius, N., Jablensky, A., Korten, A., Ernberg, G., Anker, M., Cooper, J. E., et al. (1986). Early manifestations and first-contact incidence of schizophrenia in different cultures: A preliminary report on the initial evaluation phase of the WHO Collaborative Study on Determinants of Outcome of Severe Mental Disorders. *Psychological Medicine, 16*, 909–928.

Sar, V., Akyuz, G., & Dogan, O. (2007). Prevalence of dissociative disorders among women in the general population. *Psychiatry Research, 149*, 169–176.

Satizabal, C. L., Beiser, A. S., Chouraki, V., Chêne, G., Dufouil, C., & Seshadri, S. (2016). Incidence of dementia over three decades in the Framingham Heart Study. *New England Journal of Medicine, 374*, 523–532. doi:10.1056/NEJMoa1504327

Saveanu, R., Etkin, A., Duchemin, A. M., Goldstein-Piekarski, A., Gyurak, A., Debattista, C., et al. (2015). The international study to predict optimized treatment in depression (iSPOT-D). Outcomes from the acute phase of antidepressant treatment. *Journal of Psychiatric Research, 61*, 1–12. doi:10.1016/j.jpsychires.2014.12.018

Saxena, S. (2015). Pharmacotherapy of compulsive hoarding. In R. O. Frost & G. Steketee (Eds.), *The Oxford handbook of hoarding and acquiring*. Oxford, England: Oxford University Press.

Sayette, M. A., Creswell, K. G., Dimoff, J. D., Fairbairn, C. E., Cohn, J. F., Heckman, B. W., et al. (2012). Alcohol and group formation. *Psychological Science, 23*, 869–878. http://doi.org/10.1177/0956797611435134

Sayette, M. C. (2017). The effects of alcohol on emotion in social drinkers. *Behaviour Research and Therapy, 88*, 76–89.

Schaefer, J. D., Caspi, A., Belsky, D. W., Harrington, H., Houts, R., Horwood, L. J., et al. (2017). Enduring mental health: Prevalence and prediction. *Journal of Abnormal Psychology, 126*(2), 212–224. doi:10.1037/abn0000232

Schecter, R., & Grether, J. K. (2008). Continuing increases in autism reported to California's Developmental Services System. *Archives of General Psychiatry, 65*, 19–24.

Scherk, H., Pajonk, F. G., & Leucht, S. (2007). Second-generation antipsychotic agents in the treatment of acute mania: A systematic review and meta-analysis of randomized controlled trials. *Archives of General Psychiatry, 64*, 442–455.

Schilder, P. (1953). *Medical psychology*. New York, NY: International Universities Press.

Schmaal, L., Veltman, D. J., van Erp, T. G. M., Samann, P. G., Frodl, T., Jahanshad, N., et al. (2016). Subcortical brain alterations in major depressive disorder: Findings from the enigma major depressive disorder working group. *Molecular Psychiatry, 21*(6), 806–812. doi:10.1038/mp.2015.69

Schmidt, N. B., Zvolensky, M. J., & Maner, J. K. (2006). Anxiety sensitivity: Prospective prediction of panic attacks and Axis I pathology. *Journal of Psychiatric Research, 40*(8), 691–699. doi:http://doi.org/10.1016/j.jpsychires.2006.07.009

Schmid, Y., Enzler, F., Gasser, P., Grouzmann, E., Preller, K. H., Vollenweider, F. X., et al. (2015). Acute effects of lysergic acid diethylamide in healthy subjects. *Biological Psychiatry, 78*, 544–553.

Schmitz, A., & Grillon, C. (2012). Assessing fear and anxiety in humans using the threat of predictable and unpredictable aversive events (the NPU-threat test). *NatureProtocols, 7*(3), 527–532. doi:http://www.nature.com/nprot/journal/v7/n3/abs/nprot.2012.001.html#supplementary-information

Schnab, D. W., & Trinh, N. G. (2004). Do artificial food colors promote hyperactivity in children with hyperactive syndromes? A meta-analysis of double-blind placebo-controlled trials. *Journal of Developmental and Behavioral Pediatrics, 25*, 425–434.

Schnack, H. G., van Haren, N. E. M., Nieuwenhuis, M., Hulshoff Pol, H. E., Cahn, W., & Kahn, R. S. (2016). Accelerated brain aging in schizophrenia: A longitudinal pattern recognition study. *American Journal of Psychiatry, 173*, 607–616. http://doi.org/10.1176/appi.ajp.2015.15070922

Schopler, E., Short, A., & Mesibov, G. (1989). Relation of behavioral treatment to "normal functioning": Comment on Lovaas. *Journal of Consulting and Clinical Psychology, 57*, 162–164.

Schramm, E., Kriston, L., Zobel, I., & et al. (2017). Effect of disorder-specific vs nonspecific psychotherapy for chronic depression: A randomized clinical trial. *JAMA Psychiatry, 74*(3), 233–242. doi:10.1001/jamapsychiatry.2016.3880

Schreiber, F. L. (1973). *Sybil*. Chicago, IL: Regnery.

Schuckit, M. A., Daeppen, J. B., Tipp, J. E., Hesselbrock, M., & Bucholz, K. K. (1998). The clinical course of alcohol-relatedproblems in alcohol dependent and nonalcohol dependent drinking women and men. *Journal of Studies on Alcohol, 59*, 581–590.

Schumacher, J. E., Milby, J. B., Wallace, D., Meehan, D. C., Kertesz, S., et al. (2007). Meta-analysis of day treatment and contingency-management dismantling research: Birmingham homeless cocaine studies (1990–2005). *Journal of Consulting and Clinical Psychology, 75, 823–828.*

Schwab, S. G., & Wildenauer, D. B. (2013). Genetics of psychiatric disorders in the GWAS era: An update on schizophrenia. *European Archives of Psychiatry and Clinical Neuroscience, 263*, 147–154. http://doi.org/10.1007/s00406-013-0450-z

Schwartz, M. B., Chambliss, O. H., Brownell, K. D., Blair, S., & Billington, C. (2003). Weight bias among health professionals specializing in obesity. *Obesity Research, 11*, 1033–1039.

Scott, K. M., Lim, C., Al-Hamzawi, A., Alonso, J., Bruffaerts, R., Caldas-de-Almeida, J. M., et al. (2016). Association of mental disorders with subsequent chronic physical conditions: World mental health surveys from 17 countries. *JAMA Psychiatry, 73*(2), 150–158. doi:10.1001/jamapsychiatry.2015.2688

Scott, L. N., Wright, A. G. C., Beeney, J. E., Lazarus, S. A., Pilkonis, P. A., & Stepp, S. D. (2017). Borderline personality disorder symptoms and aggression: A within-person process model. *Journal of Abnormal Psychology, 126*, 429–440. doi:10.1037/abn0000272

Searles, J. (2013, October 10). Getting into the spirit. *The New York Times*, p. TR10.

Sebaaly, J. C., Cox, S., Hughes, C. M., Kennedy, M. L. H., & Garris, S. S. (2013). Use of fluoxetine in anorexia nervosa before and after weight restoration. *The Annals of Pharmacotherapy, 47*, 1201–1205. http://doi.org/10.1177/1060028013503127

Seedat, S., Scott, K. M., Angermeyer, M., Berglund, P., Bromet, E., Brugha, T., et al. (2009). Cross-national associations between gender and mental disorders in the World Health Organization World Mental Health Surveys. *Archives of General Psychiatry, 66*, 785–795.

Seeman, P. (2013). Schizophrenia and dopamine receptors. *European Neuropsychopharmacology, 23*, 999–1009.

Segal, J. Z. (2015). The rhetoric of female sexual dysfunction: Faux feminism and the FDA. *Canadian Medical Association Journal, 187*, 915–916. doi:10.1503/cmaj.150363

Segal, Z. V. V., Kennedy, S., Gemar, M., Hood, K., Pedersen, R., & Buis, T. (2006). Cognitive reactivity to sad mood provocation and the prediction of depressive relapse. *Archives of General Psychiatry, 63*, 749–755.

Segal, Z. V., Williams, J. M. G., & Teasdale, J. D. (2003). Mindfulness-based cognitive therapy for depression: A new approach to preventing relapse. *Psychotherapy Research, 13*, 123–125.

Segal, Z. V., Williams, J. M., & Teasdale, J. D. (2001). *Mindfulness-based cognitive therapy for depression.* New York, NY: Guilford Press.

Segerstrom, S. C., & Miller, G. E. (2004). Psychological stress and the immune system: A meta-analytic study of 30 years of inquiry. *Psychological Bulletin, 130*, 601–630.

Segraves, R. T. (2010). Considerations for an evidence-based definition of premature ejaculation in the DSM-V. *Journal of Sexual Medicine, 7*, 672–679.

Seidler, G. H., & Wagner, F. E. (2006). Comparing the efficacy of EMDR and trauma-focused cognitive-behavioral therapy in the treatment of PTSD: A meta-analytic study. *Psychological Medicine, 36*, 1515–1522.

Seidman, L. J., Shapiro, D. I., Stone, W. S., Woodberry, K. A., Ronzio, A., Cornblatt, B. A., et al. (2016). Association of neurocognition with transition to psychosis: Baseline functioning in the second phase of the North American Prodrome Longitudinal Study. *JAMA Psychiatry, 73*, 1239–1248. http://doi.org/10.1001/jamapsychiatry.2016.2479

Sekar, A., Bialas, A. R., de Rivera, H., Davis, A., Hammond, T. R., Kamitaki, N., et al. (2016). Schizophrenia risk from complex variation of complement component 4. *Nature, 530*, 177–183. http://doi.org/10.1038/nature16549

Selby, E. A., Wonderlich, S. A., Crosby, R. D., Engel, S. G., Panza, E., Mitchell, J. E., et al. (2013). Nothing tastes as good as thin feels: Low positive emotion differentiation and weight-loss activities in anorexia nervosa. *Clinical Psychological Science, 2*, 514–531. doi: 10.1177/2167702613512794.

Seligman, M. E., Maier, S. F., & Geer, J. H. (1968). Alleviation of learned helplessness in the dog. *Journal of Abnormal Psychology, 73*, 256–262.

Seligman, M. E. P. (1971). Phobias and preparedness. *Behavior Therapy, 2*, 307–320.

Seligman, R., & Kirmayer, L. J. (2008). Dissociative experience and cultural neuroscience: Narrative, metaphor and mechanism. *Culture, Medicine and Psychiatry, 32*, 31–64. http://doi.org/10.1007/s11013-007-9077-8

Selling, L. S. (1940). *Men against madness.* New York, NY: Greenberg.

Selvaraj, S., Hoshi, R., Bhagwagar, Z., Murthy, N. V., Hinz, R., Cowen, P., et al. (2009). Brain serotonin transporter binding in former users of MDMA ("ecstasy"). *British Journal of Psychiatry, 194*, 355–359. http://doi.org/10.1192/bjp.bp.108.050344

Selwood, A., Johnson, K., Katona, C., Ilyketsos, C., & Livingson, G. (2007). Systematic review of the effect of psychological interventions on family caregivers of people with dementia. *Journal of Affective Disorders, 101*, 75–89.

Selye, H. (1950). *The physiology and pathology of exposure to stress.* Montreal, QC: Acta.

Sensky, T., Turkington, D., Kingdon, D., et al. (2000). A randomized controlled trial of cognitive-behavioural therapy for persistent symptoms in schizophrenia resistant to medication. *Archives of General Psychiatry, 57*, 165–172.

Seto, M. C., & Eke, A. W. (2017). Correlates of admitted sexual interest in children among individuals convicted of child pornography offenses. *Law and Human Behavior, 41*, 305–313. doi:10.1037/lhb0000240

Sewell, R. A., Poling, J., & Sofuoglu, M. (2009). The effect of cannabis compared with alcohol on driving. *American Journal on Addictions, 18*, 185–193. http://doi.org/10.1080/10550490902786934

Shackman, A. J., & Fox, A. S. (2016). Contributions of the central extended amygdala to fear and anxiety. *The Journal of Neuroscience, 36*(31), 8050–8063. doi:10.1523/jneurosci.0982-16.2016

Shackman, A. J., Salomons, T. V., Slagter, H. A., Fox, A. S., Winter, J. J., & Davidson, R. J. (2011). The integration of negative affect, pain and cognitive control in the cingulate cortex. *Nature Reviews Neuroscience, 12*, 154–167.

Shapiro, F. (1999). Eye movement desensitization and reprocessing (EMDR) and the anxiety disorders: Clinical and research implications of an integrated psychotherapy treatment. *Journal of Anxiety Disorders, 13*, 35–67.

Shapiro, J. R., Berkman, N. D., Brownley, K. A., Sedway, J. A., Lohr, K. N., & Bulik, C. M. (2007). Bulimia nervosa treatment: A systematic review of randomized controlled trials. *International Journal of Eating Disorders, 40*, 321–336. http://doi.org/10.1002/eat.20372

Sharp, C., Wright, A. G. C., Fowler, J. C., Frueh, B. C., Allen, J. G., Oldham, J., & Clark, L. A. (2015). The structure of personality pathology: Both general ("g") and specific ("s") factors? *Journal of Abnormal Psychology, 124*, 387–398. doi:10.1037/abn0000033

Shaw, D. S., Dishion, T. J., Supplee, L., Gardner, F., & Arnds, K. (2006). Randomized trial of a family-centered approach to the prevention of early conduct problems: 2-year effects of the family check-up in early childhood. *Journal of Consulting and Clinical Psychology, 74*, 1–9.

Shaywitz, B. A., Shaywitz, S. E., Pugh, K. R., Mencl, W. E., Fulbright, R. K., Skudlarski, P., et al. (2002). Disruption of posterior brain systems for reading in children with developmental dyslexia. *Biological Psychiatry, 52*, 101–110. doi:10.1016/S0006-3223(02)01365-3

Shea, M. T., Stout, R., Gunderson, J., Morey, L. C., Grilo, C. M., McGlashan, T., et al. (2002). Short-term diagnostic stability of schizotypal, borderline, avoidant, and obsessive-compulsive personality disorders. *American Journal of Psychiatry, 159*(12), 2036–2041.

Sheets, E. S., & Craighead, W. E. (2014). Comparing chronic interpersonal and noninterpersonal stress domains as predictors of depression recurrence in emerging adults. *Behaviour Research and Therapy, 63*, 36–42. doi:http://dx.doi.org/10.1016/j.brat.2014.09.001

Shenk, D. (2010). *The genius is in all of us: Why everything you've been told about genetics, talent, and IQ is wrong.* New York, NY: Doubleday.

Sher, K. J., Grekin, E. R., & Williams, N. A. (2005). The development of alcohol use disorders. *Annual Review of Clinical Psychology, 1*, 493–523.

Sher, K. J., Walitzer, K. S., Wood, P. K., & Brent, E. F. (1991). Characteristics of children of alcoholics: Putative risk factors, substance use and abuse, and psychopathology. *Journal of Abnormal Psychology, 100*, 427–448.

Sher, K. J., Wood, M. D., Wood, P. K., & Raskin, G. (1996). Alcohol outcome expectancies and alcohol use: A latent variable cross-lagged panel study. *Journal of Abnormal Psychology, 105*, 561–574.

Shic, F., Macari, S., & Chawarska, K. (2014). Speech disturbs face scanning in 6-month-old infants who develop autism spectrum disorder. *Biological Psychiatry, 75*(3), 231–237.

Shields, G. S., Bonner, J. C., & Moons, W. G. (2015). Does cortisol influence core executive functions? A meta-analysis of acute cortisol administration effects on working memory, inhibition, and set-shifting. *Psychoneuroendocrinology, 58*, 91–103. doi:10.1016/j.psyneuen.2015.04.017

Shields, G. S., Sazma, M. A., McCullough, A. M., & Yonelinas, A. P. (2017). The effects of acute stress on episodic memory: A meta-analysis and integrative review. *Psychological Bulletin, 143*, 636–675. doi:10.1037/bul0000100

Shiffman, S., Gwaltney, C. J., Balabanis, M. H., Liu, K. S., Paty, J. A., Kassel, J. D., Hickcox, M., & Gnys, M. (2002). Immediate antecedents of cigarette smoking: An analysis from ecological momentary assessment. *Journal of Abnormal Psychology, 111*, 531–545.

Shiffman, S., Paty, J. A., Gwaltney, C. J., & Dang, Q. (2004). Immediate antecedents of cigarette smoking: An analysis of unrestricted smoking patterns. *Journal of Abnormal Psychology, 113*, 166–171.

Shiffman, S., & Waters, A. J. (2004). Negative affect and smoking lapses: A prospective analysis. *Journal of Consulting and Clinical Psychology, 72*, 192–201.

Shifren, J. L., Monz, B. U., Russo, P. A., Segreti, A., & Johannes, C. B. (2008). Sexual problems and distress in United States women: Prevalence and correlates. *Obstetrics and Gynecology, 112*, 970–978.

Shiner, B., D'Avolio, L. W., Nguyen, T. M., Zayed, M. H., Young-Xu, Y., Desai, R. A., et al. (2013). Measuring use of evidence-based psychotherapy for posttraumatic stress disorder. *Administration and Policy in Mental Health, 40*(4), 311–318. doi:10.1007/s10488-012-0421-0

Shin, M., Besser, L. M., Kucik, J. E., Lu, C., Siffel, C., & Correa, A. (2009). Prevalence of Down syndrome among children and adolescents in 10 regions of the United States. *Pediatrics, 124*, 1565–1571.

Shungin, D., Winkler, T. W., Croteau-Chonka, D. C., Ferreira, T., Locke, A. E., Magi, R., et al. (2015). New genetic loci link adipose and insulin biology to body fat distribution. *Nature, 518*, 187–196. http://doi.org/10.1038/nature14132

Siegel, S. J., Irani, F., Brensinger, C. M., Kohler, C. G., Bilker, W. B., Ragland, J. D., et al. (2006). Prognostic variables at intake and long-term level of function in schizophrenia. *American Journal of Psychiatry, 163,* 433–441.

Sigman, M. (1994). What are the core deficits in autism? In S. H. Broman & J. Grafman (Eds.), *Atypical cognitive deficits in developmental disorders: Implications for brain function* (pp. 139–157). Hillsdale, NJ: Erlbaum.

Silove, D., Alonso, J., Bromet, E., Gruber, M., Sampson, N., Scott, K., et al. (2015). Pediatric-onset and adult-onset separation anxiety disorder across countries in the World Mental Health Survey. *American Journal of Psychiatry, 172*(7), 647–656. http://doi.org/10.1176/appi.ajp.2015.14091185

Silverman, K., Higgins, S. T., Brooner, R. K., Montoya, I. D., Cone, E. J., Schuster, C. R., & Preston, K. I. (1996). Sustained cocaine abstinence in methadone maintenance patients through voucher-based reinforcement therapy. *Archives of General Psychiatry, 53,* 409–413.

Simeon, D. (2009). Depersonalization disorder. In P. F. Dell & J. A. O'Neil (Eds.), *Dissociation and dissociative disorders: DSM-5 and beyond* (pp. 441–442). New York, NY: Routledge.

Simeon, D., Gross, S., Guralnik, O., Stein, D. J., Schmeidler, J., & Hollander, E. (1997). Feeling unreal: 30 cases of DSM-III-R depersonalization disorder. *American Journal of Psychiatry, 154,* 1107–1112.

Simeon, D., Knutelska, M., Nelson, D., & Guralnik, O. (2003). Feeling unreal: Depersonalization disorder update of 117 cases. *Journal of Clinical Psychiatry, 64,* 990–997.

Simmons, J. P., Nelson, L. D., & Simonsohn, U. (2011). False-positive psychology. *Psychological Science, 22*(11), 1359–1366. doi:10.1177/0956797611417632

Simon, W. (2009). Follow-up psychotherapy outcome of patients with dependent, avoidant and obsessive-compulsive personality disorders: A meta-analytic review. *International Journal of Psychiatry in Clinical Practice, 13,* 153–165.

Singh-Manoux, A., Dugravot, A., Fournier, A., et al. (2017). Trajectories of depressive symptoms before diagnosis of dementia: A 28-year follow-up study. *JAMA Psychiatry, 74,* 712–718. doi:10.1001/jamapsychiatry.2017.0660

Singh, M. K., & Gotlib, I. H. (2014). The neuroscience of depression: Implications for assessment and intervention. *Behaviour Research and Therapy, 62,* 60–73. doi:10.1016/j.brat.2014.08.008

Singh, S. P., Harley, K., & Suhail, K. (2013). Cultural specificity of emotional overinvolvement: A systematic review. *Schizophrenia Bulletin, 39,* 449–463.

Siok, W. T., Perfetti, C. A., Lin, Z., & Tan, L. H. (2004). Biological abnormality of impaired reading is constrained by culture. *Nature, 431,* 71–76.

Skeem, J. L., & Monahan, J. (2011). Current directions in violence risk assessment. *Current Directions in Psychological Science, 20,* 38–42.

Skinner, A. C., & Skelton, J. A. (2014). Prevalence and trends in obesity and severe obesity among children in the United States, 1999–2012. *Journal of the American Medical Association, Pediatrics, 168,* 561-566.

Skodol, A. E., Oldham, J. M., Hyler, S. E., Stein, D. J., Hollander, E., Gallaher, P. E., et al. (1995). Patterns of anxiety and personality disorder comorbidity. *Journal of Psychiatric Research, 29,* 361–374.

Slade, T., Chapman, C., Swift, W., Keyes, K., Tonks, Z., & Teesson, M. (2016). Birth cohort trends in the global epidemiology of alcohol use and alcohol-related harms in men and women: Systematic review and metaregression. *BMJ Open, 6,* e011827. http://doi.org/10.1136/bmjopen-2016-011827

Slater, E. (1961). The thirty-fifth Maudsley lecture: Hysteria 311. *Journal of Mental Science, 107,* 358–381.

Slavich, G. M., & Irwin, M. R. (2014). From stress to inflammation and major depressive disorder: A social signal transduction theory of depression. *Psychological Bulletin, 140,* 774–815.

Slevec, J. H., & Tiggemann, M. (2011). Predictors of body dissatisfaction and disordered eating in middle-aged women. *Clinical Psychology Review, 31,* 515–524.

Smart, R. G., & Ogburne, A. C. (2000). Drug use and drinking among students in 36 countries. *Addictive Behaviors, 25,* 455–460.

Smith, D. (2012). *Monkey mind.* New York, NY: Simon & Schuster.

Smith, D. G., & Robbins, T. W. (2013). The neurobiological underpinnings of obesity and binge eating: A rationale for adopting the Food Addiction Model. *Biological Psychiatry, 73,* 804–810.

Smith, G. T., Goldman, M. S., Greenbaum, P. E., & Christiansen, B. A. (1995). Expectancy for social facilitation from drinking: The divergent paths of high expectancy and low expectancy adolescents. *Journal of Abnormal Psychology, 104,* 32–40.

Smith, M. L., Glass, G. V., & Miller, T. I. (1980). *The benefits of psychotherapy.* Baltimore, MD: Johns Hopkins University Press.

Smith, P. J., Blumenthal, J. A., Hoffman, B. M., Cooper, H., Strauman, T. A., Welsh-Bohmer, K., et al. (2010). Aerobic exercise and neurocognitive performance: A meta-analytic review of randomized controlled trials. *Psychosomatic Medicine, 72,* 239–252. doi:10.1097/PSY.0b013e3181d14633

Smith, S. F., & Lilienfeld, S. O. (2013). Psychopathy in the workplace: The knowns and unknowns. *Aggression and Violent Behavior, 18,* 204–218.

Smith, S. F., & Lilienfeld, S. O. (2015). The response modulation hypothesis of psychopathy: A meta-analytic and narrative analysis. *Psychological Bulletin 141,* 1145–1177. doi:10.1037/bul0000024

Smith, T., Groen, A., & Wynn, J. W. (2000). Randomized trial of intensive early intervention for children with pervasive developmental disorder. *Research in Developmental Disabilities, 21,* 297–309.

Smoller, J. W. (2016). The genetics of stress-related disorders: PTSD, depression, and anxiety disorders. *Neuropsychopharmacology: Official publication of the American College of Neuropsychopharmacology, 41*(1), 297–319. doi:10.1038/npp.2015.266

Smoski, M. J., & Areán, P. A. (2015). Individual and group psychotherapy. In D. C. Steffens, D. G. Blazer, & M. E. Thakur (Eds.), *The American Psychiatric Publishing Textbook of Geriatric Psychiatry.* Washington, DC: APA.

Smyth, J., Wonderlich, S. A., Heron, K. E., Sliwinski, M. J., Crosby, R. D., et al. (2007). Daily and momentary mood and stress are associated with binge eating and vomiting in bulimia nervosa patients in the natural environment. *Journal of Consulting and Clinical Psychology, 75,* 629–638.

Sniekers, S., Stringer, S., Watanabe, K., Jansen, P. R., Coleman, J. R. I., Krapohl, E., et al. (2017). Genome-wide association meta-analysis of 78,308 individuals identifies new loci and genes influencing human intelligence. *Nature Genetics, 11,* 201. http://doi.org/10.1038/ng.3869

Snowden, L. R. (2012). Health and mental health policies' role in better understanding and closing African American–White American disparities in treatment access and quality of care. *American Psychologist, 67*(7), 524–531. doi:10.1037/a0030054

Snowling, M. J., & Hulme, C. (2011). Evidence-based interventions for reading and language difficulties: Creating a virtuous circle. *British Journal of Educational Psychology, 81*(1), 1–23. http://doi.org/10.1111/j.2044-8279.2010.02014.x

Snowling, M. J., & Melby-Lervåg, M. (2016). Oral language deficits in familial dyslexia: A meta-analysis and review. *Psychological Bulletin, 142*(5), 498–545. http://dx.doi.org/10.1037/bul0000037

Snyder, D. K., Castellani, A. M., & Whisman, M. A. (2006). Current status and future directions in couple therapy. *Annual Review of Psychology, 57,* 317–344.

Snyder, S. H. (1996). *Drugs and the brain.* New York: Scientific American Library 18.

Sobell, L. C., & Sobell, M. B. (1996). *Timeline Followback user's guide: A calendar method for assessing alcohol and drug use.* Toronto, Canada: Addiction Research Foundation.

Sobell, L. C., Sobell, M. B., & Agrawal, S. (2009). Randomized controlled trial of a cognitive-behavioral motivational intervention in a group versus individual format for substance use disorders. *Psychology of Addictive Behaviors: Journal of the Society of Psychologists in Addictive Behaviors, 23,* 672–683.

Sobell, M. B., & Sobell, L. C. (1993). *Problem drinkers: Guided self-change treatment.* New York, NY: Guilford Press.

Sofi, F., Valecchi, D., Bacci, D., Abbate, R., Gensini, G. F., Casini, A., et al. (2011). Physical activity and risk of cognitive decline: A meta-analysis of prospective studies. *Journal of Internal Medicine, 269,* 107–117.

Soto, C. J., & John, O. P. (2016). The Next Big Five Inventory (BFI-2): Developing and assessing a hierarchical model with 15 facets to enhance bandwidth, fidelity, and predictive power. *Journal of Personality and Social Psychology.* http://doi.org/10.1037/pspp0000096

Spencer, S. J., Steele, C. M., & Quinn, D. M. (1999). Stereotype threat and women's math performance. *Journal of Experimental Social Psychology, 35*, 4–28.

Spencer, T., Biederman, J., Wilens, T., Harding, M., O'Donnell, D., & Griffin, S. (1996). Pharmacotherapy of attention-deficit hyperactivity disorder across the life cycle. *Journal of the American Academy of Child and Adolescent Psychiatry, 35*, 409–432.

Spence, S. H., & Rapee, R. M. (2016). The etiology of social anxiety disorder: An evidence-based model. *Expanding the Impact of Cognitive Behaviour Therapy: A Special Edition in Honor of G. Terence Wilson, 86*, 50–67.

Sperling, R. A., Aisen, P. S., Beckett, L. A., Bennett, D. A., Craft, S., Fagan, A. M., et al. (2011). Toward defining the preclinical stages of Alzheimer's disease: Recommendations from the National Institute on Aging-Alzheimer's Association workgroups on diagnostic guidelines for Alzheimer's disease. *Alzheimer's and Dementia: The Journal of the Alzheimer's Association, 7*, 280–292.

Spitzer, R. L., Gibbon, M., Skodol, A. E., Williams, J. B. W., & First, M. B. (Eds.). (1994). *DSM-IV casebook: A learning companion to the Diagnostic and Statistical Manual of Mental Disorders* (4th ed.). Washington, DC: American Psychiatric Press.

Spoth, R. A., Guyll, M., & Day, S. X. (2002). Universal family-focused interventions in alcohol-use prevention: Cost-benefit analyses of two interventions. *Journal of Studies on Alcohol, 63*, 219–228.

Spoth, R. A., Redmond, C., Shin, C., & Azevedo, K. (2004). Brief family intervention effects on adolescent substance initiation: School-level growth curve analyses 6 years following baseline. *Journal of Consulting and Clinical Psychology, 72*, 535–542.

Sprich, S., Biederman, J., Crawford, M. H., Mundy, E., & Faraone, S. V. (2000). Adoptive and biological families of children and adolescents with ADHD. *Journal of the American Academy of Child and Adolescent Psychiatry, 39*, 1432–1437.

Stack, S. (2000). Media impacts on suicide: A quantitative review of 293 findings. *Social Science Quarterly, 81*, 957–971.

Stacy, A. W., Newcomb, M. D., & Bentler, P. M. (1991). Cognitive motivation and drug use: A 9-year longitudinal study. *Journal of Abnormal Psychology, 100*, 502–515.

Stanfield, A. C., McIntosh, A. M., Spencer, M. D., Philip, R., Gaur, S., & Lawrie, S. M. (2008). Towards a neuroanatomy of autism: A systematic review and meta-analysis of structural magnetic resonance imaging studies. *European Psychiatry, 23*(4), 289–299.

Stapinski, L. A., Abbott, M. J., & Rapee, R. M. (2010). Evaluating the cognitive avoidance model of generalised anxiety disorder: Impact of worry on threat appraisal, perceived control and anxious arousal. *Behaviour Research and Therapy, 48*(10), 1032–1040. doi:http://doi.org/10.1016/j.brat.2010.07.005

Stapinski, L. A., Bowes, L., Wolke, D., Pearson, R. M., Mahedy, L., Button, K. S., et al. (2014). Peer victimization during adolescence and risk for anxiety disorders in adulthood: A prospective cohort study. *Depression and Anxiety, 31*(7), 574–582. http://doi.org/10.1002/da.22270

Stapleton, J. A., Sutherland, G., O'Gara, C. (2007) Association between dopamine transporter genotypes and smoking cessation: A meta-analysis. *Addiction Biology 12*, 221–226.

Stark, E. A., Parsons, C. E., Van Hartevelt, T. J., Charquero-Ballester, M., McManners, H., Ehlers, A. et al. (2015). Post-traumatic stress influences the brain even in the absence of symptoms: A systematic, quantitative meta-analysis of neuroimaging studies. *Neuroscience & Biobehavioral Reviews, 56*, 207–221. doi:https://doi.org/10.1016/j.neubiorev.2015.07.007

Staugaard, S. R. (2010). Threatening faces and social anxiety: A literature review. *Clinical Psychology Review, 30*, 669–690.

Stead, L. F., Perera, R., Bullen, C., Mant, D., Hartmann-Boyce, J., Cahill, K., & Lancaster, T. (2012). Nicotine replacement therapy for smoking cessation. *Cochrane Database of Systematic Reviews, 11*. http://doi.org/10.1002/14651858.CD000146.pub4

Steadman, H. J. (1979). *Beating a rap: Defendants found incompetent to stand trial.* Chicago, IL: University of Chicago Press.

Steadman, H. J., McGreevy, M. A., Morrissey, J. P., Callahan, L. A., Robbins, P. C., & Cirincione, C. (1993). *Before and after Hinckley: Evaluating insanity defense reform.* New York, NY: Guilford Press.

Steadman, H. J., Mulvey, E. P., Monahan, J., Robbins, P. C., Appelbaum, P. S., Grisso, et al. (1998). Violence by people discharged from acute psychiatric inpatient facilities and by others in the same neighborhoods. *Archives of General Psychiatry, 55*, 393–401.

Steadman, H. J., Mulvey, E. P., Monahan, J., Robbins, P. C., Appelbaum, P. S., Grisso, T., Roth, L. H., & Silver, E. (1998). Violence by people discharged from acute psychiatric inpatient facilities and by others in the same neighborhoods. *Archives of General Psychiatry, 55*, 393–401.

Steadman, H. J., Osher, F. C., Robbins, P. C., Case, B., & Samuels, S. (2009). Prevalence of serious mental illness among jail inmates. *Psychiatric Services, 60*, 761–765.

Steele, A. L., Bergin, J., & Wade, T. D. (2011). Self-efficacy as a robust predictor of outcome in guided self-help treatment for broadly defined bulimia nervosa. *International Journal of Eating Disorders, 44*, 389–396.

Steele, C. M., & Josephs, R. A. (1988). Drinking your troubles away: 2. An attention-allocation model of alcohol's effects on psychological stress. *Journal of Abnormal Psychology, 97*, 196–205.

Steele, C. M., & Josephs, R. A. (1990). Alcohol myopia: Its prized and dangerous effects. *American Psychologist, 45*, 921–933.

Steel, Z., Silove, D., Giao, N. M., Phan, T. T., Chey, T., Whelan, A., et al. (2009). International and indigenous diagnoses of mental disorder among Vietnamese living in Vietnam and Australia. *British Journal of Psychiatry, 194*, 326–333. doi:10.1192/bjp.bp.108.050906

Steen, R. G., Mull, C., McClure, R., Hamer, R. M., & Lieberman, J. A. (2006). Brain volume in first-episode schizophrenia: Systematic review and meta-analysis of magnetic resonance imaging studies. *British Journal of Psychiatry, 188*, 510–518.

Steiger, H., Gauvin, L., Jabalpurwala, S., & Séguin, J. R. (1999). Hypersenstivity to social interactions in bulimic synromes: Relationship to binge eating. *Journal of Consulting and Clinical Psychology, 67*, 765–775.

Steinberg, D., Mills, D., & Romano, M. (2015). *When did prisons become acceptable mental healthcare facilities?* Stanford Law School Three Strikes Project, February 19, 2015. https://law.stanford.edu/publications/when-did-prisons-become-acceptable-mental-healthcare-facilities-2/).

Stein, D. J., Aguilar-Gaxiola, S., Alonso, J., Bruffaerts, R., De Jonge, P., Liu, Z., et al. (2014). Associations between mental disorders and subsequent onset of hypertension. *General Hospital Psychiatry, 36*, 142–149.

Stein, D. J., Koenen, K. C., Friedman, M. J., Hill, E., McLaughlin, K. A., Petukhova, M., et al. (2013). Dissociation in posttraumatic stress disorder: Evidence from the World Mental Health surveys. *Biological Psychiatry, 73*, 302–312.

Stein, D. J., Phillips, K. A., Bolton, D., Fulford, K. W., Sadler, J. Z., & Kendler, K. S. (2010). What is a mental/psychiatric disorder? From DSM-IV to DSM-V. *Psychological Medicine, 40*, 1759–1765.

Stein, E. A., Pankiewicz, J., Harsch, H. H., Cho, J. K., Fuller, S. A., et al. (1998). Nicotine-induced limbic cortical activation in the human brain: A functional MRI study. *American Journal of Psychiatry, 155*, 1009–1015.

Steiner, J., Walter, M., Glanz, W., Sarnyai, Z., Bernstein, H. G., Vielhaber, S., et al. (2013). Increased prevalence of diverse N-methyl-D-aspartate glutamate receptor antibodies in patients with an initial diagnosis of schizophrenia: Specific relevance of IgG NR1a antibodies for distinction from N-methyl-D-aspartate glutamate receptor encephalitis. *Journal of the American Medical Association Psychiatry, 70*, 271–278.

Steinglass, J. E., & Walsh, B. T. (2016). Neurobiological model of the persistence of anorexia nervosa. *Journal of Eating Disorders, 4*(19), 1–7. doi:10.1186/s40337-016-0106-2

Steinhausen, H.-C. (2002). The outcome of anorexia nervosa in the 20th century. *American Journal of Psychiatry, 159*, 1284–1293. http://doi.org/10.1176/appi.ajp.159.8.1284

Steinhausen, H., & Weber, S. (2009). The outcome of bulimia nervosa: Findings from one-quarter century of research. *American Journal of Psychiatry, 166*, 1331–1341.

Steketee, G., & Frost, R. O. (2003). Compulsive hoarding: Current status of the research. *Clinical Psychology Review, 23*, 905–927.

Steketee, G., & Frost, R. O. (2015). Phenomenology of hoarding. In R. O. Frost & G. Steketee (Eds.), *The Oxford handbook of hoarding and acquiring.* Oxford, England: Oxford University Press.

Stepp, S. D., Lazarus, S. A., & Byrd, A. L. (2016). A systematic review of risk factors prospectively associated with borderline personality disorder: Taking stock and moving forward. *Personality Disorders: Theory, Research, and Treatment, 7*, 316–323. doi:10.1037/per0000186

Stern, A. M. (2015). *Eugenic nation: Faults and frontiers of better breeding in modern America*. Berkeley, CA: University of California Press.

Stern, A. M., Novak, N. L., Lira, N., O'Connor, K., Harlow, S., & Kardia, S. (2017). California's sterilization survivors: An estimate and call for redress. *American Journal of Public Health, 107*, 50–54.

Stice, E. (2001). A prospective test of the dual-pathway model of bulimic pathology: Mediating effects of dieting and negative affect. *Journal of Abnormal Psychology, 110*, 124–135.

Stice, E. (2016). Interactive and mediational etiologic models of eating disorder onset: Evidence from prospective studies. *Annual Review of Clinical Psychology, 12*, 359–381. doi.org/10.1146/annurev-clinpsy-021815-093317

Stice, E., & Agras, W. S. (1999). Subtyping bulimics along dietary restraint and negative affect dimensions. *Journal of Consulting and Clinical Psychology, 67*, 460–469.

Stice, E., Becker, C. B., & Yokum, S. (2013). Eating disorder prevention: Current evidence-base and future directions. *International Journal of Eating Disorders, 46*(5), 478–485.

Stice, E., Burton, E. M., & Shaw, H. (2004). Prospective relations between bulimic pathology, depression, and substance abuse: Unpacking comorbidity in adolescent girls. *Journal of Consulting and Clinical Psychology, 72*, 62–71.

Stice, E., Davis, K., Miller, N. P., & Marti, C. N. (2008). Fasting increases risk for onset of binge eating and bulimic pathology: A 5-year prospective study. *Journal of Abnormal Psychology, 117*, 941–946.

Stice, E., Durant, S., Rohde, P., & Shaw, H. (2014). Effects of a prototype internet dissonance-based eating disorder prevention program at 1- and 2-year follow-up. *Health Psychology, 33*, 1558–1567. http://dx.doi.org/10.1037/hea0000090

Stice, E., Marti, C. N., & Rohde, P. (2013). Prevalence, incidence, impairment, and course of the proposed eating disorder diagnoses in an 8-year prospective community study of young women. *Journal of Abnormal Psychology, 122*, 445–457.

Stice, E., Marti, C. N., Spoor, S., Presnell, K., & Shaw, H. (2008). Dissonance and healthy weight eating disorder prevention programs: Long-term effects from a randomized efficacy trial. *Journal of Consulting and Clinical Psychology, 76*, 329–240.

Stice, E., Rohde, P., Shaw, H., & Gau, J. M. (2017). Clinician-led, peer-led, and Internet-delivered dissonance-based eating disorder prevention programs: Acute effectiveness of these delivery modalities. *Journal of Consulting and Clinical Psychology, 85*, 883–895. doi: 10.1037/ccp0000211.

Stice, E., Rohde, P., Shaw, H., & Marti, C. N. (2013). Efficacy trial of a selective prevention program targeting both eating disorders and obesity among female college students: 1- and 2-year follow-up effects. *Journal of Consulting and Clinical Psychology, 81*(1), 183–189.

Stice, E., Shaw, H., & Marti, C. N. (2007). A meta-analytic review of eating disorder prevention programs: Encouraging findings. *Annual Review of Clinical Psychology, 3*, 207–231.

Stice, E., & Yokum, S. (2016). Neural vulnerability factors that increase risk for future weight gain. *Psychological Bulletin, 142*, 447–471.

Stone, A. A., Schwartz, J., Neale, J. M., Shiffman, S., Marco, C. A., et al. (1998). A comparison of coping assessed by ecological momentary assessment and retrospective recall. *Journal of Personality and Social Psychology, 74*, 1670–1680.

Stone, A. A., & Shiffman, S. (1994). Ecological momentary assessment (EMA) in behavioral medicine. *Annals of Behavioral Medicine, 16*, 199–202.

Stone, J., LaFrance, W. C., Jr., Levenson, J. L., & Sharpe, M. (2010). Issues for DSM-5: Conversion disorder. *American Journal of Psychiatry, 167*, 626–627.

Stone, J., Smyth, R., Carson, A., Lewis, S., Prescott, R., Warlow, C., et al. (2005). Systematic review of misdiagnosis of conversion symptoms and "hysteria." *British Medical Journal, 331*, 989.

Stone, M. H. (1993). *Abnormalities of personality. Within and beyond the realm of treatment*. New York, NY: W. W. Norton.

Stormer, S. M., & Thompson, J. K. (1996). Explanations of body image disturbance: A test of maturational status, negative verbal commentary, and sociological hypotheses. *International Journal of Eating Disorders, 19*, 193–202.

Stossel, S. (2014, January/February). Surviving anxiety. *Atlantic Monthly*, 1–6.

Stoving, R. K., Hangaard, J., Hansen-Nord, M., & Hagen, C. (1999). A review of endocrine changes in anorexia nervosa. *Journal of Psychiatric Research, 33*, 139–152.

Strain, E. C., Bigelow, G. E., Liebson, I. A., & Stitzer, M. L. (1999). Moderate- vs low-dose methadone in the treatment of opioid dependence. *Journal of the American Medical Association, 281*, 1000–1005.

Streeton, C., & Whelan, G. (2001). Naltrexone, a relapse prevention maintenance treatment of alcohol dependence: A meta-analysis of randomized controlled trials. *Alcohol and Alcoholism, 36*, 544–552.

Streltzer, J., & Johansen, L. G. (2006). Prescription drug dependence and evolving beliefs about chronic pain management. *American Journal of Psychiatry, 163*, 594–598.

Striegel-Moore, R. H., & Franco, D. L. (2008). Should binge eating disorder be included in the DSM-V? A critical review of the state of the evidence. *Annual Review of Clinical Psychology, 4*, 305–324.

Striegel-Moore, R. H., Garvin, V., Dohm, F. A., & Rosenheck, R. (1999). Psychiatric comorbidity of eating disorders in men: A national study of hospitalized veterans. *International Journal of Eating Disorders, 25*, 399–404.

Striegel-Moore, R. H., Schreiber, G. B., Lo, A., Crawford, P., Obarzanek, E., & Rodin, J. (2000). Eating disorder symptoms in a cohort of 11 to 16-year-old black and white girls: The NHLBI Growth and Health Study. *International Journal of Eating Disorders, 27*, 49–66.

Stringer, S., Minica, C. C., Verweij, K. J. H., Mbarek, H., Bernard, M., Derringer, J., et al. (2016). Genome-wide association study of lifetime cannabis use based on a large meta-analytic sample of 32,330 subjects from the International Cannabis Consortium. *Translational Psychiatry, 6*, e769. http://doi.org/10.1038/tp.2016.36

Stritzke, W. G. K., Patrick, C. J., & Lang, P. J. (1995). Alcohol and emotion: A multidimensional approach incorporating startle probe methodology. *Journal of Abnormal Psychology, 104*, 114–122.

Strober, M., Freeman, R., Lampert, C., Diamond, J., & Kaye, W. (2000). Controlled family study of anorexia nervosa and bulimia nervosa: Evidence of shared liability and transmission of partial syndromes. *American Journal of Psychiatry, 157*, 393–401.

Strober, M., Lampert, C., Morrell, W., Burroughs, J., & Jacobs, C. (1990). A controlled family study of anorexia nervosa: Evidence of family aggregation and lack of shared transmission with affective disorders. *International Journal of Eating Disorders, 9*, 239–253.

Strub, R. L., & Black, F. W. (1981). *Organic brain syndromes: An introduction to neurobehavioral disorders*. Philadelphia, PA: Philadelphia: F. A. Davis.

Struckman-Johnson, C. (1988). Forced sex on dates: It happens to men, too. *Journal of Sex Research, 24*, 234–241.

Sturm, R. A., Duffy, D. L., Zhao, Z. Z., et al. (2008). A single SNP in an evolutionary conserved region within intron 86 of the HERC2 gene determines human blue-brown eye color. *American Journal of Human Genetics, 82*, 424–431.

Styron, W. (1992). *Darkness visible: A memoir of madness*. New York, NY: Vintage.

Substance Abuse and Mental Health Services Administration. (2016). Results from the 2015 National Survey on Drug Use and Health: Detailed tables. Retrieved from https://www.samhsa.gov/data/sites/default/files/NSDUH-DetTabs-2015/NSDUH-DetTabs-2015/NSDUH-DetTabs-2015.htm#fn1

Substance Abuse and Mental Health Services Administration (SAMHSA) (2014). Results from the 2014 National Survey on Drug Use and Health: Detailed tables. Retrieved from https://www.samhsa.gov/data/sites/default/files/NSDUH-DetTabs2014/NSDUH-DetTabs2014.htm

Suchy, Y., Eastvold, A. D., Strassberg, D. S., & Franchow, E. I. (2014). Understanding processing speed weaknesses among pedophilic child molesters: Response style vs. neuropathology. *Journal of Abnormal Psychology, 123*, 273–285.

Sue, S., Yan Cheng, J. K., Saad, C. S., & Chu, J. P. (2012). Asian American mental health: A call to action. *American Psychologist, 67*, 532–544.

Sue, S., Zane, N., Nagayama Hall, G. C., & Berger, L. K. (2009). The case for cultural competency in psychotherapeutic interventions. *Annual Review of Psychology, 60*, 525–548. doi:10.1146/annurev.psych.60.110707.163651

Sullivan, P. F., Daly, M. J., & O'Donovan, M. (2012). Genetic architectures of psychiatric disorders: The emerging picture and its implications. *Nature Reviews Genetics, 13*(8), 537–551.

Sullivan, P. F., Lin, D., Tzeng, J.-Y., van den Oord, E., Perkins, D., Stroup, T. S., et al. (2008). Genomewide association for schizophrenia in the CATIE study: Results of stage 1. *Molecular Psychiatry, 13*, 570–584. http://doi.org/10.1038/mp.2008.25

Sullivan, P. F., Neale, M. C., & Kendler, K. S. (2000). Genetic epidemiology of major depression: Review and meta-analysis. *American Journal of Psychiatry, 157*, 1552–1562.

Summers, A., & Swan, R. (2006). Sinatra: *The Life* (New York: Vintage Books).

Sun, D., Phillips, L., Velakoulis, D., Yung, A., McGorry, P. D., Wood, S. J., et al. (2009). Progressive brain structural changes mapped as psychosis develops in "at risk" individuals. *Schizophrenia Research, 108*, 85–92.

Sussman, S., Dent, C. W., McAdams, L., Stacy, A. W., Burton, D., & Flay, B. R. (1994). Group self-identification and adolescent cigarette smoking: A 1-year prospective study. *Journal of Abnormal Psychology, 103*, 576–580.

Sussman, S., Miyano, J., Rohrbach, L. A., Dent, C. W., & Sun, P. (2007). Six-month and one-year effects of project EX-4: A classroom-based smoking prevention and cessation intervention program. *Addictive Behaviors, 32*, 3005–3014. http://dx.doi.org/10.1016/j.addbeh.2007.06.016

Sutker, P. B., Uddo, M., Brailey, K., Vasterling, J. J., & Errera, P. (1994). Psychopathology in war-zone deployed and nondeployed Operation Desert Storm troops assigned grave registration duties. *Journal of Abnormal Psychology, 103*, 383–390.

Suzuki, K., Takei, N., Kawai, M., Minabe, Y., & Mori, N. (2003). Is taijin kyofusho a culture-bound syndrome? *American Journal of Psychiatry, 160*(7), 1358.

Swain, J., Koszycki, D., Shlik, J., & Bradwein, J. (2003). Pharmacological challenge agents in anxiety. In D. Nutt & J. C. Ballenger (Eds.), *Anxiety disorders* (pp. 269–295). Malden, MA: Blackwell.

Swanson, J., Hinshaw, S. P., Arnold, L. E., Gibbons, R., Marcus, S., Hur, K., et al. (2007). Secondary evaluations of MTA 36-month outcomes: Propensity score and growth mixture model analyses. *Journal of the American Academy of Child and Adolescent Psychiatry, 46*, 1002–1013.

Swanson, J., Kinsbourne, M., Nigg, J., et al. (2007). Etiologic subtypes of attention-deficit/hyperactivity disorder: Brain imaging, molecular genetic and environmental factors and the dopamine hypothesis. *Neuropsychology Review, 17*, 39–59.

Swanson, J., McBurnett, K., Christian, D. L., & Wigal, T. (1995). Stimulant medications and the treatment of children with ADHD. In T. H. Ollendick & R. J. Prinz (Eds.), *Advances in Clinical Child Psychology, 17*, pp. 265–322). New York, NY: Plenum.

Swanson, J. W., Holzer, C. E., Ganju, V. K., & Jono, R. T. (1990). Violence and psychiatric disorder in the community: Evidence from the Epidemiological Catchment Area surveys. *Hospital and Community Psychiatry, 41*, 761–770.

Swartz, J. R., Williamson, D. E., & Hariri, A. R. (2015). Developmental change in amygdala reactivity during adolescence: Effects of family history of depression and stressful life events. *American Journal of Psychiatry, 172*(3), 276–283. doi:10.1176/appi.ajp.2014.14020195

Szczypka, M. S., Kwok, K., Brot, M. D., Marck, B. T., Matsumoto, A. M., Donahue, B. A., & Palmiter, R. D. (2001). Dopamine production in the caudate putamen restores feeding in dopamine-deficient mice. *Neuron, 30*, 819–828.

Szechtman, H., & Woody, E. Z. (2004). Obsessive-compulsive disorder as a disturbance of security motivation. *Psychological Review, 111*, 111–127.

Tal, A., Niemann, S., & Wansink, B. (2017). Depicted serving size: Cereal packaging pictures exaggerate serving sizes and promote overserving. *BMC Public Health, 17*, 1103. http://doi.org/10.1186/s12889-017-4082-5

Talih, S., Balhas, Z., Eissenberg, T., Salman, R., Karaoghlanian, N., El Hellani, A., Baalbaki, R., Saliba, N., & Shihadeh, A. (2015). Effects of user puff topography, device voltage, and liquid nicotine concentration on electronic cigarette nicotine yield: Measurements and model predictions. *Nicotine & Tobacco Research, 17*, 150–157.

Tambs, K., Czajkowsky, N., Røysamb, E., Neale, M. C., Reichborn-Kjennerud, T., Aggen, S. H., et al. (2009). Structure of genetic and environmental risk factors for dimensional representations of DSM–IV anxiety disorders. *The British Journal of Psychiatry: The Journal of Mental Science, 195*(4), 301–307. doi:10.1192/bjp.bp.108.059485

Tao, K. W., Owen, J., Pace, B. T., & Imel, Z. E. (2015). A meta-analysis of multicultural competencies and psychotherapy process and outcome. *Journal of Counseling Psychology, 62*(3), 337–350. doi:10.1037/cou0000086

Tarbox, S. I., Addington, J., Cadenhead, K., Cannon, T., Cornblatt, B., Perkins, D., et al. (2013). Premorbid functional development and conversion to psychosis in clinical high-risk youths. *Development and Psychopathology, 25*, 1171–1186.

Tarrier, N., Taylor, K., & Gooding, P. (2008). Cognitive-behavioral interventions to reduce suicide behavior. *Behavior Modification, 32*, 77–108.

Task Force on Promotion and Dissemination of Psychological Procedures. (1995). Training in and dissemination of empirically-validated psychological treatments: Report and recommendations. *The Clinical Psychologist, 48*, 3–23.

Taylor, A., & Kim-Cohen, J. (2007). Meta-analysis of gene–environment interactions in developmental psychopathology. *Development and Psychopathology, 19*, 1029–1037.

Taylor, C. B., Hayward, C., King, R., Ehlers, A., Margraf, J., Maddock, R., et al. (1990). Cardiovascular and symptomatic reduction effects of alprazolam and imipramine in patients with panic disorder: Results of a double-blind, placebo-controlled trial. *Journal of Clinical Psychopharmacology, 10*, 112–118.

Taylor, C. T., & Alden, L. E. (2011). To see ourselves as others see us: An experimental integration of the intra- and interpersonal consequences of self-protection in social anxiety disorder. *Journal of Abnormal Psychology, 120*, 129–141.

Taylor, J., Iacono, W. G., & McGue, M. (2000). Evidence for a genetic etiology of early-onset delinquency. *Journal of Abnormal Psychology, 109*, 634–643.

Taylor, L. E., Swerdfeger, A. L., & Eslick, G. D. (2014). Vaccines are not associated with autism: An evidence-based meta-analysis of case-control and cohort studies. *Vaccine, 32*(29), 3623–3629.

Taylor, S. (2011). Early versus late onset obsessive-compulsive disorder: Evidence for distinct subtypes. *Clinical Psychology Review, 31*(7), 1083–1100. doi:10.1016/j.cpr.2011.06.007

Taylor, S., Asmundson, G. J., & Jang, K. L. (2011). Etiology of obsessive-compulsive symptoms and obsessive-compulsive personality traits: Common genes, mostly different environments. *Depression and Anxiety, 28*, 863–869.

Taylor, S., Thordarson, D. S., Maxfield, L., Fedoroff, I. C., Lovell, K., & Ogrodniczuk, J. (2003). Comparative efficacy, speed, and adverse effects of three PTSD treatments: Exposure therapy, EMDR, and relaxation training. *Journal of Consulting and Clinical Psychology, 71*(2), 330–338. doi:10.1037/0022-006X.71.2.330

Teachman, B. A., & Allen, J. P. (2007). Development of social anxiety: Social interaction predictors of implicit and explicit fear of negative evaluation. *Journal of Abnormal Child Psychology, 35*, 63–78.

Teasdale, J. D. (1988). Cognitive vulnerability to persistent depression. *Cognition and Emotion, 2*, 247–274.

Telch, M. J., & Harrington, P. J. Anxiety sensitivity and unexpectedness of arousal in mediating affective response to 35% carbon dioxide inhalation. Unpublished Manuscript.

Telch, M. J., Shermis, M. D., & Lucas, J. A. (1989). Anxiety sensitivity: Unitary personality trait or domain-specific appraisals? *Journal of Anxiety Disorders, 3*, 25–32.

ter Kuile, M. M., Both, S., & van Lankveld, J. J. (2012). Sexual dysfunctions in women. In P. Sturmey & M. Hersen (Eds.), *Handbook of evidence-based practice in clinical psychology, adult disorders* (Vol. 2, pp. 413–436). Hoboken, NJ: John Wiley & Sons.

ter Kuile, M. M., & Reissing, E. D. (2014). Lifelong vaginismus. In Y. M. Binik & K. S. K. Hall (Eds.), *Principles and practice of sex therapy* (5th ed., pp. 177–194). New York, NY: Guilford Press.

Terry, R. D. (2006). Alzheimer's disease and the aging brain. *Journal of Geriatric Psychiatry and Neurology, 19*, 125–128.

Thapar, A., Langley, K., Owen, M. J., & O'Donovan, M. C. (2007). Advances in genetic findings on attention deficit hyperactivity disorder. *Psychological Medicine, 37*, 1681–1692.

Thapar, A., Rice, F., Hay, D., Boivin, J., Langley, K., van den Bree, M., et al. (2009). Prenatal smoking might not cause attention-deficit/hyperactivity disorder: Evidence from a novel design. *Biological Psychiatry, 66*(8), 722–727.

Thibaut, F., De La Barra, F., Gordon, H., Cosyns, P., & Bradford, J. M. (2010). The World Federation of Societies of Biological Psychiatry (WFSBP) guidelines for the biological treatment of paraphilias. *World Journal of Biological Psychiatry, 11*, 604–655.

Thoits, P. A. (1985). Self-labeling processes in mental illness: The role of emotional deviance. *American Journal of Sociology, 92*, 221–249.

Thomas, G., Reifman, A., Barnes, G. M., & Farrell, M. P. (2000). Delayed onset of drunkenness as a protective factor for adolescent alcohol misuse and sexual risk taking; A longitudinal study. *Deviant Behavior, 21*, 181–200.

Thompson, P. M., Hayashi, H. M., Simon, S. L., et al. (2004). Structural abnormalities in the brains of human subjects who use methamphetamine. *Journal of Neuroscience, 24*, 6028–6036.

Tiefer, L., Hall, M., & Tavris, C. (2002). Beyond dysfunction: A new view of women's sexual problems. *Journal of Sex and Marital Therapy, 28*, 225–232.

Tienari, P., Wynne, L. C., Laksy, K., Moring, J., Nieminen, P., Sorri, A., et al. (2003). Genetic boundaries of the schizophrenia spectrum: Evidence from the Finnish adoptive family study of schizophrenia. *American Journal of Psychiatry, 160*, 1587–1594.

Tienari, P., Wynne, L. C., Moring, J., et al. (2000). Finnish adoptive family study: Sample selection and adoptee DSM-III diagnoses. *Acta Psychiatrica Scandinavica, 101*, 433–443.

Timko, C., Moos, R. H., Finney, J. W., & Lesar, M. D. (2001). Long-term outcomes of alcohol use disorders: Comparing untreated individuals with those in Alcoholics Anonymous and formal treatment. *Journal of Studies on Alcohol, 61*, 529–540.

Timpano, K. R., Broman-Fulks, J. J., Glaesmer, H., Exner, C., Rief, W., Olatunji, B. O., et al. (2013). A taxometric exploration of the latent structure of hoarding. *Psychological Assessment, 25*, 194–203.

Timpano, K. R., Muroff, J., & Steketee, G. (2016). A review of the diagnosis and management of hoarding disorder. *Current Treatment Options in Psychiatry, 3*(4), 394–410. doi:10.1007/s40501-016-0098-1

Tjaden, P., & Thoennes, N. (2006). Extent, nature, and consequences of rape victimization: Findings from the National Violence Against Women Survey. Washington, DC: National Institute of Justice.

Tolin, D. F., & Foa, E. B. (2006). Sex differences in trauma and posttraumatic stress disorder: A quantitative review of 25 years of research. *Psychological Bulletin, 132*, 959–992.

Tolin, D. F., Frost, R. O., Steketee, G., Gray, K., & Fitch, K. (2008). The economic and social burden of compulsive hoarding. *Psychiatry Research, 160*, 200–211.

Tolin, D. F., Frost, R. O., Steketee, G., & Muroff, J. (2015). Cognitive behavioral therapy for hoarding disorder: A meta-analysis. *Depression and Anxiety, 32*(3), 158–166. doi:10.1002/da.22327

Tolin, D. F., Kiehl, K. A., Worhunsky, P., Book, G. A., & Maltby, N. (2009). An exploratory study of the neural mechanisms of decision making in compulsive hoarding. *Psychological Medicine, 39*, 325–336.

Tolin, D. F., Stevens, M. C., Villavicencio, A. L., Norberg, M. M., Calhoun, V. D., Frost, R. O., et al. (2012). Neural mechanisms of decision making in hoarding disorder. *Archives of General Psychiatry, 69*, 832–841.

Tolin, D. F., & Villavicencio, A. (2011). Inattention, but not OCD, predicts the core features of hoarding disorder. *Behaviour Research and Therapy, 49*, 120–125.

Tolin, D. F., Worhunsky, P., & Maltby, N. (2004). Sympathetic magic in contamination-related OCD. *Journal of Behavior Therapy and Experimental Psychiatry, 35*, 193–205.

Tompkins, M. A., & Hartl, T. L. (2013). Family interventions for hoarding. *The Oxford handbook of hoarding and acquiring.* 303–315.

Tonstad, S., Tonnesen, P., Hajek, P., Williams, K. E., Billing, C. B., & Reeves, K. R. (2006). Varenicline Phase 3 Study Group. Effect of maintenance therapy with varenicline on smoking cessation: A randomized controlled trial. *JAMA, 296*, 64–71.

Topiwala, A., Allan, C. L., Valkanova, V., Zsoldos, E., Filippini, N., Sexton, C., et al. (2017). Moderate alcohol consumption as risk factor for adverse brain outcomes and cognitive decline: Longitudinal cohort study. *British Medical Journal, 357*, j2353. http://doi.org/10.1136/bmj.j2353

Torgersen, S. (1986). Genetics of somatoform disorder. *Archives of General Psychiatry, 43*, 502–505.

Torgersen, S., Lygren, S., Oien, P. A., Skre, I., Onstad, S., Edvardsen, J., et al. (2000). A twin study of personality disorders. *Comprehensive Psychiatry, 41*, 416–425. doi:10.1053/comp.2000.16560

Torgersen, S., Myers, J., Reichborn-Kjennerud, T., Røysamb, E., Kubarych, T. S., & Kendler, K. S. (2012). The heritability of cluster B personality disorders assessed both by personal interview and questionnaire. *Journal of Personality Disorders, 26*, 848–866. doi:10.1521/pedi.2012.26.6.848

Torres, A. R., Prince, M. J., Bebbington, P. E., Bhurga, D., Brugha, T. S., Farrell, M., et al. (2006). Obsessive-compulsive disorder: Prevalence, comorbidity, impact, and help-seeking in the British National Psychiatric Morbidity Survey of 2000. *American Journal of Psychiatry, 163*, 1978–1985.

Torres, U. S., Portela-Oliveira, E., Borgwardt, S., & Busatto, G. F. (2013). Structural brain changes associated with antipsychotic treatment in schizophrenia as revealed by voxel-based morphometric MRI: An activation likelihood estimation meta-analysis. *BMC Psychiatry, 13*, 139. http://doi.org/10.1186/1471-244X-13-342

Torrey, E. F. (2014). *American psychosis: How the federal government destroyed the mental illness treatment system.* Oxford, UK: Oxford University Press.

Torrey, E. F., Kennard, A. D., Eslinger, D., Lamb, R., & Pavle, J. (2010). More mentally ill persons are in jails and prisons than hospitals: A survey of the state. Treatment Advocacy Center and the National Sheriffs' Association., Washington, DC.

Torrey, E. F., Zdanowicz, M. T., Kennard, A. D., Lamb, H. R., Eslinger, D., Biasotti, M. C., & Fuller, D. A. (2014). *The treatment of persons with mental illness in prisons and jails: A state survey.* Washington, DC: Treatment Advocacy Center.

Torvik, F. A., Welander-Vatn, A., Ystrom, E., Knudsen, G. P., Czajkowski, N., Kendler, K. S., et al. (2016). Longitudinal associations between social anxiety disorder and avoidant personality disorder: A twin study. *Journal of Abnormal Psychology, 125*(1), 114–124. doi:10.1037/abn0000124

Tost, H., Champagne, F. A., & Meyer-Lindenberg, A. (2015). Environmental influence in the brain, human welfare and mental health. *Nature Neuroscience, 18*, 1421–1431. http://doi.org/10.1038/nn.4108

Toufexis, A., Blackman, A., & Drummond, T. (1996, April 29). Why Jennifer got sick. *Time.*

Touyz, S., Le Grange, D., Lacey, H., Hay, P., Smith, R., Maguire, S., et al. (2013). Treating severe and enduring anorexia nervosa: A randomized controlled trial. *Psychological Medicine, 43*, 2501–2511.

Tran, G. Q., Haaga, D. A. F., & Chambless, D. L. (1997). Expecting that alcohol will reduce social anxiety moderates the relation between social anxiety and alcohol consumption. *Cognitive Therapy and Research, 21*, 535–553.

Tran, K., Moulton, K., Santesso, N., et al. (2016). *Cognitive processing therapy for post-traumatic stress disorder: A systematic review and meta-analysis.* CADTH Health Technology Assessment, No. 141. Ottawa, ON: Canadian Agency for Drugs and Technologies in Health.

Treadway, M. T., & Pizzagalli, D. A. (2014). Imaging the pathophysiology of major depressive disorder—from localist models to circuit-based analysis. *Biology of Mood & Anxiety Disorders, 4*(1), 5. doi:10.1186/2045-5380-4-5

Treadway, M. T., & Zald, D. H. (2011). Reconsidering anhedonia in depression: Lessons from translation neuroscience. *Neuroscience and Biobehavioral Reviews, 35*, 537–555.

Treat, T. A., & Viken, R. J. (2010). Cognitive processing of weight and emotional information in disordered eating. *Current Directions in Psychological Science, 19*, 81–85.

Treynor, W., Gonzalez, R., & Nolen-Hoeksema, S. (2003). Rumination reconsidered: A psychometric analysis. *Cognitive Therapy and Research, 27*, 247–259.

Trierweiler, S. J., Neighbors, H. W., Munday, C., Thompson, E. E., Binion, V. J., & Gomez, J. P. (2000). Clinician attributions associated with the diagnosis of schizophrenia in African American and non–African American patients. *Journal of Consulting and Clinical Psychology, 68*, 171–175.

Trinder, H., & Salkovaskis, P. M. (1994). Personally relevant intrusions outside the laboratory: Long-term suppression increases intrusion. *Behaviour Research and Therapy, 32*, 833–842.

Trivedi, M. H., Rush, A. J., Wisniewski, S. R., Nierenberg, A. A., Warden, D., Ritz, L., et al. (2006). Evaluation of outcomes with citalopram for depression using measurement-based care in STAR*D: Implications for clinical practice. *American Journal of Psychiatry, 163*, 28–40.

Trull, T. J., Jahng, S., Tomko, R. L., Wood, P. K., & Sher, K. J. (2010). Revised NESARC personality disorder diagnoses: Gender, prevalence, and comorbidity with substance dependence disorders. *Journal of Personality Disorders, 24*, 412-426. doi:10.1521/pedi.2010.24.4.412

Trull, T. J., Solhan, M. B., Tragesser, S. L., Jahng, S., Wood, P. K., Piasecki, T. M., et al. (2008). Affective instability: Measuring a core feature of borderline personality disorder with ecological momentary assessment. *Journal of Abnormal Psychology, 117*, 647–661.

Tsai, D. C., & Pike, P. L. (2000). Effects of acculturation on the MMPI-2 scores of Asian American students. *Journal of Personality Assessment, 74*, 216–230.

Tsai, J. L. (2007). Ideal affect: Cultural causes and behavioral consequences. *Perspectives on Psychological Science, 2*, 242–259.

Tsai, J. L., Butcher, J. N., Vitousek, K., & Munoz, R. (2001). Culture, ethnicity, and psychopathology. In H. E. Adams & P. B. Sutker (Eds.). *The comprehensive handbook of psychopathology* (pp. 105–127). New York, NY: Plenum Press.

Tsai, J. L., Knutson, B. K., & Fung, H. H. (2006). Cultural variation in affect valuation. *Journal of Personality and Social Psychology, 90*, 288–307.

Tsai, J. L., Knutson, B. K., & Rothman, A. (2006). The pursuit of ideal affect: Variation in mood-producing behavior. *Journal of Personality and Social Psychology, 90*, 288–307.

Tsuang, M. T., Lyons, M. J., Meyer, J. M., Doyle, T., Eisen, S. A., et al. (1998). Co-occurrence of abuse of different drugs in men: The role of drug-specific and shared vulnerabilities. *Archives of General Psychiatry, 55*, 967–972.

Tully, L. A., Arseneault, L., Caspi, A., Moffitt, T. E., & Morgan, J. (2004). Does maternal warmth moderate the effects of birth weight on twins' attention-deficit/hyperactivity disorder (ADHD) symptoms and low IQ? *Journal of Consulting and Clinical Psychology, 72*, 218–226.

Turkeltaub, P. E., Gareau, L., Flowers, D. L., Zeffiro, T. A., & Eden, G. F. (2003). Development of neural mechanisms for reading. *Nature Neuroscience, 6*, 767–773. doi:10.1038/nn1065

Turkheimer, E. (2000). Three laws of behavior genetics and what they mean. *Current Directions in Psychological Science, 9*, 160–164.

Turkheimer, E., Haley, A., Waldron, M., D'Onofrio, B., & Gottesman, I. I. (2003). Socioeconomic status modifies the heritability of IQ in young children. *Psychological Science, 6*, 623–628.

Turkington, D., Kingdom, D., & Turner, T. (2002). Effectiveness of a brief cognitive-behavioural intervention in the treatment of schizophrenia. *British Journal of Psychiatry, 180*, 523–527.

Turner, C. M. (2006). Cognitive-behavioural theory and therapy for obsessive-compulsive disorder in children and adolescents: Current status and future directions. *Clinical Psychology Review, 26*, 912–948.

Turner, E. H., Matthews, A. M., Linardatos, E., Tell, R. A., & Rosenthal, R. (2008). Selective publication of antidepressant trials and its influence on apparent efficacy. *New England Journal of Medicine, 358*, 252–260.

Tyrer, H., Tyrer, P., & Barrett, B. (2013). Influence of dependent personality status on the outcome and health service costs of health anxiety. *International Journal of Social Psychiatry, 59*, 274–280.

Tyrer, P., & Bateman, A. W. (2004). Drug treatments for personality disorder. *Advances in Psychiatric Treatment, 10*, 389–398.

Tyrka, A. R., Waldron, I., Graber, J. A., & Brooks-Gunn, J. (2002). Prospective predictors of the onset of anorexic and bulimic syndromes. *International Journal of Eating Disorders, 32*, 282–290.

Uchinuma, Y., & Sekine, Y. (2000). Dissociative identity disorder (DID) in Japan: A forensic case report and the recent increase in reports of DID. *International Journal of Psychiatry in Clinical Practice, 4*, 155–160.

Uher, R., & McGuffin, P. (2010). The moderation by the serotonin transporter gene of environmental adversity in the etiology of depression: 2009 update. *Molecular Psychiatry, 15*, 18–22.

UK ECT Review Group. (2003). Efficacy and safety of electro-convulsive therapy in depressive disorders: A systematic review and meta-analysis. *The Lancet, 361*, 799–808.

Ullrich, S., & Coid, J. (2009). The age distribution of self-reported personality disorder traits in a household population. *Journal of Personality Disorders, 23*, 187–200. doi:10.1521/pedi.2009.23.2.187

Ulrich, S., Keers, R., & Coid, J. W. (2014). Delusions, anger and serious violence: New findings from the MacArthur violence risk assessment study. *Schizophrenia Bulletin, 40*, 1174–1181.

Unschuld, P. G., Buchholz, A. S., Varvaris, M., van Zijl, P. C., Ross, C. A., Pekar, J. J., et al. (2014). Prefrontal brain network connectivity indicates degree of both schizophrenia risk and cognitive dysfunction. *Schizophrenia Bulletin, 40*, 653–664.

Urada, D., Evans, E., Yang, J., Conner, B. T., et al. (2009). Evaluation of proposition 36: The substance abuse and crime prevention act of 2000: 2009 report. Retrieved from http://www.uclaisap.org/prop36/html/reports.html

U.S. Bureau of the Census. (2010). Population estimates: U. S. Census Bureau, Population Division.

U.S. Department of Education. (2013). Digest of education statistics, 2012 (Vol. NCES Number: 2014015).

U.S. Department of Health and Human Services. (1999). Mental Health: A report of the Surgeon General—Executive summary, Rockville, MD: U.S. Department of Health and Human Services, Substance Abuse and Mental Health Services Administration, Center for Mental Health Services, National Institutes of Health, National Institute of Mental Health.

U.S. Department of Health and Human Services. (2001). Mental Health: Culture, Race, and Ethnicity—A supplement to mental health: A report of the Surgeon General. Rockville, MD: U.S. Department of Health and Human Services, Substance Abuse and Mental Health Services Administration, Center for Mental Health Services.

U.S. Department of Health and Human Services. (2006). The health consequences of involuntary exposure to tobacco smoke: A report of the Surgeon General. Atlanta, GA: Department of Health and Human Services, Centers for Disease Control and Prevention, Coordinating Center for Health Promotion.

U.S. Department of Health and Human Services. (2014). *The health consequences of smoking—50 years of progress: A report of the Surgeon General*. Atlanta, GA: U.S. Department of Health and Human Services, Centers for Disease Control and Prevention, National Center for Chronic Disease Prevention and Health Promotion, Office on Smoking and Health.

U.S. Department of Health and Human Services. (2016a). *E-cigarette use among youth and young adults. A report of the Surgeon General.* Atlanta, GA: U.S. Department of Health and Human Services, Centers for Disease Control and Prevention, National Center for Chronic Disease Prevention and Health Promotion, Office on Smoking and Health.

U.S. Department of Health and Human Services. (2016b). *Facing addiction in America: The Surgeon General's report on alcohol, drugs, and health.* Washington, DC: HHS, Office of the Surgeon General.

U.S. Department of Health and Human Services Administration for Children and Families. (2010, January). *Head Start impact study. Final report.* Washington, DC.

U.S. Department of Health and Human Services (USDHHS). (2002). Supplement to Mental Health: A Report of the Surgeon General (SMA-01-3613). Retrieved July 2, 2002, from http://www.mentalhealth.org/Publications/allpubs/SMA01-3613/sma-01-3613.pdf

U.S. Department of Health and Human Services (USDHHS). (2014). 2014 National healthcare disparities report. Downloaded from https://www.ahrq.gov/research/findings/nhqrdr/2014chartbooks/effectivetx/eff-slidesmhsa.html

Valencia, M., Racon, M. L., Juarez, F., & Murow, E. (2007). A psychosocial skills training approach in Mexican outpatients with schizophrenia. *Psychological Medicine, 37*, 1393–1402.

Valenti, A. M., Narendran, R., & Pristach, C. A. (2003). Who are patients on conventional antipsychotics? *Schizophrenia Bulletin, 29*, 195–200.

Valenzuela, M. J., & Sachdev, P. (2006). Brain reserve and dementia: A systematic review. *Psychological Medicine, 36*, 441–454.

Valkanova, V., Ebmeier, K. P., & Allan, C. L. (2013). CRP, IL-6 and depression: A systematic review and meta-analysis of longitudinal studies. *Journal of Affective Disorders, 150*(3), 736–744. doi:10.1016/j.jad.2013.06.004

Vance, S., Cohen-Kettenis, P., Drescher, J., Meyer-Bahlburg, H., Pfafflin, F., & Zucker, K. (2010). Opinions about the DSM gender identity disorder diagnosis: Results from an international survey administered to organizations concerned with the welfare of transgender people. *International Journal of Transgenderism, 12*, 1–14.

Vandeleur, C. L., Fassassi, S., Castelao, E., Glaus, J., Strippoli, M.-P. F., Lasserre, A. M., et al. (2017). Prevalence and correlates of DSM-5 major depressive and related disorders in the community. *Psychiatry Research, 250*, 50–58. doi:10.1016/j.psychres.2017.01.060

van den Broucke, S., Vandereycken, W., & Vertommen, H. (1995). Marital communication in eating disorders: A controlled observational study. *International Journal of Eating Disorders, 17*, 1–23.

van der Hoeven, R. M., Broersma, M., Pijnenborg, G. H. M., Koops, E. A., van Laar, T., Stone, J., & van Beilen, M. (2015). Functional (psychogenic) movement disorders associated with normal scores in psychological questionnaires: A case control study. *Journal of Psychosomatic Research, 79*, 190–194. doi:https://doi.org/10.1016/j.jpsychores.2015.06.002

van der Leeuw, G., Gerrits, M. J., Terluin, B., Numans, M. E., van der Feltz-Cornelis, C. M., van der Horst, H. E., et al. (2015). The association between somatization and disability in primary care patients. *Journal of Psychosomatic Research, 79*, 117–122. doi:https://doi.org/10.1016/j.jpsychores.2015.03.001

Vandermosten, M., Boets, B., Poelmans, H., Sunaert, S., Wouters, J., & Ghesquiere, P. (2012). A tractography study in dyslexia: Neuroanatomic correlates of orthographic, phonological and speech processing. *Brain, 135*(Pt 3), 935–948.

van Dessel, N., den Boeft, M., van der Wouden, J. C., Kleinstäuber, M., Leone, S. S., Terluin, B., et al. (2014). Non-pharmacological interventions for somatoform disorders and medically unexplained physical symptoms (MUPS) in adults. *Cochrane Database of Systematic Reviews.* doi:10.1002/14651858.CD011142.pub2

van Erp, T. G. M., Saleh, P. A., Huttunen, M., Lönnqvist, J., Kaprio, J., Salonen, O., et al. (2004). Hippocampal volumes in schizophrenic twins. *Archives of General Psychiatry, 61*, 346–353.

van Hees, M. L. J. M., Rotter, T., Ellermann, T., & Evers, S. M. A. A. (2013). The effectiveness of individual interpersonal psychotherapy as a treatment for major depressive disorder in adult outpatients: A systematic review. *BMC Psychiatry, 13*(1), 22. doi:10.1186/1471-244x-13-22

van Lankveld, J. J., Granot, M., Weijmar Schultz, W. C., Binik, Y. M., Wesselmann, U., Pukall, C. F., et al. (2010). Women's sexual pain disorders. *Journal of Sexual Medicine, 7*, 615–631.

Van Meter, A. R., Moreira, A. L. R., & Youngstrom, E. A. (2011). Meta-analysis of epidemiologic studies of pediatric bipolar disorder. *Journal of Clinical Psychiatry, 72*(9), 1250–1256.

van Orden, K. A., Cukrowicz, K. C., Witte, T. K., Braithwaite, S. R., & Joiner, T. E. (2010). The interpersonal theory of suicide. *Psychological Review, 117*, 575–600.

van Orden, K. A., Witte, T. K., Gordon, K. H., Bender, T. W., & Joiner, T. E. (2008). Suicidal desire and the capability for suicide: Tests of the interpersonal-psychological theory of suicidal behavior among adults. *Journal of Consulting and Clinical Psychology, 76*, 72–83.

van Os, J., Kenis, G., & Rutten, B. P. (2010). The environment and schizophrenia. *Nature, 468*, 203–212.

Vanwesenbeeck, I., Bakker, F., & Gesell, S. (2010). Sexual health in the Netherlands: Main results of a population survey among Dutch adults. *International Journal of Sexual Health, 22*, 55–71.

Vanwesenbeeck, I., Have, M. T., & de Graaf, R. (2014). Associations between common mental disorders and sexual dissatisfaction in the general population. *British Journal of Psychiatry, 205*, 151–157. doi:10.1192/bjp.bp.113.135335

Varlet, V., Farsalinos, K., Augsburger, M., Thomas, A., & Etter, J. F. (2015). Toxicity assessment of refill liquids for electronic cigarettes. *International Journal of Environmental Research and Public Health, 12*, 4796–4815.

Vazire, S., Naumann, L. P., Rentfrow, P. J., & Gosling, S. D. (2008). Portrait of a narcissist: Manifestations of narcissism in physical appearance. *Journal of Research in Personality, 42*, 1439–1447.

Veale, D. (2004). Advances in a cognitive behavioural model of body dysmorphic disorder. *Body Image, 1*, 113–125.

Veehof, M. M., Oskam, M. J., Schreurs, K. M., & Bohlmeijer, E. T. (2011). Acceptance-based interventions for the treatment of chronic pain: A systematic review and meta-analysis. *Pain, 152*, 533–542.

Vemuri, P., Lesnick, T. G., Przybelski, S. A., Knopman, D. S., Mielke, M. M., Roberts, R. O., et al. (2014). Association of lifetime intellectual enrichment with cognitive decline in the older population. *JAMA Neurology, 71*, 1017–1024

Venables, N. C., Hall, J. R., Yancey, J. R., & Patrick, C. J. (2015). Factors of psychopathy and electrocortical response to emotional pictures: Further evidence for a two-process theory. *Journal of Abnormal Psychology, 124*, 319–328. http://dx.doi.org/10.1037/abn0000032

Ventura, J., Neuchterlein, K. H., Lukoff, D., & Hardesty, J. D. (1989). A prospective study of stressful life events and schizophrenic relapse. *Journal of Abnormal Psychology, 98*, 407–411.

Vervliet, B., Craske, M. G., & Hermans, D. (2013). Fear extinction and relapse: State of the art. *Annual Review of Clinical Psychology, 9*(1), 215–248. doi:10.1146/annurev-clinpsy-050212-185542

Viding, E., Blair, R. J. R., Moffitt, T. E., & Plomin, R. (2005). Evidence for substantial genetic risk for psychopathy in 7-year-olds. *Journal of Child Psychology and Psychiatry, and Allied Disciplines, 46*, 592–597. http://doi.org/10.1111/j.1469-7610.2004.00393.x

Vila-Rodriguez, F., Panenka, W. J., Lang, D. J., Thornton, A. E., Vertinsky, T., Wong, H., et al. (2013). The hotel study: multimorbidity in a community sample living in marginal housing. *American Journal of Psychiatry, 170*, 1413–1422.

Villanti, A. C., McKay, H. S., Abrams, D. B., Holtgrave, D. R., & Bowie, J. V. (2010). Smoking-cessation interventions for U.S. young adults: A systematic review. *American Journal of Preventive Medicine, 39*, 564–574.

Villemure, C., & Bushnell, M. C. (2009). Mood influences supraspinal pain processing separately from attention. *Journal of Neuroscience 29*, 705–715.

Vinkers, D. J., Gussekloo, J., Stek, M. L., Westendorp, R. G. J., & van der Mast, R. C. (2004). Temporal relation between depression and cognitive impairment in old age: Prospective population based study. *British Medical Journal, 329*, 881.

Virtanen, M., Vahtera, J., Batty, G. D., Tuisku, K., Pentti, J., Oksanen, T., et al. (2011). Overcrowding in psychiatric wards and physical assaults on staff: Data-linked longitudinal study. *British Journal of Psychiatry, 198*, 149–155.

Virués-Ortega, J. (2010). Applied behavior analytic intervention for autism in early childhood: Meta-analysis, meta-regression and dose-response meta-analysis of multiple outcomes. *Clinical Psychology Review, 30*, 387–399.

Visser, S. N., Danielson, M. L., Bitsko, R. H., Holbrook, J. R., Kogan, M. D., Ghandour, R. M., et al. (2014). Trends in the parent-report of health care provider-diagnosed and medicated attention-deficit/hyperactivity disorder: United States, 2003–2011. *Journal of the American Academy of Child and Adolescent Psychiatry, 53*(1), 34–46.e32. http://dx.doi.org/10.1016/j.jaac.2013.09.001

Vitaliani, R., Mason, W., Ances, B., Zwerdling, T., Jiang, Z., & Dalmau, J. (2005). Paraneoplastic encephalitis, psychiatric symptoms, and hypoventilation in ovarian teratoma. *Annals of Neurology, 58*, 594–604.

Vitaliano, P. P., Zhang, J., & Scanlan, J. M. (2003). Is caregiving hazardous to one's physical health? A meta-analysis. *Psychological Bulletin, 129*, 946–972.

Vitousek, K., & Manke, F. (1994). Personality variables and disorders in anorexia nervosa and bulimia nervosa. *Journal of Abnormal Psychology, 103*, 137–147.

Vittengl, J. R., Clark, L. A., Dunn, T. W., & Jarrett, R. B. (2007). Reducing relapse and recurrence in unipolar depression: A comparative meta-analysis of cognitive-behavior therapy's effects. *Journal of Consulting and Clinical Psychology, 75*, 475–488.

Vogt, D., Smith, B., Elwy, R., Martin, J., Schultz, M., Drainoni, M. L., et al. (2011). Predeployment, deployment, and postdeployment risk factors for posttraumatic stress symptomatology in female and male OEF/OIF veterans. *Journal of Abnormal Psychology, 120*, 819–831.

Vohs, K. D., & Heatherton, T. F. (2000). Self-regulatory failure: A resource-depletion approach. *Psychological Science, 11*, 249–254.

Volk, D. W., Austin, M. C., Pierri, J. N., Sampson, A. R., & Lewis, D. A. (2000). Decreased glutamic acid decarboxylase67 messenger RNA expression in a subset of prefrontal cortical gamma-aminobutyric acid neurons in subjects with schizophrenia. *Archives of General Psychiatry, 57*, 237–248.

Volkow, N. D., Wang, G. J., Fischman, M. W., & Foltin, R. W. (1997). Relationship between subjective effects of cocaine and dopamine transporter occupancy. *Nature, 386*, 827–830.

Volkow, N. D., Wang, G. J., Kollins, S. H., Wigal, T. L., Newcorn, J. H., Telang, F., et al. (2009). Evaluating dopamine reward pathway in ADHD: Clinical implications. *Journal of the American Medical Association, 302*(10), 1084–1091.

Volkow, N. D., Wang, G. J., Newcorn, J. H., Kollins, S. H., Wigal, T. L., Telang, F., et al. (2011). Motivation deficit in ADHD is associated with dysfunction of the dopamine reward pathway. *Molecular Psychiatry, 16*(11), 1147–1154.

von Krafft-Ebing, R. (1902). *Psychopathia sexualis.* Brooklyn, NY: Physicians and Surgeons Books.

Voon, V., Derbyshire, K., Ruck, C., Irvine, M. A., Worbe, Y., Enander, J., et al. (2015). Disorders of compulsivity: A common bias towards learning habits. *Molecular Psychiatry, 20*, 345–52. doi: 10.1038/mp.2014.44.

Vos, T., Allen, C., Arora, M., Barber, R. M., Bhutta, Z. A., Brown, A., et al. (2016). Global, regional, and national incidence, prevalence, and years lived with disability for 310 diseases and injuries, 1990–2013; 2015: A systematic analysis for the Global Burden of Disease Study 2015. *The Lancet, 388*(10053), 1545-1602. doi:10.1016/S0140-6736(16)31678-6

Vrshek-Schallhorn, S., Doane, L. D., Mineka, S., Zinbarg, R. E., Craske, M. G., & Adam, E. K. (2013). The cortisol awakening response predicts major depression: Predictive stability over a 4-year follow-up and effect of depression history. *Psychological Medicine, 43*(3), 483–493. doi:10.1017/S0033291712001213

Vrshek-Schallhorn, S., Mineka, S., Zinbarg, R. E., Craske, M. G., Griffith, J. W., Sutton, J., et al. (2013). Refining the candidate environment. *Clinical Psychological Science, 2*(3), 235–248. doi:10.1177/2167702613499329

Vrshek-Schallhorn, S., Mineka, S., Zinbarg, R. E., Craske, M. G., Griffith, J. W., Sutton, J., et al. (2013). Refining the candidate environment: Interpersonal stress, the serotonin transporter polymorphism, and gene–environment interactions in major depression. *Clinical Psychological Science, 2*(3), 235–248.

Vrshek-Schallhorn, S., Stroud, C. B., Mineka, S., Hammen, C., Zinbarg, R. E., Wolitzky-Taylor, K., & Craske, M. G. (2015). Chronic and episodic interpersonal stress as statistically unique predictors of depression in two samples of emerging adults. *Journal of Abnormal Psychology, 124*, 918–932. doi:10.1037/abn0000088

Wade, C. L., Kallupi, M., Hernandez, D. O., Breysse, E., de Guglielmo, G., Crawford, E., et al. (2017). High-frequency stimulation of the subthalamic nucleus blocks compulsive-like re-escalation of heroin taking in rats. *42*, 1850–1859. http://doi.org/10.1038/npp.2016.270

Wade, T. D., Bulik, C. M., Neale, M., & Kendler, K. S. (2000). Anorexia nervosa and major depression: Shared genetic and environmental risk factors. *American Journal of Psychiatry, 157*, 469–471.

Wahl, O. F. (1999). Mental health consumers' experience of stigma. *Schizophrenia Bulletin, 25*, 467–478.

Wakefield, J. C. (2011). DSM-5 proposed diagnostic criteria for sexual paraphilias: Tensions between diagnostic validity and forensic utility. *International Journal of Law and Psychiatry, 34*, 195–209. doi:10.1016/j.ijlp.2011.04.012

Wakefield, J. C. (2013). The DSM-5 debate over the bereavement exclusion: Psychiatric diagnosis and the future of empirically supported treatment. *Clinical Psychology Review, 33*, 825–845. doi:10.1016/j.cpr.2013.03.007

Wakefield, J. C. (2015). DSM-5, psychiatric epidemiology and the false positives problem. *Epidemiology and Psychiatric Sciences, 24*, 188–196. doi:10.1017/s2045796015000116

Wakefield, M., & Chaloupka, R. (2000). Effectiveness of comprehensive tobacco control programmes in reducing teenage smoking in the USA. *Tobacco Control, 9*, 177–186.

Waldinger, M. D., Quinn, P., Dilleen, M., Mundayat, R., Schweitzer, D. H., & Boolell, M. (2005). A multinational population survey of intravaginal ejaculation latency time. *Journal of Sexual Medicine, 2*, 492–497.

Walker, E. F., Davis, D. M., & Savoie, T. D. (1994). Neuromotor precursors of schizophrenia. *Schizophrenia Bulletin, 20*, 441–451.

Walker, E. F., Grimes, K. E., Davis, D. M., & Adina, J. (1993). Childhood precursors of schizophrenia: Facial expressions of emotion. *American Journal of Psychiatry, 150*, 1654–1660.

Walker, E. F., Kestler, L., Bollini, A., & Hochman, K. (2004). Schizophrenia: Etiology and course. *Annual Review of Psychology, 55*, 401–430.

Walker, E. F., Mittal, V., & Tessner, K. (2008). Stress and the hypothalamic pituitary adrenal axis in the developmental course of schizophrenia. *Annual Review of Clinical Psychology, 4*, 189–216.

Walker, E. F., Trotman, H. D., Pearce, B. D., Addington, J., Cadenhead, K. S., Cornblatt, B. A., et al. (2013). Cortisol levels and risk for psychosis: Initial findings from the North American prodrome longitudinal study. *Biological Psychiatry, 74*, 410–417.

Walker, R. D., & Bigelow, D. A. (2015). Evidence-informed, culture-based interventions and best practices in American Indian and Alaska Native communities. In P. E. Nathan & J. M. Gorman (Eds.), *A guide to treatments that work* (4th ed.) (pp. 23–54). Oxford, UK: Oxford University Press.

Walkup, J. T., Albano, A. M., Piacentini, J., Birmaher, B., Comptom, S. N., Sherrill, J. T., et al. (2008). Cognitive behavioral therapy, sertaline, or a combination in childhood anxiety. *New England Journal of Medicine, 359*, 2753–2766.

Waller, D. A., Kiser, S., Hardy, B. W., Fuchs, I., & Feigenbaum, L. P. (1986). Eating behavior and plasma betaendorphin in bulimia. *American Journal of Clinical Nutrition, 4*, 20–23.

Walsh, B. T. (2013). The enigmatic persistence of anorexia nervosa. *American Journal of Psychiatry, 170*, 477–484. doi: 10.1176/appi.ajp.2012.12081074

Walsh, B. T., Agras, S. W., Devlin, M. J., et al. (2000). Fluoxetine for bulimia nervosa following poor response to psychotherapy. *American Journal of Psychiatry, 157*, 1332–1334.

Walsh, B. T., Seidman, S. N., Sysko, R., & Gould, M. (2002). Placebo response in studies of major depression: Variable, substantial, and growing. *Journal of American Medical Association, 287*, 1840–1847.

Walsh, B. T., Wilson, G. T., Loeb, K. L., Devin, M. J., et al. (1997). Medication and psychotherapy in the treatment of bulimia nervosa. *American Journal of Psychiatry, 154*, 523–531.

Walsh, K., Hasin, D., Keyes, K. M., & Koenen, K. C. (2016). Associations between gender-based violence and personality disorders in U.S. women. *Personality Disorders: Theory, Research, and Treatment, 7*, 205–210. http://dx.doi.org/10.1037/per0000158

Walsh, T., McClellan, J. M., McCarthy, S. E., Addington, A. M., Pierce, S. B., et al. (2008). Rare structural variants disrupt genes in neurodevelopmental pathways in schizophrenia. *Science, 320*, 539–543.

Walters, G. L., & Clopton, J. R. (2000). Effect of symptom information and validity scale information on the malingering of depression on the MMPI-2. *Journal of Personality Assessment, 75*, 183–199.

Wang, P. S., Aguilar-Gaxiola, S., Alonso, J., Angermeyer, M. C., Borges, G., Bromet, E. J., et al. (2007). Use of mental health services for anxiety, mood, and substance disorders in 17 countries in the WHO World Mental Health Surveys. *The Lancet, 370*, 841–850.

Wang, P. S., Lane, M. C., Olfson, M., Pincus, H. A., Wells, K. B., & Kessler, R. C. (2005). Twelve-month use of mental health services in the United States: Results from the National Comorbidity Survey Replication. *Archives of General Psychiatry, 62*, 629–640.

Wang, P. S., Simon, G. E., Avorn, J., Azocar, F., Ludman, E. J., McCulloch, J., et al. (2007). Telephone screening, outreach, and care management for depressed workers and impact on clinical and work productivity outcomes: A randomized controlled trial. *Journal of the American Medical Association, 298*, 1401–1411.

Wansink, B., & Payne, C. R. (2009). The *Joy of Cooking* too much: 70 years of calorie increases in classic recipes. *Annals of Internal Medicine, 150*, 291.

Ward-Ciesielski, E. F., & Linehan, M. M. (2014). Psychological treatment of suicidal behaviors. In K. N. Matthew (Ed.), *The Oxford handbook of suicide and self-injury*. New York, NY: Oxford University Press.

Ward, T. B., & Beech, A. (2006). An integrated theory of sexual offending. *Aggression and Violent Behavior, 11*, 44–63.

Warwick, H. M. C., & Salkovskis, P. M. (2001). Cognitive-behavioral treatment of hypochondriasis. In D. R. Lipsitt & V. Starcevic (Eds.), *Hypochondriasis: Modern perspectives on an ancient malady* (pp. 314–328). London: Oxford University Press.

Washington, A. *Billboard*, Mar 3, 2017, http://www.billboard.com/articles/news/7710060/demi-lovato-honored-mental-health-advocacy

Waszczuk, M. A., Zavos, H. M., Gregory, A. M., & Eley, T. C. (2014). The phenotypic and genetic structure of depression and anxiety disorder symptoms in childhood, adolescence, and young adulthood. *JAMA Psychiatry, 71*, 905–916.

Waters, A., Hill, A., & Waller, G. (2001). Internal and external antecedents of binge eating episodes in a group of women with bulimia nervosa. *International Journal of Eating Disorders, 29*, 17–22.

Waters, A. M., Peters, R. M., Forrest, K. E., Zimmer-Gembeck, M. (2014). Fear acquisition and extinction in offspring of mothers with anxiety and depressive disorders. *Developmental Cognitive Neuroscience, 7*, 30–42. doi: 10.1016/j.dcn.2013.10.007.

Watkins, E. R. (2008). Constructive and unconstructive repetitive thought. *Psychological Bulletin, 134*, 163–206.

Watkins, P. C. (2002). Implicit memory bias in depression. *Cognition and Emotion, 16*, 381–402.

Watson, D., Stasik, S. M., Ro, E., & Clark, L. A. (2013). Integrating normal and pathological personality: Relating the DSM-5 trait-dimensional model to general traits of personality. *Assessment, 20*, 312–326. doi:10.1177/1073191113485810

Watson, H. J., & Rees, C. S. (2008). Meta-analysis of randomized, controlled treatment trials for pediatric obsessive-compulsive disorder. *Journal of Child Psychology and Psychiatry, and Allied Disciplines, 49*(5), 489–498. http://doi.org/10.1111/j.1469-7610.2007.01875.x

Watson, J. B., & Rayner, R. (1920). Conditioned emotional reactions. *Journal of Experimental Psychology, 3(1)*, 1–14.

Watters, E. (2010). *Crazy like us: The globalization of the American psyche*. New York, NY: Free Press.

Watt, N. F. (1974). Childhood and adolescent roots of schizophrenia. In D. Ricks, A. Thomas, & M. Roll (Eds.), *Life history research in psychopathology* (Vol. 3). Minneapolis, MN: University of Minnesota Press.

Watt, N. F., Stolorow, R. D., Lubensky, A. W., & McClelland, D. C. (1970). School adjustment and behavior of children hospitalized for schizophrenia as adults. *American Journal of Orthopsychiatry, 40*, 637–657.

Watts, A. L., Lilienfeld, S. O., Smith, S. F., Miller, J. D., Campbell, W. K., Waldman, I. D., et al. (2013). The double-edged sword of grandiose narcissism: Implications for successful and unsuccessful leadership among U.S. presidents. *Psychological Science, 24*, 2379–2389.

Weaton, M. G., & Van Meter, A. (2015). Comorbidity in hoarding disorder. In R. O. Frost & G. Steketee (Eds.), *The Oxford handbook of hoarding and acquiring*. Oxford, England: Oxford University Press.

Webster, C., Douglas, K., Eaves, D., & Hart, S. (1997). *HCR-20: Assessing risk for violence (Version 2)*. Vancouver, British Columbia, Canada: Simon Fraser University.

Webster-Stratton, C. (1998). Preventing conduct problems in Head Start children: Strengthening parenting competencies. *Journal of Consulting and Clinical Psychology, 66*, 715–730.

Webster-Stratton, C., Reid, M. J., & Hammond, M. (2001). Preventing conduct problems, promoting social competence: A parent and teacher training partnership in Head Start. *Journal of Clinical Child Psychology, 30*, 283–302.

Wechsler, D. (1968). *Escala de Inteligencia Wechsler para Adultos*. New York, NY: Psychological Corporation.

Wegner, D. M., Schneider, D. J., Carter, S. R., & White, T. L. (1987). Paradoxical effects of thought suppression. *Journal of Personality and Social Psychology, 53*, 5–13.

Wehr, T. A., Duncan, W. C., Sher, L., Aeschbach, D., Schwartz, P. J., Turner, E. H., et al. (2001). A circadian signal of change of season in patients with seasonal affective disorder. *Archives of General Psychiatry, 58*, 1108–1114.

Weickert, C. S., Fung, S. J., Catts, V. S., Schofield, P. R., Allen, K. M., Moore, L. T., et al. (2013). Molecular evidence of N-methyl-D-aspartate receptor hypofunction in schizophrenia. *Molecular Psychiatry, 18*, 1185–1192. http://doi.org/10.1038/mp.2012.137

Weierich, M. R., & Nock, M. K. (2008). Posttraumatic stress symptoms mediate the relation between childhood sexual abuse and nonsuicidal self-injury. *Journal of Consulting and Clinical Psychology, 76*, 39–44.

Weinberger, D. R. (1987). Implications of normal brain development for the pathogenesis of schizophrenia. *Archives of General Psychiatry, 44*, 660–669.

Weinberger, D. R., Berman, K. F., & Illowsky, B. P. (1988). Physiological dysfunction of dorsolateral prefrontal cortex in schizophrenia: 3. A new cohort and evidence for a monoaminergic mechanism. *Archives of General Psychiatry, 45*, 609–615.

Weinberger, D. R., Cannon-Spoor, H. E., Potkin, S. G., & Wyatt, R. J. (1980). Poor premorbid adjustment and CT scan abnormalities in chronic schizophrenia. *American Journal of Psychiatry, 137*, 1410–1413.

Weiner, B., Frieze, I., Kukla, A., Reed, L. Rest, S., & Rosenbaum, R. M. (1971). Perceiving the causes of success and failure. In E. E. Jones et al. (Eds.), *Attribution: Perceiving the causes of behavior*. Morristown, NJ: General Learning Press.

Weiner, D. B. (1994). Le geste de Pinel: The history of psychiatric myth. In M. S. Micale & R. Porter (Eds.), *Discovering the history of psychiatry*. New York, NY: Oxford University Press.

Weinstock, J., Massura, C. E., & Petry, N. M. (2013). Professional and pathological gamblers: Similarities and differences. *Journal of Gambling Studies, 29*, 205–216.

Weisberg, R. B., Brown, T. A., Wincze, J. P., & Barlow, D. H. (2001). Causal attributions and male sexual arousal: The impact of attributions for a bogus erectile difficulty on sexual arousal, cognitions, and affect. *Journal of Abnormal Psychology, 110*, 324–334.

Weisberg, R. W. (1994). Genius and madness? A quasi-experimental test of the hypothesis that manic-depression increases creativity. *Psychological Science, 5*, 361–367.

Weisman, A. G., Nuechterlein, K. H., Goldstein, M. J., & Snyder, K. S. (1998). Expressed emotion, attributions, and schizophrenia symptom dimensions. *Journal of Abnormal Psychology, 107*, 355–359.

Weiss, A. J., Bailey, M. K., O'Malley, L., Barrett, M. L., Elixhauser, A., & Steiner, C. A. (2017, June). Patient characteristics of opioid-related inpatient stays and emergency department visits nationally and by state, 2014. HCUP Statistical Brief #224. Retrieved from https://www.hcup-us.ahrq.gov/reports/statbriefs/sb224-Patient-Characteristics-Opioid-Hospital-Stays-ED-Visits-by-State.pdf

Weiss, G., & Hechtman, L. (1993). *Hyperactive children grown up* (2nd ed.). New York, NY: Guilford Press.

Weissman, A. N., & Beck, A. T. (1978, November). *Development and validation of the Dysfunctional Attitude Scale: A preliminary investigation*. Paper presented at the meeting of the Association for the Advancement of Behavior Therapy, Chicago.

Weiss, R. D., Potter, J. S., Fiellin, D. A., Byrne, M., Connery, H. S., Dickinson, W., et al. (2011). Adjunctive counseling during brief and extended buprenorphine-naloxone treatment for prescription opioid dependence: A 2-phase randomized controlled trial. *Archives of General Psychiatry, 68*, 1238–1246. http://doi.org/10.1001/archgenpsychiatry.2011.121

Weisz, J. R., McCarty, C. A., & Valeri, S. M. (2006). Effects of psychotherapy for depression in children and adolescents: A meta-analysis. *Psychological Bulletin, 132*, 132–149.

Weisz, J. R., Suwanlert, S. C., Wanchai, W., & Bernadette, R. (1987). Over- and under-controlled referral problems among children and adolescents from Thailand and the United States: The wat and wai of cultural differences. *Journal of Consulting and Clinical Psychology, 55*, 719–726.

Weisz, J. R., Weiss, B., Suwanlert, S., & Chaiyasit, W. (2003). Syndromal structure of psychopathology in children of Thailand and the United States. *Journal of Consulting and Clinical Psychology, 71*, 375–385.

Weisz, J. R., Weiss, B., Suwanlert, S., & Chaiyasit, W. (2006). Culture and youth psychopathology: Testing the syndromal sensitivity model in Thai and American adolescents. *Journal of Consulting and Clinical Psychology, 74*(6), 1098–1107. http://doi.org/10.1037/0022-006X.74.6.1098

Wells, K. C., Epstein, J. N., Hinshaw, S. P., Conners, C. K., Klaric, J. Abikoff, H. B., et al. (2000). Parenting and family stress treatment outcomes in attention deficit hyperactivity disorder (ADHD): An empirical analysis in the MTA study. *Journal of Abnormal Child Psychology, 28*, 543–553.

Wender, P. H., Kety, S. S., Rosenthal, D., Schulsinger, F., Ortmann, J., & Lunde, I. (1986). Psychiatric disorders in the biological and adoptive families of adopted individuals with affective disorders. *Archives of General Psychiatry, 43*, 923–929.

Wenzel, A., & Spokas, M. (2014). Cognitive and information processing approaches to understanding suicidal behaviors. In M. K. Nock (Ed.), *The Oxford handbook of suicide and self-injury.* New York, NY: Oxford University Press.

Wessel, L. (2017). False: Vaccination can cause autism. *Science, 356*, 368.

Westen, D. (1998). The scientific legacy of Sigmund Freud: Toward a psychodynamically informed psychological science. *Psychological Bulletin, 124*, 333–371.

Westen, D., Novotny, C. M., & Thompson-Brenner, H. (2004). The empirical status of empirically supported psychotherapies: Assumptions, findings, and reporting in controlled clinical trials. *Psychological Bulletin, 130*, 631–663.

Westman, J., Hällgren, J., Wahlbeck, K., Erlinge, D., Alfredsson, L., & Ösby, U. (2013). Cardiovascular mortality in bipolar disorder: A population-based cohort study in sweden. *BMJ Open, 3*(4), e002373. doi:10.1136/bmjopen-2012-002373

Wetherill, R. R., Jagannathan, K., Lohoff, F. W., Ehrman, R., O'Brien, C. P., Childress, A. R., & Franklin, T. R. (2014). Neural correlates of attentional bias for smoking cues: Modulation by variance in the dopamine transporter gene. *Addiction Biology, 19*, 294–304.

Whisman, M. (2007). Marital distress and DSM-IV psychiatric disorders in a population-based national survey. *Journal of Abnormal Psychology, 116*, 638–43.

Whisman, M. (2007). Marital distress and DSM-IV psychiatric disorders in a population-based national survey. *Journal of Abnormal Psychology, 116*, 638–643. doi:10.1037/0021-843X.116.3.638

Whisman, M. A., & Bruce, M. L. (1999). Marital dissatisfaction and incidence of major depressive episode in a community sample. *Journal of Abnormal Psychology, 108*, 674–678.

Whisman, M. A., Sheldon, C. T., & Goering, P. (2000). Psychiatric disorders and dissatisfaction with social relationships: Does type of relationship matter? *Journal of Abnormal Psychology, 109*, 803–808.

Whisman, M. A., & Uebelacker, L. A. (2006). Impairment and distress associated with relationship discord in a national sample of married or cohabiting adults. *Journal of Family Psychology, 20*, 369–377.

Whitaker, R. (2002). *Mad in America.* Cambridge, MA: Perseus.

Whitcomb-Smith, S., Sigmon, S. T., Martinson, A., Young, M., Craner, J., & Boulard, N. (2014). The temporal development of mood, cognitive, and vegetative symptoms in recurrent sad episodes: A test of the dual vulnerability hypothesis. *Cognitive Therapy and Research, 38*(1), 43–54. doi:10.1007/s10608-013-9577-5

White, J. W., & Smith, P. H. (2004). Sexual assault perpetration and reperpetration. *Criminal Justice and Behavior, 31*, 182–202. doi:10.1177/0093854803261342

White, S. W., Oswald, D., Ollendick, T., & Scahill, L. (2009). Anxiety in children and adolescents with autism spectrum disorders. *Clinical Psychology Review, 29*, 216–229.

Whitlock, J., Muehlenkamp, J., Eckenrode, J., Purington, A., Baral Abrams, G., Barreira, P., & Kress, V. (2013). Nonsuicidal self-injury as a gateway to suicide in young adults. *Journal of Adolescent Health, 52*(4), 486–492. doi:10.1016/j.jadohealth.2012.09.010

Whittal, M. L., Agras, S. W., & Gould, R. A. (1999). Bulimia nervosa: A meta-analysis of psychosocial and pharmacological treatments. *Behavior Therapy, 30*, 117–135.

Whittle, S., Lichter, R., Dennison, M., Vijayakumar, N., Schwartz, O., Byrne, M. L., et al. (2014). Structural brain development and depression onset during adolescence: A prospective longitudinal study. *The American Journal of Psychiatry, 171*(5), 564–571.

Widom, C. S. (2014). Longterm consequences of child maltreatment. Korbin J., Krugman R. (eds) *Handbook of Child Maltreatment.* Child Maltreatment (Contemporary Issues in Research and Policy), vol 2 (pp. 225–247). Dordrecht, Netherlands: Springer.

Wiech, K., & Tracey, I. (2009). The influence of negative emotions on pain: Behavioral effects and neural mechanisms. *NeuroImage, 47*, 987–994.

Wilcox, C. E., Pommy, J. M., & Adinoff, B. (2016). Neural circuitry of impaired emotion regulation in substance use disorders. *American Journal of Psychiatry, 173*, 344–361. http://doi.org/10.1176/appi.ajp.2015.15060710

Wildes, J. E., Emery, R. E., & Simons, A. D. (2001). The roles of ethnicity and culture in the development of eating disturbance and body dissatisfaction: A meta-analytic review. *Clinical Psychology Review, 21*, 521–551.

Wilfley, D. E., Welch, R. R, Stein, R. I., Spurrell, E. B., Cohen, L. R., et al. (2002). A randomized comparison of group cognitive-behavioral therapy and group interpersonal psychotherapy for the treatment of overweight individuals with binge eating disorder. *Archives of General Psychiatry, 59*, 713–721.

Wilhelm, S., Buhlmann, U., Hayward, L. C., Greenberg, J. L., & Dimaite, R. (2010). A cognitive-behavioral treatment approach for body dysmorphic disorder. *Cognitive and Behavioral Practice, 17*, 241–247.

Williams, J. M. G., Crane, C., Barnhofer, T., Brennan, K., Duggan, D. S., Fennell, M. J. V., et al. (2014). Mindfulness-based cognitive therapy for preventing relapse in recurrent depression: A randomized dismantling trial. *J Consult Clin Psychol., 82*(2), 275–286. doi:10.1037/a0035036

Williams, J. M. G., Watts, F. N., MacLeod, C., & Mathews, A. (1997). *Cognitive psychology and emotional disorders* (2nd ed.). New York, NY: John Wiley & Sons.

Williams, J. W., Plassman, B. L., Burke, J., Holsinger, T., & Benjamin, S. (2010). Preventing Alzheimer's disease and cognitive decline. *Evidence Report/Technology Assessment No. 193.* Rockville, MD: Duke Evidence-based Practice Center.

Williams, L. M. (2017). Defining biotypes for depression and anxiety based on large-scale circuit dysfunction: A theoretical review of the evidence and future directions for clinical translation. *Depression and Anxiety, 34*(1), 9–24. doi:10.1002/da.22556

Williams, L. M., Brown, K. J., Palmer, D., Liddell, B. J., Kemp, A. H., Olivieri, G., et al. (2006). The mellow years? Neural basis of improving emotional stability over age. *The Journal of Neuroscience, 26*, 6422–6430. doi:10.1523/jneurosci.0022-06.2006

Williams, S. S., (2016). The terrorist inside my husband's brain. *Neurology, 87*, 1308–1311.

Wills, T. A., Sandy, J. M., & Yaeger, A. M. (2002). Stress and smoking in adolescence: A test of directional hypotheses. *Health Psychology, 21*, 122–130.

Wilsnack, R. W., Vogeltanz, N. D., Wilsnack, S. C., Harris, T. R., Ahlström, S., Bondy, S., Csémy, L., Ferrence, R., et al. (2000). Gender differences in alcohol consumption and adverse drinking consequences: Cross-cultural patterns. *Addiction, 95*, 251–265.

Wilson, D. (2011, April 13). As generics near, makers tweak erectile drugs. *New York Times,* p. B11.

Wilson, G. T. (1995). Psychological treatment of binge eating and bulimia nervosa. *Journal of Mental Health (UK), 4*, 451–457.

Wilson, G. T., & Fairburn, C. G. (1998). Treatments for eating disorders. In P. Nathan & J. M. Gorman (Eds.), *A guide to treatments that work* (pp. 501–530). London, UK: Oxford University Press.

Wilson, G. T., Grilo, C. M., & Vitousek, K. M. (2007). Psychological treatment of eating disorders. *American Psychologist, 62*, 199–216. doi:http://dx.doi.org/10.1037/0003-066X.62.3.199

Wilson, G. T., Loeb, K. L., Walsh, B. T., Labouvie, E., Petkova, E., Liu, X., & Waternaux, C. (1999). Psychological and pharmacological treatment of bulimia nervosa: Predictors and processes of change. *Journal of Consulting and Clinical Psychology, 67*, 451–459.

Wilson, G. T., & Pike, K. M. (2001). Eating disorders. In D. H. Barlow (Ed.), *Clinical handbook of psychological disorders* (3rd ed., pp. 332–375). New York, NY: Guilford Press.

Wilson, G. T., Wilfley, D. E., Agras, W. S., & Bryson, S. W. (2010). Psychological treatments of binge eating disorder. *Archives of General Psychiatry, 67*, 94–101.

Wilson, G. T., & Zandberg, L. J. (2012). Cognitive–behavioral guided self-help for eating disorders: Effectiveness and scalability. *Clinical Psychology Review, 32*, 343–357.

Wilson, R. S., Scherr, P. A., Schneider, J. A., Tang, Y., & Bennett, D. A. (2007). Relation of cognitive activity to risk of developing Alzheimer's disease. *Neurology, 69*, 1191–1920.

Wilson, S., Stroud, C. B., & Durbin, C. E. (2017). Interpersonal dysfunction in personality disorders: A meta-analytic review. *Psychological Bulletin, 143*, 677–734. doi:10.1037/bul0000101

Wincze, J. P., Steketee, G., & Frost, R. O. (2007). Categorization in compulsive hoarding. *Behaviour Research and Therapy, 45*, 63–72.

Wincze, J. P., & Weisberg, R. B. (2015). *Sexual dysfunction, third edition: A guide for assessment and treatment*. New York, NY: Guilford Publications.

Wingfield, N., Kelly, N., Serdar, K., Shivy, V. A., & Mazzeo, S. E. (2011). College students' perceptions of individuals with anorexia and bulimia nervosa. *International Journal of Eating Disorders, 44*, 369–375.

Wirshing, D. W., Wirshing, W. C., Marder, S. R., Liberman, R. P., & Mintz, J. (1998). Informed consent: Assessment of comprehension. *American Journal of Psychiatry, 155*, 1508–1511.

Witkiewitz, K., & Marlatt, G. A. (2004). Relapse prevention for alcohol and drug problems: That was Zen, this is Tao. *American Psychologist, 59*, 224–235.

Wittchen, H. U., Gloster, A. T., Beesdo-Baum, K., Fava, G. A., & Craske, M. G. (2010). Agoraphobia: A review of the diagnostic classificatory position and criteria. *Depression and Anxiety, 27*, 113–133.

Wittchen, H. U., & Jacobi, F. (2005). Size and burden of mental disorders in Europe—A critical review and appraisal of 27 studies. *European Neuropsychopharmacology, 15*, 357–376.

Witthoft, M., & Rubin, G. J. (2013). Are media warnings about the adverse health effects of modern life self-fulfilling? An experimental study on idiopathic environmental intolerance attributed to electromagnetic fields (IEI-EMF). *Journal of Psychosomatic Research, 74*, 206–212. doi:10.1016/j.jpsychores.2012.12.002

Wolf, E. J., Miller, M. W., Reardon, A. F., Ryabchenko, K. A., Castillo, D., & Freund, R. (2012). A latent class analysis of dissociation and post-traumatic stress disorder: Evidence for a dissociative subtype. *Archives of General Psychiatry, 69*, 698–705.

Wolitzky, D. (1995). Traditional psychoanalytic psychotherapy. In A. S. Gurman & S. B. Messer (Eds.), *Essential psychotherapies: Theory and practice*. New York: Guilford Press.

Wolitzky-Taylor, K. B., Horowitz, J. D., Powers, M. B., & Telch, M. J. (2008). Psychological approaches in the treatment of specific phobias: A meta-analysis. *Clinical Psychology Review, 28*, 1021–1037.

Wolraich, M. L., Wilson, D. B., & White, J. W. (1995). The effect of sugar on behavior or cognition in children: A meta-analysis. *Journal of the American Medical Association, 274*, 1617–1621.

Wonderlich, S. A., Gordon, K. H., Mitchell, J. E., Crosby, R. D., Engel, S. G., & Walsh, B. T. (2009). The validity and clinical utility of binge eating disorder. *International Journal of Eating Disorders, 42*, 687–705.

Wong, Q. J. J., & Rapee, R. M. (2016). The aetiology and maintenance of social anxiety disorder: A synthesis of complimentary theoretical models and formulation of a new integrated model. *Journal of Affective Disorders, 203*, 84–100.

Woodberry, K. A., Giuliano, A. J., & Seidman, L. J. (2008). Premorbid IQ in schizophrenia: A meta-analytic review. *American Journal of Psychiatry, 165*, 579–587.

Woodmansee, M. A. (1996). The guilty but mentally ill verdict: Political expediency at the expense of moral principle. *Notre Dame Journal of Law, Ethics and Public Policy, 10*, 341–387.

Woods, S. W., Addington, J., Cadenhead, K. S., Cannon, T. D., Cornblatt, B. A., Heinssen, R., et al. (2009). Validity of the prodromal risk syndrome for first psychosis: Findings from the North American Prodrome Longitudinal Study. *Schizophrenia Bulletin, 35*, 894–908. doi:10.1093/schbul/sbp027

Woody, S. R., & Teachman, B. A. (2000). Intersection of disgust and fear: Normative and pathological views. *Clinical Psychology: Science and Practice, 7*, 291–311.

Woo, J. S., Brotto, L. A., & Gorzalka, B. B. (2011). The role of sex guilt in the relationship between culture and women's sexual desire. *Archives of Sexual Behavior, 40*, 385–394.

World Health Organization. (2012). *Global health observatory data: Suicide rates*. Geneva, Switzerland: WHO. Retrieved from http://www.who.int/gho/mental_health/suicide_rates/en/.

World Health Organization. (2015). Global health observatory data repository: Human resources data by country. Retrieved April 24, 2017, from World Health Organization. http://apps.who.int/gho/data/view.main.MHHRv

Wouda, J. C., Hartman, P. M., Bakker, R. M., Bakker, J. O., van de Wiel, H. B. M., & Schultz, W. C. (1998). Vaginal plethysmography in women with dyspareunia. *Journal of Sex Research, 35*, 141–147.

Wright, A. G. C., Krueger, R. F., Hobbs, M. J., Markon, K. E., Eaton, N. R., & Slade, T. (2013). The structure of psychopathology: Toward an expanded quantitative empirical model. *Journal of Abnormal Psychology, 122*(1), 281–294. doi:10.1037/a0030133

Wu, J., Xiao, H., Sun, H., Zou, L., & Zhu, L. Q. (2012). Role of dopamine receptors in ADHD: A systematic meta-analysis. *Molecular Neurobiology, 45*, 605–620.

Wu, Y.-T., Fratiglioni, L., Matthews, F. E., Lobo, A., Breteler, M. M. B., Skoog, I., & Brayne, C. (2016). Dementia in western Europe: Epidemiological evidence and implications for policy making. *The Lancet Neurology, 15*, 116–124. doi:10.1016/S1474-4422(15)00092-7

Wykes, T., Huddy, V., Cellard, C., McGurk, S., & Czobor, P. (2011). A meta-analysis of cognitive remediation for schizophrenia: Methodology and effect sizes. *American Journal of Psychiatry, 168*, 472–485.

Wykes, T., Steel, C., Everitt, T., & Tarrier, N. (2008). Cognitive behavior therapy for schizophrenia: Effect sizes, clinical models, and methodological rigor. *Schizophrenia Bulletin, 34*, 523–537.

Xia, J., Merinder, L. B., & Belgamwar, M. R. (2011). Psychoeducation for schizophrenia. *Schizophrenia Bulletin, 37*, 21–22.

Yaffe, K., Fiocco, A. J., Lindquist, K., Vittinghoff, E., Simonsick, E. M., Newman, A. B., et al. (2009). Predictors of maintaining cognitive function in older adults. *Neurology, 72*, 2029–2035.

Yap, M. B. H., & Jorm, A. F. (2015). Parental factors associated with childhood anxiety, depression, and internalizing problems: A systematic review and meta-analysis. *Journal of Affective Disorders, 175*, 424–440.

Yerkes, R. M., & Dodson, J. D. (1908). The relation of strength of stimulus to rapidity of habit formation. *Journal of Comparative and Neurological Psychology, 18*, 459–482.

Yilmaz, Z., Hardaway, J. A., & Bulik, C. M. (2015). Genetics and epigenetics of eating disorders. *Advances in Genomics and Genetics, 5*, 131–150. http://doi.org/10.2147/AGG.S55776

Yilmaz, Z., Zai, C. C., Hwang, R., Mann, S., Arenovich, T., Remington, G., & Daskalakis, Z. J. (2012). Antipsychotics, dopamine D2 receptor occupancy and clinical improvement in schizophrenia: A meta-analysis. *Schizophrenia Research, 140*, 214–220.

Yirmiya, N., & Sigman, M. (1991). High functioning individuals with autism: Diagnosis, empirical findings, and theoretical issues. *Clinical Psychology Review, 11*, 669–683.

Yoast, R., Williams, M. A., Deitchman, S. D., & Champion, H. C. (2001). Report of the Council on Scientific Affairs: Methadone maintenance and needle-exchange programs to reduce the medical and public health consequences of drug abuse. *Journal of Addictive Diseases, 20*, 15–40.

Yokum, S., Marti, C. N., Smolen, A., & Stice, E. (2015). Relation of the multilocus genetic composite reflecting high dopamine signaling capacity to future increases in BMI. *Appetite, 87*, 38–45.

York Cornwell, E., & Waite, L. J. (2009). Social disconnectedness, perceived isolation, and health among older adults. *Journal of Health and Social Behavior, 50*, 31–48.

Young, J., Goey, A., Minassian, A., Perry, W., Paulus, M., & Geyer, M. (2010). GBR 12909 administration as a mouse model of bipolar disorder mania: Mimicking quantitative assessment of manic behavior. *Psychopharmacology, 208*, 443–454.

Younglove, J. A., & Vitello, C. J. (2003). Community notification provisions of "Megan's Law" from a therapeutic jurisprudence perspective: A case study. *American Journal of Forensic Psychology, 21*, 25–38.

Youngstrom, E. A., Freeman, A. J., & Jenkins, M. M. (2009). The assessment of children and adolescents with bipolar disorder. *Child and Adolescent Psychiatric Clinics of North America, 18,* 353–390. doi:310.1016/j.chc.2008.1012.1002.

Yung, A. R., McGorry, P. D., McFarlane, C. A., & Patton, G. (1995). The PACE Clinic: Development of a clinical service for young people at high risk of psychosis. *Australian Psychiatry, 3,* 345–349.

Yung, A. R., Phillips, L. J., Hok, P. Y., & McGorry, P. D. (2004). Risk factors for psychosis in an ultra high-risk group: Psychopathology and clinical features. *Schizophrenia Research, 67,* 131–142.

Yung, A. R., Woods, S. W., Ruhrmann, S., Addington, J., Schultze-Lutter, F., Cornblatt, B. A., et al. (2012). Whither the attenuated psychosis syndrome? *Schizophrenia Bulletin, 38,* 1130–1134.

Zanarini, M. C., Frankenburg, F. R., Hennen, J., Reich, D. B., & Silk, K. R. (2004). Axis I comorbidity in patients with borderline personality disorder: 6-year follow-up and prediction of time to remission. *American Journal of Psychiatry, 161,* 2108–2114.

Zanarini, M. C., Frankenburg, F. R., Reich, D. B., & Fitzmaurice, G. M. (2012). Attainment and stability of sustained symptomatic remission and recovery among patients with borderline personality disorder and axis II comparison subjects: A 16-year prospective follow-up study. *American Journal of Psychiatry, 169*(5), 476–483. doi:10.1176/appi.ajp.2011.11101550

Zanarini, M. C., Skodol, A. E., Bender, D., Dolan, R., Sanislow, C., Schaefer, E., et al. (2000). The Collaborative Longitudinal Personality Disorders Study: Reliability of axis I and II diagnoses. *Journal of Personality Disorders, 14,* 291–299.

Zane, M. D. (1984). Psychoanalysis and contextual analysis of phobias. *Journal of the American Academy of Psychoanalysis, 12,* 553–568.

Zanov, M. V., & Davison, G. C. (2010). A conceptual and empirical review of 25 years of cognitive assessment using the Articulated Thoughts in Simulated Situations (ATSS) think-aloud paradigm. *Cognitive Therapy and Research, 34,* 282–291.

Zapf, P. A., & Roesch, R. (2011). Future directions in the restoration of competency to stand trial. *Current Directions in Psychological Science, 20*(1), 43–47.

Zapolski, T. C. B., Fisher, S., Hsu, W.-W., & Barnes, J. (2016). What can parents do? Examining the role of parental support on the negative relationship between racial discrimination, depression, and drug use among African American youth. *Clinical Psychological Science: A Journal of the Association for Psychological Science, 4,* 718–731. http://doi.org/10.1177/2167702616646371

Zarit, S. H., & Zarit, J. M. (2011). *Mental disorders in older adults: Fundamentals of assessment and treatment* (2nd ed.). New York, NY: Guilford Press.

Zhang, T. Y., & Meaney, M. J. (2010). Epigenetics and the environmental regulation of the genome and its function. *Annual Review of Psychology, 61,* 439–466.

Zheng, H., Sussman, S., Chen, X., Wang, Y. Xia, J., Gong, J., Liu, C., Shan, J., Unger, J., & Johnson, C. A. (2004). Project EX—A teen smoking cessation initial study in Wuhan, China. *Addictive Behaviors, 29,* 1725–1733.

Zhou, J., & Seeley, W. W. (2014). Network dysfunction in Alzheimer's disease and frontotemporal dementia: Implications for psychiatry. *Biological Psychiatry, 75,* 565–573.

Zietsch, B. P., Miller, G. F., Bailey, J. M., & Martin, N. G. (2011). Female orgasm rates are largely independent of other traits: Implications for "female orgasmic disorder" and evolutionary theories of orgasm. *Journal of Sexual Medicine, 8,* 2305–2316. doi:10.1111/j.1743-6109.2011.02300.x

Zimmerman, M., & Mattia, J. I. (1999). Differences between clinical and research practices in diagnosing borderline personality disorder. *American Journal of Psychiatry, 156,* 1570–1574.

Zimmerman, M., Rothschild, L., & Chelminski, I. (2005). The prevalence of DSM-IV personality disorders in psychiatric outpatients. *American Journal of Psychiatry, 162*(10), 1911–1918.

Zimmermann, K., Walz, C., Derckx, R. T., Kendrick, K. M., Weber, B., Dore, B., et al. (2017). Emotion regulation deficits in regular marijuana users. *Human Brain Mapping, 38,* 4270–4279. http://doi.org/10.1002/hbm.23671

Zinbarg, R. E., Mineka, S., Bobova, L., Craske, M. G., Vrshek-Schallhorn, S., Griffith, J. W., et al. (2016). Testing a hierarchical model of neuroticism and its cognitive facets: Latent structure and prospective prediction of first onsets of anxiety and unipolar mood disorders during 3 years in late adolescence. *Clinical Psychological Science, 4*(5), 805–824. doi:10.1177/2167702615618162

Zinzow, H. M., & Thompson, M. (2015). Factors associated with use of verbally coercive, incapacitated, and forcible sexual assault tactics in a longitudinal study of college men. *Aggressive Behavior, 41,* 34–43. doi:10.1002/ab.21567

Zipfel, S., Wild, B., Gross, G., Friederich, H. C., Teufel, M., Schellberg, D., et al. (2014). Focal psychodynamic therapy, cognitive behaviour therapy, and optimised treatment as usual in outpatients with anorexia nervosa (ANTOP study): Randomised controlled trial. *Lancet, 383,* 127–137.

Zohar, A. H., & Felz, L. (2001). Ritualistic behavior in young children. *Journal of Abnormal Child Psychology, 29,* 121–128.

Zubin, J., & Spring, B. (1977). Vulnerability: A new view of schizophrenia. *Journal of Abnormal Psychology, 86,* 103–126.

Zucker, K. J. (2005). Gender identity disorder in children and adolescents. *Annual Review of Clinical Psychology, 1,* 467–492. doi:10.1146/annurev.clinpsy.1.102803.144050

Name Index